MW00806652

FROM BAKSHEESH TO BRIBERY

From Baksheesh to Bribery

UNDERSTANDING THE GLOBAL FIGHT AGAINST CORRUPTION AND GRAFT

Edited by T. Markus Funk
and Andrew S. Boutros

Foreword by the
Honorable M. Margaret McKeown

OXFORD
UNIVERSITY PRESS

From Baksheesh to Bribery. T. Markus Funk and Andrew S. Boutros.
© Oxford University Press 2019. Published 2019 by Oxford University Press.

OXFORD
UNIVERSITY PRESS

Oxford University Press is a department of the University of Oxford. It furthers the University's objective of excellence in research, scholarship, and education by publishing worldwide. Oxford is a registered trademark of Oxford University Press in the UK and certain other countries.

Published in the United States of America by Oxford University Press
198 Madison Avenue, New York, NY 10016, United States of America.

© Oxford University Press 2019

All rights reserved. No part of this publication may be reproduced, stored in a retrieval system, or transmitted, in any form or by any means, without the prior permission in writing of Oxford University Press, or as expressly permitted by law, by license, or under terms agreed with the appropriate reproduction rights organization. Inquiries concerning reproduction outside the scope of the above should be sent to the Rights Department, Oxford University Press, at the address above.

You must not circulate this work in any other form
and you must impose this same condition on any acquirer.

Library of Congress Cataloging-in-Publication Data
Names: Funk, T. Markus, author. | Boutros, Andrew, author.
Title: From baksheesh to bribery : understanding the global fight against corruption and graft /
    T. Markus Funk and Andrew S. Boutros.
Description: New York : Oxford University Press, 2019. | Includes bibliographical references and index.
Identifiers: LCCN 2018038169 | ISBN 9780190232399 ((hardback) : alk. paper)
Subjects: LCSH: Corruption—Law and legislation. | Corruption—Prevention. | Bribery—Law and
    legislation. | Commercial crimes. | Corruption—Law and legislation—United States. | Corruption—
    Prevention—United States. |Bribery—Law and legislation—United States. | Commercial crimes—
    United States. | Corporations—Corrupt practices—United States.
Classification: LCC K5261 .F76 2019 | DDC 345/.02323—dc23
LC record available at https://lccn.loc.gov/2018038169

Note to Readers
This publication is designed to provide accurate and authoritative information in regard to the subject matter covered. It is based upon sources believed to be accurate and reliable and is intended to be current as of the time it was written. It is sold with the understanding that the publisher is not engaged in rendering legal, accounting, or other professional services. If legal advice or other expert assistance is required, the services of a competent professional person should be sought. Also, to confirm that the information has not been affected or changed by recent developments, traditional legal research techniques should be used, including checking primary sources where appropriate.

*(Based on the Declaration of Principles jointly adopted by a Committee of the
American Bar Association and a Committee of Publishers and Associations.)*

**You may order this or any other Oxford University Press publication
by visiting the Oxford University Press website at www.oup.com.**

Contents

About the Editors

T. Markus Funk is the Firmwide Chair of Perkins Coie LLP's White Collar & Investigations Practice. Prior to joining the law firm, Markus served as a decorated federal prosecutor in Chicago, Section Chief with the U.S. State Department-Balkans, clerk with the federal court of appeals and federal district court, and law professor at institutions including Oxford University, the University of Chicago, and Northwestern University. Since 2010, he has served as the Founding Co-Chair of the ABA's Global Anti-Corruption Committee. Markus, who successfully tried dozens of federal and state civil and criminal jury cases and has directed more than 400 investigations (including over 100 related to transnational corruption), regularly advises public and private entities and individuals on challenging ethics and compliance matters and leads transnational internal investigations.

In addition to authoring more than 100 law-related academic and popular articles, as well as chapters on a wide variety of topics, Markus haspenned a number of books, including: *Stemming the Suffering: Victims' Rights and the International Criminal Court* (Oxford University Press, 2nd edition, 2016); *Child Exploitation and Human Trafficking: Examining the Global Challenges and US Responses* (Rowman Littlefield, 2nd edition, 2016, with Chicago U.S. District Judge Virginia M. Kendall); *Mutual Legal Assistance Treaties and Letters Rogatory: A Guide for Judges* (Federal Judicial Center, 2014); *The Haiti Trial Skills Manual* (American Bar Association, 2012); and *The Kosovo Trial Skills Manual* (U.S. Department of Justice, 2005). He also carries the distinction of having received both the Department of Justice's Attorney General's Award for the Nation's top trial performance and the State Department's Superior Honor Award for service to the country.

Andrew S. Boutros is National Co-Chair of the White Collar, Internal Investigations, and False Claims practice at a major American law firm with approximately 900 lawyers across

15 domestic and foreign offices. He represents clients in challenging internal investigations and sensitive government enforcement matters. Andrew also is an early pioneer in the Foreign Corrupt Practices Act (FCPA) and a leading lawyer in criminal customs, trade, and antidumping duty fraud cases.

As a former federal prosecutor in Chicago, Andrew's investigations and prosecutions spanned the globe and have been described as among the most extensive and complex multi-district, international corporate fraud and cybercrime cases in the nation's history. Andrew uniquely was selected as the national prosecutor of the year, having earned the Federal Law Enforcement Officers Association's prestigious *National Prosecutorial Award*. He also has been elected into the American Law Institute and is the recipient of the American Bar Association's Criminal Justice Section's *Norm Maleng Minister of Justice Award*, among the highest honors the ABA can confer upon a prosecutor. The FBI, the U.S. Department of Homeland Security, and U.S. Customs and Border Protection have presented him with some of their highest honors and recognitions. The FBI has done so for his superior trial performance in a major criminal case.

Since 2011, Andrew has been teaching an advanced course on corporate criminal prosecutions and investigations at the University of Chicago Law School. A prolific writer and speaker, he has authored nearly 50 articles, thought pieces, and book chapters as well as *The ABA Compliance Officer's Deskbook* (ABA 2017, with T. Markus Funk), a best-selling book in the Criminal Justice Section. Andrew also has presented in nearly 70 domestic and international programs. He sits on the boards of numerous organizations and holds leadership positions in a variety of professional and legal associations, including being the Founding Co-Chair of the ABA Criminal Justice Section's Global Anti-Corruption Committee since 2010 and a voting Member of the ABA Criminal Justice Section Council.

Foreword

Honorable M. Margaret McKeown
Judge, United States Court of Appeals for the Ninth Circuit;
Chair, American Bar Association Rule of Law Initiative

ALTHOUGH TAKING A stand against corruption is a popular and universal theme around the world, effective legislation and enforcement remain a global challenge. The impetus to eradicate corruption, and its omnipresent variety, bribery, is a practical one: corruption hinders economic growth and development, undermines democratic and legal institutions, distorts competition, and adds uncertainty to business dealings. Indeed, there is a yin and yang to corruption; its causes are also reflected in its effects: lack of confidence in public institutions, abuse of power, lack of transparency, and a weak civil society. Fortunately, a steadily growing global commitment to anti-corruption enforcement provides a way forward. Substantial progress, however, requires political will and practical recognition by regulators and enforcers around the world. That is why this thoughtful and uniquely comprehensive publication is both well-timed and important. This book provides a framework for analyzing corruption, along with an impressive catalog of key features and comparisons of anti-corruption regimes from a wide range of countries. More importantly, the book also offers wide-ranging practical advice, ranging from internal investigations and monitoring to data privacy and the relationship between corruption and human trafficking.

Since 1977, the Foreign Corrupt Practices Act ("FCPA") has set the bar for anti-corruption enforcement around the globe. Although the FCPA recently turned forty, large FCPA settlements with the U.S. Department of Justice continue to make international headlines. The FCPA has evolved to keep pace with the increased sophistication of corruption and bribery schemes. For example, in 2018, along with the implementation of a new corporate enforcement and cooperation policy (which is detailed in Chapters 26, 27, and 28), FCPA enforcement actions generated nearly $600 million in corporate criminal fines and penalties.[1] In short, the FCPA remains, as the book's co-editor T. Markus Funk puts it in Chapter 1, "the world's preeminent anti-bribery/anti-corruption enforcement tool."

Nevertheless, as the book's title acknowledges, extraterritorial anti-corruption efforts cannot be left solely to U.S. enforcement. After all, most crimes are local. Bribery, whether domestic or foreign, is no different. Bribery and corruption are two of the most universal criminal phenomena, leaving no corner of the globe unaffected. As interested observers and defenders of the rule of law, credit should be given to ongoing efforts by the American Bar Association through its Criminal Justice Section Global Anti-Corruption Committee, as well as this book's editors and contributors, to elevate the discourse beyond the usual suspects—the FCPA and the United Kingdom's Bribery Act.

Helpfully, this book features detailed summaries authored by in-the-trenches experts on jurisdictions ranging from Australia to the UK. (Chapters 1-17). Some examples illustrate this noteworthy effort to examine corruption enforcement from a global perspective. Germany exemplifies a jurisdiction with a remarkably robust anti-bribery regime with significant extra-territorial reach. Germany also provides an example of an anti-corruption law that is at least as powerful as the FCPA and the UK Bribery Act (both in its coverage and enforcement). Yet, a quick online search underscores that the German law has largely been ignored by the English-language commentators who have what appears to be a near-surgical focus on the legislation from the United States and the United Kingdom.[2] In Chapter 8, authors Michael Malterer and Raphael Won-Pil Suh discuss Germany's increasing enforcement activity, most recently the passage of the landmark German Anti-Corruption Law (*Gesetz zur Bekämpfung der Korruption*) in November 2015. Indeed, according to the Organization for Economic Cooperation and Development (OECD), during the years 1999 - 2017, Germany led all other countries in sanctions of individuals and entities for foreign bribery offenses.[3] While the United States sanctioned a total of 224 individuals and companies, the German authorities sanctioned 327. Even though U.S. authorities sanctioned 114 more "legal persons" than Germany, this apparent anomaly largely results from the German law's rejection of a legal framework that permits criminal prosecution of a company. Put another way, and as the U.S. authorities have acknowledged through their shifting prosecution priorities, it is individuals, rather than companies, who actually commit crimes of corruption and, accordingly, must be prioritized as prosecution targets.

The United Arab Emirates (UAE) provides another example of enhanced attention to corruption. As contributing authors Lamia Matta and Ibtissem Lassoued discuss in

---

[1] Fraud Section, Criminal Div., U.S. Dep't of Justice, Fraud Section Year in Review 2018 5 (2018), available at https://www.justice.gov/criminal-fraud/file/1123566/download.

[2] *But see* T. Markus Funk, *Germany's Foreign Anti-Bribery Efforts: Second-Tier No More*, 1 Zeitschrift für Deutsches und Amerikanisches Recht, 24, 24-25 (2014) ("The . . . OECD report heaped effusive praise on Germany's recent efforts to investigate and prosecute corruption. And those enforcement efforts have, indeed, been impressive."), available at https://www.perkinscoie.com/images/content/3/2/v2/32500/04-09-2014-funk.pdf.pdf.

[3] OECD, 2017 Enforcement of the Anti-bribery Convention 5-6 tbl.1A (2018), http://www.oecd.org/daf/anti-bribery/OECD-WGB-Enforcement-Data-2018-ENG.pdf.

Chapter 16, the UAE first passed anti-bribery legislation in the late 1980s. In recent years, the UAE has enhanced penalties and expanded the scope of enforcement. Now the UAE is positioned to be a true anti-corruption leader in the Middle East. A recent enforcement action demonstrates willingness to prosecute corruption. In August 2018, the manager of a government entity was sentenced to an eighteen-month prison term and fined approximately $1.3 million as a result of her demand for bribes from domestic and foreign companies seeking construction contracts.

A final example is Indonesia. Contributors Kevin Feldis, Laode Syarif, Rasamala Aritonang, and Lakso Anindito explain in Chapter 11 that Indonesia continues to face challenges in enforcing anti-corruption legislation. However, the country has recently demonstrated an increased commitment to prosecuting those responsible for graft and bribery by prosecuting over 300 public officials for serious (though mostly domestic) corruption in the last five years.

An understanding of recent developments in anti-corruption enforcement goes beyond country-specific legislation. The World Bank Group, for example, is a key player in transnational efforts to eliminate corruption. In Chapter 23, contributors Pascale Hélène Dubois, Paul Ezzeddin, and Collin David Swan discuss how important the anti-corruption fight is to the World Bank, which works to promote economic development and reduce poverty in member countries. Because corruption removes resources from the World Bank's efforts to eliminate poverty, the World Bank has continued to enhance its efforts—especially in recent years—to fight corruption. One of the World Bank's key methods of fighting corruption is through its Office of Suspension and Debarment. A November 2015 report by the Office of Suspension and Debarment stated that the World Bank imposed 368 sanctions on firms and individuals from 2007 through June 2015. (Curiously, though, the world's largest global development bank has not explicitly deemed that using trafficked or child labor is an offense that will lead to debarment, despite various anti-trafficking pronouncements;[4] hopefully, a welcome change in their approach is on the horizon.)

Chapter 21 examines the centrality of third parties in most bribery schemes. Significant swaths of many companies' international operations rely heavily on third parties. There are many reasons for this, but it is primarily because the use of third parties can create efficiencies that a company's employees cannot. However, the use of third parties overseas also carries significant risks of corruption—and liability. Recent studies by KPMG and the OECD reveal that the use of third parties to conduct international business accounts for some 75% of foreign anti-corruption misconduct.

Turning from the "how" to the "why," this book—particularly in Chapters 21 and 29—makes the important point that bribery not only takes many forms, but also occurs for many reasons. A "one size fits all" approach does not apply to either corruption or bribery. Of course, in many instances people pay bribes and engage in related corrupt activities for personal gain, to win contracts, to avoid expenses, or, relatedly, to curry favor with high-ranking government officials. In other words, bribes are often viewed as a cheap shortcut or accelerant to improve business or the bottom line. But bribes can also arise in other contexts.

---

[4] *See, e.g.,* Megumi Makisaka, *Human Trafficking: A Brief Overview,* SOCIAL DEVELOPMENT NOTES No. 122 (detailing "The World Bank Contribution to Fighting Human Trafficking") (December 2009), available at http://siteresources.worldbank.org/EXTSOCIALDEVELOPMENT/Resources/244362-1239390842422/6012763-1239905793229/Human_Trafficking.pdf.

One such instance is in human trafficking, for which bribery and corruption go hand in hand—as analyzed by the book's co-editor T. Markus Funk in Chapter 29. Although there is certainly bribery without trafficking, trafficking almost never occurs without bribery and corruption: illegal payments to immigration officials, factory inspectors, and police.

In sum, although the FCPA remains the benchmark when it comes to anti-corruption enforcement, it is far from the only legislation triggered by bribery and corruption. Other countries and institutions are increasingly stepping up the effective enforcement of their own anti-corruption legislation. As Chapter 18 (penned jointly by co-editors Andrew S. Boutros and T. Markus Funk) points out, one method is a "carbon copy" prosecution: one country prosecutes a case involving the same set of facts as a previous enforcement action brought by another country. In other instances, cross-border enforcement actions are coordinated, whereby one jurisdiction takes the lead or both sovereigns decide to act in tandem.

Helpfully, the book contains subject-specific chapters covering important topics ranging from investigation basics (Chapter 19), mutual legal assistance treaties and letters rogatory (Chapter 20), effective third party due diligence (Chapter 21), privacy and data security (Chapter 22), monitorships (Chapter 24), voluntary disclosures (Chapter 25), deferred/non-prosecution/corporate integrity agreements (Chapter 26), company cooperation and the U.S. Sentencing Guidelines (Chapter 27), and the link between labor trafficking and corruption (Chapter 29).

The broader point, then, is that *From Baksheesh to Bribery* admirably and effectively breaks from the prevailing parochialism in addressing corruption and bribery. Funk and Boutros and their various expert contributors have undertaken a scholarly examination that finds no equal in terms of its breadth and depth, and, as a bonus, provides a very accessible go-to resource for in-house and law firm practitioners, legislators, enforcement officials, courts, and others interested in understanding the issue from a macro-perspective. It is my hope that as these dynamics become better understood, bribery and corruption will increasingly find no quarter in jurisdictions around the globe.

Acknowledgments

WE BOTH WISH to make sure to recognize the amazing patience and grit exhibited by Perkins Coie attorney Daniel Graham, who was an indispensable rock throughout this project. The wonderful Chin Sue Virnich, who kept the train on time and in motion, was similarly critical in getting this project completed. Both provided tremendous off-hour assistance, feedback, and counsel - we can't thank you enough! And, of course, both authors wish to thank their families, who lovingly supported them throughout this project.

Contributors

Jonathan Adams Baker McKenzie, Partner, Compliance & Investigations

Timur Aitkulov Clifford Chance CIS Limited, Partner (Advocate's office of Timur Aitkulov in cooperation with Clifford Chance), Regulatory Enforcement & White Collar, Litigation & Dispute Resolution

Alejandra Montenegro Almonte Miller & Chevalier Chartered, Member, International Anti-Corruption and Internal Investigations

Robert Amaee Quinn Emanuel Urquhart & Sullivan LLP, Partner, London Head of White Collar Crime & Corporate Investigations

Lakso Anindito Corruption Eradication Commission of Republic of Indonesia (KPK RI), Investigator

Rasamala Aritonang Corruption Eradication Commission of Republic of Indonesia (KPK RI), Head of Regulatory Affairs

Ignacio Andrade Aycinena Sfera Legal, Partner

Timothy D. Belevetz Holland & Knight LLP, Partner, White Collar Defense and Investigations Team

Pablo Bentes Steptoe & Johnson LLP, Managing Director, International Trade and Investment

Nikhil Bhogal Hogan Lovells, Senior Associate, Corporate Commercial and Regulatory

Kiril Bougartchev Bougartchev Moyne Associés AARPI, Partner

Andrew S. Boutros Seyfarth Shaw LLP, Partner and National Co-Chair of White Collar, Internal Investigations, and False Claims Practice

Chelsea Curfman Perkins Coie LLP, Partner, White Collar & Investigations Practice

Michael S. Diamant Gibson Dunn, Partner, White Collar Defense and Investigations Practice Group

Pascale Hélène Dubois World Bank, Integrity Vice President

Paul Ezzeddin World Bank, Senior Counsel, Legal Vice Presidency (formerly Senior Policy Officer, Office of Suspension and Debarment)

Kevin R. Feldis Perkins Coie LLP, Partner, former U.S. Department of Justice Legal Advisor at the U.S. Embassy in Jakarta, Indonesia

T. Markus Funk Perkins Coie LLP, Partner and Firmwide Chair, White Collar & Investigations Practice

María Mercedes Castro Guerra Garcia & Bodan, Senior Associate

Bingna Guo White & Case LLP, Partner, White Collar and Investigations

Michael E. Hantman Holland & Knight LLP, Partner, White Collar Defense and Investigations Team

Vaughn Harrison Hogan Lovells, Partner, Corporate Commercial and Regulatory

Tyler W. Hodgson World Bank Group, Senior Investigator (Attorney), Integrity Vice Presidency

Cori Lable Kirkland & Ellis LLP, Partner, Government & Internal Investigations

Stewart Landefeld Perkins Coie LLP, Partner, Past Firmwide Chair, Corporate Practice

Ibtissem Lassoued Al Tamimi & Company, Partner, Head of Advisory, Financial Crime

Bo Li O'Melveny & Myers LLP, Associate, White Collar Defense & Corporate Investigations

Lucinda A. Low Steptoe & Johnson LLP, Partner and Head of Compliance, Investigations, Trade and Enforcement Department

Dr. Michael Malterer Dentons Europe LLP, Partner, Corporate Team

Lamia Matta Miller & Chevalier Chartered, Member, Litigation and Global Compliance

Maria McMahon Baker McKenzie, Associate, Compliance & Investigations

Joan Meyer Baker McKenzie, Partner, Compliance & Investigations

Nathan Morin Bougartchev Moyne Associés AARPI, Junior Associate

Emmanuel Moyne Bougartchev Moyne Associés AARPI, Partner

Sébastien Muratyan Bougartchev Moyne Associés AARPI, Senior Associate

Olga Semushina Clifford Chance CIS Limited, Senior Associate, Litigation & Dispute Resolution

Lining Shan O'Melveny & Myers LLP, Senior Legal Consultant, White Collar Defense & Corporate Investigations Team

Sunil Shenoi Kirkland & Ellis LLP, Partner, Government & Internal Investigations

Michael Sink Perkins Coie LLP, Partner and Head of Denver Commercial Litigation Group

Michael Skopets Miller & Chevalier Chartered, Senior Associate, International Anti-Corruption and Internal Investigations

Juliet S. Sorensen Northwestern University Pritzker School of Law, Clinical Professor of Law, Director, Bluhm Legal Clinic

Christopher W.H. Sullivan Gibson Dunn, Of Counsel, White Collar Defense and Investigations Practice Group

Collin David Swan World Bank, Counsel, Office of Suspension and Debarment

Laode M. Syarif Corruption Eradication Commission of the Republic of Indonesia (KPK RI), Commissioner

Galina Valentirova Clifford Chance CIS Limited, Associate, Litigation & Dispute Resolution

F. Joseph Warin Gibson Dunn, Partner, Chair of Washington, D.C. Litigation Department and Co-Chair of Global White Collar Defense and Investigations Practice Group

Tarun Warriar Kirkland & Ellis LLP, Partner, Litigation

Dr. Raphael Won-Pil Suh Dentons Europe LLP, Senior Associate, Corporate Team

Alexandra Wrage TRACE, President and Founder

Robert R. Wyld Johnson Winter & Slattery, Consultant and Leader, White Collar Crime & Investigations Practice

Introduction

BACK IN 2008 your authors, both still Assistant U.S. Attorneys who happened to have first-hand experiences with anti-corruption prosecution and defense,[1] began to discuss whether we should propose

At the time, we were animated by a belief that those practitioners in the United States (and elsewhere) who were already aware of the Foreign Corrupt Practices Act (FCPA) tended to overlook the reality that other countries also have anti-bribery/anti-corruption (ABAC) regimes—including ones with extraterritorial application. One of the drivers for this cross-border interest can be found in our respective backgrounds: Markus is a German-American dual national who grew up overseas, whereas Andrew is a first-generation American with Egyptian roots. So our concern was (and still is) that many in the space were too narrowly focused only on the United States' anti-corruption regime to the exclusion of the rest of the world. In our proposal materials to the ABA, we put it this way: "This Task Force will bring together international and domestic practitioners to address the growing trend in

---

[1] In the case of Markus, he spent two years (2005–2006) as the U.S. DOJ Section Chief in post-conflict Kosovo where he, among other things, helped devise and implement Kosovo's suite of anti-corruption laws; during this time he also assisted U.S. prosecutors investigating allegations of violations of the Foreign Corrupt Practices Act (FCPA) and related anti-corruption laws. Markus and Andrew are the founding Co-Chairs, of the Criminal Justice Section's (CJS's) Global Anti-Corruption Committee.

Andrew has been handling FCPA and other anti-corruption investigations and enforcement actions since 2001 and was instrumental in helping launch and later building out the FCPA practice at a leading *Am Law* 15 firm. Prior to joining the U.S. Department of Justice, Andrew also represented major multinational companies in multiple, significant FCPA government enforcement matters, including several involving the United Nation's Oil-for-Food Program after the fall of the Saddam Hussein regime. As an Assistant United States Attorney, Andrew assisted U.S. prosecutors in their handling of FCPA and other related matters.

cross-border investigations and prosecutions, as well as engage practitioners who have a practice tailored to international white collar crime, as opposed to solely domestic."

Of course, it must be said that there were some sound reasons for the then-prevailing perspective that the United State's bribery-of-foreign-officials law was the only one that really mattered. After all, at the time U.S. FCPA prosecutions constituted some 80+ percent of the world's extraterritorial applications of ABAC laws. But what even back then was lost in this tilted view of the FCPA's global (statistical) "domination" was an appreciation that the United States was one of many countries to outlaw bribery of foreign officials.

Consider, for example, the oft-overlooked example of Germany. To many practitioners, there is the FCPA, the UK Bribery Act, and then "everything else." But the Organization for Economic Cooperation and Development's (OECD's) Working Group on Bribery characterizes Germany as assuming a "leading position" in the investigation and prosecution of bribery of foreign officials. (Though it must be said that until 1999 such bribe activity constituted a tax-deductible event under the then-prevailing German law.) Similarly, Transparency International rates Germany as having "active enforcement" of the OECD's Anti-Bribery Convention.

The OECD's June 2013 Annual Report, in fact, bears this out. Germany is ranked Number 2 among all nations since 1999 in terms of bringing bribery cases. Specifically, Germany tallied 88 cases. The United States, by contrast, pursued 139 cases and perennial client-update-favorite the United Kingdom pursued only 7.[2] Germany, in short, has quietly joined the United States as the world's leader in foreign bribery prosecutions, with the UK (surprisingly to many caught up in the initial hype surrounding the UK Bribery Act) a fairly distant third. But one would never think this was so based on the dearth of English-language articles focusing on Germany's active anti-bribery efforts.[3]

Over time, however, practitioners have become evermore aware of the reality that foreign countries are also sensitive to foreign bribery touching on their jurisdictions—and that their governments are doing something about it in terms of legislative enactments and enforcement actions (though, in this evolutionary phase of the fight against bribery and corruption, the number of nations developing or fine-tuning their anti-bribery laws far outstrips the number of nations actively pursuing suspected wrongdoers through enforcement actions).

Now—in 2019—our humble, potentially temporary "task force" has, in ABA terminology, graduated to more permanent "Committee" status. It now has multiple co-chairs, more than a thousand members, and one of the most active LinkedIn pages among all ABA Committees, and in all other respects is one of the most active committees housed under the umbrella of the ABA's Criminal Justice Section.

---

[2] In 2017, the OECD Working Group on Bribery launched its fourth phase of monitoring of Germany's implementation of the OECD Anti-Bribery Convention, so updated numbers should be available in the near future.

[3] *See* T. Markus Funk, *Germany's Foreign Anti-corruption Efforts: Second-Tier No More*, ZDAR 1/2014, *available at* https://www.perkinscoie.com/images/content/3/2/v2/32500/04-09-2014-funk.pdf.pdf.

The reason for this admittedly paternally-proud historiography of the ABA CJS Global Anti-Corruption Committee is that it in many ways reflects our (and others') ongoing efforts to promote a fuller appreciation of the wider fight against corruption, wherever in the world that democracy-destroying and rule-of-law-undermining conduct takes place. The polycentric nature of today's fight against bribery and other forms of corruption, moreover, has direct, but unfortunately oft-misunderstood, impacts on companies and individuals engaged in cross-border commerce, regardless of where in the world they are based or do business.

Which brings us to the core purpose of this book. It is our hope that the book will continue this discussion by bringing together some of the world's leading anti-corruption authorities. But instead of representing an exhaustive, country-by-country compendium of the world's anti-corruption laws (after all, today we all have the internet firmly at our disposal as a powerful research tool), our objective was to identify select, representative jurisdictions. We then asked respected practitioners to whom we owe a tremendous debt of gratitude to walk us through a deeper-dive analysis of what makes these countries' anti-corruption efforts "tick." Put another way, our goal was depth rather than breadth.

In the pursuit of our objective we note both commonalities and divergences among and between these various anti-corruption regimes, both in terms of legislative drafting and on-the-ground enforcement. Rounding out the effort, we recruited thought leaders and practitioners to pen substantive, non-geographic chapters taking on related topics such as the growing phenomenon of "carbon-copy prosecutions," cross-border third-party due diligence, internal investigations techniques and tips, monitorships, the World Bank Group's role in fighting corruption, and the function of mutual legal assistance treaties and letters rogatory.

Though we, as noted, do not intend to provide an exhaustive chronicling of the world's anti-bribery efforts, a closer examination of the jurisdictions we selected yields interesting results when it comes to the "hallmarks" of what many in the West view as an effective suite of anti-corruption laws. For example, all but two (Cuba and India) make the bribery of foreign officials a criminal offense. In fact, only Cuba lacks laws permitting extraterritorial application of anti-bribery laws. Similarly, all of the jurisdictions discussed make bribing a domestic government official a crime. Surprisingly, however, commercial/"private" bribery is, in fact, not outlawed in a number of the countries we examined (namely, Mexico, Cuba, Guatemala, and Tunisia). And although many countries impose criminal liability on *companies* involved in bribery offenses, some (Tunisia, Germany, Brazil, and Cuba) do not. Moreover, only a few countries (namely, Australia, Cuba, and Guatemala) lack laws governing financial internal controls.

Turning to the now-famous UK Bribery Act's affirmative compliance defense, having a robust compliance program only negates liability in Australia, the United Kingdom, Tunisia, and Mexico. Mexico, moreover, is also the only country that does not incentivize cooperation by giving "credit" to companies or individuals who cooperate with law enforcement. We observed a closer split when it came to a company's affirmative obligation to report potential violations of the anti-bribery laws or accounting irregularities, with Australia, Germany, Brazil, Cuba, and Guatemala *not* imposing such an obligation.

By way of a handy reference to how the selected nations' anti-corruption laws treat these central issues, consider the following summary:

Key Issue	Yes	No	Not Addressed
Is the jurisdiction subject to any international anti-corruption conventions?	Australia Brazil Canada China Cuba France Germany Guatemala India Indonesia Mexico Russia South Africa Tunisia United Arab Emirates United Kingdom United States		
Is bribery of *foreign public officials* illegal?	Australia Brazil Canada China France Germany Guatemala Mexico Russia South Africa Tunisia United Arab Emirates United Kingdom United States	Cuba India Indonesia	
Is bribery of domestic officials illegal?	Australia Brazil Canada China Cuba France Germany Guatemala		

Key Issue	Yes	No	Not Addressed
	India		
	Indonesia		
	Mexico		
	Russia		
	South Africa		
	Tunisia		
	United Arab Emirates		
	United Kingdom		
	United States		
Can the *recipient* of a bribe be prosecuted?	Australia		
	Brazil		
	Canada		
	China		
	Cuba		
	France		
	Germany		
	Guatemala		
	India		
	Indonesia		
	Mexico		
	Russia		
	South Africa		
	Tunisia		
	United Arab Emirates		
	United Kingdom		
	United States		
Is *commercial* bribery illegal?	Australia	Cuba	Tunisia
	Brazil	Guatemala	
	Canada	Mexico	
	China		
	France		
	Germany		
	India		
	Indonesia		
	Russia		
	South Africa		
	United Arab Emirates		
	United Kingdom		
	United States		

(Continued)

Key Issue	Yes	No	Not Addressed
Can *companies* be held *criminally* liable?	Australia Canada China France Guatemala India Indonesia Mexico South Africa United Arab Emirates United Kingdom United States	Brazil Germany Russia Tunisia	Cuba
Can *companies* be held *civilly* liable?	Brazil Canada China France Germany Guatemala India Mexico Russia South Africa United Kingdom United States	Australia Tunisia United Arab Emirates	Cuba
Can *individuals* be held *criminally* liable?	Australia Brazil Canada China Cuba France Germany Guatemala India Indonesia Mexico Russia South Africa Tunisia United Arab Emirates United Kingdom United States		

Key Issue	Yes	No	Not Addressed
Can *individuals* be held *civilly* liable?	Australia Brazil Canada China Cuba France Germany Guatemala India Indonesia Mexico Russia South Africa United Arab Emirates United Kingdom United States	Tunisia	
Is there a "facilitation/grease payments" exception?	Australia Germany United States	Brazil Canada China Cuba France Guatemala India Indonesia Mexico Russia South Africa Tunisia United Arab Emirates United Kingdom	
Does the subject country provide for conspiracy liability relating to violations of the anti-corruption laws?	Australia Brazil Canada Germany Guatemala India Indonesia	China Cuba France United Arab Emirates	

(Continued)

Key Issue	Yes	No	Not Addressed
	Mexico Russia South Africa Tunisia United Kingdom United States		
Does the subject country provide for: • aiding/abetting liability relating to violations of the anti-corruption laws? • attempt liability relating to violations of the anti-corruption laws?	Australia Brazil Canada China Cuba France Germany Guatemala India Indonesia Mexico Russia South Africa Tunisia United Arab Emirates United Kingdom United States		
Is failure to keep accurate books and records a criminal and/or civil offense?	Australia Canada China France Germany India Indonesia Mexico Russia South Africa United Arab Emirates United Kingdom United States	Brazil Cuba Guatemala Tunisia	

Key Issue	Yes	No	Not Addressed
Do any books-and-records violations have to involve underlying bribery proof?	Canada	Australia China France Germany India Indonesia Mexico Russia South Africa United Arab Emirates United Kingdom United States	Brazil Cuba Guatemala Tunisia
Are there laws concerning a company's financial internal controls?	Brazil China France Germany India Mexico Russia South Africa Tunisia United Arab Emirates United Kingdom United States	Australia Canada Cuba Guatemala Indonesia	
Is there an affirmative, legally mandated disclosure obligation for potential violations of the anti-bribery laws or accounting irregularities?	Canada France India Mexico South Africa Tunisia United Arab Emirates United Kingdom	Australia Brazil China Cuba Germany Guatemala Indonesia Russia United States	

(Continued)

Key Issue	Yes	No	Not Addressed
Are genuine "promotional expenses" exempt from the anti-bribery laws?	Australia Canada Germany United Arab Emirates United States	Brazil China France Guatemala India Indonesia Mexico Russia South Africa Tunisia United Kingdom	Cuba
Is the giving of gifts, entertainment, travel, meals, etc. restricted/prohibited?	Brazil Canada France Germany Guatemala India Indonesia Mexico Russia South Africa Tunisia United Arab Emirates United Kingdom United States	Australia China	Cuba
Are there any laws concerning things of value conveyed by, or to, third parties?	Brazil Canada China Cuba France Guatemala India Indonesia Mexico Russia South Africa Tunisia United Arab Emirates United Kingdom United States	Australia Germany	

Key Issue	Yes	No	Not Addressed
Are bribes tax-deductible?		Australia Brazil Canada China France Germany Guatemala India Indonesia Mexico Russia South Africa Tunisia United Kingdom United States	Cuba United Arab Emirates
Is the law applied extraterritorially?	Australia Brazil Canada China France Germany Guatemala Indonesia Mexico Russia South Africa Tunisia United Arab Emirates United Kingdom United States	India	Cuba
Is having a robust/adequate corporate compliance program an affirmative defense or way to negate liability?	Australia Canada Mexico Russia Tunisia United Kingdom United States	Brazil China France South Africa Germany Guatemala India Indonesia United Arab Emirates	Cuba

(Continued)

Key Issue	Yes	No	Not Addressed
Is there a "local law" exception/ defense?	Australia Canada United Kingdom United States	Brazil China Cuba France Germany Guatemala India Indonesia Mexico Russia South Africa Tunisia United Arab Emirates	
Is "credit" given for cooperation with authorities?	Australia Brazil Canada China Cuba France Germany Guatemala India Indonesia Russia South Africa United Arab Emirates United Kingdom United States	Mexico Tunisia	
Does the subject country have a Mutual Legal Assistance Treaty with the United States that generally covers criminal matters, including the FCPA?	Australia Brazil Canada China France Guatemala India Indonesia Mexico Russia South Africa United Kingdom	Cuba Germany Tunisia United Arab Emirates	

In terms of "big picture" observations, another emerging transnational trend we for some time have noted—and first wrote about in 2012—is the phenomenon of "carbon copy prosecutions." When Andrew coined the term back in 2012 during the ABA Annual Meeting (in Toronto, and during a panel that included Markus), we were describing the following phenomenon: "When foreign or domestic Jurisdiction A files charges based on a guilty plea or charging document from Jurisdiction B."

Since that time, the term (or derivative versions of it, such as "pile-on prosecutions" and "copy-cat prosecutions") has gained considerable currency, most recently with Deputy Attorney General (DAG) Rod Rosenstein putting it this way: "One concern is about multiple law enforcement and regulatory agencies pursuing a single entity for the same or substantially similar conduct." As globalization makes the world smaller, carbon copy prosecutions have increased in frequency, size, scope, and force. In fact, we believe carbon copy prosecutions are now a permanent part of the cross-border enforcement landscape. Simply stated, one-dimensional, single-sovereign prosecutions are a thing of a past, just like VHS tapes for watching movies.

Companies with increasing frequency are starting to reach negotiated resolutions with U.S. authorities (or some other sovereign) on international bribery-related charges—whether through a nonprosecution agreement, a deferred prosecution agreement, or a guilty plea. It is true that the authorities in any country with extraterritorial reach may well be entirely satisfied with the resolution. But the authorities in the local jurisdiction where the bribery *actually occurred* may not feel equally satiated. To the contrary, a country's incentive to vindicate its own laws is not insubstantial, especially when a company or individual has already admitted, in another proceeding (say, in the United States), to violating local law. In such transnational bribery cases, astute practitioners will recognize the very real risk that other countries will initiate prosecutions based on the same operative facts as, and admissions arising out of, the primary investigation and resolution.

DOJ and SEC FCPA settlement policies (including, most centrally, standard plea agreement language), though constantly evolving, send the clear signal that, when a company enters into a negotiated resolution with U.S. enforcers, that company is essentially powerless to subsequently defend against—much less deny—the factual basis underpinning the resolution. This all but ensures that a company that settles with the DOJ—or both the DOJ and SEC in parallel proceedings—will have little or no choice but to settle with foreign authorities, should such authorities choose to exercise jurisdiction and enforce their corollary anti-corruption laws. Accordingly, and for the reasons we lay out in our carbon-copy-prosecution chapter, both named parties and nonparties implicated in a resolution in one country ought to give due consideration to the potential impact of that resolution in another territory, especially in light of recent trends pointing to coordinated multinational cooperation and successive enforcement proceedings. Duplicative, serial enforcement actions are now part and parcel of the enforcement tapestry, even though the debate continues over the need for, and fairness of, serial enforcements, as reflected by DAG Rosenstein's echoing observations and commentary.

What we are witnessing today are efforts across the kaleidoscope of the world's sovereigns who historically share few legal, social, and political traditions and practices in common, still trying to do the same thing when it comes to fighting bribery and other forms of corruption. In doing so, the increasingly interconnected, globalized world is seeking to remove the taint of antidemocratic, harmful public (and private) corruption. If nothing else, this book demonstrates that for as far as it has come along, the global fight against corruption is only in its early stages.

It will be interesting to see whether a reader who dusts off this book in, say, 10 or 15 years will recognize and be able to trace out the various inter- and intra-nation developments charted in it. But in any event, we are confident that, as the world continues to shrink, cross-border anti-bribery laws and the agencies that enforce them will bridge the gap that has historically divided those nations serious about stopping and preventing corruption and those that have largely watched on the sidelines.

1 Geographic Chapters

1 United States—Deconstructing the FCPA

TRUE, THIS BOOK in title and concept is all about "looking beyond" the FCPA (and its English analog, the UK Bribery Act).[1] The effort here is to help the reader appreciate that the fight against corruption is truly a global, transnational effort.

That said, it is impossible to ignore the FCPA, both (1) as the world's preeminent anti-bribery/anti-corruption enforcement tool, as well (2) as the leading legislative template that is copied, either in part or in whole, by foreign countries interested in creating—or beefing up—their own anti-bribery instruments. The FCPA, therefore, serves as the world's only true anti-bribery touchstone against which subsequent enactments can be compared textually. And against which enforcement efforts can be measured substantively. To fully appreciate non-U.S. efforts to draft legislation, implement new laws, and enforce those laws, then, it is important in a project such as this to review the nuts and bolts of the anti-bribery law that "started it all."

Enacted in 1977, the Foreign Corrupt Practices Act of 1977 (FCPA) prohibits corrupt payments of money or anything of value to foreign officials in order to obtain or retain business. In 1976, the Securities and Exchange Commission (SEC) issued its groundbreaking *Report of the Securities and Exchange Commission on Questionable and Illegal Corporate Payments and Practices*, which characterized the problem of corrupt and illegal corporate payments as "serious and widespread."

In response to the report, Congress enacted the FCPA. The FCPA consists of two criminal sections that prohibit the following: (1) a company's knowing, and an individual's willful,

---

[1] This chapter was contributed by T. Markus Funk and Andrew S. Boutros.

From Baksheesh to Bribery. T. Markus Funk and Andrew S. Boutros.
© Oxford University Press 2019. Published 2019 by Oxford University Press.

violation of the Act's recordkeeping and internal-accounting-control provisions (commonly referred to as "books and records" and "internal controls" provisions); and (2) the direct or indirect payment by an issuer, American business, citizen, resident, or agent, of money or anything else "of value" to a "foreign official" or foreign political party or official thereof (or any candidate for political office) in order to influence any act or decision of that official in his or her official capacity or to secure any other improper advantage in order to obtain or retain business (commonly referred to as the "anti-bribery provision").

The FCPA is enforced by two government agencies: the SEC and the Department of Justice (DOJ). The SEC, which is responsible for civil enforcement of the FCPA, investigates and brings enforcement actions primarily against "issuers" and their officers, directors, employees, agents, or stockholders acting on the issuer's behalf. The SEC can enforce both the anti-bribery and the recordkeeping and internal controls provisions by bringing civil charges against companies. The DOJ's jurisdiction, in contrast, extends over activities of both publicly and privately held companies.

Adherence to the directives of the FCPA continues as one of the most prominent issues in corporate compliance. The consequences of a DOJ investigation for an organization can be substantial and attention-diverting, a settlement can be costly, and an indictment can be crippling.

1. FCPA Overview: How Liability Attaches

1.1 THE ANTI-BRIBERY PROVISIONS

The FCPA, at its core, makes it a crime for a person, company, or other entity to corruptly offer or provide anything of value to a foreign government official for the purpose of improperly obtaining or retaining business.[2] Put another way, the FCPA anti-bribery provisions prohibit any U.S. company (whether publicly traded or not) to engage in corrupt payments "in order to assist . . . in obtaining or retaining business, or directing business to, any person." This requirement is known as the "business purpose test" and is broadly interpreted. The anti-bribery provisions apply not only to issuers, but also to "domestic concerns" and to foreign nationals or businesses acting in the United States (or agents thereof). Domestic concerns include any citizen, national, or resident of the United States, as well as any corporation that has its principle place of business in the United States or is organized under the laws of any U.S. state. In broad strokes, then, the FCPA's anti-bribery provisions are designed to prevent an individual from directly or indirectly bribing foreign government officials.

Moving from the general (and historical) to the specific, there are five elements required to prove a violation of the anti-bribery provisions:

1. *The offer.* A real or legal "person"—an issuer, a domestic concern, or a foreign national or business acting in the United States—must act in furtherance of either (1) an offer, a payment, a promise to pay, or an authorization to pay any money; or (2) an offer, gift, promise to give, or authorization of giving anything of value.

---

[2] *See* 15 U.S.C. § 78dd-1 et seq. (2018).

2. *The (intended) recipient.* The offer, payment, promise, or authorization must be given to (1) any foreign political party or party official, (2) any candidate for foreign political office, (3) any foreign official (defined as any officer or employee of a foreign government or public international organization acting on behalf of that government or organization), or (4) any person that the "person" knows will pass the payment offer, promise, or authorization on to any of the above.

3. *Jurisdiction.* The offer, payment, promise, or authorization must be made by (1) an issuer or domestic concern and make use of any means or instrumentality of interstate commerce, (2) a national of, or an entity organized under the law of, the United States engaging in corrupt payments outside of the United States, or (3) any other person—a foreign national or business—inside the United States, but not necessarily using a means or instrumentality of interstate commerce.

4. *The purpose, Part 1.* The "person" must act for the corrupt purpose of (1) influencing an official act or decision of that foreign official, (2) inducing that foreign official to do or omit doing any act in violation of his or her lawful duty, (3) securing an improper advantage, or (4) inducing that foreign official to use his or her influence with a foreign government to affect or influence any government act or decision.

5. *The purpose, Part 2.* The act must be intended to assist the "person" in obtaining, retaining, or directing business.

However, companies should be cognizant that the DOJ may bring charges under the general conspiracy statute for conspiracy to violate the anti-bribery provisions of the FCPA, which is easier for a prosecutor to prove than the underlying anti-bribery violation itself and is also used to vitiate any statute of limitation issues. Additional items of note include the following:

- *Attempt liability.* There is no requirement that a payment actually be made or a benefit bestowed for liability to attach—all that is required is the attempt. After all, the FCPA itself also prohibits any offer, promise, or authorization to provide anything of value to a government official.
- *Broad definition of "foreign official."* The term includes anyone acting on behalf of an "instrumentality" of a non-U.S. government, department, or agency—including state-owned enterprises. "Foreign officials," therefore, include judges and court employees, police and law enforcement officers, customs agents, government employees who issue licenses or permits, and any individual elected or appointed to a political office.
- *"Thing of value" means **anything** of value.* Real or legal persons are liable for corruptly providing anything of value to a foreign official. Liability, therefore, exists from the first dollar; there is no de minimis exception. In addition to tangible items of economic value (cash for tips or bribes), "things of value" may include intangible benefits, such as gifts, entertainment, meals, trips/travel, professional training, education, loans, employment, discounted prices, and internships for relatives.
- *Political and charitable contributions.* Making political or charitable contributions also may violate the FCPA if they are made corruptly to obtain or retain business, or as part of an improper exchange of favors with a foreign official.

- *Vendors/business partners are a major compliance risk.* The FCPA also prohibits indirect corrupt payments and imposes liability if a U.S. person knowingly authorizes its third-party agent to make a corrupt payment, offer, or promise to a foreign official. Third parties can include any service provider acting on behalf of the person, such as local agents, suppliers, and distributors.
- *"Knowing" about misconduct is a deceptively low standard.* "Knowledge" is statutorily defined to mean either (1) awareness of conduct or substantial certainly that such conduct will occur, or (2) conscious disregard of a "high probability" that a corrupt payment or offer will be made. As a result, a "head in the sand" approach will not work. A real or legal person will be deemed to have knowledge of its agent's corrupt acts if the company/individual is aware of a high probability that the agent was engaged in a corrupt act and intentionally avoids confirming that fact. The net result is that solid compliance and proper investigations are no longer optional.

1.2 EXCEPTIONS AND AFFIRMATIVE DEFENSES

The FCPA provides one exception to, and two affirmative defenses for, the anti-bribery provisions. In general, the exception and the affirmative defenses should be construed extremely narrowly.

1.2.1 Facilitating or Expediting Payments

The FCPA's only exception allows for "facilitating or expediting payment[s]" to foreign officials for the purpose of "expedit[ing] or . . . secur[ing] the performance of a routine governmental action." Courts have characterized expediting and facilitating payments as " 'essentially ministerial' actions that 'merely move a particular matter toward an eventual act or decision or which do not involve any discretionary action.' " These payments may include, but are not limited to, the following: obtaining permits, licenses, or other official documents to do business in a foreign country; processing government papers; providing police protection or mail services or scheduling inspections; and providing utilities services or cargo services or protecting perishable commodities. As a practical matter, the facilitating payments exception is construed extremely narrowly. Even more, it does not exist under the laws of almost any another country, including the United Kingdom. Because it is routinely misunderstood by employees, best practices teach that it should generally not play any part in a company's anti-corruption code of conduct or trainings.

1.2.2 Local Law

The FCPA allows for an affirmative defense for what otherwise would be an anti-bribery violation if the defendant can prove that "the payment, gift, offer, or promise of anything of value that was made, was lawful under the written laws and regulations of the foreign official's, political party's, party official's, or candidate's country." The defense is statutorily limited to the written laws and regulations of a country—and very few, if any, local laws permit forms of bribery. Thus, it is never a defense to claim that the prohibited payments were made because "this is how business is done" in a particular foreign country.

1.2.3 Bona Fide Business Expenditures

An affirmative defense is also provided if "the payment, gift, offer, or promise of anything of value that was made, was a reasonable and bona fide expenditure ... incurred by or on behalf of a foreign official, party, party official, or candidate." However, the payment or gift must be "directly related to (A) the promotion, demonstration, or explanation of products or services; or (B) the execution or performance of a contract with a foreign government or agency thereof." This is the exception most likely to be invoked by companies or individuals accused of making "marginal" bribes—that is, engaging in conduct that is close to the line.

1.3 PENALTIES: CIVIL AND CRIMINAL FINES AND SENTENCES

Violation of the FCPA can result in stiff civil and criminal penalties for both entities and individuals. For criminal penalties, an entity that violates the anti-bribery provisions may be faced with a criminal fine of up to $2 million per violation or twice the loss/gain (whichever is greater), disgorgement of profits, and possible debarment/suspension. An individual who violates these provisions may face up to five years in prison, a fine of $250,000 or twice the loss/gain (whichever is greater), or both for every violation of the statute. An entity that violates the recordkeeping and internal controls provisions may be assessed criminal fines of up to $25 million. An individual who violates these provisions may be faced with a sentence of up to 20 years in prison, a fine of up to $5 million, or both. Civil actions brought against entities or individuals by the SEC under the FCPA are subject to a penalty of $10,000 per violation.

1.4 THE FCPA'S NEAR CONSTANT, COMMERCIAL-BRIBERY-PROHIBITING COMPANION: THE U.S. TRAVEL ACT

In contrast to the FCPA's singular focus on government officials, the U.S. Travel Act, which has been on the books since the early 1960s, is aimed squarely at preventing "private" or "commercial" bribery. Specifically, the Travel Act prohibits travel in interstate or foreign commerce or using the mail or any facility in interstate or foreign commerce with the intent to (1) distribute the proceeds of any unlawful activity, or (2) promote, manage, establish, or carry on any unlawful activity. "Unlawful activity," in turn, is defined to include violations of state commercial bribery laws, and "facility of interstate or foreign commerce" is defined to encompass all means of transportation and communication.

Bribery between private commercial enterprises (no matter where in the world it takes place), therefore, falls squarely within the Travel Act's proscriptions, provided the minimal jurisdictional prerequisites are met (a low bar, given that all travel or interstate or foreign communications qualify).

As the DOJ and SEC pointed out in their FCPA guidance, when a company officer, employee, or even third party pays kickbacks to an employee of another company, such private-to-private bribery threatens to invoke the specter of up to a five-year term of imprisonment and a $250,000 fine per violation.

The classic paradigm is an illegal quid pro quo: a company representative pays a bribe overseas to a foreign official in exchange for that official awarding the company a lucrative contract or granting a critical license. Often, the bribe is negotiated by a non-U.S. third-party agent working abroad, with the improper payment occurring on foreign soil. Despite the non-domestic nature of the crime, the Travel Act's *de facto* extraterritorial reach captures and prohibits precisely this type of conduct, so long as it is committed by persons, issuers, companies, or other entities that have a nexus to the United States.[3]

Of course, the kind of bribery the FCPA proscribes typically is also illegal under the local laws of the foreign country where the bribe is offered, paid, or received. In this regard, a person or company that violates the FCPA—and, particularly, that admits to such violations in the public record—risks successive prosecution *both* by the United States and another sovereign for that conduct.

1.5 RECORDKEEPING AND INTERNAL CONTROLS PROVISIONS

In addition to the anti-bribery provisions, the FCPA contains two accounting provisions: (1) the books-and-records provision, and (2) the internal controls provision. The FCPA recordkeeping and internal accounting controls provisions apply only to issuers—companies that issue stock to be traded on U.S. stock exchanges, regardless of whether the companies operate inside or outside the United States.

1.5.1 Maintain Detailed Books and Records

The books-and-records provisions require issuers to "make and keep books, records, and accounts, which, in reasonable detail, accurately and fairly reflect the transactions and dispositions of the assets of the issuer."[4] This obligation is quite extensive because "records" is defined broadly to include "accounts, correspondence, memorandums, tapes, discs, papers, books, and other documents or transcribed information of any type."

1.5.2 Create a Reasonable System of Internal Controls

The second major requirement of a public company is to create a system of internal accounting controls that provide "reasonable assurances" that transactions are (properly) authorized. The internal control provisions mandate that companies comply with several procedural requirements.

These provisions require issuers to:

[D]evise and maintain a system of internal accounting controls sufficient to provide reasonable assurances that (i) transactions are executed in accordance with

---

[3] Note, however, that the Travel Act is often charged in addition to the FCPA—in other words, these days it not infrequently performs a belt-and-suspenders function.

[4] 15 U.S.C. § 78m(b)(2)(A) (2018).

management's general or specific authorization; (ii) transactions are recorded as necessary (I) to permit preparation of financial statements in conformity with generally accepted accounting principles or any other criteria applicable to such statements, and (II) to maintain accountability for assets; (iii) access to assets is permitted only in accordance with management's general or specific authorization; and (iv) the recorded accountability for assets is compared with the existing assets at reasonable intervals and appropriate action is taken with respect to any differences.

The government considers these factors holistically. The test for compliance with the internal controls provisions is "whether a system, taken as a whole, reasonably meets the statute's specified objectives." Any violation of either the recordkeeping or the internal controls provisions will give rise to civil liability, unless it is an inadvertent mistake. For a company to be held criminally liable, it must violate these provisions knowingly.[5]

---

[5] 15 U.S.C. § 78m(b)(2) (2018). For a decision tree illustrating the flow, logic, and big picture considerations at play in a "typical" FCPA anti-bribery case, see T. Markus Funk & M. Bridget Minder, *The FCPA in 2011 and Beyond: Is Targeted FCPA Reform Really the "Wrong Thing at the Wrong Time"?*, 6 BLOOMBERG L. REPORTS—CORPORATE AND M&A L. 1, 12 (Dec. 29, 2011).

2   Australia

1. Introduction to Australia's Anti-Corruption Legislation

1.1 THE LEGAL LANDSCAPE

Australia's[1] legal landscape is divided by Commonwealth laws and by state (and territory) laws.[2] Under the *Constitution of Australia Act 1901* (Cth), the states have reserve or residual powers, while the Commonwealth has specific limited powers set out under section 51 of the Constitution. Section 51 empowers the Commonwealth Parliament, subject to the Constitution, *to make laws for the peace, order and good government* of the Commonwealth with respect to identified topics (or heads of power). In all other respects, lawmaking vests in the states save where there is a conflict and Commonwealth laws prevail over state laws.[3] Australia's anti-corruption laws are a mix of Commonwealth and state criminal laws.

The trend in interpreting the Constitution by the High Court of Australia over the last 20 years has generally been to *increase* the scope of the subject matter that is covered under section 51 of the Constitution and thereby granting the Commonwealth government increasing powers and authorities to govern for the whole of Australia.[4] Currently, the construction of

---

[1] This chapter was contributed by Johnson Winter & Slattery's Robert Wyld.

[2] The law is stated as of December 1, 2018.

[3] Section 109, Constitution of Australia Act 1901 (Cth).

[4] The Court has generally not supported the notion of a single all-embracing theory of constitutional interpretation, but rather looking to the words of the head of power and considering the extrinsic evidence concerning that power and what the natural and ordinary meaning of the statutory words covey to the reader (*see The Commonwealth v Australian Capital Territory* [2013] HCA 55 at [14]).

From Baksheesh to Bribery. T. Markus Funk and Andrew S. Boutros.
© Oxford University Press 2019. Published 2019 by Oxford University Press.

a Commonwealth or state statute, based upon a view that promotes the purpose or object of an Act, is to be preferred to a construction that does not.[5]

Criminal and civil laws have traditionally been governed by state laws. However, since the late 1990s, state governments have voluntarily transferred or agreed to Commonwealth legislative powers in relation to a wide range of topics including, relevant to bribery and corruption, the regulation and oversight of companies, and taxation and revenue laws.

1.2 THE POLITICAL LANDSCAPE

All political parties have, in general, adopted policies and laws consistent with attacking and targeting bribery and corruption at all levels in society, under domestic law and overseas (extraterritorially) in relation to any dealings with foreign governments or foreign public officials.

While there seems to be political unity in targeting bribery and corruption, in practice there has been a tendency to limit and/or reduce resources available to the criminal and civil investigators and regulators charged with responding to bribery and corruption. This lack of support for anti-corruption enforcement (as opposed to proscriptions), in turn, makes the practical, proactive enforcement of Australia's foreign bribery and anti-corruption laws that much more time-consuming and challenging.

There is, in short, an apparent contradiction between, on the one hand, the stated public government attitudes toward fighting corruption and acceptance of various international conventions and Australia's leading role in the Asia Pacific region over the last 10 to 15 years, and, on the other, what appears to be a reluctance to proactively fund a dedicated agency and to proactively aggressively enforce Australia's anti-bribery and anti-corruption laws. However, various initiatives during 2017 and 2018, including substantial proposed reforms to Australia's foreign bribery and whistle-blower protection laws (in the private sector) and a proposed deferred prosecution agreement scheme for certain Commonwealth offenses give hope for a more robust government push against corporate misconduct.

1.3 THE BUSINESS LANDSCAPE

Business interest in proactively addressing bribery and corruption risks both domestically and outside Australia have waxed and waned over the years. When significant corruption matters are in the Australian media, there is an increasing awareness of, and questioning concerning, corporate practices, corporate policies, and the offshore business risks that a company may face in conducting risky yet profitable business outside Australia. In the absence of continuous, successful enforcement efforts or company-specific issues, Australian

---

[5] Section 15AA(1) of the *Acts Interpretation Act 1901* (Cth) states that "a construction that would promote the purpose or object underlying the Act (whether that purpose or object is expressly stated in the Act or not) shall be preferred to a construction that would not promote that purpose or object." See also a paper by Justice Crennan of the High Court, speaking extra judicially—Statutes and The Contemporary Search for Meaning, February 2010, *available at* www.highcourt.gov.au.

businesses have, in the main, allocated resources away from adopting U.S.-style prophylactic anti-corruption compliance procedures and training.

That said, given the increasingly global nature of the marketplace, and the increasing exposure of Australian companies to jurisdictions where there are more aggressive regulators (particularly the United States, Germany, the UK, and some Asian countries, including Singapore, South Korea, and China), industry-leading transnational companies are increasingly addressing anti-bribery and anti-corruption laws as a sustainable issue, realizing that sustainable and long-term growth (not to mention the avoidance of business-crippling governmental intervention and potential imprisonment of employees and managers) depends upon an ethical basis of behavior that can very quickly unravel if companies and the management of companies engage in bribery and corruption.

2. Australia's Domestic Anti-Corruption Framework

2.1 AUSTRALIA'S LEGAL SYSTEM

Australia is a federation, created in 1901 when the preexisting UK colonies joined together and pursuant to the Constitution and ancillary UK legislation, created the Commonwealth of Australia.

The High Court of Australia is the ultimate court in the judicial system. Appeals to the Judicial Committee of the Privy Council were abolished in 1986.[6] The High Court has certain unlimited jurisdiction pursuant to the Constitution and other Commonwealth laws. Otherwise, it operates as the final appeal court from all state and federal courts. Applications to the High Court are by special leave (discretionary), determined by the Court where it is satisfied there is sufficient doubt arising from the lower judgments appealed from or there is sufficient public importance in the legal issues (affecting the Commonwealth or settling differences in legal views as between state appellate courts).

The Federal Court of Australia (and the Full Court of the Federal Court) exercises jurisdiction over Commonwealth laws. State Supreme Courts sit at the apex of the state judicial systems. Each state has two or three levels of courts, described as local, district (or county), and supreme courts. Each state supreme court has a court of appeal (for civil and/or criminal matters).

2.2 CRIMINAL LAW REGIME

Australia's criminal law is divided into two parts:

- Commonwealth criminal law codified in the *Criminal Code Act 1995* (Cth) ("the Criminal Code"), supported by the *Crimes Act* 1901 (Cth); and
- State criminal law, usually codified in legislation depending upon the state.[7]

---

[6] The Australia Acts 1986 (Cth).

[7] Criminal Code 2002 (ACT); Crimes Act 1900 (ACT); Crimes Act 1900 (NSW); Criminal Code Act (NT); Criminal Code Act 1899 (Qld); Criminal Law Consolidation Act 1935 (SA); Criminal Code Act 1924 (Tas); Crimes Act 1958 (Vic); and Criminal Code Act Compilation Act 1913 (WA).

Any criminal prosecution is usually commenced in a state court having the closest connection with the underlying offending conduct. The state court would either apply state criminal law for state-based criminal offenses or the Criminal Code for Commonwealth-based criminal offenses.

Each state has criminal procedure legislation, which over the recent years has streamlined and modified the criminal justice procedure systems for prosecutions. As a result, there is a much greater degree of judicial control and oversight over the criminal procedure process, and regular directions are made by courts to ensure that criminal prosecutions proceed efficiently and fairly for both the prosecutor and the accused.[8]

2.3 CIVIL LAW REGIME

Australia's civil law is a mixture of inherited English common law principles, modern civil law created through judgments of the appellate state courts of Australia and the High Court of Australia and statute, both state and Commonwealth legislation. English common law is now less applicable in Australia due to the influence of European law on English law through the European courts.

To the extent that conduct involving potential bribery and corruption may occur, and to the extent there are any civil consequences that flow from that conduct (for example, breach of statutory director and officer duties under the *Corporations Act*) such proceedings are usually commenced in the state courts.

2.4 VIEW FROM THE OUTSIDE

2.4.1 OECD Evaluation

As a signatory to the OECD *Convention on Combating Bribery of Foreign Public Officials in International Business Transactions* (OECD Convention), the OECD has subjected Australia to four Reviews. The substantive Reviews are as follows:

- Stage 1 (December 1999)—Australia; Review of implementation of the Convention and 1997 recommendation.
- Stage 2 (January 2006)—Phase 2—Report on the application of the Convention on Combating Bribery of Foreign Public Officials in International Business Transactions and 1997 Recommendation on Combating Bribery in International Business Transactions.
- Stage 3 (October 2012)—Phase 3—Report on Implementing the OECD Anti-Bribery Convention in Australia.
- Stage 4 (December 2017)—Phase 4—Report on Implementing the OECD Convention with a focus on enforcement.

---

[8] *See, e.g., Criminal Procedure Act 2009* (Vic); *Criminal Procedure Act 1986* (NSW) which for example has a more streamlined, administrative committal process, *Criminal Procedure Act 2004* (WA), and regard should be had to Supreme Court procedure rules for each state Supreme Court.

The Phase 3 Review was very critical of Australia. Between 2012 and 2015, Australia took on the extensive OECD criticisms of the country's foreign bribery record.

In June 2015, the OECD published a Follow-up Review on Australia's response to the Phase 3 Review. Australia, for its part, responded to that Follow-up Review outlining the significant developments that had occurred between 2012 and 2015.

In June 2015, the Serious Financial Crime Taskforce commenced work. While the primary agency tracking the flow of money into and out of Australia is the Australian Transaction Reports and Analysis Centre (Austrac), the Taskforce coordinates any investigations. Austrac is Australia's financial intelligence agency with regulatory responsibility for anti-money-laundering and counterterrorism financing.[9] The Taskforce has drawn on the significant resources and experience from the Australian Taxation Office (ATO) and its work on "Project Wickenby" (targeting Australian-domiciled companies and individuals involved in tax fraud and money laundering), providing an additional layer of sophisticated analysis and the tracking of the illicit financial flows that invariably derive from bribery and corruption.

The OECD Phase 4 Report was published on December 19, 2017. It recognized the substantial steps taken by the Australian government to improve its framework for detecting and investigating foreign bribery (with 19 ongoing investigations and 13 referrals under evaluation), that enforcement had increased markedly since the 2012 Phase 3 Report and a number of legislative and institutional reforms have or are designed to strengthen the focus on targeting foreign bribery. The OECD noted the significant risks of money laundering occurring in Australia's real estate sector due to the inflow of corrupt funds and the apparent lack of focus in the area.[10] Further steps were identified to focus on enforcement, addressing money laundering risks in the real estate sector and resourcing and educating companies to internally address foreign bribery risks.

2.4.2 Transparent International Corruption Perception Index Score

Transparency International (TI) and its local affiliate (TI Australia) has been a constant constructive critic of the Australian government, encouraging it to tackle foreign bribery and corruption in a proactive, robust manner.

The well-publicized TI Corruption Perceptions Index has ranked Australia as follows over the last six years: No. 8 in 2011, No. 7 in 2012, No. 9 in 2013, No. 11 in 2014, and No 13 in 2015, 2017 and 2018. The drop in rankings from 7 to 13 over seven years, a significant drop in itself, is as much explained by the mixed enforcement record in Australia as it is by the Australian

---

[9] Austrac's policies on education, enforcement, exemptions, monitoring, and reporting indicate at a high level its approach when assisting the Austrac CEO to fulfill his functions as outlined in section 212 of the *Anti-Money Laundering and Counter-Terrorism Financing Act 2006* (Cth).

[10] The OECD referred to the views of Prof. J. Sharman, of Griffith University, currently the Patrick Sheehy Professor of International Relations at Cambridge University, that Australia's failure to counter the flow of corrupt funds was more due to a lack of willingness to take action rather than a lack of capacity, given Australia's powerful anti-money laundering laws; see page 19 of the OECD Report.

government's perceived eagerness to enact laws, while doing little thereafter to actually adequately fund investigations and prosecutions to *enforce* those laws.[11]

3. Investigative and Prosecutorial Agencies
3.1 CRIMINAL LAW AGENCIES

Australia's primary criminal law enforcement agency for foreign bribery is the Australian Federal Police (AFP). The AFP is responsible for investigating allegations of foreign bribery under the Criminal Code.

In April 2012, the AFP established an internal Foreign Bribery Panel of Experts. The panel is made up of senior investigators who have been responsible for and have experience in at least one significant foreign bribery investigation and have otherwise been involved in large and complex matters that span international jurisdictions.

In February 2013, the AFP established dedicated fraud and anti-corruption teams located across Australia in the principal cities of Brisbane, Canberra, Melbourne, Sydney, and Adelaide. In September 2016, additional funding was allocated to the AFP in Perth, Melbourne, and Sydney to target foreign bribery work.

In July 2014, in answer to ongoing OECD criticism, the Australian government established the National Fraud and Anti-Corruption Center, hosted by the AFP. There is a large number of participating Australian government agencies involved in the Center[12].

The primary role of the National Fraud and Anti-Corruption Center is to strengthen the overall capability of the Australian government and criminal law enforcement agencies to respond to serious and complex fraud, foreign bribery and corruption. In addition, it provides a coordinated approach to investigation and prosecution. There is now a much more focused approach in terms of a uniform multiagency analysis of foreign bribery matters, training, the exchange of intelligence and agency secondment, and joint activities involving the agencies participating in the Center.

The Australian Criminal Intelligence Commission (formerly the Australian Crime Commission) (ACC) is a statutory body given significant inquisitorial powers for the purposes of investigating systemic and organized crime.[13] It is empowered to conduct secret enquiries and investigations, either individually or working in tandem with the AFP and/or other agencies, and it has the ability to compel those individuals who are summoned before it to produce documents, and to answer questions notwithstanding any common law privilege against self-incrimination.[14] That said, the ACC cannot compel a lawyer to produce a

---

[11] The TI *Exporting Corruption 2015* Report ranked Australia as one of six countries with moderate foreign bribery enforcement (2 prosecutions in 15 years but a much more focused process with the regulatory, investigative, and prosecutorial agencies to target foreign bribery).

[12] The agencies are the ATO, the ACC, the Australian Securities & Investments Commission (ASIC), and the Australian Transaction Report and Analysis Center (Austrac), Department of Human Services, Australian Border Force, Department of Immigration & Border Protection, Department of Foreign Affairs & Trade (DFAT,) and the Department of Defense.

[13] Australian Crime Commission Act 2002 (Cth).

[14] Section 30, ACC Act overrides the privilege against self-incrimination. Section 30(5) provides that where before giving an answer or producing a document, a person claims that by so doing he or she might be incriminated or liable to a penalty, that answer or document cannot be used against that person in any criminal proceeding,

privileged communication absent the agreement of the holder of the privilege.[15] There are substantial penalties that can be imposed on individuals or companies (1) failing to answer ACC summonses, or (2) disclosing the ACC's confidential activities, even the attendance before that body for the purposes of a secret examination.[16] While the ACC's extensive (and compulsive) investigation powers are noted, they must be exercised for a lawful purpose (proscribed by the ACC Act) and in a manner that respects an accused's rights to a fair trial.[17]

The principal prosecuting agency for criminal offenses, including foreign bribery, is the Office of the Commonwealth Director of Public Prosecutions (CDPP) under the *Director of Public Prosecutions Act 1983* (Cth) (DPP Act).[18] The role of the CDPP is to act as the independent Commonwealth prosecutor while the AFP investigates offenses.

The CDPP has published the Prosecution Policy of the Commonwealth (Prosecution Policy).[19] In general, the decision whether to prosecute will depend upon whether the evidence is sufficient to justify the institution or continuation of a prosecution. A prosecution will not proceed if, in the view of the CDPP, there is no reasonable prospect of a conviction being secured. The Prosecution Policy sets out the non-exhaustive factors for a prosecutor in determining how to conduct a prosecution. Annexure A to the Prosecution Policy applies to foreign bribery prosecutions. A prosecutor must not be influenced by considerations of national economic interest, the potential effect upon relations with another state, or the identity of the person involved in determining whether to prosecute (consistent with the terms of the OECD Convention[20]).

3.2 CIVIL LAW AGENCIES

To the extent that any civil issues arise from conduct that involve foreign bribery and may involve the activities of a company, directors or officers of a company, ASIC (Australian Securities and

---

any civil proceeding to impose a penalty, or any confiscation proceeding. See the recent judgment of the High Court in *R v Independent Broad-based Anti-corruption Commissioner* [2016] HCA 8 at [73] to [74] per Gageler J, which considered the privilege against self-incrimination under the *Independent Broad-based Anti-corruption Commission Act 2011* (Vic).

[15] Section 21D, ACC Act.

[16] Section 29B, ACC Act.

[17] Sections 29A(9) and 29A(9A) of the ACC Act make it clear that directions *must* be given by the ACC examiner to exclude or prohibit disclosure of ACC examination transcripts or evidence to investigators (the AFP) of the prosecutor (the CDPP) where to do so may prejudice a fair trial (given the accused's right to silence) if the accused has been charged or a charge is imminent. The High Court of Australia has made this clear in *Lee v The Queen* (2014) 253 CLR 455; [2013] HCA 26 at [39] to [51] per French CJ and Crennan J on the right to silence and its relationship to the statutory powers of examination in the ACC Act, in *X7 v Australian Crime Commission* (2013) 248 CLR 92 and in *X7 v The Queen* (2014) 246 A Crim R 402. These principles have been applied in state appellate courts (see *R v Seller; R v McCarthy* (2013) 232 A Crim R 249); the most recent analysis of these principles is in *Strickland (A Pseudonym) & Ors v CDPP* [2018] HCA 35 where the High Court of Australia permanently stayed four of the Securency prosecutions on the basis of egregious, illegal conduct by the investigative agencies (the ACIC and the AFP) which were incurable and materially prejudiced the defendants' rights to a fair trial.

[18] Director of Public Prosecutions Act 1983 (Cth).

[19] At www.cdpp.gov.au.

[20] Article 5, OECD Convention.

Investments Commission) is the regulator charged with overseeing the obligations of companies and directors and officers pursuant to the *Corporations Act* 2001 (Cth).

3.3 MULTIAGENCY ARRANGEMENTS

In 2011, the AFP became a member of the International Foreign Bribery Taskforce (IFBT), which was established by investigators from the AFP, the United States Federal Bureau of Investigation, the City of London Police, and the Royal Canadian Mounted Police[21].

In May 2013, the informal arrangements for cooperation was made official through the signing of a Memorandum of Understanding between the relevant IFBT agencies, enhancing their anti-corruption initiatives, cooperation, and work. The chair of the IFBT rotates between agencies each year. Australia held the chair position in 2012–2013, and will again hold the chair position in 2016–2017.

In October 2013, the AFP and ASIC entered into a Memorandum of Understanding to formalize their responsibilities and obligations in relation to investigating foreign bribery allegations. The AFP has the primary responsibility for investigating foreign bribery offenses under the Criminal Code while ASIC is responsible for investigating potential breaches of the Corporations Act. The Memorandum provides that investigations of foreign bribery offenses will be given priority over the investigation of Corporations Act offenses given the more specific alleged criminal conduct and the significant penalties that apply under the Criminal Code. Both the AFP and ASIC are agency participants in the National Fraud and Anti-Corruption Center hosted by the AFP and work closely with each other and with other agencies in evaluating all foreign bribery referrals and any investigations.

In June 2014, the AFP entered into an information sharing protocol with the Department of Foreign Affairs and Trade (DFAT). The purpose of the protocol is to support a collaborative approach between the agencies and to ensure that all information that might exist between them is properly shared and considered. In addition, all DFAT officers both in Australia and those posted overseas in Australian embassies or consulates are under an obligation to report to the AFP all allegations of foreign bribery committed by Australians and Australian companies.

The AFP has protocols in place with all state and territory authorities and police agencies to ensure that any potential offenses of foreign bribery are promptly referred to the AFP.

4. Bribery of Foreign Officials

4.1 JURISDICTION

As a general/default rule and absent specific statutory authority, Australian laws are confined to Australia and do not operate with any extraterritorial effect.[22] Unless conduct involves

---

[21] Media Release, AFP dated June 12, 2013.

[22] An example is the extraterritorial reach of Australia's anti-cartel laws, by reason of those laws applying to conduct outside Australia engaged in by Australian companies, citizens, or persons ordinarily resident in Australia; *see* section 5(1) *Competition and Consumer Act 2010* (Cth) and *Bray v F Hoffman-La Roche Ltd* [2002] FCA 243; (2002) FCR 1.

an Australian person (a company, a citizen, or a resident), with some connection or events partly occurring in Australia, then there is no basis to bring a prosecution.[23] A prosecution will depend upon conduct occurring wholly or partly in Australia by an Australian corporation, citizen, or resident.

Section 70.5 of the Criminal Code sets out the extraterritorial effect for the foreign bribery offense under Section 70.2 of the Criminal Code. There are two scenarios where the question of jurisdiction must be considered.

(a) *Conduct wholly or partly in Australia*—a person does not commit an offense (the foreign bribery offense under section 70.2 of the Criminal Code) unless the conduct constituting the alleged offense occurs either wholly or partly in Australia or wholly or partly on-board an Australian aircraft or an Australian ship.

(b) *Conduct wholly outside Australia*—a person does not commit an offense unless at the time of the alleged offense, the person is an Australian citizen, or a resident of Australia, or is a body corporate incorporated by or under a law of the Commonwealth or of an Australian state or an Australian territory.

If the conduct occurs (1) wholly outside Australia, and (2) at the time of the alleged offense, the person alleged to have committed the offense is a resident of Australia but not an Australian citizen, any prosecution requires written consent of the Australian attorney general.[24]

4.2 STATUTE OF LIMITATIONS

Prosecution for offenses under Commonwealth laws generally may be commenced as follows:

(a) for an individual:
   (i) no time limit where the maximum term of imprisonment for a first offense exceeds 6 months;
   (ii) within one year if the maximum term of imprisonment is 6 months or less; and
   (iii) within one year where the punishment is a pecuniary penalty with no imprisonment;
(b) for a corporation:
   (i) no time limit where the maximum penalty is or includes a fine of more than 150 penalty units[25] in the case of a first conviction; or
   (ii) within one year in any other case.

---

[23] See Sections 14 and 15 of the Criminal Code.

[24] Section 70.5(2) of the Criminal Code.

[25] A penalty unit is the measure used under Australian legislation to calculate a statutory fine; *see* section 4AA, Crimes Act 1914 (Cth).

These laws reflect the legal maxim *nullum tempus occurrit regi* or "time does not run against the Crown." There is no time limit for the bringing of a prosecution for the foreign bribery offense under section 70.2 of the Criminal Code or any other serious offense that may arise from the same or similar conduct as the maximum penalty in the case of an individual or a company is a substantial fine and up to 10 years imprisonment for a first offense. The Prosecution Policy includes, as a discretionary factor to be taken into account in determining whether the public interest requires a prosecution, the following (1) the passage of time since the alleged offense, considered in tandem with (2) the circumstances of the alleged offense, and (3) the timing of when the offense was discovered.

In any event, there is always a discretionary factor for the AFP and the CDPP (and ultimately the court) to evaluate if any evidence they have, or which is presented to a court, due to the passage of time, is or is not sufficiently reliable so as to question whether there is a reasonable prospect of securing a conviction.

4.3 FOREIGN BRIBERY OFFENSES

In 1999, the Criminal Code was amended to include the offense of bribing a *foreign* public official. This was Australia's response to ratifying the OECD Convention.

Section 70.2 of the Criminal Code contains the foreign bribery offense. For this offense, as with all Commonwealth offenses, the Criminal Code prescribes certain physical and fault elements of an offense, each of which must be satisfied.[26]

70.2 Bribing a foreign public official

(1) A person is guilty of an offence if:
  (a) the person:
    (i) provides a benefit to another person; or
    (ii) causes a benefit to be provided to another person; or
    (iii) offers to provide, or promises to provide, a benefit to another person; or
    (iv) causes an offer of the provision of a benefit, or a promise of the provision of a benefit, to be made to another person; and
  (b) the benefit is not legitimately due to the other person; and
  (c) the first-mentioned person does so with the intention of influencing a foreign public official (who may be the other person) in the exercise of the official's duties as a foreign public official in order to:
    (i) obtain or retain business; or
    (ii) obtain or retain a business advantage that is not legitimately due to the recipient, or intended recipient, of the business advantage (who may be the first-mentioned person).
Note: For defences see sections 70.3 and 70.4.
(1A) For the purposes of paragraph (1)(c):
  (a) the first-mentioned person does not need to intend to influence a particular foreign public official; and

---

[26] Section 3.2 generally, section 4 for physical elements, and section 5 for fault elements, Criminal Code.

(b) business, or a business advantage, does not need to be actually obtained or retained.

The terms used in the foreign bribery offense are broad.

- **Defining "Intent."** A person intends something when he or she means it or has it in mind. What is involved is the directing of the mind, having a purpose or design.[27] If intention is not proved by admission, its existence is a matter of inference from what a person actually did.[28]
- **Defining "Benefit."** The nature of the *"benefit"* that might be involved in a transaction *"includes any advantage and is not limited to property."* This is a broad definition, having the potential of encompassing any type of financial or non-financial benefit involving any amount of money/benefit.[29]
- **Defining "Legitimately Due."** What is or is not something that is *"not legitimately due"* is likely to give rise to difficulties in construction. For one, there is no definition of this phrase. Prosecutors will need to determine what is or is not "legitimate" in a foreign jurisdiction, or in turn disprove assertions made by a defendant that the conduct was "legitimate" in that jurisdiction.
- **What/Who is a "Foreign Official?"** The definition of a *"foreign public official"* is considered below.
- **Defining "Business Advantage."** What is or is not a *"business advantage"* imposes a qualification that does not appear in the US Foreign Corrupt Practices Act (**FCPA**). The Criminal Code predicates the business advantage as being something that is *"not legitimately due"* to the recipient or intended recipient. This again complicates a prosecution.[30] In contrast, the FCPA uses the phrases "payment of any money" or the "giving of anything of value" which more closely

---

[27] *Zaburoni v The Queen* [2016] HCA 12 at [6] to [9] per Kiefel, Bell & Keane JJ.

[28] In *Bahri v The Queen* [1987] HCA 16 at [2]; (1987) 162 CLR 502, the High Court of Australia noted that depending upon the nature of the particular offense the requirement of a guilty mind may involve intention, foresight, knowledge, or awareness with respect to some act, circumstance, or consequence. Where the offense charged is the commission of a proscribed act, a guilty mind exists when an intention on the part of the accused to do the proscribed act is shown. The problem then is one of proof. How does one prove the existence of the requisite intention? Sometimes there is direct evidence in the form of an admission by the accused that he intended his conduct to involve the forbidden act. More often, the existence of the requisite intention is a matter of inference from what the accused has actually done. The intention may be inferred from the doing of the proscribed act and the circumstances in which it was done; see also the High Court in *Smith v The Queen; The Queen v Afford* [2017] HCA 19 at [7] to [13].

[29] While the term "benefit" is defined in the Criminal Code, its scope has rarely been judicially considered. However, both *Moyland v State of Western Australia* [2007] WACA 52 and *R v Saba* [2013] QCA 275 considered the term included the concept of "advantage," while in *The Commissioner of the Australian Federal Police v Fysh* [2013] NSWSC 81, the Court approved *R v Pederson* [1995] NZLR 386 where the New Zealand Court of Appeal held "in its ordinary usage, 'benefits' is a wide expression."

[30] Adopting ordinary principles of statutory construction, when we look at the context and purpose of the statute, we see the phrase "not legitimately due" is likely to mean that the recipient of the benefit is not entitled to receive it, by contract or statute or any other form of legal entitlement.

connects the offending intention with the giving or offering of something of value which induces the public official to act improperly (or in breach of his or her duty).

4.4 PROPOSED NEW OFFENSE OF BRIBING A FOREIGN PUBLIC OFFICIAL

In the *Crimes Legislation Amendment (Combatting Corporate Crime) Bill 2017* (Cth) published on December 7, 2017,[31] the Australian government proposed amending the foreign bribery offense in section 70.2 of the Criminal Code (as described previously) by creating a new offense and changing some of the key concepts that have proved difficult for investigators and prosecutors to satisfy. The new proposed offense is set out below.

70.2 Bribing a foreign public official

(1) A person commits an offence if:
   (a) the person:
      (i) provides a benefit to another person; or
      (ii) causes a benefit to be provided to another person; or
      (iii) offers to provide, or promises to provide, a benefit to another person; or
      (iv) causes an offer of the provision of a benefit, or a promise of the provision of a benefit, to be made to another person; and
   (b) the first-mentioned person does so with the intention of improperly influencing a foreign public official (who may be the other person) in order to obtain or retain business or an advantage (whether or not for the first-mentioned person).

Note: See also section 70.2A. For defences see sections 70.3 and 70.4.

(2) for the purposes of paragraph (1)(b):
   (a) the first-mentioned person does not need to intend to influence a particular foreign public official; and
   (b) the first-mentioned person does not need to intend to obtain or retain particular business or a particular advantage; and
   (c) business, or an advantage, does not need to be actually obtained or retained.

The proposed amendments have made some key changes—by removing the concept of a benefit being "*not legitimately due*" and by introducing the concept that there must be the intention to "*improperly influence*" the foreign public official in the exercise of the official's duties. Whether there is or is not improper influence is a question of fact. The Bill outlines a number of factors the trier of fact may have regard to in determining whether influence is improper.[32] During the consultation phase after these reforms were announced, a number of

---

[31] The Bill was supported by the Senate Legal and Constitutional Affairs Legislation Committee in its report to the Australian Parliament on March 28, , 2018.]

[32] See proposed section 70.2A of the Criminal Code

submissions did not support the use of the term "improperly influence" as a term that is not defined or known to Australia's criminal law. Rather, the submissions favored the use of the term "*dishonesty*" as well established under Australian criminal law.[33] It remains to be seen how the courts will interpret these provisions.

The penalty for the proposed new offense remains as outlined below in Section 4.9.

4.5 PROPOSED NEW CORPORATE OFFENSE OF FAILING TO PREVENT BRIBERY

In the *Crimes Legislation Amendment (Combatting Corporate Crime) Bill 2017* (Cth) (referred to previously), the Australian government proposed a new corporate offense of failing to prevent bribery (modeled on the UK section 7 offense in the Bribery Act 2010). The offense, expressed slightly differently to the UK offense, has the following key elements:

- if an <u>associate</u> commits an offence under section 70.2 (the proposed intentional bribery of a foreign public official); or
- engages in conduct outside Australia that would constitute an offence under sections 70.2; and
- the associate does so for the profit or gain of the company.
- an "associate" means;[34]
  - o an employee, agent or contractor of the company;
  - o a subsidiary of the company within the meaning of the Corporations Act;
  - o an entity controlled by the company within the meaning of the Corporations Act; or
  - o otherwise performs services for or on behalf of the company;
- the deemed criminal liability will not apply <u>if the company proves</u> that it had in place <u>adequate procedures</u> designed to prevent such conduct; and
- the penalties are the same as for the primary offense under section 70.2 of the Criminal Code (see above).

---

[33] See the test for "dishonest" adopted in section 130.3 of the Criminal Code, which encompasses both a subjective and an objective test for offenses under chapter 7 and similar definitions in chapters 4 and 10 of the Criminal Code, which reflected the old English test set out in *R v Ghosh* [1982] QB 1053 at 1064 per Lane LJ. It should be noted that for other offenders, the common law test set out in *Peters v The Queen* (1998) 192 CLR 431 and *Macleod v The Queen* (2003) 214 CLR 230 will apply, setting out an objective test only (see *SAJ v The Queen* (2012) 225 A Crim R 528; [2012] VSCA 243 applying an objective test to dishonesty under section 184(2) of the Corporations Act where a directly acts dishonestly in the discharge of her duties, and *Vella v R; Siskos v R* [2015] NSWCCA 148 at [24] to [25] per Gleeson JA).

[34] The definition of "associate" is very broad, and while broad enough to capture incorporated subsidiaries, contractors, and agents, it may have overlooked conduct by individuals or unincorporated associations (unless they fall within the catch-all phrase as "otherwise performs services for or on behalf of the company").

The amending legislation requires the Minister of Justice to publish guidance of what is expected of companies in order to demonstrate that they have in place the necessary adequate procedures.[35]

4.6 DEFINITION OF "FOREIGN PUBLIC OFFICIAL" AND OTHER FOREIGN ENTITIES

The Criminal Code, in section 70.1 defines *"foreign public official,"* a *"foreign government body,"* a *"foreign public enterprise,"* and a *"public international organisation."* There has been no judicial consideration of these phrases by any Australian court.

foreign public official means:
(a) an employee or official of a foreign government body; or
(b) an individual who performs work for a foreign government body under a contract; or
(c) an individual who holds or performs the duties of an appointment, office or position under a law of a foreign country or of part of a foreign country; or
(d) an individual who holds or performs the duties of an appointment, office or position created by custom or convention of a foreign country or of part of a foreign country; or
(e) an individual who is otherwise in the service of a foreign government body (including service as a member of a military force or police force); or
(f) a member of the executive, judiciary or magistracy of a foreign country or of part of a foreign country; or
(g) an employee of a public international organisation; or
(h) an individual who performs work for a public international organisation under a contract; or
(i) an individual who holds or performs the duties of an office or position in a public international organisation; or
(j) an individual who is otherwise in the service of a public international organisation; or
(k) a member or officer of the legislature of a foreign country or of part of a foreign country; or
(l) an individual who:
   (i) is an authorised intermediary of a foreign public official covered by any of the above paragraphs; or
   (ii) holds himself or herself out to be the authorised intermediary of a foreign public official covered by any of the above paragraphs.

---

[35] No guidance has been published as of December 1, 2018.

foreign government body means:

(a) the government of a foreign country or of part of a foreign country; or

(b) an authority of the government of a foreign country; or

(c) an authority of the government of part of a foreign country; or

(d) a foreign local government body or foreign regional government body; or

(e) a foreign public enterprise.

foreign public enterprise means a company or any other body or association where:

(a) in the case of a company—one of the following applies:

  (i) the government of a foreign country or of part of a foreign country holds more than 50% of the issued share capital of the company;

  (ii) the government of a foreign country or of part of a foreign country holds more than 50% of the voting power in the company;

  (iii) the government of a foreign country or of part of a foreign country is in a position to appoint more than 50% of the company's board of directors;

  (iv) the directors (however described) of the company are accustomed or under an obligation (whether formal or informal) to act in accordance with the directions, instructions or wishes of the government of a foreign country or of part of a foreign country;

  (v) the government of a foreign country or of part of a foreign country is in a position to exercise control over the company; and

(b) in the case of any other body or association—either of the following applies:

  (i) the members of the executive committee (however described) of the body or association are accustomed or under an obligation (whether formal or informal) to act in accordance with the directions, instructions or wishes of the government of a foreign country or of part of a foreign country;

  (ii) the government of a foreign country or of part of a foreign country is in a position to exercise control over the body or association; and

(c) the company, body or association:

  (i) enjoys special legal rights or a special legal status under a law of a foreign country or of part of a foreign country; or

  (ii) enjoys special benefits or privileges under a law of a foreign country or of part of a foreign country;

because of the relationship of the company, body or association with the government of the foreign country or of the part of the foreign country, as the case may be.

public international organisation means:

(a) an organisation:

  (i) of which 2 or more countries, or the governments of 2 or more countries, are members; or

  (ii) that is constituted by persons representing 2 or more countries, or representing the governments of 2 or more countries; or

(b) an organisation established by, or a group of organisations constituted by:

  (i) organisations of which 2 or more countries, or the governments of 2 or more countries, are members; or

(ii) organisations that are constituted by the representatives of 2 or more countries, or the governments of 2 or more countries; or

(c) an organisation that is:

(i) an organ of, or office within, an organisation described in paragraph (a) or (b); or

(ii) a commission, council or other body established by an organisation so described or such an organ; or

(iii) a committee, or subcommittee of a committee, of an organisation described in paragraph (a) or (b), or of such an organ, council or body.

In the United States, the authorities are presently in favor of the proposition that whether an entity is an instrumentality of a government is a question of fact, focusing on the control and functions of the government and the instrumentality.[36] In Australia, it will be a matter of fact for the prosecutor to prove that any relevant person is a *"foreign public official"* (as required by section 70.2 of the Criminal Code). Importantly, the prosecutor need not prove the identity of a particular foreign public official in order to satisfy the primary offense.[37]

4.7 GIFTS, GRATUITIES, AND HOSPITALITY

The Criminal Code is silent on gifts, gratuities, and hospitality. They are not, without more, illegal or improper. There is no official guidance on these matters.

Companies and individuals are certainly entitled to give or receive gifts or gratuities or to offer or partake in commercial hospitality. The giver or receiver of a gift or gratuity or of hospitality (to, from, or involving a foreign public official) ought to, as a matter of practical reality, ensure that what is given or received, or offered, is reasonable and proportionate to the business relationship between the parties. If a gift, gratuity, or hospitality offered to a foreign public official is unreasonable, excessive in value, or otherwise disproportionate to the business relationship between the parties, the Australian authorities (like authorities elsewhere) may view such a transaction with suspicion.

4.8 (LIMITED) DEFENSES

4.8.1 Written Local Law

Under section 70.3 of the Criminal Code, where certain identified conduct (1) occurs outside Australia, and (2) is pursuant to or in accordance with written local law, a person is not guilty of an offense under section 70.2 of the Code.

---

[36] United States v. Esquenazi 752 F.3d 912 (11th Cir. 2014); see *When Does An Entity Amount to an "Instrumentality of a Foreign Government" under the Foreign Corrupt Practices Act? Emerging Judicial Trends*, Prof. Karl Boedecker, University of San Francisco, *available at* http://fcpa.stanford.edu/academic-articles/20151201-when-does-an-entity-amount-to-an-instrumentality-fcpa.pdf.

[37] See section 70.2 (1A) Criminal Code.

4.8.2 Facilitation Payments

Australia, unlike most jurisdictions other than the United States, through section 70.4 of the Criminal Code, permits facilitation payments to the extent that a payment is of a minor nature (in value) to expedite or secure the performance of a routine government action of a minor nature.

70.4 Defence—facilitation payments

(1) A person is not guilty of an offence against section 70.2 if:

    (a) the value of the benefit was of a minor nature; and

    (b) the person's conduct was engaged in for the sole or dominant purpose of expediting or securing the performance of a routine government action of a minor nature; and

    (c) as soon as practicable after the conduct occurred, the person made a record of the conduct that complies with subsection (3); and

    (d) any of the following subparagraphs applies:

        (i) the person has retained that record at all relevant times;

        (ii) that record has been lost or destroyed because of the actions of another person over whom the first-mentioned person had no control, or because of a non-human act or event over which the first-mentioned person had no control, and the first-mentioned person could not reasonably be expected to have guarded against the bringing about of that loss or that destruction;

        (iii) a prosecution for the offence is instituted more than 7 years after the conduct occurred.

Note: A defendant bears an evidential burden in relation to the matter in subsection (1). See subsection 13.3(3).

Routine government action

(2) For the purposes of this section, a ***routine government action*** is an action of a foreign public official that:

    (a) is ordinarily and commonly performed by the official; and

    (b) is covered by any of the following subparagraphs:

        (i) granting a permit, licence or other official document that qualifies a person to do business in a foreign country or in a part of a foreign country;

        (ii) processing government papers such as a visa or work permit;

        (iii) providing police protection or mail collection or delivery;

        (iv) scheduling inspections associated with contract performance or related to the transit of goods;

        (v) providing telecommunications services, power or water;

        (vi) loading and unloading cargo;

        (vii) protecting perishable products, or commodities, from deterioration;

        (viii) any other action of a similar nature; and

(c) does not involve a decision about:
    (i) whether to award new business; or
    (ii) whether to continue existing business with a particular person; or
    (iii) the terms of new business or existing business; and
(d) does not involve encouraging a decision about:
    (i) whether to award new business; or
    (ii) whether to continue existing business with a particular person; or
    (iii) the terms of new business or existing business.

Content of records

(3) A record of particular conduct engaged in by a person complies with this subsection if the record sets out:

(a) the value of the benefit concerned; and
(b) the date on which the conduct occurred; and
(c) the identity of the foreign public official in relation to whom the conduct occurred; and
(d) if that foreign public official is not the other person mentioned in paragraph 70.2(1)(a)—the identity of that other person; and
(e) particulars of the routine government action that was sought to be expedited or secured by the conduct; and
(f) the person's signature or some other means of verifying the person's identity.

What constitutes a "facilitation payment" as opposed to a bribe is a difficult-to-answer question. Section 70.4(2) states that a "routine government action" is an action of a foreign public official that:

(a) is ordinarily and commonly performed by the official; and
(b) is covered by any of the following subparagraphs:
    (i) granting a permit, licence or other official document that qualifies a person to do business in a foreign country or in a part of a foreign country;
    (ii) processing government papers such as a visa or work permit;
    (iii) providing police protection or mail collection or delivery;
    (iv) scheduling inspections associated with contract performance or related to the transit of goods;
    (v) providing telecommunications services, power or water;
    (vi) loading and unloading cargo;
    (vii) protecting perishable products, or commodities, from deterioration;
    (viii) any other action of a similar nature; and
(c) does not involve a decision about:
    (i) whether to award new business; or
    (ii) whether to continue existing business with a particular person; or
    (iii) the terms of new business or existing business; and

(d) does not involve encouraging a decision about:
   (i) whether to award new business; or
   (ii) whether to continue existing business with a particular person; or
   (iii) the terms of new business or existing business.

While the statutory language used in section 70.4(2) suggests the identified actions are the only permissible actions of a foreign public official that will amount to a *"routine government action,"* there has been no judicial consideration of these provisions by an Australian court. While section 70.4(2)(b)(viii) refers to *"any other action of a similar nature,"* the permissible action identified in sections 70.4(2)(b)(i) to (vii) are very limited in nature, and are unlikely to permit too wide a discretion in interpreting conduct falling in or out of the defense.

There has been consistent criticism of this defense as promoting the payment of small bribes and of blurring the lines between illegal bribes and permissible facilitation payments. In 2011, the Australian government issued a Consultation Paper asking whether facilitation payments as a defense to a foreign bribery charge should be maintained. In 2018, the Senate Report on Australia's Foreign Bribery Laws was strongly of the view that the facilitation payment defence should be abolished. Nothing has been said further by the government on this topic.

4.8.3 Adequate Procedures

In contrast to the UK, there is presently no formal defense to a charge of foreign bribery that a company had adequate procedures in place to prevent or minimize the risk of bribery occurring.

If the proposed new corporate offense of failing to prevent foreign bribery is enacted, then adequate procedures will be the only defense available to a company and the onus will be on the company to prove that its procedures were adequate. If the new offense is enacted, the government must publish a guidance on what constitutes "adequate procedures" by a company.

4.8.4 Corporate Culture

Corporate culture is one of those concepts that is much spoken about, but which is far harder to pin down when questions of legal liability arise. In 2001, the Criminal Code was amended to create corporate criminal liability and to specifically deal with "culture" as a factor relevant to determining potential liability. However, since then, there have been no Australian prosecutions or judgments to consider these matters.

Sections 12.1 to 12.6 of the Criminal Code set out the basis of corporate criminal liability.

There are certain features of these provisions to note.

- A company may *"expressly, tacitly or impliedly"* authorize or permit the commission of the offense, by

- o proof that the board of directors or a "*high managerial agent*"[38] intentionally, knowingly or recklessly engaged in the relevant conduct, or expressly, tacitly or impliedly authorised or permitted the commission of the offense;[39]
- o proof that a corporate culture[40] existed within the body corporate that directed, encouraged, tolerated or led to non-compliance with the relevant provision;
- o proof that the company failed to create and maintain a corporate culture that required compliance with the relevant provision.

- The statutory defense of mistake of fact (under section 9.2 of the Criminal Code) can only apply if a company can establish that either the individual who carried out the conduct was under a mistaken but reasonable belief as to facts which had they existed, would mean no offense had been committed, or if the company exercised due diligence to prevent the conduct (section 12.5(1)(a) and (b) Criminal Code).
- A failure to exercise due diligence by a company may be evidenced by the fact that the contravening conduct was substantially attributable to:
  - o inadequate corporate management, control or supervision of the conduct of one or more of a company's employees, agents or officers; or
  - o failure to provide adequate systems for conveying relevant information to relevant persons in the company.

4.9 PENALTIES

The penalties for a conviction under section 70.2 of the Criminal Code are, for each offense, as follows:

- **Individual**—imprisonment for not more than 10 years, a fine of not more than 10,000 penalty units[41] (currently AU$2,100,000), or both;

---

[38] A *high managerial agent* means an employee, agent, or officer of the body corporate with duties of such responsibility that his or her conduct may fairly be assumed to represent the body corporate's policy. This definition is broader than the traditional common law "guiding mind" principle, and is likely to more closely reflect the law in *Director of Public Prosecutions Reference No 1 of 1996* (1998) 3 VR 352 where the Court of Appeal accepted the analysis of the Privy Council in *Meridian Global Funds Management Asia Ltd v Securities Commission* [1995] 2 AC 500, to the effect that the relevant question is whose acts or omissions or state of mind are taken to be the acts or omissions or state of mind of the corporation. The Court of Appeal noted, at page 355, that sometimes "*only the board of directors acting as such or a person at or near the top of a corporation's organization will be identified as the corporation itself. On other occasions, someone lower, and perhaps much lower, in the hierarchy, will suffice.*" In *Krakowski v Eurolynx Properties Pty Ltd* (1995) 183 CLR 563; [1995] HCA 68 at [38] the High Court of Australia held that you accumulate the knowledge of all "attributable persons" of the company to ascertain the knowledge of the company.

[39] The liability arising by reason of the conduct of a high managerial agent does not apply if the body corporate proves that it exercised due diligence to prevent the conduct, or the authorization or permission; *see* section 12.3(3) Criminal Code.

[40] "Corporate culture" means an attitude, policy, rule, course of conduct, or practice existing within the body corporate generally or in the part of the body corporate in which the relevant activities takes place; *see* section 12.3(6) Criminal Code.

[41] As of July 1, 2017, one penalty unit is AU$210.00, which amount will apply until June 30, 2020, to be automatically increased by the amount of increase of the Australian Consumer Price Index (see *Crimes Amendment (Penalty Unit) Act 2017* (Cth)). The amount of the penalty is lesser the older the conduct.

- **Company**—a fine not more than the greatest of:
  - o 100,000 penalty units (currently AU$21,000,000);
  - o 3 times the value of the benefit obtained directly or indirectly from the relevant conduct, if the court can determine the value of the benefit; or
  - o if the value of the benefit cannot be determined, an amount of 10% of the annual turnover of the company during the period of 12 months ending at the end of the month which the relevant conduct occurred.

If the proposed new intentional foreign bribery offense is enacted, the scale of penalties will be as set out previously.

There are applicable sentencing principles that a court must apply when sentencing a convicted offender. These are covered in Section 7 of this chapter.

5. Bribery of Domestic Officials

5.1 JURISDICTION

Australia's domestic laws cover bribery of public officials at a Commonwealth (or federal), state, and local government level. Commonwealth laws apply throughout Australia and are focused on conduct toward or involving Commonwealth public officials.[42] Each Australian state has its own laws dealing with the bribing or corrupting of state or local government officials, and their jurisdiction is within each state.[43] This Section will cover Commonwealth laws.

5.2 BRIBERY OFFENSES

The offenses under section 141 of the Criminal Code are similar to the foreign bribery offense under section 70.2 of the Code. The offenses apply to both the *giver* (section 141.1(1)) and the *receiver* (section 141.1(3)) of the bribe.

A person is guilty of an offense under section 141.1(1) if:

1. the person dishonestly:
    - provides a benefit to another person;
    - causes a benefit to be provided to another person;
    - offers to provide, or promises to provide, a benefit to another person;
    - causes an offer or the provision of a benefit, or a promise of the provision of a benefit, to be made to another person; and

---

[42] The offense of bribing a Commonwealth public official is set out in section 141.1(4) of the Criminal Code. Section 142.3 deals with the jurisdiction for other bribery-related offenses and abuse of public office.

[43] In NSW, criminal jurisdiction covers offenses that occurred wholly or partly in the state or if wholly outside the state, had "*an effect in the State*"; *see* section 10C(2) *Crimes Act 1900* (NSW).

2. the person does so with the intention of influencing a Commonwealth public official in the exercise of the official's duties as a Commonwealth public official.[44]

All Commonwealth public officials must comply with all Australian laws and in particular, the Criminal Code.[45]

5.3 DEFINITION OF "PUBLIC OFFICIALS"

A Commonwealth public official is defined very broadly, to include politicians; public servants employed by the Commonwealth or any Commonwealth agency; judicial employees; defense, military, and police personnel, and any individual who is a contract service provider (or any employee or a corporate entity that is a service provider) to the Commonwealth.[46]

5.4 GIFTS, GRATUITIES, AND HOSPITALITY

The Criminal Code does not directly address any criminal liability arising from the giving or receiving of gifts, gratuities, or hospitality to Commonwealth public officials.

The Commonwealth APS Code of Conduct deals in some detail with gifts or benefits. While there is no concrete rule, each case must be assessed on its merits, and ethical and transparency considerations must be given priority. The Code of Conduct says the following:[47]

> When a public servant receives an offer of a gift or benefit, it is important that they consider the ethical issues involved and that there is an open and transparent process in the agency for discussing such issues. It is important to consider every offer on its merits, taking into account the relationship of the organisation making the offer with the agency.

The main risk of accepting a gift or benefit is that it may result in an actual or perceived conflict of interest. At the extreme, it could be perceived as a bribe, which is an offense under the Criminal Code and a breach of the APS Code.

5.5 DEFENSES

5.5.1 Written Local Law

There is no written law defense to a domestic bribery offense in Australia. If a payment is permissible under a contract, code of conduct, or a government agency direction, it is unlikely to constitute an offense.

---

[44] It is not necessary to prove that a defendant knew the official was a Commonwealth public official or the duties were the duties of such an official; see section 141.1(2), Criminal Code.

[45] Australian Public Service (APS) Code of Conduct states that all Commonwealth "employees have an unequivocal responsibility to comply with all applicable Australian laws." Clause 1.3(f) of the Australian Public Service Commissioner's Directions 2013 requires all public officials to report and address misconduct and any unacceptable behavior.

[46] Definition Schedule, Criminal Code.

[47] APS Code of Conduct, Chapter 4.12.

5.5.2 Facilitation Payments

There is no facilitation payment defense for any domestic bribery offense in Australia.

5.5.3 Adequate Procedures

There is no adequate procedures defense to any domestic bribery offense in Australia.

5.5.4 Corporate Culture

The corporate culture offenses in the Criminal Code apply to any domestic bribery offenses where questions of corporate culture arise in determining corporate criminal liability relevant to Commonwealth offenses. There have been no cases on this point for any domestic offense. There is no general law in the Australian states creating a corporate criminal liability offense. In NSW for example, certain environmental laws have been amended to create potential statutory liability on directors for serious offenses committed by a company, but not on companies for the conduct of its officers.[48]

5.6 PENALTIES

The penalties that might apply to domestic bribery offenses against a Commonwealth public official are the same as for foreign bribery offenses (*see* Section 4.9 of this chapter).[49]

6. Commercial Bribery
6.1 GENERAL PRINCIPLES

There are no commercial bribery offenses in Australia. However, state-based criminal laws covers conduct that may amount to commercial bribery or corruption.

6.2 STATE CRIMINAL LAWS

Each Australian state has broad prohibitions under its criminal laws to cover commercial bribery. If we take NSW as an example, we see that the *Crimes Act* 1900 (NSW) covers deception and fraud,[50] money laundering,[51] corrupt practices and corruptly receiving commissions,[52] and false and misleading information[53]. These offenses will capture any conduct at a State level that might otherwise be described as commercial bribery. While state-based anti-corruption commissions can make findings of corruption, it is then for the state DPP to determine if a prosecution can be made out. Recent prosecutions in NSW against former politicians have been based not on corruption offenses but on misconduct in public office[54].

---

[48] As an example, *see* sections 169 and 169A to 169C, *Protection of the Environment Operations Act 1997* (NSW).
[49] *See* sections 141.1(5) and (6), Criminal Code.
[50] Sections 192B to 192H, *Crimes Act 1900* (NSW).
[51] Sections 193A to 193G, *Crimes Act 1900* (NSW).
[52] Sections 249A to 249J, *Crimes Act 1900* (NSW).
[53] Sections 307A to 307C, *Crimes Act 1900* (NSW).
[54] *R v Obeid (No 12)* [2016] NSWSC 1815; on appeal at *Obeid v R* [2017] NSWCCA 221; and *R v Macdonald; R v Maitland* [2017] NSWSC 337, and *R v Macdonald; R v Maitland* [2017] NSWSC 638.

7. Sentencing Principles

7.1 GENERAL PRINCIPLES

The Commonwealth and each Australian state and territory has statutory sentencing frameworks that apply to all criminal offenses.[55]

The basic approach in Australia is to maintain broad sentencing discretions for the courts, guided by statutory factors that courts must take into account when determining a sentence for a particular offender.[56] While statutory scales of penalties or factors are set by Parliament, it is up to the sentencing judge to determine the most appropriate sentence in each individual case. A court sentencing a person for a federal offense must have regard to current sentencing practices across Australia, not to prefer practices in particular courts, and appellate courts should have regard to the judgments of other appellate courts in comparable cases unless there are compelling reasons not to do so.[57]

Australia has not favored the use of centralized sentencing guidelines such as the U.S. Federal Sentencing Guidelines. Rather, state appellate courts issue guideline judgments from time to time to assist in a consistent, coherent approach to sentencing under particular offenses.[58] While various state parliaments have bowed to public pressures to impose mandatory terms of imprisonment or minimum non-parole periods, these have been struck down by the High Court as infringing on the constitutional independence of the exercise of judicial power in the discretionary sentencing process. Thus, standard or minimum non-parole periods are but one of the factors for a sentencing judge to take into account.[59]

8. Related Criminal Offenses

8.1 CONSPIRACY

Section 11.5 of the Criminal Code creates an offense where a person enters into an agreement[60] with one or more other persons, with at least that person and one other intending[61] that an

---

[55] Crimes Act 1914 (Cth), Part 1B; Crimes (Sentencing Procedure) Act 1999 (NSW); Penalties and Sentencing Act 1992 (Qld); Criminal Law (Sentencing) Act 1988 (SA); Sentencing Act 1997 (Tas); Sentencing Act 1991 (Vic); Sentencing Act 1995 (WA); Crimes (Sentencing) Act 2005 (ACT), and Sentencing Act (NT).

[56] For example, section 21A *Crimes (Sentencing Procedure) Act 1999* (NSW) and for Commonwealth Offenses, sections 16A to 16D *Crimes Act 1914* (Cth).

[57] *The Queen v Pham* [2015] HCA 39.

[58] *See* sections 36 to 42A, *Crimes (Sentencing Procedure) Act 1999* (NSW) where sentencing guideline judgments can be published or included within an existing case at the request of the NSW Attorney General or by the Court of Criminal Appeal on its own motion; *see, e.g., R v Thomson; R v Houlton* (2000) 49 NSWLR 383; [2000] NSWCCA 309 where the Court of Criminal Appeal issued guidelines for how discounts on a sentence should be applied to pleas of guilty.

[59] *See Muldrock v The Queen* (2011) 244 CLR 120 and sections 54A to 54D, *Crimes (Sentencing Procedure) Act 1999* (NSW).

[60] An "agreement between conspirators need not be attended by any formalities"; *see R v LK* (2010) 241 CLR 177; [2010] HCA 17 at [117] and [131], approving *R v Orton* [1922] VLR 469 at 473 per Cussen J; applied in *Standen v Regina* [2015] NSWCCA 211 at [415] to [418].

[61] Recklessness as to whether a physical element of the offense exists or will exist is not sufficient to establish the requisite intent (*see R v LK* at [122] and [141]; applied in *CDPP v Brady & Ors* [2016] VSC 334 at [899] to [900]. In *Ansari v The Queen* (2010) 241 CLR 299; [2010] HCA 18, the High Court of Australia said that it is

offense[62] would be committed pursuant to the agreement, and the person and at least one other party to the agreement committed an overt act[63] pursuant to the agreement.[64] While the person can be punishable as if the offense to which the conspiracy relates had been committed, the verdict will be for conspiracy to commit that offense (not the primary offense).[65] The punishment will be the maximum penalty applicable to the underlying offense. There are a number of statutory defenses to conspiracy that can be complicated to apply.[66]

One note of caution—Australian courts have expressed concern when prosecutors file charges of conspiracy where there is, in the court's view, sufficient evidence to warrant charges for the primary offense.[67] There is a statutory power for a court to dismiss a charge of conspiracy if it thinks it is in the interests of justice to do so.[68]

8.2 ATTEMPTS

Section 11.1 of the Criminal Code creates an offense where a person attempts to commit an offense and is punishable as if the offense attempted had been committed. It is a question of fact whether the person's conduct is more than merely preparatory to the commission of the offense.[69]

8.3 AIDING AND ABETTING

Section 11.2 of the Criminal Code creates the offense of complicity and common purpose. The offense in section 11.2(1) is predicated upon a person who "aids, abets, counsels or

---

only necessary to prove that "*the accused intended that an act or acts be performed which, if carried out in accordance with the agreement, would amount to the commission of an offense.*" How that can be applied in practice is by no means easy to determine.

[62] An offense is defined in the Criminal Code Dictionary as "an offense against a law of the Commonwealth."

[63] What constitutes an "overt act" is not clear—while *R v LK* found the Criminal Code imported the established common law meaning, it seems likely that some step toward the execution of the conspiracy is required; *see* S. ODGERS, PRINCIPLES OF FEDERAL CRIMINAL LAW 227 (3d ed. 2015).

[64] The offense has been described as a "continuing offense" as it is only necessary for the Crown to prove that the accused and at least one other person said to be a party to the conspiracy were participants in an agreement to commit the offense even if it is alleged that others were party to the agreement; see *Agius v The Queen* [2013] HCA 27; 248 CLR 601 at [42]-[44], applied in *Agius v R* [2015] NSWCCA 200 at [964] to [965] per Bathurst CJ.

[65] Odgers, *supra* note 63, at 217.

[66] Sections 11.5(4) to 11.5(8); *see* Odgers, *supra* note 63, at 230–35.

[67] *R v Hoar* (1981) 148 CLR 32 at [17] "generally speaking, it is undesirable that conspiracy should be charged when a substantive offense has been committed and there is a sufficient and effective charge that this offense has been committed" per Gibbs CJ, Mason, Aickin, and Brennan JJ, although a more measured view is expressed in *Baladjam v The Queen* [2008] NSCCCA 85 at [106] per Spigelman CJ and in *McKenzie v Magistrates Court (Victoria)* [2013] VSCA 81 at [50] per Harper JA. In *CDPP v Brady & Ors* [2016] VSC 334 at [909] to [910] the Court noted the judicial caution about "those prosecuting appear to adopt the view that an accused person must be guilty of something but, rather than identifying what that something is, choose a conspiracy charge as a dragnet" (applying the words of Justice Murphy in *Gerakiteys v R* [1984] HCA 8; (1984) 153 CLR 317, 322-3).

[68] Section 11.5(6) Criminal Code.

[69] Section 11.1(2), Criminal Code.

procures" the commission of an offense by another person and who is taken to have committed that offense.

For a person to be guilty:

- the person's conduct must have in fact aided, abetted, counselled or procured the commission of the offense by the other person, which conveys[70] the concept of conduct that brings about or makes more likely the commission of an offense;[71]
- the offense must have been committed by the other person;[72]
- the person must have intended that:[73]
  o his or her conduct would aid, abet, counsel or procure the commission of any offense of the type committed by the other person; or
  o his or her conduct would aid, abet, counsel or procure the commission of an offense and was reckless about the commission of the offense that the other person in fact committed.

8.4 FALSE ACCOUNTING AND BOOKS AND RECORDS

In light of ongoing criticism of a lack of substantial false accounting laws applying throughout the Commonwealth, the Australian Parliament enacted laws that commenced on March 1, 2016, to introduce wide-ranging criminal false accounting offenses.[74] These laws create offenses for the intentionally false[75] or reckless[76] "making, altering, destroying or concealing" of an "accounting document" (defined broadly[77]) in circumstances where the person so acting intended to facilitate, conceal or disguise someone else receiving or giving a benefit to which that other person was not legitimately due and loss is suffered by another person. The prosecutor need not prove a benefit was in fact given or received or that a loss

---

[70] Section 11.2(2)(a), Criminal Code.

[71] *Handlen v The Queen* [2011] HCA 51 at [6] per French CJ, Gummow, Hayne, Crennan, Kiefel, and Bell JJ.

[72] Section 11.2(2)(b), Criminal Code.

[73] Section 11.2(3), Criminal Code.

[74] *Crimes Legislation Amendment (Proceeds of Crime and Other Measures) Act 2015* (Cth), introduces a new Part 10.9 into the Criminal Code. On February 3, 2016, a Senate Report by the Legal & Legislative Committee recommended the new laws be applied broadly to tackle financial crime and not be limited to foreign bribery cases.

[75] Section 490.1, Criminal Code.

[76] Section 490.2, Criminal Code.

[77] A document "made or required for any accounting purpose" has been defined broadly by the Courts, *see Attorney-General's Reference (No 1 of 1980)* [1981] 1 All ER 366; *R v Holt* (1983) 12 A Crim R 1 at [18] and *R v Jenkins* (2002) 6 VR 81 (applied in *R v Heinze* [2005] VSCA 124 at [80] per Nettle JA and *Adamson v O'Brien* [2008] NTSC 8 at [106] to [113] per Martin CJ). In *R v Jenkins*, the Victorian Court of Appeal held that for a document to be "required" for accounting purposes there must be a substantial connection with the accounting processes of the business or other entity, not a merely incidental connection. As to what amounted to "accounting purposes" of a business, this involved both a factual issue as to what the business actually did by way of keeping, maintaining, and preparing its accounts and a purposive issue that required consideration of the kind of information used and therefore needed for the keeping of those accounts. To determine whether a document was "required for any accounting purpose," evidence is required of the connection of the document with the relevant accounts and its requirement for that purpose.

was incurred.[78] These laws apply to conduct within and outside Australia and potentially to a wide range of commercial transactions (and are not limited to conduct amounting to foreign bribery). The penalties are severe—for an individual, imprisonment up to 10 years and/or (from July 1, 2017) a maximum fine up to AU$2,100,000 and for a company, a maximum fine up to AU$21,000,000 or three times the value of the benefit or 12 months turnover.

There are offenses under the *Corporations Act 2001* (Cth) where a company fails to keep financial records that correctly record and explain the financial position of the company in order that true and fair financial statements can be prepared,[79] or where books relating to the affairs of a company are concealed, destroyed, mutilated or falsified,[80] or where a company officer or employee provides materially false or misleading information to a director or auditor or to a financial market operator.[81]

State criminal laws contain well-established criminal law false accounting offenses.[82] They carry substantial penalties by way of imprisonment and fines and were used to prosecute former officers in the well-publicized Securency banknote printing corruption scandal.[83]

9. Cooperation and Self-Reporting

9.1 COOPERATION WITH INVESTIGATORS AND PROSECUTORS

There is no legal obligation on a person to cooperate with investigators or prosecutors.

However, there are practical and real consequences arising from a decision regarding whether to cooperate with investigators and prosecutors. The willingness of a person to cooperate is a factor to be considered in assessing the decision to prosecute.[84] In addition, under the general sentencing principles, the extent to which the offender has cooperated with investigators and prosecutors is a factor for the sentencing judge to take into account.[85]

In certain limited circumstances, the CDPP can offer an undertaking to a person in order to secure testimony against another person (often an accomplice or co-accused) for the prosecution.[86] Such undertakings:

- grant use/derivative use immunity from Commonwealth proceedings;[87]
- grant use/derivative use immunity preventing testimony given in a state of territory proceeding from use in a proceeding under a Commonwealth law;[88]

---

[78] Section 490.5, Criminal Code.
[79] Section 286, Corporations Act.
[80] Section 1307, Corporations Act.
[81] Section 1309(1) Corporations Act.
[82] For example, *see* section 83 *Crimes Act 1958* (Vic) and Part 4AA *Crimes Act 1900* (NSW).
[83] *See R v David John Ellery* [2012] VSC 349; *CDPP v Curtis* [2017] VSC 613 and *CDPP v Gerathy* [2018] VSC 289.
[84] Paragraph 2.10, Prosecution Policy of the Commonwealth.
[85] Section 16A(2)(g), *Crimes Act 1914* (Cth) where the offender pleads guilty, and section 16A(2)(h) where the offender has cooperated with investigators.
[86] Undertakings or a form of immunity can be made pursuant to sections 9(6), 9(6B), and 9(6D) of the *Director of Public Prosecutions Act 1983* (Cth). Reference should be had to the CDPP *Guidelines & Directions Manual on Undertakings, Offers of Assistance and Induced Statements*, dated Dec. 11, 2012. State DPPs have similar powers; *see* Guideline 15 of the *Prosecution Guidelines* of the NSW Office of the DPP.
[87] Section 9(6) Director of Public Prosecutions Act 1983 (Cth).
[88] Section 9(6B) Director of Public Prosecutions Act 1983 (Cth).

- grant immunity from prosecution for specified Commonwealth offenses, acts, or omissions.[89]

While the Prosecution Policy recognizes that as a general rule, all persons alleged to have committed offenses should be prosecuted and to receive reductions in sentencing due to the mitigating factor of cooperation and testimony, that cannot always occur. Undertakings will be given only where evidence necessary to secure a conviction cannot be obtained from any other source and the accomplice giving that evidence is seen as significantly less culpable than the defendant.[90] The Prosecution Policy outlines, as does the relevant statute, the criteria that are to be taken into account in making such a decision.[91]

A lesser form of protection is the "induced statement" that a witness can offer to the prosecutor in return for a "letter of comfort."[92] While these procedures do not have the statutory immunity that an undertaking grants, they can be useful for witnesses who play a minor to very minor role in any conduct and who can give evidence about the serious offending conduct that cannot otherwise be obtained by the prosecution.

9.2 SELF-REPORTING

Save for NSW,[93] there is no obligation in Australia to self-report an offense.

Under the Prosecution Policy, the CDPP may take into account the nature of any cooperation from an offender in determining whether the public interest is satisfied whether or not a prosecution should be commenced. However, the Prosecution Policy also states:

> As a matter of practical reality the proper decision in many cases will be to proceed with a prosecution if there is sufficient evidence available to justify a prosecution. Although there may be mitigating factors present in a particular case, often the proper decision will be to proceed with a prosecution and for those factors to be put to the Court at sentence in mitigation.

9.3 PLEA AGREEMENTS

There is no structured plea agreement system in Australia either for Commonwealth or state or territory criminal offenses although proposed amendments to the DPP Act are likely to see a deferred prosecution agreement scheme enacted early in 2019.

Under the Australian criminal law, the prosecutor and the defense cannot agree on a plea whereby in exchange for a certain plea, the prosecutor will accept an agreed penalty. The High

---

[89] Section 9(6D) Director of Public Prosecutions Act 1983 (Cth).

[90] Prosecution Policy paragraph 6.6.

[91] *Id.*, paragraphs 6.7 to 6.9.

[92] These are outlined in the Prosecution Policy and the Guidelines published by the CDPP and each state DPP.

[93] Section 316(1) Crimes Act 1900 (NSW) reads "If a person has committed a serious indictable offense and another person who knows or believes that the offense has been committed and that he or she has information which might be of material assistance in securing the apprehension of the offender or the prosecution or conviction of the offender for it fails without reasonable excuse to bring that information to the attention of a member of the Police Force or other appropriate authority, that other person is liable to imprisonment for 2 years."

Court of Australia has made it clear that it is not permissible under the criminal law for a prosecutor to do more than draw to the attention of the sentencing judge the facts to be found, the relevant legal principles, and what has been done in other (more or less) comparable cases.[94]

In *Barbaro v The Queen; Zirilli v The Queen*, the High Court made it clear that:[95]

> It is neither the role nor the duty of the prosecution to proffer some statement of the specific result which counsel then appearing for the prosecution (or the Director of Public Prosecutions or the Office of Public Prosecutions) considers should be reached or a statement of the bounds within which that result should fall.

Under the criminal law, it remains the duty of the sentencing judge alone to determine the sentence, applying relevant principles and considering any applicable statutory sentencing requirements.[96] However, recent judgments by experienced criminal law judges have suggested a more open approach, being a positive obligation imposed on the Crown to assist the court in the exercise of the sentencing discretion. In some cases that obligation might be discharged by the Crown indicating no dissent from a submission advanced by defense counsel that a particular sentence or range of sentences is an available sentencing outcome, or no dissent from a finding that one or more features of mitigation are present and worthy of weight in the exercise of the sentencing discretion. However the obligation is not discharged by a simple adoption of the submissions of defense counsel or, worse still, silence from the Crown Prosecutor on a range of issues of fact and law that were engaged in the sentencing exercise of all offenders.[97]

In March 2016, the Australia Attorney General's Department (AGD) issued a Consultation Paper on whether Australia should introduce a Deferred Prosecution Agreement (DPA) scheme for certain Commonwealth offenses. In March 2017, the AGD published its proposed model DPA scheme.

On December 7, 2017, the *Crimes Legislation Amendment (Combatting Corporate Crime) Bill 2017* outlined the statutory framework for the operation of the Commonwealth DPA scheme for certain Commonwealth serious offenses. The Parliamentary report recommended adoption of the proposed DPA scheme in March 2018. Since then, nothing further has occurred). It has the following key features:

- The CDPP may enter into a DPA with a company;
- Criminal proceedings must not be commenced if a DPA is approved unless the CDPP is satisfied an agreement has been contravened or that inaccurate,

---

[94] *Barbaro v The Queen; Zirilli v The Queen* (2014) 253 CLR 58; [2014] HCA 2; applied in *Commonwealth of Australia v Director, Fair Work Building Industry Inspectorate; Construction, Forestry, Mining and Energy Union v Director, Fair Work Building Industry Inspectorate* [2015] HCA 46 where the High Court ruled that the *Barbaro* principle did not apply in the context of civil penalty proceedings.

[95] *Barbaro* at [39].

[96] *Wong v The Queen* (2001) 207 CLR 584 at 611; [2001] HCA 64 at [75]; *Barbaro* at [41]; *R v MacNeil-Brown* (2008) 20 VR 677 at 711 [1320] per Buchanan JA, 716 [147] per Kellam JA; *CMB v Attorney General for New South Wales* (2015) 89 ALJR 407 where the Court held that the prosecution may submit that an identified sentence (by the trial judge) is manifestly inadequate, so avoiding appealable error by the trial judge.

[97] *R v Rajab; R v El Chami; R v B Allouche; R v E Allouche* [2017] NSWSC 975 at [88] per Fullerton J.

misleading, or incomplete information was provided in connection with the agreement and the entity supplying the information ought to have known that;

- The Commonwealth offenses to which a DPA may apply are contraventions of:
  o Australia's anti-money-laundering and anti-terrorism-financing laws;
  o The *Autonomous Sanctions Act 2011* (covering Australian sanctions);
  o The *Charter of the United Nations Act 1945* (covering UN sanctions);
  o The *Corporations Act 2001*, covering serious financial offenses;[98] and
  o The *Criminal Code 1995*, serious financial crime offenses;[99]
- A DPA must contain certain terms including an agreed statement of facts, any conditions to be satisfied, the amount of any financial penalty, and a consent to the institution of an indictment without any future committal process;
- A DPA may contain a variety of other terms concerning compensation, the implementation of a compliance program, the payment of costs, the forfeit of benefits, and any other term the CDPP "considers appropriate";
- The Commonwealth may appoint an "approving officer" (being a former judicial officer of a federal, state, or territory court) for a term of five years;
- The approving officer must review and either approve or not approve the DPA, with an approval based on the officer being satisfied the DPA is "in the interests of justice" and is "fair, reasonable and proportionate";
- Once a DPA is approved, it must be published on the CDPP's website in whole or part, and can be redacted in whole or part in the CDPP's discretion if publication would threaten public safety, prejudice ongoing investigations or the fair trial of a person, or be contrary to an order of a court;
- Any variation to a DPA must go through the same approval and publication process;
- There are limits to the admissibility into evidence of documents indicating a DPA was being negotiated or documents created solely for the purpose of negotiating a DPA (but derivative use of information so obtained may still exist); and
- There are limited rights of a Commonwealth official to disclose any information about a DPA.

---

[98] Market manipulation under s1041A, false trading and market rigging under s1041B, dissemination of information concerning illegal transactions under s1041C, false or misleading statements under 1041D, inducing persons to deal under s1041F, dishonest conduct under s1014G, prohibited conduct concerning insider information under s1043A, and the falsification of company books and records under s1307, Corporations Act.

[99] Theft under s131, obtaining property or a financial advantage by deception under s134; fraud and dishonesty under s135; bribery and/or corruption of a Commonwealth public official under ss141 and 142; forgery and forgery offenses under ss144 and 145; dealing in the proceeds of crime and the anti-money-laundering offenses under s400; the use and misuse of financial information concerning obtaining funds, credit, or financial benefits under s480; and the false and/or reckless dealings with an accounting document under s490, Criminal Code.

There are some transitional amendments to other laws, most notably the *Income Tax Assessment Act 1997* (Cth) where the nondeductibility of bribes exists as an offense, the *Crimes Act 1914* (Cth) in relation to factors to consider on sentencing, and the *DPP Act* in relation to authorizing the CDPP to negotiate, enter into, administer, and issue directions or guidelines concerning the negotiations for, the entering into, and the administration of a DPA.

On December 8, 2017, the CDPP and AFP published their Best Practice Guidelines, *Self-Reporting of Foreign Bribery and Related Offences by Corporations*.[100] This outlines how the "public interest" test in the Prosecution Policy will be applied to companies that self-report foreign bribery conduct. It sets out:

- the terms upon which a company is expected to cooperate (and what to "fully and frankly" disclose) with the AFP and the CDPP, including entering into an Investigation Cooperation Agreement;
- the confidentiality of the process, although disclosure may be made to other agencies with notice to the company;
- the factors on whether a prosecution of a self-reporting company is in the public interest;
- the grant of an indemnity (a written undertaking under the DPP Act) by the CDPP to the company making evidence given during the self-reporting process not admissible, whether directly or derivatively, against the company in any civil or criminal proceeding;
- the circumstances where an agreed statement of facts is prepared, which only applies to the prosecution and is not admissible as evidence of the truth of its contents in any other criminal or civil proceedings; and
- while the CDPP and the company can make submissions on sentencing, if a prosecution occurs, it is for the court, exercising its discretion, to impose a sentence according to established sentencing principles.

Leniency is a matter traditionally factored into by prosecutors and courts during sentencing under traditional sentencing principles and statutory sentencing requirements.

Leniency can occur in some form over the different stages in an investigation or prosecution.[101] Leniency can be shown by investigators in determining there is no case to answer, by prosecutors in negotiating charges and accepting a plea of guilty, and cooperation being a significant mitigating factor in the court showing leniency in sentencing.

---

[100] At https://www.cdpp.gov.au/publications.

[101] An example is the well-established *Immunity and Cooperation Policy for Cartel Conduct*, September 2014, published by the Australian Competition and Consumer Commission to deal with encouraging self-reporting of cartel conduct and grants of immunity or leniency depending on who is "first in the door" to report the conduct. As cartel conduct is a criminal offense, the CDPP and ACCC work together to determine the investigation scope and whether criminal or civil offenses are to be prosecuted (see the *Memorandum of Understanding between the Commonwealth Director of Public Prosecutions and the Australian Competition and Consumer Commission regarding Serious Cartel Conduct*, August 15, 2014).

10. Whistle-Blower Protection
10.1 PUBLIC SECTOR WHISTLE-BLOWER PROTECTIONS

The protections for whistle-blowers in the Commonwealth public sector were substantially reformed in late 2013.[102] There are a range of various state and territory laws governing public interest disclosures, and some have separate whistle-blower protections.[103]

The *Public Interest Disclosure Act 2013* covers all public employees, service providers under a Commonwealth contract, statutory officeholders, and individuals taken to be public officials. There has been no significant judicial analysis of this Act.[104]

Where a discloser has information, on reasonable grounds, of wrongdoing within a Commonwealth agency or by a public official or service provider on a range of broad topics that capture corruption, contraventions of the law, wastage of public funds, misconduct, maladministration, or abuse of a position, the disclosure can make a "protected disclosure" to a nominated person or agency. Once the disclosure is protected, the discloser is immune from civil, criminal, or administrative liability[105] and from reprisals or threats (with rights of compensation and if necessary, employment re-instatement).[106] The discloser's identity is protected.[107]

The discloser has limited rights to make what the Act calls "public interest" disclosures" to a wider audience if the initial disclosure has not been dealt with or if wider disclosure on public interest grounds is satisfied.[108] Care must, however, be taken with such disclosures to ensure they satisfy the statutory criteria because if they do not, the discloser is at risk. The Act sets out a regime for the investigation of disclosures. The Commonwealth Ombudsman acts as an independent reviewer of the conduct of agencies in dealing with disclosures, investigations, and reports arising from investigations.[109]

---

[102] Public Interest Disclosure Act 2013 (Cth).

[103] Public Interest Disclosures Act 1994 (NSW); Protected Disclosure Act 2012 (Vic); Public Interest Disclosure Act 2010 (Qld) and Protected Interest Disclosure Act 2010 (Qld); Whistleblower Protection Act 1993 (SA); Public Interest Disclosure Act 2002 (Tas); Public Interest Disclosure Act 2003 (WA), and Public Interest Disclosure Act 2008 (NT).

[104] One reported judgment, in *Wyatt v Cutbush* [2016] QSC 253, involved the court setting aside a default judgment, noting that given the absolute immunity the maker of a relevant disclosure had from suit under the statutory scheme, it was a significant step for a court to deny a litigant the opportunity to pursue that defense. It is not clear what occurred in that litigation.

[105] Section 10, Public Interest Disclosure Act 2013 (Cth).

[106] Sections 13 to 16, *Public Interest Disclosure Act 2013* (Cth) with offenses created in section 19, with penalties of up to two years imprisonment and/or a fine of 120 penalty units (currently, AU$21,600).

[107] Sections 20 and 21, Public Interest Disclosure Act 2013 (Cth).

[108] Division 2, Public Interest Disclosure Act 2013 (Cth).

[109] The Commonwealth Ombudsman has published the *Public Interest Disclosure Standards 2013* and the *Public Interest Disclosure Amendment (Conduct of Investigations) Standard 2014,* which requires each Commonwealth agency to ensure all public employees can properly and freely make disclosures and sets forth how internal investigations are conducted and reported upon.

10.2 PRIVATE SECTOR WHISTLE-BLOWER PROTECTIONS

Private sector protections for whistle-blowers have for many years been left largely in the hands of the private sector, with the Commonwealth and state governments showing little interest in the topic. In turn, the private sector has generally done little to protect those who blow the whistle on internal conduct to any external agency or authority. However, that has significantly changed after a decade or so of serious financial scandals and allegations of improper if not illegal conduct that only came to light because employees blew the whistle and even then, ASIC (as the Australian corporate regulator) did little if anything to act on the reports.

The Corporations Act provides a very limited statutory framework to protect whistle-blowers.[110] The key elements that must be satisfied are:

- the whistle-blower must be an officer or an employee of the company or a contractor or employee of a contractor that has a current contract to supply goods or services to the company the disclosure is about;[111]
- the disclosure must be to the company's auditor; a director, secretary, or senior manager within the company; or a person authorized by the company to receive whistle-blower disclosures or ASIC;[112]
- the whistle-blower must identify himself when making the disclosure;[113]
- the whistle-blower must have reasonable grounds to suspect that the information disclosed indicates the company or company officers may have breached the Corporations Act (or ASIC's Act);[114] and
- the whistle-blower must make the disclosure in good faith.[115].

The Corporations Act goes on to protect the disclosing person (who falls within the Act) from civil or criminal liability for making the disclosure,[116] it prohibits victimization of the disclosing person,[117] it grants rights to compensation for a victimized person,[118] and creates offenses where a confidential disclosure is made public other than in accordance with the Corporations Act.[119]

ASIC has established an Office of the Whistleblower to improve its relationship and responses to whistle-blowers and information they provide on companies regulated by ASIC. Rather than dealing directly with whistle-blowers, ASIC's Office acts as an oversight

---

[110] Pt9.4AAA, sections 1317AA to 1317AE, Corporations Act and ASIC's Information Sheet No 52, *Guidance for Whistleblowers,* published August 2015, *available at* www.asic.gov.au.

[111] Section 1317AA(1)(a) Corporations Act.

[112] Section 1317AA(1)(b) Corporations Act.

[113] Section 1317AA(1)(c) Corporations Act.

[114] Section 1317AA(1)(d) Corporations Act.

[115] Section 1317AA(1)(e) Corporations Act.

[116] Section 1317AB Corporations Act.

[117] Section 1317AC Corporations Act.

[118] Section 1317AD Corporations Act.

[119] Section 1317AE Corporations Act.

body within ASIC to ensure consistency of approach and engagement with whistle-blowers. In practice, the general consensus in Australia is that ASIC has not acted as a true friend or independent agency to protect whistle-blowers.

There is widespread dissatisfaction with the whistle-blower protection regime in the private sector. During late 2016 and 2017, the Australian Joint Parliamentary Committee on Corporations & Financial Services has been undertaking a comprehensive review of whistle-blower protection laws in the private and not-for-profit sectors. In over 70 submissions, almost all called for substantial reform, the creation of an independent agency (not ASIC, as even ASIC itself submitted[120]) to protect whistle-blowers, enhanced protections, the right to compensation, and potentially, the ability to seek a reward payment for disclosing illegal conduct.

The Parliamentary Committee delivered its report to Parliament in September 2017. In response, the Australian government published for consultation the exposure Draft *Treasury Laws Amendment (Whistleblowers) Bill 2017*. While the Bill proposed a number of important changes, particularly enhancing the anonymity of whistle-blowers and their statutory protections, it failed to address certain key weaknesses in Australia's private sector whistle-blower protection laws that were the subject of the Parliamentary Committee's Report, which mean that:

- whistle-blowers must make their own claims for compensation in court proceedings, although cost orders cannot be made against them unless a court is satisfied the claim was vexatious or made without reasonable cause;
- there is no independent authority to represent the interests of whistle-blowers or to act in their name;
- while compensation provisions are improved, there are no rewards (or U.S.-style bounties).

On December 7, 2017, the Australian government presented to Parliament the *Treasury Laws Amendment (Enhancing Whistleblower Protections) Bill 2017*. The Bill sets out the amending legislation to substantially enhance private sector whistle-blower protections. The Bill was substantially supported by a Parliamentary Committee review in its report published on March 22, 2018 which recommended certain changes. On December 6 and 7, 2018, the Government published an Amended Bill.[121] The principal amendments will all be contained in the Corporations Act and include the following:

- The Bill, once enacted (it is not yet enacted), will apply from a date to be proclaimed and will cover conduct occurring before the date of proclamation;[122]
- A disclosure may be made by an eligible whistle-blower to an eligible recipient where the discloser has reasonable grounds to suspect that the information

---

[120] Proof Committee Hansard, Parliamentary Joint Committee on Corporations and Financial Services, public hearings April 27, 2017 at page 60, noting the opening remarks of John Price, ASIC Commissioner.

[121] https://www.aph.gov.au/Parliamentary_Business/Bills_Legislation/Bills_Search_Results/Result?bId=s1120

[122] Section 2, Treasury Laws Amendment (Enhancing Whistleblower Protections) Bill 2017.

indicates that a company (or officer or employee) or a related body corporate has engaged in conduct that constitutes a contravention of any Commonwealth law that is punishable by imprisonment for a period of 12 months or more, or which represents a danger to the public or the financial system;[123]

- An eligible whistle-blower can be a current or former officer, employee, or person who supplies goods and services to the company, an associate of a company, and in respect of any individual, a dependent or spouse;[124]
- Emergency disclosures are permitted to a third party (a journalist or a member of a Parliament of the Commonwealth, state, or territory) if a disclosure has been made, a reasonable period has passed (90 days), and the discloser has reasonable grounds to believe that there is a substantial and imminent danger to a person's health and safety or the natural environment or disclosure would be in the public interest;[125]
- Confidentiality of a whistle-blower's report and his or her identity is reinforced;[126]
- Compensation rights are set out, and while a whistle-blower must still bring an individual claim, there are provisions reversing the onus of proof for certain matters and cost protections (so no adverse cost order can be made unless the discloser acted without reasonable cause);[127]
- A public company and a large proprietary company must have a whistle-blower policy in place (on or after January 1, 2019 or such later date as proclaimed by Parliament) that covers a range of matters including information about a whistle-blower's rights under the new laws;[128]
- Enhances the protections to whistle-blowers against retaliation and victimization;[129] and
- Provides protection from civil and/or criminal liability in connection with the subject matter of a disclosure made under the new laws.[130]

10.3 ATTITUDES TOWARD WHISTLE-BLOWERS

For many years, the Australian culture supported the concept that you "*do not dob in a mate.*" Individual employees go along with the herd mentality unless that person wants to put his or her head above the parapet and suffer the consequences. Is this right? Does a culture of hostility toward whistle-blowers still prevail? The extent to which Australian culture has changed remains unclear given the reluctance of all governments to properly encourage and

---

[123] Proposed section 1317AA (4) and (5), Corporations Act.

[124] Proposed section 1317AAA, Corporations Act.

[125] Proposed section 1317AAD, Corporations Act.

[126] Proposed section 1317AAE, Corporations Act.

[127] Proposed sections 1317AD (compensation and remedies), 1317AE (court orders), 1317AF (interaction between civil and criminal offenses), 1317AG (certain information not to be disclosed), and 1317AH (costs), Corporations Act.

[128] Proposed section 1317AI, Corporations Act.

[129] Proposed sections 1317AC and 1317AD, Corporations Act.

[130] Proposed section 1317AB (1), Corporations Act.

incentivize employees to blow the whistle, and when they do, to properly and proactively protect them. However, with increasing media attention on financial scandals, even ASIC is starting to accept that whistle-blowers in the private sector should be properly protected and compensated for the losses they suffer as a result of blowing the whistle.[131]

11. Key International Treaties Relating to Bribery and Corruption

11.1 OECD

In 1999, Australia ratified and became a signatory to the OECD Convention[132] and the *1997 Recommendation on Combating Bribery in International Business Transactions*. Australia's anti-corruption laws, insofar as they concern foreign public officials, are contained in the Criminal Code. These laws reflect, but are materially different from, the United States' FCPA.

Since 1999 when Australia acceded to the OECD Convention, it has been subjected to the OECD peer review process under the Convention. The 2012 Report was very critical of Australia. The 2015 Follow-Up Review and the 2017 Report each acknowledge a more focused and targeted approach taken by the Australian government combating foreign bribery. However, there still remains significant room for improvement and in particular, the political will to resource, fund, investigate, and enforce the law. These reports are available on the OECD website.

11.2 UNITED NATIONS

On December 9, 2003 Australia signed the UN Convention against Corruption, which was ratified on December 7, 2005.

11.3 OTHER TREATIES

Australia is a founding member of the Financial Action Taskforce on Anti-Money Laundering and Counter Terrorist Financing. Australia ratified the United Nations Convention against Transnational Organised Crime on May 27, 2004. Australia has played an active role in the Asia Development Bank, OECD Anti-Corruption initiative for the Asia and Pacific regions in October 2003, and in November 2004 endorsed the Asia-Pacific Economic Cooperation (APEC) Santiago commitment to fight corruption and ensure transparency.

12. Mutual Legal Assistance Treaties and Transnational Cooperation

12.1 FORMAL STATUTORY REGIME

The principal statutory scheme for mutual legal assistance and transnational cooperation is set out in the *Mutual Assistance in Criminal Matters Act* 1986 (Cth) and the *Mutual Assistance*

---

[131] *See* Strength of Organizational Whistleblowing Processes—Analysis from Australia & New Zealand, Further Results from Whistling While They Work 2, Griffith University, AJ Brown and SA Lawrence July 2017.

[132] The Organization for Economic Co-operation and Development (OECD).

in Business Regulation Act 1992 (Cth). Under each of these statutes, there is provision for formal requests of mutual legal assistance between Australia and Australian authorities and other countries and their regulatory law enforcement agencies.[133]

Regulations provide that the Mutual Assistance in Criminal Matters Act applies to a foreign country subject to any mutual assistance treaty between that country and Australia that is referred to in the Regulations. These statutory schemes are technical, cumbersome, and time-consuming but are invariably used when formal proceedings or prosecutions are contemplated by investigating agencies.

12.2 INFORMAL REGIME

Australian agencies such as the AFP, the ATO, the Australian Competition & Consumer Commission (for antitrust, cartel, and competition matters) and Australian state police agencies have numerous memoranda of understanding between themselves and counterpart agencies in a wide range of countries. These memoranda are usually available on the website of the relevant agency and facilitate the smooth and efficient exchange of information, far more productively than the cumbersome and slow process of formal mutual legal assistance under the statutory regimes.

12.3 EXTRADITION

Applications for extradition are dealt with pursuant to the *Extradition Act* 1988 (Cth). This is the statutory regime whereby authorities seek the extradition of persons to Australia and foreign countries that make application for the extradition of individuals from Australia to a foreign country.

The Act establishes procedures and confers powers upon the relevant minister for the extradition of a person from Australia to an extradition country in respect of an "extradition offence." An "extradition country" is a country declared by regulations under the Act to be an extradition country.[134] There is a statutory regime for the assessment of the underlying facts giving rise to the case for extradition and limited defenses, particularly on the grounds of persecution and/or ill health, which must be satisfied in order to defeat an application for extradition.[135]

---

[133] The legislative framework is explained in *Kennedy v Australian Securities & Investment Commission* [2005] FCAFC 32; (2005) 142 FCR 343 at [9]: approved in *Dunn v The Australian Crime Commission* [2009] FCAFC 16.

[134] For example, the *Extradition (Bribery of Foreign Public Officials) Regulations 1999* covers the extradition countries to which the Extradition Act applies subject to the OECD Convention, while the *Extradition (United States of America) Regulations* is an example of the country-specific extradition regulations made under the principal act.

[135] A useful summary of the statutory framework is set out in *Minister for Home Affairs of the Commonwealth v Zentai* [2012] HCA 28 at [12] to [17]; *see also* the earlier judgment in *Vasiljkovic v Commonwealth* [2006] HCA 40; 80 ALJR 1399; 228 ALR 447. As to a fear of persecution as a ground to oppose extradition, see *Snedden v Republic of Croatia* [2009] FCAFC 111.

13. Legal Professional Privilege
13.1 GENERAL PRINCIPLES

Legal professional privilege (LPP) is a substantive rule of law in Australia. It applies unless specifically abrogated by statute.[136] LPP applies under the common law (usually applied outside judicial or quasi-judicial proceedings) or under statute.[137]

As a general principle, LPP applies where a communication is created for the dominant purpose of the giving or receiving of legal advice (known as the *advice privilege*) or in connection with the conduct of reasonably contemplated, anticipated, or actual litigation[138] (known as the *litigation privilege*).[139] The privilege is that of the client and can be enforced by the client to prevent unauthorized disclosure of otherwise privileged communications.

LPP can be lost by the conduct of the client or the client's representatives by waiver or by voluntary disclosure, or the application of certain exceptions such as the fraud exception where a communication is found to be in furtherance of a crime or criminal offense.[140] The critical test to determine if a court will find a waiver of LPP is whether the disclosure of the privileged communication was done in circumstances inconsistent with the maintenance of confidence, as confidence is inherent in a privileged communication.[141] Whether this inconsistency arises depends upon all the circumstances at the time of the disclosure. The authorities make it clear that the question of waiver must be assessed by reference to all the facts and circumstances, and questions of "fairness" are not appropriate (despite some courts adopting that language).[142] Common interest privilege applies to communications between parties, traditionally in the context of a dispute (or litigation) where they have a material common interest in communicating with each other. Where interests are potentially adverse or selfish to each other, there will be no common interest.[143] However, current cases favor

---

[136] Daniels Corporations International Pty Ltd v ACCC (2002) 213 CLR 543 at [9]; applied in Kirby v Centro Properties Ltd (No 2) [2012] FCA 70 at [10].

[137] This requires an assessment of the facts and the application of the *Evidence Act 1995* (Cth) and other state-based Evidence Acts.

[138] The authorities require there to be a real prospect of litigation for the litigation privilege to apply; *see* Mitsubishi Electric Pty Ltd v Vic WorkCover Authority [2002] VSCA 59 at [22] per Batt JA; ACCC v Prysmian Cavi e Sistemi Energia SLR (No 2) [2012] FCA 44; Apple Inc v Samsung Electronics Co Ltd (No 2) [2012] FCA 1358 at [44] per Cowdroy J and approved in Ensham Resources Pty Ltd v Aioi Insurance Co Ltd [2012] FCAFC 191 at [56] to [57].

[139] Esso Australia Resources Ltd v Commissioner of Taxation (1999) 201 CLR 24; Daniels Corporations International Pty Ltd v ACCC (2002) 213 CLR 543 at 552; AWB Ltd v Cole (No 5) (2006) 155 FCR 30 at [41] to [44].

[140] The test of what constitutes fraud encompasses a wide species of fraud, criminal activity, or actions taken for illegal or improper purposes and extends to "trickery" and "shams." As the fraud exception is based on public policy grounds, it is sufficiently flexible to capture a range of situations where the protection of confidential communications between lawyer and client would be contrary to the public interest, see *AWB Ltd v Cole (No 5)* [2006] FCA 1234 at [210] to [212] per Young J.

[141] *Mann v Carnell* (1999) 201 CLR 1.

[142] Osland v Secretary, Dept of Justice [2008] HCA 37; British American Tobacco Australia Ltd v Secretary, Dept of Health & Aging [2011] FCAFC 107; and as an example of courts using the concept of "fairness," see Ralph Lauren 57 Pty Ltd v Byron Shire Council [2013] NSWCA 307 at [6] to [8].

[143] Ampolex Ltd v Perpetual Trustee Co (Canberra) Ltd (1995) 37 NSWLR 405 at 410 per Giles CJ; Elders Forestry Ltd v Bosi Security Services Ltd (No 2) [2010] SASC 226 at [33]; Bradley Ingram v Y Twelve Pty Ltd

a factual analysis of the circumstances causing the creation of the communication and the common interest (as a matter of fact) between the parties.[144]

13.2 APPLICATION TO INTERNAL INVESTIGATIONS

LPP applies to legal communications created by a corporate or in-house counsel, subject to certain limited reservations to ensure the "independence" of internal counsel in light of the employer-employee relationship between the internal lawyer and the corporate client employer.[145] LPP can apply to all internal investigations where communications are created for the dominant purpose of a lawyer (corporate or external counsel) providing legal advice to the client or in relation to the conduct of actual or anticipated civil and/or criminal proceedings (in Australia or overseas). Care must be taken in how documents are created, and between whom documents are communicated, as there is a risk that privilege may not exist[146] or may be waived if an appropriate privilege protocol is not put in place.

13.3 APPLICATION TO EXTERNAL INVESTIGATIONS

LPP applies to external investigations. While certain statutory authorities such as the ACC and ASIC can compel witnesses under statutory examination to answer questions and to produce documents, privilege and access or disclosure of legal advice is still protected.[147] The Commissioner of the AFP has agreed guidelines with the state Law Societies in Australia for the management of privilege claims in contested proceedings where warrants or other compulsory powers are used to seize documents from lawyers' offices (or more generally, client premises where legal records may be stored) and they include privileged communications. Urgent legal applications to courts are required to ensure, absent agreement, that privilege is protected.

[2013] NSWSC 928 where there was found to be no common interest between directors and a company when the company obtained legal advice; Marshall v Prescott [2013] NSWCA 152 at [57] to [65] per Barratt JA in relation to competing insurance claims and Schreuder v Murray (No 2) [2009] WASCA 145 at [64] to [65] per Buss JA in relation to claims for disclosure as between a trustee and a beneficiary

[144] Lane v Admedus Regen Pty Ltd [2016] FCA 864 at [27] to [30] per McKerracher J and in Equititrust Ltd (in liq); in the Matter of Equititrust Ltd (in liq) (No 3) [2016] FCA 738 at [14] per Markovic J.

[145] Seven Network Ltd v News Ltd [2005] FCA 1342; Commonwealth v Vance (2005) 157 ACTR 47 at [30]; Rich v Harrington [2007] FCA 1987; Dye v Commonwealth Securities Ltd (No 5) [2010] FCA 950.

[146] See the decision by the UK Court of Appeal in *Director, Serious Fraud Office v Eurasian Natural Resources Corporation Ltd* [2018] EWCA Civ 2006[where the court found that the investigation records of interviews created by lawyers were merely factual accounts of historical events and were privileged, under the UK litigation privilege head (as there was a reasonable apprehension of litigation in the context of a potential criminal prosecution). The court also applied this test to both anticipated civil litigation and criminal prosecutions.

[147] *Daniels Corporations International Pty Ltd v ACCC* (2002) 213 CLR 543 and *Stewart v Australian Crime Commission* [2012] FCAFC 151 at 34; *see as examples,* section 21D Australian Crime Commission Act for examinations and notices issued by the ACC and sections 196 and 197 of the *Proceeds of Crime Act 2002* (Cth) concerning examinations relating to restraining and exclusion orders on forfeiture of the proceeds of crime.

13.4 PRACTICAL ISSUES

Care must be taken to manage communications during an investigation. While LPP communications can be exchanged within a corporate group between executives or persons who need access to legal advice,[148] disclosure should be limited, subject to a written protocol, and if necessary, confidentiality undertakings. This will ensure all steps are taken to protect the inherent confidentiality in LPP communications and minimize the risk of inadvertent waiver of LPP.

14. Privacy and Data Protection

14.1 PRINCIPLES

From March 12, 2014, the Australian Privacy Principles (APPs) replaced the National Privacy Principles and Information Privacy Principles and will apply to organizations, and Australian government (and Norfolk Island government) agencies.[149] The APPs are contained in Schedule 1 of the *Privacy Amendment (Enhancing Privacy Protection) Act 2012* (Cth), which amended the *Privacy Act 1988* (Cth).

The APPs are predicated upon the use, collection, holding, and disclosure of "personal information."[150]

The APPs are as follows:[151]

- Principle 1—open and transparent management of personal information;
- Principle 2—anonymity and pseudonymity;
- Principle 3—collection of solicited personal information;
- Principle 4—dealing with unsolicited personal information;
- Principle 5—notification of the collection of personal information;
- Principle 6—use or disclosure of personal information;
- Principle 7—direct marketing;
- Principle 8—cross-border disclosure of personal information;
- Principle 9—adoption, use, or disclosure of government related identifiers;
- Principle 10—quality of personal information;
- Principle 11—security of personal information;
- Principle 12—access to personal information; and
- Principle 13—correction of personal information.

---

[148] GEC Marconi Systems v BHP [2000] FCA 593 and Wingecarribee Shire Council v Lehman Bros Australia Ltd (in liq) [2011] FCA 245.

[149] The APPs apply to Australian government agencies (and the Norfolk Island administration) and all businesses and not-for-profit organizations with an annual turnover of more than AU$3 million, subject to some statutory exceptions.

[150] "Personal information" means information or an opinion about an identified individual, or an individual who is reasonably identifiable, whether the information or opinion is true or not; and whether the information or opinion is recorded in a material form or not; see section 6 definition, *Privacy Act 1988* (Cth).

[151] Information about the application of the APPs can be found at the website of the Office of the Australian Information Commissioner at www.oaic.gov.au.

14.2 APPLICATION TO INTERNAL INVESTIGATIONS

The APPs apply to the conduct of all internal investigations where "personal information" may be obtained. Care must be taken to handle such information in accordance with the APPs. This is particularly relevant where cross-border investigations raise issues of privacy, for example, the application of European Union laws on privacy.

14.3 APPLICATION TO EXTERNAL INVESTIGATIONS

The APPs apply to the conduct of all external investigations where "personal information" may be obtained. Care must be taken to handle such information in accordance with the APPs. APP 6.2(b) and (d) permit the disclosure of personal information where the disclosure is required by law, a court order, or the activities of an enforcement agency (for example, the AFP).

14.4 NOTIFICATION OF DATA BREACHES

The *Privacy Amendment (Notifiable Data Breaches) Act 2017* establishes the "notifiable data breaches" scheme in Australia.[152] It applies from February 22, 2018, to all agencies and organizations with "personal information" security obligations under the *Privacy Act 1988*. The scheme requires an entity holding personal information to notify the Australian Information Commissioner ("the Commissioner") and affected persons of any "eligible data breach"[153] where there is unauthorized access to or disclosure of relevant information and a reasonable person would conclude that the access or disclosure is likely to result in serious harm to any individual to whom the[154] information relates. Where such a breach occurs, the entity or entities holding the information must undertake an assessment of the breach and must prepare a statement (to be disclosed to the Commissioner and affected persons).[155] While there is no private enforceable right to privacy in Australia, upon any complaint to the Commissioner arising from an eligible data breach, the *Privacy Act* grants the Commissioner powers to investigate and if necessary seek enforceable undertakings or bring proceedings for a breach of the Act.

If any unauthorized disclosure or access to personal information is detected as part of any internal or external investigation, care must be taken to assess the application of these provisions.

15. Forecast for Reforms
15.1 LEGISLATIVE REFORMS

During 2015, the Australian Senate commenced a review of Australia's foreign bribery regime. The Senate received numerous submissions the substantial majority of which call

---

[152] Included as a new Part IIIC to the Privacy Act 1988.
[153] Defined in section 26WE Privacy Act.
[154] Section 26WG Privacy Act sets out relevant matters to determine whether access or disclosure would be likely or would not be likely to result in serious harm.
[155] Section 26WK Privacy Act.

for major reforms and a commitment to proper, ongoing resourcing and targeting foreign bribery by one dedicated agency. The review was reactivated by the Senate in mid-2017 and the Senate published its extensive report in March 2018.

During December 2017, the Australian government published draft bills containing substantial reforms to Australia's foreign bribery laws and proposed Commonwealth DPA scheme together with proposed amendments to substantially enhance private sector whistleblower protections. There is widespread support for these reforms and in particular, a DPA scheme based more on the current UK model[156] than under the U.S. model (with clear independent oversight of the grant of a DPA) and with appropriately clear criteria to ensure companies can know the criteria they must satisfy in order to be able to negotiate for such an agreement.[157] It is regrettable that since early 2018, these reforms have languished save for the whistleblower reforms (with amended legislation published in December 2018). If and when they are enacted, they will not only greatly enhance the tools available to the AFP and the CDPP to target corporate misconduct, but will add pressure to all Australian companies to examine their business practices to ensure they have in place adequate procedures to avoid foreign bribery.

15.2 POLITICAL AND AGENCY ENFORCEMENT

The AFP is presently the lead agency investigating foreign bribery. While it was subject to criticism some years earlier, its overall performance has markedly improved, and a much more coordinated and focused approach is now driving Australian foreign corruption investigations.[158] For many years, the public perception in the Australian media was of a risk-averse environment amongst investigators and prosecutors and a lack of real political leadership to target all aspects of foreign bribery conduct, particularly well-connected directors and individuals. While the authorities have denied any risk-averse environment,[159] two completed criminal foreign bribery prosecutions with various guilty pleas and four prosecutions permanently stayed due to illegal conduct by investigators over 15 years, seems a remarkably small level of proactive enforcement. The Table 2.1 below outlies the cases and verdicts to December 2018.

On 6 December 2018, the Australian Parliament passed the *Telecommunications and Other Legislation Amendment (Assistance and Access) Act 2018* (Cth) in order to permit a range of enforcement and intelligence agencies to effectively require service providers to provide a means of accessing encrypted communications. The regime permits nominated Government officials to issue a "technical assistance report" and a "technical capability notice" requiring service providers to provide assistance (with the technical assistance report)

---

[156] Crime and Courts Act 2013 (UK) Schedule 17.

[157] On these, see the U.S. DOJ *Enforcement Plan and Guidance* published April 5, 2016.

[158] See the OECD Phase 4 Report on Australia, page 57, noting the "*several good practices and positive achievements by Australia*" in combating foreign bribery and enhancing enforcement.

[159] Note the submissions from the Attorney General's Department (Submission 32 dated September 2015, Overview, page 2) and the CDPP (Submission 39 dated September 30, 2015) to the Australian Senate inquiry.

TABLE 2.1

Table of Australian Foreign Bribery and Related Offenses Cases

Date	Entity/Individual and Employment Position	Offence(s)	Penalties
2012	Securency International Pty Ltd and Note Printing Australia Pty Ltd[1]	Conspiracy to bribe foreign public officials, ss11(5)(1) and 70.2 Criminal Code	Pleaded Guilty Securency fined AU$480,000 Note Printing fined AU$450,000
2013	David John Ellery, former CFO and Secretary to Securency International Pty Ltd[2]	False accounting, s83(1) Crimes Act 1958 (Vic)	Pleaded Guilty 6 months' imprisonment, wholly suspended for 2 years
2013	Radius Christanto, intermediary and agent of Securency International Pty Ltd[3]	Conspiracy to bribe foreign public officials, ss11(5)(1) and 70.2 Criminal Code	Pleaded Guilty 2 years' imprisonment. Wholly suspended for 2 years
2017	Myles Curtis, former director and CEO of Securency International Pty Ltd[4]	Conspiracy to bribe foreign public officials, ss11(5)(1) and 70.2 Criminal Code False accounting, s83(1) Crimes Act 1958 (Vic)	Pleaded Guilty 2 years, 6 months' imprisonment on Commonwealth charges, released on recognisance (due to ill health 6 months' imprisonment on State offense, suspended for 1 year
2017	John Jousif[5]	Conspiracy to bribe foreign public officials, ss11(5)(1) and 70.2 Criminal Code	Pleaded Guilty 4 years' imprisonment, non-parole period of 2 years
2017	Ibrahim Elomar[6]	Conspiracy to bribe foreign public officials, ss11(5)(1) and 70.2 Criminal Code	Pleaded Guilty 4 years' imprisonment, non-parole period of 2 years Fined AU$250,000
2017	Mamdouh Elomar[7]	Conspiracy to bribe foreign public officials, ss11(5)(1) and 70.2 Criminal Code	Pleaded Guilty 4 years' imprisonment, non-parole period of 2 years Fined AU$250,000

(*Continued*)

TABLE 2.1

Continued

Date	Entity/Individual and Employment Position	Offence(s)	Penalties
2018	Clifford Gerathy, former senior director, business development of Securency International Pty Ltd, seconded bank officer from the Reserve Bank of Australia[8]	False accounting, s83(1) Crimes Act 1958 (Vic)	Pleaded Guilty 3 months imprisonment, suspended for 6 months
2018	Tony Strickland (A Pseudonym)[9]	Conspiracy to bribe foreign public officials, ss11(5)(1) and 70.2 Criminal Code	Prosecution permanently stayed
2018	Donald Galloway (A Pseudonym)[10]	Conspiracy to bribe foreign public officials, ss11(5)(1) and 70.2 Criminal Code	Prosecution permanently stayed
2018	Edmund Hodges (A Pseudonym)[11]	Conspiracy to bribe foreign public officials, ss11(5)(1) and 70.2 Criminal Code	Prosecution permanently stayed
2018	Rick Tu (A Pseudonym)[12]	Conspiracy to bribe foreign public officials, ss11(5)(1) and 70.2 Criminal Code	Prosecution permanently stayed

[1] *CDPP v Note Printing Australia Pty Ltd and Securency International Pty Ltd* [2012] VSC 302.

[2] *Queen v Ellery* [2012] VSC 349.

[3] *CDPP v Radius Christanto* [2013] VSC 521.

[4] *CDPP v Curtis* [2017] VSC 613.

[5] R v Jousif; R v I Elomar; R v M Elomar [2017] NSWSC 1299.

[6] Ibid.

[7] Ibid.

[8] *CDPP v Gerathy* [2018] VSC 289.

[9] *Tony Strickland (a pseudonym) v Commonwealth Director of Public Prosecutions; Donald Galloway (a pseudonym) v Commonwealth Director of Public Prosecutions; Edmund Hodges (a pseudonym) v Commonwealth Director of Public Prosecutions; Rick Tu* [2018] HCA 53; the defendants the subject of the appeal in *Strickland* were John Leckenby (former Note Printing CEO), Barry Brady (former Note Printing Sales Executive), Peter Hutchinson (former Note Printing CFO) and Steven Wong (former Note Printing Australian Sales Manager).

[10] Ibid.

[11] Ibid.

[12] Ibid.

and to do acts or things (with a technical capability notice) that might be requested by the government that the decision maker is satisfied is *"reasonable, proportionate, practicable and technically feasible."* Importantly, any technical assistance notice or technical capability notice must not require a provider to implement or build <u>systemic weaknesses (a concept not defined)</u> in forms of electronic protection (a "backdoor" access to encrypted communications) nor can they prevent a provider from fixing an identified weakness or vulnerability. The overall impact of these world first reforms are unknown and have generated considerable media and industry criticism. However, politicians feel they must be strong on terror and crime, so civil liberties are again compromised because politicians tell us you can trust them if you have nothing to hide, which simply begs the questions whether anyone trusts a politician.

Yet significant legislative changes which are still on the horizon have the potential to encourage individuals to report illegal conduct, and for companies to do so more openly than has been the case in Australia in the past. Given the high public awareness of the damage caused by foreign bribery, corruption, and corporate misconduct, it is hoped that the Australian government will now take a far more proactive role to address some of the past failings in the Australian approach to tackling these issues.

15.3 POLICY AND PRACTICE

Anti-corruption initiatives are generally promoted by the Australian government and all political parties. The challenge Australia faces, like many countries facing competing budgetary pressures, is to allocate sufficient resources to properly tackle complex economic crime transactions that invariably take a long time to investigate and even longer to prosecute. Australia does not have and needs simpler processes to reform its criminal laws to encourage self-reporting and for companies to volunteer conduct in return for some certainty of result.[160] Without the proposed reforms highlighted previously, under Australia's criminal laws, there is little real incentive for companies to report potentially illegal conduct, which is invariably hard to find out about or prove in offshore countries, and which may never be detected by Australian authorities. This creates the impression that while the laws exist, enforcement is too hard, too complex, and too expensive. If that situation is allowed to continue, it acts as a great disservice to Australian society and business.

---

[160] See *Serious Fraud Office v Standard Bank plc* dated November 30, 2015, Crown Court at Southwark, Case No U20150854, the judgment in *Serious Fraud Office v Rolls-Royce plc* dated January 17, 2017, Crown Court at Southwark, Case No U20170036 and the comments of Judge Emmet Sullivan in *United States v Saena Tech Corporation; United States v Intelligent Decisions* dated October 21, 2015, encouraging the U.S. authorities to consider deferred prosecution agreements for companies and individuals where they demonstrate the real likelihood of rehabilitation.

APPENDIX

Key Issues	Australia's Approach
Is Australia subject to any international anti-corruption conventions? If so, which conventions?	Yes. OECD Convention. UN Conventions against Corruption and Organised Crime. UN Convention against Transnational Organized Crime
Is bribery of foreign public officials illegal? Do domestic anti-bribery laws apply extraterritorially?	Yes. Yes, to a limited extent.
What is the definition of a foreign public official?	See section 70.1 of the Criminal Code.
Is commercial bribery illegal?	No under Commonwealth law. Yes under Australian state criminal laws.
Is bribing domestic officials illegal?	Yes.
Can the recipient of a bribe be prosecuted?	Yes.
Can companies be held criminally liable? If so, what is the requisite intent for corporate criminal liability?	Yes. Intent is outlined in sections 12.1 to 12.6 of the Criminal Code covering corporate culture and the conduct of a company's Board of Directors and high managerial agent.
Can companies be held civilly liable? If so, what is the requisite intent for civil liability to attach?	No. Liability for foreign bribery is criminal only. If the conduct constituting the foreign bribery satisfies any other statutory offense, or civil cause of action, that may exist in favor of a plaintiff. The standard for any civil liability is on the balance of probabilities. There is no intent or "mens rea" as exists for the criminal law for civil liability. Any intention depends upon the applicable cause of action.
Can an individual be held civilly liable?	Yes. Breach of directors/officers statutory duties, see sections 180–184 Corporations Act 2001 (Cth)
If there a "facilitation payment" defense?	Only to the offense of foreign bribery; see section 70.4 of the Criminal Code.

Key Issues	Australia's Approach
Do conspiracy laws apply to anti-corruption offenses?	Yes.
Does Australia provide liability for: (a) aiding and/or abetting liability (b) attempt liability (c) for anti-corruption laws?	Yes. See sections 11.1 and 11.2 of the Criminal Code.
Is the failure to keep accurate books and records a criminal or civil offense?	Yes. See sections 1307 and 1309 of the Corporations Act for civil offences, section 490 of the Criminal Code for false and reckless dealings with accounting documents, and state criminal laws for false accounting offenses (for example, sections 192F, 192G, and 192H Crimes Act 1900 (NSW)).
Do any books and records offenses involve proof of an underlying bribery offense?	No.
Are there Australian laws concerning a company's financial internal controls? If so, are those laws applicable to public and/or private companies?	No. But see sections 12.1 to 12.6 of the Criminal Code dealing with "corporate culture" as a factor in determining corporate criminal liability.
Is there an affirmative disclosure obligation for potential violations of anti-corruption laws or accounting irregularities?	No But see section 316 Crimes Act 1900 (NSW).
Are "promotional expenses" exempt from Australia's anti-corruption laws?	They are not covered by anti-corruption laws.
Is the giving of gifts, entertainment, travel, meals, or other gratuities restricted or prohibited by anti-corruption or other laws?	No

(Continued)

Key Issues	Australia's Approach
Are there any Australian laws concerning things, property, or benefits of value conveyed by, or to, third parties?	No
Are bribes tax deductible?	No
	See section 26-52 of the *Income Tax Assessment Act 1997* (Cth).
Is Australia's anti-corruption laws applied extraterritorially?	Yes to a limited degree.
	See sections 14, 15 and 70.5 of the Criminal Code.
Is a robust corporate compliance program an affirmative defense or a factor to negate liability or reduce penalties?	No as a matter of law.
	Yes as a factor the AFP considers as to whether to prosecute or by a court in mitigation at sentencing upon a conviction.
	Yes if new corporate offences of failing to prevent bribery is enacted (proposed sections 70.5A (1), the offense and section 70.5A (5), the adequate procedures defense).
Is there a "local law" exception or defense to Australia's anti-corruption laws?	Yes.
	See section 70.3 of the Criminal Code.
Is "credit" given for cooperation with authorities? If so, how and in what form?	Yes
	See Commonwealth Prosecution Policy as a discretionary factor to apply when determining whether to prosecute, and section 16A Crimes Act 1914 (Cth) as a factor relevant to sentencing by a court.
	See CDPP Guidelines, Self-Reporting of Foreign Bribery and Related Offending by Corporations, Dec 2017
Does Australia have mutual legal assistance with the United States that covers criminal matters, including anti-corruption conduct?	Yes
	See *Extradition (Bribery of Foreign Public Officials) Regulations 1999* covering the extradition countries to which the Extradition Act applies subject to the OECD Convention and the *Extradition (United States of America) Regulations* for extradition as between Australia and the United States.

Key Issues	Australia's Approach
What are the potential penalties/sanctions for criminal and civil violations of Australia's anti-corruption laws?	The penalties are criminal as the foreign bribery offenses are criminal, not civil. Disgorgement of profit arises under the *Proceeds of Crime Act 2002* (Cth). Civil proceedings may arise if criminal proceedings cannot be supported on the evidence (e.g., directors or officers in breach of duty, with disqualification and fines as penalties). **Criminal Penalties for Individuals (from July 2017)** Imprisonment of not more than 10 years, a fine of not more than 10,000 penalty units (currently AU$2,100,000). or both. **Criminal Penalties for Companies (from July 1, 2017)** A fine of not more than the greater of: • 100,000 penalty units (currently AU$21,000,000); or • 3 times the value of the benefit derived directly or indirectly from the relevant conduct; or • if the value of the benefit cannot be determined, an amount of 10 percent of the annual turnover of the company during the period of 12 months ending at the end of the month in which the relevant conduct occurred.

3 Brazil

1. Introduction to Brazil's Anti-Corruption Legislation

Brazil[1] continues to step up its efforts to combat bribery and corruption through a combination of new legal instruments, increased domestic enforcement, and enhanced international cooperation. The most notable development in recent years was the enactment of Brazil's first anti-bribery statute applicable to companies, Law 12,846/2013 (the "*Clean Company Act*"). The statute essentially provides for strict civil and administrative liability of companies for "acts against the public administration, national or foreign," which includes bribery, bid-rigging, fraud in the execution and performance of contracts with the government, and obstruction of audits, inspections, and investigations by public officials.

These legislative developments have been accompanied by a more aggressive enforcement strategy, particularly at the federal level, spearheaded by the Brazilian Federal Police and by the Federal Prosecutor's Office ("Ministério Público Federal"). One early example of this new trend was the Mensalão trial, which in 2012 resulted in the imprisonment of 25 individuals for their participation in a congressional vote-buying scheme. Among the criminal defendants who have served prison sentences as a result of the Mensalão trial are former Chief of Cabinet José Dirceu and former Speaker of the House João Paulo Cunha.

Drawing on the lessons learned during the Mensalão prosecution, in 2014 the Federal Prosecutor's Office launched Operação Lava Jato ("Car Wash" in Portuguese). Lava Jato unveiled a corruption scheme in which Brazil's largest construction companies colluded to

---

[1] This chapter was contributed by Steptoe & Johnson LLP's Lucinda A. Low and Pablo Bentes.

From Baksheesh to Bribery. T. Markus Funk and Andrew S. Boutros.
© Oxford University Press 2019. Published 2019 by Oxford University Press.

inflate the price of contracts with majority state-owned oil producer Petrobras, and used intermediaries to pay kickbacks of between 1 and 5 percent of the price of those contracts to financial operators, lobbyists, and politicians responsible for the appointment of Petrobras's executives. At the time of this writing, Lava Jato has resulted in 2,476 different criminal proceedings, leading to the indictment of 347 individuals for corruption, crimes against the international financial system, racketeering, and money laundering.[2] As many as 300 provisional arrest warrants have been issued during the course of investigations. Among those arrested, there are senior executives of Brazil's largest construction companies, Petrobras's senior management, and high-profile politicians such as former Chief of Staff José Dirceu (who in 2012, as noted earlier, had been convicted for corruption in connection with the *Mensalão* vote-buying scheme), and former Labor Party Treasurer João Vaccari Neto. These results stem in part from the federal prosecutors' aggressive use of plea bargains, a relative novelty in Brazilian criminal enforcement. As many as 183 individuals have signed agreements to cooperate with the *Lava Jato* investigations, and have agreed to disgorge a total of R $6.4 billion (U.S. $1.7 billion) in bribes, in exchange for reduced sentences.[3]

Another distinctive feature of *Lava Jato* is its multijurisdictional character. In the course of the investigations, Brazilian authorities have to date issued a total of 269 requests for information to 45 different jurisdictions, and have initiated proceedings against a number of foreign companies, such as Skanska and SBM Offshore.[4] Information obtained in the course of *Lava Jato* also has resulted in investigations in other jurisdictions, such as the United States, Norway, and the Netherlands.

2. Brazil's Domestic Anti-Corruption Framework

Brazil has long had criminal anti-bribery statutes that apply to individuals, both on the supply (the giving of bribes) and demand (the asking for bribes) sides, and these remain in place following the enactment of the *Clean Company Act*. Brazil, like many civil law countries, does not have corporate *criminal* liability.

On the supply side, the Brazilian Criminal Code defines the crime of "active corruption" as "the offer or promise to offer any undue advantage to a public official so that he may act, omit, or delay any official act."[5] Individuals found guilty of active corruption are subject to between 2 and 12 years imprisonment, plus fines. The sanctions may be increased by one-third if as a result the public official infringes the law or delays an act otherwise due. Active corruption was the main criminal charge against the *Mensalão* and *Lava Jato* defendants, and the Federal Prosecutor's Office and the Solicitor General have been successful in obtaining the condemnation of high-profile politicians, businessmen, and lobbyists involved in the payment of bribes to public officials in both proceedings.

On the demand side, Brazilian law provides for the crime of "passive corruption," defined as "soliciting or receiving, directly or indirectly, and undue advantage . . . by virtue of a public

---

[2] http://lavajato.mpf.mp.br/ (last visited January 28, 2019).
[3] *Id.*
[4] *Id.*
[5] Article 333 of the Brazilian Criminal Code.

function, or accepting the promise of such advantage."[6] Individuals found guilty of passive corruption are subject to the same sentences as the crime of active corruption—2 to 12 years imprisonment, plus fines. Brazilian law also sanctions the conduct of agents who solicit bribes on behalf of public officials. The crime of "influence peddling" is defined as the "solicitation . . . of an advantage or promise thereof, under the pretense of influencing an official act by a public official."[7] Influence peddling is sanctioned with two to five years imprisonment plus fines, and the sentence increases by half if the agent represents or implies that the advantage is destined to a public official.

With the advent of the *Clean Company Act*, Brazilian law began providing for *corporate* non-criminal liability for acts of corruption. The statute entered into force on January 29, 2014, and provides for civil and administrative penalties for any "acts against the national or foreign public administration."[8] Corporate liability for an agent's conduct is "strict," because liability is independent from any administrative or judicial showing of culpability.[9] Corporate liability is independent of the liability of individuals for acts of corruption, although any criminal or civil liability for individuals will depend upon judicial showing of culpability.[10]

"Acts against the public administration" within the meaning of the *Clean Company Act* encompass not just corrupt conduct, but a variety of improper practices and anti-competitive behavior by legal entities in their dealings with the government. Among the sanctioned conduct are bribery, the financing of corrupt acts, the hiding of funds or interests, bid-rigging, fraud in the execution and performance of government contracts, and obstruction of audits, inspections, and investigations by public officials.[11] Companies liable for acts against the public administration are subject to fines of up to 20 percent of their gross revenue in the preceding year, publication of the condemnatory decision, and disgorgement.[12] In establishing the amount of the fine, Brazilian authorities will consider factors such as the amount of the undue advantage, the degree of injury caused to the public administration, the amount of the contract at issue, and the economic situation of the investigated entity. In addition to the existence of adequate compliance procedures, the cooperation of the investigated entity may also be a mitigating circumstance that may reduce penalties.

Until recently, Brazil was perceived as a low enforcement jurisdiction. The 2015 report of Transparency International on the Enforcement of the OECD Convention on Combating Foreign Bribery, for example, classified Brazil as a country with "little or no enforcement."[13] The subsequent 2018 report recognized the progress in enforcement attained by Brazil since Lava

---

[6] Article 317 of the Brazilian Criminal Code.

[7] Article 332 of the Brazilian Criminal Code.

[8] Law 12,846/2013, Article 1.

[9] Law 12,846/2013, Article 2.

[10] Law 12,846/2013, Article 3, paras.1 and 2.

[11] Law 12,846/2013, Article 5.

[12] Law 12,846/2013, Article 6.

[13] Exporting Corruption, Report on the Enforcement of the OECD Convention on Combating Foreign Bribery, 2015, *available at* http://www.transparency.org/exporting_corruption.

Jato, thus upgrading the country from the "low" to the "moderate," along with Portugal and Sweden.[14]

In 2014, the OECD Working Group on Bribery published Brazil's Phase 3 Report, in which it evaluated and made recommendations regarding Brazil's enforcement of the OECD Convention on Combating the Bribery of Foreign Public Officials in International Business Transactions and related instruments. The Report commended Brazil for improvement in discrete areas, in particular the enactment of the *Clean Company Act*, but criticized Brazil for its low level of enforcement of foreign bribery. The 2017 Follow-Up Phase 3 Report commended Brazil for the progress it has made in both its level of enforcement and in its ability to proactively investigate and prosecute foreign bribery, but identified asset recovery, money laundering, accounting and auditing as key areas for further improvement.[15]

Increased enforcement has led to a deterioration in the perception about corruption in Brazil. Brazil fell 20 positions in the Transparency International Corruption Perceptions Index,[16] passing from the 76th position in 2015 to the 96th position in 2017.

3. Investigative and Prosecutorial Agencies

The *Clean Company Act* adopted a decentralized structure for the enforcement of corporate liability for acts of corruption. At the federal level, the highest authority of each organ of the executive, legislative and judicial branches has original jurisdiction to investigate and administratively prosecute companies for any acts against the public administration within the meaning of the law.[17] Administrative cases are adjudicated by the same authority that investigates the conduct. The *Clean Company Act* provided the General Comptroller's Office (Controladoria Geral da União—"CGU") with concurrent jurisdiction to prosecute companies for any acts against the federal public administration.[18] The law also provided the CGU with *exclusive* jurisdiction to investigate, prosecute, and adjudicate any cases involving acts against any *foreign* public administration.[19] In an effort to provide the CGU with higher hierarchical status, the office was converted into the Ministry of Transparency and General Comptroller's Office, with similar competencies.[20]

At the state and municipal levels, each entity of the federation has the authority to establish its own agencies to investigate and prosecute companies for any acts against the public administration that occur within their respective jurisdictions. The City of São Paulo, for example, decided to mirror the federal structure and conferred upon the recently created Municipal Comptroller's Office the authority to investigate, prosecute, and adjudicate

---

[14] Exporting Corruption, Report on the Enforcement of the OECD Convention on Combating Foreign Bribery, 2018, *available at* https://www.transparency.org/whatwedo/publication/exporting_corruption_2018.

[15] Follow-Up to The Phase 3 Report & Recommendations (Feb. 2017), available online at http://www.oecd.org/corruption/anti-bribery/Brazil-Phase-3-Written-Follow-Up-Report-ENG.pdf.

[16] *Available at* https://www.transparency.org/news/feature/corruption_perceptions_index_2017#table

[17] Law 12,846, Article 8.

[18] Law 12,846/2013, Article 8, second para.

[19] Law 12,846/2013, Article 9.

[20] Law 13,341/2016.

corporate liability for acts against the São Paulo municipal administration. At the time of this writing, as many as 16 different jurisdictions in Brazil had regulated the *Clean Company Act* and created their own agencies to investigate and prosecute acts against the public administration as defined in the *Clean Company Act* that have occurred within their respective jurisdictions.

With respect to the criminal prosecution of individuals, the Brazilian Federal Constitution bestowed upon the Public Prosecutor's Office (Ministério Público) the authority to bring criminal suits against individuals.[21] The Federal Public Prosecutor's Office (Ministério Público Federal) is responsible, inter alia, for prosecuting crimes that involve entities of the Federal Public Administration in any capacity. Such lawsuits fall within the original jurisdiction of the federal courts.[22] The State Public Prosecutor's Office (Ministério Público Estadual) has residual authority to prosecute crimes on all matters not falling within the original jurisdiction of federal courts.[23]

The enactment and entry into force of the *Clean Company Act* in 2014 enhanced the need for cooperation among the various enforcement agencies that have authority over corruption matters, in particular with respect to leniency agreements that are executed under that statute and may involve individual liability as well as antitrust liability. In order to resolve any ambiguities as to the authority of the various prosecutorial agencies, on December 18, 2015, the executive branch published Provisional Measure 703/2015. It amended Articles 15 and 16 of the *Clean Company Act* to provide more clearly that the CGU, the Federal Prosecutor's Office, and the Attorney General retain concurrent jurisdiction at the federal level to negotiate and enter into leniency agreements, and that the Federal Court of Accounts (Tribunal de Contas da União—TCU) has exclusive authority to determine whether the terms of any restitution are sufficient to reimburse the National Treasury.[24] At this writing, Provisional Measure 703/2015 has not been converted into law and therefore has expired. Also in 2015, Federal Decree 8,420 was published to regulate administrative proceedings under the *Clean Company Act*.

4. Bribery of Domestic and Foreign Officials

The *Clean Company Act* does not distinguish between the bribery of domestic and foreign public officials,[25] other than to establish that the authority to prosecute acts against the foreign public administration rests within CGU.[26] As noted earlier, the *Clean Company Act* sanctions a wide variety of corrupt and anti-competitive practices, such as bribery, the financing of corrupt acts, the hiding of funds or interests, bid-rigging, fraud in the execution and performance of government contracts, and obstruction of audits, inspections, and investigations by public officials.[27] Bribery, in particular, is defined as to "promise, offer

---

[21] Article 129 of the Brazilian Federal Constitution.
[22] Article 109 of the Brazilian Federal Constitution.
[23] Article 125 of the Brazilian Federal Constitution.
[24] Provisional Measure 703/2015, Article I (amending Article 16 of Law 12,846/2013).
[25] Law 12,846/2013, Articles 1 and 5.
[26] Law 12,846/2013, Article 9.
[27] Law 12,846/2013, Article 5.

or give, directly or indirectly, an undue advantage to a public official, or to a related third party."[28]

Any legal entities, Brazilian or foreign, headquartered, having subsidiaries or representative offices, or temporarily established, in Brazil are subject to liability for acts of corruption under the *Clean Company Act*.[29] The law also expressly provides for successor liability in cases of mergers or acquisitions. Successor liability is, however, limited to the amount of the injury caused to the public administration, up to the net worth acquired by the successor.[30] Controlled and related entities are jointly liable for any acts against the public administration performed by the parent or related entity.[31]

The statute of limitations for acts against the domestic or foreign public administration is five years, counted from the date of the act or, in case of continued conduct, the date of cessation of the conduct.[32]

The *Clean Company Act* does not contain any definition of a "domestic public official." Brazilian criminal law, however, defines a public official as "any person who holds a public position, employment or function, albeit transitorily or without remuneration."[33] Employees of state-owned enterprises are also public officials for purposes of Brazilian criminal law.[34]

The *Clean Company Act* adopts a similar approach in defining *foreign* public officials. The law defines "foreign public administration," as any "body or state entity or diplomatic representation of a foreign country, at any level of government, as well as legal entities directly or indirectly controlled by the government of a foreign state."[35] International organizations are deemed foreign public administration for purposes of the law.[36] Foreign public officials, in turn, are "any person that has a position, employment or function, albeit temporarily or without remuneration, with a foreign governmental body or entity, with a diplomatic representation, or with any legal entity that is controlled, directly or indirectly, by a foreign state."[37]

The offer of gifts, gratuities, and hospitality to a public official may constitute an "undue advantage" within the meaning of the *Clean Company Act*. In October 2015, the CGU published its "Integrity Programs—Guidelines For Legal Entities" ("CGU Guidelines") establishing the minimum requirements for compliance programs of companies subject to the *Clean Company* Act. Although the CGU expressly recognizes that gifts, gratuities, and hospitality may be a legitimate business expense necessary for the promotion of a company's products or services, it requires that companies adopt policies to make sure that these types of expenses do not constitute improper payments to public officials. According to the CGU Guidelines, companies need to put in place procedures to ensure that any such expenses are

---

[28] *Id.*, Article 5, Section I.

[29] *Id.*, Article 1, sole paragraph.

[30] *Id.*, Article 4, first paragraph.

[31] *Id.*, Article 4, second paragraph.

[32] *Id.*, Article 25.

[33] Article 327 of the Brazilian Criminal Code.

[34] Article 327 of the Brazilian Criminal Code, first paragraph.

[35] Law 12,846/2013, Article 5, Section V, first paragraph.

[36] Law 12,846/2013, Article 5, Section V, second paragraph.

[37] Law 12,846/2013, Article 5, Section V, third paragraph.

reasonable, and in accordance with local legislation.[38] Brazilian law, for example, stipulates a limit of R $100 (about 25–30 U.S. dollars) for gifts and gratuities to federal public officials.[39] In addition, any such expenses cannot be provided with "unreasonable frequency" to the same recipient.[40] Invitations involving travel and related expenses must be clearly associated with the promotion of products or services.[41] The CGU recommends further that companies develop indicators so that employees can develop their critical ability to assess the reasonableness of an offer of gift, gratuity, or hospitality to a public official, and clearly communicate to their employees the responsible person to whom questions in this regard should be addressed.[42]

The *Clean Company Act* does not provide for any affirmative defenses, but the existence of adequate compliance procedures constitutes a mitigating factor in establishing a company's penalties for acts against the public administration. The CGU Guidelines provide that compliance programs must rest on the following five "pillars": (1) commitment and support from senior management, (2) an internal department provided with resources to ensure the implementation of the program, (3) assessment of the company's risk profile, (4) a proper framework and structure to ensure compliance, and (5) continuous monitoring and implementation. Although emphasizing that there is no one-size-fits-all compliance program, the CGU Guidelines highlight anti-corruption measures and policies related to: (1) interactions with government entities, (2) offering gifts and hospitality, (3) accounting records and controls, (4) hiring of third parties, (5) mergers and acquisitions, and (6) sponsorships and donations. The CGU Guidelines also underscore the need for policies that include proper communication and training, appropriate reporting channels, adequate disciplinary and remediation actions, and continuous monitoring within a company. These elements will be familiar to business with compliance programs in the United States and UK.

5. Commercial Bribery

Brazilian law does not impose criminal or administrative sanctions for bribery between private parties. The payment of kickbacks on private contracts is typically subject to restitution under civil law, and gives rise to "just cause" for dismissal of the employee under Brazilian labor law. However, any actions by the recipient to disguise the origin of funds obtained through commercial bribery may constitute the crime of money laundering, as discussed further below.

6. Related Criminal Offenses

In addition to the *Clean Company Act*, in recent years Brazil also enacted legislation that improved its anti-money-laundering framework, and created the crime of

---

[38] CGU Guidelines, p. 17.
[39] Brazilian Code of Conduct for Federal Employees, Article 9, sole paragraph, Section II.
[40] CGU Guidelines, p. 17.
[41] *Id.*
[42] *Id.*

"criminal organization" to combat widespread corruption at all levels of government. "Money laundering" in Brazil is defined as conduct designed to "hide or disguise the nature, origin, provenance, disposition, movement or property of assets, rights, or values obtained, directly or indirectly, from a criminal offense."[43] Money laundering is sanctioned with 3 to 10 years imprisonment, and fines. Sentences may be increased by up to two-thirds if the crimes are committed repeatedly, or through a criminal organization.

The crime of "criminal organization," in turn, is the "association of 4 or more individuals structurally coordinated and characterized by the division of tasks, albeit informally, with the objective of obtaining any advantage, directly or indirectly, through criminal offenses whose maximum jail sentences are greater than 4 years in prison."[44] Individuals participating in a criminal organization, or which hinder investigations related to a criminal organization, are subject to between three to eight years in prison, and fines, without prejudice of any sentences for the underlying criminal offenses.[45] The sentence is increased by up to one-sixth if a public official aids or abets the criminal organization, if the criminal organization is transnational, or if it is connected with international criminal organizations.[46]

7. Cooperation and Self-Reporting

Taking a page out of Brazil's competition law enforcement book, the *Clean Company Act* provides for a leniency program that gives authorities discretion to reduce fines by two-thirds for the first entity that cooperates with investigations, admits to wrongdoing, and ceases any misconduct. On December 8, 2015, the executive branch enacted Provisional Measure 703/2015, which amended the *Clean Company Act* so as to eliminate the requirements that companies admit to any wrongdoing and be the first to enter into leniency agreements with the CGU.[47] Provisional Measure 703/2015 also conferred concurrent jurisdiction on the CGU, the Federal Prosecutor's Office, and the attorney general to negotiate and enter into leniency agreements. Any restitution agreed in the context of a leniency agreement needs to be approved by the Federal Court of Accounts—TCU.[48] At the time of this writing, Congress had not converted Provisional Measure 703/2015 into law within the prescribed four-month period, and it has therefore expired.

Modern criminal statutes have introduced plea bargains into Brazilian law. Traditionally, as with many continental law jurisdictions, judges and prosecutors were prohibited from transacting with cooperating witnesses or criminal defendants in exchange for their cooperation, because this would constitute a violation of prosecutorial duties. Since the enactment of the "heinous crimes" law in the 1990s, however, criminal statutes began expressly providing judges and prosecutors with the authority to reduce jail sentences and fines in exchange for the defendants' cooperation with investigations. For example, the law that instituted Brazil's

---

[43] Law 12,863/2012, Article 2, amending Law 9,613/1998, Article 1.

[44] Law 12,850/2013, Article 1.

[45] Law 12,850/2013, Article 2, first paragraph.

[46] *Id.*, Article 2, fourth paragraph.

[47] *Id.* Provisional Measure 703/2015, Article I (amending Article 16 of Law 12,846/2013).

[48] *Id.*

witness protection program provides the judge with the authority to grant a judicial pardon and extinguish the criminal liability of a criminal defendant who, having no prior criminal conviction, effectively and voluntarily cooperates with the investigation.[49]

Similarly, the statute creating the criminal organization offense provides that the judge may reduce by up to two-thirds the sanctions of defendants who effectively and voluntarily cooperate with the investigation and criminal prosecution, provided that such cooperation leads to the identification of co-actors and crimes committed by them, the hierarchical structure and division of tasks in the criminal organization, recovery of assets, or localization of victims with their physical integrity preserved.[50] The judge may not participate in negotiations between the Public Prosecutor's Office, cooperating witnesses, and their legal counsel, but must nonetheless review and approve the collaboration agreement.[51] In case of retraction, any self-incriminating evidence may not be used in court against the criminal defendant.[52]

Criminal prosecutions resulting from the *Lava Jato* investigations have been largely based on a series of successive plea bargains that were struck with criminal defendants. First, the Public Prosecutor's Office entered into collaboration agreements with former Petrobras executives Pedro Barusco and Paulo Roberto Costa, followed by a collaboration agreement with financial operator Alberto Youssef. The evidence they provided in turn led to a series of plea bargains with the lobbyists, executives of construction companies, Petrobras suppliers, and ultimately with politicians such as former Senate leader Delcidio Amaral. At this writing, more than 176 collaboration agreements have been executed between criminal defendants and Public Prosecutors in the context of *Lava Jato*. The evidence that these collaborators produced has led to the imprisonment and ultimate conviction of very prominent individuals, such as the Chief Executive Officer of Construtora Odebrecht S.A., Marcelo Odebrecht, convicted in 2016 and sentenced to 19 years and 4 months in prison for active corruption, money laundering, and criminal organization. The collaboration agreement by former majority Senate leader Delcidio Amaral implicated both former president Lula and Dilma Rousseffin the alleged use of diverted Petrobras funds to finance their successful presidential bids. Separately, former President Lula was charged and convicted on different corruption charges and is now serving time in prison. In the 2018 Presidential campaign, he was launched as a candidate by the Labor's Party, and gathered great popular support until his candidacy was overruled by the Superior Electoral Court based on Brazil's Clean Record Law.[53]

8. Whistle-blower Protection

Brazilian law does not provide for whistle-blower protection. Nongovernmental organizations (NGOs) such as Transparency International and others have urged Brazilian authorities to adopt

---

[49] Law 9,807/99, Article 13.

[50] Law 12,850/2013, Article 4.

[51] Law 12,850/2013, Article 4, paragraph 6.

[52] Law 12,850/2013, Article 4, paragraph 10.

[53] Supplementary Law 135/2010.

legislation providing for whistle-blower protection following the Transparency International whistle-blower principles and the Organization of American States Model Law.[54]

9. Key International Treaties relating to Bribery

Brazil is a party to the United Nations' Convention Against Corruption,[55] the Inter-American Convention Against Corruption of the Organization of the American States,[56] and the OECD Convention on Combatting Bribery of Foreign Public Officials in International Business Transactions.[57]

10. Mutual Legal Assistance

Brazil has an extensive network of treaties providing for mutual international assistance in criminal matters. Brazil has ratified 20 bilateral treaties on this topic, with the following countries: Belgium,[58] Canada,[59] China,[60] Colombia,[61] Cuba,[62] France,[63] Honduras,[64] Italy,[65] Mexico,[66] Nigeria,[67] Panama,[68] Peru,[69] Portugal,[70] South Korea,[71] Spain,[72] Suriname,[73] Switzerland,[74] Ukraine,[75] the United Kingdom,[76] and the United States.[77]

Brazil has also joined several multilateral treaties on mutual legal assistance on criminal matters, such as the Inter-American Convention on Mutual Assistance in Criminal Matters[78]

---

[54] *See, e.g.*, http://blog.transparency.org/2015/11/12/brazil-needs-effective-protection-for-witnesses-and-victims-of-corruption (last visited Dec. 13, 2018).

[55] Legislative Decree 348/2005and Presidential Decree 5,687/2006.

[56] Legislative Decree 152/2002 and Presidential Decree 4,410/2002.

[57] Legislative Decree 125/2000 and Presidential Decree 3,678/2000.

[58] Decree 9.130/2017.

[59] Decree 6.747/2009.

[60] Decree 6.282/2007.

[61] Decree 3.895/2001.

[62] Decree 6.462/2008.

[63] Decree 3.324/1999.

[64] Decree 8.046/2013.

[65] Decree 862/1993.

[66] Decree 7.595/2011.

[67] Decree 7.582/2011.

[68] Decree 7.596/2011.

[69] Decree 3.988/2001.

[70] Decree 1.320/1994.

[71] Decree 5.721/2006.

[72] Decree 6.681/2008.

[73] Decree 6.832/2009.

[74] Decree 6.974/2009.

[75] Decree 5.984/2006.

[76] Decree 8.047/2013.

[77] Decree 3.810/2001.

[78] Decree 6.340/2006.

(Nassau Convention), the Managua Protocol complementing it,[79] and the Protocol of Mutual Legal Assistance in Criminal Matters or Mercosur (San Luis Protocol),[80] to which Bolivia and Chile have also subsequently adhered.[81]

11. Legal Profession Privilege

Traditionally, attorney-client communications were seen as confidential in Brazil, and generally protected from judicial discovery. In part, this broad understanding of the legal profession privilege stemmed from the federal constitution, which generally protects the secrecy of information that is necessary for the fulfillment of a regulated profession,[82] and enshrines the principle of "sanctity" of acts and manifestations of lawyers in the exercise of the legal profession.[83] Similarly, criminal and civil statutes penalize the violation of professional secrecy,[84] and exempt lawyers from producing evidence in both criminal and civil proceedings.[85]

The regulation of the legal profession similarly provides that a lawyer's place of work; instruments; communications (including written, phone, or digital correspondence) are privileged, *provided that these are related to the lawyer's professional activities.*[86] The proviso was a response to Portaria 1,288/2005 of the Ministry of Justice, which interpreted the privilege as not applying to judicially authorized searches and seizures of law firms whenever there were indicia that the lawyer possessed "documents or data necessary for elucidation of the facts." Currently, therefore, attorney-client communications are generally protected from judicial discovery, provided that the information relates exclusively to the attorney's professional activities. Information in furtherance of illegal activities or the concealment of the proceeds thereof are therefore not privileged.

12. Privacy and Data Protection

Brazilian law protects the right to intimacy and the privacy of personal data. The federal constitution identifies the right to privacy as a fundamental right of individuals,[87] and enshrines the principle of "sanctity" of data and telephone communications, except with judicial authorization.[88] Similarly, the internet civil framework requires telecommunications operators to safeguard and protect the privacy of personal data.[89] Beyond these general principles,

---

[79] Decree 6.340/2006.
[80] Decree 3.468/2000.
[81] Mercosur/CMC/Dec. n. 12/01.
[82] Article V, para. XIV of the Federal Constitution.
[83] Article 133 of the Federal Constitution.
[84] Article 154 of the Criminal Code.
[85] Article 207 of the Criminal Procedure Code.
[86] Law 8,906/1994, Article 7, section II, as amended by Law 11,767/2008.
[87] Federal Constitution, Article 5, X.
[88] *Id.*, Article 5, XII.
[89] Law 12,965/2014, Article 3, III.

Brazil has recently adopted a specific statute regulating the issue of privacy and data protection, known as New General Data Privacy Law (LGPD).[90]

Inspired by the European Union's General Data Privacy Regulation (GDPR), it grants broad protection to user data in Brazil in terms of privacy and intimacy.[91] It also includes specific protection to sensitive data, such as those related to political opinions. Notwithstanding, the new legislation is not applicable to activities related to criminal investigation,[92] which could be the case of corruption investigations. The new regulation will only come into effect into 2020, 18 months after being signed, giving a reasonable amount of time for companies to adapt. In practice, the new law does not resolve all the ambiguities of the previous more general legislation. Similar to the application of GDPR in Europe, the implementation of LGPD will depend on the interpretation of concepts that allow for the treatment of personal data, such as the user's "explicit and specific informed consent"[93] to be granted by the user or the "concrete and legitimate interest" of the entity controlling the data (also called the operator).[94]

13. Forecast for Reforms

In the medium term, one can still expect significant legislative activity on anti-corruption in Brazil. With the expiration of Provisional Measure 703/2015, one can reasonably expect leniency agreements to be the subject of further regulation in the near future.

Politically, the scenario is a bit murkier. The *Clean Company Act* and the *Lava Jato* investigation unquestionably represent a paradigm shift in anti-corruption enforcement in Brazil, and have the potential to change the way in which companies do business with the Brazilian government, as well as the manner in which political campaigns are financed. At the time of this writing, however, questions remained as to whether the ruling political establishment will act to undermine progress achieved in anti-corruption enforcement. After President Rousseff's impeachment (for unrelated fiscal misconduct charges), draft legislation seeking to criminalize "abuse of power" by public prosecutors in anti-corruption matters esd introduced in Congress. The interim Temer administration also is said to have thwarted draft legislation that would criminalize off-the-book campaign financing and unjust enrichment by public officials. Despite such efforts to undermine enforcement, 9 in every 10 Brazilians support *Lava Jato*, making it quite unlikely that any congressional backlash against it will succeed in the near future. The newly elected Brazilian President, Jair Bolsonaro, ran in part on an anti-corruption platform and has appointed Sergio Moro, the judge who oversaw *Lava Jato,* as his Justice Minister.

---

[90] Law 13,709/2018.
[91] Law 13,709/2018. Article 2.
[92] *Id.* Article 4, III, d.
[93] *Id.* Article 6.
[94] *Id.* Article 10.

APPENDIX

Key Issues	Brazil's Approach
Is jurisdiction subject to any international anti-corruption conventions? If so, which? (OECD, UN Convention Against Corruption, etc.)	Brazil is a party to the UN Convention Against Corruption; the Inter-American Convention Against Corruption of the Organization of the American States, and the OECD Convention on Combatting Bribery of Foreign Public Officials in International Business Transactions.
Is bribery of foreign public officials illegal (do domestic anti-bribery laws provide for extraterritorial application)?	Yes. Articles 1 and 5 of Law 12,846/2013 ("*Clean Company Act*") prohibit the payment of bribes by companies in Brazil to foreign officials.
What is the definition of foreign public officials?	Article 5, first paragraph, of the *Clean Company Act* defines a "foreign public administration" as "State organs or entities or diplomatic representations of a foreign country, at any level or sphere of government, as well as entities controlled, directly or indirectly, by a foreign public administration." Paragraph 2 provides that international public organizations shall also be deemed a "foreign public administration" for purposes of the law.
Is commercial bribery illegal?	Commercial bribery is not sanctioned criminally, but may be "just cause" for termination under Brazilian labor laws.
Is bribing domestic officials illegal?	Yes. Articles 1 and 5 of the *Clean Company Act* provide for strict corporate liability for bribes to both domestic and foreign public officials.
Can the receipt of a bribe be prosecuted?	Yes. Article 317 of the Criminal Code provides for the crime of "passive corruption."
Can companies be held criminally liable? If so, what is the requisite intent for criminal liability to attach?	Brazil does not provide for corporate criminal liability.
Can companies be held civilly liable?	Yes. Article 1 of Law 12,846/2013 (*Clean Company Act*) provides for administrative and civil liability of companies for acts against the public administration.

(*Continued*)

Key Issues	Brazil's Approach
Can individuals be held civilly liable?	Yes. Article 3 of the *Clean Company Act* establishes that corporate liability does not exclude individual liability for acts of corruption.
Is there a "facilitation/grease payments" exception?	No.
Does the subject country provide for conspiracy liability relating to violations of the anti-corruption laws?	Brazil does not have a statute that is precisely equivalent to U.S. conspiracy law. Organized conspiracies to undertake corrupt acts can be the subject of prosecution under the "organized crime" ("crime organizado") legislation, which requires four or more persons as an element of the offense.
Does the subject country provide for: (a) aiding/abetting liability relating to violations of the anti-corruption laws? (b) attempt liability relating to violations of the anti-corruption laws?	(a) Brazilian criminal law sanctions co-participants and accomplices in all crimes, which includes the crimes of active and passive corruption. (b) Attempts also generate criminal liability, including for crimes of corruption.
Is failure to keep accurate books and records a criminal and/or civil offense?	The *Clean Company Act* does not provide for separate liability for books-and-records violations, but the CGU Guidelines identify proper accounting and control as one of the elements of adequate compliance procedures.
Do any books and records violations have to involve underlying bribery proof?	Not Applicable.
Are there laws concerning a company's financial internal control? If so, are those laws applicable to private and public companies or just public companies?	Yes, both private and public companies are subject to corporate laws that contain accounting and bookkeeping provisions.
Is there an affirmative disclosure obligations for potential violations of the anti-bribery laws or accounting irregularities?	No, but the early disclosure of violations is a mitigating factor in the context of leniency agreements under the *Clean Company Act*.
Are "promotional expenses" exempt from the anti-bribery laws?	No, but the CGU Guidelines establish that reasonable expenses incurred in the promotion of the company's businesses ordinarily would not give rise to liability.

Key Issues	Brazil's Approach
Is the giving of gifts, entertainment, travel, meals, etc. restricted/prohibited?	Yes. The Brazilian Code of Conduct for Federal Employees establishes that gifts shall not exceed R $100 (about U.S. $30).
Are there any laws concerning things of value conveyed by, or to, third parties?	On the supply side, third parties are subject to the same limitations that apply to the parties they represent with respect to any dealings with public officials. There are no legal restrictions on gifts to private third parties.
Are bribes tax deductible?	No.
Is the law applied extraterritorially?	Yes. Brazilian law applies to conduct in Brazil and abroad of any companies that are headquartered, have affiliates, or representative offices in Brazil.
Is having a robust corporate compliance program an affirmative defense or way to negate liability?	No. However, the existence of adequate compliance programs constitutes a mitigating factor in establishing the penalties under the *Clean Company Act*.
Is there a "local law" exception/defense?	No.
Is "credit" given for cooperation with authorities? If so, how and in what form?	Yes, Article 7 of the *Clean Company Act* directs authorities to take into account cooperation with authorities when establishing the penalties under the law.
Does the subject country have a Mutual Legal Assistance Treaty with the United States that generally covers criminal matters, including FCPA?	Yes.
What are the potential penalties/sanctions both for civil and criminal violations?	Civil violations: fine of up to 20 percent of the company revenues, disgorgement, publication of condemnatory sentence, and disbarment. Criminal violations: both active (supply) and passive (demand) corruption convictions carry jail sentences of between 2 and 12 years, plus fines.

4 Canada

1. Introduction: The Rising Tide of Enforcement in Canada

On December 7, 1998, Canada,[1] in fulfillment of its obligations as signatory to the Organization of Economic Co-Operation and Development (OECD) *Convention on Combating Bribery of Foreign Public Officials in International Business Transactions*, adopted the *Corruption of Foreign Officials Act* (CFPOA).[2] The CFPOA became law on February 14, 1999.[3]

For the next 12 years, not much happened in Canada in relation to the investigation or prosecution of domestic or foreign bribery offences. The sole prosecution under the CFPOA was in relation to the bribery of an American customs official to facilitate the entry of employees of a waste disposal firm into the United States. The corporation received a fine of $25,000.[4] Perhaps not surprisingly, in the March 2011, Phase 3 OECD Working Group Report for Canada, it was observed that local law enforcement in some parts of Canada lacked a basic awareness of the CFPOA.[5]

---

[1] This chapter was contributed by the World Bank's Tyler Hodgson, who authored this chapter in his personal capacity The views expressed in this chapter do not reflect the position of the World Bank or any other organization. The author would like to thank Swetha Popuri and Josh Zelikovitz for their invaluable contribution in the preparation of this chapter.

[2] *Corruption of Foreign Public Officials Act*, SC 1998, c. 34 (Can.).

[3] *Corruption of Foreign Public Officials Act*, SC 1998, c. 34 (Can.).

[4] *R. v. Watts*, [2005] A.J. No. 568 (QB).

[5] OECD, Phase 3 Report on Implementing the OECD Convention in Canada, para. 92.

From Baksheesh to Bribery. T. Markus Funk and Andrew S. Boutros.
© Oxford University Press 2019. Published 2019 by Oxford University Press.

The enforcement trend in Canada in relation to foreign corrupt practices began to change later that same year. In June, 2011, Niko Resources pleaded guilty to bribing a foreign public official under the CFPOA, received a fine of $9.5 million, and was placed on probation for a period of three years.[6] Less than two years later, Griffiths Energy pled guilty to bribing a foreign public official in relation to illicit payments made to the Chadian ambassador's wife and paid a fine of $10.35 million.[7] In May 2014, the first individual successfully prosecuted under the CFPOA was sentenced to three years imprisonment following trial.[8]

Beginning in 2013, several former executives of the Quebec engineering company SNC Lavalin and a Bangladeshi politician were charged with criminal offenses under the CFPOA. These allegations relate two distinct sets of accusations: the first, concern bribing foreign public officials in Bangladesh in relation to the moribund Padma Bridge project; the second relate to bribing members of the Gadafi family in Libya. The corporation itself was subject to a search warrant and, in February 2015, was charged with bribing Libyan government officials to the tune of nearly $48 million.[9]

Charges against two of the five individuals charged in relation to the Padma Bridge project were withdrawn or stayed prior to trial.[10] Litigation concerning the criminal case against the three remaining former SNC-Lavalin executives charged in relation to the Padma Bride project were recently withdrawn during trial following a protracted legal battle that ended up before the Supreme Court of Canada in relation to a third-party record application brought by the defendants to obtain a copy of the investigative file of the Integrity Vice Presidency (INT) of the World Bank Group.[11] INT some of the information from its investigation with the Royal Canadian Mounted Police (RCMP) in relation to the Padma Bridge project. The RCMP had in turn commenced its own criminal investigation and used the information provided by INT as the basis for obtaining criminal search warrants and wiretap authorizations. On a third-party records application to obtain INT's complete investigative file, the trial judge ruled that INT had waived any privileges and immunities associated with its archives by providing selective investigative information to the RCMP.[12] The Supreme Court allowed the appeal and reversed the findings of the trial judge, ruling that under the Articles of Agreement for the World Bank Group (of which Canada was a signatory), the privileges and immunities associated with the World Bank Group were inviolable.[13]

---

[6] *R.* v. *Niko Resources*, [2011] A.J. No. 1586 (QB).

[7] *R.* v. *Griffiths Energy*, [2013] A.J. No. 412 (QB.).

[8] *R.* v. *Karigar*, [2014] O.J. No. 2490 (SC): conviction appeal affirmed [2017] O.J. No. 3530 (CA); leave to appeal denied [2017] S.C.C.A. No. 385.

[9] The company was charged with one count of bribing a foreign public official, contrary to section 3(1) of the CFPOA; and one count of criminal fraud, contrary to section 380 of the *Criminal Code*.

[10] Criminal charges against Mohammad Ismail, a former engineer at SNC-Lavalin, were stayed in November 2015. Charges against Abdul Hasan Chowdhury, the former state minister of foreign affairs for Bangladesh, were stayed for want of jurisdiction by the Superior Court of Justice (Ontario): *Chowdhury* v. *Canada*, [2014] O.J. No. 2004.

[11] *World Bank Group* v. *Wallace*, 2016 SCC 15.

[12] *Wallace* v. *Canada*, [2014] O.J. No. 6534 (SC), paras. 29–55: reversed, *World Bank Group* v. *Wallace*, 2016 SCC 15.

[13] *World Bank Group* v. *Wallace*, 2016 SCC 15, paras. 66–67.

After the matter was remitted back to the trial judge by the Supreme Court, the trial judge proceeded to throw out the wiretap evidence underlying the Crown's case for being obtained in an unconstitutal manner.[14] The charges were subsequently withdrawn by the Crown.

The criminal charges against a former SNC Lavalin executives[15] and the corporation itself[16] in relation to the Libyan allegations remain outstanding and are proceeding to trial. Riadh Ben Aissa, the former head of the construction unit for SNC Lavalin, pleaded guilty to bribing the former son of Muammar Al Gathafi in Switzerland and was subsequently extradited to Canada.[17]

In one of the more significant recent developments, in June 2014, the RCMP laid their first charges against foreign nationals—one British and two American citizens—for bribing a foreign public official under the CFPOA (see Figure 4.1).[18]

On the domestic front, Senator Mike Duffy was charged with numerous counts of criminal fraud, breach of trust, fraud on the government, and bribing a judicial officer in relation to various claims submitted by Duffy in relation to Senate expenses. In a very high-profile decision, Senator Duffy was acquitted by the Ontario Court of Justice of all charges in early 2016.[19] Additionally, several former SNC Lavalin executives were charged in relation to a bid rigging scheme associated with the construction of a super hospital in Montreal. Pierre Duhaime, SNC Lavalin's former CEO, pleaded guilty to criminal breach of trust and is awaiting sentence.[20]

This notable increase in recent enforcement activity led Transparency International to conclude that Canada is one of the most improved nations in relation to anti-bribery enforcement.[21] As the remaining SNC Lavalin prosecutions continue to wind their way through the Canadian court system, all indications remain that enforcement activity will continue unabated in Canada.

2. Jurisdiction

2.1 TERRITORIALITY PRINCIPLE

Canada's *Criminal Code* contains a presumption *against* extraterritoriality.[22]

As a general rule, for an offense to be subject to the jurisdiction of Canadian courts, there must be a "real and substantial link" between the offense and Canada.[23] While the threshold

---

[14] *Wallace* v. *Canada*, [2017] O.J. No. 708 (SC).

[15] A motion to stay the charges for unreasonable delay brought by Sami Bebawi was denied: *R. c. Bebawi*, [2018] J.Q. No. 2990 (SC).

[16] The corporation was unable to reach a Deferred Prosecution Agreement with the Crown: "SNC Lavalin stock plunges after federal prosecutors decline to negotiate a deal," The Canadian Press, October 10, 2018: https://globalnews.ca/news/4534301/snc-lavalin-stock-plunges-after-federal-prosecutors-decline-to-negotiate-a-deal/.

[17] "Former SNC-Lavalin executive Riadh Ben Aissa pleads guilty to corruption charges", Financial Post, October 1, 2014: https://business.financialpost.com/news/fp-street/snc-riadh-ben-aissa-pleads-guilty.

[18] RCMP Press Release: "RCMP Charge Individuals with Foreign Corruption" (http://www.rcmp-grc.gc.ca/ottawa/ne-no/pr-cp/2014/0604-corruption-eng.htm).

[19] *R. v. Duffy*, 3026 ONCH 220.

[20] "Former SNC Lavalin CEO Pierre Duhaime pleads guilty for role in hospital bribery", February 1, 2019, The Canadian Press: https://globalnews.ca/news/4915064/former-snc-lavalin-ceo-pierre-duhaime-pleads-guilty-for-role-in-hospital-bribery/.

[21] 2012 Report Card.

[22] RSC 1985, c C-46, s 6(2) [*Code*] provides as follows: "Subject to this Act or any other Act of Parliament, no person shall be convicted or discharged under section 730 of an offence committed outside Canada."

[23] *Libman* v. *The Queen*, [1985] 2 SCR 178, 1985 CanLII 51 at para. 74.

Canada's Corruption of Foreign Public Officials Act

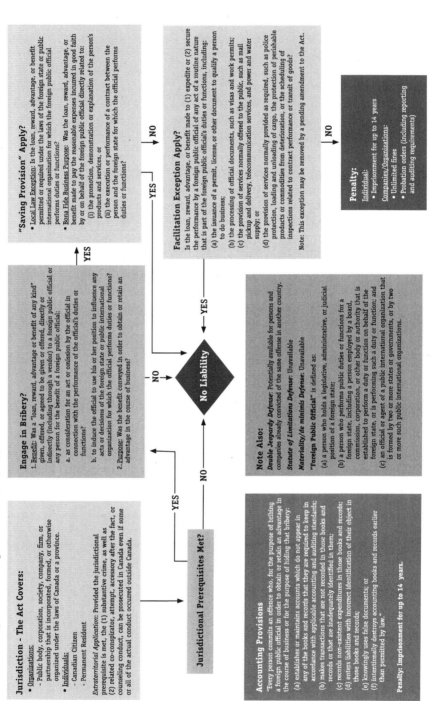

Jurisdiction - The Act Covers:

Organizations:
- Public body, corporation, society, company, firm, or partnership that is incorporated, formed, or otherwise organized under the laws of Canada or a province.

Individuals:
- Canadian Citizen
- Permanent Resident

Extraterritorial Application: Provided the jurisdictional prerequisite is met, the (1) substantive crime, as well as (2) related co-conspirator, attempt, accessory after the fact, or counseling conduct, can be prosecuted in Canada even if some or all of the actual conduct occurred outside Canada.

Jurisdictional Prerequisites Met?

Engage in Bribery?

1. **Benefit:** Was a "loan, reward, advantage or benefit of any kind" given, offered, or agreed to be given or offered, directly or indirectly (including through a vendor) to a foreign public official or any person for the benefit of a foreign public official:

   a. as consideration for an act or omission by the official in connection with the performance of the official's duties or functions?

   b. to induce the official to use his or her position to influence any acts or decisions of the foreign state or public international organization for which the official performs duties or functions?

2. **Purpose:** Was the benefit conveyed in order to obtain or retain an advantage in the course of business?

"Saving Provision" Apply?

- **Local Law Exception:** Is the loan, reward, advantage, or benefit permitted or required under the laws of the foreign state or public international organization for which the foreign public official performs duties or functions?
- **Bona Fide Business Purpose:** Was the loan, reward, advantage, or benefit made to pay the reasonable expenses incurred in good faith by or on behalf of the foreign public official directly related to:
  (i) the promotion, demonstration or explanation of the persons products and services, or
  (ii) the execution or performance of a contract between the person and the foreign state for which the official performs duties or functions?

Facilitation Exception Apply?

Is the loan, reward, advantage, or benefit made to (1) expedite or (2) secure the performance by a foreign public official of any act of a routine nature that is part of the foreign public official's duties or functions, including:

(a) the issuance of a permit, license, or other document to qualify a person to do business;

(b) the processing of official documents, such as visas and work permits;

(c) the provision of services normally offered to the public, such as mail pickup and delivery, telecommunication services, and power and water supply; or

(d) the provision of services normally provided as required, such as police protection, loading and unloading of cargo, the protection of perishable products or commodities from deterioration, or the scheduling of inspections related to contract performance or transit of goods?

Note: This exception may be removed by a pending amendment to the Act.

No Liability

Note Also:

Double Jeopardy Defense: Potentially available for persons and companies already convicted of the same offense in another country.

Statute of Limitations Defense: Unavailable

Materiality/de minimis Defense: Unavailable

"Foreign Public Official" is defined as:

(a) a person who holds a legislative, administrative, or judicial position of a foreign state;

(b) a person who performs public duties or functions for a foreign state, including a person employed by a board, commission, corporation, or other body or authority that is established to perform a duty or function on behalf of the foreign state, or is performing such a duty or function; and

(c) an official or agent of a public international organization that is formed by two or more states or governments, or by two or more such public international organizations.

Accounting Provisions

"Every person commits an offence who, for the purpose of bribing a foreign public official in order to obtain or retain an advantage in the course of business or for the purpose of hiding that bribery:

(a) establishes or maintains accounts which do not appear in any of the books and records that they are required to keep in accordance with applicable accounting and auditing standards;

(b) makes transactions that are not recorded in those books and records or that are inadequately identified in them;

(c) records non-existent expenditures in those books and records;

(d) enters liabilities with incorrect identification of their object in those books and records;

(e) knowingly uses false documents; or

(f) intentionally destroys accounting books and records earlier than permitted by law."

Penalty: Imprisonment for up to 14 years.

Penalty:

Individual:
- Imprisonment for up to 14 years

Companies/Organizations:
- Unlimited fines
- Probation orders (including reporting and auditing requirements)

YES / **NO**

This chart was prepared by Perkins Coie Partner T. Markus Funk (MFunk@perkinscoie.com). Markus retains the copyright to this chart.

FIGURE 4.1 Canada's Corruption of Foreign Public Officials Act

for a "real and substantial link" is certainly met if a significant portion of the activities constituting the offense took place in Canada, the outer limit of what is captured by this jurisdictional test is still uncertain.[24] Recent judicial trends, especially in the area of foreign bribery, indicate that the test was "never applied rigidly" by Canadian courts to preclude prosecutions of criminal activity committed in whole or in part in another jurisdiction.[25] The Ontario Court of Appeal has held that the "real and substantial" link test may be satisfied where Canada is the only country that has an interest in ensuring compliance with a Canadian court order, even where the prohibited conduct occurred entirely outside of the territory of Canada.[26]

The scope of Canada's territorial jurisdiction was clarified in 2013 when Nazir Karigar challenged his liability under the CFPOA on the basis that Canada lacked the territorial jurisdiction to try his case.[27] Karigar was a Canadian resident operating as a paid agent for Cryptomentrics Canada, a Canadian corporation. Karigar was eventually charged for his role in a conspiracy to bribe India's Minister of Civil Aviation in order to ensure that Cryptometrics Canada was successful in its bid for a biometric contract with Air India.[28] As all acts of bribery took place outside of Canada—either in India or the United States— Karigar argued that there was no "real and substantial link" between the offense and Canada.

Relying on Canada's commitment to combat international bribery as a signatory of the OECD convention, the Court found that a rigorous or narrow approach to jurisdictional issues was unwarranted. The Court determined that a real and substantial link to Canada can exist even where none of the essential elements of the offense occur on Canadian soil.[29] In rejecting Karigar's argument, the Court relied on the fact that Cryptometrics Canada is a Canadian company based in Ottawa and that Karigar had been a Canadian resident for many years. The Court also noted that if the bid had been successful, Canadian employees would have been responsible for a large portion of the work required by the contract.[30] Accordingly, even if none of the essential elements of a criminal offense occurred in Canada, there was a sufficient nexus to the country for the court to assume jurisdiction over the transactions in question.[31]

2.2 NATIONALITY PRINCIPLE

In 2013, the CFPOA was amended to allow Canadian Courts to establish jurisdiction over CFPOA offenses on the basis of the nationality principle. According to this principle, every legal or natural person of a defined category who commits an act or omission outside Canada

---

[24] *Id.* at paras. 74, 76.

[25] *R. v. Karigar*, 2013 ONSC 5199 (SC), para. 39.

[26] *R v. Rattray*, 2008 ONCA 74 at paras. 34-35 citing *R v. Greco*, 2001 CanLII 8608 (ON CA) at paras., 41–42.

[27] *R. v. Karigar*, 2013 ONSC 5199: affirmed [2017] O.J. No. 3530 (CA).

[28] *Id.*; several Air India officials were also implicated in the conspiracy. At the time Air India was a government-controlled entity.

[29] *Id.*; see also *R v. Karigar*, [2012] OJ No 6531 (SC): motion to quash indictment for want of territorial jurisdiction.

[30] *Id.*

[31] *R. v. Karigar*, [2017] O.J. No. 3530 (CA) at para. 30. The Ontario Court of Appeal appears to find that it is not necessary that an essential element of the offense take place in Canada for Canadian courts to assume territorial jurisdiction over CFPOA matters. See also *R. v. Barra*, [2018] O.J. No. 2471 (SC).

that would constitute an offense under the CFPOA if it had been committed in Canada is *deemed* by law to have committed that act or omission *in* Canada. That said, this principle applies only if the person is a Canadian citizen, permanent resident (who, after the commission of the act or omission, is present in Canada), or an entity, such as a corporation or partnership, organized under the laws of Canada.[32]

The fact that the extraterritorial application of the CFPOA under the nationality principle is limited to Canadian nationals and corporations has been used by Canadian courts as a strong indicator that any extraterritorial application of the Act to foreign nationals and corporations must be tempered. In the case of *Chowdhury v. Canada*, the Ontario Superior Court found this approach to be consistent with notions of international comity and the rebuttable presumption that Parliament does not intend to infringe state sovereignty or the norms of international law.[33]

3. Limitations

There are three general categories of offenses in Canada: indictable offenses (typically the most serious criminal offenses), summary conviction offenses (generally minor offenses with simplified procedures), and hybrid offenses, where the Crown may elect to proceed either by indictment or by way of summary conviction. Under Canadian law, hybrid offenses are considered indictable offenses unless and until the Crown elects to proceed by way of summary conviction.[34]

All foreign and domestic bribery offenses in Canada are indictable offenses, though some related offenses are hybrids.

Summary conviction offenses have a six-month limitation period.[35] By contrast, indictable offenses do *not* have any limitation period in Canada. This would include *all* bribery and corruption offenses under both the *Criminal Code* and the CFPOA.[36]

While the Canadian *Charter of Rights and Freedoms* affords an accused charged with an offense the right be tried within a reasonable time,[37] the absence of a limitation period is

---

[32] *Bill S-14; Follow-Up Report.* Section 5, CFPOA.

[33] *Chowdhury v. Canada,* 2014 ONSC 2635 (CanLII) at para. 43. While the nationality principle, working in conjunction with the territoriality principle described previously, has extended the scope of Canadian jurisdiction over CFPOA offences, the Ontario Superior Court in the *Chowdhury* decision recently clarified that there is a distinction between the concepts of jurisdiction over the person and jurisdiction over the offense. Canadian jurisdiction properly established over a CFPOA offense does not necessarily mean that Canada has the legal means necessary to compel a party (jurisdiction over the person) to be subject to its judicial process (jurisdiction over the offense); *R* v. *Chowdary,* 2014 ONSC 2635 (CanLII) at para. 54.

[34] *R.* v. *Paul-Marr,* 2005 NSCA 73 (CAo, paras. 17–34).

[35] *Criminal Code, supra,* s 786(2).

[36] For hybrid offenses laid outside of the six-month limitation period, the Crown may proceed by indictment: *R v. Dudley,* [2009] 3 SCR 570. As the vast majority of offenses contained in the *Criminal Code* are either indictable or hybrid, this effectively means that there is no applicable statute of limitations for the majority of offenses.

[37] Part I of the Constitution Act, 1982, being Schedule B to the *Canada Act 1982* (UK), 1982, c 11, ss 7, 11(b). Generally, the s. 11(b) clock begins to tick when a charge is laid. There is very limited constitutional protection against pre-charge delay: *R.* v. *Kalanj,* [1989] 1 SCR 1594.

particularly impactful for CFPOA offenses as the complexity and scope of these offenses often preclude both timely detection and resolution. For example, on February 19, 2015, the RCMP laid charges against SNC-Lavalin Group Inc. for conduct taking place as far back as 14 years earlier.[38]

4. Enforcement Framework

Under the constitutional division of powers in Canada, the power to pass criminal legislation in Canada rests exclusively with the federal government.[39] Accordingly, the *Criminal Code of Canada* has effect throughout the country, as does any legislation enacted by the federal Parliament under the criminal law power. This includes, for example, the *Corruption of Foreign Public Officials Act*. The enforcement of criminal legislation in Canada, however, is another matter.

While the federal government enjoys exclusive jurisdiction to promulgate criminal legislation, the administration of justice falls within the jurisdiction of the provinces and territories. In practice, this has meant that the enforcement for the majority of criminal offenses has been delegated to the provinces and territories. Additionally, the provinces and territories have jurisdiction over matters involving property and civil rights[40] and can pass laws that have penal consequences relating to property and civil rights.[41]

As a result, a mixture of federal and provincial (including municipal) police forces are tasked with enforcing the criminal law in Canada. The federal prosecution service (known as the Public Prosecution Service of Canada or PPSC) enjoys concurrent jurisdiction with the various provincial attorney general offices over the majority of *Criminal Code* offenses, including those relating to terrorism, criminal organizations, fraud, money laundering, and proceedings of crime.[42] The PPSC also has the exclusive jurisdiction to prosecute offenses under federal statutes that protect the public welfare, ranging from environmental and natural resources to the country's economic and social health.[43] This includes the offenses of bribing a foreign public official or attempting to hide that bribe under the CFPOA.

In practice, the federal police force (the Royal Canadian Mounted Police) has the exclusive jurisdiction to investigate and lay criminal charges under the CFPOA. The International Anti-Corruption Unit based in Ottawa and Calgary is in charge of investigations involving the bribery of foreign public officials. Civil asset forfeiture proceedings in relation to bribery offenses, however, may be instituted by the provinces or territories in which the property is located.[44]

---

[38] Royal Canadian Mounted Police, RCMP Charges SNC-Lavalin (Feb. 2015), *available at* http://www.rcmp-grc.gc.ca/ottawa/ne-no/pr-cp/2015/0219-lavalin-eng.htm.

[39] *British North America Act*, s. 91(27).

[40] *British North America Act*, s. 92(13).

[41] There can be obvious overlap between laws of a criminal nature and laws involving property and civil rights: *Chaterjee* v. *Ontario (Attorney General)*, [2009] 1 SCR 19.

[42] Public Prosecution Service of Canada 2013–2014 Departmental Performance Report, p. 5.

[43] *Id.* at 5.

[44] *See, e.g.*, the *Civil Remedies Act (Ontario)*, ss. 2–3.

5. Domestic Bribery Offenses

5.1 DEFINITION OF DOMESTIC OFFICIALS

The domestic bribery offenses found in Part IV of the *Criminal Code* address offenses against the administration of law and justice. The term "official" is broadly defined under this part of the *Code* to include any person who is elected or appointed to discharge a public duty.[45] This includes municipal officials,[46] members of the Legislative Council,[47] provincial legislators,[48] and cabinet ministers.[49]

The offense provisions in the *Criminal Code* that deal with bribery and corruption can be broken down into two categories: first, offenses involving domestic public officials; and second, commercial bribery or secret commissions. Although there is a trend toward increased enforcement, these offenses have historically received relatively little judicial consideration.

5.2 BRIBES

Broadly speaking, sections 119 and 120 of the *Code* prohibit the bribing of officials and employees of Canada and of the Canadian provinces and territories.

Section 119 penalizes bribing politicians or judges, while section 120 makes it an offense to bribe anyone "employed in the administration of criminal law." Specifically, section 119 makes it an offense to corruptly offer or accept a benefit[50] in respect of any act or omission by a judicial officer, a member of Parliament, or a legislator of a provincial/territorial legislature in relation to an official capacity. Section 120 penalizes the payment of a bribe to any party employed in the criminal justice system to interfere with the administration of justice.[51]

In order to be found liable, both sections require that an accused act "corruptly." The use of the benefit is not relevant: it is not a defense that the benefit was merely for the reimbursement of expenses.[52] In the cases involving cabinet ministers, there is a rebuttable presumption that the minister acts in an official capacity when taking actions connected to his or her department.[53]

---

[45] Section 118, *Code*. Under the same section, "office" is defined to include an office or appointment under government, a civil or military commission, or a position or employment in a public department.

[46] *R v. Sheets*, [1971] SCR 614.

[47] *Martineau v. R*, [1966] SCR 103, 1965 CarswellQue 23 at para. 30 [hereinafter *Martineau*].

[48] *R v. Fillion*, 2006 QCCA 244.

[49] *R v. Sommers*, [1960] SCR 678. Members of private organizations that provide government services, however, have been held to not fall within the ambit of the definition of an "official" for the purposes of section 118 of the *Criminal Code: R v. Kay*, 1998 CarswellOnt 5149 (Ct Jus).

[50] Offering a benefit includes directly or giving, offering, or agreeing to give a loan, reward, advantage, or benefit. Accepting a benefit means directly or indirectly demanding, accepting, or offering to accept a loan, reward, advantage, or benefit.

[51] This includes bribery with the intent to procure or facilitate the commission of an offense, to protect from detection or punishment a person who has committed or intends to commit an offense or, more generally, anything intended to interfere with the administration of justice.

[52] *R v. Yanakis*, 64 CCC (2d) 374 (Que CA), 1993 CarswellQue 248 at para. 93.

[53] *R v. Arseneau*, [1979] 2 SCR 136, 1979 CarswellNB 15 at paras. 30–31.

5.3 FRAUDS AGAINST THE GOVERNMENT

Section 121 of the *Code* addresses frauds against the government.

Unlike sections 119 and 120, corruption is not a requirement of any of the offenses under section 121. In enacting section 121, Parliament's intention was to prevent harm to the *appearance of integrity*. This is because, as stated by the Supreme Court of Canada (SCC) in *R v. Hinchley*:

> Protecting these appearances is more than a trivial concern. This section recognizes that the democratic process can be harmed just as easily by the appearance of impropriety as with actual impropriety itself.[54]

Section 121(1)(a) makes it an offense to offer a benefit to an official, or for an official to accept a benefit as consideration for any cooperation with the transacting of government business. An offense is committed if an offer is *for the purpose of gaining an advantage*—there is no requirement that an official actually assist or even be able to assist the party that offers or gives the bribe. Further, when seeking a conviction under this section it is not necessary to prove that the conduct was committed in an official capacity.[55]

Section 121(1)(b) makes it an offense for a person who has dealings with the government to pay a benefit to an employee or official of the government, unless consent in writing has been obtained from the government. The accused must intend to confer benefits with respect to dealings with government.[56]

Section 121(1)(c) makes it an offense for an official or employee of the government to accept a benefit from a person who has dealings with the government, unless the official/employee has consent in writing from the head of the applicable branch of government. The offense is only made out if the person offering the benefit has commercial dealings with government at the time the offense is committed.[57] However, the offense does not require a quid pro quo; it is sufficient for the employee/official to receive a benefit while holding their position, even if nothing is expected in return.[58]

Influence peddling is prohibited by sections 121(1)(d) and (e). The former prohibits accepting a benefit for assisting in government dealings or appointments; the latter prohibits offering a benefit for the same. Further, section 121(2) prohibits influencing an election or promoting a political candidate or party in furtherance of obtaining government contracts.[59]

5.4 MUNICIPAL CORRUPTION AND BUYING OF OFFICE

Section 123 of the *Code* makes it an offence for anyone to offer a municipal official a benefit, or for any municipal official to accept a benefit, as consideration for voting for or against any

---

[54] [1996] 3 SCR 1128 at para. 17.

[55] *Martineau v. R, supra* note 47.

[56] *R v. Cooper*, [1978] 1 SCR 860, 1977 CarswellOnt 29 at para. 21.

[57] *R v. Hinchey*, [1996] 2 SCR 1128, 1996 CanLII 157 at para. 51.

[58] *R v. Greenwood*, 5 OR (3d) 71, 1991 CarswellOnt 118 (ON CA) at para. 61 [hereinafter *Greenwood*].

[59] In addition to the *Criminal Code* provision, Canada has strict campaign finance laws under the *Canada Elections Act*, SC 2000, c 9 (and similar provincial legislation), including a complete ban on all corporate

measure, helping or preventing the adopting of any measure, or anything else related to the performance of an official act.

Section 124 prohibits the buying and selling of any public office, while section 125 makes it an offense to accept a benefit as consideration for assistance or influence to secure the appointment to an office, to negotiate in respect of such an appointment or a resignation from office, or to keep a place for transacting or negotiating business in public offices. Corrupt intent is not a requirement for these offenses.[60] The "benefit" received can include a political benefit, such as a promise to be appointed to a public board in exchange for withdrawal from an election.[61]

5.5 BREACH OF TRUST BY A PUBLIC OFFICER

Section 122 of the *Criminal Code* makes it an offense for any official to commit fraud or breach of trust in connection with her or his duties of office.[62] The accused's act or omission must breach the standard of responsibility and conduct demanded by the nature of the office in a manner that is a serious and marked departure from the standards.[63] To meet the mens rea requirement, the accused must have intended to use his or her public office for a purpose other than the public good.[64]

5.6 SECRET COMMISSIONS

Section 426 of the *Criminal Code* prohibits secrets commissions. It makes it an offense to corruptly offer to an agent or accept as an agent a benefit as consideration for an act or omission with relation to the affairs of the business of the agent's principle or to be privy to such an offer. Unlike other bribery or corruption offenses in the *Criminal Code*, this offense does not necessarily involve a public official. The gravamen of this offense is proposing or making a secret agreement with an agent to the detriment of a principal. Accordingly, liability under this section can be potentially be avoided with adequate and timely disclosure.[65]

5.7 GIFTS, GRATUITIES, AND HOSPITALITY

Public officeholders in Canada are prohibited from accepting gifts from anyone having dealings of any kind with the government. Because sections 121(1)(b) and 121(1)(c) of the *Code* do not require a quid pro quo, it is an offense for an employee or officer to accept a

---

and union donations to federal political parties and candidates (section 363(1)). Further, section 477.9 of the *Canada Elections Act* makes it an offense for a federal political candidate to accept an advantage that might reasonably be seen to have been given to influence that person in his or her future duties, if elected.

[60] *R v. Auger*, 78 CCC 126, 1942 CarswellQue 290 (Que Sessions of the Peace) at para. 16.

[61] *R v. O'Brien*, 2009 CarswellOnt 7803 (ON SC).

[62] Section 336 of the *Criminal Code* addresses a criminal breach of trust for trustees.

[63] *R v. Boulanger*, 2006 SCC 32 at para. 58. *See R. v. Duffy, supra* note 19, para. 1230: In the absence of "comparator" evidence concerning similarly situated officials, it may be difficult for the prosecution to prove a serious and marked departure from the applicable standard of care.

[64] *R v. Boulanger*, 2006 SCC 32 at para. 58.

[65] *R v. Arnold*, [1992] 2 SCR 208.

"commission, reward, advantage or benefit" even if the employee or official doesn't intend to do anything in return.[66]

The *Conflict of Interest Act* prohibits federal "public office holders" (a category that includes Members of Parliament, cabinet ministers and their staff, and certain top ministerial and department advisors) from accepting any gift that might reasonably be seen to influence the exercise of an official power, duty, or function.[67]

Similarly, the federal government's *Policy on Conflict of Interest and Post-Employment* advises Canada's public servants not to accept any gifts, hospitality, or other benefits that may have a real, apparent, or potential influence on their objectivity in carrying out their official duties and responsibilities, including free or discounted admission to sporting and cultural events, travel, or conferences.[68] However, employees may accept gifts and hospitality that have no such real, apparent, or potential influence on the carrying out of official duties so long as those gifts are infrequent, of minimal value, or arise within the normal standards of courtesy.[69]

Public servants at other levels of government are subject to analogous restrictions. For example, Ontario's civil servants may not accept gifts that could reasonably be perceived as influencing them unless the gifts are of nominal value, given as an expression of courtesy or hospitality, and reasonable in the circumstances.[70]

5.8 DEFENSES

"Adequate Procedures" and Corporate Culture:

Neither the presence of adequate procedures nor the state of corporate culture are in and of themselves positive defenses to Canada's domestic anti-corruption laws. However, both are connected to how and when a corporation can be found to be criminally liable.

Organizations (including, but not limited to, corporations) are party to an offense if, with the intent of at least in part benefiting the organization, one or more of its senior officers: (1) acts within the scope of their authority in the offense, (2) has the mens rea to be a party to the offense, (3) acts within their authority and directs work so that the offense is committed, or, (4) knowing that a representative of the organization is party to the offense, does not take all reasonable measure to stop that person from committing it.[71]

---

[66] *R* v. *Greenwood, supra* note 58, at para. 64.

[67] SC 2006, c 9, s 11. Exceptions to this prohibition include (1) gifts permitted under the *Canada Elections Act*, (2) gifts given by family or friends, or (3) gifts that are a normal expression of courtesy or protocol: s. 11(2), *Conflict of Interest Act*.

[68] *Policy on Conflict of Interest and Post-Employment* (Dec. 15, 2011), *available at* Treasury Board of Canada Secretariat www.tbs-sct.gc.ca.

[69] *Policy on Conflict of Interest and Post-Employment* (Dec. 15, 2011), *available at* Treasury Board of Canada Secretariat www.tbs-sct.gc.ca.

[70] *Conflict of Interest Rules for Public Servants (Ministry) and Former Public Servants (Ministry)*, O Reg 381/07, s 4.

[71] Section 22.2, *Criminal Code*.

The latter is similar to section 7 of the UK *Bribery Act*, with the notable difference being that failing to stop a bribe in the UK (unlike Canada) is a strict liability offense. By contrast, in Canada, a senior officer must either commit the offense or know that an organizational representative is party to the offense and *fail to stop* the offense from occurring.[72]

A "senior officer" is not restricted to members of senior management but instead captures any representative who plays an important role in the establishment of an organization's policies or is responsible for managing an important aspect of the organization's activities and, in the case of a body corporate, includes a director, chief executive officer and chief financial officer.[73]

6. Foreign Bribery Offenses

The CFPOA is exclusively a criminal statute, attaching penal liability to two primary prohibitions: (i) the act of bribing foreign public officials, and (ii) keeping false or inaccurate books and records relating to that bribery. The CFPOA is a separate statute from Canada's *Criminal Code* and one that is capable of expansion to accommodate additional international obligations with respect to anti-corruption.[74] However, as discussed previously, both CFPOA offenses are indictable offenses and *Criminal Code* provisions relating to indictable offenses apply to the CFPOA.[75]

6.1 THE CFPOA ANTI-BRIBERY OFFENSE

Section 3(1) of the CFPOA provides as follows:

3

(1) Every person commits an offence who, in order to obtain or retain an advantage in the course of business, directly or indirectly gives, offers or agrees to give or offer a loan, reward, advantage or benefit of any kind to a foreign public official or to any person for the benefit of a foreign public official

(a) as consideration for an act or omission by the official in connection with the performance of the official's duties or functions; or

---

[72] Although a corporation can be liable for offenses of negligence (as opposed to fault) under Canadian criminal law (see s. 22.1, *Criminal Code*), the domestic bribery and corruption offenses do not engage considerations of negligence. Rather, they are full mens rea offenses.

[73] *Criminal Code*, s 2.

[74] *Canada Review of Implementation and 1997 Recommendation*, Organization for Economic Co-Operation and Development, *available at* https://www.oecd.org/daf/anti-bribery/anti-briberyconvention/2385703.pdf (last visited Dec. 15, 2018), at pt. A ["*1997 Recommendation*"]; the *1997 Recommendation* stated that there is room for the Act to grow to accommodate new legislative provisions falling under this heading should Canada, in the future, undertake to sign and ratify additional international conventions.

[75] *Interpretation Act*, RSC 1985, c. I-21, at s. 34(2); *Criminal Code*, RSC, 1985, c. C-46 at s. 8(3).

(b) to induce the official to use his or her position to influence any acts or decisions of the foreign state or public international organization for which the official performs duties or functions.[76]

6.1.1 "Every Person"

The CFPOA offence is intended to apply to "every person."[77] In addition to the natural person, "every person" encompasses legal persons in the broadest sense, including organizations, public bodies, corporations (including not-for-profit corporations), societies, companies, partnerships, trade union, municipalities, or association of persons created for a common purpose with an operation structure that holds itself out to the public as an association of persons.[78] While "every person" may include foreign nationals, the wording of section 3 of the CFPOA does not confer extraterritorial jurisdiction over foreign nationals located outside of Canada.[79]

6.1.2 "In Order to"

The CFPOA does not explicitly refer to intent as a requirement for establishing liability under its anti-bribery offense. However, as the provision states that the accused must commit bribery of a foreign public official "in order to" gain something in return, the language of the provision imparts an intentional element to the offense.[80]

As CFPOA offenses are indictable offenses under the *Criminal Code*, proof of mens rea is required.[81] Sufficient mens rea to commit bribery of a foreign public official will be established in instances of willful blindness but not negligence.[82] An individual will be said to be willfully blind where the evidence demonstrates that he or she saw the need to make further inquiries, but deliberately chose not to do so.[83]

6.1.3 "Directly or Indirectly"

The use of "directly or indirectly" implies that the CFPOA anti-bribery offense covers bribes given through intermediaries.[84] In addition to resulting in liability for the "originator" of the bribe, indirect bribes may render intermediaries liable depending upon their degree of knowledge of the bribe.

6.1.4 "Loan, Reward, Advantage, or Benefit"

The CFPOA anti-bribery offense prohibits the giving or offering of a "loan, reward, advantage or benefit of any kind" to a foreign public official.[85] This language covers a broad range

---

[76] *Corruption of Foreign Public Officials Act*, SC 1998, c. 34 (Can.) at s. 3(1).

[77] *Corruption of Foreign Public Officials Act*, SC 1998, c. 34 (Can.) at s. 3(1).

[78] *Criminal Code*, s. 2

[79] *Chowdhury* v. *Canada*, [2014] O.J. No. 2004, paras. 42-46.

[80] *Corruption of Foreign Public Officials Act*, SC 1998, c. 34 (Can.). at s. 3(1).

[81] *Interpretation Act*, RSC 1985, c. I-21, at s. 34(2); *Criminal Code*, RSC, 1985, c. C-46 at s. 8(3).

[82] *1997 Recommendation* at pt. 1.1.2.

[83] *R* v. *Briscoe*, 2010 SCC 13.

[84] *Corruption of Foreign Public Officials Act*, SC 1998, c. 34 (Can.) at s. 3(1); *see also H.M.Q.* v. *Griffiths Energy International Inc.*, 2013 AJ No. 412.

[85] *Corruption of Foreign Public Officials Act*, SC 1998, c. 34 (Can.) at s. 3(1).

of possible advantages and includes intangible and non-monetary benefits.[86] Within the context of the offense of committing a fraud on the government, contrary to section 121(c) of the *Criminal Code*, the Ontario Court of Justice has observed that "the disappearance of a political embarrassment" could constitute an intangible benefit.[87]

6.1.5 "Foreign Public Official"

Numerous categories of persons fall under "foreign public official" in Canadian law, including those who hold a legislative, administrative, or judicial position of a foreign state or political subdivision of the state.[88] Persons who exercise a public function for an agency of a foreign state or subdivision of a foreign state will also meet the definition of a "foreign public official," regardless of their official status.[89] However, individuals who have not yet been elected or appointed to their public position will likely not be considered "foreign public officials" for the purposes of the CFPOA.[90] As such, candidates for public office and their political parties will generally not come within the scope of the CFPOA.

6.1.6 "Acting in Relation the Performance of Official Duties"

The CFPOA anti-bribery offense provides two alternative means to ground liability under the section: either the bribe is intended to influence the public official in connection with the exercise of his or her official duties (section 3(1)(a)); *or*, the bribe is intended to induce the public official to use his or her position to influence the acts of decisions of their foreign state or NGO (section 3(1)(b)), irrespective of whether the public official acts or omits to act within the scope of his or her authorized duties.[91] Thus it would not appear the definition of bribery captured by section 3(1)(b) is not necessarily restricted to the actions of a public official in the exercise of his or her official duties or functions.

6.2 THE CFPOA RECORD-KEEPING OFFENSE

It is an offense under the CFPOA to keep inaccurate records or to destroy records in furtherance of bribing a foreign public official or hiding that bribe. Although this section has yet to be considered by the judiciary, based on the clear language of the provision the offense is tied to committing or concealing a bribe.[92]

---

[86] *1997 Recommendations* at pt. 1.1.7; *R* v. *Hinchey, supra* note 57 at 1130.

[87] *R* v. *Duffy, supra* note 19, para. 1209

[88] *Corruption of Foreign Public Officials Act*, SC 1998, c. 34 (Can.) at s. 2.

[89] *Corruption of Foreign Public Officials Act*, SC 1998, c. 34 (Can.) at s. 2.

[90] *Corruption of Foreign Public Officials Act*, SC 1998, c. 34 (Can.) at s. 2; *1997 Recommendations* at pt. 1.1.6.

[91] *Corruption of Foreign Public Officials Act*, SC 1998, c. 34 (Can.) at s. 3(1); *see also H.M.Q.* v. *Griffiths Energy International Inc.*, 2013 AJ No. 412.

[92] Various *Criminal Code* and other legislative provisions already allow for the criminal prosecution that may involve falsification of books and records in Canada. For example, crimes involving false pretense, forgery, trafficking, or possessing a forged document, and fraud affecting the market relating to securities are all criminal offenses punishable by law: *Criminal Code* at s. 361–362, 366–367, 368, 380, 397. In situations where a charge could lie under both section 4 of the CFPOA and an applicable *Criminal Code* provision for the same

This prohibition extends to anyone who:

- Establishes or maintains accounts which do not appear in any of the books and records required to be kept in accordance with the applicable accounting and auditing standards;
- Makes transactions that are not recorded in those books and records or that are inadequately identified in them;
- Records nonexistent expenditures in those books and records;
- Enters liabilities with incorrect identification of their object in those books and records;
- Knowingly uses false documents; or
- Intentionally destroys accounting books and records earlier than permitted by law.[93]

6.3 DEFENSES

The CFPOA provides for several defenses that were influenced in large part by the OECD Commentaries on the 1999 Convention and parallel anti-corruption legislation in other jurisdictions.[94] As a result, CFPOA defenses are similar in structure—if not content—to those found in other national anti-corruption statutes.

6.3.1 Local Law

An act will not be considered bribery of a foreign public official for the purposes of the CFPOA in instances where a "loan, reward, advantage or benefit" is "permitted or required under the laws of the relevant foreign state or public international organization."[95] Notably,

---

transaction, the *Kienapple* principle would serve to avoid dual punishment for the same dereliction: see *R v. Kienapple,* [1975] 1 SCR 729, 1974 CanLII 14 (SCC).

[93] *Corruption of Foreign Public Officials Act*, SC 1998, c. 34 (Can.) at s. 4(1). In addition to the CFPOA, the *Criminal Code* provisions relating to attempt, aiding and abetting, counseling, and conspiracy apply to the anti-bribery and recordkeeping offenses under the CFPOA (ss 21, 22(1), 24(1), 465(1)(c)). These provisions expand the scope of behavior captured by the CFPOA that is subject to criminal prosecution. In Canadian criminal law, a person who attempts to commit an offense is guilty of a criminal attempt and typically liable for up to half the penalty as if the offense had been committed: s. 463, *Criminal Code*. A person who aids or abets in the commission of an offense is a party to that offense and liable for the full penalty. Likewise, a person who conspires with another to commit an indictable offense is liable for the same penalty as if that person had committed the offense. Unlike in American law, Canadian law generally does not require that an overt act be taken for a conspiracy to exist; the offense is complete upon an agreement between the parties: R v. J.F., [2013] 1 SCR 565 at para. 44. Canada's conspiracy prohibition contains extraterritorial components: anyone who conspires in Canada to do something abroad that would be an indictable offense in Canada is deemed to have conspired in Canada, and anyone who conspires abroad to commit an indictable offense in Canada is deemed to have conspired in Canada. *See Criminal Code*, ss 24(1), 465ss. (3) and (4).

[94] *1997 Recommendations* at pt. A; *see also Commentaries on the Convention on Combatting Bribery of Foreign Public Officials in International Business Transactions,* General, paragraphs 8–9.

[95] *Corruption of Foreign Public Officials Act*, SC 1998, c. 34 (Can.) at s. 3(3)(a).

unwritten local laws as well as all regulations potentially fall within the scope of this CFPOA exception.[96] This is in contrast to the FCPA local law exception, which requires that the local law be written.[97]

6.3.2 Reasonable Expenses Occurred in Good Faith

Reasonable business expenses are excluded from the offense of bribery of a foreign public official.[98] The CFPOA categorizes a loan, reward, advantage, or benefit as a reasonable business expense when it is a payment related to the "promotion, demonstration or explanation of the person's products and services" or "the execution or performance of a contract between the person and the foreign state for which the official performs duties or functions."[99]

Under the CPFOA, the defendant has an evidentiary burden of asserting that a loan, reward, advantage, or benefit is a reasonable business expense. Once a defendant is successful in doing so, the onus shifts to the prosecution to prove "beyond a reasonable doubt that the defence does not apply."[100] By contrast, under the FCPA, reasonable and bona fide business expenses are framed as an affirmative defense.[101] As such, the burden of proof under the FCPA remains on the defendant to show that a particular payment is reasonable and bona fide.[102]

6.3.3 Facilitation Payments

Facilitation payments are payments made "to expedite or secure the performance by a foreign public official of any act of a routine nature that is part of the foreign public official's duties or functions."[103] The CFPOA confines the scope of an "act of routine nature" by specifying that such an act does not include a decision to award new business, continue business, or influence the terms of business with a particular party.[104]

The CFPOA also provides guidance as to the kind of payments that would constitute a facilitation payment. Facilitation payments include: the issuance of a permit, license, or other document to qualify a person to do business; the processing of official documents, such as visas and work permits; and the provision of services normally offered to the public, such as mail pickup and delivery, telecommunications services, and power and water supply.[105]

When adopted in 1997, the OECD's Convention on Combating Bribery of Foreign Public Officials did not prohibit facilitation payments. Instead of levying criminal sanctions on companies engaged in such practices, it was determined that these payments that

---

[96] *1997 Recommendations* at pt. 1.1.4.

[97] See *Foreign Corrupt Practices Act of 1977*, Pub. L. No. 95-213, 91 Stat. 1494 (codified as amended at 15 U.S.C. ss. 78m, 78dd-1-78-dd-3, 78ff (2013)).

[98] *Corruption of Foreign Public Officials Act*, SC 1998, c. 34 (Can.) at s. 3(3)(b).

[99] *Corruption of Foreign Public Officials Act*, SC 1998, c. 34 (Can.) at s. 3(3)(b).

[100] *1997 Recommendations* at pt. 1.1.4; *Phase 3 Report* at p. 25.

[101] See *Foreign Corrupt Practices Act of 1977*, Pub. L. No. 95-213, 91 Stat. 1494 (codified as amended at 15 U.S.C. ss. 78m, 78dd-1-78-dd-3, 78ff (2013)).

[102] *1997 Recommendations* at pt. 1.1.4; *Phase 3 Report* at p. 25.

[103] *Corruption of Foreign Public Officials Act*, SC 1998, c. 34 (Can.) at s. 3(4).

[104] *Corruption of Foreign Public Officials Act*, SC 1998, c. 34 (Can.) at s. 3(5).

[105] *Corruption of Foreign Public Officials Act*, SC 1998, c. 34 (Can.) at s. 3(4); other examples include the provision of services normally provided as required, such as police protection, loading and unloading of cargo, the

"induce public officials to perform their functions" should be eliminated through supporting programs of good governance.[106] In November 2009, the OECD changed its position and recommended that member countries encourage companies to prohibit or discourage the use of facilitation payments given their *"corrosive effect."*[107]

In response to the OECD's change in position, Canada introduced a bill on February 2013 that aimed to eventually eliminate facilitation payments as an exception to the anti-bribery provisions.[108] Minister of Foreign Affairs John Baird commented that facilitation payments, which he described as a younger sister of bribery, perhaps should not have been included as an exemption in the original version of the CFPOA. Despite these statements, the bill's provisions relating to the elimination of facilitation payment did not come into force when it received Royal Assent.[109] Rather, the removal of the exception for facilitation payments were set to come into effect on a day to be fixed by order of the Governor in Council.[110] This finally occurred on October 31, 2017.[111] As this constitutes a substantive change to Canadian criminal law, it is likely that the judiciary would allow the defense of facilitation payments to continue to be available for any offense that is alleged to have occurred prior to October 31, 2017.[112]

6.3.4 Common Law Defenses

As discussed previously, the provisions of the *Criminal Code* apply mutatis mutandis to the CFPOA. Under the *Criminal Code*, all common law defenses, such as duress and the defense of necessity, continue to apply.[113] It should be noted, for example, that Transparency International permits the payment of bribes when the life and safety of the payer is in jeopardy.[114] A successful common law defense can, therefore, exculpate individuals from offenses under the CFPOA.

7. Privacy and Data Protection

The main statute that governs the use and collection of personal information in Canada is the *Personal Information Protection and Electronic Documents Act (PIPEDA)*.[115] *PIPEDA* applies

---

protection of perishable products or commodities from deterioration, or the scheduling of inspections related to contract performance or transit of goods.

[106] OECD, *Convention on Combatting Bribery of Foreign Public Officials in International Business Transactions* at 15.

[107] OECD, *Convention on Combatting Bribery of Foreign Public Officials in International Business Transactions* at 20.

[108] *See* Robin MacKay, *Bill S-14: An Act to Amend the Corruption of Foreign Public Officials Act, Legislative Summary,* February 28, 2013, s. 1.3, *available at* https://lop.parl.ca/sites/PublicWebsite/default/en_CA/ResearchPublications/LegislativeSummaries/411S14E.

[109] *See id.*

[110] *See id.*

[111] Canada Gazette, Vol. 151, No. 23.

[112] See *R. v. Dineley,* [2012] 3 SCR 272.

[113] *Interpretation Act*, RSC 1985, c. I-21, at s. 34(2); *Criminal Code*, RSC, 1985, c. C-46 at s. 8(3).

[114] Transparency International, *The Anti-corruption Plain-Language Guide,* July 28, 2009, *available at* http://www.transparency.org/whatwedo/publication/the_anti_corruption_plain_language_guide.

[115] Many provinces also have privacy legislation that applies to health information (for example, the *Personal Health Information Protection Act* in Ontario or the *Personal Health Information Act* in Newfoundland

to any organizations in Canada or with a substantial connection to Canada (including foreign corporations) that collect, use, or disclose personal information in the course of commercial activities or in relation to federal works, undertakings, or business.[116] Commercial activity is broadly defined under the Act to include any transaction or conduct of a commercial character.[117]

The cornerstone of the Act is the prohibition against the collection, use, or disclosure of personal information without the knowledge or consent of the individual, subject to limited exceptions.[118] Personal information is information about an identifiable individual.[119] This can have obvious implications for internal corporate investigations. The individual's consent is often obtained at the time that the information is first collected.[120] Without the consent of the individual the Act prohibits personal information from being used or disclosed for purposes other than those for which it was collected.[121] Accordingly, where possible consent should be obtained from employees at that time that their personal information is collected that permits the information to be used for corporate investigations, as necessary.

PIPEDA does not create any police search and seizure powers.[122] However, an organization can use personal information without the knowledge or consent of the subject if it has reasonable grounds to believe that the information "could be useful" to the investigation of a contravention of a law of Canada or a foreign jurisdiction that has been, is being, or is about to be committed.[123] Similarly, an organization can disclose personal information without the knowledge or consent of the subject if it is presented with a valid subpoena or warrant or other lawful authority to obtain such information by a government institution that is conducting an investigation relating to the enforcement of the laws of Canada or a foreign jurisdiction.[124]

8. Sentencing and Penalties

8.1 GENERAL PRINCIPLES

All of the domestic corruption offenses in Canada are indictable offenses punishable by imprisonment of up to five years.[125]

---

and Labrador; additionally, some provinces have private sector privacy laws that are substantially similar to PIPEDA, including the *Personal Information Protection Act* of Alberta. *See* the Office of the Privacy Commissioner of Canada, *Overview of Privacy Legislation in Canada*, January 2018, *available at* https://www.priv.gc.ca/en/privacy-topics/privacy-laws-in-canada/02_05_d_15/.

[116] PIPEDA, s. 4. The application of the statute to federal works is restricted to personal information about an employee (or application for employment) for applicable organizations: s. 4(1)(b). A federal work, undertaking, or business includes any subject matter over which the federal Parliament has legislative authority, including authorized foreign banks: s. 2.

[117] PIPEDA, s. 2.

[118] Schedule 1 (CAN/CSA-Q830-96), 4.3 (Principle 3—Consent).

[119] S. 2.

[120] Schedule 1, 4.3.1.

[121] Schedule 1, 4.5 (Principle 5—Limiting Use, Disclosure and Retention).

[122] *R* v. *Spencer*, [2014] SCR 212, para. 71.

[123] PIPEDA, s. 7(2)(a).

[124] PIPEDA, s. 7(3)(c) and (c.1).

[125] *See* sections 119, 121–125, and 426 of the *Criminal Code*.

Every person found to be in violation of foreign corruption offenses under the CFPOA faces a penalty of up to 14 years imprisonment.[126] Monetary penalties may also be imposed at the discretion of the Court; there is no upper limit to the fine that may be levied.[127] Where the fine is directed at an individual, the Court is required to consider the individual's ability to pay.[128] In contrast, when determining the appropriate fine to impose upon an organization, there is no obligation to consider that organization's ability to pay.[129]

Further, in instances where an organization is charged, the court may use its discretion to impose additional conditions of probation,[130] including the following: making restitution; mandatory public disclosure; implementing and communicating new policies, standards, and procedures; and any other conditions "that the court considers desirable to prevent the organization from committing subsequent offences or to remedy the harm caused by the offence."[131]

Finally, all proceeds resulting from a violation of the CFPOA, or the domestic corruption offenses noted above, may be forfeited under either the Criminal Code or under applicable provincial civil forfeiture statutes.[132]

8.2 RANGES OF DOMESTIC PENALTIES

The range of sentences imposed by courts for domestic crimes of fraud and corruption have historically been subject to significant variation, ranging from conditional sentences (house arrest) to four years imprisonment. The maximum penal sentence for frauds against the government is five years imprisonment.

Canadian courts view frauds against the government as serious offenses, because the purpose of section 121 of the *Code* is to ensure and maintain the complete integrity of the public service.[133] It is a well-established principle of Canadian law that in cases involving the corruption of public officials, the most important sentencing objectives are general deterrence and denunciation.[134]

Although it is difficult to give a range of likely penalties under these sections due to a paucity of case law, it can be said with some confidence that the tariff for an offense of corruption likely involves a penitentiary sentence, sometimes even in cases with significant mitigating factors.[135]

By way of example, in *R v. Woon*, an adjudicator of immigration tribunals was found guilty of accepting money in exchange for rendering favorable decisions in relation to refugee applications. The court held that the tarnishing of the reputation of the legal process

---

[126] *Corruption of Foreign Public Officials Act*, SC 1998, c. 34 (Can.) at s. 3(2).

[127] *Criminal Code* at s. 734, 735(1)(a).

[128] *Criminal Code* at s. 734(2).

[129] *Id.*

[130] *Criminal Code* at s. 732(3.1).

[131] *Id.*

[132] *Criminal Code* at s. 462.37(1).

[133] *R v. Cooper, supra* note 56, at para. 6.

[134] *R v. Serré*, 2005 CanLII 53776 (QC CQ) at para. 28 citing *R v. Hinchey, supra* note 57.

[135] *Id.* para. 28. A penitentiary sentence is a sentence of two or more years of imprisonment.

is a severe aggravating factor in sentencing that strikes at "the very foundation of Canadian democracy."[136] The accused was sentenced to three years imprisonment for his role in this and other crimes.

In another recent case, *R v. Serré*, a senior manager at Citizenship and Immigration Canada was found guilty of 27 offenses relating to fraud on the government and breach of trust. She was sentenced to four years imprisonment.[137] Serré's accomplice, who was not a civil servant, pled guilty to seven counts of frauds against the government, in addition to related fraud, tax evasion, and obstruction charges. He was sentenced to two years and nine months imprisonment.[138]

In *R v. Rudge*, a police officer was convicted of breach of trust contrary to section 122 after he provided confidential police documents to a criminal organization. The officer was sentenced to four years imprisonment.[139]

If the fraud on the government preys upon vulnerable people or individuals in dire circumstances, this will also be considered an aggravating factor for sentencing purposes.[140]

The courts have sometimes imposed lighter sentences such as conditional sentencing or fines in instances with strong mitigating factors such as following the orders of a senior official,[141] entering a guilty plea,[142] or lacking dishonesty or corrupt intent.[143]

8.3 RANGES OF PENALTIES FOR FOREIGN CORRUPTION

Despite its early introduction relative to anti-corruption legislation in other jurisdictions, due to tepid enforcement activity the CFPOA had only minimal impact during its first decade.[144] As discussed previously, in 2013 Canada introduced amendments to significantly strengthen the CFPOA, including raising the maximum penalty for CFPOA offenses from 5 to 14 years.[145] These legislative developments coincided with increased efforts by Canadian authorities to enhance the role of Canada's national police force, the Royal Canadian Mounted Police (RCMP), to investigate CFPOA offenses.[146]

---

[136] 2005 CanLII 53776 (QC CQ) at paras. 30–31. Amongst other offenses, the accused was found to have conspired with a sitting member of the Immigration Refugee Board to render beneficial decisions for applications in exchange for money.

[137] 2013 ONSC 1732.

[138] *Id*. para. 58.

[139] 2013 ONSC 5010.

[140] *Id*. para. 25.

[141] *R v. Power*, 1992 CarswellNS 133 (NS County Ct) at para. 19.

[142] *R v, Bedard*, 2000 NWTSC 73 at para. 10.

[143] *R v. Currie*, 1994 CarswellOnt 2990 (ON Ct Jus) at para. 31.

[144] *Phase 3 Report on Implement in the OECD Anti-Bribery Convention in Canada*, Organization for Economic Co-Operation and Development, March 2011, *available at* http://www.oecd.org/canada/ Canadaphase3reportEN.pdf, at pp. 15–24, 121, 133–35 [hereinafter *Phase 3 Report*].

[145] *Canada: Follow-up to the Phase 3 Report & Recommendations*, Organization for Economic Co-Operation and Development, May 2013, *available at* http://www.oecd.org/daf/anti-bribery/ CanadaP3writtenfollowupreportEN.pdf [hereinafter *Follow-up Report*].

[146] *Canada: Follow-up to the Phase 3 Report & Recommendations*, Organization for Economic Co-Operation and Development, May 2013, *available at* http://www.oecd.org/daf/anti-bribery/CanadaP3writtenfollowupreportEN. pdf ["*Follow-up Report*"].

These measures signal Canada's commitment to anti-corruption efforts and are in line with international trends increasingly condemning foreign bribery and enforcing rules against it.

Further, the sentences handed down in a series of recent cases have demonstrated Canadian courts' increased willingness to exercise their sentencing powers under the CFPOA in order to deter foreign corrupt practices. In 2011, Niko Resources Ltd. was fined $9.5 million after pleading guilty to violating the CFPOA.[147] In 2013, Griffiths Energy International Inc. was fined $10.3 million, also having pleaded guilty to violating the CFPOA.[148] In 2014, the Ontario Superior Court imposed the first prison sentence under the CFPOA, sentencing Nazir Karigar to three years.[149]

8.4 OTHER POSSIBLE SANCTIONS

Violating the CFPOA may result in administrative and civil sanctions. These "legal disabilities" fall short of criminal penalties but may compound the economic consequences of noncompliance with the CFPOA.[150]

Persons or organizations that have been convicted or discharged within the last three years of the CFPOA offenses of "bribery of a foreign public official" or the "falsification of books and documents" are automatically rendered ineligible to do business with the government of Canada for a period of 5-10 years.[151]

The CFPOA is exclusively a criminal statute. The fact that it does not directly permit civil penalties or causes of action has been a subject of criticism.[152] Nonetheless, accused that are subject to proceedings under the CFPOA may be subject to civil forfeiture proceedings under either federal or provincial legislation. While a criminal conviction (including a conviction under the CFPOA) is necessary to institute forfeiture proceedings in relation to the proceeds of crime,[153] under most provincial civil forfeiture legislation a criminal conviction is not necessary for the province or territory to seize property within its boundaries. Instead, all that is required to trigger forfeiture is proof on a balance of probabilities that the property in question was used or is the result of "unlawful activity."[154]

9. Whistle-Blower Protections

Compared to other jurisdictions, whistle-blower protection in Canada is still in its nascent stages. There are relatively few civil or criminal cases. Canada, generally speaking, does not have equivalents of the qui tam provisions of the U.S. False Claims Act.[155]

---

[147] *R* v. *Niko Resources Ltd.*, [2011] 101 WCB (2d), 118 (Can Alta. QB.).

[148] *H.M.Q.* v. *Griffiths Energy.* 2013 AJ No. 412.

[149] *R* v. *Karigar*, 2013 ONSC 5199.

[150] *Canada: Follow-up to the Phase 3 Report & Recommendations*, Organization for Economic Co-Operation and Development, May 2013, *available at* http://www.oecd.org/daf/anti-bribery/CanadaP3writtenfollowupreportEN.pdf.

[151] Ineligibility and Suspension Policy, Government of Canada: https://www.tpsgc-pwgsc.gc.ca/ci-if/politique-policy-eng.html

[152] OECD Working Group.

[153] *Criminal Code*, s. 462.37.

[154] *Chatterjee* v. *Ontario*, [2009] 1 SCR 629.

[155] 31 U.S.C. §§ 3729–3733.

Section 425.1 of the *Code* makes it a criminal offense for an employer or a person in a position of power to discipline or retaliate against an employee who reports or intends to report the breach of any law to federal or provincial law enforcement. The provision applies to both private and public sector employers.

There are no reported cases where an individual was charged or convicted with a breach of section 425.1.[156]

9.1 PUBLIC SECTOR WHISTLE-BLOWER PROTECTIONS

The *Public Service Disclosure Protection Act* protects federal civil servants who report wrongdoings in or related to the public sector, including contraventions of law, misuse of public funds, gross mismanagement, and/or serious breaches of the public service's code of conduct.[157] The Act protects civil servants from reprisals, and in many cases, protects them from being identified.[158]

Protection of whistle-blowers under the *Public Service Disclosure Protection Act* is managed by the Public Service Integrity Commission. However, two recent reports by Canada's Auditor General have revealed significant shortcomings within the Public Service Integrity Commission, including gross mismanagement in the investigations of alleged wrongdoing, lengthy delays, and serious violations of the Values and Ethics Code for the Public Service by the Commission itself.[159]

Some of Canada's provinces and territories have legislation similar to the *Public Service Disclosure Protection Act* with respect to their own public servants.[160]

9.2 PRIVATE SECTOR WHISTLE-BLOWER PROTECTIONS

In addition to the general protections under section 425.1 of the *Code*, the Supreme Court of Canada has held that private sector employees have the right not to be retaliated against for "up the ladder" reporting of wrongdoing.[161] This system, wherein employees report wrongdoing to successively higher levels of their organization, balances an employee's duty of loyalty to his or her employer with the public interest in the suppression of unlawful activity.[162]

---

[156] There have, however, been numerous prosecutions under provincial legislation pertaining to anti-retaliatory provisions for reporting health and safety violations.

[157] SC 2005, c 46, s 8.

[158] *Id.*, ss 19–21, 43–44.1.

[159] Office of the Auditor General of Canada, *Report of the Auditor General of Canada under the Public Servants Disclosure Protection Act: Office of the Public Sector Integrity Commissioner of Canada, Case Reports 1 and 2*, April 2004 at 14, 18; *see generally* Office of the Auditor General of Canada, *Report of the Auditor General of Canada: The Public Sector Integrity Commissioner of Canada*, Dec. 2010.

[160] *See, e.g., Public Service of Ontario Act, 2006*, SO 2006, c 35, Sched A as ss 108–150; *Public Interest Disclosure (Whistleblower Protection) Act*, SA 2012, c P-39.5.

[161] *Merk v. International Association of Bridge, Structural, Ornamental and Reinforcing Iron Workers, Local 771*, [2005] 3 SCR 425, 2005 SCC 70 at paras. 42–47.

[162] *Id.* para. 23.

The Ontario Securities Commission (OSC), which is the largest securities administrator and regulator in Canada, has recently adopted a comprehensive whistle-blower protection.[163] Under the OSC whistle-blower program, whistle-blowers who report information that leads to an OSC administrative proceeding resulting in monetary sanctions and/or voluntary payments of $1 million or more may be eligible for a financial award up to $5 million.[164] The whistle-blower policy encourages, but does not require whistle-blowers to engage in "up-the-ladder" internal reporting.[165] Employers are prohibited from retaliating or initiating reprisals against whistle-blowers,[166] and the OSC established the Office of the Whistleblower in July, 2016.[167]

The Canada Revenue Agency's Offshore Tax Informant Program allows individuals to confidentially provide information related to major international tax noncompliance that leads to the collection of taxes owing.[168] Individuals who provide sufficient, specific, and credible facts not already know to the CRA, which result in the recovery of more than $100,000, are eligible to receive a reward of 5–15 percent of the recovery.

Lawyers in Ontario may not typically disclose wrongdoing protected by solicitor-client privilege unless disclosure is necessary to prevent an imminent risk of death or serious bodily harm.[169] Even then, disclosure is permitted but not required. However, because lawyers may not themselves engage in dishonesty, fraud, or illegal activity, a lawyer who becomes aware of certain wrongdoing within an organization must progressively report such wrongdoing "up the ladder."[170] If the organization, despite the lawyer's advice, continues the wrongful conduct, the lawyer must withdraw.[171]

9.3 ATTITUDE TOWARD WHISTLE-BLOWERS

Generally, whistle-blower retaliation/protection is not an issue that has attracted a great deal of attention in the public consciousness in Canada.

Whistle-blower protections do not typically provide protection for civil servants who alert the public to actions by the government that attract controversy but that are not overtly

---

[163] *Whistleblower Program*, OSC Policy 15-601 (Oct. 28, 2015) [15-601]; *Proposed Framework for an OSC Whistleblower Program*, OSC Policy 15-401 (Feb. 3, 2015).

[164] 15-601, *id.* at 7–9. *See* definition of "award eligible outcome."

[165] *Id.* at 9.

[166] *Whistleblower Program*, OSC Policy 15-601, *supra* note 163, at 7, para. 13. *See also* Securities Act (Ontario), s. 121.5.

[167] Press Release, OSC Launches Office of the Whistleblower (July 14, 2016), *available at* http://www.osc.gov.on.ca/en/NewsEvents_nr_20160714_osc-launches-whistleblower.htm.

[168] Canada Revenue Agency, *Offshore Tax Information Policy*, last accessed December 1, 2018, and *available at* http://www.cra-arc.gc.ca/gncy/cmplnc/otip-pdife/menu-eng.html.

[169] Law Society of Ontario, *Rules of Professional Conduct*, r 3.3-3. In a recent amendment to its Whistleblower Policy, the Ontario Securities Commission clarified that in-house counsel who report information under the Policy in violation of applicable provincial or territorial bar or law society rules will not be eligible for a whistleblower award: October 4, 2018, OSC Notice of Police Amendment to OSC Policy 15-601 Whistleblower Program: http://www.osc.gov.on.ca/en/SecuritiesLaw_rule_20181004_15-601_whistleblower-program.htm.

[170] *Id.*, r 3.2-8.

[171] *Id.*, r 3.2-8(c); *id.*, r 3.2 commentary [5].

illegal. Nor do whistle-blower protections typically provide cover for civil servants who, rather than expose wrongdoing, publicly criticize government policies.[172]

In 2013, for example, a senior government lawyer was suspended without pay for disclosing to the public that the Minister of Justice was failing to properly review the constitutionality of draft legislation.[173] In 2007, a public servant was terminated, arrested, and charged with breach of trust after he leaked government plans to withdraw from the Kyoto Protocols.[174] In 2013, a federal civil servant was suspended without pay after leaking documents that showed the federal government had set recovery quotas for employment insurance fraud investigators, a claim that had previously been denied by the government.[175]

Irrespective of section 425.1 of the *Code*, Canadians are, from time to time, terminated for disclosing wrongdoing by government authorities. For example, in 2011, a professional engineer was fired from a leading energy company after he disclosed to the National Energy Board regulatory noncompliance by a leading energy company.[176] The engineer had attempted "up the ladder" disclosure prior to informing the regulator.[177] The noncompliance was largely substantiated by a subsequent investigation by the National Energy Board.[178] The company did not face charges for its apparent breach of section 425.1.

10. Self-Reporting

Self-reporting of corporate misconduct is formally encouraged through the use of policies and initiatives in two Canadian contexts: securities regulation of public companies and regulation of competition under the *Competition Act*. In the securities context, several provincial securities regulators have introduced programs that recognize and, at least in theory, reward self-reporting.[179] For example, the OSC has a formal Credit for Cooperation

---

[172] *Fraser* v. *PSSRB*, [1985] 2 SCR 455, 1985 CanLII 14 at paras. 28–44 (for clarity, civil servants continue to enjoy many protections of free expression; however, these rights are balanced against their duty to uphold the impartiality, neutrality, fairness, and integrity of the civil service).

[173] Roderick MacDonell, *The Whistleblower*, NATIONAL (CANADIAN BAR ASS'N MAG.) (Nov.–Dec. 2013), *available at* http://www.nationalmagazine.ca/Articles/November/The-whistleblower.aspx.

[174] *Government Trying to "Bully" Public Servants: Accused Leaker*, CBC NEWS (May 10, 2007), *available at* http://www.cbc.ca/news/canada/government-trying-to-bully-public-servants-accused-leaker-1.685884.

[175] *EI Whistleblower Suspended without Pay*, CBC NEWS (July 20, 2013), *available at* http://www.cbc.ca/news/canada/british-columbia/ei-whistleblower-suspended-without-pay-1.1407761.

[176] *TransCanada Whistleblower's Complaints Validated by NEB*, CBC NEWS (Feb. 25, 2014), *available at* http://www.cbc.ca/news/canada/edmonton/transcanada-whistleblower-s-complaints-validated-by-neb-1.2550175.

[177] Charles Rusnell Timothy Sawa & Joseph Loiero, *Whistleblower Forced Investigation of TransCanada Pipelines*, CBC NEWS (Oct. 17, 2012), *available at* http://www.cbc.ca/news/canada/whistleblower-forced-investigation-of-transcanada-pipelines-1.1146204.

[178] *See* in general (October 17, 2012): https://www.cbc.ca/news/canada/whistleblower-forced-investigation-of-transcanada-pipelines-1.1146204.

[179] *See* Ontario's "Credit for Cooperation" Program, Staff Notice 15-702—Credit for Cooperation (Mar. 13, 2014) 37 OSCB 2583 [hereinafter *Credit for Cooperation*]; *see* British Columbia's "Credit for Assistance in Investigations" program, BC Securities Commission 2002/41—Credit for Assistance in Investigations, *available at* https://www.bcsc.bc.ca/Securities_Law/Policies/PolicyBCN/PDF/2002-41__BCN_/ [hereinafter *Credit for Assistance*].

program that provides incentives to those respondents who "self-police, self-report and self-correct matters that may involve breaches of Ontario securities law or other types of misconduct that would be considered contrary to the public interest."[180] In exchange for cooperation, the OSC offers to narrow the scope of the enforcement measures taken against the respondent, reduce the recommended sanctions in connection with the enforcement proceeding, or propose the resolution of the matter on the basis of a settlement agreement. In limited circumstances, the OSC allows for the resolution of an enforcement proceeding by way of a settlement agreement in which the respondent makes no admissions of fact or liability (i.e., a no-contest plea).[181]

Similarly, the Competition Bureau, the body responsible for the administration and enforcement of the *Competition Act,* encourages self-reporting through the use of two programs: the Immunity Program and the Leniency Program. Under the Immunity Program, a party who self-reports potentially criminal anti-competitive activity that may be found to violate the *Competition Act* may gain immunity if their circumstances meet a list of requirements set out by the Bureau.[182] In the event that the self-reporting party is a company that qualifies for immunity, the current directors, officers, and employees who admit their involvement in the illegal anti-competitive activity will also gain access to the immunity.[183] Under the Leniency Program, cooperating parties who provide "full, frank, timely and truthful" disclosure of anti-competitive activity, may qualify for a recommendation of leniency by the Bureau to the Public Prosecution Service of Canada and the Courts (PPSC).[184] Where leniency is warranted, the Bureau usually recommends a reduction to the applicable fine. The degree of discount recommended is considered on an individual basis with regard to the extent of the party's cooperation.[185]

There are no formal programs or even guidelines that incentivize the self-reporting of con-duct that may breach the CFPOA. However, self-reporting may have some impact at the sentencing level once parties are convicted of a CFPOA offense. Two recent cases demon-strate the potential impact of self-reporting: *R v. Niko Resources Inc.* and *R v. Griffiths Energy International Inc.*[186] In *Niko,* Niko Resources Inc. cooperated with the RCMP investigation, but did not self-report. The result was that Niko Resources Inc. was fined $9.5M for pro-viding gifts to a foreign public official amounting to approximately $200,000 in value.[187] In *Griffiths Energy,* a new board of directors and management team discovered that the com-pany had previously paid an amount in excess of $2 million in connection with a foreign

---

[180] *See Credit for Cooperation, supra* note 179; *see Credit for Assistance, supra* note 179.

[181] *See Credit for Cooperation, supra* note 179; *see Credit for Assistance, supra* note 179.

[182] Competition Bureau, *Immunity Program under the Competition Act,* (June 7, 2010), http://www.competitionbureau.gc.ca/eic/site/cb-bc.nsf/eng/03248.html.

[183] *Id.*

[184] Competition Bureau, Leniency Program (Sept. 29, 2010), *available at* http://www.competitionbureau.gc.ca/eic/site/cb-bc.nsf/eng/03288.html#s3_7_3.

[185] *Id.*

[186] *R v. Niko Resources Ltd.,* [2011] 101 WCB (2d) 118 (Can Alta. QB.); *H.M.Q.* v. *Griffiths Energy International Inc.,* 2013 AJ No. 412.

[187] *R. v. Niko Resources Ltd.,* [2011] 101 WCB (2d) 118 (Can Alta. QB.).

public official.[188] In response, the company immediately began an internal investigation, self-reported to the police, and shared with the police the results of its internal investigation. On a plea, Griffiths Energy International Inc. was fined $10.35 million.[189] In the end result, while the monetary value of the bribe in *Griffiths Energy* was more than 10 times the bribe in *Niko*, Griffiths Energy International Inc. received by way of sentence a fine in a similar amount as *Niko*. Undoubtedly, the fact that Griffiths Energy self-reported its misconduct had some role to play in achieving this result.

Nevertheless, while self-reporting may have some positive impacts at the sentencing level in cases involving CFPOA offenses, the absence of a formal program promoting either immunity or leniency leaves potential respondents with no benchmarks to accurately predict the consequences of their cooperation.

Key Issues	Canada's Approach
Is Canada subject to any international anti-corruption conventions? If so, which conventions?	Yes. OECD Convention. UN Conventions against Corruption and Organised Crime. OAS Inter-American Convention against Corruption (IACAC)
Is bribery of foreign public officials illegal? Do domestic anti-bribery laws apply extraterritorially?	Yes. Yes (under the CFPOA)
What is the definition of a foreign public official?	A Foreign Official is defined in the CFPOA as: (a) a person who holds a legislative, administrative or judicial position of a foreign state; (b) a person who performs public duties or functions for a foreign state, including a person employed by a board, commission, corporation or other body or authority that is established to perform a duty or function on behalf of the foreign state, or is performing such a duty or function; and (c) an official or agent of a public international organization that is formed by two or more states or governments, or by two or more such public international organizations. (*agent public étranger*)

---

[188] *H.M.Q. v. Griffiths Energy International Inc.*, 2013 AJ No. 412.
[189] *H.M.Q. v. Griffiths Energy International Inc.*, 2013 AJ No. 412.

Key Issues	Canada's Approach
Is commercial bribery illegal?	Yes. Section 426 of the *Criminal Code* makes it an offense for someone to offer or for an agent to accept a secret commission as consideration for doing or not doing any act relating to the affairs or business of the agent's principal. Unlike the CFPOA, the *Criminal Code* (including the secret commission offense) generally does not have extraterritorial jurisdiction.
Is bribing domestic officials illegal?	Yes.
Can the recipient of a bribe be prosecuted?	Yes.
Can companies be held criminally liable? If so, what is the requisite intent for corporate criminal liability?	Yes. In relations to corporations, the *Criminal Code* distinguishes between offenses of negligence and offenses of fault. As bribery is an offense of fault, an "organization" (which includes a corporation) can be found liable if (a) one of its senior officers, (b) acting with the intent to benefit the organization at least in part (c) is (i) a party to the offense while acting within the scope of his or her authority, or (ii) directs other representatives of the organization to commit an act or omission while having the mental state to be a party to the offense and acts within the scope of his or her authority; or (iii) does not take all reasonable measures to stop a representative of the organization that the senior officer knows is or is about to be a party to an offense.
Can companies be held civilly liable?	Yes, although not under the CFPOA.
Can an individual be held civilly liable?	Yes, although not under the CFPOA.
If there a "facilitation payment" defense?	No. As of October 31, 2017, the facilitation defense was removed from the CFPOA.
Do conspiracy laws apply to anti-corruption offenses?	Yes
Does Canada provide liability for: (a) aiding and/or abetting liability (b) attempt liability (c) for anti-corruption laws?	Yes.

(*Continued*)

Key Issues	Canada's Approach
Is the failure to keep accurate books and records a criminal or civil offense?	It is a criminal offense pursuant to section 4 of the CFPOA
Do any books and records offenses have to involve proof of an underlying bribery offense?	In order to secure a conviction for the CFPOA books and records offense (section 4), the prosecution must establish that the offense occurred "for the purpose of bribing a foreign public official in order to obtain or retain an advantage in the course of business or for the purpose of hiding that bribery."
Are there Canadian laws concerning a company's financial internal controls? If so, are those laws applicable to public and/or private companies?	Public companies may be subject to internal control requirements under various provincial securities regulations. Additionally, although internal controls are not a legal requirement or obligation under the CFPOA, section 4(1) of the CFPOA makes it a criminal offense to record incorrect entries in books and records if done so for purposes of committing or hiding a bribe. This would apply to public and private companies.
Is there an affirmative disclosure obligation for potential violations of anti-corruption laws or accounting irregularities?	Potentially. To date, there is no national securities law regulator in Canada. Various provincial securities law regimes may require a public company to disclose corporate misconduct or an investigation into such alleged misconduct as part of its continuous disclosure obligations. For example, under the *Securities Act (Ontario)* if misconduct or an investigation into misconduct is a material fact (defined as a fact that would reasonably be expected to have a significant effect on the market price or value of the securities), the company may be under disclosure obligations.
Are "promotional expenses" exempt from Canada's anti-corruption laws?	An expense related to the promotion, demonstration, or explanation of products or services are exempt from punishment under the CFPOA, provided the impugned expenses were made to pay the reasonable expenses incurred in good faith by or on behalf of a foreign public official.
Is the giving of gifts, entertainment, travel, meals, or other gratuities restricted or prohibited by anti-corruption or other laws?	Yes, if done to obtain or retain an advantage in the course of business.

Key Issues	Canada's Approach
Are there any Canadian laws concerning things, property, or benefits of value conveyed by, or to, third parties?	The CFPOA prohibits bribing a foreign public official directly or indirectly, which would include payments or benefits made to third parties.
Are tax bribes deductible?	No.
Is Canada's anti-corruption laws applied extraterritorially?	Yes. The books and records offense as well as the offense of bribing a foreign public official under the *CFPOA* have extraterritorial application under the nationality principle.
Is a robust corporate compliance program an affirmative defense or a factor to negate liability or reduce penalties?	A compliance program is not an affirmative defense although it can function as a mitigating factor in sentence.
Is there a "local law" exception or defense to Canada's anti-corruption laws?	Yes. It is a defense to a charge under the CFPOA if the act is permitted or required under the laws of the foreign state or public international organization for which the foreign public official performs duties or functions.
Is "credit" given for cooperation with authorities?	To a limited extent. This is one of the factors that the court may, but is not obliged to, take into account, when sentencing a legal person.
If so, how and in what form?	There is no fixed criteria defining credit for cooperation in relation to the CFPOA.
Does Canada have mutual legal assistance with the United States that covers criminal matters, including anti-corruption conduct?	Yes.
What are the potential penalties/sanctions for criminal and civil violations of Canada's anti-corruption laws?	The CFPOA is a strictly criminal statute. It does not have civil liability. **Individuals** Individuals who contravene the books and records offense or the offense of bribing a foreign public official under the CFPOA are liable to 14 years imprisonment. **Companies** There is no limit to a fine that may be imposed on a company for a CFPOA contravention.

5   China

1. Introduction to China's Anti-Corruption Legislation

China's[1] anti-corruption legislation prohibits both official corruption and commercial bribery. China is a civil law country. It does not have a uniform national anti-corruption law yet, and the relevant anti-corruption legal provisions are mainly in the PRC Criminal Law and the PRC Anti-Unfair Competition Law. In addition to these two key legislations, there are also regulations and judicial interpretations issued by relevant government agencies and the Supreme People's Court to address implementation issues under the law.

Since China's president, Jinping Xi, came to power in 2012, China has launched an anti-corruption campaign. The Chinese Communist Party's (CCP) 18th Party Congress in 2012 emphasized the urgency and significance of fighting against corruption. Following the Congress, the Supreme People's Court and the Supreme People's Procuratorate have issued a series of judicial interpretations and rules to strengthen enforcement against bribery. China's anti-corruption campaign has significant impact on multinational companies' operations in China. UK drug company GlaxoSmithKline PLC (GSK) was accused of bribing Chinese doctors, hospitals, and government officials in an effort to sell more drugs at higher prices. In September 2014, GSK was found by the Chinese People's Court to be guilty of bribery and was fined nearly RMB 3 billion (approximately U.S. $500 million). Five of the company's

---

[1] This chapter was contributed by White & Case's Bingna Guo and O'Melveny & Myers's Lining Shan and Bo Li.

From Baksheesh to Bribery. T. Markus Funk and Andrew S. Boutros.
© Oxford University Press 2019. Published 2019 by Oxford University Press.

executives, including its then CEO, Legal Director, Vice President, and Operation Manager, Vice President and Human Resource Director, and Business Development Manager, were convicted of the criminal charge of bribery.

The 19th CCP Congress in 2017 continues to send strong signals to fight against corruption. The Party's statement from the conference reaffirms the Party's zero tolerance for corruption. The Party announced it will set up the National Supervisory Commission, which will consolidate the supervision and enforcement powers of the People's Procuratorate, Ministry of Supervision, and National Bureau of Corruption Prevention. Within one month from the 19th CCP Congress, China's Central Commission for Discipline Inspection (CCDI) announced 23 officials were under investigation.

2. China's Domestic Anti-Corruption Framework

Chinese anti-corruption rules are scattered across multiple resources. The primary statutes are the Criminal Law and the Anti-Unfair Competition Law (AUCL), which are supplemented by other anti-corruption related laws, regulations and guidelines, and judicial interpretations. In addition, the ruling CCP and the government have issued internal rules prohibiting corruption among personnel of government offices or party offices.

2.1 CRIMINAL LAW REGIME

The Criminal Law was first enacted in 1979 and later revised in 1997. It has been amended 10 times since 1997. The Criminal Law criminalizes bribery of Chinese "state functionaries" (a term similar to the concept of "officials" under the U.S. Foreign Corrupt Practices Act (FCPA), but could be narrower in scope); and bribery of "close relatives" or "close associates" of "state functionaries," as well as serious cases of bribery of foreign public officials and bribery of nonstate functionaries (often referred to as "commercial bribery"). The Criminal Law also criminalizes bribery of public entities.

Breach of the prohibitions of bribery under the Criminal Law could result in prison term, a fine for individuals, and a fine for a company if the company is convicted.

2.2 CIVIL LAW REGIME

The AUCL was first promulgated in 1993, targeting unfair and anti-competitive practices in the course of market behavior. On November 4, 2017, China's National People's Congress (NPC) passed and published revisions to the 1993 AUCL (the "AUCL (2017 Revision)"), which came into effect on January 1, 2018.

The revised AUCL, among other things, prohibits businesses from bribing (1) any employee of the counterparty to a transaction; (2) any entity or individual authorized by the counterparty to a transaction to handle relevant affairs; and (3) any entity or individual that is likely to take advantage of powers or influence to affect a transaction (often referred to as "commercial bribery"). Businesses found to be in violation are subject to an administrative fine, confiscation of illegal gains, and in serious cases revocation of business license. The injured businesses may sue for damages before the courts.

In addition to the AUCL, the laws regulating certain industries also contain anti-bribery provisions for the industries concerned, such as the Commercial Bank Law, Insurance Law, and Drug Administration Law.

2.3 INTERNAL RULES BY THE CCP AND THE GOVERNMENT

The internal anti-corruption rules issued by the CCP and the government govern the conduct of personnel of the Party or government offices. These internal rules are enforced by the CCDI and the Ministry of Supervision and their local offices respectively. These rules are of great reference value to businesses for their compliance programs, such as setting the monetary thresholds on gifts and business hospitality. For example, the Central Committee of the CCP and the State Council jointly issued multiple anti-corruption rules in 1993, stating that recipients are allowed to keep gifts from a foreign party that do not exceed RMB200 (approximately U.S. $30) in value; if the market value of a gift exceeds RMB200, the recipient is required to turn it over to the government.[2] Many companies take this threshold into consideration when deciding their gift and entertainment polices for their China operations.

2.4 VIEW FROM THE OUTSIDE

2.4.1 OECD Evaluation

China is not a party to the OECD Convention on Combating Bribery of Foreign Public Officials in International Business Transactions (the "OECD Anti-Bribery Convention"), thus the OECD does not monitor China on the implementation of the Convention.

2.4.2 Transparency International Corruption Perception Index Score

The Transparency International Corruption Perception Index has ranked China as follows over the last five years: No. 80 in 2012, No. 80 in 2013, No. 100 in 2014, No. 83 in 2015, and No. 79 in 2016.

In recent years, China has beefed up its anti-corruption efforts on catching "tigers and flies"—corrupt public officials big and small—and its scores and ranking have improved, though not substantially. Transparency International appears to suggest that civil society and the private sector in China have not been involved adequately in the campaign against corruption. Transparency International also recommends that China should join the OECD Anti-Bribery Convention.

---

[2] Item 2 of the *Notice of the General Office of the Central Committee of the Communist Party and the General Office of the State Council on Implementing the Provisions of the State Council of the People's Republic of China on Giving and Receiving Gifts in Official Functions Involving Foreigners*, issued on December 16, 1993.

3. Investigative and Prosecutorial Agencies

3.1 ADMINISTRATIVE ENFORCEMENT AGENCIES

The AUCL is enforced by the State Administration of Industry and Commerce (SAIC) and local AICs at the county level and above. The SAIC administers the registration and incorporations of business entities and enforces competition law in China at the central level. Local AICs perform these functions at the local level.

The SAIC and local AICs may impose administrative penalties in case of anti-competition conduct including commercial bribery that do not constitute crimes. If the bribery conduct under investigation constitutes a crime, the case needs to be referred to the criminal law agencies for investigation.

As mentioned previously, some laws regulating certain industries may also contain anti-corruption or anti-bribery provisions. Some of these laws may endow the industry regulators with enforcement rights over corruption and bribery conduct within their industries.

3.2 CRIMINAL LAW AGENCIES

China's criminal law enforcement agencies include the police and the procuratorate. The police are responsible for investigating bribery crimes committed by nonstate functionaries and handing over the cases to the procuratorate for prosecution once the investigation is completed. The procuratorate investigates and prosecutes bribery crimes committed by state functionaries. It is worth noting that bribery of foreign public officials is investigated by the police—not the procuratorate.

3.3 MULTIAGENCY ARRANGEMENTS

In December 2012, the SAIC, the Ministry of Public Security, and the Supreme People's Procuratorate jointly issued the *Opinions on Several Issues concerning Strengthening Coordination and Cooperation between Administrative Enforcement and Judicial Enforcement*. The *Opinions* provide for various enforcement coordination mechanisms, including joint investigation by the police and AICs of serious and complicated cases suspected of constituting a crime, and enforcement of an information-sharing platform and interagency panel among AICs, the police, and the procuratorate.

4. Bribery of Foreign Officials

4.1 JURISDICTION

As a general rule and absent specific statutory authority, Chinese laws are confined to China and do not have exterritorial jurisdiction.

According to the Criminal Law, if the conduct or outcome of a crime happens within China's territory, a prosecution can be brought in China.[3] Foreign companies and individuals can be prosecuted in China for bribery occurring within China or impacting China. Bribery

---

[3] Article 6 of the Criminal Law.

crimes under the Criminal Law committed outside China by a Chinese citizen can also be prosecuted in China.[4]

4.2 STATUTE OF LIMITATIONS

Prosecution for offenses under the Criminal Law generally may be commenced as follows:[5]

- within five years where the maximum penalty is imprisonment of less than five years;
- within 10 years where the maximum penalty is imprisonment of no less than five years and less than 10 years;
- within 15 years where the maximum penalty is imprisonment of no less than 10 years; or
- within 20 years where the maximum penalty is life imprisonment or death penalty.

The Criminal Law does not distinguish crimes committed by individuals and crimes committed by entities (often termed "entity crime") in terms of the statute of limitations. Under the Criminal Law, as a general rule, if a company is convicted, the company will be subject to a fine and the persons directly in charge and other persons directly responsible for the crime are also convicted.[6] Court practices indicate that the statutory limitations for entity crimes is based on the penalty to the individuals convicted in the entity crimes.

For the crime of bribery of foreign officials, the same statutory limitations apply to both individuals and entities: 5 years or 15 years depending on the gravity of the offenses.

4.3 FOREIGN BRIBERY OFFENSES

In 2011, China amended the Criminal Law to include the offense of bribing a foreign public official ("Foreign Bribery Offense") in efforts to implement its treaty obligations under the UN Convention Against Corruption. China ratified the convention in October 2005.

The amended Article 164 of the Criminal Law provides that "whoever gives any property to a functionary of a foreign country or an official of an international public organization for any improper commercial benefit shall be punished according to the provision of the preceding paragraph" (the "Foreign Bribery Offense"). The Foreign Bribery Offense provision criminalizes serious cases of giving "money and property" to a "functionary of a foreign country" or an "official of an international public organization" for the purpose of seeking "improper commercial benefits." Serious cases are cases in which the "money or property" involved constitute a "relatively large amount."

The meaning of the terms used in the Foreign Bribery Offense provision are discussed as follows:

> *"Money and property"*: The Supreme People's Court (SPC) and Supreme People's Procuratorate (SPP) define "money and property" very broadly to include cash,

---

[4] Article 7 of the Criminal Law.

[5] Article 87 of the Criminal Law.

[6] Article 31 of the Criminal Law.

articles, and property interests. Property interests include material benefits that can be converted into money, such as home renovation, debt relief, etc. and other benefits that require the payment of money, such as membership services, travel, etc.[7]

"Relatively large amount": Under the 2016 Judicial Interpretation, the conviction threshold—a "relatively large amount"—refers to (1) not less than RMB60,000 or (2) not less than RMB20,000 and less than RMB60,000, if there exists any of the following circumstances:[8]

- offering bribes to more than three persons;
- using illicit income for offering bribes;
- seeking a promotion or position adjustment by offering bribes; or
- the amount of economic losses caused is not less than RMB500,000 but less than RMB1million.

"Functionary of a foreign country" and "official of an international public organization": please see later on in this Section.

"Improper commercial benefits": "Improper commercial benefits" are not defined in law or in judicial interpretations. However, the SPC and SPP have defined "improper benefits" to be benefits, favor, or convenience in violation of laws, regulations, government department rules or policies, and competitive advantages in violation of the principle of fairness in commercial activities such as biddings and government procurement.[9]

4.4 "FOREIGN PUBLIC OFFICIALS" DEFINED

"Foreign public official" and "official of an international public organization" are not defined in the Criminal Law. However, it can be reasonably inferred that the definitions of these two terms under the UNCAC will be followed by the Chinese judicial authorities. The two terms are defined under the UNCAC as follows:[10]

"'Foreign public official' shall mean any person holding a legislative, executive, administrative or judicial office of a foreign country, whether appointed or elected; and any person exercising a public function for a foreign country, including for a public agency or public enterprise."

"'Official of an international public organization' shall mean an international civil servant or any person who is authorized by such an organization to act on behalf of that organization."

---

[7] Article 12 of the Interpretations of the Supreme People's Court and the Supreme People's Procuratorate on Several Issues concerning the Application of Law in Handling Criminal Cases Involving Corruption and Bribery ("2016 Judicial Interpretation").

[8] Article 11 of the 2016 Judicial Interpretation.

[9] Article 9 of the interpretations of the Supreme People's Court and the Supreme People's Procuratorate on Several Issues concerning the Application of Law in Handling Criminal Cases of Commercial Briberies [hereinafter 2008 Judicial Interpretation].

[10] Article 2 of UNCAC.

4.5 GIFTS, GRATUITIES, AND HOSPITALITY

Gifts, gratuities, and hospitality are covered under the term "money and property." The Criminal Law does not prohibit companies and individuals from giving customary, reasonable, and non-excessive gifts, gratuities, or hospitality to foreign public officials.

The 2008 Judicial Interpretation, though it predates the Foreign Bribery Offense provision, provides guidance on how to distinguish bribes from legitimate gifts, gratuities, and hospitality. The factors to be considered include:[11]

- the background for the offering, such as whether the giver and the taker are friends or relatives, and the status and extent of their previous contacts;
- value of the things provided;
- cause, timing and method of the provision of things and whether the giver requests favor from the taker related to the taker's position; and
- whether the taker takes advantage of his own position to seek benefits for the giver.

4.6 DEFENSES

4.6.1 Written Local Law

The U.S. FCPA-style written local law defense is not available under the Criminal Law.

4.6.2 Facilitation Payments

The U.S. FCPA-style facilitation payment exception is not available under the Criminal Law.

4.6.3 Adequate Procedures

The Criminal Law does not provide for an adequate procedures defense.

4.6.4 Corporate Culture

The Criminal Law does not provide for a corporate culture defense.

4.7 PENALTIES

The penalties for a conviction of Foreign Bribery Offense under Article 164 are as follows:[12]

- Individual: imprisonment of not more than three years or criminal detention and a fine in a case where a "relatively large amount" of bribe is involved; imprisonment of not less than three years and not more than 10 years and a fine in a case where a "huge amount" of money or property is involved.

[11] Article 10 of the 2008 Judicial Interpretation.
[12] Article 164 of the Criminal Law.

Please refer to Section 4.3 above for the current judicial interpretation on a "relatively large amount." The 2016 Judicial Interpretation also defines a "huge amount" to be (i) not less than RMB2 million and less than RMB10 million; or (ii) not less than RMB1 million and less than RMB2 million, if there exists any of the following circumstances:

  o   offering bribes to more than three persons;
  o   using illicit income for offering bribes;
  o   seeking a promotion or position adjustment by offering bribes; or
  o   other serious circumstances
- Entity: a fine imposed on the entity; the persons indirectly in charge or other persons directly responsible for the crime shall be punished the same way as individual convicts.

According to the 2016 Judicial Interpretation, a fine imposed on entities or individuals should be RMB100,000 up to twice the amount of the bribe.[13]

In addition, if the bribe giver confesses the bribery voluntarily prior to prosecution, it may be given a mitigated punishment or be exempt from punishment.

5. Bribery of Domestic Officials

5.1 JURISDICTION

See Section 4.1 above.

5.2 STATUTE OF LIMITATIONS

For the general principles of statute of limitations under the Criminal Law, please refer to Section 4.2 above.

Prosecution of bribery of domestic officials committed by individuals may be commenced within 10 years, 15 years, or 20 years depending on the seriousness of the crimes.[14]

Prosecution of bribery of domestic officials committed by entities may be commenced within 10 years.[15]

5.3 OFFENSES OF BRIBERY OF DOMESTIC OFFICIALS

Articles 389 and 390 of the Criminal Law criminalize bribery of domestic officials by individuals. Article 393 criminalizes bribery of domestic officials by entities.

5.3.1 Offenses Committed by Individuals

Articles 389 and 390 of the Criminal Law criminalize:

- cases of giving "money or property" to "state functionaries" for the purpose of seeking "improper benefits";

---

[13] Article 19 of the 2016 Judicial Interpretation.
[14] Articles 87 and 390 of the Criminal Law.
[15] Articles 87 and 393 of the Criminal Law.

- cases of giving a "relatively large amount" of "money and property" to "state functionaries" in "economic dealings," in violation of state regulations; and
- cases of giving rebates or handling fees in various names to "state functionaries" in violation of the state regulations.

Article 389 further provides that giving money or property to a state functionary under extortion but gaining no illegitimate benefits shall not be regarded as offering bribes.

5.3.2 Offenses Committed by Entities

Article 393 of the Criminal Law criminalizes cases of entities giving bribes to "state functionaries" for the purpose of seeking improper benefits or serious cases of entities giving "state functionaries" rebates or handling fees in violation of state regulations.

The meaning of terms used in the above domestic official bribery provisions are now discussed:

"*Money and property*": "Money and property" are interpreted very broadly by the judicial authorities. For details, please refer to Section 4.3.

"*State functionaries*": Please see Section 5.4.

"*Improper benefits*": The SPC and SPP have interpreted "improper benefits" in domestic official bribery offenses to be benefits, favor, or convenience in violation of laws, regulations, government department rules or policies, or industry norms. Competitive advantages in economic and personnel management activities in violation of the principles of fairness and justice are also considered as "improper benefits."[16]

"*Economic Dealings*": Though there is no official judicial interpretation on this term, it could include any monetary transaction.

5.4 DEFINITION OF DOMESTIC OFFICIALS

The definition of "state functionaries" in the Criminal Law is broad and vague. "State functionaries" are defined as "persons who perform public service in state organs. Persons who perform public service in state-owned companies or enterprises, institutions or people's organizations, and persons who are assigned by state organs, state-owned companies, enterprises or institutions to companies, enterprises or institutions that are not owned by the State or people's organizations to perform public service and the other persons who perform public service according to law shall all be regarded as State functionaries."[17]

The SPC has interpreted "public service" to include the organization, supervision, and management functions on behalf of a state organ, state-owned companies, enterprises,

---

[16] Article 12 of the Interpretations of the Supreme People's Court and the Supreme People's Procuratorate on Several Issues concerning the Application of Law in Handling Criminal Cases of Offering Bribes [hereinafter 2012 Judicial Interpretation].

[17] Article 93 of the Criminal Law.

institutions, or civil associations.[18] Therefore, executives and officers of state-owned companies and public institutions may be considered as state functionaries for the purpose of the Criminal Law.

According to the 2008 Judicial Interpretation, doctors in state-owned hospitals taking bribes in exchange for prescriptions are treated as nonstate functionaries, and teachers from state-owned schools taking bribes in exchange for textbooks and reference materials for students are treated as nonstate functionaries.[19]

5.5 GIFTS, GRATUITIES, AND HOSPITALITY

The 2008 Judicial Interpretation by the SPC and SPP provides guidance on distinguishing a bribe from legitimate gifts, gratuities, and hospitality. Please refer to Section 4.5.

5.6 DEFENSES

As explained above in Section 4.6.

5.6.1 Written Local Law

The U.S. FCPA-style written local law defense is not available under the Criminal Law.

5.6.2 Facilitation Payments

The U.S. FCPA-style facilitation payments exception is not available under the Criminal Law.

5.6.3 Adequate Procedures

The Criminal Law does not provide for an adequate procedures defense.

5.6.4 Corporate Culture

The Criminal Law does not provide for a corporate culture defense.

5.7 PENALTIES

Penalties for a conviction of domestic official bribery crimes are as follows:[20]

- Individual
  (1) Imprisonment of not more than five years or criminal detention and a fine.

---

[18] Item 1.(4) of the Notice of the Supreme People's Court on Issuing the Minutes of the National Courts Symposium on Trial of Economic Crime Cases.

[19] Articles 4 and 5 of the 2008 Judicial Interpretation.

[20] Articles 390 and 393 of the Criminal Law.

According to the 2016 Judicial Interpretation, this level of penalty applies to the following cases:[21]

a) the amount of the bribe is not less than RMB30,000; or

b) the amount of the bribe is not less than RMB10,000 and less than RMB30,000, if there exists any of the following circumstances:

  (i) offering bribes to more than three persons;

  (ii) using illicit income for offering bribes;

  (iii) seeking a promotion or position adjustment by offering bribes;

  (iv) offering bribes to any state functionary with supervisory and administrative functions in terms of food, drugs, work safety, and environmental protection for the purpose of conducting illegal activities;

  (v) offering bribes to judicial officers, which affects judicial justice; or causing economic losses of not less than RMB500,000 but less than 1 million yuan.

(1) Imprisonment of not less than five years and not more than ten years and a fine in the cases of "serious circumstances" or causing "serious loss to the state."

According to the 2016 Judicial Interpretation, "serious circumstances" refer to:[22]

a) the amount of the bribe is not less than RMB1 million and less than RMB5 million;

b) the amount of the bribe is not less than RMB500,000 and less than RMB1 million, if there exists any of the circumstances described under items (1).b.(i) to (1).b.(v) above; or

c) other serious circumstances.

The 2016 Judicial Interpretation defines "serious loss to the state" as causing economic loss of not less than RMB1 million and less than RMB5 million.

(3) Imprisonment of not less than 10 years or life imprisonment, and concurrent fine or confiscation of property in the cases of "especially serious circumstances" or causing "especially serious loss to the state."

The 2016 Judicial Interpretation defines "especially serious circumstance" as below:[23]

a) the amount of the bribe is not less than RMB5 million; or

b) the amount of the bribe is not less than RMB2.5 million and less than RMB5 million, if there exists any of the circumstances described under items (1).b.(i) to (1).b.(v); or

c) other especially serious circumstances.

---

[21] Article 7 of the 2016 Judicial Interpretation.

[22] Article 8 of the 2016 Judicial Interpretation.

[23] Article 9 of the 2016 Judicial Interpretation.

The 2016 Judicial Interpretation defines "especially serious loss to the state" as causing economic loss of not less than RMB5 million to the state.

- Entity: a fine imposed on the entity; the persons directly in charge and the persons directly responsible for the crime shall be subject to imprisonment of not more than five years or criminal detention and a fine.[24]

The SPP has set the prosecution threshold for bribery of state functionaries by entities at RMB200,000 in terms of the value of the bribe.[25]

According to the 2016 Judicial Interpretation, fines imposed on individuals or entities should be set between RMB100,000 up to twice the amount of the bribe.

6. Bribery of Influential People

The Criminal Law was amended in 2015 to include criminalization of bribery of "close relatives" or "close associates" of state functionaries or former state functionaries for the purpose of seeking improper benefits.

6.1 JURISDICTION

See Section 4.1 of this chapter.

6.2 STATUTE OF LIMITATIONS

The offenses of bribery of influential people committed by individuals may be prosecuted within 5 years, 10 years, or 15 years depending on the gravity of the crimes. The offenses committed by entities may be prosecuted within 5 years.[26]

6.3 OFFENSES OF BRIBERY OF INFLUENTIAL PEOPLE

Article 390 of the Criminal Law criminalizes bribery of "close relatives" or "close associates" of state functionaries or former state functionaries for the purpose of seeking improper benefits. However "close relatives" and "close associates" are not defined in the Criminal Law or judicial interpretation of Article 390.

However, the Criminal Procedural Law may offer some reference on the term "close relatives." The Criminal Procedure Law defines "close relatives" to include spouses, parents, children, and siblings.[27]

---

[24] Article 393 of the Criminal Law.
[25] Article 9 of the Provisions of the Supreme People's Procuratorate on Case Initiation Threshold on Bribe-Giving Crimes.
[26] Articles 87 and 390 of the Criminal Law.
[27] Article 108 of the Criminal Procedure Law.

A reference point to "close associates" could be the term "particular related person" adopted by the SPC and SPP in 2007 in the context of crimes of taking bribes by state functionaries. The term is defined by SPC and SPP to include a person who has such a relationship such as a close relative, lover, or any other common interest with a state functionary.[28]

6.4 GIFTS, GRATUITIES, AND HOSPITALITY

The 2008 Judicial Interpretation by the SPC and SPP provides guidance on distinguishing a bribe from legitimate gifts, gratuities, and hospitality. Please refer to Section 4.5 of this chapter.

6.5 DEFENSES

6.5.1 Written Local Law

The U.S. FCPA-style written local law defense is not available under the Criminal Law.

6.5.2 Facilitation Payments

The U.S. FCPA-style written facilitation payments exception is not available under the Criminal Law.

6.5.3 Adequate Procedures

The Criminal Law does not provide for an adequate procedures defense.

6.5.4 Corporate Culture

The Criminal Law does not provide for a corporate culture defense.

6.6 PENALTIES

Penalties for a conviction of the crime of bribery of influential people are as follows:[29]
- Individual
  (1) imprisonment of not more than three years or criminal detention and a fine;
  (2) Imprisonment of not less than three years and not more than seven years and a fine in cases with serious circumstances or causing serious loss to the state.
  (3) Imprisonment of not less than seven years and not more than 10 years and a fine in cases with specially serious circumstances or causing especially serious loss to the state.

---

[28] Article 11 of the Notice of the Supreme People's Court and the Supreme People's Procuratorate on Issuing the Opinions on Issues concerning the Application of Law in the Handling of Criminal Cases Involving the Acceptance of Bribes (2007 Judicial Interpretation).

[29] Article 390 of the Criminal Law.

The 2016 Judicial Interpretation provides that the standards for conviction and sentencing for the offense of bribing domestic officials may apply, mutatis mutandis, to the crime of bribery of influential people.[30]

- Entity: a fine imposed on entity; the person directly in charge and the person directly responsible for the crime are subject to imprisonment of not more than three years or criminal detention and a fine.

According to the 2016 Judicial Interpretation, the conviction threshold of the entity crime of bribing influential people is RMB200,000 in terms of the value of the bribe.[31]

7. Bribery of Public Entities

Article 391 of the Criminal Law criminalizes bribery of public entities.

7.1 JURISDICTION

See Section 4.1 of this chapter.

7.2 STATUTE OF LIMITATIONS

The crime of bribery of public entities committed by individuals or entities may be prosecuted within five years.

7.3 OFFENSE OF BRIBERY OF PUBLIC ENTITIES

Article 391 of the Criminal Law criminalizes cases of giving money or property to state organs, state-owned companies, state-owned enterprises, institutions, or people's organizations for the purpose of seeking improper benefits, and cases of giving rebates or handling fees to state organs, state-owned companies, state-owned enterprises, institutions, or people's organizations in economic dealings in violation of state regulations.

7.4 GIFTS, GRATUITIES, AND HOSPITALITY

The 2008 Judicial Interpretation by the SPC and SPP provides for guidance on distinguishing bribes from legitimate gifts, gratuities, and hospitality. Please refer to Section 4.5 of this chapter.

7.5 DEFENSES
7.5.1 Written Local Law

The U.S. FCPA-style written local law defense is not available under the Criminal Law.

---

[30] Article 10 of the 2016 Judicial Interpretation.
[31] Article 10 of the 2016 Judicial Interpretation.

7.5.2 Facilitation Payments

The U.S. FCPA-style written facilitation payments exception is not available under the Criminal Law.

7.5.3 Adequate Procedures

The Criminal Law does not provide for an adequate procedures defense.

7.5.4 Corporate Culture

The Criminal Law does not provide for a corporate culture defense.

7.6 PENALTIES

Penalties for a conviction of public entities bribery offenses are as follows:

- Individuals: imprisonment of not more than three years or criminal detention and a fine.
- Entity: a fine imposed on the entity; the persons directly in charge and the persons directly responsible for the crime are subject to imprisonment of not more than three years or criminal detention and a fine.

8. Commercial Bribery

Commercial bribery is generally considered as an unfair method of competition affecting trade and commerce. Under Chinese law, commercial bribery is sanctioned by both administrative law and criminal law.

8.1 JURISDICTION

Please refer to Section 4.1 of this chapter.

8.2 STATUTE OF LIMITATION

The Administrative Penalty Law provides a two-year statute of limitation, counted from the date the unlawful act is committed. This two-year statute of limitation means if an unlawful act is not discovered within two years, an administrative penalty will not be imposed, except as otherwise prescribed by law. However, if an act is ongoing or continuous, the date shall be counted from the date on which the act ends.[32] The element of continuity is interpreted as to mean committing several independent unlawful acts of the same type with the same intent.

As to the statute of limitation for a criminal offense, the general statute of limitation under the Criminal Law applies. Please refer to Section 4.2 of this chapter.

---

[32] Article 29 of the Administrative Penalty Law.

8.3 COMMERCIAL BRIBERY OFFENSES

In China, the general prohibition against commercial bribery appears in Article 7 of the Anti-Unfair Competition Law ("the AUCL (2017 Revision)"), which provides that "business operators shall not resort to bribery by offering money, property, or by other means, to any of the following entities or individuals, in order to pursue business opportunities or competitive advantages:

- any employee of the counterparty to a transaction;
- any entity or individual authorized by the counterparty to a transaction to handle relevant affairs; and
- any entity or individual that is likely to take advantage of powers or influence to affect a transaction.

If a violation constitutes a crime, commercial bribery could also trigger criminal liability.[33] The Criminal Law penalizes giving money or property in a relatively large amount to any employee of a company, enterprise, or other organization for the purpose of seeking illegitimate benefits.[34]

8.4 GIFTS, GRATUITIES, AND HOSPITALITY

For an administrative offense, the SAIC Interim Regulation defines "property" used in committing commercial bribery to include cash, and other objects in the name of promotional fees, research fees, consultation fees, etc. "Bribery by other means" includes offering all kinds of overseas and domestic travels of various descriptions, or inspection tours, etc.

For criminal offense, the SPC and SPP define "money and property" to include cash, articles, and property interests. "Property interests" include material benefits that can be converted into money, such as home renovation, debt relief, etc., and other benefits that require the payment of money, such as membership services, travel, etc.[35]

8.5 VICARIOUS LIABILITY TO THE BUSINESS FOR EMPLOYEE MISCONDUCT

Article 7 of the revised AUCL adopts a rebuttable presumption of vicarious liabilities, that is, an employee's misconduct is attributable to the employer, unless the employer can prove that such misconduct is not related to seeking business opportunities or competitive advantages for the employer. In practice it would probably be difficult for employers to distance themselves from their employees' misconduct, as bribes paid by employees are ostensibly to win businesses or competitive advantages relating to their employers' businesses, even

---

[33] Article 31 of the Anti-Unfair Competition Law.
[34] Article 164 of the Criminal Law.
[35] Article 12 of the Interpretations of the Supreme People's Court and the Supreme People's Procuratorate on Several Issues concerning the Application of Law in Handling Criminal Cases involving Corruption and Bribery [hereinafter 2016 Judicial Interpretation].

if the employees also stand to gain personally. It is worth monitoring how regulators will enforce this provision and what evidence regulators will accept to rebut the presumption of liability of employers.

We note that the existing SAIC Interim Rules Prohibiting Commercial Bribery ("the SAIC Interim Rules") provide that employees' commercial bribery acts for selling or purchasing commodities for their employers should be deemed as acts of their employers. Therefore, it is worth monitoring whether SAIC will amend the SAIC Interim Rules or issue new rules to conform with the revised AUCL.

8.6 DEFENSES

Chinese law does not provide defenses such as written local law, facilitation payments, adequate procedures, or corporate culture. Nevertheless, the AUCL and the SAIC Interim Regulation have considered the following circumstances as legitimate practices. Specifically:

- Express Discount or Intermediary Commission. The AUCL permits for "express" discounts (i.e., included in the contract terms) or commissions to "intermediaries" provided that they are accurately recorded on the books and records. The SAIC Interim Regulation defines "discount" as a concessionary price expressly offered by a business operator in the contract. This can take two forms: a deduction at the time of the purchase or a rebate.
- Nominal promotional gifts. The SAIC Interim Regulation allows giving nominal promotional gifts based on common commercial practice.
- Service fee for sales promotion. According to the Administrative Measures on Fair Trading between Retailers and Suppliers, it is permissible for manufacturers or distributors to pay service fees charged by retailers for sales promotions, such as publishing promotional brochures and posters. A retailer must obtain its supplier's consent and explicitly stipulate the promotional activities and service fee standards in a contract.

8.6.1 Written Local Law

Not applicable.

8.6.2 Facilitation Payments

Not applicable.

8.6.3 Adequate Procedures

Not applicable.

8.6.4 Corporate Culture

Not applicable.

8.7 PENALTY

For an administrative offense, the AICs may impose a fine of not less than RMB100,000 but not more than RMB3 million in light of the circumstances, and confiscate the illegal gains, if any. Where the circumstance is serious, a business operator's business license could be revoked.[36]

For a criminal offense, an individual giving a bribe in a relatively large amount shall be sentenced to imprisonment of not more than 3 years or detention and concurrently sentenced to a fine; if the amount involved is huge, the bribe-giver shall be sentenced to imprisonment of not less than 3 years but not more than 10 years and concurrently sentenced to a fine.[37]

According to the 2016 Judicial Interpretation, "relatively large amount" refers to bribes exceeding RMB60,000, or the total bribe ranges between RMB20,000 and RMB60,000 if it also has an aggravating factor; and "huge amount" refers to total bribes ranges between RMB2 million to RMB10 million, or the total bribes range between RMB1 million and RMB2 million if it also has an aggravating factor.[38]

If an entity commits the crime, it shall be fined, and the persons who are directly in charge and other persons who are directly responsible for the crime shall be sentenced according to the above standards. Any bribe-giver who confesses the bribery voluntarily prior to prosecution may be given a mitigated punishment or be exempted from punishment.[39]

9. Sentencing Principles

9.1 GENERAL PRINCIPLES

Chinese Criminal Law provides statutory sentencing guidelines (i.e., normally setting maximum and minimum punishment) that applies to each of the criminal offenses. When it comes to sentencing, judges are required to consider the facts, the nature, and the circumstances of the crime, as well as the degree of harm to society.[40] If the circumstances of a crime call for a heavier or lighter punishment under the provisions of the Criminal Law, the criminal can be sentenced to a heavier or lighter punishment within the limits of the prescribed punishment.[41]

There are certain general aggravating or mitigating factors, such as voluntary surrender, that allow the judge to rule beyond the statutory sentencing standards. The judge may sentence a criminal to a punishment less than the statutory punishment if the mitigating factors so require.[42] Furthermore, even if there is no mitigating factor, upon the approval of the

---

[36] Article 19 of the AUCL.
[37] Article 164 of the Criminal Law.
[38] Article 11 of the 2016 Judicial Interpretation.
[39] Article 164 of the Criminal Law.
[40] Article 61 of the Criminal Law.
[41] Article 62 of the Criminal Law.
[42] Article 62 of the Criminal Law.

SPC, based on the special situation of the case, a criminal may be sentenced to a punishment below the statutory standards.[43]

Sentencing Rules for Criminal Cases of Corruption and Bribery

Below is a summary table for the sentencing rules in criminal cases of corruption and bribery.

Offence	Threshold	Sentencing
Accepting a bribe by a state-functionary	"Relatively large amount" (RMB30,000 but less than RMB200,000; or between RMB10,000 to RMB30,000 if it also has an aggravating factor [44] listed under Article 1 of the 2016 Judicial Interpretation)	Imprisonment of not more than three years or detention and a concurrent fine.
	"Huge amount" (RMB200,000 but less than RMB3 million, or between RMB100,000 and RMB200,000 if it also has an aggravating factor)	Imprisonment of not less than three years but not more than 10 years and a concurrent fine or confiscation of property
	"Especially huge amount" not less than RMB3 million, or between RMB1.5 million and RMB3 million if it also has an aggravating factor	Imprisonment of not less than 10 years or life imprisonment and a concurrent fine or confiscation of property
	"Especially huge amount" with especially serious loss to the interests of the state and the people	Life imprisonment or the death penalty and confiscation of property
Accepting bribe by a nonstate functionary[45]	"Relatively large amount" (RMB60,000 but less than RMB400,000; or between RMB20,000 and RMB60,000 if it also has an aggravating factor listed under Article 1 of the 2016 Judicial Interpretation)[46]	Imprisonment of not more than five years or detention.
	"Huge amount" (RMB400,000 but less than RMB6 million, or between RMB200,000 and RMB400,000 if it also has an aggravating factor)	Imprisonment of more than five years, and/or confiscation of property.

(*Continued*)

---

[43] Article 63 of the Criminal Law.

[44] Article 1 of the 2016 Judicial Interpretation.

[45] Article 163 of the Criminal Law.

[46] The monetary threshold for prosecution of the crime of giving bribes to nonstate functionaries is set at two times the amount of the threshold for the crime of giving bribes to state functionaries. See Article 11 of the Judicial Interpretation.

Offence	Threshold	Sentencing
Giving a bribe to a state functionary	Over RMB30,000, or between RMB10,000 and RMB30,000 if it also has an aggregating factor specified in Article 7 of the 2016 Judicial Interpretation	Imprisonment of not more than five years or detention and a concurrent fine
	"Serious circumstance" (bribes range between RMB1 million to RMB5 million, or between RMB500,000 and RMB1 million if it also has an aggravating factor)[47]	Imprisonment of not less than 5 years but not more than 10 years and a concurrent fine
	"especially serious circumstance" (bribes over RMB5 million, or between RMB2.5 million and RMB5 million if it also has an aggravating factor)[48]	Imprisonment of not less than 10 years or life imprisonment and a concurrent fine or confiscation of property.
Giving a bribe to a nonstate functionary	"Relatively large amount" (Over RMB60,000, or between RMB20,000 to RMB60,000 if it also has an aggregating factor specified in Article 7 of the 2016 Judicial Interpretation)[49]	Imprisonment of not more than three years or detention and a concurrent fine
	"Huge amount" (between RMB2 million to RMB10 million or RMB1 million to RMB2 million if it also has an aggregating factor)	Imprisonment of not less than 3 years but not more than 10 years and a concurrent fine

9.1.1 Aggregating Factors

For the crime of accepting a bribe, the aggregating factors include:

- extortion of bribes repeatedly;
- interests of public property, the state, and the people; or
- seeking job promotion or post adjustment.[50]

For the crime of giving a bribe, the aggregating factors include:

- offering bribes to three or more persons;
- offering bribes with illegal gains;

---

[47] Article 8 of the 2016 Judicial Interpretation.
[48] Article 9 of the 2016 Judicial Interpretation.
[49] Article 11 of the 2016 Judicial Interpretation.
[50] Article 1 of the 2016 Judicial Interpretation.

- offering bribes with the purpose of seeking job promotion or post adjustment;
- offering bribes to a state-functionary responsible for the supervision and administration of food, drugs, work safety, environmental protection, and so on to conduct illegal activities;
- offering bribes to a judicial officer that affects judicial justice; or
- causing economic losses of not less than RMB 500,000 but less than RMB 1 million.[51]

9.1.2 Mitigating Factors

In terms of the mitigating factors, for the crime of giving bribes to state-functionaries, Article 390 of the Criminal Law provides that if the circumstances of the crime are relatively minor and the briber plays a critical role in detecting a major case or if he/she performs any major meritorious services, he/she may be given a mitigated punishment or be exempted from punishment.[52]

The 2016 Judicial Interpretation defines "relatively minor" as a crime that may be sentenced to imprisonment of not more than three years, subject to the facts and circumstances of the crime.[53] "Playing a critical role in detecting a major case" on the other hand means voluntarily:

- providing new evidence not previously obtained for a major ongoing case,
- providing evidence that helps officials detect a new major case,
- providing facts related to bribery that are critical for the collection of evidence for a major case, or
- providing evidence that is critical to capturing a fugitive or illegally acquired assets/ property in a major case.

In addition, in the event of giving bribes by an entity, such entity or its responsible person who decides to confess voluntarily the act of giving bribes before being prosecuted may be given a mitigated punishment or exempted from the punishment. A responsible person who is entrusted to directly handle the bribe-giving of the entity but voluntarily confesses such act of bribe-giving that he/she knew before being prosecuted may be given a mitigated punishment or exempted from the punishment as well.[54]

9.2 STATE/REGIONAL SENTENCING APPROACH

Not applicable

---

[51] Article 7 of the 2016 Judicial Interpretation.

[52] Article 390 of the Criminal Law.

[53] Article 14 of the 2016 Judicial Interpretation.

[54] Article 7 of the Interpretations of the Supreme People's Court and the Supreme People's Procuratorate on Several Issues concerning Application of Law for Handling Criminal Cases of Bribe Offering [hereinafter 2012 Judicial Interpretation].

9.3 FEDERAL SENTENCING APPROACH

Not applicable

9.4 DOMESTIC VERSUS FOREIGN BRIBERY

Not applicable

10. Related Criminal Offenses

10.1 CONSPIRACY

Not applicable

10.2 ATTEMPT

Attempt is a type of inchoate crime under the Criminal Law, and also exists in the crime of corruption or bribery. Criminal attempt occurs when a crime has already begun to be carried out but is not consummated because of factors independent from the will of the criminal.[55]

In terms of the sentencing for criminal attempt, the criminal who attempts to commit a crime may, in comparison against one who consummates the crime, receive a lesser punishment or a mitigated punishment.[56]

10.3 AIDING AND ABETTING

The Criminal Law incorporates the doctrine of aiding and abetting in the commission of a crime. Article 29 of the Criminal Law allows the court to pronounce guilty a criminal for aiding and abetting according to the role that criminal plays in the joint crime.

It is worth noting a specific application of aiding and abetting doctrine in the crime of corruption. Article 392 of the Criminal Law penalizes the act of introducing a bribe to state-functionaries under serious circumstances. Punishment can be imprisonment of not more than three years or detention and a concurrent fine.[57]

10.4 FALSE ACCOUNTING AND BOOKS AND RECORDS

Under Chinese law, false accounting and books and records is not considered as constituting the crime of bribery. As for administrative liability, the revised AUCL requires a business to faithfully make an entry in its accounting book of a discount or a commission to an intermediary. The business receiving the discount or commission shall also faithfully enter it into its accounting book.

---

[55] Article 23 of the Criminal Law.
[56] Article 23 of the Criminal Law.
[57] Article 392 of the Criminal Law.

As for companies that are obliged to disclose information to their shareholders or the general public, criminal liability may also arise if such a company provides false financial and accounting statements, conceals any important facts in such statements, or fails to disclose any other important information that shall be disclosed according to law, and severely damaged the interests of the shareholders or any other person. In such case, the persons directly in charge and other directly responsible persons shall be sentenced to imprisonment of not more than three years or detention, and shall be jointly or individually fined RMB20,000 to RMB200,000.[58]

10.5 MONEY LAUNDERING

Under the Criminal Law, if a person obviously knows that the income is obtained from corruption or bribery, and still launders the money to disguise or conceal the origin or nature thereof, such person commits the crime of money laundering.[59] Corporate criminal liability extends to money laundering activity as well.

The activities of money laundering include:

- providing any capital account;
- assisting the transfer of property into cash, financial instruments, or negotiable securities;
- assisting the transfer of capital by means of transfer accounts or any other means of settlement;
- assisting the remittance of funds to overseas; or
- disguising or concealing the origin or nature of any crime-related income or the proceeds generated therefrom by any other means.

"By any other means" in the above-mentioned provision include:

- assisting in the transfer or conversion of criminal gains and the proceeds thereof by pawning, leasing, trading, investing or otherwise dealing with such gains;
- assisting in the transfer or conversion of criminal gains and the proceeds thereof by mixing such gains and proceeds with operating income from a shopping mall, restaurant, place of entertainment, or other cash-intensive place;
- assisting in the conversion of criminal gains and the proceeds thereof into "legal" property by means of fictitious transactions, nominal obligations or liabilities, false guarantees, overstated income, or other means;
- assisting in the conversion of criminal gains and the proceeds thereof by trading lottery tickets, etc.;
- assisting in the conversion of criminal gains and the proceeds thereof into gambling profits by means of gambling;

---

[58] Article 161 of the Criminal Law.
[59] Article 191 of the Criminal Law.

- assisting in the carriage, transport, or mailing of criminal gains and the proceeds thereof across borders; or
- assisting in the transfer or conversion of criminal gains and the proceeds thereof by any means other than those stipulated above.[60]

A person who commits money laundering shall be sentenced to imprisonment of not more than five years or criminal detention, and shall be jointly or individually imposed a fine of 5 percent to 20 percent of the amount of laundered money. His incomes obtained from the money laundering as well as the proceeds generated therefrom shall be confiscated. If the circumstances are serious, the sentence of imprisonment shall be upgraded to not less than 5 years but not more than 10 years.

10.6 TAX AND OTHER FRAUDS

Not applicable

11. Cooperation and Self-Reporting

11.1 POWER OF INVESTIGATORS AND PROSECUTORS

Commercial bribery cases under the AUCL are investigated by the AICs. The AIC's investigation powers include:

- accessing the business premises involved in a suspected unfair competition act for inspection;
- questioning the business operator under investigation, any interested party, or any other related entity or individual, and requiring them to explain relevant situations or provide other materials in relation to the investigated act;
- inquiring into and copying the contracts and agreements, account books, vouchers, documents, records, business correspondence, and other materials related to a suspected unfair competition act;
- sealing up and/or seizing the property involved in a suspected unfair competition act; and
- inquiring into the bank account of a business operator that is suspected of an unfair competition act.

It is worth noting that for sealing or seizures, a written decision needs to be delivered on the spot, as required under the PRC Administrative Compulsion Law.

Criminal bribery cases are investigated by the public security bureaus or the procuratorates. In order to investigate criminal activities, police officers or prosecutors are empowered to

---

[60] Article 2 of the Interpretation of the Supreme People's Court on Several Issues concerning the Application of Laws to the Hearing of Money Laundering and Other Criminal Cases.

interrogate, inquest, and examine the sites, objects, and people relevant to a crime; search, seal, and seize material evidence and documentary evidence; and question the witnesses or use other technical investigation measures.[61] According to the circumstances of a criminal case, police officers or prosecutors may also compel the appearance of the criminal suspect or defendant, and order him to obtain a guarantor pending trial or subject him to residential surveillance.[62]

11.2   COOPERATION WITH INVESTIGATORS

When enforcement authorities are inspecting unfair competition acts, which include commercial bribery, the business operator, interested persons, and witnesses under investigation are obliged to truthfully provide relevant materials or particulars.[63]

11.3   SELF-REPORTING

In a criminal investigation, there is no legal obligation on a suspect to cooperate or self-report. However, to incentivize cooperation and self-reporting, Chinese law provides certain mechanisms in exchange for mitigated punishment, which will be discussed in more detail in Section 11.5 on leniency.

11.4   PLEA AGREEMENT

Historically, China does not have a plea bargain mechanism in its judicial proceedings. Facing an increasing caseload, China decided to test a plea bargain mechanism. On September 3, 2016, China's legislative body approved the SPC and SPP's proposal of creating a pilot program under which criminal suspects and defendants are allowed to voluntarily plead guilty before trial in exchange for lighter punishments. This pilot program took effect on September 4, 2016, in 18 cities including Beijing, Tianjin, Shanghai, Chongqing, Shenzhen, Xiamen, and Guangzhou.[64]

Pursuant to this decision, the SPC, the SPP, the Ministry of Public Security, the Ministry of State Security, and the Ministry of Justice jointly released Measures for Carrying Out the Pilot Program for the System of Leniency for Guilty Pleas and Punishment Acceptance for Criminal Cases in Certain Areas (the "Guilty Plea Measures"). Article 1 provides that suspects and defendants who plead guilty voluntarily, raise no objection to the criminal facts they are accused of, agree to sentencing proposals, and sign depositions may be given

---

[61] Section II of Chapter II of the Criminal Law

[62] Article 66 of the Criminal Procedure Law.

[63] Article 14 of the AUCL.

[64] Decision of the National People's Congress Standing Committee on Authorizing the Supreme People's Court and the Supreme People's Procuratorate to Implement in Certain Areas the Piloting of Plea Bargaining for Criminal Cases.

mitigated punishments in accordance with the law.[65] Where a suspect confesses the fact of an alleged crime voluntarily and faithfully renders meritorious services or the case involves major state interests, upon approval by the SPP, the prosecutor may decide not to institute a prosecution.[66]

11.5 LENIENCY

In general, a court may grant leniency to a criminal suspect or defendant if he/she voluntarily and truthfully confesses to his or her crime, , admits to the facts of the crime that he/she is charged with, and is willing to accept punishment for such crime.[67]. The same treatment applies to a situation where a suspect performs meritorious services such as exposing an offense committed by another, which is verified through investigation, or producing important clues for solving other cases.[68] Where a defendant admits guilty and accepts punishment for the crime he/she is charged with, subject to applicable conditions and the consent of such defendant, such defendant can be tried by a single judge pursuant to the fast-track sentencing procedure prescribed in the Criminal Procedure Law.[69]

For the crime of giving bribes, if the suspect "plays a critical role in detecting a major case," he will receive mitigated punishment. In addition, if the suspect voluntarily and truthfully confesses to the facts of the alleged crime or commits any meritorious act, or if such crime involves any significant national interest, with the approval of the SPP: (a) the public security bureaus has the discretion to dismiss the case; and (b) the procuratorate has the discretion to decide not to initiate prosecution or not to prosecute one or more alleged crimes that such suspect is being charged with.[70] In the event of giving bribes by an entity, such entity or its responsible person who decides to confess voluntarily the act of giving bribes before being prosecuted may be given a mitigated punishment or exempted from the punishment. A responsible person who is entrusted to directly handle the bribe-giving of the entity but voluntarily confesses such act of bribe-giving before being prosecuted may be given a mitigated punishment or exempted from the punishment as well.

12. Whistle-Blower Protection

Whistle-blower protection in China exists in criminal cases but has not been extended to administrative enforcement actions. The Criminal Procedure Law requires the public security authorities, the procuratorates, and the courts to safeguard the security of whistle-blowers and their close relatives.[71] Upon request by the whistle-blowers, the authorities

---

[65] Article 1 of the Guilty Plea Measures.
[66] Article 13 of the Guilty Plea Measures.
[67] Article 15 of the Criminal Procedure Law.
[68] See, for instance, Article 182 of the Criminal Procedure Law.
[69] Article 222 of the Crinimal Procedure Law.
[70] Article 182 of the Crinimal Procedure Law.
[71] Article 111 of the Criminal Procedure Law.

shall not make their names and acts of reporting, complaining, or informing known to the public.[72]

Reprisal for tipping-off from any official of a state organ is also a criminal offense that carries a sentence of imprisonment of not more than two years or criminal detention. If the circumstances are serious, the official abusing the power shall be sentenced to imprisonment of not less than two years but not more than seven years.[73]

12.1 PUBLIC SECTOR WHISTLE-BLOWER PROTECTIONS

The protection of a whistle-blower for reporting crimes involving abuse of power was substantially improved in 2016. On March 30, 2016, the SPP, the Ministry of Public Security, and the Ministry of Finance jointly released Several Provisions on Protecting and Rewarding Whistleblowers for Reporting Crimes Involving Abuse of Power. The new rules offer greater protection to whistle-blowers providing tips about state functionaries committing crimes such as corruption, official bribery, embezzlement, and malfeasance.

Consistent with the general principle, the protection covers both the whistle-blower and his/her close relatives. The new rules offered seven measures plus one catch-all provision to safeguard confidentiality of the whistle-blowing, from accepting a tip-off through responding to the whistle-blower.[74] For example, the tip-off must only be heard by designated personnel and the information will be stored in encrypted computers. It also requires that when the prosecutor's office receives real-name reporting, it has to assess the risks from the report and develop whistle-blower protection plans to prevent acts of retaliation against the whistle-blower.[75]

The new rules define retaliation broadly to include not only threats to the safety or property of the whistle-blowers and their close relatives, but also employment termination, withholding benefits payable, disciplinary sanctions, etc.[76]

Moreover, the new rules incentivize whistle-blowing by increasing the amount of monetary reward. Depending on the nature and circumstances of the crimes against which tip-offs are lodged, the value of the clues contained therein, and other factors, a whistle-blower in general can receive a monetary reward up to RMB200,000. A whistle-blower who has made significant contributions may upon approval by the relevant provincial procuratorate receive a monetary reward between RMB200,000 to RMB500,000. With the SPP's approval, there is no ceiling for rewards given to "extraordinarily significant contributions."[77]

Further, rather than putting all relevant authorities into the same basket without naming the responsible organ, the new rules clarify it is the prosecuting bodies' responsibility to protect whistle-blowers and their close relatives, with the police offering assistance.[78]

---

[72] *Id.*

[73] Article 254 of the Criminal Law.

[74] Article 5 of the Several Provisions on Protecting and Rewarding Whistleblowers for Reporting Duty Crimes.

[75] *Id.*, Article 6.

[76] *Id.*, Article 7.

[77] *Id.*, Article 16.

[78] *Id.*, Article 9.

12.2 PRIVATE SECTOR WHISTLE-BLOWER PROTECTIONS

Whistle-blower protection in the private sector is left to private companies' internal policies, and there is no official guideline or requirement for setting up a whistle-blower hotline or no-retaliation policy.

12.3 ATTITUDES TOWARD WHISTLEBLOWERS

Officially, with the campaign against corruption and bribery as well as the new whistle-blower protection rules in the public sector, the Chinese government welcomes and incentivizes whistle-blowers to stand out and participate in this effort. There have been a lot of real-name whistle-blowing reporting that led to the discovery of high-profile corruption cases.

In the private sector, the business environment in China has largely improved in recent years. Companies in China are embracing the concept of compliance and have realized the harm corruptive conduct and bribery can cause. In light of these factors, the private sector's attitude toward whistle-blowers is also positive.

13. Key International Treaties Relating to Bribery and Corruption

13.1 UNITED NATIONS CONVENTION AGAINST CORRUPTION

China signed the United Nations Convention against Corruption (the "Convention") on December 10, 2003, and submitted ratification on January 13, 2006. The Convention has been in effect in China since February 12, 2006, subject to a reservation under article 66(2), that is, declining to accept the jurisdiction of the International Court of Justice over any disputes arising under the Convention between two or more states parties.[79] The SPP is the designated central authority to receive requests for mutual legal assistance and other related issues pursuant to Article 46.13 of the Convention. The Convention also applies to Hong Kong Special Administrative Region and Macau Special Administrative Region. The Convention serves as the legal basis for cooperation on extradition (surrender of accused and convicted persons) between China (including Hong Kong SAR and Macao SAR) and other states parties to the Convention.

Since joining the Convention, China has proactively developed its domestic laws to meet the requirements under the Convention. Examples include the establishment of the crime of bribery of foreign public officials and officials of public international organizations and the introduction of confiscation procedure into the Criminal Procedure Law.

13.2 OTHER TREATIES

China has been a member of Financial Action Task Force since 2007, and is also a member of the Eurasian Group on Combating Money-laundering and Financing of Terrorism, as well as the Asia/Pacific Group on Money Laundering.

---

[79] More information about the Convention and China's reservation is available at https://treaties.un.org/Pages/ViewDetails.aspx?src=IND&mtdsg_no=XVIII-14&chapter=18&clang=_en#EndDec (Last visited Dec. 10, 2018).

14. Mutual Legal Assistance Treaties and Transnational Cooperation

14.1 MUTUAL LEGAL ASSISTANCE

Article 18 of the Criminal Procedure Law provides that international treaties or the principle of reciprocity are the grounds for Chinese and foreign judicial authorities to request legal assistance on criminal matters.

According to the statistics published by the Ministry of Justice, by the end of September 2018, China has reached 44 agreements on mutual legal assistance in criminal matters with multiple countries including the United States, Canada, France, Australia, Japan, the United Kingdom, etc.[80]

If we take the agreement between China and the United States as an example, we see it designates the Central Authority of each party to make and receive requests pursuant to the agreement. China has been consistently designating this responsibility to the Ministry of Justice. The agreement also sets forth the limitations on assistance, formality requirement for the requests, and the execution and postponement of requests.[81]

14.2 EXTRADITION

By the end of September 2018, China had reached 54 extradition agreements, among which 37 agreements have come into effect.[82] Nevertheless, there is no extradition agreement between China and the United States or Canada or Australia. The absence of extradition treaties with these countries makes them the top destinations for fugitives from China.

14.3 TRANSNATIONAL COOPERATION

China has been proactively seeking transnational cooperation in repatriating corrupt fugitives and recovering assets they transferred overseas. China has code-named its international manhunt of corrupt fugitive officials as Operation Sky Net. According to published statistics, Operation Sky Net has been steadily obtaining excellent results. In 2016 alone, the Operation Sky Net led to the capture of 1,032 fugitives from over 70 countries and the recovery of about RMB2.4 billion.[83]

In addition to this multiagency effort, the Ministry of Public Security also launched Operation Fox Hunt targeting suspects of all economic crimes. Since the campaign against

---

[80] "我国对外缔结司法合作类条约" ("China's foreign judicial cooperation treaties"), *available at* http://www.fmprc.gov.cn/web/ziliao_674904/tytj_674911/wgdwdjdsfhzty_674917/t1215630.shtml (Last visited Dec. 10, 2018).

[81] Judicial Assistance Agreement between the United States of America and China (signed in Beijing on June 19, 2000), *available at* https://www.state.gov/documents/organization/126977.pdf

[82] "我国对外缔结司法合作类条约" ("China's foreign judicial cooperation treaties"), *available at* http://www.fmprc.gov.cn/web/ziliao_674904/tytj_674911/wgdwdjdsfhzty_674917/t1215630.shtml (Last visited December 10, 2018).

[83] "'天网2017'行动启动" ("Kicking off 'Operation Sky Net'"), *available at* http://csr.mos.gov.cn/content/2017-03/09/content_46584.htm (Last visited Dec. 10, 2018).

corruption continues in China, it is expected that China will explore more transnational co-operation on repatriation of fugitives.

On October 26, 2018, the Standing Committee of the NPC adopted the Law of the People's Republic of China on International Criminal Judicial Assistance (ICJA), which came into effect on October 10, 2018.

The ICJA provides as a general principle that China and foreign countries may provide criminal judicial assistance to each other under the principles of equality and reciprocity, subject to the condition that such judicial assistance does not: (a) damage China's sovereignty, security, and public interests; or (b) violate any fundamental principles of Chinese law. Without the approvals of the competent authorities: (i) no foreign institution, organization, or individual may conduct any activities in China relating to criminal judicial proceedings prescribed by the ICJA; and (ii) no domestic institution, organization, or individual (including multinational companies' subsidiaries) may provide evidentiary materials or any assistance prescribed under the ICJA to foreign countries.[84]

The criminal judicial assistance activities prescribed by ICJA includes (a) service of documents, (b) investigation and evidence collection, (c) arrangement for witness's testimony and assistance, (d) search and seizure, (e) confiscation and transfer of illegal proceeds, (f) transfer of sentenced person, and (g) other assistance. In order to seek criminal judicial assistance in China, a foreign country will need to file a written request satisfying the requirements provided by the applicable criminal judicial assistance treaty or, in the absence of such a treaty or if such a treaty does not provide any specific requirements concerning the written request, the requirements prescribed under the ICJA should be followed.[85] As a general limitation, the ICJA expressly provides that China's assistance in serving judicial documents under the ICJA does not amount to any recognition of the legal force of such judicial documents, and China has no obligation to assist in the service of any summons or subpoena requiring any Chinese citizen to attend an interrogation or appear in a court as a defendant.[86]

15. Legal Professional Privilege
15.1 GENERAL PRINCIPLES

China does not have Western-style attorney-client privilege or attorney work product doctrine. What the law provides is a confidentiality obligation for Chinese lawyers. According to Article 38 of the Law on Lawyers as well as Article 43 of the Administrative Measures for Practice by Lawyers, "Lawyers shall keep confidential any state secret or business secret known to them in the practicing activities, and may not disclose any privacy of the party concerned."[87] In addition, lawyers shall "keep confidential any situation or information he/she known from the practice that the principal and others are unwilling to be disclosed [...]."[88] Article 46 of

---

[84] Article 4 of The Law of the People's Republic of China on International Criminal Judicial Assistance.

[85] Article 13 of The Law of the People's Republic of China on International Criminal Judicial Assistance.

[86] Article 22 of The Law of the People's Republic of China on International Criminal Judicial Assistance.

[87] Article 38 of the Law on Lawyers; Article 43 of the Administrative Measures for Practice by Lawyers.

[88] *Id.*

the Criminal Procedure Law further provides that the "defense lawyer shall have the right to maintain confidentiality of the relevant circumstances and information of the client that have come to his knowledge during his practice."[89]

In addition to the above confidentiality obligation or right, all three aforementioned laws set forth an exception requiring lawyers to "timely report a crime being contemplated or carried out that endangers national security or public security, or gravely threatens the personal safety of other persons."[90] The Criminal Procedure Law also imposes an obligation to testify on anyone that has knowledge of the case.[91]

15.2 APPLICATION TO INTERNAL INVESTIGATION

As noted previously, because of the lack of attorney-client privilege, communication with lawyers, regardless where they are admitted, is not privileged for purposes of Chinese law.

15.3 APPLICATION TO EXTERNAL INVESTIGATION

If a company in China faces an administrative investigation initiated by Chinese authorities, it cannot assert attorney-client privilege to withhold documents or information.

15.4 PRACTICAL ISSUES

When a company faces a multijurisdiction investigation, it shall be careful in using non-lawyers to conduct or assist in the investigation. It is also worth noting a lot of the in-house counsels in Chinese companies are not licensed lawyers. In any event, a company needs to think ahead to which jurisdiction its investigation result or communication with government authorities may be exposed, and whether lawyers licensed in a specific jurisdiction need to be involved for the purpose of preserving the attorney-client privilege.

16. Privacy and Data Protection

Chinese law recognizes the right to privacy, yet it does not have an omnibus data protection law to regulate the collection, use, and storage of personal information. In addition to upholding the right to privacy in principle by the Constitution and the civil law, the personal information protection regime in China consists of a patchwork of sector-specific laws[92] and guidelines and stand-alone provisions in broader laws. In the recent enacted Cyber Security Law, which became effective on June 1, 2017, personal information

---

[89] Article 48 of the Criminal Procedure Law.

[90] Article 38 of the Law on Lawyers; Article 43 of the Administrative Measures for Practice by Lawyers.

[91] Article 62 of the Criminal Procedure Law.

[92] Such as the Circular of the People's Bank of China on Improving Personal Financial Information Protection by Banking Financial Institutions; Administrative Measures for Online Trading; Administrative Regulation on Logistics Service User's Personal Information.

is defined as all kinds of information recorded in electronic or other formats that can be used to independently identify or be combined with other information to identify natural persons' personal identity. Such information includes, but is not limited to, names, dates of birth, ID numbers, biological identification information, addresses and telephone numbers, etc.[93]

In general, collection of personal information requires consent from the information owner before collection and notifying the subject of the purpose, method, and scope of the collection. In addition to the rules regarding collection, there is a variety of civil and criminal laws and regulations that restrict disclosure and transfer of personal information. For example, Chinese law provides that an employer must keep personal information of its employees confidential and prohibits the disclosure of personal information without prior written consent.[94] Moreover, although it has not been finalized yet, it is expected that network operators in China need to conduct a security assessment before exporting personal information and important data collected and generated in China.[95]

16.1 PRINCIPLES

Not applicable

16.2 APPLICATION TO INTERNAL INVESTIGATIONS

Usually, companies have internal policies that any information saved on corporate computers or other electronic devices belong to the companies. In practice, it is still advisable for companies to obtain employees' written consent before data collection, which in most cases will deal with personal information the employees may have saved on their corporate computers. Most companies seek such written consent in advance in their employment contracts and/or employee handbooks.

If an internal investigation involves cross-border data transfer, consent from the information owner must be obtained for transfer of personal information. Also, for companies that fall within the category of critical information infrastructure operators, personal information and important data gathered and produced during operations in China cannot be transferred overseas.[96] Further, if the internal investigation may involve state secrets, a term broadly defined,[97] the document review must be conducted within the mainland China. Without permission of competent authorities, no carrier of state secrets can be exported.[98]

---

[93] Article 76 of the Cyber Security Law.

[94] Article 13, The Regulation on Employment Service and Employment Management.

[95] Draft Security Assessment Measures for Exporting Personal Information and Important Data (April 11, 2017), *available at* http://www.cac.gov.cn/2017-04/11/c_1120785691.htm

[96] Article 37 of the Cyber Security Law.

[97] Articles 2 and 9 of the Law on Protecting the State Secrets.

[98] Article 25 of the Law on Protecting the State Secrets.

16.3 APPLICATION TO EXTERNAL INVESTIGATIONS

If a company is facing an external investigation initiated by Chinese government authorities, in principle the company is obligated to provide any information, including personal information it obtains, to the relevant authorities. If facing an external investigation by foreign government authorities, before handing over or voluntarily disclosing any information, a company needs to ensure compliance with Chinese data protection and privacy laws as mentioned above. Improper production of evidence of other documents may trigger criminal liabilities in China.

17. Forecast for Reforms and Parting Thoughts

17.1 LEGISLATIVE REFORMS

China has amended its existing laws to conform to the requirements of international treaties it signed, such as the United Nations Convention against Corruption, and has also issued new rules and judicial interpretations to strengthen its fight against corruption. China has issued the National Supervision Law, which is considered a national anti-corruption law, effective from March 20, 2018. The National Supervision Law applies to individuals exercising public power, and provides that the state supervision authority has the power to retain in custody suspects abuse-of-power crimes (including but not limited to corruption and bribery) for a maximum period of six months.[99]

17.2 POLITICAL AND AGENCY ENFORCEMENT WILL

The reform of the national supervision system is considered as being part of China's overall political reform aimed at strengthening the inner-Party as well as national supervision against corruption. The report of the 19th CCP Congress says the pilot supervision reform, which was launched in Beijing, and Shanxi and Zhejiang provinces in December 2016, will be extended nationwide, in order to deepen the national supervision system reform. This shows the Chinese CCP and government's sustained efforts to fight against corruption.

17.3 POLICY AND PRACTICE

China's president Jinping Xi repeatedly emphasized that corruption is a threat to the CCP's survival. As of 2016, China's anti-corruption campaign has disciplined and convicted over 120 high-ranking officials, including about a dozen high-ranking military officers, several senior executives of state-owned companies, and some national leaders. The Chinese government and judicial authorities have also issued a series of amendments to existing laws and new regulations and judicial interpretations to overhaul the country's regulatory framework and enforcement regarding official and commercial bribery, and bring positive updates to address increasingly complicated bribery schemes. These developments have significant implications for companies doing business in China.

---

[99] Article 22 and Article 43 of the National Supervision Law.

APPENDIX

Key Issues	China's Approach
Is jurisdiction subject to any international anti-corruption conventions? If so, which? (OECD, UN Convention against Corruption, etc.)	China is a party to the United Nations Convention Against Corruption. Please refer to Section 13.
Is bribery of foreign public officials illegal?	Yes. Please refer to Section 4.
Do domestic anti-bribery laws provide for extraterritorial application?	Yes, to the extent that the crime is committed by a Chinese citizen or a Chinese entity.
What is the definition of foreign public officials?	Not defined under Chinese law
Is commercial bribery illegal?	Yes. Please refer to Section 8.
Is bribing domestic officials illegal?	Yes. Please refer to Section 5.
Can the receipt of a bribe be prosecuted?	Yes, if the amount of bribe meets the monetary threshold for criminal prosecution. Please refer to Section 9.
Can companies be held criminally liable?	Yes.
If so, what is the requisite intent for criminal liability to attach?	The intent of seeking improper benefits is generally required; but no intent is required in serious cases of giving "state functionaries" rebates or handling fees in violation of state regulations.
Can companies be held civilly liable?	Yes.
If so, what is the requisite intent for civil liability to attach?	The intent of pursuing business opportunities or competitive advantages is required under the AUCL (2017 Revisions).
Can individuals be held civilly liable?	Yes.
Is there a "facilitation/grease payments" exception?	No.
Does the subject country provide for conspiracy liability relating to violations of the anti-corruption laws?	No.

Key Issues	China's Approach
Does the subject country provide for: (a) aiding/abetting liability relating to violations of the anti-corruption laws? (b) attempt liability relating to violations of the anti-corruption laws?	(a) Yes. Please refer to Section 10.3. (b) Yes. Please refer to Section 10.2.
Is failure to keep accurate books and records a criminal and/or civil offense?	Both. False accounting and books and records may trigger liabilities under the AUCL. Criminal liability may also arise if a company that is obliged to disclose information to its shareholders or the general public provides false financial and accounting statements, conceals any important facts in such statements, or fails to disclose any other important information that shall be disclosed according to law. Please refer to Section 10.4. In addition, failure to keep accurate books and records is also a violation of the Securities Law of the PRC.
Do any books and records violations have to involve underlying bribery proof?	No.
Are there laws concerning a company's financial internal controls? If so, are those laws applicable to private and public companies or just public companies?	Yes. Chinese law requires all companies, including both private and public companies, to establish their financial and accounting policies. There are more detailed rules specifically for public companies. But violation of these rules would not automatically be considered as violation of the anti-corruption rules.
Is there an affirmative disclosure obligations for potential violations of the anti-bribery laws or accounting irregularities?	Overall, there is no affirmative disclosure obligation. Disclosure obligation may arise if a listed company commits violations of the anti-bribery laws or accounting irregularities that constitute a material event.
Are "promotional expenses" exempt from the anti-bribery laws?	No FCPA-style equivalent of "promotional expense exception," but promotional gifts of nominal value based on common commercial practice is permitted. Please refer to Section 8.6.
Is the giving of gifts, entertainment, travel, meals, etc. restricted/prohibited?	No.

(*Continued*)

Key Issues	China's Approach
Are there any laws concerning things of value conveyed by, or to, third parties?	Yes. The AUCL (2017 Revisions) prohibits bribing (i) any entity or individual authorized by the counterparty to a transaction to handle relevant affairs; and (ii) any entity or individual that is likely to take advantage of powers or influence to affect a transaction. Please refer to section 8.3. The Criminal Law also prohibits bribing influential people. Please refer to Section 6.
Are bribes tax deductible?	No.
Is the law applied extraterritorially?	Yes, to the extent that the crime is committed by a Chinese citizen or a Chinese entity.
Is having a robust corporate compliance program an affirmative defense or way to negate liability?	No affirmative defense for corporate compliance program.
Is there a "local law" exception/defense?	No. Please refer to Section 8.6.
Is "credit" given for cooperation with authorities? If so, how and in what form?	No guidelines on "credit" for cooperation with authorities. For criminal matters, in general, a bribe-giver who voluntarily surrenders himself to law enforcement authority and truthfully confesses his crime may receive a lighter or mitigated punishment. If the circumstances of crime are relatively minor and the bribe-giver plays a critical role in detecting a major case. or if the bribe-giver performs any major meritorious services, he may be given a mitigated punishment or be exempted from punishment. Where a company offering bribes voluntarily confesses to bribery upon a collective decision of the entity or a decision of the person in charge of the entity before a criminal investigation is initiated against the entity, the entity and relevant liable persons may receive a mitigated punishment or be exempted from punishment. Where a directly liable person who directly handled the bribery on behalf of the entity voluntarily confesses to the entity's bribery in his or her knowledge before a criminal investigation is initiated against the entity, the directly liable person may receive a mitigated punishment or be exempted from punishment.

Key Issues	China's Approach
Does the subject country have a Mutual Legal Assistance Treaty with the United States that generally covers criminal matters, including the FCPA?	Yes. China and the United States have an Agreement on Mutual Legal Assistance in Criminal Matters, which should cover the FCPA. But the scope of application and the types of assistance are limited. For example, the agreement does not include an arrangement on extradition. Please refer to Section 14.

What are the potential penalties/ sanctions both for civil and criminal violations?	**Individuals**
	Penalties for criminal violations
	• Commercial bribery and bribery of foreign public officials: imprisonment of not more than 10 years and fine
	• Bribery of domestic officials: maximum imprisonment of more than 10 years or life imprisonment, and fine or confiscation or property
	• Bribery of influential people: imprisonment of not more than 10 years and fine.
	• Bribery of public entity: imprisonment of more than three years or criminal detention, and fine
	Companies
	Penalties for civil violations under the AUCL (2017 Revisions): a fine between RMB100,000-3,000,000; confiscation of illegal gains; and revocation of business license in serious cases.
	Penalties for criminal violations:
	• Companies: fine
	• The person directly in charge and the person directly responsible for the crime within the company:
	  o imprisonment of not more than 10 years and fine in case of commercial bribery or bribery of foreign public officials;
	  o imprisonment of not more than three years or criminal detention and fine in case of bribery of public entities or influential people;
	  o imprisonment of not more than five years or criminal detention and fine in case of bribery of domestic officials.

6 Cuba

1. Introduction

Cuba[1] has long been saddled with a culture of corruption. A lengthy history of colonialism and a state-controlled economy have produced a country with a weak economy, product shortages, low wages, and an understanding that taking a little for oneself is not only acceptable but, in many cases, necessary to get by.

In socialist Cuba, the extent of centralized control is higher than in many other parts of the world. Because authority is concentrated in one official political party—the Communist Party of Cuba—and the state manages most elements of economic activity, including nearly every significant business enterprise, the opportunities for public corruption are ubiquitous. Scarcity and rationing of resources have led to an environment where obtaining goods and services requires grease payments, workers steal items from their employers to sell on the black market, and employees are often absent so that they can earn extra money from side jobs. At the same time, poorly paid bureaucrats, business managers, and even high-level government officials have become accustomed to supplementing their income through the illicit use of their position. The centralization of power along with strict government control of the media and lax compliance oversight have led to a lack of transparency and accountability.

Although high-level corruption on a large scale is less common in Cuba than in other parts of the world, including elsewhere in Latin America, lower-level corruption, borne out of an understanding that breaking the rules (really, the law) is necessary for survival, is widespread.

---

[1] This chapter was contributed by Holland & Knight's Timothy D. Belevetz and Michael E. Hantman.

From Baksheesh to Bribery. T. Markus Funk and Andrew S. Boutros.
© Oxford University Press 2019. Published 2019 by Oxford University Press.

Against this backdrop, over the years the ruling Castro regime has taken a number of approaches to curbing corruption that have led to the current set of laws and institutions aimed at reducing corrupt conduct as well as controlling fraud, waste, abuse, and cronyism.

2. Criminal Law Regime

Based on the European continental tradition, Cuba's legal system is the product of a number of influences. A former Spanish colony, Cuba uses a civil law system, where written codes, rather than court-decided precedent, serve as the primary source of law.[2] As a further reflection of its colonial past, it employs an inquisitorial system in criminal cases like those used in Spain and France.[3] Vestiges of the U.S. occupation from 1898 to 1902 include Anglo-American legal traditions such as habeas corpus and a more robust decoupling of courts and prosecutors than usual for a Marxist nation.[4] In addition, more than a half-century of Marxism and extensive Soviet influence have endowed the Cuban legal system with socialist features that seek to promote ideology through the use of the law.[5]

Among the codes that comprise Cuba's written law is the Penal Code, which defines criminal conduct and establishes applicable penalties. Under Cuban law, an act is a crime if it is prohibited by law and is considered socially dangerous or harmful. An offense that does not meet the requisite level of social harm is considered a non-criminal infraction for which an offender is issued a citation.[6]

Cuban law with regard to bribery is not well developed. Unlike the extensive legal regimes in places such as the United States, Germany, and the United Kingdom, which have a broad set of laws, ample official guidance, well-publicized judicial decisions, and well-established enforcement institutions, Cuba has limited legislation, no meaningful official guidance or even reporting of cases, and spotty enforcement.

Corrupt practices, both large-scale and petty, have long been a reality in Cuba. Publicly, the Castro regime has consistently condemned corruption and in fact has offered resistance to it as a basis for the revolution that culminated in the establishment of the Castro regime in 1959. For example, in a 1993 speech to the Eighth Science and Technology Forum, then-President Fidel Castro proclaimed:

> I was telling you how the world was greatly in need of a vaccine against corruption. Fortunately, the Revolution, through its sense of morality, through its sense of responsibility, immunized the main cadres against corruption.[7]

---

[2] Ray Michalowski, *World Factbook of Criminal Justice Systems: Cuba*. WORLD FACTBOOK. BUREAU OF JUSTICE STATICS 1 (1997) Web. (Mar. 3, 2016), *available at* http://www.bjs.gov/content/pub/pdf/wfbcjsc.pdf (last visited Mar. 3, 2018).

[3] *Id.*

[4] *Id.*

[5] *Id.*

[6] *Id.*

[7] Speech of Fidel Castro at the Closing Session of the Eighth National Forum of Science and Technology on Dec. 17, 1993, *available at* http://www.cuba.cu/gobierno/discursos/1993/esp/f171293e.html (last visited Mar. 30, 2016).

In reality, however, the Castro government's response to corruption over the years has been varied.

For the first three decades of the Castro regime, the Soviet Union propped up the Cuban economy through massive subsidies in the form of sales of low-cost oil and purchases of Cuban sugar at inflated prices.[8] This generous support served to conceal the inefficiencies of the Cuban economy, including those attributable to corrupt practices. In the late 1970s and early 1980s, the Soviet Union began to adopt more market-based economic policies and prompted Cuba to do the same. Castro made a halfhearted effort to follow the lead of the Soviet Union and other Eastern European nations by decentralizing certain aspects of the economy such as the sales of excess products by private farmers and artisans' handicrafts.[9] That effort did not last long, however, and in mid-1986, Castro cited a burgeoning capitalist class, unrestrained consumerism, and middlemen seeking profits as the justification for a new set of reforms that came to be known as "rectification."[10] As part of the rectification campaign, Castro denounced managers who engaged in corruption, cronyism, waste, and fraud.[11]

By the mid-1990s, Castro began to adopt a more focused approach to eliminating corruption and promoting efficiency. In his view, corrupt practices contributed to the collapse of the Soviet Union. Out of concern the same thing could happen in Cuba, Castro sought to strengthen the government's anti-corruption enforcement efforts.[12] Over the next few years, the regime instituted a set of initiatives to accomplish that goal, including new anti-corruption legislation, a code of ethics for public officials, a public campaign to crack down on graft, the establishment of a Ministry of Auditing and Control (later consolidated into the Comptroller General's Office), and enhanced accounting procedures.

A set of new laws anchored the effort by amending or creating new criminal statutes. Decree-Law No. 149, enacted in 1994, gives the government broad authority to seize funds and items individuals acquired by means of "undue enrichment." The legislation was intended to deter and punish those profiting from a lucrative black market for goods. Decree-Law No. 150, enacted at about the same time, criminalizes "illicit enrichment" by both public officials and ordinary citizens and provides for prison sentences, fines, and seizure of illegally obtained funds and goods. Decree-Law No. 175, which was enacted in 1997, amended the criminal laws by, among other things, increasing the penalties for white collar offenses and making bribery and influence peddling illegal. These legislative initiatives have been codified

---

[8] Clyde H. Farnsworth, *Soviet Said to Reduce Support for Cuban Economy*. N.Y. TIMES, Mar. 15, 1998, *available at* http://www.nytimes.com/1988/03/16/world/soviet-said-to-reduce-support-for-cuban-economy.html?module=Slide&region=SlideShowTopBar&version=SlideCard-2&action=Click&contentCollection=T%20Magazine&slideshowTitle=Google%20and%20Apple%E2%80%99s%20New%20Headquarters%20Resemble%20Hippie%20Communes&currentSlide=2&entrySlide=1&pgtype=imageslideshow (last visited Mar. 15, 2016).

[9] Jorge F. Pérez-López, *Rectification at Three: Impact on the Cuban Economy*. 25(3) STUDIES IN COMPARATIVE INT'L DEV. 8–9 (1990).

[10] *Id.* at 10.

[11] *Id.* at 11.

[12] *Cuba Creates New Anti-Corruption Ministry*. CARIBBEAN DEALS. PARADISE NEWS/REUTERS, May 3, 2001, *available at* http://www.onepaper.com/deals/?v=d&i=&s=Caribbean:Paradise+News&p=37042 (last visited Mar. 30, 2016).

in the Penal Code. But that these new laws are less than 25-years old tells the tale of an anti-corruption legal system still seeking to find its legs.

Generally speaking, economic crimes are penalized by means of a term of incarceration with a statutorily fixed minimum and maximum, a fine range expressed in increments called cuotas, and forfeiture of ill-gotten gains. A cuota is a unit of fine with a value that varies. For example, an individual may be subject to a fine of a certain number of cuotas at the rate of one peso per cuota while another may be subject to a fine of the same number of cuotas at the rate of two pesos per cuota. Under Article 35, section 2, one cuota is not less than 1 peso and not more than 50 pesos.

Perhaps less realized is that Cuba is also a party to the United Nations Convention Against Corruption (UNCAC), a multilateral and legally binding international agreement that requires signatories to adopt specific anti-corruption measures.[13] The purpose of the convention is to foster the implementation of steps to prevent domestic and foreign bribery, embezzlement, influence peddling, and money laundering. Cuba signed the convention in 2005 and ratified it in 2007.[14]

3. Civil Law Regime

The Cuban judicial system is comprised of courts at the municipal, provincial, and Supreme Court levels.[15] Anti-corruption measures in Cuba are enforced by law enforcement officials, but there are a few important civil mechanisms. In Cuba, a court can declare void a contract arising out of corrupt conduct. In addition, under Article 70 of the Penal Code, a defendant found guilty of an act of corruption may be civilly liable for damages caused by the offense. Courts can order return of the property at issue in the offense. If the defendant fails to make the victim whole, the court may impose an additional term of incarceration of three to six months.

3.1 INVESTIGATIVE AND PROSECUTORIAL AGENCIES

In 2009, Cuba established the Comptroller General's Office, part of the mission of which is to receive and investigate citizen complaints regarding the misuse of public funds and other forms of corruption. It has authority over all government ministries and reports directly to the president of the Council of State, the 31-member body that exercises legislative authority between sessions of the National Assembly, Cuba's legislature, and the supreme organ of state authority.

---

[13] *United Nations Convention against Corruption (UNCAC)*, United Nations Office on Drugs and Crime (2004), *available at* https://www.unodc.org/documents/treaties/UNCAC/Publications/Convention/08-50026_E.pdf (last visited Mar. 30, 2016); *United Nations Convention against Corruption Signature and Ratification Status as of 1 December 2015*, United Nations Office on Drugs and Crime, *available at* https://www.unodc.org/unodc/en/treaties/CAC/signatories.html (last visited Mar. 20, 2016).

[14] *Id.*

[15] *Country Reports on Human Rights Practices for 2011*, U.S. Department of State, Bureau of Democracy, Human Rights & Labor, *available at* http://www.state.gov/documents/organization/186717.pdf (last visited Apr. 22, 2016).

The Office of the Attorney General of the Republic is responsible for prosecuting criminal offenses. It is subordinate to the National Assembly and its Council of State. Prosecutors from the provincial office of the Attorney General handle the prosecution of felonies, including bribery and related offenses. All charges are taken to trial as there is no mechanism for plea bargaining.

4. Transparency International Corruption Perception Index Score

Every year, Transparency International, a nongovernmental organization that monitors international corporate and political corruption, rates nations with regard to how corrupt their public sectors are perceived to be. The ranking, known as the Corruption Perception Index, relies on opinion surveys and expert assessments by several well-recognized research organizations. It is widely viewed as the benchmark ranking of corruption across the globe. In its 2017 survey, Transparency International placed Cuba 62nd among the 180 countries it ranked from best to worst.[16] Cuba received a score of 47 on a scale where 0 is the most corrupt and 100 is the most transparent and accountable, thereby placing it among the more than two-thirds of the countries on the list that are on the more corrupt side of the spectrum.

5. Bribery of Foreign Officials

Despite a mandate under the UNCAC to make it illegal, bribery of foreign officials is not regulated under Cuban law.[17]

6. Bribery of Domestic Officials

Article 152 of the Cuban Penal Code makes bribery of public officials a criminal offense.[18] Section 4 of the article prohibits paying or offering to pay a bribe to a public official. It

---

[16] Transparency International, 2015 Corruption Perception Index, *available at* https://www.transparency.org/country/#CUB_DataResearch_SurveysIndices (last visited Mar. 21, 2016).

[17] UNCAC, Art. 16 states:

1. Each State Party shall adopt such legislative and other measures as may be necessary to establish as a criminal offence, when committed intentionally, the promise, offering or giving to a foreign public official or an official of a public international organization, directly or indirectly, of an undue advantage, for the official himself or herself or another person or entity, in order that the official act or refrain from acting in the exercise of his or her official duties, in order to obtain or retain business or other undue advantage in relation to the conduct of international business.

2. Each State Party shall consider adopting such legislative and other measures as may be necessary to establish as a criminal offence, when committed intentionally, the solicitation or acceptance by a foreign public official or an official of a public international organization, directly or indirectly, of an undue advantage, for the official himself or herself or another person or entity, in order that the official act or refrain from acting in the exercise of his or her official duties.

[18] Código Penal, La Republica de Cuba, Ministerio de Justicia, Capitulo IV: Cohecho, Exaccion Ilegal Y Negociaciones Ilicita Art. 152, §§ 1–4 (Gaceta Oficial 1987) [hereinafter Penal Code], *available at* http://www.gacetaoficial.cu/html/codigo_penal.html#A8 (last visited Mar. 24, 2016).

includes providing "an advantage or benefit." The penalties for a violation are two to five years' imprisonment, a fine of 500 to 1,000 cuotas, or both.

Article 152 also makes it illegal for a public official to accept a bribe. The penalties are tiered according to the degree of the official's involvement. Under section 1, an official who receives a bribe, including "an advantage or benefit," is subject to a term of imprisonment of 4 to 10 years. That section also makes it illegal to receive a bribe directly or indirectly and to receive the bribe not only for the official but also for someone else. An official who merely accepts an offer of a bribe without ever receiving it is subject under section 2 to a penalty of two to five years of incarceration, a fine of 500 to 1,000 cuotas, or both. Section 3 provides for a penalty of 8 to 20 years' imprisonment for a public official who actively solicits a bribe.

Cuban law makes a distinction between bribes paid to public officials in more senior positions that involve greater responsibility and authority and those paid to public employees who do not occupy such positions. Under Article 152, section 6, public employees who are found guilty of soliciting, accepting, or agreeing to accept a bribe may be sentenced to terms of imprisonment half as long as the statutory minimums for public officials.

In addition, under Article 152, section 8, forfeiture, or as the Penal Code puts it, "confiscation," may also be ordered.

The government's recent efforts to combat public corruption have led to several high-profile prosecutions.[19] In 2011, the president of Empresa de Telecomunicaciones de Cuba S.A., a state-run telecommunications monopoly, along with several other senior executives, were arrested on corruption charges.[20] The president and most of the company's vice presidents were suspended.

Fifteen public officials and businessmen, all employed by either the Cubana de Aviacion, a state-owned airline, or Sol y Son, a tourism company jointly owned by the Cuban government and Chilean investors, were convicted in 2011 for receiving or paying bribes.[21] They received sentences of 3 to 15 years in prison.

Two executives of Coral Capital Group, a British investment company involved in the redevelopment of a luxury Havana hotel, were charged and convicted in 2013 for undisclosed bribery offenses. Both were released from prison shortly after the trial but only after serving months in pretrial detention.[22]

In 2014, 17 Cuban government officials, including the vice president of the sugar ministry, executives of joint venture partners, and a Canadian businessman, were sentenced to as many as 20 years in prison for their role in a scheme to steer lucrative contracts to a Canadian automotive equipment company.[23]

---

[19] Details about the cases are limited as Cuba's government-run media does not report on corruption scandals.

[20] *Cuba Arrests Telephone Executives in Corruption Sweep*. REUTERS, Aug. 9, 2011, *available at* http://www.reuters.com/article/cuba-telecoms-corruption-idUSN1E7780N620110809 (last visited Mar. 5, 2016).

[21] *Cuba: Outcome of Airline Corruption Trial Revealed*, INTER PRESS SERVICE, June 7, 2011, *available at* http://www.ipsnews.net/2011/06/cuba-outcome-of-airline-corruption-trial-revealed/ (last visited Mar. 15, 2016).

[22] *Cuba Corruption Case Britons Fakhre and Purvis Freed*, BBC NEWS. June 21, 2013, *available at* http://www.bbc.com/news/uk-23000845 (last visited Mar. 15, 2016).

[23] *Exclusive: Gifts for Cubans End in 15-Year Sentence for Canadian CEO*, REUTERS, Oct. 3, 2014, *available at* http://www.reuters.com/article/us-cuba-corruption-canada-exclusive-idUSKCN0HS0UG20141003 (last visited Mar. 15, 2016).

7. Commercial Bribery

With regard to commercial bribery, Cuban law prohibits making a bribe but not receiving one. Article 152, section 4's prohibition on paying or offering to pay bribes applies to instances where the recipient is a commercial manager or employee just as it does in cases where the recipient is a government official. The penalties for the offense are two to five years' in prison, a fine of 500 to 1,000 cuotas, or both.

Cuban law does not regulate receiving bribes where the recipient is a commercial manager or employee. In Cuba, however, where the government owns virtually all businesses and means of production, the line between a commercial actor and a public official can be hard to discern. The payment of a kickback to what appears to be a corporate manager may in fact be considered a bribe to a public official if that manager is employed by a state-owned enterprise.

8. Related Criminal Offenses

The Penal Code, in accord with the UNCAC, criminalizes a number of related offenses.

Attempt. Article 12 criminalizes the unconsummated attempt to commit an offense. Generally the penalties are the same as those for the offense itself had it been successful, although the court may reduce the sentence by as much as one-third below the statutory minimum. Under Article 13, an individual who spontaneously ends or prevents an attempt to commit an offense is not criminally liable.

Aiding and Abetting. Article 18 extends liability to those who "participate," or aid and abet, in a criminal act. Individuals who organize a criminal offense, induce others to participate in it, advise others with respect to its execution, or conceal evidence of it are included. Under Article 19, as with attempt, a participant in a criminal act who spontaneously prevents its execution is not criminally liable.

Influence Peddling. The Cuban Penal Code prohibits influence peddling, or trading in influence. Article 151 makes it illegal to use influence, directly or indirectly, on a public official or employee. Under section 1 of that article, the penalties are a term of incarceration of three to eight years imprisonment and forfeiture of any ill-gotten gains.

Money Laundering. More than 55 years of U.S. economic sanctions, nationalized banks, and few opportunities for private enterprise have impeded Cuba's full participation in the international banking system. As a result, there is a low incidence of money laundering in Cuba. Nonetheless, under Article 346 of the Penal Code, laundering the proceeds of a crime is illegal but only with regard to specific predicate offenses that do not include crimes related to corruption.

Tax Evasion. Under Article 343, section 1, evading or attempting to evade the payment of assessed taxes is a crime punishable by two to five years in prison, a fine of 500 to 1,000 cuotas, or both. Under section 2, if the conduct involves false accounting, including concealing, altering, or omitting relevant financial information, the penalties are increased to three to eight years imprisonment. Section 3 criminalizes failure to pay over taxes that have been withheld and provides for penalties of two to five years imprisonment, a fine of 500 to 1,000 cuotas, or both.

Illicit Enrichment. Article 150 makes illegal illicit enrichment, defined under the UNCAC as the "significant increase in the assets of a public official that he or she cannot reasonably explain in relation to his or her lawful income."[24] Under Article 150, section 1, an "authority or official" who engages in illicit enrichment is subject to three to eight years in prison. If the offense is committed by someone other than an authority or official, under Article 150, section 2, the penalties are two to five years imprisonment, a fine of 300 to 1,000 cuotas, or both. In addition, under section 3, forfeiture may be ordered regardless of who commits the offense.

Abuse of Functions. Several sections of the Penal Code criminalize abuse of functions, defined under the UNCAC as "the performance of or failure to perform an act, in violation of laws, by a public official in the discharge of his or her functions, for the purpose of obtaining an undue advantage for himself or herself or for another person or entity."[25] Under Article 225, an individual who, without authorization, uses or allows another to use materials, equipment, or the services of workers under that individual's authority is subject to one to three years in prison, a fine of 300 to 1,000 cuotas, or both. The prohibition applies to public officials as well as private individuals.

Article 153, section 1 makes it illegal for a public official or employee to require payments to the government knowing that they are improper or more than required. The penalties are one to three years imprisonment, a fine of 300 to 1,000 cuotas, or both. In addition, a public official or employee who, by virtue of his or her position, intervenes in any contract, negotiation, decision, business, or operation in order to obtain a benefit for him- or herself or for another is subject, under Article 153, section 2, to a term of imprisonment of three to eight years. Under section 3, forfeiture also applies.

Similarly, Article 133 prohibits a public official from exercising his or her authority unlawfully for the purpose of harming another or obtaining an illegal profit. The penalties are one to three years imprisonment or a fine of 300 to 1,000 cuotas, provided the conduct does not constitute "a crime of greater significance."[26]

Embezzlement. The Penal Code criminalizes embezzlement. Under Article 336, section 1, an individual who misappropriates assets owned by the government or a political, social, or mass[27] organization or personal property in the care of a "State economic activity" is subject to a term of three to eight years imprisonment. Under section 2, the term of imprisonment is 8 to 20 years if the misappropriated assets are "of considerable value." By contrast, if the assets are "of limited value," section 3 provides for a term of imprisonment of six months to two years, a fine 200 to 500 cuotas, or both. An individual who makes payments, including employee salaries, in excess of the authorized amount, is subject to six months to two years in prison and a fine of 200 to 500 cuotas. section 5 extends the prohibitions and penalties to managers and employees of private entities.

---

[24] UNCAC, Art. 20.

[25] UNCAC, Art. 19.

[26] The Penal Code does not define "a crime of greater significance."

[27] An organization to mobilize mass support for the Communist Party.

9. Cooperation

The Penal Code explicitly recognizes cooperation with law enforcement as a mitigating factor with regard to criminal sanctions. Article 52 provides for such consideration in instances where an individual has admitted his or her role in the crime or has provided authorities with other facts related to the offense.

As noted previously, the Cuban criminal justice system does not allow for pretrial guilty pleas. All criminal cases are resolved through trial.

10. Whistle-Blower Protection

Although the Comptroller General's Office accepts citizen complaints related to the misuse of public resources, generally there is little protection for whistle-blowers in Cuba. The Cuban constitution limits freedom of speech and press to matters consistent with "the objectives of socialist society."[28] In addition, access to broad communication channels is restricted because the state owns and operates all mass media outlets, including television, radio, and print businesses. Internet access is also tightly controlled. Accordingly, a vital tool in the effort to detect and prevent bribery, the misuse of government funds, fraud, and other types of corruption is largely missing.

11. Key International Treaties Relating to Bribery and Corruption

As noted previously, Cuba is a signatory to the United Nations Convention against Corruption.[29] Divided into eight parts, the UNCAC's articles are: (1) general provisions, (2) preventive measures, (3) criminalization and law enforcement, (4) international cooperation, (5) asset recovery, (6) technical assistance and information exchange, (7) mechanisms for implementation, and (8) final provisions.[30] Cuba has adopted a number of the UNCAC's provisions.[31] For instance, active bribery of national public officials (Article 15 of the UNCAC) is covered by Article 152, Paragraph 4, of the Penal Code, and illicit enrichment is criminalized at Article 150 of the Penal Code (Article 20 of the UNCAC). In other areas, however, Cuba has failed to implement laws prohibiting conduct addressed in the UNCAC. For example, the bribery of foreign public officials and officials of public international organizations (Article 16 of the UNCAC) is not illegal in Cuba.

---

[28] Constitution of the Republic of Cuba, Art. 53, *available at* http://www.constitutionnet.org/files/Cuba%20 Constitution.pdf(last visited Dec. 14. 2018).

[29] https://www.unodc.org/documents/treaties/UNCAC/Publications/Convention/08-50026_E.pdf (last visited Dec. 7 , 2018).

[30] *Id.*

[31] Conference of the States Parties to the United Nations Convention against Corruption, Sept. 13, *available at* https://www.unodc.org/documents/treaties/UNCAC/WorkingGroups/ImplementationReviewGroup/ ExecutiveSummaries/V1386376e.pdf.

Cuba is also a signatory to United Nations Convention against Transnational Organized Crime UNCATO). The UNCATO recognizes the importance of close international cooperation to tackle those problems associated with organized crime. Ratifying nations commit to the adoption of a series of measures against transnational organized crime, including the creation of domestic criminal offenses such as participation in an organized criminal group, money laundering, corruption, and obstruction of justice; the adoption of a framework for extradition, mutual legal assistance, and law enforcement cooperation; and an effort to provide training and technical assistance for building or upgrading the capacity of national authorities. In addition, Cuba has outlawed money laundering through the adoption of Article 346 of the Penal Code, which covers laundering the proceeds of crime. And Article 338 of the Criminal Code criminalizes the acquisition, the possession, and the use of the proceeds of crime.

Despite Cuba's adoption of the UNCAC and the UNCATO, Cuba has failed to ratify other international treaties intended to root out corruption and bribery. For instance, Cuba is not a signatory to the OECD Convention on Combating Bribery of Foreign Public Officials in International Business Transactions (the "OECD Convention").[32] The OECD Convention establishes standards to criminalize bribery of foreign public officials in cross-border business transactions. The focus of the OECD Convention concerns the supply side of bribery transactions.[33]

12. Mutual Legal Assistance, Treaties, and Transnational Cooperation

Cuba is not a party to any mutual legal assistance treaties with other countries.

In recent years, Cuba has cooperated with a small number of left-leaning allies such as Venezuela and Bolivia, particularly in areas such as oil-for-labor and national defense.[34] Cuba has also demonstrated a renewed interest in outreach to other nations such as Mexico. In 2013, Mexico and Cuba announced the relaunch of relations between the two countries, including the strengthening of trade, financial, and other cooperation agreements and forgiveness of 70 percent of Cuba's debt to Mexico.[35]

For decades, transnational cooperation between the United States and Cuba has been very limited—and exceedingly strained. The primary instance where the two nations

---

[32] http://www.oecd.org/daf/anti-bribery/WGBRatificationStatus.pdf (last visited Dec. 7, 2018).

[33] http://www.oecd.org/investment/anti-bribery/anti-briberyconvention/oecdantibriberyconvention.htm (Last visited Dec. 7, 2018).

[34] Javier Corrales, Amherst College. "The Logic of Extremism: How Chávez Gains by Giving Cuba So Much" Center for Latin American and Caribbean Studies, University of Connecticut, *available at* http://archive.thedialogue.org/PublicationFiles/CubaVenezuelaandtheAmericasAChangingLandscape.pdf (last visited Dec. 7, 2018).

[35] *Cuba; Mexico: Relationship Re-Launched, Agreements Signed*, Global Legal Monitor—Library of Congress, Nov. 8, 2013.

have cooperated is on drug enforcement issues and providing information on movements of suspected drug boats through the Caribbean.[36] Greater cooperation between the United States and Cuba, however, has begun with progress on normalizing diplomatic relations.[37] Efforts are already underway between the United States and Cuba to cooperate on law enforcement. For instance on May 17, 2016, the two nations conducted bilateral meetings to reinforce the benefits of law enforcement cooperation and address areas of cooperation in counterterrorism, counternarcotics, transnational crime, cybercrime, secure travel and trade, and fugitives.[38] However the efforts to normalize relations under President Obama have taken a step back under President Trump. President Trump has imposed new restrictions on travel and remittances, but diplomatic relations remain intact.[39]

13. Legal Professional Privilege

Although the attorney-client privilege theoretically exists in Cuba,[40] the country's legal industry is dominated by the government.[41] Independent legal practices in Cuba are nonexistent,[42] because all Cuban lawyers work for the government or state-owned law firms.[43] In addition, Cuban lawyers have different ethical obligations than lawyers in Western, industrialized nations (including a very limited and arguably nonexistent attorney-client privilege).[44] Nonetheless, there is anecdotal evidence that Cuban lawyers do respect the attorney-client privilege.[45]

---

[36] *In Fight against Drugs, Cuba and U.S. on Same Team*, WASH. POST, Jan. 5, 2015, *available at* https://www.washingtonpost.com/world/the_americas/in-fight-against-drugs-cuba-and-us-on-same-team/2015/01/05/6416305a-90fc-11e4-a66f-0ca5037a597d_story.html.

[37] *United States and Cuba to Hold Second Law Enforcement Dialogue in Havana, Cuba*, May 13, 2016, *available at* http://www.state.gov/r/pa/prs/ps/2016/05/257195.htm.

[38] *Id.*

[39] "Trump cancels Obama's 'one-sided deal' with Cuba," June 17, 2007 available at https://news.sky.com/story/trump-cancels-obamas-one-sided-deal-with-cuba-10918100 (last visited Dec. 7, 2018).

[40] *Privacy in Cuba*, UNIVERSITY OF CHICAGO LAW SCHOOL CHICAGO UNBOUND. Nov. 3, 2015, *available at* http://chicagounbound.uchicago.edu/cgi/viewcontent.cgi?article=1006&context=international_immersion_program_papers.

[41] *A New Dawn for Cuba as It Opens for Business*, ABA J., June 1, 2016, *available at* http://www.abajournal.com/magazine/article/a_new_dawn_for_cuba_as_it_opens_for_business/.

[42] *Id.*

[43] *Cuba's Legal Composite: A Blend of the Familiar and the Foreign*, BENCH & BAR MINN. (Jan. 11, 2012). Available at http://mnbenchbar.com/2012/01/cubas-legal-composite/.

[44] Fatema Merchant & Lisa Mays, *Hotels and Hospitality in Cuba: OFAC and Obama Paving the Way*, GLOBAL TRADE LAW BLOG (Apr. 20, 2016), *available at* http://www.globaltradelawblog.com/2016/04/20/hotels-and-hospitality-in-cuba-ofac-and-obama-paving-the-way/.

[45] *A New Dawn for Cuba, supra* note 41.

14. Privacy and Data Protection

As with the attorney-client privilege, Cubans theoretically enjoy a number of privacy rights. For example, the Cuban Constitution provides certain protections concerning searches and seizures, stating:

> ARTICLE 56—The home is inviolable. Nobody can enter the home of another against his will, except in those cases foreseen by law.
>
> ARTICLE 57—Mail is inviolable. It can be seized, opened and examined only in cases prescribed by law. Secrecy is maintained on matters other than those which led to the examination. The same principle is to be applied in the case of cable, telegraph and telephone communication.
>
> ARTICLE 58—Freedom and inviolability of persons is assured to all those who live in the country. Nobody can be arrested, except in the manner, with the guarantees and in the cases indicated by law. The person who has been arrested or [who is a] prisoner is inviolable in his personal integrity.[46]

However, as observed by Human Rights Watch, "Cuba often disregards the constitutional right to freedom from arbitrary arrest and search, and the privacy of correspondence and telephone communications. Cuba's utter lack of judicial and prosecutorial independence contributes to these abuses."[47]

According to the U.S. State Department, "In practice . . . the [Cuban] government routinely and systematically monitored correspondence and communications between citizens, surveilled their movements, and entered homes without legal authority and with impunity. Police searched homes and seized personal goods without the legally required documentation."[48] Cuban police routinely violate procedural laws and fail to provide legally required documentation during arbitrary detentions and searches.[49] Although police brutality is forbidden, security forces employ aggressive and physically abusive tactics. There is no known mechanism to investigate government abuses.

Although Article 53 of the Cuban Constitution provides that Cuban citizens enjoy "freedom of speech and of the press," the law regulates the exercise of these freedoms—they must be consistent with the "objectives of socialist society"—and media organizations cannot be owned privately.[50] The government tolerates little to no criticism, with even prominent

---

[46] The Constitution of the Republic of Cuba, 1976 (as Amended to 2002), *available at* http://www.constitutionnet.org/files/Cuba%20Constitution.pdf.

[47] III. Impediments to Human Rights in Cuban Law, Human Rights Watch, *available at* http://www.hrw.org/reports/1999/cuba/Cuba996-03.htm#P621_87226 (last visited Dec. 7, 2018).

[48] *Country Reports on Human Rights Practices for 2011*, *supra* note 15.

[49] *2010 Country Reports on Human Rights Practices*, U.S. Department of State, Bureau of Democracy, Human Rights and Labor, Apr. 8, 2011, *available at* http://www.state.gov/j/drl/rls/hrrpt/2010/wha/154501.htm.

[50] The Constitution of the Republic of Cuba, 1976, *supra* note 46.

figures facing punishment for speaking out against the regime.[51] In addition, Cubans can be incarcerated for criticizing the government or for organizing groups to challenge political power.[52]

And although "Cuba's constitution purportedly protects privacy rights, government interference and pervasive monitoring of communications are commonplace. Personal data rights, for example, are not recognized under Cuban law."[53] There are significant restrictions on access to the internet, and reports suggest that the government monitors email and internet chat rooms and browsing. The government, in short, controls virtually all internet access.[54]

While it has not been implemented, there has been progress in Cuba of adopting a new Constitution which would, among other things, provide greater private property rights.[55] Whether this new Constitution would appreciably affect privacy and data protection is unclear.

15. Forecast for Reforms and Parting Thoughts

If past is prologue, there is evidence that Cuba may be moving in the right direction to root out corruption and strengthen the rule of law. The relatively recent creation of the Comptroller General's Office (in 2009), partly meant to receive and investigate citizen complaints about corruption, was a significant step in this regard. These efforts have resulted in Cuba's ranking of 62 among the 180 countries ranked in the 2017 Transparency Index from best to worst, a far better result than many would expect.

The good news for the business community and those who want Cuba to begin respecting the rule of law is the improved diplomatic relations between Cuba and the United States. Although these two nations have had little communication or cooperation since the early 1960s, those relations have begun to thaw, most notably with the December 2014 announcement that the United States intended to normalize relations with the island nation.[56] Since that time, a number of positive steps have been taken:

- An April 2015 face-to-face meeting between Presidents Barack Obama and Raúl Castro, and a visit by President Obama to Cuba in March 2016;[57]

---

[51] *Country Reports on Human Rights Practices for 2011*, *supra* note 15.

[52] *Country Profile: Cuba*, Library of Congress—Federal Research Division, Sept. 2006 at 25, *available at* https://www.loc.gov/rr/frd/cs/profiles/Cuba.pdf.

[53] *Data Protection Law in Spain and Latin America: Survey of Legal Approaches*, Aldo M. Leiva, 41(4).

[54] *Country Reports on Human Rights Practices for 2011*, *supra* note 15.

[55] "Cuba sets out new constitutional reforms." BBC News. 2018-07-15. https://www.bbc.com/news/world-latin-america-44836358 (Last visited Dec. 7, 2018).

[56] ADD CITE, *available at* https://www.whitehouse.gov/the-press-office/2014/12/17/statement-president-cuba-policy-changes (last visited February 17, 2019).

[57] Julie Hirschfeld Davis & Randal C. Archibold, *Obama Meets Raúl Castro, Making History*, N.Y. TIMES, Apr. 11, 2015, *available at* http://www.nytimes.com/2015/04/12/world/americas/obama-cuba-summit-of-the-americas.html; Merchant & Mays, *supra* note 44.

- Removal of Cuba from the state sponsor of terrorism list in May 2015 thereby allowing United States' banks to give loans to companies wanting to do business in Cuba;[58]
- A February 2016 agreement to re-establish commercial air travel between the United States and Cuba;[59]
- Approval for an American company to construct a plant in Cuba to assemble tractors for sale to Cuban farmers;[60]
- Permission from the United States to allow companies to export products that benefit private and cooperative farmers in Cuba;[61]
- Doubling of the number of public Wi-Fi access spots to more than 100 across the country in 2016 and bringing broadband internet to a small number of Cuban homes (where it was previously illegal);[62]
- Permission for United States' banks to directly access the Cuban financial system;[63] and
- The Cuban government allowing for the privatization of more than 9,000 restaurants.[64]

Despite the fact that some progress has been made, few are celebrating just yet. President Donald Trump could undo President Obama's executive actions. Also, there is scant evidence that the Cuban government has strengthened the rule of law, private land ownership is quite limited, and the Cuban government is a majority owner in nearly all businesses. As for U.S. companies, in order to do business in Cuba, they must receive authorization from the Office of Foreign Assets Control and, once that tedious process is complete, must work with burdensome Cuban regulations and bureaucracies, and will likely be faced with government-controlled counterparties.

APPENDIX

Key Issues	Cuba's Approach
Is jurisdiction subject to any international anti-corruption conventions? If so, which? (OECD, UN Convention against Corruption, etc.)	Cuba is a signatory to the UN Convention against Corruption.

---

[58] *A New Dawn for Cuba, supra* note 41.

[59] *Id.*

[60] Michael Weissenstein, *The Obama Administration Has Approved the First U.S. Factory in Cuba in More than Half a Century, Allowing a Pair of Former Software Engineers to Build a Plant Assembling as Many as 1,000 Small Tractors a Year*, U.S. NEWS & WORLD REPORT, Feb. 15, 2016, *available at* http://www.usnews.com/news/business/articles/2016-02-15/apnewsbreak-us-oks-first-factory-in-cuba-since-revolution.

[61] *Id.*

[62] *Id.*

[63] *Key Points from the President's Announcement on Cuba Sanctions.* A publication of PwVC's financial services regulatory practice (Dec. 18, 2014), *available at* http://www.pwc.com/us/en/financial-services/regulatory-services/publications/assets/2014-cuba-sanctions.pdf.

[64] *A new dawn for Cuba, supra* note 41.

Key Issues	Cuba's Approach
Is bribery of foreign public officials illegal (do domestic anti-bribery laws provide for extraterritorial application)?	No.
What is the definition of foreign public officials?	N/A
Is commercial bribery illegal?	While there is no express prohibition on commercial bribery, the fact that most individuals in Cuba work for the state means the laws against bribery of public officials extend to bribery of those who would appear to be commercial parties.
Is bribing domestic officials illegal?	Yes, bribing and offering to bribe domestic officials is illegal.
Can the receipt of a bribe be prosecuted?	Yes.
Can companies be held criminally liable? If so, what is the requisite intent for criminal liability to attach?	*Unclear.*
Can companies be held civilly liable? If so, what is the requisite intent for criminal liability to attach?	*Unclear.*
Can individuals be held civilly liable?	Yes, individuals may be held civilly liable for damages caused by the offense.
Is there a "facilitation/grease payments" exception?	There is nothing to suggest that facilitation, or "grease," payments are legal.
Does the subject country provide for conspiracy liability relating to violations of the anti-corruption laws?	There does not appear to be any law regarding this.
Does the subject country provide for: (a) aiding/abetting liability relating to violations of the anti-corruption laws? (b) attempt liability relating to violations of the anti-corruption laws?	Yes, there is aiding and abetting liability for violations of anti-corruption laws. Yes, there is liability for attempting corruption offenses.
Is failure to keep accurate books and records a criminal and/or civil offense?	There does not appear to be any law regarding this, but false accounting with regard to tax matters is a criminal offense.
Do any books and records violations have to involve underlying bribery proof?	There does not appear to be any law regarding this.

(Continued)

Key Issues	Cuba's Approach
Are there laws concerning a company's financial internal controls? If so, are those laws applicable to private and public companies or just public companies?	There does not appear to be any law regarding this.
Is there an affirmative disclosure obligation for potential violations of the anti-bribery laws or accounting irregularities?	There does not appear to be any law regarding this.
Are "promotional expenses" exempt from the anti-bribery laws?	There does not appear to be any law regarding this.
Is the giving of gifts, entertainment, travel, meals, etc. restricted/prohibited?	There does not appear to be any law regarding this.
Are there any laws concerning things of value conveyed by, or to, third parties?	There is no law explicitly making payment of a bribe indirectly illegal. Receiving a bribe, including "an advantage or benefit," directly or indirectly is illegal.
Are bribes tax deductible?	There does not appear to be any law regarding this.
Is the law applied extraterritorially?	*Unclear.*
Is having a robust corporate compliance program an affirmative defense or way to negate liability?	*Unclear.*
Is there a "local law" exception/defense?	No.
Is "credit" given for cooperation with authorities? If so, how and in what form?	Yes, cooperation is recognized as a mitigating factor. Credit is given where an individual has admitted his or her role in a crime or has provided authorities with other facts related to the offense.
Does the subject country have a Mutual Legal Assistance Treaty with the United States that generally covers criminal matters, including the FCPA?	No.
What are the potential penalties/sanctions both for civil and criminal violations?	Bribing domestic officials is punishable by two to five years in prison. Accepting a bribe as a domestic official is punishable by 4 to 10 years in prison, while soliciting such a bribe is punishable by 8 to 20 years in prison. In addition, violators are subject to a fine of up to 50,000 Cuban pesos along with forfeiture.

7 France

1. Introduction to France's Anti-Corruption Legislation

Since the Law No. 2000-595 of 30 June 2000 amending the Penal Code and the Code of Criminal Procedure with regard to the fight against corruption introduced the offense of bribery of foreign public officials, France[1] has made undeniable progress in combating corruption.

Over the last several years, numerous reforms have been adopted that testify to France's determination to effectively fight corruption. For example, the Law No. 2007-1598 of 13 November 2007, relating to the fight against corruption expanded the scope of criminal prosecution. On July 9, 2010, it was supplemented by Law No. 2010-768, which focuses on facilitating the seizure and confiscation of assets in criminal matters. The French criminal prosecution arsenal was thereafter reinforced by Law No. 2013-1117 of 6 December 2013, on combating major economic and financial crimes. This law significantly increased possible penalties,[2] and concurrently created the office of the National Financial Prosecutor, having special jurisdiction in economic and financial matters, and particularly over those relating to corruption, as well as exclusive jurisdiction over stock market offenses. In addition, the 2013 Act authorized certain anti-corruption organizations to exercise the rights of a civil claimant

---

[1] This chapter was contributed by Bougartchev Moyne Associé's lawyers Kiril Bougartchev, Emmanuel Moyne, Sebastien Muratyan and Nathan Morin.

[2] In particular, the possible fines for bribery of French and foreign public officials were increased from €150,000 to €1,000,000 for individuals and from €750,000 to €5,000,000 for legal entities.

From Baksheesh to Bribery. T. Markus Funk and Andrew S. Boutros.
© Oxford University Press 2019. Published 2019 by Oxford University Press.

(*partie civile*) before a criminal court and, therefore, to initiate prosecution; gone, in short, was the Public Prosecutor's sole dominion in this field.

Nevertheless, the OECD was particularly critical of France in its 2012 Phase 3 Report on Implementing the OECD Anti-Bribery Convention in France. Despite subsequently considerably softening its tone and welcoming the various reforms France had adopted when it published its follow-up to the Phase 3 report,[3] on October 23, 2014, the OECD expressed its *"serious concerns for France's limited efforts"* to combat bribery in international transactions.[4]

As so often happens with the OECD, it is not the current legal framework, which is quite comprehensive, but it is its *implementation* that draws forth the OECD's criticisms. In fact, it is true that the number of French prosecutions and convictions on the grounds of corruption is relatively low. In this regard, in 2014 the OECD pointed out that since the OECD Convention had come into force in France, only 58 proceedings had been initiated for bribery of foreign public officials, of which 31 had been closed with no further action or dismissed, or had ended in discharge.

However, the necessity to combat corruption must not be confused with an obligation to obtain convictions. Such an approach would disregard the fundamental principle of a right to a fair trial.

Moreover, the French legislator recently took such criticism into account and strove to make further progress in preventing, detecting and punishing corruption in order to reach the highest international standards. Law No. 2016-1691, known as "Sapin II law," was signed on December 9, 2016 and came into force with regard to most of its provisions on December 11, 2016. The most significant reforms regarding the fight against corruption brought about by the Sapin II law are:

- The obligation, for certain legal entities[5] and their executives (chairman, chief executives and managers), to set up an effective compliance program to prevent and detect corruption and influence peddling in France and abroad;
- The creation of a new anti-corruption agency, which replaced the current Central Service of Corruption Prevention, and is notably tasked with ensuring the implementation of these compliance programs and sanctioning the legal entities and their executives that would have not complied with the obligation of setting up effectively this compliance program;
- The introduction of a true settlement procedure for legal entities, called the "public interest judicial convention" (*convention judiciaire d'intérêt public*), with no acknowledgment of guilt;
- The implementation of a general status for whistle-blowers, protecting them from a broad range of retaliatory measures;
- The creation of a national register of lobbyists.

---

[3] France: Follow-up to the Phase 3 Report and Recommendations, December 2014.

[4] Statement of the OECD Working Group on Bribery on France's implementation of the Anti-Bribery Convention, 23 October 2014.

[5] Legal entities that have at least 500 employees or that belong to a group whose parent company's headquarters are located in France and has a workforce of at least 500 employees, and whose turnover or consolidated turnover exceeds €100 million.

Last, a recent case shows the French courts' determination to severely punish corruption offenses, provided they are properly proved. In that case, the Paris Court of Appeal convicted no fewer than five persons, including two legal entities, for bribing foreign public officials, as well as two individuals for aiding and abetting the bribery of foreign public officials. The penalties imposed on the legal entities range from €300,000 to €750,000, the maximum possible fine at the time of the relevant events, and the individuals were ordered to pay fines ranging from €15,000 to €75,000.[6] On March 14, 2018, the Court of Cassation rejected the appeals lodged against the Paris Court of Appeal's decision by the above mentioned companies and individuals.[7]

2. French Domestic Anti-corruption Framework

2.1 CRIMINAL LAW REGIME

Under the French criminal law, an offense is comprised of (1) a physical element, and (2) a mental element and, in certain cases, the additional requirement of (3) a "prior condition."

The "prior condition," which the Penal Code requires for each offense of corruption, is defined as an indispensable prerequisite in order to commit the offense,[8] and in corruption matters concerns the status of the person corrupted.

The physical element concerns the prohibited act itself, while the mental element refers to the intent to commit the offense. The mental element usually includes a general intent (*dol général*), which requires that the perpetrator of the offense (1) be aware that he is acting in violation of the law, and (2) possess the will to commit the prohibited act, as well as (3) a special intent (*dol spécial*), which requires an intention to achieve a specific objective.

As is the case for individuals, legal entities may be criminally liable even if not expressly provided by law.[9] Legal entities are criminally liable only for offenses committed "on their behalf" by their "corporate bodies or representatives," but such liability does not preclude individuals from also being liable if they are perpetrators of or accomplices to an offense.[10]

On March 27, 2017, the French Parliament introduced a duty of due diligence for parent companies and subcontracting enterprises.[11] This new law amended the French Commercial Code and requires certain companies[12] to adopt and implement a forward-looking "due diligence plan" regarding human rights, environmental, and health and safety issues in their

---

[6] CA Paris, 26 February 2016, No. 13/09208. Although no jail sentence was imposed in this case, this ruling shows criminal courts' intent to effectively combat corruption.

[7] Cass. crim., 14 March 2018, No. 16-82.117.

[8] For example, receiving the proceeds of an offense may only be prosecuted if such proceeds are the product of a felony or misdemeanor.

[9] Until the Law No. 2004-204 of March 9, 2004, adapting the justice system to changes in criminal behavior, a specific provision was required in order to extend criminal liability to legal entities for a given offense.

[10] Penal Code, article 121-2.

[11] Law No. 2017-399 of March 27, 2017 on the duty of due diligence for parent companies and subcontracting companies.

[12] Limited companies (*sociétés anonymes*), Simplified limited companies (*sociétés par actions simplifiées*) and Limited partnership with shares (*sociétés en commandite par actions*) that at the end of two consecutive financial years employ at least 5,000 workers within the company and its direct or indirect subsidiaries and whose

supply chains. The purpose of such plan is to set up reasonable due diligence measures to identify and prevent the occurrence of the severe violation of human rights and fundamental freedoms, serious environmental harm or severe health and safety breaches against persons, generated by their own activities and those of the companies they control, directly or indirectly, as well as by the activities of the subcontractors or suppliers with which they have an established business relationship.[13] Such plan as well as a report on its implementation are required to be made public and would be included in the company's annual report.

In the case of noncompliance with these landmark obligations, any person with standing would be permitted to sue to request a court directing the company to adopt a vigilance plan. Last, in the event of damage, any person with standing to sue could seek to hold the legal entity civilly liable to obtain compensation for his loss and to order that the court's decision be published.[14] Suffice it to say that this legal regime is a true game changer.

The French Penal Code bases the prosecution of bribery on the status of the person bribed, creating a specific offense for each type of person. Thus, French law criminalizes bribery of domestic public officials,[15] bribery of domestic judicial staff,[16] and bribery of domestic private individuals.[17] Since the aforementioned Law of June 30, 2000, the French criminal law also punishes the offense of bribery of foreign or international public officials[18] and bribery of foreign or international judicial staff.[19]

In each situation, French law distinguishes between active bribery and passive bribery. The existence of distinct offenses allows the possibility of prosecuting the bribe-giver separately from the bribe-taker because proof of the offense of passive bribery does not require proof of the offense of active bribery, and vice versa.

Active bribery is the act of (1) unlawfully proposing, at any time, directly or indirectly, any offer, promise, donation, gift, or advantage to a person (public official, private individual, or judicial official), for the benefit of such person or of a third party, to induce such person to perform or refrain from performing, or because such person has performed or refrained from performing, any act pertaining to her position, duties, mandate or activities, or facilitated thereby; or (2) accepting the proposal of such person who unlawfully requests, at any time, directly or indirectly, such advantages in exchange for such acts.

---

registered office is located in France, or who employ at least 10,000 workers within the company and its direct or indirect subsidiaries, and whose registered office is located in France or abroad.

[13] The plan is to include (1) a mapping that identifies, analyses and ranks risks, (2) procedures to regularly assess the situation of subsidiaries, subcontractors or suppliers with whom the company maintain an established business relationship, (3) appropriate action to mitigate risks or prevent severe violations, (4) an alert mechanism that enables employees to report existing risks and (5) a monitoring scheme to follow up on the measures implemented and their efficiency.

[14] It is to be noted that as voted by Parliament, in the case of non-compliance with this obligation, the bill provided for a civil fine of €10 million. However, on March 23, 2017, the Constitutional Court deemed that the provisions setting out the basis on which such civil fines could be imposed was not clear enough and violated the Constitution.

[15] Penal Code, articles 433-1 and 432-11.

[16] Penal Code, article 434-9.

[17] Penal Code, articles 445-1 and 445-2.

[18] Penal Code, articles 435-1 and 435-3.

[19] Penal Code, articles 435-7 and 435-9.

Passive bribery, in contrast, is the act whereby a person (public official, private individual, or judicial staff) unlawfully requests or accepts advantages as defined above, at any time, directly or indirectly, on his own behalf or on behalf of a third party, to perform or refrain from performing, or because such person has performed or refrained from performing, any act pertaining to his position, duties, mandate, or activities, or facilitated thereby.

Therefore, the prerequisite for the offenses of bribery is the status of the person bribed, which is specific to each bribery offense.

The physical element is requesting or accepting any advantage (passive bribery) or proposing or agreeing to grant an advantage (active bribery).

Last, the mental element is deduced from the unlawful nature of the advantage conferred or received and from the fact that the request, proposal, agreement, or acceptance are necessarily intentional acts (general intent), as well as from the objective sought, that is, for the bribe-taker, to perform or refrain from performing an act to obtain an advantage and, for the bribe-giver, conferring an advantage to obtain the benefit of such performance or nonperformance (special intent).

The mere fact of making a proposal or accepting a request for an advantage suffices for the commission of the offense of active bribery, and the mere fact of requesting or accepting a proposed advantage suffices for the commission of the offense of passive bribery. The results expected by the perpetrators need not occur for the offenses to have been committed. In other words, neither the performance of the act nor the receipt of the advantage are required elements of the offense. For this reason, French law does not expressly criminalize attempted bribery.

For example, without calling into question his presumption of innocence, a former president of the French Republic was recently placed under judicial examination (*mis en examen*) and could be sent to trial on the grounds of active bribery, active influence peddling (for this case, see Section 13 of this chapter), and receiving the proceeds of a breach of professional secrecy. The allegation is that the former president, inter alia, contemplated assisting in procuring for a third party—in this case a senior judge—a prestigious position in exchange for a service to be performed by that judge.

To clarify some ambiguous language of the French legislature in the aforementioned Law No. 2000-595 of June 30, 2000, Law No. 2011-525 of May 17, 2011, to simplify and improve the quality of the law, confirmed the principle that concluding a corruption pact[20] need not precede the act or nonperformance intended for an offense of corruption to have been committed. Case law had already established such principle before the legislature acted.

These tools for prosecuting corruption are usefully supplemented by the criminalization of active and passive influence peddling, which refers to the situation in which a person abuses his actual or supposed influence with a view to obtaining a distinction, job, contract, or any other favorable decision from an individual (whose status varies depending on the case), or from a legal entity.

---

[20] It is to be noted that concluding a corruption pact does not necessarily require an express agreement.

2.2 CIVIL LAW REGIME

The French civil liability regime offers victims of an offense two distinct alternatives:

- A civil action for compensation of losses sustained that is brought before the civil courts on the grounds of article 1240 of the Civil Code (former article 1382 of the Civil Code); or
- A civil action before the criminal courts in which the victim is a party to the proceedings. Persons who have personally suffered a loss caused directly by an offense may bring an action before the criminal courts, which enables them not only to obtain compensation for their loss, but also to initiate prosecution if the Public Prosecutor does not take the initiative.[21]

Although the Criminal Chamber of the Court of Cassation recognizes that individuals may sustain a direct and personal loss for which they are entitled to obtain compensation before the criminal courts in corruption cases,[22] compensating the victims is problematic in practice due to evidentiary difficulties. This is particularly true in the civil courts because corruption is most frequently concealed, and in civil cases French law does not have a procedure equivalent to the discovery tools available in U.S. courts.

Nevertheless, there has been progress in French law on this point. Law No. 2013-1117 of December 6, 2013, on combating tax fraud and major economic and financial crimes, abolished the Public Prosecutor's monopoly to commence prosecution of offenses of bribery of foreign or international public officials and of foreign or international court staff. Since then, civil claimants are enabled to initiate prosecution, regardless of the type of bribery offense in question. This law also authorizes accredited anti-corruption organizations to exercise the rights of a civil claimant for a certain number of offenses, in particular for various corruption offenses.[23]

Last, French civil law considers corruption pacts and influence peddling agreements to be void on the grounds that their consideration or purpose is immoral and illegal, fraudulent, or contrary to French public policy.[24]

2.3 VIEW FROM THE OUTSIDE

2.3.1 OECD Evaluation

When it published its Phase 3 Report on Implementing the OECD Anti-Bribery Convention in France, the OECD working group was particularly critical of the French system.[25]

---

[21] Code of Criminal Procedure, articles 1 and 2.

[22] Cass. crim., 1 December 1992.

[23] Code of Criminal Procedure, article 2-23. However, even before this law was adopted, in the "ill-gotten gains" case, a case in which persons were prosecuted for bribery-related offenses, the Court of Cassation granted Transparency International France standing to sue, despite the fact that it was not accredited by law, since the offenses prosecuted were likely to cause the association a direct and personal damage due to the specificity of its duty's goal and purpose (Cass., crim., 9 November 2010, No. 09-88.272).

[24] Cass. com., 7 March 1961, Bull. civ. III.

[25] Of 33 recommendations, the OECD working group considered that 4 had been fully implemented, 17 had been partially implemented, and 12 were still awaiting implementation.

The shortcomings of the French legislation the OECD working group pointed out concerned, in particular, (1) the dual-criminality requirement for prosecuting acts committed abroad, (2) the specific status of the Public Prosecutor's office in its relations with the executive branch, (3) the fact that influence peddling involving foreign public officials was not punishable, (4) the requirements for imposing criminal liability on legal entities, and (5) the amount of the penalties provided by law and of the penalties imposed in practice, with the OECD regretting, more generally, the low number of prosecutions and convictions.

Although the OECD softened its tone in its follow-up to the Phase 3 report, it nevertheless stated that *"France* [was] *insufficiently in compliance with the Anti-Bribery Convention."*[26]

We deem certain of these criticisms to be unjustified, in particular because the anti-corruption framework has been significantly strengthened since the Phase 3 report. Therefore, although the French law still has some imperfections, in particular in implementing the existing legislative arsenal, France's efforts in this area are difficult to deny.

2.3.2 Transparency International Corruption Perceptions Index Score

In its 2018 Corruption Perceptions Index, Transparency International gave France a score of 72, which ranks France 21st worldwide among the countries perceived to be the least corrupt.[27]

This is a slight improvement over 2014, when France was in 26th place worldwide with a score of 69.[28] Overall, France's score has been relatively stable in recent years. As Transparency International France explained, the fact that reforms adopted do not have an immediate impact is normal because *"there is always a transitional period before amendments to the legal framework are reflected in actual changes in behavior."*[29]

Notwithstanding the above considerations, Transparency International ranked France in the category "Limited Enforcement" in the report "Exporting Corruption 2018" published on September 12, 2018 which aims to assess the enforcement of the OECD Anti-Bribery Convention.

Given the first public interest judicial conventions that have been concluded in anti-corruption matters, one of them having seen the sentencing of a major French financial institution to pay a fine of €250,150,755 in France and the same amount to the DOJ in June 2018, it is questionable to read such a critic.

3. Investigative and Prosecutorial Agencies

3.1 ADMINISTRATIVE AGENCIES

In French law, corruption offenses may be prosecuted before the criminal courts only. No administrative authority is empowered to impose civil penalties, as the U.S. Securities and Exchange Commission (SEC) may do.

However, Sapin II law lead to the creation of a French Anticorruption Agency (AFA), whose main duty is to make sure that certain legal entities (see Section 1 above) implement

---

[26] Statement of the OECD Working Group on Bribery on France's Implementation of the Anti-Bribery Convention, 23 October 2014.

[27] Transparency International, Corruption Perceptions Index 2018.

[28] Transparency International, Corruption Perceptions Index 2014, p. 4.

[29] Transparency International France, 2013 Report on Combating Corruption in France, p. 7.

programs to prevent and detect corrupt acts. The AFA has been empowered to send warnings to non-compliant companies and to refer cases to its Sanctions Committee so as to prosecute and punish legal entities—the fine is up to €1,000,000—and their representatives—who can be punished by fines up to €200,000—who breach the prevention and detection obligations prescribed by the law.

The AFA has been granted other duties, such as issuing non-legally binding recommendations on how to prevent and detect acts of bribery, influence-peddling, misappropriation or embezzlement of public funds, unlawful taking of interest and favouritism, or monitoring the execution of the new penalty and the judicial convention mentioned below. The AFA published its recommendations on December 21, 2017.

In order to accomplish these missions, AFA agents have been empowered to require the production of any document, as well as any helpful information, and to keep a copy thereof. The Sapin II law introduced an offense of obstruction, sanctioning persons impeding AFA's agents carrying out a control. The fine incurred is up to €30.000.

Since October 2017, the AFA has undertaken dozens of controls notably within companies acting in the energy, aerospace, defence and banking sectors.

It is to be noted that well before the Sapin II law and the creation of the AFA, various entities already played a relatively important role in preventing and fighting corruption.

This was the case with the Central Service of Corruption Prevention (SCPC), which was replaced by the AFA.[30]

In addition, Tracfin, the agency charged with dealing with and taking action against illegal financial circuits, is the sole center for collecting suspicions reported by the regulated professions subject to the anti-money-laundering measures. In that capacity, it receives all reports of suspicions that may concern corrupt acts.[31]

These agencies, as well as the High Authority for Transparency in Public Life, which was created by the Laws of 11 October 2013 on transparency in public life, and the Public Finance General Directorate, play a fundamental role in detecting offenses, in particular corruption offenses. They deal with the office of the Public Prosecutor, which gives instructions to the enquiry services and ensures they cooperate fully.

3.2 CRIMINAL LAW AGENCIES

In French criminal law, the Public Prosecutor's office is the key to prosecution as it is empowered to decide whether it is appropriate to institute proceedings, although civil claimants may also initiate prosecution (see Section 2.2 above).

---

[30] The SCPC was an independent inter-ministerial institution under the authority of the Minister of Justice whose duties were to (1) centralise the information necessary to detect and prevent corruption, (2) advise administrative authorities and assist the judicial authorities before which corruption cases are brought and (3) carry out awareness-raising and training actions for French companies to enable them to detect and combat corruption. In this regard, the SCPC published guidelines on compliance policies for companies.

[31] Tracfin was at the origin of the investigations and prosecutions that led to the aforementioned decision of the Paris Court of Appeal of 26 February 2016.

The Public Prosecutor, as well as the ordinary criminal courts when the Public Prosecutor brings cases before them, has jurisdiction to handle corruption cases. However, this general jurisdiction is shared with specific prosecutorial agencies and specialized courts.

On February 1, 2014, a National Financial Prosecutor, specialized in economic and financial matters, and more specifically in corruption and tax fraud matters, was added to the judicial system.

The National Financial Prosecutor—and consequently the investigating magistrates of the financial division of the Paris High Court (*Tribunal de grande instance*)—were granted inter alia (1) exclusive jurisdiction to investigate and prosecute stock market offenses; (2) concurrent jurisdiction with the ordinary high courts over the offenses of bribery of foreign public officials, as well as the offense of bribery of private individuals if the matter is highly complex due to the large number of perpetrators, accomplices, or victims of the offense or due to the offense's geographical scope; and (3) concurrent jurisdiction with the Inter-regional Specialised Courts in economic and financial matters and the ordinary high courts over cases involving bribery in the public sector, influence peddling, unlawful taking of interests, favoritism if such matters are particularly complex, and related money laundering activities.[32]

The circular of January 31, 2014, gives a clearer picture of the objective to be achieved, that is, to grant a specialized prosecutorial body jurisdiction over the matters that are the most complex or *"likely to generate significant national or international impact."*[33]

However, the specific powers granted to the National Financial Prosecutor and the investigating magistrates of the financial division of the Paris High Court do not foreclose the expanded territorial jurisdiction granted to the eight Inter-regional Specialised Courts, which also continue to have concurrent jurisdiction with local courts over a certain number of economic and financial offenses, including some corruption offenses, if they are highly complex.[34]

These various prosecutorial bodies are assisted by a specialized investigative service, the Central Office for Fight Against Corruption and Financial and Tax Offenses (*Office Central de Lutte contre la Corruption et les Infractions Financières et Fiscales* (OCLCIFF)), which was created in October 2013. OCLCIFF has significant resources and specialized officers to act in matters involving offenses to probity, tax fraud, and, more broadly, financial offenses, either on its own initiative or pursuant to a request for judicial assistance (*commission rogatoire*). In addition, this unit may assist the National Police or National Gendarmerie in their investigations. It is also tasked with leading and coordinating, at the national and operational levels, police investigations in criminal matters and enquiries within its remit. Last, it

---

[32] Code of Criminal Procedure, article 705.

[33] On January 19, 2015, Éliane Houlette, the National Financial Prosecutor, stated at the formal sitting to mark the beginning of the Paris High Court's judicial year: *"To date, 353 proceedings have been referred to the office of the Financial Prosecutor, of which 207 are currently pending. Thirty-two were closed with no further action, 35 were transferred to other prosecutorial offices, 28 were joined with cases already initiated and 40 involve requests for international judicial assistance in criminal matters. Fifty-one concern stock market offenses, 70 concern offenses to probity and 74 concern tax fraud, of which 23 involve VAT fraud."*

[34] Code of Criminal Procedure, article 704.

is in a position to continue its investigations abroad, and its relations with foreign authorities are facilitated by the fact that it is *"the central point of contact in international exchanges."*[35]

Finally, an Agency for the Management and Recovery of Seized and Confiscated Assets in criminal matters (*Agence de Gestion et de Recouvrement des Avoirs Saisis et Confisqués en matière pénale*, (AGRASC)) was created by the aforementioned Law of 9 July 2010. AGRASC's duties include recovering assets seized in the course of criminal proceedings and conducting prejudgment sales of confiscated assets when they are no longer needed as evidence or if they may lose value.

For example, in the "ill-gotten gains" case,[36] AGRASC auctioned nine luxury cars owned by the son of the president of an African country, which had been seized during the proceedings, for an amount of €2.8 million.

3.3 MULTIAGENCY ARRANGEMENTS

Whereas relations between the SEC and the U.S. Department of Justice are governed by agreement, there is currently no equivalent arrangement in French law.

However, the AFA already cooperates with the National Financial Prosecutor, with whom it concluded an agreement governing their relationship, and any other entity with jurisdiction to prosecute and punish corruption, it being specified that it has been entitled to inform the Public Prosecutor about any acts of corruption it might become aware of. The Agency has already used this power to inform the National Financial Prosecutor that opened a criminal investigation notably on public and private corruption grounds in the so called electricity control case, which is pending.

4. Bribery of Foreign Officials

4.1 JURISDICTION

Generally, criminal proceedings may be initiated in France against the author of a misdemeanour if:

- **French Law.** French law is applicable, which is the case if:
  o **Territory.** The offense is committed in France;[37]
  o **Territory, Part II.** Any of the constituent elements of the offense is committed in France;[38]
  o **Nationality and Dual Criminality.** The perpetrator of the offense is French and a similar offense exists in the country in which it is committed;[39]
  o **Victim.** The victim is French;[40] or

---

[35] Decree No. 2013-960 of 25 October 2013 creating the Central Office for Fight Against Corruption and Financial and Tax Offenses.

[36] Cass. crim., 30 June 2010, No. 09-83.689.

[37] Penal Code, article 113-2.

[38] *Id.*

[39] Penal Code, article 113-6.

[40] Penal Code, article 113-7.

- *International Convention.* An international convention designates the French courts.[41]

The Sapin II law extended the French judges' jurisdiction over acts of bribery and influence peddling committed abroad by removing the two usual criteria governing proceedings against French citizen for acts committed outside France. Indeed, the dual criminality requirement of Article 113-6 of the Penal Code for bribery committed abroad is not required anymore for these offenses. Furthermore, for this type of offenses, Article 113-8 of the Penal Code, which authorizes the Prosecutor to initiate prosecution for offenses committed abroad by a French citizen only if the victim has filed a claim or if the authorities of the country in question have lodged an official complaint is not applicable.[42]

As stated previously, the Paris High Court has concurrent jurisdiction with the ordinary courts to prosecute and judge[43] the offense of bribery of foreign public officials.[44]

4.2 STATUTE OF LIMITATIONS

Until recently, the limitation period expired three years after the request or acceptance (in cases of passive bribery), and three years after the proposal or agreement (in cases of active bribery).[45]

Law No. 2017-242 of February 27, 2017, which came into force as of March 1, 2017, increased the limitation period from three years to six years following the day of commission, as described above.

However, this period is tolled and begins to run anew each time that a different act is performed pursuant to the corruption pact, whether an act pertaining to the position of the foreign public official or his acceptance of any advantage. Therefore, if the corruption pact is performed over time, the limitation period will really only begin to run from the last of the fraudulent acts committed.

The starting point of the limitation period is also delayed for occult and concealed offenses to the day the offense was discovered in circumstances enabling prosecution.[46] Thus, this new law enshrined in legislation the ruling of the Court of Cassation rendered on the principle to which the limitation periods shall not run against those who are not in a position to take action (*contra non valentem agere non currit praescriptio*).[47] However, in order to avoid the

---

[41] *See* Code of Criminal Procedure, articles 689, 689-1, and 689-8, which refer to the Convention on the protection of the European Communities' financial interests of 27 September 1996 and the Convention against corruption involving officials of the European Communities or officials of member states of the European Union of 26 May 1997.

[42] Penal Code, articles 435-6-2 and 435-11-2.

[43] Before the 32nd Criminal Chamber of the Paris High Court.

[44] Code of Criminal Procedure, article 705.

[45] Penal Code, article 8.

[46] Penal Code, article 9-1.

[47] Before the aforementioned law indeed, if the limitation period for bribery had expired, prosecution of the bribe-giver was still possible on the grounds of misuse of corporate assets since, for that offense, the Criminal Chamber ruled that the three years limitation period began to run as from the date on which the offense was discovered under circumstances enabling prosecution (Cass. crim., 7 December 1967, Bull. crim. No. 321). In a

risk of imprescriptibility of offenses, the French legislator specified that prosecution against offenses such as bribery would in any event be time-barred 12 full years following the day on which the offense was committed.

4.3 FOREIGN BRIBERY OFFENSES

French criminal law has prohibited active bribery of foreign public officials since the aforementioned Law of 30 June 2000[48] and the passive bribery by such officials since the Law of 13 November 2007 discussed previously.[49] Bribery of foreign and international judicial staff is also prohibited and is the subject of separate provisions.[50]

These tools for prosecuting corruption are usefully supplemented by the criminalization of active and passive influence peddling involving officials of public international organizations and influence peddling involving international judicial staff as well as, following Sapin II law, active and passive influence peddling involving foreign public officials.[51]

4.4 DEFINITION OF FOREIGN PUBLIC OFFICIALS

French criminal law prohibits active or passive bribery and influence peddling involving persons who:

- Hold public authority; or
- Have a public service mission; or
- Hold a public elected office.

In addition, such persons must perform their duties:

- In a foreign state; or
- Within a public international organization, which includes organizations created pursuant to the European Union treaty.

Any irregularity in the public official's situation—for example, due to the manner in which he was appointed—is irrelevant, and the position he holds may be permanent or temporary. The law also prohibits the active and passive bribery of any:

- Person who holds a judicial position in a foreign state or with an international court;
- Civil servant with the registry of a foreign court or international court;

---

decision dated May 6, 2009, the Criminal Chamber transposed its case law applicable to misuse of corporate assets to bribery (Cass. crim., 6 May 2009, No. 08-84.107).

[48] Penal Code, article 435-3.
[49] Penal Code, article 435-1.
[50] Penal Code, articles 435-7 and 435-9.
[51] Penal Code, articles 435-2 and 435-4.

- Expert appointed by any such court or by the parties;
- Person appointed to act as a conciliator or mediator by any such court; and
- Arbitrator who performs his duties under the arbitration law of a foreign state.[52]

Similarly, the French criminal law prohibits active and passive influence peddling involving a person who holds a position on or with an international court or who has been appointed by such a court.[53]

4.5 GIFTS, GRATUITIES, AND HOSPITALITY

The scope of the French Penal Code is very broad and includes offers, promises, donations, gifts, or advantages, without any restriction as to the magnitude of the advantage offered.

This list covers a great many possibilities, which makes it difficult for companies to know what comes within the scope of the offense. Unlike the Bribery Act, French law does not include any tools that assist in identifying acts that may be prohibited. However, the AFA has published guidelines for companies to assist them in setting up prevention and detection programs. In this respect, it recommends identifying risks, by focusing inter alia on the issues of gifts, accommodations, or entertainment; customer travel; donations; sponsorships; and "facilitation" payments.[54]

The decisions rendered in cases involving bribery of domestic public officials provide several illustrations of prohibited acts. Bribes may of course consist of a sum of money and may take the form of a percentage on a contract awarded[55] or a commission. It may also be a non-cash benefit—such as an apartment[56] or a car[57]—or even a service, such as a safari,[58] a trip,[59] or a fine wines tasting.[60]

4.6 DEFENSES

4.6.1 Written Local Law

The French anti-bribery laws do not provide for any specific defenses.

---

[52] Penal Code, articles 435-7 and 435-9.

[53] Penal Code, article 435-8.

[54] AFA, Recommendations on how to prevent and detect acts of bribery, influence-peddling, misappropriation or embezzlement of public funds, unlawful taking of interest and favouritism, December 21, 2017.

[55] Cass. crim., 12 September 2012, No. 11-87.281.

[56] Cass. Crim., 27 October 1997, No. 96-83.698.

[57] Cass. crim., 30 June 2010, No. 09-83.689.

[58] Cass. crim., 19 September 2007, No. 07-80.593

[59] Cass. crim., 31 October 2012, No. 12-84.220.

[60] Cass. crim., 30 June 2010, No. 09-83.689.

4.6.2 Facilitation Payments

Facilitation payments are not a defense under French law, and a conviction may be obtained even if the amounts at stake are small.

However, if the amounts at issue are small, it may be considered to be a mitigating factor by a court when it determines the quantum of the penalty to be imposed.

For example, the Social Chamber of the Court of Cassation invalidated the dismissal of an employee due to the low value of a gift he had received, in that case a ticket to a football match with a value of €28.[61]

4.6.3 Adequate Procedures

A conviction may also be obtained even if corruption prevention and/or detection procedures have been set up.

However, if adequate procedures have been implemented, courts may prove lenient in applying the law. That said, the Circular dated January 31, 2018 on the presentation and implementation of the criminal provisions provided for by the Sapin II law states, with regard to the public interest judicial convention, that the existence of such adequate procedures should not be taken into account when assessing the amount of the public interest fine to be pronounced.

4.6.4 Corporate Culture

Even before the Sapin II law implementation, a significant number of major French companies had set up corruption prevention and/or detection procedures, in particular to protect themselves against the penalties that Anglo-American courts may otherwise impose on them.

As stated above, the Sapin II law introduced a new duty, for certain companies, their chairmen, chief executives and managers, to prevent bribery and influence peddling by setting up a comprehensive compliance program to prevent such offenses. Compliance measures, which had to be implemented by June 1, 2017, include:

– The adoption of a code of conduct;
– An internal whistle-blowing system to allow employees to report acts or behaviours that violate the company's code of conduct;
– A regularly updated risk mapping where risks of external solicitations would be outlined according to the line of business and the geographic area concerned;
– Assessment procedures evaluating clients, suppliers and intermediaries based on the risk mapping;
– Accounting controls to spot any act of bribery or influence peddling;
– Training sessions for risk-exposed personnel;
– A disciplinary policy; and
– An internal monitoring scheme for all measures implemented.

---

[61] Cass. soc., 23 June 2010, No. 09-40.254.

4.6.5 Penalties

Bribery is severely punished by French law. Individuals who commit the offenses of active bribery[62] and passive bribery[63] may be imprisoned for a term of up to 10 years, the maximum penalty for misdemeanors (*délits*), as well as be ordered to pay a fine of €1 million. The fine may be increased to an amount equal to double the proceeds generated by the offense.

Other penalties may also be imposed on such persons: they may be prohibited from holding public office or from engaging in the professional or social activity in the performance of which, or in connection with the performance of which, the offense was committed, for a period of up to five years,[64] or they may be barred from France if the offense was committed by a foreigner. Last, publication of the judgment may be ordered and the item that was used or was intended to be used to commit the offense, or any item that is a proceed of the infraction, may be confiscated.

Active bribery of foreign public officials committed by a legal entity[65] is subject to a fine of €5 million, which may be increased to an amount equal to double[66] the proceeds generated by the offense.[67] Supplemental penalties are also provided.[68]

The Sapin II law introduced a new ancillary penalty which can be imposed by judges on legal entities convicted for bribery or influence peddling. This penalty would oblige the legal entity to implement a compliance program for up to five years, in accordance with the measures mentioned above and under the supervision of the AFA.[69] Should this penalty not to be implemented, individuals may be imprisoned for up to two years and ordered to pay a €50,000 maximum fine, while legal entities are subject to a maximum fine of €250,000.

---

[62] Penal Code, article 435-3.

[63] Penal Code, article 435-1.

[64] Penal Code, article 435-14.

[65] French law does not exclude the possibility that a foreign public official who accepts a bribe may be a legal entity, for example a foreign state-owned company. If the courts were to hold otherwise, these legal entities could nevertheless be prosecuted for aiding and abetting, in which case the possible penalties would be the same as for the offense of active bribery.

[66] However, the SCPC considered that this amount may be increased to 10 times the proceeds generated by the offense.

[67] Penal Code, article 435-15.

[68] *Id.* The following penalties may be imposed: (i) a prohibition against directly or indirectly performing, for a period of up to five years, one or more professional or social activities; (ii) placement under judicial supervision for a period of up to five years; (iii) the closure, for a period of up to five years, of the establishments, or of one or more of the establishments, of the company used to commit the offense; (iv) exclusion from public contracts, for a period of up to five years; (v) a prohibition against offering financial instruments to the public or of having its financial instruments admitted to trade on a regulated market, for a period of up to five years; (vi) a prohibition against issuing cheques other than those enabling the drawer to withdraw funds from the payee or that are certified, or against using payment cards, for a period of up to five years. Last, the Penal Code provides for confiscation of assets and publication of the judgment handed down. The judicial supervision referred to previously involves the appointment of a person assigned to monitor activities related to the offense. At least every six months, a report on this judicial supervision is submitted to the judge charged with the enforcement of sentences. Based on that report, the judge may transfer the matter before the court that imposed the judicial supervision so that it may impose a new penalty, including, if appropriate, issuing an order for further judicial supervision, or end the judicial supervision.

[69] Penal Code, article 131-39-2.

The penalties provided for active bribery of foreign or international judicial officials are the same as for bribery of foreign public officials.

In cases of influence peddling involving foreign public officials, [70] officials of a public international organization[71] or international judicial staff,[72] individuals are liable for a term of imprisonment of up to five years and a fine of €500,000—which may be increased to an amount equal to double the proceeds generated by the offense—as well as various supplemental penalties.[73] Legal entities are liable for a fine of €2.5 million—which may be increased to an amount equal to double[74] the proceeds generated by the offense—as well as various supplemental penalties.[75]

In the past, few of the convictions handed down in corruption cases were on the grounds of bribery of foreign public officials. For example, in an important case involving bribery of foreign public officials in which the trial court had held a legal entity liable to pay a fine of €500,000, the Court of Appeal acquitted the legal entity on the grounds that no evidence showed that the company had risked losing the contract and that, therefore, there was insufficient proof that the payments were intended as a bribe.[76]

Courts now seems to judge more severely cases on the ground of corruption of public officials. More recently, the Paris Court of Appeal, in the aforementioned decision, reversed the trial court and convicted various legal entities and individuals for bribery of foreign public officials and for aiding and abetting the commission of such offense. In that case, one of the legal entities was ordered to pay a fine of €750,000.[77] This sentence was confirmed by the Court of Cassation on March 14, 2018.

5. Bribery of Domestic Officials

5.1 JURISDICTION

The ordinary jurisdictional rules apply to cases of bribery of domestic public officials. However, as stated previously, the National Financial Prosecutor and the investigating magistrates of the financial division of the Paris High Court have concurrent jurisdiction with the Inter-regional Specialised Courts and the ordinary courts to handle cases of bribery in the public sector that are particularly complex. The Inter-regional Specialised Courts themselves have expanded jurisdiction and, therefore, have concurrent jurisdiction with the ordinary courts over cases of bribery of domestic public officials if they are highly complex.

The matters handled by the National Financial Prosecutor and the investigating magistrates of the financial division of the Paris High Court are judged, if the matters are committed for trial before the criminal court, by the 32nd criminal chamber of the Paris

---

[70] Penal Code, articles 435-2 and 435-4.

[71] Penal Code, articles 435-2 and 435-4.

[72] Penal Code, articles 435-8 and 435-10.

[73] Penal Code, article 435-14.

[74] The SCPC considers that this amount may be increased to 10 times the proceeds generated by the offense.

[75] Penal Code, article 435-15.

[76] CA Paris, 7 January 2015, No. 12/08695.

[77] CA Paris, 26 February 2016, No. 13/09208.

High Court. Other matters that are assigned to other public prosecutor's offices and ordinary investigating magistrates will be judged by the courts that have territorial jurisdiction over them.

5.2 STATUTE OF LIMITATIONS

The rules on limitation periods are the same as for the offense of bribery of foreign public officials (see Section 4.2 above).

5.3 DOMESTIC BRIBERY OF OFFICIALS OFFENSES

The French criminal law prohibits active and passive bribery of domestic public officials, as well as active and passive influence peddling involving such officials. Bribery of domestic judicial staff is also prohibited and is the subject of separate provisions.[78] The same applies to influence peddling involving domestic judicial staff.[79]

5.4 DEFINITION OF DOMESTIC OFFICIALS

Similarly to bribery of foreign public officials, French law is very broad and applies to all persons who:

- Hold public authority;
- Have a public service mission; or
- Hold a public elected office.

The French criminal law also prohibits bribery of judicial staff, which includes judges, court clerks, experts, mediators and arbitrators.

5.5 GIFTS, GRATUITIES, AND HOSPITALITY

With respect to bribery of domestic public officials, the Penal Code also applies to offers, promises, donations, gifts, and advantages.

5.6 DEFENSES

5.6.1 Written Local Law

The section on this point regarding bribery of foreign public officials also applies to the offense of bribery of domestic public officials (see Section 4.6.1 above).

---

[78] Penal Code, article 434-9.
[79] Penal Code, article 434-9-1.

5.6.2 Facilitation Payments

See Section 4.6.2 above.

5.6.3 Adequate procedures

See Section 4.6.3 above.

5.6.4 Corporate Culture

See Section 4.6.4 above.

5.7 PENALTIES

Active or passive bribery of domestic public officials and judicial staff by an individual is punishable by a 10-year term of imprisonment and a fine of €1 million—which may be increased to an amount equal to double the proceeds generated by the offense—as well as supplemental penalties similar to those described above (see Section 4.6.5 above). In addition, this offense is also punishable by a prohibition against exercising a commercial or industrial profession, or directing, administering, managing or controlling a company in any capacity, permanently or for a period of up to 15 years. Legal entities are liable for a fine of €5 million—which may be increased to an amount equal to double[80] the proceeds generated by the offense—and supplemental penalties similar to those discussed earlier (see Section 4.6.5 above).

An increasing number of elected officials have been sanctioned. For example, on August 19, 2013, the mayor of a French town was convicted of embezzlement of public funds, favoritism, forgery, and passive bribery of a public official, and sentenced to a four-year term of imprisonment, one year of which was suspended, and a fine of €50,000, as well as being barred from holding office for five years. This conviction became final after the defendant abandoned his appeal. Similarly, on June 12, 2018, the Paris Court of Appeal sentenced the former director of Lyon's judicial police, on the grounds notably of passive bribery and influence peddling to four years' imprisonment (among which 18 months suspended) and to a permanent ban on practising in police ranks.[81] Lastly, On November 22, 2017, the Aix-en-Provence Court of Appeal sentenced a former deputy prefect to three years' imprisonment and a fine of €20,000 for passive bribery involving a public official.[82]

Similar penalties are provided for influence peddling involving domestic public officials or judicial staff.[83]

For example, on March 8, 2017, the Court of Cassation approved the Paris Court of appeal's ruling of 15 September 2016, sentencing an individual to three years imprisonment, including eighteen months' probation, a fine of €15,000 and ten years ban on managing or administrating for, among other things, active influence peddling toward a domestic public

---

[80] The SCPC considers that this amount may be increased to 10 times the proceeds generated by the offense.

[81] CA Paris, 12 June 2018; this decision has, to our knowledge, become final.

[82] CA Aix-en-Provence, 22 November 2017; this decision is not final.

[83] Penal Code, articles 432-11, 433-1, 433-2, and 434-9-1.

official. [84] In another case, a former judge in Béthune (France) was convicted by the Paris Court of Appeal, on April 13, 2018, for influence-peddling and sentenced to five years forfeiture of civic and civil rights as he made money out of complacent judgments in 2010. Seven other defendants who had sought interventions in their favour or the judge's clemency, were also sentenced on the ground of influence-peddling. [85]

Bribery of domestic judicial staff for the benefit or to the detriment of a person who is the subject of criminal prosecution is punishable by a 15-year term of imprisonment.[86]

6. Commercial Bribery

6.1 JURISDICTION

The Inter-regional Specialised Courts do not have expanded jurisdiction over the offense of bribery of private individuals. However, they have jurisdiction over related offenses, such as misuse of corporate assets and, therefore, these courts may hear cases involving bribery of private individuals. Moreover, for highly complex matters, the National Financial Prosecutor and the investigating magistrates of the financial division of the Paris High Court have concurrent jurisdiction with the ordinary courts to conduct enquiries or investigate matters that are particularly complex.[87]

6.2 STATUTE OF LIMITATIONS

The same rules as those discussed previously (see Section 4.2 above) apply here as well.

6.3 COMMERCIAL BRIBERY OFFENSES

The Penal Code prohibits both active and passive bribery of private individuals.

The bribe-taker must not be a person who holds public authority, or who has a public service mission, or who holds a public elected office. Moreover, such person must, in connection with a professional or corporate activity, hold a management position with or be employed by an individual, a legal entity, or any type of organization. Therefore, the scope of the law encompasses all managers and employees, but also covers the members of the learned professions and volunteers. The structure to which such person is attached may be a legal entity or individual, but also a group without legal personality.

Law No. 2011-2012 of 29 December 2011 to reinforce the health safety of medicines and health products was adopted in order to extend the scope of the so-called anti-gift law of January 27, 1993, which regulates the relationships between companies that market health products and health professionals, to students training to become health professionals and to the associations that represent them. Under these provisions, a certain number of health

---

[84] Cass. Crim. Ch., 8 March 2017, No. 15-85.820.
[85] Paris Court of Appeal, 13 April 2018, No. 17/00067; this decision has, to our knowledge, become final.
[86] Penal Code, article 434-9.
[87] Code of Criminal Procedure, article 705.

professionals are prohibited from receiving cash or non-cash benefits from companies that provide services or produce or market products covered by the mandatory social security plans.[88]

Influence peddling involving private individuals is also prohibited.[89]

6.4 GIFTS, GRATUITIES, AND HOSPITALITY

For these purposes, the Penal Code also applies to offers, promises, donations, gifts, and advantages. On this topic, the Court of Cassation has held that the advantages in question may be in the form of percentages of financial transactions[90] or a stake in the capital of a company.[91]

6.5 DEFENSES

6.5.1 Written Local Law

Similarly to other corruption offenses, French laws prohibiting bribery of private individuals do not provide for any specific defenses (see Section 4.6.1 above).

6.5.2 Facilitation Payments

See Section 4.6.2 above.

6.5.3 Adequate procedures

See Section 4.6.3 above.

6.5.4 Corporate Culture

See Section 4.6.4 above.

6.6 PENALTIES

Active and passive bribery of private individuals by individuals is punishable by a five-year term of imprisonment and a fine of €500,000—which may be increased to an amount equal to double the proceeds generated by the offense[92]—as well as supplemental penalties,[93] whereas legal entities are liable for a fine of €2.5 million—which may be increased to an

---

[88] Public Health Code, article L. 4113-6.

[89] Penal Code, article 433-2.

[90] Cass. crim., 19 June 2013, No. 12-83.031.

[91] Cass. crim., 18 September 2001, No. 01-80.716.

[92] Penal Code, articles 445-1 and 445-2.

[93] Penal Code, article 445-3.

amount equal to double[94] the proceeds generated by the offense, as well as supplemental penalties.[95]

Influence peddling involving private individuals is punishable by similar penalties.[96]

In a decision dated June 20, 2015, that has become final, a former European elected official was convicted of active influence peddling for having interceded with the vice president of a region in order to enable the manager of a construction company to obtain authorization to operate an asbestos removal site. The company manager was convicted of passive influence peddling and sentenced to two years imprisonment to be served under electronic supervision, while the other defendant was sentenced to a six-month suspended prison sentence and a fine of €50,000.[97]

7. Sentencing Principles

7.1 GENERAL PRINCIPLES

The discretion of judges to determine penalties is one of the fundamental principles of the French criminal law. The judge has full discretion to choose, from among the penalties applicable to the offense, those he deems appropriate in light of the nature of the acts and the personality of the defendant. Accordingly, the judge may impose only one of the possible penalties.[98] The judge also has significant discretion to determine the quantum of the penalty, with the only restriction being the maximum prescribed by law (the law does not provide for minimum sentences).[99]

However, the judge must in all cases explain the grounds for his decision if he imposes a prison sentence that is not suspended and provides for no adjustments to the penalty, which partly explains the low number of non-suspended prison sentences handed down to date in corruption cases.[100]

Furthermore, a basic principle of French law is that sentences are not consecutive, which means that if several penalties of the same type are possible because more than one offense has been committed, only one penalty of such type may be imposed, up to the highest statutory maximum penalty.[101]

7.2 STATE/REGIONAL SENTENCING APPROACH

France is not a federal country. Therefore, the distinction between the state/regional approach and federal approach is not relevant with respect to French law.

---

[94] The SCPC considered that this amount may be increased to 10 times the proceeds generated by the offense.

[95] Penal Code, article 445-4.

[96] Penal Code, articles 433-2, 433-22, and 433-23.

[97] CA Aix-en-Provence, 30 June 2015, No. 2015/268.

[98] Penal Code, article 132-17.

[99] Penal Code, articles 132-19 and 132-20.

[100] Penal Code, article 132-19.

[101] Penal Code, articles 132-2 and 132-3.

The 2017 AFA report has shown that prosecutors handled 758 proceedings relating to probity offenses in 2016, that amongst those the most frequently prosecuted offenses were bribery (134 prosecutions), misappropriation of public property (91 prosecutions), illegal taking of interest (64 prosecutions) and influence-peddling (23 prosecutions). Eventually, in 2016, there were 253 convictions for offenses to probity. 44% of them resulted in the imposition of a fine and 67% resulted in a prison sentence. Of the 67% prison sentences handed down, 22% were non-suspended.[102]

As seen previously, the French parliament has provided stiff penalties for acts of corruption. However, the dissuasive effect of these penalties is attenuated by the low number of prosecutions and convictions, and by the fact that the penalties actually imposed in the event of a conviction are significantly lower than the statutory maximums.

Nevertheless, the decision rendered on February 26, 2016, that was discussed above (see Section 4.6.5 above) suggests that the courts will be increasingly severe in the future.[103]

7.3 FEDERAL SENTENCING APPROACH

See Section 7.2 above.

7.4 DOMESTIC VERSUS FOREIGN BRIBERY

It is the intent of the French legislature to punish bribery of foreign public officials as severely as bribery of domestic public officials. Moreover, the required elements of these two offenses are nearly identical.

Few of the convictions handed down in corruption cases were on the grounds of bribery of foreign public officials. The follow-up to the Phase 3 report for France, which was published in 2014, shows that since the OECD Convention came into force, only 58 procedures have been initiated for bribery of foreign public officials, of which 24 new procedures were initiated since the publication of the Phase 3 report in 2012. It also shows that between 2012 and 2014, only three individuals were convicted, resulting in fines ranging from €5,000 to €20,000, and that 11 new cases concerning legal entities had been closed with no further action or dismissed, or had ended in discharge.

8. Related Criminal Offenses

8.1 CONSPIRACY

For certain offenses, the French criminal law provides for an aggravation of the possible penalty if the offense is committed by an organized gang,[104] such as in cases involving money laundering or receiving the proceeds of an offense. Such a provision does not exist for corruption offenses.

---

[102] AFA, Anual Activity Report, 2017.

[103] CA Paris, 26 February 2016, No. 13/09208.

[104] An organized gang is any group formed or any arrangement made for preparation purposes, which is established by one or more material elements of one or more offenses (Penal Code, article 132-71).

8.2 ATTEMPT

Attempted bribery is not specifically criminalized because the offense of bribery is committed merely by a request or proposal, as well as by mere agreement or acceptance—a corruption pact creates a link, in the mind of the perpetrator of the offense, between the advantage requested or offered and the act expected of the bribe-taker, but such pact does not necessarily require an express agreement between the bribe-giver and the bribe-taker—without the need for the advantage offered or requested to be actually conferred or the subsequent act to be performed (see Section 2.1 above).

8.3 AIDING AND ABETTING

Under French law, an individual or legal entity who knowingly, by providing aid or assistance, facilitates the preparation or commission of an offense, or any person who through a gift, promise, threat, order or abuse of authority or power induces the commission of an offense or who gives instructions to commit an offense, is considered to be an accomplice to such offense.[105] The accomplice is subject to the same penalties as the principal perpetrator of the offense.[106]

For example, the Court of Cassation convicted an individual for aiding and abetting bribery for having acted as an intermediary by depositing checks into his own bank account on behalf of a mayor who had accepted bribes.[107]

8.4 FALSE ACCOUNTING/BOOKS AND RECORDS

Corruption offenses committed by legal entities generally lead them to devise accounting stratagems enabling them to conceal, in their financial statements, the benefits obtained or paid by using fake invoices, whether the invoice changes the amount of a transaction or is for a nonexistent transaction, which means the financial statements do not accurately reflect the company's results.

It is an offense for the chairman, directors, or executive officers of a joint-stock company to publish or present to the shareholders, even if no dividends are distributed, annual financial statements that do not provide, for each financial year, an accurate view of the results of the company's operations during the financial year or of its financial position and assets at the end of such period.[108]

---

[105] Penal Code, article 121-7.

[106] Penal Code, article 121-6.

[107] Cass. crim., 20 May 2009, No. 08-87.354.

[108] Article L.241-3 of the Commercial Code also provides that managers of limited liability companies (SARL) are liable for a term of imprisonment of up to five years and a fine of up to €375,000 for presenting to the shareholders, even if no dividends are distributed, annual financial statements that do not provide, for each financial year, an accurate view of the results of the company's operations during the financial year or of its financial position and assets at the end of such period, with a view to concealing the company's true situation.

· Individuals convicted for this offense are liable for a fine of up to €375,000 and supplemental penalties,[109] and legal entities risk a fine of up to €1,875,000.[110]

Last, companies whose securities are admitted to trade on a regulated market may also be prosecuted by the French Financial Markets Authority (*Autorité des Marchés Financiers* (AMF)) if they disclose financial information that is false, inaccurate, or deceptive. Such acts are punishable by a financial penalty of €100 millions or ten times the amount of gains generated.[111]

8.5 MONEY LAUNDERING

French law defines money laundering as the act of facilitating, by any means, the false legitimation of the origin of the assets or income of the perpetrator of a felony or misdemeanor that generated a direct or indirect gain for him. Money laundering also comprises the act of assisting in investing, concealing, or converting the direct or indirect proceeds of a felony or misdemeanor.

If committed by an individual, this offense is punishable by up to five years imprisonment and a fine of €375,000.[112] These penalties are increased to 10 years imprisonment and a fine of €750,000 in cases of aggravated money laundering, that is, if money laundering is committed regularly, by taking advantage of the facilities procured by the exercise of a professional activity or by an organized gang.[113] Supplemental penalties[114] may also be imposed.

Moreover, the fine may be increased to half the value of the assets or funds involved in the money laundering transactions. Furthermore, if the underlying offense is punishable by a term of imprisonment that is longer than that provided for money laundering, money laundering is punishable by the penalties applicable to the offense of which the perpetrator was aware. However, if such offense carries aggravating circumstances, the money launderer will be subject only to the penalties applicable to the aggravating circumstances of which he was aware.[115]

Legal entities are liable for a fine of up to €1,875,000, which may be doubled in cases of aggravated money laundering, as well as supplemental penalties.[116]

---

[109] Commercial Code, articles L. 242-6 and L. 242-30. Article L. 249-1 of the Commercial Code provides that individuals convicted of this offense may also incur supplemental penalties, such as being prohibited from holding public office or from engaging in the professional or corporate activity in the performance of which, or in connection with the performance of which, the offense was committed, or being prohibited from engaging in a commercial or industrial profession, or from directly or indirectly directing, administering, managing, or controlling in any capacity, on their own behalf or on behalf of a third party, a commercial or industrial business or a commercial company. These prohibitions against engaging in various types of activities may be imposed cumulatively.

[110] Penal Code, article 131-38.

[111] AMF General Regulation, article 223-1, and Monetary and Financial Code, articles L. 621-15 and L. 621-14.

[112] Penal Code, article 324-1.

[113] Penal Code, article 324-2.

[114] Penal Code, article 324-7.

[115] Penal Code, article 324-4.

[116] Penal Code, article 324-9.

The aforementioned Law of 6 December 2013 facilitated prosecution of this offense by reversing the burden of proof. Now, assets or income are presumed to be the direct or indirect proceeds of a felony or misdemeanor if the physical, legal, or financial circumstances of an investment, concealment, or conversion operation can be explained only by the intent to conceal the origin or actual beneficiary of such assets or income.[117]

Last, it bears noting that the offense of money laundering is a stand-alone offense. In a case involving a person prosecuted on these grounds for having regularly transferred, circulated, and converted the proceeds of active and passive bribery committed in Nigeria, the Court of Cassation held that the laws that define the offense of money laundering do not require the underlying offense that generated the sums that were laundered to have been committed in France or that the French courts have jurisdiction to prosecute such underlying offense.[118]

In the "ill-gotten gains" case, the 32nd Criminal Chamber of the Paris High Court recently sentenced the Vice-President of an African country to three years imprisonment and to pay a fine of €30 million, both sentences being suspended, notably for laundering of the proceeds of corruption. The court also ordered the seizure of many assets in France, for an amount of several millions.[119] This judgment is currently on appeal.

8.6 TAX AND OTHER FRAUDS

The General Tax Code expressly provides that sums paid or benefits granted, directly or through intermediaries, to a public official or a third party to induce such official to act or refrain from acting in the performance of her official duties, with a view to obtaining or retaining a contract or other improper advantage in international commercial transactions, are not deductible from taxable income.[120] The Conseil d'État—the highest French administrative court—recently applied this statute in a case in which a French company had paid €140 million to the U.S. authorities. In that case, the administrative judge stated that if the offense of bribery is committed by an employee of a legal entity, the culpable intent of the legal entity is not required for the sums paid to a public official to be added back into its taxable income.[121]

In addition, prosecution for tax fraud is a possibility because the bribe-giver and the bribe-taker may have an interest in concealing benefits paid or received from the French tax authorities for purposes of calculating tax owed.

Tax fraud is a criminal offense defined as the act, by any person, of fraudulently avoiding or attempting to fraudulently avoid the calculation or payment of all or part of his taxes, or of intentionally failing to file his tax return within the required time periods, or of intentionally

---

[117] Penal Code, article 324-1-1.

[118] Cass. crim., 24 February 2010, No. 09-82.857.

[119] Trib. corr., 32nd ch., 27 October 2017. It is to be noted that for one of the assets, a luxurious apartment bought for €25 million, the seizure will have to wait the outcome of a proceeding pending before the International Court of Justice.

[120] General Tax Code, article 39.

[121] Conseil d'État, 4 February 2015, No. 364708.

concealing any of the sums subject to tax, or of arranging his insolvency or hindering the collection of tax by other maneuvers, or by acting in any other fraudulent manner.

Individuals convicted of tax fraud are subject to a fine of €500,000 and five years imprisonment, in addition to applicable tax penalties. In addition, they are also subject to supplemental penalties.[122] Legal entities are liable for a fine of €2,500,000.[123]

8.7 OTHER KEY RELATED CRIMINAL LAWS

Payments made in connection with corrupt acts may constitute other offenses.

First, use of a company's funds and assets for illicit purposes is necessarily inconsistent with the corporate interest and is therefore a misuse of corporate assets.[124] Under the French criminal law it is an offense for the chairman, directors, or executive officers of a limited company (*société anonyme*),[125] as well as for the de facto managers, in bad faith, to use the assets or credit of a company for purposes they know are contrary to the corporate interest, for personal purposes, or to benefit another company or business is which they have a direct or indirect interest.[126] Individuals are subject to a five-year term of imprisonment and a fine of €375,000, as well as supplemental penalties,[127] whereas legal entities are subject to a fine of €1,875,000.

Second, recipients of the proceeds of corrupt acts, other than the bribe-taker himself, may be prosecuted for receiving the proceeds of an offense. The French criminal law defines this offense as (1) the act of concealing, holding, or transferring an item, or acting as an intermediary in order to transfer such item, with knowledge that such item is the product of a felony or misdemeanor; or (2) the act of knowingly benefitting, in any manner, from the proceeds of an offense. Individuals are subject to a five-year term of imprisonment and a fine of €375,000.[128]

This offense is punishable by ten years imprisonment and a fine of €750,000 if it is committed regularly, by taking advantage of the facilities procured by the exercise of a professional activity or by an organized gang. These fines may be increased to up to half the value of the assets concealed. If the offense that generated the asset concealed is punishable by a longer prison sentence, the defendant is subject to the penalties applicable to such offense if

---

[122] General Tax Code, article 1741. Penalties are increased to a fine of €2,000,000 and seven years imprisonment if the offense is committed by an organized gang or is carried out or facilitated by (1) accounts opened or contracts entered into with organizations established abroad; (2) the interposition of individuals or legal entities or any organization, trust, or comparable institution established abroad; (3) the use of a false identity, forged documents, or any other type of falsification; or (4) a fictitious or artificial tax domicile abroad.

[123] Penal Code, article 131-38.

[124] Cass. crim., 19 September 2007, No. 07-80.533.

[125] Similar provisions apply to other corporate forms.

[126] Commercial Code, article L 242-6.

[127] This offense is punishable by seven years imprisonment and a fine of €500,000 if it is carried out or facilitated by accounts opened or contracts entered into with organizations established abroad, or the interposition of individuals or legal entities or any organization, trust, or comparable institution established abroad.

[128] Penal Code, article 321-1.

she is aware thereof and, if such offense carries aggravating circumstances, she will be subject to the penalties applicable only to the aggravating circumstances of which she was aware.[129]

Legal entities are liable for a fine of €1,875,000, as well as for supplemental penalties.[130]

Last, prosecution for laundering of the proceeds of misuse of corporate assets is also theoretically possible.

9. Cooperation and Self-Reporting

9.1 POWERS OF INVESTIGATORS AND PROSECUTORS

The aforementioned Law of 6 December 2013 considerably enhanced the efficiency of enquiries, prosecutions, and investigative procedures in corruption cases by extending the scope of extraordinary procedural measures, which were originally intended for combating organized crime and delinquency, to corruption offenses. Now, in corruption cases, investigators and prosecutorial agencies may take advantage of measures such as surveillance, infiltration, wiretapping, recording conversations, and filming certain premises or vehicles.[131]

9.2 COOPERATION WITH INVESTIGATORS

The French criminal law does not provide for any special treatment of perpetrators of offenses who cooperate with investigators. However, the cooperation of the accused during the investigation stage and throughout the proceedings and, in the case of legal entities, the adoption of measures intended to reinforce internal anti-corruption systems, may be considered to be mitigating factors by a court when it determines the quantum of the penalty to be imposed. It is to be noted that in the first public interest convention concluded on October 30, 2017, the lack of cooperation of the concerned legal entity with the judicial authorities, as well as the circumstance that it did not report the facts by itself, were stressed out by the National Financial Prosecutor. However, at the time of the investigation, there was no legal incentive to cooperate, which explains why it has not been taken into account in this case. Therefore, it is to be expected that the lack of cooperation will be taken into account by Prosecutors while assessing the amount of the public interest fine to be pronounced.

9.3 SELF-REPORTING

The aforementioned Law of 6 December 2013 introduced the possibility for the perpetrators of, or the accomplices to, an offense of bribery or of influence peddling of public officials or judicial staff[132] to have their penalties reduced by half if, by having informed the administrative or judicial authorities, they enabled putting a stop to the offense or identifying other perpetrators or accomplices, if any.[133] At this time, customs agents have a much greater

---

[129] Penal Code, article 321-2.

[130] Penal Code, article 321-12.

[131] Code of Criminal Procedure, article 706-1-1.

[132] This provision is not available in cases of bribery of private individuals.

[133] Penal Code, articles 432-11-1, 433-2-1, 434-9-2, 435-6-1 and 435-11-1.

incentive to act as informants because the law exempts them from the penalties, fines, and confiscations prescribed by the Penal Code if they report acts of corruption they have committed.[134]

9.4 LENIENCY

French law does not provide any leniency measure, subject to what is provided for self-reporting. However, the court is free to adjust the fine by reference to various factors.

In a decision rendered on December 15, 2015, the Court of Cassation held in the "ill-gotten gains" case that the immunity from jurisdiction that a foreign head of state may have cannot be validly asserted in a case involving an offense he committed for personal purposes before he took office.[135]

9.5 PLEA AGREEMENTS

First of all, Law No. 2011-1862 of 13 December 2011 on the distribution of litigation files and the streamlining of certain court procedures extended the scope of the "appearance pursuant to a prior admission of guilt" procedure (*comparution sur reconnaissance préalable de culpabilité* (CRPC)) to corruption offenses. This procedure allows the Public Prosecutor's office to offer directly and without a trial, of its own initiative or at the request of the accused or his lawyer, one or more penalties to a person who acknowledges the acts of which he is accused.[136] If the accused accepts the penalty(ies) proposed, the presiding judge of the High Court must then approve such penalty(ies). Use of this procedure results in a criminal conviction because the aforementioned court judgment approving the penalty(ies) is deemed a conviction.

Second, as stated previously, the Sapin II law introduced a true settlement procedure, inspired by the US deferred prosecution agreement (DPA), with no acknowledgment of guilt. Called the "public interest judicial convention," this new alternative dispute resolution mechanism is solely available for legal entities suspected of acts of bribery or influence peddling, laundering of tax fraud proceeds and related offenses. Since the entry into force of Law No. 2018-898 of 23 October 2018 relating to the fight against fraud, it is also available for legal entities suspected of tax fraud. This settlement procedure is an option made available for the Public Prosecutor before the opening of criminal proceedings as well as to the Investigating Magistrate before the closing of his investigation, at the request of or in agreement with the Public Prosecutor. Should this procedure be initiated, the accused legal entity may be offered to:

- Pay a fine, called "public interest fine," in proportion to the advantages gained from the offenses within the limit of 30% of the annual average turnover calculated on the basis of the last three turnovers available, with the possibility to spread the fine over a maximum of one year, and/or

---

[134] Customs Code, article 59.

[135] Cass. crim., 15 December 2015, No. 15-83.156.

[136] Code of Criminal Procedure, article 495-7.

- Set up, under the AFA's supervision, a compliance program for up to three years in line with the measures described previously; and, if necessary
- Compensate the victims for their loss. In this respect, Article 41-1-2 of the Code of Criminal Procedure provides that, when the victim is identified, "the agreement also provides for the amount and methods of compensation for a damage caused by the offense."

During a subsequent validation hearing, the President of the High Court decides whether or not to validate the proposed agreement by carrying out a substantial review. Once validated, the legal entity has 10 days to retract. Then, the validation as well as the public interest fine amount and the agreement itself will be published on the AFA's website.

Public prosecution would only be precluded once all obligations have been performed, it being specified that the victim would retain the ability to claim compensation for his/her loss before the civil courts and that the legal entity's executives and employees would remain criminally liable before the criminal jurisdictions.

On October 30, 2017, the Swiss branch of a British bank concluded the first public interest judicial convention—validated by the High Court of Paris on November 4, 2017—with the National Financial Prosecutor's office and agreed to pay €300 million (a €158 million fine and €142 million to the French state as damages) to settle a long-running investigation into tax evasion by French citizens in Switzerland. The amount of the public interest fine was based on two elements: the restitution of the profits derived from the breaches and an additional penalty based on the exceptional gravity of the facts. It should be noted that the additional penalty was not provided for by the Sapin II law. To justify this complementary penalty, the National Financial Prosecutor indicated that the bank *"did not disclose the facts to the French judicial authorities or acknowledge its criminal responsibility during the judicial investigation"* and that it also *"provided minimal cooperation in investigations"*, but stressed out that at the time of the judicial investigation, there was no incentive mechanism to cooperate under French law.

Several conventions have been concluded since then, among which three matters of corruption with French companies.

For example, two French companies have concluded with the Prosecutor of Nanterre, respectively on February 14 and 15, 2018, public judicial interest conventions in relation to domestic bribery acts. They agreed to pay a public interest fine of €2,700,000 and €800,000 respectively as well as to implement a compliance program within respectively a 18-month and 2-year period under the AFA's supervision. Each of them also agreed to pay an amount of €30,000 for compensation of the damages undergone by a third company. In this case, the two French companies were found to have corrupted one employee of a third company, by offering the latter trips and payment of expenses in order to conclude and maintain commercial contracts with the said company. Both conventions were validated by the High Court of Nanterre on February 23, 2018.

More recently, on May 24, 2018, a public interest judicial convention was concluded with a French bank concerning bribery of Lybian public officials. The convention was validated by the High Court of Paris on June 4, 2018. This is the first convention negotiated in cooperation with the US Department of Justice. Indeed, the two prosecuting authorities coordinated their action in order to reach simultaneously the conclusion of a public interest judicial convention and a deferred prosecution agreement (with respect to the Lybian and IBOR matters). Therefore, the French bank has agreed to pay $1.34 billion to resolve the disputes in the United States and France, the sanctions in France being a public interest fine of €250,150,755 and a 2-year supervision of its compliance program by the AFA.

10. Whistle-Blower Protection

10.1 PUBLIC SECTOR WHISTLE-BLOWER PROTECTIONS

Article 40 of the Code of Criminal Procedure requires all public officials and civil servants who, in the performance of their duties, become aware of a felony or misdemeanor to inform the Public Prosecutor's office and provide it with all information in relation thereto.

Well before the adoption of the Sapin II law, French law provided a protective mechanism for public sector whistle-blowers.[137] Since then, a general status for whistle-blowers has been created, protecting them from a broad range of retaliatory measures (see Section 10.3 below).

10.2 PRIVATE SECTOR WHISTLE-BLOWER PROTECTIONS

Statutory auditors are required, under criminal penalties if they do not, to report to the Public Prosecutor criminal acts of which they become aware, and incur no criminal liability for doing so, including on the grounds of making malicious accusations. They are also required to report to Tracfin transactions involving sums that they know, suspect, or have good reason for suspecting originate from an offense punishable by a prison sentence of more than one year or that contribute to financing terrorism (see Section 13.1).[138]

The Sapin II law enhanced the existing protective mechanism[139] for private sector whistle-blowers (see Section 10.3 below).

---

[137] Since the aforementioned Law of 6 December 2013, reporting felonies and misdemeanours committed in the civil service was not only a duty, but also a right. The protective system created provided that no measure concerning inter alia recruitment, tenure, training, evaluation, discipline, promotion, assignment or transfers may be taken against any civil servant because he has in good faith reported or testified about acts that are the constituent elements of a felony or misdemeanour of which he becomes aware in the performance of his duties. Any contrary provision or act was automatically void (Article 6 ter A of the Law of 13 July 1983, as amended by Law No. 2013-1117 of 6 December 2013).

[138] Commercial Code, articles L. 823-12 and L.820-7.

[139] The aforementioned Law of 13 November 2007 added a provision to the French Employment Code that prohibited any person from being denied employment, an internship, or training, or being disciplined, dismissed, or discriminated against, directly or indirectly, for having in good faith reported or testified, to his employer or the judicial or administrative authorities, about acts of corruption of which he becomes aware in the performance of his duties. Any contrary termination of an employment contract and, more broadly, any contrary provision or act was automatically void (Employment Code, article L. 1161-1). In the same way, the aforementioned Law of 6 December 2013 provided additional protections for whistle-blowers by extending this protective mechanism to all felonies and misdemeanours that a person reported and of which he becomes aware of in the performance of his duties. The new provisions added to the Employment Code provided that such report may be made to any person, including the press (Employment Code, article L. 1132-3-3.)

10.3 ATTITUDE TOWARD WHISTLE-BLOWERS

The efforts of the French legislature have not yet led to a total change in the historical French reticence to such "informant" mechanisms.

Nevertheless, many major companies, well before the introduction of the Sapin II law provisions, had already set up whistle-blower systems notwithstanding the lack of legislative provisions thereon. Such systems are seen, above all, as a tool to prevent the financial and reputational risks that a company could face if criminal acts are made public.

In whistle-blowing cases, certain courts ruled in favor of the whistle-blower, including in a situation to which the Law of 6 December 2013 was not yet applicable.[140] Thus, in a decision rendered on May 21, 2015, the Grenoble Court of Appeal invalidated the dismissal of an employee that occurred after he reported acts of corruption to his supervisors.[141]

As stated previously, the Sapin II law provides enhanced protection for whistle-blowers by creating (1) a general status for whistle-blowers; (2) an obligation for public and private companies that employ at least 50 employees to adopt an internal whistle-blowing system; and (3) a new specific protection for whistle-blowers in the financial sector.

Under this new system, whistle-blowers, when fulfilling with certain conditions, will benefit from immunity against discriminatory and retaliatory measures committed by their employer[142] as well as against criminal prosecution for breach of secrecy,[143] except with regard to secrets that concern national defence, lawyer-client privilege and medical confidentiality.[144]

In order to be illegible to the protective mechanism, the person reporting an unlawful act has to:

- Match with the definition provided by the Sapin II law, that is, "*an individual who reports, selflessly and in good faith, a crime or an offense, a serious and obvious breach of an international commitment duly ratified or approved by France, of a unilateral act from an international organization issued on the basis of such commitment, of law or regulation, or a serious threat or harm to the public interest, of which he has personal knowledge;*"[145]
- Comply with the reporting procedure.[146]

Should these conditions be met, any person obstructing the escalation of the alert shall be punishable by up to one year of imprisonment and a €15,000 fine. Moreover, any

---

[140] CA Basse-Terre, 13 October 2014, No. 13/00225.

[141] CA Grenoble, 21 May 2015, No. 12/04109.

[142] Employment Code, article L. 1132-3-3.

[143] Penal Code, article 122-9.

[144] Sapin II law, article 6.

[145] Sapin II law, article 6.

[146] The alert needs to be reported in priority to the supervisor, the employee or any designated adviser. In the absence of response from the latter within a reasonable time, this alert can be sent to the judicial authority, the administrative authority or professional bodies. That said, a further lack of response from authorities within three months enables the whistle-blower to make the alert publicly available. As an exception, this process can be bypassed in case of serious and imminent danger or risk of irreversible damage (Sapin II law, article 8).

discriminatory or retaliatory measure taken by an employer against a whistle-blower will be null and void under French labor law.[147] Defamation complaints are also discouraged since the maximum fine that may be ordered against plaintiffs for abusive or dilatory complaints are increased from €15,000 to €30,000.[148]

Lastly, the identity of the whistle-blower and of the person referred to in the alert, as well as the information received, must remain confidential. The unlawful disclosure of an information that could lead to the identification of a whistle-blower is punishable by up to two years of imprisonment and a fine of up to €30,000.[149]

11. Key International Treaties Relating to Bribery and Corruption

To a great extent, the French anti-corruption legal framework is the result of the transposition by France of the anti-corruption international conventions it has ratified, that is:

- The European Union convention on the fight against corruption involving officials of the European Communities or officials of member states;[150]
- The OECD Convention on Combating Bribery of Foreign Public Officials in International Business Transactions;[151]
- The Council of Europe criminal and civil law conventions on corruption of 27 January 1999 and 4 November 1999, respectively;[152]
- The additional protocol to the Council of Europe criminal law convention on international corruption;[153]
- The United Nations Convention against Corruption.[154]

12. Mutual Legal Assistance Treaties and Transnational Cooperation

France is a party to numerous multilateral and bilateral judicial cooperation agreements in criminal matters, and recent cases prove the effectiveness of this cooperation. As the OECD itself noted in its Phase 3 report, requests for assistance in corruption matters are successfully handled, although the response times are generally long.[155]

Unless otherwise agreed, requests submitted by national authorities to their foreign counterparts go through the Ministry of Justice's Office of Assistance in Criminal Matters,

---

[147] Employment Code, articles L. 1332-3 and L. 1332-4.

[148] Sapin II law, article 13.

[149] Sapin II law, article 9.

[150] Signed on May 26, 1997, before its ratification was authorised by Law No. 99-423 of 27 May 1999.

[151] Signed by France on December 17, 1997 before its ratification was authorised by Law No. 99-424 of 27 May 1999.

[152] The ratification of which was authorised by France by the Law of 25 April 2008.

[153] Signed on May 15, 2003 before its ratification was authorised by Law No. 2007-1154 of 1 August 2007.

[154] Signed by France on October 31, 2003 before its ratification was authorised by Law No. 2005-743 of 4 July 2005.

[155] Phase 3 Report on Implementing the OECD Anti-Bribery Convention in France, p. 64.

whereas requests from foreign authorities are transmitted through diplomatic channels.[156] These formalities result in relatively long response times. In fact, the transmission of mutual assistance requests is usually slightly faster within the European Union because judicial authorities can communicate directly with each other.[157]

If offenses are prosecuted by the British or American authorities pursuant to the Bribery Act or Foreign Corrupt Practices Act, the French criminal law does not prevent parallel criminal prosecutions in France. For example, parallel investigations were conducted in France and the United States in the "ill-gotten gains" case. Actually, the PNF is developing international cooperation in many matters. The public interest judicial convention above-mentioned concluded on June 2018 is a perfect example of such international cooperation.

13. Legal Professional Privilege
13.1 PRINCIPLES

Lawyers are bound by professional confidentiality and incur criminal liability if they breach such confidentiality.[158]

To make this professional confidentiality truly effective, Article 434-1 of the Penal Code exempts lawyers from the duty to report felonies and misdemeanors. However, lawyers have an ethical obligation to withdraw from a matter in the event of doubt about the legality of their client's transaction, and they can be lawfully prosecuted if they take part in an offense.

Order No. 2009-104 of 30 January 2009 to prevent the use of the financial system for purposes of money laundering and the financing of terrorism has shrunk this principle somewhat. Similarly to banks, investment service providers, chartered accountants, and statutory auditors, lawyers are required to report transactions involving sums that they know, suspect, or have good reason for suspecting originate from an offense punishable by a prison sentence of more than one year or that contribute to financing terrorism. Such report is submitted to the president of the Bar Association, who will decide whether the report should be forwarded to Tracfin.

However, lawyers are not required to submit such reports if their actions are in relation to a court procedure or if they are providing a legal consultation.[159]

13.2 APPLICATION TO INTERNAL INVESTIGATIONS

French law does not recognize the concept of an in-house lawyer. The professional secrecy only covers the relationship between a lawyer (admitted to the local Bar) and his client.[160]

---

[156] Code of Criminal Procedure, article 694.

[157] Code of Criminal Procedure, article 695-1.

[158] Penal Code, article 226-13.

[159] Monetary and Financial Code, articles L. 561-1 to L. 561-4.

[160] On December 11, 2014, a bill containing a provision for the extension of the duty of professional secrecy to in-house lawyers was submitted to the National Assembly but was ultimately rejected.

Lawyers, as well as auditors, however, can intervene as internal investigators since this activity falls within the scope of the lawyer profession.[161] In this respect, the Paris Bar Council formulated precise ethics rules pertaining to internal investigations.

13.3 APPLICATION TO EXTERNAL INVESTIGATION

Article 66-5 of the law of 31 December 1971 protects any written communication addressed by a lawyer to his client (correspondence, meeting notes, and generally all documents forming parts of the client's file) or by a lawyer to his opposing counsels.

In civil and commercial matters, the doctrine of privilege is binding and respected by regulatory and other investigative bodies, which cannot order the production of, nor rely upon, documents protected by professional confidentiality while investigating and carrying out checks. In criminal, customs, and tax matters, subject to one condition provided by the Code of criminal procedure (see Section 13.4), documents protected by professional confidentiality cannot be seized during searches.

13.4 PRACTICAL ISSUES

Professional confidentiality is not an absolute protection. Therefore, it cannot be validly asserted against the judicial authorities if the lawyer is suspected of having taken part in an offense.

A lawyer's telephone may also be tapped if her client is suspected of having taken part in a felony or misdemeanor, and such measure will be upheld. For example, the Court of Cassation recently upheld wiretap measures employed against two lawyers in a case in which they themselves could potentially be bothered—a decision that caused quite a stir.[162]

Furthermore, lawyers must be particularly vigilant in connection with their advisory work or if they handle funds.

14. Privacy and Data Protection

14.1 PRINCIPLES

Further to the Code of Criminal Procedure, the French judicial authorities may order any person, establishment, or organization, whether public or private, or any public services likely to possess any documents relevant to the inquiry in progress, including those produced from a registered computer or data processing system, to provide them with these documents.[163] The duty of professional secrecy may not be given, without legitimate grounds, as a reason for noncompliance.[164] Where such orders relate notably to lawyers, the transfer of these documents may only take place with their consent.

---

[161] Paris Bar Council deliberation dated March 8, 2016.

[162] Cass. crim., 22 March 2016, No. 15-83.207.

[163] Code of Criminal Procedure, articles 60-1, 77-1-1 and 99-3.

[164] According to the Cour de cassation (Cass. crim., 15 March 2016: No. 15-90023), it is only in "exceptional circumstances" that it would be possible not to comply with a judicial order on the grounds of the duty of

With the abovementioned exception, the failure to respond to such an order as quickly as possible is punished by a fine of €3,570 for individuals and €17,850 for legal persons.

Moreover, further to the Penal Code, the Public Prosecutor, an investigating magistrate, or a court to which a matter has been referred may obtain necessary financial or tax information from the parties, any government body, any financial institution, or any other person holding funds of the accused, and no confidentiality obligation may be asserted in opposition thereto.[165]

Therefore, banking secrecy[166] and, more broadly, business secrecy cannot be asserted against the judicial authorities in criminal matters. Legal privilege has been dealt with in Section 13 of this chapter.

Moreover, no one may invoke the intimacy of private life or the secrecy of correspondence against the judicial authorities in criminal matters (see Section 14.3 below).

However, French law specifically protects information classified as a national defense secret, which is defined as information which if disclosed or accessed would be detrimental to the national defense or could lead to discovery of a national defense secret.[167] Accordingly, the Penal Code prohibits the act, by any person, of destroying, misappropriating, stealing, reproducing, granting access to any non-qualified person or disclosing to the public, or allowing such disclosure, including through carelessness or negligence, of any process, object, document, information, computer network, computer data, or file that has been classified as a national defense secret.[168]

Defense secrecy may be asserted against any person, including magistrates investigating acts of corruption. However, such magistrates may request that the National Defence Secrecy Advisory Commission (*Commission Consultative du Secret de la Défense Nationale* (CCSDN)) lift defense secrecy. The CCSDN will give its opinion to the competent Minister, who has sole discretion to decide whether information should be declassified.

Last, the Law of 26 July 1968, as amended, prohibits any person from requesting, searching for, or disclosing, in writing, orally, or in any other form, economic, commercial, industrial, financial, or technical documents or information for use as evidence in foreign judicial or administrative proceedings or in connection therewith outside the framework of international treaties and agreements as well as statutes and regulations in force. A similar prohibition applies if the disclosure of such information would be detrimental to France's sovereignty, security, or essential economic interests, or to public order. Violations of this prohibition are punishable by a prison sentence of six months and a fine of €18,000, or by one of these penalties only.[169] Legal entities are subject to a fine of €90,000. One of AFA's duty is to ensure proper implementation of the French bloking statutes.

---

professional secrecy. However, to the best of our knowledge, there is to date no case law on the subject that would allow determining what these "exceptional circumstances" could be.

[165] Penal Code, article 132-22.

[166] Monetary and Financial Code, article 511-33.

[167] Penal Code, article 413-9.

[168] Penal Code, articles 413-10 and 413-11.

[169] Law No. 68-678 of 26 July 1968, as amended, on the disclosure of documents and information of an economic, commercial, industrial, financial, or technical nature to foreign individuals or legal entities.

14.2 APPLICATION TO INTERNAL INVESTIGATIONS

Inside a company, the employee's intimacy of private life and the right to the secrecy of his/her correspondence is protected. Under French law, any emails sent or received by an employee from or on his or her employer-provided-device—as well as files stored on a company-owned computer—are presumed to be of a professional nature and can be checked or disclosed by the employer, unless they are clearly identified as "personal" or "private." In that case, French law affords considerable protection of the confidentiality of such employees' personal correspondence/files to which an employer can access under very strict conditions only.

A company could seek to obtain, before any trial and under certain conditions, a court order that would authorize a bailiff to retrieve and secure evidence stored on a hard drive if that evidence is necessary to establish the facts upon which the resolution of the case depends.[170]

14.3 APPLICATION TO EXTERNAL INVESTIGATIONS

Under French law, an employer, when requested by a judicial authority by way of a judicial order to provide its employees' private emails, cannot refuse to comply with such order by arguing that it would be violating the secrecy of private correspondence.

A company could seek to obtain the abovementioned court order toward another company.

14.4 PRACTICAL ISSUES

In some criminal matters such as the "Taiwanese frigates" case,[171] the competent Ministers have refused to lift defense secrecy. However, in many others, such secrecy was lifted.

In a decision dated December 12, 2007, the Criminal Chamber affirmed a Court of Appeal decision that imposed a €10,000 fine on a French lawyer for having searched, in France, for information about the conditions surrounding the takeover of a U.S. insurance company for use as evidence in U.S. proceedings outside the framework of international treaties and agreements.[172]

15. Forecast for Reforms and Parting Thoughts

15.1 LEGISLATIVE REFORMS

As described previously, the Sapin II law is a huge step for France in its fight against bribery. Consequently, it is quite early to expect any new legislative reform in this field of law. However, Mr Charles Duchaine, a former investigating magistrate recently appointed as President of the AFA, is already promoting the expansion of the AFA's jurisdiction over foreign legal entities' subsidiaries since under the Sapin II law, it has jurisdiction only regarding French companies and their subsidiaries.

---

[170] Code of Civil Procedure, article 145.

[171] "*The Bunker of Defence Secrecy*," L'EXPRESS, August 5, 2008.

[172] Cass. crim., 12 December 2007, No. 07-83.228.

15.2 POLITICAL AND AGENCY ENFORCEMENT WILL

The various reforms adopted in 2013, as well as the Sapin II law quite clearly demonstrate the determination of the France to combat corruption.

All of the various authorities in charge of fighting corruption have shown a similarly strong resolve. Éliane Houlette, the National Financial Prosecutor, as well as Charles Duchaine have on several occasions expressed their intent to effectively combat corruption. The same is true of the criminal courts, as illustrated by recent cases. Furthermore, the conclusion of the first public interest judicial conventions illustrate this trend.

Moreover, civil agencies demonstrate their activism on a daily basis, in particular by the various guidelines they have published for companies or whistle-blowers.

APPENDIX

Key Issues	France's Approach
Is jurisdiction subject to any international anti-corruption conventions? If so, which? (OECD, UN Convention against Corruption, etc.)	Yes: • the European Union convention on the fight against corruption involving officials of the European Communities or officials of member states • the OECD Convention on Combating Bribery of Foreign Public Officials in International Business Transactions • the Council of Europe criminal and civil law conventions on corruption of 27 January 1999 and 4 November 1999, respectively • the additional protocol to the Council of Europe criminal law convention on international corruption • the United Nations Convention against Corruption
Is bribery of foreign public officials illegal (do domestic anti-bribery laws provide for extraterritorial application)?	Yes
What is the definition of foreign public officials?	The law covers any person who holds public authority, has a public service mission, or holds a public elected office. Furthermore, these persons must perform their duties in a foreign state or within an international organization, which includes organizations created pursuant to the European Union treaty.
Is commercial bribery illegal?	Yes

(Continued)

Key Issues	France's Approach
Is bribing domestic officials illegal?	Yes
Can the receipt of a bribe be prosecuted?	Yes
Can companies be held criminally liable? If so, what is the requisite intent for criminal liability to attach?	Yes A legal entity is criminally liable for offenses committed by its corporate bodies or representatives on its behalf.
Can companies be held civilly liable? If so, what is the requisite intent for civil liability to attach?	Yes
Can individuals be held civilly liable?	Yes
Is there a "facilitation/grease payments"' exception?	No
Does the subject country provide for conspiracy liability relating to violations of the anti-corruption laws?	No
Does the subject country provide for (a) aiding/abetting liability relating to violations of the anti-corruption laws? (b) attempt liability relating to violations of the anti-corruption laws?	(a) Yes (b) NA, the offense of corruption is constituted by mere solicitation or by the acceptance of an offer
Is failure to keep accurate books and records a criminal and/or civil offense?	Yes
Do any books and records violations have to involve underlying bribery proof?	No
Are there laws concerning a company's financial internal controls? If so, are those laws applicable to private and public companies or just public companies?	Yes They are applicable to both private and public companies.

Key Issues	France's Approach
Is there an affirmative disclosure obligation for potential violations of the anti-bribery laws or accounting irregularities?	Yes
Are "promotional expenses" exempt from the anti-bribery laws?	No
Is the giving of gifts, entertainment, travel, meals, etc. restricted/prohibited?	Not specifically prohibited but restricted in practice.
Are there any laws concerning things of value conveyed by, or to, third parties?	Yes
Are bribes tax deductible?	No
Is the law applied extraterritorially?	Yes
Is having a robust corporate compliance program an affirmative defense or way to negate liability?	No
Is there a "local law" exception/defense?	No
Is "credit" given for cooperation with authorities? If so, how and in what form?	The law provides that persons who report acts of corruption they have committed may receive reduced penalties.
Does the subject country have a Mutual Legal Assistance Treaty with the United States that generally covers criminal matters, including the FCPA?	France concluded a bilateral treaty on mutual assistance in criminal matters with the United States on December 10, 1998. That treaty does not specifically concern the FCPA.
What are the potential penalties/sanctions both for civil and criminal violations?	For each corruption offense, fines and terms of imprisonment may be imposed, as well as supplemental penalties. In addition, the perpetrators of the offense may be ordered to compensate the loss caused to the victims. Corrupt acts are deemed null and void.

8   Germany

1. Introduction to Germany's Anti-Corruption Legislation

1.1 INTRODUCTION

One of the largest corruption scandals in German corporate history found its end in 2008 leading to an aftermath milestone judgment of the Munich District Court in December 2013 setting out the key requirements necessary for the effective fight against corruption in the German corporate world.[1] The affected German conglomerate company had claimed civil damages in the amount of EUR 15 million against its former CFO who was responsible for the company's compliance system at the relevant time. The judges set out in great detail how a compliance management system needs to be set up in order to prevent bribery of foreign officials. Further, the judges stated that the functioning of a compliance management system lies in the sole and ultimate responsibility of the management board. If a board member simply delegates the compliance responsibility to a compliance organization without close monitoring, supervision, and guidance, he is—per the court—in breach of his organizational duty as a board member to ensure legal conduct by the company. In case of failure of the compliance system, all board members are then jointly and severally liable for damages resulting from a violation of this obligation. This important judgment was another wake-up call for the German companies to re-enforce and double-check the efficiency of their compliance management systems in order to fight corruption effectively—and to protect the board members from personal liability.

---

[1] This chapter was contributed by Dentons' Michael Malterer and Raphael Won-Pil Suh.

From Baksheesh to Bribery. T. Markus Funk and Andrew S. Boutros.
© Oxford University Press 2019. Published 2019 by Oxford University Press.

1.2   NEW GERMAN ANTI-CORRUPTION LAW

In 2015, the German government has made noticeable efforts in its fight against corruption. Notably in November 2015, the German parliament passed the new German Anti-Corruption Law (*Gesetz zur Bekämpfung der Korruption*). The new law amends a number of provisions of the German Criminal Code (GCC) with a view to adjusting German law to European and international law requirements. Key elements are—among others—the extension of the criminal offense of taking and giving bribes in commercial business, the expansion of the criminal offense of bribing public officials, and the extraterritorial applicability of German bribery laws.

1.3   DRAFT BILL FOR ANTI-CORRUPTION LAW IN THE
HEALTHCARE SECTOR

Further, in October 2015, the German government adopted a draft proposal for the implementation of a new criminal offense of taking and giving bribes in the healthcare sector in section 299a GCC (*Bestechlichkeit und Bestechung im Gesundheitswesen*). These legislative efforts were essentially triggered by a decision of the German Federal Court of Justice (*Bundesgerichtshof*) on March 29, 2012. In this decision, the court ruled that contract doctors in private practice (*niedergelassene Vertragsärzte*) were not to be classified as "public officials" or "agents" in light of German criminal law. Hence, illegal benefits granted by representatives of the pharmaceutical industry to such doctors in order to encourage them to prescribe certain drugs currently do not fall under German criminal anti-corruption law. Section 299a GCC now eliminates this disparity and penalizes active and passive bribery of medical professionals with the intent to achieve a favorable treatment of the respective drugs in domestic or foreign competition.

1.4   NEED FOR IMPROVEMENTS IN THE FIGHT AGAINST CORRUPTION

Despite these legislative efforts in the fight against corruption, according to the Executive Opinion Survey for 2015 of the World Economic Forum the reputation of the German corporate world with regard to its integrity seems to take constant damage. Edda Müller, Chairperson of Transparency International in Germany, states that Germany should not be dazzled by the rise in the 2015 Corruption Perceptions Index. In fact, she points out that the recent compliance and corruption scandals in the automobile, sports, and financial services sectors in Germany have proven the opposite and hence, there is much work to be done regarding integrity.

1.5   OVERVIEW

This chapter will give an overview on Germany's current fight against corruption on a corporate, political, and legislative level. It serves to give the reader from a non-German jurisdiction a first impression on the current environment in Germany regarding the fight against corruption.

2. Germany's Domestic Anti-Corruption Framework

The criminal law regime on anti-corruption in Germany is mainly codified in the German Criminal Code (*Strafgesetzbuch*—StGB) and the Law on Combating International Bribery (*Gesetz zur Bekämpfung internationaler Bestechung*—IntBestG). Further, provisions are contained in the Administrative Offenses Act regarding corporate liability.

2.1.1 New Anti-Corruption Law in 2015

The key provisions on bribery and corruption are stipulated in sections 299 and 331 et. seq. of the German Criminal Code (GCC). These and further provisions in the GCC were amended in November 2015 when the German parliament enacted the Law on Fighting Corruption (*Gesetz zur Bekämpfung der Korruption*). The new law not only extends the applicability of bribery in the commercial and public sector, it also provides for extraterritorial enforcement by the German authorities for bribery of foreign officials. With the new law, the German parliament finally made a big step toward implementing international regulations on fighting corruption into German law.

2.1.2 German Criminal Code

Sections 299 and 331 et. seq. GCC prohibit the accepting and granting of a benefit or a bribe in the commercial and in the public sector:

   (i) Section 299 GCC prohibits active and passive bribery in the commercial sector. This section was amended in November 2015.

  (ii) Section 331 GCC prohibits German and European public officials from accepting or accepting a promise for a benefit for himself/herself or for a third party in exchange for the execution of a legal public service (passive bribery).

 (iii) Section 332 GCC prohibits German and European public officials from requesting, accepting, or accepting a promise for a benefit for himself/herself or for a third party in exchange for the execution of a public service leading to a violation of his/her official duties (passive bribery).

  (iv) Section 333 GCC is the counterpart to Section 331 GCC and prohibits any individual from offering, promising, or granting a benefit to a German or European public official in exchange for the execution of a legal public service (active bribery).

   (v) Section 334 GCC is the counterpart to Section 332 GCC and prohibits any individual from offering, promising, or granting a benefit to a German or European public official in exchange for the execution of a public service leading to a violation of his/her official duties (active bribery).

  (vi) Section 335a GCC extends the criminal liability resulting from sections 331 and 334 to foreign public officials.

2.1.3 Bribery of Legislative Bodies

The Law on Combatting International Bribery (IntBestG) provides for criminal liability for any individual who with the intention to obtain an undue benefit in the international commercial business offers or grants a benefit to a member of a foreign legislative body. This must occur in exchange for the execution of a service related to the respective position. According to section 3 of the Law on Combating International Bribery, to trigger criminal liability it is not relevant where the offense is committed. Decisive is the fact that the offender is a German national.

2.1.4 Personal Criminal Liability

The person who bribes or accepts a bribe can be criminally sanctioned based on the GCC to either pay a monetary fine (calculated based on his personal income and the severity of the offense) or imprisonment of up to 10 years.

2.1.5 Corporate Liability

2.1.5.1 No Corporate Criminal Liability—But Administrative Fines

2.1.5.1.1 LIABILITY UNDER OWIG. Under current German law, corporations as such cannot be held criminally liable, that is, cannot be charged as a criminal defendant. In fact, corporations only face liability for administrative offenses according to the German Administrative Offences Act (*Ordnungswidrigkeitengesetz*—OWiG) leading to administrative fines. Such corporate liability can occur for certain compliance violations committed by the company's management members or for the failure of the management to prevent violations committed by the company's employees through adequate supervision. Such violations include bribery, fraud, money laundering, falsification of books and records, or any crime sanctioned under German law. This also includes violations committed and sanctioned under foreign law (e.g., committed by employees of foreign subsidiaries).

2.1.5.1.2 FINE UNDER OWIG. Prior to June 2013, the maximum administrative fine that could be imposed on a corporation was capped at EUR 1 million in case of intentional misconduct and at EUR 500,000 in case of negligent misconduct. In effect as of June 30, 2013, the maximum fine was increased tenfold to EUR 10 million for intentional conduct and to EUR 5 million for negligent conduct.

The maximum fine can be exceeded without limitation if and to the extent the company's benefits derived from the misconduct exceed such maximum (e.g., profits made under a contract obtained by bribery). Hence, the disgorgement of profits may easily exceed the mere administrative fine amount by multiple times.

2.1.5.1.3 APPLICABILITY. The German Administrative Offenses Act is applicable to all companies with business activities in Germany. In particular, it affects companies operating through Germany-based legal entities, German branches of foreign entities, or foreign persons that have committed crimes or administrative offenses in Germany.

2.1.5.1.4 INCONSISTENT APPROACH REGARDING AFFIRMATIVE DEFENSE AS A WAY TO MITIGATE LIABILITY. The German Administrative Offences Act itself does not stipulate the acknowledgment of adequate compliance management systems as a defense or mitigating factor to decrease the administrative fines. In fact, the respective court or enforcement authority exerts its discretion in each case as to whether to consider factors such as a robust corporate compliance program when deciding whether to charge a corporation or in the assessment of the administrative fine amounts. Statistics have shown that due to lack of a statutory guidance, the enforcing authorities substantially deviate in the consideration of compliance efforts as an affirmative defense.

2.1.5.1.5 DRAFT BILL TO IMPLEMENT AFFIRMATIVE DEFENSE IN OWIG. Hence, in April 2014, the German Association of In-House Counsels (*Bundesverband der Unternehmensjuristen e.V.*) introduced a draft bill that proposed to amend the German Administrative Offences Act, however this draft bill has not yet been accepted by the German legislation. The draft bill aimed to avoid a criminal liability of corporations due to the fact that such corporate criminal liability is nonexistent under German law. Rather, its objective was to implement a statutory defense line for corporations by setting up an effective compliance management system. If the corporation complies with the key compliance elements set out in the draft bill, the authorities shall exert their discretion and take such efforts into consideration when determining the monetary fine.

2.1.5.2 Draft Bill of Law to Establish Corporate Criminal Liability in Germany (Verbandsstrafrecht)

2.1.5.2.1 CORPORATE CRIMINAL LIABILITY. The OECD had criticized Germany that its corporate administrative fines (although increased to EUR 10 million in 2013) are not a sufficient deterrent to corporate misconduct and do not provide enough incentives for companies to establish adequate compliance management systems. Hence, in light of these criticisms, there have been long-standing debates regarding the implementation of criminal prosecution of corporations.

On November 14, 2013, the Conference of Ministers of Justice of the German states resolved to introduce a bill for a Corporate Criminal Code (*Verbandsstrafgesetzbuch*) under which—for the first time—criminal sanctions should be imposed directly against corporations.

2.1.5.2.2 CRIMINAL SANCTIONS. The bill of the Corporate Criminal Code provides for a number of corporate criminal penalties such as monetary fines, loss of subsidies, debarment from public tenders, and—in cases of repeated noncompliance—the dissolution of the company. Especially, the monetary fine could rise to up to 10 percent of the average total revenue of the corporation (i.e., can rise to substantially higher amounts than the statutory administrative maximum fine of EUR 10 million).

2.1.5.2.3 AFFIRMATIVE DEFENSE AS A WAY TO MITIGATE LIABILITY. The bill also proposes that the court may completely waive criminal sanctions if the corporation has adopted adequate organizational measures to prevent similar corporate misconduct in the future. The court may especially waive the criminal sanction if the corporation has materially contributed to have the corporate misconduct uncovered by voluntary disclosure and provided solid evidence to the enforcement authorities, provided, however, that such voluntary disclosure was made prior to the opening of criminal proceedings.

If this bill is enacted, German law would—for the first time—expressly acknowledge the establishment of effective and adequate compliance management systems to prevent future violations and cooperation as mitigating factors to decrease fines, or even to prevent corporate liability for employees' misconduct.

2.2 CIVIL LAW REGIME

In 1999, Germany signed the Civil Law Convention on Corruption that was adopted by the Council of Europe. The convention was designed to ensure that effective civil remedies existed in the laws of the European member states for persons and corporations that had suffered damage as a result of corruption. Germany still has not ratified this convention. However, German civil, tort, and corporate law provides for several legal instruments for the compensation of damages resulting from corruption.

2.2.1 Civil and Tort Law

Corporations that suffered damages due to corruption can claim damages against the contractual partner if an employee of the contractual partner paid bribes to an employee of the bribed corporation. Also, a company can claim damages under civil law and undertake the disciplinary measures under employment law against its employee that committed the corruption offense. Further, German tort law provides for damage claims of bribed companies against the company whose employee committed the offense.

2.2.2 Corporate Law

Corporations that suffer damages due to corruption can also claim civil damages against their own management board members for breaching their managerial duties. This has been reaffirmed by a landmark judgment of the District Court Munich I in December 2013. The court based the damage claim of the claiming company against its former CFO on section 93 para. 2 of the German Stock Corporation Act (*Aktiengesetz*—AktG) which states that "management board members who breach their duties are obliged to compensate the damages the company suffered thereof."

The court stated that such duty comprises the obligation of the management board members to comply with the laws, and further obliges the management board members to provide for an organizational system in the company that prevents violations of the law by its employees. Hence, the management board must establish an efficient compliance system tailored to the specific risk profile of the company. If it fails to do so, the management board members can be held personally and severally liable for respective damages.

The court stated that the management board had—despite numerous indications—not undertaken the necessary measures to prevent the slush funds established for bribing foreign public officials. By omitting to take active steps in investigating any suspected law violations and to take the respective measures, the management board members had violated their board duties, leading to damage claims of the company.

2.3 VIEW FROM THE OUTSIDE
2.3.1 OECD Evaluation

In April 2013, the OECD issued its Follow-Up to the Phase 3 report on Germany's efforts regarding the implementation of the OECD Convention on Combating Bribery of Foreign Public Officials in International Business Transactions. The follow-up report provides information on the progress made by Germany in implementing the recommendations of its Phase 3 report. Whereas the OECD Working Group has appreciated Germany's active corruption enforcement efforts made since 2013 including the increase of the maximum administrative fine from EUR 1 million to EUR 10 million, it has criticized Germany that a number of OECD recommendations have not yet been implemented, for example, a clear definition of facilitation payments and the statutory protection of whistle-blowers.

2.3.2 TI CPI Score

In the 2015 and 2016 Corruption Perceptions Index of Transparency International, Germany each obtained 81 points and ranked 10th place together with Great Britain and Luxembourg. In comparison to 2014, Germany improved by two points and two ranks. This improvement may be due to the German government's noticeable efforts in its fight against corruption. For example, Germany has finally ratified the United Nations Convention against Corruption. Further, the criminal liability in connection with corruption of and with elected officials and political representatives (*Mandatsträger*) was increased.

3. Investigative and Prosecutorial Agencies
3.1 CIVIL LAW AGENCIES

There are no civil law agencies competent for the prosecution of corruption offenses in Germany.

3.2 CRIMINAL LAW AGENCIES

In Germany, the public prosecution offices are the competent criminal law agency for the prosecution of bribery and corruption. These are hierarchically structured. Each German federal state (16 in all) has an independent public prosecution office. The public prosecution office is organized parallel to the respective courts, which means that the territorial competence of public prosecutors is governed by the territorial jurisdiction of the court where the public prosecution office has been established.

In addition, many of the public prosecution offices have additional special units that are exclusively dealing with white collar crime (so called "*Schwerpunktstaatsanwaltschaften*"). These special units have been established on the basis of section 143 para. 4 of the German Court Constitution Act enabling the setup of such specialized public prosecution offices. The objective is to support the units that require specialized know-how and increased manpower (such as e-discovery specialists) with regard to white-collar crime enforcements.

3.3 MULTIAGENCY ARRANGEMENTS

There are no multiagency arrangements regarding the prosecution of corruption offenses in Germany.

4. Bribery of Foreign Officials

4.1 JURISDICTION

Bribing foreign public officials is prohibited under German law. The German Criminal Code sanctions active and passive bribery of foreign public officials.

4.2 STATUTE OF LIMITATIONS

The statute of limitation for bribing foreign officials is a maximum of 10 years and begins after the offense has been completed. The statute of limitation for offenses under the German Administrative Offences Act is a maximum three years.

4.3 FOREIGN BRIBERY OFFENSES

According to sections 331 to 335a of the German Criminal Code, active and passive bribery of foreign public officials is prohibited if the offense concerns a future official act. It is not required that the public act—that is requested in exchange for the bribe—is a legal act or violates the public duties of the foreign official.

4.4 "FOREIGN PUBLIC OFFICIALS" DEFINED

The definition of foreign public official is contained in section 335a GCC.

4.4.1 Definition of Foreign Public Official regarding Bribery Leading to a Legal Public Service

With regard to offenses according to section 331 and 333, section 335a para. 2 GCC stipulates that (1) a member of the International Court of Justice shall be treated as a German judge (*Richter*), and (2) a public servant of the International Court of Justice shall be treated as a public official (*Amtsträger*) in the meaning of German law.

4.4.2 Definition of Foreign Public Official regarding Bribery Leading to an Illegal Public Service

With regard to offenses according to section 332 and 334, section 335a para. 1 GCC stipulates that (1) a member of a foreign or international court shall be treated as a German judge, and (2) the following shall be treated as a foreign public official in the meaning of German law:

(i) a public servant of a foreign country and a person who is authorised to fulfil public tasks for a foreign country,

(ii) a public servant of an international organization and a person who is authorised to fulfil tasks for an international organization, and

(iii) a soldier of a foreign country and a soldier who is authorized to fulfil tasks for an international organization.

4.4.3 Implications

Section 335a GCC was newly implemented in November 2015. Whereas the IntBestG previously only prohibited the active bribery of foreign public officials (i.e., the donor of the bribe committed the crime, not the foreign public official receiving the bribe), section 335a GCC now also criminalizes the acceptance of such bribes by the foreign public official (passive bribery).

As a result of this change, non-German public officials may be prosecuted by German prosecution authorities if they accept a benefit in return for a violation of an official duty associated with a future official act: for example, a Russian customs officer illegally gives preferential treatment to a shipment of a German company in return for a cash payment.

It is expected that the enforcement authorities will continue to focus on active bribery of foreign public officials. But it remains to be seen to what extent German prosecution authorities can and will make use of this additional far-reaching power to prosecute foreign public officials for receiving bribes.

Because the main challenge of this new law will be that the German prosecutors and courts will have to assess the foreign law as to whether (1) the receiver of the bribe is to be classified as a foreign public official, and if yes, (2) he or she actually violated one of its public duties according to the local law. Only when the first foreign public official is convicted by a German court for passive bribery under German law, can we state that the expansion of the law really had an effect.

4.5 GIFTS, GRATUITIES, AND HOSPITALITY

Gifts, gratuities, and hospitality granted to foreign public officials may constitute a benefit within the meaning of German anti-bribery offenses. There is no law or official guidance as to minimum value thresholds in Germany (such as in the United States or UK). Hence, as a result of increased compliance awareness most German companies prohibit any gifts to foreign public officials.

However, German case law provides for an exception if the benefit is deemed "socially acceptable." This term is quite broad and depends upon a variety of factors such as the nature of the gift, or the timely proximity between granting the gift and the generated business. In general, a benefit in the amount of up to EUR 30 is regarded as socially acceptable. Due to the gray area, German prosecutors tend to follow a strict approach and German companies tend to implement internal guidelines that strictly prohibit receiving or granting gifts or invitations of any kind (in particular to public officials).

4.6 DEFENSES

4.6.1 Written Local Law

According to German law, there is no express provision that recognizes defense measures that a company can take to avoid or minimize criminal or administrative fines. Adequate procedures such as a functioning compliance management system are not yet finally recognized as a mean to limit and mitigate the expected sanctions. The new law proposals regarding corporate liability introduce such corporate defense, and we are waiting to see if such proposals become law. Currently, the prosecuting authorities exert their individual discretion on whether to recognize existing adequate procedures in their assessment of the fine.

4.6.2 Facilitation Payments

Facilitation payments, that is, payments for the performance of lawful acts, made to foreign public officials, are not prohibited under German law.

4.6.3 Adequate Procedures

Unlike under the UK Bribery Act, German law does not yet provide for the implementation of adequate procedures in the company to constitute a defense. In fact, management is held fully responsible in cases of corruption even executed on low levels of the company hierarchy. However, there are efforts to introduce adequate procedure benefits into German legislation. As of now, the guidelines for anti-corruption policies in Germany mainly stem from the compliance management system standard called IDW PS 980. This standard was developed by the Institute of German Accountants and consists of seven steps. Number one of these steps and thus the framework for all compliance measures is the "corporate culture." This means that the top management must implement adequate procedures in the company in order to convey an atmosphere of zero tolerance against corruption ("tone from the top"). However, an exemplary corporate culture currently does not (yet) grant the company's management any benefits.

4.6.4 Corporate Culture

As mentioned previously, corporate culture is part of a functioning compliance management system as required under the current standards in Germany. However, the sane corporate culture does still not constitute a defense, and hence, does not prevent the company from being held responsible for acts of corruption.

4.7 PENALTIES

The penalties for bribery of foreign public officials are monetary fines (based on the income and the severity of the offense) and imprisonment of up to 10 years for the acting individual.

Further, the company for which the individual was acting may be sanctioned with an administrative fine of up to EUR 10 million plus disgorgement of the generated profits.

5. Bribery of Domestic Officials

5.1 JURISDICTION

The bribery of domestic officials is stipulated in sections 331 to 334 of the German Criminal Code. The German Criminal Code sanctions active and passive bribery of German public officials.

5.2 STATUTE OF LIMITATIONS

The statute of limitation for bribing German officials is a maximum 10 years and begins after the offense has been completed. The statute of limitation for offenses under the German Administrative Offences Act is a maximum three years.

5.3 DOMESTIC BRIBERY OF OFFICIALS OFFENSES

According to sections 331 to 334 of the German Criminal Code, active and passive bribery of German public officials is prohibited irrespective of whether the public official violates his/her official duties when executing the public act.

5.4 DEFINITION OF DOMESTIC OFFICIALS

5.4.1 Definition

The term "domestic public official" (*Amtsträger*) is defined in section 11 para. 1, no. 2 GCC and includes (1) civil servants and judges, (2) individuals who carry out public official functions, and (3) individuals who have otherwise been appointed to serve with a public authority or agency or have been commissioned to perform public administrative services regardless of the organizational form chosen to fulfill such duties.

5.4.2 State-Owned Entities

The term "domestic public official" also includes employees of private companies that are state-owned. A private company is regarded as being state-owned if the respective state can factually control the business. This is regularly the case if more than 50 percent of the shares are held by the state. However, if private investors have a blocking minority for fundamental matters of the private company, German case law denies factual control held by the state and hence, no state-owned company is given.

5.4.3 Medical Doctors

According to a judgment of the German Federal Court of Justice (*Bundesgerichtshof*), in 2012 contract doctors in private practice (*niedergelassene Vertragsärzte*) were not to be classified as "public officials" or "agents" in light of German criminal law. Hence, illegal benefits granted by pharmaceutical companies to such doctors in order to incentivize them to prescribe their drugs previously did not fall under German anti-corruption law.

The German government adopted a draft proposal in October 2015 for the implementation of a new criminal offense that makes active and passive bribery in the healthcare sector a criminal offense (see section 299a GCC).

5.4.4 European Public Officials

Under the new law, in addition to "public officials" (*Amtsträger*), "European public officials" (*Europäische Amtsträger*) are explicitly included in the criminal offenses of bribing public officials under sections 331 to 334 GCC. Further, section 11 para. 1, no. 2a GCC now contains a legal definition of the term "European public officials" that includes members of the European Commission; the European Central Bank; the European Court of Auditors, and any other court of the European Union; officials and other servants of the European Union; and individuals mandated to execute tasks for the European Union.

5.5 GIFTS, GRATUITIES, AND HOSPITALITY

Also with regards to gifts, gratuities, and hospitality granted to German public officials, there is no official guidance as to the allowed amounts. As a result all gifts, gratuities, and invitations (even of low value) in general may constitute a benefit within the meaning of German anti-bribery offenses. However, the German courts have established case law according to which certain circumstances must be given for the gift to be unlawful. Especially, the gift or any other benefit, in order to be allowed, must be able to be regarded as socially acceptable (*sozial-adäquat*). This may depend on various factors such as the nature of the gift, the occasion. and the role and function of the recipient. Generally, a benefit worth not more than EUR 30 is widely regarded as socially acceptable.

5.6 DEFENSES

5.6.1 Written Local Law

As stated above according to German law, there is no express law that recognizes defense measures that a company can take to avoid or minimize criminal or administrative fines. The new law proposals regarding corporate liability introduce such corporate defense and it is to be awaited if such proposals become law.

5.6.2 Facilitation Payments

Facilitation payments, that is, payments made to German officials for the performance of lawful acts, are prohibited under German law. Especially, section 333 GCC (*"giving bribes"*) states that *"whosoever offers, promises or grants a benefit to a public official, a person entrusted with special public service functions or a soldier in the Armed Forces for that person or a third person for the discharge of a duty shall be liable to imprisonment not exceeding three years or a fine."* That is, it is sufficient to give any benefit (no matter the value). German case law is very restrictive and includes facilitation payments.

5.6.3 Adequate Procedures

The same principles apply as for bribery of foreign public officials. Hence, German law does not yet provide for the implementation of adequate procedures in the company to constitute a defense. Rather, management is held fully responsible in cases of corruption even executed on low levels of the company hierarchy.

5.6.4 Corporate Culture

As mentioned previously, corporate culture is part of a functioning compliance management system as required under the current standards in Germany. However, the sane corporate culture does still not constitute a defense and hence, does not prevent the company from being held responsible for acts of corruption.

5.7 PENALTIES

The penalties for bribery of German public officials are monetary fines and imprisonment of up to 10 years for the acting individuals.

Further, the company for which the individual was acting may be sanctioned with an administrative fine of up to EUR 10 million next to disgorgement of the generated profits.

6. Commercial Bribery

6.1 JURISDICTION

Commercial bribery is stipulated in section 299 of the German Criminal Code. The German Criminal Code sanctions active and passive bribery in commercial business. This also applies to offenses committed abroad.

6.2 STATUTE OF LIMITATIONS

The statute of limitation for commercial bribery is a maximum of 10 years and begins after the offense has been completed. The statute of limitation for offenses under the German Administrative Offences Act is maximum of three years.

6.3 COMMERCIAL BRIBERY OFFENSES

In Germany, passive and active bribery in private business transactions is prohibited under section 299 GCC.

Section 299 GCC contains two offenses of commercial bribery. It (1) prohibits benefits requested, promised, or provided in exchange for an undue preference in domestic or foreign competition ("*Wettbewerbsmodell*"), and (2) prohibits benefits that are provided in violation of the recipient's obligations vis-á-vis his or her employer ("*Geschäftsherrenmodell*").

6.3.1 First Offense of Bribery in Commercial Sector

The first offense of bribery in the commercial sector (see section 299 para. 1, no. 1 GCC) makes the request, acceptance of a promise for or acceptance of a benefit, a crime if this is made in return for providing an unfair advantage in a business competition. Likewise, the offering, promising, or granting of a benefit to an employee or an agent of a commercial organization is a crime if made in return for obtaining an unfair advantage in a business competition. The objective of this provision is the protection of fair competition.

Thus, section 299, para. 1, no. 1 GCC covers, for example cases where an employee in the procurement department selects a service supplier that did not submit the most economically advantageous offer compared to its competitors, but gave the employee in the procurement department a personal benefit in return for his selecting that supplier.

6.3.2 Second Offense of Bribery in Commercial Sector

Effective as of November 26, 2015, a second offense was implemented in section 299 GCC. The newly implemented provision makes the request, acceptance of a promise for or acceptance of a benefit, a crime if this is made in return for a breach of duty toward the commercial organization. Likewise, the offering, promising, or granting of a benefit to an employee or an agent of a commercial organization is a crime if made in return for a breach of duty toward the commercial organization.

This offense is linked to a specific duty owed by the employee to its employer; hence, it is called the employer model ("*Geschäftsherrenmodell*"). This new provision was implemented by the German legislature in order to meet international requirements.

The key element of the new law is that the criminal offense of taking and giving bribes in commercial practice now extends to acts that lie beyond the competition realm. The new offense triggers criminal liability irrespective of whether the criminal act was committed in the context of (unfair) competition. According to the explanatory notes to the law, the new provision aims at protecting the employer's interests in the loyal and unbiased performance of duties by its employees and agents.

6.3.2.1 Critics to Employer Model

In Germany, the new provision has led to criticism that there are uncertainties as to which specific acts would qualify as a breach of duty and thus fulfill the elements of the crime. Further, it has been criticized that the employer—by setting up the duties owed by the employees—would be in a position to determine the likelihood of criminal offenses by its employees who breach such duties.

According to explanatory notes provided by the legislature, a violation of a company's internal compliance guidelines or concealing the acceptance of a benefit received by the employee from the commercial organization by itself may, however, not be sufficient to establish a breach of duty. Rather, the benefit provided or accepted must be specifically made in return for acts or omissions that violate duties toward that employer relating to the commercial transaction.

6.3.2.2 Implications for Compliance in Companies

These modifications of the current law call for a review of corporate conduct guidelines and compliance controls as well as tailored communication to relevant and responsible employees in order to reassure and refresh awareness of risks associated with the expanded commercial bribery statutes in Germany.

6.3.2.3 Requirement of a Formal Demand for Prosecution

However, the risk of investigations against employees and contractual partners of companies based on the new provision is mitigated by the fact that violations of section 299 GCC arising from a breach of duties to companies may only be prosecuted upon a formal demand (*Strafantrag*) of the company, unless the public prosecution authority exceptionally considers prosecution necessary due to a special public interest. As regards violations of section 299 GCC due to obtaining an unfair advantage in competition, the position remains the same as under the previous legislation, that is, a formal demand for prosecution may be filed by competitors of the "donor" as well as by the company of the "receiver."

6.4 GIFTS, GRATUITIES, AND HOSPITALITY

The Highest Court in Germany (*Bundesgerichtshof*—BGH) has issued an important judgment in 2008 that provides guidance regarding the assessment whether a gift, gratuity, or hospitality is allowed. According to the underlying case, the question whether a gift granted to a public official leads to a criminal offense is subject to the following factors:

(a) The corporate position, role and function of the public official in the corporation;
(b) The timely proximity between granting the gift and the generated business;
(c) The type of the gift and its transparency;
(d) The social adequacy of the gift; and
(e) The purpose for the granting of the gift.

German courts take these factors into account on a case-by-case basis.

6.5 DEFENSES

6.5.1 Written Local Law

The recognition of corporate defense measures follows the same principles as set out with regard to bribery of foreign and domestic officials.

6.5.2 Facilitation Payments

Facilitation payments are uncommon in commercial business because the receiver of the benefit at the company is not under any official obligation to undertake a public (legal) task. In fact, any low payment, resembling facilitation payments in the public sector, can be regarded as a benefit and hence, as a bribe in the commercial sector and can be sanctioned.

6.5.3 Adequate Procedures

The same principles apply as for bribery of foreign public officials and domestic officials. Hence, German law does not yet provide for the implementation of adequate procedures in the company to constitute a defense. Rather, management is held fully responsible in cases of corruption even executed on low levels of the company hierarchy.

6.5.4 Corporate Culture

As mentioned previously, corporate culture is part of a functioning compliance management system as required under the current standards in Germany. However, the sane corporate culture does still not constitute a defense and hence, does not prevent the company from being held responsible for acts of corruption.

6.6 PENALTIES

The penalties for commercial bribery are monetary fines and imprisonment of up to 10 years for the acting individuals.

Further, the company for which the individual was acting may be sanctioned with an administrative fine of up to EUR 10 million next to disgorgement of the profits generated by the tainted contract.

7. Sentencing Principles

In Germany, there is no such sentencing guidance for corruption and bribery violations as, for example, the U.S. Sentencing Guidelines regarding the FCPA. In fact, the prosecution and the practice of legal sanctions is inconsistent among the prosecution offices in Germany. Law proposals regarding uniform sentencing principles are still missing.

8. Related Criminal Offenses

8.1 CONSPIRACY

Conspiracy is not classified as a criminal offense under German law. That is, plotting to commit a crime without commencement of the criminal act itself is not deemed illegal. However, German law prohibits the formation of and membership in a criminal organization (paragraph 129 GCC). It is required that the criminal organization be established for a long term and that its sole purpose is to commit a series of crimes.

8.2 ATTEMPT

The attempt of committing active or passive bribery of public officials is illegal and penalized equally to the actual offense. However, the court may in its discretion grant a milder punishment for attempted crimes (see section 23, para. 2 GCC).

8.3 AIDING AND ABETTING

Aiding and abetting a crime constitutes a criminal offense according to section 27 GCC. Its punishment is equal to the punishment for committing the actual crime, at least in cases where the abetting significantly contributed to the perpetrator's resolution to commit the crime. It is in the court's discretion to grant a milder punishment (see section 27, para. 2 GCC).

8.4 FALSE ACCOUNTING/BOOKS AND RECORDS

False accounting is illegal under German law. Members of the representative body or the supervisory board of a company can be prosecuted in cases where they wrongly state the company's financial accounts in the opening balance, the annual financial statement, or the progress report. To qualify, a false statement must be remarkably false and untenable. These are, for example, dubious outstanding accounts, fictive values, omission of balance sheet items, or arbitrary over- or underrating.

8.5 MONEY LAUNDERING

Money laundering is considered a crime under German law. "Laundering money," channeling money generated in illegal activities such as arms trafficking, drug dealing, or tax evasion into the economic circle usually occurs in the context of organized crime. Corruption is a suitable predicate offense for money laundering according to the new anti-corruption law of 2014.

8.6 TAX AND OTHER FRAUDS

Tax fraud in connection with bribery is stipulated to be a criminal offense.

9. Cooperation and Self-Reporting

9.1 POWERS OF INVESTIGATORS AND PROSECUTORS

The prosecutors in Germany are equipped with a range of investigatory tools. Two of the most important ones in terms of investigation in bribery matters are the search warrant and the seizure of relevant material. The prosecutor must have reasonable grounds for his suspicion that the company in question is involved in corruption and bribery in order to obtain the search warrant from the relevant judge.

9.2 COOPERATION WITH INVESTIGATORS

Companies that are subject to investigation by the German prosecutors are well advised to cooperate with the investigation teams. Especially in case of dawn raids, the company should refrain from destroying material or deleting data. Good cooperation with the investigators does not guarantee favorable treatment. However, noncooperation triggers tremendous detrimental effects.

9.3 SELF-REPORTING

In Germany, there does not exist any obligation for self-reporting if a company becomes aware of a corruption-related law violation within its business. However, laws of countries in which the respective German company operates might have such disclosure laws, and therefore the situation must be assessed in detail. Further, contractual obligations to self-report might be stipulated in compliance agreements that the company enters with its customers and business partners. However, German companies are well advised to self-report in the future in order to benefit from proposed leniency programs.

9.4 PLEA AGREEMENTS

9.4.1 Please Agreements according to Section 257c StPO

Plea agreements are permissible under certain requirements as set out in section 257c of the German Code of Criminal Procedure (*Strafprozessordnung*—StPO). Section 257c StPO sets out that the court and the parties to the proceeding can enter into a plea agreement as proposed by the court. This plea agreement must not address the verdict of guilty and is restricted only to setting out the penalty to be imposed on the defendant. The defendant is typically obliged to make a confession. All discussions and negotiations on this plea agreement must be documented in writing and made public.

9.4.2 Termination under Conditions according to Section 153a StPO

As the transparency and documentation obligations under Section 257c StPO may be burdensome to the parties, there is the tendency to conclude criminal proceedings by applying section 153a StPO, which allows for termination of a trial without judgment under certain conditions. These conditions may include restitution or paying a certain amount of money. Usually this provision is applied with respect to minor offenses. However, in August 2014 the regional court of Munich terminated a corruption trial against Bernie Ecclestone, the chief of Formula One, pursuant to Section 153a StPO against a record-setting payment of U.S. $100 million. The payment by Ecclestone is the largest payment by an individual in German court history to allow severe individual corruption charges to be abandoned. Ecclestone had originally been accused of having bribed a former executive of the State Bank of Bavaria by paying more than EUR 30 million in connection with the sale of a majority stake in Formula One, which was at that time held by the State Bank of Bavaria.

9.5 LENIENCY

9.5.1 No Official Leniency Program

German law does not provide for leniency programs in case of corruption violations. Hence, German companies that have a well-functioning compliance system and did thorough investigations on possible violations within their business are currently reluctant to disclose their findings to the authorities because they cannot rely on receiving credit for it. This is due to the fact that possible fine decreases based on compliance efforts still lie in the sole discretion of the respective prosecution authorities and courts. There are no sentencing principles that give the prosecutors and judges reliable guidance on whether and how to acknowledge compliance efforts. In fact, companies disclosing their findings to the authorities run the risk of having high fines imposed on them and possible debarment of public tenders despite their compliance efforts.

9.5.2 Draft Bill to Implement Affirmative Defense in OWiG

Hence, in April 2014, the German Association of In-House Counsels has introduced a draft bill on amending the German Administrative Offences Act. The draft bill sets out—among others—a leniency clause stating that a fine against a self-disclosing company can be waived if the company voluntarily and comprehensively reports the internal misconduct to the relevant authority and also sets out how recognized weak points in its control system have been remediated with regard to the future. The draft bill explains that this leniency program shall incentivize corporations to reinforce their compliance efforts. Possible incentives such as "deferred prosecution agreements" (DPAs) similar to the ones in the United States or UK are discussed. Such DPAs would oblige a company to remediate identified compliance deficits within a certain period of time. In case these deficits have been remediated successfully, a fine could be waived completely.

10. Whistle-Blower Protection

10.1 PRIVATE SECTOR WHISTLE-BLOWER PROTECTION

10.1.1 No Specific Law on Whistle-Blower Protection

In Germany, there is no specific legislation in place relating to whistle-blowing. There have been several legislative initiatives to introduce specific protection for whistle-blowers from retaliation; however, these initiatives have not been successful (i.e., there is currently no statutory protection of whistle-blowers in Germany).

10.1.2 Protection under the German Dismissal Protection Act

Whistle-blowers are, however, protected under the German Dismissal Protection Act (*Kündigungsschutzgesetz*—KSchG).

The KSchG provides that employees may only be terminated for a specific reason. Such reason can be, for example, the employee's (mis)conduct or a serious breach of her employment contract. Blowing the whistle internally in relation to a matter of legitimate concern does not constitute a valid reason for dismissal. But blowing the whistle externally, for example, to an authority, without trying to resolve the matter internally first, with the potential consequence of damaging the employer's reputation, may be regarded as a valid reason for termination. However, such initial external whistle-blowing may be justified if the employee is reporting a criminal offense committed by the employer. Hence, whether there is a reason for termination in the specific case must be assessed on a case-by-case basis. The courts take various factors into account when making this assessment such as the employee's constitutional right to free speech, the employee's contractual duty of loyalty, and the employer's right to protect its reputation and interest to keep certain efficiencies within the sphere of the company.

10.2 PUBLIC SECTOR WHISTLE-BLOWER PROTECTION

10.2.1 Similar Principles as in the Private Sector

In general, the principles and laws for employees in the private sector also apply to German public officials. However, there are special laws in the public sector that provide for a disclosure obligation for public officials.

10.2.2 Special Laws in the Public Sector

According to the German Act on Federal Officials (*Bundesbeamtengesetz*—BBG) and the German Act on Status Rights of Officials (*Beamtenstatusgesetz*—BeamtStG) public officials are released from confidentiality and called to report if there exists reasonable ground for suspicions of corruption offenses as set out in sections 331 to 335a GCC.

10.3 ATTITUDE TOWARD WHISTLE-BLOWERS

The term "whistle-blower" cannot be accurately translated into German and is also not yet very well known in the German public. Further, the concept of reporting wrongdoing, even for the benefit of the community, can have a negative connotation due to Germany's history.

However, since 2003, the OECD had requested that Germany improve its private sector whistle-blower protections, and in April 2013 the OECD asked Germany to provide a written report on its progress within a year. In addition, the G20 and the Council of Europe are requesting legal improvements of whistle-blower protections. But Germany still continues to rely on its labour law regulations, constitutional requirements and relevant case law to provide for protection of whistle-blowers.

Until today there is no express law for the protection of whistle-blowers. The political party that overruled the draft laws on whistle-blower protection argues that the existing legal system provides for sufficient protection.

Despite the absence of whistle-blowing culture in Germany, many German corporations have set up and implemented sophisticated whistle-blowing systems. Especially, after the landmark judgment by the District Court of Munich I in December 2013, German corporations will need to re-enforce these efforts. The court ruled that an efficient compliance management system falls within the responsibility of the respective management. Failure leads to personal liability. The court will only deem a compliance management system to be effective if it not only provides for whistle-blowing hotlines but also grants maximum protection to the whistle-blowers acting in compliance with the law. If the employees notice that the corporation does not provide maximum whistle-blower protection, wrongdoings remain undisclosed, leading the compliance system to fail—hence, the management is liable.

11. Key International Treaties Relating to Bribery and Corruption

In addition to various bilateral and multilateral agreements, Germany has signed a number of international anti-corruption conventions:

(1) the OECD Anti-Bribery Convention;
(2) the United Nations Convention against Corruption (UNCAC);
(3) the United Nations Convention against Transnational Organized Crime (CTOC); and
(4) the Council of Europe Criminal Law Convention on Corruption.

Although Germany was among the first signatories of the UNCAC in 2003, the UNCAC had not been ratified until 2014 because Germany had not amended the criminal offenses of electoral bribery in accordance with the UNCAC. This has only changed following the enactment of stricter anti-bribery laws in relation to electoral bribery as of September 2014. The UNCAC has now been ratified.

Further, Germany is a member of the Group of States against Corruption that was established in 1999 by the Council of Europe to monitor states' compliance with the organization's anti-corruption standards.

12. Mutual Legal Assistance Treaties and Transnational Cooperation

There is only a limited number of legal assistance treaties between Germany and other countries. Hence, cooperation with public prosecutors from other jurisdictions is mainly supported by Transparency International based in Berlin. Transparency International focuses on a structural approach, which means that it strives to establish the awareness and structures that are necessary to support cooperation between the different prosecutorial bodies.

13. Legal Professional Privilege

Legal privilege of documents prepared in the course of internal investigations by external counsel has been subject to a number of court decisions in the past few years. There is a noticeable development toward strengthening the German legal privilege.

13.1 DECISION OF DISTRICT COURT OF HAMBURG IN 2010

In 2010, the District Court of Hamburg had taken a very narrow approach to the attorney-client-privilege and permitted the seizure of documents that were prepared by external counsel in their offices, arguing that the attorney-client relationship between the law firm and its corporate client in the specific case was different from the relationship between a criminal defense lawyer (*Strafverteidiger*) and his client. According to the court, only the latter relationship enabled the attorney-client privilege. Hence, only documentation that was held by criminal attorneys representing individuals was protected from prosecutorial measures. In the specific case, the District Court of Hamburg allowed memoranda from the internal investigation prepared by external counsel to be seized by German law enforcement authorities.

13.2 DECISION OF DISTRICT COURT OF MANNHEIM IN 2012

In 2012, the District Court of Mannheim took a different standpoint and granted full legal privilege for documents created during an internal investigation. The court stated that section 160a para. 1 of the German Code of Criminal Procedure (*Strafprozessordnung*—StPO) provides for information that was entrusted to an attorney to be subject to legal privilege. In the specific case, the court held that the investigation report that was prepared by and in the possession of an external law firm engaged by the corporate client to conduct the internal investigation was protected from seizure by the German prosecutorial authorities. However, the court clarified that this protection would no longer be given if the client had passed over the documents to its external counsel with the willful intent to shield them from seizure.

13.3 DECISION OF DISTRICT COURT OF BRAUNSCHWEIG IN 2015

In July 2015, the District Court of Braunschweig rendered a key decision that further strengthens the legal privilege regarding documents that were prepared in the course of internal investigations. The court held that documents that were prepared by external counsel for the purpose of defending a corporate client against potential future proceedings by enforcement authorities are protected against seizure under the German attorney-client privilege set out in Section 148 para. 1 of the German Code of Criminal Procedure.

The court decided that documents prepared by legal counsel for the purpose of defending the corporate client against potential investigation proceedings are exempt from seizure, irrespective of their place of custody (at the office of the client or its external counsel) and irrespective of the time of their preparation (before or after investigatory proceedings have been initiated).

Also, the protection against seizure does not depend upon the nature of the investigatory proceedings as criminal or administrative. In the same decision the court clarified that the legal privilege does not extend to documents that have been prepared by a corporation for purposes other than its potential defense in a criminal or administrative matter. In the specific case, a document held to fall outside of the protected attorney-client privilege was an internal audit report.

13.4 CONCLUSION

The decision of the Regional Court of Braunschweig goes above and beyond the prior two decisions as for the legal privilege to apply it neither requires a threatening criminal or administrative proceeding nor the privileged documents being in the physical custody of external counsel. While this decision does not have any binding effect on other German courts, it clearly indicates the trend toward an increased protection of reports and working documents prepared by external counsel in the course of an internal investigation by legal privilege against government seizure. This is a welcome development for companies that rely on external counsel to help conduct internal investigations.

14. Privacy and Data Protection

In 2010, the German government had considered significant changes to the German Federal Data Protection Act (*Bundesdatenschutzgesetz*) through the proposed Act to Regulate the Data Protection of Employees (*Gesetz zur Regelung des Beschäftigtendatenschutzes*). The amendments were meant to significantly impact a corporation's ability to conduct internal investigations and implement effective compliance controls over employees.

Due to the heavy political and legal discussion about the proposed amendments, the law could not be passed during the legislative period in 2010.

The General Data Protection Regulation (GPDR) taking effect on 25 May 2018 dramatically changed the legal requirements for employers to access, monitor and review an employee's email correspondence in the course of an internal investigation. While an express consent from the employee regarding the access to its emails may form a legal basis of data processing under GDPR, such consent must be given freely. Due to the imbalance of power between employer and employee, it is oftentimes unlikely that such consent has truly been given voluntary. Hence, alternatively the employer can rely on the legal basis of a "legitimate interest," that is, the need to investigate an employee's conduct due to genuine suspicion of misconduct or even illegality. Such suspicion should be based on specific and documented facts. Also, the processing of the data must be necessary to achieve the legitimate interest of the employer. In any event, the employer must inform the employee of its right to object in the data processing. Where there are compelling reasons to override the individual's objection (e.g., in case of serious suspected offences), the employer may continue to process their data for the specific purposes.Under the new regime of the GDPR, employers should—in the course of an internal investigation— provide its employees a privacy notice that describes in detail, amongst others, the legal basis on which the employer is processing their personal data, the purposes for which their personal data is processed and their right to object to the processing of their personal data. Regarding the actual processing of the personal data, the employer needs to comply with the GDPR's basic principles (i) processing must take place in a transparent manner, (ii) processing is limited to what is absolutely necessary in relation to the purpose of the investigation and (iii) the data is not to be used beyond the purpose for which it was collected.

15. Forecast for Reforms and Parting Thoughts

The fight against corruption in Germany and its corporate world has again picked up speed between 2015 and 2018. Especially, various law proposals regarding anti-corruption have been passed due to international requirements. German courts recognize and appreciate that corporations have established sophisticated compliance systems in order to manage corruption and compliance risks. Those companies that fail to implement efficient compliance systems risk drastic enforcement by the local authorities and substantial business detriments. Various verdicts have repeatedly demonstrated the efficient enforcement of corruption and bribery in the German business world.

German companies have reinforced their compliance efforts and are well advised to continue improving their compliance management systems in order to adhere to local and international law requirements.

Especially, the U.S. $100 million Ecclestone settlement opens a new chapter in the German anti-corruption law arena. While prior OECD working groups noted "*that the level of sanctions applied to both legal and natural persons may not always be fully effective, proportionate and dissuasive,*" the Ecclestone settlement is a landmark example of how the German court's view has changed over the last years and will develop in the future toward more vigorous enforcements against offenders in corruption-related matters.

APPENDIX

Key Issues	Germany's Approach
Is jurisdiction subject to any international anti-corruption conventions? If so, which? (OECD, UN Convention against Corruption, etc.)	Germany is subject to the following international anti-corruption conventions: Council of Europe Criminal Law Convention on Corruption of 27 January 1999 and its additional protocol of 15 May 2003; Council of Europe Framework Decision 2003/568/JHA of 22 July 2003 on combating corruption in the private sector; United Nations Convention against Corruption of 31 October 2003 (UNCAC); United Nations Convention against Transnational Organized Crime (CTOC); OECD Convention on Combating Bribery of Foreign Public Officials in International Business Transactions dated 21 November 1997.
Is bribery of foreign public officials illegal (do domestic anti-bribery laws provide for extraterritorial application)?	Yes, bribery of foreign public officials is prohibited under German criminal law. The German Criminal Code provides for extraterritorial application regarding active and passive bribery of foreign public officials. Whereas the German prosecution offices have vast experience in enforcing active bribery of foreign public officials, it remains to be seen how active the enforcement authorities will be in charging foreign public officials for German law violations.
What is the definition of foreign public officials?	Under German law, the following are regarded as "foreign public officials": members of the European Commission, European Central Bank, European Court of Auditors and any other court of the European Union; officials and other servants of the European Union and individuals mandated to execute tasks for the European Union; members of the International Court of Justice; public servants of the International Court of Justice; members of a foreign or international court; public servants of a foreign country who are authorized to fulfil public tasks for a foreign country; public servants of an international organization; individuals who are authorized to fulfill tasks for an international organization; soldiers of a foreign country and soldiers who are authorized to fulfill tasks for an international organization.

Key Issues	Germany's Approach
Is commercial bribery illegal?	Yes, section 299 German Criminal Code contains two offenses of commercial bribery. First, it prohibits benefits requested, promised, or provided in exchange for an undue preference in domestic or foreign competition ("*Wettbewerbsmodell*"). Second, it prohibits benefits that are provided in exchange for an action that violates the recipient's obligations vis-á-vis his or her employer ("*Geschäftsherrenmodell*").
Is bribing domestic officials illegal?	Yes, according to sections 331 to 334 of the German Criminal Code, active and passive bribery of German officials is illegal. If the active or passive bribery leads to an act of the public official where he or she violates his/her official duties, the maximum imprisonment term is five years (instead of three years in case of legal public acts).
Can the receipt of a bribe be prosecuted?	Yes, German criminal law prohibits passive bribery of domestic and foreign public officials. The prosecution of foreign public officials for passive bribery is not (yet) common, however, although possible under German law. German authorities face legal challenges such as (1) the determination of whether the bribe receiver is to be classified as a public official under German law, and (2) the assessment of whether the provided public act occurred under a violation of official duties.
Can companies be held criminally liable? If so, what is the requisite intent for criminal liability to attach?	Corporate entities cannot be held criminally liable under German law. They are only subject to administrative law, which—however—can lead to substantial administrative fines being imposed. Draft law proposals to implement corporate criminal liability in Germany have been introduced, however they have not yet been passed.
Can companies be held civilly liable? If so, what is the requisite intent for civilly liability to attach?	Companies whose employees have violated anti-corruption provisions can be held civilly liable. For example, corporations that suffered damages due to corruption can claim damages against the violating contractual partner based on civil, contract, and tort law.
Can individuals be held civilly liable?	Yes, especially management board members can be held personally liable for damages suffered by corporations based on corruption offenses in the business. This has been reaffirmed by the milestone judgment of the District Court Munich I in December 2013. The court based the damage claim of the company against its former CFO mainly on the failure of the CFO to manage an efficient compliance system that would have prevented the bribery offenses.

(Continued)

Key Issues	Germany's Approach
Is there a "facilitation/ grease payments" exception?	Facilitation payments made to foreign public officials are not prohibited under German law. However, facilitation payments made to German officials are prohibited under German law.
Does the subject country provide for conspiracy liability relating to violations of the anti-corruption laws?	Yes.
Does the subject country provide for: (a) aiding/abetting liability relating to violations of the anti-corruption laws? (b) attempt liability relating to violations of the anti-corruption laws?	(a) Yes (b) Yes
Is failure to keep accurate books and records a criminal and/or civil offense?	The failure to keep accurate books and records is a criminal offense according to section 283 of the German Criminal Code if it occurs in connection with insolvency proceedings.
Do any books and records violations have to involve underlying bribery proof?	No.
Are there laws concerning a company's financial internal controls? If so, are those laws applicable to private and public companies or just public companies?	Yes, private and public companies.

Key Issues	Germany's Approach
Is there an affirmative disclosure obligation for potential violations of the anti-bribery laws or accounting irregularities?	No.
Are "promotional expenses" exempt from the anti-bribery laws?	Yes, but only if these expenses are at arm's length, transparent, and there is no quid-pro-quo "criminal agreement" (*"Unrechtsvereinbarung"*) regarding expected business dealings.
Is the giving of gifts, entertainment, travel, meals, etc. restricted/ prohibited?	There is no law or official guidance as to minimum value thresholds for allowed gifts and entertainment in Germany. Hence, gifts and entertainment granted to foreign and German public officials may constitute a benefit within the meaning of German anti-bribery offenses.
	However, German case law provides for an exception if the benefit is deemed "socially acceptable." Whether a gift is socially acceptable depends upon factors such as the nature of the gift or the timely proximity between granting the gift and the generated business. In general, a benefit in the amount of up to EUR 30 is regarded as socially acceptable. German courts take these factors into account on a case-by-case basis.
Are there any laws concerning things of value conveyed by, or to, third parties?	German law does not (yet) provide for attributable liability of a company if a mandated third party (e.g., agent) conveys things of value and violates anti-bribery laws. This lack of law has been criticized by the European Commission.
Are bribes tax deductible?	No, not anymore (since 1998).
Is the law applied extraterritorially?	Yes.
Is having a robust corporate compliance program an affirmative defense or way to negate liability?	No. However, despite lacking guidance German courts and prosecution offices consider robust compliance programs in their legal assessment. New law proposals provide for robust corporate compliance as an efficient way to minimize liability.
Is there a "local law" exception/defense?	No.

(*Continued*)

Key Issues	Germany's Approach
Is "credit" given for cooperation with authorities? If so, how and in what form?	Whether credit is given for cooperation lies in the discretion of the respective enforcement authority and hence is dependent on a case-by-case analysis. Credit can be given, for example, in a lower administrative fine.
Does Germany have a Mutual Legal Assistance Treaty with the United States that generally covers criminal matters, including the FCPA?	No.
What are the potential penalties/sanctions both for civil and criminal violations?	Criminal sanctions include monetary fines (calculated based on the personal income of the offender and the severity of the offense) or imprisonment between 5 and 10 years.

9   Guatemala

1. Introduction to Guatemala's Anti-Corruption Legislation

1.1 THE LEGAL LANDSCAPE

Guatemala[1] is one of several countries in Latin America (others being Mexico, Colombia, Brazil, and Argentina) that has significantly strengthened its anti-corruption legislation in recent years.[2] The centerpiece of this effort came in 2012 through Decree 31-2012, which introduced new criminal offenses relating to the bribery of foreign officials,[3] revised other criminal offenses related to public corruption, and increased penalties for certain acts of bribery.[4] Other amendments enacted in 2012 also expanded the concept of criminal liability for corporate offenses, with penalties including fines and dissolution of the corporate entity.

As part of its reform efforts, Guatemala also modified Decree 55-2010, which provides for disgorgement and seizures of assets obtained through criminal activity, including products of corruption. The modifications permit disgorgement and seizure of assets as a civil remedy separate and apart from criminal proceedings. Other efforts included reforms to the Public Procurement Law[5] and the codification of collusion as a recognized criminal offense.

---

[1] This chapter was contributed by Miller & Chevalier's Alejandra Montenegro Almonte and Michael Skopets, Asensio Andrade Flores' Ignacio Andrade Aycinena, and Garcia & Bodan's María Mercedes Castro Guerra.

[2] Notably, Guatemala's Criminal Code has contained anti-corruption provisions since its inception in 1973, including a prohibition on the bribery of public officials.

[3] For the purposes of this chapter, note that in Guatemala, as in many other legal systems, "active bribery" refers to the giving of a bribe, while "passive bribery" refers to the receipt of a bribe.

[4] Decree 31-2012, Articles 22 and 23.

[5] Decree 46-2016 (reforming the Ley de Contrataciones del Estado, formerly enacted via Decree 57-92).

From Baksheesh to Bribery. T. Markus Funk and Andrew S. Boutros.
© Oxford University Press 2019. Published 2019 by Oxford University Press.

The legal landscape of Guatemalan anti-corruption legislation will likely continue to expand following the public corruption scandals (known as "La Linea") that surfaced in 2015 and 2016 and led to the arrests of over 300 private citizens and public officials—including the indictment and criminal prosecution of then-president Otto Pérez Molina, the former vice president, and other high-level officials.

Notably, the investigation and prosecution of the "La Linea" corruption schemes resulted from close collaboration between Guatemala's Public Prosecutor Service (Fiscalía General de la Nación) and the UN-backed International Commission Against Impunity in Guatemala ("Comisión Internacional contra la Impunidad en Guatemala" or "CICIG"), which assisted the Public Prosecutor Service in investigating and prosecuting many of these high-profile corruption cases. Their success has engendered political and popular support for the country's anti-corruption efforts.

1.2 THE POLITICAL LANDSCAPE

In the 1996, Guatemala emerged from decades of civil war and has since that time made significant progress in building its democratic institutions. The country has democratic elections and the peaceful transition of power between political parties.

In 2015, during the administration of President Otto Pérez Molina (elected in 2012), Guatemala suffered a political crisis resulting from corruption at the highest levels of the government. The La Linea corruption scandal caused the resignation and criminal prosecution of then-president Pérez Molina and his vice president. Elections were held in 2015 resulting in the election of current-president Jimmy Morales, who was sworn into office in January 2016.

Today, Guatemala has a democratic multiparty political system, albeit a fragmented one. No clear majority has been in place in the country's legislature since 2004. As a result, the checks and balances among the executive, legislative, and judicial branches have remained weak. Against this backdrop, the public perception of corruption in Guatemala, both domestically and internationally, has remained high.

1.3 THE BUSINESS LANDSCAPE

In recent years, Guatemala has seen strong economic growth. According to the World Bank, Guatemala has enjoyed a 3.0 percent GDP growth since 2012 and is expected to grow by 3.2 percent in 2017.[6] Guatemala's economy is based on export of agricultural commodities such as coffee, sugar, bananas, palm oil, and cardamom, and apparel and textiles, with the service sector growing rapidly, particularly in the call-center sector. Foreign remittances remain a strong source of economic growth for the country, accounting for 10 percent of Guatemala's GDP in 2016.[7]

---

[6] http://www.worldbank.org/en/country/guatemala/overview (last visited Dec. 19, 2018).

[7] http://www.centralamericadata.com/en/article/home/Guatemala_Record_Remittances_in_2016 (last visited Dec. 19, 2018).

2. Guatemala's Domestic Anti-Corruption Framework

2.1 GUATEMALA'S LEGAL SYSTEM

Guatemala has been a sovereign nation since its independence from Spain in 1821. It adopted its current constitution in 1985, which established three equal and independent branches of government—the judiciary, legislative, and executive. The Supreme Court is the highest court of the land, with ultimate appellate jurisdiction over civil, administrative, and criminal matters, and special jurisdiction over constitutional matters involving Ministers of State. The Supreme Court is composed of 13 magistrates who are elected by Congress to serve a term of 5 years.

Lower courts are divided into Criminal Courts and Civil Courts. Criminal Courts have jurisdiction over all criminal offenses, including those related to corruption and bribery. Jurisdiction over offenses related to organized crime and high-profile cases may, at the request of the Public Prosecutor Service and upon approval by the Supreme Court, be judged by "High-Risk Courts" ("*Juzgados de Mayor Riesgo*"). These courts have special security measures and are all located in Guatemala City. Their jurisdiction spans high-risk cases occurring anywhere in the country.

All criminal cases that involve a potential penalty exceeding one year are tried by District Criminal Courts in the respective department, based on the country's political and geographic division into departments. Lesser offenses are judged by Criminal Justices of the Peace at the municipal level.

Appellate Courts are divided by subject jurisdiction, such as Administrative Panel Courts for administrative cases, Juvenile Appeals Courts for cases involving minors, Government Accounts Courts, and others.

Lower courts have jurisdiction over Constitutional Matters in the first instance, and all such cases are subject to appeal before the Constitutional Court. The Constitutional Court is an independent tribunal that acts to protect the constitutional order and to protect citizens from arbitrary government actions by evaluating the legality of laws and governmental acts under the Constitution.

2.2 CRIMINAL LAW REGIME

Guatemala's criminal laws are codified in the *Código Penal* or Criminal Code. The Code was enacted by Congress on January 1, 1974, and has been amended numerous times since 1981.

The Criminal Code governs all criminal offenses. Bribery-related offenses are contained under Title XI of the Criminal Code ("Offenses against the Public Administration"). The Criminal Code is modified by Congressional Decrees, such as Decree 31-2012, which do not themselves have the force of law but are incorporated into the Criminal Code itself.

All criminal cases are brought by the Public Prosecutor Office and assigned to district attorneys, section attorneys, and agency attorneys, depending on the jurisdiction and subject matter of the case. In addition, the Public Prosecutor may appoint Special District Attorneys for higher profile or sensitive cases, such as those involving CICIG.

2.3 CIVIL LAW REGIME

Guatemala is a civil law country, in which Congressional Codes and legislation constitute the primary sources of law. Judicial precedent applies in two limited circumstances: (1) when the Supreme Court has issued the same judgment in five cases; or (2) when the Constitutional Court has issued the same judgment in three cases.

As discussed previously, all bribery and corruption offenses are governed by Guatemala's Criminal Code. However, the Public Prosecutor's Office includes a specialized unit created for the purpose of enforcing the asset forfeiture proceedings introduced through Decree 31-2012. Asset forfeiture procedures are civil causes of action that may be initiated separate and apart from criminal procedures—even when no criminal liability has been established.

2.4 VIEW FROM THE OUTSIDE

2.4.1 OECD Evaluation

Guatemala is not a signatory to the OECD Convention on Combating Bribery of Foreign Public Officials in International Business Transactions ("OECD Convention").[8] While Guatemala's role with respect to the OECD Convention is under discussion by the Guatemalan Congress, as of the date of this publication, the Convention has not been approved or ratified. Nonetheless, Guatemala's accession to other treaties has compelled the country to implement heightened standards against bribery and corruption.

2.4.2 OAS Evaluation

Guatemala is a Permanent Member of the Organization of American States (OAS) and a signatory to the Inter-American Convention against Corruption (IACAC). Guatemala anti-corruption legislation is under review under the Mechanism for Follow-up on the Implementation of the Inter-American Convention against Corruption (MESICIC), an inter-governmental body established by the OAS. Each round of review focuses on member states' implementation of specific provisions in the IACC and evaluates progress in adopting policy recommendations by the MESICIC in prior rounds.[9] The most recent report on Guatemala was issued in 2013.[10] The report acknowledged Guatemala's efforts to prevent corruption,[11] but also noted that many reforms recommended by MESICIC in prior reviews remained outstanding (introduction of conflicts of interest regulations, income and asset disclosure requirements by public officials, coordination among domestic oversight bodies, and cooperation with foreign authorities).[12]

---

[8] "OECD" stands for Organization for Economic Co-operation and Development.

[9] Organization of American States (OAS), Secretariat of Legal Affairs (SLA).

[10] http://www.oas.org/juridico/english/gtm.htm

[11] MESICIC, FINAL REPORT ON THE REPUBLIC OF GUATEMALA (2013).

[12] See id. at 56–59.

2.4.3 Transparency International Corruption Perception Index Score

Transparency International (TI) has consistently ranked Guatemala amongst the countries with high levels of perceived corruption. In the last five years, Guatemala has dropped even further in its ranking (from number 113 out of 176 countries in 2012 to number 136 in 2016[13]). The drop in rankings over the past five years reflects the nature and scope of the corruption scandals involving former president Pérez Molina and his ministers and associates, including a kickback scheme at the customs agency, receipt of bribes in exchange for public contracts, abuse of public funds, and illicit campaign finance.[14]

Despite the large scale of these corruption schemes and the consequential harm to the public, TI and its local affiliate, Acción Ciudadana, lauded the resignation and imprisonment of the former president sending "a strong warning" to corrupt individuals that money and power no longer guarantee impunity.[15] Public confidence in anti-corruption enforcement also appears to have risen as a result. According to the Latin America Corruption Survey conducted by the law firm Miller & Chevalier, after the Molina scandals in 2015, there is a notable increase in the percentage of Guatemalans who believe an offender of anti-corruption laws is likely to be locally prosecuted.[16]

3. Investigative and Prosecutorial Agencies

3.1 CRIMINAL LAW AGENCIES

Guatemala's Public Prosecutor Service (known as both the Fiscalía General de la República[17] and the Ministerio Público[18]) is the government organ responsible for prosecuting all criminal offenses in Guatemala. It acts in criminal cases regarding bribery and corruption via five subagencies: the Prosecutor for Administrative Crimes, which is in charge of all prosecutions of crimes committed by public officials or against public funds or goods; the Prosecutor for Organized Crime; the Prosecutor against Money Laundering; the Special Prosecutor against impunity, which is the point of contact with CICIG and the government's main prosecution arm in cases within CICIG's jurisdiction; and the Prosecutor for Asset Forfeiture.

CICIG was created in 2006 through agreement between the UN Secretary General and the Public Prosecutor Service. CICIG operates under Guatemalan laws but remains a politically, organizationally, and financially independent international body.[19] It is tasked with

---

[13] *See* https://www.transparency.org/news/feature/corruption_perceptions_index_2016 (last visited Dec. 19, 2018).

[14] *See, e.g.*, Michael Lohmuller, *Guatemala's Government Corruption Scandals Explained*, INSIGHT CRIME (June 21, 2016), http://www.insightcrime.org/news-analysis/guatemala-s-government-corruption-scandals-explained.

[15] Transparency International, *The Americas: How 2015 Was a Warning to the Corrupt* (Jan. 27, 2016), http://blog.transparency.org/2016/01/27/the-americas-how-2015-was-a-warning-to-the-corrupt.

[16] *See* Miller & Chevalier, 2016 Latin America Corruption Survey. The percentage of Guatemalan respondents who believe an offender is likely to be locally prosecuted went up from 36 percent in 2012 to 65 percent in 2016. As comparison, the regional average in Latin America is 59 percent.

[17] Commonly translated as "Attorney General's Office."

[18] Commonly translated as "Public Ministry."

[19] CICIG is autonomously funded, with its funding obtained mostly through cooperation efforts of the international community. CICIG has diplomatic prerogatives and immunity from prosecution in Guatemala's courts.

assisting the Public Prosecutor Service and other state institutions in the investigation and prosecution of certain types of criminal cases.[20] CICIG is authorized to conduct criminal proceedings in Guatemalan courts and to serve as an "Adjunct to Prosecution."[21] CICIG is currently operating under a four-year mandate, which is slated to expire in 2019, but may be renewed by the UN Security Council and the Guatemalan government.

The State Comptroller also has enforcement authority over matters involving the use of public funds and goods.[22] The State Comptroller also has enforcement authority with respect to civil, administrative, and criminal liability of public officials. The State Comptroller refers all administrative and corruption violations identified within the scope of its duties to the Public Prosecutor's Office.

3.2 CIVIL LAW AGENCIES

The Solicitor General (Procuraduría General de la Nación) is the primary advisor to and representative of the Guatemalan government. In that capacity, the Solicitor General has standing in cases involving matters of public interest or that cause harm to the state, for example, misuse of public goods or other criminal activities by public officials.

3.3 MULTIAGENCY ARRANGEMENTS

Multiagency arrangements appear to be increasingly common in Guatemala. For example, the Public Prosecutor Service (in conjunction with CICIG) executed several cooperation agreements with the Banking Superintendency, the Tax Administration Superintendency, and the State Comptroller. The agreements cover various areas of criminal activity, including corruption.

4. Bribery of Foreign Officials

4.1 JURISDICTION

As a general rule, Guatemalan criminal laws only reach criminal conduct occurring within Guatemala. Article 5 of the Criminal Code, however, contains an extraterritoriality provision, which extends jurisdiction to the following scenarios:

(a) A criminal offense committed outside of the country by a Guatemalan public official, if it has not been adjudicated in the country in which the criminal offense was committed.

Its installations have immunity, and CICIG's commissioner has a diplomatic status similar to that of UN personnel in Guatemala.

[20] *See* http://www.cicig.org/index.php?page=mandate (last visited Dec. 19, 2018) for a more complete description of CICIG's mandate.

[21] The "Adjunct to Prosecution" figure is a special characteristic of Guatemala's legal system, which allows certain entities and victims to collaborate in criminal proceedings.

[22] *See* Section 2.3, *supra*.

(b) A criminal offense committed in a Guatemalan ship, aircraft, or another means of transportation, if it has not been adjudicated in the country in which the criminal offense was committed.

(c) A criminal offense committed by a Guatemalan outside of Guatemala, when his or her extradition has been denied.

(d) A criminal offense committed outside of Guatemala against a Guatemalan citizen, if it has not been adjudicated in the country in which the criminal offense was committed, provided that the Public Prosecutor Service has issued a formal charge and the accused is in Guatemala.

(e) A criminal offense that in accordance with a treaty or convention must be sanctioned in Guatemala even when not committed in its territory.

(f) A criminal offense committed outside of Guatemala against the security of the state, the constitutional order, or its territorial integrity, as well as forgery of the president's signature or counterfeiting or forgery of currency or bank notes, legal tender, bonds, and other securities and credit documents.

4.2 STATUTE OF LIMITATIONS

Under Guatemalan law, the statute of limitations generally depends on the maximum penalty of the particular criminal offense. Under the Criminal Code, the statute of limitations for criminal offenses related to the Bribery of Foreign Officials is generally one and a third of the maximum available penalty.[23]

4.3 FOREIGN BRIBERY OFFENSES

4.3.1 Active Transnational Bribery

One of the most significant changes introduced by Decree 31-2012 was the criminalization of "Active Transnational Bribery."

Article 24 of the Decree (codified in Article 442 Bis of the Criminal Code) prohibits:

(a) Any person subject to the jurisdiction of Guatemalan law;

(b) from offering a gift or presenting, promising, or giving any pecuniary or other benefit;

(c) either directly or indirectly;

(d) to a public official of another state or an international organization, for that official or for another person;

(e) with the aim that said public official act or refrain from acting in the performance of his or her functions, to obtain or retain a business or some other undue advantage of an economic or commercial nature.

Another important change of Decree 31-2012 was the modification of corporate liability. Corporations may be held criminally liable if any of their directors, managers, executives,

---

[23] *See* Criminal Code, Article 107.

representatives, administrators, officers, or employees engage in Active Transnational Bribery for the company's benefit.[24]

4.3.2 Passive Transnational Bribery

Article 25 of the Decree introduced a new "Passive Transnational Bribery" criminal offense as Article 442 Ter of the Criminal Code. The new Article 442 Ter makes it a crime for foreign public officials or employees to solicit or accept, directly or indirectly, anything of value in exchange for carrying out, ordering, or refraining from performing an act within that person's official functions.

4.4 DEFINITION OF "FOREIGN PUBLIC OFFICIAL"

Decree 31-2012 defines "Foreign Public Official" as "any person in a legislative, executive, administrative, or judicial position of a foreign country, whether appointed or elected; and any person that exercises a public function for a foreign country, including a government instrumentality and state owned enterprise."[25]

4.5 GIFTS, GRATUITIES, AND HOSPITALITY

Guatemalan legislation prohibits gifts, gratuities, or hospitality of any value if they are given to foreign public officials with the purpose of obtaining an undue advantage.

4.6 DEFENSES
4.6.1 Written Local Law

The Guatemalan Criminal Code does not provide any exceptions from liability under Article 442 Bis or Article 442 Ter for payments permitted under local law, nor does the Code provide an affirmative defense for such payments.

4.6.2 Facilitation Payments

Guatemalan law does not provide any exceptions from liability for facilitation payments that would otherwise violate Article 442 Bis or Article 442 Ter.

4.6.3 Adequate Procedures

Many Guatemalan companies recognize the importance of maintaining procedures to prevent bribery and corruption. The law, however, does not recognize the existence of such procedures as a defense to a charge of bribery or corruption.

---

[24] Decree 31-2012, Article 2.
[25] Criminal Code, General Provisions, Article I (as modified by Decree 31-2012).

4.6.4 Corporate Culture

The demonstration of a corporate culture that does not condone illicit bribery may help in support of a defense against corporate criminal liability, but is not a defense to a charge of bribery or corruption.

4.7 PENALTIES

4.7.1 Active Transnational Bribery

Active transnational bribery is punishable by imprisonment for 5 to 10 years and by a fine of between 50,000 and 500,000 quetzals.[26]

4.7.2 Corporate Liability

Under Guatemalan anti-bribery laws, a corporation engaging in active transnational bribery may be subject to a fine ranging between 100,000 and 750,000 quetzals.[27] In the event of a repeat offense, corporate dissolution may be ordered.

4.7.3 Passive Transnational Bribery

Passive transnational bribery is punishable by 5 to 10 years imprisonment and a fine of 50,000 to 500,000 quetzals.

5. Bribery of Domestic Officials

5.1 JURISDICTION

As described in Section 4.1, *supra*, the jurisdiction of Guatemala's Criminal Code is territorial, with the exception of extraterritorial provisions set forth in Article 5 of the Code. Therefore, unless a bribery offense falls within one of the exceptions under Article 5, the offense may only be charged if the conduct occurred within Guatemala.

5.2 DOMESTIC BRIBERY OFFENSES

The Criminal Code sets forth three criminal offenses related to the provision of payments or other benefits to domestic public officials:

(a) Passive Bribery;
(b) Active Bribery; and
(c) Illicit Acceptance of Gifts.

---

[26] Criminal Code, Article 442 Bis (as modified by Decree 31-2012). As of July 1, 2017, this fine amount is equal to approximately U.S. $6,817 to $68,165.

[27] As of July 1, 2017, this fine amount is equal to approximately U.S. $13,633 to $102,248.

Under Article 439 of the Code, the offense of passive bribery occurs when a public official or employee intentionally solicits or accepts, directly or indirectly, any object of pecuniary value or another benefit, such as a favor, gift, present, promise, or advantage for him- or herself or another person, in exchange for carrying out or refraining from performing an act within the scope of said public official's or employee's official functions.[28] The Code expressly states that the criminal offense of passive bribery applies to arbitrators, experts, or any other persons who exercise, whether occasionally or permanently, a public function or role.[29]

It follows therefore, that the offense of active bribery occurs when a person intentionally offers or provides, directly or indirectly, to a public official or employee any object of economic value or another benefit, such as a favor, a promise of a gift or a present, or an advantage, for him- or herself or another person, in exchange for the official carrying out or refraining from performing an act within the scope of his or her official functions.[30]

Article 443 of the Code also includes an offense for the illicit acceptance of gifts, which is triggered when an official or public employee accepts gifts, presents, offers, or promises from persons who have any pending matter before the public official or employee.[31]

The effect of Article 443 is to permit the prosecution of officials where the element of intent required under Article 439 is not proven (e.g., that the gift, present, offer, or promise was provided *in exchange for carrying out or refraining from performing some act*). Under Article 443 it is sufficient to prove that the gift-giver had some matter pending before the official.

5.3 STATUTES OF LIMITATIONS

The statutes of limitations for passive domestic bribery and active domestic bribery are the same as those set forth in Section 4.2 of this chapter. The statute of limitation for the illicit acceptance of gifts is four years.[32]

5.4 DEFINITION OF "DOMESTIC PUBLIC OFFICIALS"

Decree 31-2012 defines "Public Official" as any person in a legislative, executive, administrative, or judicial position, whether appointed or elected, permanent or temporary, paid or honorary.[33] A "Public Official" is also any person who exercises a public function, including for a government instrumentality or state owned enterprise, or provides a public service.[34]

Notably, Article 441 of the Criminal Code extends the applicability of domestic bribery offenses (i.e., active and passive bribery) to arbitrators, experts, and "other persons who exercise a public function or role."[35] However, arbitrators, experts, and "other persons who

---

[28] Criminal Code, Article 439.

[29] Criminal Code, Article 441. Note that no definition is provided for "public function."

[30] Criminal Code, Article 442.

[31] Criminal Code, Article 443.

[32] *See* Criminal Code, Article 107.

[33] Criminal Code, General Provisions, Article I (as modified by Decree 31-2012).

[34] Criminal Code, General Provisions, Article I (as modified by Decree 31-2012).

[35] Criminal Code, Article 441. Note than no definition is provided for "public function."

exercise a public function or role" are not covered by the illicit acceptance of gifts provision in Article 443 of the Criminal Code.

5.5 GIFTS, GRATUITIES, AND HOSPITALITY

Guatemalan law does not prohibit giving gifts, gratuities, or other hospitality to domestic officials. Rather, the propriety of the gift, gratuity, or hospitality turns on whether the gift, gratuity, or hospitality was provided to influence the official to carry out or refrain from performing an act benefitting the giver of the gift, gratuity, or hospitality.

Article 443 of the Criminal Code, however, prohibits domestic officials from accepting any gifts—regardless of purpose—from persons who have a matter pending before him or her.

5.6 DEFENSES

5.6.1 Facilitation Payments

Facilitation payments are not a defense or exception to any of the bribery offenses under the Criminal Code.

5.6.2 Adequate Procedures

Corporations may be held criminally liable for acts of bribery or corruption by their directors, managers, executives, representative's administrators, officials, or employees if the corporation failed to "control or supervise" the conduct its administrators, officials, or employees or authorized the conduct. However, the existence of adequate procedures to prevent the risk of bribery is not recognized as an affirmative defense to a domestic bribery charge.

5.6.3 Corporate Culture

The demonstration of a corporate culture that does not condone illicit bribery may help in support of a defense against corporate criminal liability, but is not a defense to a charge of domestic bribery or corruption.

5.7 PENALTIES

The penalty structure discussed in Section 4.7 of the chapter also applies to cases of domestic bribery.

Domestic officials who solicit or induce an improper gift are subject to imprisonment of 12 to 60 months and to a fine of 100 to 3,000 quetzales.[36]

The illicit acceptance of gifts is punishable by a term of imprisonment between one and three years and to a fine of between 5,000 and 25,000 quetzales.[37]

---

[36] Criminal Code, Article 439.

[37] Criminal Code, Article 443. As of July 1, 2017, this fine amount is equal to approximately U.S. $682 to $3,408.

In addition, under Decree 55-2010, the government can seek the forfeiture of any direct or indirect proceeds of passive or active bribery.[38] Asset forfeiture is a civil remedy that can be initiated, separate and apart from any criminal prosecution, when no criminal conviction has been sought or obtained.

Asset forfeiture proceedings may be initiated by the Public Prosecutor if an investigation concludes that there is a credible and reasonable basis to believe that the assets in question are the result of criminal conduct as defined in Article 4 of Decree 55-2010. Within the proceedings, the burden of proof rests with the defendant to establish that the assets were not the product of criminal conduct.

6. Commercial Bribery

There is no commercial bribery offense under Guatemalan law.

7. Sentencing Principles
7.1 GENERAL PRINCIPLES

In Guatemala, sentencing guidelines are codified in the Criminal Code.[39] The guidelines provide a range (minimum and maximum) for offenses enumerated in the Criminal Code. Judges may take certain mitigating and aggravating factors under consideration, such as:

- The danger posed by the defendant;
- The defendant's criminal history;
- The history of the victim; and
- The extent of the harm caused.

8. Related Criminal Offenses
8.1 CONSPIRACY

The crime of conspiracy was introduced in Guatemala through Decree 21-2006. "Conspiracy" is defined as acting in concert with one or more persons toward the commission of one or more offenses enumerated in Article 3 of the Decree.[40] The applicable penalty for conspiracy is the same as that for the underlying offense, and it is independent of the penalty for the underlying offense.[41]

8.2 ATTEMPTS

The attempt to commit an unlawful act is codified as a crime in Articles 14 and 15 of the Criminal Code.

---

[38] *See* Decree 55-2010, Article 2(a.5).

[39] Criminal Code, Article 65.

[40] Decree 21-2006, Article 3.

[41] *Id.*

Article 14 provides that an attempt exists when the execution of a criminal offense is commenced, but is frustrated by causes independent of the actor's will.

Under Article 15, an attempt exists even if the would-be criminal offense is sought to be committed through means that would make the realization of the crime impossible.

8.3 AIDING AND ABETTING

Article 37 of the Criminal Code, criminalizes aiding and abetting by creating criminal liability for those who:

- Encourage another in his/her resolve to commit a crime;
- Promise to assist or cooperate after a crime is committed;
- Provide information or obtain the resources for the commission of a crime;
- Act as a conduit or an intermediary between participants of a crime to facilitate coordination; or
- Provide cover to those who commit a crime.

8.4 FALSE ACCOUNTING AND BOOKS AND RECORDS

Guatemalan legislation does not include a crime for false accounting entries or inaccurate books and records.

9. Cooperation and Self Reporting

9.1 COOPERATION WITH INVESTIGATORS AND PROSECUTORS

Guatemala's criminal system provides cooperation credit to individuals who have participated in criminal conduct but provides "effective collaboration" to an investigation or prosecution of organized crime, including bribery offenses.[42]

Collaboration is deemed effective when it leads to any of the following results:

- Avoids the continuation or consummation of the crime or decreases its scope;
- Provides a better understanding of the planning or execution of the crime;
- Identifies the architects or perpetrators of the crime that has been committed or will be committed, or identifies leaders of a criminal organization;
- Identifies the members of a criminal organization and its operations permitting the authorities to dismantle it, reduce its membership, or detain one or more of its members;
- Assists in tracking or locating the instruments, goods, products, or earnings generated by the criminal activity as well as the sources financing the criminal organization;
- Delivers instruments, goods, products, or earnings generated by of the criminal activities.[43]

---

[42] Articulo 90 Ley contra la Delincuencia y Crimen Organizado.
[43] Decree 21-2006, Article 91.

The following benefits may be granted for effective cooperation:

- Suspension of criminal prosecution;
- Withdrawal of charges or termination of criminal proceedings;
- Reduction in prison sentence.

Whether cooperation credit will be granted at all depends on the effectiveness of the cooperation and on the materiality or importance of the cooperation to the prosecution. For cooperation credit to be granted for testimony against the defendant, corroboratory evidence must also be presented.[44]

9.2 SELF-REPORTING

There is no formal self-reporting mechanism in Guatemala, nor is there formal mitigation credit for those who self-report.

9.3 PLEA AGREEMENTS

Plea agreements are available, but only with relation to crimes with sentences of fewer than five years.

9.4 LENIENCY

Guatemalan law does not permit judges to apply leniency in sentencing. However, the Guatemalan constitution does grant the president of Guatemala the ability to issue pardons and thereby suspend sentences.

10. Whistle-Blower Protection

Guatemala does not offer whistle-blower protections.

11. Relevant International Treaties
11.1 OECD

Guatemala, as noted above, is not a signatory to the OECD Convention on Combating Bribery of Foreign Public Officials in International Business Transactions.

11.2 UNITED NATIONS

Guatemala is bound by two conventions sponsored by the United Nations (UN) to combat criminal syndicates and promote anti-corruption measures. On December 12, 2000,

---

[44] Decree 21-2006, Article 92.

Guatemala signed the UN Convention against Transnational Organized Crime, which was ratified on September 25, 2003. On December 9, 2003, Guatemala signed the UN Convention against Corruption, which was ratified on November 3, 2006.

11.3 OTHER TREATIES AND INITIATIVES

As an OAS member country, Guatemala ratified the Inter-American Convention against Corruption (IACAC) on June 12, 2001. Guatemala was subject to four rounds of reviews by OAS experts assessing its implementation of the IACAC. In 2011, Guatemala joined the Extractive Industry Transparency Initiative (EITI), a global standard promoting the open and accountable management of oil, gas, and mineral resources. In 2014, Guatemala was declared compliant with EITI Rules set out in 2011. It is yet to be assessed against the upgraded 2016 EITI Standard.[45] In addition, Guatemala has participated in the Open Government Partnership (OGP) since 2011. OGP is an international platform launched in 2011 to foster government transparency and accountability. Participating countries must develop action plans with concrete commitments to promote transparency, conduct independent reporting on progress, and engage civil society in the process. Having completed two reporting cycles with 62 commitments, Guatemala is currently working to fulfill 22 new commitments under its third action plan.[46]

12. Transnational Cooperation
12.1 MUTUAL LEGAL ASSISTANCE TREATIES

Guatemala adopted two OAS conventions relating to mutual legal assistance in fighting corruption.

The first is the Inter-American Convention against Corruption, which Guatemala ratified in 2001. That Convention requires signatory states to "afford one another the widest measure of mutual assistance . . . in conformity with their domestic laws" in the investigation and prosecution of corrupt acts.[47]

The second is the Inter-American Convention on Mutual Assistance in Criminal Matters, ratified by Guatemala in 2003. It requires signatory states to assist with notification of rulings and judgments, taking of testimony, summoning of witnesses, freezing of assets, searches and seizures, and transmittal of documents, among other things.[48] Application of the convention is limited to crimes "punishable by one year or more of imprisonment" in the state requesting assistance.[49]

---

[45] Extractive Industry Transparency Initiative (EITI).

[46] Open Government Partnership (OGP).

[47] Inter-American Convention against Corruption Article 14, Mar. 29, 1996, S. Treaty Doc. No. 105-39, 35 I.L.M. 724.

[48] *Id.* Article 7.

[49] *Id.* Article 6.

12.2 EXTRADITION

12.2.1 Domestic Laws

The Law Regulating Extradition Procedures, Congressional Decree 28-2008 (the "Extradition Law") is the principal regulatory scheme for extradition. It covers (1) active extradition, whereby the Guatemalan government seeks extradition of persons to Guatemala from another state; and (2) passive extradition, whereby the Guatemalan government receives a request from another state to surrender fugitives.

With regard to passive extradition, the Extradition Law stipulates that the judicial branch shall be solely responsible for deciding the admissibility of passive extraditions presented by the Public Prosecutor Service.[50] It further states that a refusal to grant extradition requires the State of Guatemala to bring criminal actions when it is permissible under a treaty, convention, international arrangement, or domestic law.[51]

The Extradition Law also allows the foreign state seeking extradition to request the Guatemalan government to place the person sought under preventive custody, provided that the foreign state demonstrates the existence of an arrest warrant and presents a formal extradition request within the deadline set in the international arrangement.[52]

With regard to active extradition, the Extradition Law instructs the Ministry of Foreign Affairs, at the request of the Public Prosecutor's Office, to issue a request for preventive custody or formal extradition to the foreign state, when a Guatemalan court has ordered the arrest of the person sought and the person has been convicted and sentenced to prison.[53]

Finally, the Extradition Law establishes the "preeminence of international treaties dealing with extradition." When an international treaty ratified by Guatemala sets out different extradition procedures than those in the Law, "the treaty provisions shall prevail."[54]

Article 8 of the Criminal Code echoes the preeminence of international treaties:

Extradition may only be requested or granted for common crimes. In cases involving extradition covered by international treaties, it may only be granted if there is reciprocity.

In no case may extradition be sought or granted for political crimes or for related common crimes.

With respect to the extradition of Guatemalan citizens, the Guatemalan constitution provides that "Guatemalans may not be extradited for political crimes, nor may they be surrendered to a foreign government under any circumstances, except under treaties or conventions pertaining to crimes against humanity or against international law."[55]

---

[50] The Law Regulating Extradition Procedures, Congressional Decree 28-2008, Article 10.

[51] *Id.*

[52] *Id.* Article 14.

[53] *Id.* Article 31.

[54] *Id.* Article 34.

[55] Guatemalan Constitution, Article 7.

12.2.2 Extradition Treaties

Guatemala has bilateral extradition treaties with Belgium, Spain, the United States of America, Great Britain, and Mexico.[56] Guatemala also ratified the 1933 Montevideo Convention on Extradition along with Argentina, Chile, Columbia, the Dominican Republic, Ecuador, El Salvador, Honduras, Mexico, Nicaragua, Panama, and the United States.[57]

In addition, Guatemala is a party to the Inter-American Convention Against Corruption and the United Nations Convention against Corruption, both which contain extradition obligations for individuals involved in corruption. In fact, as a signatory to these two Conventions, Guatemala has sought extradition of Guatemalan public officials who have arrest warrants for corrupt acts that took place in Guatemala.

Guatemala is also a party to the following treaties in Matters of International Criminal cooperation, elements of which bear on its extradition obligations: Treaty of Reciprocal Assistance in Criminal Matters between Guatemala and Mexico of February 1996, Treaty of Reciprocal Assistance in Criminal Matters between the Republics of Central America of 1993, Inter-American Treaty of Reciprocal Assistance, and the Interamerican Convention of Criminal Reciprocal Assistance of 1992.

12.3 TECHNICAL COOPERATION

Guatemala has benefited from several bilateral and multilateral assistance programs to strengthen its legal institutions and promote public accountability. Most notable among them is the International Commission against Impunity in Guatemala (CICIG), a UN-sponsored independent body charged with investigating and prosecuting serious crimes in Guatemala. CICIG played a crucial role in exposing corruption schemes involving the former president, Otto Pérez Molina, and supporting the prosecution of high officials by Guatemala's Public Prosecutor Service.[58] In addition, CICIG provides technical assistance to public institutions such as the Public Prosecutor Service and the National Civilian Police to build longer-term capacity to combat organized crime.[59] Other technical cooperation programs undertaken by Guatemala include the Transparency and Integrity Project with USAID, the bilateral aid agency run by the U.S. government, and with the World Bank, the Project for Tax Administration Transparency and Efficiency.[60]

13. Forecast for Reforms

13.1 LEGISLATIVE REFORMS

Guatemala has taken important steps to strengthen the design and implementation of its anti-corruption legislation. The anti-corruption law of Decree 31-2012 enacted

---

[56] Ministry of Foreign Affairs, Republic of Guatemala, *Extradition Procedure in Guatemala*.

[57] Convention on Extradition (Inter-American), Dec. 26, 1933, 49 Stat. 3111.

[58] Kevin Casas-Zamora & Miguel Carter, Beyond the Scandals: the Changing Context of Corruption in Latin America 21 (2017).

[59] CICIG Brochure, available at http://www.cicig.org/uploads/documents/broshure/broshure_en.pdf (last visited Dec. 19, 2018).

[60] In a press release dated January 18, 2017, the World Bank announced a $55 million project loan to improve the transparency and efficiency of the tax administration in Guatemala.

important modifications and new felonies for the Criminal Code, and the Law against Organized Crime.

In addition, in 2015, Guatemala introduced significant reforms to increase the transparency of the public procurement process.

13.2 POLITICAL AND AGENCY ENFORCEMENT

Since the corruption scandal of 2015, the fight against corruption has been at the forefront of CICIG activities in Guatemala and a hallmark of the Public Prosecutor Service's agenda. Through their collective efforts, the CICIG and the Public Prosecutor Service have uncovered other corruption scandals, and promoted criminal prosecution against a number of public officials. Currently family members of the president have been arraigned and are pending trial. Most of the corruption prosecutions have involved little relationship with bribery, but have nevertheless increased awareness of the need to counter corruption in all of its forms.

13.3 POLICY AND PRACTICE

Despite the efforts of the CICIG and Public Prosecutor Service, Guatemala's executive branch has not introduced any policy changes related to bribery or corruption. Regrettably, this inaction continues to fuel public skepticism regarding the extent and effectiveness of the reforms.

However, in practice, the president of Guatemala ran a campaign that included anti-corruption platforms and, since taking office, has supported the efforts of CICIG and the Public Prosecutor Service. There is hope, therefore, that the tide in Guatemala is changing and that greater efforts will be made at all levels and across all branches to fight corruption.

APPENDIX

Key Issues	Guatemala's Approach
Is Guatemala subject to any international anti-corruption conventions? If so, which conventions?	Yes. UN Convention against Corruption. UN Convention against Transnational Organized Crime. Inter-American Convention against Corruption. The Extractive Industry Transparency Initiative. Open Government Partnership.

Key Issues	Guatemala's Approach
Is bribery of foreign public officials illegal?	Yes, under Decree 31-2012 the existing bribery felony was expanded.
Do domestic anti-bribery laws apply extraterritorially?	The jurisdiction of Guatemala's Criminal Code is territorial, with the exception of extraterritorial provisions set forth in Article 5 of the Code (Article 5's proscriptions are outlined in the substantive chapter on Guatemala). Therefore, unless a bribery offense falls within one of the exceptions under Article 5, the offense may only be charged if the conduct occurred within Guatemala.
What is the definition of a foreign public official?	Decree 31-2012 defines "Foreign Public Official" as "any person in a legislative, executive, administrative, or judicial position of a foreign country, whether appointed or elected; and any person that exercises a public function for a foreign country, including a government instrumentality and state owned enterprise."
Is commercial bribery illegal?	No.
Is bribing domestic officials illegal?	Yes, and is punishable by imprisonment for 5 to 10 years and by a fine of between 50,000 and 500,000 quetzals.
Can the recipient of a bribe be prosecuted?	The recipient of a bribe may be prosecuted for violating the Criminal Codes prohibition against "passive bribery." which occurs when a public official or employee intentionally solicits or accepts, directly or indirectly, any object of pecuniary value or another benefit, such as a favor, gift, present, promise, or advantage for him- or herself or another person, in exchange for carrying out or refraining from performing an act within the scope of said public official's or employee's official functions.
Can companies be held criminally liable? If so, what is the requisite intent for corporate criminal liability?	Yes. Corporations may be held criminally liable if any of their directors, managers, executives, representatives, administrators, officers, or employees engage in active transnational bribery for the company's benefit.

(*Continued*)

Key Issues	Guatemala's Approach
Can an individual be held civilly liable?	Yes.
Is there a "facilitation payment" defense?	No, there is no facilitation payment defense.
Do conspiracy laws apply to anti-corruption offenses?	Yes. "Conspiracy" is defined as acting in concert with one or more persons toward the commission of one or more offenses enumerated in Article 3 of the Decree.[61] The applicable penalty for conspiracy is the same as that for the underlying offense, and it is independent of the penalty for the underlying offense.
Does Guatemala provide liability for: aiding and/or abetting liability attempted liability for anti-corruption laws?	Yes.
Is the failure to keep accurate books and records a criminal or civil offense?	No.
Do any books and records offenses have to involve proof of an underlying bribery offense?	N/A
Are there Guatemalan laws concerning a company's financial internal controls? If so, are those laws applicable to public and/or private companies?	No.
Is there an affirmative disclosure obligation for potential violations of anti-corruption laws or accounting irregularities?	No.
Are "promotional expenses" exempt from Guatemala's anti-corruption laws?	No.
Is the giving of gifts, entertainment, travel, meals, or other gratuities restricted or prohibited by anti-corruption or other laws?	Guatemalan law does not prohibit giving gifts, gratuities, or other hospitality to domestic officials. Rather, the propriety of the gift, gratuity, or hospitality turns on whether the gift, gratuity, or hospitality was provided to influence the official to carry out or refrain from performing an act benefitting the giver of the gift, gratuity, or hospitality. However, Article 443 of the Criminal Code prohibits domestic officials from accepting any gifts—regardless of purpose—from persons who have a matter pending before him or her.

---

[61] Decree 21-2006, Article 3.

Key Issues	Guatemala's Approach
Are there any Guatemalan laws concerning things, property, or benefits of value conveyed by, or to, third parties?	Yes.
Are tax bribes deductible?	No.
Are Guatemala's anti-corruption laws applied extraterritorially?	The jurisdiction of Guatemala's Criminal Code is territorial, with the exception of extraterritorial provisions set forth in Article 5 of the Code. Therefore, unless a bribery offense falls within one of the exceptions under Article 5, the offense may only be charged if the conduct occurred within Guatemala.
Is a robust corporate compliance program an affirmative defense or a factor to negate liability or reduce penalties?	No.
Is there a "local law" exception or defense to Guatemala's anti-corruption laws?	No.
Is "credit" given for cooperation with authorities? If so, how and in what form?	Guatemala's criminal system provides cooperation credit to individuals who have participated in criminal conduct but provides "effective collaboration" to an investigation or prosecution of organized crime, including bribery offenses. Whether cooperation credit will be granted at all depends on the effectiveness of the cooperation and on the materiality or importance of the cooperation to the prosecution. For cooperation credit to be granted for testimony against the defendant, corroboratory evidence must also be presented.
Does Guatemala have a mutual legal assistance agreement with the United States that covers criminal matters, including anti-corruption conduct?	Yes. See the Inter-American Convention on Mutual Assistance in Criminal Matters for mutual assistance provisions and procedures. See also the U.S.-Guatemala bilateral extradition treaty, which covers "embezzlement or criminal embezzlement of public funds" in the list of crimes eligible for extradition."[62]

(*Continued*)

---

[62] Treaty between the United States and the Republic of Guatemala for the Mutual Extradition of Fugitives from Justice, Feb. 27, 1903, 33 Stat. 2147, T.S. 425.

Key Issues	Guatemala's Approach
What are the potential penalties/sanctions for criminal and civil violations of Guatemala's anti-corruption laws?	**"Active" Transnational Bribery**
	Active Transnational Bribery is punishable by imprisonment for 5 to 10 years and by a fine of between 50,000 and 500,000 quetzals.[63]
	Corporate Liability
	Under Guatemalan anti-bribery laws, a corporation engaging in active transnational bribery may be subject to a fine ranging between 100,000 and 750,000 quetzals.[64] In the event of a repeat offense, corporate dissolution may be ordered.
	"Passive" Transnational Bribery
	Passive Transnational Bribery is punishable by 5 to 10 years imprisonment and a fine of 50,000 to 500,000 quetzals.

[63] Criminal Code, Article 442 Bis (as modified by Decree 31-2012). As of July 1, 2017, this fine amount is equal to approximately U.S. $6,817 to $68,165.

[64] As of July 1, 2017, this fine amount is equal to approximately U.S. $13,633 to $102,248.

10 India

1. Introduction to India's Anti-Corruption Legislation

On May 26, 2014, Narendra Modi took office as India's current prime minister.[1] Modi had won a landslide victory after campaigning on a few key platform items, chief among these his pledges to reinvigorate the Indian economy, and to eradicate the corruption hindering legitimate economic growth. In November 2016, Modi undertook the most high-profile anti-corruption measure of his administration to date, when he announced to the country that India immediately would remove from circulation all 500- and 1,000-rupee notes. The goal of demonetization was to remove "black money" from the Indian economy that Modi and others viewed as underpinning graft, kickbacks, tax evasion, and associated offenses.

The demonetization campaign was a global media sensation, with some praising Modi's bold stroke and others expressing concern that it might be a triumph of style over substance. Just over a year post-demonetization, feelings continue to be mixed—and this is also an apt assessment of the larger Indian anti-corruption landscape. Although there have been a number of high-profile prosecutions against politicians and businesspersons in recent years, anti-corruption enforcement in the country remains constrained and often painstakingly slow: the Indian Prevention of Corruption Act criminalizes bribery of Indian government officials, but no analogous legislation exists criminalizing commercial bribery or bribery of foreign government officials. Similarly, India saw its first conviction under the Prevention of Money Laundering Act (PMLA) in 2017—but this came 15 years after the law was enacted.

---

[1] This chapter was contributed by Kirkland & Ellis's Cori Lable, Sunil Shenoi, and Tarun Warriar.

From Baksheesh to Bribery. T. Markus Funk and Andrew S. Boutros.
© Oxford University Press 2019. Published 2019 by Oxford University Press.

Notwithstanding the current prime minister's reform agenda, and although a number of legislative reforms to expand the scope of current anti-corruption laws are pending in the Indian parliament, there is much ground to make up before India can be viewed as a global leader in the fight against bribery.

2. Domestic Anti-Corruption Framework

2.1 CRIMINAL LAW REGIME

India has several criminal laws that prohibit bribery and corruption. The primary legislation penalizing corruption as a criminal offense is the Prevention of Corruption Act, 1988 (PCA), which principally prohibits government officials from accepting bribes, although recent 2018 amendments to the PCA now also have criminalized paying bribes intended to influence government officials. Corruption may also constitute criminal offenses under certain provisions of the Foreign Contribution Regulation Act 2010 (FCRA) and the Indian Penal Code 1860 (IPC), both of which apply to government officials and private citizens.

In contrast to anti-corruption laws of other countries, such as the United States or United Kingdom, bribe-giving is not an offense under the FCRA or the IPC, and traditionally was not targeted by the PCA either. With the recent amendments to the PCA, bribe-givers may now be prosecuted for giving or offering an "undue advantage" with the intent of "inducing" or "rewarding" a public servant to improperly perform a public duty. Under the IPC, a bribe-giver can be prosecuted for "cheating," as discussed in Section 5.3.1.2. Further, India does not currently have any legislation that criminalizes bribery of foreign officials, focusing only on bribes accepted by Indian public officials.

Other 2018 amendments to the PCA have brought the statute more in line with international laws such as the U.S. Foreign Corrupt Practices Act (FCPA) and the UK Bribery Act (UKBA). In particular, the amended PCA now makes clear that it is "immaterial" whether bribes are paid directly or through a third party, and allows for prosecution of indirect bribery schemes. The amendments also created corporate liability for "commercial organizations" (defined to include companies formed outside of India, but operating within the country), and permits the acts of such organizations' "associated persons" (presumptively including employees, and defined as including all others who "perform services for or on behalf of the commercial organization") to be imputed to them. Corporate officers found to have consented to or acted in furtherance of corporate corrupt conduct also may be found personally liable. However, similar to the UKBA, the PCA also now allows companies to raise an "adequate procedures" defense, such that vicarious liability for the acts of associated persons may be defeated if the company is able to demonstrate it has implemented appropriate internal controls. Given how new these changes are, it remains to be seen how the amended PCA may affect India's enforcement landscape.

2.2 CIVIL LAW REGIME

Like many jurisdictions, India's civil law regime consists of several sets of laws that prohibit corruption. Where India is notably different from other jurisdictions is that its civil laws addressing corruption tend to focus on regulating the conduct of government officials, not corrupt acts committed by private citizens. Certain types of laws apply to different levels of government officials, such as the Central Civil Services (Conduct) Rules, 1964, which apply to nearly every civil service employee of the central government; and the All India Services (Conduct) Rules, 1968, which apply to Central and state government employees, such as members of the Indian Administrative Service, the Indian Police Service, and the Indian Forest Service. Other laws focus on particular types of employees, such as the Indian Foreign Service (Conduct and Discipline) Rules, 1961 and the Railway Services (Conduct) Rules. These laws are discussed in greater detail in Section 5.3.1.3.

2.3 VIEW FROM THE OUTSIDE

2.3.1 OECD Evaluation

Despite being one of the world's largest economies, India is one of only five G20 members that have not signed the OECD Anti-Bribery Convention, which aims to reduce corruption in developing countries by establishing sanctions against the bribery of foreign government officials in international business transactions. Nevertheless, India has signed the United Nations Convention Against Corruption (UNCAC), and recent developments by the current Modi government of India suggest a desire to reduce corruption.

2.3.2 Transparency International Evaluation

India has consistently fared poorly in Transparency International's (TI's) evaluations of corruption. In particular, India has been ranked quite low in TI's well-known Corruption Perception Index (CPI), finishing between 76th and 95th each year from 2011 to 2017. TI also recently published a special report on corruption in the Asia-Pacific region, in which India was found to have the highest bribery rate of the 16 countries that were surveyed.[2] Nearly 7 in 10 people examined by TI acknowledged payment of a bribe in connection with access to public services. Survey respondents also ranked India the highest with respect to the frequency of bribes paid in connection with public schools, public hospitals, IDs and voting rights, utilities, and police. At the same time, the TI report also provides cause for cautious optimism, as survey respondents ranked India among the top three countries regarding the government's efforts to fight corruption.

3. Investigative and Prosecutorial Agencies

3.1 CENTRAL BUREAU OF INVESTIGATION (CBI) AND ANTI-CORRUPTION BUREAU (ACB)

The CBI and ACB are the principal government agencies in India tasked with investigating offenses under the PCA. The CBI has jurisdiction over the central government and union territories, and usually takes on high-profile national cases involving substantial sums. For example, it is leading the investigation into the "2G" scandal, which involves allegations of a previous government allocating the 2G mobile frequency spectrum to certain private

---

[2] Transparency International, People and Corruption: Asia Pacific—Global Corruption Barometer, Mar, 7, 2017.

companies at heavily discounted prices, at an alleged loss of approximately U.S. $27 billion;[3] and the "Coalgate" scandal, in which it is alleged that a previous government allocated India's coal deposits to selected private companies at less than fair market value, at an alleged loss of approximately U.S. $170 billion.[4]

The ACB has branches in every state, which investigate potential violations within those specific states. For example, the Delhi Branch of the ACB is leading the investigation into conglomerate Reliance Industries, in relation to allegations that the company colluded with officials at the Oil Ministry in Delhi to fix the price of natural gas.[5] That branch office is also investigating alleged corruption at the Delhi Jal Board, which is the municipal body charged with administering Delhi's water supply.[6]

3.2 CENTRAL VIGILANCE COMMISSION (CVC)

The CVC was established in 1964 to address governmental corruption. Although it is an independent agency, free from executive authority, the CVC only conducts investigations relating to civil works of the Indian government, such as construction and infrastructure. For all other potential crimes, including corruption under the PCA, the CVC exercises supervisory jurisdiction over the Central Bureau of Investigation (CBI) and assists the CBI with technical matters.

Although the CVC's investigative powers are limited, the CVC also provides a valuable public function by providing the public with information about enforcement efforts and initiatives. For example, the CVC has issued guidelines for government agencies when initiating corruption cases against judicial or quasi-judicial officers.[7] Likewise, the CVC provides an annual report to Parliament sharing statistics on government corruption. In 2017, the CVC reported that complaints against public servants had increased 67 percent from 2015 to 2016, a substantial portion of which still are pending investigation.[8]

3.3 ENFORCEMENT DIRECTORATE

Although not directly related to policing anti-corruption laws, the Enforcement Directorate is charged with investigating and prosecuting cases relating to the Prevention of Money

---

[3] http://indiatoday.intoday.in/story/what-is-the-2g-scam-all-about/1/188832.html (Oct. 19, 2012) (last visited Dec. 14, 2018).

[4] http://www.thehindu.com/news/national/whats-the-coal-scam-about/article6983434.ece (Mar. 12, 2015) (last visited Dec. 14, 2018).

[5] https://economictimes.indiatimes.com/industry/energy/oil-gas/anti-corruption-branch-calls-reliance-industries-executive-director-for-questioning/articleshow/60963409.cms (Oct.6, 2017) (last visited Dec.14, 2018).

[6] http://www.thehindu.com/news/national/other-states/ACB-asks-Mishra-to-join-investigation/article14999910.ece (Sept.26, 2016) (last visited Dec.14, 2018).

[7] http://indianexpress.com/article/india/india-news-india/central-vigilance-commissions-new-guidelines-to-take-action-against-judicial-officers-4387688/ (Nov.21, 2016) (last visited Dec.14, 2018).

[8] https://economictimes.indiatimes.com/news/politics-and-nation/67-jump-in-corruption-complaints-railways-tops-cvc/articleshow/58167812.cms (Apr.13, 2017) (last visited Dec.14, 2018).

Laundering Act 2002 and the Foreign Exchange Management Act 1999. It is common for the Enforcement Directorate to refer a matter to the CVC or CBI if it identifies evidence suggesting that a related crime has been committed under the PCA.[9]

3.4 SERIOUS FRAUD INVESTIGATION OFFICE (SFIO)

The SFIO was established under the Companies Act, 2013, and is devoted to detecting, investigating, and prosecuting white-collar crime and fraud. The SFIO is expected to investigate three types of cases: (1) complex cases with multidisciplinary involvement; (2) cases of substantial public interest, based on size or monetary impact; or (3) investigations that could lead to clear improvement in India's systems, laws, or procedures. Significantly, SFIO investigations preempt investigations by other government agencies.[10]

Recently, the SFIO's prosecutorial powers expanded to include the authority to arrest people for violations of the Companies Act, 2013, and in late August 2017, the Corporate Affairs Ministry finally promulgated rules effectuating the SFIO's arrest authority. [11] Given that the SFIO has initiated more than 300 investigations in the last three years, SFIO enforcement activity may increase now that SFIO can also carry out arrests.

3.5 COMPTROLLER AND AUDITOR GENERAL OF INDIA (CAG)

The CAG is a constitutional authority responsible for auditing the income and expenses of the Indian central and state governments, all government-affiliated companies and corporations, and all other bodies substantially financed by the government. Although it has no prosecutorial powers, the CAG has played an increasingly prominent role in recent years, as its reports have been used by citizens in "public interest litigations" seeking court orders to investigate suspected corruption. For example, it was a CAG report that ultimately led to the investigation into the alleged allotment of telecom bandwidth spectrum at improperly low valuations (the "2G" scandal).

3.6 LOKPAL AND LOKAYUKTA

Pursuant to the Lokpal and Lokayuktas Act, 2013, independent ombudsmen at central (Lokpal) and state (Lokayukta) level were created to investigate and prosecute corruption by public officials. The impact of these ombudsmen has been uncertain, however, as the office of the Lokpal is currently vacant, and the investigative activity of both the Lokpal and the Lokayukta has been minimal.

---

[9] *See, e.g.,* the ED's referral to the CBI related to an investigation of Moin Qureshi (http://indianexpress.com/article/india/india-news-india/cbi-examines-reference-from-ed-to-probe-moin-qureshi-meat-exporter-corruption-beef-ban-4381342/) (Nov. 18, 2016) (last visited Dec. 14, 2018).

[10] s.212(3) Companies Act.

[11] https://economictimes.indiatimes.com/news/economy/policy/now-serious-fraud-investigation-office-has-powers-to-arrest/articleshow/60244268.cms (Aug.27, 2017) (last visited Dec.14, 2018).

4. Bribery of Foreign Officials

Unlike many other global jurisdictions, India does not have legislation prohibiting bribery of foreign officials. Although legislation to address this area has been proposed, such proposals have stalled, which may be attributable to the Indian government's current focus on reducing domestic corruption.

5. Bribery of Domestic Officials

India's anti-bribery regime consists of both criminal and civil laws designed to prohibit bribery of Indian government officials. India's criminal offenses are set out in the PCA, FCRA, IPC, and the Companies Act. The PCA specifically criminalizes the taking of bribes by "public servants," as well as the abetment of corruption by public servants. The FCRA makes it an offense for certain specified categories of public officials and government employees to accept contributions or hospitality from foreign sources. Corruption may also be considered a "criminal conspiracy," "criminal breach of trust," or "cheating" under the Indian Penal Code. Finally, bribery may also constitute "fraud" for the purposes of the Companies Act.

In addition to India's criminal prohibitions on bribery, government officials involved in bribery are subject to civil penalties under several sets of laws, including the Central Civil Services (Conduct) Rules, 1964; the All India Services (Conduct) Rules, 1968; and the Indian Foreign Service (Conduct and Discipline) Rules, 1961.

Despite the numerous laws that prohibit bribery, the PCA is the primary mechanism used by Indian regulatory authorities to investigate and prosecute bribery offenses. Accordingly, this chapter will focus on the PCA, while also discussing those other criminal laws' penalties for bribery. To a lesser extent, this chapter will briefly cover relevant civil laws against bribery.

5.1 JURISDICTION

The PCA applies throughout the territory of India, with the exception of the State of Jammu and Kashmir, and also applies to citizens of India residing outside India.[12] Unlike the FCPA and UKBA, the PCA does not apply to conduct occurring outside India, nor does it apply to bribes paid to foreign (i.e., non-Indian) government officials. Although it is a national law, special judges appointed by either the central government or any state government may adjudicate enforcement actions pursuant to the PCA.[13]

Other laws relating to corruption have broader geographic reach than the PCA. For example, the FCRA applies throughout India and to citizens of India who are not in India, as well as to companies registered or incorporated in India.[14] Although the FCRA is silent on whether its jurisdiction extends to conduct outside India, the definition of "foreign

---

[12] Section 2, PCA.
[13] Section 3, PCA.
[14] Section 1, FCRA.

hospitality" in the statute suggests that improper hospitality given to an Indian official in a foreign country would be prohibited. The IPC is more explicit, applying to all acts by Indian citizens, both within and outside India.[15] The Companies Act takes a similar approach with respect to companies registered or incorporated in India, but also applies to companies registered or incorporated outside India that have a place of business in India or that conduct business in India, provided that such companies are 50 percent or more owned by Indian citizens or parent companies that are themselves required to comply with the Companies Act.[16]

5.2 STATUTE OF LIMITATIONS

None of the PCA, FCRA, or Companies Act specifies a time limit for the prosecution of offenses or the completion of trials involving offenses under these statutes. However, under the Code of Criminal Procedure, complaints regarding criminal offenses under the IPC and other statutes must be filed within a limitations period,[17] which is based on the maximum penalty of the offense at issue: six months for offenses punishable by fine, one year for offenses subject to a maximum one-year prison term, and three years for offenses with a maximum one- to three-year prison term.[18] Notably, the Code of Criminal Procedure does not define a limitation period for offenses with a prison term of more than three years, so many bribery offenses technically may not be subject to any statute of limitations, although Indian courts have not specifically ruled on this issue.

5.3 DOMESTIC BRIBERY OFFENSES

5.3.1 Offenses by Officials

5.3.1.1 PCA

The PCA prohibits "public servants" from accepting, obtaining, agreeing to accept, or attempting to obtain a monetary or non-monetary bribe, referred to as a "gratification." This prohibition is implemented through a series of specific criminal offenses that forbid public servants from: (1) taking gratification other than legal remuneration in respect of an official act (section 7), (2) taking gratification by corrupt or illegal means in order to influence a public servant (section 8), (3) taking gratification for exercise of personal influence with a public servant (section 9), and (d) obtaining a valuable thing without consideration from a person involved in a proceeding or business transaction with such public servant (Section 11).[19]

---

[15] Section 4, IPC.

[16] Section 1, 2(42), 379, Companies Act.

[17] Live Law News Network, *In Criminal Cases, Period of Limitation Starts from the Date of Complaint, Not from Date of Cognizance: Constitution Bench*, LIVELAW.IN (Nov. 27, 2013), *available at* http://www.livelaw. in/in-criminal-cases-period-of-limitation-starts-from-the-date-of-complaint-not-from-date-of-cognizance-constitution-bench/ (describing the Indian Supreme Court's holding in Sarah Mathew v. Institute of Cardio Vascular Diseases & Ors. 2014(2) SCC 62, that "the relevant date is the date of filing of the complaint or the date of institution of prosecution and not the date on which the Magistrate takes cognizance").

[18] Section 468(2), Code of Criminal Procedure.

[19] Sections 7, 8, 9, 11, PCA.

The PCA also outlaws certain forms of "habitual" corruption (sections 13 and 14), as well as other forms of self-enrichment through bribery deemed as criminal misconduct (section 13).[20] Notably, the PCA does not contain the concept of a "facilitation" or "expediting" payment exception that is present in some international anti-bribery laws; thus, any such payment would be considered an illegal gratification under the PCA.[21]

Those prosecuted under the PCA face a potentially high hurdle: if the prosecution proves that the public servant accepted, agreed to accept, or attempted to obtain a bribe, whether monetary or non-monetary, the court then applies a rebuttable presumption that the purpose of the bribe was to take one of the prohibited actions described above (e.g., to influence a public official).[22] However, in January 2016, the Supreme Court of India significantly weakened the effect of this presumption. In *Krishan Chander v. State of Delhi*, a police constable allegedly demanded a Rs. 5,000 bribe to release the complainant's brother on bail.[23] After the complainant paid the first installment and his brother was released, the complainant worked with the Anti-corruption Bureau to use marked bills for the second installment.[24] Following the constable's acceptance of the second payment, which included the marked bills, the constable was arrested, convicted under sections 7 (accepting a bribe in exercise of official capacity) and 13 (criminal misconduct) of the PCA, and sentenced to two years in jail and a Rs. 500 fine.[25] The constable eventually appealed his conviction to the Supreme Court of India, which held that, notwithstanding the rebuttable presumption, proof of payment of the bribe was insufficient to support a conviction under the PCA; rather, the prosecution must also prove the additional element that the public servant had made a corrupt demand.[26] Although the *Krishan Chander* case involved only two anti-bribery provisions of the PCA, the court's narrow interpretation could present an obstacle for future anti-bribery enforcement in India.

5.3.1.2 Other Criminal Laws

The Foreign Contribution Regulation Act (FCRA) was enacted to consolidate and regulate the law on acceptance and utilization of foreign contributions or hospitality by certain specified individuals and organizations, on the ground that these activities are detrimental

---

[20] Section 13 of the PCA prohibits a public servant from: (i) habitual acceptance of bribes, (ii) habitual acceptance of things of value from people involved in transactions with the public servant, (iii) misappropriating property under his control as a public servant, (iv) obtaining monetary or non-monetary value by corrupt or illegal means or by abusing his position as a public servant, (v) obtaining monetary or non-monetary value without any public interest, (vi) possessing moneys disproportionate to his known source of income. Similarly, Section 14 criminalizes habitual corruption under Sections 8, 9, or 12 (abetment of Sections 7 or 11).

[21] Nishith Desai Associates, A Comparative View of Anti-corruption Laws of India: A Legal, Regulatory, Tax and Strategic Perspective 4, *available at* http://www.nishithdesai.com/fileadmin/user_upload/pdfs/Research%20Papers/A_Comparative_View_of_Anti-Corruption_Laws_of_India.pdf. (June 2016) (last visited Dec. 14, 2018).

[22] Section 20, PCA.

[23] Krishan Chander v. State of Delhi, India Supreme Court (Jan. 6, 2016).

[24] *Id.*

[25] *Id.*

[26] *Id.*

to India's national interest.[27] The FCRA outlaws two broad categories of conduct that could constitute bribery. First, the FCRA prohibits certain types of government officials from accepting a "foreign contribution" and prohibits residents of India and nonresident citizens from, directly or indirectly, accepting or delivering, foreign contributions on behalf of government officials.[28] Second, the FCRA prohibits certain categories of government officials from receiving any "foreign hospitality."[29]

Like anti-corruption laws in other jurisdictions, the term "foreign contribution" is broadly defined and includes the giving of any article valued above a certain threshold, currently set by the Indian government at Rs. 25,000 (U.S. $500).[30] "Foreign hospitality" means any offer that is not "purely casual" and is "made in cash or kind by a foreign source for providing a person with the costs of travel to any foreign country or territory, free boarding, lodging, transport, or medical treatment.[31] "Foreign source" includes any foreign company, trust, foundation, or citizen.[32] Compliance with the FCRA is administered by the Ministry of Home Affairs.

Acceptance of a bribe, or attempted participation in bribery, may also constitute a crime under the provisions of the Indian Penal Code 1860 (IPC).[33] Specifically, acts of corruption by a "public servant" may also amount to a "criminal conspiracy" when two or more persons agree to undertake or cause the commission of an illegal act.[34] In addition, corruption can constitute a "criminal breach of trust," in which a person entrusted with property dishonestly misappropriates or converts to his own use that property, or dishonestly uses or disposes of that property in violation of legal instructions.[35] Further, the IPC broadly defines an offense called "cheating," which includes inducing a person to deliver property that would not have been given without deception.[36] The broad nature of the above-described offenses under the IPC often results in parallel charges under the IPC and PCA for bribery-related conduct.[37]

---

[27] Recitals, FCRA.

[28] Section 3, FCRA.

[29] Sections 3 and 6, FCRA.

[30] Section 2(1)(h). FCRA.

[31] Section 2(1)(i), FCRA.

[32] Section 2(1)(j), FCRA.

[33] The Indian Penal Code defines bribery offenses that are similar to the PCA, but that are limited to the bribes in connection with the "exercise of electoral rights," which are defined as "the right of a person to stand, or not to stand as, or to withdraw from being, a candidate or to vote or refrain from voting at any election." Section 171 A of the IPC. Given the overlap of the PCA and the IPC's electoral bribery offenses, this chapter focuses on the PCA and other broadly applicable bribery laws.

[34] Section 120A, IPC.

[35] Section 409, IPC. The Supreme Court has held that a minister functions as a trustee with respect to public property, and failure to administer such property fairly could render him or her liable for criminal breach of trust. K.D. GAUR, TEXTBOOK ON THE INDIAN PENAL CODE 712 (4th ed. 2009) (describing the holding of *Shiva Sagar Tiwari v. Union of India* (1996) 6 SCC 558).

[36] Section 415, IPC.

[37] *See, e.g., Chargesheet against 11 Assam Officials*, THE TELEGRAPH (May 27, 2017), *available at* https://www.telegraphindia.com/1170527/jsp/northeast/story_153737.jsp (reporting that the vigilance and anti-corruption bureau of Assam charged officers of the Indian Administrative Service in Assam with violations of the PCA and IPC for bribery-related conduct); *see also* Alore Tikku, *Ex-Air Force Chief SP Tyagi, 8 Others Named in Chopper Scam Chargesheet*, NDTV (Sept. 1, 2017), *available at* https://www.ndtv.com/india-news/

Acceptance of a bribe may also constitute "fraud" under the Indian Companies Act, as "fraud" is defined to include "any act, omission, concealment of any fact of abuse of position committed by any person ... with intent to deceive, to gain undue advantage from, or to injure the interests of, the company or its shareholders or its creditors or any other person."[38]

5.3.1.3 Civil Laws

Although several sets of civil laws prohibit corruption, the scope of these laws is limited. For example, certain types of civil laws regulate improper conduct, including corruption, by government officials, such as the Central Civil Services (Conduct) Rules, 1964, which apply to nearly every civil service employee of the central government. Similarly, the All India Services (Conduct) Rules, 1968 apply to central and state government employees, including members of the Indian Administrative Service, the Indian Police Service, and the Indian Forest Service. Other civil laws focus on particular government agencies, such as the Indian Foreign Service (Conduct and Discipline) Rules, 1961 and the Railway Services (Conduct) Rules.

All of these various civil service rules contemplate anti-corruption compliance by requiring civil servants to meet standards of integrity and duty in the course of their employment.[39] Specifically, the rules contain restrictions on family members accepting employment with a private undertaking having official dealings with the government,[40] receipt of gifts with a value exceeding specific thresholds,[41] and acceptance of lavish or frequent hospitality from commercial organizations or persons having official dealings with the relevant civil servant.[42] However, acceptance of casual meals, transport, or hospitality is permitted.[43]

5.3.2 Offenses by Private Actors

5.3.2.1 PCA

One of the significant differences between the PCA and international anti-bribery laws such as the FCPA and UKBA involves the treatment of the bribe-*givers*. Until the 2018 amendments expanding the scope of the PCA, the statute only allowed for the prosecution of a bribe-giver for abetting a public servant's bribery offense,[44] and such prosecutions had been limited, if they occurred at all.[45] A significant factor undercutting the enforcement of the PCA against bribe-givers was the PCA itself— the prior section 24 of the PCA exempted a bribe-giver from prosecution if he or she agreed to provide evidence that he or she offered or agreed to offer the bribe in criminal proceedings against the accused public servant.[46]

---

ex-air-force-chief-sp-tyagi-9-others-named-in-chopper-scam-chargesheet-1745035 (reporting the prosecution of the former Air Force Chief, SP Tyagi, and AgustaWestland executives in connection with alleged payments to secure a contract for the supply of helicopters).

[38] Section 447, Companies Act.

[39] *See, e.g.*, Rule 3(2), Services Rules.

[40] *See, e.g.*, Rule 4(2)(b), Services Rules.

[41] *See, e.g.*, Rule 11(1), Services Rules.

[42] *See, e.g.*, Rule 11(3), Services Rules.

[43] *See, e.g.*, Rule 11(1), Services Rules.

[44] Section 10, PCA.

[45] NISHITH DESAI ASSOCIATES, *supra* note 21, at 3–4.

[46] Section 24, PCA.

In addition to this historic safe harbor, one Indian court previously held that bribe-givers can only be prosecuted if they are co-conspirators to the bribery. In other words, bribe-givers could not be prosecuted unless they affirmatively sought to, rather than were forced to, give a bribe. In *Akilesh Kumar v. CBI & Anr*, the appeal of a conviction for corruption under the PCA, the appellant's counsel argued that the evidence of two prosecution witnesses should be disregarded because they aided and abetted the crime. The High Court of Kerala rejected this argument, concluding that the witnesses did not intend to give a bribe: because abetment required the agreement of two or more people to engage in a conspiracy to do an illegal act, an individual who gave a bribe under duress lacked the requisite intent to aid and abet.[47]

The PCA now has changed the scope of these protections, and now only immunizes the conduct of bribe-givers who are deemed to be the victims of "coercive bribery" —that is, those who have been forced to pay bribes. In order to qualify for such immunity, the bribe-giver must report his or her payment and the circumstances to law enforcement or a relevant investigative agency within seven days. In addition, the PCA allows for the prosecution of intermediaries or "middle men" involved in facilitating bribery of public servants. Specifically, a person violates the PCA if he or she "accepts or obtains or agrees to accept or attempts to obtain, from any person, for himself or any other person, any gratification whatever, as a motive or reward for inducing, by the exercise of personal influence, any public servant."[48]

5.3.2.2 Other Relevant Laws

Although the PCA until recently allowed for prosecution of private bribe-givers only in limited circumstances, private bribe-givers have been subject to other criminal laws prohibiting bribery. As described previously, non-Indian nationals physically present in India and citizens of India residing outside India may also be prosecuted under the FCRA for delivering and/or receiving foreign contributions on behalf of government officials.[49] Similarly, the "criminal conspiracy" and "cheating" provisions of the IPC and the "fraud" provisions of the Companies Act allow for prosecution of private actors involved in bribery. Nevertheless, the PCA remains the primary enforcement mechanism for prosecuting corruption in India.

5.4 DEFINITION OF DOMESTIC OFFICIALS
5.4.1 PCA

As described previously, the PCA's prohibitions primarily apply to Indian domestic officials. "Public servants" are broadly defined under the law to include any: (1) person employed by the central, state, or local government; (2) person employed by a government entity; (3) judge or other person authorized to perform duties in connection with the administration of justice; (4) arbitrator; (5) election official; (6) other officer performing any public duty; (7) officer of a registered cooperative society that receives aid from the government; (8) member or

---

[47] 2011 (4) KLJ 471.
[48] Section 9, PCA.
[49] Section 3(2)(a), FCRA.

employee of a government commission or board; (9) university officials and employees; and (10) any other officer or employee of an institution receiving government aid.

Consistent with the PCA's explanatory note that the law should be broadly construed to encompass all individuals acting in a quasi-public manner,[50] the judiciary has afforded the definition of "public servant" extensive reach. For example, in *Central Bureau of Investigation v. Ramesh Gelli*, the Supreme Court of India held that the chair and executive director of a private sector bank should be considered public servants for purposes of the PCA.[51] The court reasoned that one of the underlying purposes of the PCA was to expand upon the definition of public servant used in prior laws, and that the two employees at issue would be considered public servants under the Banking Regulation Act of 1949, the statute under which the bank at issue was licensed.[52] Similarly, the Delhi High Court has held that employees of an insurance company formed by an act of Parliament were automatically considered public servants, regardless of their role or responsibilities.[53]

Despite its wide-ranging definition, certain parties fall outside the scope of the definition of "public servant." For example, unlike the FCPA, the PCA does not restrict payments made to members of public international organizations such as the United Nations or International Red Cross, political parties, or political candidates.[54]

5.4.2 Other Relevant Laws

Although certain parties fall outside the PCA's definition of public servant, some of those same parties are subject to the restrictions of the FCRA. Under the FCRA, the prohibition on accepting "foreign contributions" applies to candidates for election, judges, government servants, employees of government-owned or controlled bodies, members of the legislature, political parties, or political organizations.[55] In addition, employees of newspapers and companies that broadcast news via radio or television can also be subject to the prohibition on accepting foreign contributions.

In contrast, FCRA's prohibition on accepting "foreign hospitality" is applied more narrowly and only encompasses those traditionally viewed as government officials, such as members of the legislature, judges, government employees, and employees of state-owned or—controlled corporations.[56] The IPC's definition of "public servant" is similarly limited and covers only government employees, military officers, police, judges and officers of a Court of Justice, and employees of any local authority established by a central or state Act.[57] The key factor under the

---

[50] Section 2, PCA, Explanation 2 ("Wherever the words 'public servant' occur, they shall be understood of every person who is in actual possession of the situation of a public servant, whatever legal defect there may be in his right to hold that situation.").

[51] CBI v. Ramesh Gelli & Ors, 2016 (3) SCC 788 [Central Bureau of Investigation, Bank Securities & Fraud Cell v. Ramesh Gelli & Ors., Crl. App. 1077-1081 of 2013 decided on February 23, 2016.]

[52] CBI v. Ramesh Gelli & Ors, 2016 (3) SCC 788, at [7].

[53] Bhupinder Singh Sikka v. CBI Crl. App. No. 124 of 2011, Delhi High Court, decided on Mar. 25, 2011.

[54] http://www.luthra.com/admin/presentation_images/Challenges%20and%20Compliance%20under%20 Indian%20Anti-corruption%20Laws%20-%20Mohit%20Saraf%20-%20June%208.ppt (last visited Dec. 14, 2018).

[55] Section 3 FCRA.

[56] Section 6, FCRA.

[57] Section 21, IPC.

IPC is whether the individual functions as a public servant, not whether the individual is appointed by the government.[58]

5.5 PROCEDURAL CONCERNS

Although the scope of the parties and conduct covered by the PCA is broad, certain of the PCA's procedural requirements present challenges to enforcement. In particular, the PCA requires police officers below a certain rank to obtain a magistrate's order in advance before investigating any alleged offenses under the PCA.[59] In Delhi, this requirement applies to those below the rank of an Inspector of Police, whereas in other states, the requirement applies to all those below an Assistant Commissioner of Police. The one exception to this rule is that Inspectors of Police or higher-ranking officers may investigate violations of the PCA upon authorization from the applicable state government.

Even after a police investigation into violations of the PCA has begun, an additional procedural hurdle exists: Before a case against a public servant can be tried in court, a governmental body with authority to remove the public servant from office must sanction the prosecution.[60] For example, in order for a court to hear a case involving a central government official charged with violating the PCA, the central government must first approve the action's proceeding.[61] Similar requirements exist for employees of state and local governments.[62]

This pre-approval requirement has proven to be an obstacle to PCA enforcement actions.[63] Indeed, in 2012, the Supreme Court cited evidence that nearly 40 percent of requests to authorize litigation under the PCA were still pending approval from the applicable governmental authority.[64] Nevertheless, certain developments have helped ameliorate the potential obstacle posed by the pre-approval scheme. At the state level, Uttar Pradesh amended the PCA such that if a local authority in Uttar Pradesh has refused to sanction a case against a local public servant, the state government may step in to provide the required approval.[65] Furthermore, the Supreme Court has limited the application of the pre-approval requirement to situations when the public servant is still employed by the same governmental entity in connection with which the allegedly illegal conduct occurred.[66] If the public servant has left that office, then the pre-approval requirement does not apply, even if the individual continues to be employed by a different governmental entity.[67]

---

[58] Section 21, Explanation 1 and Explanation 2, IPC.

[59] Section 17, PCA.

[60] Section 19, PCA.

[61] Section 19, PCA.

[62] Section 19, PCA.

[63] NISHITH DESAI ASSOCIATES, *supra* note 21.

[64] *Id.*

[65] Section 19(d), PCA.

[66] L Narayana Swamy v. State of Karnataka (2016(8) SCALE 560); *see also* http://www.internationallawoffice.com/Newsletters/White-Collar-Crime/India/Shardul-Amarchand-Mangaldas-Co/Supreme-Court-rules-on-prior-approval-for-prosecution-of-public-servants?redir=1 (Oct.17, 2016) (last visited Dec.14, 2018).

[67] L Narayana Swamy v. State of Karnataka (2016(8) SCALE 560); see also http://www.internationallawoffice.com/Newsletters/White-Collar-Crime/India/Shardul-Amarchand-Mangaldas-Co/Supreme-Court-rules-on-prior-approval-for-prosecution-of-public-servants?redir=1 (Oct.17, 2016) (last visited Dec.14, 2018).

5.6 DEFENSES

The PCA has no affirmative defenses other than the newly introduced corporate "adequate procedures" defense—although as described in Section 5.3.1.1 of this chapter, the recent *Krishnan Chander* case illustrates that defendants also may argue that the prosecution has not proven that the public servant demanded a bribe.[68] Although *Krishnan Chander* involved only two anti-bribery provisions of the PCA, the court's narrow interpretation of the language of those provisions suggests that defendants charged under other sections of the PCA potentially could raise analogous ambiguity defenses. For example, defendants charged under section 14 of the PCA (habitual corruption) may challenge allegations that their conduct is "habitual," since the PCA does not define that term.

Neither the FCRA nor the Companies Act provide for affirmative defenses. However, the IPC sets forth several affirmative defenses, some of which are present in other jurisdictions, such as mistake of fact, justification, and coercion.[69]

5.7 PENALTIES

5.7.1 PCA

All convictions under the PCA require a term of imprisonment, with most of the anti-bribery provisions requiring a term ranging from six months to 10 years.[70] If an individual is convicted under section 13 of the PCA (criminal misconduct), then the minimum term of imprisonment increases to one to seven years.[71] If an individual is convicted under Section 14 of the PCA (habitual corruption), then the length of imprisonment changes again, this time to a term of two to seven years.[72] Imprisonment is required even when an individual has been convicted of an attempt to violate the PCA. In such cases, the PCA does not contain a minimum term, only a maximum term of three years.[73]

Individuals convicted under the PCA will also be fined, regardless of the provision under which they are convicted.[74] For most of the anti-bribery offenses, the statute provides no guidance about the magnitude of the potential fine or the criteria a court should use in calculating an appropriate one. However, if a public servant is found guilty of possessing monetary resources disproportionate to his income, a court is required to "take into account the pecuniary resources or property . . . [for] which the accused person is unable to account."[75] For all other convictions under sections 13 or 14, the court must "take into consideration

---

[68] Krishan Chander v. State of Delhi, India Supreme Court (Jan. 6, 2016).

[69] Sections 76–106, IPC.

[70] PCA, Sections 7–12.

[71] PCA, Section 13.

[72] PCA, Section 14.

[73] PCA, Section 15.

[74] *See* PCA Section 7 ("and shall also be liable to fine"); Section 8 (same); Section 9 (same); Section 10 (same); Section 11 (same); Section 12 (same); Section 13 (same); Section 14 (same); Section 15 ("shall be punishable . . . with fine").

[75] PCA, Section 16.

the amount or the value of the property, if any, which, the accused person has obtained by committing the offence."[76]

Although the PCA does not provide a remedy involving the seizure of assets tainted by bribery, investigating agencies can attach tainted property in the course of their investigation and trial processes.[77] Thus, parties conducting transactions in India must also conduct appropriate due diligence on their counterparties and such parties' historical conduct, and how that conduct might affect the status of real assets.[78]

5.7.2 Other Relevant Laws

The FCRA sets forth a two-tier penalty system. Those found guilty of contravening FCRA's prohibition on accepting "foreign contributions" can be sentenced to imprisonment for up to five years or a fine, or both,[79] while the penalty for contravening the prohibition on accepting "foreign hospitality" is imprisonment for up to one year, or a fine, or both.[80] Investigating agencies can also seize property or currency from individuals if they have reason to believe it was received in contravention of the Act.[81] In the event that such individual is found guilty of violating the FCRA, seized property can be permanently confiscated.[82]

Under the IPC, the penalties vary depending on how the corrupt conduct was charged. For example, participation in a criminal conspiracy to commit bribery may incur a penalty of up to six months' imprisonment or a fine, or both;[83] conviction for criminal breach of trust could result in imprisonment for up to three years, a fine, or both;[84] and a conviction for cheating is punishable by up to seven years' imprisonment, plus a compulsory fine.[85]

As described previously, bribery of government officials also may constitute "fraud" under the Companies Act, which offense carries a term of imprisonment from six months to 10 years. Where fraud involves "public interest," the minimum term of imprisonment is three years. A fraud conviction under the Companies Act results in a compulsory fine that is not less than the amount involved in the fraud, but may extend up to three times such amount.

Significantly (and unlike the PCA), neither the FCRA nor the IPC contain any criteria or other guidance that a court should consider in determining the appropriate sentence for a given crime under these statutes.

---

[76] PCA, Section 16.
[77] NISHITH DESAI ASSOCIATES, *supra* note 21, at 4.
[78] *Id.*
[79] Section 35, FCRA.
[80] Section 37, FCRA.
[81] Section 25, FCRA.
[82] Section 28, FCRA.
[83] Section 120B, IPC.
[84] Section 406, IPC.
[85] Section 420, IPC.

6. Commercial Bribery

One noteworthy difference between the Indian anti-corruption framework and anti-corruption laws in foreign jurisdictions is that there is no legislation in India specifically prohibiting commercial bribery between private actors. The text of the PCA limits its enforcement to public-sector corruption: Even the recent precedent holding that certain individuals traditionally viewed as private actors may be within the scope of the PCA,[86] those rulings have been based on reasoning that such individuals are performing functions akin to public servants. Although several recent proposed statutes have included the criminalization of private bribery, none of these have become law.

Nevertheless, bribes paid to secure contracts in the private sector are not free from recourse. *See supra* Section 5.4.2.2 for a description of how private bribery may be proscribed under the anti-fraud provisions of the IPC and the Companies Act.

7. Sentencing Principles

Indian judges are vested with broad discretion in imposing sentences for violation of criminal statutes.[87] Although judges are required to consider any sentencing factors that are enumerated in the relevant statute, they are not limited by structured sentencing guidelines issued by either the legislature or judiciary, and are directed to consider "the facts and circumstances of each case" when deciding a sentence.[88] Yet despite the lack of formal sentencing guidance, the Supreme Court of India has noted that judges' sentencing determinations should consider several traditional criminal law principles, such as proportionality (including aggravating and mitigating factors), deterrence, and rehabilitation.[89]

8. Related Criminal Offenses
8.1 CONSPIRACY, ATTEMPT, AIDING AND ABETTING

As set forth previously, the PCA prohibits attempts to obtain a monetary or non-monetary bribe, as well as abetting a bribe of a public servant, and the IPC criminalizes conspiracy. Although the IPC does not define "attempt" as a substantive offense, Indian courts have criminalized attempted crimes by identifying certain elements that meet the conspiracy standard.[90]

---

[86] *See supra* Section 5.3.2.1.

[87] *See, e.g.*, Code of Criminal Procedure, No. 2 of 1974, Section 235(2) ("If the accused is convicted, the Judge shall . . . hear the accused on the question of sentence, and then pass sentence on him according to law."); *id.* at Section 248(2) ("Where, . . . the Magistrate finds the accused guilty, . . . he shall, after hearing the accused on the question of sentence, pass sentence upon him according to law.").

[88] State of M.P. v. Bablu Natt, (2009) 2 S.C.C. 272, para. 13.

[89] Soman v. State of Kerala, (2013) 11 S.C.C. 382, para. 13–14.

[90] ASHOK SAGAR & SUMEET KACHWAHA, KACHWAHA & PARTNERS, BUSINESS CRIME 2018: INDIA, *available at* https://iclg.com/practice-areas/business-crime-laws-and-regulations/india (Sept. 12, 2018) (last visited Dec. 14, 2018).

8.2 FALSE ACCOUNTING/BOOKS AND RECORDS

Like several other jurisdictions, India requires companies to abide by a detailed accounting regime. Under the Companies Act, companies are required to keep books and records and prepare financial statements that "give a true and fair view of the state of affairs of the company."[91] As has been seen in corruption settlements in foreign jurisdictions, companies alleged to have engaged in bribery or corrupt conduct are sometimes found liable under applicable recordkeeping and financial statement requirements. In India, such violations can expose the company's board of directors, officers, and employees to criminal liability, including a prison term of up to one year and a fine between INR 50,000 (approximately U.S. $770) and INR 500,000 (approximately U.S. $7,700).

Alongside the requirement to maintain accurate books and records, companies are required to maintain adequate internal financial controls, responsibilities for which are shared by several parties. For example, directors of a publicly listed company must state in the company's financial statements that the company has implemented effective internal financial controls.[92] The financial statements must also include an auditor's report, which must specify whether the company has adequate internal financial controls and if they are effective.[93] Similarly, the company's audit committee is also required to evaluate the strength of the company's internal controls.[94] The company's independent directors also must satisfy themselves regarding the integrity of financial information and financial controls.[95]

Payments made in connection with an illegal purpose, including corrupt conduct, cannot be deducted as expenses under the Income Tax Act of 1961.[96] Accordingly, recording bribe payments, or describing transactions inaccurately to obscure bribe payments, could lead to tax evasion and subject company officers and employees to prison sentences and fines.

8.3 MONEY LAUNDERING

The Prevention of Money Laundering Act, 2002, as amended in 2012 (PMLA) is India's principal legislation aimed at preventing money laundering. Under the PMLA, money laundering includes "any process or activity connected with the proceeds of crime including its concealment, possession, acquisition or use and projecting or claiming it as untainted property."[97] The predicate offenses include violations of the PCA and several other statutes.[98] Penalties for violating the PMLA include a term of imprisonment from 3 to 10 years, a fine, or both.

---

[91] Section 128-129, Companies Act of 2013.

[92] Companies Act, 2013, Section 134(5)(e).

[93] Companies Act, 2013, Section 143(3)(i).

[94] Companies Act, 2013, Section 177(4)(vii).

[95] Companies Act, Schedule IV.

[96] *See* Section 37, Explanation 1 ("For the removal of doubts, it is hereby declared that any expenditure incurred by an assessee for any purpose which is an offence or which is prohibited by law shall not be deemed to have been incurred for the purpose of business or profession and no deduction or allowance shall be made in respect of such expenditure.").

[97] Section 3, PMLA.

[98] Schedule, PMLA.

Despite the PMLA's coming into force in 2005, and subsequent amendments to the legislation in 2005, 2009, and 2012, more than a decade passed before the first conviction was secured under the statute. In January 2017, the Enforcement Directorate successfully prosecuted former Jharkhand minister Hari Narayan Rai for misappropriating public funds and laundering those funds through two construction companies and a dairy company for his own benefit.[99] Rai was found guilty of laundering INR 37.2 million and was sentenced to seven years of imprisonment and fined INR 500,000.[100] Notably, a special CBI court also found Rai guilty of violating the PCA's prohibition on misusing his public office for personal gain, and separately sentenced him to five years imprisonment.[101]

Since the landmark case against Rai, the Enforcement Directorate appears to have become more active in prosecuting offenses under the PMLA, in part by following the CBI's lead in prosecuting corruption cases. Recently, after the CBI filed a case charging violations of the PCA by several individuals, including Karti Chidambaram, son of former finance minister P. Chidambaram, the Enforcement Directorate filed its own action against the same parties for violations of the PMLA.[102] Likewise, following the ACB's initiation of a case against former Maharashtra minister Chhagan Bhujbal, and his nephew and former MP Samir Bhujbal, for violating the PCA, the Enforcement Directorate charged the Bhujbals with violating the PMLA.[103] The Enforcement Directorate also continues to investigate officials of the Goan state government and employees of U.S. construction management firm Louis Berger International Inc. ("Louis Berger"), following Louis Berger's 2015 bribery settlement with U.S. regulators, which included allegations of U.S. $976,630 in bribes paid to officials of the Goan government.[104] These cases suggest that future prosecutions of corrupt conduct in India will be more likely to involve both PCA and PMLA actions.

8.4 OTHER CRIMINAL OFFENSES

In addition to the laws addressing corruption discussed previously, certain other laws may be used to prosecute companies or individuals engaged in corrupt conduct. For example,

---

[99] *Former Jharkhand Minister Becomes the First to Be Convicted under Prevention of Money Laundering Act*, HUFFINGTON POST (Jan. 31, 2017), *available at* http://www.huffingtonpost.in/2017/01/31/former-jharkhand-minister-becomes-the-first-to-be-convicted-unde_a_21703740/.

[100] *Id.*

[101] *Ex-minister Gets 5-Year RI in Assets Case- Graft Empire in Power Unravels; Wife & Brother also Convicted for Abetment*, THE TELEGRAPH (Dec. 15, 2016), *available at* https://www.telegraphindia.com/1161215/jsp/frontpage/story_124863.jsp.

[102] *ED Files PMLA Case against Karti Chidambaram*, THE TIMES OF INDIA (May 19, 2017), *available at* https://timesofindia.indiatimes.com/india/ed-files-pmla-case-against-karti-chidambaram/articleshow/58747232.cms.

[103] *Money Laundering: PMLA Court Extends Custody of Chhagan Bhujbal, Nephew till May 25*, ZEE NEWS (May 11, 2016) (involving parallel complaints by the Enforcement Directorate for money laundering and the Maharastran Anti-Corruption Bureau for several criminal offenses, but none under the PCA), *available at* http://zeenews.india.com/news/maharashtra/money-laundering-pmla-court-extends-custody-of-chhagan-bhujbal-nephew-till-may-25_1884080.html.

[104] *Louis Berger Bribery Case: ED Files Money Laundering Case*, THE ECONOMIC TIMES (Aug. 7, 2015), *available at* http://economictimes.indiatimes.com/news/politics-and-nation/louis-berger-bribery-case-ed-files-money-laundering-case/articleshow/48393956.cms.

in 2015, India enacted the Black Money Act, which taxes assets held abroad and penalizes the failure to disclose foreign assets and income.[105] Together with the Benami Transactions (Prohibition) Act, 1988 ("Benami Act"), which prohibits the purchase of property in the name of another person who does not pay for the property,[106] prosecutors could initiate cases by focusing on how bribe recipients are claiming (or masking) the proceeds of corruption, similar to that of the PMLA. Likewise, the nexus between certain corrupt conduct and anti-competitive practices suggests that a company engaged in corrupt conduct could be investigated by the Competition Commission of India (CCI), the regulator charged with examining abuse of dominance and cartel-like behavior under the Indian Competition Act, 2002.[107] Nevertheless, the PCA, IPC, Companies Act, and PMLA remain the primary tools used by Indian authorities to prosecute corrupt behavior.

9. Cooperation and Self-Reporting

Currently, investigating authorities in India do not have any formal policies regarding "cooperation credit" for those who self-report potential violations of anti-corruption laws or otherwise cooperate with investigations. Likewise, none of India's corruption legislation, including the PCA, FCRA, PMLA, IPC, and the Companies Act, contains leniency provisions for individuals or entities who self-report violations relating to corruption.[108]

In the event that an individual or entity voluntarily self-reports criminal conduct, a court may grant leniency in the form of a pardon, particularly where the party making the disclosure is an accomplice to other, more culpable parties involved in the offense.[109] Pardons may be granted for bribery offenses under the PCA,[110] but certain limitations exist. During the investigation phase, a magistrate can grant a pardon, provided that the offense involves a potential term of imprisonment of seven years or more, and the party to be pardoned both has made a full disclosure to the magistrate and agreed to serve as a trial witness.[111] Once a case has been committed for trial, the pardon power shifts from the magistrate to the Sessions or Special Judge, but no other limitations apply.[112]

A self-reporting or cooperating party also may seek a plea bargain. The accused must first submit a plea bargain application, and then is subject to an in camera examination by the court. If the court is satisfied that the application was submitted voluntarily, the accused

---

[105] The Black Money (Undisclosed Foreign Income and Assets) and Imposition of Tax Act, 2015.

[106] Section 3, Benami Act.

[107] NISHITH DESAI ASSOCIATES, *supra* note 21, at 14.

[108] SAGAR & KACHWAHA, *supra* note 90. This section distinguishes between leniency and immunity. As discussed in Section 5.3.2.1, section 24 of the PCA provides a person accused of abetment with immunity if that person makes a statement in proceedings initiated against the public servant, provided that that person only paid to the bribe to entrap the public servant after approaching the authorities.

[109] Sections 306–307, Code of Criminal Procedure.

[110] Ashok Km, *Magistrate Can Grant Tender of Pardon in Respect of Cases Triable by Special Judge under Prevention of Corruption Act; SC*, LIVELAW.IN, *available at* http://www.livelaw.in/magistrate-can-grant-tender-pardon-respect-cases-triable-special-judge-prevention-corruption-act/ (May 14, 2016) (last visited Dec. 14, 2018).

[111] Section 306, Code of Criminal Procedure.

[112] Section 307, Code of Criminal Procedure.

and the prosecutor will then be afforded time to work out a resolution.[113] Plea bargains are not available to those who have been previously charged with the same offense, or in cases when the predicate offense is punishable by more than seven years of imprisonment.[114] Furthermore, the predicate offense cannot be an offense that "affects the socio-economic condition of the country."[115] Although the central government has not yet defined the set of offenses that might have such a socioeconomic effect, the Supreme Court of India has held that cases involving "serious offences, including those under [Indian Penal Code] or offences of moral turpitude under special statutes, like [the PCA] . . . may not be sanctioned for settlement."[116]

10. Whistle-Blower Protection

10.1 WHISTLE BLOWERS PROTECTION ACT, 2011 ("WHISTLE BLOWERS ACT")

The Whistle Blowers Act establishes a mechanism for individuals to report attempted or actual violations of the PCA, other abuses of power resulting in a loss to the government or a wrongful gain to a public servant or third party, or attempted or actual criminal offenses.[117] Depending on the subject of the report, complaints must be made to a specified authority.[118] For example, a report of corruption regarding an employee of the central government must be sent to the Central Vigilance Commission, whereas a report about a judge below the level of the High Court must be reported to the applicable High Court.[119]

The Whistle Blowers Act does not allow anonymity: In order for the applicable governmental authority to act on a whistle-blower's complaint, the complainant must disclose his or her identity.[120] Nevertheless, the government must keep the complainant's identity secret,[121] except in very limited circumstances.[122] A 2013 decision by the Supreme Court of India further narrowed these exceptions, holding that a whistle-blower's identity cannot be disclosed to an individual being prosecuted under the PCA.[123] Even where the complaint does not relate to the PCA, a complainant's identity may only be disclosed with his or her prior written consent.[124] The penalty for revealing the identity of a whistle-blower is imprisonment of up to three years accompanied by a fine of INR 50,000.[125]

---

[113] Section 265B of the Code of Criminal Procedure.

[114] Section 265A, 265B of the Code of Criminal Procedure.

[115] Section 265A of the Code of Criminal Procedure. Plea bargains are also not available for offenses against a woman or a child below the age of 14. *Id.*

[116] Gian Singh v. State of Punjab (2012) 10 SCC 303; *see also* NISHITH DESAI ASSOCIATES, *supra* note 21, at 4.

[117] Whistle Blowers Act, Sections 3(d), 4(1).

[118] Whistle Blowers Act, Section 3(b).

[119] *Id.*

[120] Whistle Blowers Act, Section 4(6).

[121] Whistle Blowers Act, Section 5(1)(b).

[122] Whistle Blowers Act, Section 5(4).

[123] *SC: Can't Tell Accused Who Whistleblower Is*, THE TIMES OF INDIA (Aug. 23, 2013), *available at* https://timesofindia.indiatimes.com/india/SC-Cant-tell-accused-who-whistleblower-is/articleshow/21987081.cms.

[124] Whistle Blowers Act, Section 5(4).

[125] Whistle Blowers Act, Section 16.

The Whistle Blowers Act's protection of a complainant goes beyond merely not revealing his or her identity. Indeed, the central government is required to *ensure* that a complainant is not victimized in connection with submission of a complaint or providing assistance to a governmental authority in connection with an investigation related to the Whistle Blowers Act.[126] Further, if retaliation against the complainant occurs, the whistle-blower may apply for relief before the government authority to which the initial complaint was submitted.[127] In such a hearing, the allegedly retaliating party has the burden of proof to establish that the complainant was not victimized.[128]

10.2 VIGIL MECHANISMS

In addition to the Whistle Blowers Act, publicly listed companies, companies that accept deposits from the public, and companies that have borrowed more than INR 50 crores are required to establish a "vigil mechanism" for directors and employees to submit their concerns.[129] These companies are further required to provide adequate safeguards against retaliation toward complainants utilizing the vigil mechanism.[130] However, no statutory or regulatory penalties exist under the Companies Act for failure to provide sufficient safeguards.

11. Key International Treaties Relating to Bribery and Corruption

India is a signatory to the United Nations Convention against Corruption (UNCAC), which requires signatories to "prevent and criminalize different corrupt practices, promote international cooperation, cooperate for the recovery of stolen assets and enhance technical assistance and information exchange."[131] The convention does not subject individuals or entities to civil or criminal liability; instead, it simply commits the government to certain objectives and initiatives.

Unlike many countries, India is not a signatory to the OECD Convention on Combating Bribery of Foreign Public Officials in International Business Transactions. Nevertheless, India participates in other anti-corruption initiatives, including the Financial Action Task Force, the OECD Anti-corruption Initiative for Asia, and the Asia/Pacific Group on Money Laundering.

---

[126] Whistle Blowers Act, Section 11(1).

[127] Whistle Blowers Act, Section 11(2).

[128] Whistle Blowers Act, Section 11(2).

[129] Companies Act, Section 177(9); Rule 7 of the Companies (Meetings of Board and its Powers) Rules, 2014; *see also* Regulation 22 of Securities and Exchange Board of India (Listing Obligations and Disclosure Requirements) Regulations, 2015.

[130] Companies Act, Section 177(10); Rule 7(4) of the Companies (Meetings of Board and Its Powers) Rules, 2014; *see also* Regulation 22 of Securities and Exchange Board of India (Listing Obligations and Disclosure Requirements) Regulations, 2015.

[131] INDIA: GOVERNMENT RATIFIES TWO UN CONVENTIONS RELATED TO TRANSNATIONAL ORGANIZED CRIME AND CORRUPTION, UNITED NATIONS OFFICE ON DRUGS AND CRIME, *available at* https://www.unodc.org/southasia/en/frontpage/2011/may/indian-govt-ratifies-two-un-conventions.html (last visited Dec. 14, 2018).

12. Mutual Legal Assistance Treaties and Transnational Cooperation

India has also signed the United Nations Convention on Transnational Organised Crime (UNTOC), which commits the country to take measures to "prevent and control transnational organized crime, including (i) the criminalizing of the participation in an organized criminal group, of money laundering, related corruption and obstruction of justice and (ii) the adoption of frameworks for extradition, mutual legal assistance and international co-operation."[132] Like UNCAC, the UNTOC itself does not subject individuals or entities in India to civil or criminal liability.

In furtherance of its commitments under UNTOC, India has (as of this writing) entered into 39 individual mutual legal assistance treaties with other countries, including the United States, UK, Canada, France, and Russia.[133] Further, India recently joined the Multilateral Competent Authority Agreement on Automatic Exchange of Financial Account Information (MCAA), which will allow Indian authorities to receive information about Indian citizens' assets held abroad from more than 90 other member countries.[134]

In addition to its transnational agreements, the PMLA also contains procedures for India and other countries to exchange evidence, transfer an accused person, and attach, seize and/ or release property in connection with investigations of anti-money-laundering laws.[135] The PMLA also permits the central government to enter into agreements with other countries to exchange information intended to prevent violations of anti-money-laundering laws in India or the partner country, or to investigate violations of the PMLA in India.[136]

In recent years, India has cooperated with foreign authorities on a number of issues, in particular relating to money laundering. For example, Switzerland recently ratified an agreement providing for the automatic exchange of financial account information with India to combat tax evasion and money laundering.[137] Further, current prime minister Narendra Modi has informally sought the UK's assistance in extraditing high-profile fugitive businessmen Vijay Mallya and Lalit Modi back to India, so that the men could be tried for a variety of economic offenses.[138]

---

[132] *Id.*

[133] MINISTRY OF EXTERNAL AFFAIRS, GOVERNMENT OF INDIA, MUTUAL LEGAL ASSISTANCE IN CRIMINAL MATTERS, *available at* http://www.mea.gov.in/mutual-legal-assistance-in-criminal-matters.htm (May 31, 2016) (last visited Dec. 14, 2018).

[134] *Automatic Exchange Portal: International Framework for the CRS*, OECD, *available at* http://www.oecd.org/tax/automatic-exchange/international-framework-for-the-crs/ (last visited Dec. 14, 2018); Signatories of the Multilateral Competent Authority Agreement on Automatic Exchange of Financial Account Information and Intended First Information Exchange Date, OECD, *available at* http://www.oecd.org/tax/automatic-exchange/international-framework-for-the-crs/MCAA-Signatories.pdf (Oct. 29, 2018) (last visited Dec. 14, 2018).

[135] PMLA, Sections 57–60.

[136] PMLA, Section 56.

[137] SWITZERLAND RATIFIES AUTOMATIC EXCHANGE OF INFORMATION WITH INDIA, THE HINDU (June 16, 2017), *available at* http://www.thehindu.com/business/Economy/switzerland-agrees-to-share-black-money-data-with-india/article19087914.ece

[138] *PM Seeks UK's Help in Return of Vijay Mallya, Lalit Modi*, OUTLOOK (July 8, 2017), *available at* https://www.outlookindia.com/newsscroll/pm-seeks-uks-help-in-return-of-vijay-mallya-lalit-modi/1094439.

13. Legal Professional Privilege

Indian law embodies legal professional privilege concepts similar to those found in many other jurisdictions. Although not expressly labeled as the attorney-client privilege, the Indian Evidence Act, 1872 prohibits advocates[139] from disclosing communications with their clients and from disclosing the contents of legal documents in the attorney's possession related to the attorney-client relationship.[140] As in other jurisdictions, an exception to this prohibition exists for communications made in furtherance of an illegal purpose, or facts showing that a crime or fraud has occurred following the establishment of the attorney-client relationship.[141] One potentially key difference from other jurisdictions is that communications between advocates and third parties working at their direction, such as accountants, are not always protected from disclosure.[142]

Other significant differences relate to the role of foreign and in-house counsel. Foreign attorneys are not allowed to practice law in India if they are not registered as advocates under the Indian Advocates Act, 1961. However, foreign attorneys are allowed to practice *foreign* law in India on a "fly-in/fly-out" basis to advise on foreign law issues.[143] In such cases, the legal professional privileges of the foreign attorneys' legal system apply to that advice.

Whether attorney-client privilege applies to communications with in-house counsel in India is unsettled, because in-house counsel may not qualify as an "advocate." The issue is whether the in-house counsel is merely a full-time employee who performs non-advocate work, in which case the individual ceases to be an advocate (even if registered as an advocate).[144] Nevertheless, employment contracts with in-house counsel typically contain a

---

[139] Advocates are attorneys registered under the Indian Advocates Act, 1961 and consequently are the only group of persons entitled to practice law in India. *See* Section 29 of the Indian Advocates Act, 1961.

[140] Indian Evidence Act, Section 126.

[141] Indian Evidence Act, Section 126.

[142] *See* ABHAY TIWARI, LEGAL PROFESSIONAL PRIVILEGES IN INDIA, *available at* http://www.academia.edu/6663577/Legal_professional_privileges_in_india (last visited Dec.14, 2018). ("Unlike the position in England, no privilege is available for communications made by parties or their Advocates and third parties for the specific purpose of pending or contemplated litigation"). *But see* GAURI KULKARNI, PRIVILEGED LEGAL COMMUNICATIONS, *available at* http://www.legalserviceindia.com/articles/pc.htm (last visited Dec. 14, 2018). ("This immunity may extend to third parties, such as consultants who are recruited to help with the preparation of the case for trial.").

[143] A.K. Balaji v. Government of India and Ors., (2012) 35 KLR 290 (Mad.); *see also* VYAPAK DESAI ET AL, NIDHI DESAI ASSOCIATES, PRACTICE OF FOREIGN LAW IN INDIA FOREIGN LAWYERS CAN "FLY- IN AND FLY- OUT," *available at* http://www.indialawjournal.org/archives/volume5/issue_1/special_story.html(2012) (last visited Dec.14, 2018).

[144] *See, e.g.*, Satish Kumar Sharma v. Bar Council of Himachal Pradesh, 2001 1 SCR 34 ("[I]f a full-time employee is not pleading on behalf of his or her employer, or if terms of employment are such that he or she does not have to act or plead but is required to do other kinds of functions, then he or she ceases to be an advocate. The latter is then a mere employee of the body corporate."); Deepak Agarwal v. Keshav Kaushik, 2013 5 SCC 277 (noting that "the key aspect is whether such employment is consistent with his practising as an advocate"). *But see* Municipal Corporation of Greater Bombay v. Vijay Metal Works (AIR 1982 Bom 6) (holding that "a salaried employee who advises his employer on all legal questions and also other legal matters would get the same protection as others, viz., barrister, attorney, pleader or vakil, under Ss.126 and 129, and, therefore, any

confidentiality clause that protects the disclosure of communications between employees and in-house counsel.[145]

14. Privacy and Data Protection

In 2011, India's Ministry of Communications and Information Technology promulgated the Information Technology (Reasonable security practices and procedures and sensitive personal data or information) Rules, 2011 ("IT Rules"). The IT Rules defined two categories of protected information: "personal information," and "sensitive personal data or information" (the latter hereafter referred to as "sensitive personal information").[146] Personal information is broadly defined as *any* information that is capable of identifying a person, whereas sensitive personal information is limited to eight specific categories of information, including, but not limited to, passwords, financial information, health information, and biometric data.[147]

Significantly, the IT Rules set forth different requirements relating to the handling of the two categories of information. Organizations are required to establish a privacy policy with respect to both personal information and sensitive personal information.[148] The IT Rules, however, impose more stringent requirements relating to the collection, disclosure, and transfer of sensitive personal information, all of which typically require consent from the providers of such information unless disclosure is permitted by contract or is required to comply with a legal obligation, such as disclosure to government authorities in connection with an investigation or prosecution of a criminal offense.[149] Data only may be transferred to parties in India or in other countries if the recipient provides the same level of data protection as the disclosing party.[150]

15. Forecast for Reforms and Parting Thoughts

As mentioned at the beginning of this chapter, there is strong public support in India for anti-corruption reform efforts and increased prosecution of corruption. India also has a large number of existing statutes that, to varying degrees, prohibit bribery and related offenses. The existing enforcement regime faces challenges, however, in many of those laws' procedural impediments to the speedy investigation and prosecution of corruption crimes, coupled with the realities of the oversubscribed and delayed dockets of the Indian judicial system. Prime Minister Modi commented about his demonetization campaign that, "This is not an end. I have more projects in mind to make India corruption-free." The international community will be watching India in the years to come to see if the country can indeed turn that rhetoric into reality.

---

communication made in confidence to him by his employer seeking his legal advice or by him to his employer giving legal advice should get the protections of Ss.126 and 129").

[145] Shardul S. Shroff, Amarchand & Mangaldas & Suresh A. Shroff & Co., *In-House Counsel and the Attorney-Client Privilege* (2007), *available at* www.lexmundi.com/Document.asp?DocID=1936.

[146] IT Rules, Section 2(i), 3.

[147] IT Rules, Section 3.

[148] IT Rules, Section 4.

[149] IT Rules, Section 6.

[150] IT Rules, Section 7.

APPENDIX

Key Issues	India's approach
Is jurisdiction subject to any international anti-corruption conventions? If so, which? (OECD, UN Convention against Corruption, etc.)	Yes. India is a signatory to the UN Convention against Corruption.
Is bribery of foreign public officials illegal (do domestic anti-bribery laws provide for extraterritorial application)?	No. India's anti-bribery laws are limited to bribery by domestic officials.
What is the definition of foreign public officials?	N/A
Is commercial bribery illegal?	Not specifically. However, it may constitute "fraud" under the Companies Act, 2013 or a "criminal conspiracy" or "cheating" for the purposes of the Indian Penal Code, 1860 (IPC).
Is bribing domestic officials illegal?	Yes. The Prevention of Corruption Act, 1988 (PCA) permits the prosecution of both "public servants" who accept a bribe, as well as those who abet corruption by public servants.
Can the receipt of a bribe be prosecuted?	Yes. The receipt of a bribe can be criminally prosecuted under the PCA and the Foreign Contribution Regulation Act 2010 (FCRA). Additionally, government officials can also be subject to civil penalties for bribery pursuant to certain civil service conduct rules.
Can companies be held criminally liable? If so, what is the requisite intent for criminal liability to attach?	Yes. The same intent applies to companies as it does to individuals.
Can companies be held civilly liable?	Yes.
Can individuals be held civilly liable?	Yes.
Is there a "facilitation/grease payments" exception?	No.
Does India provide for conspiracy liability relating to violations of the anti-corruption laws?	Yes. Participation in corruption may amount to a "criminal conspiracy" or "cheating" for the purposes of the IPC.

(Continued)

Key Issues	India's approach
Does India provide for: (a) aiding/abetting liability relating to violations of the anti-corruption laws? (b) attempt liability relating to violations of the anti-corruption laws?	Yes. The PCA allows for the prosecution of the bribe-giver for abetting a public servant's bribery offense, as well as for attempted bribery.
Is failure to keep accurate books and records a criminal and/or civil offense?	Failure to keep accurate books and records can subject a company's board, officers, or employees to criminal liability.
Do any books and records violations have to involve underlying bribery proof?	No.
Are there laws concerning a company's financial internal controls? If so, are those laws applicable to private and public companies or just public companies?	Yes. Directors of a publicly listed company must state in the company's financial statements that the company has implemented internal financial controls and that they are effective. The auditor's report must also specify whether the company has adequate internal financial controls and whether they are effective. The audit committee is also required to evaluate the company's internal controls. Finally, independent directors need to satisfy themselves on the integrity of financial information and financial controls.
Is there an affirmative disclosure obligation for potential violations of the anti-bribery laws or accounting irregularities?	Yes. If a company's auditor has reason to believe a fraud has occurred, he is required to submit a report to the central government or to the Audit Committee, depending on whether the amount of the fraud at issue.
Are "promotional expenses" exempt from the anti-bribery laws?	No.
Is the giving of gifts, entertainment, travel, meals, etc. restricted/prohibited?	Yes. Section 11 of the PCA bars public servants from obtaining value without consideration. Section 6 of the FCRA prescribes that no members of the legislature, office bearer, judge, government servant, or any other government-controlled body shall accept foreign hospitality when travelling abroad without prior permission from the Central Government. The Indian civil service rules also impose thresholds on receipt of gifts and hospitality.

Key Issues	India's approach
Are there any laws concerning things of value conveyed by, or to, third parties?	Yes. The PCA prohibits a third party from taking gratification by corrupt or illegal means in order to influence a public servant (Section 8) and taking gratification for exercise of personal influence with a public servant (Section 9).
Are bribes tax deductible?	No.
Is the law applied extraterritorially?	No.
Is having a robust corporate compliance program an affirmative defense or way to negate liability?	Yes. The PCA now provides for an "adequate procedures" defense.
Is there a "local law" exception/defense?	No.
Is "credit" given for cooperation with authorities? If so, how and in what form?	Yes. The PCA exempts a bribe-giver from prosecution if he or she, within seven days of making a "coercive" or compelled bribe payment, reports being the victim of such coercion to law enforcement or an appropriate investigative agency.
Does the subject country have a Mutual Legal Assistance Treaty with the United States that generally covers criminal matters, including the FCPA?	Yes, India and the United States have a Mutual Legal Assistance Treaty with the United States that generally covers criminal matters, but does not specifically reference the FCPA.
What are the potential penalties/sanctions both for civil and criminal violations?	Criminal violations are usually punishable by imprisonment and a compulsory fine. Civil offenses are punishable by a fine. The potential length of imprisonment and the potential amount of any fine varies based on the specific criminal offense at issue.

11 Indonesia

1. Introduction to Indonesia's Anti-Corruption Legislation

1.1 CURRENT OVERVIEW

Recent high-level graft and bribery cases in Indonesia[1] vividly demonstrate both the continued pervasiveness of the public corruption problem throughout government and the increased commitment to investigating and prosecuting those responsible. Indonesia's *Reformasi* era, beginning in 1998, has included a slow but steady series of institutional reforms, new laws, and new institutions, that along with an increasingly active civil society, have allowed significant progress to be made in the fight against corruption. In the last five years, well over 300 public officials have been prosecuted for serious corruption, including judges, ministerial officials, and national legislators.[2] There have been set-backs, questions about commitment and political will, and missed opportunities to do more, but suggestions that Indonesia is not making progress in combatting corruption would be premature. In fact, what is arguably the country's most sweeping corruption investigation in history began in 2017 and continues to determinedly progress in 2019, thus far resulting in seven high profile convictions and jail sentenes, including a fifteen year sentenced imposed on the Speaker

---

[1] This chapter was contributed by Perkins Coie's Kevin R. Feldis and the Komisi Pemberantasan Korupsi's Laode M. Syarif, Rasamala Aritonang, and Lakso Anindito.

[2] Anti-Corruption Clearing House, https://acch.kpk.go.id/id/statistik/tindak-pidana-korupsi/tpk-berdasarkan-profesi-jabatan (last visited Dec. 14, 2018).

From Baksheesh to Bribery. T. Markus Funk and Andrew S. Boutros.
© Oxford University Press 2019. Published 2019 by Oxford University Press.

of Parliament (DPR), for their roles in a scheme to pocket over U.S. $170 million in government funds.[3]

The Indonesian National Police and the Attorney General's Office must play a central role if Indonesia is going to be successful at combatting corruption in the long-term, but for now, it is Indonesia's independent Corruption Eradication Commission (Komisi Pemberantasan Korupsi or KPK) that is at the forefront of investigating and prosecuting corruption. In 2018 alone, the KPK opened 126 corruption investigations, and over the last 14 years has convicted over 915 individuals, including 229 federal, provincial, and local lawmakers for corruption.[4] Perhaps due to this success, the KPK has gained popular support but also significant opposition, and there have been efforts to diminish its independence and authority, as exemplified by the inquiry into the KPK launched by Parliament in 2017.[5]

One of the most important developments in the legal landscape in recent years, and one that has the potential to have a measurable positive impact if implemented wisely, is the adoption of a new regulation on corporate criminal liability. In December 2016, the Indonesian Supreme Court adopted *Perma No. 13*, a regulation that confirmed the legality authority to prosecute companies under existing criminal laws and provided much needed procedural guidance on how companies could be held accountable for the actions of their employees and agents. Indonesia's Corruption Eradication Commission is well aware that the authority to prosecute corporate entities can be a powerful tool in the fight against corruption, and Indonesian companies are well advised to take note of their potential liability for encouraging, allowing, or failing to stop their employees from engaging in bribery or other acts of corruption on behalf of their employers.

1.2 HISTORICAL PERSPECTIVE

Indonesia is made up of more than 17,000 islands inhabited by over 300 distinct ethnic groups. With a population of over 260 million people, Indonesia is world's fourth most populous nation and the world's most populous Muslim-majority country.[6] Its capital city, Jakarta, contains 30 million people within its metropolitan area, making it one of the largest on earth, with a density of 39,000 people per square mile.[7] Indonesia is a complex, diverse, and multifaceted country, and it is important to place its current levels of corruption and efforts to combat them in historical, geographical, and political context.

The Republic of Indonesia declared independence from the Netherlands in 1945, and adopted its first Criminal Code (KUHP) in 1946.[8] While the Criminal Code generally prohibits corrupt acts, Indonesia recognized early on that additional protections were

---

[3] Ulla Fionna, *Jokowi's Struggle to Crack Down on Corruption*, TODAY, Oct. 13, 2017, https:todayonline.com/world/jokowis-struggle-crack-down-corruption (last visited Dec. 14, 2018).

[4] Anti-Corruption Clearing House, https://acch.kpk.go.id/id/statistik/tindak-pidana-korupsi and https://acch.kpk.go.id/id/statistik/tindak-pidana-korupsi/tpk-berdasarkan-profesi-jabatan (last visited Dec. 14, 2018)

[5] Dams Alexander Sinaga & Markus Junianto Sihaloho, *KPK Receives Widespread Support after Lawmakers Attempt to Weaken Its Authority*, JAKARTA GLOBE, July 16, 2017, https://jakartaglobe.id/news/kpk-receives-widespread-support-lawmakers-attempt-weaken-authority/, (last visited Dec. 14, 2018).

[6] http:http://worldpopulationreview.com/countries/indonesia-population/ (last visited Jan. 23, 2018).

[7] *Id.*

[8] Law No. 1 of 1946.

necessary to combat public corruption. During the initial years of Indonesia's political independence, there were a number of unsuccessful attempts to adopt anti-corruption legislation. Ultimately, President Soekarno, Indonesia's first president, issued *Government Regulation in Lieu of Law (Perppu) No. 24 of 1960 on the Investigation, Prosecution and Questioning of Corruption Crimes*. Rather than follow the ordinary lawmaking process, President Soekarno issued this regulation under the presidential authority, which still exists today, to adopt regulations in limited emergency circumstances that have the force of law but are not reviewed and approved by Parliament.[9] This early anti-corruption effort recognized the need for financial transparency in government by requiring suspects to provide information about their personal and family assets when requested to do so by the prosecutor.[10] During the period of President Soekarno's leadership, from 1946 to 1966, several different asset inspector and supervising bodies were also created with the purpose of investigating unexplained income, preventing the loss of state assets, and prosecuting corruption.[11]

In 1967, President Soeharto, Indonesia's second president, publicly criticized the previous administration for being incapable of eradicating corruption. In 1971, Indonesia adopted its first stand-alone anti-corruption law effectively replacing the 1960 anti-corruption regulation.[12] In 1980, Indonesia also adopted a separate and new anti-bribery law.[13] President Soeharto's regime, often referred to as the New Order, ran from 1966 to 1998 and also supported the creation of several anti-corruption agencies such as the Corruption Eradication Team (*Tim Pemberantasan Korupsi*) formed in 1967 and led by the Attorney General, and Operation Order (Operasi Keteriban) launched in 1977.[14] These entities and initiatives had some success in increasing the prosecution of corruption matters and saving state funds, but have been criticized for focusing only upon minor corruption and not going after significant political or military targets. Overall, the New Order anti-corruption mechanisms were ineffective at best, and commentators have observed that public corruption actually grew during this time period.[15] By 1998, Indonesia was ranked number 80 out of 85 on Transparency International's Corruption Perception Index, placing it among the most corrupt countries in the world. That same year, economic troubles and political instability led to President Soeharto's resignation, ushering in a new period of reform.

The era of *Reformasi* (reform) has brought a reversal of some of the more authoritarian aspects of the Sueoarto New Order regime and an emphasis on democratization and decentralization of authority. It also ushered in a renewed focus to combatting public corruption.[16] Dissatisfied with the level of cronyism that many believed existed in government,

---

[9] Denny Indrayana, *Don't Kill KPK*, Published by Intrans Publishing in collaboration with Indonesia Corruption Watch and the Center for Anti-Corruption Studies Faculty of Law (2016) at 7.

[10] *Id.* at 3–7.

[11] *Id.* at 8–16.

[12] Law No. 3 of 1971 (anti-corruption).

[13] Law No. 11 of 1980 (anti-bribery).

[14] Presidential Decree Number 228 of 1967; Indrayana, *supra* note 9, at 16–23.

[15] Joanna MacMillan, Reformasi *and Public Corruption: Why Indonesia's Anti-Corruption Agency Strategy Should be Reformed to Effectively Combat Public Corruption*, 35 EMORY INT'L L. REV. 591–94 (2011).

[16] *Id.* at 588.

Indonesia passed Law No. 28 of 1999 on *Government Executives Who Are Clean and Free from Corruption, Collusion and Nepotism*, as well as Law No. 31 of 1999 on the *Eradication of Criminal Acts of Corruption* (the 1999 Anti-Corruption Law replaced law No. 3 of 1971).[17] The 1999 Anti-Corruption Law (as amended in 2001) is still in force today. It defines corruption broadly, provides significant penalties, and generally provides a solid legal framework for prosecuting corruption. Recognizing that having a good anti-corruption law was not enough, and that past enforcement efforts had been insufficient, the government also decided it was necessary to create a new independent anti-corruption agency with broad powers.[18] In 2002, separate legislation was adopted mandating the formation of the Corruption Eradication Commission (KPK), which as mentioned previously, has grown in importance and impact ever since.[19] Under the same law, Indonesia also established a separate Anti-Corruption Court. In 2006, Indonesia ratified the UN Convention against Corruption, and actively looks to the convention for guidance.[20]

2. Indonesia's Domestic Anti-Corruption Framework

2.1 LEGAL SYSTEM

The Republic of Indonesia has a unitary national system of government with a civil-code-based legal regime.[21] In fact, Indonesia is the largest civil law jurisdiction in the world. Inherited from the Dutch model, Indonesia's legal system was built upon the inquisitorial approach that characterizes civil law systems as they first developed in Continental Europe. Indonesia adopted a constitution when it declared independence in 1945, and while the Indonesian Constitution remains at the top of the legal hierarchy, the majority of legal authority flows from statutes adopted by the House of Representatives (abbreviated as DPR and also referred to as the Parliament). Presidential decrees, government regulations, provincial regulations, and local municipal ordinances are also part of the modern Indonesian legal framework. The process for adopting each type of law and regulation, at each level of government, and the relative supremacy of each, is set forth in *Law No. 12 of 2011 Concerning the Making of Rules*.

During Indonesia's current Reform era, there has been a marked and purposeful effort to provide greater regional autonomy to the many local governments that make up what is the world's largest archipelago.[22] Accordingly, to fully understand Indonesia's legal landscape, it is also important to note that each of Indonesia's 34 provinces has some independence and authority to run their local governments, pass local laws, and manage the affairs and resources in their region. The same is true for the many district, sub-district, and village level

---

[17] Law No. 28 of 1999 and Law No. 31 of 1999 (Anti-Corruption Law); Law No. 20 of 2001 on Changes in Law No. 31 of 1999 (Amendments to Anti-Corruption Law).

[18] MacMillan, *supra* note 15, at 597; SIMON BUTT, CORRUPTION AND LAW IN INDONESIA 22–25 (2012).

[19] Law No. 30 of 2002 [hereinafter the KPK Law].

[20] Law No.7 Year 2006 on Ratification of UNCAC (UNCAC Ratification Act).

[21] Indonesia's Constitution 1945 (*Undang-Undang Dasar 1945*) (Indonesia's Constitution 1945), Article 1.

[22] Michael Buehler. Decentralisation and Local Democracy in Indonesia: The Marginalisation of the Public Sphere. In E. Aspinall & M. Mietzner (Eds.), Problems of Democratisation in Indonesia: Elections, Institutions and Society. ISEAS–Yusof Ishak Institute (2010) at 267–267.

authorities as well. National presidential elections have been held since 1998, and likewise, the majority of local governors and mayors are elected by direct election. While this positive step forward for democracy is to be lauded, for purposes of this writing, it is also important to note that this decentralization of power has provided opportunities for local cronyism and corruption, and in some ways made it harder for national anti-corruption efforts to succeed.

Indonesia has an independent judicial branch of government. District Courts are trial level courts of general jurisdiction, and their rulings can be appealed to High Courts. Cases are heard by a panel of three judges, and there are no jury trials. There are specialized juvenile courts, human rights courts, commercial courts, fisheries courts, and anti-corruption courts, among others. Indonesia's special Anti-Corruption Courts were created under the same law that created the KPK, and they started operating in 2004.[23] In recognition of the fact that corruption had invaded the judicial system, as it had every other branch of government, the Anti-Corruption Courts are required to have a large five-judge panel that includes two senior career judges, and three ad hoc judges who are outside legal experts drawn from academics, practicing, retired judges, or other legal experts.[24] The Indonesian Supreme Court (Mahkamah Agung) is the highest authority court in the country, serving as the final court of appeals for both civil and criminal matters.[25] In addition, Indonesia has an independent Constitutional Court with responsibility over constitutional questions, as well as matters relating to political parties and elections.

Indonesia does not have a common law tradition, and as a result, the decisions of one court do not serve as binding legal precedent. What this often means in practice is that those seeking to understand the legal landscape, including law enforcement, cannot rely upon past court decisions to help predict how future courts will apply the law, even when faced with similar circumstances.[26]

2.2 CRIMINAL LAW REGIME

Consistent with civil law jurisdictions, Indonesia's criminal law regime is drawn from the Indonesian Criminal Code and the many separate criminal statutes that have been adopted by Parliament criminalizing specific offenses.[27] The Indonesian Criminal Code was carried over from the Dutch Penal Code (*Wetboek van Strafrecht*) that was used during the colonial period and that in turn drew many principles from the French Napoleonic *Code Pénal*.[28] The Criminal Code includes some corruption-related offenses, including bribery of public officials (Article 209), bribery of judges (article 210), and extortion of public officials (Article 452). These code provisions have been updated and greatly expanded upon

---

[23] BUTT, *supra* note 18, at 32.

[24] *Id.* at 33.

[25] Indonesia's Constitution, Article 24.

[26] Tim Lindsey & Simon Butt, *Indonesian Law*, Oxford University Press (2018) at 73–74; Benjamin B. Wagner & Leslie Gielow Jacobs, *Retooling Law Enforcement to Investigate and Prosecute Entrenched Corruption: Key Criminal Procedure Reforms for Indonesia and Other Nations*, 30 U. Pa. J. Int'l L. 183 (2008) at 213.

[27] MOELJATNO, PRINCIPLES OF CRIMINAL LAW (ASAS-ASAS HUKUM PIDANA) 28 (rev. ed. 2015).

[28] L UTRECHT, CRIMINAL LAW (HUKUM PIDANA) 49 (1958) and P.J.P TAX, THE DUTCH CRIMINAL JUSTICE SYSTEM 25 (2008).

by Indonesia's more recent anti-corruption statute, which preempts the Criminal Code to the extent there is overlap. Since 1999, Indonesia's primary anti-corruption law has been Law No. 31 of 1999 on the Eradication of Corruption, as amended by Law No. 20 of 2001 (referred to as the Anti-Corruption Law). This broad law greatly increased the penalties for corruption crimes, and covers a wide range of corrupt conduct that can be generally summarized to include:

- Unjust enrichment at the expense of the state (Articles 2 and 3)
- Bribery of public officials (Article 5)
- Bribery/corruptly influencing a judge (Article 6)
- Embezzlement by a civil servant (Article 8)
- Falsification of official books and records (Article 9)
- Destruction of public records (Article 10)
- Gratuities to civil servant (Article 11)
- Other corrupt acts (Article 12)

Significantly, the Anti-Corruption Law, as well as a separate Anti-Money Laundering Law, include clear guidance that prohibits aiding and abetting, conspiring and attempting to violate these laws, and punishes them the same as the principal offender.[29] Moreover, the Anti-Corruption Law states that where corruption is committed by or on behalf of a corporation, prosecution and sentencing may be conducted against the corporation and/or its managers.[30]

An important part of Indonesia's criminal law regime is the Criminal Procedure Code (KUHAP) that was adopted in 1981, replacing and revoking the Dutch colonial era procedural rules (*Herzien Indonesisch Reglement*) that initially formed the basis for much of Indonesian law.[31] The Criminal Procedure Code divides the criminal process into three separate stages. The investigation phase is led by the police, the prosecution phase is led by the public prosecutors, and the judicial phase is led by judges. Criminal cases follow a fairly rigid process under which the police prepare a dossier during the investigation phase (further divided into pre-investigation and investigation phase) that is then presented to the prosecutors and ultimately to the judge. The dossier contains witness statements, reports, and relevant documents that judges use to exercise their inquisitorial role that includes questioning the defendant and witnesses during trial. The Criminal Procedure Code recognizes five different categories of evidence: (1) testimony of witnesses, (2) testimony of experts, (3) documentary evidence, (4) "indication" evidence in the form of documents of witness testimony that tends to establish that an offense occurred or the identity of the perpetrator, and (5) testimony of the defendant. To secure a conviction, prosecutors must present testimony from at least two witnesses or evidence from at least two different categories.

Significant and commendable work has gone into drafting an updated Criminal Procedure Code, and/or proposing amendments that would both assist law enforcement and clarify

---

[29] Anti-Corruption Law, Article 15; Anti-Money Laundering Law.
[30] Anti-Corruption Law, Article 20.
[31] Law No. 8 Year 1981 on Law of Criminal Procedure (Criminal Procedure Code), section of consider; *Staatsblad* No. 44 Year 1941.

protections for defendants. For example, the current code does not include a right against self-incrimination or provide a mechanism for seeking to exclude illegally obtained evidence.[32] Nor does the code specifically reference electronic evidence, or create mechanisms to allow for sentencing reductions, plea agreements, or immunity for cooperating witnesses: tools that would greatly assist with the investigation and prosecution of corruption cases. In the absence of a new procedure code, numerous more recent criminal laws specifically add and define procedural components to assist with their enforcement. Most notably, the Anti-Corruption Law includes procedural provisions for limited asset recovery, evidentiary presumptions (referred to as reverse burden of proof), investigative techniques, and the admission of electronic evidence.[33]

2.3 CIVIL LAW REGIME

Similar to Indonesia's criminal law system, the primary source of civil law in Indonesia is the Indonesian Civil Code (Kitab Undang-Undang Hukum Perdata or KUHP) adopted from the Dutch Civil Code (*burgerlijk wetboek voor Indonesie*).[34] In addition to the strong Dutch tradition, civil laws in Indonesia are influenced by both customary and Islamic Law. Private plaintiffs can bring civil cases in the public courts based upon civil statutory violations. As noted previously, the district courts and high courts are courts of general jurisdiction, hearing both criminal and civil cases. Victims of crimes can also file civil suits seeking compensation for losses arising out of acts that are the subject of criminal prosecution by the state. [35] In addition, Article 98 of the Criminal Procedure Code allows a victim to request that his or her civil suit for compensation be joined with the criminal case. The district court handling the criminal case shall consider its competence to adjudicate the compensation claim, along with the veracity of the claim, in determining whether to grant joinder.[36] In cases where the national Victim and Witness Protection Agency recognizes and individual as a crime victim, prosecutors may also seek restitution for a victim by including a claim for compensation in the criminal indictment.[37]

   Indonesia's Anti-Corruption law also provides two separate civil remedies that the state can pursue to recover stolen assets linked to corruption. First, prosecutors can pursue civil cases seeking compensation from individuals where an investigation shows that a corruption offense has resulted in the deprivation of state assets, but the evidence is not sufficient to support a criminal prosecution.[38] Second, in cases where the suspect in a corruption investigation dies, prosecutors can file a civil suit seeking to recover stolen state assets.[39]

---

[32] Robert R. Strang, "More Adversarial, but not Completely Adversarial": Reformasi of the Indonesian Criminal Procedure Code, Fordham International Law Journal Volume 32, Issue 1 (2008) at 197.

[33] Law No. 31 of 1999 on Eradication of the Criminal Act of Corruption (Anti-Corruption Act), as amended by Law No. 20 Year 2001. Law No. 30 Year 2002 on Corruption Eradication Commission (KPK Law).

[34] *Staatsblaad* No. 23 Year 1847.

[35] Civil Code, Article 1365.

[36] Criminal Code, Article 99.

[37] Law No. 31 Year 2014 on Witness and Victim Protection, Article 7A.

[38] Anti-Corruption Law, Article 32.

[39] Anti-Corruption Law, Article 34.

2.4 VIEWS FROM THE OUTSIDE

2.4.1 OECD Evaluation

Although Indonesia is not a member country of the Organization for Economic Cooperation and Development (OECD), it has worked in partnership with the OECD since 2007, participating in seven different OECD bodies/committees and adhering to more than 10 OECD legal instruments.[40] Indonesia also uses the OECD Anti-Corruption Convention as a model, but as a nonmember, the OECD has not conducted an evaluation of Indonesia. The OECD is however actively supporting the government of Indonesia in implementing reforms in many areas, including economic policy, tax, investment, trade, regulation, and anti-corruption. A recent OECD publication, *Active with Indonesia (2016)*, highlights the positive steps Indonesia is taking to coordinate with the OECD to implement reforms in these areas, including working toward accession to the OECD Anti-Bribery Convention. At present, the OECD noted that Indonesia lacks legislation prohibiting the bribery of foreign public officials.[41] The OECD also identified public procurement as a specific risk area for Indonesia, and has invited Indonesia to coordinate more closely on efforts to increase transparency and accountability of public procurement systems.[42]

2.4.2 Transparency International Corruption Perception Index Score

In 2017, Indonesia's Corruption Perception Index (CPI) score was 37, the same score it received in 2016. While not an improvement over the year prior, Indonesia's CPI score has been on an positive trend for the last five years. In terms of overall ranking, Indonesia was in a 7-way tie for 96th place in 2017, a bit of a decline from its 90th place ranking in 2016, but again a marked improvement from its ranking of 118 in 2012.[43] Indonesia looks to the CPI as an important tool and one of the measurements used to evaluate the success of its National Strategy of Prevention and Eradication Corruption in Indonesia (see Table 11.1).[44]

TABLE 11.1

Corruption Perception Index

Indonesia	2012	2013	2014	2015	2016	2017
Score	32	32	34	36	37	37
Rank	118	114	107	88	90	96

[40] OECD, ACTIVE WITH INDONESIA 3 (2016).

[41] *Id.* at 32.

[42] *Id. at* 33.

[43] Transparency International, *Corruption Perception Index* https://www.transparency.org/news/feature/corruption_perceptions_index_2017#table (last visited Dec. 20, 2018).

[44] Presidential Regulation No. 55 Year 2012 on the National Strategy of Prevention and Eradication of Corruption in Indonesia (Presidential Regulation on the National Strategy of Prevention and Corruption Eradication).

3. Investigative and Prosecutorial Agencies

3.1 CRIMINAL LAW AGENCIES

The Indonesian National Police force (INP or POLRI) is responsible for law enforcement throughout Indonesia, and is made up of more than 400,000 police officers and civilian employees. The Chief of Police is appointed by the president. Under the Criminal Procedure Code, criminal investigations are controlled by the police. Although Indonesia is a civil law country, it no longer has investigating magistrates.[45] Prosecutors play little or no role in the majority of criminal investigations until the completed dossier is presented to them for the purpose of preparing an indictment. The INP has the authority to investigate corruption, as it does with all other crimes, but as will be discussed, high-level corruption cases are also investigated and prosecuted by Indonesia's Corruption Eradication Commission.

The Attorney General's Office is the national prosecuting authority in Indonesia. Similar to the police, there are regional prosecutors' offices throughout the country, and they all report up through a highly centralized chain of command.[46] Prosecutors must review dossiers presented by the police within seven days and may return cases for further investigation if they find them insufficient for prosecution.[47] Once a case is accepted, the prosecutor prepares a bill of indictment that is presented to the court along with the dossier. The Attorney General's Office has authority to prosecute all corruption cases, and it has a specialized Anti-Corruption Unit within its Special Crimes Division.

Indonesia's Corruption Eradication Commission (the KPK) has the unique power and authority to both investigate and prosecute major corruption cases that meet any of the following three statutory criteria spelled out in the 2002 law that created the commission: (1) corruption cases involving law enforcement officers or government executives, (2) corruption cases involving a state loss of at least 1 billion rupiah (U.S. $75,000), and (3) corruption cases involving matters of wide-spread public notoriety.[48] In practice, this means that the KPK does not have authority over low-level bribery or minor corruption cases. The KPK was established under the authority of Law No. 30 of 2002 (the KPK Law) with the explicit recognition that the INP and Attorney General's Office had not been functioning effectively and efficiently in eradicating corruption.[49] The KPK began operations in 2003, and has steadily increased the number of corruption cases it investigates each year.

The KPK is an independent government institution, and executes its duties and authorities without oversight from the executive, judicial, or legislative branches.[50] The

---

[45] Strang, *supra* note 32, at 195.

[46] Wagner, *supra* note 26, at 201.

[47] Criminal Procedure Code, Articles 110 and 138.

[48] Corruption Eradication Act, Article 11.

[49] Corruption Eradication Commission Act, Elucidation Paragraph 3 that mentions law enforcement with regards to the eradication of corruption so far has been lackluster. In order to improve conditions, we must enhance law enforcement methods by forming a special agency that will be allowed a wide authority that is independent as well as free from the influence of notorious powers in the effort to combat graft in a coordinated effort that is implemented optimally, intensively, effectively, professionally, and continuously.

[50] Anti-Corruption Law, Article 3, states that the KPK is to be a state agency that will perform its duties and authority independently, free from any and all influence. According to the article elucidation, "powers and influence" shall be construed as any power that could affect the tasks and authority of the KPK or members of

KPK is required to report periodically to the president, the House of Representatives, and the State Audit Board, and is also required to provide the public with open access to information so the community can directly monitor the progress of its corruption eradication efforts.[51] The KPK has five commissioners, four of whom supervise one of the four KPK departments (Enforcement, Prevention, Information and Data, Internal Supervision and Community Complaints), and one of whom is the chairperson. The KPK uses an outside recruitment service and a rigorous hiring process to select its own criminal investigators and prosecutors in order to insure they are qualified and have the highest standards of integrity. Importantly, the KPK also has the authority to take over ongoing corruption investigations or prosecutions from the police or Attorney General's Office (AGO) if the case has stalled or there are other indications that the matter is not being actively pursued.

3.2 CIVIL LAW AGENCIES

While corruption matters are largely handled by criminal law agencies as described previously, Indonesia's Anti-Corruption Law provides that criminal investigators may refer matters for civil enforcement in cases where they do not find sufficient evidence of corruption to support a criminal prosecution. Specifically, investigators may submit an investigatory case file to the civil enforcement attorneys within the Government Law Office of the AGO or to the aggrieved institution to file a civil action seeking to recover government assets.[52] The Business Competition Supervisory Commission (Komisi Pengawas Persaingan Usaha or KPPU) also has civil authority to conduct investigations into certain unfair business practices, and to impose penalties on business actors who engage in anticompetitive activities that violate Indonesia's Anti-Monopoly Act.[53]

Indonesia also has a very capable Financial Transaction Reporting and Analysis Center (Pusat Pelaporan dan Analisis Transaksi Keuangan or PPATK) that serves as Indonesia's Financial Intelligence Unit and is a member of the international EGMONT group of FIUs.[54] PPATK is not a law enforcement agency, but is authorized to provide information and data on financial transactions related to money laundering, corruption, and other criminal offenses.[55] Law enforcement agencies may specifically request assistance, or the PPATK

---

the Commissioners of the KPK individually, from any executive, judiciary, legislative, and any other entities connected to a corruption case, or any other circumstances and situation.

[51] *Id.*, Article 20.

[52] Anti-Corruption Law, Article 32. The same process of civil referral is used in cases where the criminal suspect dies. Articles 2–3.

[53] Law No. 5 Year 1999 on Prohibition of Monopolistic Practices and Unfair Business Competition (Anti-Monopoly Act). Article 22 states that business actors shall be prohibited from conspiring with other parties with the aim of determining the awardees of tenders that may cause unfair business competition.

[54] The EGMONT Group is an international group of FIUs that cooperate to combat money laundering, terrorist financing, and other transnational crime. https://egmontgroup.org/en/content/about (last visited, Dec. 14, 2018).

[55] Anti-Money Laundering Law, chapter VI, describes the function and authority of Indonesian Financial Transaction Reports and Analysis Center (PPATK).

may proactively provide information to the police, prosecutors, or the KPK that raises suspicion of criminal violations. It should also be noted that in addition to criminal enforcement authority, the KPK has a wide scope of non-criminal responsibilities including prevention, research, and monitoring the implementation of good governance practices across ministries.[56]

3.3 MULTIAGENCY ARRANGEMENTS

Indonesian law enforcement agencies have been increasingly working together to tackle corruption in a more coordinated fashion. While some institutional barriers exist, and there have been significant tensions between agencies in the past, the KPK is dedicated to working with police and prosecutors to handle corruption cases. The KPK Law instructs that the KPK was formed with the purpose of improving the effectiveness and efficiency of efforts to eradicate criminal acts of corruption, and that the KPK should coordinate with other institutions to fight corruption.[57] This practical guidance is due to the fact that the KPK is centralized in Jakarta and has only a small fraction of the number of investigators and prosecutors compared to the hundreds of thousands of INP officers and many thousands AGO prosecutors located around the country. It is also consistent with how the KPK approaches its mission. The KPK regularly provides training and leadership in pursuing corruption investigations and prosecutions, and in advocating for new laws and regulations to advance the ability of law enforcement to handle public corruption cases.

3.4 ANTI-CORRUPTION COURTS

In addition to the police, prosecutors, and the KPK, as well as the PPATK, the special Anti-Corruption Courts play a central role in Indonesia's anti-corruption regime. Indonesia's Anti-Corruption Courts were created under the same law that created the KPK.[58] The KPK Law requires that this specialized court include ad hoc judges to sit alongside career judges who would be specifically chosen based upon their experience. The purpose of establishing Anti-Corruption Courts was to promote efficiency, integrity, and expertise.[59] Specialized Anti-Corruption Courts are now located in every province, examining and deciding all corruption cases both prosecuted by the KPK or by prosecutors under the authority of the AGO. If there is an objection to the verdict imposed by the Anti-Corruption Court, an appeal, cassation or review may be filed.

---

[56] KPK Law, Article 6.

[57] BUTT, *supra* note 18, at 31; Law No. 30 of 2002 (the KPK Law) Articles 4 and 6.

[58] KPK Law, Article 53; *see also* Law No. 46 Year 2009 on Anti-Corruption Courts.

[59] *See* Matthew C. Stephenson & Sofie A. Schutte, *Specialized Anti-Corruption Courts: A Comparative Mapping,* (U4Anti-Corruption Resource Centre, 2016 No. 7), 10, https://www.u4.no/publications/specialised-anti-corruption-courts-a-comparative-mapping.pdf (last visited, Dec. 14, 2018).

4. Bribery of Foreign Officials

Indonesia does not currently have legislation addressing the bribery of foreign public officials in international business transactions. This gap in Indonesia's anti-corruption framework is well recognized by the government as well as by civil society in Indonesia, and steps are being taken to close it. Indonesia has included prohibitions on bribing foreign officials in drafts of a new updated Criminal Code that has been in development for some time. Although the updated Criminal Code has the support of the president, its passage remains uncertain and controversial among some in government.[60] As a result, there is also discussion about including foreign bribery prohibitions in amendments to the Anti-Corruption Law that have also been proposed by the KPK and others. The OCED has also invited Indonesia to participate in its Working Group on Bribery as a way of moving toward compliance with the OECD Anti-Bribery Convention.[61]

5. Bribery of Domestic Officials

5.1 JURISDICTION

Indonesia's Criminal Code provides that the criminal laws of Indonesia apply to any person who commits a criminal offense within the territory of Indonesia.[62] This includes violations of Indonesia's Anti-Corruption Law. Based on the principle of nationality applied in Indonesia, the Criminal Code also states that any Indonesian public official who commits a criminal act outside the territory of Indonesia can also be prosecuted.[63] Moreover, the Anti-Corruption Law states that any person (including corporations) outside the territory of Indonesia that renders assistance, opportunities, means, or information to enable the commission of a criminal act of corruption shall also be liable guilty of corruption and be subject to the same penalties provided for under the law.[64]

5.2 STATUTE OF LIMITATIONS

A 12-year statute of limitations applies for the crime of bribery of domestic officials.[65] Article 78 of the Criminal Code explains the right to prosecute shall lapse after a period of years depending on the severity of the offense as measured by the maximum sentence that may be imposed. As a result, the same 12-year limitations period applies for all other violations of Indonesia's Anti-Corruption Law, with the exception of any violations for which life

---

[60] Robertus Belarminus, Corruption Crimes Is Regulated by Criminal Code: Efforts to Delegitimize KPK, *available at* http://nasional.kompas.com/read/2017/06/15/21220381/pidana.korupsi.diatur.kuhp.dinilai. sebagai.upaya.mendelegitimasi.kpk (last visited Dec. 28, 2017).

[61] Active with Indonesia, OECD 2016.

[62] Penal Code, Article 2.

[63] Penal Code, Article 7.

[64] Anti-Corruption Law, Article 16.

[65] Criminal Code, Article 78.

imprisonment or capital punishment may be imposed. In such case, the statute of limitations is 18 years.[66]

5.3 BRIBERY OF DOMESTIC OFFICIALS

Indonesia's Anti-Corruption Law identifies the broad range of corruption offenses that apply in Indonesia today, including bribery of domestic officials.[67] The law criminalizes bribery of public officials on the part of both the giver and the recipient, and also prohibits bribery involving judges and advocates.[68]

While there are a number of relevant anti-corruption provisions in the Anti-Corruption Law, including embezzlement by public officials, creating false records, destruction of evidence, and accepting gratuities, Article 5 addresses bribery of public officials and prohibits anyone from:

(a) giving or promising something to a public official or state apparatus with the aim of persuading the official to do something or not to do something because of his/her position which would violate his/her obligations;

(b) giving something to a civil servant or state apparatus because of or in relation to something in violation of his/her obligation whether or not it is done because of his/her position.[69]

Article 6 similarly addresses bribery of judges or lawyers by prohibiting anyone from:

(c) giving or promising something to a judge with the aim of influencing the decision of the case;

(d) giving or promising something to an individual who according to legislation is appointed as a lawyer to attend a trial session with the aim of influencing the advice or views on the case given to the court.[70]

5.4 DEFINITION OF DOMESTIC OFFICIALS

Indonesia's Anti-Corruption Law defines a civil servant or public official broadly to include:

- a civil servant as defined in the Civil Servants Law;
- a civil servant as defined in the Indonesian Criminal Code;
- a person who receives a salary or wage from the finances of the state or the regions;
- a person who receives a salary or wage from a corporation that receives support from the finances of the state or the regions (i.e., a state-owned enterprise); or

---

[66] *Id.*

[67] Anti-Corruption Law, Articles 5, 6, 11, 12a–d and 13.

[68] Anti-Corruption Law, Articles 5 and 6.

[69] Anti-Corruption Law, Article 5.

[70] Anti-Corruption Law, Article 6.

- a person who receives a salary or wage from another corporation that uses capital or facilities from the state or the public.

To the extent that they do not conflict with the Anti-Corruption Law, several other statutes also have definitions for civil servants. The Civil Servant Law defines civil servants as Indonesian citizens who are hired to fulfill a duty of an office of the state or are given other stately duties and are salaried in accordance with the prevailing laws and regulations. This comprises central and regional government officials, members of the armed forces, and members of the police. The Indonesian Criminal Code defines civil servants as all persons who have been elected or who, by reason other than as a result of election, are members of a legislative body, a government body, or a body of the peoples' representatives formed by or on behalf of the government. The Criminal Code also states that judges, chairpersons, and members of religious councils, and any person who joins the armed forces, will also be viewed as a civil servant.

5.5 GIFTS, GRATUITIES, AND HOSPITALITY

Indonesia's Anti-Corruption Law prohibits gifts, gratuities, and hospitality. Article 12B provides that any gratification/gratuity given to a civil servant or public official in relation to his or her position and contrary to his or her official duties and obligations shall be considered a bribe. The Anti-Corruption Law defines "gratuity" broadly as a gift to a civil servant or state apparatus in the widest sense of the term, including the giving of money, goods, discounts, commission, non-interest-bearing loans, travel tickets, accommodation facilities, free medical care, and other facilities. The restriction applies to both those providing and receiving such benefits.[71] Moreover, if the gratuity involved is greater than 10 million rupiahs (U.S. $750), the recipient has the burden of proving it is not a bribe.[72]

5.6 DEFENSES

Indonesia does not have any statutory or affirmative defenses to bribery or corruption crimes, and does not recognize exceptions for facilitation payments or adequate procedures. Civil servants and public officials who wish to accept gratuities not related to their employment must report the gratuity to the KPK within 30 days of receipt seeking a determination as to its legality. The KPK has 30 days to review and make a decision. Other than this process, Indonesia's Anti-Corruption Law does not provide for exceptions.

---

[71] A gratuity would include the giving of money, goods, discounts, commissions, non-interest-bearing loans, travel tickets, accommodation, facilities, free medical care, and other facilities, whether these are given in Indonesia or abroad, by electronic or non-electronic means; see Corruption Eradication Act, Elucidation Article 12B.

[72] Anti-Corruption Law, Article 12B(1)a.

5.7 FACILITATION PAYMENTS

Indonesia's Anti-Corruption Law does not specifically address facilitation payments but can be broadly interpreted to prohibit such payments. The Law essentially penalizes the act of giving or promising something to a civil servant or a state apparatus with the aim of persuading him/her to do something or to refrain from doing something that would violate his obligations, or because of or in relation to something in violation of his or her obligations, whether or not it is done because of his position; including providing a "gratuity" to a civil servant or public official in relation to his or her position in return for a favor. Accordingly, no facilitation payment exceptions or defenses exist.

5.8 PENALTIES

Violations of Indonesia's Anti-Bribery provisions are subject to a minimum of one year and a maximum of five years in prison, and a minimum fine of 50 million rupiah up to 250 million rupiah.[73] Violations of other portions of the Anti-Corruption Law, such as the Unjust Enrichment/Gratuity provisions, can be penalized by fines of between 50 million rupiah and 1,000 million rupiah, and by imprisonment for up to 20 years. Under special circumstances, life imprisonment or the death penalty can be imposed.[74] Corporate entities (companies, unincorporated associations, partnerships, etc.) may also be prosecuted for corruption offenses.[75] Fines for corporations are increased by one-third. In addition, Indonesia's Anti-Money Laundering Law provides broad authority to seize and forfeit the proceeds of criminal activity, including corruption.[76]

6. Commercial Bribery
6.1 GENERAL PRINCIPLES

Indonesia does not have a commercial bribery law. Other laws, such as the Anti-Money Laundering Law or Criminal Code prohibition on fraudulent acts may be applied to acts related to commercial bribery or corruption in the context of bribery in the private sector.[77]

7. Sentencing Principles

The Indonesian Criminal Code provides that no act shall be punished unless by virtue of a statutory penal provision.[78] Other than this broad requirement that courts imposes

---

[73] Anti-Corruption Law, Article 5.

[74] Anti-Corruption Law, Articles 2–12.

[75] Anti-Corruption Law, Article 20(7).

[76] Law No. 8 Year 2010 Regarding Counter Measures and Eradication of Money Laundering. (Anti-Money Laundering Law), Articles 2 and 3.

[77] Criminal Code, Article 378 (fraudulent acts).

[78] Penal Code, Article 1.

sentences consistent with the range detailed in the statute, Indonesian law does not require judges to consider any specific sentencing factors, and there are no sentencing guidelines. As a result, the fines and terms of imprisonment imposed within the range authorized by law can vary widely. Moreover, Indonesia does not have any alternative forms of punishment such as home or community confinement, community service, or other alternative noncustodial sentences. Nor does the criminal justice system provide mechanisms for treatment or rehabilitation.

8. Related Criminal Offenses

8.1 ATTEMPT, AIDING AND ABETTING, AND CONSPIRACY

Indonesia's Anti-Corruption Law provides that any person attempting, abetting, or maliciously conspiring to commit criminal acts of corruption shall be liable for the same penalties as the principal persons committing the crime.[79] This language is more clear and arguably broader than the liability imposed on various types of criminal participants under the Criminal Code, which penalizes anyone who "causes others to perpetrate" or "intentionally provokes" the criminal act, as well as those who "deliberately aid" in the commission of a crime.[80] The Anti-Corruption Law also punishes attempt, aiding and abetting, and conspiracy to the same extent as the completed crime and principal actor. This differs from the Criminal Code that reduces by one-third the penalty imposed for those convicted of acting in complicity.[81]

8.2 FALSE ACCOUNTING/BOOKS AND RECORDS

The Anti-Corruption Law makes it a crime for any person to refuse to provide information or to provide false information related to corruption investigations.[82] In addition, Indonesia's Criminal Code makes it a crime to forge or falsify certain types of records, to include any writings related to titles, contracts, or a release from debt. The Code also makes it a crime to deliberately make use of such a false writing as if it were genuine (knowing it is false.)[83] Other Criminal Code provisions prohibit additional specific types of false statements and writings, including false medical records, travel permits, and title documents.[84]

---

[79] Anti-Corruption Law, Article 15.
[80] Penal Code, Article 55; *See also* P.A.F LAMINTANG, FOUNDATIONS OF CRIMINAL LAW IN INDONESIA (DASAR-DASAR HUKUM PIDANA DI INDONESIA) 4TH EDITION (2011) 634.
[81] Penal Code, Article 55.
[82] Anti-Corruption Law, Article 22.
[83] Criminal Code, Articles 263 and 264.
[84] Criminal Code, Articles 266 to 275.

8.3 MONEY LAUNDERING

Indonesia has a broad Anti-Money Laundering Law and has been steadily increasing its anti-money laundering regime to comply with international standards.[85] This includes broad know-your-customer rules, the reporting of suspicious transactions, and prohibitions on bulk cash smuggling.[86] In addition to the KPK, customs, the National Narcotics Agency, the tax authority, and the police who investigate money laundering, Indonesia's Financial Intelligence Unit (PPATK) plays an engaged and important monitoring and reporting role.[87] The most recent Anti-Money Laundering law, adopted in 2010, makes it illegal for anyone to:

1. Place, transfer, forward, spend, pay, grant, deposit, take abroad, or change the form or currency of any asset that is recognized or reasonably alleged to be proceeds of criminal action;

2. Hide, or disguise the origin, source, location, purpose, transfer of right or true ownership of any asset that is known or reasonably alleged to be proceeds of criminal action;

3. Accept or take control of the placement, transfer, payment, grant, deposit, exchange or utilize any asset that is known or reasonably alleged to be proceeds of criminal action.[88]

As such, Indonesia's law encompasses what Indonesia describes as both the active passive participants and passive participants in money laundering, so long as they know or reasonably suspect that the assets involved are proceeds of criminal activity. The Anti-Money Laundering Law specifically includes corporations as potential defendants,[89] and it criminalizes attempt, aiding, and conspiracy.[90] The maximum penalty is 20 years in prison, and 5 billion rupiah in fines.[91] The fine for corporations is up to 100 billion rupiah, and in addition corporations are subject to having their business suspended, licenses revoked, assets confiscated, and even having the company being taken over by the state.[92] Assets can also be confiscated and sold if the company cannot pay fines imposed.[93] In the event that the defendant's assets are insufficient to pay the fine, up to one year in jail can be substituted for the fine.[94]

Moreover, the Anti-Money Laundering law allows assets to be frozen temporarily during the investigation, and to later be forfeited without the need for a criminal conviction in the

---

[85] Law No. 8 Year 2010 (Anti-Money Laundering Law), Articles 3–5; Indonesia has been working to fully comply with the Financial Action Task Force (FATF) Recommendations for anti-money laundering.

[86] Anti-Money Laundering Law, Articles 18–22 (Know Your Customer), Articles 23–30 (Reporting), Articles 33–36 (Cash Smuggling).

[87] Anti-Money Laundering Law, Articles 37–46 (PPATK Duties, Function and Authority).

[88] Anti-Money Laundering Law, Articles 3–5.

[89] Anti-Money Laundering Law, Article 6.

[90] Anti-Money Laundering Law, Article 10.

[91] Anti-Money Laundering Law, Articles 3, 4, and 5.

[92] Anti-Money Laundering Law, Article 7.

[93] Anti-Money Laundering Law, Article 9.

[94] Anti-Money Laundering Law, Article 8.

event that the alleged perpetrator and/or third party fails to object within a specified time period.[95] This Non-Conviction Based (NCB) forfeiture mechanism seeks to create a presumption that would place the burden of proof on the party objecting to show that the assets were not involved in money laundering, but in practice the implementation of this type of forfeiture has been unclear.[96] Seeking to establish improved procedures for NCB forfeiture, the Supreme Court issued guidance for judges on how to handle NCB forfeiture by issuing Supreme Court Regulation No. 1 Year 2013.[97]

A few examples demonstrate the scope of Indonesia's Anti-money laundering law, and the power it has given to law enforcement. In 2013, Djoko Susilo, a famous general with the Indonesian National Police, was convicted of money laundering and obligated to pay more than Rp 32 billion (more than U.S. $ 2,3 million).[98] In 2015, Fuad Amin, an important and influential political figure in East Java and mayor of Bangkalan, was convicted of money laundering and ordered to pay more than Rp.222 billion (more than U.S. $15.47 million).[99] As for corporate penalties, the KPK confiscated shares of the company Nazarudin that had a value of more than Rp. 55 billion (more than U.S. $40,590,000).[100]

More recently, corporations have also been investigated and convicted of Money Laundering. For example, in 2017, the Indoensia contruction company PT Beringin Bangun Utamawas convicted of laundering the proceeds of corruption and sentenced to pay a fine of Rp. 750,000,000,- (U.S. $50,000).[101] In that case, the owner of company was also convicted for his role in using the corporation to layer and hide the true source of his illegally obtained funds. The owner was sentenced to 5 years in prison, a fine of Rp. 500,000,000,- (U.S. $33,333) and a penalty of Rp. 3,276,596,619,30 (U.S. $218,439).[102] In early 2018, the KPK announced a still ongoing money laundering investigation into PT TRADHA, a construction company owned by the mayor of Kebumen Regency. That investigation is looking into the role of both the corporation and it owner in the awarding of lucrative government procurement projects, to include the laundering of alleged illegal gratuities paid by contractors and the purchase of luxury items by the owner in the name of the corporation.[103]

---

[95] Anti-Money Laundering Law, Article 67.

[96] *Id.*

[97] Supreme Court Regulation No. 1 Year 2003 on Guidance for Settlement Wealth Related with Money Laundering and other crimes.

[98] Djoko Susilo v. Republic of Indonesia, Supreme Court Decision No. 537 K/Pid.Sus/2014.

[99] Fuad Amin v. Republic of Indonesia, Supreme Court Decision No. 980 K/Pid.Sus/2016.

[100] Nazarudin v. Republic of Indonesia, The Jakarta Pusat's Special Dictrict Court for Corruption Decision No. 159_Pid.SUS_TPK_2015_PN.Jkt.Pst.pdf.

[101] P.T. Beringin Bangun Utama v. Republic of Indonesia, The Bengkulu's Special Court for Corruption Decision No. 64/Pid.Sus/TPKl2016/PN.Bgl.

[102] Christoper O. Dewabrata v. Republic of Indonesia, The Bengkulu's Special Court for Corruption Decision No. 10/PID.SUS.TPK/2017/PN.Bgl.

[103] Naufal Mamduh, KPK investigates PT TRADHA as money laundering's suspect, 2018, May 18, 2018, https://tirto.id/kpk-tetapkan-pt-tradha-sebagai-tersangka-kasus-pencucian-uang-cKJA (last visited, Dec. 14, 2018); Tempo.co, KPK Names Kebumen Regent Suspect in Money Laundering https://en.tempo.co/read/918579/kpk-names-kebumen-regent-suspect-in-money-laundering (last visited Dec. 21, 2018).

8.4 TAX AND OTHER FRAUDS

Under Indonesia's tax law, taxpayers are required to properly record transactions, and it is a crime to create false accounting records or books. Other tax crimes include failure to comply with administrative tax reporting obligations, tax evasion, and engaging in acts to impede tax inspection or audit.[104] Indonesia also has a separate Public Accountant Law that makes it a crime for an accountant to intentionally manipulate accounting records.[105]

Law enforcement officers in Indonesia are well aware of the connection between tax evasion and corruption. In 2016, the KPK prosecuted an officer from the Tax Department who helped a taxpayer evade taxes owed. In this case, the tax official received gratification of more than U.S. $659,800 connected with laundering more than U.S. $3,500,000.[106] The KPK also prosecuted a tax official who accepted a bribe of over U.S. $140,000 from a corporation.[107]

8.5 OTHER OFFENSES RELATED TO CORRUPTION

Obstruction of justice, witness tampering, and destruction of evidence are also crimes under Indonesia's Anti-Corruption Law. Any person who intentionally prevents or obstructs, or indirectly sabotages investigations, prosecutions, or the examination of witnesses faces a sentence of between 3 and 12 years.[108] Any who refuse to give a statement as a witness could be punished with the same punishment as if they made a false statement, with the exclusion of someone with a family relationship such as father, mother, grandfather, grandmother, sibling, husband or wife, child, and grandchild, who are excluded.[109] Anyone who has a professional obligation to keep a secret is waived from the obligation to give statements.[110] The Anti-Corruption law also makes it a crime to destroy evidence, including documents or anything that would be admissible as evidence, with a penalty of between two and seven years in prison.[111]

8.6 CRIMES BY LAW ENFORCEMENT OFFICERS

Indonesia's Criminal Code has long penalized criminal conduct by a government official with a sentence one-third longer than ordinary people.[112] The Anti-Corruption Law picks up on these prohibitions and also makes it a crime for anyone to destroy or alter evidence, or

---

[104] Law No. 16 Year 2009 on General Provision of Tax (Tax Act), Articles 38, 39, and 39A, 41A, 41B, and 41C.

[105] Constitutional Court Decision No. 84/PUU-IX/2011; Law No. 5 Year 2011 on Public Accountant, Article 55.

[106] Gayus Tambunan v. Republic of Indonesia, Supreme Court Decision No. 1198_K_PID.SUS_2011.pdf.

[107] Priska Sari Pertiwi, *Former Tax Department Official Has* Been *sentenced to 10 Years, available at* https://www.cnnindonesia.com/nasional/20170724132651-12-229912/eks-pejabat-pajak-handang-soekarno-divonis-10-tahun-penjara (last visited Dec. 14, 2018).

[108] Anti-Corruption Law, Article 21.

[109] Criminal Code, Article 174; Anti-Corruption Law, Article 35.

[110] Anti-Corruption Law, Article 36.

[111] *Id.*, Article 10.

[112] Criminal Code, Article 52.

file a false report.[113] Moreover, it is illegal for investigators, prosecutors, and other employees of the KPK to engage in conflicts of interest, with penalties up to a maximum of five years.[114]

9. Cooperation and Self-Reporting

Indonesia's Anti-Corruption framework does not include any mechanism for cooperation or self-reporting, and there is no system of plea bargaining. Proposed revisions of the Criminal Procedure Code, as well as proposed amendments to the Anti-Corruption Law, include options that would allow sentencing reductions and potential immunity, as these steps are recognized as necessary to fully comply with the UN Convention against Corruption.

Similarly, Indonesia does not currently have a set of sentencing guidelines or policy considerations that specifically provide consideration or sentencing mitigation for corporate compliance programs. However, as noted elsewhere, new Supreme Court guidance on corporate criminal liability describes factors that judges may consider in assessing a corporation's culpability. Perma No. 13 of 2016 discusses preventative measures, the benefits derived by corporations from the criminal activity, and whether the corporation allowed or tolerated the criminal activity. The KPK is also currently considering the development of law enforcement guidance specifically related to corporate compliance programs, and factors that separate genuine efforts from superficial ones.

10. Whistle-Blower Protection
10.1 PUBLIC SECTOR WHISTLE-BLOWER PROTECTION

Indonesia's Law on Witness and Victim Protection was adopted in 2006, and amended in 2014.[115] Under the law, the Witness and Victim Protection Agency (LPSK) has authority to provide protections and services to victims and witnesses in criminal cases, including corruption. Overall, however, contradictions with other laws, gaps in the protections provided, and other legal uncertainties result in this law falling far short of providing the comprehensive whistle-blower protection required by the UN Convention against Corruption.[116]

---

[113] Corruption Eradication Act, Article 23.

[114] Corruption Eradication Commission Act, Articles 65 and 66.

[115] Law No. 13 Year 2006, as amended by Law No. 31 Year 2014. Under Article 15 Law No. 30 Year 2002, the Corruption Eradication Commission also has the authority to protect the witness and victim to dismantle corruption, but this authority does not equate to whistle-blower protection.

[116] There are also other contradictions in the current legal framework that discourage whistle-blowing. Government Regulation No. 42 Year 2004 on Ethical Conduct of Indonesia's Public Sector (Government Regulation No. 42 on Ethical Conduct and Law No. 5 Year 2014 on Public Official (Public Official Act). Under Government Regulation, public servants are obliged to support and implement policies taken by their superiors (stipulated in Article 9 of the regulation). This regulation contradicts the Public Official Act that requires public servants to hold the principle of public integrity, which involves neutrality, accountability, professionality, openness, and so on. In upholding this principle, public officials have to be independent from any political pressure, and are required to defend legality and due process, which are critical to the public interest (Mulgan 2008, at 350). This contradicting regulations reduces the incentive to disclose corrupt conduct in public sectors.

For example, Indonesia's criminal defamation law can be manipulated by those who have the political or financial power to instigate defamation charges against whistle-blowers who make allegations of corruption, fraud, or misconduct against them. The case of Khairiansyah Salman, a former auditor of the Supreme Audit Agency (BPK), is a good example. He was prosecuted after reporting the results of an investigation he conducted that revealed rampant corruption within the General Election Commission (KPU) that administered legislative and presidential elections in 2004.[117]

10.2 PRIVATE SECTOR WHISTLE-BLOWER PROTECTION

There is no specific legislation in Indonesia providing private sector whistle-blower protection. As noted previously, individuals who are determined to be witnesses or victims in criminal cases have some limited protections, but not to the extent envisioned by most whistle-blower protection laws or required by the UNCAC. Although no legislation exists, some private sector companies have implemented policies that protect whistle-blowers who report fraud, misconduct, and ethics violation.[118]

11. Key International Treaties Relating to Bribery and Corruption

Indonesia signed the UN Convention against Corruption (UNCAC) in 2003 and ratified it by Law No. 7 of 2006.[119] UNCAC plays an important role in Indonesia as a tool to measure the adequacy of its anti-corruption legislation as a part of the national strategy of prevention and eradication of corruption. Furthermore, UNCAC provides a mechanism for robust cooperation on law enforcement matters between member countries.[120] Indonesia is also a member of the Asia/Pacific Group on Money Laundering (APG) and is an active at the international level in promoting anti-money-laundering initiatives.[121] Moreover, Indonesia is a G20 country and is an active member of the G20 Anti-Corruption Working Group.

12. Mutual Legal Assistance Treaties and Transnational Cooperation

Indonesia provides mutual legal assistance and transnational cooperation with other countries pursuant to treaties and, mutual legal assistance agreements, based upon general

---

[117] THE JAKARTA POST, Oct. 19, 2012.

[118] For instance, one of Indonesia airline companies, Garuda Indonesia, has an internal policy for whistle-blower protection. Under the board of director decree No. kpts-15/C0000/2012-So, the whistle-blower protection policy also applies in PT. Pertamina (Persero) (the Indonesian oil and gas company).

[119] UNCAC Ratification Act.

[120] Presidential Regulation on the National Strategy of Prevention and Corruption Eradication.

[121] FATF, Members of APG, *available at* http://www.fatf-gafi.org/countries/#APG (last visited Dec. 14, 2018).

principles of reciprocity.[122] Law No. 1 of 2006 on Mutual Legal Assistance defines the scope of assistance to include:

(a) identifying and locating persons;
(b) obtaining statements or other forms thereof;
(c) providing documents or other forms thereof;
(d) making arrangements for persons to provide statements or to assist in the investigation;
(e) delivering letters;
(f) executing the inquiry of search warrant and seizure;
(g) the forfeiture of proceeds of crime;
(h) the recovery of pecuniary penalties in respect to the crime;
(i) the restraining of dealings in property, the freezing of property that may be recovered or confiscated, or that may be needed to satisfy pecuniary penalties imposed, in respect to the crime;
(j) locating property that may be recovered, or may be needed to satisfy pecuniary penalties imposed, in respect to the crime, and/or
(k) other assistance in accordance with this Law.[123]

Indonesia recognizes that good cooperation between countries is important to combatting corruption, and has experience providing mutual legal assistance using treaties, and more informally. For example, Indonesia cooperated with the UK Serious Fraud Office between 2015 and 2017 related to the Roll Royce Cases. Several of the charges being investigated related to the procurement of engines for Indonesia's national airline, Garuda Indonesia.[124] After a lengthy investigation Roll Royce entered into a deferred prosecution agreement in the UK and paid more than £497,252,645.[125] In Indonesia, the KPK thereafter designated the former Director of Garuda Indonesia as a suspect in alleged corruption.

Indonesia's Extradition Act came into force in 1979.[126] Just like MLA, extradition can be done with or without a treaty.[127] Indonesia will only consider extradition for offenses included in the list of crimes allowed under the Extradition Act, and after the proper court process.[128] Requests for extradition must be made through Indonesia's Central Authority within the Ministry of Law and Human Rights. If the requirements for filing an extradition request are met, the Ministry of Law and Human Rights forwards the request to the attorney general and the chief of police who will locate and present the subject to the Court for a final decision.[129]

---

[122] Law No. 1 Year 2006 on Mutual Legal Assistance, Article 5 (Mutual Legal Assistance law provides that (1) Assistance may be provided based on a Treaty. (2) In the absence of treaty as referred to in paragraph (1), the Assistance may be provided based on a good relationship under the reciprocity principles).

[123] *Id.*, Article 3 (2).

[124] Peggy Hollinger, Ben Bland & Catherin Belton, *Indonesia Probes Corruption Related to Rolls Royce and Airbus*, FIN. TIMES, Jan. 19, 2017.

[125] DPA Rolls Royce v. SFO 2017.

[126] Law No. 1 Year 1979 about Extradition (Extradition Act).

[127] *Id.*, Article 2,

[128] *Id.*, Articles 4 and 5.

[129] *Id.*, Articles 32–33.

One interesting example of Indonesia seeking extradition from another country is the Adrian Kiki Case. Adrian Kiki was convicted of corruption related to Bank Indonesia Liquidity Assistance Fund but escaped to Australia.[130] The attorney general of Indonesia requested extradition of Kiki from Australia. Kiki filed a plea with Australia's District Court arguing he had been tried in Indonesia in absentia, and that the prison system in Indonesia had potential for abuse of power. However, in 2013, the Supreme Court of Western Australia granted Indonesia's extradition request.

13. Legal Professional Privilege
13.1 GENERAL PRINCIPLES

Indonesian law recognizes a legal professional privilege that is based upon a lawyer's obligation to keep secret what they learn or acquire from a client based upon their professional relationship. Unlike the attorney-client privilege applied in the United States that can only be waived by the client, the legal professional privilege in Indonesia takes the form of a lawyer's professional obligation to maintain the confidentiality of what that lawyer learns from his or her client.[131] This professional obligation is mandated by Indonesia's Law on Advocates as follows:

> *(1) Advocates should keep secret things that are known or obtained from their Clients because of their professional relationships, except as determined otherwise by law. (2) Advocates have the right of confidentiality related to the Client, including the protection of files and documents upon the foreclosure or investigation and protection from the interception of Advocates' electronic communications.[132]*

It is important to be aware, however, that there are limits and exceptions to the protections provided by the legal professional privilege, including the possibility that items can be seized by law enforcement or presented at trial with an appropriate court order, regardless of any confidentiality requirements. The Criminal Procedure Code, Article 43, provides that the seizure of documents or other written materials from those who are "obligated to keep them confidential" may be carried out by authority of a special warrant signed by the head of the local District Court. In addition, Article 170 provides a mechanism whereby "a person under obligations of confidentiality" because of that person's occupation may ask the court to excuse that person from the obligation so he or she can testify as a witness concerning matters entrusted to that person.[133] Both of these procedural mechanisms are potential avenues for the legal protection privilege to be overcome in the context of a criminal case. The Law

---

[130] Adrian Kiki v. Republic of Indonesia, High Court Decision No.71/PID/2003/PT.DKI.

[131] The two main sources of the legal professional privilege are the Law on Advocates and the Advocates Code of Ethics (which is not a law, but a set of professional standards). The Advocates Code of Ethics, Section 4(h) provides that "advocates are obliged to hold their professional confidentiality regarding matters disclosed by the clients in trust and they are obligated to maintain such confidentiality after the relationship between advocate and client ends."

[132] Law No. 18 Year 2003, Article 19.

[133] Criminal Procedure Code, Article 170.

on Advocates seems also to acknowledge exceptions to confidentiality when it states that advocates should keep secret things that are known or obtained from their clients because of their professional relationships, *except as determined otherwise by law*.[134]

In the specific context of corruption cases, the KPK Law provides authority for the KPK to pursue investigative steps without the requirement of a court order (the police and prosecutors do not have this unilateral authority). This includes the authority for the KPK to wiretap and record conversations as part of the investigatory process, without any statutory requirement that they provide any special protections for attorney-client communications. In addition, although the KPK cannot interview a suspect's lawyer and ask that person to reveal client secrets, it may separately investigate a lawyer who is suspected of being involved with the criminal activity. In this way, a lawyer may not use the legal professional privilege to hide or facilitate criminal activity. In addition, the Anti-Corruption Law requires those called to testify as witnesses, including those who "according to occupation" are obligated to maintain confidentiality.[135]

Notaries in Indonesia also have a duty to keep information secret. Article 16 paragraph (1) f of Law No. 2 of 2014 states that a notary should keep all secrets related to the deed made and any information obtained in making the deed according to the oath of office, except when laws determine something else. Article 66 of the same notary law also states that an investigator, public prosecutor, or judge may only take photocopies of deeds and letters in the notary's depository, and call the notary to attend the examination after obtaining the approval of the honorary board of notaries.[136]

13.2 APPLICATION TO INTERNAL INVESTIGATIONS

The same requirement to keep client information secret under the Law on Advocates would appear to apply where a corporation is the client. That would support the position that internal investigations conducted by lawyers may be kept confidential. Uncertainty exists, however, because Indonesia's statutory framework does not specifically address internal investigations. Indonesia is just recently beginning to focus on enforcing corporate criminal liability, and therefore also has less practical experience with investigating and prosecuting companies, and likewise less experience with internal investigations being conducted. The biggest consideration with internal investigations would likely be recognizing, as described previously, that under certain circumstances items and information can still be seized by law enforcement as part of a criminal investigation, and witnesses required to testify.

13.3 APPLICATION TO EXTERNAL INVESTIGATIONS

As with internal investigations, the same requirement to keep client information secret under the Law on Advocates would appear to apply to external investigations where a

---

[134] Law No. 18 Year 2003, Article 19.
[135] Anti-Corruption Law, Article 36.
[136] Law No. 2 Year 2014.

corporation is the client. Here again, uncertainly exists, because Indonesia's statutory framework does not specifically address external investigations. Indonesia is just recently beginning to focus on enforcing corporate criminal liability, and therefore also has less practical experience with investigating and prosecuting companies, and likewise less experience with companies hiring outside counsel to conduct investigations. The biggest consideration with internal investigations would likely be recognizing, as described previously, that under certain circumstances items and information can still be seized by law enforcement as part of a criminal investigation, and witnesses called upon to testify.

13.4 PRACTICAL ISSUES

Although Indonesia's Law on Advocates provides a statutory mandate that *Advocates should keep secret things that are known or obtained from their Clients*, there are many unanswered questions about how the law will be applied in different circumstances, as well as a number of legal exceptions that create additional uncertainties. Even where the privilege should otherwise apply, in practice the police and prosecutors may not respect the legal professional privilege, and there is little recourse if the privilege is invaded. At present, Indonesia's Criminal Procedure Code does not include an exclusionary rule, or any pretrial mechanism for preventing even illegally obtained evidence from being presented in court.

On the other hand, law enforcement is understandably suspicious that the protection given by the law to the profession of advocates and notaries may be used for shelter in the practice of crime. The KPK has seen examples of corruption cases where advocates or notaries have acted as "gatekeepers."

Another practical problem is the lack of supervision by Indonesia's professional organizations, including advocate and notary associations. There are still few cases of ethical violations examined with the violator then found guilty by the professional associations. In practice, even an advocate who is investigated and convicted by his organization then seeks to join other advocate organizations. This is possible because in Indonesia there is more than one organization or association of advocates established and managed independently.

14. Privacy and Data Protection

14.1 PRINCIPLES

Indonesia's Constitution recognizes a strong right to privacy. At the same time, the Constitution also recognizes that in exercising his/her rights and freedoms, every person must also accept the restrictions established by law for the purpose of respecting the rights and freedoms of others and satisfying the demands of morality, religious freedom, security, and public order in a democratic society.[137] In 1999, in the beginning of the Reform Era,

---

[137] Indonesia's Constitution, Article 28J.

Indonesia adopted a Human Rights Act that addressed privacy, including electronic communications, by stating:

> *No one shall be subject to arbitrary interference with his correspondence, including electronic communications, except upon the order of a court or other legitimate authority according to prevailing legislation.*[138]

In 2016, Indonesia adopted an updated Electronic Information and Transactions Law (referred to as the ITE Law).[139] The new law prohibits anyone from sharing personal data of another person online (or through any electronic media) without the consent of that person. It also creates a private right of action that allows anyone whose rights are infringed under the act to file a claim for damages.[140] Additional provisions of the same law include a "right to be forgotten" clause that provides a mechanism for anyone to seek a court order requiring internet service providers to permanently delete information about them that is no longer "relevant."[141] While this provides an avenue for a person to potentially remove or limit the personal information that can be kept electronically, the requirement of a court order may create a significant procedural barrier for many, and there may likely be debate over what person information is no longer "relevant" as required under the law.

The ITE Law gives the Indonesian government additional authorities and powers as well. This includes government authority to block certain internet content, or order internet services providers to remove content that contains "prohibited electronic information" to include immoral content such as pornography.[142] It also makes it a crime to spread misleading information, hate speech, and defamation.[143] Reaction to the new law has been mixed, with some groups voicing concern that powers granted to the government under the ITE law and the continued ability to prosecute defamation could be used to restrict or chill freedom of speech and expression.[144] Historically, one of the more controversial privacy issues in Indonesia has been the government's authority to intercept electronic communications. The ITE law includes expanded powers for the KPK, police, or prosecutors to conduct electronic interceptions (wiretaps, interception of digital communications, recording of conversations) without a warrant when investigating crimes under this law.[145] As a practical matter, law enforcement in Indonesia already has broad authority to conduct searches and to intercept wire communications, and multiple other statutes address what types of electronic interceptions may be conducted by different government authorities investigating different types of criminal activity. These laws include: (1) the Anti-Corruption Law, (2) the KPK Law, (3)

---

[138] Law No. 39 Year 1999 on Human Rights, Article 36.

[139] Law No. 19 Year 2016, amending Law No. 11 Year 2008.

[140] ITE Law, Article 26.

[141] ITE Law, Article 40.

[142] ITE Law, Article 45.

[143] ITE Law, Article 27.

[144] Ina Parlina, *Newly Revised ITE Law Still Draconian*, JAKARTA POST, Nov. 29, 2016, *available at* http://www.thejakartapost.com/news/2016/11/29/newly-revised-ite-law-still-draconian.html) (last visited Jan. 25, 2018).

[145] Wahyudi Djafar, *Protection of Privacy Rights in Digital Era (Perlindungan Hak Privasi diera Digital), available at* http://referensi.elsam.or.id/2014/10/memastikan-perlindungan-hak-atas-privasi-di-era-digital/ (last visited Dec. 28, 2017).

the Intelligence Act,[146] (4) the Drugs Act,[147] (5) the Eradication of Terrorism Act,[148] (6) the Judicial Commission Act,[149] (7) the Anti-Human Trafficking Act,[150] and (8) the Telecommunication Act.[151]

14.2 APPLICATION TO INTERNAL AND EXTERNAL INVESTIGATIONS

Under the ITE Law, companies are not authorized to allow access to personal information without permission of the person involved. In practice, however, employers require employees to provide consent as part of their work contracts or as part of the terms of using their company computer systems.

15. Forecast for Reforms

15.1 LEGISLATIVES REFORMS

In December 2016, the Indonesian Supreme Court adopted a new regulation on Corporate Criminal Liability.[152] This regulation did not modify the substantive laws currently in force, but rather, clarified the procedures that may be used under existing law to indict, try, and convict corporations for criminal acts. With these clarifications now in place, uncertainties that previously prevented investigators and prosecutors from pursuing corporate wrongdoing have been eliminated, and law enforcement now has a clear path that will allow for corporate prosecutions to proceed. It was not long after the new Supreme Court regulation was issued that the KPK announced it was investigating companies for corruption. The ability to hold corporations accountable under the criminal laws for the corrupt acts of their agents and employees has the potential the greatly deter criminal conduct and to encourage Indonesian companies to heighten their focus on corporate due diligence and compliance. Along these lines, however, additional guidance is needed, whether in the form of policy, regulation, or law, that will provide a framework for evaluating and recognizing the strength and effectiveness of corporate compliance programs as part of either the charging or sentencing considerations for corporations.

While efforts to tackle corporate corruption are significant, and are expected to greatly decrease the incentives for companies to engage in bribery and other forms of corruption, additional reforms to Indonesia's anti-corruption framework remain pending. The most pressing legislative reforms that are needed include amending the current Anti-Corruption Law or passing a new statute that prohibits: (1) commercial bribery/bribery in the private sector, (2) bribery of foreign officials, (3) illicit enrichment, and (4) trading in influence. These provisions are not only important to fill current gaps, but also necessary to comply with the requirements of UNCAC.[153]

---

[146] Law No. 17 Year 2011 on Intelligence (Intelligence Act).

[147] Law No. 35 Year 2009 on Drugs (Drugs Act).

[148] Law No. 15 Year 2003 on Eradication Terrorism (Eradication Terrorism Act).

[149] Law No. 18 Year 2011 on Judicial Commission (Judicial Commission Act).

[150] Law No. 21 Year 2007 on Eradication Human Trafficking (Anti-Human Trafficking Act).

[151] Law No. 36 Year 1999 on Telecommunication (Telecommunication Act).

[152] Supreme Court of the Republic of Indonesia, Perma No. 13 of 2016.

[153] United Nations Convention against Corruption, Article 16 (Bribery of Foreign Public Officials), Article 18 (Trading in Influence), Article 20 (Illicit Enrichment), Article 21 (Bribery in the Private Sector).

At least two separate legislative proposals are currently being discussed in Indonesia that have the potential to address these legislative gaps. The first is a revision of the Criminal Code, and the second is an amendment to the Anti-Corruption law. While both of these possible legislative reforms have positive potential, there is also a concern among some that any new legislation could also be used to undermine anti-corruption measures that are working. In particular, there are some in government who want to weaken the authority of the KPK, which would be a significant step backward for Indonesia.

15.2 POLITICAL WILL

Indonesia's current president, Joko "Jokowi" Widodo, was elected in 2014 on a platform of reform that promised a clean government that was not tainted by the corruption of the past.[154] As the governor of Jakarta, Jokowi established himself as an efficient leader who was free from corruption,[155] and expectations were high for his presidency. Coming to the end of his five-year term, and facing an re-election race in April 2019, some commentators point to the corruption scandals that continue to unfold in Indonesia and suggest that Jokowi has not been serious about his commitment to reform. This suggestion is mistaken. Despite potential political backlash from a long list of politically powerful figures being arrested for corruption during the last four years, Jokowi has not hesitated in his support for the KPK, or been personally linked to any improper conduct. The president has also taken steps to implement other anti-corruption reforms, such as electronic procurement systems, and established a task force to identify and address fraud and corruption in the growing national healthcare system.[156] At the same time, the stark reality is that corruption remains a major problem in Indonesia, and progress has been slower than many had hoped. The success of the KPK has also brought political enemies, and recent attempts by the Parliament to alter the current anti-corruption landscape or exert authority over the KPK are largely viewed as attempts to weaken the ability of Indonesia's independent anti-corruption agency to remain independent. The ongonig electronic identification (eKTP) corruption investigation, implicating dozens of senior politicians for stealing hundreds of millions of U.S. dollars, may help to explain the intensity of the current effort to undermine the KPK.[157] Now more than ever, it will take political willpower to continue to keep current anti-corruption efforts on course, and even stronger leadership from the president to add wind to the sails of positive change.

---

[154] Neil Thompson, *Indonesia's Unfolding Corruption Scandal*, THE DIPLOMAT, Apr. 3, 2017, *available at* https://thediplomat.com/2017/04/indonesias-unfolding-corruption-scandal/ (last visited Dec. 14, 2018).

[155] Scott Edwards, *Indonesia's Struggle to End Corruption Is Hitting Snag after Snag*, University of Birmingham, *available at* https://www.birmingham.ac.uk/research/perspective/indonesia-corruption.aspx (last visited Dec. 14, 2018).

[156] *Id.*

[157] Thompson, *supra* note 154.

15.3 POLICY AND PRACTICES

Indonesia's *Reformasi* era is less than 20 years old. Great progress has been made during that time to discard old practices, adopt new laws, build new agencies, and reform institutions. Change takes time, and there are certainly wealthy and powerful forces in Indonesia that have benefited from corruption and who will fight against reform.[158] Investigating and prosecuting corruption is also a resource intensive, costly, and time-consuming process. Add the sheer geographic size, inherently porous borders, and an increase in regional autonomy among local governments spread across 34 provinces, and the complexity of combatting corruption in Indonesia becomes even more apparent. Despite these obstacles, hundreds of corrupt public officials have been convicted, removed from office, and sent to jail. During 2017 amd 2018 alone, the KPK has investigated and prosecuted a Constitutional Court judge, the Speaker and multiple members of Parliament, prominent regional governors, ministerial officials, and many dozens of other government officials for corruption related offenses. .

Other positive signs of progress also exist. The once frosty relationship between the Indonesian National Police and the KPK seems to have thawed. This is an important development for many reasons, including that the KPK's budget is 1 percent that of the national police, and at about 1,000 total employees, has an even smaller relative workforce.[159] In addition to its limited budget and people power, the purpose of the KPK was never to replace or compete with the police or prosecutors office. Instead, as the KPK Law envisioned, the agency also has a coordinating and supporting role to play. In addition, as other commentators have observed regarding other nations around the world, a successful anti-corruption campaign must take a multiagency approach. Stepping up to the challenge, the Indonesian National Police recently announced the creation of a specialized Anti-Corruption Detachment, perhaps modeled on its very successful Detachment 88 of counterterrorism officers. In announcing the new anti-corruption unit, Police Chief General Tito Karnavian noted that the purpose of the new unit was not to compete with the KPK, but rather to boost the capacity to handle graft cases. In another positive sign, the police have invited the Attorney General's Office to join together in forming an anti-corruption task force to make it easier for police and prosecutors to share information and work together, something that is historically challenging.[160]

Perhaps the biggest challenge to tackling corruption in Indonesia is sustaining the commitment to keep fighting. At present, public support is high for anti-corruption efforts, and there are many people inside and outside of the Indonesian government committed to success.

---

[158] https://globalanticorruptionblog.com/2015/03/20/gecko-v-crocodile-round-three-indonesias-ongoing-fight-between-the-police-and-the-kpk/ (last visited Jan. 25, 2018).

[159] Jeffrey Hutton, *How This Agency Is Waging War against Corruption in Indonesia, and Winning*, THIS WEEK IN ASIA, July 22, 2017.

[160] Nurul Fitri Ramadhani, *National Police to Form Special Anti-Graft Squad*, JAKARTA POST, July 18, 2017.

APPENDIX

Key Issues	Indonesia's Approach
Is jurisdiction subject to any international anti-corruption conventions? If so, which conventions?	Yes. UN Convention Against Transnational Organized Crime
Do domestic anti-bribery laws apply extraterritorially?	Yes, to a limited extent.
What is the definition of a foreign public official?	Indonesia has no specific regulation/definition on foreign bribery.
Is commercial bribery illegal?	Yes, in limited offenses that are regulated in Law No. 11 Year 1980.
Is bribing domestic officials illegal?	Yes.
Can the recipient of a bribe be prosecuted?	Yes.
If so, what is the requisite intent for corporate criminal liability?	Corporations can be held vicariously liable for the acts of their agents and employees.
Can individuals be held civilly liable?	Yes.
If there a "facilitation payment" defense?	No.
Do conspiracy laws apply to anti-corruption offenses?	Yes.
Does the subject country provide for: (a) aiding/abetting liability relating to violations of the anti-corruption laws? (b) attempt liability relating to violations of the anti-corruption laws?	Yes. Anti-Corruption Law, Article 15
Is the failure to keep accurate books and records a criminal or civil offense?	It is a criminal offence as regulated under Indonesia's Criminal Code (KUHP) and the Tax Act. The Anti-Corruption Law has no specific article of this matter.
Do any books and records offenses involve proof of an underlying bribery offense?	No.
If so, are those laws applicable to public and/or private companies?	Yes.
Is there an affirmative disclosure obligation for potential violations of anti-corruption laws or accounting irregularities?	No.

Key Issues	Indonesia's Approach
Are "promotional expenses" exempt from Indonesia's anti-corruption laws?	No, but see definition of "gratification" in Anti-Corruption Law.
Is the giving of gifts, entertainment, travel, meals, or other gratuities restricted or prohibited by anti-corruption or other laws?	Yes. In some circumstances, for example attending a seminar/conference, it is allowed as long as all of the participants get the same meals or souvenir and the value of the meals or souvenir does not exceed the limit prescribed by the KPK Gratification Regulations (around U.S. $50).
Are there any Indonesia laws concerning things, property, or benefits of value conveyed by, or to, third parties?	Yes, Indonesia recognizes the concept of controlling personnel in the Eradication of Money Laundering Act and has several regulations about beneficial owners.
Are bribes tax deductible?	No.
Is Indonesia's anti-corruption laws applied extraterritorially?	See Anti-Corruption Law, Article 16
Is a robust corporate compliance program an affirmative defense or a factor to negate liability or reduce penalties?	No. There is no specific law about compliance programs. However, robust prevention programs and compliance plans can be used by the accused as a defense or as a mitigating factor at sentencing.
Is there a "local law" exception or defense to Indonesia's anti-corruption laws?	No.
If so, how and in what form?	There is not a specific law, but in practice yes.
Does Indonesia have mutual legal assistance with the United States that covers criminal matters, including anti-corruption conduct?	Yes, Indonesia cooperates with the United States on law enforcement matters. Indonesia does not have an MLA agreement with the United States, but in practice Indonesia has very good cooperation with the U.S. DOJ. Indonesia also has an agreement with FinCEN (Financial Crimes Enforcement Networ) for the exchange of information.

(Continued)

Key Issues	Indonesia's Approach
What are the potential penalties/sanctions for criminal and civil violations of Indonesia's anti-corruption laws?	If the corruptions are followed by money laundering, the offender will be punished by the money laundering act, which provides for heavier fines than do corruption offenses.

12 Mexico

ON JULY 12, 2015,[1] Joaquín "el Chapo" Guzmán made one of the best-known jail-breaks in recent history.[2] He is known as one of the key leaders of the Mexico-U.S. drug trade, reportedly having moved more than 500 tons of Colombian cocaine to the United States by the time of his arrest just over a year before his escape.[3] El Chapo follows in the steps of other colorful Latin American outlaws who attempt to gain popular following by minimizing the harm they do in their home countries and tapping into social discontent and grievances.[4]

As many suspected from the outset, el Chapo managed to escape by bribing and corruptly influencing Mexican government officials.[5] He had escaped from prison once before,

---

[1] This chapter was contributed by Baker McKenzie's Joan Meyer, Maria McMahon and Jonathan Adams.

[2] Silvia Otero, "*El 'Chapo' vuelve a fugarse* [El Chapo escaped again]" UNIVERSAL (Mexico City), Jul. 12, 2015, *available at* https://www.eluniversal.com.mx/articulo/nacion/seguridad/2015/07/12/el-chapo-vuelve-fugarse#imagen-1 (last visited Dec. 10, 2018).

[3] Eric Lichtblau, "*El Chapo Faces Array of Drug Charges in United States,*" N.Y. TIMES, Jan. 10, 2016, *available at* https://www.nytimes.com/2016/01/11/world/americas/extradition-of-el-chapo-to-us-is-neither-certain-nor-simple.html (last visited Dec. 10, 2018).

[4] *Pueblo natal de El Chapo lamenta su captura* [El Chapo's hometown mourns his capture]," EL ECONOMISTA, Jan. 11, 2016, *available at* http://eleconomista.com.mx/sociedad/2016/01/11/pueblo-natal-chapo-lamenta-su-captura (last visited Dec. 20, 2016); Vicente Gutiérrez *El Chapo un héroe para la cultura mexicana* [El Chapo is a hero of Mexican culture], EL ECONOMISTA, Jan. 10, 2016, *available at* http://eleconomista.com.mx/entretenimiento/2016/01/10/chapo-heroe-cultura-mexicana (last visited Dec. 20, 2016).

[5] Lilia Gonzalez, Lilia, *La IP Pide esclarecer fuga del Chapo Guzmán* [The private sector requests to shed light on El Chapo's escape], EL ECONOMISTA, Jan. 10, 2016, *available at* http://eleconomista.com.mx/sociedad/2016/01/10/ip-pide-esclarecer-fuga-chapo-guzman (last visited Dec. 20, 2016); *Equipo del chapo para fuga en prisión*

From Baksheesh to Bribery. T. Markus Funk and Andrew S. Boutros.
© Oxford University Press 2019. Published 2019 by Oxford University Press.

in 2001.[6] That time, he remained at large for over 13 years. This time, his freedom lasted less than six months.[7] Ironically, it appears that el Chapo's attempt to sculpt his public image through Hollywood interviews caused him to let down his guard, and allowed the Mexican Marines to find and recapture him.[8]

While el Chapo is one of the recent beneficiaries of government corruption in Mexico, there have been other colorful public figures who have served time in prison for corruption. Elba Esther Gordillo represents a different face of corruption in Mexico. From her origins in the tropical southern Mexican state of Chiapas, she came to Mexico City in the 1970s as a teachers' union leader and in the 1980s as a federal congresswoman from the neighboring State of Mexico. In 1987, she briefly served as Speaker of the Mexican lower house at the federal level, the Chamber of Deputies. She led the Institutional Revolutionary Party (PRI, by its Spanish acronym) from 2002 to 2005, but throughout her career, her power base has been a teachers' union that continues to be at the center of controversial social movements in Mexico. In 2013, Gordillo was arrested for the use of illicitly obtained funds, organized crime and tax evasion. Evidence showed that she had purchased over US $2 million of luxury clothing, had plastic surgeries in California, and purchased a private jet and at least 10 properties in the United States, one of which was worth nearly US $5 million. She also reportedly purchased 59 Hummer SUVs for her political followers in the teachers' union.[9]

These two contrasting stories illustrate how corruption in Mexico bridges the spectrum from sophisticated criminals to leading political figures.

The current political and social climate in Mexico should be viewed in the context of its fractured past. By the early nineteenth century, long-standing Spanish influence and government oppression, combined with the poverty of the region, created a social underclass yearning for independence. The Mexican Revolution of 1910–1917 marked an important watershed in Mexican history. From a social and legislative perspective it was arguably even more important than independence from Spain. One of the most important and lasting legacies of the Mexican Revolution is the Constitution of 1917, which has been widely recognized as the first modern constitution in the world because of its aspirational social dimensions and detailed attention to the economic and social aspects of national life. Under this Constitution, the PRI ruled for 70 years until it relinquished power in 2000. In the 12 years that followed, the National Action Party (PAN, by its Spanish acronym) waged what

[El Chapo's team that facilitated his escape], EL ECONOMISTA, Jan. 8, 2016, *available at* http://eleconomista. com.mx/sociedad/2016/01/08/equipo-chapo-fuga-prision-pgr (last visited Dec. 20, 2016).

[6] Dalia Ramirez, *Se fuga joaquin el chapo guzman del altiplano* [Joaquín El Chapo Guzman escapes from Altiplano], EXCELSIOR, July 12, 2015, *available at* http://www.excelsior.com.mx/nacional/2015/07/12/1034212 (last visited Dec. 20, 2016).

[7] Dalia Ramírez, *"Se fuga Joaquín 'El Chapo'" Guzmán del Altiplano* [Joaquín El Chapo guzmán escapes from Altiplano], EXCELSIOR, July 12, 2015, *available at* http://www.excelsior.com.mx/nacional/2015/07/12/1034212 (last visited Dec. 10, 2018).

[8] *Una película biográfica delató El Chapo* [A biographical movie gave El Chapo away], EL ECONOMISTA, Jan. 8, 2016, *available at* http://eleconomista.com.mx/sociedad/2016/01/08/pelicula-biografica-delato-chapo-pgr (last visited Dec. 20, 2016).

[9] Jo Tuckman, *Elba Esther Gordillo—Mexico's Famed Union Boss—Accused of Embezzlement*, THE GUARDIAN, Feb. 27, 2013, *available at* https://www.theguardian.com/world/2013/feb/27/elba-esther-gordillo-mexico-union-embezzlement (last visited Dec. 20, 2016).

for some amounted to a civil war against the underclass, fostering a drug trafficking culture in Mexico. The PRI returned to power in 2012 with a promise of fighting corruption and other government abuses. In May 2015, Congress and the states approved a constitutional amendment that created a new National Anti-Corruption System. It left many of the specifics to the implementing legislation, which was adopted on July 18, 2016. While the legislative framework for combating corruption is still being finalized, it is undeniable that the Mexican government is now much more sensitive to corruption and its overall impact on the daily life of its citizens, and has made substantial advances to enhance its anti-corruption regime.

This chapter examines the current domestic anti-corruption framework in Mexico, and conducts an in-depth analysis of the most relevant provisions. Sections 1-7 provide an overview of Mexico's domestic anti-corruption framework comprising criminal, civil, and administrative legislation, as well as international viewpoints on the matter. They also discuss the elements of anti-bribery legislation in various contexts, and examine related criminal offenses. Sections 8 and 9 introduce mitigating factors and whistleblower protections. Section 10 summarizes key international treaties on corruption and transnational cooperation. Sections 11 and 12 addressee privacy and data protection issues, and attorney-client privilege. The chapter closes with a Section dedicated to a forecast for reforms and other final thoughts.

1. Mexico's Domestic Anti-Corruption Framework

Corruption and bribery have been crimes under the Mexico's Federal Criminal Code since its first publication in 1931.[10] However, and as discussed in more detail later in the chapter, the nonpublic nature of most criminal prosecutions in Mexico has made it hard to determine when and if the law is being enforced. Anecdotal accounts from criminal defense lawyers and government officials indicate prosecution has been practically nonexistent.

Other than the political variety, which has long been a contentious issue, corruption in Mexico did not become a major candidacy issue until Felipe Calderón's presidential candidacy in 2004. The Manifesto Anti-Corruption Efforts promulgated at the time focused on accounting and fiscal reform, educational content, regulatory simplification, promotion of transparency, institutional accountability, and professionalization of public service.[11] During his administration, President Felipe Calderón proposed, and succeeded in enacting, an administrative law that for the first time defined specific activities that would be sanctioned as corruption. Because of defendant protections in the criminal procedure law in Mexico, many perceived that an administrative law would be easier to use for uprooting corruption. The new law, the Federal Law Against Corruption in Government Procurement of 2012, had one significant shortcoming that became immediately apparent: as its name indicates, it covers corruption activities only in the context of public bids. In addition, the results of the administrative actions related to procurement proceedings are only partially public, and those that are published focus almost exclusively on technical shortcomings of bidders. Requests for

---

[10] *Código Penal Federal* [hereinafter Federal Criminal Code], Art. 217, published on Jan. 2, 1931, *available at* http://www.diputados.gob.mx/LeyesBiblio/ref/cpf/CPF_orig_14ago31_ima.pdf (last visited Dec. 10, 2018).

[11] BRIAN P. LOUGHMAN & RICHARD A. SIBERY, BRIBERY AND CORRUPTION (2012).

further data from the National Institute of Transparency (INAI, by its Spanish acronym) did not result in any additional information.

The ruling party from 1928 to 2000, PRI, had largely been assumed to be corrupt. After 12 years of PAN rule from 2000 to 2012, the PRI was poised to make a comeback, but had to address its perceived corruption problems. So PRI presidential candidate Enrique Peña Nieto made anti-corruption an integral part of his election campaign and touted a "new-and-improved" PRI that would fight corruption. After concentrating on reforming the national petroleum company during his first two years in office, President Peña pushed through a constitutional transparency amendment in 2014 and a constitutional anti-corruption amendment in 2015. The anti-corruption amendment was implemented in July 2016 by means of a series of laws: the General Law on the National Anti-Corruption System, the Organic Law for the Federal Tribunal on Administrative Justice, and the General Law of Administrative Responsibilities.[12]

The National Anti-Corruption System and most of the provisions of the ancillary laws entered into full force and effect in July 2017. The Senate subsequently discussed the proposed budget of approximately U.S. $7.5 million for the implementation of the National Anti-Corruption System.[13] Also, the Commission for the Selection for the Citizen Participation Committee reviewed the qualifications of 59 candidates to fill the five open positions in the Committee.[14] This committee is part of the National Anti-Corruption System.

1.1 CRIMINAL LAW REGIME

Both individuals and legal entities are criminally liable for bribery of public officials in Mexico. Until late 2014, as was the case with most Latin American jurisdictions, bribery and all other crimes in Mexico could only be committed by individuals. Practitioners were of the opinion that the *scienter* element of criminal liability made it impossible for a legal entity to be liable for a crime. In other words, a company does not have a mind of its own and, therefore, cannot possibly have the necessary *mens rea* to commit a crime. There has always been an article of the Federal Criminal Code and many local criminal codes allowing, in some cases, sanctions imposed on a company under certain circumstances.[15] However, the criminal offense itself was not attributed to the company. Rather, the company was treated as a tool or

---

[12] On July 18, 2016, as published in a special evening edition of the *Daily Federal Gazette*, Congress also approved modifications to the Federal Criminal Code, the Organic Federal Public Administration Law, the Audit Law, the Tax Coordination Law, the General Accounting Law, and the Organic Law of the Attorney General of the Republic, *available at* http://dof.gob.mx/index.php?year=2016&month=07&day=18&edicion=VES (last visited Dec. 10, 2018).

[13] *Solicitan 143 mdp para Sistema Nacional Anticorrupción* [143 million pesos requested for National Anti-Corruption System], EXCELSIOR, Oct. 3, 2016, *available at* http://www.excelsior.com.mx/nacional/2016/10/03/1120327 (last visited Dec. 20, 2016).

[14] Alonso Urrutia, *Sistema anticorrupción anuncia a aspirantes a comité ciudadano* [Anti-Corruption system announces candidates for citizens committee], JORNADA, *available at* http://www.jornada.unam.mx/ultimas/2016/12/15/sistema-anticorrupcion-anuncia-a-aspirantes-para-comite-ciudadano (last visited Dec. 15, 2016).

[15] Federal Criminal Code, Art. 11 bis.

means for carrying out a crime, for example, like an automobile or other property confiscated by the authorities because it was used in the commission of the crime.

In November 2014, the Mexico City Legislative Assembly passed modifications to the criminal code making bribery (and all other crimes) offenses that can be committed by both individuals and legal entities.[16] Mexico City legislature took an innovative approach to the challenge of imposing penalties on legal entities by creating a framework to calculate those penalties. It was based on establishing a sanction equivalent to a prison sentence imposed upon an individual. Historically, monetary sanctions in Mexican law had been calculated based on the officially defined daily minimum wage, which is currently approximately U.S. $5. Even when multiplied by thousands, these sanctions were rarely material or dissuasive for companies with large concentrations of capital. Instead of using the daily minimum wage as a starting point for penalty calculations, the Mexico City legislature set out that the equivalent penalty for a corporation of a year in prison for an individual shall be 920 times the daily net profit of a legal entity.[17] Now, penalties are based on daily company profits commensurate with the prison time to which an individual would have been sentenced for the same crime, with 920 days of profits to be assessed for each year of a prison sentence. This innovative approach to calculating penalties greatly increased potential penalties payable by legal entities in Mexico City.

The Mexico City criminal law came into effect in late 2014, but there have been few cases where companies have actually been found criminally liable. However, the authorities have shown that they will not hesitate to impose multimillion-dollar sanctions on companies and find them liable in the most egregious cases.[18] For example, in August 2015, Mexico City settled criminal charges against a gas transportation company assessing a significant penalty. The company had been charged in connection with an explosion near a children's hospital in Cuajimalpa, in the southwest of Mexico City. Five people died and 16 were severely injured, in addition to the significant property damage caused by the explosion.[19]

While the constitutional anti-bribery amendment of 2015 did not require per se creating criminal liability for corporate entities, some practitioners speculated that this law enforcement tool could be added to the federal arsenal, especially in light of the Mexico City legislation of 2014. And in fact, without any public fanfare, about one month before the rest of the implementing legislation for the anti-bribery amendment was enacted, Congress amended the Federal Criminal Code in June of 2016 to allow corporate criminal liability for certain crimes. As a result, bribery of public officials by both individuals and legal entities is now prohibited under the Federal Criminal Code.[20] Legal theorists still debate over the specifics

---

[16] *Código Penal para la Ciudad de México* [hereinafter Mexico City Criminal Code], Arts. 27 bis, 277, 278.

[17] Mexico City Criminal Code, Article 38 bis.

[18] David S. Vela, *Finaliza litigio contra Gas Expres Nieto por explosión en Cuajimalpa* [Litigation against Gas Expres Nieto for explosión in Cuajimalpa comes to an end], EL FINANCIERO, Aug. 19, 2015, http://www.elfinanciero.com.mx/nacional/finaliza-litigio-contra-gas-expres-nieto-por-explosion-en-cuajimalpa.htm (last visited Dec. 20, 2016).

[19] Filiberto Cruz, *Termina Gas Express Nieto proceso por explosión en Cuajimalpa* [Gas Express Nieto ends process for explosión in Cuajimalpa], EXCELSIOR, Aug. 25, 2015 , http://www.excelsior.com.mx/comunidad/2015/08/25/1042064 (last visited Dec. 20, 2016).

[20] Federal Criminal Code, Article 222.

of implementation of this novel approach to criminal law, and it is still too early to gauge its effectiveness, but the potential for change is clear. One item that Congress will still need to address is sanctions. The maximum criminal penalty for federal bribery offenses committed by companies is currently approximately U.S. $3,000, which is not a significant deterrent for most companies.

I.2 CIVIL AND ADMINISTRATIVE LAW REGIMES

Civil actions based on government corruption are not common in Mexico and the law is not well developed in this area. If a civil action were to be filed, Mexican law contemplates shareholder actions against directors and officers for breach of duty of care or loyalty.[21] Mexican statutes provide for the filing of such civil actions but they are not used in practice. Mexican civil courts have not traditionally applied civil law standards to issues such as torts when criminal legislation covers the matter. For example, if a civil court were to be presented with an action based on director or officer breach of duty of care in a government corruption case, it would likely require a criminal conviction against an individual before considering the derivative action.

The Mexican Federal Law Against Corruption in Government Procurement (2012) establishes judicial and administrative sanctions for individuals and legal entities that engage in bribery of public officials in the context of government contracts.[22] The law also prohibits engaging in any activity with a government official to obtain an undue advantage in a federal public bid, even in the absence of a bribe.[23] Finally, the law prohibits using economic pressure to obtain documentation from a government official to gain an advantage in a public bid.[24] Sanctions can reach up to the equivalent of U.S. $6 million.[25]

In July 2016, Congress approved a new law as part of the secondary legislation to implement the Constitutional Anti-Corruption Amendment of May 2015.[26] This law, the General Law of Administrative Responsibilities (GLAR),[27] will punish both individuals and legal entities for any bribery of government officials, whether in the government procurement context or otherwise, and whether at the federal level or any other government level in Mexico.[28] The law will also punish individuals who use influence or other improper means to obtain an undue advantage in any federal, state, or local government bid.[29] Regardless of

---

[21] *Ley General de Sociedades Mercantiles* [hereinafter General Commercial Companies Law], Arts. 142 to 163, governs director obligations and liability.

[22] Art. 8(I).

[23] Art. 8(II).

[24] Art. 8(VII).

[25] Art. 27.

[26] *Gaceta Parlamentaria* (Parliamentary Gazette), http://gaceta.diputados.gob.mx/PDF/63/2016/jul/20160706-III.pdf, (last visited July 9, 2016).

[27] *Ley General de Responsabilidades Administrativas* [hereinafter General Law of Administrative Responsibilities], *Diario Oficial de la Federación* (Official Federal Gazette), July 18, 2016, http://dof.gob.mx/nota_detalle.php?codigo=5445048&fecha=18/07/2016 (last visited Dec. 12, 2018).

[28] Art. 66.

[29] Art. 70.

any overlap with antitrust legislation, any agreement between two or more persons to gain an undue advantage will also be punishable by this law.[30] Finally, these prohibitions also apply to interactions of Mexican persons subject to this law with foreign public officials.[31]

The GLAR also prohibits any person from engaging the services of a public servant during the first year after his/her public service ends, if the public servant had access to information that would give an undue advantage to the persons engaging him/her, and makes it available to them.[32] Evidentiary issues will undoubtedly be difficult in these cases, particularly given the formalistic approach of Mexican law.

The most controversial part of the GLAR was the requirement that public officials disclose their property and economic interests, and tax filings[33] that applied to all federal, state, and local government officials.[34] This requirement created great controversy in Congress and drew strong resistance from traditionally left-leaning parties that wanted to apply the same transparency requirements to private companies that engage in business with the government. President Peña vetoed the extension as to private parties, and the law went into effect stipulating disclosures for public officials only.

1.3 EXTERNAL VIEWPOINTS

1.3.1 OECD Evaluation

Mexico has been a member of the OECD Convention on Combating Bribery of Foreign Officials in International Business Transactions since 1999. The OECD Anti-Bribery Convention establishes a requirement to criminalize bribery of foreign officials and provides for a number of related measures that make the bribery prohibition effective. The implementation of the OECD Anti-Bribery Convention is being monitored in phases through a peer review process.

The OECD evaluation of Mexico's implementation of the OECD Anti-Bribery Convention was carried out in October 2011 by a peer review team from Slovenia and Spain.[35] The team focused per the OECD directive on foreign corruption, and found some progress but urged further action. Foreign bribery was outlawed in Mexico as a result of its ratification of the OECD Anti-Bribery Convention, but there has been little evidence of actual prosecutions, and stricter enforcement was recommended. Additionally, the review team recommended that Mexico enhance its anti-corruption and anti-money-laundering legislation, increase maximum sanctions for books and records offenses, enact whistle-blower protections, and continue to promote corporate compliance measures, with emphasis on Mexican companies that are not subject to the U.S. Foreign Corrupt Practices Act (FCPA). When the focus shifted to domestic bribery as a point of reference, the review team found

---

[30] *Id.*

[31] *Id.*

[32] Art. 72.

[33] Arts. 32 to 48.

[34] Art. 3(XXV).

[35] Phase 3 Report on Mexico by the OECD Working Group on Bribery, October 14, 2011, *available at* http://www.oecd.org/daf/anti-bribery/Mexicophase3reportEN.pdf (last visited Dec. 20, 2016).

little action in this regard as well. The review team noted that Mexico should give greater priority to the criminal enforcement of its bribery laws.

A follow-up review in 2014 showed limited progress.[36] The working group noted that Mexico fully implemented only 4 out of 22 recommendations made in 2011, and still had no prosecutions or convictions for foreign bribery, although it had conducted a number of investigations that resulted in domestic bribery charges. Information on convictions was not available.

1.3.2 Transparency International Corruption Perception Index Score

Mexico's score in the 2017 Transparency International Corruption Perception Index is 29 out of 100, with 0 being the most corrupt and 100 being the least corrupt. On the rank scale among countries from cleanest (first) to most corrupt (last), Mexico ranks 135 out of 180, just above countries such as Bangladesh, Guatemala and Kenya, and below Ukraine, Sierra Leone and Myanmar. It is below Brazil (96), India (81) and China (77), and is viewed as corrupt as Russia (also 135). Mexico's Corruption Perception Index ranking has consistently reflected perceptions of significant corruption at all levels of its government.

2. Investigative and Prosecutorial Agencies

2.1 ADMINISTRATIVE LAW AGENCIES

Each Mexican government agency has the authority to enforce its own administrative laws on anti-corruption. Ultimately, if these government agencies fail to enforce their laws, the Secretary of Public Administration has jurisdiction to investigate and issue administrative sanctions or refer a case to the Attorney General for criminal prosecution.[37] The Tribunal for Tax and Administrative Justice has jurisdiction when administrative cases are appealed.[38]

Under the new Federal Law of Administrative Responsibilities of Public Servants, internal bodies of each government agency are responsible for investigating, substantiating, determining, and imposing sanctions for minor administrative offenses. In case of serious offenses by either public servants or private entities, the Superior Federal Court on Administrative Justice has jurisdiction to impose sanctions.[39]

2.2 CRIMINAL LAW AGENCIES

The main agency involved in investigating crimes, including bribery, is the Attorney General, which investigates crimes at the federal level (*Procuraduría General de la República*) and at the state level (e.g., *Procuraduría General Judicial*).

---

[36] Follow up to the Phase 3 Report & Recommendations, June 16, 2014, *available at* http://www.oecd.org/daf/anti-bribery/MexicoPhase3WrittenFollowUpEN.pdf (last visited Dec. 20, 2016).

[37] Federal Law of Administrative Responsibilities of Public Servants, Art. 4.

[38] Federal Law of Administrative Responsibilities of Public Servants, Art. 25.

[39] Federal Law of Administrative Responsibilities of Public Servants, Art. 12.

The agency's report from 2015 contains a section on crimes committed by public servants and against the administration of justice. However, this section does not include any statistics or data as to the efficacy of the agency's investigations.[40] It only refers to the Special Unit for the Investigation of Crimes Committed by Public Servants and against the Administration of Justice (*Unidad Especializada en la Investigación de Delitos Cometidos por Servidores Públicos y contra la Administración de Justicia*), and its mission to combat corruption and impunity of public servants.

2.3 MULTIAGENCY ARRANGEMENTS

Mexico is a member of the OECD and, as mentioned in Section 1.3.1., a signatory to the OECD Anti-Bribery Convention. Mexico is also a signatory to the OAS Convention Against Corruption and the UN Convention Against Corruption.

3. Sentencing Principles

There is no official guidance on sentencing in Mexico other than the criteria established by law. Very limited information on convictions and sentencing is public in Mexico. Beginning in 2015, some sentences have been made public, for example, some sentencing rulings have been published online but the names of the accused and their representatives have been redacted.

The Federal Court for Administrative Justice provides on its website a database with the names, positions, offenses, and sanctions of public servants.[41] In addition, it makes available copies of public sentences issued from August 2015 to date.[42] Even though these sentencing rulings can be used to develop legal arguments in similar cases, they are not binding. The judge in each particular case may consider previous sentencing decisions, but the weight given to these decisions is discretionary.

As this area of law continues to evolve, so will the sentencing principles and their application to new cases.

4. Bribery of Foreign Officials

In August 2016, the U.S. Securities and Exchange Commission charged a Houston-based oil field services company Key Energy Services, Inc. with violating the FCPA's internal controls

---

[40] 3rd Report of Labor of the Federal Attorney General (2015), *available at* http://pgrarchivos.blob.core.windows.net/informe-de-labores/2015.pdf (last visited Dec. 10, 2018).

[41] Database of Public Servants Sanctioned by the Federal Court of Administrative Justice, *available at* http://www.tfja.gob.mx/servicios/firm-sanc/ (last visited Dec. 10, 2018).

[42] Database of Public Sentences by the Federal Court of Administrative Justice, http://www.tfjfa.gob.mx/servicios/consulta_sentencia/ (last visited Dec. 10, 2018).

and books-and-records provisions as a result of bribes paid to an employee of Pemex, the Mexican state-owned oil company.[43] Key Energy agreed to disgorge U.S. $5 million to settle the case with the SEC. In addition, the company stated it would exit the Mexican market by the end of 2016.[44]

The Key Energy case is noteworthy because it involves one of the most prominent Mexican state-owned companies, which has been accused of corruption for decades. It has been alleged that Key Energy Mexico made multiple payments totaling approximately U.S. $561,000 to a purported consulting firm to assist in closing Pemex contracts.[45] The company hired the consulting firm in 2011, but failed to do any due diligence. Key Energy Mexico recorded payments to the consulting firm as legitimate business expenses.[46] This case illustrates two points critical in anti-corruption compliance: third-party liability, and importance of due diligence, self-monitoring, and auditing. While considering the sanctions, the SEC noted that Key Energy cooperated and took remedial action.[47]

4.1 JURISDICTION

As noted previously, Mexican law established its prohibition against bribery of foreign officials, similar to the FCPA, at the insistence of the OECD in 1999. The Mexican foreign bribery offense covers payments, offers, or promises to pay to "foreign public officials" for the purposes of receiving illicit benefits. The law defines public officials broadly to include employees of government-owned companies and officials of international organizations.[48] There are no specific jurisdictional long-arm statutes in Mexico, so the standard rules of jurisdiction under Mexican law apply. Mexican law is strictly territorial, so the person or entity would generally need to be present in the national territory at the time the crime is committed.

4.2 STATUTE OF LIMITATIONS

The National Code of Criminal Procedure (2014) provides that the action must be filed no later than three years after the date on which the last act that constitutes the crime is committed.[49]

---

[43] Richard L. Cassin, *Key Energy Pays $5 Million to Settle FCPA Offenses in Mexico*, FCPA BLOG, Aug. 12, 2016, *available at* http://www.fcpablog.com/blog/2016/8/12/key-energy-pays-5-million-to-settle-fcpa-offenses-in-mexico.html (last visited Dec. 20, 2016).

[44] *Id.*

[45] *Id.*

[46] *Id.*

[47] *Id.*

[48] Federal Criminal Code, Art. 222 bis.

[49] *Código Nacional de Procedimientos Penales* [hereinafter National Code of Criminal Procedure], Arts. 102, 105.

4.3 FOREIGN BRIBERY OFFENSES

A violation occurs when a payment, or an offer or promise to make any payment or give any gift, is made to a foreign public official with the purpose of obtaining or retaining an undue advantage in the course or as a result of international commercial transactions.[50]

4.4 "FOREIGN PUBLIC OFFICIALS" DEFINED

A "foreign public official" is defined as any individual that: (1) has an employment, charge, or commission with legislative, executive, or judicial powers; (2) is employed by an autonomous public body at any level of a foreign government, whether appointed or elected; (3) has a position with an authority in a public agency or public company or a company that has public participation in a foreign country; or (4) holds a position of an official or agent in a public international agency or organization.[51]

4.5 GIFTS, GRATUITIES, AND HOSPITALITY

A bribe can include money or any gift, in the form of goods or services. Mexico does not have specific rules regarding gifts, gratuities, or hospitality. Whether a gift, gratuity, or hospitality expense could be considered bribery would need to be determined on a case-by-case basis, taking into account the circumstances, type, and size of the expense.

4.6 DEFENSES

4.6.1 Written Local Law

The Mexican law does not establish any affirmative defenses that are specific to foreign bribery. However, the standard defense of avoiding a greater evil may be used in cases of endangerment of human life.[52] In addition, although there is no express defense for cases where a gift or payment was allowed by local law, the advantage sought must be "undue," which implies that if the gift or payment is legal under local law in the jurisdiction where the gift was given or the payment was made, it would not be illegal under Mexican law because it would not have conferred an undue advantage.

4.6.2 Facilitation Payments

There is no exception for facilitation payments in the context of foreign bribery.

---

[50] Federal Criminal Code, Art. 222 bis.

[51] *Id.*

[52] Federal Criminal Code, Art. 15(V).

4.6.3 Adequate Procedures

There is no affirmative defense for adequate procedures to negate corporate liability in Mexico. The ability to demonstrate the established adequate procedures in the form of a compliance program would be useful, however, in proving that an employee involved in wrongdoing was not acting on behalf of the company, thus limiting the potential liability of the company.

The existence of a compliance program is a mitigating factor for determining appropriate sanctions under the Federal Criminal Code.[53] Having a compliance structure (called a permanent control organ or *órgano de control permanente*) in place at the time of the commission of the crime can reduce sanctions by up to 25 percent. So far, there has been no track record of the application of this potential mitigating factor.

4.6.4 Corporate Culture

With respect to bribery of foreign officials, it should be noted that Mexican companies with operations outside of Mexico have almost exclusively focused their foreign activities on the Latin American region. Mexican executives generally consider other Latin American cultures to be substantially similar to their own home culture. To the extent that their corporate practices in Mexico are improving (see our discussion in Section 5.6.4 below), these improvements tend to be region-wide. However, when Mexican companies operate in cultures outside Latin America, especially in emerging markets, they tend to accept the customs and practices of these countries more readily because of their own past experiences with corruption. In addition, outside the region, it is more difficult for employees of Mexican entities to see the effects of foreign bribery as detrimental for them or their companies.

4.7 PENALTIES

Penalties for foreign bribery are limited to the equivalent of approximately U.S. $4,000 for both individuals and corporate entities.[54] For individuals, up to 14 year' imprisonment may be imposed, and for both legal entities and individuals, up to eight years prohibition on contracting with any federal public authority may also be imposed. Additionally, if a court determines that an individual was effectively using the company as an alter ego, the company can be ordered to have its operations suspended or even be dissolved.[55] This provision is distinct from the formal criminal liability of companies that was enacted in June 2016, and has been on the books for decades, but has been rarely invoked.

---

[53] Art. 11 bis(B).
[54] Throughout the chapter the exchange rate is MXN$18/U.S. $1.
[55] Federal Criminal Code, Art. 11.

5. Bribery of Domestic Officials

5.1 JURISDICTION

Jurisdiction under Mexican criminal law is generally territorial at the federal and state levels.[56] Because criminal law has traditionally focused on individuals and on violent crime, the concept of cross-border crimes has not been significantly developed. However, the Federal Criminal Code includes jurisdiction over crimes that either have effects in Mexico or are committed by or against Mexican nationals abroad, when the act committed is illegal in the foreign jurisdiction but the suspect has not been prosecuted abroad.[57]

5.2 STATUTE OF LIMITATIONS

For misdemeanors (crimes punishable by fines only), the federal statute of limitations is one year from the date of the offense.[58] For public offenses that merit removal from office, the statute of limitations is two years.[59] For serious offenses punishable by imprisonment, the statute of limitations is half of the maximum jail sentence available under law, with a minimum of three years.[60]

5.3 DOMESTIC BRIBERY OF OFFICIALS OFFENSES

The Mexican Federal Criminal Code has outlawed bribery since its enactment in 1931, during the aftermath of the Mexican Revolution.[61] Bribery of public officials (*cohecho*) is prohibited by the Mexican Federal Criminal Code, Article 222. The crime of bribery is defined to cover federal officials and some state officials.[62] State criminal codes include similar offenses that cover state and local officials.[63] Definitions of bribery crimes are generally consistent across the state and federal legislation.[64]

Bribery is committed both by public servants who solicit or receive a bribe and by private individuals who offer to pay or make a payment to corrupt a public servant:

> The public servant who, directly or indirectly, solicits or receives unduly for the public servant or another person, money or any other gift, or accepts a promise, to do or refrain from doing any just or unjust act in relation to the public servant's functions, and

---

[56] Federal Criminal Code, Arts. 1–5.

[57] Federal Criminal Code, Arts. 1–4.

[58] Federal Criminal Code, Arts. 101–104.

[59] Federal Criminal Code, Art. 106.

[60] *Id.*

[61] *Código Penal para el Distrito y Territorios Federales* [hereinafter Criminal Code for the District and Federal Territories], *available at* http://www.diputados.gob.mx/LeyesBiblio/ref/cpf/CPF_orig_14ago31_ima.pdf (last visited July 9, 2016).

[62] Federal Criminal Code, Arts. 1 to 5.

[63] *Cf.* Mexico City Criminal Code, Art. 272.

[64] *Cf. id.*

Whoever promises or gives any benefit to any of the persons described in the foregoing paragraph, to cause any public servant to do or refrain from doing an act related to the public servant's function, employment, charge or commission.[65]

There is also a related crime of embezzlement, called *"peculado,"* which is committed when a public official uses government funds for unauthorized use. It also covers individuals who receive a benefit from this unauthorized use, and so could apply to private individuals who make payments to government entities, with the knowledge that the proceeds will be diverted by a public official, and receive a benefit in exchange.[66] We are not aware of any private individual who has been convicted of this crime. This crime has not been extended to corporate entities by the June 2016 reforms.[67]

As noted previously, in November 2014, the legislature for Mexico City (formerly known as the Federal District) revised the Mexico City Criminal Code to explicitly provide for criminal liability for corporate entities. As part of the definition of the crime, it stipulates that the required intent will be considered as that of the individual acting on behalf of the company.[68]

5.4 DEFINITION OF DOMESTIC OFFICIALS

The Mexican Federal Criminal Code broadly defines "public servant" to include any individual who has employment, position or charge of any type in the central Public Federal Administration, Mexico City, decentralized organs, government majority-owned companies, organizations or entities that have been assimilated to these (such as public trusts, autonomous constitutional organs, Federal Congress, Federal Judiciary, or Federal District Judiciary), or entities that manage federal economic resources. State governors, officials in local legislatures, and magistrates in local tribunals are also considered public servants.[69]

5.5 GIFTS, GRATUITIES, AND HOSPITALITY

Mexican law does not establish any guidelines for private citizens for the giving of gifts, gratuities, or hospitality to domestic government officials. An administrative law provides a guideline for federal government officials in that they can receive from the same person up to 10 times the federal daily minimum wage (for a total of approximately U.S. $50) per year in personal gifts.[70] However, this limit should not be interpreted as a limit on the value of meals or hospitality that can be provided to an official in relation to attending government business. As long as the hospitality is provided in connection with legitimate business interactions with the government, reasonable hospitality does not violate the law.

---

[65] Federal Criminal Code, Art. 222.

[66] Federal Criminal Code, Art. 223.

[67] Federal Criminal Code, Art. 11 bis.

[68] Mexico City Criminal Code, Art. 27.

[69] Federal Criminal Code, Art. 212.

[70] Federal Law of Administrative Responsibilities of Public Servants, Art. 45.

5.6 DEFENSES

5.6.1 Written Local Law

If all elements of bribery are established under Mexican law, there are no affirmative defenses available other than the standard defenses of duress, mistake, or self-defense.[71] However, one state court (Chiapas) has interpreted its own state criminal code to require proof that the person giving the bribe acted on his or her own initiative, and not in response to a request or demand by the public official involved.[72] Because it would be difficult for the state to prove that no initial request was made, it is most likely that a defendant would need to provide at least some evidence of a request by the public official. Under Mexican evidentiary rules, which in some cases do not even admit evidence in the form of emails, this would be a challenge.

Until recent amendments, the Federal Criminal Code had similar language to that of the state of Chiapas regarding spontaneity (i.e., giving a bribe voluntarily rather than upon request or demand), so some commentators have suggested that the "spontaneity" should be interpreted in the federal criminal context the same way as the Chiapas court interpreted it in connection with the Chiapas criminal code. However, in the 10 years since the Chiapas court decision, we are not aware of any court having addressed the "spontaneity" issue or having followed the Chiapas court's interpretation, so that decision may have been an anomaly. The recent amendments to the Federal Criminal Code appear to indicate that Congress does not agree with the Chiapas court interpretation.

5.6.2 Facilitation Payments

Mexican law does not include an exception or defense for facilitation payments.

5.6.3 Adequate Procedures

Although adequate procedures do not function as a defense against a federal charge, the advantage of having established adequate procedures in the form of a compliance program is that it would be useful in proving that an employee involved in any wrongdoing was not acting on his or her company's behalf. A corporate defendant may apply for a reduction of up to 25 percent of the applicable sanctions if it can be shown that it had adequate procedures in place.[73] As noted previously, Mexico City's law also establishes corporate criminal liability and stipulates that one of the elements to establish guilt when lower-level employees are involved is the lack of proper oversight of culpable employees.[74] The company should, therefore, establish a compliance program to mitigate any potential corporate criminal liability.[75] The existence of a compliance program is also a mitigating factor under the General Law of Administrative Responsibilities as noted further.

---

[71] Federal Criminal Code, Art. 15.

[72] Second Circuit Court of the Twentieth Collegiate. Protection review 227/2005. 24 August 2006. Unanimously decided. Relator: Marta Olivia Tello Acuña. Secretary: Bayardo Raúl Nájera Díaz.

[73] Federal Criminal Code, Art. 11 bis.

[74] Mexico City Criminal Code, Art. 27 bis.

[75] Mexico City Criminal Code, Art. 27 quintus.

Under the General Law of Administrative Responsibilities, having a compliance program can act in essence as an affirmative defense. The compliance program, referred to as an "integrity policy" (*política de integridad*) in the GLAR, must contain the following characteristics, which are generally consistent with those of the DOJ/SEC 2012 Resource Guide[76]:

(a) A clear and complete organizational and procedural manual that clearly defines the functions and responsibilities of each part of the company, and specifies clearly the chains of command and leadership for each corporate structure.

(b) A code of conduct that is duly published and made known to every person in the organization and that has systems and mechanisms for effective implementation.

(c) Adequate and effective controls, monitoring, and auditing systems that ensure compliance on a continuous and periodic basis throughout the organization.

(d) Adequate whistle-blowing systems for internal reports also allowing for reporting to authorities, as well as disciplinary processes with clear and specific consequences for those who act contrary to internal company policies or to Mexican legislation.

(e) Adequate systems and processes for training on ethics standards.

(f) Human resources policies to avoid hiring employees who could be a risk to the integrity of the company. These policies cannot enable discrimination on the basis of ethnicity, nationality, gender, age, disabilities, social status, health status, religion, political opinion, sexual orientation, marital status, or any other ground that compromises human dignity or curtails human rights and liberties.

(g) Mechanisms to ensure transparency and disclosure of interests (avoiding conflicts of interest) at all times.[77]

Because the GLAR has not been fully implemented until July 2017, there is no track record yet on the criteria that the administrative courts may use to evaluate compliance programs or "integrity policies." There is no guidance by the enforcement authorities on how they may use evidence of compliance programs in decisions on whether to bring enforcement actions.

5.6.4 Corporate Culture

In the conduct of daily affairs, Mexican residents often use intermediaries to navigate the bureaucracies responsible for issuing licenses and permits. Among other informal names, these intermediaries are sometimes called "*gestores.*" *Gestores* are generally believed to engage in low-level corruption to achieve their clients' objectives. Small privately owned companies formed to assist with licensing usually follow the practices established by their owners and managerial employees, and it is not in fact uncommon for them to be involved in low-level corruption when obtaining licenses and permits. Foreign companies operating in Mexico often either adopt local practices or hire local employees who conduct themselves as they

---

[76] *SEC and Justice Department Release FCPA Guide*, Nov. 14, 2012, *available at* https://www.sec.gov/News/PressRelease/Detail/PressRelease/1365171485784 (last visited Dec. 20, 2016).

[77] GLAR, Art. 25.

would in a privately held company. Mexican companies doing business abroad often follow a similar path. However, the global anti-corruption movement has significantly changed the playing field over the last 10 years, and as a result these practices are now receiving greater scrutiny.

In many cases, Mexican companies have made significant progress in eliminating corruption in their ranks, especially to the extent they are part of multinational organizations or supply chains. As multinational companies headquartered in the United States and other countries with extraterritorial application of anti-corruption law become more consistent in applying their internal policies overseas, many Mexican companies have been forced to follow suit, and some are even beginning to see compliance as a business advantage instead of a burden. As a result, some companies are slowly eradicating their corrupt cultures. However, companies doing business in Mexico should be aware of lingering practices, such as the use of shell companies to hide payments to family members of government officials and the making of small "grease" payments in connection with obtaining or maintaining licenses and permits.

In our experience, many Mexican companies are either not yet aware of the modifications to the Mexico City Criminal Code or believe that enforcement of this law will be lacking, so they may continue to adhere to their old behaviors.

5.7 PENALTIES

The Mexican Federal Criminal Code establishes the same penalties for public officials as for individuals who corrupt public officials, whether under *cohecho* or under *peculado*. The penalties are the following:

- Up to 14 years in jail
- A fine of up to approximately U.S. $4,000
- Removal from public office, if applicable
- Up to 14-year prohibition from holding public office[78]

If the perpetrator is an elected public official or a public official whose appointment requires ratification by Congress, the penalties may be increased by up to one-third.[79] As with all crimes, punishment includes restitution.[80]

In addition to the recently enacted criminal liability for companies, if prosecutors can show that a legal entity was used as an instrumentality for the commission of a crime and that it benefitted from the crime, the suspension of operations or dissolution of the entity can be ordered if the judge deems it necessary for public safety. This provision has been in Mexican law for many decades but it is not commonly used by courts.[81]

---

[78] Arts. 222, 223, Federal Criminal Code.
[79] Federal Criminal Code, Art. 212.
[80] Federal Criminal Code, Arts. 29, 30.
[81] Federal Criminal Code, Art. 11.

For activities that are deemed criminal bribery offenses, there are also administrative sanctions in the public procurement context for both individuals and companies.[82] The penalties are as follows:[83]

For individuals:

- Fines up to approximately U.S. $304,000, or 35 percent of the value of the contract, whichever is greater
- Debarment for up to eight years

For companies:

- Fines up to approximately U.S. $12.2 million, or 35 percent of the value of the contract, whichever is greater
- Debarment for up to 10 years

In Mexico City, the individual fines are similar to those established at the federal level, and prison sentences can be up to nine years.[84] For companies, however, the Mexico City Criminal Code establishes sanctions based on multiples of daily net profits. As noted in Section 1.1, for a crime that would entail a prison sentence of one year for an individual, the law prescribes the equivalent of 920 days of its net daily profit for a company.[85]

6. Commercial Bribery

6.1 JURISDICTION

Jurisdiction is predicated on territoriality, as described in Section 4.1 above.

6.2 STATUTE OF LIMITATIONS

For commercially significant amounts, the statute of limitations is at least three years, and longer in cases with aggravating circumtances.[86]

6.3 COMMERCIAL BRIBERY OFFENSES

Commercial bribery per se is not penalized in Mexico. There are, however, several crimes that could potentially be charged in cases of private or commercial bribery, such as fraud, forgery, theft, and abuse of trust, which is similar to embezzlement.[87] An employee who receives a bribe from a third party could be liable for fraud or theft, and for justified

---

[82] *Ley Federal Anticorrupción en Contrataciones Públicas* [hereinafter Federal Law against Corruption in Government Procurement].

[83] Federal Law against Corruption in Government Procurement, Art. 27.

[84] Federal Criminal Code, Art. 272.

[85] Mexico City Criminal Code, Art. 38 bis.

[86] Federal Criminal Code, Arts. 104–106.

[87] Federal Criminal Code, Arts. 386 ff, 243 ff, 367 ff, 382 ff.

termination of employment. However, we have not seen these mechanisms used in practice, and experienced practitioners consider their successful application to commercial bribery cases unlikely.

6.4 GIFTS, GRATUITIES, AND HOSPITALITY

There are no specific guidelines for gifts, gratuities, or hospitality in the commercial context. In Mexico, it has long been customary to give gifts for the holidays or on the occasion of a birthday, wedding, or other important family event such as the wedding of a recipient's son or daughter. These have not been traditionally seen as quid pro quo or improper activities, but part of the traditions in the business community. In recent years, the practice has diminished due to corporate rules at multinational companies, but remains strong in family-run businesses.

6.5 DEFENSES

6.5.1 Written Local Law

The defenses to crimes such as those described in Section 6.3 above are the common defenses available under Mexican law. See Section 5.6 above.

6.5.2 Facilitation Payments

Mexican law does not include an exception or defense for facilitation payments.

6.5.3 Adequate Procedures

Although adequate procedures do not function as a defense against a federal charge, the advantage of having established adequate procedures in the form of a compliance program is that it would be useful in proving that an employee involved in any wrongdoing was not acting on his or her company's behalf. A corporate defendant may apply for a reduction of up to 25 percent of the applicable sanctions if it can be shown that it had adequate procedures in place.[88] Mexico City's law also establishes corporate criminal liability and stipulates that one of the elements to establish guilt when lower-level employees are involved is the lack of proper oversight of culpable employees. The company should, therefore, establish a compliance program to mitigate any potential corporate criminal liability. The existence of a compliance program is also a mitigating factor under the General Law of Administrative Responsibilities as noted previously.[89]

6.5.4 Corporate Culture

Commercial bribery and kickbacks are common in Mexican businesses, whether local or multinational. They are most common in family-owned businesses where the owners often

---

[88] Art. 11 bis(B).

[89] *See* Section 5.6.3, above.

engage in other unethical practices, such as tax evasion, commercially dishonest practices, and abuse of workers' rights. Companies that desire to avoid and resist these practices should establish robust compliance structures with clear policies, training, monitoring, and audit programs, both for employees and for third parties. They should take into account that employees and third parties acting on behalf of the company will likely encounter situations where they will receive illegal and improper solicitations from government employees at the local, state, and federal levels. Employees and third parties should know how to respond in such situations.

6.6 PENALTIES

The penalties for the crimes listed in this section (fraud, theft, and abuse of trust) are up to 12 years in prison and up to U.S. $4,000 in fines.[90]

7. Related Criminal Offenses
7.1 CONSPIRACY

The Federal Criminal Code prohibits conspiracy to commit any crimes. This offense is punishable by up to nine years in prison and up to approximately U.S. $556 in fines.[91]

7.2 ATTEMPT

An attempt to commit a crime is punishable at the discretion of the judge depending on the degree to which the accused completed the elements of the crime and whether the lack of consummation was due to his/her own volition or to the actions of others.[92]

7.3 AIDING AND ABETTING

Anyone who engages in aiding and abetting (as this term is used in U.S. jurisdictions) is considered to be liable for the crime committed.[93]

7.4 FALSE ACCOUNTING/BOOKS AND RECORDS

The Federal Tax Code requires keeping accurate and complete books and records.[94] The fines for violating this requirement are approximately U.S. $750.

---

[90] *Cf.* Federal Criminal Code, Arts. 367ff, 382, 386.
[91] Federal Criminal Code, Art. 141.
[92] Federal Criminal Code, Art. 12.
[93] Federal Criminal Code, Art. 13(VI).
[94] *Código Fiscal de la Federación* [hereinafter Federal Tax Code], Arts. 83, 84.

7.5 MONEY LAUNDERING

Money laundering is prohibited by the Federal Criminal Code.[95] Penalties are up to 15 years in prison and up to approximately U.S. $40,000 in fines. A new anti-money laundering law enacted in 2012 requires anyone engaging in certain transactions in cash, including real estate and corporate transactions, to notify the Mexican Tax Authorities.[96]

7.6 TAX AND OTHER FRAUDS

Tax fraud is committed by anyone who evades taxes intentionally, and includes nonpayment of tax on income from illicit activities.[97] Penalties include imprisonment of up to nine years and fines depending on the amount of unpaid tax.[98]

8. Cooperation and Self-Reporting
8.1 POWERS OF INVESTIGATORS AND PROSECUTORS

The Attorney General of Mexico (*Produraduría General de la República*) has enforcement responsibilities and investigatory powers over federal crimes.[99] It has established an Assistant Attorney General for Federal Crimes, which includes a Special Unit for Investigation of Crimes Committed by Public Servants and against Public Administration of Justice, charged with investigating corruption.[100] In this Special Unit, there is a Special Prosecutor for Combating Corruption in Federal Public Service, an office created in 2004.[101] This Special Prosecutor also investigates foreign bribery and money laundering.[102] State attorneys generally have enforcement obligations and investigatory powers over state anti-corruption laws.[103]

The Attorney General of Mexico also has supervisory powers over the police conducting anti-corruption investigations, and can request search warrants from the judicial authority.[104] Any public prosecutor may begin a corruption investigation and indict a suspect.

Mexican law has also established the Secretary of Public Administration to investigate, sanction administratively, and recommend criminal prosecution for acts of corruption.[105]

---

[95] Federal Criminal Code, Art. 400 bis.

[96] *Ley Federal para la Prevención e Identificación de Operaciones con Recursos de Procedencia Ilícita* [hereinafter Federal Law for the Prevention and Identification of Transactions Using Resources of Illegal Source].

[97] Federal Tax Code Art. 108.

[98] Federal Tax Code, Art. 21.

[99] *Ley Orgánica de la Procuraduría General de la República* [hereinafter Organic Law of the Mexican Attorney General], Art. 4.

[100] Organic Law of the Mexican Attorney General, Art. 9.

[101] Organic Law of the Mexican Attorney General, Art. 10 bis.

[102] Organic Law of the Mexican Attorney General, Art. 10 ter.

[103] *Cf. Ley Orgánica de la Procuraduría General de Justicia del Distrito Federal* [hereinafter Organic Law of the Attorney General for the Federal District], Art. 2.

[104] Organic Law of the Mexican Attorney General, Art. 4.

[105] *Ley Orgánica de la Administración Pública Federal* [hereinafter Organic Law of the Federal Public Administration], Art. 37.

Finally, the General Law on the National Anti-Corruption System, adopted in July 2016, created the National Anti-Corruption System, which is tasked with coordinating the anti-corruption activity of all government and state agencies responsible for the prevention, detection, and prosecution of corruption.[106] After being designated for elimination in 2009 by President Calderón, the Secretary of Public Administration got a new life and new relevance in President Peña's anti-corruption reforms, as the chief enforcer of the National Anti-Corruption System.[107]

8.2 COOPERATION WITH INVESTIGATORS

Mexican criminal law does not establish any incentives for cooperation with investigators. However, the laws of Mexico City and some states provide for the cooperation to be taken into account in determining the guilt of the party charged.[108]

8.3 SELF-REPORTING

There is no incentive for self-reporting under federal criminal law. Mexico City law includes an express provision containing an incentive for self-reporting by reducing penalties for bribery by one-third, at the discretion of the judge.[109]

In the administrative realm, the 2016 General Law of Administrative Responsibilities has introduced the concept of a whistle-blower in the anti-corruption space.[110] Under this concept, a person who has committed a serious administrative offense, which includes corruption, can admit liability and fully and continuously cooperate with the authorities in exchange for a potential sanction reduction of 50 to 70 percent, or suspension of temporary ineligibility to participate in government procurement processes.

8.4 PLEA AGREEMENTS

Plea agreements are not formally used in the criminal legal system in Mexico.

8.5 LENIENCY

As discussed elsewhere, judges in Mexico have been legislatively delegated discretion to impose penalties within the bounds established by law. However, due to the lack of publicly available sentencing data, information regarding the use of leniency is only anecdotal.

---

[106] *Ley General del Sistema Nacional Anticorrupción* [hereinafter General Law on the National Anti-Corruption System], Art. 6.

[107] Organic Law of the Federal Public Administration, Art. 37 (cf. paras. XXV, XXVI).

[108] Mexico City Criminal Code, Art. 27 quintus.

[109] Mexico City Criminal Code, Art. 278.

[110] Art. 88.

9. Whistle-Blower Protection

9.1 PUBLIC SECTOR WHISTLE-BLOWER PROTECTIONS

Although Mexican criminal procedure law[111] and some administrative laws require parties who know about criminal conduct to report it,[112] there are no formal protections or anti-retaliation provisions in place for whistle-blowers. In addition, there are no monetary rewards available for whistle-blowers. The provision requiring reporting is not actively enforced.

9.2 PRIVATE SECTOR WHISTLE-BLOWER PROTECTIONS

There are no legally mandated private sector whistle-blower protections in Mexico, but multinational companies have begun to establish whistle-blower protections based on policies and laws of other countries, which may be applicable to Mexican residents by virtue of their employment. In our experience, many companies are generally not sure how to implement such protections. The lack of information regarding implementation extends to human resources and legal professionals who are charged with oversight of whistle-blower policies in Mexican subsidiaries of multinational companies.

9.3 ATTITUDE TOWARD WHISTLE-BLOWERS

Attitudes toward whistle-blowers continue to be largely negative in Mexico because the reporting of misconduct is believed to reflect disloyalty to co-workers. Mexico is still a relatively homogenous country with a coherent and internally consistent set of social mores and cultural values. Mexicans expect each other to share basic points of view on many matters, and immigrants are expected to assimilate as fully as possible. Mexico has a strong cultural memory of being conquered by a relatively small number of Spaniards in the sixteenth century due at least in part to disunity among its indigenous groups. Some of these groups sided with the Spaniards, and later repented bitterly for having done so. This may explain, in part, the general abhorrence to reporting on co-workers to higher authorities. Reporting on a fellow employee, especially to a foreign employer, is justifiable in the eyes of most Mexicans only in cases of extreme abuse or corruption.

10. Key International Treaties Relating to Bribery and Corruption, Mutual Legal Assistance Treaties, and Transnational Cooperation

Mexico has ratified the United Nations Convention against Corruption (2004), the OECD Anti-Bribery Convention (1999), and the Inter-American Convention Against Corruption (1997).

---

[111] Federal Code of Criminal Procedure, Art. 116.
[112] Federal Law of Administrative Responsibilities of Public Servants, Art. 8.

United Nations Convention Against Corruption

The goals of this Convention are:

(a) To promote and strengthen measures to prevent and combat corruption more efficiently and effectively;

(b) To promote, facilitate and support international cooperation and technical assistance in the prevention of and fight against corruption, including in asset recovery;

(c) To promote integrity, accountability and proper management of public affairs and public property.[113]

OECD Anti-Bribery Convention

The OECD Anti-Bribery Convention establishes legally binding standards to criminalize bribery of foreign public officials in international business transactions and provides for a host of related measures that make it effective. It is the first and only international anti-corruption instrument focused on the "supply side" of the bribery transaction.[114]

Inter-American Convention Against Corruption

The purposes of this Convention are:

(a) To promote and strengthen the development by each of the States Parties of the mechanisms needed to prevent, detect, punish and eradicate corruption; and

(b) To promote, facilitate and regulate cooperation among the States Parties to ensure the effectiveness of measures and actions to prevent, detect, punish and eradicate corruption in the performance of public functions and acts of corruption specifically related to such performance.[115]

Mexico is also a party to several treaties on mutual legal assistance and transnational cooperation, including mutual legal assistance treaties with Australia, Canada, Chile, Colombia, Costa Rica, Cuba, El Salvador, Spain, the United States, France, Great Britain and Northern Ireland, Guatemala, Nicaragua, Panama, Peru, Portugal, Venezuela, and the Bahamas.[116] It has also ratified the Inter-American Convention on Mutual Assistance in Criminal Matters as of 2003.[117]

11. Legal Professional Privilege

11.1 PRINCIPLES

Generally, legal professional privilege is the right of a client to maintain confidentiality with regard to communications with the client's legal counsel. The right belongs to the client, and

---

[113] United Nations Convention against Corruption, New York 2004, *available at* https://www.unodc.org/documents/brussels/UN_Convention_Against_Corruption.pdf (last visited Dec. 20, 2016).

[114] OECD Convention on Combating Bribery of Foreign Official in International Business Transactions, *available at* http://www.oecd.org/corruption/oecdantibriberyconvention.htm (last visited Dec. 20, 2016).

[115] Inter-American Convention against Corruption, *available at* http://www.oas.org/en/sla/dil/inter_american_treaties_B-58_against_Corruption.asp (last visited Dec. 20, 2016).

[116] https://www.oas.org/juridico/mla/sp/mex/sp_mex-mla-gen-list.pdf (last visited Dec. 10, 2018).

[117] *Id.*

the client can prohibit counsel from disclosing those communications. This is to be distinguished from the obligation to maintain professional confidences or secrets. Although there are similarities in the concepts, a simple example serves to distinguish them. If a client is approached by a government authority and required to divulge certain information or documentation, it can claim that the information or documentation is part of its communications with counsel in the rendering of legal advice in contemplation of legal action. The attorney can claim the same, on behalf of the client. For the attorney, claiming that he cannot divulge a document or information because it is a client secret can end in a similar result: denying access to the government authority. However, the ground is different: here the attorney is bound by a duty instead of asserting a right on behalf of the client. To clarify the point, the client cannot claim vis-à-vis a government authority that information or documentation is protected as a professional secret or confidence—such information or documentation is only a professional secret or confidence in the hands of a professional legal advisor.

While Mexican law recognizes the principle of professional secrets, it does not recognize the concept of legal professional privilege. As a practical matter, raids on clients cannot be limited by claims of professional secrets or confidences. These arguments are only available to attorneys, who are rarely, if ever, raided to obtain information about their clients.

11.2 PRACTICAL ISSUES

In practice, the only information that can be claimed as exempt from collection or subpoena by government authorities is trade secrets or sensitive personal data.

12. Privacy and Data Protection
12.1 PRINCIPLES

Mexico enacted the Federal Law on the Protection of Personal Information in Possession of Private Persons (the Data Privacy Law) in 2010. The Data Privacy Law defines personal information as any information about an identified or identifiable person. It further defines sensitive personal information as information that affects the most intimate sphere of the person or that, if used improperly, can lead to discrimination or serious damage.[118] The law requires providing notice to individuals prior to accessing their personal information and allowing them to opt out if they object to the treatment of their information by the private parties involved.[119] Initially, the applicability of the law to employees was not clear, but the agency charged with enforcing the law has clarified its applicability and provided additional guidance.[120]

---

[118] *Ley Federal de Protección de Datos Personales en Posesión de los Particulares* [hereinafter Federal Law on the Protection of Personal Information in Possession of Private Persons], Art. 3.

[119] Federal Law on the Protection of Personal Information in Possession of Private Persons, Arts. 16 and 17.

[120] *Guía para cumplir con los principios y deberes de la Ley Federal de Protección de Datos en Posesión de Particulares* [Guidelines to comply with the principles and duties of the Federal Law on the Protection of Personal Information in Possession of Private Persons] http://inicio.ifai.org.mx/DocumentosdeInteres/Guia_obligaciones_lfpdppp_junio2016.pdf (last visited July 12, 2016).

12.2 APPLICATION TO INTERNAL INVESTIGATIONS

Employers can collect employee data from company-owned equipment if they have provided a general notice to employees on the use of personal data on company-owned equipment. Although the law creates a category of sensitive personal information the treatment of which requires written consent, employers can generally tailor their investigations to avoid handling sensitive personal information inappropriately.

The Data Privacy Law does not focus on territorial borders or establish European-style requirements for legislation of receptor countries. Instead of establishing country-specific requirements, it requires any transfers of data between legal entities to be covered by contractual obligations to observe the commitments of the original custodian of the personal data.[121]

12.3 APPLICATION TO EXTERNAL INVESTIGATIONS

To the extent that external investigators are authorized by the company to conduct an investigation, they act as company agents and are covered by the notice provided by the company to its employees and third parties, as long as they have an agreement in place that guarantees treatment of personal data that is commensurate with the treatment guaranteed in the company's notice.

13. Forecast for Reforms and Parting Thoughts

13.1 LEGISLATIVE REFORMS

As previously discussed, in May 2015, Mexico amended its Constitution to create a new framework for combatting corruption. Congress passed the implementing legislation on July 18, 2016. Specifically, Congress reformed the Federal Criminal Code to enact criminal liability for legal entities at the federal level for the first time in Mexican history. In addition, Congress approved major new legislation that fulfills the disappointed promise of the 2012 anti-corruption law, which only applied in the government procurement context. This law, the General Law of Administrative Responsibilities, represents an important step forward by way of increasing the fines, strengthening enforcement mechanisms, and mandating significant personal financial disclosure requirements for public officials.[122] Additionally, the General Law of Administrative Responsibilities establishes the principle of taking into consideration compliance programs as part of the determination of guilt[123] as well as the imposition of sanctions.[124] Penalties for companies for violations of this law include double disgorgement, and up to U.S. $6 million in fines.[125] The law also establishes the concept of piercing the corporate veil.[126] These concepts are unprecedented in Mexican law, and so it

---

[121] Federal Law on the Protection of Personal Information in Possession of Private Persons, Arts. 36 and 37.

[122] *Gaceta Parlamentaria* [Parlamentary Gazette], http://gaceta.diputados.gob.mx/PDF/63/2016/jun/20160616-I.pdf (last visited July 10, 2016), Arts. 26 to 42.

[123] General Law of Administrative Responsibilities, Art. 25.

[124] General Law of Administrative Responsibilities, Art. 81.

[125] *Id.*

[126] *Id.*

is presently not clear how they will be implemented. Although the law is administrative in nature, it calls for establishing guilt beyond a reasonable doubt.[127] This burden of proof is unprecedented in an administrative setting, so it is also not clear how this will be implemented. Finally, the law establishes significant benefits for self-reporting,[128] which will potentially be a watershed in Mexican anti-corruption environment.

13.2 POLITICAL WILLPOWER AND AGENCY ENFORCEMENT

Political scandals, many corruption-related, continue to surface regularly, with little apparent effect on corruption prosecution. The political will to amend the Constitution was a promising sign, which has been followed by significant progress in implementing legislation. Enforcement officials have until now been loath to impose criminal sanctions for corrupt behavior, but the Secretary of Public Administration has shown much more willingness to enforce its administrative legislation. Because the new law is administrative in nature and is overseen by the Secretary of Public Administration, there are good prospects for enforcement.

While prosecutors have been somewhat reluctant to enforce anti-corruption laws against individuals, they may be more willing to do so now that much larger fines are available against companies, particularly at the Mexico City level. Indeed, as noted previously, significant fines have been imposed against Mexico City companies for egregious crimes, in amounts far in excess of what would have been available against individuals.

13.3 POLICY AND PRACTICE

There has been very little enforcement of anti-corruption legislation by Mexican authorities to date. Local improvements are largely the result of multinational company initiatives driven by U.S. FCPA concerns.

Using data from the Foreign Corrupt Practices Act Clearinghouse at Stanford Law School, enforcement actions statistics from the DOJ and the SEC involving Latin America for the period 2006–2016, shows that there were 54 cases involving FCPA violations in the region, mostly originating from Mexico (12), Argentina (10), Venezuela (8), and Brazil (8).[129]

Based on FCPA enforcement actions and investigations in Mexico, it appears that pharmaceuticals, oil and gas, construction, and banking are the industries where corrupt practices have been flourishing in Mexico, although no industry is immune to prosecution given the realities of day-to-day life and business practices on the ground.

Third parties remain the single greatest area of corruption risk in Mexico. Consultants, "*gestores*" (intermediaries dealing with administrative bureaucracy on behalf of clients), family members of state-owned customers, fictitious service providers, shell companies, and various intermediaries have been used to pay bribes in FCPA cases involving Mexico.

---

[127] General Law of Administrative Responsibilities, Art. 135.
[128] General Law of Administrative Responsibilities, Art. 89.
[129] http://fcpa.stanford.edu/resources-academic.html (last visited Dec. 10, 2018).

Company executives operating in Mexico pled guilty for their participation in corruption schemes.[130] Major government institutions, such as *Petroleos Mexicanos* (Pemex[131]), *Comisión Federal de Electricidad* (Lindsay Manufacturing[132]), *Mexican Policía Federal Preventiva, Mexican Coordinación General de Transportes Aéreos Presidenciales* (BizJet[133]), and the Mexico Social Security Institute (Stryker[134]), have been implicated in settled FCPA cases. Improper gifting and excessive hospitality amounting to corruption have also been a recurrent issue in Mexico, particularly with medical companies.[135] Obtaining licensing and permits is another major area that lends itself to corruption, particularly given the immense bureaucracy in Mexico (Walmart[136]). Another recurrent theme presented in these cases is

---

[130] https://www.justice.gov/opa/pr/former-chief-executive-officer-lufthansa-subsidiary-bizjet-pleads-guilty-foreign-bribery (last visited Dec. 10, 2018).

[131] Hewlett Packard pled guilty in 2014 and agreed to pay over U.S. $108 million for FCPA violations on a worldwide basis. In Mexico, it allegedly paid nearly U.S. $1.5 million through an overpaid "channel partner" to win a Pemex IT contract worth approximately U.S. $6 million. One of the Pemex officials reportedly received U.S. $125,000. *See* https://www.justice.gov/opa/pr/hewlett-packard-russia-agrees-plead-guilty-foreign-bribery (last visited July 9, 2016).

[132] Lindsay Manufacturing and its senior employees were convicted in 2011 for bribing officials at the Comisión Federal de Electricidad, Mexico's state-owned electric utility, subsequently, a U.S. District Court overturned the conviction on the grounds that the Lindsay prosecution had been tainted. Prosecutors had originally sought U.S. $24 million in criminal fines for bribes in relation to supply contracts. *See* http://blogs.wsj.com/corruption-currents/2012/05/29/u-s-drops-appeal-in-lindsey-manufacturing-fcpa-case/ (last visited July 9, 2016).

[133] In 2012, Bizjet agreed to pay a U.S. $11.8 million criminal penalty to resolve charges of illegal payments to officials at the Mexican Policía Federal Preventiva, the Mexican Coordinación General de Transportes Aéreos Presidenciales, the air fleet for the Gobierno del Estado de Sinaloa, and the air fleet for the Gobierno del Estado de Sonora, as well as Panamanian officials. The payments were to secure aircraft maintenance contracts. It paid bribes both directly to the foreign officials or through a shell company owned and operated by a BizJet sales manager. *See* https://www.justice.gov/opa/pr/bizjet-international-sales-and-support-inc-resolves-foreign-corrupt-practices-act (last visited July 9, 2016).

[134] According to the SEC, in Mexico Stryker paid U.S. $46,000 in bribes through a law firm to the Mexican Social Security Institute to obtain medical device sales worth U.S. $2.1 million. Brought by the SEC, the case was based solely on the books and records provisions of the FCPA. Stryker agreed to pay U.S. $13.2 million to settle the charges. https://www.sec.gov/News/PressRelease/Detail/PressRelease/1370540044262, https://www.sec.gov/litigation/admin/2013/34-70751.pdf (last visited July 9, 2016).

[135] As part of a $623 million 2016 settlement with the DOJ, Olympus Corporation of the Americas agreed to pay $22.8 million and submit to a three-year DPA to resolve criminal FCPA allegations. In seven countries in Latin America, including Mexico, Olympus paid money and provided free medical education travel, free or heavily discounted equipment, and other things of value to doctors working at government hospitals and clinics to induce purchase of Olympus products. *See* https://www.justice.gov/opa/pr/medical-equipment-company-will-pay-646-million-making-illegal-payments-doctors-and-hospitals (last visited Dec. 10, 2018).

[136] In 2012, the *New York Times* published articles that claimed that top officials at Walmart Mexican hid a widespread corruption scheme from the company's headquarters. It was alleged that Walmart personnel had paid over $24 million in bribes for expedited and controversial construction permits throughout Mexico, including one location in the shadow of the Teotihuacan pyramids. After Walmart had spent over U.S. $600 million on a compliance investigation, the *Wall Street Journal* reported that the investigation was winding down without finding major wrongdoing. *See* http://www.wsj.com/articles/wal-mart-bribery-probe-finds-little-misconduct-in-mexico-1445215737 (last visited July 9, 2016). As of August 2018, Walmart reported that it has spent about U.S. $900 million on legal fees and other costs stemming from the investigation, including a

the hiring of government officials' relatives and falsifying documentation on services allegedly provided by such relatives (Tyson Foods, Paradigm[137]). Payments of percentages of profits on government contracts and other kickbacks are also widespread in Mexico (Orthofix[138]).

In fiscal year 2016, the U.S. Securities and Exchange Commission's Office of the Whistleblower received tips from 67 non-U.S. countries, including 29 complaints from Mexico (which is double the amount of complaints from Mexico in 2015).[139] Given the recent trends and growing whistle-blower activism, FCPA enforcement involving Mexico will likely continue unabated.

APPENDIX

Key Issues	Mexico's Approach
Is jurisdiction subject to any international anti-corruption conventions? If so, which? (OECD, UN Convention against Corruption, etc.)	Mexico is a member of the OECD and a signatory to the OECD Anti-Bribery Convention. It is also a signatory to the OAS Convention Against Corruption and the UN Convention against Corruption.
Is bribery of foreign public officials illegal (do domestic anti-bribery laws provide for extraterritorial application)?	Yes.
What is the definition of foreign public officials?	The law defines public officials broadly to include government-owned companies and officials of international organizations. Lack of enforcement precludes further definition based on court rulings.

(Continued)

---

global overhaul of its internal compliance system. https://www.bloomberg.com/news/articles/2018-08-02/walmart-is-said-to-be-deadlocked-with-u-s-over-bribery-probe, (last visited Dec. 14, 2018). The matter is still ongoing.

[137] Paradigm's hiring of the brother of an official from Pemex, which arguably resulted in Paradigm being awarded a contract, was prosecuted as an FCPA offense. *See* http://www.fcpablog.com/blog/tag/paradigm#sthash.cpphJRrg.dpuf (last visited Dec. 10, 2018).

[138] In 2012, Orthofix agreed to pay U.S. $7.4 million and submit to a deferred prosecution agreement, partially based on allegations in Mexico of payments to Mexico Social Security officials of percentages of profits on government contracts. *See* https://www.justice.gov/sites/default/files/criminal-fraud/legacy/2012/08/15/2012-07-10-orthofix-info.pdf (last visited July 9, 2016); https://www.sec.gov/News/PressRelease/Detail/PressRelease/1365171483164 (last visited July 9, 2016).

[139] SEC, 2016 Annual Report to Congress on the Dodd-Frank Whistleblower Program (2016), *available at* https://www.sec.gov/reports.

Key Issues	Mexico's Approach
Is commercial bribery illegal?	No. However, the activities constituting commercial bribery may qualify as other crimes, such as fraud, fraudulent administration, theft, etc.
Is bribing domestic officials illegal?	Yes.
Can the receipt of a bribe be prosecuted?	Yes.
Can companies be held criminally liable? If so, what is the requisite intent for criminal liability to attach?	Yes. The requisite intent will be considered as that of the individual acting on behalf of the company.
Can companies be held civilly liable? If so, what is the requisite intent for criminal liability to attach?	Yes, administratively. The element of intent is imputed to the company if it is demonstrated that: a) crimes are committed in its name, on its behalf, for its benefit or using means that it provides; and b) due control was not exercised in the company.
Can individuals be held civilly liable?	Yes.
Is there a "facilitation/grease payments" exception?	No.
Does the subject country provide for conspiracy liability relating to violations of the anti-corruption laws?	Yes.
Does the subject country provide for: (a) aiding/abetting liability relating to violations of the anti-corruption laws? (b) attempt liability relating to violations of the anti-corruption laws?	A person aiding and abetting, as this term is understood in U.S. jurisdictions, would be directly liable under Mexican law. An attempt is punishable as a lesser offense.
Is failure to keep accurate books and records a criminal and/or civil offense?	The Federal Tax Code requires keeping accurate and complete books and records. Failure to comply is usually a civil/administrative offense, although in some cases it can qualify as a crime.
Do any books and records violations have to involve underlying bribery proof?	No.

Key Issues	Mexico's Approach
Are there laws concerning a company's financial internal controls? If so, are those laws applicable to private and public companies or just public companies?	Yes. All businesses must keep accounting records in accordance with the requirements of the Commercial Code (Articles 33 to 38). The Tax Code provides that failure to keep accurate books and records for tax purposes is punishable as a crime (Article 111). Publicly traded companies have additional obligations with respect to internal controls under the Stock Exchange Law (*Ley de Mercado de Valores*).
Is there an affirmative disclosure obligations for potential violations of the anti-bribery laws or accounting irregularities?	For all crimes, there is a general obligation to report, but there are no sanctions for failure to do so, and in practice there are no mechanisms to enforce such reporting. For accounting irregularities, the tax authorities frequently provide amnesty to encourage reporting.
Are "promotional expenses" exempt from the anti-bribery laws?	No.
Is the giving of gifts, entertainment, travel, meals, etc. restricted/prohibited?	Not specifically, but giving of these may qualify as a bribe if certain conditions are met, such as circumstances indicating a corrupt intent.
Are there any laws concerning things of value conveyed by, or to, third parties?	Yes, to the extent third parties are acting on behalf of companies to obtain an undue advantage or acting for government officials to accept a bribe on their behalf.
Are bribes tax deductible?	No.
Is the law applied extraterritorially?	Yes.
Is having a robust corporate compliance program an affirmative defense or way to negate liability?	For infractions by lower-level employees in Mexico City it can be a defense, but otherwise it is only a mitigation for sanctions.
Is there a "local law" exception/defense?	No.
Is "credit" given for cooperation with authorities? If so, how and in what form?	Generally no, but the Mexico City law provides for credit in the form of a reduction of penalties by one-third at the discretion of a judge. Also, under the General Law of Administrative Responsibilities, a person who commits a serious administrative offense, which includes corruption, will be able to admit liability and fully and continuously cooperate with the authorities in exchange for a potential sanction reduction of 50 to 70 percent.

(Continued)

Key Issues	Mexico's Approach
Does the subject country have a Mutual Legal Assistance Treaty with the United States that generally covers criminal matters, including the FCPA?	Yes.
What are the potential penalties/ sanctions both for civil and criminal violations?	Criminal: Up to 14 years in jail; and fines up to approximately U.S. $4,000. Civil/Administrative: Up to approximately U.S. $12.2 million, or 35 percent of the value of the contract, whichever is greater; and Debarment for up to 10 years.

13 Russia

1. Introduction to Russia's Anti-Corruption Legislation

1.1 THE LEGAL LANDSCAPE

Russian[1] anti-corruption legislation includes the following:

(a) The universally recognized principles and norms of international law;

(b) The Constitution of the Russian Federation, which sets down the fundamental general principles of Russian law;

(c) International treaties and agreements to which Russia is party, including the following anti-corruption conventions:

- the United Nations Convention against Corruption of 31 October 2003 (the "UN Convention");
- the OECD Convention on Combating Bribery of Foreign Public Officials in International Business Transactions of 21 November 1997 (the "OECD Convention");
- the Council of Europe Criminal Law Convention on Corruption of 27 January 1999; and
- the Council of Europe Convention on Laundering, Search, Seizure and Confiscation of the Proceeds from Crime of 8 November 1990;

(d) Federal laws, inter alia:

- the Criminal Code of the Russian Federation—No. 63-FZ of 13 June 1996 (the "Criminal Code");

---

[1] This chapter was contributed by Clifford Chance's Timur Aitkulov, Olga Semushina, and Galina Valentirova.

From Baksheesh to Bribery. T. Markus Funk and Andrew S. Boutros.
© Oxford University Press 2019. Published 2019 by Oxford University Press.

- the Administrative Offenses Code of the Russian Federation—No. 195-FZ of 30 December 2001 (the "Administrative Offenses Code");
- Federal Law No. 230 of 3 December 2012 on Monitoring Expenditures by Public Officials and Other Persons for Commensurateness with Income (the "Expenditures Law");
- Federal Law No. 273-FZ of 25 December 2008 On Combating Corruption (the "Anti-Corruption Law"); and
- Federal Law No. 115-FZ of 7 August 2001 On Preventing the Legalisation (Laundering) of the Proceeds of Crime and the Financing of Terrorism (the "AML Law").
- Recent developments in Russian legislation have been generally aimed at stiffening the penalties for corruption-related offenses.
- Also, a number of anti-corruption bills are pending at the moment, including:
- amendments to the Anti-Corruption Law that are aimed at making organizations carry out their anti-corruption duties more effectively and protecting whistle-blowers; and
- amendments to the Criminal Code to increase liability for corruption;

(e) Orders (in Russian: *ukazi*) of the President of the Russian Federation.

The president issues orders based on the RF Constitution and Federal Laws, with which, therefore, his orders must comply. Presidential orders in the area of corruption include:

- Order No. 378 of 29 June 2018 on the National Plan for Combating Corruption in 2018–2020;
- Order No. 925 of 21 July 2010 on Measures to Implement Certain Provisions of the Federal Law on Combating Corruption; and
- Order No. 815 of 19 May 2008 on Measures to Combat Corruption.

(f) Decrees (in Russian: *postanovleniya*) of the Government of the Russian Federation (RF).

The government issues Decrees based on the RF Constitution, federal laws, and orders of the president. In the area of corruption, these include:

- Decree No. 1405 of 18 December 2014 on Certain Issues Related to Combating Corruption; and
- Decree No. 96 of 26 February 2010 on Anti-Corruption Expert Assessments of Normative Acts and Draft Normative Acts.

(g) Regulations of other federal state agencies (the ministries, the General Prosecutor's Office, the RF Central Bank, etc.), which must comply with all of the above-mentioned sources of law;

(h) Regulations of the regions and republics of the Russian Federation and local authorities; and

(i) Decrees of the Plenum of the Supreme Court of the Russian Federation.

The Plenum of the Supreme Court of the Russian Federation periodically issues decrees in which it clarifies provisions of the anti-corruption legislation and provides guidance for the lower courts. Such clarifications are crucial for practice and are binding on the lower courts. For instance, the decrees clarify the elements of a crime that the law enforcement authorities will have to prove and criteria for situations in which criminal liability should not be imposed. The Plenum of the Supreme Court of the Russian Federation has issued, among other things, the following clarification relating to corruption offenses:

(1)   Decree of the Plenum of the Supreme Court of the Russian Federation No. 24 of 9 July 2013 on Court Practice in Cases of Bribery and Other Corruption-Related Offenses; and

(2)   Decree of the Plenum of the Supreme Court of the Russian Federation No. 19 of 16 October 2009 on Court Practice in Cases of Abuse of Public Office and Authority.

These two decrees of the Plenum of the Supreme Court give examples involving, inter alia, international public officials, and clarify the elements that the law enforcement authorities will need to prove to successfully prosecute a bribery case.

1.2   THE POLITICAL LANDSCAPE

Combating corruption is a very popular topic for political discussion in Russia. For instance, the majority of Russian political parties unanimously proclaim combating corruption to be one of the cornerstones of their political programs.[2] According to Russia's foremost political party, United Russia (in Russian: *Edinaya Rossiya*), "[c]*ombating corruption must be made a truly nationwide concern.*"[3]

The last few years have seen a significant increase in corruption-related investigations against Russian public officials. Recent major cases have seen custodial sentences (accompanied, amongst other things, by significant fines) being imposed against the following individuals:

(a)   Alexei Ulyukaev, ex-Minister of Economic Development, for accepting a bribe of U.S. $2 million;

(b)   Nikita Belykh, ex-governor of the Kirov region, for accepting a bribe of EUR 400,000; and

(c)   Alexander Khoroshavin, ex-governor of the Sakhalin Region, for accepting a bribe totaling more than RUB 522 million (approximately U.S. $8 million).

There are also ongoing court proceedings and investigations against Dmitry Zakharchenko, the former deputy chief of the "T" Department[4] of the Anti-Corruption Directorate of the RF Ministry of Internal Affairs, in connection with several allegations of bribe-taking. In the course of the investigation, the law-enforcement

---

[2] The political programs of Russia's main political parties are available at: United Russia—http://er.ru/party/presidential_election/; Liberal Democratic Party of Russia—https://ldpr.ru/party/Program_LDPR/; Communist Party of the Russian Federation—https://kprf.ru/party/program.

[3] United Russia's political programme is available at http://er.ru/party/presidential_election/.

[4] A unit that focuses on offenses in the fuel and energy sector.

authorities seized assets, including cash, worth of a total of more than RUB 9 billon (approximately U.S. $136 million).

1.3 THE BUSINESS LANDSCAPE

Russian law enforcement authorities tend to bring criminal cases against public officials, rather than the senior management of private companies. The criminal cases that have been covered in the Russian media, moreover, have involved investigations into the acceptance of relatively small bribes. This might be because the authorities are focusing on corruption in the public sector. Also, and in practice, cases that start out as bribery cases can later be reclassified as fraud or "abuse of powers" cases.

As a matter of Russian law, companies are obliged to implement certain measures in order to comply with anti-corruption laws. Recent research by PricewaterhouseCoopers produced in 2017[5] showed that in 2017, Russian companies have demonstrated a higher level of compliance with anti-corruption legislation than they did in 2016. This research involved analyzing publicly available information about anti-corruption measures taken by 125 leading Russian companies from different sectors. According to the research, these Russian companies have been implementing the following measures:

(a) the creation of separate compliance departments;
(b) the adoption of special anti-corruption policies, regulations, and codes of conduct;
(c) compliance and KYC procedures; and
(d) the setting up of "hotlines" that employees can use to report corruption-related issues.

According to the research, pharmaceutical, and telecommunications companies have demonstrated the highest level of compliance.

Recent trends in Russian legislation have been aimed at combating corruption in the commercial sector more effectively. For instance, Federal Law No. 208-FZ of 26 December 1995 on Joint-Stock Companies was amended in July 2018 to oblige public joint-stock companies to put in place a risk-management and internal control system by, among other things, adopting an appropriate policy and conducting an internal audit to assess the reliability and effectiveness of their risk-management and internal control system.

2. Russia's Domestic Anti-Corruption Framework

2.1 CRIMINAL LAW REGIME

In Russia, all criminal offenses and penalties are dealt with in the Criminal Code. The procedural rules for the law enforcement authorities' criminal investigations are set down in the Criminal Procedure Code.

As a matter of Russian criminal law, only individuals may be criminally liable; the Criminal Code does *not* establish criminal liability for corporate/commercial entities (which are

---

[5] *Available at* https://www.pwc.ru/ru/publications/assets/anticorruption-2017.pdf.

subject to administrative liability, please see Section 2.3). However, from time to time, draft laws providing for corporate criminal liability are considered by state bodies, including the RF State Duma. For instance, a draft law on corporate criminal liability submitted to the Russian State Duma in March 2015 proposed criminal liability for legal entities (both Russian and international) for corruption-related and other offenses. However, in mid-2015 the government gave a negative response to the bill and it was not adopted. At the moment, an initiative to amend the Criminal Code to establish corporate criminal liability is still being extensively debated. For example, in October 2017, the Chairman of the Russian Investigative Committee, Alexander Bastrykin, proposed that the Russian State Duma should draft and submit a new bill on corporate criminal liability.

The Criminal Code applies on the basis of the principle of territoriality, that is, as a rule, any individual who commits a crime in the territory of the Russian Federation,[6] including its territorial seas and airspace, will be criminally liable under the Criminal Code.[7]

The extraterritorial application of the Criminal Code is based on the following principles:[8]

2.1.1 Principle of Nationality

Russian citizens and stateless persons who permanently reside in Russia will be criminally liable under the Criminal Code if they commit a crime outside Russia, (1) if the act (crime) is in violation of the interests protected by the Criminal Code, and (2) if there is no foreign court judgment relating to the crime.[9]

2.1.2 Principle of Special Mission (Protective Approach)

Russian military personnel based outside the Russian Federation who have committed a crime in the territory of a foreign state are criminally liable under the Criminal Code, unless otherwise established by an international treaty to which Russia is party.[10]

2.1.3 Principle of Universal Jurisdiction

Foreign nationals and stateless persons who do not permanently reside in Russia and have committed a crime outside Russian territory may also be criminally liable under the Criminal Code.[11] The test is as follows: (1) the crime is against the interests of the Russian Federation or against a Russian citizen or a stateless person who permanently resides in Russia, or (2) the crime is provided for by an international treaty to which the Russian Federation is party (or another international document setting out obligations recognized by the Russian

---

[6] Law of the Russian Federation No. 4730-1 of 1 April 1993 on the State Border of the Russian Federation.

[7] Articles 11(1) and 11(2) of the Criminal Code. The Criminal Code also applies to crimes committed in the exclusive economic zone and on the continental shelf of the Russian Federation; onboard a vessel or aircraft registered in the Russian Federation that is on the open seas or in the air outside the borders of the Russian Federation, unless otherwise established by an international treaty or agreement of the Russian Federation; or onboard a military vessel or aircraft of the Russian Federation, regardless of location (Articles 11(2) and 11(3) of the Criminal Code).

[8] G.A. ESAKOV COMMENTARY TO THE CRIMINAL CODE OF THE RUSSIAN FEDERATION (7th ed. 2017).

[9] Article 12(1) of the Criminal Code.

[10] Article 12(2) of the Criminal Code.

[11] Article 12(3) of the Criminal Code.

Federation in the sphere of relations governed by the Criminal Code) and the person in question has not been convicted in a foreign state and is facing criminal charges in Russia.

The Criminal Code establishes criminal liability for accepting/giving a bribe,[12] commercial bribery,[13] small-scale bribery/commercial bribery,[14] acting as an intermediary for a bribe or a commercial bribe,[15] and incitement of a bribe or a commercial bribe.[16] The Criminal Code also provides criminal liability for corruption-related offenses, which include money laundering,[17] false accounting,[18] and others.

Penalties include imprisonment, fines, disqualification from certain posts or activities for a certain period of time, community service, compulsory work, and deprivation of liberty (for more details on the penalties for bribery and commercial bribery see Sections 4.7, 5.7, and 6.6).

According to the Criminal Code the offense can be committed by several persons, with specific roles and responsibilities.[19] The criminal liability of each such person will depend on his/her actual role in the commission of the offense (orchestrator, instigator, accessory, or principal).[20] For certain crimes, the Criminal Code provides criminal liability for persons who have specific status (e.g., public officials). If the crime is committed by several persons and not all of them have that status, those people will still be liable under the Criminal Code but as orchestrator, instigator, or accessory only.[21]

The Criminal Code stipulates the limitation periods for criminal liability.[22] These limitation periods depend upon the gravity of the crime and are as follows:

(a) two years after the commission of a minor offense (deliberate and negligent offenses with a maximum penalty of three years' imprisonment);[23]

(b) six years after the commission of a moderately serious offense (deliberate offenses with a maximum penalty of five years' imprisonment and negligent offenses with a maximum penalty of three years' imprisonment);[24]

(c) ten years after the commission of a grave offense (deliberate offenses with a maximum penalty of ten years' imprisonment);[25] and

(d) fifteen years after the commission of a particularly grave offense (deliberate offenses punishable by imprisonment for more than ten years or a more severe penalty).[26]

---

[12] Articles 290 and 291 of the Criminal Code.

[13] Article 204 of the Criminal Code.

[14] Articles 291.2 and 204.2 of the Criminal Code.

[15] Articles 291.1 and 204.1 of the Criminal Code.

[16] Article 304 of the Criminal Code.

[17] Articles 174 & 174.1 of the Criminal Code.

[18] Article 172.1 of the Criminal Code.

[19] Article 32 of the Criminal Code.

[20] Article 34(1) of the Criminal Code.

[21] Article 34(4) of the Criminal Code.

[22] Article 78 of the Criminal Code.

[23] Article 15(2) of the Criminal Code.

[24] Article 15(3) of the Criminal Code.

[25] Article 15(4) of the Criminal Code.

[26] Article 15(5) of the Criminal Code.

2.2 CIVIL LAW REGIME

As a rule, the damage suffered as a result of a crime is recovered in the course of the criminal proceedings. The grounds for claims are Articles 15 and 1064 of the Civil Code, which provide general rules for obtaining compensation for damage in civil law cases. It, moreover, is possible to claim both actual damage and lost profit. However, according to court practice, in cases in which compensation is sought for damage suffered as a result of crime, only actual damage is recoverable. The claim may be brought either in separate proceedings[27] or as a stand-alone claim in the course of the criminal proceedings against the individual accused of a corruption offense.[28]

As a matter of Russian law, both a transaction that by itself constitutes bribery[29] and a transaction entered into as a result of bribery[30] may be ruled invalid by the court.

Also, according to the Expenditures Law, in cases in which it is established that expenditure by a public official or his/her spouse and children is not commensurate with their income, the General Prosecutor has the power to bring a lawsuit against them to have their assets seized by the state if there is no evidence that the assets in question were obtained with legitimate income. It should also be noted that, as was demonstrated in the case against Dmitri Zakharchenko (please see Section 1.2), such lawsuits can be brought not only against a public official's spouse and children but also against his/her parents, siblings, and civil partners.

2.3 ADMINISTRATIVE OFFENSES LAW REGIME

As a rule, offenses are administratively punishable if they do not constitute a crime under the Criminal Code because they pose a low risk to the public. Administrative offenses and penalties are set out in the Administrative Offenses Code.

In the majority of cases the Administrative Offenses Code applies based on the principle of territoriality. Administrative penalties include warnings, administrative fines, administrative arrest, administrative deportation of foreign citizens or stateless persons, disqualification, etc. Also, as a rule, the limitation periods are short, for instance the limitation period for the majority of administrative offenses is two months from the date that the administrative offense was committed.

As legal entities are not subject to criminal liability, the Administrative Offenses Code provides for significant fines for them in certain cases, and this could, arguably, be considered "quasi-criminal liability for legal entities."

Specifically, the Administrative Offenses Code envisages[31] administrative liability for providing, offering, or promising unlawful remuneration on behalf or in the interests of a legal

---

[27] Appellate Ruling of the Court of the Rostov Region of 6 September 2016 in case No. 33-15491/2016.

[28] Article 44(2) of the Criminal Procedure Code.

[29] Appellate ruling of the Court of the Novosibirsk Region of 6 October 2016 in case No. 33-9919/2016; Appellate ruling of the Court of the Primorskiy Krai of 7 June 2017 in case No. 33-5637/2017.

[30] *See, e.g.*, Appellate Ruling of the Supreme Court of the Karachayevo-Cherkess Republic of 8 February 2017 in case No. 33-87/17.

[31] The Administrative Offenses Code also provides liability for hiring a state or municipal employee who occupies or has occupied certain offices under an employment agreement or entering into a civil contract with such an

entity or other legal entity related to that legal entity to a public official, foreign public official, official of an international organization, or a person exercising management functions at a commercial or other organization in return for performing an act (or omitting to act) for the benefit of the legal entity or other legal entity related to that legal entity, where these actions (or omissions) are part of the work duties of the official/person.[32]

If a legal entity is found guilty of a bribery offense, the maximum possible administrative penalty is a fine equal to 100 times the value of the bribe (but not less than RUB 100 million (approximately U.S. $1.5 million)), accompanied by confiscation of the money, securities, or other assets that constituted the bribe.

The limitation period for the above offense is six years from the date that the administrative offense was committed. Also, a legal entity that has committed the above offense outside the territory of the Russian Federation is subject to administrative liability under the Administrative Offenses Code if (1) the offense is against the interests of the Russian Federation, or (2) it is provided for by an international treaty of the Russian Federation and the legal entity has not been held liable in a foreign state (it appears that this is the only exception from the principle of territorial application of the Administrative Offenses Code).

In practice, the Russian law enforcement authorities tend to open administrative proceedings against legal entities where a manager or employee is convicted of bribery. Criminal proceedings against an individual and administrative proceedings against the entity may be based on the same facts[33] and can be heard in parallel.

2.4 VIEW FROM THE OUTSIDE

2.4.1 OECD Evaluation

The OECD has been cooperating with the Russian Federation since 1992. The legal framework for relations between the Russian Federation and the OECD is set out in the Declaration on Co-operation and the Agreement on Privileges and Immunities granted to the OECD in the Russian Federation, both dated June 8, 1994. The Russian Federation made an official request for OECD membership in 1996 and,[34] although it is still not a member, it has the status of an observer within the OECD. Also, in March 2014, the OECD suspended the OECD accession process for the Russian Federation.[35]

In February 2012, Russia joined the OECD Convention on Combating Bribery of Foreign Public Officials in International Business Transactions. This resulted in amendments to Russian legislation—please see Section 4.3.

---

employee for works or services in breach of the Anti-Corruption Law (Article 19.29 of the Administrative Offenses Code).

[32] Article 19.28 of the Administrative Offenses Code.

[33] Item 28 of Decree of the Plenum of the RF Supreme Court No. 24 of 9 July 2013.

[34] http://www.oecd.org/russia/therussianfederationandtheoecd.htm (accessed on 17 December 2018).

[35] http://www.oecd.org/newsroom/statement-by-the-oecd-regarding-the-status-of-the-accession-process-with-russia-and-co-operation-with-ukraine.htm (accessed on 17 December 2018).

Also, the Working Group on Bribery has been monitoring how well Russia is implementing the requirements of the Convention. In March 2016, the OECD Working Group on Bribery found that a large majority of its recommendations were still not or only partially being implemented by the Russian Federation.[36]

2.4.2 Transparency International Corruption Perception Index Score

In 1999, the Centre for Anti-Corruption Research and Initiative Transparency International Russia was founded in Russia.

Although Russia has significantly amended its anti-corruption legislation and put in place numerous measures to combat corruption, it is still ranked very low by Transparency International. Over the last five years, the Transparency International Corruption Perception Index has ranked the Russian Federation as follows: No. 133 in 2012,[37] No. 127 in 2013,[38] No. 136 in 2014,[39] No. 119 in 2015[40] and No. 131 in 2016,[41] and No. 135 in 2017.[42]

3. Investigative and Prosecutorial Agencies

3.1 CRIMINAL LAW AGENCIES

As a matter of Russian criminal-procedural law, the majority of cases are investigated by investigators of the Investigative Committee of the Russian Federation. The Federal Security Service, the Russian Foreign Intelligence Service, police, and other officers of the RF Ministry of Internal Affairs and the customs and military authorities are also empowered to investigate certain crimes.

Pretrial investigations of the majority of corruption-related criminal offenses are conducted by investigators of the RF Investigative Committee and officers of the RF Ministry of Internal Affairs.

Operational units of certain state bodies (the Federal Security Service, the Russian Foreign Intelligence Service, the police, customs, etc.) listed in Federal Law No. 144-FZ of 12 August 1995 on Operational-Search Activities play an important role in detecting and investigating criminal offenses. These units are entitled to carry out operational-search activities both before and after the criminal cases (investigations) are officially opened.

Operational units are empowered to conduct, among other things, disclosed or undisclosed: interrogations, enquiries, test purchases, examinations of items and documents, the interception of telephone conversations, postal items, and other kinds of communications and searches of premises, buildings, sites, and vehicles.

---

[36] http://www.oecd.org/russia/russia-oecdanti-briberyconvention.htm (accessed on 17 December 2018).

[37] https://www.transparency.org/cpi2012/results (accessed on 17 December 2018).

[38] https://www.transparency.org/cpi2013/results (accessed on 17 December 2018).

[39] https://www.transparency.org/cpi2014/results (accessed on 17 December 2018).

[40] https://www.transparency.org/cpi2015/results#results-table (accessed on 17 December 2018).

[41] https://www.transparency.org/news/feature/corruption_perceptions_index_2016#table (accessed on 17 December 2018).

[42] https://www.transparency.org/news/feature/corruption_perceptions_index_2017 (accessed on 17 December 2018).

The results of operational-search activities can be used as evidence in criminal proceedings only provided that they comply with the law, including the Criminal Procedure Code. There is also a specific procedure for making the results of operational-search activities available to investigators, enquiries agencies, and the courts.[43]

As a rule, operational-search activities relating to corruption-related criminal offenses are conducted by the General Directorate for Economic Security and Combating Corruption of the RF Ministry of Internal Affairs[44] and the relevant departments of regional bodies of the RF Ministry of Internal Affairs.

Operational-search activities can also be conducted upon a specific request, among other things, for verification of whether (1) information submitted by individuals applying for/occupying certain public offices is complete and true, and (2) individuals occupying certain public offices comply with the rules for preventing and managing conflicts of interests.

Prosecutors, too, take part in criminal proceedings, with broad powers. Prosecutors supervise the investigators (e.g., they are empowered to revoke certain decisions by investigators, including decisions to open or terminate an investigation) at the pretrial stage and represent the state in the course of criminal proceedings in court (see also Section 9.1).

3.2 ADMINISTRATIVE LAW AGENCIES

Administrative cases are opened and considered by the state body that has competence in the area to which the offense relates (e.g., the Federal Antimonopoly Service commences and considers administrative cases relating to breaches of antimonopoly legislation). Certain cases can be examined by the courts only.

Administrative proceedings relating to corruption-related administrative offenses are commenced by prosecutors and considered by the courts.

3.3 MULTIAGENCY ARRANGEMENTS

Russian law provides for the creation of a variety of bodies focused on cooperation and the provision of advice in the area of corruption. These bodies may include representatives of the federal authorities and regional authorities and other persons.

For instance, such bodies can be set up by the president;[45] the Presidential Council for Countering Corruption (the "Presidential Council") was established in May 2008.[46] The Presidential Council is headed by the president and includes the General Prosecutor, the Chairman of the RF Investigative Committee, the Director of the Federal Security

---

[43] Order of the RF Ministry of Internal Affairs & Others No. 776 of 27 September 2013 on the Adoption of the Instruction Establishing the Procedure for Making the Results of Operational-Search Activities Available to Enquiries Agencies, Investigators and Courts.

[44] https://xn--b1aew.xn--p1ai/mvd/structure1/Glavnie_upravlenija/Glavnoe_upravlenie_jekonomicheskoj_bezop (accessed on 17 December 2018).

[45] Article 5(5) of the Anti-Corruption Law.

[46] Order of the RF President No. 815 of 19 May 2008 on Measures to Counter Corruption.

Service, and the Chairman of the RF Constitutional Court. The Presidential Council is responsible for:

(a) proposing to the President initiatives relating to the development and realization of state anti-corruption policy;

(b) coordinating the anti-corruption efforts of the federal executive authorities, regional executive authorities, and local bodies; and

(c) overseeing the realization of the National Plan for Countering Corruption.

Also, the General Prosecutor and his/her subordinate prosecutors coordinate the anti-corruption activities of internal affairs bodies, bodies of the Federal Security Service, and the customs and other law enforcement authorities.[47] To this end, prosecutors are empowered to convene coordination meetings, set up working groups, request statistical and other data, and so on.[48]

4. Bribery of Foreign Officials

4.1 JURISDICTION

The principles of territorial and extraterritorial application for the Criminal Code and Administrative Offenses Code referred to in Sections 2.1 and 2.3 above apply in cases of bribery of foreign officials. Rules in international treaties to which Russia is party are also applicable. Specifically, according to Article 4(3) of the OECD Convention, when more than one state has jurisdiction over the bribery of a foreign public official, the states involved shall, at the request of one of them, consult with a view to determining the most appropriate jurisdiction for the prosecution.

4.2 STATUTE OF LIMITATIONS

The limitation periods referred to in Sections 2.1 and 2.3 above apply.

To be specific, the limitation period for accepting or giving a bribe in an amount not exceeding RUB 25,000 (approximately U.S. $380) and for small-scale bribery (not exceeding RUB 10,000 (approximately U.S. $151)), which are minor offenses, is two years from the day that the offense was committed.

The limitation period for giving a bribe in an amount exceeding RUB 25,000 (approximately U.S. $380) but not exceeding RUB 150,000 (approximately U.S. $2,270) or acting as an intermediary for bribery in the absence of aggravating circumstances, which are moderately serious offenses, is six years from the day that the offense was committed.

The limitation period for accepting or giving a bribe in return for committing unlawful actions or acting as an intermediary for a bribe in an amount exceeding RUB 150,000

---

[47] Article 5(6) of the Anti-Corruption Law and Article 8(1) of Federal Law No. 2202-1 of 17 January 1992 on the Public Prosecutor's Office of the Russian Federation.

[48] Article 8(2) of Federal Law No. 2202-1 of 17 January 1992 on the Public Prosecutor's Office of the Russian Federation.

(approximately U.S. $2,270) but not exceeding RUB 1 million (approximately U.S. $15,150), which are grave offenses, is 10 years from the day that the offense was committed.

The limitation period for accepting or giving a bribe in an amount exceeding RUB 150,000 (approximately U.S. $2,270) or acting as an intermediary for a bribe in an amount exceeding RUB 1 million (approximately U.S. $15,150), which are extremely grave offenses, is 15 years from the day that the offense was committed.

4.3 FOREIGN BRIBERY OFFENSES

In 2011, Russian legislation was amended following Russia's ratification of the UN Convention and the OECD Convention. The Criminal Code was amended to criminalize the following foreign bribery offenses: (1) acceptance of a bribe by a foreign public official/official of an international organization, (2) giving a bribe to a foreign public official/official of an international organization, and (3) acting as an intermediary for a bribe if the bribe is being passed on to a foreign public official/official of a public international organization. The Administrative Offenses Code was amended[49] to extend administrative liability to legal entities for providing, offering, or promising unlawful remuneration to foreign public officials or officials of international organizations.

In 2016, the Criminal Code was further amended to criminalize incitement of a bribe in relation to a foreign public official/official of an international organization.[50]

4.4 "FOREIGN PUBLIC OFFICIAL" DEFINED

In Russian criminal and administrative law, the definitions of *"foreign public official"* and *"official of an international organisation"* are in line with the OECD Convention.

Specifically, a *"foreign public official"* is an individual who holds legislative, executive, administrative, or judicial office in a foreign country, whether appointed or elected, and any person who exercises duties of public office of a foreign country, including at a public agency or public enterprise.[51] The Plenum of the RF Supreme Court has clarified that ministers, mayors, judges, and public prosecutors are to be recognized as foreign public officials.[52]

Accordingly, an *"official of an international organisation"* is an international civil servant or any person who is authorized by an international organization to act on behalf of that organization.[53] The Plenum of the RF Supreme Court has clarified that a member of a parliamentary assembly of an international organization to which Russia is party, an individual who holds judicial office at an international court the jurisdiction of which is recognized by Russia, etc. are to be recognized as officials of international organizations.[54]

---

[49] Federal Law No. 97-FZ of 4 May 2011 on Amendments to the RF Criminal Code and Administrative Offenses Code in Development of Anti-Corruption Legislation.

[50] Article 304 of the Criminal Code.

[51] Note 2 to Article 290 of the Criminal Code and Note 3 to Article 19.28 of the Administrative Offenses Code.

[52] Item 1 of Decree No. 24 of 9 July 2013 of the Plenum of the RF Supreme Court.

[53] Note 2 to Article 290 of the Criminal Code & Note 3 to Article 19.28 of the Administrative Offenses Code.

[54] Item 1 of Decree of the Plenum of the RF Supreme Court No. 24 of 9 July 2013.

4.5 GIFTS, GRATUITIES, AND HOSPITALITY

Russian anti-bribery law gives no specific guidance on gifts, gratuities, and hospitality provided to foreign public officials or officials of international organizations. As a matter of Russian law, each payment must be assessed using the criteria for corruption offenses, whether criminal or administrative.

4.6 DEFENSES

4.6.1 Written Local Law

The written law defenses are the same for bribery of both foreign and local officials.

The Criminal Code establishes several specific cases in which an individual can be released from criminal liability for bribery of public officials (in addition to the general grounds for release from criminal liability applicable to minor and moderately serious offenses, such as active remorse (in Russian: *deyatelnoe raskayanie*) and settlement with the injured party). To be specific, an individual who has given a bribe or acted as an intermediary for a bribe may be released from criminal liability if (1) he/she actively assists in detecting or investigating the crime, and (2) he/she voluntarily reported the crime to the competent authorities or the bribe was extorted from him/her.

Active assistance in detecting and/or investigating the crime can be demonstrated by, for example, actions aimed at bringing other individuals involved in committing the crime (bribe-taker, bribe-giver, intermediary) to justice and tracing the property transferred as a bribe.

The Plenum of the RF Supreme Court has provided certain examples of when a bribe-giver, bribe-taker, or an intermediary for a bribe should not be held criminally liable for bribery.[55] For instance, the head of a federal or local institution should not be held criminally liable for accepting a bribe if he/she accepts sponsor support for the benefit of the institution in return for his/her acting for the benefit of the sponsor (although such actions can be treated as a criminally punishable abuse of power or exceeding of power if there are grounds to do so). Also, a bribe-giver or an intermediary for a bribe should not be held criminally liable if that person believed that the "bribe" was not intended for the unlawful enrichment of a public official or his/her relatives or close friends.

In addition, the Criminal Code lists circumstances that mitigate criminal liability (a full confession, pregnancy, etc.).

The Administrative Offenses Code similarly provides several specific cases in which a legal entity can be released from administrative liability for providing, offering, or promising unlawful remuneration on behalf or in the interests of a legal entity (in addition to the general grounds for release from administrative liability such as the minor nature of the offense or extreme necessity).[56] A legal entity can be released from administrative liability for committing the abovementioned offense if (1) it assists in the detection, investigation of

---

[55] Item 23 of Decree of the Plenum of the RF Supreme Court No. 24 of 9 July 2013.
[56] Article 19.28 of the Administrative Offenses Code.

the offense and/or detection, investigation of a crime relating to the offense or (2) the unlawful remuneration was extorted from the legal entity. It should be noted that this defense does not apply if the unlawful remuneration was provided, offered or promised to a foreign public official or an official of a public international organization in connection with a commercial transaction.

The Administrative Offenses Code also lists circumstances that mitigate administrative liability, which include the voluntary termination of the unlawful activity and the voluntary reporting of the offense.

4.6.2 Facilitation Payments

There is no specific exemption under Russian law for facilitation payments. Each payment must be assessed using the criteria for corruption offenses, whether criminal or administrative.

4.6.3 Adequate Procedures

If an entity is charged with an administrative offense, it may be a defense to show that it has taken all possible and reasonable steps to prevent the offense and comply with the relevant statutory requirements (please see also Section 1.3).

4.7 PENALTIES

In the Criminal Code, the penalties for bribery offenses depend on the amount of the bribe and whether there are any aggravating circumstances (conspiracy, an offense by an organized group, accepting a bribe through extortion, etc.). Penalties do not depend on whether the bribe-taker is a local or foreign official.

The list of penalties for bribery offenses in the Criminal Code is extensive. The maximum penalties for bribery of public officials are as follows:

(a) for accepting a bribe of an extremely large amount (exceeding RUB 1 million (approximately U.S. $15,150))—imprisonment for up to 15 years, with or without a fine equal to 70 times the value of the bribe and/or disqualification from certain positions or certain activities for up to 15 years;

(b) for giving a bribe in an extremely large amount—imprisonment for up to 15 years, with or without a fine equal to 70 times the value of the bribe and/or disqualification from certain positions or certain activities for up to 10 years;

(c) for acting as an intermediary for a bribe of an extremely large amount—imprisonment for up to 12 years, with or without a fine equal to 70 times the value of the bribe and/or disqualification from certain positions or certain activities for up to 7 years;

(d) for small-scale bribery—imprisonment for up to three years; and

(e) for incitement to bribe—imprisonment for up to five years, with or without disqualification from certain positions or certain activities for up to three years.

According to the Administrative Offenses Code, the maximum administrative penalty for legal entities is a fine equal to 100 times the value of the bribe (but not less than RUB

100 million (approximately U.S. $1.5 million)), accompanied by confiscation of the money, securities, or other assets that constituted the bribe.

5. Bribery of Domestic Officials

5.1 JURISDICTION

The principles of territorial and extraterritorial application for the Criminal Code and Administrative Offenses Code referred to in Sections 2.1 and 2.3 above apply in cases of bribery of domestic officials.

5.2 STATUTE OF LIMITATIONS

The limitation periods referred to in Section 4.2 above apply.

5.3 BRIBERY OFFENSES

The Criminal Code envisages the following bribery offenses: accepting and giving a bribe, acting as an intermediary for a bribe, small-scale bribery, and incitement to bribe.

Legal entities are subject to administrative liability for providing, offering, or promising unlawful remuneration to public officials.

5.4 DEFINITION OF "PUBLIC OFFICIALS"

A *"public official"* is defined as an individual who, on a permanent or temporary basis or by special authority, performs the functions of a representative of the state or fulfills organizational and management or administrative functions at state or local authorities, state or municipal enterprises, state corporations, state companies, state or municipal unitary enterprises, joint-stock companies in which the Russian Federation or a constituent entity or a municipality holds a controlling stake, or the military.[57]

The Plenum of the RF Supreme Court has provided some clarification of elements of the definition of *"public official,"* including the following:[58]

5.4.1 Functions of a Representative of the State

These functions are performed by individuals who exercise functions of legislative, executive, and judicial bodies or law enforcement and supervisory authorities, where they are entitled to exercise their powers with respect to persons not subordinated to them or to render binding decisions.

In view of the above, functions of a representative of the state are performed by judges, ministers, governors, etc.

---

[57] Note 1 to Article 285 of the Criminal Code.
[58] Item 1 of Decree of the Plenum of the RF Supreme Court No. 24 of 9 July 2013 and Items 3–5 of Decree of the Plenum of the RF Supreme Court No. 19 of 16 October 2009.

5.4.2 Organizational and Management Duties

These duties include a public official's powers to exercise management functions with respect to the staff of a state body or a state or municipal institution (or a department of such a body or institution), or certain employees subordinated to them, to determine staff composition and employees' duties, to apply incentives and impose disciplinary measures, etc.

Organizational and management duties also include powers to make decisions that have legal effect and certain legal implications (the powers of medical professionals issuing an official sick-leave certificate or an official when issuing a license or making an entry in the register of legal entities).[59]

5.4.3 Administrative Duties

Administrative duties include managing and disposing of assets and/or monetary funds on the balance sheet and/or accounts of organizations, institutions or military units, and administering payroll and the payment of bonuses.

5.4.4 Performance of Public Official's Duties "By Special Authority"

"Special authority" means that an individual performs any of the duties mentioned in items 5.4.1–5.4.3 in this Section by operation of law or by order or decree of a superior official or another authority (e.g., the duties of a member of a jury).[60]

5.5 GIFTS, GRATUITIES, AND HOSPITALITY

Under the Civil Code, it is prohibited "to donate gifts, except for common gifts, worth up to RUB 3000 [approximately U.S. $45] to persons holding public offices of the Russian Federation, public offices of constituent entities of the Russian Federation or municipal offices, or to state employees, municipal employees or employees of the Bank of Russia in connection with their official capacity or in connection with the performance of their official duties."[61]

This restriction does not apply to cases in which gifts are donated in connection with official entertainment, business trips, and other official events. If the value of the gifts exceeds RUB 3,000 (approximately U.S. $45), they should be deemed state, regional, or local property, and officials must hand them over to the body for which the official works.

Public officials are required to report any gifts received in connection with official entertainment, business trips, and other official events that they take part in as a public official, to the authority they work for.[62] This duty applies to people holding public office, state and

---

[59] N.I. Biryukov, O.N. Vedernikova, S.A. Vorozhtsov et al. Commentary to Decrees of the Plenum of the Supreme Court of the Russian Federation on Criminal Cases (V.M. Lebedev ed. 3d ed. 2014).

[60] Item 6 of Decree of the Plenum of the RF Supreme Court No. 19 of 16 October 2009.

[61] Article 575 of the Civil Code.

[62] Item 4 of Decree of the Government of the Russian Federation No. 10 of 9 January 2014.

municipal employees, employees of the Bank of Russia, the RF Pension Fund, the RF Social Insurance Fund, the RF Federal Compulsory Medical Insurance Fund, and other organizations established by federal laws, and organizations established to perform the functions of federal state authorities.[63]

5.6 DEFENSES

5.6.1 Written Local Law

The defense available is the same as that in Section 4.6.1 above.

5.6.2 Facilitation Payments

The regime is the same as that in Section 4.6.2 above.

5.6.3 Adequate Procedures

The regime is the same as that in Section 4.6.3 above.

5.7 PENALTIES

The penalties are the same as those in Section 4.7 above.

6. Commercial Bribery

6.1 JURISDICTION

The principles of territorial and extraterritorial application for the Criminal Code and Administrative Offenses Code in Sections 2.1 and 2.3 above apply in cases of commercial bribery.

6.2 STATUTE OF LIMITATIONS

Limitation periods for criminally punishable commercial bribery offenses vary with the gravity of the offense (see Section 2.1).

The limitation period for accepting a bribe in an amount not exceeding RUB 25,000 (approximately U.S. $380), giving a bribe in an amount exceeding RUB 150,000 (approximately U.S. $2,270), acting as an intermediary for bribery in an amount exceeding RUB 25,000 (approximately U.S. $380) but not exceeding RUB 150,000 (approximately U.S. $2,270) or for small-scale commercial bribery (in an amount not exceeding RUB 10,000 (approximately U.S. $150)), which are minor offenses, is two years from the day that the offense was committed.

The limitation period for accepting a bribe in an amount exceeding RUB 150,000 (approximately U.S. $2,270) but not exceeding RUB 1 million (approximately U.S. $15,150),

---

[63] *Id.* Items 1 and 4.

giving a bribe in an amount exceeding RUB 1 million (approximately U.S. $15,150) or acting as an intermediary for bribery in an amount exceeding RUB 1 million (approximately U.S. $15,150), which are grave offenses, is 10 years from the day that the offense was committed.

The limitation period for accepting a bribe in an amount exceeding RUB 1 million (approximately U.S. $15,150), an extremely grave offense, is 15 years from the day that the offense was committed.

In relation to administrative liability, the limitation periods in Section 2.3 above apply.

6.3 COMMERCIAL BRIBERY OFFENSES

Commercial bribery offenses include giving and accepting commercial bribes,[64] acting as an intermediary in commercial bribery,[65] small-scale commercial bribery,[66] and incitement of commercial graft.[67]

Russian criminal law defines commercial bribery as:

"[G]iving unlawful remuneration (in the form of money, securities or other property, services or property rights) to a person exercising management functions at a commercial or other organisation (including when unlawful remuneration is given to another individual or legal entity on the instruction of such person) in return for performing an act (or omitting to act) for the benefit of the bribe-giver or other individuals or legal entities if these actions (or omissions) are part of the work duties of the person or the person may contribute to these actions (or omissions) due to his/her position"; and

"[T]he acceptance of unlawful remuneration by a person exercising management functions at a commercial or other organisation."[68]

An example of a bribe-taker is a CEO, a member of the board of directors, or the head of a particular department responsible for certain approvals, where he/she performs organizational and management duties or administrative duties (for further details please see Section 5.4.2 and 5.4.3).

6.4 GIFTS, GRATUITIES, AND HOSPITALITY

Russian anti-bribery legislation does not provide special rules for donations to persons exercising management functions at a commercial or other organization. In practice, restrictions in this regard may be set down by a company's bylaws.

---

[64] Article 204 of the Criminal Code.

[65] Article 204.1 of the Criminal Code.

[66] Article 204.2 of the Criminal Code.

[67] Article 304 of the Criminal Code.

[68] Article 204 of the Criminal Code.

6.5 DEFENSES

6.5.1 Written Local Law

The Criminal Code establishes several specific cases in which an individual may be released from criminal liability for commercial bribery:

(a) an individual who gave a commercial bribe, including a small-scale one, or acted as an intermediary for a commercial bribe may be released from criminal liability if he/she actively assists in detecting and/or investigating the crime and voluntarily reported the crime to the competent authorities;[69] and

(b) an individual who gave a commercial bribe, including a small-scale one, may be released from criminal liability if he/she actively assists in detecting and/ or investigating the crime and the commercial bribe was extorted from this individual.[70]

Please see also Section 4.6.1.

6.5.2 Facilitation Payments

The regime is the same as that in Section 4.6.2 above.

6.5.3 Adequate Procedures

The regime is the same as that in Section 4.6.3 above.

6.6 PENALTIES

In the Criminal Code, the penalties for bribery offenses depend on the amount of the bribe and whether there are any aggravating circumstances (conspiracy, an offense by an organized group, accepting a bribe through extortion, etc.).

The list of penalties for bribery offenses in the Criminal Code is extensive. The maximum penalties for commercial bribery are as follows:

(a) for accepting a bribe in an amount exceeding RUB 1 million (approximately U.S. $15,150)—imprisonment for up to 12 years, with or without a fine equal to 50 times the value of the bribe and/or disqualification from certain positions or certain activities for up to 6 years;

(b) for giving a bribe in an amount exceeding RUB 1 million (approximately U.S. $15,150)—imprisonment for up to eight years, with or without a fine equal to 40 times the value of the bribe and/or disqualification from certain positions or certain activities for up to five years;

---

[69] Note 2 to Article 204, note to Article 204.1 and note to Article 204.2 of the Criminal Code.
[70] Note to Article 204 and note to Article 204.2 of the Criminal Code.

(c) for acting as an intermediary in commercial bribery in an amount exceeding RUB 1 million (approximately U.S. $15,150)—imprisonment for up to seven years, with or without a fine equal to 40 times the value of the bribe and/or disqualification from certain positions or certain activities for up to six years;

(d) for small-scale commercial bribery committed by a person with a criminal record for any type of commercial bribery—imprisonment for up to one year;

(e) for incitement of commercial graft—imprisonment for up to five years, with or without disqualification from certain positions or certain activities for up to three years.

For administrative penalties please see Section 4.7.

7. Sentencing Principles
7.1 GENERAL PRINCIPLES

In Russia, statutory sentencing frameworks apply to all criminal and administrative offenses.[71]

As a rule, a penalty for a crime must be fair and within the limits established by the Criminal Code; a more severe penalty (within those envisaged) may be imposed only if the less severe penalty could not achieve the purpose of the penalty.

When imposing a criminal penalty, the court must consider the nature and degree of public danger that the crime posed; the character of the convicted person, including any mitigating or aggravating circumstances; and the impact of the penalty, in terms of reforming the convicted person and upon his family's living conditions. According to clarification from the Plenum of the RF Supreme Court, details of the convicted person's character include his or her marital and financial status, physical condition, behavior in everyday life, and question as to whether he/she has underage children or other dependants (a spouse, parents, other close relatives).[72]

If the possible penalties for a corruption-related offense include a fine, the courts should consider factors indicating whether he or she will be able to pay the fine (e.g., his/her financial position and earning capacity and his/her family's financial position).[73]

If the possible penalties for a corruption-related offense include disqualification from certain positions or activities for a certain period, the courts should consider whether the convicted person can be permitted to retain the right to hold the position or engage in the activities in question.[74]

According to publicly available court statistics relating to bribery for 2017,[75] in 2017, 1,475 custodial sentences were handed down (out of 17,334 sentences in total), most of which were for five years or less; 4,326 sentences included a fine as the principal punishment, and 929

---

[71] Chapter 10 of the Criminal Code and Chapter 4 of the Administrative Offenses Code.

[72] Item 1 of Decree of the Plenum of the RF Supreme Court No. 58 of 22 December 2015.

[73] Item 36.1 of Decree of the Plenum of the RF Supreme Court No. 24 of 9 July 2013.

[74] *Id.* Item 36.2 and Article 47(3) of the Criminal Code.

[75] *Available at*: http://www.cdep.ru/index.php?id=150 (accessed on 17 December 2018).

imposed a fine as an additional punishment; 107 sentences included disqualification from certain positions or certain activities as the principal punishment, and 1,174 disqualified the offender as an additional punishment.

8. Related Criminal Offenses

8.1 CONSPIRACY

Conspiracy does not constitute a separate crime in Russian criminal law but it is usually an aggravating circumstance. The doctrine defines conspiracy as the mutual agreement of accomplices to commit a crime. Conspiracy can be in verbal or any other form, for example, by gesture.

Conspiracy is a feature of the three forms of criminal complicity set down in the Criminal Code: (1) the commission of a crime by a group of persons in a conspiracy, (2) the commission of a crime by an organized group, and (3) the commission of a crime by a criminal community (criminal organization). If a crime is committed with complicity, the offender is subject to a severe penalty.

8.2 ATTEMPTS

The Criminal Code establishes criminal liability for preparing for a crime and attempting a crime. Preparation for a crime is defined as an individual's looking for, manufacturing, or adapting means or instruments for committing a crime; finding accomplices for a crime; conspiring to commit a crime or any other deliberate creation of the conditions for committing a crime, where the crime was not committed by reason of circumstances beyond the individual's control. Only preparing to commit a grave or particularly grave crime is criminally punishable (for definitions of grave and particularly grave crimes see Section 2.1).

Attempting a crime is defined as deliberate actions or omissions by an individual that are aimed directly at committing a crime, where the crime was not committed by reason of circumstances beyond the individual's control. Attempt is criminally punishable irrespective of the gravity of the crime that the offender attempted to commit, although the length or amount of the penalty must not exceed three-quarters of the length or amount of the stiffest penalty that the Criminal Code provides for the crime that was attempted.

If a public official or a person exercising management functions at a commercial or other organization has declined to accept a bribe, the person who attempted to give the bribe will be criminally liable for attempt to bribe or to be an intermediary in bribery. If bribery or commercial bribery was not actually committed by reason of circumstances beyond the control of the individuals who attempted to give or accept the bribe, these actions are also classed as an attempt to give or accept a bribe or be an intermediary in bribery.[76]

---

[76] Paragraph 12 of Decree of the Plenum of the RF Supreme Court No. 24 of 9 July 2013.

8.3 AIDING AND ABETTING

In Russia a crime may be committed with complicity, that is, due to the deliberate joint participation of two or more individuals in committing a deliberate crime. Aiding and abetting are two types of criminal complicity in Russian law (which also has the concepts of organizer and actor).

According to the Criminal Code, an abettor is an individual who incites another individual to commit a crime by persuasion, bribery, duress, or in any other way.[77]

According to the Criminal Code, an aider is an individual who:

(a) procures the commission of a crime through advice, instructions, the provision of information, means or instruments for committing the crime or the removal of obstacles to the crime,

(b) promises beforehand to conceal the offender, means and instruments of the commission of the crime, traces of the crime or objects criminally obtained, or

(c) promises beforehand to acquire or sell objects criminally obtained.[78]

Criminal liability for aiding and abetting depends on the nature of the crime and the actual involvement of the aider or abettor in the crime.

8.4 MONEY LAUNDERING

The Criminal Code establishes criminal liability for the legalization (laundering) of the proceeds of crime committed by other persons and by the offender himself.[79]

In the Criminal Code, the legalization (laundering) of the proceeds of crime is defined as the performance of financial operations and other transactions involving monetary funds or other assets obtained by illegal means in order to impart a legitimate appearance to the possession, use, and disposal of the monetary funds or other assets.

The maximum penalty for legalizing (laundering) the proceeds of crime in an amount exceeding RUB 6 million (approximately U.S. $91,000) is imprisonment for up to seven years, with or without (1) a fine equal to RUB 1 million (approximately U.S. $15,150) or the salary or other income of the convicted person for a period up to five years, or (2) deprivation of liberty for up to three years, or (3) disqualification from certain positions or certain activities for up to five years.

8.5 FALSE ACCOUNTING

The Criminal Code establishes criminal liability for false accounting[80] by certain financial institutions, such as lending institutions (e.g., banks), insurance companies, and professional securities market participants. The maximum penalty for this crime is imprisonment for up

---

[77] Article 33(4) of the Criminal Code.
[78] Article 33(5) of the Criminal Code.
[79] Articles 174 and 174.1 of the Criminal Code.
[80] Article 172.1 of the Criminal Code.

to four years, with or without disqualification from certain positions or certain activities for up to three years.

The falsification of accounts and other documents is a crime if the actions in question were taken when there were signs of bankruptcy and caused significant damage (in an amount exceeding RUB 2,250,000 (approximately U.S. $34,000)).[81] However, actions like this can also be classed as an administrative offense if, for example, the damage is less than RUB 2,250,000 (approximately U.S. $34,000), under Article 14.13 of the Administrative Offenses Code. Some other violations of accounting law can lead to administrative liability (Article 15.11 of the Administrative Offenses Code).

8.6 OTHER CORRUPTION-RELATED OFFENSES

As a matter of Russian law, other corruption-related offenses include bribery in public procurement,[82] i.e.:

(1) bribe-giving / bribe-taking in relation to the following persons representing interests of the customer in the procurement of goods, services or works for state or municipal needs:
(a) contracting service employees,
(b) contracting administrators,
(c) persons responsible for the acceptance of goods, services or works and
(d) other authorized representatives.
The offense here is acting (or omitting to act) in the interests of a bribe-giver or other person in connection with the procurement of goods, services or works for state or municipal needs (in the absence of elements of the offense of bribery[83] or commercial bribery[84]).
The maximum penalty for giving a bribe in public procurement is imprisonment for up to eight years, with or without a fine of 40 times the value of the bribe and / or disqualification from certain positions or certain activities for up to five years.
(2) The maximum penalty for accepting a bribe in public procurement is imprisonment for up to 12 years, with or without a fine of 50 times the value of the bribe and / or disqualification from certain positions or certain activities for up to seven years incitement of a bribe in public procurement.

Other corruption-related offenses in Russian law may include, depending on circumstances, fraud (in different sectors, e.g., credit and insurance fraud)[85] and abuse of powers (by public officials and the management of commercial organizations).[86]

---

[81] Article 195 of the Criminal Code.
[82] Articles 200.5 and 304 of the Criminal Code.
[83] Articles 290 and 291 of the Criminal Code.
[84] Article 204 of the Criminal Code.
[85] Articles 159 and 159.1–159.6 of the Criminal Code.
[86] Articles 201 and 286 of the Criminal Code.

In practice, if the law enforcement authorities are not able to prove all of the elements of bribery (that an official accepted a bribe relating to the performance of his/her duties or a person accepted a bribe relating to the performance of administrative duties, etc.), which is not always a straightforward exercise, they can reclassify the crime as fraud or abuse of power.

The maximum penalty for fraud in an amount exceeding RUB 1 million (approximately U.S. $15,150) is imprisonment for up to 10 years, with or without (1) a fine equal to RUB 1 million (approximately U.S. $15,150) or the convicted person's salary or other income for a period of up to three years, or (2) deprivation of liberty for up to two years.

The maximum penalty for abuse of power by public officials and in commercial organizations if it has had severe consequences is imprisonment for up to 10 years together with disqualification from certain positions or certain activities for up to 3 years.

9. Cooperation and Self-Reporting
9.1 POWERS OF INVESTIGATORS AND PROSECUTORS

The Criminal Procedure Code gives investigators broad powers in the investigation of criminal cases. They are empowered to conduct preliminary enquiries (the stage that precedes the official opening of a criminal case), to open a criminal case, to terminate a criminal case, to direct the course of the investigation themselves and to decide whether to take investigative or other procedural action (with a few exceptions, e.g., when a court judgment is required).[87]

Prosecutors are also actively involved in criminal proceedings. However, they are mainly empowered to monitor compliance with the law by investigators, enquiries agencies, and bodies conducting operational-search activities; and to represent the state in the criminal proceedings in court.[88] Prosecutors are empowered, among other things, to:[89]

(a) Oversee compliance with federal statutory requirements regarding the acceptance, registration, and consideration of reports of crimes;
(b) Approve an indictment (a document prepared by the investigator after the pretrial investigation) if there is sufficient evidence of a crime; and
(c) Consider a motion to enter into a pretrial cooperation agreement and an investigator's decree on the matter, to enter into a pretrial cooperation agreement, and to issue a decree amending or terminating such an agreement.

Importantly, from September 2007, the powers of prosecutors were substantially restricted: prosecutors are no longer entitled to personally conduct investigations or participate in investigative actions.

---

[87] Article 38(2) of the Criminal Procedure Code.
[88] Article 1(2) of Federal Law No. 2202-1 of 17 January 1992 on the Public Prosecutor's Office of the Russian Federation.
[89] Article 37(2) of the Criminal Procedure Code.

9.2 COOPERATION WITH INVESTIGATORS AND PROSECUTORS

Russian criminal procedural law does not specifically impose an obligation to cooperate with investigators and prosecutors. However, an individual may be summoned for interrogation by an investigator in the course of a criminal case, in which case, the individual is obliged to appear before the investigator and answer the investigator's questions; otherwise he/she may be detained or subjected to other coercive measures.[90] Witnesses and injured parties may be held criminally liable if they refuse to provide evidence for the investigator or knowingly give false evidence,[91] although a person is entitled to refuse to give evidence against him/herself, a spouse, or close relatives.[92]

If an accused person actively assists in the investigation, including in the tracing of illegally obtained property, etc., the court has to take this into consideration as a mitigating circumstance when imposing sentencing.[93] As a rule, in such cases, the accused should not be sentenced to a penalty that exceeds two-thirds of the maximum penalty established by the Criminal Code (if there are no aggravating circumstances). Please see also Section 9.4.

9.3 SELF-REPORTING

Self-reporting[94] is defined as a voluntary report by an individual (i.e., not because he/she has been detained on suspicion of a crime) of a crime committed by him/her or with his/her participation, given in writing or orally.[95]

The Criminal Code establishes that self-reporting is a mitigating circumstance. As a rule, in such cases, the accused should not be subject to a penalty that exceeds two-thirds of the maximum penalty established by the Criminal Code (if there are no aggravating circumstances).[96]

Self-reporting should also be treated as a condition that can exempt an individual from criminal liability for corruption-related offenses (*see* Sections 4.6.1, 5.6.1, and 6.5.1).

9.4 PLEA AGREEMENTS

Russian criminal procedural law does not include the concept of a plea agreement. However, the Criminal Procedure Code gives the accused the opportunity to enter into a pretrial cooperation agreement with the prosecutor.

---

[90] Article 188(3) of the Criminal Procedure Code.

[91] Articles 307 and 308 of the Criminal Code.

[92] Note to Article 308 of the Criminal Code.

[93] Article 61(1)(i) of the Criminal Code.

[94] *Id.*

[95] Article 142(1) and (2) of the Criminal Procedure Code and Item 29 of Decree of the Plenum of the RF Supreme Court No. 58 of 22 December 2015.

[96] Articles 62(1) and 64 of the Criminal Code.

The accused is entitled to file a motion with the prosecutor asking to enter into a pretrial agreement, between the time that the criminal prosecution is commenced and the time that the preliminary investigation is completed.[97]

A pretrial cooperation agreement may be amended or terminated by the prosecutor if, among other things, the accused reports only his/her own participation in the crime or gives information that was already known to the law enforcement authorities.[98]

A case against an accused person who has entered into a pretrial agreement is tried through a special, expedited process (without, inter alia, a preliminary hearing or the examination and evaluation of evidence) if the court ascertains that (1) the prosecutor has confirmed that the accused has complied with the terms of the pretrial agreement, and (2) the pretrial agreement was entered into voluntarily and with the participation of a defense attorney.[99]

If the accused enters into a pretrial agreement in addition to self-reporting, active assistance in the investigation, etc., the penalty may not exceed half the most severe penalty established by the Criminal Code.[100] At the court's discretion, the accused may be sentenced to a less severe penalty, given a conditional sentence, or released from serving his/her sentence.[101]

9.5 LENIENCY

As a matter of Russian law, the jury can decide that the court should show leniency. However, a jury can only be involved in a very limited number of cases, and that list does not include corruption-related offenses.

The Criminal Code also establishes mitigating factors (e.g., the accused is a minor or pregnant, or has self-reported) that should be taken into account when sentencing.[102] The list of these mitigating factors is not exhaustive. There can also be leniency if the accused has entered into a pretrial cooperation agreement or has pleaded guilty.

Under certain circumstances (e.g., self-reporting or active cooperation with investigators), an individual may be released from criminal liability for corruption-related offenses (*see* Sections 4.6.1, 5.6.1, and 6.5.1).

10. Whistle-Blower Protection
10.1 PUBLIC SECTOR WHISTLE-BLOWER PROTECTIONS

Currently there is no special regulation of protection for whistle-blowers in Russia. However, there are general provisions on state protective measures that may apply

---

[97] Article 317.1(2) of the Criminal Procedure Code.

[98] Article 317.4(5) of the Criminal Procedure Code.

[99] Article 317.6(2) of the Criminal Procedure Code.

[100] Article 62(2) of the Criminal Code.

[101] Article 317.7(5) of the Criminal Procedure Code.

[102] Article 61 of the Criminal Code.

to (1) injured persons, witnesses, and other parties to criminal proceedings;[103] and (2) judges and public officials from the law enforcement authorities or supervising authorities.[104]

State and municipal employees are obliged to report to their employer, the prosecutor's office, or another state authority if they have been approached for the purpose of inciting them to commit a corruption-related offense.[105] Also, there is a general concept that such employees and those who have reported cases in which other public or municipal officials have committed corruption-related offenses or have provided untrue or incomplete details of income and assets must be protected by the state. However, to date, state protection covers injured persons, witnesses, other parties to criminal proceedings, judges, and public officials from the law enforcement authorities and supervising authorities only. A draft law envisaging state protection for state and municipal employees if they report corruption-related offenses is still pending in the Russian State Duma.

10.2 PRIVATE-SECTOR WHISTLE-BLOWER PROTECTIONS

There are no specific rules regarding protection for private-sector whistle-blowers. A whistle-blower may enjoy state protection only if he/she is a party to the criminal proceedings (see Section 10.1). A draft law establishing state protection for private-sector employees reporting corruption-related offenses is currently being reviewed by the Russian State Duma.

11. Key International Treaties Relating to Bribery and Corruption
11.1 OECD

On February 1, 2012, Russia became party to the OECD Convention. As matters now stand, Russia is still not a member of the OECD but it is, from time to time, subjected to a peer review process by the OECD Working Group on Bribery (see Section 2.4.1).

11.2 UNITED NATIONS

The United Nations conventions relating to corruption to which Russia is party include the UN Convention against Corruption (ratified on March 8, 2006, without reservations), the United Nations Convention against Transnational Organized Crime of 15 November 2000 (ratified on April 26, 2004, without reservations), and the International Convention for the Suppression of the Financing of Terrorism of 9 December 1999 (ratified on July 10, 2002, without reservations).

---

[103] Federal Law No. 119-FZ of 20 August 2004 on State Protection of Injured Persons, Witnesses and Other Parties to Criminal Proceedings.

[104] Federal Law No. 45-FZ of 20 April 1995 on State Protection for Judges and Public Officials from Law Enforcement Authorities and Supervising Authorities.

[105] Article 9(1) of the Anti-Corruption Law.

On July 25, 2006, Russia ratified the Criminal Law Convention on Corruption of 27 January 1999 without reservations and automatically became a member of the Group of States Against Corruption (GRECO), which, inter alia, monitors its members' compliance with Council of Europe anti-corruption standards.

The Council of Europe Convention on Laundering, Search, Seizure and Confiscation of the Proceeds from Crime of 8 November 1990 was ratified by Russia on May 28, 2001, with certain reservations in relation to confiscation.

The Council of Europe Convention on Laundering, Search, Seizure and Confiscation of the Proceeds from Crime and on the Financing of Terrorism of 16 May 2005 was ratified by Russia on September 28, 2017, with a number of reservations, including reservations concerning the application of confiscation measures only in relation to certain crimes in the Criminal Code and the adoption of legislation requiring offenders to demonstrate the origin of alleged proceeds or other property liable to confiscation.

12. Mutual Legal Assistance Treaties and Transnational Cooperation

The international legal framework for transnational cooperation between the Russian courts and law enforcement authorities and foreign competent authorities on criminal issues comprises, among other things:

(a)   the European Convention on Mutual Assistance in Criminal Matters (Strasbourg, April 20, 1959), ratified by Russia on October 25, 1999;

(b)   the European Convention on Extradition (Paris, December 13, 1957), ratified by Russia on October 26, 1999;

(c)   the European Convention on the Transfer of Proceedings in Criminal Matters (Strasbourg, May 15, 1972), ratified by Russia on October 30, 2007;

(d)   the Convention on the Transfer of Sentenced Persons (Strasbourg, March 21, 1983), ratified by Russia on August 28, 2007; and

(e)   the Minsk Convention on Legal Assistance and Legal Relations in Civil, Family and Criminal Matters (Minsk, January 22, 1993), ratified by Russia on August 4, 1994.

The Russian Federation also has numerous bilateral international agreements on legal assistance in criminal matters. For instance, on June 17, 1999, it entered into the Agreement on Mutual Legal Assistance in Criminal Matters with the United States of America.

The Russian law enforcement authorities cooperate with foreign authorities in criminal matters by entering into multiagency agreements. There are many such agreements, entered into by the RF Ministry of Internal Affairs, the RF General Prosecutor's Office, the RF Investigative Committee, and other authorities.

Russia is a member of the International Criminal Police Organization (INTERPOL) and an INTERPOL National Central Bureau for Russia has been established.

Also, where there is no international agreement, legal assistance in criminal matters can be sought and provided on the basis of reciprocity.[106]

13. Legal Professional Privilege

13.1 GENERAL PRINCIPLES

Generally, Russian law does not provide for legal professional privilege. The closest concept in Russian law is "advocate secrecy." According to Federal Law No. 63-FZ of 31 May 2002 on Advocacy and the Bar in the Russian Federation ("Advocacy Law") and the Code of Professional Ethics for Advocates,[107] advocates cannot be asked to produce information and documents obtained in the course of rendering legal services to their clients; this right is unwaivable.[108]

An advocate may not be interrogated as a witness regarding circumstances that became known to him/her while rendering legal services to his or her client. Operational-search activities and investigative actions may be conducted against an advocate (including searches of residential and business premises occupied by an advocate for his or her professional activities) by court order only.

Advocate secrecy applies only to advocates, that is, to lawyers who have qualified and been registered as attorneys with the Russian registry of Russian advocates. A breach of advocate secrecy can lead to a number of sanctions, including removal from the registry of advocates.

Advocate secrecy does not apply to clients of advocates, who may be asked to produce documents and information and any advice obtained from the advocate.

14. Privacy and Data Protection

14.1 PERSONAL DATA

Personal data protection is mainly regulated by Federal Law No. 152-FZ of 27 July 2006 on Personal Data (the "Personal Data Law").

The Personal Data Law sets out only the general principle for determining what personal data is: information that directly or indirectly concerns an individual.[109] According to the practice of the Russian courts and state authorities, personal data comprises but is not limited to an individual's forename(s), surname, date of birth, and ID details, as well as the terms of their employment, for example, job title, salary, and other payments.

The Personal Data Law applies, among other things, to persons (individuals, companies, etc.) that "process personal data." The "processing of personal data" includes, among other things, obtaining, recording, systematizing, compiling, storing, modifying (updating, amending), extracting, using, transferring (disseminating, furnishing, providing access to), anonymizing, blocking, deleting, and destroying personal data.[110]

---

[106] Articles 453, 457, 460, 462, and 469 of the Criminal Procedure Code.

[107] The Code of Professional Ethics for Advocates was adopted by the 1st Russian Congress of Advocates on 31 January 2003.

[108] Articles 6(4)(5) and 8 of the Advocacy Law.

[109] Article 3 of the Personal Data Law.

[110] *Id.*

Those who process personal data must keep this data confidential and must not disseminate it or give third parties access to it without the individual's consent.[111] Such consent (amongst other things) must stipulate the purpose for which the personal data may be processed.[112]

Also, as a rule, when collecting personal data (e.g., via the internet), persons who process personal data are obliged to ensure that the personal data of Russian citizens is recorded, systematized, compiled, stored, modified (updated, amended), and extracted using databases located on the territory of Russia.[113]

The Personal Data Law sets down certain cases in which an individual's consent might not be required for personal data to be processed.[114] For example, an individual's personal data may be processed without his/her consent where it is necessary in connection with the individual's participation in criminal court proceedings.[115]

Failure to comply with the Personal Data Law can result in criminal, administrative, and civil liability.

14.2 SECRECY OF CORRESPONDENCE

The secrecy of correspondence is a fundamental right guaranteed by the Russian Constitution[116] and Federal Law No. 126-FZ of 7 July 2003 On Communications (the "Communications Law").[117]

These secrecy of correspondence provisions guarantee privacy of correspondence, telephone conversations, and postal, telegraph, and other communications.[118] According to Russian court practice, both the content of communications and information about the addressees must be protected.

The right to secrecy of correspondence may be restricted only in the cases established by law (see Section 14.4).

Violations of secrecy of correspondence are criminally punishable.

14.3 INTERNAL INVESTIGATIONS

The rules on personal data protection and secrecy of correspondence mentioned in Sections 14.1 and 14.2 also apply to the conduct of internal investigations.

14.4 EXTERNAL INVESTIGATIONS

The rules on personal data protection and secrecy of correspondence mentioned in Sections 14.1 and 14.2 apply to the conduct of external investigations, with certain exceptions, including the following.

---

[111] Article 7 of the Personal Data Law.
[112] Article 9(4) of the Personal Data Law.
[113] Article 18(5) of the Personal Data Law.
[114] Article 6 of the Personal Data Law.
[115] Article 6(1)(3) of the Personal Data Law.
[116] Article 23 of the RF Constitution.
[117] Article 63 of the Communications Law.
[118] Article 63(1) of the Communications Law.

An individual's personal data may be processed without his/her consent in connection with the individual's participation in constitutional, civil, administrative, or criminal court proceedings or proceedings in the *arbitrazh* (state commercial) courts.[119]

The authorities conducting criminal proceedings and/or operational-search activities may restrict an individual's right to secrecy of correspondence under a court judgment.[120]

15. Forecast for Reforms

15.1 LEGISLATIVE REFORMS

Recent legislative initiatives include draft laws[121] that are currently pending before the Russian State Duma, aimed (amongst other things) at aligning the Criminal Code with the GRECO recommendations. These bills, if adopted, would incorporate the following amendments into the Criminal Code:

(a) stiffening criminal liability for corruption-related offenses by:

    (i) establishing criminal liability for the following offenses: (1) commercial bribery committed by or in relation to an employee of a commercial or other organisation, (2) promising, proposing or requesting participation in commercial bribery, (3) a promise, proposal or request for a bribe to be taken or given and (4) abuse of influence in return for unlawful remuneration; and

    (ii) extending the maximum main penalty for accepting and giving a bribe[122] from three and two years' imprisonment, respectively, to four years' imprisonment, where there are no special aggravating circumstances and the bribe does not exceed RUB 25,000 (approximately U.S. $380). The amendments would, if adopted, reclassify these crimes, now minor offenses, as moderately serious offenses and, therefore, extend the limitation period for criminal prosecution from two years to six years.

(b) criminalizing the giving and taking of intangible bribes (in Russian: *nematerialniye vzyatki*) by broadening the definitions of bribery and commercial bribery; and

(c) criminalizing commercial bribery committed by Russian and foreign arbitrators.

At the moment, the Russian State Duma is also considering a bill of amendments to the Anti-Corruption Law that would introduce measures to protect employees who report corruption offenses.[123]

---

[119] Article 6(1)(3) of the Personal Data Law.

[120] Articles 13 and 186 of the Criminal Procedure Code and Articles 6, 8, and 9 of Federal Law No. 144- FZ of 12 August 1995 on Operational-Search Activities.

[121] *Available at* http://sozd.parlament.gov.ru/bill/235984-7 and http://sozd.parliament.gov.ru/bill/232807-7 (accessed on 17 December 2018).

[122] Articles 290(1) and 291(1) of the Criminal Code.

[123] *Available at* http://sozd.parlament.gov.ru/bill/286313-7 (accessed on 17 December 2018).

15.2 POLITICAL AND AGENCY ENFORCEMENT WILL

Recent years have seen a general trend in enforcement characterized by the Russian law enforcement authorities' focusing on investigating corruption offenses committed by public officials, rather than in commercial sectors. A number of such investigations have been extensively covered in the media (see Section 1.2). In line with this trend, there has also been an increase in the verification of data on the income, material liabilities, expenditures, etc. of public officials and certain of their close relatives, with the materials from such verification exercises being provided to the law enforcement authorities if violations are identified.

APPENDIX

Key issues	Russia's Approach
Is Russia subject to any international anti-corruption conventions? If so, which? (OECD, UN Convention against Corruption, etc.)	Yes. See Sections 1.1, 2.4, and 11.
Is bribing foreign public officials illegal? Do domestic anti-bribery laws apply extraterritorially?	Yes. Yes, to a limited extent.
What is the definition of a foreign public official?	A "*foreign public official*" is an individual who holds legislative, executive, administrative, or judicial office in a foreign country, whether appointed or elected, and any person who exercises duties of a public office of a foreign country, including at a public agency or public enterprise.
Is commercial bribery illegal?	Yes.
Is bribing domestic officials illegal?	Yes.
Can the recipient of a bribe be prosecuted?	Yes.
Can companies be held criminally liable? If so, what is the requisite intent for corporate criminal liability?	No, but they may be subject to administrative liability (see Section 2.3).
Can companies be held civilly liable?	Yes. As discussed in Section 2.3, administrative liability may also be available.
Can an individual be held civilly liable?	Yes.
If there a "facilitation payment" defense?	No.

Key issues	Russia's Approach
Do conspiracy laws apply to anti-corruption offenses?	Yes.
Does Russia impose: a) aiding and/or abetting liability and/or b) attempt liability relating to violations of anti-corruption laws?	Yes.
Is the failure to keep accurate books and records a criminal or civil offense?	There is criminal and administrative liability for offenses that include the falsification of books and records (see Section 8.5).
Do any books and records offenses require proof of an underlying bribery offense?	No.
Are there Russian laws concerning a company's financial internal controls? If so, are those laws applicable to public and/or private companies?	Yes. These laws are applicable to both private and public companies.
Is there an affirmative disclosure obligation for potential violations of anti-corruption laws or accounting irregularities?	No.
Are "promotional expenses" exempt from Russia's anti-corruption laws?	There is no specific exemption under Russian law for promotional expenses. Each payment must be assessed using the criteria for corruption offenses, whether criminal or administrative.
Is the giving of gifts, entertainment, travel, meals, or other gratuities restricted or prohibited by anti-corruption or other laws?	Yes, to a limited extent.
Are there any Russian laws concerning things, property, or benefits of value conveyed by or to third parties?	Yes.
Are bribes tax deductible?	No.
Is Russia's anti-corruption law applied extraterritorially?	Yes, to a limited extent.

(Continued)

Key issues	Russia's Approach
Is having a robust corporate compliance program an affirmative defence or a factor to negate liability or reduce penalties?	If an entity is charged with an administrative offense, it may be a defense to show that it has taken all possible and reasonable steps to prevent the offense and comply with the relevant statutory requirements.
Is there a "local law" exception or defense to Russia's anti-corruption laws?	No, each payment must be assessed using the criteria for corruption offenses, whether criminal or administrative. Regarding available defenses, please see Sections 4.6.1, 5.6.1, and 6.5.1.
Is "credit" given for cooperation with the authorities? If so, how and in what form?	Yes, see Sections 9.2, 9.3, 9.4, and 9.5.
Does Russia have a Mutual Legal Assistance Treaty with the United States that generally covers criminal matters, including the FCPA?	There is the Agreement on Mutual Legal Assistance in Criminal Matters, which the Russian Federation and the United States of America entered into on June 17, 1999.
What are the potential penalties/sanctions for criminal and civil violations of Russia's anti-corruption laws?	The maximum criminal penalty for individuals is imprisonment for up to 15 years, with or without a fine equal to 70 times the value of the bribe and/or disqualification from certain positions or certain activities for up to 15 years (see Sections 4.7, 5.7, and 6.6). The maximum administrative penalty for legal entities is a fine equal to 100 times the value of the bribe (but not less than RUB 100 million (approximately U.S. $1.5 million)), accompanied by confiscation of the money, securities, or other assets that constituted the bribe. As regards civil penalties, individuals and legal entities may be obliged to reimburse damages.

14 South Africa

1. Introduction to South African Anti-Corruption Landscape

Before understanding the South African legal regime regarding bribery and anti-corruption, it is vitally important to understand how the South African legal regime operates as well as the hierarchy of law in South Africa.[1]

South Africa is one of the few countries in the world in which criminal law has not been set out in a single uniform Act of Parliament or code.

Accordingly, South African criminal law is sourced from three avenues, namely:

(a) Legislation (Act's and Regulations of Parliament duly promulgated);
(b) case law; and
(c) the common law.

During apartheid, South Africa was a parliamentary sovereign nation, and a court's powers were limited to interpreting statutes adopted by Parliament. However, since democracy was attained on April 27, 1994, and when Nelson Mandela became South Africa's first democratically elected president, South Africa became a constitutional democracy, which means that all laws must comply with the provisions of the Constitution of the Republic of South Africa (the "Constitution"). This naturally is also applicable to legislation governing criminal law.

---

[1] This chapter was contributed by Hogan Lovells's Vaughn Harrison and Nikhil Bhogal.

From Baksheesh to Bribery. T. Markus Funk and Andrew S. Boutros.
© Oxford University Press 2019. Published 2019 by Oxford University Press.

Further, South Africa's common law originates from Roman Dutch Law, which has, over a number of years, been adopted and reinforced by the South African judiciary. This is of significant importance as the Constitution provides that a court of law is to follow the principle of judicial precedent when adjudicating cases (there are, however, a number of exceptions to this rule, such as where the decision of the court *a quo* is manifestly wrong).

2. South Africa's Domestic Anti-Corruption framework

2.1 CRIMINAL LAW REGIME

In South Africa, criminal law emanates from three sources, namely common law, case law, and statute.

As with all common law jurisdictions, common law offenses can be varied, or abolished, by statute, and, for example, the common law offense of bribery was repealed by the Corruption Act 94 of 1992 (the "Corruption Act"), which created a new offense of corruption. The Corruption Act was subsequently repealed by the Prevention and Combating of Corrupt Activities Act 12 of 2004, as amended ("PRECCA").

Further, criminal prosecutions are generally a public affair, and a crime committed against an individual is considered a crime against the state; hence, in criminal law cases, the citation of the court *a quo* will always be styled as the *"State v. [Name of the Defendant]."*

Although South Africa does not have a unified Act of Parliament catering to the substantive aspects of criminal law, the procedural aspects are governed in terms of the Criminal Procedure Act 51 of 1977.

In order to secure a conviction, evidence presented by the prosecution must be of such a nature as to be *"beyond a reasonable doubt"* that the defendant committed the crime in question.

South Africa's jury system was abolished in 1969 by the Abolition of Juries Act and all trials are concluded before either a judge of the High Court or a magistrate of a district court, or a regional magistrate of a regional court, all depending on the severity of the offense committed.

2.2 CIVIL LAW REGIME

South Africa's civil law elements were introduced as a result of its colonial history, but can best be described as a hybrid between common law, statute, and judicial precedent.

Civil liability may arise in many forms such as a breach of a legal or contractual duty. Where one has been found to have committed a civil wrong, such person is said to have committed a "delict," also known as a tort in other jurisdictions.

It is commonly recognized that an actionable wrong or delict has five elements or requirements, namely:

    (a) the commission or omission of an act (actus reus);
    (b) which is unlawful or wrongful (wrongfulness);
    (c) Committed negligently or with a particular intent (*culpa* or fault);
    (d) which results in or causes the harm (causation); and
    (e) the suffering of injury, loss, or damage (harm).

Unlike criminal law, each court has its own procedure with respect to civil litigation.

2.3 VIEW FROM THE OUTSIDE—OECD EVALUATION

As with all participants to the Organisation for Economic Co-operation and Development (OECD) Convention on Combatting Bribery of Foreign Public Officials in International Business Transaction (the "OECD Convention"), South Africa subjected itself to three OECD reviews. The three substantive reviews were as follows:

(a) Phase 1 (June 2008)—Review of the implementation of the OECD Convention and 1997 revised recommendations;

(b) Phase 2 (July 2010)—Report on the application of the OECD Convention on Combatting Bribery of Foreign Public Officials in International Business Transactions and the 2009 recommendation for Further Combatting Bribery of Foreign Public Officials in International Business Transactions; and

(c) Phase 3 (March 2014)—Report on Implementing the OECD Anti-Bribery Convention in South Africa.

The Phase 3 report was highly critical of South Africa, noting that South Africa was required to take urgent steps to proactively investigate and prosecute foreign bribery. As of the date of the report, no foreign bribery cases had been prosecuted since South Africa joined the OECD Convention in 2007.

The OECD Working Group on Bribery made some of the following recommendations to improve South Africa's fight against foreign bribery:

(a) Significantly increase efforts to proactively detect, investigate, and prosecute foreign bribery;

(b) Ensure that national economic interests and identities of natural or legal persons involved do not influence the investigation or prosecution of foreign bribery cases;

(c) Increase the financial resources available to law enforcement agencies;

(d) Ensure enhanced cooperation between the police and prosecutors; and

(e) To urgently raise awareness that people who report suspected acts of foreign bribery are in practice afforded the protections guaranteed by law.

The Phase 3 report, however, also highlighted several other positive aspects regarding South Africa's fight against foreign bribery. This included South Africa's well-drafted corruption legislation, and broad and flexible corporate liability regime, as well as additional steps taken to strengthen public-listed and state-owned enterprises internal controls, and ethics, and compliance measures for the purpose of both detecting and preventing foreign bribery.

2.4 VIEW FROM THE OUTSIDE—TRANSPARENCY INTERNATIONAL CORRUPTION PERCEPTION INDEX SCORE

Corruption is not a problem unique to South Africa, but it is one of the country's major challenges.

Although South Africa slightly improved its score in the Corruption Perceptions Index (CPI) for 2016, as published in January 2017, from 44 to 45, South Africa's rank with regard to CPI fell from 61 to 64, in relation to all 176 countries under review.

Transparency International notes that this is concerning as a score below 50 signifies that such a country is a country with a corruption problem.

Further, Transparency International's 2013 Global Corruption Barometer reflected that 47 percent of South African respondents had paid a bribe in that year to a public or police official.

3. Investigative and Prosecutorial Agency

The South African Police Service (SAPS) is the first avenue of redress where one is to report an issue pertaining to any crime. Also forming a part of the SAPS is a specialist body established by the South African Government, being the police's directorate for priority crime investigations, otherwise known as the "Hawks."

In addition to the SAPS and Hawks, the Special Investigations Unit (SIU) and the Asset Forfeiture Unit (AFU) are creatures of statute specifically mandated to investigate organized crime and money laundering.

The National Prosecuting Authority (NPA), South Africa's centralized prosecuting authority, is mandated to prosecute individuals on behalf of the state.

The Anti-Corruption Inter-Ministerial Committee (ACIMC), *at an executive level,* exercises oversight over all public and private sector anti-corruption initiatives and comprises the following nine cabinet ministers, whose portfolios directly contribute to combatting corruption:

(a) The Minister of Justice and Correctional Services;
(b) The Minister of State Security;
(c) The Minister of Police;
(d) The Minister of Co-operative Governance and Traditional Affairs;
(e) The Minister of Public Service and Administration;
(f) The Minister of Finance;
(g) The Minister of Home Affairs;
(h) The Minister of Social Development; and
(i) The Minister for Planning, Monitoring and Evaluation in the Presidency.

At an *operational level,* working under the oversight of the ACIMC, the Anti-Corruption Task Team (ACTT) has been established as the central body to implement the government's anti-corruption strategy.

The South African Reserve Bank (SARB) (the South African equivalent of the American Central Bank or Federal Reserve Bank) is mandated to supervise the South African banking financial sector as well as administering and enforcing exchange control policies and local currency.

Although SARB supervises the banking financial sector, the Financial Services Board (FSB) is responsible for supervising the nonbanking financial services sector such as pension funds, collective investment schemes, and the insurance sectors. In the event of any contravention, the FSB's enforcement committee has the necessary enforcement powers to ensure compliance.

The Auditor-General of South Africa (AGSA) is one of South Africa's "Chapter 9 Institutions." All Chapter 9 Institutions are guaranteed independence and are subject only to the Constitution and the law and must be impartial while exercising their power, without fear, favor, or prejudice. The AGSA is appointed by the South African Parliament and has its independence guaranteed by the Constitution. As a Chapter 9 Institution, the AGSA is accountable to the National Assembly and must report on their activities and the performance of its functions to the National Assembly at least once a year. In fulfilling its reporting obligation to Parliament, AGSA does so through the Standing Committee on Public Accounts (SCOPA).

AGSA is constitutionally mandated, and obliged, to audit and report on the accounts, financial statements, and financial management of:

(a) national and provincial state departments and administrations;
(b) all municipalities; and
(c) any other institution or accounting entity required by national or provincial legislation to be audited by the AGSA.

The South African Revenue Service (SARS) (the South African equivalent of the American Internal Revenue Service (IRS) is tasked with collecting tax revenues and ensuring compliance with South African tax laws. SARS has a specialized task team that works in collaboration with both local and foreign law enforcement agencies to investigate tax fraud.

Like the AGSA, the Office of the Public Protector is also a Chapter 9 institution and accordingly is afforded the same protections and guarantees of independence as the AGSA and has the power to:

(a) investigate any conduct in state affairs, or in the public administration in any sphere of government, that is alleged or suspected to be improper or to result in any impropriety or prejudice;
(b) to report on that conduct; and
(c) to take appropriate remedial action.

4. South Africa's Domestic Anti-Corruption Framework

Generally, all forms of corruption, whether domestic or commercial, are governed by PRECCA.

PRECCA was written to bring South African's legislation in line with the United Nations (UN) Convention against Corruption and the African Union (AU) Convention on Preventing and Combating Corruption.

4.1 CRIMINAL LAW REGIME

South Africa is party to a number of international agreements and conventions aimed at combatting corruption. Examples of these conventions include:

(a) The UN Convention against corruption;
(b) The AU Convention on preventing and combatting corruption;
(c) The OECD Anti-Bribery Convention; and
(d) The Southern African Development Community (SADC) Protocol against corruption.

South Africa is a dualist country, which means that there is a difference between national law and international law. International law needs to be translated into national law, and without this translation, the international law does not apply. However section 39 of the Constitution provides that when interpreting the Bill of Rights of the Constitution, a court, tribunal, or forum must consider international law; and may consider foreign law.

Arising from these various protocols and conventions, South Africa has obligations to take various steps to stamp out corruption. These include:

(a) Establishing an independent anti-corruption agency;
(b) Ensuring that steps are taken to investigate and prosecute corruption;
(c) Preventing corruption by removing the opportunities for corruption;
(d) Educating the public on the harm caused by corruption;
(e) Ensuring transparency and access to information when combatting corruption;
(f) Establishing mechanisms that encourage participation by the media, civil society, and nongovernmental organizations (NGOs) in the fight against corruption; and
(g) Adopting measures that address corruption in the public and private sectors and cooperating and assisting with other states in criminal matters.

Accordingly, and in line with South Africa's obligations in terms of the protocols and conventions discussed previously, South Africa has adopted various pieces of legislation concerning anti-corruption measures. The main anti-corruption law relevant for the purposes of this chapter is PRECCA.

PRECCA creates a general offense of corruption, which is defined in section 3 as—

Any person who, directly or indirectly—
  (a) Accepts or agrees or offers to accept any gratification from any other person, whether for the benefit of himself or herself or for the benefit of another person; or
  (b) Gives or agrees or offers to give to any other person any gratification, whether for the benefit of that other person or for the benefit of another person,
  in order to act, personally or by influencing another person so as to act, in a manner—
    (i) that amounts to the—
      (aa) illegal, dishonest, unauthorised, incomplete, or biased; or

> (bb) misuse or selling of information or material acquired in the course of the exercise, carrying out or performance of any powers, duties or functions arising out of a constitutional, statutory, contractual or any other legal obligation;
>
> (ii) that amounts to the—
>
> (aa) the abuse of a position of authority;
>
> (bb) a breach of trust; or
>
> (cc) the violation of a legal duty or a set of rules,
>
> (iii) designed to achieve an unjustified result; or
>
> (iv) that amounts to any other unauthorised or improper inducement to do or not to do anything, is guilty of the offence of corruption.

The term "gratification" is defined in the Act to include

> (a) money, whether in cash or otherwise;
>
> (b) any donation, gift, loan, fee, reward, valuable security, property or interest in property of any description, whether movable or immovable, or any other similar advantage;
>
> (c) the avoidance of a loss, liability, penalty, forfeiture, punishment or other disadvantage;
>
> (d) any office, status, honour, employment, contract of employment or services, any agreement to give employment or render services in any capacity and residential or holiday accommodation;
>
> (e) any payment, release, discharge or liquidation of any loan, obligation or other liability, whether in whole or in part;
>
> (f) any forbearance to demand any money or money's worth or valuable thing;
>
> (g) any other service or favour or advantage of any description, including protection from any penalty or disability incurred or apprehended or from any action or proceedings of a disciplinary, civil or criminal nature, whether or not already instituted, and includes the exercise or the forbearance from the exercise of any right or any official power or duty;
>
> (h) any right or privilege;
>
> (i) any real or pretended aid, vote, consent, influence or abstention from voting; or
>
> (j) any valuable consideration or benefit of any kind, including any discount, commission, rebate, bonus, deduction or percentage;

South Africa is a common law jurisdiction, and as such, when South Africa's statutes are silent on a particular area, the courts refer to the provisions of the common law.

With regard to an offeror, the offense of corruption therefore has four principle elements, namely, the act of the offeror:

(a) offering gratification (as defined); to an

(b) offeree (regardless of whether or not the offeree accepts the gratification);

(c) with the intention of such offered gratification being aimed at inducing the offeree to perform or not to perform an act or series of acts;

(d) contrary to the offeree's legal obligations to perform, or not to perform such act or series of acts.

It is worth noting that PRECCA applies to both the public and private sectors and South Africa does not have separate legislation governing these sectors.

A reference in PRECCA to any act includes an omission, and "acting" shall be construed accordingly. Further a reference in PRECCA to any person includes a person in the private sector.

The common law crime of bribery was repealed by PRECCA and a new statutory offense of corruption has accordingly been created.

Later in this chapter we will deal with the definitions of what constitutes a foreign public official, as well as a domestic public official, and the relevance of this distinction.

5. Bribery of Foreign Officials

5.1 JURISDICTION

The preamble to PRECCA provides that the purpose of PRECCA is to, inter alia, provide for extraterritorial jurisdiction with respect to the offense of corruption and offenses relating to corrupt activities.

In this regard, section 35(1) of PRECCA provides that even if the act alleged to constitute an offense under PRECCA occurred outside the borders of South Africa, a South African court will, irrespective of whether or not the act constitutes an offense at the place of its commission, have jurisdiction in respect of that offense if the person to be charged

(a) Is a South African Citizen;
(b) Is ordinarily resident in South Africa;
(c) Was arrested in South Africa;
(d) Is a company, incorporated or registered as such under any law in South Africa; or
(e) Any body of persons, corporate or unincorporated, in South Africa.

Further, section 35(2) of PRECCA provides that any act alleged to constitute an offense under PRECCA and that is committed outside the borders of South Africa by a person, other than a person contemplated in subsection (1), will, irrespective of whether or not the act constitutes an offense at the place of its commission, *be deemed to have been committed in South Africa* if that—

(a) act affects or is intended to affect a public body (as defined), a business or any other person in South Africa;
(b) such person is found to be in South Africa; *and*
(c) such person is for one or other reason not extradited by South Africa, or if there is no application to extradite that person.

Accordingly, the above three factors constitute factual inquiries, and must all be met before such an act is to be "deemed" to have occurred in South Africa.

Section 35(3) of PRECCA goes on to note that any offense committed in a country outside of South Africa as contemplated in subsections (1) or (2), is, for the purpose of determining jurisdiction of a court to try the offense, deemed to have been committed:

(a) at the place where the accused is ordinarily resident; or
(b) at the accused person's principal place of business.

5.2 STATUTE OF LIMITATIONS

South Africa does not have a statute of limitations with regard to criminal offenses.

5.3 FOREIGN BRIBERY OFFENSES

Section 5 of PRECCA provides the following:

> *(1) Any person who, directly or indirectly gives or agrees or offers to give any gratification to a foreign public official, whether for the benefit of that foreign public official or for the benefit of another person, in order to act, personally or by influencing another person so to act, in a manner—*
>> *(a) that amounts to the—*
>>> *(i) illegal, dishonest, unauthorised, incomplete, or biased; or*
>>> *(ii) misuse or selling of information or material acquired in the course of the, exercise, carrying out or performance of any powers, duties or functions arising out of a constitutional, statutory, contractual or any other legal obligation;*
>> *(b) that amounts to—*
>>> *(i) the abuse of a position of authority;*
>>> *(ii) a breach of trust; or*
>>> *(iii) the violation of a legal duty or a set of rules;*
>> *(c) designed to achieve an unjustified result; or*
>> *(d) that amounts to any other unauthorised or improper inducement to do or not to do anything,*
> *is guilty of the offence of corrupt activities relating to foreign public officials.*
> *(2) Without derogating from the generality of section 2(4), "to act" in subsection (1) includes—*
>> *(a) the using of such public official's or such other person's position to influence any acts or decisions of the foreign state or public international organisation concerned; or*
>> *(b) obtaining or retaining a contract, business or an advantage in the conduct of business of that foreign state or public international organisation.*

The term "gratification" has already been considered on the first page of this chapter.

5.4 "FOREIGN PUBLIC OFFICIALS" DEFINED

PRECCA defines the term *"Foreign Public Official"* to mean:

> *(a) any person holding a legislative, administrative or judicial office of a foreign state;*
> *(b) any person performing public functions for a foreign state, including any person employed by a board, commission, corporation or other body or authority that performs a function on behalf of the foreign state; or*
> *(c) an official or agent of a public international organization.*[2]

---

[2] Section 1 of the Prevention and Combatting of Corrupt Activities Act, 2004, as amended.

5.5 GIFTS, GRATUITIES, AND HOSPITALITY

PRECCA does not prescribe a statutory cap on corporate gifts, hospitality, and/or entertainment. However, it is important to note that the definition of *"gratuity"* does include, inter alia, gifts.

As discussed previously in this chapter, where one offers a gift without the intention of inducing improper conduct, such an offeror will not be guilty of the statutory offense of corruption.

However, offerors are discouraged from offering "gratification" or "gifts" that may be at risk of being considered as *"extravagant."*

5.6 DEFENSES

5.6.1 Written Local Law

Section 25 of PRECCA provides that where a person is charged with an offense in terms of PRECCA, it is not a valid defense for the accused person to contend that he or she

(a) did not have the power, right or opportunity to perform or not to perform the act in relation to which the gratification was given, accepted or offered; or

(b) accepted or agreed or offered to accept, or gave or agreed or offered to give gratification without intending to perform or not to perform the act in relation to which the gratification was given, accepted or offered; or

(c) failed to perform or not to perform the act in relation to which the gratification was given, accepted or offered.

5.6.2 Presumptions

Section 24(1) provides for a presumption against all persons in that this section provides that *where one is charged with the offense* of corruption, proof that that person, or someone else at the instance of that person

(a) *accepted or agreed or offered to accept any gratification from; or*

(b) *gave or agreed or offered to give any gratification to, any other person—*

(i) *who holds or seeks to obtain a contract, licence, permit, employment or anything whatsoever from a public body, private organisation, corporate body or other organisation or institution in which the person charged was serving as an official;*

(ii) *who is concerned, or who is likely to be concerned, in any proceedings or business transacted, pending or likely to be transacted before or by the person charged or public body, private organisation, corporate body, political party or other organisation or institution in which the person charged was serving as an official; or*

(iii) *who acts on behalf of a person contemplated in subparagraph (i) or (ii), and, if the State can further show that despite having taken reasonable steps, it was not able with reasonable certainty to link the acceptance of or agreement or offer to accept or the giving or agreement to give or offer to give the gratification to any lawful authority or excuse on the part of the person charged, and in the absence of evidence to the contrary which raises reasonable doubt, is sufficient evidence that the person charged accepted or agreed or offered to accept such gratification from that person or gave or agreed or offered to give such gratification to that person in order to act, in a manner—*

(aa) *that amounts to the—*

    (aaa) *illegal, dishonest, unauthorised, incomplete, or biased; or*

    (bbb) *misuse or selling of information or material acquired in the course of the, exercise, carrying out or performance of any powers, duties or functions arising out of a constitutional, statutory, contractual or any other legal obligation;*

(bb) *that amounts to—*

    (aaa) *the abuse of a position of authority;*

    (bbb) *a breach of trust; or*

    (ccc) *the violation of a legal duty or a set of rules;*

(cc) *designed to achieve an unjustified result; or*

(dd) *that amounts to any other unauthorised or improper inducement to do or not to do anything.*

Though section 24(1) of PRECCA notes this presumption, it is still for the prosecution to show beyond a reasonable doubt that the gratification was offered/accepted with the intent of inducing the defendant to act in the manner as discussed.

Section 24(2) of PRECCA caters for further presumptions against *public officers*. A *public officer* is generally any person who is a member, an officer, an employee or servant of a public body (as defined earlier in this chapter), with the exception of (1) members of parliament, (2) judges and magistrates, and (3) members of the NPA (these persons are included in section 24(1) of PRECCA).

Section 24(2) provides that where a public officer whose duties include detention, investigation, prosecution, or punishment of offenders is charged with an offense involving the acceptance of gratification, arising from

(a) the arrest, detention, investigation or prosecution of any person for an alleged offense;

(b) the omission to arrest, detain or prosecute any person for an alleged offense; or

(c) the investigation of an alleged offense.

It is not necessary for the prosecution to prove that the accused believed that an offense contemplated in paragraphs (a)–(c) or any other offense had been committed.

This section is peculiar as the definition of public officer specifically excludes members of the prosecution as well as members of the judiciary, but section 24(2) seems to contemplate members of the prosecution as well as members of the judiciary. The position is accordingly presently unclear.

5.6.3 Facilitation Payments

Though not specifically addressed in PRECCA, a facilitation payment, or *"grease payment"* would be considered as *"gratification"* under PRECCA and would likely amount to the offense of corruption under PRECCA.

5.6.4 Adequate Procedures

There is no adequate procedures defense to any domestic bribery offense in South Africa.

5.6.5 Corporate Culture

South Africa has yet to prosecute a case involving foreign bribery offenses notwithstanding South Africa's strongly drafted legislation in this regard. It is unfortunate that the enforcement mechanisms and political and corporate will to enforce such offenses is currently lacking.

5.6.6 Penalties

Section 26[3] provides that where a person is convicted of an offense of corrupt activities relating to foreign public officials under section 5 of PRECCA, such person

  (a) *in the case of a sentence to be imposed by a High Court, is subject to a fine or to imprisonment up to a period for imprisonment for life;*
  (b) *in the case of a sentence to be imposed by a regional court, is subject to a fine or to imprisonment for a period not exceeding 18 years; or*
  (c) *in the case of a sentence to be imposed by a magistrates court, is subject to a fine or to imprisonment for a period of imprisonment not exceeding 5 years.*

Further, in addition to any fine, a court may impose a fine equal to five times the value of the gratification involved in the subject offense.

6. Bribery of Domestic Officials

6.1 JURISDICTION

Courts have full jurisdiction on matters related to bribery of domestic officials, and the court first hearing the case will be determined by the geographic location of the person accused of committing an offense in terms of PRECCA.

6.2 STATUTE OF LIMITATIONS

As mentioned earlier in this chapter, South Africa does not have a statute of limitations concerning criminal offenses.

6.3 DEFINITION OF DOMESTIC OFFICIALS

PRECCA does not define the term *"Domestic Official."* However, the term *"official"* is defined to mean:

> *any director, functionary, officer or agent serving in any capacity whatsoever in a public body, private organisation, corporate body, political party, institution or other*

---

[3] Section 26 of the Prevention and Combating of Corrupt Activities Act 12 of 2004.

employment, whether under a contract of service or otherwise, and whether in an executive capacity or not.[4]

The term "*public body*" is defined to mean:

(a) any department of state administration in the national or provincial sphere of government or any municipality in the local sphere of government; or

(b) any other functionary or institution when—

  (i) exercising a power or performing a duty or function in terms of the Constitution or provincial constitution; or

  (ii) exercising a public power or performing a public duty or function in terms of any legislation.[5]

6.4 DOMESTIC BRIBERY OF OFFICIALS OFFENSES

Much like the offense in terms of section 5 of PRECCA (an offense of corrupt activities relating to foreign public officials), section 3 of PRECCA provides the following:

Any person who, directly or indirectly—

  (a) accepts or agrees or offers to accept any gratification from any other person, whether for the benefit of himself or herself or for the benefit of another person; or

  (b) gives or agrees or offers to give to any other person any gratification, whether for the benefit of that other person or for the benefit of another person,

  in order to act, personally or by influencing another person so to act, in a manner—

  (i) that amounts to the-

    (aa) illegal, dishonest, unauthorised, incomplete, or biased; or

    (bb) misuse or selling of information or material acquired in the course of the exercise, carrying out or performance of any powers, duties or functions arising out of a constitutional, statutory, contractual or any other legal obligation;

  (ii) that amount to—

    (aa) the abuse of a position of authority;

    (bb) a breach of trust; or

    (cc) the violation of a legal duty or a set of rules;

  (iii) designed to achieve an unjustified result; or

  (iv) that amounts to any other unauthorised or improper inducement to do or not to do anything,

  is guilty of the offence of corruption.

---

[4] Section 1 of the Prevention and Combatting of Corrupt Activities Act, 2004, as amended.

[5] Prevention and Combating of Corrupt Activities Act 12 of 2004,

6.5 GIFTS, GRATUITIES, AND HOSPITALITY

The principles applying to foreign public officials relating to "gratuities" are equally applicable to domestic public officials.

The codes of conduct for public officials are chiefly governed by the Executive Members' Ethics Act[6] (EMA).

Section 2 of EMA provides that the president must, after consultation with Parliament, by proclamation, publish a code of ethics (the "Code") prescribing standards and rules aimed at promoting open, democratic, and accountable government and with which public officials must comply in performing their official responsibilities.

Accordingly, the Code published in terms of EMA section 2 is binding on all domestic public officials.

Further, section 2(2)(c) provides that the Code muse require domestic public officials to disclose to an official in the office of the premier concerned—

> *"any financial interests acquired after their assumption of office, including any gifts, foreign travel, pensions, hospitality and other benefits of a material nature received by them or by such person having a family or other relationship with them as may be determined in the [Code] . . ."*

With regard to the "office of the Premier," it is important to note that South African Parliament has a bicameral Parliament that is supported by a joint administration. The National Assembly is the House directly elected by the voters while the National Council of Provinces (NCOP) is elected by the provinces and represents them to ensure that provincial interests are taken into account in the national sphere of government. Each respective province will elect a "Premier" that is the head of the relevant province's delegation to the NCOP.

The Code caters for enhanced disclosures relating to "gifts" received.

Paragraph 4 of the Code provides that a domestic public official may not solicit or accept a gift or benefit that

(a) *Is in return for any benefit received from the domestic official in the domestic public official's official capacity;*

(b) *Constitutes improper influence on the domestic public official; or*

(c) *Constitutes an attempt to influence the domestic public official in the performance of such person's duties.*

Further, when a domestic public official, in the course of such person's duties, has received or has been offered a gift with a value of more than R1000 (approximately U.S. $75), such domestic public official may request permission from the president or premier, as the case may be, to retain or accept the gift.

If the permission is granted, the domestic public official may retain/accept the gift but must disclose particulars thereof as prescribed in the Code.

---

[6] Executive Members' Ethics Act 82 of 1998, as amended.

However, where permission was not requested or granted the domestic public official must either:

(a) Return the gift or decline the offer; or
(b) Donate the gift to the state.

It must be noted that for the purposes of paragraph 4 of the Code, the term "gift" does not include travel facilities or hospitality arising from attendance at meals, functions, meetings, cocktail parties, conventions, conferences, or similar events attended by domestic public officials as part of such person's executive duties. However, this is catered for elsewhere in the Code.

6.5.1 Disclosures in Terms of the Code

Paragraph 6 of the Code provides that domestic public officials must disclose the following interests and details:

(a) **Shares** *and other financial interests in companies and other corporate entities by indicating*:
   (i) *The number, nature and nominal value of shares of any type in any public or private company;*
   (ii) *The name of that company; and*
   (iii) *The nature and value of any other financial interests held in any company or any other corporate entity.*
(b) *Sponsorships*:
   (i) *The source and description of direct financial sponsorship or assistance from any source other than the domestic public official's party that benefits the member in his or her personal and private capacity; and*
   (ii) *The amount or value of the sponsorship or assistance.*
(c) **Gifts and hospitality** *other than that received from a spouse or permanent companion or family member.*
   A description, including the value and source of—
   (i) *any gift with a value of more than R350 [approximately U.S. $26)];*
   (ii) *gifts received from a single source which cumulatively exceed the value of R350 in any calendar year;*
   (iii) *hospitality intended as a personal gift with a value of more than R350; and*
   (iv) *hospitality intended as a gift and received from a single source, and which cumulatively exceeds the value of R350 in any calendar year.*
      In this regard, permission must be sought from the President or Premier, as the case may be, where one wishes to accept/retain a gift worth more than R1000. Where a gift is between R350 and R1000, the relevant domestic public official need not seek permission but is merely required to disclose that such gift was received. Where a gift is less than R350, no permission nor disclosure is required.
(d) *Benefits*:
   (i) *The nature and source of any other benefit of a material nature; and*
   (ii) *The value of that benefit.*

Interestingly, it is unclear what is considered as a *"benefit of a material nature"* and whether the term *"material"* is to be judged on an objective or subjective standard.

An example would be something that may be insignificant and of little financial value but may offer material symbolic value.

A further example would relate to a mining right for an undeveloped piece of land in a foreign country, though the mining right may initially be of low value, it no doubt has potential to attract value.

> (e) **Foreign travel** *other than personal visits paid for by the domestic public official, or official travel paid for by the state, or travel paid for by the domestic public official's political party*:
>   (i) *A brief description of the journey abroad; and*
>   (ii) *Particulars of the sponsor.*

It is noteworthy that this point only caters for international travel and does not address the issue of local travel. This is relevant given that certain upmarket hotels in South Africa charge US$ 800 per night, or more.

However, domestic travel will more than likely be covered as a "benefit" or as a "gift/hospitality" and will no doubt need to be disclosed as such.

> (f) **Land and immovable property**, *including land or property outside South Africa*:
>   (i) *a description of and the extent of the land or property;*
>   (ii) *the area in which it is situated; and*
>   (iii) *the nature and value of the interest in the land or property.*
> (g) *Pensions*:
>   (i) *The source of any pension; and*
>   (ii) *The value of the pension.*

6.6 DEFENSES

There are no specific defenses that avail themselves in relation to an offense committed in terms of section 5 of PRECCA, though the presumptions detailed above remain applicable.

6.7 CORPORATE CULTURE

It is unfortunate that there is a perception amongst both corporate bodies and citizens that the current government is susceptible to corruption.

However, this perception is not unfounded as should one open an informed newspaper in South Africa on any given day of the week, allegations of corruption are difficult to avoid.

It is not uncommon to see that certain public tenders are often awarded to persons who directly/indirectly are connected with influential domestic public officials.

6.8 PENALTIES

The penalties applicable to the commission of an offense relating to foreign public officials are equally applicable to domestic public officials.

Section 47 of the Constitution further provides that where a person is convicted of an offense and sentenced to more than 12 months imprisonment without the option of a fine, such person is disqualified from being a member of the South African Parliament.

This disqualification ends five years after the sentence has been completed.

7. Commercial Bribery

7.1 COMMERCIAL BRIBERY OFFENSES

7.1.1 Failure to Act

Section 34 of PRECCA creates a duty to report corrupt transactions.

Generally, no liability attaches to a person for a failure to act. However, where there is a duty to act and such person fails to perform his or her duty, then liability against such person could well arise.

Section 34 is an instance that creates such a duty to act.

Section 34(1) of PRECCA provides as follows:

> *(1) Any person who holds a position of authority and who knows or ought reasonably to have known or suspected that any other person has committed*
>> *(a) an offence under Part 1, 2,3 or 4, or section 20 or 21 (in so far as it relates to the aforementioned offences of Chapter 2; or*
>> *(b) the offence of theft, fraud, extortion, forgery or uttering a forged document, involving an amount of R100 000 or more, must report such knowledge or suspicion or cause such knowledge or suspicion to be reported to any police official.*

The offenses referred to in section 34(1)(a) relate to the offenses of:

(a) Part 1—The General offense of corruption; and
(b) Part 2—Corrupt activities relating to
    (i) Public Officers;
    (ii) Foreign Public Officials;
    (iii) Agents;
    (iv) Members of the legislature;
    (v) Judicial officers; and
    (vi) Members of the NPA.
(c) Part 3—Offenses of receiving or offering of unauthorised gratification by a party, or to a party, in order to facilitate an employment relationship;
(d) Part 4—Offenses in respect of corrupt activities relating to specific matters such as—
    (i) Witnesses and evidential material during certain proceedings;
    (ii) Contracts;

(iii) Procuring and withdrawal of tenders;
(iv) Auctions;
(v) Sporting events; and
(vi) Gambling games or games of chance.
(e) Section 20—Accessory to or after an offense,[7] and
(f) Section 21—The attempt, conspiracy and inducing another person to commit an offense.[8]

7.1.2 Section 12 of PRECCA—Offenses in Respect of Corrupt Activities Relating to Contracts

Section 12(1) of PRECCA provides as follows:

(1) Any person who, directly or indirectly—

(a) accepts or agrees or offers to accept any gratification from any other person, whether for the benefit of himself or herself or for the benefit of that other person or of another person; or

(b) gives or agrees or offers to give any other person any gratification, whether for the benefit of that other person of for the benefit of another person—

   (i) in order to improperly influence, in any way—

      (aa) the promotion, execution or procurement of any contract with a public body, private organisation, corporate body or any other organisation or institution; or

      (bb) the fixing of the price, consideration or other moneys stipulated or otherwise provided for in any such contract; or

   (ii) as a reward for acting as contemplated in paragraph (a),

is guilty of the offence of corrupt activities relating to contracts.

7.1.3 "Bid Rigging"

Section 13(1) of PRECCA provides as follows:

(1) Any person who, directly or indirectly, accepts or agrees or offers to accept any gratification from any other person, whether for the benefit of himself or herself or for the benefit of another person, as—

(a) an inducement to, personally or by influencing any other person so to act-

   (i) award a tender, in relation to a contract for performing any work, providing any service, supplying any article, material or substance or performing any other act, to a particular person; or

   (ii) upon an invitation for such contract, make a tender for that contract which has as its aim to cause the tenderee to accept a particular tender; or

   (iii) withdraw a tender made by him or her for such contract; or

(b) a reward for acting as contemplated in paragraph (a)(i) (ii) or (iii),

is guilty of the offence of corrupt activities relating to procuring and withdrawal of tenders."

---

[7] This will be discussed later.
[8] This will be discussed in-depth later in this chapter.

Further, if one is found to have contravened the provisions of section 13(1) of PRECCA there may be room for one to argue that such person has contravened the provisions of section 4(1)(b)(iii) of the Competition Act 89 of 1998 (the "Competition Act").

Section 4(1)(b)(iii) of the Competition Act provides as follows:

> *An agreement between, or concerted practice by firms or a decision by an association of firms is prohibited if it is between parties in a horizontal relationship and if it involves collusive tendering.*

Collusive tendering, commonly called "bid rigging," is therefore an agreement amongst competitors not to compete on the bids they submit after being invited to tender. For these purposes, firms will be regarded as competitors if they are in the same sector of business.

The South African Competition Commission's website notes that bid rigging can take many forms, for example instances of:

Complementary Bidding	Bid Suppression	bid rotation
Where firms reach an agreement to submit bids that involve a competitor agreeing to submit a bid that is higher than the designated winner, a competitor submits a bid that is known to be too high to be accepted, or a competitor submits a bid that contains special terms that are known to be unacceptable to the purchaser. Cover bidding or complementary bidding is designed to give the appearance of genuine competition.	Entails agreements amongst competitors in which one or more companies agree to refrain from bidding or to withdraw a previously submitted bid so that the designated winner's bid will be accepted;	In bid rotation schemes, conspiring firms continue to bid but they agree to take turns being the winner (i.e., lowest qualifying) bidder.

The South African Competition Commission further notes that collusive tendering is often accompanied by an agreement to cede portions of a tender to the losing bidder, should the tenders not be awarded, and as had been agreed upon by the bidding firms involved.

It may well be argued that the cession of the relevant portion of the tender may be considered to be a "gratuity," given the broad definition PRECCA ascribes to this term.

Section 13(2) of PRECCA goes on to provide that:

> (2) *Any person who, directly or indirectly—*
> > (a) *gives or agrees or offers to give any gratification to any other person, whether for the benefit of that other person or the benefit of another person, as—*
> > > (i) *an inducement to, personally or by influencing any other person so to act, award a tender, in relation to a contract for performing any work,*

> *providing any service, supplying any article, material or substance or*
> *performing any other act, to a particular person; or*
>> *(ii) a reward for acting as contemplated in subparagraph (i); or*
>
> *(b) with the intent to obtain a tender in relation to a contract for performing any*
> *work, providing any service, supplying any article, material or substance or*
> *performing any other act, gives or agrees or offers to give any gratification to*
> *any person who has made a tender in relation to that contract, whether for the*
> *benefit of that tenderer or for the benefit of any other person, as—*
>> *(i) an inducement to withdraw the tender; or*
>> *(ii) a reward for withdrawing or having withdrawn the tender,*
>
> *is guilty of the offence of corrupt activities relating to procuring and withdrawal of tenders.*

7.1.4 OECD and the Companies Act 71 of 2008 (the "Companies Act")

In terms of the Companies Act Regulations, a company's social and ethics committee is required to monitor the company's activities, having regard to any relevant legislation, other legal requirements, or prevailing codes of best practice, with regard to matters relating to, inter alia,

(a) the 10 principles set out in the United Nations Global Compact Principles (which include anti-corruption); and

(b) the OECD recommendations regarding corruption.[9]

In this regard, it should be noted that the Companies Act does not require all companies to establish a social and ethics committee. However, where one is:

(a) a public company (i.e., a company which may raise capital from the general public and whose securities may be freely transferred by its shareholders);

(b) a state owned company; or

(c) a company whose public interest score[10] is above 500 points in any two of the previous five years,

such company is statutorily obliged to establish a social and ethics committee.[11]

7.1.4.1 Adequate Procedures

There is no adequate procedures defense to any corporate bribery offense in South Africa.

7.1.4.2 Corporate Culture

Political will to fight domestic corruption, to date, has meant that many offenders have tended to be unconcerned about the possible repercussions that may occur as a result of committing an offense in terms of PRECCA.

---

[9] Regulation 43(5) of the Companies Act Regulations.

[10] The scope of how a company's public interest score is determined is beyond the scope of this book.

[11] Regulation 43 of the Companies Act Regulations.

South Africa's citizenry further often believe that "there is no point" in reporting a matter to the SAPS as there is a perception that the SAPS has inadequate will, skills, and capacity to properly investigate the relevant complaint.

In recent months, and following the appointment of President Ramaphosa at the beginning of 2018, attitudes are changing, and capacity, leadership, and funding of the NPA is being enhanced, commissions of enquiries have been appointed by the president to investigate corruption and criminal prosecutions of high level persons are expected to follow.

7.2 PENALTIES

7.2.1 Failure to Report

Section 34(2), when read with the provisions of section 26(1)(b) of PRECCA, provides that where one fails to comply with the provisions of section 34(1) (i.e., failing to report the offense when required to do so), then such person is liable:

(a) *In the case of a sentence to be imposed by a High Court, or a regional court, to a fine or to imprisonment for a period not exceeding ten (10) years; or*

(b) *In the case of a sentence to be imposed by a magistrates court, to a fine or to imprisonment for a period not exceeding three (3) years.*

7.2.2 Sections 12 and 13 of PRECCA—Offenses in Respect of Corrupt Activities Relating to Contracts and "Bid Rigging"

Section 26 provides that where one is convicted of an offense in respect of corrupt activities relating to foreign public officials under section 12 or 13 of PRECCA, such person—

(a) *in the case of a sentence to be imposed by a High Court, is subject to a fine **or** to imprisonment for a period for up to imprisonment for life;*

(b) *in the case of a sentence to be imposed by a regional court, is subject to a fine or to imprisonment for a period not exceeding 18 years; or*

(c) *in the case of a sentence to be imposed by a magistrates court, is subject to a fine or to imprisonment for a period not exceeding 5 years.*

Further, in addition to any fine, a court may impose a fine equal to five times the value of the gratification involved in the offense.

The Competition Act goes on to provide that where one is found to have knowingly participated in the process of "bid rigging," the Competition Tribunal may impose an administrative penalty of up to 10 percent of the relevant firm's annual turnover in South Africa and its exports from South Africa during the relevant firm's preceding financial year.

8. Sentencing Principles

8.1 GENERAL PRINCIPLES

Unlike countries such as the United States, South Africa does not have distinguishable federal and regional laws, as it is not a federal system.

Accordingly, whether a crime is committed in one province or another province will not affect the penalty associated with such crime.

Subject to what is set out below, sentencing is considered the primary prerogative of the relevant court in South Africa, and such trial courts are given a wide discretion as to the criminal sanction that a convicted individual may receive with regard to white collar crime—including corruption—and subject to the limitations set out in various applicable statutes.

Further, this discretion is often guided by judicial precedent as well as certain factors that Parliament or previous judgments may have pronounced upon.

However, in sentencing an individual, courts apply what has become known as the *"triad of Zinn,"* which was established in one of South Africa's most important jurisprudential cases of *S v. Zinn*.[12] The court found that when sentencing an individual, three primary considerations need to be taken into account, these being:

(a) the nature of the crime;
(b) the nature of the offender; and
(c) public interest, including a deterrence factor.

Though South Africa does not have sentencing guidelines such as those applied in countries such as the United States, a mandatory minimum sentencing regime was investigated based on recommendations made to the Minister of Justice by a special committee enacted to review such.

The Minister of Justice appointed a further committee to review South Africa's sentencing regime, and in calendar year 2000, this special committee concluded that a "Sentencing Council" be formed to develop, inter alia, sentencing guidelines. Notwithstanding this recommendation, the South African Parliament has yet to take this matter further.

9. Related Criminal Offenses

9.1 ACCESSORY TO OR AFTER THE OFFENSE, ATTEMPT, CONSPIRACY, AIDING, AND ABETTING

Section 20 of PRECCA deals with accessories to the offense and provides as follows:

Any person who, knowing that property or any part thereof forms part of any gratification which is the subject of an offence in terms of Part 1, 2, 3 or 4, or section 21 (in so far as it relates to the aforementioned offences) of this Chapter, directly or indirectly, whether on behalf of himself or herself or on behalf of any other person—
(a) enters into or causes to be entered into any dealing in relation to such property or any part thereof; or

---

[12] State v. Zinn 1969 (2) SA 537 (A).

(b) *uses or causes to be used, or holds, receives or conceals such property or any part thereof,*
is guilty of an offence.

Section 21 of PRECCA applies to those who attempt, conspire, induce, or aid and abet one to commit an offense in terms of PRECCA and provides as follows:

Any person who—
    (a) *attempts;*
    (b) *conspires with any other person; or*
    (c) *aids, abets, induces, incites, instigates, instructs, commands, counsels or procures*
        another person,
to commit an offence in terms of this Act, is guilty of an offence.

In both these instances, where one is tried and convicted, such person may be subject:

    (a) *In the case of a sentence to be imposed by a High Court or a regional court, to a fine or*
        to imprisonment for a period not exceeding ten (10) years; or
    (b) *In the case of a sentence to be imposed by a magistrates court, to a fine or to imprison-*
        ment for a period not exceeding three (3) years.

9.2 FALSE ACCOUNTING/BOOKS AND RECORDS

This issue is dealt with in the Companies Act under section 214 and provides that it is an offense to, inter alia:

    (a) Be a party to falsifying accounting records;
    (b) Fraudulently providing false or misleading information; or
    (c) Being a party to a prospectus containing "untrue" statements;

Further, an omission from a prospectus or written statement of any matter that, in the context, is calculated to mislead the reader, shall constitute the making of an untrue statement in that prospectus or written statement, irrespective of whether the Companies Act requires that matter to be included in the prospectus or written statement.

A person is considered to *"be a party"* if—

    (a) *the relevant document/record includes or is otherwise based on a scheme, structure or*
        form of words or numbers devised, prepared or recommended by that person; and
    (b) *the scheme, structure or form of words is of such a nature that the person knew, or*
        ought reasonably to have known, that its inclusion or other use in connection with the
        preparation of the document would cause it to be false or misleading.

Where one is found to have contravened the provisions of section 214 of the Companies Act, such person, upon conviction, may be subject to a fine and/or to imprisonment for a period not exceeding 10 years.

9.3 MONEY LAUNDERING

There are three key pieces of legislation governing money laundering in South Africa, namely:

(a) the Prevention of Organised Crime Act[13] (POCA);
(b) the Financial Intelligence Centre Act[14] (FICA); and
(c) the Protection of Constitutional Democracy Against Terrorist and Related Activities Act[15] (POCDATARA).

9.3.1 POCA

POCA's money laundering offenses relate to:

(a) racketeering; and
(b) the proceeds of unlawful activities which include:
   (i) money laundering;
   (ii) assisting another person to benefit from the proceeds of unlawful activities; and
   (iii) acquiring, possessing or using the proceeds of unlawful activities.

The penalties for contravening the provisions of POCA are harsh and depending on the offense can be as extreme as:

(a) a fine of R1000 million[16] [approximately U.S. $75 million]; or
(b) to imprisonment for a period between 30 years to life.[17]

POCA also provides for the forfeiture of illegal proceeds to the state.

9.3.2 FICA

FICA attempts to combat money laundering and terrorist financing activities or to prevent the commission of money laundering or terrorist financing offenses by imposing specific duties on institutions that may or could be used for money laundering or terrorist financing purposes.

FICA penalties range from 15 years imprisonment and/or a fine of up to R100 000 000 (approximately U.S. $ 7.6 million).

9.3.3 POCDATARA

POCDATARA creates the offense of terrorism and a number of terrorist-related offenses, including terrorist financing offenses.

The penalties imposed by POCDATARA can be a fine within the jurisdiction of the court in which the matter is heard, or imprisonment of between five years to life.

---

[13] Prevention of Organised Crime Act 38 of 1998.
[14] Financial Intelligence Centre Act 38 of 2001.
[15] Protection of Constitutional Democracy Against Terrorist and Related Activities Act 33 of 2004.
[16] Section 3 of the Prevention of Organised Crime Act 38 of 1998.
[17] *Id.*

10. Cooperation and Self-Reporting

10.1 COOPERATION WITH INVESTIGATORS

Generally, there is no legal obligation to cooperate with investigators during their respective investigations, and usually suspects are not obliged to incriminate themselves. However, where an investigator duly obtains a *subpoena* to be issued against an individual, and in respect of specific legislation such an individual is prima facie obliged to assist the investigator in respect of the details of such subpoena.

This subpoena may entail providing written and/or oral testimony on oath and/or entail the relevant individual subpoenaed to provide documents to the investigator such as bank accounts, email correspondence, letters, and minutes of meetings.

The concept of legal professional privilege, discussed at Section 14 of this chapter, remains applicable with regard to subpoenas.

10.2 SELF-REPORTING

Generally, and unless provided otherwise elsewhere, there is no obligation for one to self-report. As mentioned earlier, it is a corporate offense under section 34 of PRECCA not to report.

10.3 PLEA AGREEMENTS

This aspect is governed by the provisions of the Criminal Procedure Act No 51 of 1977 (CPA).

With regard to plea and sentence agreements, a prosecutor and accused may only enter into a plea and sentence agreement where certain requirements and formalities have been adhered to. The prosecutor may only enter into a plea and sentence agreement with the accused where such prosecutor:

(a) Has obtained the prior written consent from the NDPP in this regard;
(b) After consulting the investigation office in charge of investigating the relevant case;
 (i) This requirement may be dispensed with if the prosecutor is satisfied that consultation with the person charged with the investigation of the case will delay the proceedings to such an extent that it could—
  (A) cause substantial prejudice to the prosecution, the accused, the complainant or his or her representative; *and*
  (B) adversely affect the administration of justice.
(c) After considering, at least—
 (i) the nature of and circumstances relating to the offense;
 (ii) the personal circumstances of the accused;
 (iii) the previous convictions of the accused, if any; and
 (iv) the interests of the community;
(d) after affording the complainant or his or her representative, where it is reasonable to do so and taking into account the nature of and circumstances relating to

the offense and the interests of the complainant, the opportunity to make representations to the prosecutor regarding-

   (i)   the contents of the agreement; and

   (ii) the inclusion in the agreement of a condition relating to compensation or the rendering to the complainant of some specific benefit or service in lieu of compensation for damage or pecuniary loss.

Further, section 105A(2) of the CPA provides that all plea and sentence agreements must, at the very least:

(e) Provide written confirmation that the accused, before entering into the agreement, has been informed that he or she has the right

   (i)   to be presumed innocent until proven guilty beyond a reasonable doubt;

   (ii) to remain silent and not to testify during the legal proceedings; and

   (iii) not to be compelled to give self-incriminating evidence.

(f) Provide fully the terms of the agreement, the substantial facts of the matter, all other facts relevant to the sentence agreement and any admissions made by the accused;

(g) Be signed by the relevant prosecutor, the relevant accused and his or her legal representative; and

(h) If the accused has negotiated with the prosecutor through an interpreter, contain a certificate by the interpreter to the effect that he or she interpreted accurately during the negotiations and with respect to the contents of the agreement.

   The prosecutor is required, before the accused is required to plead, inform the trial court that a plea and sentence agreement in terms of section 105A of the CPA has been entered into and the court shall then—

(i) require the accused to confirm that such an agreement has been entered into; and

(j) satisfy itself that the prosecutor has consulted the investigating officer in charge of the case and afforded the complainant an opportunity to make representations.

   If the court is not satisfied that the prosecutor has consulted the investigating officer in charge of the case and afforded the complainant an opportunity to make representations, the court shall—

(k) inform the prosecutor and the accused of the reasons for noncompliance; and

(l) afford the prosecutor and the accused the opportunity to comply with the requirements concerned.

   If the court is satisfied that the prosecutor has consulted the investigating officer in charge of the case, afforded the complainant an opportunity to make representations and that the plea and sentence agreement complies with the prescribed requirements, the court shall require the accused to plead to the charge and order that the contents of the agreement be disclosed in court.

   After the contents of the agreement have been disclosed, the court shall question the accused whether—

(m) he or she confirms the terms of the agreement and the admissions made by him or her in the agreement;

(n) with reference to the alleged facts of the case, he or she admits the allegations in the charge to which he or she has agreed to plead guilty; and

(o) the agreement was entered into freely and voluntarily in his or her sound and sober senses and without having been unduly influenced.

After this inquiry, if the court is not satisfied that the accused is guilty of the offense with respect to which the agreement was entered into, or it appears to the court that the accused does not admit an allegation in the charge sheet, or that the accused has incorrectly admitted any such allegation, or that the accused has a valid defense to the charge, or for any other reason the court is of the opinion that the plea of guilty by the accused should not stand, the court shall record a plea of not guilty and inform the prosecutor and the accused of the reasons therefor.

If the court has recorded a plea of not guilty, the trial shall start de novo before another presiding officer, provided that the accused may waive his or her right to be tried before another presiding officer.

If the court is satisfied that the accused admits the allegations in the charge and that he or she is guilty of the offense in respect of which the agreement was entered into, the court shall proceed to consider the relevant plea and sentence agreement.

If the court is satisfied that the sentence agreement is just, the court shall inform the prosecutor and the accused that the court is so satisfied, whereupon the court shall convict the accused of the offense charged and sentence the accused in accordance with the sentence agreement.

10.4 LENIENCY

In accordance with the "triad of Zinn" discussed earlier under Section 8 of this chapter, a court will consider mitigating factors with regard to all three legs of the triad.

To reiterate, the triad of Zinn constitutes the following:

(a) the nature of the crime;

(b) the nature of the offender; and

(c) public interest.

With regard to the first prong, that is, the nature of the crime, courts will likely, but are not obliged to, be more lenient on instances where the offender has been convicted of attempted offenses, bona fide errors, and cases relating to possible entrapment.

Concerning the second prong, that is, the nature of the offender, entails that the punishment fit the offender, as one of the aims of the South African criminal justice system is to reform the offender. Accordingly, the following factors, being a non-exhaustive list, are considered mitigating factors that a court may consider in sentencing an individual:

(a) age—both youth and elderly;

(b) previous convictions;

(c) bad health;

(d) interests of dependents (if any);

(e) whether the offender is the sole breadwinner of their relevant household;

   (f) diminished capacity[18] and/or intelligence;
      (a) remorse; and
      (b) whether the offender rendered a guilty plea.

The final prong of the triad of Zinn, being public interest, incorporates for purposes of punishment in the South African criminal justice system, the elements of, rehabilitation, retribution, and deterrence.

The chief mitigating factor considered by a court with regard to the interests of the public relate to the balancing exercise of whether a lengthy period of incarceration may be outweighed by the detriment that the community may suffer should the accused serve a lengthy period in prison: for instance, if the offender is the sole breadwinner in a household and dependents of the offender will likely suffer should the offender be imprisoned.

11. Whistle-Blower Protection

There are several items of legislation that ensure whistle-blowers are protected in the event that they disclose certain information or expose alleged or suspected criminal or irregular activity.

The following Acts of Parliament have been enacted to protect whistle-blowers:

   (a) The Protected Disclosures Act, 2000;
   (b) The Companies Act. 2008;
   (c) The Labour Relations Act 1995;
   (d) Protection From Harassment Act, 2011; and
   (e) The Witness Protection Act, 1998.

For the purposes of this Chapter we will only concern ourselves with the provisions of the Protected Disclosures Act.

The Protected Disclosures Act was enacted on August 1, 2000, as it was acknowledged that neither South African common law nor statutory law made provision for mechanisms or procedures in terms of which employees could, without fear of reprisals, disclose information relating to suspected or alleged criminal or other irregular conduct by their employers, whether in the private or the public sector.

It is noteworthy that this Act is applicable to both public and private sector employees.

Section 3 of the Protected Disclosures Act provides that:

No employee may be subjected to any occupational detriment by his or her employer on account, or partly on account, of having made a protected disclosure.

Further, the term *"occupational detriment"* is defined to include instances of, inter alia,

   (a) being subjected to any disciplinary action;
   (b) being refused transfer or promotion;

---

[18] However, where the offender voluntarily created the circumstance of his or her mental state being non compos mentis, a court may consider this to be an aggravating factor.

(c) being dismissed, suspended, demoted, harassed or intimidated; and
(d) being otherwise adversely affected in respect of his or her employment, profession or office, including employment opportunities and work security.

In the event an employee is found to be in breach of section 3 of the Protected Disclosures Act, such an employee will be found to have committed an unfair labor practice against the relevant whistle-blower, and the employer may have a judgment recorded against them whereby they are to make reparations to the relevant employee, and the relevant court may also make an order interdicting (the equivalent of an injunction) the employer from subjecting the whistle-blower to an *occupational detriment*.

A disclosure is defined to mean any:

> *. . . disclosure made concerning the conduct of an employer, or of an employee of that employer, made by any employee who has reason to believe that the information concerned shows or tends to show one or more of the following-*
>   (a) *That a criminal offence has been committed, is being committed or is likely to be committed;*
>   (b) *that a person has failed, is failing or is likely to fail to comply with any legal obligation to which that person is subject;*
>   (c) *that a miscarriage of justice has occurred, is occurring or is likely to occur;*
>   (d) *that the health or safety of an individual has been, is being or is likely to be endangered;*
>   (e) *that the environment has been, is being or is likely to be damaged;*
>   (f) *unfair discrimination as contemplated in the Promotion of Equality and Prevention of Unfair Discrimination Act, 2000 (Act No. 4 of 2000); or*
>   (g) *that any matter referred to in paragraphs (a) to (f) has been, is being or is likely to be deliberately concealed.*[19]

11.1 WHAT IS CONSIDERED AS A "PROTECTED DISCLOSURE"

It is only where a disclosure is categorized as a *"Protected Disclosure"* that the relevant employee will be afforded the cloak of protection granted to a whistle-blower in terms of the Protected Disclosure Act.

11.2 DISCLOSURES TO LEGAL ADVISERS

Where a disclosure is made

(a) to a legal practitioner or to a person whose occupation involves the giving of legal advice; and
(b) with the object of and in the course of obtaining legal advice.

such a disclosure will be considered a *"protected disclosure."*[20]

---

[19] Section 1 of the Protected Disclosures Act.
[20] Section 5 of the Protected Disclosures Act.

11.3 DISCLOSURES TO EMPLOYERS

Where a disclosure is made in good faith

(a) substantially in accordance with any procedure prescribed, or authorised by the employee's employer for reporting or otherwise remedying the alleged impropriety concerned; or

(b) to the employer of the employee, where there is no procedure as contemplated in paragraph (a),

such a disclosure will be considered a *"protected disclosure."*[21]

Further, any employee who, in accordance with a procedure authorized by his or her employer, makes disclosure to a person other than his or her employer, is deemed, for the purposes of the Protected Disclosures Act, to be making the disclosure to his or her employer.[22]

11.4 DISCLOSURES TO A MEMBER OF THE CABINET OR EXECUTIVE COUNCIL

Any disclosure made in good faith to a member of the Cabinet or of the Executive Council of a province is a protected disclosure if the employee's employer is

(a) an individual appointed in terms of legislation by a member of Cabinet or of the Executive Council of a province;

(b) a body, the members of which are appointed in terms of legislation by a member of Cabinet or of the Executive Council of a province; or

(c) an organ of state falling within the area of responsibility of the member concerned.[23]

11.5 DISCLOSURES TO CERTAIN PERSONS OR BODIES

Any disclosure made in good faith to

(a) the Public Protector;

(b) the Auditor-General; *or*

(c) a person or body prescribed for purposes of this section; and in respect of which the employee concerned reasonably believes that-

   (i) the relevant impropriety falls within any description of matters which, in the ordinary course are dealt with by the person or body concerned; *and*

   (ii) the information disclosed, and any allegation contained in it, are substantially true,

such a disclosure will be considered a *"protected disclosure."*[24]

---

[21] Section 6(1) of the Protected Disclosures Act.

[22] Section 6(2) of the Protected Disclosures Act.

[23] Section 7 of the Protected Disclosures Act.

[24] Section 8(1) of the Protected Disclosures Act.

11.6 GENERAL PROTECTED DISCLOSURES

Section 9 of the Protected Disclosures Act provides for *"General Protected Disclosures,"* which relate to instances where the disclosure is not covered by the aforementioned provisions.

Generally, this provision provides that where a disclosure is:

(t)   made in good faith; and
(u)   the employee is of the genuine belief that it is substantially true.

such disclosure is to be construed as a *"protected disclosure."*
Further factors that are to be considered include, inter alia:

(v)   the seriousness of the impropriety;
(w)   whether the impropriety is continuing or is likely to occur in the future; and
(x)   the public interest.

11.7 ATTITUDE TOWARDS WHISTLE-BLOWERS

Notwithstanding the plethora of legislation enacted to protect whistle-blowers from unfair discrimination, whistle-blowers often are treated unfairly, and accordingly, the act of whistle-blowing is taking place less frequently.

PricewaterhouseCoopers conducted a study in 2014 that found that only 30 percent of South Africans felt safe to "blow the whistle."

As a practical matter, although the law in theory protects "whistle-blowers," in reality a whistle-blower must still approach a court of law to enforce his or her legal rights. Practically speaking, employers have the power, and often do, to prolong court cases, which in turn often results in the whistle-blower's financial resources being depleted.

12. Key International Treaties Relating to Bribery and Corruption

As mentioned earlier, South Africa has ratified a number of international treaties aimed at combatting corruption, and these include:

(a)   The United Nations Convention against Corruption (UNCAC)—ratified on November 22, 2004;
(b)   The African Union Convention on Preventing and Combatting Corruption ("AU Convention")—ratified on May 31, 2004;
(c)   The OECD Anti-Bribery Convention (OECD)—Ratified on June 19, 2007; and
(d)   The SADC Protocol against Corruption—adopted in August 2001.

Although South Africa may ratify a treaty it does not automatically result that such treaty has the effect of law. As a dualist country, in order for international law to have the effect of law domestically, South Africa must enact legislation that explicitly incorporates the international law into South Africa's domestic law.

PRECCA was adopted for this very purpose.

The South African Constitution further provides that Parliament is required to ratify international treaties.

12.1 UNCAC

Under UNCAC, South Africa is obliged to help other parties to the convention to prevent and fight corruption, by providing technical assistance, where necessary.

Amongst the requirements to criminalize corruption, prevent corruption, and coordinate with other countries in the fight against corruption, UNCAC requires parties to such convention to adopt legislation to provide whistle-blowers protection against unjustified treatment.

12.2 THE AU CONVENTION

The AU convention requires signatories to establish, maintain, and strengthen independent national anti-corruption authorities or agencies.

12.3 OECD

South Africa is a non-member country of the OECD but as of 2007 has been a party thereto. The OECD establishes legally binding standards to criminalize bribery of foreign public officials in cross-border business transactions.

12.4 SADC PROTOCOL AGAINST CORRUPTION (THE "PROTOCOL")

The Protocol was the first regional anti-corruption treaty in Africa and provides for the prevention, detection, and punishment of corruption.

The Protocol further covers cooperation between member states in relation to corruption in both the public and private sectors.

13. Mutual Legal Assistance Treaties and Transnational Cooperation

The Extradition Act[25] provides that the president may enter into an agreement with any foreign state, providing for the surrender on a reciprocal basis of persons accused or convicted of the commission within the jurisdiction of South Africa or any territory under the sovereignty or protection of such state, of an extraditable offense or offenses specified in such agreement, and may likewise agree to any amendment or revocation of such agreement.

The agreements referred to are treaties, and under each treaty there are provisions for formal requests of mutual assistance between, on the one hand, South Africa, and the South African authorities, and on the other hand the relevant foreign state and such foreign state's authorities.

---

[25] Extradition Act 67 of 1962, as amended.

The Extradition Act further provides for certain formalities and powers conferred upon the South African Minister of Justice, as well as magistrates in relation to issuing and executing warrants of arrest.

South Africa currently has extradition agreements and Mutual Legal Assistance in Criminal Matters Treaties with numerous countries. In addition, there are numerous other Mutual Legal Assistance in Criminal Matters Treaties that are either currently under negotiation or have yet to be ratified by either South Africa or the relevant foreign state.

14. Legal Professional Privilege

Like many commonwealth jurisdictions, legal professional privilege (LPP) in South Africa consists of two components: namely

(a) Legal Advice Privilege (LAP); and
(b) Litigation Privilege (LP).

LAP generally protects communications between legal advisers and their clients provided that:

(a) The attorney in question acted in their professional capacity as a legal professional;
(b) Such communication was made in confidence and was for the purpose of obtaining/giving legal advice; and
(c) The advice in question was not sought for an illegal purpose.

LP protects communications, in whatever form, between legal advisers and/or their clients on the one hand and third parties on the other, provided that:

(a) The above three requirements in relation to LAP are met;
(b) The communication in question was made for the sole purposes of being placed before the legal adviser in order to enable such legal adviser to advise; and
(c) The communication was made for the sole purpose of intended or contemplated litigation.

14.1 WHAT IS COVERED BY LPP

Provided that the communication, in whatever form, has satisfied the requirements detailed previously, such communication is protected by LPP. Merely providing an attorney with a document of a confidential nature does not mean that such communication will be protected by LPP, if such communication was not for the purpose of obtaining legal advice.

14.2 APPLICATION TO EXTERNAL OR INTERNAL INVESTIGATIONS

Though an external or internal investigator may subpoena certain communications, the contents of such communications need not be disclosed if such communications are subject to LPP.

However, one is required to disclose the existence of such communication and merely note that the communication is protected by LPP.

Further, LPP can only be waived by the client concerned, which can occur either expressly or implicitly. Where implicit, the test is an objective test.

15. Privacy and Data Protection

This area is for the time being not regulated in South Africa, as the Protection of Private Information Act 4 of 2013 (POPI) is still not yet fully in force.

However, the provisions of POPI that were signed by the president indicate that much of POPI is akin to the UK Data Protection Act, and generally compliance with the latter will result in compliance with the former.

16. Forecast for Reforms and Parting Thoughts

Although the South African Constitutional Court has reviewed and requested amendments to the South African Police Service Act 68 of 1995, to amend various provisions therein, in order to ensure that the SAPS and NPA has the necessary structural and operational independence to fulfill their mandate without undue influence, the revised Act has yet to be passed, and other concerns with regard to the independence of investigation and prosecution remain unaddressed.

Further, although not scientific, many South African's are of the view that the NPA is an organization that very often makes its decisions for political reasons and without properly considering the merits of the relevant matter.

These perceptions are as a result that many of the NPA heads have either resigned (sometimes after receiving a golden handshake) or been declared "unfit to hold office" by a court of law.

In cases of resignation, such resignation occurred in respect of NPA investigations either into alleged corrupt activities involving the president himself or alleged corrupt activities involving persons in high places, or persons who are politically well connected.

Legislation in this regard and political will are probably the most important reform needed in order to address issues of enforcement with regard to cases involving corruption. The head of the NPA should be a protected appointment who can only be removed by an order of court or a special majority in Parliament (unlike the simple majority currently required in terms of statute), and such head should be able to act independently and without fear or favor. Unfortunately, this requires political will to effect such a change, and at this moment in time, there is a weak separation of powers in this regard.

Further, and as Phase 3 of the OECD Report notes, although South Africa has strongly drafted legislation with respect to whistle-blowers, few persons are aware of protections afforded by the relevant legislation, no concrete steps have been taken to ensure that reporting can occur without fear of reprisal or retaliatory action, and as indicated previously, whistle-blowers do not properly receive the protection they are entitled to. So, in this regard, there is room for improvement.

In Addition, during the course of November 2017, the South African government invited the public to provide comments on a draft bill (the "Bill") that seeks to introduce a number of amendments to PRECCA, including the following:

(1) As discussed previously in this chapter, the term *"facilitiation payment"* is not currently defined in PRECCA but should, in the author's opinion, be considered to be a form of *"gratification."* In this regard, the Bill aims to define the term *"facilitation payment"* to mean:

> *. . . a payment made to an official, a foreign public official or any third party that acts as incentive for the official to complete some action or process expeditiously, or to provide the party making the payment or another party an unfair or unlawful advantage.*

The Bill further seeks to introduce facilitation payments as an offence by including it in the definition of the term *"gratification."*

(2) Further, the Bill seeks to introduce a form of immunity for whistle-blowers under the section 34 duty to report, and provides that:

> *A court may find that any person who bona fide filed a report as contemplated in subsection (1) may not be held liable to any civil, criminal or disciplinary proceedings in respect of the content of such report.*

It should be noted that courts are still provided with a discretion in order to determine whether the relevant person submitting report should be granted immunity. In this regard, the Bill is silent as to what criteria a court should consider in making such determination.

(3) Currently, only individuals can be found to have contravened the provisions of PRECCA and there are no aspects relating to corporate liablity. In this regard, the Bill seeks to introduce an element of corporate liability and the sentencing of a corporate entity as well as imposing maximum fines. However, the Bill fails to provide when a corporate entity should be held liable and when it's agent may be held liable.

(4) In addition, though there are is no defense in respect of *"adequate procedures"* in PRECCA, the Bill proposes introducing an obligation on persons in a position of authority (as defined in section 34(4) of PRECCA to include senior management and the company's board of directors), to *"implement appropriate internal compliance programmes in order to ensure that offenses . . . are in fact detected and reported."* It is however unfortunate that neither PRECCA nor the Bill provides any clarity on what should be considered to be an *"appropriate internal compliance programme"* nor what the consequences should be in the event that such programs are not put in place.

(5) With regard to extraterritorial jurisdiction, the Bill seeks to extend the extraterritorial application of PRECCA and provides that *". . . the South African authorities shall, regardless of whether or not the act constitutes an offence at its place*

of commission, have jurisdiction to investigate and prosecute, if appropriate, that offence."

Further, the Bill seeks to extend the extraterritorial application of PRECCA to:

(a) a corporate body that *"de facto exercises control over any corporation or body of persons located outside the Republic irrespective of the nationalities of such foreign corporation or body;"* and

(b) *"a foreign public official or other foreign individual or entity who solicited or accepted a gratification in contravention of [PRECCA]";*

In terms of PRECCA, extraterritorial jurisdiction is only afforded to courts, while the Bill seeks to extend the extraterritorial application to all *"South African authorities,"* which must include investigatory bodies such as the SAPS, the Hawks, the SIU and the AFU.

APPENDIX

Key Issues	South Africa's Approach
Is South Africa subject to any international anti-corruption conventions? If so, which conventions?	Yes. OECD Convention. UN Conventions Against Corruption and Organised Crime. AU Convention on Preventing and Combatting Corruption. The SADC Protocol Against Corruption.
Is bribery of foreign public officials illegal? Do domestic anti-bribery laws apply extraterritorially?	Yes. Yes.
What is the definition of a foreign public official?	A Foreign Official is defined in PRECCA as: a) any person holding a legislative, administrative or judicial office of a foreign state; b) any person performing public functions for a foreign state, including any person employed by a board, commission, corporation, or other body or authority that performs a function on behalf of the foreign state; or c) an official or agent of a public international organization.
Is commercial bribery illegal?	Yes, to a limited extent.
Is bribing domestic officials illegal?	Yes.

Key Issues	South Africa's Approach
Can the recipient of a bribe be prosecuted?	Yes.
Can companies be held criminally liable? If so, what is the requisite intent for corporate criminal liability?	Yes and No. In general, where a statute does not provide for criminal corporate liability, a corporation cannot be held criminally liable. In terms of PRECCA, a corporation cannot be held criminally liable; however, draft legislation has been introduced to amend this position. Any form of "dolus" will be enough to secure a conviction.
Can companies be held civilly liable?	Yes. Companies can be held civilly liable for offenses relating to bribery and the principles applicable to delict (also known as tort outside of South Africa) relating to natural persons apply equally to juristic entities. Accordingly, the individual concerned, may upon the relevant court granting the relevant order, be held liable separately, for civil damages and this applies to both direct and consequential losses. South African courts have adopted the principle that the relevant wrongdoer is required to place the "plaintiff" in the financial position that he or she would have been in had the relevant wrongful act not been committed.
Can individual be held civilly liable?	Yes.
If there a "facilitation payment" defense?	No.
Do conspiracy laws apply to anti-corruption offenses?	Yes.
Does South Africa provide liability for: (a) aiding and/or abetting liability (b) attempt liability (c) for anti-corruption laws?	Yes.
Is the failure to keep accurate books and records a criminal or civil offense?	Yes, in certain circumstances.
Do any books and records offenses have to involve proof of an underlying bribery offense?	No.

(Continued)

Key Issues	South Africa's Approach
Are there South African laws concerning a company's financial internal controls?	Yes.
	Applicable to all public companies and certain "large" private companies, depending on the relevant private companies "public interest score."
If so, are those laws applicable to public and/or private companies?	
Is there an affirmative disclosure obligation for potential violations of anti-corruption laws or accounting irregularities?	Yes, see section 34 of PRECCA.
Are "promotional expenses" exempt from South Africa's anti-corruption laws?	If the promotional expense can be categorized as a "gratuity," such an expense may be construed as a bribe.
Is the giving of gifts, entertainment, travel, meals, or other gratuities restricted or prohibited by anti-corruption or other laws?	Yes.
Are there any South African laws concerning things, property, or benefits of value conveyed by, or to, third parties?	Yes.
Are tax bribes deductible?	No, in terms of South African common law, one cannot profit from their own wrong doing.
Is South Africa's anti-corruption laws applied extraterritorially?	Yes, to a limited degree.
Is a robust corporate compliance program an affirmative defense or a factor to negate liability or reduce penalties?	No.
Is there a "local law" exception or defense to South Africa's anti-corruption laws?	No.
Is "credit" given for cooperation with authorities?	To a limited extent. This is one of the factors that the court may, but is not obliged to, take into account, when sentencing an individual.
If so, how and in what form?	
Does South Africa have mutual legal assistance with the United States that covers criminal matters, including anti-corruption conduct?	Yes.

Key Issues	South Africa's Approach
What are the potential penalties/ sanctions for criminal and civil violations of South Africa's anti-corruption laws?	**Individuals** a) In the case of a sentence to be imposed by a High Court, to a fine **or** to imprisonment for a period for imprisonment for life; b) in the case of a sentence to be imposed by a regional court, to a fine or to imprisonment for a period not exceeding 18 years; or c) in the case of a sentence to be imposed by a magistrates court, to a fine or to imprisonment for a period of imprisonment not exceeding 5 years. Further, in addition to any fine, a court may impose a fine equal to five times the value of the gratification involved in the offense committed **Companies** Where one holds a sufficiently senior position within a company and ought reasonably to have known that an amount involving R100 000 or more was utilized in relation to a "bribe" and such person fails to report it to the SAPS, the points (a)–(c) previously mentioned are applicable to the individual concerned. With relation to collusive tendering, the Competition Tribunal may impose an administrative penalty of up to 10 percent of the relevant firm's annual turnover in South Africa and its exports from South Africa during the relevant firm's preceding financial year. Further, a court may impose a fine equal to five times the value of the gratification involved in the offense committed.

15 Tunisia

1. Introduction to Tunisia's Anti-Corruption Legislation

After ruling Tunisia[1] for more than 23 years, Zine el-Abidine Ben Ali abdicated the presidency in 2011 in the face of mass demonstrations sparked by a single act of defiance in the face of corruption—a fruit seller's refusal to pay off an extortionate local official. After Ben Ali's flight, the interim government moved quickly to prosecute the former president and his wife, now living in exile in Saudi Arabia, on charges of corruption. On June 20, 2011, a Tunisian court sentenced them in absentia to 35 years in prison for embezzlement and misuse of public money, and also levied a $65 million fine against the former first family.

In spite of the Ben Ali verdict, Tunisians remained concerned that the revolution would present yet another opportunity for corrupt officials to exploit their power. In a series of focus groups conducted by the National Democratic Institute in the wake of the Arab Spring, Tunisian youth stated that corruption and unemployment should be the top priorities of the assembly formed to draft a new constitution.[2] As a result of these concerns, voiced strongly by the Tunisian youth associations and the anti-corruption NGO OpenGovTN, members of the Constituent Assembly voted to include in the country's constitution a clause guaranteeing transparency and open government. Article 10 of the Tunisian Constitution, adopted on January 26, 2014, is the result. Article 10 provides that "The state shall ensure

---

[1] This chapter was contributed by Professor Juliet Sorensen, Northwestern Pritzker School of Law.
[2] *Voices of a Revolution: Conversations with Tunisia's Youth, available at* https://www.ndi.org/files/conversations-with-tunisia-youth-apr-2011.pdf (last visited Dec. 14, 2018).

From Baksheesh to Bribery. T. Markus Funk and Andrew S. Boutros.
© Oxford University Press 2019. Published 2019 by Oxford University Press.

the proper use of public funds and take the necessary measures to spend it according to the priorities of the national economy, and prevent corruption and all that can threaten national resources and sovereignty."[3]

Whether and to what extent the state has complied with Article 10 is the subject of this chapter, which summarizes the entrenched corruption of the former authoritarian regime, and evaluates current anti-corruption laws, the reforms and challenges related to corruption, and transparency since the Jasmine Revolution. It concludes with specific recommendations for increased transparency and accountability in Tunisia.

1.1 PRE-REVOLUTION TUNISIA: CORRUPTION AND THE BEN ALI REGIME

Dictatorship and cronyism in pre-revolution Tunisia led to high-level, "grand" corruption as a way of life. Corrupt aspects of the old regime included an executive branch not subject to meaningful checks and balances; "opaque" political party funding, especially for the dominant political party, the Democratic Constitutional Rally; severely restricted freedom of the press; and public contracts awarded without a transparent review process, based on nepotism and a "spoils" system.[4] In 2010, the 220 businesses that were confiscated the following year from members of the family of the former president, Zine El Abidine Ben Ali, accounted for more than 20 percent of profits in the entire economy.[5]

Since the Arab Spring of 2011, Tunisia has undergone a series of reforms aimed at accountability and transparency. These include a new constitution, formed through a democratic process; a series of legal reforms, outlined later in the chapter; and elections that were widely found to be free and fair.[6] However, if the Jasmine Revolution did away with the inherent "grand corruption" of dictatorship, petty corruption has filled the void left by an omnipresent president. According to Samir Annabi, the former director of the National Anti-Corruption Authority founded in late 2011, corruption was formerly equated with Ben Ali. Today, the country is in the process of implementing a democracy that seeks to minimize grand corruption. Indeed, grand corruption has diminished for two reasons, according to Annabi: first, large government projects have lessened since the Revolution, and second, those that do take place are under closer supervision.[7] Acts of petty corruption, however, have "prospered."[8]

---

[3] Article 10, Tunisia's Constitution of 2014, *available at* https://www.constituteproject.org/constitution/Tunisia_2014.pdf.

[4] *See* The New Constitution of Tunisia: Choices and Decisions: The Wilberforce Society University of Cambridge (2012).

[5] *All in the Family: State Capture in Tunisia*, Bob Rijkers et al., http://documents.worldbank.org/curated/en/440461468173649062/All-in-the-family-state-capture-in-Tunisia (2014) (last visited Dec. 14, 2018).

[6] FREEDOM HOUSE 2015 COUNTRY REPORT: TUNISIA (HTTPS://FREEDOMHOUSE.ORG/REPORT/FREEDOM-WORLD/2015/TUNISIA) (last visited Dec. 14, 2018) ("International and local observers concluded that the 2014 elections were free and fair"), https://freedomhouse.org/report/freedom-world/2015/tunisia.

[7] *Tunisian Economy "Plagued by Petty Corruption," Experts Say*, AGENCE FRANCE-PRESS, Oct. 2, 2015.

[8] *Id.*

2. Tunisia's Domestic Anti-Corruption Framework

2.1 CRIMINAL LAW REGIME

Tunisia's legal system is based on a civil code. The primary sources of law are the Constitution, laws passed by Parliament, and international law. The anti-corruption legal framework consists of the Penal Code, the Code of Criminal Procedure, and Act No. 2003-75 of 10 December 2003 on supporting international efforts to combat terrorism and suppress money laundering (the "LBC Act").[9] Tunisia's Penal Code includes 11 articles that address corruption, including elements, definitions, and penalties.

One significant cause for concern about the sincerity of Tunisia's commitment to address corruption is a bill proposed in September 2015 that would offer amnesty to those convicted of corruption. Dubbed the "economic and financial reconciliation" bill, it offers amnesty to those businessmen and civil servants accused of corruption who confess and return misappropriated funds. Critics assert that the law does not have a clear way to reveal the full amount stolen, nor ways to prevent fraud, leaving open the opportunity for the corrupt to hide their wealth.[10]

2.2 CIVIL LAW REGIME AND ETHICAL STANDARDS

In order to establish ethical values in the public sector, a Code of Conduct for Public Officials was recently developed. Every public official in Tunisia receives a copy of the Code upon entering office and is required to review it.[11] Tunisia has also recently approved a new decree on the regulation of public procurement and created "Tuneps," an e-procurement system. Public tenders require bidders to provide a sworn statement that they have not and will not, either themselves or through a third party, make any promises or give gifts with a view to influencing the outcome of the tender and realization of the project.[12] Moreover, public officials in the same office that is awarding the contract are precluded from receiving the contract.[13]

2.3 ACCESS TO INFORMATION

Tunisia's post-revolution Constitution guarantees access to information,[14] bolstered by a public decree stating that the public has the right to request information from

---

[9] Conference of the States Parties to the United Nations Convention Against Corruption, Convention Implementation Review Group, Executive Summary: Tunisia, Nov. 2015.

[10] Samti, *In Tunisia, A New Reconciliation Law Stokes Protest and Conflict Instead,"* FOREIGN POLICY, Sept. 15, 2015.

[11] OECD 2014, "Renforcer l'Integrite en Tunisie: L'elaboration des norms pour les agents publics et le renforcement du systeme de declaration de patrimoine."

[12] Department of State Bureau of Economic and Business Affairs, 2014 Investment Climate Statement—Tunisia.

[13] Decree 3158 of 2002; Decree 3018 of 2009.

[14] Article 32, Tunisia's Constitution of 2014, *available at* https://www.constituteproject.org/constitution/Tunisia_2014.pdf.

the government.[15] However, exceptions are reportedly so broad as to undermine the Constitution's promise of transparency and accountability.[16] An online tool, Marsoum 41,[17] has been set up to enable citizens to directly access public information and to allow an independent commission to monitor compliance.

2.4 VIEW FROM THE OUTSIDE

2.4.1 OECD Evaluation

In the view of the OECD, foreign direct investment in the country continues to be deterred by corruption and related issues. Institutional barriers reflective of grand corruption in the old regime persist. Coupled with security concerns, these have a chilling effect on foreign direct investment. For example, foreigners are not allowed to purchase agricultural land or to hold a majority interest in a joint venture in the agri-food sector, and there are restrictions in other sectors, including transport, communications, construction, tourism, and information technology services.[18] An ongoing lack of effective institutions to ensure public sector accountability, the rule of law, and checks and balances on power in Tunisia results in weak protection of property rights, corruption, and barriers to entry in the Tunisian markets.[19]

In the framework of the OECD Integrity Scan of Tunisia, business associations suggested that the integrity of companies has declined since the recent political changes, partly owing to the degradation of the state control environment. The OECD has urged Tunisia to promote integrity and fight corruption by "systematically implementing UNCAC's provisions," including "*i)* ensure the effective implementation and dissemination of the Code of Conduct, *ii)* establish a tailored legal framework for reform whistleblowing protection, *iii)* strengthen the asset-declaration system, *iv)* fully implement the new e-procurement system Tuneps and *v)* simplify control systems, with a stronger focus on internal control and audit functions."[20]

2.4.2 Transparency International Corruption Perception Index Score

Tunisia ranks 74th out of 180 countries in the 2017 Transparency International Corruption Perception Index. It scores 42 out of 100 "good government" points in the same index, a

---

[15] *Marsoum 41 Promotes Freedom of Information in Tunisia, available at* http://www.tunisiait.com/article,nbsptounesa_lance_marsoum_41,12730.html (last visited Dec. 14, 2018).

[16] TUNISIA FREEDOM OF THE PRESS 2015 REPORT, *available at* https://freedomhouse.org/report/freedompress/2015/tunisia (last visited Feb. 4, 2019).

[17] www.marsoum41.org.

[18] *"Tunisia: A Reform Agenda to Support Competitiveness and Inclusive Growth*, OECD, Mar. 2015, *available at* https://www.oecd.org/countries/tunisia/Tunisia-a-reform-agenda-to-support-competitiveness-and-inclusive-growth.pdf.

[19] *Towards a New Economic Model for Tunisia: Identifying Tunisia's Binding Constraints to Broad-Based Growth*, AFRICAN DEVELOPMENT BANK (2013).

[20] OECD and Clean Gov Biz, *Integrity Scan of Tunisia,*" June 2013, *available at* https://www.oecd.org/cleangovbiz/Tunisia-Integrity-ScanEN.pdf, June 2013.

slight improvement from the two previous years, in which it scored 41 (2016) and 38 (2015), respectively.[21]

3. Investigative and Prosecutorial Agencies

A range of executive agencies address aspects of corruption in Tunisia. The National Anti-Corruption Authority, created by Decree Law 2011-120 of 14 November 2011, is the preeminent post-revolution anti-corruption agency in Tunisia. The Independent Commission to Investigate Corruption, also created in 2011, focuses on abuse of power in the Ben Ali regime. Other government agencies include the Ministries of Justice, Foreign Affairs, and Property and Land Effects, which work together in investigations abroad; the Judicial and Financial Unit at the Tunis Court of First Instance; and the Tunisian Financial Analysis Committee at the Central Bank.[22]

In addition, Tunisia is a member of the Arab Anti-Corruption and Integrity Network (ACINET)[23], established in 2008 and considered to be the overarching participatory mechanism for anti-corruption related capacity development, information exchange, and policy dialogue in the region.

4. Bribery of Foreign Officials
4.1 JURISDICTION

Extraterritorial jurisdiction applies to cases of international bribery in Tunisia.[24]

4.2 STATUTE OF LIMITATIONS

The statute of limitations in Tunisia is 10 years for felonies, 3 years for misdemeanors, and 1 year for "petty offenses."[25] All corruption-related crimes in Tunisia are either felonies or misdemeanors.[26] Article 6 of the Code of Criminal Procedure provides that the statute of limitations may be interrupted by any investigative measure or any step in criminal proceedings, even with regard to targets who are not directly implicated by such step.

4.3 FOREIGN BRIBERY OFFENSES

According to Article 307 bis of Tunisia's Code of Criminal Procedure, "bribing a foreign official is illegal."[27]

---

[21] 2017 Corruption Perception Index, https://www.transparency.org/news/feature/corruption_perceptions_index_2017#table (last accessed Dec. 14, 2018).

[22] Conference of the States Parties, *supra* note 9.

[23] *Govenmental Members of the Arab Anti-Corruption and Integrity Network, available at* http://www.arabacinet.org/index.php/en/structure/official-members (last visited Dec. 14, 2018).

[24] *Id.*

[25] Code of Criminal Procedure Arts. 3, 4, and 5.

[26] Conference of the States Parties, *supra* note 9.

[27] Global Integrity, *African Integrity Indicators, available at* https://www.globalintegrity.org/research/reports/global-integrity-report/global-integrity-report-2008/gir-scorecard-2008-tunisia-/ (last visited Dec. 14, 2018).

4.4 "FOREIGN PUBLIC OFFICIALS" DEFINED

"Foreign public official" is not defined in the Penal Code.

4.5 GIFTS, GRATUITIES, AND HOSPITALITY

The Penal Code reflects no exception for facilitation payments, or any allowance for marketing and promotional expenses, although gifts are considered distinct from bribes on the basis of corrupt intent. Article 83 provides that "Any person having the quality of civil servant who accepted, directly or indirectly, for himself or for the benefit of someone else, gifts, donations, promises or any kind of advantage, to accomplish an action related to his position, will be given 10 years in prisons and fined 10,000 Tunisian Dinars." According to Article 37 of Tunisia's Penal Code, where the law systematically sets the criminal gift or gratification in context with a deed requested or offered, gifts or gratification that have been given or taken without consideration are not considered bribery.

4.6 DEFENSES

Defenses to the crime of bribery of a foreign public official are not defined as distinct from other forms of bribery.

4.7 PENALTIES

According to the Penal Code, the offense of bribery or "offering, promising or giving any undue pecuniary or other advantage to a Tunisian public official," directly or through an intermediary, carries a 10-year prison sentence and a fine equal to twice the amount of the bribe received or promised; the minimum fine is TND 10,000 (approximately U.S. $6,000). No separate penalty is identified for the crime of bribing a foreign public official.

A well-known international corporate bribery case involving Tunisian public officials resulted in the Swiss Office of the Attorney General issuing a 2011 summary punishment order against Alstom Network Schweitz AG for failing to take reasonable measures to prevent bribery of foreign public officials in Tunisia, Latvia, and Malaysia. Alstom was sentenced to a fine of 2.5 million Swiss francs and a "compensatory penalty" in the amount of 36.4 million Swiss francs. The basis for the order was the admission by Alstom that consultants in these countries, acting on Alstom's behalf, had paid considerable bribes to public officials in order to retain business.[28]

---

[28] Jacinta Oduor et al., Left out of the Bargain: Settlements in Foreign Bribery Cases and Implications for Asset Recovery, Stolen Asset Recovery Series (2014).

5. Bribery of Domestic Officials

5.1 JURISDICTION

Domestic criminal law applies to bribery offenses committed within the territory of the country, irrespective of the nationality of the perpetrator.[29]

5.2 STATUTE OF LIMITATIONS

The statute of limitations in Tunisia is 10 years for felonies, 3 years for misdemeanors, and 1 year for "petty offenses."[30] All corruption-related crimes in Tunisia are either felonies or misdemeanors.[31] Article 6 of the Code of Criminal Procedure provides that the statute of limitations may be interrupted by any investigative measure or any step in criminal proceedings, even with regard to targets who are not directly implicated by such step.

5.3 DOMESTIC BRIBERY OF OFFICIALS: OFFENSES

The Penal Code, Articles 15, 16, 18, 21, and 83–94, criminalizes active and passive bribery, that is, both paying and accepting bribes,[32] using public resources for private gain, trading in influence, or "the actions of receiving or giving rewards to public officials for the purpose of influencing the official's decision-making in the discharge of his/her public function."[33]

5.4 DEFINITION OF DOMESTIC OFFICIALS

"Public official" is defined in Article 82 as "any person who is granted official powers or who is employed by an agency of the State, a local authority, a public institution or any other entity responsible for the management of a State facility."

5.5 GIFTS, GRATUITIES, AND HOSPITALITY

As stated previously, the Penal Code reflects no exception for facilitation payments, or any allowance for marketing and promotional expenses, although gifts are considered distinct from bribes on the basis of corrupt intent. Article 83 provides that "Any person having the quality of civil servant who accepted, directly or indirectly, for himself or for the benefit of someone else, gifts, donations, promises or any kind of advantage, to accomplish an

---

[29] MENA-OECD Investment Programme, "Business Ethics and Anti-bribery Policies in Selected Middle East and North African Countries," *available at* https://www.oecd.org/mena/competitiveness/36086689.pdf (last visited Dec. 14, 2018).

[30] Code of Criminal Procedure Arts. 3, 4, and 5.

[31] Conference of the States Parties, *supra* note 9.

[32] It should be noted that the Penal Code currently does not define of the offense of "active bribery" (Arts. 91–93).

[33] MENA-OECD Investment Programme, *supra* note 29, at 22.

action related to his position, will be given 10 years in prisons and fined 10,000 Tunisian Dinars." According to Article 37 of Tunisia's Penal Code, where the law systematically sets the criminal gift or gratification in context with a deed requested or offered—that is, a quid pro quo—gifts or gratification that have been given or taken without consideration are not considered bribery.

5.6 DEFENSES

As stated previously, under Article 37 of the Penal Code where the law requires a quid pro quo as an element of the offense, gifts or gratification that have been given or taken without consideration are not considered bribery.

Article 93 of the Penal Code provides that individuals involved in corruption conduct are absolved if they come forward regarding the conduct and provide evidence thereof before the commencement of any investigation.

5.7 PENALTIES

According to the Penal Code, the offense of bribery or "offering, promising or giving any undue pecuniary or other advantage to a Tunisian public official," directly or through an intermediary, carries a 10-year prison sentence and a fine equal to twice the amount of the bribe received or promised; the minimum fine is TND 10,000 (approximately U.S. $6,000).

6. Commercial Bribery

Commercial bribery does not appear to be addressed by Tunisia's Penal Code.

7. Sentencing Principles

Penalties for corruption offenses including sentences of imprisonment ranging from 1 to 20 years, in addition to fines and other penalties. Under article 56 of the General Civil Service Regulations, a civil servant who commits a crime shall be suspended from official duties immediately. Removal from public office is a penalty that must be imposed in cases of active or passive bribery, and an optional penalty in cases of abuses of power, misappropriation of public funds, and money laundering. Violation of conflict of interest laws are subject to a maximum of three years imprisonment.[34]

8. Related Criminal Offenses

Related offenses include money laundering and extortion. Tunisian law also addresses conflict of interest in a range of statutes, including the requirement that public

---

[34] Penal Code, Sec. 97 bis.

employees shall not have private employment without the permission of the employee's public office.[35]

Finally, Tunisian law provides for asset forfeiture.[36] Conspiracy and attempt are also criminalized.[37]

9. Cooperation and Self-Reporting

9.1 SELF-REPORTING

Article 93 of the Penal Code provides that bribers or intermediaries who notify the public authorities of the offense before criminal charges are brought against them will be exempted from punishment.[38] This article applies only to a narrow category of corruption offenses, and not to related offenses such as money laundering, concealment, embezzlement, abuse of functions, or obstruction of justice.[39]

9.2 COOPERATION WITH INVESTIGATORS

Tunisia does not have an institutional basis to encourage persons who have participated in the offense to cooperate with investigators in order to recover the proceeds of an offense.[40]

9.3 PLEA AGREEMENTS/LENIENCY

Tunisian law does not provide for the reduction of sentences for a person who cooperates with law enforcement.[41]

10. Whistle-Blower Protections

Tunisia does not provide an integrated system of protection for whistle-blowers.[42]

11. Key International Treaties Related to Bribery and Corruption

As for multilateral treaties, Tunisia signed the United Nations Convention against Corruption in 2004 and ratified the UNCAC in 2008.[43] It signed the United Nations Convention Against Transnational Organized Crime in 2000, and ratified the UNTOC

---

[35] Law 112, Sec. 5.

[36] Penal Code, Arts. 5, 28, 29, 94, and 98.

[37] *Id.*

[38] August 2015, *Transparency International Condemns Draft Bill in Tunisia That Would Set the Corrupt Free,* (Transparency International Secretariat), Aug. 2015, *available at* http://www.transparency.org/news/pressrelease/transparency_international_condemns_tunisian_draft_law_that_would_set_the_c.

[39] Conference of the States Parties, *supra* note 9.

[40] *Id.*

[41] *Id.*

[42] *Id.*

[43] *Signatories to the United Nations Convention against Corruption, available at* https://www.unodc.org/unodc/en/treaties/CAC/signatories.html (last visited Dec. 14, 2018) .

in 2003.[44] Tunisia is not party to either the OECD Anti-Bribery Convention or the African Union Convention on Preventing and Combating Corruption.

Weeks before the Jasmine Revolution, the League of Arab States issued the first official pan-Arab anti-corruption instrument— the Arab Convention to Fight Corruption (ACAC)—which was signed on December 21, 2010, by 21 Arab countries, including Tunisia. The preamble of the ACAC affirms that the fight against corruption is not limited to the official authorities, as people and civil society have a crucial role to play.[45] It reiterates the need for international cooperation in the extradition of criminals, mutual legal assistance, and asset recovery.[46] The convention is based on the principles of "Islam and other Religions of the Book," the Charter of the Arab league, the UN Charter, and all regional and international conventions related to fighting corruption that Arab states have signed, including the UNCAC.[47]

The ACAC requires states parties to take a number of anti-corruption steps. Article 2 states that it aims to prevent and repress all forms of corruption through reinforcing Arab cooperation, particularly in the recovery of stolen assets, and emphasizes the goal of enhancing the role of individuals and civil society to achieve these goals.[48] With regard to the crimes that constitute corruption, the article describes 13 such actions, including bribery of national and international public officials, corruption in public and private sectors, money laundering, illicit enrichment, abuse of functions, embezzlement of property in the private and in public sectors, trading in influence, and obstruction of justice.[49] Article 10 states the importance of prevention and criminalization of corruption and outlines measures which states parties should implement to ensure the participation of citizens in the fight against corruption, including standards for transparency and competition in public procurement, and encourages signatories to develop codes of conduct and ethics standards for public employees.[50] The importance of raising awareness about corruption amongst citizens is highlighted in Article 11, which suggests that states parties should include fighting corruption in education curricula, as well as advertising anti-corruption institutions to which citizens can send their complaints.[51] Finally, Article 14 of the Convention urges each state party to protect witnesses, experts, victims, and whistle-blowers.

Tunisia is a founding member of the Middle East and North Africa Financial Action Task Force, which combats money laundering and terrorist financing. It is also a member of the Arab Anti-Corruption and Integrity Network (ACINET), which in April 2013 issued the Beirut Declaration Against Corruption, a document entitled "Reconciling Hopes with

---

[44] *Signatories to the UN Convention against Transnational Crime and Its Protocols, available at* https://www.unodc.org/unodc/en/treaties/CTOC/signatures.html (last visited Dec. 14, 2018).

[45] Arab Anti-Corruption Convention, *available at* https://star.worldbank.org/star/sites/star/files/Arab-Convention-Against-Corruption.pdf (last visited Dec. 14, 2018).

[46] *Id.*

[47] Transparency International, *A Glance at the Arab Convention to Fight Corruption,* Aug. 21, 2012.

[48] *Id.*

[49] *Id.*

[50] *Id.*

[51] *Id.*

Realities in the Fight against Corruption: Paving the Way for Innovation," which calls for a renewed commitment from the Arab states to meaningfully address corruption.

12. Mutual Legal Assistance Treaties and Transnational Cooperation

Neither an MLAT nor an extradition treaty exists between Tunisia and the United States. However, Tunisia does have Major Non-NATO Ally (MNNA) status, granted by the United States in 2015.[52] There is also a consular convention between the two countries, which establishes clear obligations with respect to matters such as notification of consular officers of the arrest and detention of nationals and protection of the rights and interests of nationals of their countries (1992),[53] and a Convention between the government of the United States of America and the government of the Tunisian Republic for the Avoidance of Double Taxation and the Prevention of Fiscal Evasion with Respect to Taxes on Income (1990).[54]

13. Legal Professional Privilege

Under Tunisian law, attorney-client privilege is referred to as "professional secrecy." The bar requires that lawyers take an oath of professional secrecy as a condition to practicing law.[55] Violation of the privilege is subject to criminal prosecution and up to six months imprisonment.[56] The privilege may be waived with the consent of the client unless the disclosure of the secret "threatens public policy or morality."[57]

14. Privacy and Data Protection

Article 24 of the Constitution provides that "the state protects the right to privacy, the sanctity of domiciles, the confidentiality of correspondence and communications, and personal data." However, Tunisia's 2004 Personal Data Protection Law, a relic of the Ben Ali regime, gives state authorities the power to process and collect personal data without the supervision of an independent body.[58] Under the same law, public institutions are not required to obtain consent from data subjects when collecting or processing data.[59] Data subjects are also barred from accessing information possessed by public authorities.[60]

---

[52] *Designation of Tunisia as a Major Non-NATO Ally, available at* http://www.state.gov/r/pa/prs/ps/2015/07/244811.htm (last visited Dec. 14, 2018).

[53] *Consular Convention with the Republic of Tunisia, available at* https://www.congress.gov/treaty-document/101st-congress/12 (last visited Dec. 14, 2018).

[54] Tax Convention with Tunisia, *available at* https://www.irs.gov/pub/irs-trty/tunisia.pdf (last visited Dec. 14, 2018).

[55] Law n° 89-87, Chapter II, Article 5 (attorney registration conditions), Sept. 7, 1989.

[56] Penal Code, Art. 254.

[57] *Id.*

[58] Law No. 2004-63 on Personal Data Protection.

[59] *Id.*

[60] *Id.*

15. Forecast for Reforms and Parting Thoughts

Tunisia continues its active efforts to address corruption. Moreover, many Tunisian companies, especially publicly traded ones and companies with foreign interests, are introducing codes of conduct and internal controls on a voluntary basis and are taking other measures to improve their own integrity. Business associations also take an active role in promoting integrity measures and an active part in the MENA-OECD Business Integrity Network, "a forum for business to engage in peer-learning and knowledge-sharing from the region and beyond, in view of promoting stronger, cleaner and fairer business environments."[61] However, the former president of the national anti-corruption agency, Samir Annabi, has declared that it will take "generations" to eradicate corruption in the mentality, behavior, and institutions of Tunisia.[62]

The absence of corruption does not automatically result in democracy, but meaningful participatory democracy cannot exist where corruption thrives. As stated in the Preamble of the United Nations Convention against Corruption, "problems and threats posed by corruption . . . undermin[e] the institutions and values of democracy, ethical values and justice."[63] Conversely, democratic systems that permit freedom of speech and association tend to reduce corruption. The adversarial nature of a multiparty system also chills corruption: competitive elections may both incentivize politicians to reveal the untrustworthy behavior of their opponents and to earn the public trust.[64]

The Nobel Peace Prize for 2015 was awarded to a coalition of Tunisian labor union leaders, businesspeople, lawyers, and human rights activists "for its decisive contribution to the building of a pluralistic democracy in Tunisia in the wake of the Jasmine Revolution of 2011." The Norwegian Nobel Committee specifically cited the effort made by the "Tunisian Quartet" to support the work of the constitutional congress and the constitutional process in 2014, resulting in a Constitution that was approved by that country's national assembly and signed by President Moncef Marzouki. In a country with a history of corruption and kleptocracy, Article 10 of the Tunisian Constitution and the legal reforms that have followed are a strong declaration of intent to change course. History will judge if they fulfill their promise.

---

[61] Practices to Strengthen Business Integrity In the MENA Region, *available at* http://www.oecd.org/mena/competitiveness//PracticesBusinessIntegrity.pdf (last visited Dec. 14, 2018).

[62] UNDP, *Appui a l'Etablissment d'un Systeme National d'Integrite en Tunisie*, Jan.–June 2015.

[63] Preamble, United Nations Convention against Corruption, https://www.unodc.org/documents/treaties/UNCAC/Publications/Convention/08-50026_E.pdf (last visited Dec. 14, 2018).

[64] Juliet Sorensen, *Ideals without Illusions: Corruption and the Future of a Democratic North Africa*, 10 Nw. J. INT'L HUM. RTS. 202 (2012), *available at* http://scholarlycommons.law.northwestern.edu/njihr/vol10/iss4/3.

APPENDIX

Key Issues	Tunisia Approach
Is jurisdiction subject to any international anti-corruption conventions? If so, which? (OECD, UN Convention against Corruption, etc.)	Yes, most notably, the UNCAC, the UNTOC, and the ACAC.
Is bribery of foreign public officials illegal (do domestic anti-bribery laws provide for extraterritorial application)?	Yes. According to Article 307 bis of Tunisia's Code of Criminal Procedure, "bribing a foreign official is illegal." GLOBAL INTEGRITY, *African Integrity Indicators, available at* https://www.globalintegrity.org/research/reports/global-integrity-report/global-integrity-report-2008/gir-scorecard-2008-tunisia-/.
What is the definition of foreign public officials?	"Foreign public official" is not defined in the Penal Code. However, "public official" is defined in Article 82.
Is commercial bribery illegal?	Commercial bribery does not appear to be addressed by Tunisia's Penal Code.
Is bribing domestic officials illegal?	Yes. According to Tunisia's Penal Code Article 91, "offering a bribe (i.e., active corruption) is illegal." Source: GLOBAL INTEGRITY, *African Integrity Indicators, available at* https://www.globalintegrity.org/research/reports/global-integrity-report/global-integrity-report-2008/gir-scorecard-2008-tunisia-/.
Can the receipt of a bribe be prosecuted?	Yes. Article 83 provides that "Any person having the quality of civil servant who accepted, directly or indirectly, for himself or for the benefit of someone else, gifts, donations, promises or any kind of advantage, to accomplish an action related to his position, will be given 10 years in prisons and fined 10,000 Tunisian Dinars." Source: GLOBAL INTEGRITY, *African Integrity Indicators, available at* http://aii.globalintegrity.org/indicator-details?country=tunisia&num=10&year=2015.

(Continued)

Key Issues	Tunisia Approach
Can companies be held criminally liable?	No. "[M]ost MENA countries' laws do not adopt the principle of criminal responsibility of legal persons (e.g., corporations) for bribery." Source: http://www.oecd.org/mena/competitiveness//36086689.pdf at page 28.
Can companies be held civilly liable?	No.
Can individuals be held civilly liable?	No.
Is there a "facilitation/grease payments" exception?	No.
Does the subject country provide for conspiracy liability relating to violations of the anti-corruption laws?	Yes. According to the Penal Code, "conspiracy to commit a crime (i.e., organized crime) is illegal." Source: GLOBAL INTEGRITY, *African Integrity Indicators, available at* https://www.globalintegrity.org/research/reports/global-integrity-report/global-integrity-report-2008/gir-scorecard-2008-tunisia-/.
Is there an affirmative disclosure obligations for potential violations of the anti-bribery laws or accounting irregularities?	Yes. Article 29 of Tunisia's Code of Criminal Procedure provides that "any constituted authority, any public official or employee who, in the exercise of his duties, becomes aware of an offence is required to report this fact immediately to the State prosecutor, together will all relevant information, records and documents." Source: http://www.oecd.org/mena/competitiveness//36086689.pdf at page 32.
Are "promotional expenses" exempt from the anti-bribery laws?	No.
Is the giving of gifts, entertainment, travel, meals, etc. restricted/prohibited?	Only where there is corrupt intent. According to article 37 of Tunisia's Penal Code, where the law systematically sets the criminal gift or gratification in context with a deed requested or offered, gifts or gratification that have been given or taken without consideration are not considered bribery. Source: http://www.oecd.org/mena/competitiveness//36086689.pdf at page 24.

Key Issues	Tunisia Approach
Are there any laws concerning things of value conveyed by, or to, third parties?	Yes. Article 91 of the Penal Code provides that third-party intermediaries are liable under anti-bribery laws to the same extent as the principals.
Are bribes tax deductible?	No. All bribes are illegal and hence are not tax deductible. 19 NO. 7 Middle E. Executive Rep. 16, 18.
Is the law applied extraterritorially?	Yes. Pursuant to article 307 bis of Tunisia's code of criminal procedure, Tunisian criminal law applies to crimes and offenses, including the offense of bribing a public official, committed outside Tunisia by Tunisian nationals. However, the exercise of extraterritorial jurisdiction is nevertheless sometimes subject to procedural requirements that can make it difficult to apply in cases of bribery of foreign public officials by the country's own nationals. Tunisia's criminal code requires that criminal charges be preceded by the filing of a complaint by the victim or an official "denunciation" by the country where the offence was committed. Source: http://www.oecd.org/mena/competitiveness//36086689.pdf at page 35.
Is having a robust corporate compliance program an affirmative defense or way to negate liability?	Yes, where corporate compliance includes voluntary, affirmative disclosure. Article 93 provides that individuals involved in corruption conduct are absolved if they come forward regarding the conduct and provide evidence thereof before the commencement of any investigation.
Is there a "local law" exception/defense?	No.
What are the potential penalties/sanctions both for civil and criminal violations?	The range of punishments are reflected in Chapter III of the Penal Code. Bribery is punished by 10 years imprisonment and a fine of double the gain. Judicial corruption is punished by 20 years in prison where the case involves a potential sentence of life imprisonment or death and the judge accepts a bribe in exchange for a particular judgment.

(Continued)

Key Issues	Tunisia Approach
Is failure to keep accurate books and records a criminal and/or civil offense?	No.
Are there laws concerning a company's financial internal controls?	Yes. Law n° 2003-75 of 10 December 2003 requires companies to implement "know-your-customer" policies and establish internal controls . . . " Source: http://www.oecd.org/mena/competitiveness//36086689.pdf at page 17.

JULIET S. SORENSEN is a clinical professor at Northwestern Pritzker School of Law, where she teaches public corruption.

16 The United Arab Emirates

1. Introduction to UAE's Anti-Corruption Legislation

The United Arab Emirates (UAE)[1] passed its first anti-bribery legislation in the late 1980s, and over the years, has developed a wide-ranging framework that targets corruption, bribery, and even facilitation payments. The laws, which appear in legislative initiatives regulating a variety of industries and areas, create a robust system to combat both public and private-sector corruption and bribery. As a result, the UAE leads the Middle East as one of the least corrupt countries in which to do business in the region.[2]

Although anti-bribery legislation passed in the last 30 years focused primarily on combating domestic government corruption, the UAE government has recently passed laws penalizing the bribery of foreign officials and enhancing penalties for private-sector corruption. In addition, 2016 amendments to the Federal Penal Code strengthened the legal framework against public corruption, fraud, and embezzlement with a view to further protecting the public trust. For example, the UAE has now expanded the definition of a public official to include employees of entities owned in whole or in part by the government (both local and federal). In addition, the Penal Code now provides for fines of up to 500,000 AED (approximately U.S. $135,000) increased from 50,000 AED (approximately U.S. $13,600)

---

[1] This chapter was contributed by Miller & Chevalier's Lamia Matta and Al Tamimi & Company's Ibtissem Lassoued. Adam Wolstenholme, Senior Associate in the Dubai office of Al Tamimi & Company, provided invaluable research assistance.

[2] Pursuant to Transparency International's 2016 Corruption Perception Index https://www.transparency.org/news/feature/corruption_perceptions_index_2016#table.

From Baksheesh to Bribery. T. Markus Funk and Andrew S. Boutros.
© Oxford University Press 2019. Published 2019 by Oxford University Press.

against private companies whose officers or agents seek to obtain a benefit by paying a government employee to misuse his or her public position.

The recent changes follow the recommendations of a September 2013 report[3] by the Implementation Review Group of the United National Convention against Corruption (UNCAC or "the Convention"), which identified gaps in the UAE's legal framework against corruption (discussed in detail in Section 2.3 of this chapter). The UAE has since sought to address those gaps and, in a number of announcements, has affirmed its commitment to transparency and accountability.

2. UAE's Domestic Anti-Corruption Framework

Formed in 1971, the UAE is a federation of seven emirates made up of Abu Dhabi, Ajman, Dubai, Fujairah, Ras al Khaimah, Sharjah, and Umm al Quwain. Abu Dhabi, the second most populous city, serves as the capital. The country follows a civil law system, where the primary source of law is found in a system of codes (penal and civil, with sharia law governing certain areas, such as inheritance and personal status) and in legislation. By contrast, common law prevails in the free zones, out of which most multinationals operate.[4] In all criminal matters, however, whether in the free zones or without, the federal penal provisions apply.

The Ministry of Justice appoints all federal judges, while judges for each emirate are appointed by the rulers of each emirate. The courts consist of a court of first instance, a court of appeals, and a court of cassation. Within each of these, there is a criminal division, a civil division, and a sharia division. The Federal Supreme Court sits in Abu Dhabi.

There are common law courts operating in two of the UAE's free zones which deal only with commercial disputes: the DIFC Courts in Dubai and the Abu Dhabi Global Markets Courts. These courts can hear local or international commercial disputes as long as all parties consent to the courts' jurisdiction.

The laws that address corruption in the UAE are distributed in numerous legislative instruments. Sections 2.1 and 2.2 describe the primary laws that apply.

2.1 CRIMINAL LAW REGIME

The UAE's criminal law is predominantly regulated through federal provisions that apply throughout the UAE. In addition these criminal provisions apply within the

---

[3] https://www.unodc.org/documents/treaties/UNCAC/WorkingGroups/ImplementationReviewGroup/ExecutiveSummaries/V1386204e.pdf.

[4] Free zones are special economic zones that offer very attractive business conditions to expatriate investors. Depending on the free zone, these can include tax concessions, duty-free imports, freedom from currency restrictions, and complete foreign ownership and control. As of July 2017 there are more than 40 free zones operating in the UAE. These economic zones are governed by a special framework of rules and regulations applicable to each individual trade zone. The largest of these is the Dubai International Financial Center ("DIFC") which has its own independent regulator (the Dubai Financial Service Authority), judicial system (DIFC Courts), and global financial exchange.

free zones, which usually operate under a civil and administrative framework separate from the federal provisions. The relevant federal criminal laws are contained within the following:

- UAE Federal Penal Law No. 3 of 1987 as amended by Emiri Decree No. 7 of 2016 ("Penal Code");
- UAE Federal Law No. 4 of 2002 on the Criminalization of Money Laundering as amended by Federal Law No. 9 of 2014 ("AML Law").

Abu Dhabi and Dubai have their own Penal Codes (Abu Dhabi Penal Code No. 1 of 1970 and Dubai Penal Code Law No. 1 of 1970) that also contain anti-bribery provisions (Articles 41–42 and Articles 118–122, respectively). The anti-bribery provisions in the Abu Dhabi and Dubai penal codes were passed prior to the federal anti-bribery laws, and today they apply only to the extent that they do not conflict with the Federal Penal Code. The Codes of Abu Dhabi and Dubai are utilized by Public Prosecutors where there are no associated provisions in the Federal Code. As such and since the Federal Code covers anti-bribery laws, the Abu Dhabi and Dubai Codes that relate to bribery are redundant as they provide no greater protection than the federal provisions.

2.2 CIVIL LAW REGIME

The UAE's civil anti-bribery regime operates at the federal level through Federal Decree Law No. 11 of 2008 as amended by Federal Decree Law No. 9 of 2011 and Federal Decree Law No. 17 of 2016, ("Federal Human Resources Law"). The bribery provisions in the Federal Human Resources Law are outlined in Chapter 10 of the law and govern he conduct of civilian employees working in federal entities.

In addition to the federal law, Abu Dhabi and Dubai have implemented their own civil codes that can be utilized to combat corruption, namely:

- Abu Dhabi Law No. 6 of 2016 concerning Human Resources in the Emirate of Abu Dhabi;
- Abu Dhabi Law No. 1 of 2006 concerning Civil Service in the Emirate of Abu Dhabi;
- The Dubai Government Human Resources Management Law No. 27 of 2006, which tackles government corruption in Dubai;
- Dubai Recovery of Public Funds Law No. 37 of 2009, relating to unlawful use of public funds in Dubai.

2.3 VIEW FROM THE OUTSIDE

2.3.1 OECD Evaluation

The UAE is not party to the OECD Convention on Combating Bribery of Foreign Public Officials in International Business Transactions.

2.3.2 The UNCAC Implementation Review Group Evaluation

The UAE signed onto UNCAC on August 10, 2005, and ratified it on February 22, 2006.[5] A peer-review process called the Implementation Review Mechanism evaluates the implementation of the Convention into domestic law by states that are parties. The Review Mechanism is non-punitive and non-adversarial and has no ranking system. However, it results in the publication by the Implementation Review Group of a country review report that—while drafted in close cooperation with the state being reviewed—nonetheless offers insight into challenges the country has faced in implementing the Convention as well as successes and good practices. The first cycle of the Review Mechanism started in 2010 and covers the UNCAC chapters on criminalization, law enforcement, and international cooperation. The second cycle, which was launched in November 2015, will cover the UNCAC chapters on preventive measures and asset recovery.

The Implementation Review Group conducted its UAE assessment in January 2013. The UAE's self-assessment and the full report have not been made available, but the Executive Summary of the Implementation Review Group's report is publicly available.[6] In the category of "successes and good practices," the Review Group found that the UAE has a robust legal regime against money-laundering and it praised two distinct provisions of the Penal Code relating to the crime of concealment and to demand-side bribery in the private sector. As for the category of "challenges," among the Implementation Group's recommendations were that the UAE (1) continue to implement Article 16 of UNCAC, which prohibits bribery of foreign public officials and officials of public international organizations; (2) expand the long-arm jurisdiction of UAE courts; (3) criminalize active bribery in the private sector, (4) criminalize illicit enrichment in the public sector; (5) prevent bank secrecy from becoming an obstacle to investigations; and (6) provide greater legal protections to whistle-blowers.

As noted in Section 1 of this chapter, the UAE has taken steps to implement the Implementation Review Group's recommendations. For instance, the UAE expanded the definition of "bribery" to include foreign public officials, amended the Penal Code to create the offense of causing a loss to public funds by negligence,[7] and expanded the government's extraterritorial reach to prosecute bribery offenses that are committed outside the UAE. Although there are a number of recommendations that have not yet been implemented, the UAE has taken significant steps since the issuance of the 2013 report to expand the reach and scope of its anti-corruption laws.

2.3.3 Transparency International Corruption Perception Index Score

Transparency International (TI), which measures the perceived levels of public sector corruption in countries and territories around the world,[8] began evaluating the perception of

---

[5] https://www.unodc.org/unodc/en/treaties/CAC/signatories.html

[6] As of December 2018, the Executive Summary was accessible at the following link: http://www.unodc.org/documents/treaties/UNCAC/WorkingGroups/ImplementationReviewGroup/ExecutiveSummaries/V1386204e.pdf.

[7] Penal Code Article (227).

[8] According to TI, "[t]he annual Corruption Perceptions Index reflects the perceptions of business people, academics and risk analysts, both resident and non-resident." The data from these sources is analyzed by independent statisticians and data specialists. https://www.transparency.org/research/cpi/cpi_2003/0/.

corruption in the UAE in 2003. At that time, the UAE ranked number 37 out of 133 countries evaluated. Finland, which ranked at number 1 that year, was deemed to have the lowest levels of perceived corruption. Bangladesh, which that year ranked the lowest at 133, was described by TI as a country "where corruption is perceived to be pervasive." The rank of the UAE has changed over the years, going from as low as 35 in 2008 to as high as 21 in 2017. TI published its most recent annual Corruption Perceptions Index in 2017, in which, as noted earlier, it ranked the UAE 21st out of 176 countries, giving it the highest rank that year of any country in the Middle East and North Africa.

3. Investigative and Prosecutorial Agencies

As bribery and corruption are criminal offences under UAE law, the main investigative agencies are criminal agencies.

3.1 CRIMINAL LAW AGENCIES

At a federal level, the following government entities are involved in the enforcement and regulation of anti-corruption:

- The police;
- The Public Prosecutor's Office;
- The Ministry of Justice.

The police are generally responsible for the initial investigation of allegations of corruption and bribery. The police have the authority to refer matters to the Public Prosecutor's Office for decisions relating to criminal complaints and prosecution.

The Public Prosecutor oversees the investigation, gathers evidence, questions witnesses, and determines whether a crime has been committed. Once such a decision has been made, the prosecutor files the indictment and transfers the case to the applicable court.

The Ministry of Justice has supervisory responsibility for the judiciary. Under the investigative approach of the state authorities, the Ministry of Justice supervises all parties responsible for the investigation and prosecution of criminal matters, including but not limited to judges, prosecutors, and the courts.

3.2 CIVIL LAW AGENCIES

The UAE's State Audit Institution (SAI), a civil law agency that has independent status within the UAE, has investigative authority in relation to public sector financial transactions. The SAI is the supreme audit authority in the UAE and its aim is to provide financial oversight and increase the accountability of federal entities. SAI's "Department of Anti-Corruption and Investigation of Financial Violations" investigates those cases of public sector fraud, corruption, and fiscal mismanagement detected by its auditors or referred to it by its president. Where appropriate, the SAI refers cases of fiscal crimes to the Public Prosecutor's office.

Where no crime has been committed, the SAI has the authority to recommend disciplinary sanctions.

At the state level, His Highness Sheikh Mohammed bin Zayed Al Nahyan, Crown Prince of Abu Dhabi and Deputy Supreme Commander of the UAE Armed Forces, issued directives in May 2015 to the Abu Dhabi Accountability Authority (ADAA) to create an Anti-Corruption Unit (ACU) within the ADAA. The ACU's mandate is to investigate financial irregularities and corruption and to identify gaps in internal controls and propose legislation and internal audit regulation to address them. This Unit was intended to work in conjunction with state and federal criminal law agencies and to have investigative powers in relation to financial irregularities and corruption. However, to date, the Unit has not been as proactive as had been envisioned.

3.3 MULTIAGENCY ARRANGEMENTS

Federal Law No. 39 of 2006 Concerning International Judicial Cooperation in Criminal Matters was passed to facilitate the UAE's cooperation with foreign and international judicial authorities. This law empowers federal courts and the Ministry of Justice, under enumerated circumstances, to provide information to foreign authorities regarding the identity and whereabouts of an individual, search persons and premises, seize property, and obtain information and evidence that might assist their foreign counterparts in conducting investigations or making extradition arrangements.

The UAE Central Bank's Anti-Money Laundering and Suspicious Cases Unit (AMLSCU) has similarly entered into over 40 memoranda of understanding with foreign Financial Intelligence Units in an attempt to affect improved exchange of information and assistance in combatting financial crimes.

In the League of Arab States, the well-established Riyadh Arab Agreement for Judicial Cooperation of 1983 ("Riyadh Agreement") also encourages greater cooperation between signatory countries. It provides for the mutual recognition and enforcement of court judgments among contracting states as well as, among other areas, the exchange of information between the ministries of justice of contracting states and the extradition of persons accused or convicted in contracting states.

Joining the global fight against corruption, the League of Arab States issued the Arab Convention to Fight Corruption on December 21, 2010. The UAE, in conjunction with 20 other Arab countries, signed on to the convention, which provides in Article 10, paragraph 9, for cooperation between signatory states as well as cooperation between signatory states and relevant international and regional organizations.

4. Bribery of Foreign Officials
4.1 JURISDICTION

In October 2016, the anti-bribery provisions of the UAE Federal Penal Code were amended to include foreign public officials and employees of international organizations. Pursuant to Article 237 of the Penal Code, as amended, it is now a violation of UAE law to bribe a foreign public official as well as officials of public international organizations. Pursuant to Article 234 of the Penal Code, as amended, it is also a crime for foreign public officials or employees of international organizations to solicit or accept (whether directly or indirectly) for themselves or for others, "a gift, benefit or other grant that is not due or a promise or anything in order to commit or omit an act in violation of the duties of his or her function." The UAE may assert jurisdiction over foreign officials if the bribe was committed in the UAE or if the effects of the bribe were intended to be in the UAE.

Article (239) (bis) (1), as amended, provides extraterritorial jurisdiction over any offenses involving bribery, even if committed outside the territory of the UAE:

> The provisions of this Law shall apply on whoever commits one of the crimes set forth in this Chapter outside the State, or if the perpetrator or the victim is a national of the country, or if the crime is committed by an employee of the public or private sector of the State or affects a public property.[9]

4.2   STATUTE OF LIMITATIONS

The October 2016 amendment to the Penal Code has removed all statutes of limitation as they relate to bribery in the UAE. Specifically, Article 239 (2) (bis), as amended, states that although certain predicate offenses may have statutes of limitations, these will not apply in cases of bribery or corruption, either for a criminal or civil claim:

> The criminal action shall not abate upon the lapse of the term in one of the crimes provided for in this Chapter and the adjudged sentence shall not abate. The civil actions that arise from or are connected to such action shall not abate upon the lapse of the term.[10]

4.3   FOREIGN BRIBERY OFFENSES

Articles 234–239 of the Penal Code, as amended, relate to bribery offenses, including foreign bribery, and are contained in Part Two of the Penal Code, which covers Crimes against Public Administration.

4.4   "FOREIGN PUBLIC OFFICIALS" DEFINED

The law defines Foreign Public Officials expansively at Article 6 (bis) (1) of the Penal Code:

> A foreign public official in accordance with this Law shall be: any person who occupies a legislative, executive, administrative or judicial position in another country, whether

---

[9] The official language of the UAE is Arabic, and all legislation is written in Arabic. Translations provided in this article are unofficial translations taken in large part from Westlaw© Middle East.

[10] Article 239 (2) (bis).

permanent or temporary, and whether he is elected or appointed, with or without a salary, and any person entrusted with public service functions.

The same section of the Penal Code also provides an expansive definition of an "employee of an international organization" as "any person who occupies a position in an international organization or is authorized by such organization to act on its behalf."

Through the implementation of such inclusive definitions, the Penal Code now applies to far more individuals than had previously been affected by anti-corruption legislation, and accordingly has strengthened the general anti-corruption framework in the UAE.

4.5 GIFTS, GRATUITIES, AND HOSPITALITY

When it comes to foreign officials, UAE law requires that there be an underlying intent to bribe on the part of the gift-giver before a gift can be characterized as a bribe. What constitutes proof of intent will depend of the specific facts of each case. In determining whether the requisite intent existed, courts and prosecutors consider a number of factors including the context in which the gift is given (for example, if the gift is given as a wedding gift), the frequency with which gifts were given, the value of the gift, the timing of the gift, the custom of the parties, and the ability of the recipient to affect the gift-giver's position with regard to winning or retaining business.

There is no minimum threshold under UAE law for the valuation of gifts. A subjective assessment involving the above context is undertaken by the authorities when reviewing the value of the gift that is involved and subject to review.

4.6 DEFENSES

Pursuant to Article 239 of the Penal Code, a person who offers a bribe to a government official "shall be exempt from punishment if he informs the judicial or administrative authorities of the crime before the crime is discovered." The protections of Article 239 do not extend to the individual who receives or accepts the bribe.

Save for the exception of voluntary self-reporting, there are no statutory defenses available in the Penal Code.

4.7 PENALTIES

Article 234 of the Penal Code, which makes it illegal for a foreign public official to accept, directly or indirectly, a gift, benefit or other grant, provides a statutory minimum punishment of 3 years imprisonment, while the maximum, pursuant to Article 68 of the Penal Code, is 15 years imprisonment.

With regard to supply-side bribery of foreign public officials, Articles 237 and 237 (bis) provide a minimum sentence of three years' imprisonment and a maximum of 5 years imprisonment.

In addition to imprisonment, Article 238 provides a punitive financial penalty as follows:

A convict shall be ordered to pay a fine equivalent to what has been demanded or offered or accepted, in all cases shown in the preceding Articles of this chapter, provided that the fine shall not be less than five thousand Dirhams.

A judgment shall also be passed for the confiscation of a gift accepted by or offered to the public official or the person entrusted with public service functions.

5. Bribery of Domestic Officials

5.1 JURISDICTION

Articles 234–239 of the Penal Code govern bribery offenses relating to both foreign and domestic officials. In addition, Article 239 (bis) (1) of the Federal Penal Code provides jurisdiction over crimes of bribery (both demand-side and supply-side bribery) where the crime was committed outside the UAE but the act affects UAE public funds, or was committed by a national of the UAE or any person employed in either the public or private sector in the UAE.

5.2 STATUTE OF LIMITATIONS

As noted previously, the October 2016 amendments to the Penal Code removed statutes of limitation as they relate to bribery in the UAE. For offenses committed prior to October 2016, however, the 20-year statute of limitations still applies to limit liability.

5.3 DOMESTIC BRIBERY OF OFFICIALS OFFENSES

As noted above, Articles 234–239 of the Penal Code govern bribery offenses. In addition, the Federal Human Resources Law provides guidance relating to the personal conduct of domestic officials, and specifically addresses conduct in relation to gifts, bribes, and conflicts of interest.

5.4 DEFINITION OF DOMESTIC OFFICIALS

A "public official" as defined in Article 5 of the Penal Code is "any person occupying a federal or local job, whether legislative, executive, administrative, or judicial, and whether he is appointed or elected." The definition includes:

(a) persons entrusted with the public authority,
(b) employees working in ministries and governmental departments,
(c) members of the Armed Forces,
(d) employees of the state's security apparatus,
(e) members of the judiciary,

(f) members of legislative, consultative and municipal councils,

(g) whomever is delegated by any of the public authorities to perform a specific assignment within the limits of the work entrusted to him,

(h) members of boards of directors, managers and all other employees working in associations, public corporations and companies partially or wholly owned by the federal government or the local governments, and

(i) members of boards of directors, managers and all other employees working in associations and public welfare institutions.

Article 5 further provides that those not included in the categories described in the "preceding paragraphs but who perform work connected to public service in accordance with instructions issued to him from a public official having the authority to give such an instruction according to prescribed laws or regulations, concerning the work assigned to him, shall be considered *ipso jure* (that is, by operation of law) to be entrusted with public service functions."

5.5 GIFTS, GRATUITIES, AND HOSPITALITY

Article 70 of the UAE Federal Human Resources Law prohibits any government employee from receiving "any gifts, except for those that bear the logo and name of the presenting party." The article further prohibits individuals from making or distributing gifts except in the name of the federal ministry and, more specifically, the organizational unit approved by the ministry to distribute gifts.

5.6 DEFENSES

As noted previously, Article 239 extinguishes criminal liability where the bribe payer discloses the criminal activity to the authorities. With the exception of that provision, there are no other defenses available under the Penal Code.

5.7 PENALTIES

Article 234 of the Penal Code, which makes it illegal for a public servant to accept, directly or indirectly, a gift, benefit, or other grant, provides a statutory minimum punishment of 3 years imprisonment, while the maximum, pursuant to Article 68 of the Penal Code, is 15 years imprisonment.

With regard to offering, whether directly or indirectly, a thing of value to a public servant, in order for such employee to commit or omit and act in violation of the duties of his or her function, Articles 237 and 237 (bis) provide a minimum sentence of three years imprisonment and a maximum of five years imprisonment. As noted previously, in addition to imprisonment, Article 238 contemplates a financial penalty not less than 5,000 Dirhams (around $U.S. 1,350) or the equivalent amount of the bribe offered. Furthermore, the authorities will confiscate any gift provided.

6. Commercial Bribery

6.1 JURISDICTION

Although the anti-corruption provisions of the Penal Code—Articles 234–239—govern bribery of both domestic and foreign officials, they also apply in the private sector context.

6.2 STATUTE OF LIMITATIONS

As noted previously, all statutes of limitation as they relate to bribery in the UAE have now been repealed.

6.3 COMMERCIAL BRIBERY OFFENSES

Pursuant to UAE law, demand-side bribery involving purely commercial enterprises, that is, accepting gifts or money from the agents or employees of potential contractors or partners in exchange for securing an advantage over business competitors, constitutes a crime under Article 236 (bis) and 236 (bis) (2).

UAE, however, does not criminalize supply-side commercial/private bribery. Accordingly, the act of offering a gift, or benefit, in exchange for obtaining an advantage over competitors is not encompassed in the legislation and is therefore legal. As noted in Section 2.3 of this chapter, the UN Implementation Review Group recommended in its September 2013 Executive Summary that the UAE pass legislation criminalizing supply-side bribery in the private sector. Although there have been recent developments relating to the UAE's anti-bribery provisions, these developments have not addressed the proffering of gifts under purely commercial/private agreements.

6.4 DEFENSES

As noted previously, save for any voluntary self-disclosure, there are no defenses available to those who accept a bribe.

6.5 PENALTIES

In the UAE, a wronged party who has suffered damage as a result of a crime may be joined to criminal proceedings as a claimant to effect temporary compensation to gain restitution for the harm committed.

The amount of the restitution may be decided by the criminal courts and may include restitution and compensation for damages. However, the matter must be referred to the civil courts following conviction of the accused.

7. Sentencing Principles

7.1 GENERAL PRINCIPLES

Authorities take a zero-tolerance approach to bribery in the UAE, and since October 2016, there has been a general increase in judicial sentencing powers for such crimes. For example, the penalty for offering a bribe to a public official (either domestic or foreign) has increased from a period of imprisonment of at least a year and a fine of not less than 10,000 AED (approximately U.S. $2,723) to imprisonment for three to five years and a fine equal to the amount offered, but not less than 5,000 AED (U.S. $1,350).[11] However, courts and judges in the UAE do not exercise a great deal of discretion in determining sentences. In the UAE, the sentence ranges are defined by statute. There is nothing akin to the U.S. Federal Sentencing Guidelines or any similar set of rules that set out a uniform sentencing policy. A judge can exercise discretion only in determining whether the sentence will be at the low or high end of the statutory range.

7.2 DOMESTIC VERSUS FOREIGN BRIBERY

As a general rule, the UAE has taken domestic bribery very seriously and has developed a robust set of laws that criminalize bribery and that define what is appropriate behavior for a public servant. We now await case law related to the recently introduced legislation making it illegal to bribe foreign officials. The implementation of the October 2016 amendments is, however, a clear statement of intent by the UAE authorities that they will maintain a robust approach to bribery in all of its forms.

8. Related Criminal Offenses
8.1 CONSPIRACY

Although the UAE Penal Code contemplates the common law concept of conspiracy as it relates to violent crimes, there are no specific articles in the criminal law that encompass conspiracy as it would relate to bribery-related criminal offenses.

8.2 ATTEMPT

Under UAE law an attempt is defined as "the commencement of the execution of an act with the intention to commit a crime, if its effect is prevented for reasons beyond the control of the felon."[12]

The term commencement refers to the "[c]ommitment of an act, if in itself it is regarded as a constituent part of the practical element of the crime or gives rise to it immediately and directly." Neither having the intent to commit a crime nor carrying out preparatory deeds constitutes an attempt to commit a crime unless the law provides otherwise. It is a question of fact whether the person's conduct is preparatory or rises to the level of having "commenced" to commit a crime.

Unless the law provides otherwise, the penalty for "attempt" is as follows:

(a) Imprisonment for life if the penalty designated for the crime is the death sentence.
(b) Imprisonment for a certain term if the penalty designated for the crime is life imprisonment.

---

[11] Penal Code Article (237) (bis).
[12] Penal Code Article (34).

(c) Imprisonment for a period not exceeding half of the maximum penalty provided for the crime, or detention if the penalty provided for is imprisonment for a certain term.[13]

8.3 AIDING AND ABETTING

The UAE Penal Code recognizes two kinds of criminal complicity, direct and by causation. Article 44 of the Penal Code provides that principals and accomplices to a crime are equally responsible before the law. Moreover, accomplices to crimes face the same criminal liability as the principal under the UAE Penal Code.

For a person to be a direct accomplice, a person must (1) join another person in committing the crime, and (2) take part in committing the crime by intentionally committing any of its constituent acts. An accomplice shall be equally liable for the crime whether he contacts the principal directly or through an intermediary. If the accomplice utilizes another person to execute any of the constituent acts of the crime, and the latter person is, for any reason, not criminally responsible for those actions, the accomplice will be deemed liable.[14]

To be an accomplice by causation, a person must (1) encourage a crime that then occurs in accordance with the encouragement, or (2) collude with others to commit a crime and the crime occurs in accordance with the plan, or (3) provide a third person with a weapon, tool, or any material support that is then used to knowingly carry out a crime, or (4) willfully assist a third party by any means to prepare for, facilitate, or complete a crime.[15] An accomplice by causation who is found at the scene of a crime with the intent to commit the crime shall be considered a direct accomplice if the crime is not committed by another person.[16]

Article (51) of the Penal Code provides that a direct or causative accomplice to a crime shall receive the penalty of the crime that has actually been committed, even if it is other than that intended to be committed, whenever the crime that took place is a probable consequence of the complicity that has happened.

8.4 FALSE ACCOUNTING/BOOKS AND RECORDS

The UAE does not have a law like the FCPA under which companies and individuals can be prosecuted for failure to maintain accurate financial records. Pursuant to the UAE Federal Law No. 2 of 2015 ("Commercial Companies Law"), companies that are publicly traded on the UAE stock market have disclosure obligations and, at certain periods of the fiscal year, must file final audited financials with the Emirates Securities and Commodities Authority (ESCA), the Department of Economic Development (DED), and the relevant stock exchange. Both ESCA and DED may impose penalties for failure to maintain

---

[13] Penal Code Article (35).
[14] Penal Code Article (44).
[15] Penal Code Article (45).
[16] Penal Code Article (46).

accounting records that accurately reflect the financial position of the company.[17] With a few exceptions, private companies, on the other hand, are not required to make such filings.

Because the Commercial Companies law creates reporting obligations,[18] the mischaracterization of expenditures on a company's financials could conceivably be deemed a violation of the law. Typically, however, the UAE authorities do not pursue a bribery or fraud case using the financial disclosure laws as its prosecutorial vehicle.

8.5 MONEY LAUNDERING

In 2002, the UAE passed an AML Law that criminalizes any acts involving the transfer, conversion, deposit, concealment, or disguise of any property related to criminal offenses, or the source of the same. The 2014 amendment (Federal Law No. 9 of 2014) established the UAE's Financial Information Unit, a body that is responsible for money laundering offenses and suspicious transactions in the UAE.

In addition to federal laws and regulations, the UAE Central Bank issues circulars to reflect local, regional, and global changes in the anti-money laundering and countering terrorist financing (AML/CTF) framework, and there are mandatory AML/CTF procedures issued by various supervisory bodies such as the Dubai Financial Services Authority (DFSA), the independent financial regulatory agency of the DIFC. The DFSA's regulatory mandate is laid out in Law No. 12 of 2004 ("UAE Regulatory Law of 2004"), which among other things, empowers the DFSA to set policy and make rules regarding matters delegated to its authority. Among the matters under its jurisdiction is the issuing of policy and rules relating to anti-money laundering in the DIFC. To implement that mandate, the DFSA adopted as part of its Rulebook an Anti-Money Laundering module that is "designed to provide a single reference point for all persons and entities . . . who are supervised by the DFSA for Anti-Money Laundering (AML), Counter-Terrorist Financing (CTF) and sanctions compliance."[19] The DFSA's civil guidance and regulation with respect to AML is meant to supplement AML/CFT provisions under federal criminal law. Note, however, that although the DFSA has the jurisdiction to regulate rules and policy, any prosecution relating to criminal AML/CFT issues would be brought by the federal authorities applying the federal AML/CFT law.

8.6 TAX AND OTHER FRAUDS

There are no specific tax laws in the UAE that relate to fraud. However, Chapter VI of the Penal Code, entitled "Embezzlement and Damage to Public Property," provides a maximum penalty of five years for "any public official or a person assigned to public service and having concern with the collection of taxes, fees, fines or the like, who knowingly seeks to take what is not due, or in excess of what is due."[20]

---

[17] Commercial Companies Law, Article 344.
[18] Commercial Companies Law, Article 236.
[19] http://dfsa.complinet.com/net_file_store/new_rulebooks/d/f/DFSA_CP89_App1.pdf.
[20] Penal Code Article (226).

The UAE introduced its own value added tax (VAT) law on January 1, 2018,[21] and in July 2017, the UAE issued Federal Law No. 7 of 2017, which sets out the rights and obligations between the UAE's Federal Tax Authority and taxpayers, and also completes the framework to implement VAT and other taxes.

9. Cooperation and Self-Reporting

9.1 POWERS OF INVESTIGATORS AND PROSECUTORS

The powers of investigative authorities are governed by the UAE Penal Procedures Law (Federal Law No. 35 of 1992).

Initial investigations in the UAE are usually conducted by the police, who will assess the strength of the evidence and will interview the accused. Once this initial investigation has been concluded, the suspect may be arrested and detained for an initial period of up to 48 hours.

Should there be grounds for suspicion and further detention the suspect will be transferred to the Public Prosecutor's Office. The Public Prosecutor's Office has 24 hours to decide whether to arrest the suspect, remand him with or without bail, or release him without charge.[22]

Both the police and the Public Prosecutor's Office have the authority to investigate necessary evidence in order to indict a suspect. The Public Prosecutor's Office has a supervisory role and has greater power in regards to this investigation than the police. As an example of the Public Prosecutor's greater powers, in the UAE the police do not have the right to search a suspect's domestic residence without prior written authorisation from the Public Prosecutor's Office. Once a suspect has been charged, the Public Prosecutor may direct the police to collect further evidence to assist with their enquiries.

9.2 COOPERATION WITH INVESTIGATORS

As noted previously, under Article 239 of the Penal Code, a Public Prosecutor has the discretion to dismiss a criminal report or abstain from prosecuting a briber or intermediary if the individual informs the judicial or administrative authorities of the crime or confesses her crime before it is discovered. This provision does not provide automatic immunity to the person who has reported such a crime, but it does permit the authorities to exercise discretion as to how to proceed.

9.3 SELF-REPORTING

There is an affirmative obligation under UAE law to disclose a criminal act to authorities. Article 274 of the Penal Code requires individuals to disclose any information they have of a criminal act:

> Whoever becomes aware of a crime and abstains from informing the concerned authorities shall be punished by a fine not exceeding one thousand Dirhams

---

[21] https://www.mof.gov.ae/En/budget/Pages/VATQuestions.asp.
[22] UAE Penal Procedures Law, Article 47.

[approximately U.S. $272]. Exemption from such a penalty may be granted if the person concerned is a spouse of the offender or one of his descendants, ascendants, brothers, sisters or persons having the same degree of relationship by marriage.

Furthermore pursuant to the AML Law, employees of financial, commercial, and economic establishments are legally required to report any offenses related to money laundering or the financing of terrorism to the UAE's Financial Information Unit.[23]

9.4 PLEA AGREEMENTS

There are no provisions in the UAE legal or judicial systems that enable prosecution authorities to accept plea agreements.

9.5 LENIENCY

Save for the provisions of Article 239 of the Penal Code (discussed in Section 9.2 of this chapter), there are no established principles relating to prosecutorial exercise of leniency under UAE law.

10. Whistle-Blower Protection

10.1 GENERAL PRINCIPLES

Notwithstanding recent efforts to include greater whistle-blower protections in the AML Law, there is currently no federal law protecting the rights of whistle-blowers in the UAE. As noted in Section 9.3 of this chapter, Article 274 of the UAE Penal Code imposes a positive obligation on individuals who become aware of a crime to report that crime to the authorities. If the crime is not reported, the individual could face prosecution and a financial penalty.[24] UAE privacy laws, however, conflict with the UAE's statutory reporting obligation. For example, if the information being disclosed constitutes commercial or personal confidential information, the individual could be accused of violating his or her employment contract, or worse, risk prosecution and face imprisonment for a minimum period of one year (Article 379 of the Penal Code). Where trade secrets are disclosed, an individual may also face civil liability.

In its September 2013 Executive Summary, the UN Implementation Review Group specifically recommended that the UAE consider enacting legislation aimed "at protecting reporting persons from retaliation or other unjustified treatment," in line with Article 33 of the UN Convention that requires that each state party consider incorporating into its domestic legal system appropriate measure to provide protections to whistle-blowers.

---

[23] AML Law, Article 15.
[24] Moreover, there are no financial rewards or incentives in the UAE for disclosure of criminal acts.

Although the government has not introduced legislation that protects whistle-blowers as a category, the 2014 amendment to the AML law introduced protection for individuals who blow the whistle on matters relating specifically to money laundering and terrorism. The AML Law exempts from prosecution and civil and administrative liability any person who violates a legislative, contractual, regulatory, or administrative provision while providing the authorities information relating to money laundering or terrorism, provided the report is not false, made in bad faith, or with the intent to prejudice third parties.

More recently, in April 2016, the Emirate of Dubai introduced Dubai Law No. 4 of 2016 ("Law 4 of 2016"), which first, establishes the Dubai Economic Security Centre ("the Centre") and second, provides explicit protections to any whistle-blower who submits an allegation to the Centre. Pursuant to Law 4 of 2016, the role of the Centre is to provide economic security to Dubai by monitoring fraud and financial irregularities in the Emirate. When an individual discloses an allegation of wrongdoing to the Centre, the Centre is required to ensure the freedom, protection, and security of the whistle-blower, including from confidentiality rules to which the whistle-blower may have agreed. It is currently not clear whether a whistle-blower would receive the same protection if the report were made to a government body other than the Centre, but answers to these and other questions will become clear as the law is applied in practice.

10.2 ATTITUDE TOWARDS WHISTLE-BLOWERS

Whistle-blowing is uncommon in the Middle East. As noted previously, in the UAE whistle-blowers risk civil or criminal prosecution for violating data privacy laws or for damaging the reputation of persons they have accused of wrongdoing. Recent developments, however, indicate that the UAE government is taking steps to protect those who wish to report a crime, at least in the AML context. Dubai's recent move to protect whistle-blowers will likely result in greater federal protection in the coming years and thus more incentive to blow the whistle on fraud and corruption.

11. Key International Treaties Relating to Bribery and Corruption

The UAE is party to various international treaties and has adopted the following:

- The United Nations Convention against Corruption, adopted by the UN General Assembly in October 2003, was signed by the UAE in August 2005 and ratified it in February 2006, through Federal Decree No. 8 of 2006;
- The United Nations Convention against Transnational Organized Crime, adopted by the UN General Assembly on November 15, 2000, was signed by the UAE in December 2002 and ratified on May 9, 2007;
- The Arab Convention for Combating Corruption was signed by the UAE in December 2010.

12. Mutual Legal Assistance Treaties and Transnational Cooperation

UAE is signatory to a number of international conventions that provide grounds for legal assistance with other signatory parties for crimes covered by the convention, including but not limited to the following:

- United Nations Convention against Corruption;
- Arab Convention to Fight Corruption;
- Arab League Treaty for Recognition and Enforcement of court decisions;
- Arab League Treaty on International Judicial Co-operation in Criminal Matters;
- Riyadh Arab Agreement for Judicial Co-operation;
- Arab League Convention on Extradition; and
- Arab League Committee on Anti-Money Laundering.

13. Legal Professional Privilege

Like many civil law jurisdictions in the Middle East, the legal system in the UAE does not recognize the common law concept of legal professional privilege. However, in the UAE, lawyers are bound by a duty of confidentiality to their clients that operates, in many ways, like the common law concept of legal privilege. For example, legal representatives may not disclose a client's confidential information, and a client may seek recourse if such disclosure is made. Pursuant to Article 379 of the UAE Penal Code, it is a crime to disclose documents containing secrets or confidences where the documents were fraudulently obtained or where they were entrusted to a party because of that party's profession or position.

In regards to civil matters in the free zones, as noted previously, there are currently two common law courts operating in the UAE, the DIFC Courts in Dubai and the ADGM Courts in Abu Dhabi. These courts have their own laws, regulations, and independent judicial authority, where the concept of legal privilege is relied upon by the parties. However, as also noted previously, even in the free zones, jurisdiction over criminal matters is reserved to the federal courts.

14. Privacy and Data Protection

In the UAE, there is no single, comprehensive federal law regulating the collection and use of personal data. The UAE Penal Code makes it an offense to publish, through any means, news, pictures, or comments pertaining to the secrets of people's private or familial lives. It also makes it an offense for anyone who is entrusted with a secret, by reason of profession, craft, circumstance, or art, to disclose the secret, or use it for his or her own benefit, or that of another, unless such disclosure or use is permitted by law or by the consent of the person to whom the secret pertains.

There are, however, data protection laws that govern businesses registered and operating in the DIFC and other free zones. Those legal provisions are generally consistent with data protection laws from other jurisdictions (specifically, the EU Data Protection Directive 95/46/EC and the UK Data Protection Act 1998). They regulate the collection, handling, disclosure, and use of personal data in the DIFC, as well as the rights of individuals to whom the data belongs.

The DIFC data protection rules require that personal data be processed fairly, lawfully, securely, and for a specified and legitimate purpose. They also contain restrictions on data transfer from within the DIFC to places outside.

15. Forecast for Reforms and Parting Thoughts

The recent amendments to the Penal Code are a clear demonstration of the intention of the UAE legislature to widen the scope of the anti-corruption legislation and increase the protections available to both public and private entities.

On a practical level and in addition to the above, in January 2016 the UAE Ministry of Interior started the "My Job Is a Trust" Campaign raising awareness about avoiding corruption and the abuse of power.[25] The police authorities have also shown their intent to maximize the application and implementation of the anti-bribery provisions by advertising the use of a website, aman.gov.ae, that serves as a confidential reporting portal to allow users to anonymously report any suspicions of corruption.

The Dubai police authorities have also recently shown their intent to pursue criminals to the fullest extent of the law regardless of the amount of the bribe offered. In August 2018, the Dubai Court of First Instance issued a six-month prison sentence for an official of the Road Transport Authority, who accepted a bribe of 5,000 Dirhams (U.S. $1,361) from a driving student in exchange for passing the student on his driving examination. That same month, a Dubai Court of Appeals sentenced a manager of a government-owned entity to 18 months in prison and fined her 4.8 million Dirhams (U.S. $1.3 million) for demanding bribes of construction company executives seeking to win construction tenders. The construction company managers also received one-year prison terms as well as fines in the amount of the bribes paid.

APPENDIX

Key Issues	UAE's Approach
Is the UAE subject to any international anti-corruption conventions?	Yes.
	• UN Conventions Against Corruption and Organized Crime
If so, which conventions?	• UN Convention Against Transnational Organized Crime
	• Arab Convention for Combatting Corruption
Is bribery of foreign public officials illegal?	Yes.
Do domestic anti-bribery laws apply extraterritorially?	Yes.

(Continued)

---

[25] https://www.moi.gov.ae/en/media.center/news/news1k20160126.aspx.

Key Issues	UAE's Approach
What is the definition of a foreign public official?	A foreign public official is defined in Article 6 (bis) of the Penal Code as "[a]ny person who occupies a legislative, executive, administrative or judicial position in another country, whether permanent or temporary, and whether he is elected or appointed, with or without a salary, and any person entrusted with public service functions." The anti-bribery laws also make it a crime to bribe an "employee of an international organization." That term is defined in Article 6 (bis) of the Penal Code as "any person who occupies a position in an international organization or is authorized by such organization to act on its behalf."
Is commercial bribery illegal?	Yes, but only passive bribery is illegal. That is, it is illegal to accept gifts or money from the agents or employees of others in exchange for securing an advantage over business competitors.
Is bribing domestic officials illegal?	Yes.
Can the recipient of a bribe be prosecuted?	Yes.
Can companies be held criminally liable? If so, what is the requisite intent for corporate criminal liability?	Yes. Respondeat superior liability applies.
Can companies be held civilly liable?	No.
Can individual be held civilly liable?	Yes.
If there a "facilitation payment" defense?	No.
Do conspiracy laws apply to anti-corruption offenses?	No.
Does the UAE provide liability for: a) aiding and/or abetting liability relating to violations of the anti-corruption laws? b) attempt liability relating to violations of the anti-corruptions laws?	a) Yes. b) Yes.

Key Issues	UAE's Approach
Is the failure to keep accurate books and records a criminal or civil offense?	It is a civil offense under the Commercial Companies Law for publicly traded companies to fail to maintain accounting records that accurately reflect the company's financial position.
Do any books and records offenses have to involve proof of an underlying bribery offense?	This is not applicable in the UAE context.
Are there UAE laws concerning a company's financial internal controls? If so, are those laws applicable to public and/or private companies?	Yes, the UAE Commercial Companies Law imposes disclosure obligations on publicly traded companies that, at certain periods of the fiscal year, must file final audited financials with the Emirates Securities and Commodities Authority (ESCA), the Department of Economic Development (DED), and the relevant stock exchange. The laws are applicable only to companies that are publicly traded on the UAE stock exchange.
Is there an affirmative disclosure obligation for potential violations of anti-corruption laws or accounting irregularities?	Yes under both the Penal Code and the AML law.
Are "promotional expenses" exempt from UAE's anti-corruption laws?	Yes, Article 70 of the UAE Federal Human Resources Law prohibits any government employee from receiving "any gifts, except for those that bear the logo and name of the presenting party".
Is the giving of gifts, entertainment, travel, meals, or other gratuities restricted or prohibited by anti-corruption or other laws?	Yes.
Are there any UAE laws concerning things, property, or benefits of value conveyed by, or to, third parties?	Yes.
Are tax bribes deductible?	There are no business tax laws governing this area. The only tax that applies in the United Arab Emirates in the Value Added Tax.
Are the UAE's anti-corruption laws applied extraterritorially?	Yes. where the crime was committed outside the state but where the act affects UAE public funds or was committed by a national of the UAE or an employee in either the public or private sector of the UAE.

(Continued)

Key Issues	UAE's Approach
Is a robust corporate compliance program an affirmative defense or a factor to negate liability or reduce penalties?	No.
Is there a "local law" exception or defense to UAE's anti-corruption laws?	No.
Is "credit" given for cooperation with authorities? If so, how and in what form?	Credit may be given at the discretion of the Public Prosecutor's Office solely in relation to voluntary self-reporting.
Does the UAE have mutual legal assistance with the United States that covers criminal matters, including anti-corruption conduct?	No.
What are the potential penalties/sanctions for criminal and civil violations of the UAE's anti-corruption laws?	Article 234 of the Penal Code, which makes it illegal for a public servant to accept, directly or indirectly, a gift, benefit or other grant, provides a statutory minimum punishment of 3 years, while the maximum, pursuant to Article 68 of the Penal Code, is 15 years. With regards to offering, whether directly or indirectly, a thing of value to a public servant, in order for such employee to commit or omit and act in violation of the duties of his or her function, Article 237 and 237 (bis) provide a minimum sentence of three years imprisonment and a maximum of five years imprisonment. As noted previously, in addition to imprisonment, Article 238 contemplates a financial penalty in both instances.

17 United Kingdom

1. Introduction to the United Kingdom's Anti-Corruption Legislation

Since the late nineteenth century the United Kingdom[1] has implemented a series of anti-corruption laws targeting corrupt behavior and the proceeds of criminal activity, whether they within the UK or abroad. It, indeed, was one of the first countries in the world to have explicit statutory provisions outlawing bribery, and has had a long-standing legislative framework prohibiting fraud and misconduct in public office.[2]

These laws were, however, rarely used. And prosecutions were few and far between.[3] One impediment to more robust enforcement was the complexity and overlapping nature of the various pieces of legislation addressing bribery, which seemingly had evolved as a result of piecemeal reforms over time. Following recommendations by the Organisation for Economic Cooperation and Development (OECD), the UK adopted its first comprehensive anti-corruption legislation in the form of the Bribery Act 2010 ("Bribery Act"), which went into force in July 2011. The Bribery Act is now considered arguably one of the most stringent anti-corruption statutes in the world, criminalizing both public and commercial bribery.

---

[1] This chapter was contributed by Quinn Emanuel Urquhart & Sullivan's Robert Amaee.

[2] Including, the Public Bodies Corrupt Practices Act 1889, Prevention of Corruption Act 1906, Prevention of Corruption Act 1916 and the Criminal Law Act 1977, the Anti-terrorism Crime and Security Act 2001, and the Proceeds of Crime Act 2002.

[3] Prior to the Bribery Act, there had been only one successful prosecution for overseas bribery in 2008, when an individual was sentenced to prison for conspiring to corrupt U.S. officials.

From Baksheesh to Bribery. T. Markus Funk and Andrew S. Boutros.
© Oxford University Press 2019. Published 2019 by Oxford University Press.

In spite of the adoption of the Bribery Act (to great fanfare—in particular in the United States), very few prosecutions of note had until recently been brought under the Bribery Act. The main agency responsible for enforcing the Bribery Act, the Serious Fraud Office (SFO) had, compared to its counterpart in the United States, the Department of Justice (DOJ), secured very few corporate criminal convictions or significant financial settlements.

That said, the introduction of deferred prosecution agreements (DPAs) in February 2014 and the UK government's renewed emphasis on combatting financial crime, (illustrated by legislative proposals to expand the scope of existing financial crime legislation[4] and public consultations on amendments to the test for corporate criminal liability[5]), has led to the emergence of a more proactive and seemingly more aggressive approach to enforcement. The SFO's DPA with Rolls Royce Plc in January 2017 resulted in a record-breaking £497 million settlement, putting it on a par with the more headline-grabbing settlements achieved by the DOJ and comprehensively refuting the criticism that the SFO is not prepared to push for substantial financial penalties.

2. The United Kingdom's Domestic Anti-Corruption Framework
2.1 CRIMINAL LAW REGIME

The primary piece of legislation criminalizing bribery in the UK, the Bribery Act, was enacted on April 8, 2010, and came into force on July 1, 2011. It was introduced along with guidance issued by the Ministry of Justice ("MOJ Guidance") on its compliance implications for companies.[6] The Bribery Act abolished the existing common law and statutory offences dealing with bribery and corruption and introduced new offenses of "bribing another person" (whether in the private or public sector) and "being bribed," a novel corporate offence of failure to prevent bribery, and a separate offense of bribery of foreign public officials. The Bribery Act applies only to offences that occurred after the date it came into force. Prior to the Bribery Act, bribery offenses were contained in a variety of legislation, primarily the Prevention of Corruption Act 1906.[7] For acts and offenses that predate July 1, 2011, these statutes remain relevant.

Notwithstanding the new, toothy legislative framework, the UK government has acknowledged that it is difficult under English law to prosecute companies for criminal offenses committed by their employees or agents. This is, in large part, due to the current

---

[4] The Criminal Finances Bill (first read in Parliament in 2016) introduces a new corporate offense of failure to prevent the facilitation of tax evasion. Similar to section 7 of the Bribery Act, the new offense will hold corporations liable for the actions of employees and agents. It is expected to enter into force in 2017.

[5] *See* call for evidence to consider reforms in relation to corporate criminal liability, launched on January 13, 2017. The aim is to "consider whether existing laws sufficiently hold companies to account for the criminal wrongdoing of their staff. For example, it will look at whether successful convictions are being hindered by prosecutors needing to prove the 'directing mind and will' of businesses undertaking criminal activity." Source: https://www.gov.uk/government/news/new-crackdown-on-corporate-economic-crime (last visited Dec. 19, 2018).

[6] Ministry of Justice Guidance on the Bribery Act 2010, published March 30, 2011.

[7] *See also* the Public Bodies Corrupt Practices Act 1889, the Prevention of Corruption Act 1916, and the Anti-Terrorism, Crime and Security Act 2001.

state of the law on corporate criminal liability, which requires prosecutors to show that those at board level or other senior officers acting as the company's "directing mind and will" were involved in the criminal conduct.[8] This can be difficult to prove, particularly in relation to large organizations in which decision-making is often decentralized.[9] As an example, there was considerable public debate regarding the hurdles prosecutors face in establishing corporate criminal liability following the SFO's inability to prosecute any of the banks implicated in its investigation of LIBOR rate manipulation.

Following calls from prosecutors and others for reform to this area of the law, the UK government introduced a new corporate offense of failing to prevent tax evasion (Part 3 of the Criminal Finances Act 2017, which came into force on 30 September 2017), and in January 2017 announced a public consultation to consider wider reforms.[10] There is little doubt that the UK is moving toward an enhanced corporate criminal liability framework. The only question remains whether there will be wholesale reform toward a U.S.-style "Respondeat Superior" model—in which the company can be held liable for the wrongful acts of an employee or agent, if such acts occur within the scope of the employment or agency—or an extension of the "failure to prevent" model, first introduced by the Bribery Act, to economic crimes other than bribery and tax evasion.

2.2 CIVIL LAW REGIME

Those who have suffered loss as a result of bribery have recourse in the civil courts to recover damages from the person who received the bribe, as well the person offering or advancing it. Both corporates and individuals can be held liable. Civil causes of action arise in scenarios in which a payment is made to an agent without the knowledge or consent of the principal. Common law definitions of bribery have consistently prescribed the following elements of the civil tort of bribery:

(a) An agency relationship.
(b) A payment made, or benefit provided, to the agent by a person dealing with the principal.
(c) Knowledge on the part of the person making the payment or advancing the benefit of the agency relationship.
(d) The payment made to the agent is not disclosed to the principal.[11]

---

[8] The requirement is referred to as the "identification principle." *See Tesco Supermarkets Ltd v Nattrass* [1971] UKHL.

[9] For this reason, to date, the SFO has primarily had success in prosecuting smaller organizations. For example, the conviction of Smith & Ouzman for foreign bribery offenses in December 2014. The company concerned was small and family owned.

[10] *See* the Government's Corporate Liability for Economic Crime: Call for Evidence, announced on January 13, 2017, *available at* https://consult.justice.gov.uk/digital-communications/corporate-liability-for-economic-crime/.

[11] See *Petrotrade Inc v Smith* [2000] 1 Lloyd's Rep 486 and *Novoship (UK) Ltd and others v Mikhaylyuk and others* [2012] EWHC 3586 (Comm).

A claimant would, therefore, need to prove the payment of a bribe, that the bribe was paid to an agent, that the bribe was secret, and that the defendant knew that the recipient agent acted for the claimant. To assist claimants English law has developed a number of irrebuttable assumptions. It is assumed that there was a corrupt motive in relation to the bribe[12] and also that the agent was influenced by it.[13] It is also irrelevant whether the parties believed what they doing was wrong,[14] nor is it necessary to demonstrate the principal suffered any loss as a result of the bribe.[15]

Separate to civil claims for bribery brought by private persons, prosecutors, including the SFO, can use their powers under Part V of the Proceeds of Crime Act 2002 (POCA) to apply for a Civil Recovery Order (CRO) in respect of "criminal property," the benefits resulting from bribery offenses. These powers are reserved to the state and cannot be used by private individuals to recover damages. CROs can be deployed even without a criminal conviction and have been used by the SFO in a number of settlements with companies that were deemed to be in possession of the criminal property.[16]

The SFO has an additional civil power in the form of Serious Crime Prevention Orders (SCPOs), introduced by the Serious Crime Act 2007.[17] SCPOs are a form of injunction that may be imposed by an English court against individuals or corporates found to be involved in serious crime (committed in the UK or elsewhere). They are designed to prevent, restrict, or disrupt involvement in serious crime.[18] The SFO must show to the court that there is a real or significant risk that the defendant will commit further offenses. Prohibitions, restrictions, or requirements (or other terms the court considers appropriate) may be imposed. For example, a restriction may be imposed on an individual's financial dealings or his freedom to travel within or outside the UK. Although a civil order with a civil standard of proof, violation of a SCPOs amounts to a separate criminal offense that is punishable in addition to the underlying criminality. SCPOs are, however, intended to protect the public and address the risk of additional criminal offending, and are not intended to punish. In March 2009, the SFO obtained its first SCPO against an individual for his involvement in a boiler room fraud.[19]

---

[12] *Anangel v IHI* [1990] 1 Lloyd's Rep 167.

[13] *Shipway v Broadwood* [1899] 1 QB 369.

[14] *Id.*

[15] *Parker v McKenna* (1874) 10 Ch App 96.

[16] For example, CROs have been imposed by the SFO on companies including Mabey Engineering, Oxford University Press, Macmillan Publishers Limited, KBR Haliburton, and DePuy/Johnson & Johnson.

[17] The SFO may apply for a SCPO to the High Court or the Crown Court. Applications are made to the Crown Court if a person has been convicted of a serious offense, or to the High Court on a "stand-alone" application if the person has been "involved" in serious crime. *See* CPS Guidance on SCPOs, *available at* http://www.cps. gov.uk/legal/s_to_u/serious_crime_prevention_orders_(scpo)_guidance/ (last visited Dec. 19, 2018).

[18] A corporation or an individual is treated as having being involved in "serious crime" if he: (1) has a conviction for a serious offense (including Bribery Act and money laundering offenses), (2) has facilitated the commission by another person of a serious offense, or (3) he has conducted himself in a way that was likely to facilitate the commission by himself or another person of a serious offense in the UK.

[19] SFO press release dated March 20 2009, *available at* http://webarchive.nationalarchives.gov.uk/ 20090606100924/http://www.sfo.gov.uk/news/prout/pr_616.asp?id=616.

2.3 VIEW FROM THE OUTSIDE

2.3.1 Organisation for Economic Cooperation and Development

In December 2001, the UK enacted aspects of the OECD's Convention on Combatting Bribery of Foreign Public Officials in International Transactions (the OECD Convention) by implementing certain provisions in the Anti-Terrorism, Crime and Security Act 2001 (ATCSA). The ATCSA confirmed the reach of the UK's jurisdiction to bribery committed abroad by its nationals and enhanced existing bribery laws to include foreign public officials, two key requirements of the OECD Convention.

In March 2003 the OECD Working Group on Bribery in International Business Transactions published a report that, while acknowledging that significant steps had been taken, was critical of a number of aspects of the UK's legislative framework (highlighting the patchwork of overlapping statutes and common law offenses) and recommended that a comprehensive law be implemented.

Following the UK government's failure to address the highlighted issues, the OECD issued another report in 2005 (the OECD Report), which required the UK to enact "at the earliest possible date" wholesale legislation, including bribery of foreign public officials.[20] The OECD Report also specifically noted that no individual or corporation had been indicted or tried for the offense of bribing a foreign public official since the UK ratified the OECD Convention in 1998.[21] These deficiencies were finally addressed some five years later with the introduction of the Bribery Act.[22]

Notwithstanding this protracted process, the OECD has praised the Bribery Act, describing it as "essential to securing the credibility of the UK legal framework to fight bribery.[23] In response to the Working Group's recommendations and as a demonstration of its commitment to the OECD Convention, the Bribery Act includes a stand-alone offense dedicated to the bribery of foreign public officials.

2.3.2 Transparency International

Transparency International's Corruption Perceptions Index for 2016,[24] on a scale of zero (highly corrupt) to 100 (very clean), ranks the UK in 10th place out of 168 countries globally, placing it alongside Germany and Luxembourg as one of the countries with the least bribery

---

[20] Working Group Report, United Kingdom: Phase 2 Report on the Application of the Convention on Combating Bribery of Foreign Public Officials in International Business Transactions and the 1997 Recommendation on Combating Bribery in International Business Transactions, at paragraph 248, *available at* https://www.oecd.org/daf/anti-bribery/anti-briberyconvention/34599062.pdf (last visited Dec. 19, 2018).

[21] *Id.* para. 249.

[22] The Working Group repeated its recommendations in 2007 in its Follow-Up Report on the Implementation of the Phase 2 Recommendations, dated June 21, 2007. Source: http://www.oecd.org/daf/anti-bribery/anti-briberyconvention/38962457.pdf, and in 2008 with its Phase 2bis Report, dated October 16, 2008. Source: http://www.oecd.org/daf/anti-bribery/anti-briberyconvention/41515077.pdf.

[23] Press Release, OECD, OECD Secretary-General Angel Gurría Welcomed the Introduction into the UK Parliament of a New Bribery Bill (Nov. 23, 2009).

[24] Published on Jan. 25, 2017. Source: http://www.transparency.org/news/feature/corruption_perceptions_index_2016.

(or, at least, the lowest public perception of bribery—which may not be the same thing[25]). Transparency International has noted that the UK's scores have improved "significantly" in recent years, recognizing the UK's rise in the rankings from a pre-Bribery Act 20th position in 2010.[26] This progress is in large part due to the enactment of the Bribery Act, arguably the most far-reaching anti-corruption statute of all the OECD Convention signatory countries, and the increased focus of the UK government and enforcement agencies on combatting corruption.

3. Investigative and Prosecutorial Agencies

Bribery offences that are serious, complex or have a multijurisdictional dimension are investigated and prosecuted by the Serious Fraud Office (SFO). In cases of suspected corruption, the SFO has unique pre-investigation powers to compel disclosure of information that is used to assist the agency in determining whether to commence an investigation.[27] The same powers are also available to the SFO in all its cases, once it accepts a matter for investigation.[28] Less serious, or complex allegations of bribery that do not fall within the remit of the SFO, are investigated by the police force in the UK and, when appropriate, referred to the Crown Prosecution Service (CPS) for prosecution.

The SFO works closely with other agencies, including the National Crime Agency (NCA) (successor to the Serious Organised Crime Agency). The NCA leads the UK's international effort in relation to serious and organized crime of all kinds, including bribery and corruption. It works closely with other investigative agencies, regulators, and prosecutors in the UK, and its Economic Crime Command is tasked with coordinating the country's approach to financial crime. The NCA is also the agency to which organizations operating in the "regulated sector" and others will submit suspicious activity reports for the purposes of complying with the requirement of the Proceeds of Crime Act 2002.

Within the NCA, the International Corruption Unit (ICU) is a specialist division created in May 2015 as part of the UK government's 2014 Anti-Corruption Plan to work alongside the SFO, with a focus on investigating allegations of bribery of foreign officials and related money laundering offenses.[29] The ICU is also responsible

---

[25] *See generally* T. Markus Funk & Caryn Trombino, *Triple-Barrelled Critique of US Foreign Anti-corruption Efforts—But Is There Cause for Concern?* ABA CRIMINAL JUSTICE SECTION NEWSLETTER (Winter, 2011) (Although the media tends to imbue TI's Index with a quasi-scientific legitimacy, in reality, the Index relies on nonstandardized and frequently imprecise surveys, many of which vary dramatically in terms of completeness and methodology. TI's fine print reflects an appreciation of the Index's shortcomings: "Year-to-year changes in a country/territory's score can result from a change in the perceptions of a country's performance, a change in the ranking provided by original sources or changes in the methodology resulting from TI's efforts to improve the index."), *available at* https://www.perkinscoie.com/images/content/2/3/v2/23196/11-02-funk.pdf.

[26] *See* Transparency International's Summary, *Europe and Central Asia: Why Anti-corruption Laws Are Not Stopping the Corrupt.*

[27] Section 2A of the Criminal Justice Act 1987.

[28] *Id.* at section 2.

[29] The ICU combined the remits of the Metropolitan Police Proceeds of Corruption Unit, the City of London Police Overseas Anti-Corruption Unit, and elements of the Economic Crime Command.

for supporting foreign law enforcement agencies with international anti-corruption investigations, and the UK authorities with enforcement of financial sanctions, among other responsibilities.

Additionally, there are a number of cross-agency initiatives aimed at enhancing collaboration among the various agencies that have been tasked, to varying degrees, with combating financial crime. The Joint Financial Analysis Centre (JFAC), initially set up last year in response to the leak of the Panama Papers and the subsequent setting up of a Panama Papers Taskforce by the government, is one such initiative. JFAC brings together the SFO, the NCA, Her Majesty's Customs & Revenue, and the Financial Conduct Authority (FCA).[30]

Unlike the SFO and the NCA, the FCA, which regulates many financial services firms operating in the UK, is not mandated to enforce bribery and corruption legislation. It is, however, responsible for ensuring the integrity of the financial markets of the UK and has the power to investigate and impose penalties on the companies it regulates.[31] Regulated entities within the UK are required to maintain effective systems and controls to counter the risk of bribery and other financial crime, and the FCA has levied a number of sizeable fines on financial services firms that it deemed to have failed to maintain adequate systems and controls. The role of the FCA is of particular importance in ensuring effective enforcement. Financial institutions are viewed as "gatekeepers" to the UK's financial system, and markets are often targeted by those seeking to launder or move funds derived from corrupt activity.[32]

The FCA has had some success in enforcing anti-money-laundering compliance and, more generally, market integrity. It has imposed substantial financial penalties against UK and non-UK banks for money laundering breaches and for foreign currency exchange manipulation.[33] In January 2017, it fined Deutsche Bank AG £163 million, marking the largest financial penalty for anti-money-laundering controls failings imposed by the FCA to date.[34] However, perhaps its most significant enforcement success is the £1.1 billion in total fines levied against Citibank, HSBC Bank plc, JPMorgan Chase Bank NA, The Royal Bank of Scotland plc, and UBS AG in 2014 for failing to control business practices connected to their foreign exchange trading operations.[35] In addition to sizeable financial penalties, it launched an industry-wide remediation program to address "root causes" of the failings.

The FCA has also prosecuted other types of crime committed by those working within the financial services sector, most notably targeting individuals involved in insider dealing.[36] In

---

[30] *See* https://www.gov.uk/government/news/taskforce-launches-criminal-and-civil-investigations-into-panama-papers (last visited Dec. 19, 2018).

[31] https://www.fca.org.uk/firms/financial-crime (last visited Dec. 19, 2018).

[32] The role and importance of "gatekeepers" is explained in the Financial Action Task Force's report on Laundering the Proceeds of Corruption, July 2011.

[33] With respect to anti-money laundering, the FCA took enforcement action against Barclays Bank plc Final Notice, dated 25 November 2015, and Sonali Bank (UK) Limited (the UK subsidiary of Sonali Bank, which is ultimately owned by the Bangladesh government) Final Notice dated 12 October 2016, amongst others.

[34] Deutsche Bank AG Final Notice, dated 30 January 2017.

[35] Press Release, FCA, FCA Fines Banks £1.1 Billion for FX Failings and Announces Industry-Wide Remediation Programme" (Nov. 12, 2014).

[36] The FCA has the power to prosecute the criminal offense of insider dealing under Part V of the Criminal Justice Act 1993. It also has the power to prosecute criminal offenses related to insider dealing under Part 7 of

November 2016, following a high-profile two-year-long investigation it secured convictions against two individuals, one of which was the longest ever sentence handed down for insider dealing in a case brought by the FCA.[37] According to the FCA's statistics, it secured penalties totaling £884.6 million against regulated firms and individuals in 2015/2016.[38] Its approach to its wide range of enforcement powers, including criminal, civil, and regulatory penalties, are set out in its Enforcement Guide.[39]

4. Bribery of Foreign Officials

Section 6 of the Bribery Act provides a stand-alone offense of bribing a foreign public official. A "Foreign Public Official" is defined as an individual who holds a legislative, administrative, or judicial position (whether appointed or elected) or who exercises a "public function" for or on behalf of a foreign country. It also includes an individual who exercises a public function for a public agency or enterprise in a foreign country, such as state-owned companies. The broad definition includes officials or agents of international public organizations, whose members are countries, governments or other public organizations (such as the United Nations and the World Bank).[40] Foreign political parties and their officials, on the other hand, are not included within the scope of the definition, nor are prospective public officials.[41]

A person will be guilty of the offense if he or she offers, promises, or gives a financial or other advantage to a foreign public official or a third party, and the intention of the payer is to influence someone in his or her capacity as a foreign public official. In addition, the payer must also intend to obtain or retain business or an advantage in the conduct of business.[42] There is, however, no express requirement for the payer to intend to induce the public official to act improperly, although in practice this likely will be an ingredient of any charge brought under this section.[43]

Companies seeking to pay legitimate expenses for or provide hospitality to foreign public officials will need to be mindful of the lower threshold to establishing liability under section 6, as opposed to that under section 1 (see Section 5 "Commercial Bribery" in this chapter),

---

the Financial Services and Markets Act 2012, including the offenses of making false or misleading statements, creating false or misleading impressions, and making false or misleading statements or creating a false or misleading impression in relation to specified benchmarks.

[37] Press Release, FCA, Insider Dealers Sentenced in Operation Tabernula Trial (Nov. 30, 2016), *available at* https://www.fca.org.uk/news/press-releases/insider-dealers-sentenced-operation-tabernula-trial.

[38] FCA's Enforcement Annual Performance Account 2015/2016, Section 14, *available at* https://www.fca.org.uk/enforcement-annual-performance-account-2015-16/14-enforcement-statistics.

[39] FCA's Enforcement Guide, *available at* https://www.handbook.fca.org.uk/handbook/EG/1/1.html (last visited Dec. 19, 2018)

[40] Sections 6(5) and 6(6) of the Bribery Act.

[41] Bribes paid to or received by such persons could fall under sections 1 or 2 of the Act.

[42] Section 6(2) of the Bribery Act.

[43] Unlike offenses under the U.S. FCPA, the Bribery Act does not require the payer to have "corruptly" intended to influence the actions or decisions of the foreign public official.

and implement safeguards within their compliance programs to mitigate the increased risks.[44]

In that connection, the SFO has published guidance (SFO Guidance), which states that "bona fide hospitality, promotional or other legitimate business expenditure is recognised as an established and important part of doing business," and notes that the SFO will look to standard prosecution guidance, which incorporates public interest considerations, to determine whether to prosecute.[45] The MOJ Guidance goes further and states that "it is not the intention of the [Bribery] Act to criminalise such behaviour. The Government does not intend the Bribery Act to prohibit reasonable and proportionate hospitality and promotional or other expenditure."[46] As to what will be reasonable and proportionate will depend on the circumstances, but the MOJ Guidance does provide some indicators. The more lavish the hospitality or the higher the expenditure, the greater the inference that it is intended to influence the official, although the level of expenditure is not the only consideration.[47]

An additional consideration when dealing with foreign public officials is the fact that, unlike the U.S. Foreign Corrupt Practices Act 1977 (FCPA), the Bribery Act does not provide any exceptions for reasonable payments made to foreign public officials that are related to the promotion, demonstration, or explanation of goods or services, or the performance of a relevant contract.[48] Similarly, the Bribery Act does not provide an exemption for making payments to expedite or secure routine governmental actions, permitted in the FCPA as facilitating payments. The SFO Guidance states that such payments are a type of bribe under the Bribery Act, and were considered to be bribes even prior to the coming into force of the Bribery Act.[49]

In terms of territorial application, the offense of bribing a foreign public official can apply to acts or omissions forming part of the offense which take place in the UK, as well as those committed overseas, where the acts or omissions are committed by a person with a "close connection" to the UK (e.g., a British citizen, a person ordinarily resident in the UK, or a body incorporated in the UK).[50]

Penalties for bribing a foreign public official under the Bribery Act include a maximum prison sentence of 10 years (in the case of individuals) and/or an unlimited fine, and an unlimited fine for companies.

---

[44] The Bribery Act provides for a local law exemption, likely to be of limited utility, but in theory relevant to circumstances where a written law permits or requires the foreign public official to be influenced (e.g., a payment made to benefit the local community as part of a tender process).

[45] *See* SFO's Bribery Act Guidance on facilitation payments and business expenditure, revised in October 2012, *available at* https://www.sfo.gov.uk/publications/guidance-policy-and-protocols/bribery-act-guidance/.

[46] Ministry of Justice Guidance on The Bribery Act, published March 2011, at 12.

[47] *Id*. at 13.

[48] Title 15, Commerce and Trade, Chapter 2B, §§ 78dd-1(c), 78dd-2(c) and 78dd-3(c).

[49] *See* SFO's Bribery Act Guidance on facilitation payments and business expenditure, revised in October 2012, *available at* https://www.sfo.gov.uk/publications/guidance-policy-and-protocols/bribery-act-guidance/.

[50] Section 12 of the Bribery Act.

5. Commercial Bribery (Including Bribery of Domestic Officials)

Sections 1 and 2 of the Bribery Act prohibit the "bribing of another person" (whether in the public or private sector), and "being bribed." The offenses under these provisions can be committed as follows:

(a) offering, promising or giving a financial or other advantage, with the intention of inducing "improper performance;"

(b) being bribed, either by requesting, agreeing to receive or accepting a financial or other advantage, with the intention of inducing improper performance on the part of the recipient of a "relevant function or activity."

While "financial or other advantage" is not defined in the Bribery Act, any payment, gift, or other form of benefit, including corporate hospitality and promotional expenditure, could amount to such an advantage. "Function or activity" is defined, albeit broadly, to include that which is to be performed in good faith, impartially, or where the person performing it is in a position of trust.[51] It also includes any function of a public nature and any activity that is connected with a business, performed in the course of a person's employment, and any activity performed by or on behalf of a corporate or unincorporated body of persons.[52]

The Bribery Act sets out a two-limb test to determine whether a "financial or other advantage" is intended to induce "improper performance" by the recipient. Conduct will be deemed improper if it amounts to a breach of an expectation that a person will act in good faith, impartially, or in accordance with a position of trust.[53] These expectations are to be assessed with regard to "what the reasonable person in the UK would expect in relation to the performance of the type of function or activity concerned." This is an objective test, and is to be applied even if the function or activity occurs outside the UK.[54]

In terms of territorial application, the offenses can apply to acts or omissions forming part of the offense that take place in the UK, as well as those committed overseas, where the acts or omissions are committed by a person with a "close connection" to the UK (e.g., a British citizen, a person ordinarily resident in the UK, or a body incorporated in the UK).[55]

These offenses carry a maximum prison sentence of 10 years (in the case of individuals) and/or an unlimited fine, and an unlimited fine in the case of companies.[56]

---

[51] Section 3(1) of the Bribery Act.

[52] *Id.* section 3(2).

[53] *Id.* section 4.

[54] *Id.* section 5.

[55] *Id.* section 12.

[56] There is no limitation period for the prosecution of offenses under the Bribery Act. However, for individuals, the Human Rights Act 1998 provides a right to a fair and public hearing within a reasonable time.

6. Failure to Prevent Bribery; A Corporate Offense

The Bribery Act created a novel offense aimed at commercial organizations that fail to prevent bribes being paid on their behalf.[57] The offense will be committed if an "associated person" bribes another person (under Sections 1 or 6 of the Bribery Act) to obtain or retain business or an advantage in the conduct of business for a relevant commercial organization. An "associated person" is someone who performs services for or on behalf of the relevant commercial organization.[58]

A commercial organization can defend itself against a charge of having failed to prevent bribery, by proving, on the balance of probabilities, that it had in place at the time of the offending "adequate procedures" designed to prevent associated person from engaging in bribery. The Bribery Act provides no definition of what constitutes "adequate procedures," but the associated MOJ Guidance outlines six principles to assist companies in implementing such internal controls.[59] The U.S. DOJ and SEC have also released "A Resource Guide to the FCPA" (discussed in more detail elsewhere in this book) setting out 10 hallmarks of an effective FCPA compliance program.[60]

7. Sentencing Principles

The first Bribery Act convictions were secured by the Crown Prosecution Service (CPS) against individuals in relation to domestic bribery offenses. Although the offenses are perhaps less serious than those that fall within the SFO's remit, the sentences imposed have been fairly robust. The CPS secured the first conviction under the Bribery Act, within months of its introduction, against a court clerk for requesting and receiving a bribe of £500 in exchange for "fixing" speeding charges. The sentencing court viewed his offending as serious, handing down a term of six years imprisonment, reduced to four on appeal. This case and others since, including the taxi driver who offered a bribe to a licensing officer to pass his driving test and a university student who tried to bribe his tutor to change his grade, indicate a range of corrupt behavior that the CPS has been successful in prosecuting.

Following these early convictions, The Sentencing Council's Fraud, Bribery and Money Laundering Offences Definitive Guide (the Sentencing Guidelines) were introduced to assist the court in determining sentences to be applied. The Sentencing Guidelines apply to individuals and organizations sentenced on or after October 1, 2014, irrespective of the date of the offense. The Sentencing Guidelines introduced, for the first time, comprehensive

---

[57] *Id.* section 7.

[58] There is a rebuttable presumption that an employee acts in such a capacity. In other circumstances, the issue will be determined by reference to all of the circumstances.

[59] Ministry of Justice Guidance published March 2011, p. 15. The six principles are as follows: proportionate procedures, top-level commitment, risk assessment, due diligence, communication (including training), monitoring, and review.

[60] Source: https://www.justice.gov/sites/default/files/criminal-fraud/legacy/2015/01/16/guide.pdf (last visited Dec. 19, 2018).

guidance on the sentencing of corporate offenders for financial crimes, and mark a move toward a sentencing approach that has long existed in the United States. However, unlike the United States' Federal Sentencing Guidelines for Corporations, the UK's Sentencing Guidelines do not specify numerical adjustments or calculations for any sentence that may be imposed against a party that cooperates with authorities. The Sentencing Guidelines ultimately leave a great deal of discretion in the hands of the presiding judge, but do offer the prospect of greater consistency in sentencing decisions.

The Sentencing Guidelines also seek to take account of the impact of the offending on victims, with the level of culpability (assessed as a first step) to increase if there are a large number of victims or there is deliberate targeting of a vulnerable victim. Next, the impact of the offending, including actual or intended gain, is considered to establish the harm caused. The level of culpability and harm are then used to calculate the length of the sentence (for individuals), or level of fine. Aggravating and mitigating factors are applied to increase or decrease the penalty length or amount. The judge is then asked to "step back" and consider whether the sentence is adequate before considering need for confiscation, compensation, or other orders, such as disqualifying an individual from acting as a company director.

8. Related Criminal Offenses

8.1 CONSPIRACY

In England and Wales, the Criminal Law Act 1977 states that a person (including a corporate body) is guilty of conspiracy to commit an offense if he or she "agrees with any other person or persons that a course of conduct shall be pursued which will necessarily amount to or involve the commission of any offence or offences by one or more of the parties to the agreement if the agreement is carried out in accordance with their intentions."[61] The required "agreement" does not need to be explicit. But the parties must agree and each form an intention to perform some role in pursuing the course of conduct in question.[62] Conspiracy offenses apply to any offense that, if it were undertaken, would be triable in England and Wales, including bribery offenses.[63] By their very nature, conspiracy offenses can result in the conviction of multiple parties.

In March 2010, Innospec Ltd pleaded guilty to conspiracy to corrupt contrary to the Criminal Law Act 1977. A number of executives and agents who worked for the company were also found guilty of conspiracy to corrupt. More recently, Rolls Royce entered into a DPA with the SFO to settle several counts of conspiracy to corrupt involving a number of agents and intermediaries across multiple jurisdictions. The SFO has stated that its investigation into the individuals involved is ongoing.

---

[61] Section 1 Criminal Law Act 1997.

[62] *R v Anderson* [1986] AC 27.

[63] Similar provisions for Northern Ireland are found in the Criminal Attempts and Conspiracy Order 1983. Common law conspiracy offences and the offense of aiding, abetting, counseling, procuring, or inciting an offense under the Criminal Procedures (Scotland) Act 1995, Section 293 will apply. See further: https://www.oecd.org/unitedkingdom/46883138.pdf (last visited Dec. 19, 2018).

8.2 AIDING AND ABETTING

It is an offense under English common law to aid, abet, counsel, or procure an offense, including offenses under the Bribery Act. In addition, the Accessories and Abettors Act 1861 provides that any person who does so may be prosecuted as if he or she were the principal offender. The Serious Crime Act 2007 also provides that it is an offense to encourage or assist an offense under the Bribery Act, regardless of whether the underlying bribery offense has been committed.

8.3 ATTEMPT

The Criminal Attempts Act 1981 provides that a person is guilty of attempting to commit an offense if he or she has the intent to commit the offense and commits an act that is "more than merely preparatory" to the commission of the offense. The attempt offense applies to any offense that would be triable in England and Wales as an indictable offense, including domestic or foreign bribery.

8.4 FALSE ACCOUNTING/BOOKS AND RECORDS

Unlike the FCPA, the UK Bribery Act does not specify a freestanding "books and records" requirement, where the failure to maintain these would amount to a separate criminal offense. When a company is suspected of failing to prevent bribery contrary to section 7 of the Bribery Act, in determining whether to bring Bribery Act charges the SFO will assess the adequacy of the company's procedures. The SFO must establish a bribery offense has taken place as it cannot pursue enforcement action under the Bribery Act purely based on any failures in a company's internal compliance controls.

Nonetheless, in respect of a suspected failure to keep adequate accounting records, prosecutors have in the past resorted to bringing actions under the provisions of the Companies Acts of 1985 and 2006. In 2010, for example, following an extensive SFO investigation into overseas corruption, BAE Systems ("BAE") pleaded guilty to failing to keep accurate accounts, contrary to section 221 of the Companies Act 1985.[64] The company notably did not plead guilty to bribery offenses.

A separate offense of false accounting exists under section 17 of the Theft Act 1968. A person commits the offense if he or she intentionally falsifies, alters, or submits false, inaccurate, or deceptive records for accounting purposes. Accounts can be of a personal or corporate nature, and can involve tax or any other records necessary to prepare accounts. False accounting was brought to the attention of the British public following a highly publicized inquiry into Members of Parliament (MPs) who were alleged to have falsely claimed reimbursement for expenses they had not incurred. A number were investigated and some were eventually convicted of false accounting.

---

[64] Now replaced, in substantially the same form, by the sections 386 and 387 of the Companies Act 2006.

8.5 MONEY LAUNDERING

The Proceeds of Crime Act 2002 (POCA), so far as is relevant for the purposes of this chapter, criminalizes the act of money laundering, as well as the failure of those operating in the "regulated sector" to report suspicions of another's money laundering.[65] Under the POCA, it is an offense to:

(a) conceal, disguise, convert, or transfer the proceeds of crime (referred to as "criminal property" under the POCA),[66]

(b) enter into or become concerned in an arrangement in which a person knows or suspects the retention, use or control of the proceeds of crime; or

(c) acquire, use, or possess the proceeds of crime.[67]

Offenses committed under the Bribery Act, which give rise to the proceeds of crime, can therefore also result in a separate offense under the POCA. As a defense, organizations within and outside the "regulated sector" can seek consent from the NCA to undertake an activity that would otherwise amount to a money laundering offense under the POCA, for example, retaining or using the proceeds of crime.[68]

8.6 TAX AND OTHER FRAUDS

In addition to the more general criminal offenses related to fraud, both under common law and the Fraud Act 2006, there are a number of statutes that specifically criminalize fraudulent activity in relation to tax, principally tax evasion. In addition, a new corporate offense of failure to prevent the facilitation of tax evasion was introduced by Part 3 of the Criminal Finances Act 2017, which came into force on 30 September 2017.[69]

8.6.1 The Fraud Act 2006

The Fraud Act 2006 provides for an overarching fraud offense, which can be committed in the following ways: (1) fraud by false representation,[70] (2) fraud by failing to disclose information where there is a legal duty to do so,[71] and (3) fraud by abuse of position.[72] For each offense, the defendant must have intended to make a gain or cause a loss to another

---

[65] Persons within the "regulated sector" for the purposes of the Proceeds of Crime Act primarily include: FCA regulated firms (such as banks and investment advisers), lawyers, accountants, and tax advisers. Those caught by this requirement are required to file suspicious activity reports (SARs) to the National Crime Agency in circumstances where they have knowledge and suspicion of money laundering; see section 338 POCA. The SAR regime is likely to be subject to some future modification via the Criminal Finances Bill.

[66] "Criminal property" is defined in the POCA as any benefit from criminal conduct, or any property representing the same. It will include the profits or financial gains arising from bribery.

[67] Sections 327, 328, and 329 of the POCA respectively.

[68] An "authorised disclosure" under section 338 POCA.

[69] Subject to the "reasonable prevention procedures" defense.

[70] Section 2 of the Fraud Act 2006.

[71] *Id.* section 3.

[72] *Id.* section 4.

(although no gain or loss needs actually to have occurred), and his conduct must be dishonest. The Fraud Act was introduced to enable prosecutors to use "modern and flexible statutory offences of fraud," however, the controversial common law offense of conspiracy to defraud remains in use.

8.6.2 Conspiracy to Defraud

The common law offense of conspiracy to defraud consists of an agreement by two or more people to dishonestly deprive another of a proprietary right to which he or she is entitled. The offense has been criticized for being too broad, uncertain in application, and too complicated for juries to understand.[73] It was intended that with the introduction of the Fraud Act, the common law offense of conspiracy to defraud would fall away. Despite this and because of its potentially wide application, it remains in use by prosecutors. As a consequence, soon after the implementation of the Fraud Act 2006, the attorney general issued specific guidelines on the use of the common law offense, which required prosecutors to first consider whether the offense concerned could be prosecuted under statute.[74] Nonetheless, the offense can still be charged in certain circumstances.[75]

8.6.3 Fraudulent Evasion of Value Added Tax

It is an offense for a person to knowingly be concerned in, or take steps with the aim of, fraudulently evading the payment of Value Added Tax (VAT) owed by such a person (or another if relevant).[76] Even if tax is eventually paid, the offense will still be committed if it is not paid when it is due. The offense can also be committed by someone who is not liable to pay the tax owed.

8.6.4 Fraudulent Evasion of Income Tax

A person who is "knowingly concerned" in the evasion of income tax commits an offense under the Taxes Management Act 1970. This offense does not extend to other forms of tax, but the "knowingly concerned" element causes it to capture conduct of others involved, not just the person who is liable to pay the tax (for example, those who pay cash for services will be guilty of the offense if they have the necessary knowledge).

---

[73] *See* the Law Commission Consultation Paper No.155, Legislating the Criminal Code: Fraud and Deception, http://www.lawcom.gov.uk/wp-content/uploads/2015/03/cp155_Legislating_the_Criminal_Code_Fraud_and_Deception_Consultation.pdf (last visited Dec. 19, 2018) The Fraud Act 2006 was introduced in light of this report.

[74] Use of the Common Law Offence of Conspiracy to Defraud, guidance issued by the Attorney General's Office, published in 2007 and updated Nov. 29, 2012, *available at* https://www.gov.uk/guidance/use-of-the-common-law-offence-of-conspiracy-to-defraud-6#issues-to-be-considered-in-using-the-common-law-offence.

[75] Specific examples are provided in the Attorney General's guidance, including circumstances where there is evidence of several different kinds of criminality, several jurisdictions and/or organized crime networks.

[76] Section 72(1) of the Value Added Taxes Act 1994.

8.7 FINANCIAL SANCTIONS

The UK imposes financial sanctions against a specified list of governments, entities, and individuals, for the purposes of exerting pressure to bring about improvements in certain countries. Sanctions typically include asset freezing to prohibit the transfer of funds to a sanctioned party (described as a "designated person" in the relevant statutory instruments). They can also restrict others from dealing with the funds or economic resources of a designated person. Criminal penalties may be imposed by the Office of Financial Sanctions Implementation, which is responsible for the enforcement of the UK's financial sanctions regime.[77] Regulatory penalties may also apply to those regulated by the FCA.[78]

The UK financial sanctions regime is made up of a series of statutory instruments and directly effective EU regulations, which together implement sanctions initiated by the UK as well as those imposed by the UN and the EU. In addition to UN, EU, and UK sanctions, companies in the UK should also consider those imposed by the U.S. Regulations issued by the U.S. Office of Foreign Assets Control (OFAC) feature a broad definition of "US person," which can include companies operating in the United States, regardless of where they are registered, as well as the non-U.S. branches of U.S. companies. The OFAC regulations also apply to any transaction denominated in U.S. dollars, as such a transaction will eventually connect with the U.S. banking system. OFAC has also typically enforced sanctions more vigorously than its EU or UK counterparts.

9. Cooperation and Self-Reporting
9.1 POWERS OF INVESTIGATORS AND PROSECUTORS

In April 2006, the Serious Organised Crime and Police Act 2005 (SOCPA) introduced a statutory framework to the preexisting common law that affords prosecutors, including the SFO and the FCA, the power to confer criminal immunity.[79] SOCPA does not confer a right on the offender to receive leniency in return for his or her assistance, thereby maintaining the convention that sentencing remains the responsibility of the judiciary (see further discussion on SOCPA under "Leniency" at Section 8.5 of this chapter).

More recently, in February 2014, the SFO was granted the power to invite cooperating corporate offenders to enter into a court-sanctioned DPA as further incentive for companies to work with the SFO and to avoid prosecution (see "Plea Agreements" at Section 8.4 of this chapter).[80]

---

[77] The Office of Financial Sanctions Implementation is part of HM Treasury and is responsible for the implementation and enforcement of the financial sanctions regime in the United Kingdom.

[78] As with bribery, the FCA is not specifically responsible for enforcing compliance with asset freezes or sanctions, however, it does expect regulated entities to have systems and controls sufficient to mitigate the risk of financial crime and to ensure they meet their financial sanctions obligations. *See* the FCA's summary on its approach and relevant guidance for regulated firms, *available at* https://www.fca.org.uk/firms/financial-crime/financial-sanctions (last visited Dec. 19, 2018).

[79] Sections 71–73 of the Serious Organised Crime and Police Act.

[80] DPAs were first introduced in the UK in February 2014 by the Crime and Courts Act 2013. In contrast, DPAs in the United States, at the federal level, were first used between the DOJ and Salomon Brothers in 1992. The DPA process was then formalized in the *U.S. Attorneys' Manual*.

9.2 COOPERATION WITH INVESTIGATORS

As illustrated by its comments in relation to the UK's first DPAs, the SFO considers full co-operation as a key precondition to any potential settlement, and it has made clear that a self-report is not sufficient in the absence of such cooperation.[81] Commenting on the Standard Bank DPA, which involved an early self-report by the company to the SFO, the General Counsel of the SFO stated, "it should . . . be obvious from a cursory review of the public policy guidance that we will not enter into a DPA with a company that has not cooperated with us. Our Director . . . has repeatedly emphasized this point . . . The Standard Bank case shows how this can be made to work in practice. . . . Their conduct was an object lesson in how to cooperate."[82]

The DPA Code of Practice 2014 also lists cooperation first and foremost as a public interest factor against prosecution.[83] It provides examples of cooperation, including "identifying relevant witnesses," "providing a report in respect of any internal investigation," and "where practicable . . . making the witnesses available for interview when requested."[84]

The Rolls Royce DPA, in particular, provides the clearest guidance yet on the degree of cooperation the court seemingly would expect to see before a DPA will be approved. The "extraordinary" cooperation provided by the company to the SFO was a significant factor in the court's decision to approve the DPA in spite of the evidence amassed by the SFO indicating long-standing and serious instances of bribery by the company, and resulted in the company being awarded a 50 percent reduction in the financial penalty imposed. This outcome is all the more noteworthy as the company did not in fact self-report the allegation to the SFO, but only began its cooperation after *being contacted* by the SFO.[85] Sir Brian Leveson, the presiding judge, acknowledged this, and explained that "the fact that an investigation was not triggered by a self-report would usually be highly relevant in the balance but the nature and extent of the cooperation provided by Rolls Royce in this case has persuaded the SFO not only to use the word 'extraordinary' to describe it but also to advance the argument that, 'in the particular circumstances of this case, [the Court] should not distinguish between its assistance and that of those who have self-reported from the outset.' "[86]

As a further complicating factor, there has recently been considerable debate as to whether the level of cooperation required by the SFO necessitates a waiver of legal privilege. The

---

[81] *See* speech by Ben Morgan, Joint Head of Bribery and Corruption at the SFO, at the Annual Anti-Bribery and Corruption Forum, October 29, 2015, "you [companies] don't have to cooperate, but if you say you want to—back it up, really do it; don't say one thing, but really work to a different agenda. We see straight through that and it doesn't work. Self-reporting alone is not sufficient," *available at* https//www.sfo.gov.uk/2015/10/29/ben-morgan-at-the-annual-anti-bribery-corruption-forum/.

[82] *See* speech by Alun Milford, SFO General Counsel, at the European Compliance and Ethics Institute, Prague, Mar. 29, 2016, *available at* https://www.sfo.gov.uk/2016/03/29/speech-compliance-professionals/.

[83] Paragraph 2.8.2(i) of the DPA Code.

[84] Paragraph 2.8.2(i) of the DPA Code.

[85] Applying the Sentencing Guidelines, the court calculated the aggregate penalty for the 12 counts on the indictment, resulting in an aggregate penalty of £478 million. It applied a 50 percent discount, bringing the penalty to £239 million. Rolls Royce also agreed to pay £258 million in disgorgement of profits attributable to the wrongdoing.

[86] *SFO v Rolls Royce*, Approved Judgment, 17 January 2017, at paragraph 22.

Director of the SFO has been clear in his view that the companies seeking a DPA "should not hide behind legal privilege." (see also "Legal Professional Privilege" at Section 12 of this chapter).

9.3 SELF-REPORTING

There is no legal obligation on corporations or individuals to report instances or suspicions of bribery to authorities in the UK; however, there may be benefits in doing so.[87] Self-reporting by companies is strongly encouraged by both the SFO and the FCA, both of which consider an open and cooperative approach by those looking to report to be a significant factor when determining what further action to take, and may result in mitigation of any penalty imposed (see "Leniency" at Section 8.5 of this chapter).[88] Self-reporting has, therefore, at least until the emergence of the Rolls Royce DPA, been a key element in settlement arrangements.

The SFO's approach to self-reporting has evolved since the publication of its guidance in 2009 ("2009 Guidance"). The 2009 Guidance sought to encourage companies to self-report instances of overseas bribery by suggesting that in certain "appropriate cases" civil rather than criminal penalties would be applied.[89] However, in 2012, following the appointment of a new Director, the SFO promptly withdrew the 2009 Guidance, and in its revised policy statement made clear that "self-reporting is no guarantee a prosecution will not follow."[90]

Since then, authorities in the UK have consistently sought to encourage companies to self-report (both publically and in the context of direct SFO contacts). The FCA has gone so far as to publicly describe the nature of a firm's overall relationship with the regulator as an "important consideration before an enforcement investigation and/or action is taken forward."[91] For its part, the SFO will consider the nature and extent of a company's self-report, including how early such a report is made when considering whether to enter into DPA negotiations.[92] As a further point encouraging self-reporting, failure to report wrongdoing within a reasonable period after the offense comes to light is regarded by prosecutors as a public interest factor in favor of prosecution.[93] This is reinforced by the Sentencing Council's

---

[87] Certain exceptions apply, such as the anti-money-laundering reporting obligations that place obligations on entities operating in the regulated sector. Proceeds of Crime Act 2002 s 7(d).

[88] An additional consideration when dealing with the FCA is the obligation of regulated entities to abide by the FCA's "Principles for Businesses." Principle 11, in particular, requires that: "A firm must deal with its regulators in an open and cooperative way, and must disclose to the appropriate regulator appropriately anything relating to the firm of which that regulator would reasonably expect notice."

[89] The 2009 Guidance was published after the SFO's settlement with Balfour Beatty plc in 2008. Following the company's self-report of overseas corruption, a civil recovery order was imposed rather than criminal penalties. The 2009 Guidance is not currently publicly available. The Guidance had received stern criticism in a report by the OECD for appearing to prefer civil penalties to criminal sanctions.

[90] Source: https//www.sfo.gov.uk/publications/guidance-policy-and-protocols/corporate-self-reporting/ (last visited Dec. 19, 2018).

[91] See the FCA's Enforcement Guide at paragraph 2.32.

[92] See the DPA Code at paragraphs 2.9.1 and 2.9.3.

[93] Guidance on Corporate Prosecutions, issued by the Director of Public Prosecutions, the Director of the Serious Fraud Office, and the Director of the Revenue and Customs Prosecutions Office, at p.7.

Fraud, Bribery and Money Laundering Offences Definitive Guide, which states that an attempt to conceal misconduct is a factor that will increase the seriousness of the offense and will likely result in harsher penalties being imposed.[94] As the January 2017 Rolls Royce DPA clearly demonstrates, however, the absence of a self-report does not preclude the SFO from entering into a DPA, provided other factors (including the level of cooperation) argue in favor of such an outcome.

9.4 PLEA AGREEMENTS

Formal negotiated plea agreements in the UK are, unlike in the United States, relatively new and limited to prosecutions involving serious and complex fraud. Following its introduction in May 2009, the UK Attorney General's *Guidelines on Plea Discussions in Cases of Serious or Complex Fraud* permit pleas to be agreed, prior to any charge being brought, and may occur following a self-report by a prospective defendant or as a result of an SFO investigation.[95] Prosecutors' discretion not to pursue prosecution is set out in the Code for Crown Prosecutors, which makes clear that any relevant guidance must be followed when considering an "out of court disposal," and that such a determination must be in the public interest.[96]

Plea agreements have attracted some criticism from the judiciary, highlighting the tension that exists between the constitutional principle that the judiciary is responsible for sentencing defendants and the move toward negotiated plea agreements as an efficient enforcement method. This tension was brought into sharp focus in *R v Innospec*, a case in which the SFO, the U.S. authorities, and the company had reached an agreement on the level of fines prior to entering court for a sentencing hearing. The presiding judge, Lord Justice Thomas, found the $12.7 million agreed fine that the defendant was due to pay in the UK to be "wholly inadequate."[97] He went further to state that the SFO did not have the power to enter into such agreements and that it should not do so again. This criticism and clear steer that the courts will not simply consent to agreements entered into by the SFO was responsible, in large part, for persuading the UK government of the need to introduce a formal mechanism that would allow such agreements, leading to the introduction of deferred prosecution agreements (DPAs) in the UK.

DPAs were first introduced in the UK in February 2014 by the Crime and Courts Act 2013. Their introduction provided prosecutors, in particular the SFO, with a powerful new tool with which to tackle corporate criminality.

DPAs are a court-approved, voluntary agreement between a designated prosecutor (currently the Director of the SFO and the Director of Public Prosecutions) and a body corporate, a partnership, or an unincorporated partnership. Unlike in the United States, DPAs are not available to individuals in the UK. Additionally, the UK's version of the

---

[94] Sentencing Council's Fraud, Bribery and Money Laundering Offences Definitive Guide, at p.50.

[95] *See Innospec* and *BAE* respectively.

[96] *See* the Code for Crown Prosecutors https://www.cps.gov.uk/publications/code_for_crown_prosecutors/, (last visited Dec. 19, 2018), at p.12.

[97] In *R v Innospec* [2010] EW Misc 7 (EWCC).

DPA, in contrast with the U.S. version, requires a presiding judge to be involved in overseeing the progress of the DPA negotiations from an early stage through to final resolution.

As with the DPA system in the United States, the prosecutor will defer (and where a DPA is fully complied with, ultimately discontinue) the criminal prosecution of a corporation, in exchange for that organization's compliance with certain requirements. Such requirements may include, but are not limited to, the following:

(a) pay to the prosecutor a financial penalty;

(b) compensate victims of the alleged offense;

(c) donate money to a charity or other party;

(d) disgorge any profits made from the alleged offense;

(e) implement a compliance program or to make changes to an existing compliance program relating to the organization's policies or employee training, or both;

(f) cooperate in any investigation related to the alleged offense; and/or

(g) pay any reasonable costs of the prosecutor in relation to the alleged offense or the DPA.[98]

The DPA Code of Practice 2014 ("DPA Code") makes clear that whether a DPA will be offered to an organization is at the *sole discretion* of the prosecutor and cannot be requested by the organization.[99]

As to the level of discount available that may be applied to a financial penalty imposed, the DPA Code has provided some clarity. A possible one-third discount is to be applied where the "circumstances are equivalent to that of an early guilty plea."[100] Despite this and illustrating judicial discretion, two of the three DPAs granted to date in the UK have applied a 50 percent discount.[101]

9.5 LENIENCY

The UK Sentencing Council's *Fraud, Bribery and money Laundering Offences: Definitive Guideline* ("Sentencing Guidelines") provides a list of factors, including voluntary self-reporting, which could reduce the seriousness of the offense concerned, or otherwise reflect mitigation, thereby reducing the sentence imposed.[102] Introduced in October 2014, the *UK Sentencing Guidelines* provide a long-overdue structure for the sentencing of corporate offenders in the UK for the first time.

The mitigating factors specified in the *Sentencing Guidelines* are not, however, attributed to set numerical values, which would make calculation of any penalty mitigation more

---

[98] Paragraph 5(5) of Schedule 17 to the Crime and Courts Act 2013.

[99] *See* paragraph 1 of the DPA Code.

[100] The DPA Code states: "a financial penalty [for a DPA] must provide for a discount equivalent to that which would be afforded by an early guilty plea. Current guidelines provide for a one third discount for a [guilty] plea at the earliest opportunity."

[101] DPAs with XYZ Ltd (July 2016) and Rolls Royce plc (Jan. 2017).

[102] The UK Sentencing Guidelines are effective from October 1, 2014.

precise (as is the case with the U.S. *Federal Sentencing Guidelines for Corporations*). It is solely within the judge's discretion to determine how much weight should be attributed to any mitigating factors, including self-reporting and cooperation.[103]

Significantly, self-reporting does not guarantee that prosecution will not follow, particularly in cases of more serious wrongdoing and where prosecutors determine that proceeding to prosecution is the in the public interest. The SFO can decide to prosecute at any stage, including after the commencement of DPA negotiations where a cooperating company may have already provided crucial information to the SFO, thereby assisting in building the case against itself.

In respect of individuals, SOCPA established a statutory framework to regulate agreements made with offenders who assist the investigation or prosecution of others. Under these powers a specified prosecutor can make a formal agreement:

(a) not to prosecute an offender (Immunity Notice);[104]
(b) not to use certain evidence (Restricted Use Undertaking);[105]
(c) setting out terms under which an offender, who wishes to secure a reduced sentence, will cooperate with an investigation or prosecution (Reduction in Sentence);[106] or
(d) setting out terms under which a prosecutor agrees to refer a case back to court for a review of sentence (Review of Sentence).[107]

The SFO, the CPS, and the FCA, among others, have the power to confer immunity upon an individual under Section 71. As an alternative to offering immunity, a prosecutor may, in the appropriate circumstances, offer a deal pursuant to section 73, whereby the court will be invited to assess the degree of leniency that should be awarded for the cooperation offered by the individual.

The court, in the case of *R v Blackburn*, was the first, following the coming into force of the section 73 power, to be invited to make such an assessment.[108] It held that, while sentencing will be at the discretion of the presiding judge and dependent upon the facts of each case, typically a discount of 50–66 percent should apply to the sentence that otherwise would have been handed down, with discounts of 75 percent or more reserved for the "most exceptional" cases. The subsequent case of *R v Dougall*,[109] which dealt with a white collar defendant who had cooperated with the SFO, went further and countenanced the offering of higher discounts in cases in which the final outcome, after applying the *Blackburn* discount, was still not deemed to be sufficiently favorable to the cooperating defendant, in view of his

---

[103] Currently, there is no indications that the UK Sentencing Guidelines will move towards a U.S. approach to sentencing. The United States has in fact recently taken further steps to increase the certainty of potential leniency for cooperators with the introduction of the DOJ's Pilot Program in April 2016 to standardize cooperation credit in FCPA cases.

[104] Section 71 of SOCPA.

[105] *Id.* section 72.

[106] *Id.* section 73.

[107] *Id.* section 74.

[108] *R v Blackburn* [2007] EWCA 2290.

[109] *R v Dougall* [2010] EWCA 1048.

or her level of cooperation and the value of encouraging similarly placed defendants to assist prosecutors. Subsequent cases have tended to support the offering of discounts over and above those advocated by *Blackburn*, in appropriate cases.[110,111,112]

10. Whistle-Blower Protection
10.1 PUBLIC AND PRIVATE SECTOR WHISTLE-BLOWER PROTECTIONS

The Public Interest Disclosure Act 1998 (PIDA) provides robust protection for whistleblowers in the workplace, both in the public and private sector, against being subject to any form of "detriment" following a disclosure.[113] The PIDA was implemented following a series of public inquiries into a number of health and safety disasters and the collapse of major financial institutions in which it was established that workers had been aware of contributory risks or wrongdoing.[114] The inquiries also found that employees who had spoken up at the time were ignored or felt that they were unable to voice concerns. The whistleblowing charity Public Concern at Work (PCaW) campaigned for new legislation to be implemented, which culminated in the introduction of the PIDA.

The PIDA covers all workers across all sectors and refers to disclosures regarding criminal offenses, as well as a range of acts that might constitute wrongdoing.[115] Such "qualifying disclosures" are protected under the PIDA if they are made in the public interest.[116] Unusually, when the whistle-blowing regime under PIDA was first introduced it did not include a public interest test, which allowed claimants to seek protection for disclosures that related to personal disputes regarding breaches of their contracts of employment.[117] The PIDA was amended in 2013 to include a public interest condition.[118]

The UK has taken further steps to enhance protections for workplace disclosures. In addition to the PIDA, the UK's Corporate Governance Code requires companies listed on the London Stock Exchange to ensure arrangements are in place for staff to raise concerns in confidence.[119] The FCA Handbook also recommends that regulated entities implement whistle-blowing procedures.[120] In April 2016, the FCA went a step further and introduced rules to require all UK banks, building societies, and certain insurance and large investment

---

[110] *R v Ford* [2011] EWCA 473.

[111] The sentencing of Bruce Hall. *See* https://www.sfo.gov.uk/cases/victor-dahdaleh-bruce-hall/ (last visited Dec. 19, 2018).

[112] *R v Papachristos* [2014] EWCA 1863.

[113] Section 47B PIDA.

[114] For example, the Clapham rail disaster in 1988 and the collapse of the BCCI banking group in 1991.

[115] Described as "disclosures qualifying for protection" at section 43B of the Public Interest Disclosure Act.

[116] The public interest test was introduced by the Enterprise Regulatory Reform Act 2013.

[117] This trend was initiated following a ruling in *Parkins v Sodexho Ltd* [2002] IRLR 109, which held that an employee could make a qualifying disclosure about a past, current, or putative breach of his own contract of employment, regardless of the lack of public interest.

[118] The meaning of public interest is potentially very wide-ranging as the claimant need only demonstrate that he reasonably believed that his disclosure was in the public interest.

[119] *See* C.3.4 of the Corporate Governance Code.

[120] Chapter SYSC 4.1.2 of the FCA Handbook.

firms to implement enhanced internal procedures designed to encourage and protect whistle-blowers who make reports internally within their institutions. These changes include the appointment of a senior level employee as a "whistleblower's champion," among other protections, and were introduced following recommendations by the Parliamentary Commission on Banking Standards.[121]

By way of further practical measures to encourage reports of corruption, the MOJ Guidance provides a suggested list of compliance procedures to prevent bribery, including reporting and whistle-blowing procedures and expects "tone from the top" management statements demonstrating a commitment to preventing bribery to also refer to "confidential reporting of bribery."[122]

10.2 ATTITUDE TOWARD WHISTLE-BLOWERS

The UK has made significant legislative strides in enhancing whistle-blower protections, acknowledging that their role is vital in alerting authorities of serious compliance issues and/or criminal offenses within organizations. But the UK government has encountered criticism for not doing more to promote public awareness of the importance of whistle-blowing. In its November 2013 report, the PCaW cited evidence that less than half of employees surveyed were even *aware* of a whistle-blowing policy in their workplace.[123] This lack of awareness is a potential hindrance to the effectiveness of legislative protections and also potentially indicates a lack of engagement by companies to encourage reporting. It also stands at odds with public attitudes toward whistle-blowers.[124]

For its part, the FCA has also sought to strengthen whistle-blower protections. It undertook a review of its own whistle-blowing procedures and resources for external reports with positive results, as illustrated by an increase in disclosures made to it between 2007/2008 and 2014/2015.[125] However, an increase in disclosures does not necessarily mean an increase in enforcement as a result of those reports. The SFO launched its "SFO Confidential" whistle-blowing hotline in 2011, but has yet to report that *any* investigation

---

[121] *See* relevant amendments to the FCA Handbook, principally those within Chapter SYSC 18.

[122] *See* paragraphs 1.7 and 2.3 of the MOJ Guidance, *available at* https://www.justice.gov.uk/downloads/legislation/bribery-act-2010-guidance.pdf (last visited Dec. 19, 2018).

[123] Report on the effectiveness of existing arrangement for workplace whistleblowing in the UK, published by PCaW, November 2013, p. 9. The PCaW was set up (prior to the implementation of the PDA) as an independent commission to review all aspects of whistle-blowing. Source: http://www.pcaw.org.uk/files/WBC%20Report%20Final.pdf

[124] Academic research conducted by Dr. Wim Vandekerckhove of the University of Greenwhich, dated November 15, 2012, titled *UK Public Attitudes to Whistleblowing*, indicates that four out of five people in the UK think that people should be supported for revealing serious wrongdoing, even where it means revealing inside information, *available at* http://www.academia.edu/2134339/UK_Public_Attitudes_to_Whistleblowing_Survey_2012.

[125] The Financial Services Authority (the FCA's predecessor) received 138 whistle-blower reports in 2007/2008, as compared with 1,340 disclosures received by the FCA in 2014/2015. See FCA Press Release (Apr. 19, 2016), *available at* https://www.fca.org.uk/news/press-releases/fca-introduces-new-rules-whistleblowing.

has been launched using information derived from any of the thousands of tips it has reportedly received to date.[126]

Unlike in the United States, whistle-blowers in the UK are not provided with financial incentives to make reports.[127] There is an ongoing debate as to the efficacy of offering rewards for providing good quality information, but there do not appear to be any signs that authorities will introduce these, at least in the near future. A public consultation conducted in 2013, and a subsequent statement published by the FCA and the Prudential Regulation Authority in 2014, both found that the majority of respondents did not consider it appropriate to introduce financial incentives.[128] Citing the U.S. model, reasons given included concerns as to whether incentives necessarily lead to an increase in the number or the quality of whistle-blower reports.[129]

The UK government, however, apparently remains open to the idea of providing financial incentives for whistle-blowers, stating in its *Anti-Corruption Action Plan* published in December 2014 that while there is "limited support for financial incentives these should not be ruled out in all cases" and expressed a commitment to continue to consider whether more could be done to incentivize and support whistle-blowers.[130]

For the time being at least, the approach in the UK appears to be focused on improving the ability to report as well as employment protections, rather than introducing rewards for reporting. It may well be some time before we see financial incentives offered to whistle-blowers in the UK, if recent comments of the Director of the SFO are any guide; when asked whether whistle-blowers should be rewarded he stated, "Well it's not for me to say, but I think there is something slightly grubby about it . . . [y]ou have to balance that grubbiness with the incentive don't you?"[131]

11. Key International Treaties Relating to Bribery and Corruption

The UK is a signatory to a number of anti-corruption conventions, including:

(a) the United Nations International Convention against Corruption (signed in December 2003 and ratified in February 2006);

---

[126] Jamie Dunkley, *Serious Fraud Office Failing to Follow-Up on Thousands of Tip-Offs,* THE INDEPENDENT, Apr. 6, 2015, *available at* http://www.independent.co.uk/news/business/news/serious-fraud-office-failing-to-follow-up-thousands-of-tip-offs-10158889.html.

[127] Section 922 of the Dodd-Frank Wall Street Reform and Consumer Protection Act, signed into law in July 2010, provides that the SEC shall pay awards to eligible whistle-blowers who voluntarily provide the SEC with original information that leads to a successful enforcement action yielding monetary sanctions of over $1 million. Reports are made to the SEC's Office of the Whistleblower. *See* https://www.sec.gov/whistleblower/ (last visited Dec. 19, 2018).

[128] *See The Whistleblowing Framework Call for evidence: Government Response* (June 2014), *available at* https://www.gov.uk/government/uploads/system/uploads/attachment_data/file/323399/bis-14-914-whistleblowing-framework-call-for-evidence-government-response.pdf, and the FCA and PRA's Note for the Treasury Select Committee on Financial Incentives for Whistle Blowers (July 2014), *available at* https:// www.fca.org.uk/publication/financial-incentives-for-whistleblowers.pdf.

[129] *See* the FCA and PRA's Note for the Treasury Select Committee on Financial Incentives for Whistle Blowers (July 2014), at 2.

[130] Anti-Corruption Plan (Dec. 2014), at paragraph 3.6.

[131] MLEX Market Insights Interview with David Green QC, Jan. 2017.

(b) the United Nations Convention against Transnational Organised Crime (signed in December 2000 and ratified in February 2006);

(c) the OECD Convention on Combating Bribery of Foreign Public officials in International Business Transactions (signed in December 1997 and ratified in December 1998);

(d) the Council of Europe Criminal Law Convention on Corruption (signed in January 1999 and ratified in December 2003);[132]

(e) the Council of Europe Civil Law Convention on Corruption (signed in June 2000, but as of the time of writing has yet to be ratified);

(f) the European Union Convention on the Protection of the European Communities" Financial Interests and Protocols (adopted by member states in July 1995 and entered into force in October 2002); and

(g) the Convention on the Fight against Corruption involving Officials of the European Communities or Officials of Member States of the European Union (adopted by Member States in May 1997 and ratified by the UK in April 1999).

12. Mutual Legal Assistance Treaties and Transnational Cooperation

Complex financial crime invariably crosses national borders, making the operation of Mutual Legal Assistance (MLA) to assist cooperation and the sharing of intelligence between various national agencies vitally important. MLA can be requested and provided through informal procedures between national agencies (e.g., letters of request), the operation of multilateral conventions, agreements or treaties, bilateral agreements, or domestic legislation such as the UK's Crime (International Cooperation) Act 2003 (CICA).[133]

CICA is the primary legislation providing for MLA in criminal investigations and prosecutions, within and on behalf of the UK. It provides for the exercise of search and seizure powers, obtaining of evidence, and the transfer of offenders to assist with criminal proceedings in other jurisdictions.[134] The Home Office UK Central Authority (UKCA) is responsible for receiving MLA requests in England, Wales, and Northern Ireland. The guidance governing the UKCA states that, provided the specified criteria are met, the UK accedes to most requests received.[135]

Alongside the UKCA, the International Crime Bureau (UKICB) is responsible for facilitating day-to-day cooperation between domestic and international agencies via MLAs. The UKICB is a division within the National Crime Agency and primarily acts as the point of contact for international agencies such as INTERPOL and Europol for the exchange of information.[136]

---

[132] The UK made a number of reservations.

[133] The SFO, for its part, has long-standing information sharing links with various prosecutors in other jurisdictions, including the U.S. DOJ.

[134] Part I of the CICA 2003.

[135] Requests for Mutual Legal Assistance Criminal Matters—Guidelines for Authorities Outside of the United Kingdom (12th ed. 2015), *available at* https://www.gov.uk/government/uploads/system/uploads/attachment_data/file/415038/MLA_Guidelines_2015.pdf, at page 15.

[136] Similar to INTERPOL, Europol is responsible for EU criminal intelligence, including the exchange of information.

At the European Union level, the European Judicial Network, based in The Hague, leads the operation of the various MLA treaties relevant to the UK throughout the EU.[137] This is further supported by the EU's judicial cooperation unit, Eurojust. Comprised of prosecutors, magistrates, and police officers acting as representatives for each member state, Eurojust is tasked with working "to support and strengthen coordination and cooperation between national investigating and prosecuting authorities in relation to serious crime affecting two or more Member States."[138]

13. Legal Professional Privilege
13.1 PRINCIPLES

Certain confidential communications between a lawyer and a client are protected by legal professional privilege (LPP), and as a result are not disclosable to another party, including enforcement agencies and prosecutors. The LPP protection can only be overridden in limited circumstances, although it can be lost entirely and irrevocably if LPP is waived by the client.

Under English law, LPP only protects confidential communications (and any evidence of those communications) that fall under one of two categories of privilege:

(a) *legal advice privilege*—confidential communications for the purpose of seeking and receiving legal advice, but excluding communications with third parties (as these communications would not be confidential); and

(b) *litigation privilege*—confidential communications between a lawyer and his or her client and/or a third party, or between the client and a third party that have been created for the dominant purpose of obtaining legal advice, evidence, or information in preparation for legal proceedings which are already underway, or that are reasonably imminent.

LPP applies to advice provided by both external and in-house lawyers, provided that the party advising is acting in his or her capacity as a lawyer and not as, for example, a member of the board or in a general compliance capacity. In the context of a routine internal investigations and in the absence of imminent litigation, legal advice privilege is the most likely to apply.

Under English law, LPP will only apply to communications between a lawyer and the individuals specifically responsible for seeking and obtaining legal advice, whether from internal or external lawyers.[139] Unlike the position in the United States, the "client" does not extend to all employees within the organization, or even a whole team or division. Communications between a lawyer and employees outside the "client" team will, therefore, generally not be afforded the protection of LPP. For this reason, it is important that the client is clearly defined at the outset of any investigation. The establishment of an investigation committee may assist with this.

---

[137] Including, the Schengen Convention and the EU Convention on Mutual Assistance in Criminal Matters 1959.

[138] Article 86 of the Lisbon Treaty, which sets out Eurojust's scope of responsibilities.

[139] *Three Rivers District Council v Governor and Company of the Bank of England (No. 5)* [2003] EWCA Civ 474.

There has been increasing debate as to whether full cooperation with authorities in the UK may require a waiver of privilege. The SFO and the FCA[140] have both stated that in their view companies are "letting legal privilege become an unnecessary barrier" in sharing information arising out of internal investigations.[141] Both agencies have increasingly challenged circumstances in which privilege has been asserted by companies under investigation. The SFO has stated that it "will view as uncooperative false or exaggerated claims of privilege" while simultaneously praising "a company's decision to structure its investigation in such a way as not to attract privilege claims" as a "significant mark of cooperation."[142]

The SFO's guidance on self-reporting also makes clear that "in considering whether a self-reporting corporate body has been genuinely proactive, prosecutors will consider whether it has provided sufficient information, including making witnesses available and disclosing the details of any internal investigation."[143] This appears to envisage access to information and materials associated with a company's internal investigation: material that typically would be considered legally privileged. As an example, in the Rolls Royce DPA case, the company was praised for and arguably rewarded for providing the SFO with details of witness interviews conducted as part of its internal investigation, and for providing a limited waiver of privilege in relation to internal investigation materials.[144]

At the same time, the High Court in the recent decision in *Re the RBS Rights Issue Litigation* ruled that transcripts, notes, and other records of witness interviews prepared by in-house and external counsel as part of an internal investigation are not protected by legal advice privilege where those communications are not between the client (within the strict definition above) and its lawyers.[145] This contrasts sharply with the approach of the U.S. DOJ and the Securities and exchange Commission (SEC), both of which have policies that prevent them from requesting a waiver of privilege.[146]

This position has developed considerably from U.S. prosecutors' original position, which was similar to the UK's current views on legal privilege. Under the Holder Memo issued in 1999, prosecutors were advised to consider "a waiver of the attorney-client and work product protections" as a factor in evaluating whether to charge a corporation with a criminal offense.[147] This approach hardened with the publication of the Thompson Memo,

---

[140] For further details on the FCA's stated expectations in relation to the managing of internal investigations by regulated firms and the treatment of privileged information see the FCA's Enforcement Guide within its Handbook at EG 3.11.12.

[141] Jamie Symington, Director of Enforcement, FCA, speech at Pinsent Masons Regulatory Conference, Nov. 5, 2015, *available at* http//www.fca.org.uk/news/speeches/internal-investigations-by-firms-.

[142] Speech by Alun Milford, SFO General Counsel, speaking at the European Compliance and Ethics Institute, Prague, Mar. 29, 2016, *available at* https://www.sfo.gov.uk/2016/03/29/speech-compliance-professionals/.

[143] *See* SFO Guidance on Corporate Self-Reporting, revised Oct. 2012, *available at* https://www.sfo.gov.uk/publications/guidance-policy-and-protocols/corporate-self-reporting/.

[144] *SFO v Rolls Royce plc*, Case no: U20170036, 17 January 2017, at paragraph 20.

[145] *Re the RBS Rights Issue Litigation* [*2016*] EWHC 3161 (Ch). The decision affirmed the definition of "client" as set out in *Three Rivers*.

[146] Title 9-28.710 of the U.S. ATTORNEY'S MANUAL.

[147] Eric H. Holder, *Principles of Federal Prosecution of Business Organisations* (June 16, 1999), *available at* https://www.justice.gov/sites/default/files/criminal-fraud/legacy/2010/04/11/charging-corps.PDF.

which made consideration of the waiver of privilege (among other factors) compulsory for prosecutors.[148] This hard-line approach was heavily criticized and gradually evolved further still, culminating in the release of subsequent memos.[149] The position changed significantly toward U.S. prosecutors' current position with the publication of the Filip Memo in 2008, which expressly states that a company's cooperation credit no long relies on a waiver of privilege and restates that "waiving the attorney-client and work product protections has never been a prerequisite ... for a corporation to be viewed as cooperative."[150]

Privilege(s) in Jeopardy in the UK? Thoughts on the *Eurasia Natural Resources* Case [Contributed by Gina LaMonica and Courtney Roldan—Adapted from "U.K. Criminal Prosecutors Obtain Disclosure of Internal Investigation Documents, Prompting Privilege Concerns" (Bloomberg-BNA).

In a controversial ruling, London's High Court has held that interview notes and other documents created by outside legal counsel and forensic accountants as part of an internal investigation into foreign bribery allegations are not protected by the legal professional privilege. While the appeals process is already underway, the May 8, 2017. decision by the Honourable Mrs. Justice Andrews is a noteworthy victory for the SFO.

Eurasian Natural Resources Corporation (ENRC), the UK division of a multinational mining conglomerate operating in the Middle East and Africa, is the subject of an on-going SFO criminal investigation. ENRC was allegedly first made aware of possible criminal problems back in December 2010, when it received a whistle-blower complaint alleging bribery and corruption in its Kazakhstan subsidiary. At times, following the SFO's involvement, ENRC appears to have been in a cooperation posture with the enforcement agency; but then the SFO filed a petition seeking to force ENRC to produce confidential internal investigation documents the company claimed were privileged. The London High Court agreed with the SFO, ruling that almost all of the documents at issue were not privileged and should be disclosed to the SFO.

The SFO's petition sought four categories of documents on the basis they were not subject to any type of privilege protections under UK law:

(a) ENRC's outside counsel's notes of interviews with employees, former employees, and other third parties;
(b) Forensic accountants' reports and analyses;
(c) Slides and investigation-related materials presented to ENRC's board; and
(d) Email exchanges between an ENRC senior executive and an in-house mergers and acquisitions department attorney.

ENRC claimed the UK's "litigation privilege" attached to all four categories of documents. Alternatively, ENRC asserted that the UK's "legal advice privilege" also attached to each of the categories, with the exception of the forensic accountant's books and records reports.

---

[148] Larry D. Thompson, *Principles of Federal Prosecution of Business Organisations* (Jan. 2003).

[149] Rebecca C.E. McFadyen, *The Thompson Memo: Its Predecessors, Its Successor, and Its Effect on Corporate Attorney-Client Privilege*, 8 J. Bus. & Sec. L. (2007).

[150] Mark Filip, *Principles of Federal Prosecution of Business Organisations* (Aug. 28, 2008), *available at* https://www.justice.gov/sites/default/files/dag/legacy/2008/11/03/dag-memo-08282008.pdf.

Ultimately, the London High Court ruled that only one category of documents—outside counsel's communications with the ENRC board of directors—was protected by the legal professional privilege. The court ordered that the rest of the documents must be turned over to the SFO, and ENRC has already taken steps to appeal the decision.

The London High Court ruled that virtually all documents at issue in the case were not privileged, ordering troves of documents created by ENRC's outside counsel and forensic accountants during the internal investigation to be turned over to the SFO. In reaching this decision, the High Court discussed at length whether the various categories of documents could qualify for protection under either the litigation or advice privilege.

First, the Court found that the litigation privilege could not apply because prosecution was not "reasonably contemplated" by ENRC at the time the documents were created. Mrs Justice Andrews cited the fact that certain documents were created before ENRC was even under investigation, and other documents were created while ENRC was cooperating with the SFO. In the words of Mrs Justice Andrews, a "fear of prosecution on a 'worst case scenario' is not good enough" to invoke the litigation privilege. In addressing legal advice privilege, Mrs Justice Andrews found the first category, attorney interviews, could not be protected because it is "wholly artificial to treat the employees as 'instructing' the [attorney] on the client's behalf . . . when they are plainly not standing in the shoes of the client for the purpose of obtaining the legal advice." Thus, the court found that interviews with various individuals did not constitute communications with the "client"—invoking a very narrow interpretation of that term as only applying to individuals who are expressly authorized to obtain legal advice on a company's behalf. Likewise, the court found that communications between ENRC's executive and in-house merger and acquisitions lawyer could not be protected because the lawyer was acting in his role as a businessman, and not as a legal advisor. In fact, the only category of documents that the court held were protected under the legal advice privilege were the slides and materials presented to ENRC's board at its request for legal advice. Mrs Justice Andrews found that the slides were prepared by outside counsel, with the sole purpose to provide legal advice to ENRC, even though the slides contained some factual information. Because the slides were "part and parcel of the confidential solicitor-client communication" legal advice privilege protected the material.

ENRC has promised seek permission to appeal the decision, after Mrs Justice Andrews declined the company's initial request to do so. Although the ENRC decision raises concerns for multinationals, the SFO has long maintained a strong stance against what it considers to be "spurious" claims of legal privilege. In the past, SFO director David Green has criticized privilege claims that "amount to a strategy of deliberate obstruction," and indicated that the SFO will scrutinize assertions of privilege over materials created during an internal investigation. Moreover, in the civil litigation context, UK courts have recently issued other decisions rejecting claims of privilege over outside counsel's employee interview notes and witness statements.

In contrast to these developments in the UK, the U.S. DOJ has generally not pushed for such narrow confines on attorney-client privilege, especially in the context of corporate internal investigations. Further, the DOJ's assessment of cooperation credit does not currently hinge on the disclosure of documents and communications protected by the privilege. Nonetheless, multinationals should remain vigilant to take proper steps during internal investigations to maximize privilege protections, while at the same time structuring cooperation with government authorities in a productive manner—wherever such investigations are based.

14. Privacy and Data Protection

Data privacy legislation in the UK is fairly comprehensive and will be relevant to the conduct of internal and external investigations in which personal data is likely to be reviewed and possibly also transferred and/or disclosed outside the jurisdiction. A detailed overview of the legislative framework for data privacy is beyond the scope of this chapter; instead this Section aims to provide an overview of the key legislative provisions and some of the practical issues that may be encountered in the course of an investigation.

The use of personal data is governed by the Data Protection Act 1998 (DPA 1998), which implemented the DON'T Data Protection Directive 95/46/EEC.[151] The DPA 1998 imposes obligations on those who collect personal data, such as employers, and grants a range of rights to individual data subjects. The DPA applies to circumstances in which "personal data"[152] (and where relevant, "sensitive personal data"[153]) is subject to "processing,"[154] with both terms broadly defined. Those who maintain and process personal data must comply with a number of obligations regarding the handling and use of personal data. The DPA 1998 sets out a number of data protection principles (Data Protection Principles), which require amongst other things, that data must be obtained only for specified lawful purposes, maintained securely, only be processed in accordance with the rights of data subjects, and not be transferred outside the European Economic Area (EEA).[155]

A breach of the DPA 1998 can result in criminal as well as civil liability. The consequences of failing to comply with the requirements of the DPA 1998 are, ironically, demonstrated by the SFO's own breach of the DPA 1998 while investigating BAE Systems and allegations into its arms deals with Saudi Arabia. In March 2015, the ICO fined the SFO £180,000 after evidence, which included personal and sensitive personal data, was mistakenly sent to the wrong witness. When announcing the fine, the ICO stated that "this was an easily preventable breach that does not reflect well on the organisation. All law enforcement agencies should see this penalty as a warning that their legal obligations to look after people's information continue even after their investigation has concluded."[156]

---

[151] The Data Protection Directive is due to be replaced by the General Data Protection Regulation in 2018.

[152] "Data subject" is defined as any individual about whom data is processed.

[153] "Sensitive personal data" is data relating to individuals that is particularly private, including racial or ethnic origin of the data subject, his or her political opinions and religious beliefs, his or her physical or mental health, and sexual life. This category of personal data is afforded a higher level of protection by the DPA 1998.

[154] "Processing" is broadly defined to include obtaining, recording, holding, using, disclosing or erasing data, section 1(1) DPA.

[155] Except where the destination country ensures an adequate level of protection for the rights of the data subject. Significantly, this does not include the United States.

[156] See the ICO's notice of action taken against the SFO dated 30 March 2015, available at https://ico.org.uk/action-weve-taken/enforcement/serious-fraud-office/.

Bearing in mind the potential penalties, the Data Protection Principles present some practical challenges to those conducting internal investigations involving the collection of data, as well as those disclosing data or otherwise cooperating as part of an external investigation. The Information Commissioner's Office (ICO), the independent authority in the UK responsible for enforcing and upholding individuals' privacy rights, has not published specific guidance on the operation of the DPA 1998 in the context of an investigation, but has published guidance on related issues, such as employee monitoring.[157]

There are a number of aspects of the DPA 1998 to bear in mind when conducting investigations. First, the proportionality principle that underpins the DPA 1998 requires that where personal data is collected it shall be "adequate, relevant and not excessive in relation to the purpose or purposes for which they are processed."[158] For example, the collection of an employee's emails during the course of an investigation should be limited to that which is relevant to the review and should not include documents that are clearly personal. Where possible, steps should be taken to ensure that personal emails are not inadvertently collected. Document review protocols should also clearly address how those reviewing data should handle personal data.

Second, any personal data collected should be kept securely throughout the investigation and afterward, to the extent that the data is to be retained.[159] Access to electronic personal data can more easily be monitored and made secure with the use of password-protected review platforms.

The transfer of personal data, particularly outside the EEA, for example, to a parent company or regulator in the United States, presents further challenges. The DPA 1998 prohibits the transfer of personal data outside the EEA, except in limited circumstances and subject to fairly onerous conditions.[160] Such a transfer must also be processed fairly and lawfully. In practice, to comply with this the data controller should explain the purpose for processing the personal data to the data subject at the time of collection.[161] At the same time and to facilitate a transfer outside the EEA in accordance with the DPA 1998, consent to the transfer of personal data is often sought from the data subject. Consent must be freely given and can be withdrawn at any time.[162] This inevitably conflicts with the need to conduct an investigation as unobtrusively as possible and in many cases reliance is placed upon an employee's agreement to IT Use or other policies that address the possible uses of data by the company.

Where consent cannot be relied upon there are other methods available to facilitate the transfer of data outside the EEA, including Binding Corporate Rules and contractual clauses. These methods are deemed to amount to "adequate safeguards" under the DPA 1998

---

[157] The Information Commissioner's Employment Practices Code, published November 2011.

[158] Principle 3, Schedule 1 of the DPA 1998.

[159] Principle 7, Schedule 1 of the DPA 1998 requires that "appropriate technical and organisations measures shall be taken against unauthorised or unlawful processing of personal data and against accidental loss or destruction of, or damage to, personal data." Where personal data is retained, Principle 5 should also be borne in mind. It requires that personal data "shall not be kept for longer than is necessary."

[160] Principle 8, Schedule 1 of the DPA 1998.

[161] *Id.* Principle I.

[162] There has been some debate as to whether such consent can ever be freely given in the employment context, on the basis that an employee cannot be expected to freely give consent in his or her subordinate position.

whereby the rights of data subjects continue to be protected even after their data has been transferred outside the EEA. Organizations in the United States were, until October 2016, able to rely on a self-certification process known as the Safe Harbor regime to meet the adequate safeguards' requirement to lawfully transfer data from the EU to the United States.[163] However, following reports in 2013 of U.S. government surveillance of individuals (which included gathering data on EU citizens from companies that were part of the Safe Harbor regime) the scheme was declared invalid by the EU in October 2015 and eventually replaced with the EU-U.S. Data Privacy Shield ("the Privacy Shield") in July 2016.[164] The Privacy Shield operates in a broadly similar way to the Safe Harbour scheme, but with enhanced rights and protections for data subjects. The future of the Privacy Shield is, however, already in doubt. In January 2017, U.S. president Trump signed an executive order that effectively removed the privacy rights of non-U.S. citizens.[165] At the time of writing, the implications of the Executive Order and its practical impact remain to be seen for the approximately 1,500 companies that rely on the Privacy Shield to transfer data.[166]

Data protection legislation in the EU will be subject to further change with the introduction of the General Data Protection Regulation (GDPR), which member states must comply with by May 2018.[167] Many of the principles set out in the GDPR are broadly similar to those set out in the Data Protection Directive, but importantly, the GDPR is expected to harmonize data protection legislation across the EU, thereby making it easier for companies in the EU and non-EU companies dealing with EU citizens' data that are now drawn into its ambit to comply.[168]

The ICO has published guidance for organizations to assist them with preparing for the GDPR.[169] The conditions for data transfers outside the EEA remain largely unchanged, although the ability of organizations to rely on a data subject's consent to facilitate a transfer is more limited, with express rather implied consent being required. The GDPR does appear to make it easier for corporations to validly transfer data, with new justifications for transfers

---

[163] To join the Safe Harbour scheme a U.S. organization had to be monitored or regulated by an independent statutory body that the EU deemed as having appropriate safeguards in place to protect personal privacy and that has jurisdiction to investigate complaints. The U.S. Department of Commerce and the Department of Transportation were recognized by the EU Commission as two such statutory bodies.

[164] EU Court of Justice decision in *Maximillian Schrems v Data Protection Commissioner*, Case C-362/14.

[165] Executive Order: Enhancing Public Safety in the Interior of the United States, dated 27 January 2017, at section 14, which reads: "Agencies shall, to the extent consistent with applicable law, ensure that their privacy policies exclude persons who are not United States citizens or lawful permanent residents from the protections of the Privacy Act regarding personally identifiable information."

[166] *See* the Privacy Shield List via the U.S. Department of Commerce's website, available at https://www. privacyshield.gov/list (last visited Dec. 19, 2018).

[167] "Regulation (E.U.) 2016/679 on the protection of natural persons with regard to the processing of personal data and on the free movement of such data," commonly referred to as the General Data Protection Regulation.

[168] The Data Protection Directive requires member states to implement a minimum set of legislative rights and requirements, but provided these standards are met, individual member states may implement additional rights and/or restrictions. The GDPR will automatically apply across the EU, without the need for member states to implement on an individual basis.

[169] Preparing for the General Data Protection Regulation (GDPR), 12 Steps to Take Now, published by the ICO in Mar. 2016.

introduced.[170] The preexisting model contracts and binding corporate rules to transfer data are also addressed, with model contracts no longer requiring authorization from the relevant data authority (such as the ICO in the UK) and binding corporate rules now formally enshrined in statute (whereas previously they were based on guidance issued by national data authorities). Alongside these changes, the GDPR introduces significant penalties for breach, with fines of up to €20 million or 4 percent of annual worldwide turnover, whichever is greater.

15. Forecast for Reforms and Parting Thoughts

The enforcement landscape in the UK is shifting toward a more active and potentially more aggressive phase. The UK government has made concerted efforts to enhance the legislative framework to expand the ways in which criminal liability can attach, in particular to corporations. These and expected future developments in the law on corporate criminal liability are aimed at overcoming the well-documented inherent obstacles that currently stand in the way of prosecutors being able to bring a successful prosecution against companies accused of having engaged in criminal conduct. The introduction of a new offense of failure to prevent tax evasion and the UK government's consultation on reform of the law relating to corporate criminal liability for economic crimes clearly demonstrate the UK government's intended direction in this area of the law. The increased exposure that corporations will face as a result of these changes could lead to a greater number of prosecutions, but is also likely to act as a catalyst to increasing the number of settlements (a phenomenon readily visible in the United States).

For its part, the SFO has shown its commitment and appetite to pursuing lengthy and often expensive investigations against large corporations. This has not always been fruitful, as the absence of prosecutions against banks implicated in alleged LIBOR manipulation illustrated. Since then however, the SFO has secured three DPAs, the last of which with Rolls Royce resulted in a record financial penalty, on a scale comparable to the fines typically imposed by the U.S. DOJ and SEC.[171] Although not a conviction, its significance should not be underestimated. It is a clear indication of the level of fine the SFO is prepared and able to impose, as well as the level of cooperation that the SFO and the courts expect from a company that wishes to settle a particular issue by way of a DPA. The Director of the SFO, David Green QC, who has overseen the SFO's successful early use of DPAs, The Director of the SFO, Sir David Green QC, who oversaw the SFO's successful early use of DPAs, stated at the time that "the SFO is ready, willing and able to play its part in the fight against economic crime . . . we are well equipped and confident in that exacting role and mission." In August 2018, Lisa Osofsky, took on the role of Director of the SFO for a five-year term. Ms. Osofsky, a lawyer with prior experience in the private sector and as a U.S. federal

---

[170] For example, data transfers are permitted where the data importer has signed up to appropriate industry codes of conduct or obtained certification, Articles 40–43 and 46 of the GDPR.

[171] In some ways the size of the Rolls Royce penalty may be seen as a harbinger of the type of "uniform" application of penalties in cases of corruption in the United States and the UK that was advocated by Lord Justice Thomas in *R v Innospec*. In his judgment he stated that *"[a]lthough there may be reason to differentiate the custodial penalties imposed for corruption between the US and England and Wales, no-one was able to suggest any reason for differentiating in financial penalties. Indeed there is every reason for states to adopt a uniform approach to financial penalties for corruption of foreign government officials so that the penalties in each country do not discriminate either favourably or unfavourably against a company in a particular state."*

prosecutor, has given every indication that she intends to target corrupt practices with same vigor as her predecessor, but there is every reason to expect that the SFO would continue to target corrupt practices with the same vigor under his successor. As David Green has stated, "the SFO is ready, willing and able to play its part in the fight against economic crime . . . we are well equipped and confident in that exacting role and mission."[172]

APPENDIX

Key Issues	United Kingdom's Approach
Is the UK subject to any international anti-corruption conventions? If so, which? (OECD, UN Convention against Corruption etc.)	The UK is a signatory to a number of anti-corruption conventions, including the United Nations International Convention against Corruption and the United Nations Convention against Transnational Organised Crime, among others (see "Key International Treaties Relating to Bribery and Corruption" at Section 10).
Is bribery of foreign public officials illegal (do domestic anti-bribery laws provide for extraterritorial application)?	Yes. The Bribery Act 2010 has broad extraterritorial application. An offense under section 6 of the Bribery Act (the offering, promising or giving of a bribe to a foreign public official) will be committed even if the activity comprising the offense takes place outside the UK, provided a person whose acts or omissions has a "close connection" with the UK.
What is the definition of foreign public officials?	The Bribery Act defines a "foreign public official" as an individual who holds a legislative, administrative, or judicial position (whether appointed or elected) or who exercises a public function for or on behalf of a foreign country. It will also include an individual who exercises a public function for a public agency or enterprise in a foreign country, such as state-owned companies. The definition includes officials or agents of international public organizations, whose members are countries, governments, or other public organizations (such as the United Nations and the World Bank).[173] Foreign political parties and their officials are not included within the scope of the definition, nor are prospective public officials.
Is commercial bribery illegal?	Yes, see "Commercial Bribery" at Section 5 of this chapter.
Is bribing domestic officials illegal?	Yes, see "Commercial Bribery" at Section 5 of this chapter.

---

[172] Speech by David Green CB QC, Director of the SFO, at the Cambridge Symposium on Economic Crime, Sept. 5, 2016, *available at* https://www.sfo.gov.uk/2016/09/05/cambridge-symposium-2016/.

[173] Sections 6(5) and 6(6) of the Bribery Act.

Key Issues	United Kingdom's Approach
Can the receipt of a bribe be prosecuted?	It is an offense to request, agree to receive, or accept a bribe, regardless of whether the recipient actually receives it.[174]
Can companies be held criminally liable?	Companies can be held criminally liable for offenses under the Bribery Act.
If so, what is the requisite intent for criminal liability to attach?	Whether or not corporate liability will arise under the general offenses set out in the Bribery Act (sections 1, 2, and 6), is determined by the "identification principle." This principle provides that the acts of those who represent the "directing mind and will" of the company (i.e., board directors and senior officers) can be attributed to the company itself. The identification principle is a significant hurdle for prosecutors in the UK in establishing corporate criminal liability. Companies can also be held liable for failure to prevent bribery under section 7 of the Bribery Act.
Can companies be held civilly liable?	Yes, see the "Civil Law Regime" at Section 2.2 of this chapter.
Can individuals be held civilly liable?	Yes, see the "Civil Law Regime" at Section 2.2 of this chapter.
Is there a "facilitation/grease payments" exception?	No. English law does not distinguish "facilitation" or "grease" payments from other forms of bribery. There is no exception or defense for such payments.
Does the UK provide for conspiracy liability relating to violations of the anti-corruption laws?	Yes, see Section 8.1 of this chapter.
Does the UK provide for: (a) aiding/abetting liability relating to violations of the anti-corruption laws? (b) attempt liability relating to violations of the anti-corruption laws?	Yes, see Sections 8.2 and 8.3 of this chapter.
Is failure to keep accurate books and records a criminal and/or civil offense?	Unlike the FCPA, the failure to maintain accurate "books and records" is not an offense under the Bribery Act. Criminal penalties may apply under The Companies Act 2006 and other statutes (see "False Accounting/Books and Records" at Section 8.4 of this chapter.

(Continued)

---

[174] *Id.* section 2.

Key Issues	United Kingdom's Approach
Do any books and records violations have to involve underlying bribery proof?	Accounting violations are not offenses under the Bribery Act, but may be prosecuted under different statutes that do not require underlying bribery proof (see "False Accounting/Books and Records" at Section 8.4 of this chapter.
Are there laws concerning a company's financial internal controls? If so, are those laws applicable to private and public companies or just public companies?	Save for obligations on FCA-regulated companies, private companies are not subject to specific legislation regarding internal financial controls. Private companies are, however, required to comply with requirements set out at section 471(2) of the Companies Act 2006 regarding the preparation and audit of company accounts and directors' responsibilities. Companies whose securities are admitted to trading on a market operated by the London Stock Exchange are subject to rules relating to internal controls pursuant to the Listing Rules, the Disclosure and Transparency Rules and the AIM Rules, as appropriate.[175]
Is there an affirmative disclosure obligation for potential violations of anti-bribery laws or accounting irregularities?	There are no positive obligations on companies or their officers to report potential violations of anti-bribery laws. However, entities regulated by the FCA are subject to a broad and ongoing requirement to deal with their regulators in an open and cooperative way.[176] Firms must disclose to the FCA anything relating to the firm of which it would reasonably expect notice, which may in certain circumstances, include reports of bribery offenses and/or accounting irregularities.
Are "promotional expenses" exempt from the anti-bribery laws?	Unlike the FCPA, there is no exemption or affirmative defenses for promotional expenses under the Bribery Act (see "Bribery of Foreign Officials" at Section 4 and "Commercial Bribery" at Section 5 of this chapter).
Is the giving of gifts, entertainment, travel, meals, etc., restricted/prohibited?	Not specifically, but if disproportionate they could constitute a bribe under the Bribery Act. The Bribery Act does not aim to prohibit reasonable and proportionate hospitality and promotional or other expenditure. As to what will be reasonable and proportionate will depend on the circumstances.

[175] The application of the rules will vary depending on the nature of a company's listing and the business sector in which a company operates.

[176] Principle 11 of the Principles for Business as set out in the FCA Handbook.

Key Issues	United Kingdom's Approach
Are there any laws concerning things of value conveyed by, or to, third parties?	The Bribery Act will apply to payments or things of value (where they constitute a bribe) conveyed by, or to, third parties on behalf of another.
Are bribes tax deductible?	There is no express provision prohibiting the deduction of bribes from tax. However, the Corporation Taxes Act 2009 and the Income (Trading and Other) Act 2005 prohibit tax deductions for any payment relating to a criminal offense in the UK.[177]
Is the law applied extraterritorially?	The Finance Act 2002 extends this prohibition on tax deduction of bribes to include payments that take place outside the UK.
Is having a robust corporate compliance program an affirmative defense or way to negate liability?	A robust corporate compliance program is a defense to the strict liability offense under section 7 of the Bribery Act (failing to prevent bribery).
Is there a "local law" exception/defense?	In relation to the offense of bribing a foreign public official, prosecutors are also required to prove that the official concerned was not permitted or required to be influenced by local written law to accept a payment or advantage.[178] (See "Bribery of Foreign Officials" at Section 4 of this chapter).
Is "credit" given for cooperation with authorities? If so, how and in what form?	In contrast to the United States, cooperation credit is a more recent and less predictable concept in the UK. The UK Sentencing Guideline makes clear that early admissions by a company or early self-reporting will reduce the seriousness of the offense or otherwise indicate mitigation, thereby reducing the sentence imposed. Any "credit" granted is at the discretion of the sentencing judge. (See "Sentencing Principles" at Section 6 of this chapter).
Does the UK have a Mutual Legal Assistance Treaty with the United States that generally covers criminal matters, including the FCPA?	The Bribery Act's criminal penalties against natural persons for foreign bribery are sufficient for the UK to seek and provide extradition.

(Continued)

---

[177] Sections 1304 and 55 respectively.
[178] Section 6(7) of the Bribery Act.

Key Issues	United Kingdom's Approach
What are the potential penalties/sanctions both for civil and criminal violations?	Criminal sanctions for bribery offenses include a maximum prison sentence of 10 years (in the case of individuals) and/or an unlimited fine. Prosecutors can also seize criminal property under Part II of the Proceeds of Crime Act 2002. Corporate offenders may also be permanently barred from government contracts across the EU by virtue of the Public Contracts Regulations 2015. Individuals who hold directorships could also be disqualified under the Companies Directors Disqualification Act 1986 for up to 15 years. The FCA also has the power to impose sanctions against companies it regulates for failing to maintain effective systems and controls to counter bribery risk, as required by the FCA Handbook.[179] Civil claims can also be brought by individuals and companies for damages for loss caused by bribery.

---

[179] For example, Aon Ltd, which was fined £5.25 million by the FCA in 2009.

2 Subject-Specific Chapters

18 "Carbon-Copy Prosecutions": A Multi-Dimensional Enforcement Paradigm that is Here to Stay

ONE EMERGING TRANSNATIONAL trend we have observed for some time—and first wrote about in 2012—is the phenomenon of "carbon-copy prosecutions."[1] Since Mr. Boutros first coined the term "carbon-copy prosecution" back in 2012,[2] the term has gained considerable currency, most recently with Deputy Attorney General Rod Rosenstein speaking about it in similar terms: "One concern is about multiple law enforcement and regulatory agencies pursuing a single entity for the same or substantially similar conduct."[3]

1. Carbon-Copy Basics

On occasion, a company will reach a negotiated resolution with U.S. authorities on international bribery-related charges—whether through a nonprosecution agreement, a deferred

---

[1] This chapter was contributed by Andrew S. Boutros and T. Markus Funk. Portions of this chapter are adapted with permission from an article by the same name first published in the *The University of Chicago Legal Forum*, Volume 2012, as well as ANDREW S. BOUTROS, T. MARKUS FUNK ET AL., THE ABA COMPLIANCE OFFICER DESKBOOK, ch. 5 (American Bar Association, 2017).

[2] Boutros coined the term "carbon-copy prosecutions" during a presentation delivered with Mr. Funk in Toronto, Canada, in the summer of 2011. *See* Juliet S. Sorensen, *The Globalization of Anti-Corruption Law*, FCPA PROFESSOR BLOG (Aug. 16, 2011), *available at* http://www.fcpaprofessor.com/2011/08/page/3 (last visited Jan. 30, 2019) (summarizing the 2011 ABA Annual Meeting Presidential Showcase Panel, which included the authors, and noting Mr. Boutros's coining of the term "carbon-copy prosecutions").

[3] *Available at* http://fcpaprofessor.com/fcpa-relevant-deputy-ag-rosensteins-concern-multiple-law-enforcement-regulatory-agencies-pursing-single-entity-conduct/ (last visited Jan. 30, 2019).

From Baksheesh to Bribery. T. Markus Funk and Andrew S. Boutros.
© Oxford University Press 2019. Published 2019 by Oxford University Press.

prosecution agreement, or a guilty plea. Although in those cases the U.S. authorities may be perfectly satisfied with the resolution, the authorities in other countries where the bribery (and harm) actually occurred may not feel vindicated. In those situations, there exists a bona fide risk that the other countries will initiate prosecutions based on the same operative facts as, and admissions arising out of, the U.S. investigation and resolution.

The next result is that, if an individual corporate officer is even tangentially involved or implicated in a U.S.-negotiated resolution, that corporate officer—even if not named at all in the resolution—faces potential criminal charges overseas. The officer, therefore, has a strong incentive to ensure that the resolution does not name him or her and that it describes the officer's conduct in the most positive light (or at least neutrally).

The net effect of DOJ and SEC FCPA settlement policies is that when a company enters into a negotiated resolution with U.S. enforcers, it is essentially powerless to defend against— much less deny—the factual basis on which the resolution is based. This all but ensures that a company that settles with the DOJ—or both the DOJ and SEC in parallel proceedings— will have little or no choice but to settle with foreign authorities, should such authorities choose to exercise jurisdiction and enforce their corollary anti-corruption laws.

A country's incentive to vindicate its own laws is not insubstantial, especially when a company or individual has already admitted, in another proceeding (say, in the United States), to violating local law. Accordingly, both named parties and nonparties implicated in a resolution in one country ought to give due consideration to the potential impact of that resolution in another territory, especially in light of recent trends pointing to coordinated multinational cooperation and successive enforcement proceedings.

The old (indeed, perhaps "ancient") days of one-dimensional government investigations appear to be over. Duplicative serial enforcement actions are now part and parcel of the enforcement landscape, despite a healthy ongoing debate over the need for, and fairness of, serial enforcements. Carbon-copy prosecutions have already left their seemingly permanent mark and are already part and parcel of the international vernacular dealing with cross-border corruption matters. Our prediction is that, as globalization continues to shrink the world, carbon-copy prosecutions will continue to increase in frequency, size, scope, and force.

2. The Halliburton Example

In February 2009, oilfield services giant Halliburton Company settled with U.S. authorities for a record-breaking $579 million to put an end to charges that one of its former units bribed Nigerian officials to obtain multibillion dollar contracts to build liquefied natural gas facilities on Bonny Island, Nigeria.[4] The resolution no doubt brought a sigh of relief to those Halliburton executives who had been under investigation but who, at the conclusion of the U.S. probe, had not been criminally or civilly charged. For many of them, however, that relative calm ended on December 7, 2010, when Nigerian anti-corruption authorities

---

[4] The resolution was reached with the following three Halliburton-related entities: (1) Kellogg, Brown & Root LLC (KBR); (2) its parent company, KBR, Inc; and (3) Halliburton Company ("Halliburton"), which was the former parent company of KBR, Inc. *See* https://www.law.com/almID/1202428219124/Halliburton-and-KBR-to-Pay-579-Million-in-Penalties-in-Nigerian-Bribe-Case/ (last visited February 4, 2019).

released a 16-count criminal complaint against Halliburton, several related companies, and many of their C-suite executives for conduct that mirrored—and that the companies to a great extent had already publicly admitted to being part of—the resolved U.S. criminal and administrative cases.[5]

Even more, the announcement garnered worldwide headlines due to its inclusion of former U.S. vice president Richard Cheney, the one-time Halliburton CEO.[6] Nigerian authorities also sought extradition of the defendants (including Vice President Cheney), invoking its long-standing extradition treaty with the United States.[7] Within two weeks, Halliburton settled the Nigeria case.[8] But the message sent by the actions of the Nigerian authorities was loud and clear. First, if a corporation reaches a negotiated resolution with U.S. authorities on international bribery-related charges—whether through a nonprosecution agreement, a deferred prosecution agreement, or a guilty plea—there is a bona fide risk that other countries will initiate prosecutions based on the same facts as, and admissions arising out of, the U.S. investigation and resolution. Second, if an individual corporate officer is even peripherally implicated in a U.S.-negotiated resolution, that person could face potential criminal charges overseas. The officer, therefore, is incentivized to ensure that the resolution either does not name him or her or that it describes the officer's conduct in the most positive light.

3. Carbon-Copy Prosecutions

3.1 CARBON-COPY PROSECUTIONS: A NEW FIXTURE IN THE INTERNATIONAL ENFORCEMENT ARENA

3.1.1 A Definition and an Explanation of Carbon-Copy Prosecutions

We use the term "carbon-copy prosecutions"[9] to refer to successive, duplicative prosecutions by multiple sovereigns for conduct transgressing the laws of several nations, but arising out of the same common nucleus of operative facts. Although it may have been an "emerging" trend in the mid-2000s, today, we view carbon-copy prosecutions as a seemingly permanent fixture in the equation used to conduct and resolve international anti-corruption investigations.

For years—especially during the early gestational period of cross-border corruption enforcement actions—corporate targets concerned themselves primarily with whether they

---

[5] *See* Sam Olukoya, *Nigeria Charges Dick Cheney with Corruption,* Tucson Sentinel (Dec. 7, 2010), *available at* www.tucsonsentinel.com/nationworld/report/120710_cheney_corruption/nigeria-charges-dick-cheney-with-corruption/ (last visited Jan. 30, 2019).

[6] *See, e.g., Nigeria Plans to Charge Cheney in Case of Bribery,* N.Y. Times (Dec. 3, 2010), A12.

[7] *See* Caryn L. Trombino, *Nigeria Gets a Piece of the Halliburton Pie* (American Bar Association Criminal Justice Section, Global Anti-Corruption Task Force), *available at* https://www.perkinscoie.com/en/news-insights/nigeria-gets-a-piece-of-the-halliburton-pie.html (last visited Jan. 30, 2019). The United States and Nigeria entered into an extradition treaty on December 22, 1931, which went into effect on June 24, 1935. *See* 47 Stat. 2122 (1931), codified at 18 U.S.C. §§ 3181–3196 (2018).

[8] *See* Bruce Zagaris, *UK National Pleads Guilty to Nigerian Bribes in KBR Joint Venture and Nigeria Reaches Agreement with Halliburton,* 27 Int'l Enf't L. Reporter 563 (Feb. 2011).

[9] *See* Sorensen, *supra* note 2 ("Boutros also pointed out an increased trend in what he termed 'carbon copy' prosecutions, a phenomenon where foreign authorities rely on the factual findings emerging out of US enforcement actions to vindicate the local laws of their own jurisdiction—often the site of the bribe payment or bribe receipt.").

would face liability from *both* the DOJ and SEC for overseas conduct violating the FCPA. However, exposure to liability from a single sovereign is no longer the singular concern. Now, companies and their executives and agents cannot afford to focus exclusively on the enforcement arms of the DOJ and SEC, both acting on behalf of the unitary, monolithic sovereignty of the United States. Today's international enforcement picture is much more complex.[10]

First, an increasing number of nations are enacting—or at least contemplating—enhanced anti-corruption laws. For example, China, Russia, and the United Kingdom have passed new (or at least "newer") and enhanced anti-corruption legislation, while India continues to make headway.[11] Indonesia, Jordan, Morocco, Taiwan, and Ukraine, furthermore, are among those countries also to have recently proposed or adopted anti-corruption measures.[12] More important for purposes of this chapter, and as more recent foreign enforcement actions demonstrate, more and more nations are actively *enforcing* their own local anti-corruption laws.[13] As such, serious consideration must be given to the increasing possibility of successive prosecutions by multiple sovereigns for the same core conduct that gives rise to U.S. liability.

Of course, an important distinction must be made between the theoretical risk of prosecution and a foreign nation's actual, demonstrated willingness to prosecute.[14] To be sure, for years companies and others have known and understood—at least on a theoretical level—that from an international jurisdictional standpoint an illegal act committed in one nation could give rise to liability in another nation that prohibits the same or a similar act

---

[10] For example, in addition to civil and criminal liability, wrongdoers face debarment under the World Bank's antifraud and corruption policy. *See World Bank Sanctions Procedures* § 9.01 (World Bank Group, Jan. 1, 2011), *available at* http://go.worldbank.org/G9UW6Y0DC0 (last visited Jan. 30, 2019). *See also* Pascale Dubois, *Domestic and International Administrative Tools to Combat Fraud & Corruption: A Comparison of US Suspension and Debarment with the World Bank's Sanctions System*, 2012 Univ. Chi. Legal Forum 195, 227–28 (2012).

[11] *See* PRC Anti-Unfair Competition Law Art. 8 (People's Republic of China 2003); PRC Criminal Law Art. 164 and Amend. 8 (People's Republic of China 2011) (criminalizing the payment of bribes to non-PRC government officials and international public organizations); *Federal Law on Amendments to the Criminal Code and the Code of Administrative Offences of the Russian Federation to Improve State Anti-corruption Management*, *available at* http://eng.kremlin.ru/news/2164 (last visited Jan. 30, 2019) (raising fines to up to 100 times the amount of the bribe given or received with a cap of 500 million rubles, or approximately $18.3 million); Bribery Act 2010, c 23 (UK).

[12] *See* F. Joseph Warin et al., *2011 Mid-Year FCPA Update* (Gibson Dunn 2011), *available at* https://www.gibsondunn.com/2011-mid-year-fcpa-update/ (last visited Jan. 30, 2019).

[13] *See* F. Joseph Warin et al., *2008 Year-End FCPA Update* (Gibson Dunn 2009), *available at* https://www.gibsondunn.com/2008-year-end-fcpa-update/ (last visited Jan. 30, 2019) (quoting the DOJ's then-acting assistant attorney general as stating that the "United States is not the only player at the table" when it comes to "fighting global corruption").

[14] Indeed, the statistics show that foreign enforcements continue to considerably lag behind U.S. enforcement activities. *See* T. Markus Funk & M. Bridget Minder, *The FCPA in 2011 and Beyond*, 6 Bloomberg L. Reports—Corporate and M&A L. 10; this is a reference to page 10 of the article, see here: https://www.perkinscoie.com/images/content/2/6/v2/26382/lit-12-01funkminderfcpayear-in-review.pdf ("[A]lthough the world may, indeed, be . . . passing more local anti-corruption legislation . . . its collective zeal to actually enforce anti-corruption laws continues to significantly lag.").

(or conduct facilitating the commission of the illegal act).[15] For example, a bribe paid overseas by a U.S. agent to a foreign official not only offends the FCPA and the U.S. Travel Act,[16] but it almost certainly violates the local laws where the bribe was paid and accepted. Even more, with the proliferation of extraterritorial provisions in the criminal laws of nations that prohibit international bribery, a single improper payment can trigger liability not only in the United States under the FCPA *and* in the country where the bribe took place, but also in *every* jurisdiction that claims a codified interest in putting an end to foreign bribery by those that carry on a business, or part of a business, within its territories.[17]

But the phrase "carbon-copy prosecutions" does not refer to questions of overlapping jurisdiction among nations, nor does it implicate hypothetical enforcement opportunities arising out of the quilt-like pattern of overlapping foreign laws that prohibit international bribery. Instead, it describes the real-world, burgeoning—and now here-to-stay—phenomenon of consecutive prosecutions (or at least investigations) in multiple jurisdictions for the same (or similar) underlying conduct.[18] Indeed, two key features of these prosecutions are (1) the *timing* in which often foreign governments bring their follow-on actions, and (2) the *subject matter* of these enforcement actions.

If we turn from the general to the specific, we see that more recent enforcement trends tell a story of foreign countries initiating largely *similar* (if not nearly identical) foreign proceedings with increased frequency *after* a company has already resolved its FCPA liability with U.S. authorities, whether by way of a non-prosecution agreement, a deferred prosecution agreement, or a guilty plea. In this regard, one organization, the Socio-Economic Rights and Accountability Project (SERAP), has petitioned the Nigerian government to "urgently take steps to seek adequate damages and compensation against multinational corporations who have been found guilty in the US of committing foreign bribery in Nigeria."[19] In fact, in an effort to provide specific, actionable information to the Nigerian government in support of

---

[15] *See, e.g.,* David C. Weiss, Note, *The Foreign Corrupt Practices Act, SEC Disgorgement of Profits, and the Evolving International Bribery Regime: Weighing Proportionality, Retribution, and Deterrence,* 30 MICH. J. INT'L L. 471, 493–94 & n.118 (2009) (identifying and collecting the jurisdictional provisions of at least 17 countries that are said to "employ broad jurisdiction that could result in an individual or firm facing foreign bribery charges and being subject to prosecution in multiple jurisdictions for the same underlying conduct").

[16] 18 U.S.C. § 1952 (2018).

[17] *See* Weiss, *supra* note 15, at 493–94. One such example is the UK Bribery Act, which includes a jurisdictional provision that captures within its reach all entities and partnerships that "carr[y] on a business, or part of a business, in any part of the United Kingdom," even if the improper payment itself has no territorial connection to the United Kingdom. Bribery Act 2010, c 23 s 7(5) (UK). *See generally* T. Markus Funk, *Understanding the UK Bribery Act as It Relates to Organizations (Section 7)* (Perkins Coie 2011), *available at* http://www.perkinscoie. com/files/upload/LIT_11_12FlowChart_UKBriberyAct.pdf (last visited Jan. 30, 2019).

[18] Carbon-copy prosecutions are also to be distinguished from global resolutions across countries, such as the global settlements (or proposed global settlements) involving (1) Siemens (resolution with United States and Germany), (2) BAE Systems PLC (resolution with the United States and United Kingdom), and (3) Innospec Inc. (resolution with the United States and United Kingdom). *See, e.g.,* Claudius O. Sokenu, *2010 FCPA Enforcement Year-End Review,* 43 BNA SEC. REG. & L. REPORTER 12 (Mar. 21, 2011) (describing BAE's and Innospec's efforts and tribulations in entering into a global settlement with U.S. and UK authorities).

[19] Marcus Cohen, David Elesinmogun & Obumneme Egwuatu, *Will Nigeria Take Another Bite?,* THE FCPA BLOG (Aug. 4, 2011). *See also* Chinyere Amalu, *Bribery: SERAP Asks EFCC to Seek Damages against Halliburton, Others,* LEADERSHIP (Mar. 8, 2011), *available at* http://www.leadership.ng/nga/articles/3165/ 2011/08/03/bribery_serap_asks_efcc_seek_damages_against_halliburton_others.html (last visited Sept. 10,

its petition, SERAP identified by name those companies that had already admitted to having committed FCPA violations in Nigeria, yet had received no or, in SERAP's views, too little punishment, under Nigerian law.[20] According to SERAP:

> While settlement by Halliburton Co and Kellogg Brown & Root LLC (KBR) in Nigeria has amounted only to US $35 million, the corporation has paid over $727 million in settlement and damages in the US. Similarly, Technip SA has paid $338 million in settlement in the US, but has not paid any damages in Nigeria. Snamprogetti Netherlands BV and ENI SpA paid only $32.5 million in Nigeria, but has [sic] paid $365 million in the US.
>
> JGC Corp paid $28.5 million in Nigeria but paid $218.8 million in the US; MW Kellogg paid no damages in Nigeria, but has paid £7 million in the UK. Also, Julius Berger Nigeria Plc has paid only $29.5 million in Nigeria, while Willbros International has paid over $41 million in the US but has made no payment in Nigeria. Panalpina paid $82 million in US, but no payment has been made in Nigeria. The Royal Dutch Shell Plc has paid only $10 million in Nigeria whereas it has paid $48.2 million in the US.
>
> . . . Pride International paid $56.1 million in the US but made no payment in Nigeria; Noble Corp has paid $8.1 million in the US but no payment made in Nigeria; Tidewater Inc has paid $15.7 million in the US but no payment in Nigeria; Transocean Inc made payment of $20.6 million in the US but no payment made in Nigeria; Shell Nigerian Exploration and Production Co. Ltd paid $18 million in the US but no payment in Nigeria; and Siemens AG paid only $46 million in Nigeria, whereas it paid $800 million in the US.[21]

Similarly—although with the carbon-copy request being directed to U.S. authorities—the highly influential international corruption watchdog organization Transparency International not-so-long-ago asked the DOJ to "examine" Oklahoma-based Walters Power International's $20 million fraud conviction in Pakistan and to "take action against" it and other U.S. firms under the FCPA based on the Pakistani Supreme Court's findings of guilt.[22]

2012) (summarizing SERAP's petition). But as some have observed, "[m]any Nigerians, both those serving in public office as well as those on the street, may not want to pursue multinational corporations already dinged for FCPA violations" because to do so "may scare off foreign companies willing to invest in Nigeria" and lead to "loss of jobs ultimately, *if unintentionally*, punishing the Nigerian people." *See* Cohen, Elesinmogun & Egwuatu, *supra* (emphasis in original).

[20] Amalu, *supra* note 19.

[21] *Id.* For another list identifying companies that have entered into foreign resolutions for bribe-related conduct also resolved by way of U.S.-based FCPA enforcement actions, see Richard L. Cassin, *Who Paid FCPA-Related Fines Overseas?*, THE FCPA BLOG (Aug. 8, 2011), *available at* http://www.fcpablog.com/blog/2011/8/8/who-paid-fcpa-related-fines-overseas.html (last visited Sept. 10, 2012).

[22] *See* Usman Manzoor, *US Urged to Take Action against RPP Firm for $20m Fraud*, THE NEWS INT'L (Apr. 10, 2012) ("Transparency International Pakistan requests Chief, Fraud Section U.S. Department of Justice Criminal Division to kindly examine this case and take action against the US firms under the anti-bribery provisions of the FCPA Act 1977.").

When faced with such serial, linear enforcement proceedings, companies can be expected to resolve their successive enforcement actions in a manner similar to their original resolution.

3.1.2 Carbon-Copy Prosecutions: Their Practical Implications

When a company enters into a negotiated resolution with the DOJ, it must allocute; that is, it must admit, accept, and acknowledge responsibility for the underlying conduct that gave rise to liability. In the case of a guilty plea, a court is not permitted to accept a guilty plea unless it "determine[s] that there is a factual basis for the plea."[23] Moreover, a district court's acceptance of a guilty plea is a "factual finding" that a defendant is guilty of the charge.[24]

In contrast, and until January 2012, the SEC had a long-standing policy of settling cases by allowing a party neither to admit nor deny the agency's allegations in the civil injunctive complaint or administrative order.[25] But on January 7, 2012, the SEC announced a modification to the "settlement language [appropriate] for cases involving criminal convictions where a defendant [ ] admit[s] violations of the criminal law."[26] "[T]he new policy does not require admissions or adjudications of fact beyond those already made in criminal cases, but

---

[23] FED. R. CRIM. P. 11(b)(3).

[24] *See, e.g.,* United States v. Hildenbrand, 527 F.3d 466, 475 (5th Cir. 2008) ("[The Fifth Circuit] regards the district court's acceptance of a guilty plea as a factual finding to be reviewed for clear error."). *See also* Gray v. Comm'r of Internal Revenue, 708 F.2d 243, 246 (6th Cir. 1983) (stating that a "guilty plea is as much a conviction as a conviction following jury trial" and explaining further in the tax context that "[n]umerous federal courts have held that a conviction for federal income tax evasion, either upon a plea of guilty, or upon a jury verdict of guilt, conclusively establishes fraud in a subsequent civil tax fraud proceeding through application of the doctrine of collateral estoppel").

[25] *See* SEC Release No 33-5337 (Nov. 28, 1972), 37 Fed. Reg. 25224-01 (Nov. 29, 1972) (formally permitting respondent to avoid admitting or denying the allegations). *See also* 17 C.F.R. § 202.5; SEC v. Citigroup Global Mkts., Inc., 2011 WL 5903733, at *4 (S.D.N.Y. 2011) (describing as "long-standing" the SEC's policy "of allowing defendants to enter into Consent Judgments without admitting or denying the underlying allegations"); SEC v. Vitesse Semiconductor Corp, 771 F. Supp. 2d 304, 308–10 (S.D.N.Y. 2010) (examining the history of the SEC policy). In recent years, this policy has led to increasing criticism and scrutiny by the federal courts. *Compare* Citigroup Global Mkts., Inc., 2011 WL 5903733 at *2 ("[T]he Court concludes that it cannot approve [the Consent Judgment], because the Court has not been provided with any proven or admitted facts upon which to exercise even a modest degree of independent judgment."), *with* SEC v. Citigroup Global Mkts., Inc., 673 F.3d 158, 169 (2d Cir. 2012) (granting a stay of the district court's proceedings on the ground that the SEC and Citigroup had made a "strong showing of likelihood of success in setting aside the district court's rejection of their settlement"). *See also* Letter to Counsel, SEC v. Koss Corp., No 11-C-991, *1–2 (E.D. Wis. Dec. 20, 2011) (relying on the district court's decision in SEC v. Citigroup Global Markets, Inc., to reject an SEC settlement with Koss Corporation and requesting "a written factual predicate" for the settlement); Adam S. Hakki, Christopher R. Fenton & Brian G. Burke, *The Impact of the Financial Crisis on the Regulatory Landscape and the Resulting Implications for Securities Class Action Litigation,* 1950 PLI/Corp 81, 94 (Apr. 26, 2012); SEC v. Bank of America Corp., 653 F. Supp. 2d 507, 508 (S.D.N.Y. 2009) (denying an SEC-proposed $33 million settlement with Bank of America because, in part, Bank of America neither admitted nor denied the allegations in the Consent Judgment and took the position in its court submission that "the proxy statement in issue was totally in accordance with the law").

[26] Robert Khuzami, *Public Statement by SEC Staff: Recent Policy Change* (SEC, Jan. 7, 2012), *available at* http://www.sec.gov/news/speech/2012/spch010712rsk.htm (last visited Jan. 31, 2019). *See also* Edward Wyatt, *S.E.C. Changes Policy on Firms' Admissions of Guilty,* N.Y. TIMES (Jan. 7, 2012), B1.

eliminates language that may be construed as inconsistent with admissions or findings that have already been made in the criminal cases."[27] The policy applies regardless of whether the criminal resolution comes in the form of a conviction, deferred prosecution agreement, or nonprosecution agreement.[28] Naturally, then, the statement of facts in a criminal plea agreement—especially in those cases with parallel SEC enforcement exposure—can prove to be the most negotiated (and contested) portion of such a resolution.

Similarly, when a company admits to the factual basis in a DOJ-based deferred prosecution agreement (DPA) or nonprosecution agreement (NPA), the terms of the agreement typically bar the company from making any public statement contradicting the factual basis.[29] Moreover, these agreements ordinarily empower the DOJ alone to determine whether a company has breached its agreement and taken a position contradicting the factual basis.[30]

The net effect of these DOJ and SEC policies is that when a company enters into a negotiated resolution with the DOJ—particularly in those cases with parallel SEC enforcement actions—it is essentially powerless to defend against, much less deny, the factual basis on which the resolution is based.[31] This all but ensures that a company that settles with the DOJ—or both the DOJ and SEC in parallel proceedings—will have little or no choice but to settle with foreign authorities, should such authorities choose to exercise jurisdiction and enforce their corollary anti-corruption laws.

Historically—and even more so today—the principal reason that companies meticulously negotiate the factual statements included in out-of-court settlements is to blunt the onslaught of potential follow-on derivative and employment lawsuits, tort and contract law claims, securities fraud actions, and private actions under the Racketeer Influenced

---

[27] Khuzami, *supra* note 26. As the SEC noted, the new policy change "does not affect [the SEC's] traditional 'neither admit nor deny' approach in settlements that do not involve criminal convictions or admissions of criminal law violations." *Id.*

[28] *Id.* The SEC has recently expanded its settlement vehicles to include deferred prosecution and nonprosecution agreements. *See* ENFORCEMENT MANUAL §§ 6.2.3–6.2.4 at 129–33 (SEC Nov. 28, 2017), *available at* http://www.sec.gov/divisions/enforce/enforcementmanual.pdf (last visited Jan. 31, 2019). *See also* SEC, Press Release, Tenaris to Pay $5.4 Million in SEC's First-Ever Deferred Prosecution Agreement (May 17, 2011), *available at* http://www.sec.gov/news/press/2011/2011-112.htm (last visited Jan. 31, 2019).

[29] *See* F. Joseph Warin et al., *2009 Year-End Update on Corporate Deferred Prosecution and Non-Prosecution Agreements* (Gibson Dunn 2010), *available at* https://www.gibsondunn.com/2009-year-end-update-on-corporate-deferred-prosecution-and-non-prosecution-agreements/ (last visited Jan. 31, 2019) (observing that "the terms and conditions of DPAs and NPAs have become more homogenous over the past few years" and that "the vast majority of DPAs and NPAs contained provisions . . . prohibiting the company for making any statement that contradicts the facts as laid out in the agreement"). *See also* Khuzami, *supra* note 26 ("Under the new approach . . . we will . . . [r]etain the current prohibition on denying the allegations of the Complaint/[Order Instituting Proceedings] or making statements suggesting the Commission's allegations are without factual basis.").

[30] *See* Warin et al., *supra* note 29 (observing that pretrial diversion agreements routinely "giv[e] DOJ sole discretion to determine whether the agreement has been breached by the company").

[31] *See* F. Joseph Warin & Andrew S. Boutros, *Response, Deferred Prosecution Agreements: A View from the Trenches and a Proposal for Reform*, 93 VA. L. REV. BRIEF 121, 128–29 (2007) (describing FirstEnergy's predicament of potentially violating its DPA because of a "highly nuanced, legalistic argument" it made in submitting a claim for insurance coverage).

and Corrupt Organizations Act.[32] By keeping the factual statement as simple as possible, companies position themselves to be able to defend themselves more vigorously against these piggyback civil actions, while at the same time avoiding claims that they are contradicting the negotiated factual statements. In today's international anti-corruption climate, however, such concerns transcend civil liability and reach the very real possibility of sequential liability to foreign sovereigns.[33]

3.2 NOTEWORTHY EXAMPLES OF CARBON-COPY PROSECUTIONS

The concept of carbon-copy prosecution may be something that we "codified"—or perhaps stated differently, bottled up like vitamins for others to ingest and draw knowledge and power from, here—but its real-world manifestation is certainly not new.

3.2.1 Alcatel-Lucent

Take, for example, Alcatel-Lucent SA ("Alcatel-Lucent")—a case involving a *double dose* of carbon-copy prosecutions. In January 2010, the French-based telecommunications equipment and services provider agreed to pay $10 million to the Costa Rican government to settle charges that it had paid some $7 million in kickbacks to Costa Rican government officials (including $800,000 that went directly to former Costa Rican president Miguel Angel Rodriguez) to win a 2001 cellular telephone equipment contract valued at $149 million.[34] The settlement "marked the first time in Costa Rica's history that a foreign corporation agreed to pay the government damages for corruption."[35]

---

[32] *See id.* at 129. The authors explain:

> As should be obvious, the whole point of a DPA is that companies may not be able to weather the storm of an indictment without it; upon indictment, companies are likely to face fundamental instability, downgrading of creditworthiness, loss of market share, diminution of stock value, market and reputational damage, debarment from certain industries, regulatory proceedings, and class actions.

Id.

[33] For a discussion of the interplay and potential implications of the United Nations Convention Against Corruption (UNCAC) on successive multi-sovereign enforcement actions, see Mary Shaddock-Jones & Thomas Fox, *The United Nations Convention Against Corruption: A New Focus?—Part II*, FCPA COMPLIANCE & ETHICS BLOG (Sept. 8, 2011), *available at* http://tfoxlaw.wordpress.com/category/united-nations-convention-against-corruption-uncac/ (last visited Jan. 31, 2019). Shaddock-Jones and Fox explain:

> An enforcement action based upon Article 53 could allow a country such as Nigeria to come into a U.S. court and seek compensation from a U.S. company which has committed bribery in Nigeria or require the DOJ/SEC to recognize a foreign country which has ratified the UNCAC as the "legitimate owner" of profits disgorged or fines and penalties paid to the U.S. government as a result of a FCPA violation.

Id.

[34] Leslie Josephs, *Update 1—Alcatel-Lucent to Pay $10 Mln in Costa Rica Case* (Reuters 2010), *available at* http://www.reuters.com/article/2010/01/21/alcatellucent-costarica-idUSN2121041320100121 (last visited Jan. 31, 2019). *See also* Sokenu, *supra* note 18.

[35] DOJ, Press Release, Alcatel-Lucent S.A. and Three Subsidiaries Agree to Pay $92 Million to Resolve Foreign Corrupt Practices Act Investigation (Dec. 27, 2010), *available at* http://www.justice.gov/opa/pr/2010/December/10-crm-1481.html (last visited Jan. 31, 2019).

Less than a year later, in December 2010, U.S. authorities announced that Alcatel-Lucent and three of its subsidiaries had resolved a pending six-year FCPA investigation.[36] As part of this resolution, Alcatel-Lucent agreed to pay a combined $137.4 million to the DOJ and SEC to resolve a variety of FCPA violations arising from millions of dollars of improper payments to foreign officials in Costa Rica, Honduras, Malaysia, and Taiwan.[37] Specifically, to settle the SEC's civil complaint, Alcatel-Lucent agreed to pay $45.4 million in disgorgement to the SEC and also consented to an injunction from future violations of the FCPA's anti-bribery, books-and-records, and internal controls provisions.[38]

To resolve its criminal case with the DOJ, Alcatel-Lucent agreed to proceed by way of criminal information (as opposed to indictment) and entered into a three-year deferred prosecution agreement that included a more than 40-page statement of facts chronicling years of improper payments and lax controls.[39] Significantly, as part of its deferred prosecution agreement, Alcatel-Lucent also agreed to cooperate with foreign authorities in their investigations.[40] Specifically, Alcatel-Lucent's DPA stated:

> At the request of the Department, and consistent with applicable law and regulations ... Alcatel-Lucent shall also cooperate fully with such other domestic or foreign law enforcement authorities and agencies, as well as the Multilateral Development Banks ("MDBs"), in any investigation of Alcatel-Lucent, or any of its present and former officers, directors, employees, agents, consultants, contractors, subcontractors, and subsidiaries, or any other party, in any and all matters relating to corrupt payments, related false books and records, and inadequate internal controls, and in such manner as the parties may agree.[41]

Alcatel-Lucent also agreed that:

> With respect to any information, testimony, documents, records or other tangible evidence provided to the Department pursuant to this Agreement, Alcatel-Lucent consents to any and all disclosures, subject to applicable law and regulations . . . to other governmental authorities, including United States authorities and those of a

---

[36] *See* Government's Memorandum in Support of the Proposed Plea Agreement and Deferred Prosecution Agreement, United States v. Alcatel-Lucent, SA, Nos. 10-CR-20906-Cooke, 10-CR-20907-Cooke, at *10, *16–17 (S.D. Fla. May 23, 2011) (available on Westlaw at 2011 WL 2038436). Those subsidiaries were Alcatel-Lucent Trade International, AG; Alcatel-Lucent France, SA; and Alcatel Centroamerica, SA. *See id.*

[37] DOJ, *supra* note 35. *See also* SEC v. Alcatel-Lucent, SA, Litigation Release No. 21795 (SEC Dec. 27, 2010), *available at* http://www.sec.gov/litigation/litreleases/2010/lr21795.htm (last visited Jan. 31, 2019).

[38] SEC, Press Release, Company to Pay More than $137 Million to Settle SEC and DOJ Charges (Dec. 27, 2010), *available at* http://www.sec.gov/news/press/2010/2010-258.htm (last visited Sept. 10, 2012). *See also* SEC v. Alcatel-Lucent, SA, *supra* note 37.

[39] Deferred Prosecution Agreement, United States v. Alcatel-Lucent, SA, No. 10-CR-20907-Moore (S.D. Fla. Dec. 27, 2010) [hereinafter Alcatel-Lucent DPA]. *See also* DOJ, supra note 35.

[40] Alcatel-Lucent DPA, *supra* note 39, at *4.

[41] *Id.*

foreign government, and the MDBs, of such materials as the Department, in its sole discretion, shall deem appropriate.[42]

Three of Alcatel-Lucent's subsidiaries resolved their criminal cases by pleading guilty to charges of conspiring to violate the FCPA, and each agreed to a 43-page consolidated statement of facts.[43] As part of their plea agreements, the Alcatel-Lucent subsidiaries agreed that, "at the request of the Department," the subsidiaries would "cooperate fully with foreign law enforcement authorities and agencies."[44]

Two days later, Honduran authorities responded to the news of Alcatel-Lucent's U.S. resolution by announcing that they would *reopen* their investigation against Alcatel-Lucent and, more specifically, into the now-admitted conduct that occurred in Honduras and gave rise to Alcatel-Lucent's U.S. liability.[45] According to news reports, "Honduran anti-corruption prosecutor Henry Salgado said Honduras will ask the U.S. Securities and Exchange Commission to supply the information on which the settlement was based, [in order] to identify those [in Honduras who were] involved."[46] According to Mr. Salgado, "[i]n this case, international assistance should be asked for, in order to access the file and see who made the payments to [the Honduran government officials]. . . . If we accept the guilt, there must be people's names. We expect international collaboration."[47] Such collaboration, according to the news reports, meant that the "plan" would be to "petition" the SEC and DOJ for information.[48] This news came despite the fact that the "Alcatel relationship had already been investigated [ ] by the Honduran High Court of Auditors, who found no improprieties."[49]

3.2.2 Nigerian-Based Carbon-Copy Prosecutions

(a) *The Bonny Island Prosecutions: Halliburton.* Although carbon-copy prosecutions appear to be a globally emerging trend, the movement has been especially pronounced

---

[42] *Id.* at *5.

[43] *See* Plea Agreement, United States v. Alcatel Centroamerica, SA, No. 10-CR-20906-Martinez (S.D. Fla. Dec. 27, 2010).

[44] *Id.* at *3.

[45] Associated Press, *Honduras Reopens Alcatel Bribe Case on SEC ruling*, MERCURY NEWS (Dec. 29, 2010), *available at* https://www.mercurynews.com/2010/12/29/honduras-reopens-alcatel-bribe-case/ (last visited Jan. 31, 2019). Malaysian authorities are also said to be investigating Alcatel-Lucent for bribes it paid to its government officials. *See* Sokenu, *supra* note 18 ("Following the company's $137 million settlement with the Justice Department and the Commission, officials in Malaysia and Honduras, two countries mentioned in the U.S. settlement, announced that they were investigating Alcatel-Lucent's conduct in their respective countries."). Even without a carbon-copy prosecution out of Malaysia, Alcatel-Lucent is believed to have served a one-year ban on participating in Malaysian government-related vendor bids, including tender offers, contracts, and joint ventures. *See* Melissa Chua, *Alca-Lu Barred from Axiata, TM Bids* (TELECOM ASIA, Mar. 25, 2011), *available at* http://www.telecomasia.net/content/alca-lu-barred-axiata-tm-bids (last visited Jan. 31, 2019).

[46] Mercury News, *supra* note 45.

[47] *Honduran Court of Auditors Investigated Alcatel-Lucent* (HONDURAS NEWS, Dec. 29, 2010), online at http://www.hondurasnews.com/auditors-investigate-alcatele/ (last visited Jan. 31, 2019).

[48] *Id.*

[49] *Id.* Indeed, the manager of the Honduran State telephone company, Hondutel, was quoted as saying that "[t]he information we have from the Hondutel legal counsel is that they did research Alcatel, but it ended with

in Nigeria.[50] Take, for example, the case of the earlier-mentioned Bonny Island joint venture, in which the TSKJ consortium[51] paid some $182 million in third-party consulting fees, with the expectation that some of those fees would be used to pay bribes to Nigerian officials.[52] Three of the joint venture participants are of particular relevance here: Halliburton/KBR, Inc./KBR;[53] Snamprogetti and its parent company ENI SpA; and JGC.[54]

When, in February 2009, Halliburton's former subsidiary KBR pleaded guilty to five counts of violating the FCPA, it admitted to being part of the TSKJ consortium that had paid at least $182 million in consulting fees.[55] As discussed previously, these fees were used in part to pay bribes to Nigerian government officials between 1995 and 2004, with the goal of securing engineering, procurement, and construction contracts to build liquefied natural gas facilities. The contracts were valued at approximately $6 billion and led to KBR profits of approximately $235.5 million. As part of its plea agreement, KBR agreed to pay a $402 million criminal fine.[56] Simultaneously, KBR's current and former parent companies—KBR, Inc., and Halliburton, respectively—entered into civil settlements with the SEC based on alleged internal control failures and falsified corporate books and records.[57] The two entities agreed to disgorge jointly $177 million in profits derived from the FCPA violations.[58] In

---

nothing, they found no liability at the time." *Id.* (stating also that "[t]he Honduras TSC [the Tribunal Superior de Cuentas or Secretary General of The Court of Accounts] revealed that they had investigated the administration of former Hondutel manager, Luis Alonso 'Chitin' Valenzuela, and found no civil or criminal liability between the years 2004 and 2005").

[50] Despite this fact, "the total amount of fines levied by the [Nigerian] Economic and Financial Crimes Commission (EFCC) . . . equates to less that 4% of the total penalties fines [sic] imposed by the United States, Germany, and the United Kingdom." *See* Cohen, Elesinmogun & Egwuatu, *supra* note 19. *See also* Amalu, *supra* note 19 (providing a detailed breakdown of the payouts made by multinational companies to resolve their Nigerian-related FCPA liability without a corresponding payout to the Nigerian government).

[51] The TSKJ consortium consisted of four companies from four different countries: (1) Technip, SA, a French company; (2) Snamprogetti Netherland BV, a Dutch company; (3) Halliburton Company, a U.S. company; and (4) JGC Corporation, a Japanese company. DOJ, Press Release, JGC Corporation Resolves Foreign Corrupt Practices Act Investigation and Agrees to Pay a $218.8 Million Criminal Penalty (Apr. 6, 2011), *available at* http://www.justice.gov/opa/pr/2011/April/11-crm-431.html (last visited Jan. 31, 2019).

[52] *Id.*

[53] *See* note 4.

[54] On January 17, 2012, Japan's Marubeni Corporation resolved FCPA liability by agreeing to pay a $54.6 million criminal fine for its role as an agent of the TSKJ consortium. *See* DOJ, Press Release, Marubeni Corporation Resolves Foreign Corrupt Practices Act Investigation and Agrees to Pay a $54.6 Million Criminal Penalty (Jan. 17, 2012), *available at* http://www.justice.gov/opa/pr/2012/January/12-crm-060.html (last visited Jan. 31, 2019).

[55] *See* Plea Agreement, United States v. Kellogg, Brown & Root LLC, Case No. 09-CR-71, *38 (S.D. Tex. Feb. 11, 2009).

[56] *See id.*

[57] SEC v. Halliburton Co., Litigation Release No. 20897 (SEC Feb. 11, 2009), *available at* http://www.sec.gov/litigation/litreleases/2009/lr20897.htm (last visited Jan. 31, 2019).

[58] *Id.*

total, Halliburton, KBR, Inc., and KBR agreed to a total payment package of $579 million to resolve their FCPA matters.[59]

Less than two years later, in early December 2010—*after* Halliburton, KBR, Inc., and KBR had resolved their Bonny Island criminal and civil liability in the United States—Nigeria's anti-corruption agency, the Economic and Financial Crimes Commission, filed a 16-count criminal complaint, based on the *same* Bonny Island activities, against KBR, Halliburton, and current and former executives of each.[60] The charges against KBR's then-current CEO were lodged notwithstanding KBR's claim that the CEO joined KBR *after* the conclusion of the conduct associated with the Bonny Island projects.[61]

Similarly, the Nigerian government charged Vice President Cheney even though, according to Vice President Cheney's lawyer, "[t]he Department of Justice and the Securities and Exchange Commission investigated that joint venture extensively and found no suggestion of any impropriety by Dick Cheney in his role of CEO of Halliburton."[62] Despite this, news outlets reported that, according to Nigerian authorities, an arrest warrant for Vice President Cheney (and presumably others) would be "issued and transmitted through Interpol," typically the first step in an extradition process.[63]

According to some, "[i]t is believed the Nigerian authorities want to probe the case further *from their perspective*," notwithstanding the U.S. investigation.[64] Others speculated that the Nigerian probe was politically motivated: "There could [have] be[en] political calculations at play in the new charges. Nigerian President Goodluck Jonathan face[d] a[n] [up]coming primary election in the nation's ruling party against former Vice President Atiku Abubakar," and "the charges c[a]me as the election loom[ed]."[65] Either way, at the time, KBR

---

[59] *Id.*

[60] Elisha Bala-Gbogbo, *Nigeria to Charge Dick Cheney in Pipeline Bribery Case* (BLOOMBERG, Dec. 1, 2010), *available at* https://www.bloomberg.com/news/articles/2010-12-01/nigeria-to-file-charges-against-former-u-s-vice-president-over-bribery (last visited Jan. 31, 2019). Those charged included, among others, former Vice President Cheney (Halliburton's onetime CEO), Halliburton then-CEO David Lesar, Halliburton Nigeria Limited, former KBR CEO Albert "Jack" Stanley, KBR then-CEO William P. Utt, and TSKJ Nigeria Limited. *See Nigeria Files Bribery Charges against Dick Cheney* (Dec. 9, 2010), *available at* http://www.domain-b.com/economy/worldeconomy/20101209_bribery_charges.html (last visited Jan. 31, 2019). *See also* Jon Gambrell, *Nigeria Charges Dick Cheney in Halliburton Bribery Case* (NBCNEWS, Dec. 7, 2010), *available at* http://www.nbcnews.com/id/40555171/ns/world_news-africa/t/nigeria-charges-dick-cheney-halliburton-bribery-case/#.XFNXLKpKhdw (last visited Jan. 31, 2019).

[61] *See* KBR, Press Release, KBR Statement Regarding Latest Nigerian FCPA Charges (Dec. 7, 2010), *available at* http://investors.kbr.com/investors/press-releases/Press-Release-Details/2010/kbr-statement-regarding-latest-nigerian-fcpa-charges/default.aspx (last visited Jan. 31, 2019) ("No one on KBR's current executive team was involved in the FCPA violations.").

[62] *See* Gambrell, *supra* note 60 (further stating that "[a]ny suggestion of misconduct on [Mr. Cheney's] part, made now, years later, is entirely baseless").

[63] Bala-Gbogbo, *supra* note 60. *See also* Gambrell, *supra* note 60. Gambrell quoted a Nigerian spokesperson as stating that "[w]e are following the laws of the land. We want to follow the laws and see where it will go . . . . We're very convinced by the time the trial commences, we'd make application for appropriate court orders to be issued." *Id. See generally supra* note 7.

[64] *Nigeria Files Bribery Charges against Dick Cheney, supra* note 60 (emphasis added).

[65] Gambrell, *supra* note 60. *See also Halliburton Settles Nigeria Bribery Claims for $35 Million* (CNN, Dec. 21, 2010), *available at* http://www.cnn.com/2010/WORLD/africa/12/21/nigeria.halliburton/index.html (last visited Jan. 31, 2019) ("Many observers in Nigeria regarded the charges as a publicity stunt by the financial

insisted that it would "continue to vigorously defend itself and its executives if necessary, in th[e] matter" and it described the actions of the Nigerian government as "wildly and wrongly asserting blame."[66]

Less than two weeks later, however, KBR's fight ended when Halliburton agreed to pay $35 million to the Nigerian authorities to settle bribery allegations of "distribution of gratification to public officials."[67] According to Halliburton's statement on the issue:

> Pursuant to [the settlement] agreement, all lawsuits and charges against KBR and Halliburton corporate entities and associated persons have been withdrawn, the [Federal Government of Nigeria (FGN)] agreed not to bring any further criminal charges or civil claims against those entities or persons, and Halliburton agreed to pay US$32.5 million to the FGN and to pay an additional US$2.5 million for FGN's attorneys' fees and other expenses.[68]

Halliburton also "agreed to provide reasonable assistance in the FGN's effort to recover amounts frozen in a Swiss bank account of a former . . . agent [associated with the Bonny Island projects] and affirmed a continuing commitment with regard to corporate governance."[69]

(b) *Snamprogetti & JGC Corporation.* A similar pattern ensued with Snamprogetti and JGC Corporation, two additional members of the TSKJ consortium. In July 2010, the Italian energy company ENI SpA and its Dutch subsidiary Snamprogetti resolved FCPA charges arising out of their shares of bribes paid in connection with the Bonny Island projects.[70] ENI and Snamprogetti jointly settled their civil cases with the SEC and agreed to disgorge $125 million in profits.[71] Snamprogetti also entered into a deferred prosecution agreement with the DOJ to resolve two criminal counts of FCPA-related violations and agreed to pay a $240 million criminal fine.[72] Less than five months later, Snamprogetti agreed to pay $32.5 million to settle a carbon-copy prosecution brought by Nigerian authorities for the same conduct

---

crimes commission ahead of national elections in April and as a symbolic effort to display resolve against government corruption.").

[66] *Id.*

[67] Halliburton, Press Release, *Halliburton Confirms Agreement to Settle with Federal Government of Nigeria* (Dec. 21, 2010), *available at* https://star.worldbank.org/corruption-cases/sites/corruption-cases/files/documents/arw/Halliburton_Nigeria_Settlement_Company_Press_Release_Dec_21_2010.pdf (last visited Jan. 31, 2019). *See also Halliburton Settles Nigeria Bribery Claims, supra* note 65.

[68] Halliburton, *supra* note 67.

[69] *Id.*

[70] DOJ, Press Release, Snamprogetti Netherlands B.V. Resolves Foreign Corrupt Practices Act Investigation and Agrees to Pay $240 Million Criminal Penalty (July 7, 2010), *available at* http://www.justice.gov/opa/pr/2010/July/10-crm-780.html (last visited Jan. 31, 2019).

[71] SEC v. ENI, SpA, and Snamprogetti Netherlands, BV, Litigation Release No. 21588 (SEC, July 7, 2010), *available at* http://www.sec.gov/litigation/litreleases/2010/lr21588.htm (last visited Jan. 31, 2019).

[72] *Id.* Snamprogetti was charged by criminal information with (1) conspiracy to violate the FCPA, and (2) aiding and abetting an FCPA violation. *See* Criminal Information, United States v. Snamprogetti Netherlands BV, Case No. 4:10-CV-2414 (S.D. Tex. July 7, 2010).

that gave rise to its FCPA liability.[73] In return, the "Federal Government of Nigeria agreed to dismiss all charges against Snamprogetti . . . and to renounce to [sic] any civil claims and criminal charges in any jurisdiction" against the company.[74]

Similarly, in January 2011, JGC Corporation agreed to pay $28.5 million to Nigerian authorities to resolve its portion of the bribes paid by the TSKJ consortium.[75] But in a reversal of the typical order of enforcement proceedings, four months later, JGC Corporation entered into a deferred prosecution with the DOJ to resolve criminal FCPA charges.[76] As part of its U.S.-based resolution, JGC Corporation agreed to pay a $218.8 million criminal fine.[77]

   (c) *Shell and Siemens.* In 2010, the Nigerian Economic and Financial Crimes Commission brought additional carbon-copy prosecutions against FCPA defendants that had resolved international bribery cases with U.S. authorities.[78] First, Royal Dutch Shell Plc (Shell) paid $10 million to Nigerian authorities in December 2010[79] after already having paid $48.15 million in criminal fines, disgorgement of profits, and interest to U.S. authorities in November 2010.[80]

---

[73] ENI Saipem SpA, Press Release, Snamprogetti Netherlands BV Enters Agreement with Federal Government of Nigeria (Dec. 10, 2010), *available at* https://star.worldbank.org/corruption-cases/sites/corruption-cases/files/documents/arw/Snamprogetti_Nigeria_Settlement_Company_Statement_2013pr_10-12-20_TSKJ.pdf (last visited Jan. 31, 2019). Specifically, Snamprogetti announced that it had "entered into a settlement and non-prosecution agreement with the Nigerian authorities" and agreed "to the payment of a criminal penalty of $30 million and of $2.5 million as reimbursement for legal costs and expenses incurred by the Nigerian authorities." *Id. See also* Samuel Rubenfeld, *Eni Unit Reaches $32.5 Million Settlement with Nigeria*, CORRUPTION CURRENTS BLOG (WALL ST. J., Dec. 20, 2010), *available at* http://blogs.wsj.com/corruption-currents/2010/12/20/eni-unit-reaches-325-million-settlement-with-nigeria/ (last visited Jan. 31, 2019).

[74] *See* ENI Saipem SpA, *supra* note 73.

[75] *See* JGC Corporation, *Consolidated Financial Statements—Summary* (May 13, 2011), *available at* http://www.jgc.com/en/05_ir/financial_s_summary.html#t2010.

[76] DOJ, *supra* note 51.

[77] *Id.*

[78] In addition to the enforcement actions brought by Nigerian authorities described previously, there is believed to be at least one remaining open carbon-copy Nigerian-led investigation. *See* Sokenu, *supra* note 18, citing Joe Palazzolo, *2011: The Year of the FCPA Piggyback?*, CORRUPTION CURRENTS BLOG (WALL ST. J., Dec. 29, 2010), *available at* https://blogs.wsj.com/corruption-currents/2010/12/29/2011-the-year-of-the-fcpa-piggyback/ (last visited Jan. 31, 2019) ("Panalpina [Group] . . . is also under investigation in Nigeria. . . ."). Panalpina, as part of its plea agreement in the United States, has already agreed to "cooperate with the Department and with any other federal, state, local, or foreign law enforcement agency subject to and consistent with any applicable laws and regulations." *See* Plea Agreement, United States v. Panalpina, Case No. 10-CR-765, *5 (S.D. Tex. Nov. 4, 2010) (available on Westlaw at 2010 WL 4523728). It has also "consent[ed] to any and all disclosures consistent with applicable law and regulation to other governmental authorities, including United States authorities and those of a foreign government, of such materials as the Department, in its sole discretion, shall deem appropriate." *Id.*

[79] *See* Elisha Bala-Gbogbo, *Shell Pays $10 Million Fine to Nigerian Government* (BLOOMBERG, Dec. 22, 2010), *available at* http://www.bloomberg.com/news/2010-12-22/shell-pays-10-million-fine-to-nigerian-government-update1- (last visited Jan. 31, 2019).

[80] *See* DOJ, Press Release, Oil Services Companies and a Freight Forwarding Company Agree to Resolve Foreign Bribery Investigations and to Pay More than $156 Million in Criminal Penalties (Nov. 4, 2010), *available at*

Second, Siemens AG paid $46.5 million to Nigerian authorities in November 2010[81] after having paid $800 million to U.S. authorities to resolve the largest-ever FCPA matter in U.S. history and $569 million to the Munich, Germany, Public Prosecutor's Office—for a total combined payment of nearly $1.4 billion—in December 2008.[82]

Indeed, Siemens has been the subject of a variety of other anti-corruption carbon-copy enforcement actions and debarment proceedings besides its resolutions with U.S., German, and Nigerian authorities. For example, on March 9, 2009, Siemens was notified by the Vendor Review Committee of the United Nations Secretariat Procurement Division (UNPD) that it was being suspended from the UNPD vendor database for a minimum period of six months.[83] Siemens's suspension "stemmed from [its] guilty plea in December 2008 to violations of the U.S. Foreign Corrupt Practices Act."[84] Although Siemens sought to lift the suspension on December 22, 2009, it remained disqualified from United Nations contracting opportunities until January 14, 2011, at which point Siemens was invited to re-register with the UNPD.[85]

---

http://www.justice.gov/opa/pr/2010/November/10-crm-1251.html (last visited Jan. 31, 2019). Shell's deferred prosecution agreement obligated it to:

> At the request of the Department, and consistent with applicable law and regulations . . . cooperate fully with other domestic or foreign law enforcement authorities and agencies as well as the Multilateral Development Banks ("MDBs"), in any investigation of [Shell], or any of its present and former directors, employees, agents, consultants, contractors, subcontractors, subsidiaries, affiliates, or any other party, in any and all matters relating to corrupt payments and related false books, records, and inadequate internal controls.

See Deferred Prosecution Agreement, United States v. Shell Nigeria Exploration and Production Co., No. 10-CR-767, at *4–7 (S.D. Tex. Nov. 4, 2010). Shell's deferred prosecution agreement also contained a consent provision that provided that Shell "consent[ed] to any and all disclosures consistent with applicable law and regulation to other governmental authorities, including United States authorities and those of a foreign government, and the MDBs, of such materials as the Department, in its sole discretion, shall deem appropriate." *Id.* at *6–7. BizJet International Sales and Support, Inc.'s FCPA-predicated deferred prosecution agreement with the DOJ contains another more recent—yet virtually identical—cooperation obligation. *See* Deferred Prosecution Agreement, United States v. BizJet Int'l Sales & Support, Inc., No. 12-CR-61, at *3–5 (N.D. Okla. Mar. 14, 2012).

[81] *See Recent Domestic Bribery Enforcement Developments in Nigeria*, TRACEBLOG (TRACE, Dec. 23, 2010), *available at* https://www.traceinternational.org/blog/566/Recent_Domestic_Bribery_Enforcement_Developments_in_Nigeria (last visited Jan. 31, 2019).

[82] *See* DOJ, Press Release, Siemens AG and Three Subsidiaries Plead Guilty to Foreign Corrupt Practices Act Violations and Agree to Pay $450 Million in Combined Criminal Fines (Dec. 15, 2008), *available at* http://www.justice.gov/opa/pr/2008/December/08-crm-1105.html (last visited Jan. 31, 2019). Specifically, Siemens agreed to pay a criminal fine of $450 million to the Department of Justice and $350 million in disgorgement of profits to the SEC. In the German prosecution, Siemens agreed to pay €395 million (approximately $569 million), in addition to the €201 million (approximately $287 million) it paid in October 2007 to settle another related enforcement action brought by the Munich Public Prosecutor. *Id.*

[83] Siemens AG, Press Release, Q2 Legal Proceedings (May 4, 2011), *available at* http://www.siemens.com/press/pool/de/events/2011/corporate/2011-q2/2011-q2-legal-proceedings-e.pdf (last visited Jan. 31, 2019).

[84] *Id.*

[85] *Id.*

Similarly, on July 2, 2009, "in the wake of the company's acknowledged past misconduct in its global business," Siemens entered into global settlement with the World Bank Group in which it agreed to pay $100 million over the next 15 years to support anti-corruption work.[86] Siemens also agreed to up to a four-year debarment for its Russian subsidiary and a voluntary two-year cease-and-desist from bidding on World Bank business for Siemens AG and all of its consolidated subsidiaries and affiliates.[87] In addition, in February 2012, Siemens agreed to pay the Greek government €270 million (approximately $336 million) to resolve bribes dating back to the 1990s.[88] The Greek Parliament approved the settlement on April 5, 2012.[89] Despite the fact that Siemens has resolved these matters, it continues to "remain[ ] subject to corruption-related investigations in several jurisdictions around the world."[90]

4. Carbon-Copy Prosecutions: Evaluating the Cost-Benefit Considerations

The recent trend toward transnational carbon-copy prosecutions has created some unavoidable forks in the road for those mired in internal investigations and follow-on government-led actions. At the initial stage of disclosure, for example, companies now must evaluate not only whether to voluntarily disclose potential FCPA violations to U.S. authorities,[91] but also whether, and to what extent, to make simultaneous—or nearly simultaneous—*front-end* self-disclosures to foreign authorities. Of course, real costs and benefits inform this analysis.

4.1 POTENTIAL BENEFITS OF EARLY MULTI-SOVEREIGN DISCLOSURES TO U.S. AND FOREIGN AUTHORITIES

4.1.1 Front-End Considerations

On one side of the ledger, simultaneous multi-disclosures to U.S. and foreign officials ensure that the very entity that presumably benefited from the improper payments, or on whose behalf the improper payments were made, promptly and directly delivers the bad news to

---

[86] World Bank Group, Press Release, Siemens to Pay $100m to Fight Corruption as Part of World Bank Group Settlement (July 2, 2009), *available at* http://web.worldbank.org/WBSITE/EXTERNAL/NEWS/0,,contentMDK:22234573~pagePK:34370~piPK:34424~theSitePK:4607,00.html (last visited Jan. 31, 2019).

[87] *Id.*

[88] Siemens AG, Press Release, Siemens and the Hellenic Republic Reach a Settlement Agreement and Mark a New Beginning (Apr. 5, 2012), *available at* http://www.siemens.com/press/en/pressrelease/?press=/en/pressrelease/2012/corporate/axx20120420.htm (last visited Jan. 31, 2019). *See also Siemens' Settlement with Greece Is Now Official*, TRACEBLOG (TRACE Apr. 10, 2012), *available at* https://www.traceinternational.org/blog/470/Siemens_settlement_with_Greece_is_now_official (last visited Jan. 31, 2019).

[89] Siemens AG, *supra* note 88.

[90] Siemens AG, *supra* note 83. For a list of the remaining country-specific investigations of Siemens, see https://www.traceinternational2.org/compendium/view.asp?id=124.

[91] *See* DOJ, *Principles of Federal Prosecutions of Business Organizations* § 9-28.300, 3–5 (2008), *available at* http://www.justice.gov/opa/documents/corp-charging-guidelines.pdf (last visited Jan. 31, 2019) (instructing prosecutors to consider, among other things, "the corporation's timely and voluntary disclosure of wrongdoing and its willingness to cooperate in the investigation of its agents," and "to replace responsible management, to discipline or terminate wrongdoers, to pay restitution, and to cooperate with the relevant government

interested government authorities. Multi-sovereign disclosures also ensure that foreign governments are—or, at least, can be said to be—treated equally to the U.S. government. Indeed, early multi-disclosures are an acknowledgment at some level that the foreign jurisdiction that is the site of the crime, and whose government officials may have actually been corrupted, has at least an equally great interest in vindicating its own local laws.[92]

Moreover, U.S. authorities may favorably view such transnational disclosures. Such disclosures demonstrate a corporate commitment to making aggrieved sovereigns whole, or, at a minimum, reflect respect for the local jurisdictions. Prompt and direct local disclosures also avoid a scenario in which foreign governments are caught off guard with headline-grabbing news of corrupt conduct committed by their own officials. Multi-front disclosures enable local governments to get ahead of a potential media crisis[93] and are likely to place the company in better stead with the local jurisdictions. In short, early disclosures empower local authorities to gain control of a situation, to remove or otherwise contain corrupt public officials earlier rather than later in the process, and to respond proactively to allegations of government corruption.

Multi-front disclosures also tend to reduce the likelihood of duplicative investigatory work, both for law enforcement authorities and private counsel, and thus have the potential to lead to economies of scale. Early multi-sovereign disclosures ensure that potentially interested foreign and domestic governments are consulted from the beginning on matters relating to the investigation, including, for example, how the investigation can be conducted, what additional follow-up items might be pursued, and what local legal or factual concerns should be addressed during an otherwise U.S.-focused investigation. Such disclosures also make it more likely that foreign governments will be willing to cooperate and coordinate *both* with U.S. authorities *and* with company counsel in their collective efforts to interview

---

agencies"). For a discussion of the effect of the Dodd-Frank Whistleblower Protection Act on that calculus, see T. Markus Funk, *Another Landmark Year*, 3 BLOOMBERG L. REPORT—WHITE COLLAR CRIME 5.

[92] For example, Nigerian-based SERAP asked the SEC "to establish a process enabling foreign government entities victimized by FCPA violations, on a case-by-case basis, to apply for some or all of the [FCPA] civil penalties and disgorgement proceeds companies agree to pay to settle SEC investigations."Alexander W. Sierck, *African NGO Asks for Distribution of FCPA Recoveries*, THE FCPA BLOG (Mar. 16, 2012), *available at* http://www.fcpablog.com/blog/2012/3/16/african-ngo-asks-for-distribution-of-fcpa-recoveries.html (last visited Jan. 31, 2019), citing Alexander W. Sierck, *Letter to Robert S. Khuzami re FCPA Civil Penalty and Disgorgement Proceeds* *1. According to SERAP, "victimized foreign government entities bear the cost of bribery and corruption of their officials." Sierck, *Letter to Robert S. Khuzami, supra*, at *2. As such, in its request, SERAP proposed a variant of the carbon-copy prosecution concept: "[A]fter, and only after, public notice of an FCPA settlement agreement, the victim foreign government entity . . . [should be allowed] to file a request that the Enforcement Division pay some or all of the agreed payment proceeds to or for the benefit of the victim government entity or to a home country-based or US-based NGO." *Id.* at *4. In SERAP's own words, its "proposal would only come into play after an FCPA matter has been resolved, typically as a result of a settlement with the company." *Id.* In May 2012, the SEC responded to SERAP's proposal by pointing out that "the framework of [U.S.] securities laws requires a proximate connection to the harm caused by a particular violation." Benjamin Kessler, *Giving Back to the Victims*, THE FCPA BLOG (May 2, 2012), *available at* http://www.fcpablog.com/blog/2012/5/2/giving-back-to-the-victims.html (last visited Jan. 31, 2019), citing Robert S. Khuzami, *Letter to Alexander Sierck* *1 (Apr. 25, 2012).

[93] *See* F. Joseph Warin & Andrew S. Boutros, *FCPA Investigations: Working through a Media Crisis*, 22 BNA WHITE-COLLAR CRIME REPORT 3 (Nov. 29, 2007).

witnesses, obtain permission to enter the local jurisdictions, and otherwise obtain and export relevant material from the local jurisdictions to the United States.[94]

4.1.2 Back-End Considerations

At the back-end, early multi-sovereign disclosures are also more likely to lead to global settlements, with the benefits of coordinated resolutions and across-the-board finality.[95] For example, coordinated worldwide disclosures and ensuing investigations generally increase the likelihood that a corporation can successfully petition U.S. authorities for one-for-one credit for any compensatory or penal payment made to local authorities as part of a global resolution.[96] The converse is also true; by cooperating and complying with local authorities from the beginning of an investigation, a company might be more successful in its effort to dissuade a foreign government, even the United States, from bringing a carbon-copy prosecution.[97] Even beyond questions of prosecutorial discretion, however, the substantive laws of other nations and other related treaty obligations may well create serious advantages that favor—or disadvantages that cut against—early front-end multi-sovereign disclosures.

4.1.3 International Double Jeopardy as a Consideration

As a matter of U.S. law, "[t]he Constitution of the United States has not adopted the doctrine of international double jeopardy."[98] That is, "prosecution by a foreign sovereign does not preclude the United States from bringing criminal charges,"[99] nor does the double jeopardy clause "prevent extradition from the United States for the purpose of a foreign prosecution following prosecution in the United States for the same offense."[100] But the same rule

---

[94] One example of a law that makes removal of material from a jurisdiction difficult is China's law on the protection of state secrets.

[95] *See* Sokenu, *supra* note 18 ("While such settlements offer closure, they can be incredibly tricky to negotiate and even trickier to get approved through courts that are not familiar with U.S.-style settlement.").

[96] *See* Warin et al., *supra* note 13 (summarizing comments made by the Department of Justice's then FCPA Chief Mark Mendelsohn and citing "the 2006 Statoil and 2007 Akzo Nobel prosecutions as examples in which DOJ has credited penalties paid in foreign jurisdiction against those to be paid in the United States").

[97] *See id.* (quoting former FCPA Chief Mendelsohn as stating, "[t]here are other cases that are not public where we have elected to do nothing in deference to ongoing foreign investigations—or to sit back and wait to see what the outcome of that foreign investigation will be"). *See also id.* ("If that foreign investigation results in some enforcement action, we may elect to do nothing. On the other hand, if . . . that foreign prosecution never gets off the ground, we may step in and proceed with our investigation.").

[98] United States v. Martin, 574 F.2d 1359, 1360 (5th Cir. 1978). *See also* Chua Han Mow v. United States, 730 F.2d 1308 (9th Cir. 1984) (describing a contrary argument as "frivolous").

[99] United States v. Richardson, 580 F.2d 946, 947 (9th Cir. 1978). As the Supreme Court stated in the context of successive state-state prosecutions, "[w]hen a defendant in a single act violates the peace and dignity of two sovereigns by breaking the laws of each, he has committed two distinct offences," and as such, "it cannot be truly averred that the offender has been twice punished for the same offence; but only that by one act he has committed two offences, for each of which he is justly punishable." Heath v. Alabama, 474 U.S. 82, 93 (1985).

[100] Elcock v. United States, 80 F. Supp. 2d 70, 75 (E.D.N.Y. 2000). *See also In re* Ryan, 360 F. Supp. 270, 274 (E.D.N.Y. 1973), *aff'd*, 478 F.2d 1397 (2d Cir. 1973) ("There is no constitutional right to be free from double jeopardy resulting from extradition to the demanding country.").

does not hold true in other nations—"[t]here are [ ] limitations on multiple prosecutions by different sovereign jurisdictions established by treaty or [foreign] domestic laws."[101]

For example, Richard Alderman, while then the Director of the United Kingdom's Serious Fraud Office (SFO), discussed key differences between the U.S. and the UK approaches to the double jeopardy doctrine, as well as the doctrine's effects on the UK's ability to bring a carbon-copy prosecution.[102] Using the BAE Systems enforcement action to expound upon the operation and application of the UK double jeopardy doctrine, Director Alderman candidly explained that when BAE "agreed to plead guilty to offences brought by the US Department of Justice[,] [t]hat plea of guilty had consequences so far as the SFO's investigation was concerned."[103] According to Director Alderman, because BAE "pleaded guilty in the US to offences relating to Central and Eastern Europe[,] [u]nder the UK law of double jeopardy, it was no longer possible for the SFO investigation relating to Central and Eastern Europe to continue."[104] Given that "the law on double jeopardy differs as between the US and the UK," Director Alderman stated rather explicitly that "the SFO needed to terminate the investigations relating to Central and Eastern Europe once [BAE's] plea of guilty was entered in the US."[105]

Director Alderman next explained that the UK double jeopardy analysis depends not on the offense charged by the original charging jurisdiction, but rather on the underlying facts used to support the offense, regardless of the offense itself.[106] Specifically, Director Alderman responded as follows when presented with a question regarding the SFO's prosecution of BAE after BAE entered into its resolution with U.S. authorities:

> [Question]: As to the double jeopardy issue, the offense BAE pleaded guilty to in the U.S. was not a corruption offense, but rather a charge of conspiracy to make false statements to the U.S. government including as to its compliance with the

---

[101] See Linda E. Carter, *The Principle of Complementarity and the International Criminal Court: The Role of Ne Bis in Idem*, 8 Santa Clara J. Int'l L. 165, 172–73 (2010). *See, e.g.*, Treacy v. Director of Public Prosecutions [1971] AC 537 (HL) (Diplock LJ). *See also* Lisa Griffin, *Two Sides of a "Sargasso Sea": Successive Prosecution for the "Same Offence" in the United States and the United Kingdom*, 37 Univ. Richmond L. Rev. 471, 490 (2002). Griffin explains:

> Protection against successive prosecution under United Kingdom law is afforded in two different ways: first, there is a core "same-elements" protection that is based on the pleas of autrefois acquit and autrefois convict; second, this narrow protection is supplemented by a broad judicial discretion to stay successive prosecutions under the doctrine of "abuse of process."

Id.

[102] Richard Alderman stepped down as the SFO Director on April 20, 2012. *See* Lindsay Fortado, *U.K. Serious Fraud Chief Walks Away from Agency in Flux* (Bloomberg, Apr. 20, 2012), *available at* http://www.bloomberg.com/news/2012-04-20/u-k-serious-fraud-office-chief-walks-away-from-agency-in-flux.html (last visited Sept. 10, 2012).

[103] Mike Koehler, *A Conversation with Richard Alderman Regarding BAE*, FCPA Professor Blog (Mar. 15, 2011), *available at* http://www.fcpaprofessor.com/a-conversation-with-richard-alderman-regarding-bae (last visited Jan. 31, 2019) (linking to a transcript of the interview).

[104] *Id.*

[105] *Id.*

[106] *Id.*

provisions of the FCPA.... [C]ertain of the factual allegations supporting this non-corruption offense related to Central and Eastern Europe. Are you suggesting that simply because facts are alleged in a U.S. prosecution to support a non-corruption charge, that the U.K. is thereby prohibited from bringing a corruption charge as to those facts?

[Director Alderman's Answer]: Yes. [The UK] double jeopardy law looks at the facts in issue in the other jurisdiction and not the precise offence. Our law does not allow someone to be prosecuted here in relation to a set of facts if that person has been in jeopardy of a conviction in relation to those facts in another jurisdiction. As a result I could not continue to consider whether to prosecute BAE for an offence relating to Central and Eastern Europe once BAE had pleaded guilty in the US.[107]

Thus, in deciding whether to make front-end or back-end multi-sovereign disclosures, careful consideration should be given to the double jeopardy doctrine and practices of the local jurisdiction (and of any other interested nation with extraterritorial anti-corruption jurisdictional reach).

4.2 POTENTIAL COSTS OF EARLY MULTI-SOVEREIGN DISCLOSURES TO U.S. AND FOREIGN AUTHORITIES

Early multi-sovereign disclosures—and the cascading consequences that flow from them—are also not without distinct potential drawbacks. To state the obvious, such disclosures have the prospect of exponentially complicating investigations. They could necessitate that resources be allocated across different continents, with teams of professionals simultaneously interacting with different government personalities, constituents, cultures, and priorities. They could require organizations to staff and coordinate worldwide investigations moving at different paces, with different scopes and focuses, and responding to varying levels of governmental sophistication.

Parallel cross-border investigations can also implicate conflicting substantive laws, procedural rules, modes of evidence gathering, and data privacy rights. They can expose *persons*—not just companies—to sequential prosecutions by multiple sovereigns, absent a treaty or local law to the contrary.[108] They could lead foreign sovereigns to charge—and seek the extradition of—U.S. executives or non-U.S. personnel before the completion of the U.S. investigation. They have the potential to cause local persons implicated in the underlying conduct—or even material witnesses with relevant information—not to cooperate with a joint U.S.-local sovereign investigation. And, in the view of some, early disclosures to—and coordinated efforts on the part of—foreign governments may all but ensure that foreign sovereigns bring their own tag-along enforcement actions, as proof positive of their commitment to fight

---

[107] Koehler, *supra* 103.

[108] *See* United States v. Jeong, 624 F.3d 706, 711–12 (5th Cir. 2010) (upholding a defendant's sequential U.S.-based conviction following his South Korean conviction for the same conduct and holding that Article 4.3 of the OECD's Anti-Bribery Convention "does not prohibit two signatory countries [such as the United States and South Korea] from prosecuting the same offense," because the OECD Convention only requires countries with concurrent jurisdiction to consult with one another upon request).

corruption and to secure concrete, tangible results for their early involvement in, and assistance with, the U.S. investigation. In fact, in investigations of potentially improper payments in multiple jurisdictions, one foreign government might choose to break away from the pack and strike first, insisting on settling its matters first, even in those cases where the global investigation is, as a whole, far from complete.[109]

Quarterbacking these myriad issues—much less doing so in a seamless and efficient manner—poses serious challenges at a variety of levels. As one practitioner summarized, "[i]nterest from law enforcement agencies from other countries significantly increases the complexities surrounding when, and to whom, to self-report, how and when to conduct internal investigations, what to do with the results of the internal investigation, and how to structure global settlements with multiple countries with conflicting legal jurisprudence."[110]

5. Not to Be Overlooked: The Potential Collateral Estoppel Effects of Foreign Judgments

As a historical matter, the critical issue of the potential collateral estoppel effects of carbon-copy prosecutions often receives inadequate attention. By way of illustration, assume a company's employee brings a whistle-blower retaliation action in India. The case is fully and fairly litigated between the company and the employee, and the employee prevails. There is a very real chance that—barring something improper about the India-based litigation—if the employee also brings a whistle-blower action in a U.S. court, key factual disputes may be deemed to have been resolved in the foreign litigation.

5.1 THE NUTS AND BOLTS OF COLLATERAL ESTOPPEL

Collateral estoppel, also known as "issue preclusion," is a common law estoppel doctrine that prevents a party from relitigating an issue. Put another way, once a court has decided an issue of fact or law necessary to its judgment, collateral estoppel precludes relitigation of the same *issue* in a different suit involving the parties to the first case.[111] In contrast, res judicata, also known as "claim preclusion," bars litigation of the same *case* between the same parties.[112]

---

[109] Alcatel-Lucent's resolution with Costa Rican authorities, which occurred nearly a year before Alcatel-Lucent settled its FCPA case with U.S. authorities, might be one such example. *See supra* note 34.

[110] Sokenu, *supra* note 18.

[111] *See* Muegler v. Bening, 413 F.3d 980 (9th Cir. 2005) (holding that collateral estoppel can be used to prevent a debtor from relitigating the issue of fraud in a nondischargeability action in bankruptcy court).

[112] *See* Allen v. McCurry, 449 U.S. 90, 94 (1980). As the Court explained:

> Under res judicata, a final judgment on the merits of an action precludes the parties or their privies from relitigating issues that were or could have been raised in that action. Under collateral estoppel, once a court has decided an issue of fact or law necessary to its judgment, that decision may preclude relitigation of the issue in a suit on a different cause of action involving a party to the first case.

Id.

Collateral estoppel can also apply to criminal cases.[113] Unlike double jeopardy, which generally requires a prior acquittal or conviction to preclude the proceedings, collateral estoppel is not similarly limited. To the contrary, "collateral estoppel is applicable in criminal cases only when double jeopardy is not."[114] And for issues resolved in foreign proceedings, provided the foreign proceedings were fair, impartial, and compatible with U.S. conceptions of due process of law, facts resolved in foreign courts can have a preclusive effect on subsequent proceedings in U.S. courts.[115] What follows is a brief discussion of the steps involved in determining whether the relitigation of a particular issue is likely to be collaterally estopped.

5.2 "STANDARD" TWO-STAGE COLLATERAL ESTOPPEL ANALYSIS

The question of whether collateral estoppel bars relitigation of certain factual disputes requires two analytical steps.

5.2.1 Does the United States Recognize the Foreign Judgment?

In U.S. courts, the full faith and credit clause of the U.S. Constitution dictates whether a court in one state will recognize the judgment issued in the court of another state.[116] Judgments of foreign nations' courts and tribunals, in contrast, can potentially be recognized domestically under federal law by resorting to the (somewhat "squishy") doctrine of comity—a principle more akin to courtesy than compulsion.[117] Judge Richard Posner, in the case of United States v. Kashamu,[118] summarized the concept of comity as "a doctrine of deference

---

[113] *See, e.g.*, Ashe v. Swenson, 397 U.S. 436, 443–46 (1970) (holding that the state, which prosecuted the defendant for multiple robberies, was collaterally estopped from relitigating the issue of identity). *See also* United States v. Bailin, 977 F.2d 270, 275–76 (7th Cir. 1992) (applying the principle of collateral estoppel to a criminal case).

[114] *Bailin*, 977 F.2d at 275. *See also* United States v. Stauffer Chem. Co., 464 U.S. 165 (1984) (applying collateral estoppel to bar contempt proceeding where parties had litigated identical issues in a prior proceeding to quash a warrant); United States v. Shenberg, 89 F.3d 1461, 1479 (11th Cir. 1996) ("We agree with the Seventh Circuit and hold that the Double Jeopardy Clause does not limit the application of collateral estoppel to only cases in which double jeopardy applies."); Kraushaar v. Flanigan, 45 F.3d 1040, 1050 (7th Cir. 1995) (discussing the application of collateral estoppel where a state court judge had previously dismissed criminal charges for lack of probable cause).

[115] *See* Gabbanelli Accordions & Imports, LLC v. Gabbanelli, 575 F.3d 693, 697 (7th Cir. 2009) ("It is true that American courts apply the American doctrine of res judicata even to a foreign judgment of a nation like Italy that would not treat an American judgment the same way."). *See also* Oneac Corp. v. Raychem Corp., 20 F. Supp. 2d 1233, 1242–43 (N.D. Ill. 1998) ("The UK decision itself demonstrates that the issues [sought to be relitigated in U.S. District Court] were actually decided and necessary for the final decision. Lastly, neither this court nor the parties question the fairness of the proceedings in the United Kingdom."); Northlake Marketing & Supply, Inc. v. Glaverbel SA, 986 F. Supp. 471, 475–76 (N.D. Ill. 1997) (applying collateral estoppel based on the factual finding of a Belgian court because Belgian procedures were "fundamentally fair" and the accused patent infringer had a full and fair opportunity to litigate the factual issues).

[116] *See* Williams v. North Carolina, 325 U.S. 226, 229 (1945) ("In short, the Full Faith and Credit Clause puts the Constitution behind a judgment, instead of the too fluid, ill-defined concept of 'comity.'").

[117] *See, e.g.*, Verlinden BV v. Central Bank of Nigeria, 461 U.S. 480, 486 (1983) ("[F]oreign sovereign immunity is a matter of grace and comity."). *See also* Nat'l City Bank of New York v. Republic of China, 348 U.S. 356, 362 n.7 (1955) (explaining that foreign sovereign immunity derives from "standards of public morality, fair dealing, reciprocal self-interest, and respect for the power and dignity of the foreign sovereign") (internal quotations omitted).

[118] 656 F.3d 679 (7th Cir. 2011).

based on respect for the judicial decisions of foreign sovereigns (or of U.S. states, which are quasi-sovereigns)."[119] But commentators, as well as Supreme Court decisions, have criticized the doctrine of comity because of its elusive definition.

Under the doctrine of comity, foreign judgments are entitled to recognition if they:

- Were made upon appropriate notice;
- Arose from the opportunity for a full and fair presentation of evidence;
- Were before a foreign court of competent jurisdiction, which operated in a legal system likely to provide for the impartial administration of justice in disputes between the citizens of that foreign nation and other nations; and
- Did not prejudice the litigants' rights as U.S. citizens or otherwise contravene U.S. public policy.[120]

Conversely, then, reasons for *not* recognizing a foreign judgment include:

- The rendering foreign court lacked jurisdiction;
- The judgment offended U.S. public policy;
- The judgment was tainted by fraud; or
- The judgment prejudiced the rights of U.S. citizen-litigants by failing to accord them due process or to adhere to generally accepted notions of jurisprudence.[121]

Once a litigant has cleared the foreign-judgment-recognition hurdle, the inquiry shifts to whether the scope of the preclusive effect of the foreign judgment is governed by the laws of the rendering foreign state, the United States, or its states. The Restatement, commentators, and courts have been unable to reach consensus on this question.

5.2.2 What Is the Scope of the Judgment's Preclusive Effect?

The decision concerning which jurisdiction's collateral estoppel rules apply to a foreign judgment is complicated by the fact that the full faith and credit clause does not compel the outcome. Some courts avoid answering this difficult conflict-of-laws question altogether, either by finding a perceived conflict or by adopting the parties' choice of law (the latter, for obvious reasons, making this step particularly easy).

(a) *Minority practice: default to rendering state's issue preclusion law.* The minority practice is simply to default to the rendering foreign state's issue preclusion law.

---

[119] *Id.* at 683.

[120] *See* Hilton v. Guyot, 159 U.S. 113, 202–03 (1895) (holding that, where "comity of this nation" calls for recognition of a judgment rendered abroad, "the merits of the case should not . . . be tried afresh . . . upon the mere assertion . . . that the judgment was erroneous in law or in fact"). *See also* RESTATEMENT (SECOND) OF CONFLICT OF LAWS § 106 (AM. LAW INST. 1977) ("A judgment will be recognized and enforced in other states even though an error of fact or of law was made in the proceedings before judgment."); *id.* § 106 cmt. a ("Th[is] rule is . . . applicable to judgments rendered in foreign nations.").

[121] *See generally* RESTATEMENT (THIRD) OF FOREIGN RELATIONS LAW OF THE UNITED STATES §§ 481–482 (AM. LAW INST. 1987).

Reasons supporting this approach include that it treats the foreign court no differently than one domestic court would treat another domestic court and that it prevents unfair surprises to litigants who formed their expectations based on litigation in a particular legal regime.[122]

(b) *Majority practice: apply U.S. collateral estoppel rules to the foreign judgment.* There are valuable benefits from applying U.S. rules of collateral estoppel to foreign judgments. Applying U.S. issue preclusion rules is administratively easier for U.S. courts and arguably less costly for parties. To the extent that U.S. rules are broader than foreign rules of issue preclusion, moreover, the U.S. rules better advance the underlying rationale for claim and issue preclusion.[123] Finally, application of domestic preclusion rules protects the interests of U.S. citizens, who might have been involuntarily hauled into, and successfully defended against a case filed in, a foreign court.[124]

5.3 THE COLLATERAL ESTOPPEL TAKEAWAY

To avoid costly collateral estoppel mistakes or oversights, practitioners should understand the complex and intricate collateral estoppel principles of the rendering foreign state, and should concurrently evaluate the possible follow-on impact of foreign litigation and any potentially applicable collateral estoppel rules. Regardless of whether a U.S. court follows the minority or prevailing approach to evaluating the collateral estoppel effects of foreign judgments, the practitioner should be prepared to explain precisely how adopting or declining to follow the collateral estoppel principles of a rendering foreign jurisdiction advances the underlying rationales of collateral estoppel, res judicata, comity, and U.S. public policy.

6. Conclusion

The phenomenon of carbon-copy prosecutions arrived a decade or so ago and staked a claim in the international anti-corruption enforcement paradigm. We observed it, wrote about it, and in doing so, helped bring attention to a practice that has continued to gain in momentum over time.

A country's incentive to vindicate its own laws is not insubstantial, especially when a company or individual has already admitted, in a foreign proceeding, to violating local law.

---

[122] *See* Robert C. Casad, *Issue Preclusion and Foreign Country Judgments: Whose Law?*, 70 IOWA L. REV. 53, 70 (1984).

[123] *See* Scott A. Storey, *Mutuality of Collateral Estoppel in Multi-State Litigation: An Evaluation of the Restatement (Second) of Conflict of Laws*, 35 WASH. & LEE L. REV. 993, 1003 (1978).

[124] *See* Alfadda v. Fenn, 966 F. Supp. 1317, 1329 (S.D.N.Y. 1997) (concluding that a federal court "should normally apply" U.S. federal or state law to decide the scope of the preclusive effect of a foreign judgment, but recognizing additional factors that are particularly relevant to determining the preclusive effect of foreign judgments). *See also* Hurst v. The Socialist People's Libyan Arab Jamahiriya, 474 F. Supp. 2d 19, 32–33 (D.D.C. 2007).

Accordingly, both named parties and nonparties implicated in a resolution in one country ought to give due consideration to the potential impact of that resolution in another territory, especially in light of recent trends pointing to coordinated multinational cooperation and successive enforcement proceedings. The days of one-dimensional government investigations appear to be over for good. Duplicative, serial enforcement actions are now part and parcel of the enforcement landscape, despite a healthy ongoing debate over the need for, and fairness of, serial enforcements. Our continued prediction is that, as globalization makes the world smaller, what we call carbon-copy prosecutions will increase in frequency, size, scope, and force—as the past decade has ably demonstrated.

19 The Delicate Task: Guide to Investigating Allegations of Company-Internal Misconduct

LAWYERS ARE NOT acrobats.[1] But the series of balancing acts internal investigations require are unique even among legal professionals. True, the search for the truth (or, at least, an approximation thereof) is obviously the most immediate goal of any internal investigation. But that observation offers little more than spotting the pig in the python. In the complicated real world occupied by today's companies, the search for the truth finds itself in constant tension with other important, and often outcome-determinative, considerations. And this pressure is felt from the day the investigation is launched.

As practitioners whose daily job it is to investigate allegations of wrongdoing of all types (bribery, fraud, breach of fiduciary duties, theft, hostile work environment, cybercrime, sexual harassment, etc.), your authors have learned most of our lessons the hard way. But our at-times painful experiences are your gain. Our goal, here, is to mine our collective experiences so that you will be prepared to answer the most common questions when facing the tricky task of investigating claims that an employee—and, not infrequently, someone at or near "the top" of the company—may have engaged in wrongdoing.

1. Why Investigations Are Worth the Cost (and Headache)

Unquestionably, investigations can be resource-intensive and expensive. But when facing claims of misconduct—especially claims of misconduct by members of the board

---

[1] This chapter was contributed by T. Markus Funk and Perkins Coie LLP's Stewart Landefeld and Chelsea Curfman.

From Baksheesh to Bribery. T. Markus Funk and Andrew S. Boutros.
© Oxford University Press 2019. Published 2019 by Oxford University Press.

or management—it is critical that companies conduct an appropriately scaled, appropriately overseen investigation. In particular, consider these "benefits" of internal investigations:

- **Shore up employee/company morale.** When allegations of wrongdoing are overlooked by company leadership—or are *perceived* as having been overlooked—company morale inevitably suffers. This is especially true where the allegations of wrongdoing concern members of company leadership. Conversely, when companies appropriately and swiftly address such allegations, the message to company personnel and other stakeholders is that they are working at a place where compliance, good judgment, and accountability are not only valued, but are also even-handedly enforced (no matter on which rung of the corporate ladder the wrongdoer happens to be perched).
- **Safeguard your brand: Protect your company's hard-earned reputation.** Public relations experts will tell you that getting ahead of a developing problem/scandal is the most important step a company can take. A company that, with deliberate speed, launches an investigation into allegations of wrongdoing is in the best position to protect its brand and address PR/reputational issues that may arise. That said, jumping the gun and making a public announcement before the company has a true understanding of the scope of the problem can be dangerous. So our bottom line is that a properly conducted investigation in which the interim results are shared with the PR/HR/management teams is the best way to protect what for most companies is the one asset they can't afford to lose, namely, the public's and the customers' trust and respect.
- **Potential liability—Get ahead of it!** If, say, a whistle-blower makes claims of wrongdoing against members of management and threatens to take those claims public, the best thing a company can do is to conduct an internal investigation in order to (1) know more than the whistle-blower, and (2) as appropriate, seize any first-mover advantage by going to the public or the regulators first. This, in turn, helps control exposure to a myriad of legal risks such as governmental/regulatory enforcement actions, shareholder derivative suits, and civil lawsuits and whistle-blower claims.

We are not trying to be cynical, but the truth is that whistle-blowers and plaintiff's attorneys, no matter how genuine their concern, often know enough to be dangerous, but they rarely know the "whole story." By developing the full factual picture and determining the scope of any potential liability, the company will be in a better position to both frame/contextualize the issues in the public sphere and outmaneuver the opposition in the case of threatened or filed lawsuits.

- **Remove problem actors to reduce risk of future issues (and demonstrate remediation).** Stated simply, one central benefit of investigations is that they more often than not help root out problem actors within the company. Taking an active role in disciplining/removing such individuals sends the right message to stakeholders and allows the company to "do the right thing" (and to be *seen* doing the right thing), while reducing its risk of repeat problems in the future.

- **Signal and pursue constant improvement.** In virtually every investigation, the client-company will learn of weaknesses in the company's internal controls, processes, and/or governance structure that can be improved. These improvements not only reduce future legal risk, but also result in more efficient and streamlined operations within the company.

- **Show board ownership of issues and reflect an appropriate "tone at the top."** An appropriately handled investigation sends a message that the board has its hand on the ethical tiller. It also reflects a promising "tone at the top," because the board demonstrates substantive engagement and oversight.

2. Balancing Investigative Objectives with Business Realities

So far we have painted a fairly rosy picture of why investigations are important and beneficial to companies. But the truth is that the objectives of company management, the in-house legal department, internal audit, the board, or outside counsel in conducting a properly designed internal investigation often are in tension with the day-to-day realities of running a business. Here, by way of example, are some of the most common areas where investigative objectives and business realities may be in conflict:

Laudable Objective	"But . . ."
Maximize Applicable Privileges	*Running a Company Requires Transparency*
A primary objective during any investigation is to maximize protection of all applicable legal privileges. As a result, absolute confidentiality is key.	• Key stakeholders want (and sometimes need) to know about the purpose and progress of the investigation and whether "bad apples" or bad acts have been identified. They, accordingly, expect periodic updates concerning the investigation, including the status, preliminary findings, etc.
	• Nobody—let alone a member of management or the board—wants to be "left in the dark" while the investigation appears to drag on with no end in sight.

(Continued)

Laudable Objective	"But . . ."
Protect Employee Morale The company cannot afford to allow employee and management morale to erode during a stressful, often painful, and/or longer-than-expected investigative process. And the mere fact of a confidential investigation itself can make employees and management lose faith in the company and worry about their positions. As a result, company-internal members of an investigation team often want to provide real-time investigation updates or preliminary observations to company management/employees.	**Necessary Limitations to Knowledge Circle** • The sharing of preliminary observations just to appease employee or management concerns risks informational leaks, and can foster an appearance that the investigators are "playing favorites," are aligned with any person or group, or otherwise are merely using the "independent investigation" as a pretext to reach a predetermined result. • Only if all appropriate investigative steps occur—including, among other things, interviews, transaction testing, document collection, and review—will the investigation produce robust and defensible findings and a sensible remediation plan.
Retaining Familiar Counsel When it comes to outside counsel, companies often wish to engage counsel that "know the company," have helped the company with many different legal issues through the years, and appreciate the company's culture and values (and sometimes these factors even cause companies to retain "house counsel" not experienced in internal investigation matters).	**Retaining Independent Counsel with Investigative Expertise** • Enforcement agencies, courts, and other stakeholders will expect to see experienced, specialized internal investigators conducting sensitive investigations. • The more the retained investigators can demonstrate objectivity and a lack of conflicts of interest (such as "keeping the CEO happy"), the better for the company.
Using In-House Counsel to Investigate It likely will, in the first instance at least, be easier, quicker, and cheaper to have in-house counsel handle the investigation.	**Hiring Experienced Outside Counsel for Potentially Serious Matters Maximizes Privilege** • There is a happy median. Many jurisdictions (notably, EU countries) will not recognize privilege in communications with in-house counsel, as they do not view in-house counsel as independent from their employer (the company). These jurisdictions, therefore, do not protect in-house counsel communications with privilege. Outside counsel, in contrast, can engage in privileged communications.

Laudable Objective	"But . . ."
Operating Transparently and Quickly to Report Any Actual or Potential Issues to the Authorities	*Protecting the Company's Interests—and Reporting Only When Necessary*

Operating Transparently and Quickly to Report Any Actual or Potential Issues to the Authorities

Many responsible companies rush to self-report potential issues to authorities. Key stakeholders (including government agencies) will expect self-reporting, transparency, and openness about the investigation's results. In fact, the DOJ has built entire divisions around self-reporting and the incentives that flow therefrom.

Protecting the Company's Interests—and Reporting Only When Necessary

- In the absence of a third-party/whistleblower threat, unnecessary or premature reporting and self-disclosure can result in huge headaches for the company.
- Companies must, within the confines of legality, protect against costly and avoidable shareholder suits, overzealous enforcers or regulators, etc.

Loyalty toward Members of Management and the Board

Company values often include showing loyalty toward employees, members of management, and the board. Companies, therefore, often feel that they should protect "their people" against overzealous government enforcers, regulators, shareholders, and investigating counsel.

Protecting the Company Comes First

- The board's duty is to protect the company's long-term interests by identifying employees and management with potential criminal or civil exposure.
- The days of "circling the wagons" and sticking together have been undone by an entirely new incentive structure that rewards the company or employee who arrives first at the prosecutor's office.
- In this legal environment, companies are expected to mitigate risk by (as part of a broader remediation plan) strictly disciplining or terminating individuals, and/or turning them over to the authorities. At times, these individuals may be viewed by some as having done little more than made mistakes or exhibited judgment errors.

3. A Few Preliminary Words on the Role of the Board When Management (Or a Board Member) Is Implicated

We all understand that the fundamental obligation of any board is to ensure that company management is acting in the long-term best interests of the corporation and its shareholders. The natural result of this understanding is that credible allegations of misconduct by management require prompt attention, particularly when (as is often the case) the accused members of management also sit on the board. When such a potential role-based conflict of interest exists, the board's independent directors must be actively involved in the investigation.

Generally, this means creating a special committee of the board comprised of independent directors to direct and oversee the investigation.

Under the standard established in the Delaware Chancery Court's landmark 1996 decision of *In re Caremark International Inc. Derivative Litigation* (later adopted by the Delaware Supreme Court in *Stone v. Ritter* and the U.S. District Court for the District of New Jersey in *Palkon v. Holmes*), directors have the responsibility to do more than passively receive information. Instead, the expectation is that directors will actively monitor the business of the corporation, including overseeing the creation and implementation of internal controls and overseeing internal investigations.

If directors utterly fail to implement any reporting or information system or controls or, having implemented a system of controls, consciously fail to monitor or oversee the system's operation, they may face liability for a failure of oversight. In contrast, the board, by having a committee investigate a particular matter, will demonstrate that it is monitoring risk and discharging its fiduciary obligations.[2]

4. The Basic Investigative Steps

Assume that someone inside your company has made an allegation of company-internal misconduct—what next? The following practical steps are adaptable to almost all internal investigation contexts, no matter the subject matter, scope, or geography:

(a) **From Day 1 Handle Complaints (and Complainants) Appropriately.** How a company handles the initial complaint and complainant, including how the complaint is escalated and evaluated, can have a tremendous impact on the company's potential legal risk exposure. It is crucial, therefore, that companies develop an effective process to recognize complaints, "triage" or assess which complaints require escalation, and then evaluate whether, and to what degree, investigation is required.
Handling Complaints (the Right Way)—Evaluating Sources of Information
- Complaint need not come through formal channels
    o Anonymous letters
    o Reports to supervisors
    o Whistle-blower emails, hotline, and media reports
- Not always in writing
- No "magic words" needed to trigger investigation
    o Knowledge of potential misconduct may be enough to trigger need to investigate
- Not all complaints require investigation
    o A robust "intake and triage" process should be in place to identify for which complaints an investigation will be appropriate

---

[2] *See Stone v. Ritter*, 911 A.2d. 362, 370 (Del. Supr. 2006); *see also* Reiter *ex rel.* Capital One Fin. Corp. v. Fairbank et al., No. 11693-CB, 2016 WL 6081823 (Del. Ch. Oct. 18, 2016) (dismissing claims of personal liability against the Capital One board, finding that they did not consciously disregard their responsibility to oversee compliance with the Bank Secrecy Act and related anti-money-laundering laws).

- o Credibility of source and nature and seriousness of allegations is key
- o Does complaint involve:
  - Government, Regulatory, Ethical, or Safety Violations (corruption/bribery/FCPA/trafficking/child labor)?
  - Company's Code of Conduct/Handbook?
  - Harassment, Discrimination, Retaliation, Violence?
  - Conflict of Interest (financial, administrative)?
  - Misappropriation of Trade Secrets/Confidential Information?
  - Breaches of Contractual Agreements?
  - Violations by an Executive Officer?

(b) **Hire Outside Counsel Carefully.** Once a company determines that investigation is justified—because of a credible whistle-blower complaint, internal complaint, audit findings, or some other source—the company must select an appropriate investigator. While some complaints warrant investigation by company-internal functions such as human resources, internal audit, or the in-house legal department, in selected cases, the company (typically through the Audit Committee or a special committee of the board) should look to hire experienced and independent outside counsel to conduct the investigation. Counsel's independence (in the sense of not having very close personal or business relationships with management) can be particularly important where the allegations involve management or board members. In those cases, counsel's ability to demonstrate that they have little prior involvement with the company or the board can help stave off later questions about whether counsel's potential conflicting interests (in protecting a long-term client) may have influenced the results of their investigation.

Choosing an Investigator
- Things to Consider:
  - o Type of complaint being investigated
  - o Positions, personalities, and backgrounds of the people being investigated
  - o Number of investigators
- **Possible Investigators/Escalation Decision**:
  - o HR
  - o In-house legal counsel
  - o Internal auditors
  - o Outside investigators
- **When Is Board Investigation Required?**
  - o If allegations involve conduct of senior management who could have influence (or appearance of influence) over internal investigation
  - o If allegations may be material to the company
  - o If needed to satisfy external auditor, government regulators, prosecutor, stockholders, or other audience
  - o Outside counsel generally involved when board or committee oversee investigation

(c) **Engagement Letter.** For investigations that require board or committee oversight, the committee should enter into a separate engagement letter with counsel for the investigation. The engagement letter should clearly define who the client is (the board? Special committee of the board?), and specify to whom outside counsel reports (generally the chair of the committee), as blurring lines in that area can lead to accidental waiver of legal privilege. In addition, internal counsel and investigators may also be directed to report, with respect to this particular matter, directly to the chair of the committee, in order to give the committee additional control over the independence of the investigation.

(d) **Clearly Define Objectives.** To avoid any ambiguity concerning what falls within the investigator's purview, the company should work with outside counsel to clearly define the investigatory objectives, both in terms of the scope of the issues to be reviewed and the type of investigative tasks to be performed.

(e) **Briefing the Committee: Committee and Chair Updates.** When a board committee is involved, inside and outside counsel and the committee chair should decide on a plan for keeping the committee abreast of the investigation. This will generally involve frequent (perhaps weekly) updates to the committee chair, and less frequent (when there are material issues to report) briefings of the full committee. Counsel should work with the committee chair to ensure that materials are sent in a way that preserves privilege, and screened from anybody at the company who could be a possible subject of the investigation. This often will mean that the materials should be delivered to directors not through the regular board portal, but directly from outside counsel.

(f) **Auditor Section 10A Review.** The committee chair and outside counsel should also work with the company's outside auditors, who will have an obligation under Section 10A of the Securities Exchange of Act of 1934 to review any illegality or impropriety. Under Section 10A of the Exchange Act, auditors who detect or otherwise become aware of information that an illegal act "has or may have occurred" must undertake certain prescribed actions. These actions include determining: (1) whether it is likely that an illegal act has occurred, (2) whether that act is material to the company, and (3) the possible effect the act may have on the company's financial statements. Auditors generally look to the company and its counsel to investigate and evaluate any suspected wrongdoing. Because Section 10A requires the auditors to determine whether management and the board have taken "timely and appropriate remedial action," the auditors also will expect to shadow the company's investigation, and will expect the investigation to be independent of those who may be found responsible for any wrongdoing or shortcomings in controls or procedures. In this process, the auditors will work closely with outside counsel and expect to have access to nonprivileged information in connection with the Section 10A review.

(g) **Demonstrated Objectivity Right Out of the Gate.** Everyone involved in an investigation must be prepared in advance for the reality that any allegation involving a director or member of upper management must be addressed with complete objectivity. As with any investigation where the stakes are high, start by assuming nothing, let experienced investigators follow the facts, remain appropriately involved without getting in the way, and then address the implications of what has been found. Fear or concern about perception have no place in the investigative process.

Effective Investigations—Maintaining Credibility and Confidence

- Neutrality and fairness of approach
- Necessary witnesses interviewed and properly advised
- Appropriate follow-up with all relevant parties
- Confidentiality is maintained
- Investigation has (and is *viewed* as having) integrity—results are reliable and evidence-based
- Any remedial actions are supported by evidence (documents, facts)
- Effective remedial action taken to address conduct and deter similar conduct

(h) **Avoiding the Dreaded "Runaway Investigation"—Maintaining Discipline in the Form of a Carefully Devised Investigative Work Plan.** We have all seen investigations that appear to be all thrust, no vector. So it is not surprising that a company's management or board may have misgivings about unleashing independent counsel on an investigation. Fortunately, those concerns can largely be addressed through a bit of advance planning and proper oversight. To ensure alignment within the investigative team, and to ward against unpleasant surprises, a critical first step in any investigation is designing a practical and appropriately detailed investigative work plan and budget. The tone and level of granularity for such a work plan will differ based on (1) the nature and scope of the allegation(s), (2) whether vendors such as forensic accountants are involved, and (3) the level of experience the company has with investigations generally.

Preparing for an Investigation—Ensuring Alignment

- Written investigative work plans define scope; ensure alignment
- Work plan should address/include:
  - o Summary of the issues being investigated
  - o Scope and scale of investigation – consider date range, corporate entities, employees/vendors of interest
  - o Sources of evidence:
    - *Custodians*—Who may have relevant information?
    - *Forms of evidence*—Email, other electronic records, hard-copy files, voicemail, accounting records, company policies, etc.
  - o Plan for preserving, collecting, and reviewing evidence
  - o Potential interviews
  - o Process and format for reporting findings
  - o Need for experts or other service providers
  - o Confidentiality/privilege
- Work plan should also establish tentative investigation schedule
- Budget can be developed out of work plan
- Board Committee can approve work plan and budget
- Work plan can be revised as investigation progresses

(i) **The Nuts and Bolts of Internal Investigations, Part I—Evidence Collection and Review.** Once a work plan is in place, the next step in any investigation is to collect and review potentially relevant evidence. Evidence can take many forms, but in larger investigations or investigations alleging misconduct by a board member or senior management, employee emails and communications stored on company-issued computers and mobile devices are often a prime source of relevant information. Companies anticipating an investigation should take appropriate steps to preserve these and other sources of evidence, such as issuing document preservation notices or interrupting the company's regular data retention/deletion practices.

(j) **The Nuts and Bolts of Internal Investigations, Part II—(Document-Based) Interviews.** Experienced investigators typically divide interviews into (1) "scoping" interviews and, thereafter, (2) document-based interviews. In an ideal world, even during the scoping phase you will have at least some documents (perhaps maybe just the allegations) in hand to run by your witnesses in order to gain a better understanding of the context of the allegations/conduct and narrow the focus on who else you should be talking with. Once the scoping phase is complete and document review has commenced you can start getting down to brass tacks by preparing for the more in-depth document-based interviews.

Effective Interviewing—Preparation
- Determine who to interview
  - Only people with relevant information (minimize business disruptions)
  - Include management/gatekeepers
  - Beware of privilege risks if interviewing former employees/vendors
  - Determine Order of Interviews:
  - Most important witnesses to least important? Background witnesses first? "Scoping" phase interviews?
  - Consider witness availability
- Address interview logistics:
  - Format—In person? Phone?
  - Location—On company premises? Offsite? (private setting needed)
  - Interviewer—Proper pairing based on personality/cultural considerations
  - Notice period—May be a benefit to the element of surprise
- Prepare an Interview Outline:
  - Outline should identify key topics to be covered; key documents; key questions
  - Not a script
- Anticipate pre-interview issues:
  - Accuser abandons complaint
  - Witness refuses to do interview, or appears but refuses to answer questions (any fiduciary/contractual obligation to cooperate?)
  - Witness wants time to prepare (do not permit delay)
  - Witness retains counsel and demands info/updates

Evidence Collection and Review
- Identify potential sources of data
  - Data custodians—who is likely to have relevant information? (consider current/former employees, assistants, supervisors)

- o Sources of data—company email, share files, voicemail, company-issued computers/mobile devices, hard-copy files
- o Also consider policies/procedures, internal audit files, vendor due diligence files, contracts, personnel files, expense reports/invoices/other accounting data
- Data preservation
  - o Is a legal hold/document preservation notice needed? Consider nature of issues; likelihood of data loss or litigation
  - o Interrupt regular data retention practices
- Data collection
  - o Who will perform collection—is vendor assistance needed?
  - o Where will data be hosted?
  - o Permission—local data privacy laws may limit access to data
- Data review
  - o Target potentially relevant data—use keyword search terms for electronic records
  - o Prepare and follow review protocol to ensure consistency between reviewers
  - o Develop method of tracking/summarizing key evidence
  - o Document everything—what was reviewed, when, by whom, any technical issues, etc.

Effective Interviewing—Preparation

- Determine who to interview
  - o Only people with relevant information (minimize business disruptions)
  - o Include management/gatekeepers
  - o Beware of privilege risks if interviewing former employees/vendors
- Determine order of interviews:
  - o Most important witnesses to least important? Background witnesses first? "Scoping" phase interviews?
  - o Consider witness availability
- Address interview logistics:
  - o Format—In person? Phone?
  - o Location—On company premises? Offsite? (private setting needed)
  - o Interviewer—Proper pairing based on personality/cultural considerations
  - o Notice period—May be a benefit to the element of surprise
- Prepare an interview outline:
  - o Outline should identify key topics to be covered; key documents; key questions
  - o Not a script
- Anticipate pre-interview issues:
  - o Accuser abandons complaint
  - o Witness refuses to do interview, or appears but refuses to answer questions (any fiduciary/contractual obligation to cooperate?)
  - o Witness wants time to prepare (do not permit delay)
  - o Witness retains counsel and demands info/updates

Effective Interviewing—Structure and Approach

- Do not record interview or allow audio or video recording
- Initiation of interview:
  - o Explain purpose of meeting (only necessary facts)
  - o Provide "*Upjohn* advisements"— represent the company; privilege; etc.
  - o Reference "no retaliation" policy
  - o Confirm interviewee understands advisements
  - o Be prepared for "Do I need a lawyer" and other questions
- Body of interview:
  - o Start with employee background—establish comfort
  - o Ask open-ended questions; don't assume facts (who, what, where, when, why, how?)
  - o Get precise answers to questions—do not permit evasion
  - o Use documents to corroborate
  - o Allow interviewee to explain documents/facts
    - o Avoid prejudgment
    - o Probe answers that seem suspect and circle back for inconsistencies – use interviewee's answers
  - o Avoid confrontation—maintain neutrality
- Conclusion of the interview:
  - o Ask if everything relevant has been covered
  - o Request suggestions of people to talk to, evidence to obtain
  - o Inform interviewee the company is working to resolve issue
  - o Reassure employee regarding lack of retaliation
  - o Encourage witness to contact you with additional comments ("face-saver")
  - o Thank witness for his/her time

Effective Interviewing—Memorializing What You Learned

- During the interview
  - o Take clear and copious notes
  - o Note time of interview, length, people present, location
  - o Include only facts and observations—do not interpret
  - o Observe and note witness behavior (evasion, delays, discomfort)
  - o Note use of documents
- After the interview
  - o Promptly after the interview, prepare summary (formal or informal)
- Basic elements of a memorandum of interview (MOI):
  - o Circumstances and logistics (time, location, purpose, attendees, *Upjohn* advisements)
  - o Facts gathered (chronological or by subject)
  - o Wrap-up
  - o Attachments/Exhibits

5. Avoiding Investigation Pitfalls (Data Privacy, Whistle-Blower Statutes, and Uncooperative Employees)

(a) **Understanding Data Privacy Regimes *Outside* of the United States.** Notions of an individual's right to privacy are hardly new. U.S. courts have long ensured the constitutional right to privacy, and beyond U.S. borders, the right to privacy is enshrined in both the Universal Declaration of Human Rights (which was adopted by the United Nations General Assembly in 1948), and the European Union's Charter of Fundamental Rights (which became legally binding in 2009 as part of the Lisbon Treaty and included the right to respect for a person's "private and family life, home and communications"). That said, today's means of storing, duplicating, accessing, and distributing information poses very real challenges to our ability to protect sensitive information. Put another way, simply locking a file cabinet or setting up basic internal security controls will not do it. In response, recent years have seen a proliferation of data privacy regimes across the globe. As of this writing, more than 80 countries have devised comprehensive national data privacy laws. What is more, our domestic U.S. laws tend to be relatively lenient compared to the strict data regimes of many of the countries in which U.S. companies do business. It is therefore a nonstarter for investigative counsel to take a blanket approach to obtaining company data from foreign jurisdictions. Instead, investigative counsel must from day 1 educate themselves about local data privacy laws in the jurisdiction(s) involved to avoid costly missteps.

(b) **Complying with Whistle-Blower Protection Statutes.** As discussed in detail elsewhere in this book, whistle-blower protection statutes—like data privacy regimes—are increasingly gaining currency outside of the United States. Understanding what statutes exist in the jurisdictions in which you do business is, therefore, a critical early step in any cross-border investigation.

(c) **Taking Preemptive Steps to Encourage Cooperation and Access to Evidence— Some of our "Biggies."** In many investigations, the investigators will encounter a board member, CEO, CFO, or other employee-witness who, for whatever reason, is reluctant or refuses to cooperate with the investigation, meet with counsel, be interviewed, etc. There are a number of preemptive steps companies can take to ensure they are well-positioned to address such objections when, and if, they arise:

- **Ensuring Cooperation through Service Agreements.** One of the best ways to avoid (or combat) refusals to cooperate is for companies to implement corporate governance guidelines stating that all board members and management, consistent with their fiduciary duties, are expected to cooperate with investigations (it is even better if this clause appears in the individual manager, employee, or board member's service agreement). Ideally, the guidelines/agreement will include simple, direct language requiring the individual to fully cooperate in any internal or external investigation involving events occurring during the individual's tenure with the company or of which he or she has personal knowledge. The agreement also should specify that cooperation includes expeditiously turning over any requested documents and communications within the individual's possession, custody, or control, including personal phone records, email account information, text messages, and so forth. The company should also specify that the duty to cooperate remains even after an individual resigns or is terminated from the company. Of course, the individual employee, board member, or member of management may push back against such language, but this can be managed, in part, by including a reciprocal duty by the company to cooperate. Companies may also wish to explain, as part of a director training program, the benefit each individual derives from indemnification, the business judgment rule, insurance, and any other protections specific to the company. Put another way, the company can message to the director/manager that it is not asking the individual for more than the company itself is willing to provide.

- **Informing Reluctant Management-Level Employees of the "Free-Standing Duty to Cooperate."** While having language in service agreements mandating cooperation with investigations is consistent with best practices, many companies may not have thought of that until it is too late. So what should those companies do when a board member, manager, or employee simply refuses to cooperate with an investigation? In the face of such a refusal (which is, in fact, fairly common), it can be helpful to politely point out to the individual or that person's counsel that board members, managers, and even employees owe a fiduciary duty to their companies, including a duty of care and a duty of loyalty. These duties, in turn, have been judicially interpreted to include a duty to cooperate with an internal investigation. It is important to note, however, that such a duty to cooperate is not explicit in the Model Business Corporation Act, nor is it settled as a matter of law.[3] As a result, this tactic is best used as a second line of defense. It is always preferable to include duty-to-cooperate language in service agreements, before any allegations arise.

- **Thoughtfully Devising Company Data Policies and Considering the Use of Company-Issued Communication Devices (Laptops, Phones, Tablets, Etc.).** Companies should also consider whether to issue company-owned communication devices (laptops, phones, etc.) and company email addresses to board members, and to require directors to use these devices for all company business. This requirement can be included in procedures adopted by the board, or in individual service agreements, and would give the independent investigators access to these communications in the event of an internal investigation.[4] This requirement has two additional benefits: (1) it can provide an independent ground for removal if a board member fails to follow company instructions about using the designated

---

[3] Note that Section 302 of SOX (codified at 15 U.S.C. § 7241) lends support to the argument that directors' fiduciary duties include a duty to cooperate with investigations. Section 302 imposes upon officers a responsibility to ensure that they have accurately reported to the company's auditors and to the company's audit committee any fraud, whether or not material, that involves (1) directors, (2) management, or (3) other employees who have a significant role in the issuer's internal controls. In short, these provisions incentivize (or, at least, *should* incentivize) CEOs and CFOs to diligently investigate any known or suspected wrongdoing brought to their attention; a failure to do so may subject them to liability.

[4] This presumes that the company has in place data privacy policies that state explicitly that all information stored on or transferred through a company-owned device is company property and subject to review at any time

communication services or devices, and (2) it may prevent the inadvertent waiver of privileged information. For instance, if a board member communicates with the company's outside counsel using a non-company email account (that is monitored, for example, by the board member's employer), there is a risk that the attorney-client privilege otherwise applicable to that communication may be deemed waived.

That said, a muted word of caution is in order: while requiring the use of company-issued communication devices or email accounts may be helpful when investigating a recalcitrant board member, it also puts a greater burden on the company in the event of an external investigation. Specifically, the company will be required to maintain and preserve the information and may be subject to sanctions if, for instance, it doesn't take steps to preserve text messages once litigation is reasonably anticipated. Additionally, board members may reject any service agreement that allows the company unlimited access to their communications.

6. Concluding an Investigation

Inevitably, the most challenging and time-consuming stages of any investigation are evidence collection and review and interviews. But when that process is complete, clients want to know, "so, what did you find?"

(a) **Collecting, Analyzing, and Sharing the Investigative Findings**. As discussed previously, the investigative work plan should dictate when, and in what format, investigation findings will be conveyed to the client. In any investigation, it is important to ensure that findings are factually accurate, appropriately limited, and conveyed in a manner that maximizes protection of legal privileges.

(b) **Report-out to Committee and Board**. In board or committee-led investigations, counsel's final task will be to brief the committee and its chair on the results both of the investigation and recommended remediation steps. The committee should have ample opportunity to raise questions. Counsel and the committee chair should work to ensure that outside experts, including forensic accountants or internal audit personnel as needed, are available for the committee meeting. Minutes of the meeting should be privileged and maintained separately, in the company's books and records, from those that will be reviewed and reviewable by auditors.

(c) **Briefing the Auditors**. At the conclusion of the investigation, counsel will brief the company's independent auditors on any nonprivileged outcome of the investigation. This Section 10A briefing should be verbal and carefully calibrated to ensure that privilege is maintained. For example, counsel will wish to take care to not share with the auditors the search terms or other key elements that counsel used in

---

without notice to the board member. Such policies, while ubiquitous among U.S. companies, may not be in place in foreign companies or subsidiaries.

the investigation that could be privileged and the disclosure of which could jeopardize the maintenance of the privilege.

Relaying Findings and Protecting Privilege

- Determine form of reporting (privilege)
  - o Written report, verbal readout, or presentation—written reports should avoid legal conclusions
  - o Do results warrant readout to auditors, shareholders, creditors, regulators?
- Substance of report—are facts in dispute?
  - o Corroborate, corroborate, corroborate
  - o If facts are conflicting, be ready to present mixed well-documented findings
- Use best judgment to assess witness credibility
  - o Timing of complaint
  - o Motivation of complainant
  - o Veracity and motivation of witnesses
- Final report (regardless of format) should address:
  - o Parties involved in the investigation and their roles
  - o What was, and was not, reviewed (limitations to the investigative scope)
  - o Create a chronology of tasks—complaint, preparation, evidence review, interviews, findings, and remediation

(d) **Designing an Effective Remediation Plan.** Assuming the investigation corroborated the initial complaint or identified other misconduct or a failure of internal controls, a key final step in any investigation is preparing and implementing an effective remediation plan. Remediation plans can take many forms depending on the nature and severity of the misconduct and the company's goals for punishing wrongdoers or deterring similar acts in the future. An effective remediation plan may also help reduce corporate fines or damage awards in regulatory actions or litigation brought against the company related to the underlying misconduct.

Designing an Effective Remediation Plan

- Did investigation identify misconduct or governance/internal controls issues?
- If yes, consider:
  - o Desires of complainant (and reaction of authorities/board members/management/jurors)
  - o Risk of regulatory action or civil litigation
  - o Existence of similar violations within the company/industry
  - o Client goals (deterrence, punishment, restitution)
- Structure remediation plan around existing company policies and procedures
- Possible Remedies:
- Written warnings/reprimand
- Acknowledgment of wrongdoing
- Administrative leave
- Reduction/elimination of bonus
- Additional training
- Transfer
- Suspension
- Termination
- Reporting to authorities

(e) **Findings Short of "Cause"—Options for Replacing a Nonfunctioning Director(s).**[5] Even if the conduct identified during the internal investigation does not support a for-cause termination, the board may still decide that the investigation has shown that a particular board member or manager is no longer right for the job. To the extent a board or nominating and governance committee, in fulfilling its responsibility to nominate and evaluate directors, determines that a director needs to be removed, it has only a few tools at its disposal. Both Delaware law and the Model Business Corporation Act (MBCA) follow the general rule that shareholders (acting by majority vote), rather than the board, have the power to remove a director. In short, while directors may have a responsibility to monitor board health, shareholders have the primary power to remove directors or elect replacement directors. A company and its board have many tools to deal with a director who needs to be removed.

7. Parting Thoughts

Conducting any type of internal investigation into allegations of employee misconduct can be tricky, and the stakes—and sensitivities—only get higher when the allegations target board members or members of management. As outlined previously, the key to tackling these challenges is to break the meta-tasks into individual, digestible process steps. With a well-defined plan and an investigative team that remains independent and focused on the ultimate goal, companies can achieve robust and reliable investigative findings (see Figure 19.1).

8. Investigation Protocol
8.1 STEP I: INTAKE

(a) Ethics and Compliance (E&C) or other internal non-board Committee members (regardless of nomenclature) are alerted to a potential compliance issue via one of the company's intake mechanisms (hotline, website, manager complaint, legal, etc.). For reports initiated through human resources or the legal department, a member of the E&C Committee will gather as much information from the informant as possible and enter the information into the compliance database (usually a site intake form).

---

[5] Note that, for many companies, removing a director will likely trigger an obligation to file a current report on Form 8-K with the U.S. Securities and Exchange Commission (SEC). Under Item 5.02 of Form 8-K, a company must file a Form 8-K when a director retires, resigns, is removed, or refuses to stand for re-election. If the director's resignation or removal results from a disagreement with the management of the company, or is for cause, the filing is made under Item 5.02(a); all other disclosures fall under Item 5.02(b). A company must file a current report on SEC Form 8-K within four business days after a disclosable event has occurred. As relevant here, a disclosable event includes a notice, written or verbal, from the director to the company of his or her decision to resign, retire, or refuse to stand for re-election (but because decisions such as this take time, thought, and discourse, the mere discussion or consideration of resignation, retirement, or refusal to stand does not require disclosure).

Generic Key Internal Investigation Steps

Initial Intake—Common Triggers
- Government actions, subpoena, search warrant, and witness interview.
- Whistle-blower complaint
- Media report
- Shareholder demand
- Civil suit
- Informal channels ("gossip," advocacy group pressure, etc.)

First-Level Case Assessment & Initial "Escalation Decision"
- How credible is the source of the allegation?
- How serious is the alleged misconduct?
- Criminal/regulatory issues implicated?
- Management or public image involved?
- Likelihood of detection and reputational damage?
- History of similar problems?

Internal Audit
- May be experienced investigators
- Should be independent
- Report to management (concern about management inhibiting full disclosure)
- Communication will likely not be covered by attorney-client privilege
- More appropriate in routine matters

In-House Counsel
- Experience with investigations varies
- May be seen as less independent by third parties (i.e., the government)
- Risk that some communications will be deemed business communications not covered by attorney-client privilege
- More appropriate in routine matters

Regular Outside Counsel
- Lawyers' independence could be questioned, depending on relationship/history with management
- Attorney-client privilege will apply
- Should not investigate senior management or persons with whom the firm regularly works

Regular Outside Counsel
- Required in certain sensitive situations
- Attorney-client privilege will apply
- May have special expertise in internal investigations
- May have less familiarity with business than regular outside counsel

Create the Investigation Plan
- Define purpose and scope of investigation
- Identify major tasks:
  - Document preservation, collection, and review
  - Need for litigation hold and forensic analysis
  - Privilege and *Upjohn* issues
  - Budget
  - Investigatory fact-development phases and deadlines

Second-Level Evaluation of Allegations and Evidence: Understanding Who, What, Where, and When?

POTENTIALLY CREDIBLE

NOT POTENTIALLY CREDIBLE

Document rationale for not pursuing matter further at this juncture

Summarize Factual Findings & Legal Conclusions
- Meet with "need to know" legal/management/HR team to discuss findings & preliminary analysis
- Develop recommendations and any remedial action and implementation plan
- Written or oral presentation?

Close-Out
- Secure all records
- Retain final version of memoranda and reports
- Determine with whom to share results
- Legal holds removed?
- Self-reflection—compliance gaps identified?

Steps to Protect Privilege

Is Substantial Purpose of Communications to Seek Legal Advice?

Practical Pointers:

- Easier to protect outside counsel communications because in-house counsel often provide (and are perceived as providing) business advice
- Ensure that the appropriate person in organization requests investigation—consider reciprocal engagement letters setting forth nature of representation and interest in protecting privilege
- Key reason to protect privilege is so company can control outgoing flow of information
- Non-lawyers acting at a lawyer's direction may be engaging in privileged communications (see *Kovel*)
- Applies only to communication about facts, not the facts themselves

YES ↓

Person Receiving Information Authorized to Do So?

Practical Pointers:

- Document shared understanding of privilege protection plan
- Labeling *privileged* or *attorney work product* is necessary, but without more does not create protection

YES ↓

Communications Intended to Be Confidential?

Practical Pointers:

- Avoid unintentional joint-representation waiver by flawed *Upjohn* admonitions
- Include carefully drafted summary of purpose of overall representation in engagement letter
- If client has parents, subsidiaries, or affiliates, take steps to make explicit that they are also covered by privilege
- Think carefully about who will receive your findings and whether the findings should be written or oral
- No disclosure to third parties

YES ↓

Confidentiality in Fact Preserved?

Practical Pointers:

- Ensure that you never cc or bcc a non-lawyer unless person is unquestionably in the "need to know" group—and ensure that client does the same
- Exercise caution when sharing with others (including outside audit)

YES →

— NO → **Privilege Likely Does Not Apply**

— NO →

— NO →

How to Protect Company/Client Interests in the Written Work Plan

Before assignment of an internal legal investigation to in-house or outside attorney, prepare written plan that includes:

- Objective of the legal advice
- Who within the company "needs to know" the legal advice
- Scope/task of the legal investigation
- Statement concerning need to preserve confidentiality
- Steps taken to ensure investigation is conducted consistent with existing corporate employee/employer policies
- Shared understanding of interview preamble, including *Upjohn* admonitions to all employees:
  - I am the company lawyer and not your lawyer
  - I can tell the company what you tell me
- What you tell me is confidential, protected by the attorney-client privilege between me and the company
- Only the company can waive the privilege and disclose what you have told me to others
- What you tell me may be given to regulators, law enforcement and/or public officials—and therefore must be truthful
  - Document consent to continue interview
- Immediate task:
  - Consider drafting and issuing litigation holds to all relevant employees

Note: If no anticipation of litigation, no work-product privilege applies

---

Communication Likely Privileged

This chart was prepared by Perkins Coie Partner T. Markus Funk (MFunk@perkinscoie.com). Markus retains the copyright to this chart.

FIGURE 19.1 Key Internal Investigation Steps

(b) If a report of an actual or potential violation of the company's E&C program comes in via the E&C hotline, the outside vendor personnel receiving the call shall forward the report to the E&C Committee for review by email.

(c) If the report comes in any other way, any member of the E&C committee receiving the report should email a summary of the report to the rest of the E&C Committee. The E&C Committee will assign an investigator (a member of the E&C Committee). If a report requires immediate investigation, the chair of the E&C Committee will assign an investigator and communicate the decision to the E&C Committee.

8.2 STEP 2: VALIDITY DETERMINATION

(a) The investigator will decide if the complaint is valid and requires investigation. If it is determined to be invalid, the investigator will enter his or her reasoning into the compliance database. The investigation ceases.

A valid complaint has the following qualities:

(b) Reasonable basis in fact (evidence exists)

(c) Involves a violation of corporate policy

On the other hand, an invalid complaint has these characteristics:

(d) A lack of specificity

(e) Vague

(f) Willful harassment of employer (reasonable person standard: Does the complaint express a genuine concern about a workplace violation, or is it intended merely to annoy or irritate the employer?)

8.3 STEP 3: BOARD OVERSIGHT

(a) Most investigations will be overseen by the non-board E&C Committee.

(b) But the Board itself (generally through the Audit Committee or a special committee) should take over oversight if: a senior executive (CEO, CFO, CLO/GC) may be implicated; or an outside auditor, governmental investigator or other stakeholder would expect an independent board-led investigation; or because of the prominence of the issue, the risk to the company, or another reason that makes the matter of keen interest to the board.

8.4 STEP 4: PLANNING

(a) If the complaint is considered valid, the investigator notifies the appropriate stakeholders and works with the E&C Committee or board committee to develop an investigative plan involving the appropriate resources (e.g., legal, human resources, security, internal audit).

(b) The E&C Committee should determine whether others will be included in directing and performing the investigative plan. Other stakeholders may be included by considering the apparent nature of the report, such as the following:

- Matters relating to financial concerns may include the Chief Financial Officer (CFO).
- Matters relating to employee conduct may include the global vice president of human resources.
- Matters relating to potential violations of state or federal law may include the General Counsel.

8.4.1 In Writing (Putting Together the "Investigative Work Plan")

The investigator should begin an investigation with a written objective and investigative plan. The investigative plan should be informed, at a minimum, by the following questions:

- What happened?
- When did the company know what happened?
- What was the response to what happened?

Invariably, both the objective of the investigation and the investigative plan will need to be updated or revised as more information is obtained in the course of the investigation. Such changes may lead to a broadening of the scope of the investigation and therefore of the relevant team (including going from a situation where the investigation can be competently handled internally to one where an outside firm may be needed for expertise, staffing numbers, or independence). There can also be cases in which the investigation becomes less complex than originally thought. It is always more efficient to deal with these issues via a written plan.

The investigator shall update the claims reporting database within the network system as appropriate.

8.5 STEP 5: COLLECTION OF RELEVANT INFORMATION

As this Section will relate, the investigator should gather information through document review, electronic forensics, and interviews (including complainant, subject of complaint, and witnesses.

8.5.1 Purpose of the Compliance Investigation: Determine the Facts

The purpose of a compliance investigation is to determine the relevant facts, not to "prove" a case. Addressing the relevant facts through corrective or disciplinary action is a separate part of the compliance process, once the facts are established.

Compliance investigations must be conducted in a professional manner by individuals with appropriate backgrounds, including certain technical expertise (production, manufacturing, distribution, finance, etc.), to the extent those issues are relevant to the investigation.

There are circumstances in which investigations must be conducted by outside firms (such as potential conflicts of interest, need for additional resources or expertise, etc.), and they will be subject to certain procedures. However, it is more common that investigations will be conducted wholly or primarily by internal staff. Internal investigations are the primary focus of this hotline process.

8.5.2 Interviews and *Upjohn* Advisements

If an interview is conducted by attorneys and there is any question that the interviewee may think that the attorney represents the interviewee rather than, or in addition to, the company, the so-called *Upjohn* advisements (amended as appropriate for non-U.S. jurisdictions) should be provided. (Note that we use the term "advisements," rather than the more threatening "Upjohn *Warnings*"). They can at a very high level be summarized as follows:

- The interviewers represent the company only, not the interviewee.
- Information provided in the interview is protected by the company's attorney-client privilege, which is controlled by the company, not the interviewee.
- Information shared with the interviewers may be used by the company against the interviewee.
- The company may decide whether to waive the privilege and disclose information from the interview to third parties, including the government.

8.5.3 Preparation/Securing Documents

Once a matter is identified for investigation, the investigator should log the information into the case management database and the lead investigator (and investigation team) should be identified.

The investigation should, in addition to identifying all possible internal witnesses, be prepared to consider other relevant documents, such as emails, memos, individual and department files, expense reports including company credit card records and receipts, travel reports, time sheets, and electronic log-in data. Care should be exercised before reviewing such documents without the knowledge or consent of the involved employee. Asking an individual to provide such documents often results in cooperation, even in cases where the information provided is unflattering to the individual providing it.

However, there can be instances in which an individual is not cooperative and the company may need to exercise its right to review such documents according to its rights under company policies and any applicable local, state, or national laws. Those rights, such as reviewing emails without knowledge or consent of the author or recipient, are normally best exercised on as limited a basis as necessary (both in terms of the scope, meaning the date range/subject matter, and the individuals who actually review the emails) to meet the needs of the investigation.

In some situations involving potentially very serious issues in which outside counsel is taking the lead, a process in which documents are secured before interviews may be appropriate. However, judgment should be exercised in less serious cases.

8.5.4 Number of Interviewers and Style of Interview

In the vast majority of cases, interviews should be done in the presence of at least two persons besides the interviewee. Both interviewers should take notes, although one should have the primary responsibility for doing so. It is fine if only one of the interviewers asks questions. The interview and the notes should be discussed among the interviewers as soon as possible after the interview to ensure completeness and accuracy.

Although nervousness and anxiety are commonplace in internal investigation interviews, most people are inclined to be forthcoming if questioned politely. It is normally most effective to allow the interview to be conversational in tone and allow the interviewee to speak for as long as he wishes about whatever he wishes. An interviewer should have an outline of topics to be addressed, but that outline should only serve as a guide. All of the topics should be covered eventually, but not necessarily in the order in which the interviewer has written them. Resist the notion of "controlling" the interview in the same sense that a lawyer would want to control testimony during cross-examination in a trial. Rather, interviewees are more likely to give candid, truthful, accurate, and useful information if they are allowed to speak naturally and at their own pace as opposed to following a questioner's list, which may give the interviewee an opportunity to pause and be more calculating in his or her responses. Of course, there are also people who will lie or conveniently "forget" material information, particularly if they believe that it is damaging to them personally. Thorough, professional investigations will nonetheless often result in documentation or other witness statements to establish the truth.

8.6 STEP 6: FACTUAL AND LEGAL ANALYSIS

The investigator organizes and analyzes the gathered information in preparation for reporting and presentation. After presentation of the facts, the E&C Committee determines policy and legal implications of the findings in consultation with the legal department.

8.6.1 The Investigation Itself Must Be Conducted in Accordance with the Company's Code of Conduct

At the outset, the interviewers will obviously want to introduce themselves and explain who they are, their relationship to the company, and their role in the interview (e.g., company management has requested that we review the procurement operations for this location). This would also be the time to indicate, as applicable, that the interview constitutes company confidential information, that the interviewee is obligated under the company's code of conduct to cooperate with the investigation, and that the interviewee is not to speak with others about the interview (subject to exceptions in the case of the interviewee obtaining their own personal counsel or other personal advisors). If the interviewee is not the target of the investigation (and reasonably appears unlikely to become a target), it may be useful to inform that person in order to make the interview more relaxed.

Investigations must be undertaken in a professional manner in accordance with the company's code of conduct and its provisions regarding respect for individuals. Tactics such as lying to interviewees, being unduly harsh or aggressive with interviewees, implying that one can make a "deal" with an interviewee, and so forth are not permissible.

In addition, the following principles should be observed and participants in the investigation should be informed of them, unless it is apparent that they are already aware:

- An investigation does not presume any wrongdoing or any other facts. The objective of the investigation is to determine the facts as best as possible.
- Employees are expected to cooperate with internal investigations.
- There is no stigma attached to being questioned during an internal investigation.
- There is no stigma attached to being the target of an investigation if no wrongdoing is found.
- Confidentiality of the investigation must be preserved by the investigators, sharing information only on a need-to-know basis.
- Individuals interviewed or requested to provide documents as part of an investigation must maintain confidentiality, and not discuss the subject of the interview with others (although they may need to let their supervisor know that they were requested to participate in a confidential internal investigation).
- The company's policy prohibiting retaliation against individuals providing evidence of misconduct will apply.

8.7   STEP 7: REPORTING TO STAKEHOLDERS

The E&C Committee reports—or asks outside counsel to report—findings to the appropriate stakeholders.

8.7.1   Conclusions: Investigation Report

It is not unusual for facts that completely change the tenor of the investigation to arise late in the investigations process. For this reason and to avoid the disruption of giving out misleading or incorrect information that may be acted upon prematurely, the investigators should avoid making conclusions before the investigation is complete. It may be necessary to advise a small number of managers of the progress of an investigation before it is complete, but the audience of such reports should be limited to a need-to-know basis, and such progress reports should be clear that all the facts or document review are not complete.

Once the investigation is complete, the facts should be memorialized, usually in a written report. But sometimes it may be more appropriate to deliver the report orally at a meeting in which the conclusions are set forth and to keep the written report for internal-use only (this, among other things, helps reduce the odds of inadvertent privilege waiver and can also avoid issues if a party-opponent later seeks discovery). The length and content of the report can be tailored for the circumstances, but the report should identify the subject and scope of the investigation, date and duration, any limitations on the investigations process (if applicable), and conclusions. Depending on the audience of the investigation report, the identification of individuals interviewed, and supporting documents might not be shown in the report, but the investigator should have such information readily available in written form in case it becomes necessary to produce later.

8.8 STEP 8: CORRECTIVE ACTION

The company should implement corrective action as necessary (e.g., written warning, verbal warning, coaching, training, final warning, termination). The individual assigned to investigate and prepare the report shall conduct his/her investigation and report findings to the E&C or Board Committee, who shall then determine whether any action is necessary.

8.9 STEP 9: CLOSE-OUT AND FOLLOW-UP

Update the status on the compliance database and give a description of the final determination as well as corrective action. When the investigation report is concluded and the investigation is closed, those facts should be logged onto the case management ledger. The E&C or Board Committee or other responsible department, which might well be someone different from the lead investigator, should then follow up to ensure that any corrective or disciplinary action determined as a result of the investigation is actually carried out:

(a) Upon completing any recommended action, the individual assigned to investigate the report shall save any related documentation.

(b) The individual assigned to investigate the report shall investigate as appropriate and complete the following fields:
  - *Disposition*: Enter a brief description of the findings and conclusion of the matter.
  - *Date Closed*: Enter the date the matter was closed or resolved.

20 The Key Tools of the Trade in Transnational Bribery Investigations and Prosecutions: Mutual Legal Assistance Treaties (MLATs) and Letters Rogatory

1. Introduction

The investigation of corruption, bribery, and similar transnational criminal conduct, like the discovery process for transnational civil proceedings, often involves gathering evidence located in foreign countries.[1] However, national sovereignty, international treaties, and international law preclude U.S. law enforcement officials from simply flying to a foreign country to conduct searches, question suspects, obtain documents, and proceed with arresting individuals for trial in the United States. In the absence of a foreign country's agreement to cooperate in a criminal investigation, U.S. prosecutors or civil litigation counsel have limited options. For this reason, transnational cooperation and collaboration is an integral component of contemporary justice systems—and is something that must be understood by those involved in prosecuting, investigating, or defending bribery/corruption cases involving extraterritorial application of the bribery laws, in which case evidence is almost by definition going to be located in a foreign jurisdiction.[2]

---

[1] This chapter was contributed by T. Markus Funk. Portions of this chapter are adapted with permission from T. Markus Funk, Federal Judicial Center, Mutual Legal Assistance Treaties and Letters Rogatory: A Guide for Judges (2014).

[2] See generally Lita M. Grace, The United States and Canadian Border: An Attempt to Increase Bi-Lateral Cooperation for the Prevention of Transnational Crime, Colum. J. Int'l Aff. (July 23, 2012), https://jia.sipa. columbia.edu/online-articles/united-states-and-canadian-border-attempt-increase-bi-lateral-cooperation-prevention ("[M]ultiple federal law enforcement agencies have begun to observe a statistical increase in the committing of transnational crime. The United States understands that it will take cooperation with more than one country in order to deter transnational crime . . . .").

From Baksheesh to Bribery. T. Markus Funk and Andrew S. Boutros.
© Oxford University Press 2019. Published 2019 by Oxford University Press.

There are two primary means of obtaining evidence for use in transnational criminal proceedings: a Mutual Legal Assistance Treaty (MLAT) and a letter rogatory (counsel in civil proceedings are limited to the latter). Evidence obtained from abroad through these tools may be presented as part of court proceedings, requiring U.S. judges to be familiar with the legal issues implicated by transnational requests for assistance.[3] In addition, diplomacy, executive agreements, and information exchange through informal communications also play an important role in transnational criminal investigations and civil litigation.[4]

Requests for transnational assistance requiring judicial oversight most commonly involve activities necessary for proceeding with a criminal investigation or prosecution or a transnational civil proceeding, such as serving subpoenas, locating evidence and individuals, and taking testimony. The court's role in reviewing these requests will vary depending upon the applicable treaties and foreign law.[5]

The MLAT is a treaty-based mechanism for seeking foreign law enforcement cooperation and assistance in support of an ongoing criminal investigation or proceeding.[6] The MLAT process, and its benefits, are available only to government officials, typically prosecutors.[7] MLATs do not apply to civil litigants or proceedings. Supervising the execution of *incoming* MLATs—requests for assistance from foreign jurisdictions—requires direct federal district court oversight and involvement.[8] In contrast, the courts play no part in initiating or processing *outgoing* MLAT requests. That is the province of the executive branch.

Letters rogatory, on the other hand, have a considerably broader reach than MLATs: they can be issued by U.S. federal and state courts as part of criminal, civil, and administrative

---

[3] This chapter focuses on obtaining evidence and assistance in criminal matters. The Hague Convention on the Taking of Evidence Abroad in Civil or Commercial Matters [hereinafter the Hague Evidence Convention]—codified at 28 U.S.C. § 1781 under the auspices of the Hague Conference on Private International Law, and enforced since 1972—sets forth the procedures for obtaining evidence and assistance in civil cases by its over 50 signatory countries (including the United States).

[4] *See generally* Virginia M. Kendall & T. Markus Funk, Child Exploitation and Trafficking: Examining the Global Challenges and U.S. Responses 231–34 (2012) ("Although formal MLATs, letters rogatory, and conventions may be the 'public face' of the world's cooperative law enforcement community, a comparable amount of exchange of information occurs through tried-and-tested informal [channels]."); Dan Webb et al., Corporate Internal Investigations § 13.08 (2010) (noting the various informal channels of foreign-based evidence gathering in light of the "past two decades [of exploding] international trade and commerce").

[5] For example, 28 U.S.C. § 1782 (2018) expressly states that "a person may not be compelled to give his testimony or statement or to produce a document or other thing in violation of any applicable privilege," which may include foreign privilege. *See In re* Comm'r's Subpoenas, 325 F.3d 1287, 1292 (11th Cir. 2003) (noting that 28 U.S.C. § 1782's "legally applicable privilege" language "embraces privileges recognized by foreign law"), *abrogated on other grounds by* Intel Corp. v. Advanced Micro Devices, Inc., 542 U.S. 241, 260–63 (2004).

[6] *See generally* U.S. Department of State, 7 Foreign Affairs Manual [hereinafter FAM] § 962.1, www.state.gov/m/a/dir/regs/fam/ ("MLATs have become increasingly important. They seek to improve the effectiveness of judicial assistance and to regularize and facilitate its procedures.").

[7] *See id.* § 962.5.

[8] However, state courts do not help in the processing of incoming MLAT requests. If evidence located abroad is needed as part of a prosecution in state courts, local prosecutors may enlist the MLAT process and work with the foreign judicial system. *See* Morgenthau v. Avion Res. Ltd., 49 A.D.3d 50, 59, 849 N.Y.S.2d 223, 230 (2007).

proceedings; and they can be sent to U.S. federal and state courts by any foreign or international tribunal or "interested person."[9]

Letters rogatory (also known as "letters of request" when presented by a nonparty "interested person"[10]) were first used to facilitate cooperation among the courts of the several states of the pre-Revolutionary American Union. Today, the letter rogatory process is used internationally and is codified at 28 U.S.C. §§ 1781[11] and 1782 (2018) (the "Judicial Assistance Statute").[12]

Letters rogatory are available to prosecutors, defendants, and civil litigants once formal proceedings have commenced; they typically cannot issue during the *investigative* stage of criminal proceedings.[13] The process for letters rogatory is more time-consuming and unpredictable than that for MLATs. This is in large part because the enforcement of letters rogatory is a matter of comity between courts, rather than treaty-based.

For these reasons, prosecutors typically consider letters rogatory an option of last resort for accessing evidence abroad, to be exercised only when MLATs are not available. In contrast, because MLATs are never available to private parties, defense counsel and civil litigants must rely on letters rogatory to gather evidence located abroad. This disparity in access to evidence may result in delayed proceedings and cause the defense to raise access-to-justice issues.

Requests from abroad ("incoming requests") for legal assistance are directed to a country's designated "central authority," usually the Department (or Ministry) of Justice. The central

---

[9] *See* 28 U.S.C. § 1782(a) (2018) ("The order may be made pursuant to a letter rogatory issued, or request made, by a foreign or international tribunal or upon the application of any interested person and may direct that the testimony or statement be given, or the document or other thing be produced, before a person appointed by the court.").

[10] *See generally In re* Letter of Request from Crown Prosecution Serv. of United Kingdom, 870 F.2d 686, 687 (D.C. Cir. 1989) (involving a request by a foreign government for information for use in an underlying criminal investigation).

[11] Title 28 U.S.C. § 1781(a) provides that the U.S. State Department is empowered to (1) use formal channels to transmit letters rogatory from foreign or international tribunals to the appropriate U.S. court, and receive and return them after execution; and (2) transmit letters rogatory from U.S. courts to the applicable foreign or international tribunal, officer, or agency, and receive and return them after execution. Notably, section 1781(b) also expressly states that U.S. courts or foreign or international tribunals may skip the middleman (to wit, the U.S. State Department) and send their requests directly to the foreign tribunal, officer, or agency.

[12] Title 28 U.S.C. § 1782(a) allows any litigant involved in a "proceeding in a foreign or international tribunal" to apply to a U.S. court to obtain evidence for use in the non-U.S. civil or criminal proceeding. This avenue for obtaining evidence from inside the United States is, thus, unrestricted in terms of (1) the type of proceeding, and (2) the foreign countries from which such requests can issue, and, therefore, overlaps—and, indeed, exceeds—the subject matter of the Hague Evidence Convention. What is more, unlike the Hague Evidence Convention, section 1782 does not require the foreign litigant to first request the discovery from the non-U.S. tribunal.

[13] *See In re* Letter of Request from Crown Prosecution Serv. of United Kingdom, 870 F.2d at 692 (suggesting that letters rogatory are available prior to the initiation of formal proceedings only if there is a reliable indication that there is a likelihood that proceedings will be instituted within a reasonable time); *see also* 28 U.S.C. § 1782(a) (providing that, with the exception of criminal investigations, the section only covers "testimony or statement or . . . documents or other things for use in a *proceeding* in a foreign or international tribunal . . .") (emphasis added).

authority, in turn, transmits the MLAT or letter-rogatory-related communication to the appropriate court or government entity. When a federal prosecutor appears before a U.S. district court requesting assistance on behalf of a foreign state or provides notice that the U.S. government will seek assistance from a foreign state, the prosecutor acts at the direction of the U.S. Department of Justice's Office of International Affairs (OIA). OIA is the United States' central authority and de facto functional hub for all outgoing and incoming requests for transnational investigation and litigation assistance. Its attorneys process the paperwork for incoming and outgoing requests for assistance, issue guidance, and draft the form motions used by federal prosecutors. If the court has questions or concerns about the request, the judge may address them directly to OIA, typically through the local U.S. Attorney's Office.

This chapter provides an overview of the statutory schemes and procedural matters that distinguish MLATs and letters rogatory, and it discusses legal issues that arise when the prosecution, the defense, or a civil litigant seeks to obtain evidence from abroad as part of a criminal or civil proceeding. Table 20.1 is a chart that compares the two processes. The chapter also discusses informal channels for information exchange in Part IV.

2. Mutual Legal Assistance Treaties

2.1 OVERVIEW

MLATs are the principal vehicle through which law enforcement officials make transnational requests for assistance relating to evidence gathering and other law enforcement activities. They are available for use by law enforcement officials involved in criminal investigations and proceedings (or in some civil matters where the case is related to a criminal matter).[14] MLATs are legally binding negotiated commitments. Nonetheless, courts review specific requests for assistance and may deny them if they fail to comply with applicable domestic law or procedure.[15]

2.1.1 Scope

MLATs provide for mutual cooperation between nations in the investigation and prosecution of transnational crime, and they do so through explicitly enumerated categories of law

---

[14] *See generally* 7 FAM § 962.5, *supra* note 6.

[15] *See generally In re* Request from the United Kingdom Pursuant to the Treaty between the Government of the U.S. and the Government of the UK on Mutual Assistance in Criminal Matters *in re* Dolours Price, 718 F.3d 13, 21–23 (1st Cir. 2013) (holding that district courts retain the inherent authority to quash subpoenas issued under the U.S.–UK MLAT on grounds of relevance); United States v. Rommy, 506 F.3d 108, 129 (2d Cir. 2007) (holding that "when securing evidence without MLAT authorization, foreign government officials lacking diplomatic immunity must conduct themselves in accordance with applicable 'domestic laws.'"); *see also* Kimberly Prost, *Breaking Down the Barriers: International Cooperation in Combating Transnational Crime*, INFO. EXCHANGE NETWORK FOR MUTUAL ASSISTANCE CRIM. MATTERS & EXTRADITION, http://www.oas.org/juridico/mla/en/can/en_can_prost.en.html (last visited Jan. 31, 2019) ("For mutual assistance to succeed, the operative principle must be that requests will be executed in accordance with the law of the requested state and to the extent not prohibited by that law, will be provided in the manner sought by the requesting state. In other words, while authorities in a requested state must always meet the standards prescribed by domestic law, unless the rendering of assistance in the form sought would constitute a violation of that law, it should be provided.").

TABLE 20.1

Comparison of an MLAT and a Letter Rogatory

Issue	MLAT	Letter Rogatory
Nature of instrument?	Bilateral cooperation treaty	Issued by state and federal courts as a matter of comity (and with the expectation of reciprocity)
Scope of use?	The primary method of obtaining foreign evidence and other assistance	Available to all parties in criminal and civil matters
Nature of judicial involvement?	U.S. district courts supervise issuance and execution only of incoming requests	Federal and state judiciaries supervise issuance and execution of outgoing and incoming requests
Available to criminal defendants?	No (except pursuant to the first three MLATS the United States signed)	Yes; in fact, is the primary formal means for defendants to obtain foreign evidence
Available to civil litigants?	No	Yes
Available to prosecutors?	Yes	Yes
Must a case have been filed for assistance to be available?	No	Yes
Available pre-indictment (during investigative phase)?	Yes	No
Efficient method of obtaining evidence?	Relatively speaking, yes	No, generally slow and cumbersome
Processed through diplomatic channels?	Always	Almost always

enforcement assistance unique to each treaty.[16] The types of assistance MLATs usually provide for include the following:

- serving judicial or other documents;
- locating or identifying persons or things;

---

[16] *See In re* Comm'r's Subpoenas, 325 F.3d 1287, 1291 (11th Cir. 2003) ("Despite the apparent versatility of 28 U.S.C. § 1782, law enforcement authorities found the statute to be an unattractive option in practice because it provided wide discretion in the district court to refuse the request and did not obligate other nations to return the favor that it grants. MLATs, on the other hand, have the desired quality of compulsion, as they contractually obligate the two countries to provide to each other evidence and other forms of assistance needed in criminal cases while streamlining and enhancing the effectiveness of the process for obtaining needed evidence."), *abrogated on other grounds by* Intel Corp. v. Advanced Micro Devices, Inc., 542 U.S. 241, 260–63 (2004).

- taking testimony;
- examining objects and sites;
- requesting searches and seizures;
- obtaining documents or electronic evidence;
- identifying, tracing, and freezing or confiscating proceeds or instrumentalities of crime and/or other assets;
- transferring persons in custody for testimonial purposes or to face charges, as in extradition cases;
- freezing assets; and
- any other assistance permitted by the foreign law and specified in the applicable treaty.[17]

Most MLATs also include a catch-all provision authorizing the transfer of any evidence not prohibited by the requested nation's law.[18]

The United States has bilateral MLATs in force with every European Union member state, many of the Organization of American States member states, and many other countries around the world. An MLAT is negotiated by the U.S. Department of Justice in cooperation with the U.S. Department of State. The secretary of state formally submits the proposed MLAT, typically together with a report detailing the function and purposes of the MLAT's key provisions,[19] to the president of the United States for transmittal to the U.S. Senate. Following the advice and consent of the Senate, the president signs the treaty and directs the secretary of state to take the actions necessary for the treaty to enter into force. Once signatory countries have complied with entry-into-force provisions, the MLAT becomes binding under international law.[20]

In February 2010, the United States and the European Union (through its 56 member states) entered into a historic MLAT. This multiparty MLAT seeks to enhance and modernize cross-border law enforcement and judicial cooperation. The terms of the EU–U.S. agreement include standard areas of assistance, such as identifying financial account information, finding and seizing evidence, and taking testimony. This MLAT also includes provisions addressing bank secrecy, joint criminal investigations, use of videoconferencing for taking testimony, and assistance to administrative agencies, such as the Securities and Exchange Commission and the Federal Trade Commission.[21]

---

[17] *See generally* Hon. Virginia M. Kendall & T. Markus Funk, *The Role of Mutual Legal Assistance Treaties in Obtaining Foreign Evidence*, 40 A.B.A. LITIG. J. 1, 1–3 (2014) (listing standard types of assistance).

[18] DAVID LUBAN ET AL., INTERNATIONAL AND TRANSNATIONAL CRIMINAL LAW 376 (2009).

[19] *See, e.g.,* S. Exec. Doc. No. 109-14 (2006); S. Treaty Doc. No. 111-6 (2010).

[20] *See, e.g.,* S. Exec. Doc. No. 110-14 (2008); *see also* U.S. Gov't Accountability Office, GAO-11-730, Tax Administration: *IRS's Information Exchanges with Other Countries Could Be Improved through Better Performance Information* (2011).

[21] LUBAN ET AL., *supra* note 18, at 386.

2.1.2 Procedure

When a foreign country requests assistance pursuant to an MLAT, the U.S. court must determine whether (1) the terms of the MLAT prescribe practices or procedures for the taking of testimony and production of evidence, (2) the Federal Rules of Procedure and Evidence apply, or (3) the MLAT requires some sort of a hybrid approach. It is also acceptable to follow specified practices and procedures of the requesting country—*provided* they are consistent with U.S. law, including the rules relating to privilege. MLATs executed in the United States must follow U.S. constitutional requirements, including the protection of Fourth Amendment[22] and Fifth Amendment[23] rights. That said, U.S. legal standards do not apply to the seizure of evidence overseas when the foreign country is conducting the investigation independently and seizes evidence later introduced in a U.S. court,[24] nor does the Sixth Amendment right to counsel attach to civil depositions.[25]

---

[22] U.S. CONST. amend. IV (providing freedom from "unreasonable searches and seizures").

[23] *Id.* amend. V. Witnesses deposed in the United States or in a foreign country retain the Fifth Amendment privilege against self-incrimination, regardless of whether they are U.S. citizens or foreign nationals. *See generally In re* Terrorist Bombings of South Africa, 552 F.3d 177, 199 (2d Cir. 2008) ("[R]egardless of the origin—i.e., domestic or foreign—of a statement, it cannot be admitted at trial in the United States if the statement was 'compelled.' Similarly, it does not matter whether the defendant is a U.S. citizen or a foreign national: 'no person' tried in the civilian courts of the United States can be compelled 'to be a witness against himself.'") (citation omitted). *See also* United States v. Jefferson, 594 F. Supp. 2d 655, 670 n.25 (E.D. Va. 2009); David Cole, *Are Foreign Nationals Entitled to the Same Constitutional Rights as Citizens?*, 25 JEFFERSON L. REV. 367, 388 (2003) (analyzing the issue and finding that U.S. and foreign citizens enjoy the same general privileges and protections under the U.S. Constitution).

[24] United States v. Behety, 32 F.3d 503 (11th Cir. 1994) (holding that U.S. authorities' presence during Guatemalan officials' search of a U.S. vessel and action of tipping Guatemalan authorities that the vessel may contain cocaine insufficient to constitute "substantial participation," which would have triggered the Fourth Amendment reasonableness standard for evaluating the search); United States v. Rosenthal, 793 F.2d 1214, 1230–31 (11th Cir. 1986) ("Evidence obtained by foreign police officers from searches carried out in their own countries is generally admissible in American courts regardless of whether the search complies with the Fourth Amendment. . . . There are two exceptions to the general rule. The first . . . provides for exclusion of the evidence if the conduct of the foreign officers shocks the conscience of the American court. The second exception . . . provides that if American law enforcement officials substantially participate in the foreign search, or if the foreign authorities actually conducting the search were acting as agents for their American counterparts, the exclusionary rule can be invoked."); United States v. Ramcharan, No. 04-20065-CR, 2008 WL 170377, at *9 (S.D. Fla. Jan. 14, 2008) (holding the Fourth Amendment did not apply where the evidence did "not establish that the DEA [Drug Enforcement Agency] substantially participated in the Bahamian wiretap of [defendant's] telephones or that the Bahamian authorities were acting as agents of the DEA when they undertook this electronic monitoring").

[25] Civil depositions do not trigger the Sixth Amendment. *See generally* Perez v. Pima Cnty. Superior, 50 F. App'x 368, 370 (9th Cir. 2002) ("The right to counsel attaches only upon the initiation of criminal judicial proceedings against the defendant, or when the government's role otherwise shifts from investigation to accusation."); United States v. Hayes, 231 F.3d 663, 674 (9th Cir. 2000) (holding that the right to counsel had not attached, even after the government had sought to obtain material witness depositions for use at the defendant's trial).

2.1.3 Contents

To assist the U.S. court in reviewing an incoming MLAT request, the following information is usually included (or should be made available by the assistant U.S. attorney handling the matter):

2.1.4 Basic Information

- the name of the authority conducting the investigation, prosecution, or other proceeding to which the request relates;
- a description of the subject matter and the nature of the investigation, prosecution, or proceeding, including the specific criminal offenses that relate to the matter;
- a description of the evidence, information, or other assistance sought; and
- a statement of the purpose for which the evidence, information, or other assistance is sought.

2.1.5 Assistance-Specific Details

- information concerning the identity and location of any person from whom evidence is sought;
- information concerning the identity and location of a person to be served, that person's relationship to the proceeding, and the manner in which service is to be made;
- information on the identity and whereabouts of a person to be located;
- a precise description of the place or person to be searched and items to be seized;
- a description of the manner in which any testimony or statement is to be taken and recorded;
- a list of questions to be asked of a witness; and
- a description of any particular procedure to be followed in executing the request.

An MLAT request containing this information provides the district court with a general basis for evaluating the request for assistance. If necessary, the court may ask the assigned prosecutor to provide additional information (typically through OIA).

2.2 STATUTORY SCHEME

1. 28 U.S.C. § 1782

Originally enacted in the mid-nineteenth century to encourage reciprocal assistance with transnational litigation, the statute now codified at 28 U.S.C. § 1782 permits federal courts to provide cross-border assistance via MLATs.[26] It sets forth specific procedures courts and prosecutors must follow:

---

[26] *See, e.g.,* Intel Corp. v. Advanced Micro Devices, Inc., 542 U.S. 241, 247–49 (2004) (detailing the history of section 1782).

a) The district court of the district in which a person resides or is found *may* order him to give his testimony or statement or to produce a document or other thing for use in a proceeding in a foreign or international tribunal, including criminal investigations conducted before formal accusation. . . . The order may prescribe the practice and procedure, which may be in whole or part the practice and procedure of the foreign country or the international tribunal, for taking the testimony or statement or producing the document or other thing. To the extent that the order does not prescribe otherwise, the testimony or statement shall be taken, and the document or other thing produced, in accordance with the Federal Rules of Civil Procedure.[27]

Section 1782 allows any "interested person" from any country who is involved in a "proceeding in a foreign or international tribunal" to apply—whether through an MLAT or letter rogatory—to a U.S. court to obtain evidence for use in that non-U.S. civil or criminal proceeding. Section 1782 is broader than the Hague Evidence Convention and does not require the foreign litigant to first request the discovery from the non-U.S. tribunal.[28] Section 1782 gives courts discretion as to "whether, and to what extent, to honor a request for assistance."[29]

2. 18 U.S.C. § 3512

The Foreign Evidence Efficiency Act, codified at 18 U.S.C. § 3512 (2018), was enacted to help streamline the MLAT process, making it "easier for the United States to respond to requests by allowing them to be centralized and by putting the process for handling them within a clear statutory system."[30]

The assistance contemplated by section 3512 includes, but is not limited to

(a) a search warrant, as provided under Rule 41 of the Federal Rules of Criminal Procedure;[31]

(b) a warrant or order for contents of stored wire or electronic communications or for records related thereto, as provided under section 2703 of this title;

(c) an order for a pen register or trap and trace device, as provided under section 3123 of this title; or

---

[27] 28 U.S.C. § 1782(a).

[28] *See In re* Premises Located at 840 140th Ave., NE, Bellevue, Wash., 634 F.3d 557, 571 (9th Cir. 2011) ("We hold that requests for assistance via the U.S.–Russia MLAT utilize the procedural mechanisms of § 1782 without importing the substantive limitations of § 1782. In particular, the parties to the treaty intended that the district courts would not possess the normal 'broad discretion,' conferred by § 1782, to deny requests for assistance.").

[29] *See id.* at 563.

[30] 155 CONG. REC. S6810 (daily ed. June 18, 2009) (statement of Sen. Whitehouse).

[31] Note, however, that a district court's authorization to issue search warrants under this section is subject to certain restrictions, namely, that the foreign offense for which the evidence is sought involves conduct that, if committed in the United States, would be considered an offense "punishable by imprisonment for more than one year under [f]ederal or [s]tate law." 18 U.S.C. § 3512(e).

    (d) an order requiring the appearance of a person for the purpose of providing testimony or a statement, or requiring the production of documents or other things, or both.[32]

To process the foreign request for assistance, the assistant U.S. attorney will review and approve the request, and then, pursuant to 18 U.S.C. § 3512, will file it with the U.S. district court

    (a) in the district where the person who may be required to appear resides or is located or in which the documents or things to be produced are located;
    (b) in cases in which the request seeks the appearance of persons or production of documents or things that may be located in multiple districts, in any one of the districts in which such a person, documents, or things may be located; or
    (c) in any case, the district in which a related Federal criminal investigation or prosecution is being conducted, or in the District of Columbia.[33]

As it does under 28 U.S.C. § 1782, the court has discretion under 18 U.S.C. § 3512 over whether to issue the requested order.[34]

    The application to provide the requested assistance, like all such filings, may be submitted ex parte and under seal.[35] Section 3512 also permits the appointment of an outside individual—sometimes referred to as a "commissioner"[36]—"to direct the taking of testimony or statements or of the production of documents or other things, or both."[37] A commissioner may pursue requests in multiple judicial districts, eliminating the need for judges in different districts to appoint separate commissioners and otherwise duplicate their efforts.[38] Section 3512 also permits judges to oversee and approve subpoenas and other orders (but not search warrants) outside of their district.

    Under section 3512, federal judges continue to serve as gatekeepers for search warrants, wiretaps, and other methods of obtaining evidence, ensuring that the collection of requested

---

[32] 18 U.S.C. § 3512(a)(2).

[33] *Id.* § 3512(a) & (c).

[34] *Id.* § 3512(a)(1) (providing that "a Federal judge *may* issue such orders as may be necessary to execute a request from a foreign authority") (emphasis added); *id.* § 3512(a)(2) ("Any order issued by a Federal judge pursuant to paragraph (1) *may* include the issuance of [non-exhaustive list of orders].") (emphasis added).

[35] *See generally* ROBERT TIMOTHY REAGAN, FEDERAL JUDICIAL CENTER, SEALING COURT RECORDS AND PROCEEDINGS: A POCKET GUIDE (2010) (noting the court's wide discretion in whether to grant an ex parte motion to seal).

[36] While the statute does not require the commissioner to be a lawyer or prosecutor, *see* 18 U.S.C. § 3512(b)(1) ("In response to an application for execution of a request from a foreign authority as described under subsection (a), a Federal judge may also issue an order appointing *a person* to direct the taking of testimony or statements or of the production of documents or other things, or both.") (emphasis added), courts routinely appoint an assistant U.S. attorney to be the commissioner, *see, e.g.*, United States v. Trs. of Boston Coll., 831 F. Supp. 2d 435 (D. Mass. 2011) (appointing an assistant U.S. attorney as the commissioner); *In re* Request from United Kingdom Pursuant to Treaty, 685 F.3d 1 (1st Cir. 2012) (same).

[37] 18 U.S.C. § 3512(b)(1), (2).

[38] *See id.* § 3512(b)(2), (f).

foreign evidence meets the same standards as those required in U.S. cases (such as, for example, the probable cause standard, specificity in warrants, and protection of attorney-client, physician-patient, and other recognized privileges).[39]

2.3 JUDICIAL REVIEW OF REQUESTS FOR MUTUAL LEGAL ASSISTANCE

Although there is a presumption in favor of honoring MLAT requests,[40] the district court must still review the terms of each request, checking that they comply with the terms of the underlying treaty and comport with U.S. law.[41] For example, in *United Kingdom v. United States*,[42] appellants awaiting trial in England requested disclosure of law enforcement documents they claimed were requested by British law enforcement officials pursuant to the U.S.–UK MLAT. The Eleventh Circuit denied the motion, finding that the underlying UK request for evidence did not conform to the specific protocol set forth in the treaty and, accordingly, no valid MLAT request had been made.[43]

U.S. courts will also consider constitutional challenges to a request for legal assistance. Although such cases are rare, "a district court may not enforce a subpoena that would offend a constitutional guarantee," such as a subpoena that would result in an "egregious violation of human rights."[44]

2.4 LEGAL ISSUES

While the majority of requests for assistance pursuant to an MLAT proceed uneventfully, courts sometimes are called upon to resolve related legal issues, such as dual criminality, the defense's access to evidence located abroad, delays, and statutes of limitations.

2.4.1 Dual Criminality

Unlike extradition treaties enforced in U.S. courts, MLATs do not require dual criminality— that the offense for which the foreign state seeks assistance also constitutes a crime in the requested state. The utilitarian reason for this deviation from the norm is to facilitate responsiveness.

---

[39] *See, e.g.*, 28 U.S.C. § 1782(a) ("A person may not be compelled to give his testimony or statement or to produce a document or other thing in violation of any legally applicable privilege."); *In re* Request from United Kingdom Pursuant to Treaty Between Government of U.S. & Government of United Kingdom on Mutual Assistance in Criminal Matters *in re* Dolours Price, 718 F.3d 13 (1st Cir. 2013) (conducting a relevancy analysis of subpoenaed materials); *cf.* McKevitt v. Pallasch, 339 F.3d 530, 531 (7th Cir. 2003) ("Section 1782(a) of the Judicial Code authorizes federal district courts to order the production of evidentiary materials for use in foreign legal proceedings, provided the materials are not privileged.").

[40] *In re* Premises Located at 840 140th Ave. NE, Bellevue, Wash., 634 F.3d 557, 571 (9th Cir. 2011) ("When a request for assistance under the MLAT arrives before a district court . . . almost all the factors already would point to the conclusion that the district court should grant the request.").

[41] *See* Kendall & Funk, *supra* note 17, at 2 (discussing the role of district courts as gatekeepers).

[42] 238 F.3d 1312, 1315 (11th Cir. 2001).

[43] *Id.* at 1317.

[44] *In re* Premises, 634 F.3d at 572.

MLATs, after all, are intended to improve law enforcement cooperation between countries, and the United States' law enforcement objectives often depend upon timely assistance from treaty signatories. The United States has committed to responding to requests under MLATs even if the doctrine of dual criminality exists as part of the requesting country's domestic law.[45] This approach establishes a high standard of responsiveness, enabling the United States to "urge that foreign authorities respond to our requests for evidence with comparable speed."[46] Most MLATs expressly state that the dual criminality principle does not apply.[47]

Some MLATS, however, are drafted to include limitations that are triggered if the requested assistance requires a court warrant or other compulsion and the underlying offense is not a crime in the requested country. In jurisdictions where domestic law requires dual criminality for international treaties, the MLAT is often drafted to include a nonexclusive list of covered offenses that allow for mutual legal assistance.

2.4.2 Defense Access to Evidence Located Abroad

The MLAT process was created to facilitate international cooperation in the investigation and prosecution of criminal cases. Each treaty's terms apply only to the contracting nations' parties, and the benefits conferred are available only to the government officials of those nations.

The first three MLATs signed by the United States—those with Switzerland,[48] Turkey, and the Netherlands—include provisions granting defense counsel permission to access evidence pursuant to an MLAT. Subsequent MLATs do not include comparable provisions.[49]

Thus, access to evidence through an MLAT is restricted to prosecutors, government agencies that investigate criminal conduct, and government agencies that are responsible for matters ancillary to criminal conduct, including civil forfeiture. In fact, the vast majority of MLATs signed by the United States explicitly *exclude* nongovernment access to

---

[45] United States v. Trs. of Boston Coll., 831 F. Supp. 2d 435, 450 (D. Mass. 2011), *aff'd in part sub nom. In re* Request from United Kingdom Pursuant to Treaty between Government of United States and Government of United Kingdom on Mut. Assistance in Criminal Matters *In re* Dolours Price, 718 F.3d 13 (1st Cir. 2013); *In re* Request from United Kingdom Pursuant to Treaty, 685 F.3d 1 (1st Cir. 2012).

[46] *Trs. of Boston Coll.*, 831 F. Supp. 2d at 450 (quoting 155 CONG. REC. S6810 (daily ed. June 18, 2009) (statement of Sen. Whitehouse)).

[47] *In re* Comm'r's Subpoenas, 325 F.3d 1287, 1299 (11th Cir. 2003). *See also* sources cited at *supra* note 4.

[48] In a case involving the MLAT between the United States and Switzerland, defense counsel requested the government's assistance with securing witness testimony via the MLAT process. Agreeing with the defense argument that the proffered evidence was important to its case, the court ordered the Department of Justice to provide the requested assistance. United States v. Sindona, 636 F.2d 792 (2d Cir. 1980). The reasoning of this case is limited to MLATs that provide for defense access to evidence abroad, such as those with Switzerland, Turkey, and the Netherlands. All other MLATs include language explicitly restricting defense access. *See also* L. Song Richardson, *Convicting the Innocent*, 26 BERKELEY J. INT'L L. 62, 84 (2008); United States v. Chitron Electrs. Co., 668 F. Supp. 2d 298, 306 (D. Mass. 2009) (discussing U.S.–China MLAT).

[49] *See* United Kingdom v. United States, 238 F.3d 1312, 1317 (11th Cir. 2001).

U.S. processes.[50] Criminal defendants, like civil litigants, must use letters rogatory to secure evidence located abroad, a process that is less efficient and less reliable.[51]

Federal prosecutors increasingly rely on extraterritoriality provisions in federal law, such as those incorporated into the Foreign Corrupt Practices Act,[52] to bring cases in which much of the physical evidence and most potential witnesses are located overseas. Because the MLAT process is only available to the prosecution, the defendant's ability to collect and present evidence is limited.

Commentators have noted that the lack of compulsion parity between prosecutors and the defense in obtaining foreign evidence has due process implications.[53] Counsel for the defense may argue that a vital piece of exculpatory evidence is located overseas and the MLAT process is the only realistic way of obtaining it. Counsel may request that the government provide assistance with accessing this evidence through the MLAT process, and if the prosecution refuses, counsel may petition the court for relief.[54] However, few, if any, courts have been receptive to such petitions in the absence of language in the MLAT that provides for defense access to evidence abroad.

---

[50] *See* United States v. Duboc, 694 F.3d 1223, 1229 (11th Cir. 2012) ("[T]here is a presumption that international agreements do not create private rights or private causes of action in domestic courts, even when the agreement directly benefits private persons. This presumption and the plain terms of the MLAT show that Duboc, as a private party, may not use the MLAT as a defense to the forfeiture of the Thailand condos.") (citing United States v. Valencia-Trujillo, 573 F.3d 1171, 1180–81 (11th Cir. 2009)); United States v. Meza, No. 15cr3175 JM, 2017 WL 1321383, at *2 (S.D. Cal. Apr. 7, 2017) (quoting United States v. Sedaghaty, 728 F.3d 885, 917 (9th Cir. 2013) ("[T]he district court had no authority to order the Executive Branch to invoke the [MLAT] treaty process to obtain evidence abroad for a private individual.")).

[51] *See generally United Kingdom*, 238 F.3d at 1314 (explaining that there is no MLAT provision for private parties, such as individual criminal defendants in the English (or American) courts, to request the production of information).

[52] 15 U.S.C. §§ 78dd-1, *et seq.* (2018). *See generally* T. Markus Funk & Bo Dul, *Regrouping and Refocusing: 2013 FCPA Year-in-Review and Enforcement Trends for 2014*, BLOOMBERG BNA SEC. REG. & L. REP., 46 SRLR 121 (Jan. 20, 2014).

[53] *See* Daniel Huff, *Witness for the Defense: The Compulsory Process Clause as a Limit on Extraterritorial Criminal Jurisdiction*, 15 TEX. REV. L. & POL. 129, 160–61 (2010); Robert Neale Lyman, *Compulsory Process in a Globalized Era: Defendant Access to Mutual Legal Assistance Treaties*, 47 VA. J. INT'L L. 261, 273 (2006); Richardson, *supra* note 48, at 84–85; Ian R. Conner, *Peoples Divided: The Application of United States Constitutional Protections in International Criminal Law Enforcement,* 11 WM. & MARY BILL RTS. J. 495, 503–04 (2002); Frank Tuerkheimer, *Globalization of U.S. Law Enforcement: Does the Constitution Come Along?*, 39 HOUS. L. REV. 307, 357–73 (2002). *See also* United States v. Theresius Filippi, 918 F.2d 244, 247 (1st Cir. 1990) (implicating the due process clause by not requesting Special Interest Parole from the Immigration and Naturalization Service).

[54] If the Department of Justice refuses to use an MLAT to execute a Federal Rule of Criminal Procedure 15 court order authorizing a criminal defendant to take a deposition abroad (instead telling the defendant to seek enforcement of the order through a letter rogatory), the defendant may contend that the refusal violates the defendant's rights under the compulsory process clause of the Sixth Amendment. Defendants may also cite the International Covenant on Civil and Political Rights, to which the United States became a party in 1992. The Covenant provides, in part: "In the determination of any criminal charge against him, everyone shall be entitled to the following minimum guarantees in full equality . . . . To examine or have examined, the witnesses against him and to obtain the attendance and examination of witnesses on his behalf under the same conditions as witnesses against him." International Covenant on Civil and Political Rights, Dec. 16, 1966, S. Treaty Doc. No. 95-20, 6 I.L.M. 368 (1967), 999 U.N.T.S. 171 (referring to art. 14, sec. 3).

In *United States v. Mejia*, the defendants were involved in a cross-border drug-trafficking organization run out of Costa Rica. A grand jury in the District of Columbia indicted the Colombian nationals, charging them with conspiracy to distribute cocaine.[55] Panamanian authorities arrested two of the defendants, turning the men over to the custody of the United States. During pretrial proceedings, the two defendants petitioned the trial court to require that the government produce tape recordings made during the Costa Rican trial of one of their alleged (non-testifying) coconspirators. The defendants conceded that the tapes were not within the U.S. government's "possession, custody, or control" within the meaning of Rule 16, but argued that the prosecution had "the power" to secure the trial tapes or transcripts from the Costa Rican government via the U.S.–Costa Rican MLAT.[56] The trial court rejected the defendants' request, ruling that the government had no obligation to use its "best efforts" through the MLAT to obtain the tapes.[57]

On appeal, the D.C. Circuit found that the government satisfied its sole obligation: compliance with Rule 16. The court did note that, pursuant to 28 U.S.C. § 1781(b)(2), the defendants "could have asked the district court to issue letters rogatory to the Costa Rican court to obtain any tapes or transcripts that may have existed, [but did] not do so."[58] This language may leave open the argument that had the defendants first sought the requested evidence using the letter rogatory process, the outcome (or at least the analysis) might have been different.[59]

Courts have consistently held that MLATs create no private rights permitting an individual defendant to force the government to request evidence pursuant to an MLAT, even when the defendant invokes constitutional concerns.[60] In *United States v. Jefferson*, Jefferson argued that the Sixth Amendment required the government to utilize the MLAT process to obtain depositions for the defense.[61] The district court disagreed, stating that "it is clear that defendant is not entitled to make use of the MLAT and that this result does not violate defendant's constitutional right to compulsory process."[62]

Likewise, the Eleventh Circuit rejected a challenge to a forfeiture order by a defendant who asserted that the government did not follow the provisions of the MLAT between Thailand and the United States.[63] The court noted the "presumption that international agreements do not create private rights," and held that the defendant, as a private party, could not use the MLAT as a defense to the forfeiture.[64] The First Circuit similarly rejected an argument

---

[55] United States v. Mejia, 448 F.3d 436 (D.C. Cir. 2006).

[56] *Id.* at 444.

[57] *Id.*

[58] *Id.* at 445.

[59] *See id.* (citing United States v. Sensi, 879 F.2d 888, 899 (D.C. Cir. 1989)). *But see* Euromepa v. R. Esmerian, Inc., 51 F.3d 1095, 1098 (2d Cir. 1995) (declining to engraft a "quasi-exhaustion requirement" into section 1782 that would force litigants to seek "information through the foreign or international tribunal" before requesting discovery from the district court); *In re* Republic of Kazakhstan for an Order Directing Discovery from Clyde & Co. LLP Pursuant to 28 U.S.C. section 1782, 110 F. Supp. 512, 517 (S.D.N.Y. 2015) (same); *In re* Veiga, 746 F. Supp. 2d 8, 24 (D.D.C. 2010) (same).

[60] *See, e.g.*, United States v. Jefferson, 594 F. Supp. 2d 655, 674 (E.D. Va. 2009).

[61] *Id.* at 673.

[62] *Id.*

[63] United States v. Duboc, 694 F.3d 1223, 1229 (11th Cir. 2012).

[64] *Id.* at 1229–30.

that an MLAT allowed for a private right of action, citing both the language of the U.S.–UK MLAT itself and the fact that other courts have "uniformly" ruled that no such private right exists under the language of similar MLATs.[65]

2.4.3 Delay

Obtaining evidence through the use of formal MLATs between nations can be time-consuming and may result in government requests for additional time. The main difficulties are the required level of legal formality and the availability of resources, such as staff and funding. In more complex cases, as well as those involving technology, another potential cause of delay is the limited capacity of some foreign law enforcement agencies to conduct the sophisticated forensic analysis needed to comply with an MLAT request.[66]

In other cases, the foreign country may simply have more limited experience with the evidence-gathering process. *United States v. $93,110.00 in U.S. Currency,*[67] for example, in-volved an action for civil forfeiture with evidence located in Mexico. Although the case had been pending for almost three years, the U.S. government requested additional time to gather evidence, citing the "significant challenges" in obtaining formal discovery from Mexico de-spite numerous inquiries. Noting the government's due diligence, the court granted the re-quest, but also stated that it would rely on its inherent authority to control the scheduling of pretrial proceedings and deny any future MLAT-based extension requests.[68]

Although district courts are involved in overseeing incoming MLAT requests, they have no direct oversight over requests sent *from* the United States to a foreign country. A court may sometimes become indirectly involved in an outgoing MLAT process, however, such as when delays in processing have an impact on the management of a domestic case or present speedy trial issues. If an MLAT request issued by the Department of Justice threatens to re-sult in unacceptable delays in or burdens on a court proceeding, the court may suggest that the government either (1) forgo obtaining certain evidence, or (2) limit its request to essen-tial evidence, thereby ensuring that requests are processed expeditiously.

2.4.4 Statute of Limitations

When the government seeks evidence from abroad prior to the return of an indictment, the government files an ex parte application with the court to toll the statute of limitations pur-suant to 18 U.S.C. § 3292 (2018). The court must find by a preponderance of the evidence that "it reasonably appears" the evidence is located in the foreign country,[69] and the tolling of the statute may not exceed three years.[70] The suspension of the statute of limitations begins on

---

[65] *In re* Request from United Kingdom Pursuant to Treaty, 685 F.3d 1 (1st Cir. 2012).

[66] *See generally* KENDALL & FUNK, *supra* note 4, at 215 (suggesting that, because of these challenges, it is often preferable to request that the foreign authorities "simply ship the entire seized hard drive to the United States").

[67] No. CV-08-1499-PHX-LOA, 2010 WL 2745065 (D. Ariz. July 12, 2010).

[68] *Id.*

[69] 18 U.S.C. § 3292(a)(1); *see also* United States v. Trainor, 376 F.3d 1325, 1336 (11th Cir. 2004) ("[T]he Government must present some evidence—something of evidentiary value—that it reasonably appears the requested evi-dence is in a foreign country.").

[70] 18 U.S.C. § 3292(c)(1); *see, e.g.,* United States v. Lyttle, 667 F.3d 220, 224 (2d Cir. 2012) (holding that sec-tion 3292 "requires a district court to suspend the running of a statute of limitations upon an appropriate

the date that the MLAT request is made; it ends when the foreign government takes its final action on the request.[71] Section 3292 does not provide the defendant with a right to notice that the statute of limitations is being suspended or a hearing on the issue.[72]

In *United States v. Lyttle*, the court rejected the defendant's claim that tolling the statute of limitations was improper, because the documents in question could have been obtained through the U.S. branch of a Hungarian bank via domestic subpoena duces tecum, rather than the more time-consuming MLAT process.[73] Looking at the "plain text" of section 3292, the court found no requirement that the foreign evidence be obtainable *only* through diplomatic channels in order for the statute of limitations to be tolled.[74]

Although section 3292 incorporates a low evidentiary threshold, the court must nevertheless scrutinize government requests to have the statute of limitations tolled. In *United States v. Wilson*,[75] the defendant was indicted in 1998 for an international money laundering conspiracy involving the Bahamas. The defendant filed a motion to dismiss, arguing that the prosecution was time-barred. Contesting this motion, the government pointed to a 1994 court order suspending the limitations period beginning in 1993, when OIA made an official request for Wilson's financial records from a Nassau bank, pursuant to the U.S.–Bahamas MLAT. Wilson challenged the government's assertion, arguing that the proffered copy of the letter of request and the government's "representation" that the letter was sent were inadequate.[76] The Fifth Circuit ruled that the evidence raised a factual issue concerning whether the government actually sent the discovery request to the Bahamas, and the court remanded the case for an evidentiary hearing.[77]

On remand, the government failed to produce any documentary evidence that the letter of request was sent; nor did it offer testimony of individuals who issued or received the letter.[78] The district court, nevertheless, again denied Wilson's motion to

---

application showing: (1) that evidence of an offense being investigated by a grand jury is in a foreign country; and (2) that such evidence has been officially requested. According to the statute, the preponderance-of-the-evidence standard applies when determining whether the United States has made an official request. When deciding whether the evidence is in a foreign country, however, a lower standard applies: a court must find by a preponderance of the evidence . . . that it reasonably appears, or reasonably appeared at the time the request was made, that such evidence is, or was, in a foreign country.").

[71] 18 U.S.C. § 3292(b).

[72] *See* DeGeorge v. U.S. Dist. Court for Cent. Dist. Cal., 219 F.3d 930, 937 (9th Cir. 2000). *See also* United States v. Hoffecker, 530 F.3d 137, 168 (3d Cir. 2008) ("We find that there was nothing improper about the ex parte nature of the proceeding before the grand jury judge."); United States v. Wilson, 249 F.3d 366, 371 (5th Cir. 2001) ("An application to toll the statute of limitations under § 3292 is a preindictment, ex parte proceeding."), *abrogated by* Whitfield v. United States, 543 U.S. 209 (2005).

[73] 667 F.3d at 224–25.

[74] *Id.* at 225.

[75] 249 F.3d 366 (5th Cir. 2001). *See also* United States v. Torres, 318 F.3d 1058, 1061 (11th Cir. 2003) ("Under § 3292, the government may apply, ex parte, for suspension of the statute of limitations when it seeks evidence located in a foreign country.").

[76] *Wilson*, 249 F.3d at 372.

[77] *Id.* at 373.

[78] The government introduced the testimony of a paralegal who did not work on the Wilson case but "claimed familiarity with the office policies and procedures in place in 1993 when OIA allegedly sent the MLAT request." United States v. Wilson, 322 F.3d 353 (5th Cir. 2003).

dismiss. The court of appeals, in turn, for a second time reversed the district court's decision, pointing to the absence of "consistent procedures or practices at OIA during the time in question," and concluding that the district court improperly tolled the statute of limitations.[79]

3. Letters Rogatory

Letters rogatory are formal requests for judicial assistance made by a court in one country to a court in another country.[80] Once issued, they may be conveyed through diplomatic channels, or they may be sent directly from court to court.[81] Letters rogatory are often used to obtain evidence, such as compelled testimony, that may not be accessible to a foreign criminal or civil litigant without judicial authorization. They are used primarily by nongovernment litigants, who do not have access to the MLAT process. "While it has been held that federal courts have inherent power to issue and respond to letters rogatory, such jurisdiction has largely been regulated by congressional legislation."[82]

3.1 OUTGOING

The letter rogatory process is less formal than pursuing evidence through an MLAT, but its execution can be more time-consuming. Outgoing letters rogatory—requests for assistance with obtaining evidence abroad, made by counsel through the U.S. court— are issued by the U.S. State Department pursuant to 28 U.S.C. § 1781, and provided for under Federal Rules of Civil Procedure 28(b) and 4(f)(2)(B). Section 1781(b), however, also allows for a district court (and, for that matter, a foreign court) to bypass the State Department and transmit the outgoing letter rogatory directly to the "foreign tribunal, officer, or agency."[83]

---

[79] *Id.* at 362.

[80] The rules for enforcement of letters rogatory were promulgated as part of the Hague Convention Relating to Civil Procedure, which was ratified by more than 60 countries, including the United States. *See* Hague Convention Relating to Civil Procedure, http://www.jus.uio.no/english/services/library/treaties/11/11-02/civil-procedure.xml (last visited Jan. 31, 2019). *See also* Eileen P. McCarthy, *A Proposed Uniform Standard for U.S. Courts in Granting Requests for International Judicial Assistance*, 15 FORDHAM INT'L L.J. 772, 778 (1991) ("Letters rogatory can be more effective than commissions because the executing courts have recourse to their own procedures to compel recalcitrant or reluctant witnesses to comply with their judicial decrees.").

[81] 28 U.S.C. § 1781 (2018). Letters rogatory and accompanying documents may be submitted to ATTN: Judicial Assistance Officer, U.S. Department of State, Office of Legal Affairs, (CA/OCS/L), SA-17, 10th Floor, 2201 C Street, NW, Washington, D.C., 20522-1710. *See generally Preparation of Letters Rogatory*, U.S. Department of State, https://travel.state.gov/content/travel/en/legal/travel-legal-considerations/internl-judicial-asst/obtaining-evidence/Preparation-Letters-Rogatory.html (last visited Jan. 31, 2019).

[82] *In re* Letters Rogatory from the Justice Court, District of Montreal, Canada, 523 F.2d 562, 564 (6th Cir. 1975) (citations omitted).

[83] Title 28 U.S.C. § 1781(a) provides that the U.S. State Department is empowered to (1) use formal channels to transmit letters rogatory from foreign or international tribunals to the appropriate U.S. court and receive and return them after execution, and (2) transmit letters rogatory from U.S. courts to the applicable foreign or international tribunal, officer, or agency and receive and return them after execution.

In most cases, foreign courts honor requests issued pursuant to letters rogatory. However, international judicial assistance is discretionary, based upon principles of comity rather than treaty, and is also subject to legal procedures in the requested country. Compliance with a letter rogatory request is left to the discretion of the court or tribunal in the "requested" jurisdiction (that is, the court or tribunal to which the letter rogatory is addressed). For example, if a request for compelled testimony is granted by a foreign court, the taking of that testimony may not necessarily follow procedures similar to those of the United States, such as through depositions.

Because the letter rogatory process is time-consuming and may involve unique issues of foreign procedural law, parties seeking evidence can arrange for local counsel in the foreign country to file the letter rogatory on their behalf, a strategy that may facilitate the process. The U.S. trial proceedings may be impacted by delays flowing from the foregoing procedural and practical hurdles.[84]

3.2 INCOMING

Incoming letters rogatory—requests for judicial assistance originating in a foreign or international tribunal—are also covered by 28 U.S.C. §§ 1781 and 1782. OIA receives incoming letters rogatory from foreign or international tribunals and transmits each request to the federal court in the district where the evidence is located or witness resides.[85] After reviewing the request, the district court may order the taking of testimony or production of evidence for use in the foreign proceeding.[86] The evidence is then provided to the requesting foreign party by OIA.

The U.S. court may "prescribe the practice and procedure, which may be in whole or part the practice and procedure of the foreign country or the international tribunal, for taking the testimony or statement or producing the document or other thing."[87] Or, if nothing in the request prescribes otherwise, the court may follow the Federal Rules of Civil Procedure. Legal privileges are respected, and privileged testimony cannot be compelled. The process typically takes place ex parte, though a court has the authority to require notification of other parties in the foreign litigation prior to the issuance of an order.[88]

U.S. courts have considerable discretion when reviewing incoming letters rogatory from foreign courts.[89] The U.S. Supreme Court's decision in *Intel Corp. v. Advanced Micro Devices,*

---

[84] The following statutory provisions also govern the issuance and processing of letters rogatory: the All Writs Act, 28 U.S.C. § 1651; 28 U.S.C. §§ 1781 and 1782 (describing the transmittal of letters rogatory through the Department of State and through the district courts); 28 U.S.C. § 1696 (providing for the use of letters rogatory for service of process pursuant to a request by a foreign tribunal); and 22 C.F.R. § 92.66 (detailing the consular procedures for transmittal of letters rogatory).

[85] 28 U.S.C. § 1782 (2018).

[86] *Id.*

[87] *Id.*

[88] *See, e.g., In re* Merck & Co., 197 F.R.D. 267, 271 (M.D.N.C. 2000); Jiangsu Steamship Co., Ltd. v. Success Superior Ltd., No. 14 Civ. 9997(CM), 2015 WL 3439220, at *8 n.1 (S.D.N.Y. Feb. 5, 2015) (quoting *In re* Mereck & Co., 197 F.R.D. at 271).

[89] *See* Intel Corp. v. Advanced Micro Devices, Inc., 542 U.S. 241, 264 (2004) ("As earlier emphasized, a district court is not required to grant a § 1782(a) discovery application simply because it has the authority to do so.");

Inc.[90] involved a request to a U.S. district court for the production of documents to be used in a proceeding before a European administrative tribunal. The Supreme Court clarified the parameters of U.S. court assistance to foreign tribunals pursuant to section 1782 and reiterated that district courts have broad discretion in allowing discovery that aids foreign proceedings.

When reviewing an application made under section 1782, a court should examine the nature of the foreign tribunal, the character of the proceedings, and the foreign government's receptivity to U.S. judicial assistance. It should also consider the following:

- Is the person from whom discovery is sought a participant in the foreign proceeding? "[T]he need for § 1782(a) aid generally is not as apparent as it ordinarily is when evidence is sought from a nonparticipant."[91]
- Does the request conceal "an attempt to circumvent foreign proof-gathering restrictions or other policies of a foreign country or the United States?"[92]
- Is the request unduly intrusive or burdensome or made for the purpose of harassment?[93]

The *Intel* decision also noted that in some cases a court may modify a discovery request to make it less burdensome.[94]

3.3 CASE MANAGEMENT

In contrast to MLATs, letters rogatory are not treaty-based; there is no guarantee that the requested country or tribunal will act on a request for assistance, or if it acts, how it will act. When evaluating a defendant's request for letters rogatory to secure evidence located abroad, courts consider the following factors:

- Is the proffered evidence exculpatory?
- Is it cumulative of evidence more readily available in the United States?
- Was the request for evidence made in a timely manner?[95]

Four Pillars Enters. Co. v. Avery Dennison Corp., 308 F.3d 1075, 1078 (9th Cir. 2002) ("Congress gave the federal district courts broad discretion to determine whether, and to what extent, to honor a request for assistance under 28 U.S.C. § 1782."); HT S.R.L. v. Velasco, 125 F. Supp. 3d 211, 219 (D.D.C. 2015) ("[Under section 1782(a)] the court must first determine whether it has the authority to permit or enforce the request and then whether it should exercise its discretion to permit or enforce the request.").

[90] 542 U.S. at 241.

[91] *In re* Clerici, 481 F.3d 1324, 1334 (11th Cir. 2007) (quoting *Intel*, 542 U.S. at 264–65).

[92] *Intel*, 542 U.S. at 241.

[93] *See generally id.* at 264–65; *In re* Request for Assistance from Ministry of Legal Affairs of Trinidad & Tobago, 848 F.2d 1151, 1156 (11th Cir. 1988).

[94] *Intel*, 542 U.S. at 245 ("[I]ntrusive or burdensome requests may be rejected or trimmed.").

[95] United States v. Dearden, 546 F.2d 622, 625 (5th Cir. 1977); United States v. Jefferson, 594 F. Supp. 2d 655, 673 (E.D. Va. 2009); United States v. Rosen, 240 F.R.D. 204, 213 (E.D. Va. 2007).

If the evidence in question is necessary to ensure a fair trial, obtaining it will most likely warrant the delay inherent in the letter rogatory process.[96]

In *United States v. Jefferson*,[97] for example, Jefferson made a pretrial motion to depose witnesses located in Nigeria, arguing that their testimony would be exculpatory.[98] The witnesses would not consent to be deposed, and Jefferson sought an order requiring the government to invoke the MLAT between the United States and Nigeria, or, in the alternative, requested that the court issue a letter rogatory.[99] The court found the proffered witness testimony to be material, non-cumulative, and potentially exculpatory.[100] The government argued that Jefferson's motion should be denied because he waited nearly a year after indictment before seeking the evidence and the trial would be delayed.

Noting that the MLAT process was not available to the defense, the court agreed to issue a letter rogatory. The court found that the material nature of the evidence requested excused the delay required to obtain it. The court issued a letter rogatory to the appropriate Nigerian judicial authority, requesting that it ascertain the witnesses' willingness to waive their Fifth Amendment rights and answer questions fully in a later deposition—a compromise ruling tailored to the case.[101]

The letter rogatory process may take as long as a year, presenting courts with case management challenges. Although delays may be mitigated by transmitting a copy of the request through INTERPOL or some other more direct route, even in urgent cases such requests often take at least a month to execute. To minimize unnecessary delay, the court may choose to review outgoing letters rogatory or inquire of counsel whether steps were taken to ensure as expeditious a response as possible.

3.3.1 Preliminary Information

Courts may consider the following issues when reviewing an outgoing letter rogatory:

- Did the party requesting the assistance review the country-specific judicial assistance information on the Department of State website and U.S. state and federal law relating to the subject to determine whether the requested assistance can, in fact, be rendered?
- Does the letter include unnecessary information that may confuse a court in the receiving foreign country?
- Is the request for assistance sufficiently specific so as not to resemble a fishing expedition?
- If the party making the request believes it is preferable for foreign courts to follow particular procedures, does the letter include specific instructions in this regard

---

[96] *See* Progressive Minerals, LLC v. Rashid, No. 5:07-CV-108, 2009 WL 1789083, at *2 (N.D. W. Va. June 23, 2009); *Rosen,* 240 F.R.D. at 213.

[97] 594 F. Supp. 2d at 661.

[98] *Id.*

[99] *Id.*

[100] *Id.* at 667–73.

[101] *Id.* at 675–76.

(for example, a verbatim transcript, witness testimony under oath, or permission for U.S. or foreign counsel to attend or participate in proceedings)?

- Has the party requesting the letter consulted the country-specific information for guidance about authentication procedures for the particular country (that is, are a judicial signature and seal sufficient)?

3.3.2 Essential Elements of a Letter Rogatory

In addition, to facilitate the process, courts should ensure that the letter includes the following:

- a statement that the request for international judicial assistance is being made in the interests of justice;
- a brief synopsis of the case, including identification of the parties and the nature of the claim and relief sought, to enable the foreign court to understand the issues involved;
- the type of case (e.g., civil, criminal, or administrative);
- the nature of the assistance required (e.g., compel testimony or production of evidence, serve process);
- the name, address, and other identifiers, such as corporate title, of the person abroad to be served or from whom evidence is to be compelled, and a description of any documents to be served;
- a list of questions to be asked, where applicable (generally in the form of written interrogatories);
- a statement from the requesting court expressing a willingness to provide similar reciprocal assistance to judicial authorities of the receiving state; and
- a statement that the requesting court or counsel is willing to reimburse the judicial authorities of the receiving state for any costs incurred in executing the requesting court's letter rogatory.

Figure 20.1 outlines the typical outgoing letter rogatory process, and the Appendix presents a sample letter rogatory from the U.S. Department of Justice.

4. Information Exchange through Informal Channels

Although formal MLATs, letters rogatory, and other international conventions are the "public face" of transnational legal assistance, a significant amount of criminal investigation-related information is exchanged through informal channels: investigator to investigator, prosecutor to prosecutor, defense counsel to local counterpart. Indeed, personal, cooperative law enforcement relationships can be so informal and "off the grid" that law enforcement agencies, courts, and defendants may only learn of them by accident.

Responding to the challenges of transnational law enforcement, the FBI and other U.S. law enforcement agencies have aggressively sought to develop institutional relationships with their foreign counterparts. Teams of U.S. law enforcement officers regularly coordinate

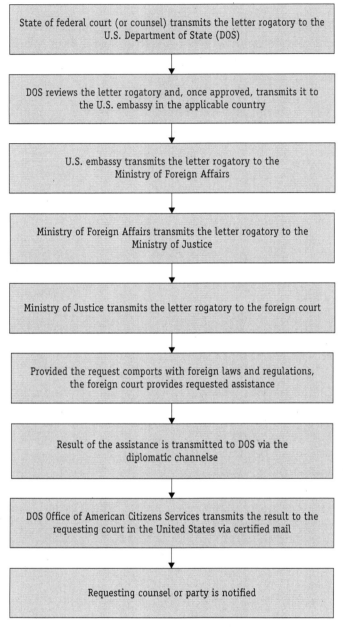

FIGURE 20.1 Submitting a Letter Rogatory for Execution by a Foreign Court

with each other and with their foreign counterparts in a task force approach, often working out of offices in U.S. embassies and missions around the world. This "bricks and mortar" outreach enables U.S. law enforcement officials to cultivate professional relationships and more readily access other sources of information in the host countries.

The U.S. Departments of State, Treasury, and Justice institutionalize cross-border cooperation through memoranda of understanding (MOU) structured to improve the handling and sharing of law enforcement information in foreign jurisdictions. Although the benefits of this cooperation are significant, the process has limitations. Courts should be aware that information gathered in the informal manner described in this Section may be incomplete and is not always tendered to prosecutors or, through the discovery process, provided to the defense.

5. Conclusion

Whether through MLATs, letters rogatory, or informal means, the process of obtaining evidence from abroad in criminal and civil cases can be time-consuming and frustrating to all parties involved, including the courts. Prepared with a basic understanding of how these transnational evidence-gathering tools operate, courts can plan for potential delays; evaluate the arguments made by the government, the defense, and civil litigants; and facilitate the evidence-gathering process in a manner that promotes fairness and conserves resources.

21 Global Developments in, and Evolution of, Third-Party Due Diligence

1. Introduction

Companies conduct anti-bribery due diligence on third parties for multiple reasons: to protect their commercial reputations; to contribute to a fair and transparent marketplace; and to avoid complicity with corruption at every level.[1]

And then, of course, there is the law. Experience and observation has taught all but the most isolated companies that prosecutions under transnational bribery laws bring with them not only substantial penalties, but also the staggering cost of investigations and cooperation. The risk of prosecution is not limited to the actions of the company; it can extend to the company's liability for the acts of third parties. Countries from the United States to China now include liability for indirect payments (through or by third parties) in their anti-bribery legislation. It is also now common that the test of a company's knowledge of corruption, such as that included in the FCPA, is not limited to actual knowledge, but can be satisfied by the failure of that company to seek out information, including information about the third parties with which it does business. And then there is the risk of consumer boycotts, advocacy group pressures, and other brand-damaging negative externalities flowing from allegations of corruption and bribery.

This increased global understanding of the bribery risks associated with third parties, and the consequent drive by companies to protect themselves, has increased focus on companies'

---

[1] This chapter was contributed by TRACE's Alexandra Wrage. The author wishes to acknowledge the contributions of Thomas Hoskins and Robert Clark to the preparation of this chapter.

From Baksheesh to Bribery. T. Markus Funk and Andrew S. Boutros.
© Oxford University Press 2019. Published 2019 by Oxford University Press.

due diligence processes of their third-party business associates. Companies may protect themselves from the likelihood of bribery occurring in the first place by implementing, executing, and maintaining a robust due diligence program. Furthermore, legal protections against investigation or prosecutions are now provided by a company having in place adequate due diligence processes. Under the UK Bribery Act 2010, for example, a company has a defense to a prosecution if it can show that it had adequate procedures in place to prevent such payments by an associated individual. While no "compliance defense" exists in the FCPA, the U.S. Sentencing Guidelines include credit for companies that maintain an effective compliance program.

Yet despite the development of this global understanding and the very real incentives to undertake due diligence, the problem of mitigating the risks posed by third parties endures. A 2015 study conducted across 64 countries by KMPG indicated that the risk associated with third parties was the biggest bribery challenge that companies faced. OECD research one year earlier indicated that over 75 percent of the 427 foreign public corruption cases sampled involved third parties.

While no company can ensure that its third parties will never bribe, this chapter provides practical steps that can be taken to reduce the likelihood of inappropriate payments by its third-party associates. It describes the roles third parties play in international business, the factors that should be considered in determining the risk posed by a third party, as well as issues relating to risk-mitigation and ongoing monitoring. It further addresses common pitfalls in the due diligence process, ways to reduce costs, and the conflict between due diligence and data privacy. The discussion is not intended to be relied upon as legal advice, but rather as a practical guide for conducting a meaningful due diligence process.

The recommendations and processes outlined in the chapter reflect the due-diligence "best practices" of more than 15 years of TRACE benchmarking across more than 300 companies active in almost all countries and in a wide variety of industries. While many of these suggestions reflect common sense, applying them rigorously and consistently will reduce risk and promote confidence that a third party is acting in accordance with the best practices promulgated by other well-run companies.

2. The Role of Third Parties

There are many reasons a company doing business internationally retains third parties instead of relying on its own employees. Third parties can help bridge the gaps of distance, time, custom, and language between the company and the local business community. They may be sales agents, consultants, distributors, suppliers, vendors, subcontractors, joint venture partners—the variety of labels is extensive.

More significant than their title is the role they perform. Third parties can help the company understand and comply with local licensing and permit requirements, or provide access to and help to build relationships with key government officials. They can allow the company to explore business opportunities in new regions without the expense of hiring new employees or relocating current ones, or can be used to temporarily expand the company's in-country presence with a minimum of financial risk. Third parties can also be retained to assist with import and export logistics or to provide local legal or accounting services. In some jurisdictions, the law simply won't allow a foreign company to conduct business without using a resident intermediary. In short, third parties often play a critical role in opening international markets to a company's products, identifying new opportunities and market trends, providing introductions to decision-makers, and responding quickly and effectively to customer concerns.

Yet it is often the very same strengths that make a third party attractive (such as access to decision-makers) that can make them a risk (bribing those same decision-makers, for example). There can be extraordinary pressure on third parties to close deals, especially deals that have required months or years of effort to develop. Many third parties work purely on commission. They may not even be reimbursed for their expenses unless and until the ink dries on the contract. This creates risky incentives for a third party to make illicit payments to government officials as a way to ensure success. For this reason, most anti-bribery laws explicitly provide that companies must not make inappropriate payments either directly *or indirectly*, namely through third parties.

3. Determining the Risk Posed by Third Parties

The risk posed by a third party depends on a number of factors. A common risk factor is the nature of the relationship between the third party and the company. A commissioned sales agent generally carries a greater bribery risk than a service provider giving legal or accounting advice because of the pressure arising from the third party relying on commission. Additional examples of deal-specific factors that affect the level of risk a third party may pose include the following aspects of the nature of that third party:

- The volume and value of the third party's business for the company in the region;
- The value of the total compensation received by the third party from the company internationally;
- The size or value of a particular government concession or contract;
- The issue of whether the third party has the exclusive right to market the company's products in the region.

Other factors depend on the structure and stability of the third party:

- Length of time the third party has been operating in the market;
- The issue of whether the third party is a publicly traded company on a recognized stock exchange;
- The financial stability of the third party.

Additional risk factors may arise by virtue of the industry in which the third party operates, for example:

- Whether the market is controlled by government officials with a reputation for corruption;
- Whether the industry itself has a reputation for corruption;

- The nature and extent of contact the third party can expect to have with government officials.

The reputation of the local market more generally also contributes to the risk of operating there through a third party. For companies seeking a relationship with a third party in an unfamiliar country, there are independent, publicly available matrices of a particular country's risk of bribery. The TRACE Matrix, for example, is specifically tailored to provide the compliance community with detailed information with which to assess the propensity for public-sector bribery. The most useful of these tables can provide companies with guidance by examining factors such as:

- Whether anti-bribery laws are enforced;
- The level of transparency in governmental practices and the civil service of that nation;
- The extent to which civil society provides genuine oversight of corruption.

A company that is just beginning to implement a due-diligence program should prioritize the vetting of third parties that represent the most significant risk. Depending on these risk factors, third parties may appropriately undergo a more streamlined due-diligence review. In certain cases, especially those where the vetting of third parties throws up significant "red flags," a heightened review may be prudent.

4. Red Flags

The review processes described in this chapter can help the company develop as complete a picture as possible of any third party's expertise, relationship to government officials, financial stability, and commitment to ethical business practices. Over the course of the review, certain "red flags" may arise. The appearance of such red flags does not necessarily mean that the third party should not be engaged. But each requires additional investigation.

Some examples of circumstances that flag up when further investigation is required include:

- The third party requests payment in cash, to a numbered account, or to an account controlled by a third party;
- The third party requests payment in another country, especially a country with limited transparency in its banking system;
- The third party requests advance or partial payment shortly before a procurement decision is to be made;
- The third party requests payment for out-of-the-ordinary, ill-defined, or last-minute expenses;
- An owner or employee of the third party also holds a government position;
- A relative of the third party holds a government position. This is particularly significant if it is a position involving procurement or other decision-making

functions or if the person holds a high-ranking position in the department toward which the third party's business efforts are directed;

- The third party refuses to disclose its owners, partners, or principals;
- The third party is government-owned;
- The third party's corporate structure involves shell companies, holding companies, or other features that disguise true ownership;
- A customer has inexplicably asked the company to use a particular specified third party;
- The third party has been recommended by one of the company's employees with an unwarranted degree of enthusiasm;
- The third party's business appears to be deficient for the proposed undertaking, for example if they are understaffed, poorly equipped, or inconveniently located;
- The third party lacks expertise in the relevant industry;
- The third party is insolvent or facing significant financial difficulties;
- The third party is ignorant of, or indifferent to, the laws and regulations governing the relevant region and the third party's proposed activities;
- A reputational or financial reference fails to respond, or answers evasively.
- There are credible rumors or media reports of corrupt behavior;
- The third party is currently under investigation or has prior convictions.

This list is far from exhaustive, but any of these "red flags" is cause for even greater concern if the third party operates in a country or in an industry that has a low level of business or financial transparency, or a high level of government interference. The appearance of such flags, especially in these contexts, may warrant increasing the level of due diligence being undertaken.

5. Selecting Third Parties

The first step in the process of vetting and retaining a third party is a methodical search for the best-qualified candidate. The business justification for selecting the third party should be clear and well-documented, and should explain why the role cannot be fulfilled by the company's existing employees, which alternative candidates were considered, and why they were unsuccessful.

The initial assessment of third-party candidates should be undertaken by the person most familiar with the company's local business strategy. To ensure impartiality, however, the assessment should then be reviewed and expressly approved by management, ideally based elsewhere.

The records should clearly identify the reasons for the selection of the particular candidate (and a third-party questionnaire can be a great starting point for such a justification). What expertise and resources will the third party bring to bear on the project? If a third party will be promoting a highly technical product, for example, what demonstrates that the successful candidate possesses the relevant technical training? Most third parties are likely to be well-positioned with respect to the local business community, but what other business advantages (over and above his or her personal connections) does that person possess? If there are few additional advantages, closer scrutiny is likely to be called for.

The business-justification record should, alongside the positive reasons for the third party's selection, also include an assessment of the level of risk associated with the third party's retention. This will, in turn, determine the appropriate level of due diligence that should be undertaken by the company. The documentation should summarize the discussions with the proposed third party, during which the company should verify that the third party understands and agrees to adhere to the company's business values, including that of anticorruption. Finally, having made the decision to retain that third party, the record should explicitly confirm that the company is unaware of any reputational, business, or other reason that would make the third party unsuitable.

Upon selection, any successful candidate must be instructed not to undertake any work on the company's behalf until the due diligence process is completed and a contract is in place. Even if the relationship is not yet formalized, the company may still be liable for any illicit payments made in an attempt to secure a benefit for the company.

What of existing third-party business associates? The company may believe that its familiarity with existing third parties makes formal review unnecessary. Enforcement authorities are unlikely to share this view. Companies should implement the same due diligence program for existing "heritage" third parties as with new ones. This has the benefit of applying the vetting process consistently and equally to all similarly situated third parties.

6. Due Diligence Procedures

The following due diligence procedures are divided into four levels, from the most basic degree of scrutiny to heightened review. These levels are cumulative. Each level should incorporate the tasks of any levels beneath it.

Each of the levels includes an internal element and an external element. The internal review involves analyzing relevant information obtained directly from the third party. Such information can often be easily obtained through questionnaires, completed by the third party itself, or by the company's compliance team based on discussions with it.

The external review incorporates further information derived from sources external to the third party, as well as independently verifying the information generated by the internal review. The external review should be conducted without assistance from either the regional business team or directly from the third party because such teams, motivated to conclude the deal, are unlikely to possess the impartiality necessary to conduct the due diligence process. Many companies outsource part or all of the due diligence procedure (subject to a nondisclosure agreement) to an independent third party to ensure impartiality.

These levels of due diligence can be adjusted to meet a particular company's compliance needs, including tailoring the questions asked or the materials requested. In making such adjustments, the goal is always to collect appropriate information that will enable the company to make an informed assessment of the reliability, trustworthiness, and transparency of its business partners. As long as adjustments are based on a sound risk-based analysis, the company's exposure to liability through a bespoke due diligence procedure should not be adversely affected.

6.1 LOW RISK LEVEL—BASIC DUE DILIGENCE

The lowest level of risk can generally be mitigated by simple searches of the entity name and the names of owners and others with significant connections to the third party under consideration. This would require, for example, that the company conduct a basic search of the names against global regulatory, watch, and sanctions lists in order to determine if they are, for example, a Denied Person (those people or entities denied export privileges for past misconduct), or a Politically Exposed Person (senior officials in foreign governments, political parties, or government-owned enterprises). Such searches can be conducted swiftly and cost effectively often with same-day results. Once access to the appropriate lists is obtained the same checks can be automated to run not only once, but at regular intervals.

6.2 MEDIUM RISK LEVEL—MORE THOROUGH CHECKS

Where the sorts of factors discussed in Section 3 indicate that a potential third party is a medium risk, the checks—and consequent review process—are a step up from basic due diligence. They can also be more easily streamlined to the specific circumstances of the relationship between the company and third party, allowing the company to select specific areas upon which to focus.

6.2.1 The Internal Review

At this level a large number of the checks and due diligence information on a third party can be gathered by the use of the above-mentioned due diligence questionnaires, which should cover:

- *Contact Information*: Full name, address, and telephone number of the company or individual, along with website and email address. This is the most basic way in which a company can obtain an idea of the countries in which the third party's services are provided (and use a relevant matrix to assess that country or region in a general sense). It may not, of course, provide the definitive answer to all the locations in which the company operates.
- *Company Structure*: Is a third party organized as a partnership? A corporation? With or without limited liability? The answers to these questions can help narrow the questions to be asked about ownership.
- *Company Ownership*: Substantial legal ownership should be identified. It may be necessary to extend the inquiry to true beneficial ownership if "red flags" are encountered during the due diligence process. It is also important for companies to appreciate that a third party's ownership can change on a regular basis, necessitating further or regularly scheduled additional checks. Ownership of publicly traded third parties changes on a daily basis, for example, and so this may be less meaningful.
- *Company Description*: What is the third party's history? Its qualifications? What services does it provide? A review of the third party's website can provide insight

into its expertise and sophistication, as well as helping to flag potential conflicts of interest and inconsistencies with the company's questionnaire responses.

- *Key Employees*: The third party should be required to identify key employees who will be acting on its behalf. These names can then be checked in the same way as company owners against global media and sanctions lists and for current or past ties to government.

- *Identifying Reputational References*: Reputational references may be obtained as part of the process of engaging a third party, whether obtained during the due diligence review or as part of the company's more general business evaluation of the third party. While the content of the references would form part of the external review, the suggestions from the third party as to who best to contact can provide insight into the entity's standing in the business community.

- *Disclosures*: Third parties should be required to disclose any prior bankruptcies, criminal convictions, or pending civil or criminal investigations, specifically whether they involve bribery, fraud, tax evasion, export violations, or antitrust issues. Third parties should also disclose whether they have ever been debarred from bidding on government contracts in any country. Alternatively, the third party should be required to certify that no such circumstance applies to them.

- *Certifications*: A company should seek a written certification directly from the third party that it is financially stable, that its books and records are maintained in accordance with internationally accepted accounting standards, and that it is in compliance with all applicable anti-bribery laws and any business registration requirements.

Of course, and as others have observed, one challenge is that a company willing to engage in bribery and related corrupt conduct will typically also be willing to provide false information in the form of due diligence questionnaire answers. That said, even providing some of the verifiable, basic information is something many corrupt vendors will simply refuse to do (in and of itself a major red flag).

6.2.2 The External Review

This level of due diligence should include the following areas of external review, geared toward uncovering adverse information that might be left undisclosed by an unethical, or even dishonest, third party during the internal review:

- *Obtaining Reputational References*: The content of the references identified by the third party is an important source of information. References should be asked about the prospective third party's effectiveness, reputation, relations with the government, and business ethics. In order to minimize subjectivity (and therefore increase the value of the reference), questions about reputation and ethics should be framed in a way that calls for a yes or no response, followed by an opportunity to elaborate.

- *Media Search*: A media search is a simple, cost-effective measure, and a crucial element in any robust compliance program. The name of the third party should be run through a global media database covering both print-based and online media for the past five years to uncover reports of any association with a bribery scandal. The same exercise should be undertaken with the names of any owners, principals, partners, and key employees of the third party.

Of course, allegations in a newspaper article are not the same as formal charges or a bribery conviction, and so carry less weight. There have, for example, been recent examples of competitors planting negative media stories simply to frustrate the engagement of third parties by seeking to delay the due diligence process. Nonetheless, uncovering such allegations remains an important starting point for further inquiry, and these must be addressed.

- *Government Databases*: A number of government organizations maintain lists of persons known to have violated various laws or regulations. Reviewing the names of potential third parties (and their owners, principals, partners, and key employees) against these lists is more than an important compliance precaution; a company that retains someone who is included on such a list may itself be breaking the law.

6.3 HIGH RISK LEVEL—RIGOROUS CERTIFICATION

This level of review, aimed at enabling the company to certify that the third party is an appropriate one with which to form a business relationship, is appropriate where the compliance risk may be considered moderate to high. It should be regarded as the due diligence standard and is appropriate, for example, for third parties such as sales agents paid on commission, or those that have frequent government interaction.

6.3.1 The Internal Review

This review requires greater detail in the third party's responses than the checks conducted of lower-risk third parties and should, in addition to those checks outlined in the previous sections, address the following:

- *Company Structure*: The company should ascertain whether business-entity third parties have any subsidiaries, affiliates, or branch offices, or are partners in any joint ventures. Certain types of businesses can, notwithstanding immediate ownership, additionally have a large number of connected entities that are potentially relevant and may also need to be investigated. This is commonly the case in freight forwarding entities, for example. If the third party has such connected entities, they should provide the names of the other owners or partners of the connected entities.
- *Company Ownership*: The inquiry here should go beyond title and requires disclosure of the third party's complete beneficial ownership. The aim is to identify the real people underlying the third party—not just parent companies, holding companies, or trusts—so as to ensure that none of them are government officials. Every person with an ownership interest in the third party should be required to disclose whether

he or she is employed by the government and whether any of his or her immediate family members are so employed.

Owners should also be required to provide citizenship information, as there are a number of countries that limit the role of noncitizen third parties. This also gives a fuller view of the connections any third party has with particular regions or countries, which may be checked against relevant matrices. In addition, this is an opportunity to ascertain whether the third party has any conflicts of interest that may render it unsuitable for business reasons, even if there appear to be no compliance issues.

- *Curricula Vitae*: The company should request a curriculum vitae for each owner, director, and key employee of the third party. These can provide a useful way to check for previous government employment, as well as to verify qualifications for the industry in which the third party will be operating. Finally, all key personnel should be asked to provide information about any other companies in which they are shareholders or partners, or for which they serve as officers or directors. This is to satisfy the company that even if the third party itself has no ties to government, there is not another entity with the same ownership that may have handled inappropriate payments on behalf of the third party.

- *Company Description*: Here, the company should obtain a more detailed picture of the third party's operations. How many years has it been in business? In which countries does it operate? How many employees does it have? What are its approximate revenues? If relevant to the work it will undertake, what are the industries in which it operates, and the nature of its facilities? As in the basic review and the medium-level checks discussed previously in this Section, the company's website can be a useful reference point for further insight and verification. In addition, the third party should be required to provide a selection of its corporate literature such as brochures or company profiles in order to assess consistency and industry competence.

- *Corporate Registration Documents*: The third party should prove that it is properly constituted and authorized to act by providing the company with copies of its corporate registration documents. These may include its articles of incorporation, or proof of registration with local tax authorities. It should also include any government agency licenses and its registration with any organizations or associations. Even if a translation is required, the document should also be included in its original language.

- *Subcontractors or additional third parties*: The third party should identify any subcontractors, intermediaries, or additional third parties it intends to engage to fulfill its obligations to the company. Due diligence should be undertaken on any such entities.

- *Local Law Requirements*: The third party should be able to identify and demonstrate familiarity with the local laws and regulations relevant to the industry in which it operates. This can signal to the company its willingness to familiarize itself with and comply with applicable laws. This enquiry should include any local laws prohibiting bribery. The company should verify the correctness of the information provided.

- *Compensation*: The reasonableness of the proposed compensation can demonstrate the third party's understanding of the local market. An overly inflated compensation figure may also indicate that monies could be intended for diversion as illicit or unlawful payments.
- *Internal Ethics Codes*: The third party should be asked what internal policies and ethics codes are already in place that specifically address the issue of bribery and corruption, and how these are disseminated to employees and any subsidiaries, affiliates, subcontractors, and additional third parties. If the third party lacks formal written procedures, it should give the company a detailed description of how it handles such issues. Enquires should also be conducted into whether there are effective internal reporting mechanisms if employees uncover compliance issues.
- *Internal Training*: The third party should be asked how regularly the management and employees undertake anti-bribery training or updates on this subject.

6.3.2 The External Review

- *Financial Reference*: The company should review the third party's audited financial records for the previous year. If those records are not available, the company should seek a financial reference from a bank, an accountant, or even one of the third party's own suppliers. Enquiries of the referee should include how long it has worked with the third party. This can help the company assess the third party's stability and depth of ties to the local business community. A reference from a local bank provides evidence that the third party banks locally, rather than in another country with a less transparent banking system. A company should also determine if the third party is a reliable client, since a third party struggling to meet its business commitments is under greater financial pressure to close a deal.
- *Media Search*: At this level of risk, the media search should be more thorough than the search under the medium-level checks outlined previously. In addition to the third party's owners, principals, partners, and key employees, the media search should also encompass any subsidiaries, joint ventures, and intermediaries the third party intends to engage.
- *Reputational References*: In order to satisfy this level of due diligence, a greater number of business references should be contacted who have had regular contact with the third party in the recent past. Whereas in the medium-level checks one or two references may be sufficient, at this higher level of certification multiple recent references should be obtained and the information each one gives should be carefully cross-referenced with the portfolio of other reputational references in order to obtain a fuller understanding of the soundness of the third party's recent interactions.

6.4 HIGHEST RISK LEVEL—FULL THIRD-PARTY REVIEW

Heightened review is the most detailed and intrusive level of due diligence, requiring both in-person interviews and facility visits. This level of scrutiny is called for in certain limited situations, such as when vetting third parties who are potential joint venture partners, acquisition targets, or third parties with significant unresolved "red flags."

6.4.1 The Internal Review

Along with the topics covered by the basic checks and due diligence certifications, the heightened review should address the following:

- *Interactions with Government Officials*: The company should ascertain how and with what frequency the third party interacts with government officials. This should include information about the third party's interactions with customs, licensing, and permitting officials, and the existence or otherwise of any government inspections of the third party. To the fullest extent possible this information should be obtained prior to the in-person interviews, thereby allowing the company to identify and prioritize specific topics for discussion.
- *Interviews with Relevant Personnel*: A review of the third party's organizational chart will help the company put together a list of the relevant personnel for interviewing. Depending on the third party's structure this may include its owners, directors, senior management, legal and compliance staff, marketing, finance and business development personnel, and employees responsible for regulatory approval and logistics. Often such interviews should be conducted by a legally trained individual with in-depth knowledge of the proposed business relationship.
- *Business Profile*: The third party should provide the company with a detailed overview of the company and the industry. This should include other companies and products with which the third party has business relationships, and the manner in which the third party markets and sells its products or services. This detailed overview should include a description of the business climate in the countries where the third party operates, which can be checked by the company against independently complied matrices dealing with the risk of bribery in those countries.
- *Licenses and Permits*: A company should obtain copies of all mandatory licenses and permits that the third party is required to possess to conduct its business. Where possible, the company should obtain, review, and analyze copies of all permits, licenses, registrations, purchase orders, and invoices with any of the third party's government customers. If a translation of these documents is required they should nonetheless also be viewed in the original language.
- *Financial Information*: In addition to the third party's most recent annual audited financial records, a company should request copies of the third party's financial statements and access to its books and records to enable a more thorough investigation into the third party's financial dealings.

- *Compliance Program*: The company should obtain and carefully review a copy of the third party's code of conduct and ethics policies. Particular attention should be paid to the content (or lack thereof) of policies and procedures governing gifts and hospitality, charitable contributions, and the third party's own due diligence practices on its business associates. The company should also review the third party's hiring and retention policies, including how it disciplines employees who violate its code of conduct or any applicable laws. The company should also determine whether any such disciplinary actions have been taken in the recent past.
- *Internal Controls*: A company should familiarize itself with the third party's internal controls, such as how it handles petty cash disbursements, invoicing, payment authorizations, and employee reimbursement.
- *Facility Visit*: A visit to the third party's place of business can demonstrate its suitability for the type of work for which it is being engaged. This is of particular importance for third parties engaged in technical or specialized work.

6.4.2 The External Review

In addition to reputational and financial references, media sources, and government databases, the following should be considered as part of a heightened review:

- *Embassy Consultation*: Where possible, the company should meet with local embassy staff or a recognized public trade promotion agency of the company's home country, for example the United States Commercial Service or UK Trade and Investment, to determine whether the embassy or trade body is familiar with the third party. They may be able to provide the company with helpful information about the third party's reputation and potentially negative compliance conduct in the past.
- *Public Records Search*: Local counsel should be engaged to conduct a search of all appropriate public records, including verification that corporate third parties have complied with the relevant local establishment and reporting requirements. A criminal-records search should also be undertaken on the third party's owners and those connected to the third party, where possible.

7. Documentation

Despite a company's due diligence and best precautions, one of its third parties may nonetheless pay or offer a bribe to a foreign government official. If this happens, it is crucial that the company be able to show a documented commitment and adherence to a sound compliance plan. This will have the effect of both minimizing reputational damage and reducing criminal or civil liability. It is essential, therefore, that a company maintain a detailed written record of its review of all current or potential third parties.

The record should include a summary of the decision to engage the third party, the basis upon which that party was chosen, and the risk assessment process by which the appropriate level of due diligence was determined, as well as all relevant documentation of that review process. A third party should not be engaged without a written agreement specifying the terms of the relationship and the scope of the third party's work. The agreement should include the following provisions:

- The third party has an obligation not to offer or give anything of value to a customer in order to secure a business advantage;
- The third party should report to the company any details of customers or potential customers who solicit any inappropriate payments;
- The third party should comply with written guidelines regarding when to seek the company's approval for any hospitality or customary gifts;
- The parties must comply with all applicable anti-bribery laws and regulations (the elements of which should be specified within the agreement);
- The third party must comply with all applicable local law, including registration and other regulatory requirements, and provide annual certification of such compliance;
- No payments will be made to the third party other than in strict accordance with the terms of the agreement;
- The engagement may be immediately terminated without compensation if the third party violates any anti-bribery laws (though some countries may restrict enforcement of such contractual clauses);
- The third party may not assign its rights to any other party that has not been subjected to the same level of due diligence by the company, nor may the third party employ any other entity to provide the contracted-for services without obtaining the company's prior approval;
- The third party must allow the company to audit its books and records upon credible allegations of misconduct or reasonable suspicion of improper payments.

The third party should be required to notify the company promptly of any change in ownership. It should also advise the company of any other changes relevant to the due diligence it has undergone, or confirm at regular intervals (by way of formally certifying, for example) that there have been no changes and all previously provided information remains accurate.

A copy of the record should be maintained for the duration of the business relationship with the third party, and thereafter in accordance with the company's document-retention policy.

8. Approval Process and Post-approval Monitoring

When internal and external elements of the appropriate level of due diligence have been completed, the legal or compliance team should prepare a statement summarizing the review that has been undertaken and drawing a reasoned conclusion about whether retaining the third party is compatible with the company's business goals and ethics. Any unresolved issues or missing information should be noted. This statement should then be reviewed and (if appropriate) approved by senior management with no direct interest in the matter.

Any effective due diligence process does not, however, end when a third party is engaged by the company. The process is ongoing. The same investigations that were conducted by the original due diligence procedure can be repeated in part or in their entirety. The extent to which the tasks outlined previously need to be refreshed will depend on the circumstances, changes in the relationship, and the level of risk present.

Some companies require their third parties to expressly attest at intervals to compliance with anti-bribery controls. Certain tasks that were undertaken in the initial due diligence process can be easily repeated, such as media monitoring and reviews of government watch lists. These can be automated to be repeated at regular predetermined intervals.

Mere repetition of previously conducted due diligence checks may not, however, be sufficient. Much can change, even in a relatively short period of time: the characteristics of the third party, its ownership or financial stability, the business relationship between the company and third party, the climate of the industry as a whole, or the circumstances of the country or region. To simply repeat previous checks as if due diligence were a train on a single track risks entirely neglecting this dynamism, and exposes the company to the same danger of liability as existed at the outset of the relationship with the third party. The company should, at regular intervals, conduct a renewed assessment of the risk that a third party poses, and so be aware of the need to tailor the previous compliance program to the new reality in which the company and third party find themselves.

By virtue of the company and third party having ongoing business interactions, previously unavailable material will be available to the company. Often this information is obtained as part of a functioning business relationship, but it can be used additionally for due diligence purposes. For example, monitoring invoices and fees is not merely a financial task; unexpected increases in cost or sudden demands for payment could be a cause of compliance concern. Regularly submitted activity reports that show, for example, unnecessarily frequent meetings between the third party and government officials could also put the company on notice that a compliance issue has arisen. Often companies need to instigate processes to ensure that documentation is shared internally so the relevant information reaches people responsible for ensuring the third party's compliance. An increasing trend is also to employ data analytics tools with the available internal data to spot concerning anomalies.

Perhaps the most powerful tool for a company to monitor its third parties' compliance is the exercise of audit clauses inserted into the contractual terms. Such audit clauses may provide for "triggered" audits upon reasonable suspicion of misconduct. While most companies don't have the resources to audit all third parties, they should prioritize their riskiest relationships.

9. A Willingness to End the Business Relationship

It is beyond the scope of this chapter to dictate the circumstances in which a company should end its business relationship with a third party for misconduct. The determination is fact specific. It is also true that there can be very profound difficulties for companies in ending business relationships. There may be concerns about a potential contract breach, because the third party has a monopoly and the company has no alternative upon termination of the relationship than to leave the market.

Despite these difficulties, however, companies should maintain a genuine commitment to the possibility of ending a business relationship in appropriate circumstances. Leslie Caldwell, Assistant Attorney General of the United States, said in May 2015:

> A company should sensitize third parties with which it interacts (for example, vendors, agents or consultants) to the company's expectation that its partners are compliant. This means more than including boilerplate language in a contract. It means taking action—including termination of a business relationship—if a partner demonstrates a lack of respect for laws and policies.

It could actually worsen a company's exposure to enforcement action if it has gone to the effort of implementing anti-bribery safeguards but then fails ultimately to abide by them. This could leave the impression to enforcement authorities, the media, judge, or jury that the company was not merely incompetent or unfortunate, but rather aware of and complicit in the delinquency of its third party's misconduct.

It is more than just a matter of protecting the company from enforcement action or reputational damage, however. Without signaling to the third party that there is a genuine willingness by the company to act on noncompliant behavior to the fullest extent possible, the message is conveyed that the compliance regime is unimportant.

10. Common Due Diligence Pitfalls

- *Lack of Internal and External Transparency and Prioritization*: While not a recent development, the failure to prioritize and publicize a robust due diligence process has stubbornly endured in many companies, serving to undermine any process put in place. The message should be clear: due diligence is a *requirement*, not merely a *recommendation*. If the "tone from the top" demonstrates a lack of prioritization, this can lead to deficient risk assessments, an inconsistent approach to the resultant due diligence process, and dangerous consequences. A lack of prioritization can also give the impression to both company employees and third parties that due diligence is nothing more than a box-ticking barrier to efficient business to which no real thought needs to be dedicated. Finally, a lack of prioritization can frustrate the development of a company's internal information flows. Information received by one department that could lead an employee in a different department to recognize a problem simply never crosses that employee's desk.
- *Failure to Effectively Implement throughout Company*: Establishing and maintaining good corporate governance requires commitment at the highest levels, but commitment alone is not sufficient. Those who are responsible for compliance need to put the company's standards into practice throughout the organization, wherever it operates. Getting buy-in on the importance of due diligence from the company's business teams (as opposed to their seeing the process as the jealously guarded preserve of the legal department) is particularly important. Of course

the process itself may need to be conducted independently of such teams to ensure impartiality, but if there is no appreciation of its importance with those who work most closely with third parties, deficiencies in the process will not be recognized and may even be exploited.

- *Absence of Active Due Diligence Procedure Management*: The lack of active management of the due diligence procedure is also a common pitfall. Often even the most well-meaning managers, daunted by the size of the task and potential penalties involved, spend their time and resources designing incredibly intricate and perfect procedures. A perfect procedure doesn't exist when human nature is in play. It is impossible to mitigate all risks of bribery, and it may even be impossible to define all risks with absolute accuracy all the time. Once a company is liberated by the knowledge that perfection is impossible, then it can throw itself into the pursuit of the best *possible* program.

- *Insufficient Oversight*: Often companies demonstrate a failure during due diligence investigations to actively manage the process. Commonly this manifests itself in things as simple as a failure to provide hard deadlines for specific information to be obtained or for checks to be completed. Some companies have a tendency to take a "hands off" approach in third-party affairs, with unrealistic reliance placed on standard contractual terms that give little practical comfort. A common example is a company's failure to inquire into or actively participate in the third party's relationships with others further down the sales and marketing chain.

- *Inadequate Documentation*: Finally, documentation deficiencies are common. While in theory the process of documentation is simple, the practicalities can be cripplingly complex. Large companies with multiple regional branches, operating across different jurisdictions, using different languages, and forming webs of relationships with myriad third parties all in a fast moving world hardly lends itself to orderly recordkeeping. The ability to ensure that there is a centralized repository without duplication of regional lists and which is organized to the extent of being usefully accessed and employed is essential to the information-intensive inquiry that is ongoing compliance. Many companies employ specialized IT solutions rather than scattering documents across many different databases. At the very least, resources need to be dedicated to the task of effectively maintaining and retaining documentation.

11. Managing Costs

A common complaint about due diligence is the cost involved. As this chapter seeks to demonstrate, companies can cut costs by taking a risk-based approach. Not every third party represents the same risks to a company, so not every third party should consume the same resources. Streamlining the process based on a rational assessment of risk, rather than applying a "one-size-fits-all" approach, should safeguard the bottom line.

Many of the costs of due diligence can be shared with the third party rather than shouldered in their entirety by the company. The most obvious costs to pass on include training of the third party's employees, the cost of adopting a code of conduct, and even (with appropriate active management by the company) the cost of additional due diligence conducted by the third party on other entities further along the supply chain.

Recent evolutions in due diligence have gone beyond shifting only these obvious costs. Costs are incurred unnecessarily when the same third party is subject to the same due diligence inquiries multiple times, but the results go to different prospective business partners. As a result the responsibility for anti-bribery vetting, and the subsequent certification of compliance, is rapidly shifting directly to the third parties or well-positioned independent entities. After all, once the third party has completed certified due diligence, that certification is portable from the point of view of the third party; a single certification can be employed with multiple trading partners as a valid business credential, saving costs and speeding up the contracting process. The third party then has a vested interest in ensuring their information is up to date and their status is maintained, for example by updating their certified due diligence annually.

In employing this tool, however, the prospective business partner should remember two things. First, that the mere fact of certification is not alone determinative. What is significant is the underlying report and analysis that lies behind the certification. Often such reports are readily available to a company considering engagement of the third party, subject to the appropriate consents. Second, the reputation of the independent provider of this certified status is crucial. From the company's perspective, however, making certification portable and allowing ownership of it by the third party transfers most of the costs and eliminates most of the delay associated with the process.

Reducing delays in the process will have consequent cost reductions. As recently as 10 years ago, a significant cause of such delays were cultural differences and misunderstandings attached to compliance, resulting in suspicion on both sides. We have now entered an era where most third parties recognize that the process is routine, and that full cooperation will cause swifter final determination. Any residual cultural differences may be overcome by a clear articulation by the company that:

The point of due diligence is not to impugn the integrity of the third party;
The company appreciates there is a burden on the third party;
There is a business advantage to the third party in handling compliance well.

As previously discussed, the uniformity of a company employing the same type of process for all current and prospective third parties also prevents the affront of a third party feeling singled out.

12. Data Privacy Considerations

A company's due diligence protocol is complicated by often competing data privacy obligations. On the one hand, permitting third-party partners to hold up a data privacy shield from the probing light of a company's due diligence investigation could reduce the effectiveness of the program. On the other hand, mishandling a thorough due diligence investigation could result in the company itself running afoul of data privacy regulations.

Data privacy rules vary by country, which presents additional challenges. Even seemingly settled alliances between jurisdictions can crumble, thereby permanently altering the terrain. For example, the European Court of Justice's October 2015 decision that the EU-U.S. Safe Harbor framework for data transfer was invalid, dismantled a 15-year agreement that had hitherto with little controversy dictated the parameters for transferring data between the two regions.

These competing interests can leave the impression of a company being stuck between a rock and a hard place. Some CEOs may feel that the only rational plan of attack is to decide which of the competing regimes they are least afraid of.

There are, however, some positives in global developments of late. Recent statements by anti-corruption enforcement agencies (even those that are most active) indicate a sensitivity to this conflict faced by companies. The U.S. Department of Justice, for example, in a February 2016 deferred prosecution agreement demonstrated an appreciation that a company under investigation has to respect its global data privacy obligations. Yet, by so doing, the enforcement agency would nonetheless regard the company as having been cooperative. The same appreciation can also be found in the U.S. Department of Justice's April 2016 guidance update. Likewise some data protection authorities and agencies possess a general appreciation of the importance of companies processing data as part of a due diligence program, especially in an anti-corruption context. The Commission Nationale de L'informatique, a French data protection authority, has previously decided that the processing of invasive personal data was justified in the context of foreign legislation (in this case American and British anti-corruption legislation) where the data subjects represented a significant risk of corruption.

Furthermore, the twin considerations of due diligence and data privacy may be reconciled when a company carefully considers the following when processing the data it encounters during its due diligence procedure:

> The company should classify the nature of the information the company will process as part of its due diligence process. For some jurisdictions the crucial distinction is between Personally Identifiable Information (PII) and information that is more general in nature. In other jurisdictions the relevant distinction is between sensitive personal data as opposed to personal data. The sensitive personal data classification (and, consequently, more regulated handling of this data set) would include financial information and biometric information (including race, ethnic origin, political opinions, or religious beliefs that could be gathered as part of a company establishing an individual's connections with public officials), even where the information was provided to a company by the data subject under a lawful contract. The patchwork of varied classifications across different countries means there is little substitute for the company taking local advice on the specific jurisdiction where the due diligence is being conducted. Companies could, however, avoid significant difficulties in swaths of due diligence documents if any irrelevant or unnecessary personal or sensitive information is removed from documents, or if the information was aggregated by the third party to allow an assessment of risk without even collecting sensitive data.

> Access to some information may, by its very nature, be prohibited because of data privacy concerns even if consent is given. In some nations even official records may be beyond reach if these documents relate to ongoing civil ligation. Other countries may have expansive frameworks of state secrecy laws that will prohibit access to information that is potentially

significant to complete due diligence work. The lack of such information, even ostensibly because of data privacy rules, should not be regarded as being a special case that allows escaping a reassessment of the level of risk that the third party may pose to a company's interests. A red flag is still a red flag even if the absence of information is due to data privacy.

Consider who the targets of the due diligence process should be. Most enforcement agencies understand the need to vet key employees, but are less patient with sweeping reviews of all employees without regard to their role at the company.

When conducting due diligence, companies should be keenly aware of the origin of the information that it collects or considers. Most companies will naturally consider whether information was obtained from a public source or a private source. But the public/private distinction may be subject to nuance. For example, seemingly public information posted on a subject's social media feed may be off limits in some countries where someone other than the data subject is responsible for posting that information. Another example is some jurisdictions' use of the test of whether the subject of that data could him- or herself access the information as allowing permissible handling, rather than relying on the public/private distinction.

Companies also should bear in mind the purposes for which the data was collected. Of special significance is whether that purpose requires that it must be transferred out of its jurisdiction of origin. The act of transferring data out of its home jurisdiction can totally alter the level of regulation the original jurisdiction can exercise over the data, and so transfer abroad may be impermissible. Additionally, if the company has obtained the information for a different purpose, it may not be able to employ it for the due diligence investigation simply by virtue of being in possession of it.

While it is often prudent to obtain the consent of the data subject for the use of the data, a company should consider carefully the terms of that consent. Does the third party have the authority to give consent on behalf of the data it is in possession of and subsequently passes on to the company for due diligence purposes? Is the consent required only of a general nature, for example the general consent by way of automated check-boxes on due diligence questionnaires? Alternatively, is specific consent required because of the nature of the data or the subject? Consider whether there has been a clear articulation by the company conducting due diligence of what data will be examined, for what purpose, and what will be done with the data.

Companies also should be aware that, as with due diligence itself, data privacy obligations are ongoing; once the data has been used it cannot simply be retained without some valid rationale. Obligations in certain jurisdictions may extend to secure storage and even requirements to destroy or preclude further access by the company to certain types of information once any legitimate due diligence purpose has been served.

So, what practical safeguards can be employed by companies? Often a total lack of protection from data privacy rules can be overcome by including within the due diligence process a mechanism to get the subject's consent to obtain, handle, and retain information. Specific data protection warnings and consent clauses should be incorporated in third-party compliance questionnaires and related forms. Exposure to data privacy can be minimized by requiring the third party to gather the relevant data itself or, alternatively, by using an independent due diligence provider. Contractual clauses or indemnifications requiring the third party to obtain consent from the original subject of the data may also provide a basic level of protection.

13. Official Guidance

Given that the extent of a company's liability depends on its showing the authorities that it had a meaningful compliance program in place, it is important to know what degree of due diligence the authorities consider sufficient. Some guidance can be obtained from official publications.

In the United States, for example, there is *A Resource Guide to the U.S. Foreign Corrupt Practices Act*, published jointly by the DOJ and the SEC (*available at* http://www.justice. gov/criminal/fraud/fcpa). Or, in the United Kingdom, one can turn to the Ministry of Justice publication entitled *The Bribery Act 2010: Guidance about Procedures Which Relevant Commercial Organizations Can Put into Place to Prevent Persons Associated with Them from Bribing* (*available at* http://www.justice.gov.uk/guidance/bribery.htm). The advice in these and similar publications tends to be fairly general in nature. For example, the amount of due diligence required in any given situation is characterized as being "reasonable," "appropriate," and "proportionate" to the risks involved.

Anything more specific than this is difficult to find. There is only limited judicial precedent, primarily because anti-bribery cases brought against companies are commonly settled rather than tried in court. What precedent does exist is often of limited assistance, given the fact-specific character of any implemented program and, consequently, its "adequacy" or "reasonableness." Nevertheless, official publications such as those that have just been identified are helpful reference points.

14. Conclusion

Due diligence can be time-consuming. But the lessons learned during the global development of a compliance consensus have taught us that deficiencies in due diligence procedures are often even more time-consuming and may be far more costly. When due diligence is done properly, third parties can respond with confidence when a customer makes an inappropriate demand, knowing that the company will support it in doing the right thing. Over time, third parties can be a local bullhorn, amplifying the company's anti-bribery message in the local market.

Third parties truly determined to violate anti-bribery laws will do so despite the best efforts of company leaders and their compliance teams. For the great majority, though, the goal is to secure legitimate business opportunities in exchange for reasonable compensation. The evolution of third-party due diligence enables commercial relationships based on this simple principle to flourish, advancing the interests and the reputations of all involved.

22 Investigations, Privacy, and Data Security Issues

1. Introduction

Internal investigations routinely require companies and investigators to gather and review wide swaths of company documents and data that may incorporate information from employees, customers, or other third parties across multiple jurisdictions.[1] These variegated forms of data likely may contain sensitive or personal information protected by privacy and data security laws. Given that privacy and data security standards vary from country to country, and within a particular country, such as the United States, may be composed of disparate and overlapping legal protections, investigators will need to be familiar not only with the categories of data they collect, but also the legal standards that govern the data's collection, use, storage, and transfer. As necessary, investigators may need to hire local or technical experts to assist with compliance with the governing standards. The following is an overview of potentially applicable U.S. laws, as well as several international privacy and data protection laws.

1.1 U.S. PRIVACY PROTECTIONS

Privacy laws in the United States seek to protect specific forms of sensitive information traceable to a specific person. Generally, personally identifiable information includes "any information about an individual maintained by an agency, including (1) any information that can be

---

[1] This chapter was contributed by Perkins Coie LLP's Michael Sink. This chapter has been adapted from *The ABA Compliance Officer's Deskbook.*

From Baksheesh to Bribery. T. Markus Funk and Andrew S. Boutros.
© Oxford University Press 2019. Published 2019 by Oxford University Press.

used to distinguish or trace an individual's identity, such as name, Social Security number, date and place of birth, mother's maiden name, or biometric records; and (2) any other information that is linked or linkable to an individual, such as medical, educational, financial, and employment information."[2] In the United States, however, there is no comprehensive national privacy framework. Rather, at the federal level, there are disparate privacy laws and regulations that govern specific industry sectors, the kinds of data collected, and particular usage. Some of the sectoral laws that companies are most likely to encounter include the following:

- **The Cable Communications Policy Act**, 47 U.S.C. § 551 (1984 Cable Act). The Cable Communications Policy Act requires cable operators to advise customers of the personally identifiable information it collects, limits the use and disclosure of that data, provides customers with the opportunity to inspect the data, and requires the deletion of the data.[3] The Federal Communications Commission (FCC) is primarily responsible for enforcing the Cable Communications Policy Act.

- **The Children's Online Privacy Protection Act** (COPPA), 15 U.S.C. §§ 6501–6506. COPPA imposes liability on website and electronic service operators for the collection of "personal information" from children.[4] The Federal Trade Commission (FTC) is the primary enforcement agency for COPPA.

- **The Communications Act**, 47 U.S.C. §§ 151 et seq. The Communications Act imposes liability on telecommunications carriers for disclosure of customer proprietary network information (CPNI), including information that relates to the quantity, technical configuration, type, destination, location, and amount of use of telecommunications services, and information contained in billing statements such as call detail and calling plan information.[5] The FCC is responsible for enforcing the Communications Act.

- **The Driver's Privacy Protection Act** (DPPA), 18 U.S.C. §§ 2721 et seq. The DPPA prohibits, among other things, any person from knowingly obtaining or disclosing personal information from a motor vehicle record without a permissible use, and from using false statements to obtain motor vehicle records.[6]

---

[2] United States Government Accountability Office, Report 08-536, Privacy: Alternatives Exist for Enhancing Protection of Personally Identifiable Information 1 n.1 (May 2008). *See also* National Institute of Standards and Technology, *Guide to Protecting the Confidentiality of Personally Identifiable Information (PII): Recommendations of the National Institute of Standards and Technology* ES-1 (Apr. 2010) (applying the GAO definition).

[3] *See, e.g.*, Scofield v. Telecable of Overland Park, Inc., 973 F.2d 874, 878–84 (10th Cir. 1992) (discussing notice requirements and appending copy of notice deemed to be sufficient).

[4] *See also* the FTC COPPA Rule, 16 C.F.R. § 312.3 (2018).

[5] 47 U.S.C. § 222(h)(1) (2014). *See also* the FCC's 2007 CPNI Order, *Implementation of the Telecommunications Act of 1996: Telecommunications Carriers' Use of Customer Proprietary Network Information and Other Customer Information, Report and Order and Further Notice of Proposed Rulemaking*, 22 FCC Rcd. 6927, 6959, para. 64 (2007) (carriers must "take every reasonable precaution to protect the confidentiality of proprietary or personal customer information"). *See, e.g.*, National Cable & Telecommc'ns Ass'n v. FCC, 555 F.3d 996, 997–1003 (D.C. Cir. 2009) (discussing CPNI restrictions and upholding the FCC 2007 CPNI Order).

[6] 18 U.S.C. § 2722 (2015). *See, e.g.*, Maracich v. Spears, 570 U.S. 48, 76–78 (2013) (attorney solicitation of clients based on personal information provided by the DMV subject to the DPPA); Kehoe v. Fidelity Fed. Bank & Trust, 421 F.3d 1209 (11th Cir. 2005) (discussing remedy provisions under the DPPA).

- **The Electronic Communications Privacy Act** (ECPA), Pub. L. No. 99–508, 100 Stat. 1848 (1986). Among its various protections, the ECPA contains three distinct privacy regimes: the Wiretap Act, 18 U.S.C. §§ 2510–2522, the Stored Communications Act, 18 U.S.C. §§ 2701–2709, 2711, and the pen register and trap and trace provisions, 18 U.S.C. §§ 3121–3127.
  - o The Wiretap Act protects all persons from the interception in transit of the content of their oral, wire, or electronic communications (or the disclosure of intercepted communications), subject to enumerated statutory exceptions.[7]
  - o The Stored Communications Act (SCA) governs electronic communications services (any services that provides users the ability to send or receive wire or electronic communications) and remote computing services (services that provide computer storage or processing services by means of an electronic communications system).[8] The SCA protects basic subscriber information (name, address, phone connection, duration records, length of service, and instrument identifier) along with the content of communications, and certain noncontent records and information, such as access and viewing history.[9] The SCA prohibits unauthorized access to stored communications and the disclosure of such communications to third parties, absent a statutory exception.[10]
  - o The pen register and trap and trace provisions protect all persons from the installation of a pen register or trap and trace device designed to capture the noncontent information of oral, wire, or electronic communications, except as authorized by statute.[11]

---

[7] 18 U.S.C. § 2511 (2015 & Supp. 2018). *See, e.g.*, Bartnicki v. Vopper, 532 U.S. 514, 527–35 (2001) (discussing disclosure restrictions and recognizing First Amendment exception for matters of public concern that were not directly intercepted).

[8] 18 U.S.C. § 2510(15) (2015) (defining "electronic communication service" as "any service which provides to users thereof the ability to send or receive wire or electronic communications"); *id.* § 2711(2) (defining "remote computing service" as "the provision to the public of computer storage or processing services by means of an electronic communications system"). *See, e.g.*, Quon v. Arch Wireless Operating Co., 529 F.3d 892, 900 (9th Cir. 2008) ("The SCA was enacted because the advent of the Internet presented a host of potential privacy breaches that the Fourth Amendment does not address."), *rev'd on Fourth Amendment grounds by City of Ontario v. Quon*, 560 U.S. 746 (2010).

[9] 18 U.S.C. § 2703 (2015 & Supp. 2018). *See also* Orin S. Kerr, *A User's Guide to the Stored Communications Act, and a Legislator's Guide to Amending It*, 72 GEO. WASH. L. REV. 1208 (2004) (describing structure of the SCA and the various categories of protected information).

[10] 18 U.S.C. § 2701 (2015) and § 2702 (2015 & 2018 Supp.). *See, e.g.*, Vista Marketing, LLC v. Burkett, 812 F.3d 954, 962–79 (11th Cir. 2016) (construing SCA penalty provisions in case involving unauthorized access to emails).

[11] 18 U.S.C. § 3121(a) (2015). *See also* 18 U.S.C. §§ 3127(3) & (4) (2015) (defining pen register and trap and trace devices). *See, e.g.*, United States v. Forrester, 512 F.3d 500, 511–13 (9th Cir. 2008) (discussing remedies under the statute).

- **The Fair Credit Reporting Act** (FCRA), 15 U.S.C. §§ 1681–1681t. Among other things, the FCRA aims to protect consumer privacy with respect to credit reports and transactions.[12] The FCRA limits the circumstances under which a "consumer reporting agency" may furnish a consumer report. In short, consumer reporting agencies may only provide credit reports to individuals or entities with a valid need.[13] A consumer reporting agency has been broadly defined as any person or entity that regularly engages in the practice of assembling or evaluating consumer credit information or providing consumer reports.[14] Consumer reports include "any written, oral, or other communication of any information by a consumer reporting agency bearing on a consumer's credit worthiness, credit standing, credit capacity, character, general reputation, personal characteristics, or mode of living" that is used to establish credit or insurance eligibility, employment, or another enumerated statutory purpose.[15] Consumers are entitled to know the information about them contained in their files as well as when a consumer report has been used to deny an application for credit.[16] Consumers also have the right to correct inaccurate information in their reports, and consumer reporting agencies are required to correct or remove inaccurate, incomplete, or unverifiable information.[17] The FCRA also prohibits the printing of either credit card numbers beyond the last five digits or the expiration date on receipts in point-of-sale transactions.[18]

- **The Family Educational Rights and Privacy Act** (FERPA), 20 U.S.C. § 1232g; 34 C.F.R. §§ 99.1–99.67. FERPA applies to educational agencies and institutions that receive funds under any program administered by the U.S. Department of Education. FERPA protects the privacy of education records that are directly related to a student and maintained by an educational agency or institution, or by a party acting for the agency or institution.[19] Ordinarily, education records may not be disclosed without written parental consent.[20] FERPA, however, does allow disclosure without consent to providers of institutional services. Institutional service providers are contractors, consultants, volunteers, or other parties to whom an agency or institution outsources functions, such as IT services or legal advice, for which the educational institution could otherwise use its own employees, provided

---

[12] *See* Safeco Ins. Co. of Am. v. Burr, 551 U.S. 47, 52 (2007) (The FCRA was passed "to ensure fair and accurate credit reporting, promote efficiency in the banking system, and protect consumer privacy.").

[13] *See* 15 U.S.C. § 1681b (2009 & 2018 Supp.).

[14] 15 U.S.C. § 1681a(f) (2009 & 2018 Supp.).

[15] *Id.* § 1681a(d)(1).

[16] *Id.* §§ 1681g(a) & 1681.

[17] *Id.* § 1681i.

[18] 15 U.S.C. § 1681c(g)(1) (2009 & 2018 Supp.); *see also* United States v. Bormes, 568 U.S. 6, 7, 19-20 (2012) (discussing the FCRA digit disclosure prohibition and holding that the Little Tucker Act does not waive sovereign immunity with respect to FCRA damages actions).

[19] 34 C.F.R. § 99.3, Education records (2018). *See also* Owasso Independent Sch. Dist. No. 1-011 v. Falvo, 534 U.S. 426, 432–36 (2002) (discussing definition of education record and holding that peer-grading by other students does not constitute an education record).

[20] 20 U.S.C. § 1232g(b)(1) (2017).

that the service provider is under the direct control of the educational institution and complies with the use and disclosure provisions of FERPA.[21] FERPA is enforced by the U.S. Department of Education.[22]

- **The Financial Services Modernization Act (or Gramm-Leach-Bliley Act) (GLBA)**, 15 U.S.C. §§ 6801–6809. The GLBA governs financial institutions and third parties that provide services for or function on behalf of financial institutions.[23] The GLBA protects any personal information collected by a financial institution in connection with providing a financial product or service, unless the information is otherwise publicly available.[24] Covered entities may not disclose such information absent customer consent, which can be obtained by notice of disclosure and the opportunity to opt out, or pursuant to the terms of the originating institution's privacy policy or other statutory exception.[25]

- **The Health Insurance Portability and Accountability Act** (HIPAA), Pub. L. No. 104–191, 110 Stat.1936 (1996).[26] HIPAA applies to healthcare clearinghouses, employer-sponsored health plans, health insurers, certain medical service providers, and their business associates, which are defined as "person or entity that performs certain functions or activities that involve the use or disclosure of protected health information on behalf of, or provides services to, a covered entity."[27] HIPAA covers "protected health information" (PHI), which is any information held by a covered entity that concerns health status, provision of healthcare, or payment for health that can be linked to an individual.[28] The HIPAA Privacy Rule (as modified by the 2013 HIPAA Omnibus Rule) prohibits a covered entity from disclosing PHI absent a patient's express written authorization or another statutory exception.[29] Business associates may receive PHI provided they put in place appropriate safeguards. HIPAA is primarily enforced by the U.S. Department of Health and Human Services (HHS).

- **The Satellite Home Viewers Extension and Reauthorization Act** (SHVERA), 47 U.S.C. § 338(i). Like the Cable Communications Policy Act, SHVERA requires satellite operators to advise customers of the personally identifiable information

---

[21] 34 C.F.R. § 99.31 (2018).

[22] 20 U.S.C. § 1232g(g) (2017). *See also* Gonzaga Univ. v. Doe, 536 U.S. 273, 276 (2002) (FERPA does not create a personal right to enforce).

[23] 15 U.S.C. § 6802(a) (2009 & 2018 Supp.). *See also* the FTC's Financial Privacy Rule, 16 C.F.R. part 313 (protecting personally identifiable financial information) (2018). *See, e.g.,* Trans Union LLC v. FTC, 295 F.3d 42, 48–52 (D.C. Cir. 2002) (upholding Financial Privacy Rule).

[24] 15 U.S.C. § 6802(a) (2009). *See, e.g.,* Dunmire v. Morgan Stanley DW, Inc., 475 F.3d 956, 960–61 (8th Cir. 2007) (discussing the nonpublic requirement).

[25] *Id.* at § 6802(b)–(e).

[26] *See also* the HHS Privacy Rule, 45 C.F.R. parts 160 & 164 subpts. A & E (2018); South Carolina Med. Ass'n v. Thompson, 327 F.3d 346, 353–55 (4th Cir. 2003) (upholding HHS regulations).

[27] 42 U.S.C. § 1320d-1(a) (2012); 45 C.F.R. §§ 160.102(a)(b) and 160-103, business associate.

[28] 45 C.F.R. § 160.103, Protected Health Information (2018). *See also* 42 U.S.C. §§ 1320d(4) (2012) (defining health information) & (6) (defining individually identifiable information).

[29] 45 C.F.R. §§ 164.510, 164.512 (2018). *See* Murphy v. Dulay, 768 F.3d 1360, 1369–71 (11th Cir. 2014) (discussing consent and statutory exceptions).

it collects, limits the use and disclosure of that data, provides customers with the opportunity to inspect the data, and requires the deletion of the data.[30] The FCC is responsible for enforcing SHVERA.

- **The Telephone Records and Privacy Protection Act** (TRAPPA), 18 U.S.C. § 1039. TRAPPA imposes liability on any person who improperly obtains or sells confidential phone records or CPNI.[31]
- **The Video Privacy Protection Act** (VPPA), 18 U.S.C. § 2710. The VPPA imposes liability for the unauthorized disclosure of "personally identifiable information" relating to a person's use or request of video materials or services from a video tape service provider.[32]

Violations of these statutes carry with them various penalties ranging from criminal penalties, fines, and other civil penalties to statutory damages, private causes of actions, and attorneys' fees, in addition to the reputational and commercial harm. These penalties can be substantial. In 2014, for example, New York and Presbyterian Hospital and Columbia University paid $4.5 million to HHS to settle a HIPAA action stemming from the release of the electronic PHI of 6,800 individuals.[33] In 2015, AT&T settled an FCC CPNI investigation for $25 million.[34]

The FTC plays a prominent role in enforcing federal privacy laws. In addition to mandates under specific privacy statutes such as COPPA and FCRA, the FTC broadly investigates privacy and data security complaints affecting consumers under section 5(a) of the Federal Trade Commission Act ("FTC Act"). Section 5(a) prohibits both unfair and deceptive acts or practices that affect commerce. The FTC has pursued failures to follow privacy policies and statements as deceptive practices.[35] The FTC has also successfully sued companies as an unfair trade practice for failing to maintain reasonable and appropriate cybersecurity measures for consumers.[36]

States also play a significant role in privacy regulation. Most states have laws that duplicate or expand upon many of the federal statutes outlined previously. In California, for example, the Online Privacy Protection Act of 2003 requires operators of websites (or online service providers) that collect information on California residents to conspicuously post a privacy policy.[37] Failure to comply with the provisions of such a privacy policy constitutes unfair

---

[30] *See, e.g.,* Padilla v. DISH Network LLC, No. 12-cv-7350, 2014 WL 539746, at *1–4 (N.D. Ill. Feb. 11, 2014) (discussing remedy provisions under SHVERA).

[31] *See, e.g.,* F.T.C. v. Accusearch Inc., F.3d 1187, 1194–95, 1201–02 (10th Cir. 2009) (discussing TRAPPA and the Federal Trade Com mission Act's prohibition against unfair trade practices).

[32] *See, e.g.,* Sterk v. Redbox Automated Retail, LLC, 672 F.3d 535, 537 (7th Cir. 2012) (construing remedies provisions under the VPPA).

[33] HHS Press Office, *Data Breach Results in $4.8 Million HIPAA Settlements* (May 7, 2014), *available at* http://www.hhs.gov/about/news/2014/05/07/data-breach-results-48-million-hipaa-settlements.html#.

[34] FCC, *AT&T To Pay $25 Million to Settle Consumer Privacy Investigation* (Apr. 8, 2015), *available at* https://www.fcc.gov/document/att-pay-25m-settle-investigation-three-data-breaches-0.

[35] *See, e.g.,* Electronic Privacy Information Center v. FTC, 844 F. Supp. 2d 98 (D.D.C. 2012) (discussing privacy policy consent decree).

[36] *See* FTC v. Wyndham Worldwide Corp., 799 F.3d 236, 243–47 (3d Cir. 2015) (upholding authority of the FTC to regulate cybersecurity under section 5 of the FTC Act).

[37] CAL. BUS. & PROF. CODE §§ 22575-79 (2018). *See also* Office of the Attorney General, State of California Department of Justice, Privacy Laws, *available at* https://oag.ca.gov/privacy/privacy-laws (last visited Dec. 14,

competition.[38] Courts have also construed other states' consumer protection acts to cover privacy practices even in the absence of a specific privacy statute.[39] Private litigants may also attempt to bring claims under state common law theories such as breach of contract, breach of warranty, fraudulent misrepresentation, negligence, or invasion of privacy torts.[40]

1.2 U.S. DATA SECURITY PROVISIONS

In the United States, data security laws often overlap with privacy protections. Several sectoral laws, such as HIPAA, FERPA, and GLBA, not only impose requirements on the collection and use of protected data but also impose detailed technical data security standards that must be adopted by companies that have access to data protected by those statutes. The HIPAA Security Rule (as modified by the 2013 HIPAA Omnibus Rule) protects electronic PHI handled by a covered entity.[41] It requires specific and appropriate administrative, physical, and technical safeguards to ensure the protection of electronic PHI. FERPA generally requires that covered educational institutions use "reasonable methods" to maintain data security[42] but does not impose specific security standards. The GLBA places an "obligation" on subject entities to protect the security of customers' data,[43] and directs the regulatory entities tasked with enforcing the Act to adopt appropriate security safeguards.[44] The FTC's Safeguards Rule broadly sets forth the elements necessary to implement "administrative, technical, and physical safeguards to protect the security, confidentiality, and integrity of customer information" under the GLBA.[45]

Sarbanes-Oxley (SOX), among other things, requires publicly held companies to assess their internal controls, report the results to the Securities and Exchange Commission (SEC), and have an independent auditor review that assessment in an effort to ensure the accuracy and reliability of corporate disclosures.[46] The audit guidelines issued by the Public Company Accounting Oversight Board (PCAOB) for SOX audits specifically include information technology controls among the internal controls that should be assessed.[47]

2016) [updated and url corrected]. See also the recently enacted California Consumer Privacy Act of 2018, Cal. Civ. Code §§ 1798.100 to 1798.198, which goes into effect January 1, 2020.

[38] Cal. Bus. & Prof. Code § 22576 (2018).

[39] *See, e.g., In re* Target Corp. Data Sec. Breach Litig., 66 F. Supp. 3d 1154, 1161–66 (D. Minn. 2014).

[40] *See, e.g., In re* Sony Gaming Networks & Customer Data Sec. Breach Litig., 996 F. Supp. 2d 942, 963–84 (S.D. Cal. 2014) (evaluating and dismissing plaintiffs' breach of warranty, misrepresentation, and negligence claims); *In re* Anthem, Inc. Data Breach Litig., No. 15-MD-02617-LHK, 2016 WL 589760, at *9–15 (N.D. Cal. Feb. 14, 2016) (evaluating and dismissing plaintiffs' breach of contract and negligence claims); *In re* Zappos.com, Inc., No. 3:12–cv–00325–RCJ–VPC, 2013 WL 4830497, at *3–5 (D. Nev. Sept. 9, 2013) (dismissing common law claims for public disclosure of private facts, breach of contract, negligence, and unjust enrichment).

[41] 45 C.F.R. pts. 160 & 164 subpts. A & C (2018).

[42] 34 C.F.R. § 99.31(a)(1)(ii) (2018).

[43] 15 U.S.C. § 6801(a) (2009 & 2018 Supp.).

[44] *Id.* § 6801(b).

[45] 16 C.F.R. § 314.1(a) (2018).

[46] 15 U.S.C. § 7262 (2009 & 2018 Supp.).

[47] Public Company Accounting Oversight Board, *Release No. 2010-004, Auditing Standard No. 12: Identifying and Assessing Risks of Material Misstatement* at para. 29 & *Release No. 2007-005A, Auditing Standard No. 5: An Audit of Internal Control over Financial Reporting That Is Integrated with an Audit of Financial Statements* at paras. 27, 36, and 47.

In addition, the SEC requires investment advisors, broker-dealers, and investment companies to "adopt written policies and procedures that address administrative, technical, and physical safeguards for the protection of customer records and information" pursuant to its authority under the GLBA.[48]

The FTC requires that companies apply reasonable and appropriate data security practices lest they commit an unfair trade practice under section 5 of the FTC Act.[49] The FTC has also enacted specific data security rules, such as the Health Breach Notification Rule, which imposes a duty on non-HIPAA personal health records vendors, including online service providers (and those that do business with them) to report to the FTC data breaches involving personal health records, and to notify affected individuals and possibly the media.[50]

States may also implement data security requirements. California, for example, requires all businesses to "implement and maintain reasonable security procedures and practices" to protect personal information gathered from California residents.[51] In addition, 47 states have data breach notification requirements for entities that transmit or store sensitive personal information about consumers, as defined by each state's statute.[52] Under such statutes, entities that have experienced a breach have, at a minimum, an obligation to provide timely notice of the breach to both the affected individuals, as well as a designated state agency.[53] Timeliness varies from state to state and, in some cases industry to industry, and can be as short as five days. States may also impose common law duties to protect consumer information entrusted to commercial entities.[54]

2. International Privacy and Data Security Regimes

International privacy and data security regimes abound. A summary of all such regimes is beyond the purview of this chapter. Three of the most significant privacy and data security provisions for U.S. companies doing business abroad, however, include those of Australia, Canada, and the European Union. In addition, the Asia-Pacific Economic Cooperation (APEC) has adopted a privacy framework recommendation for its member economies.

---

[48] Regulation S-P, 17 C.F.R. Part 248 (2018). *See* Stevens v. Interactive Fin. Advisors, Inc., No. 15-2130, 2016 WL 4056401, at *3–4 (7th Cir. July 29, 2016) (discussing requirements of Regulation S-P).

[49] *See, e.g.*, FTC v. Wyndham Worldwide Corp., 799 F.3d 236, 240–41 (3d Cir. 2015) (listing FTC's allegations regarding failure to use readily available security measures).

[50] 16 C.F.R. pt. 318 (2018).

[51] CAL. CIV. CODE § 1798.81.5(b) (2018). *See also* Massachusetts, 201 C.M.R. 17.00 (2018).

[52] National Conference of State Legislatures, Security Breach Notification Laws (Jan. 4, 2016), *available at* http://www.ncsl.org/research/telecommunications-and-information-technology/security-breach-notification-laws.aspx.

[53] For a chart summarizing each state's data breach requirements, see Perkins Coie LLP, *Security Breach Notification Chart, available at* https://www.perkinscoie.com/en/news-insights/security-breach-notification-chart.html (last updated June 2016).

[54] *See In re* Sony Gaming Networks & Customer Data Sec. Breach Litig., 996 F. Supp. 2d 942, 966 (S.D. Cal. 2014) (finding "a legal duty to safeguard a consumer's confidential information entrusted to a commercial entity" under California and Massachusetts law).

Australia's Privacy Act, as amended, requires private businesses over a certain size or in certain industries to protect Australians' personally identifiable information, regardless of whether it is private, based on a set of 13 Australian Privacy Principles (APPs).[55] The privacy principles generally require notice of collection, limit the purposes for which information can be collected and used, require consent for sensitive information or, when the use of the personal information changes, provide individuals with an anonymity option where practical and with access to, and the ability to correct their information. In addition, privacy principle 11.1 requires that a company "take reasonable steps to protect the personal information it holds from misuse, interference and loss and from unauthorised access, modification or disclosure." Privacy principle 8 also regulates the cross-border disclosure of protected information and requires that companies ensure that foreign recipients follow the APPs, while imposing liability on the sender for certain actions of the recipient. The Office of the Australian Information Commissioner has issued detailed guidance as to what steps should be taken to comply with both APPs 8 and 11.[56]

In addition to various sectoral privacy laws and province-specific privacy regulations, Canada's chief privacy statute governing the conduct of commercial activity is the Personal Information Protection and Electronic Documents Act (PIPEDA).[57] PIPEDA not only sets out 10 fair information principles, but it also prohibits the collection, use, and disclosure of Canadians' personal information by entities engaged in commercial activity in Canada without the consent of the individual. Personal information is defined broadly as "information about an identifiable individual" and has been broadly construed. If the intended use changes, consent must be obtained again. Individuals have a right to access and correct personal information. Moreover, companies must appropriately safeguard the information they collect

The European Union's (EU) Data Protection Directive establishes a minimum legal requirement that all member states must incorporate into their own national laws.[58] The Directive governs the "processing" of "personal data." Processing includes the collection, organization, storage, alteration, retrieval, disclosure, blocking, erasing, or destruction of data. Personal data is defined broadly to mean any information by which an individual can be personally identified. The Directive sets forth seven privacy principles regarding opt-out choice, onward data transfer, security, data integrity, access, and correction of data that must be followed.

The Directive remains in effect until May 25, 2018, when the General Data Protection Regulation, adopted by the European Parliament in April 2016, will supersede it.[59] The General Data Protection Regulation, among other things, incorporates the seven principles from the Directive, requires breach notification, grants rights of erasure and data porting to EU residents, and increases fines (up to 4 percent of gross global revenue). The General Data Protection Regulation applies to all foreign companies that process the data of EU residents.

---

[55] Privacy Act 1988 (Cth).

[56] *See* Office of Austl. Info. Comm'r, APP Guidelines (Apr. 2015), *available at* https://www.oaic.gov.au/agencies-and-organisations/app-guidelines/.

[57] S.C. 2000, c 5, as amended.

[58] Directive 95/46/EC of the European Parliament and the Council of 24 October 1995 on the Protection of Individuals with Regard to the Processing of Personal Data and on the Free Movement of Such Data.

[59] Regulation 2016/679, 2016 O.J. (L 119) (EU).

In July 2016, the European Commission approved the EU-U.S. Privacy Shield governing the U.S. companies' collection and receipt of EU citizens' data. Among other things, it requires U.S. companies to certify to the Department of Commerce that they comply with heightened transfer requirements, display a privacy policy on the company website, respond promptly to complaints, submit to arbitration, and cooperate with European data protection authorities. Compliance is subject to FTC enforcement.

Finally, APEC has adopted a voluntary privacy framework for its 21 member economies.[60] The privacy framework adopts nine information privacy principles about prevention of harm, notice, collection limitations, appropriate use, consumer choice, integrity of personal information, security safeguards, access and correction rights, and accountability. The privacy framework also recommends the cooperative development of cross-border privacy rules. To that end, APEC created the Cross Border Privacy Rules (CBPR) system.[61] The CBPR system requires participating businesses to implement data privacy policies that comply with the Privacy Framework. The policies must be enforceable by law and deemed compliant by independent APEC agents. Participating member economies include the United States, Mexico, Japan, and Canada. In addition, APEC and the European Union have adopted a referential that facilitates simultaneous dual certification of compliance with both privacy regimes.

3. Practical Pointers

Attorneys conducting internal investigations should consider the following practical pointers prior to commencing the discovery phase of the investigation:

3.1 IDENTIFY THE CATEGORIES OF PROTECTABLE INFORMATION NECESSARY TO, OR LIKELY TO BE COLLECTED BY, THE INVESTIGATION

A preliminary assessment of the categories of protectable information maintained by the company conducted at the outset of an investigation should determine what consumer data the company collects, how it is collected, how it is used, who has access to it, how it is stored, how it is shared, how it is destroyed, and any likely security vulnerabilities. To the extent a company has conducted a privacy audit, those reports may be useful to investigators in shaping the extent of their document and data requests, as well as how such data may be collected, stored, transferred, or destroyed during or after the investigation.

3.2 DETERMINE THE LOCATIONS WHERE SUBJECT INFORMATION IS STORED AND WHERE IT MAY BE TRANSFERRED TO FOR REVIEW

Any time a company stores data in or transfers data out of foreign countries, investigators in conjunction with the company should research any applicable data transfer protocols

---

[60] APEC, Privacy Framework (2005), *available at* https://www.apec.org/Publications/2005/12/APEC-Privacy-Framework .

[61] *See APEC Cross Border Privacy Rules (CBPR) System, available at* http://www.cbprs.org (Dec. 14, 2018).

and implement them in advance of the data transfers. In addition, the company may need to be prepared to certify compliance with those protocols to a foreign government or regulatory agency.

3.3 ASSESS ANY COMPANY POLICIES ON PRIVACY AND DATA SECURITY POLICIES

Many companies have written company-wide privacy and data security policies that cover the protected information the company handles and provide guidance on its use during security or breach incidents. These policies can contain useful information regarding company procedures and contact points. Where the procedures are set for collection, use, transfer, and destruction protocols, investigators should consider adopting them where they meet or exceed the applicable legal standards.

3.4 ASSESS PERMISSIBLE LEGAL OR INVESTIGATORY EXCEPTIONS OR CARVE-OUTS TO APPLICABLE PRIVACY AND DATA SECURITY REGULATIONS

Depending on the regulatory framework, outside legal investigators and associated vendors may be treated as an internal division of the company with the same rights and duties related to the collection, use, transfer, or deletion of data. Or, the use of data to obtain legal advice may be a permitted statutory use exempting it from the regulatory framework. In other scenarios, however, outside investigators may be considered third-party vendors who must enter into specific forms of agreements with specific data use, storage, and destruction standards that must be agreed to and followed.

3.5 RETAIN ANY NECESSARY LOCAL OR TECHNICAL EXPERTS TO ASSIST WITH REGULATORY COMPLIANCE FOR DATA GATHERING, STORAGE, USE, AND DESTRUCTION

Local or specialist legal counsel can provide guidance on applicable legal, regulatory, or industry standards, especially outside the jurisdiction of the investigators. Technical vendors, moreover, will likely be necessary to comply with any data storage, transfer, or deletion requirements that the average investigative firm will not be equipped to meet.

3.6 WHERE POSSIBLE, TAILOR INFORMATION AND DOCUMENT REQUESTS TO AVOID THE COLLECTION OF UNNECESSARY PERSONAL OR SENSITIVE INFORMATION

Rather than gathering broad categories of marginally relevant information that may contain protected sensitive information only to be subject to strict regulatory requirements regarding its use, storage, and destruction, targeted gathering of documents and information that minimize the collection of personal information can avoid costly and time-consuming regulatory burdens later in the process.

3.7 OBTAIN CONSENT FOR USE WHERE POSSIBLE

Although often impractical, occasionally investigators may have direct contact with employees or customers as witnesses regarding the subject of the investigation. If the witnesses are cooperative, consider obtaining consent for the use of specific personal information necessary to the investigation in order to avoid future any future disputes.

3.8 SECURE DATA SHARED WITH ANY THIRD PARTIES

Sensitive information collected in the course of an investigation should be shared with vetted third parties only when necessary. In addition to vetting, companies should incorporate provisions into third-party contracts requiring the third party to comply with the company's privacy and data security policies, requiring the destruction of any protected information at the end of any project, and imposing penalties and requiring indemnification in the event of a violation of those provisions.

3.9 ENSURE THE EVENTUAL DELETION OR DESTRUCTION OF SENSITIVE OR PERSONAL INFORMATION WHEN NO LONGER NECESSARY TO THE INVESTIGATION

Often an afterthought, planning for eventual data deletion or destruction can avoid logistical difficulties and costs later, especially where third parties have been provided access. In addition to ensuring regulatory compliance, prompt and thorough data deletion or destruction can help ensure the confidentiality of the investigation, as well as limit sources of potential future data breaches.

23 Increasing Accountability and Reducing Corruption: the World Bank's Anti-Corruption System

1. World Bank Institutional Introduction

1.1 GOALS AND MISSION

The World Bank Group consists of five international financial institutions, including the two that are traditionally referred to as the "World Bank"[1]: the International Bank for Reconstruction and Development (IBRD), and the International Development Association (IDA).[2] Along with the other parts of the World Bank Group, the World Bank (or "Bank") works to promote economic development and reduce poverty in its member countries. One of the world's largest sources of development financing and technical assistance for developing countries, the Bank "uses financial resources and its extensive experience to partner with developing countries to reduce poverty, increase economic growth, and improve quality of life."[3]

The Bank was conceived during World War II at an international conference in Bretton Woods, New Hampshire, with the goal of assisting Europe's reconstruction efforts. The

---

[1] This chapter was contributed by the World Bank's Pascale Hélène Dubois, Paul Ezzeddin, and Collin David Swan.

[2] The term "World Bank Group" incorporates the World Bank (IBRD and IDA) and three other agencies: the International Finance Corporation (IFC), which makes equity investments and provides loans, guarantees, and advisory services to private-sector business in developing countries; the Multilateral Investment Guarantee Agency (MIGA), which provides political risk insurance guarantees to private-sector investors and lenders; and the International Centre for Settlement of Investment Disputes (ICSID), which provides facilities for conciliation and arbitration of international investment disputes.

[3] THE WORLD BANK, A GUIDE TO THE WORLD BANK 3 (3d ed. 2011).

From Baksheesh to Bribery. T. Markus Funk and Andrew S. Boutros.
© Oxford University Press 2019. Published 2019 by Oxford University Press.

Bank issued its first loan on May 9, 1947, to France for postwar reconstruction, valued at $250 million.[4] The Bank has since evolved into a development institution working to eliminate extreme poverty and boost shared prosperity among its member countries. The Bank employs a diverse staff of economists, public policy experts, sectoral experts, lawyers, and social scientists at its headquarters in Washington, DC, and its various country offices around the globe.[5]

Today, the Bank consists of 189 member countries, or shareholders, who are represented on the Bank's Board of Executive Directors.[6] The Bank's member countries that are borrowers use Bank financing and other forms of assistance ranging from loans and grants to technical assistance and policy advice. The Bank works in partnership with a wide range of actors, including government agencies, civil society organizations, other aid agencies, and the private sector.[7]

In 2014, the World Bank Group adopted two ambitious goals: (1) eradicating extreme poverty by reducing the number of people living on less than $1.25 a day to 3 percent by 2030, and (2) promoting shared prosperity by fostering the income growth of the bottom 40 percent in every country.[8] The Bank has leveraged the strength of its institutions and their unique ability to partner with the public and private sectors to deliver customized development solutions.[9] In Fiscal Year 2018, the Bank committed $66.9 billion in financing through loans, grants, equity investments, and guarantees to its member countries and to private businesses.[10]

2. Recognizing the Need for an Anti-Corruption Regime
2.1 POLICY BASIS FOR THE BANK'S SANCTIONS SYSTEM

The Bank's Articles of Agreement require that Bank funds be used for their intended purposes and with due attention to economy and efficiency.[11] In furtherance of this fiduciary

---

[4] *The World Bank's First Loan*, WORLD BANK, *available at* http://www.worldbank.org/en/about/archives/history/exhibits/the-world-banks-first-loan (last visited Dec. 12, 2018).

[5] The World Bank currently has more than 10,000 employees in more than 120 offices worldwide. *See What We Do*, WORLD BANK, *available at* http://www.worldbank.org/en/about/what-we-do (last visited Dec. 12, 2018).

[6] IBRD consists of 189 member countries, and IDA consists of 173 member countries. *See Member Countries*, WORLD BANK, *available at* http://www.worldbank.org/en/about/leadership/members#1 (last updated July 27, 2018).

[7] The World Bank, *supra* note 3, at 3.

[8] THE WORLD BANK, THE WORLD BANK GROUP A TO Z 39 (2015).

[9] *Id.*

[10] THE WORLD BANK, WORLD BANK ANNUAL REPORT 2018 7 (2018), *available at* http://www.worldbank.org/en/about/annual-report.

[11] International Bank for Reconstruction and Development Articles of Agreement, art. III, § 5(b) (as amended, effective June 27, 2012) ("The Bank shall make arrangements to ensure that the proceeds of any loan are used only for the purposes for which the loan was granted, with due attention to considerations of economy and efficiency and without regard to political or other non-economic influences or considerations."); *see also* International Development Association Articles of Agreement, art. V, §6 (Sept. 24, 1960) ("The Association and its officers shall not interfere in the political affairs of any member; nor shall they be influenced in their decisions by the political character of the member or members concerned. Only economic considerations shall

duty, the Bank's anti-corruption measures seek to incorporate processes that ensure standards of good governance and conformity with principles of the rule of law.[12] Recognizing that fraud and corruption weaken institutions and divert essential resources from poverty-eradication efforts, over the past two decades, the Bank has introduced, enhanced, and enforced a variety of administrative instruments to combat fraud and corruption in Bank-financed projects. One of the key aspects of this effort has been the ongoing development of the Bank's suspension and debarment system. This system, often referred to as the Bank's "sanctions system" or "sanctions regime," is designed to exclude proven wrongdoers from Bank-financed operations while ensuring that accused parties are treated fairly and given a chance to mount a defense. The sanctions system also has valuable spillover effects and serves to deter certain would-be wrongdoers from engaging in misconduct, encourages prevention and compliance, and incentivizes rehabilitation.[13]

Indeed, according to Richard Thornburgh, the former UN Undersecretary General and U.S. Attorney General, the withholding of future business—that is, debarment—is a common tool used by national governments against wrongdoers "frequently in conjunction with a criminal proceeding in the national courts or a civil action for recovery of loss."[14] International institutions such as the World Bank, however, lack the ability to bring criminal proceedings, although they may refer matters to the relevant national authorities. "An international organization's likely recourse" is thus "the simple preventive action of refraining from doing any business with the firm in the future[.]"[15]

2.2 RECOGNIZING FRAUD AND CORRUPTION IN BANK-FINANCED PROJECTS

Until the mid-1990s, the Bank considered issues related to fraud and corruption to fall outside its mandate as a development organization. "For many years, corruption was seen as primarily, if not exclusively, a political problem with little or no relevance to economic development."[16] The corrosive effects of corruption and fraud on economic development were publicly highlighted by former Bank president James Wolfensohn in a 1996 speech.[17] Wolfensohn called on the institution to "deal with the cancer of corruption," setting the

---

be relevant to their decisions, and these considerations shall be weighed impartially in order to achieve the purposes stated in this Agreement.").

[12] Anne-Marie Leroy & Frank Fariello, *The World Bank Group Sanctions Process and Its Recent Reforms*, 7 (World Bank 2011), *available at* http://siteresources.worldbank.org/INTLAWJUSTICE/Resources/SanctionsProcess.pdf.

[13] Pascale Hélène Dubois, *Domestic and Administrative Tools to Combat Fraud & Corruption: A Comparison of US Suspension and Debarment with the World Bank's Sanctions System*, 2012 U. CHI. LEGAL F. 195, 217 (2012).

[14] DICK THORNBURGH, RONALD L. GAINER & CUYLER H. WALKER, REPORT CONCERNING THE DEBARMENT PROCESSES OF THE WORLD BANK 3 (Aug. 14, 2002), *available at* http://siteresources.worldbank.org/PROCUREMENT/Resources/thornburghreport.pdf.

[15] *Id.* at 4.

[16] Leroy & Fariello, *supra* note 12, at 9.

[17] James D. Wolfensohn, President, World Bank, Annual Meetings Address: People and Development (Oct. 1, 1996).

Bank on the path to a series of changes in its lending program and fiduciary processes. President Wolfensohn pledged the Bank's support for international efforts to fight corruption and establish voluntary standards of behavior.[18] Soon after, the Bank created a formal mechanism for debarring parties that engaged in fraud and corruption in connection with Bank-financed projects.[19] This new mechanism complemented long-used procurement remedies, such as declarations of misprocurement and suspension of payment for projects (or parts of projects) when fiduciary breaches were discovered.

2.3 INITIAL ONE-TIER SANCTIONS SYSTEM

The Bank's sanctions process was first formulated in a paper presented to the Bank's Board of Executive Directors in July 1996,[20] and was implemented in a January 1998 Operational Memorandum.[21] Consistent with the Board paper and the Operational Memorandum, the President established a Sanctions Committee in November 1998 to review allegations of fraud and corruption[22] and to recommend to the President sanctions to be imposed on those firms or individuals found to have engaged in fraudulent or corrupt activities.[23] The Sanctions Committee, composed of senior Bank staff, reviewed allegations of fraud and corruption by bidders, contractors, suppliers, and consultants in Bank-financed projects and recommended an appropriate sanction to the President of the Bank, who took the final decision on any sanction.[24] In August 2001, the Bank drafted detailed written procedures to govern the debarment proceedings conducted before the Bank's Sanctions Committee.[25]

---

[18] *Id.*

[19] Leroy & Fariello, *supra* note 12, at 9.

[20] The World Bank, *Fraud and Corruption—Proposed Amendments in the Bank's Loan Documents for the Purpose of Making Them More Effective in the Fight against Fraud and Corruption, World Bank Board Paper R96-112/1* (July 11, 1996).

[21] The World Bank, *Operational Memorandum on Fraud and Corruption under Bank-Financed Contracts: Procedures for Dealing with Allegations against Bidders, Suppliers, Contractors, or Consultants* (Jan. 5, 1998).

[22] The 1999 version of the Bank's *Guidelines: Procurement under IBRD Loans and IDA Credits* defined "corrupt practice" as "the offering, giving, receiving, or soliciting of any thing of value to influence the action of a public official in the procurement process or in contract execution," and "fraudulent practice" as "a misrepresentation of facts in order to influence a procurement process or the execution of a contract to the detriment of the Borrower, and includes collusive practices among bidders (prior to or after bid submission) designed to establish prices at artificial, non-competitive levels and to deprive the Borrower of the benefits of free and open competition." World Bank, *Guidelines: Procurement under IBRD Loans and IDA Credits*, § 1.15(a) (Jan. 1999).

[23] *World Bank Group Sanctions Regime: An Overview*, The World Bank, at 10, *available at* http://siteresources. worldbank.org/EXTOFFEVASUS/Resources/Overview-SecM2010-0543.pdf; *see also* The World Bank, Procurement: Sanctions Committee, *available at:* http://go.worldbank.org/BJ9P6TARY1 (last visited Feb. 23, 2016).

[24] *Id.*

[25] THE WORLD BANK OFFICE OF SUSPENSION AND DEBARMENT, REPORT ON FUNCTIONS, DATA AND LESSONS LEARNED 2007–2015: SECOND EDITION (2015) 8, *available at* http://go.worldbank.org/ E3OQKOCVP0 [hereinafter "OSD Report"].

2.4 THE THORNBURGH REPORT

In 2002, the Bank undertook a comprehensive review of the sanctions process and commissioned Richard Thornburgh to prepare a report on the Bank's process and to recommend possible reforms.[26] In his final report, Thornburgh noted in particular that "[a]ll organizations of any size occasionally find themselves victims of fraud or corruption" and that "[t]he manner in which they respond to such fraud and corruption depends to a certain degree upon the nature of the organization—in particular whether it is a business corporation, a national governmental agency, or, like the World Bank, an international organization."[27]

Noting the unique position of the World Bank as an international financial institution, the Thornburgh Report asserted that the Bank's interests would be best served "by debarment procedures that (1) would effectively and efficiently protect the monies entrusted to the Bank, and (2) would assure a fair opportunity for a firm to explain its interpretation of the facts underlying any allegations against it."[28] Among Thornburgh's many recommendations were the proposed adoption of procedures that would "(a) enable the Bank to dispose a significant proportion of cases without the necessity of a full hearing before the Sanctions Committee and (b) permit the Bank temporarily to suspend a respondent from eligibility for new Bank-financed contracts pending the final disposition of a debarment matter."[29]

2.5 DEVELOPMENT OF A TWO-TIERED SANCTIONS SYSTEM

In July 2004, in light of past experience and following a review of the recommendations made by Thornburgh, the Bank's Board of Executive Directors approved a series of significant changes to the sanctions system, including:

(a) Modifying the membership of the World Bank Group Sanctions Board ("Sanctions Board"), the successor to the Sanctions Committee, to include both World Bank staff and external members;

(b) Establishing the new staff position of IBRD/IDA Evaluation and Suspension Officer (now called the Chief Suspension and Debarment Officer or SDO) to impose temporary suspensions and provide for the early disposition of cases;

(c) Introducing measures to address a perceived need for more flexible sanctions;

(d) Explicitly recognizing cooperation as a mitigating factor in sanctions determinations; and

(e) Creating additional incentives for contractors to voluntarily disclose information about fraud and corruption in World-Bank-financed projects.[30]

---

[26] Thornburgh et al., *supra* note 14.

[27] *Id.* at 2.

[28] *Id.* at 8.

[29] *Id.* at 36.

[30] OSD Report, *supra* note 25, at 9. *See also* THE WORLD BANK GROUP, ANNUAL REPORT ON INVESTIGATIONS AND SANCTIONS OF STAFF MISCONDUCT AND FRAUD AND CORRUPTION IN BANK-FINANCED PROJECTS FISCAL 2004, WORLD BANK BOARD REPORT 31575, Appendix at 3 (Jan. 1, 2004).

The 2004 sanctions reforms also extended the coverage of the sanctions system to the International Finance Corporation (IFC) and the Multilateral Investment Guarantee Agency (MIGA), as well as the World Bank's Partial Risk Guarantee (PRG) operations.[31]

Seeking to fully implement the 2004 recommendations and continue to improve the sanctions system, the Bank undertook an in-depth review of its anti-corruption activities in 2005.[32] This review resulted in:

(a) the expansion of the sanctions system beyond procurement to cover, more generally, fraud and corruption that may occur in connection with the use of Bank loan proceeds in the preparation and/or implementation of Bank-financed investment projects;

(b) the adoption of new definitions of corrupt, fraudulent, collusive, and coercive practices;[33] and

(c) the adoption of "obstructive practices" as a separate sanctionable offense, covering both noncompliance with the World Bank's third-party audit rights and deliberate obstruction of World Bank investigations.[34]

The Board of Executive Directors approved the changes in August 2006, and new sanctions procedures were developed, with an effective date of October 15, 2006. In November 2006, the first SDO for IBRD/IDA was selected.[35]

3. Anti-Corruption Efforts: The Bank's Current Sanctions Process

Under the current system, allegations that a firm or individual has engaged in a Sanctionable Practice are investigated by the World Bank's Integrity Vice Presidency (INT).[36] If, after completing its investigation, INT believes there is sufficient evidence to support a finding that the firm or individual has engaged in misconduct, INT submits a Statement of Accusations

---

[31] The World Bank, *Sanctions Reform: Expansion of Sanctions Regime Beyond Procurement and Sanctioning of Obstructive Practices, World Bank Board Papers R2006-0149* (July 28, 2006). Today, each of IFC, MIGA, and the Bank's guarantees program has a sanctions system that closely parallels that of the Bank.

[32] The World Bank, *Sanctions Reform: Expansion of Sanctions Regime beyond Procurement and Sanctioning of Obstructive Practices—Information Note for Borrowers* (July 2006), *available at* http://siteresources.worldbank.org/PROJECTS/Resources/40940-1173795340221/SanctionsReformNoteBorrowers.pdf.

[33] For the definitions of sanctions practices as they have developed over time, *see* www.worldbank.org/sanctions, "Key and Reference Documents." The current definitions of corrupt, fraudulent, collusive, and coercive practices have been largely harmonized across the World Bank and its partner multilateral development banks. Frank Fariello & Conrad Daly, "Coordinating the Fight against Corruption among MDBs: The Past, Present, and Future of Sanctions," 45 GEO. WASH. INT'L L. REV. 253, 261 (2013).

[34] The World Bank, *Sanctions Reform—Information Note for Borrowers, supra* note 32.

[35] OSD Report, *supra* note 25, at 9. The officers responsible for suspension and debarment at IFC, MIGA and in the World Bank's guarantee operations are referred to as those institutions' "Evaluation and Suspension Officers" (EOs).

[36] *See* The World Bank Group Integrity Vice Presidency, http://www.worldbank.org/integrity (last visited Dec. 12, 2018).

and Evidence (SAE) to the Office of Suspension and Debarment (OSD).[37] The SDO reviews INT's submission and determines whether there is sufficient evidence to support a finding that it is more likely than not that the alleged misconduct occurred. If the SDO concludes that the record contains insufficient evidence to support one or more of the accusations in the SAE, the case is referred back to INT for revision and/or further investigation.[38]

If sufficient evidence is found, the SDO then applies the World Bank's Sanctioning Guidelines to determine the appropriate sanction.[39] Under the Sanctioning Guidelines, the baseline sanction is a three-year debarment with conditional release.[40] The SDO will also consider any evidence in the record of mitigating or aggravating factors (as listed in the Sanctioning Guidelines) that would result in an upward or downward adjustment to the base sanction.[41] Upon arriving at an appropriate sanction based on the Sanctioning Guidelines, the SDO issues a Notice of Sanctions Proceedings to the respondent firm and/or individual found to have engaged in the misconduct.[42] The Notice includes the allegations, evidence, and the above-mentioned sanction. Upon issuance of the Notice, the respondent is temporarily suspended from eligibility to be awarded new Bank-financed contracts pending the final outcome of the proceedings.[43] Any existing or ongoing contracts held by the respondent are not affected, although borrowers are required to "apply additional due diligence by closely supervising and monitoring any on-going contract (whether under prior or post review) executed by a firm or individual which has been sanctioned by the Bank after such contract was signed."[44]

Upon receiving a Notice of Sanctions Proceedings, the respondent may submit a written explanation (known as an "Explanation") to the SDO within 30 days after the Notice's delivery stating why the Notice should be withdrawn or the recommended sanction revised.[45]

---

[37] Bank Procedure: Sanctions Proceedings and Settlements in Bank Financed Projects § 3.A, ¶ 3.01(b) (June 28, 2016) [hereinafter World Bank Sanctions Procedures], *available at* http://siteresources.worldbank. org/EXTOFFEVASUS/Resources/3601045-1377105390925/Procedure_Bank_Procedure_Sanctions_Proceedings_and_Settlements_in_Bank_Financed_Projects(6.28.2016).pdf.

[38] *See* OSD Report, *supra* note 25, at 11. In 36 percent of cases reviewed, OSD has determined that there was insufficient evidence to support one or more accusations. *See id.* at 32.

[39] *See* World Bank Sanctioning Guidelines (Jan. 15, 2011), *available at* http://siteresources.worldbank.org/EXTOFFEVASUS/Resources/WorldBankSanctioningGuidelines.pdf.

[40] *Id.*

[41] *Id.*

[42] World Bank Sanctions Procedures § 3.A, ¶ 4.01.

[43] *Id.* ¶ 4.02(a). The World Bank may suspend respondents from eligibility during the investigation phase, prior to the submission of an SAE. INT may present to the SDO a Request for Temporary Suspension before concluding an investigation if it believes there is sufficient evidence to support a finding of at least one Sanctionable Practice against a respondent and it is likely to conclude the investigation and present an SAE to the SDO within one year. *Id.* ¶ 2.01. If the SDO determines that the evidence is sufficient to support a finding that the respondent has engaged in at least one Sanctionable Practice, the SDO may issue a Notice of Temporary Suspension and impose a temporary suspension on the respondent lasting no longer than one year.

[44] World Bank *Guidelines: Procurement of Goods, Works, and Non-consulting Services under IBRD Loans and IDA Credits & Grants*, Appendix at 1 § 8 (Jan. 2011); *see also* World Bank, *Guidelines: Selection and Employment of Consultants under IBRD Loans & IDA Credits & Grants by World Bank Borrowers*, Appendix at 1 § 8 (Jan. 2011).

[45] World Bank Sanctions Procedures § 3.A, ¶ 4.02(b).

If the respondent does not appeal to the World Bank Group's Sanctions Board, the sanction recommended by the SDO is imposed after 90 days following the Notice's delivery,[46] and a public determination—known as a "Notice of Uncontested Sanctions Proceedings"—is published on OSD's website.[47]

If the respondent wishes to further contest the allegations and/or the recommended sanction, it may file a response (known as a "Response") with the World Bank Group's Sanctions Board within 90 days following the Notice's delivery (the respondent need not have filed an Explanation beforehand).[48] The Sanctions Board is the second tier of the Bank's administrative sanctions process and is comprised of seven external members, each serving a non-renewable term of six years.[49] The Sanctions Board meets several times a year to review cases de novo after receiving pleadings from both the respondent and INT. The Sanctions Board may also hold an administrative hearing in a case if requested by INT or a respondent.[50] In deciding each case, the Sanctions Board considers "INT's allegations and evidence as presented in the Notice of Sanctions Proceedings; the respondent's arguments and evidence submitted in response to the Notice; INT's reply brief; the parties' presentations at a hearing, if applicable; and any other materials contained in the record."[51] Full decisions of the Sanctions Board have been published since 2012 and are publicly available on its website.[52]

If a respondent is found to have committed a Sanctionable Practice, the SDO or the Sanctions Board will impose one of the following sanctions: (1) debarment with conditional release, (2) fixed-term debarment, (3) conditional non-debarment, (4) letter of reprimand, or (5) restitution.[53] As stated in the Bank's Sanctioning Guidelines, the baseline sanction is a three-year debarment with conditional release,[54] meaning that the firm or individual is declared ineligible to receive new World-Bank-financed contracts for three years and will be released from debarment only upon completion of specific conditions imposed by the Integrity Compliance Officer, an independent office housed within INT.[55] Debarments and

---

[46] *Id.* ¶ 4.04.

[47] *See* Suspension and Debarment Officer Determinations in Uncontested Proceedings, http://web. worldbank.org/WBSITE/EXTERNAL/EXTABOUTUS/ORGANIZATION/ORGUNITS/ EXTOFFEVASUS/0,,contentMDK:22911816~menuPK:7926949~pagePK:64168445~piPK:64168309~th eSitePK:3601046,00.html (last visited Dec. 12, 2018) .

[48] World Bank Sanctions Procedures § 3.A, ¶ 5.01(a).

[49] WBG Policy: Statute of the Sanctions Board § 3.A, ¶ 4 (Oct. 18, 2016), *available at* http://siteresources. worldbank.org/EXTOFFEVASUS/Resources/3601045-1377105390925/WBG_Policy_Statute_of_the_ Sanctions_Board_(10.18.2016).pdf.

[50] The World Bank Group Sanctions Board Law Digest, at 19 (Dec. 2011), *available at* http://siteresources. worldbank.org/INTOFFEVASUS/Resources/3601037-1342729035803/SanctionsBoardLawDigest.pdf.

[51] *Id.*

[52] *See* Sanctions Board Decisions, http://web.worldbank.org/WBSITE/EXTERNAL/EXTABOUTUS/ ORGANIZATION/ORGUNITS/EXTOFFEVASUS/0,,contentMDK:23059612~pagePK:64168445~pi PK:64168309~theSitePK:3601046,00.html (last visited Dec. 12, 2018).

[53] World Bank Sanctions Procedures § 3.A, ¶ 9.01. These sanctions may extend to any affiliates that control, or are controlled by, the respondent. *Id.* ¶ 9.04(b).

[54] World Bank Sanctioning Guidelines (Jan. 15, 2011).

[55] World Bank Sanctions Procedures § 3.A, ¶ 9.03. *See also* The World Bank Group, *Summary of World Bank Group Integrity Compliance Guidelines*, http://siteresources.worldbank.org/INTDOII/Resources/ IntegrityComplianceGuidelines_2_1_11web.pdf (last visited Dec. 12, 2018).

other sanctions are posted on the World Bank's public website and are therefore observable by any number of interested parties conducting due diligence prior to a procurement or other business decision.[56]

The Integrity Compliance Officer has the authority to determine whether a sanctioned entity has satisfied the imposed conditions, such as implementing a corporate compliance program.[57] As noted in the Summary of the World Bank Group Integrity Compliance Guidelines, "the establishment (or improvement) and implementation of an integrity compliance program satisfactory to the [Bank] will be a principal condition to ending a debarment (or conditional non-debarment)[.]"[58] The Bank's Integrity Compliance Guidelines detail the key aspects of an acceptable integrity compliance program, including a clear prohibition of misconduct and the creation and maintenance of a "trust-based, inclusive organizational culture that encourages ethical conduct, a commitment to compliance with the law and a culture in which [m]isconduct is not tolerated."[59] The Integrity Compliance Guidelines encourage the respondent to carry out a comprehensive risk assessment and address identified shortcomings.[60] Other considerations include the development and maintenance of clear internal policies designed to "prevent, detect, investigate and remediate" misconduct, as well as internal controls, training and communication, incentives, and reporting policies.[61]

Finally, INT has the authority to enter into negotiated settlements with firms or individuals at any point prior to the completion of sanctions proceedings, including during the investigation phase. These settlements are known as Negotiated Resolution Agreements, and are subject to a number of safeguards, must be cleared with the World Bank Group General Counsel, and are reviewed by the SDO to ensure that the settlement was entered into voluntarily and that the agreed sanction does not manifestly violate the Bank's Sanctioning Guidelines.[62] INT also operates a Voluntary Disclosure Program, under which entities may voluntarily disclose to the Bank the results of an internal investigation into past misconduct on Bank-financed projects in exchange for confidentiality and continued eligibility to receive Bank-financed contracts. Among other things, participants in the Program must implement a robust internal compliance program and commit not to engage in future misconduct.[63] The Bank monitors the internal compliance programs of participants for a period of three years.[64] A firm that violates the provisions of the Voluntary Disclosure Program will be debarred for a period of 10 years.[65]

---

[56] *See* World Bank Listing of Ineligible Firms & Individuals, http://www.worldbank.org/debarr (last visited Dec. 12, 2018).

[57] World Bank Sanctions Procedures § 3.A, ¶ 9.03.

[58] The World Bank Group, *Summary of World Bank Compliance Guidelines, supra* note 55.

[59] *Id.*

[60] *Id.*

[61] *Id.*

[62] World Bank Sanctions Procedures § 3.A, ¶ 11.02. *See also* World Bank Sanctioning Guidelines (Jan. 15, 2011).

[63] *See* Voluntary Disclosure Program, http://siteresources.worldbank.org/INTVOLDISPRO/Resources/ VDPGuidelinesforParticipants.pdf (last visited Dec.13, 2018).

[64] *Id.*

[65] World Bank Sanctions Procedures § 9.01(c) n.18.

4. Cross-Debarment among Multilateral Development Banks

In 2010, the Bank entered into a cross-debarment agreement with other large multilateral development banks (MDBs) in an effort to enhance the impact of their respective debarments. This agreement provides for the mutual recognition of debarments imposed by the Bank and the African Development Bank, the European Bank for Reconstruction and Development, the Asian Development Bank, and the Inter-American Development Bank.[66] If a firm or individual is debarred by one of these MDBs for more than one year, it is debarred by the others, subject to certain limited exceptions.[67] Through June 30, 2015, the Bank had enforced more than 150 debarments imposed by other MDBs under the MDB cross-debarment agreement.

5. Criminal Action and Referrals to National Authorities

As a quasi-judicial administrative process, the Bank's sanctions system does not have the power to impose criminal or civil penalties. The sanctions system is most similar to the administrative suspension and debarment processes found in an increasing number of national procurement regimes, although there is no exact parallel.[68] Elements of a variety of existing models were used as points of reference in developing the rules of the Bank's sanctions system, including national suspension and debarment systems. But other comparisons may be equally informative, such as with various criminal and civil law regimes, other administrative law tribunals, contract and tort law, and parallel arrangements in other international organizations.[69]

The misconduct addressed by the Bank's suspension and debarment system is often of a nature that would be considered criminal in many countries, and the Bank refers such cases to national governments for their consideration and action, as appropriate.[70] When INT believes that the laws of a Bank member country may have been broken, it refers those findings to the relevant authorities.[71] Indeed, INT notes that "[r]eferring the findings of our investigations to national law enforcement authorities has been instrumental in helping countries advance their own anti-corruption work."[72] As stated in a recent INT Annual Update, INT views national anti-corruption authorities as "critical partners" in the global

---

[66] The agreement is available online at http://siteresources.worldbank.org/NEWS/Resources/AgreementForM utualEnforcementofDebarmentDecisions.pdf.

[67] S. Zimmermann & F. Fariello, "Coordinating the Fight against Fraud and Corruption: Agreement on Cross-Debarment among Multilateral Development Banks," 3 WORLD BANK LEGAL REV. 189 (2012).

[68] OSD Report, *supra* note 25, at 8; Leroy & Fariello, *supra* note 12, at 7.

[69] *See, e.g.*, Dubois, *supra* note 13.

[70] OSD Report, *supra* note 25, at 8.

[71] World Bank Group Integrity Vice Presidency, *FY13 Annual Update*, at 6 (2013), *available at* http://www-wds. worldbank.org/external/default/WDSContentServer/WDSP/IB/2013/10/16/000356161_20131016131322/ Rendered/PDF/818580BR0Intego10PUBLIC00Box379845B.pdf.

[72] The World Bank Group, *Integrity Vice Presidency Annual Update for Fiscal Year 2015*, at 14 (2015), *available at* http://siteresources.worldbank.org/EXTDOII/Resources/588920-1444050544186/INT_FY15_Annual_ Update.pdf.

fight against corruption.[73] INT has cooperated with national authorities from around the world on various anti-corruption efforts.[74] Stephen Zimmermann, former INT Director of Operations, has credited "cooperation with other entities, with our development partners, the private sector and with national authorities" as "a key enabler of success in [INT's] work."[75] The World Bank's International Corruption Hunters Alliance (ICHA) aims to enhance the dialogue among national authorities by bringing together "heads and senior officials of corruption fighting bodies from around the world . . . to share innovations, push the policy envelope, and collaborate in solving cases."[76]

6. Statistics on the Functioning of the Bank's Sanctions System

In November 2015, OSD released the second edition of its public report in an effort to share information on the functioning of the Bank's sanctions system, entitled "The World Bank Office of Suspension and Debarment: Report on Functions, Data, and Lessons Learned."[77] The second edition provides case processing data and other performance metrics related to 251 sanctions cases submitted to OSD from the office's creation in 2007 through June 30, 2015, which have resulted in 368 sanctions imposed on firms and individuals (including sanctions resulting from 52 settlement agreements between the respondent and INT).[78]

The vast majority of cases and settlements (86 percent) received by OSD from its inception through June 30, 2015 involved at least one accusation of fraudulent practice, while accusations of corruption occurred in 18 percent of cases and settlements.[79] A little less than half of the fraud cases related to accusations of forged third-party documents, such as bank guarantees, and manufacturer's authorizations.[80] OSD saw fewer instances of accusations of collusion (8 percent), obstruction (4 percent), and coercion (1 percent).[81]

OSD's report also provides a breakdown of OSD's determinations. In 96 percent of the cases that OSD reviewed through June 30, 2015, OSD determined that there was sufficient

---

[73] *See* The World Bank Group, *Integrity Vice Presidency Annual Update Fiscal Year 2014*, at 24 (2014), *available at* http://siteresources.worldbank.org/EXTDOII/Resources/588920-1412626296780/INT_Annual_Update_ FY14_WEB.pdf.

[74] *Id.* at 24–25.

[75] Stephen Zimmermann, *International Organizations Tip the Scale towards Integrity*, THE FCPA BLOG (Jan. 12, 2016), *available at* http://www.fcpablog.com/blog/2016/1/12/stephen-zimmermann-international-organizations-tip-the-scale.html.

[76] *Id.* More information on the ICHA is available at http://www.worldbank.org/en/about/unit/integrity-vice-presidency/icha.

[77] OSD Report, *supra* note 25.

[78] *Id.* at 25. Through June 30, 2015, OSD also imposed temporary suspensions on 359 firms and individuals. This includes 18 temporary suspensions that were imposed pursuant to the "early temporary suspension" (ETS) procedure. *Id.* at 26.

[79] *Id.* at 30.

[80] *Id.* at 31.

[81] *Id.* at 30. The total of the percentages exceeds 100 percent because a number of cases involved claims of more than one type of sanctionable practice (for example, payment of a bribe (corrupt practice) and the submission of false documents (fraudulent practice)).

evidence to support at least one of the claims made by INT against one or more respondents.[82] In 36 percent of the cases reviewed, OSD determined that there was insufficient evidence to support one or more of the claims made by INT, resulting in the referral of the case back to INT for revision. In a slight majority of such cases, OSD found that there was insufficient evidence for all claims against one or more of the respondents, meaning that INT was required to drop those respondents from the case. In the remainder of such cases, OSD found that there was sufficient evidence for at least one claim against all respondents, but insufficient evidence for certain other claims, meaning that INT was required to drop those claims from the case.[83]

About one-third (33 percent) of sanctions cases issued by OSD were appealed to the Sanctions Board.[84] The remaining two-thirds of cases were resolved at the OSD level, meaning that the respondents failed to submit a timely response to the Sanctions Board, and the SDO imposed the recommended sanction through a public Notice of Uncontested Sanctions Proceedings.[85]

7. Conclusion

Recent estimates put the costs of fraud and corruption to the global economy at up to 5 percent of GDP.[86] When it comes to development, this diversion of scarce resources ends up having the greatest impact on those who are supposed to benefit the most: the poor. The World Bank has worked to battle against the damage caused by corruption, both by working with its partners to deter and prevent it from occurring and by enforcing the Bank's rules through debarment when corruption is detected. From 1999 through 2015 the Bank had debarred or otherwise sanctioned more than 700 firms and individuals (not including MDB cross-debarments). The Bank has also worked hard to create a sanctions system that is efficient, effective, and fair, offering accused parties a fair process through which they can present their defense.

---

[82] *Id.* at 32.

[83] *Id.*

[84] *Id.* at 33.

[85] *Id.*

[86] *See* International Chamber of Commerce, Transparency International, the United Nations Global Compact & The World Economic Forum Partnering Against Corruption Initiative, *Clean Business Is Good Business* (2008), *available at* https://www.unglobalcompact.org/library/158.

24 Corporate Monitors and the Monitorship Process

1. Introduction

The prospect of a Foreign Corrupt Practices Act (FCPA)[1] monitor[2] and its associated cost, effort, and scrutiny is unpleasant for a company that just emerged from what likely was a long, expensive, and invasive investigation and just wants to get back to business. A creature borne entirely of the terms of a settlement with enforcement authorities, a monitorship is rarely welcomed by companies, and monitorships can, and sometimes do, go very wrong. A monitorship need not be unnecessarily contentious or expensive, however, and, when properly executed, can be a helpful endeavor that leads to a stronger company.

The monitor is an independent party usually tasked with ensuring that an offending company complies with the terms of the resolution and implements anti-corruption policies, procedures, and controls reasonably designed to detect and prevent FCPA violations. A monitor evaluates the company's anti-corruption compliance program, determines if it is reasonably designed and implemented, makes recommendations for improvement, and sets forth his or her observations in periodic written reports to the company and U.S. government. To do so, monitors interview employees, review documents, make site visits to domestic and international locations, and conduct various analyses and testing—all of which will be called for in the company's settlement papers.

---

[1] This chapter was contributed by Gibson Dunn's F. Joseph Warin, Michael Diamant, and Christopher Sullivan.
[2] Monitors can go by various names, such as "independent consultant" or "outside compliance consultant."

From Baksheesh to Bribery. T. Markus Funk and Andrew S. Boutros.
© Oxford University Press 2019. Published 2019 by Oxford University Press.

Given this book's focus on global anti-corruption laws, this chapter considers the use of corporate compliance monitors as a condition to resolving corporate FCPA enforcement actions, where U.S. prosecutors and regulators have imposed dozens of monitors; what FCPA monitorships commonly involve; and best practices for FCPA monitorships.

2. FCPA Enforcement and Compliance Monitors

2.1 BACKGROUND

Compliance monitorships have been used in a variety of settings. In the United States, monitors have been imposed in cases involving everything from accounting fraud to drug misbranding to environmental violations to obscenity. In the area of corruption, the World Bank routinely requires monitors for companies resolving allegations of misconduct, including corruption, connected to Bank-funded projects.[3] The UK Serious Fraud Office's 2009 criminal resolution with Mabey & Johnson Ltd. for corruption-related misconduct involved the appointment of a monitor. Further, Canadian courts have appointed monitors pursuant to Canada's Corruption of Foreign Public Officials Act. And, in July 2015, French Finance Minister Michel Sapin proposed legislation that would create a legal basis in France for the imposition of independent monitors.

The dual enforcers of the FCPA—the U.S. Securities and Exchange Commission (SEC) and U.S. Department of Justice (DOJ)—have frequently imposed monitors as a term of an FCPA settlement. With the SEC, a monitorship usually appears as a term of an administrative settlement or final judgment; the DOJ usually includes a monitorship as a term of a deferred prosecution agreement (DPA), nonprosecution agreement (NPA), or plea agreement.

The convergence in the rise of FCPA enforcement and the use of alternative resolution vehicles in the last decade had contributed to the rise of FCPA monitorships. FCPA enforcement exploded in 2007,[4] and corporate DPAs and NPAs have become more popular since 2003,[5] following the Arthur Andersen indictment and formation of the DOJ Corporate Fraud Task Force, which resulted in the 2003 "Thompson Memorandum" encouraging DPAs as an alternative to indictment.[6] In the last decade, the vast majority of DPAs requiring a monitor have involved FCPA allegations.

---

[3] In fact, when the French company Alstom S.A. pleaded guilty to FCPA violations and paid a $772 million criminal fine in 2014, the U.S. Department of Justice did not require a monitor because one already had been imposed pursuant to an earlier resolution with the World Bank. For a detailed analysis of the World Bank's integrity enforcement regime, see Michael S. Diamant, Christopher W.H. Sullivan & Jason H. Smith, *Sanctionable Practices at the World Bank: Interpretation and Enforcement*, 18 U. Pa. J. Bus. L. 985 (2016).

[4] *See* F. Joseph Warin, Michael S. Diamant & Veronica S. Root, *Somebody's Watching Me: FCPA Monitorships and How They Can Work Better*, 13 U. Penn. J. Bus. L. 321, 325 (2011) (explaining the rise of FCPA enforcement in the last decade).

[5] From 2002 until 2005, the DOJ entered into almost three times as many DPAs and NPAs (31) as in the previous 10 years. Since 2005, the DOJ has averaged more than 30 settlements per year. For statistics on NPAs/DPAs between 2000 and 2015, see 2015 Year-End Update on Corporate Non-Prosecution Agreements (NPAs) and Deferred Prosecution Agreements (DPAs), Gibson Dunn (Jan. 5, 2016), *available at* http://www.gibsondunn.com/publications/Pages/2015-Year-End-Update-Corporate-Non-Prosecution-Agreements-and-Deferred-Prosecution-Agreements.aspx.

[6] *See* Washington Legal Foundation, Chapter 6. Deferred Prosecution and Non-prosecution Agreements 6-2, *available at* http://www.wlf.org/upload/chapter6DPAs.pdf; Memorandum from Larry

From 2004 through 2015, 129 companies resolved FCPA enforcement actions with the DOJ and the SEC. Nearly one-third of these companies had to retain a monitor. Recent trends show the DOJ and the SEC becoming more willing to tailor monitorships in FCPA cases—relying, at least between 2012 and 2015, more on self-reporting and hybrid-monitorships. For instance, from 2004 to 2009, a monitorship was more likely than not. But the 21 corporate FCPA enforcement actions resolved in 2014 and 2015 saw just two monitorships.

DOJ and SEC guidance confirms using an FCPA monitor as an "independent third party who assesses and monitors a company's adherence to the compliance requirements of an agreement that was designed to reduce the risk of recurrence of the company's misconduct."[7] Monitors allow prosecutors and regulators to maintain ongoing supervision of the corporation and reduce the chance of backsliding, all with little to no cost or resource allocation required by the government.

2.2 FACTORS INFLUENCING THE GOVERNMENT'S DECISION TO REQUIRE AN FCPA MONITOR

The last decade of corporate FCPA enforcement reveals no single factor as decisive in whether the DOJ or the SEC will require a company to retain a monitor. The SEC and DOJ consider a mix of factors, including the following:

- The nature and size of the company;
- The seriousness, duration, and extent of the misconduct, including whether it spans multiple geographies and/or product lines; and
- The quality of the company's anti-corruption compliance program at the time of the misconduct and the company's subsequent remedial efforts.[8]

D. Thompson, Deputy Attorney Gen., to U.S. Attorneys, Regarding Principles of Federal Prosecutions of Business Organizations (Jan. 20, 2003) [hereinafter Thompson Memorandum], *available at* http://www.usdoj. gov/dag/cftf/business-organizations.pdf. Arthur Andersen was a worldwide institution with billions in annual revenues and more than 85,000 employees. By the time the Supreme Court unanimously reversed its conviction in 2005, employees were virtually gone, partnership value had vanished, and litigants were dividing up the few remaining assets. Arthur Andersen and the DOJ reportedly discussed a DPA but failed to come to an agreement.

[7] Criminal Division of the U.S. Department of Justice and Enforcement Division of the U.S. Securities and Exchange Commission, *A Resource Guide to the U.S. Foreign Corrupt Practices Act*, at 71 (Nov. 14, 2012), *available at* https://www.justice.gov/sites/default/files/criminal-fraud/legacy/2015/01/16/guide.pdf.

[8] *Id.; see also* Memorandum from Craig S. Morford, Acting Deputy Attorney General, to the Heads of Department Components & U.S. Attorneys, on Selection and Use of Monitors in Deferred Prosecution Agreements and Non-prosecution Agreements with Corporations, at 2 (Mar. 7, 2008), *available at* http://www.justice.gov/dag/ morford-useofmonitorsmemo-03072008.pdf [hereinafter Morford Memorandum]; Memorandum from Brian A. Benczkowski, Assistant Attorney General, to All Criminal Division Personnel, on Selection of Monitors in Criminal Division Matters, at 2 (Oct. 11, 2018), *available at* https://www.justice.gov/opa/speech/file/1100531/ download [hereinafter Benczkowski Memorandum].

Other factors, such as the profits generated, the nature of the misconduct, or a company's voluntary disclosure, do not appear to play a key role in determining whether a company receives a monitor.[9]

Two factors have emerged as most determinative of whether an FCPA settlement will include a monitor: (1) the systemic nature of the misconduct, and (2) the quality of the anti-corruption compliance program to prevent and detect similar issues. Misconduct that stems from a corporate culture of corruption or a deficient or nonexistent set of internal controls is more likely to earn a monitor. Because FCPA cases often reveal systemic cultural and internal controls problems at a company, it is unsurprising that the government often imposes a monitor as a term of an FCPA settlement.

2.2.1 Culture of Corruption

Misconduct that was viewed within the organization as a way of doing business weighs heavily in favor of a monitor. In contrast, where a violation results from the bad acts of an isolated set of employees in contravention of company policy, a monitor is less likely. This is intuitive, because the government understands that no anti-corruption compliance program—even one that is best in class—can prevent all misconduct.

The German corporate giant Siemens AG, which settled civil and criminal FCPA charges in 2008, allegedly made thousands of corrupt payments to third parties, totaling approximately $1.4 billion, around the world, across multiple corporate segments, and in the face of warnings to top management.[10] Despite extensive remedial efforts and an expansive internal investigation, Siemens received a monitor for four years.

By contrast, the SEC did not require Mead Johnson Nutrition to retain a monitor to resolve FCPA allegations. Certain employees of Mead Johnson's Chinese subsidiary allegedly used marketing funds to improperly compensate healthcare professionals in China. In contrast to Siemens, the conduct was limited to certain employees of the single subsidiary and was in contravention of company policy, and there was no indication that senior management was involved.

Ingrained business practices are difficult to uproot. In cases involving a pervasive culture of corruption, a monitor can serve as a transformational function, helping a company take steps to stamp out lingering pockets of noncompliance. Indeed, the DOJ's 2003 "McNulty Memorandum," which provides guidance regarding corporate offenders, advises that "the government [should] address and be a force for positive change of corporate culture [and] alter corporate behavior."[11] The SEC's "Seaboard Report" likewise advise securities enforcers

---

[9] For example, from 2004 to 2015, resolutions with a voluntary disclosure were just as likely to include a monitor as resolutions without one—nearly one-third of the time. Further, several companies resolved FCPA allegations in connection with the Oil-for-Food program (OFFP), but few of the OFFP cases resulted in monitorships. Except for Ingersoll-Rand, only companies whose enforcement action covered conduct beyond the OFFP—namely, Daimler, Innospec, Siemens, and Weatherford—received monitors.

[10] See Complaint at 2, SEC v. Siemens Aktiengesellschaft (D.D.C. Dec. 12, 2008), *available at* http://www.siemens.com/press/pool/de/events/2008-12-PK/SEC.pdf.

[11] Memorandum from Paul J. McNulty, Deputy Attorney General, U.S. Department of Justice, to Heads of Department Components, U.S. Attorneys (Dec. 12, 2006), *available at* http://www.usdoj.gov/dag/speeches/2006/mcnulty_memo.pdf.

to consider whether "a tone of lawlessness [was] set by those in control of the company."[12] Such a task is well-suited for a monitor, who is insulated from the pressures of internal politics and business demands.

2.2.2 Deficient Anti-Corruption Compliance Program

The lack of an effective anti-corruption compliance program is perhaps the most important factor in whether a company gets a monitor. The DOJ's 2008 "Morford Memorandum" specifically states that "it may be appropriate to use a monitor where a company does not have an effective internal compliance program, or where it needs to establish necessary internal controls."[13] The DOJ's 2018 "Benczkowski Memorandum" likewise provides that the DOJ should consider whether the underlying misconduct involved "the exploitation of an inadequate compliance program or internal control systems."[14] The Seaboard Report also provides that leniency is more appropriate for companies with effective compliance programs.[15]

Developing an effective program can be complex, expensive, and time-intensive. A company that has endured an enforcement action typically understands the need for anti-corruption compliance and already will have taken steps to improve its program—sometimes, building one from the ground up. In such situations, a monitor can provide the motivation to ensure that the necessary support is provided within the company to see the program implemented and functioning well—and that it becomes entrenched within the fabric of the organization.

3. Common Terms of FCPA Monitorships

In 2008, Acting Deputy Attorney General Craig S. Morford issued the "Morford Memorandum," which sets forth principles that federal prosecutors should follow in using monitors in DPAs. In addition to providing guidance on monitor selection, the Morford Memorandum discusses the scope of a monitor's duties. The Memorandum sets forth several principles:

(a) A monitor is an independent third party, not an employee or agent of the corporation or of the government;

(b) A monitor's primary responsibility should be to assess and monitor a corporation's compliance with the terms of the agreement that are specifically designed to address and reduce the risk of recurrence of the corporation's misconduct, including,

---

[12] Report of Investigation Pursuant to Section 21(a) of the Securities Exchange Act of 1934 and Commission Statement on the Relationship of Cooperation to Agency Enforcement Decisions, Exchange Act Release No. 1470, Accounting and Auditing Enforcement Release No. 1470 (Oct. 23, 2001) [hereinafter Seaboard Report], *available at* http://www.sec.gov/litigation/investreport/34-44969.htm. The SEC's Enforcement Manual also includes these concepts. *See* SEC Division of Enforcement, Enforcement Manual 97 (June 4, 2015), *available at* http://www.sec.gov/divisions/enforce/enforcementmanual.pdf.

[13] Morford Memorandum, *supra* note 8, at 2; *see* Seaboard Report.

[14] Benczkowski Memorandum, *supra* note 8, at 2.

[15] *See* Seaboard Report, *supra* note 12, at 220.

in most cases, evaluating (and, where appropriate, proposing) internal controls and corporate ethics and compliance programs;

(c) In carrying out his or her duties, a monitor will often need to understand the full scope of the corporation's misconduct covered by the agreement, but the monitor's responsibilities should be no broader than necessary to address and reduce the risk of recurrence of the corporation's misconduct;

(d) Communication among the government, the corporation, and the monitor is in the interest of all the parties;

(e) If the corporation chooses not to adopt recommendations made by the monitor within a reasonable time, either the monitor or the corporation, or both, should report that fact to the government, along with the corporation's reasons; and

(f) The agreement should clearly identify any types of previously undisclosed or new misconduct that the monitor will be required to report directly to the government. The agreement should also provide that as to evidence of other such misconduct, the monitor will have the discretion to report this misconduct to the government or the corporation or both.

These principles brought some standardization to the process, while leaving room for flexibility to account for "the varying facts and circumstances of each case."[16]

An FCPA monitorship is entirely a creation of the settlement agreement, which defines its terms. Although it is tempting to focus on the dollars associated with a settlement and the need for the organization to move on, it is important not to overlook the terms of the settlement agreement that frame the monitorship. The terms of the settlement agreement not only empower the monitor, but they also serve to protect the company from potential overreach. For instance, FCPA settlements typically provide explicitly that the monitor need not reinvestigate the conduct that led to the settlement. This enables the monitor and his or her team to test and evaluate the current anti-corruption compliance program, not investigate potential law violations.

Company counsel must closely analyze each aspect of the settlement agreement to ensure that the requirements are clearly defined. When negotiating the terms of a monitorship, the following are among the key considerations:

- The length of the monitorship;
- Ensuring that the monitorship has clear, workable timelines and that the DOJ and SEC settlement agreements are aligned;
- Ensuring that the monitor employs a risk-based approach to his or her work; and
- The monitor's certification requirements.

Other areas that are addressed in the settlement agreements include the lack of an attorney-client relationship and the reporting obligations if the monitor identifies potentially illegal conduct or encounters intentionally uncooperative employees. Settlement agreements with contradictory or imprecise language could cause a monitor to take steps that are inconsistent with the company's expectations.

---

[16] Morford Memorandum, *supra* note 8, at 2.

3.1 LENGTH OF THE MONITORSHIP

FCPA monitorships usually last between 18 and 36 months, but they have been both shorter and longer. From 2004 through 2011, the length of monitorships mandated in an FCPA enforcement action was most commonly three years. Between 2012 and 2015, the vast majority were for 18 months. The two monitorships required in corporate FCPA enforcement actions during the first quarter of 2016 are for three years.

In December 2008, Siemens resolved FCPA allegations that required a four-year monitorship—a first. The agreement also contained language allowing the monitorship to be shortened or extended in certain circumstances. This flexibility in duration was also a first. Settlement agreements entered into subsequently typically include language allowing the monitorship's time frame to be shortened or lengthened, if necessary. For instance, Weatherford International's 2013 DPA, which called for an 18-month monitorship followed by a self-reporting period, contains language allowing the monitorship or self-reporting period to be terminated early.[17]

Although an early termination has not occurred yet,[18] a company negotiating a settlement that has a monitor should push for a term that contemplates the possibility of lessening the monitorship's duration. As stated in the Morford Memorandum, "in most cases, an agreement should provide for early termination if the corporation can demonstrate to the Government that there exists a change in circumstances sufficient to eliminate the need for a monitor."[19]

3.2 WORKABLE TIMELINES

The length and composition of the monitor's review periods vary and are usually tied to the overall length of the monitorship. Most settlement agreements include a schedule on which the monitor must submit a draft work plan for review by the company, the DOJ, and the SEC, complete his or her review, and issue his or her report; and they also usually provide a timeline for the company to implement any recommendations. Such timelines help to limit the possibility that a monitor will conduct a nonstop review. For instance, Vimpelcom entered into a settlement agreement in 2016 that calls for an initial monitor review and report, followed by two follow-up reviews and reports. The monitor has 30 days to submit a draft initial work plan, after which the DOJ, the SEC, and the company have 30 days to

---

[17] Deferred Prosecution Agreement ¶ 3, United States v. Weatherford Int'l Ltd., No. 13-cr-733 (S.D. Tex. Nov. 26, 2013).

[18] On February 6, 2007, Aibel Group, along with three other subsidiaries of Vetco International Ltd., settled criminal FCPA charges. Aibel entered into a DPA with the DOJ, agreeing to engage outside "Compliance Counsel" for three years. On November 21, 2008, the DOJ announced that Aibel, after failing to meet the obligations imposed by the DPA, would plead guilty to a two-count criminal information charging conspiracy to violate the FCPA and violation of the anti-bribery provision of the FCPA. The DPA was dismissed with the government's consent, and Aibel agreed to pay a $4.2 million fine and to report annually to the DOJ for two years regarding its efforts to put in place controls and systems to comply with applicable anti-bribery laws.

[19] Morford Memorandum, *supra* note 8, at 8.

comment. The monitor then has 120 days to complete the initial review and submit the initial report, after which Vimpelcom has 120 days to implement any recommendations.

A company negotiating an FCPA resolution should closely analyze the timeline set forth in the proposed settlement documents to ensure that the milestones are internally consistent. Further, when dealing with both the DOJ and the SEC, a company may have to negotiate separately with each agency. In this situation, a company should work carefully to ensure that the respective settlement agreements are aligned with respect to the terms and timeline of the monitorship.

3.3 EMPLOYING A RISK-BASED APPROACH

The somewhat open-ended nature of an FCPA monitorship could lead to an inefficient effort to peer into every corner of the corporation. Recent FCPA settlement agreements typically include language that instructs the monitor to use a risk-based approach. For instance, Diebold, Inc., entered into a DPA in 2013 providing that "[t]he Monitor's reviews should use a risk-based approach, and thus, the Monitor is not expected to conduct a comprehensive review of all business lines, all business activities, or all markets."

Additionally, to avoid unnecessarily duplicative work, it is important for monitors to be able to rely, as appropriate, on existing internal compliance work that has already been performed by the corporation. This is another area where the Siemens settlement provides a good example: "[T]he Monitor is encouraged to coordinate with Siemens personnel including auditors and compliance personnel and, to the extent the Monitor deems appropriate, he or she may rely on Siemens processes, on the results of studies, reviews, audits and analyses conducted by or on behalf of Siemens and on sampling and testing methodologies." The more a company is able to work with the monitor—either by supplying the monitor with prior work or by assisting the monitor in the ongoing review—the more likely the monitorship will be effective and efficient.

3.4 CERTIFICATION REQUIREMENTS

The monitor may also be required to certify after each follow-up review whether the compliance program is reasonably designed and implemented. The language used in describing the monitor's responsibilities regarding the recommendations and certifications he or she must issue varies only slightly from agreement to agreement, but those minor variations can have huge significance. Like many FCPA settlements, the terms of Statoil's monitor requirement provided that during each of his follow-up reviews, Statoil's monitor must "certify whether STATOIL's anti-bribery compliance program, including its policies and procedures, is appropriately designed and implemented to ensure compliance with the FCPA."[20] This was

---

[20] United States v. Statoil, ASA, No. 06-cr-00960, at 11 (S.D.N.Y. Oct. 12, 2006), *available at* https://www.justice.gov/sites/default/files/criminal-fraud/legacy/2011/02/16/10-09-06statoil-agree.pdf; Cease-and-Desist Order, Statoil, Exchange Act Release No. 54599 (Oct. 13, 2006), *available at* www.sec.gov/litigation/admin/2006/34-54599.pdf.

somewhat in tension with the monitor's mandate to determine "whether STATOIL's policies and procedures are reasonably designed to detect and prevent violations of the FCPA." The concept that an effective program inevitably involves the detection of violations implicitly acknowledges that no compliance program, even the most effective, will prevent all misconduct. This is an unassailable contention. Like a big city with a large police force, large multinational companies will inevitably have employees who intentionally break the rules. Therefore, a word such as "ensure," which connotes total security, complicates the duty of the monitor and may lead to a more exacting review.

In its global FCPA settlement, Siemens headed off this problem by ensuring that the certification mandate for the monitor mirrored his actual review mandate: he was required to "certify whether the compliance program of Siemens, including its policies and procedures, [was] reasonably designed and implemented to detect and prevent violations within Siemens of the anti-corruption laws."[21] This simple change ensures that the program be calibrated to the level of corruption risk facing the entity and not to an unrealistic level of anti-bribery compliance. Recent FCPA settlements, such as Louis Berger International's 2015 DPA, similarly have required the monitor to certify "reasonable" design and implementation of the anti-corruption compliance program.

3.5 NO ATTORNEY-CLIENT RELATIONSHIP

Companies required to retain an FCPA monitor typically agree not to enter into an attorney-client relationship with the monitor. This was not always the case. Some earlier agreements did not strictly prohibit the company from forming an attorney-client relationship with the monitor, but any attorney-client privilege had to be waived with respect to the agency with which the company settled. Today, however, settlement agreements expressly forestall the creation of an attorney-client relationship. The most recent agreements simply state that there is no such relationship. Because this language is so explicit, companies may find it more difficult to assert attorney-client privilege if an outside party attempts to gain access to information communicated by the company to the monitor.

The lack of an attorney-client relationship between the monitor and company can pose a significant risk of further legal exposure for the company. Because the monitor is independent, actively reviews the company's policies and procedures, and reports to the government, the monitor might discover and reveal previously undisclosed wrongdoing or request, and be given, access to privileged information.

One of the reasons that settlement agreements forbid an attorney-client relationship is that it could undermine the monitor's independence. Similarly, the settlement documents typically include a "cooling off" period in which the company is prohibited from retaining the monitor for a period of time after the monitorship concludes. Even if doing so would not actually undermine the monitor's independence during the course of the monitorship,

---

[21] Final Judgment, SEC v. Siemens Aktiengesellschaft, (D.D.C. Dec. 12, 2008) (No. 1:08-cv-02167), at 10–11, *available at* http://www.siemens.com/press/pool/de/events/2008-12- PK/SEC.pdf; Statement of Offense at Attachment 2, ¶ 6, United States v. Siemens Aktiengesellschaft, No. 08-367 (D.D.C. 2008), *available at* http://www.justice.gov/opa/documents/siemens-ag-stmt-offense.pdf.

the public's perception of the effectiveness of monitors could be diminished were the company permitted to turn around and hire the very monitor who was assessing the company's compliance with the resolution agreement. Because of this, almost every company entering into a compliance monitorship has been required to agree to a provision prohibiting it from affiliating with, or hiring, a monitor for one or two years after the monitorship term expires.

3.6 DISCOVERED MISCONDUCT

The Morford Memorandum makes clear that the monitor's role is to evaluate ongoing compliance and not to "investigate historical misconduct."[22] The Morford Memorandum provides that, if additional misconduct is discovered during the monitor's term, the settlement agreement "should clearly identify any types of previously undisclosed or new misconduct that the monitor will be required to report directly to the Government."[23] Furthermore, "[t]he agreement may set forth certain types of previously undisclosed or new misconduct that the monitor will be required to report directly to the Government."[24]

Recent FCPA settlement agreements explicitly address this topic. Avon Products, Inc.'s 2014 DPA includes a framework typical of recent settlements. It provides that should the monitor discover "corrupt or otherwise suspicious payments" or "false books and records" that occurred either after the date of the settlement or that, although predating the governmental resolution, were not adequately dealt with by the company, the monitor should promptly report such activities to certain members of senior management for action. This allows the company to investigate the circumstances itself and then inform the monitor of its response, which the monitor can address in his or her reports. If the monitor believes any such misconduct may constitute a violation of the law, he or she is instructed also to report that to the government.

4. Selecting an FCPA Monitor
4.1 A MERITS-BASED PROCESS

The Morford Memorandum and Benczkowski Memorandum explain that a monitor should be selected based on his or her merits. This includes the need to avoid potential and actual conflicts of interest. To help avoid conflicts of interest, prosecutors do not select or veto a monitor candidate unilaterally; rather, the Morford Memorandum and Benczkowski Memorandum provide for the creation of a "Standing Committee on the Selection of Monitors."[25] After the committee approves a monitor candidate, the Office of the Deputy Attorney General must also approve the monitor.[26] Further, the government may decline to accept a monitor if he or she has an affiliation with the corporation, such as having a relative on the company's payroll or having conducted past work for the company. If the SEC and

---

[22] Morford Memorandum, *supra* note 8, at 6.

[23] *Id.* at 7.

[24] *Id.*

[25] Benczkowski Memorandum, *supra* note 8, at 3; *see also* Morford Memorandum, *supra* note 8, at 3.

[26] Benczkowski Memorandum, *supra* note 8, at 7.

DOJ require a monitor for related FCPA conduct, they will coordinate in both selection and the execution of the monitorship.

In the end, the government's goals are that the process "produce[s] a high-quality and conflict-free monitor" and "instill[s] public confidence."[27] The company typically plays a lead role in identifying potential monitors and obtaining approval for appointment as monitor. The Benczkowski Memorandum and FCPA settlement documents generally provide that a company should propose three monitor candidates to the government, along with its preference among the candidates, from which the government can accept or reject any candidate. SEC settlement documents can be more deferential, sometimes providing that a company "shall retain a Monitor that is not unacceptable to the Commission staff."[28] For this reason, the company should communicate regularly with the government during the process, so that the prosecutors and enforcement attorneys understand the company's methodology and its good faith in selecting an effective monitor. This is an area where the company needs to exercise the utmost caution and perform extensive due diligence. Even well-crafted settlement agreements may not guard against a monitor who becomes abusive, runs up excessive fees, or exceeds his or her mandate.

4.2 FACTORS TO CONSIDER WHEN NOMINATING A MONITOR

The company plays a key role in identifying and vetting potential candidates to ensure that it proposes a monitor who is conflict free, highly qualified and respected, and capable of creating public confidence in his or her performance. In addition to these prerequisites, the ideal candidate will have relevant industry background, experience with similar companies, a measured approach and understanding of a monitor's role, and terrific references.

4.2.1 Competency

A monitor and his or her firm should have a dynamic FCPA practice. First, any company will want to avoid having the monitor develop an understanding of the FCPA or good compliance practices on the job during the monitorship. In addition, there are benefits to considering candidates with substantive monitorship experience, either in the role of monitor or counsel to a company that has had a monitor. This past experience is critical as a predictor of future behavior. Experience with a wide variety of clients will also make it more likely that a monitor will take a measured view of an effective compliance program. A monitor must appreciate the complexities of multinational organizations and the compliance challenges that attend them. A frantic monitor who sees huge failures behind every isolated incident can cause unwarranted headaches for the company and can cause the government to lose confidence in the process.

Monitors are expected to be knowledgeable in the design and implementation of anti-corruption compliance programs. Quality monitors will offer practical, constructive suggestions that add value and efficacy to the compliance program and controls of a

---

[27] Morford Memorandum, *supra* note 8, at 3.
[28] *See, e.g.*, Consent ¶ 4, SEC v. Weatherford Int'l Ltd., No. 4:13-cv-03500 (S.D. Tex. Nov. 26, 2013).

company. Equally as important is an understanding of the business that the program seeks to safeguard. The monitor's work should reflect the risks that attend the business. What works in pharmaceuticals, for example, may not work in the oil and gas sector. Without understanding the business, developing risk-based recommendations is next to impossible. The monitor cannot effectively evaluate the controls or make suggestions to improve them unless he or she knows how they work with the business.

It is important that these attributes extend to the members of the monitor's team. A company should consider the backgrounds of the team members who will likely execute the lion's share of the fieldwork for the monitor. They should share these aforementioned qualities, as it does little good for an experienced anti-corruption practitioner to be surrounded by an inexperienced support crew who will flounder during the early stages of the monitorship.

4.2.2 Credibility

Credibility is crucial to both the company and the government. The selection process should ultimately "produce a high-quality and conflict-free monitor" that will "instill public confidence" in his or her work.[29] When considering a candidate, a company should contact as many clients and practitioners as possible to develop a clear picture of how the candidate behaves professionally.

4.3 TYPES OF FCPA MONITORS

Lawyers—particularly, ex-prosecutors—are the most common candidates to serve as FCPA monitors. But former prosecutors are not the only type of professional to have been appointed as monitors. Forensic accountants and consulting firms also have served as FCPA monitors. The Morford Memorandum even encourages prosecutors and companies to broaden their list of potential candidates to include non-lawyer professionals: "While attorneys, including but not limited to former Government attorneys, may have certain skills that qualify them to function effectively as a monitor, other individuals, such as accountants, technical or scientific experts, and compliance experts, may have skills that are more appropriate to the tasks contemplated in a given agreement."[30] In the case of Siemens, the former German Minister of Finance was appointed as monitor, supported by Gibson, Dunn & Crutcher LLP.

5. FCPA Monitors in Practice

5.1 ENGAGEMENT LETTER

The company should enter into an engagement letter with the monitor. Key issues to be addressed in an engagement letter include budgets and staffing, as well as mechanisms to protect the confidentiality of information.

Because the company retains the compliance monitor, it pays the costs of the monitorship. Monitorship fees and expenses can amount to millions of dollars, and, without clear

---

[29] Morford Memorandum, *supra* note 8, at 3.

[30] *Id.* at 4.

guidelines, it can be very difficult to limit the cost of a monitorship. Some monitors may claim that any attempt at budgeting or capping fees will undermine their independence. But a monitorship is different from an investigation or litigation—it is largely predictable. Like an auditor, the monitor should be able to provide a detailed budget that reflects his or her vision for the engagement. A detailed timeline is also important for controlling costs. By pegging a timeline to the budget, the company and the monitor can better manage costs and increase transparency.

It is entirely reasonable for a company to request from the monitor fee estimates and budgets in advance of specific undertakings associated with the engagement. The monitor's budget should include projected costs associated with key planned activities of the monitorship, such as international site visits and report writing. After the monitorship is underway, it is reasonable for the monitor to provide periodic updates regarding fees. This allows the monitor and company to discuss potential cost overruns or unanticipated activities. If certain tasks appear to be unreasonably expensive, a company can work with the monitor to discuss strategies to reduce their cost. The goals here should be to avoid surprises and ensure that the monitor's work is being conducted efficiently.

As discussed earlier, a monitorship also can make certain information vulnerable to discovery by third parties. Because the monitor does not have an attorney-client relationship with the company, provision of certain privileged materials to the monitor risks waiver. The company and monitor should work together to minimize this risk, as such risk undermines the monitorship in addition to hurting the company. At a minimum, the monitor's retention letter should include a non-waiver agreement.[31]

5.2 THE RELATIONSHIP: COOPERATIVE NOT ADVERSARIAL

Both the monitor and the company must strive whenever possible to have a cooperative—not an adversarial—relationship. The goal should be to add real value to the organization by enhancing its compliance program. To achieve this goal, the monitor must take steps to ensure that the company, including the board of directors and senior management, supports the monitor's work throughout the monitorship process.

A monitorship can result in steep indirect costs to the company and its personnel. The monitor's work may lead to costly implementation of additional compliance policies and procedures, and it may become a drain on company resources, as personnel are diverted to assist the monitor with any ancillary follow-up work. It often is helpful to identify a knowledgeable individual or group of people within the company to serve as the monitor's primary point of contact and to assist with the monitor's work. To avoid surprises for the monitor and company, constant communication is imperative and should include iterative work plans, planning meetings, update meetings, fixed timelines and deliverables, and task-based budgets.

FCPA settlements normally provide that certain disputes will be resolved by the government. Indeed, the DOJ's 2010 "Grindler Memorandum," which supplements the Morford

---

[31] *See supra* Section 5, discussing the confidentiality of monitor reports.

Memorandum, provides that settlement agreements should explain the DOJ's role in re-solving disputes that may arise between the monitor and the company.[32] Because successful monitorships run on trust and cooperation, monitors and companies should try to avoid resorting to this where possible. When a dispute is raised to the SEC or DOJ, the rela-tionship may be damaged. Monitors and companies should therefore try to work out any differences and align their understandings of the monitorship mandate well in advance of fieldwork or report writing.

5.3 THE MONITOR'S WORK

The cardinal rule for any monitor is that he or she must, at all times, abide by the terms of the agreements with the DOJ and the SEC. As discussed previously, the settlement agreements contain many of the key components of the specific monitorship: the length of the monitor-ship, when and for how long the monitor will conduct reviews, any certifications that a mon-itor may have to make, the nature and general structure of fieldwork, and any work product that the monitor must submit to the government and the company.

Once selected, the monitor will review the anti-corruption compliance program; conduct analyses, studies, and testing; review documents and policies; interview employees; make on-site inspections and observations; make recommendations for improvement; and issue reports.

Most FCPA settlement agreements require an initial report and subsequent follow-up reports. In addition to formal reports, FCPA settlement agreements include language requiring meetings among the company, the monitor, and the government to ensure that the monitorship is progressing well.

5.3.1 Work Plans

Recent FCPA settlement agreements require monitors to submit written work plans that "identify with reasonable specificity the activities the Monitor plans to undertake in execu-tion of the Mandate, including a written request for documents."[33] An effective work plan clearly sets forth the monitor's planned activities. Further, the monitor typically must allow the company and government to review and comment on the draft work plan.

A sufficiently detailed work plan will address all of the core activities that the monitor anticipates in that review period. It typically will include the following:

- An overview of the monitor's role and objectives;
- A proposed timeline for the review period based on the settlement agreements, including the date on which the monitor will submit a final report to the government and company;

---

[32] Memorandum from Gary G. Grindler, Deputy Attorney General, U.S. Department of Justice, Additional Guidance on the Use of Monitors in Deferred Prosecution Agreements and Non-prosecution Agreements with Corporations (May 25, 2010), *available at* https://www.justice.gov/usam/criminal-resource-manual-166-additional-guidance-use-monitors-dpas-and-npas.

[33] *See, e.g.*, Deferred Prosecution Agreement, Attach. D ¶ 11, United States v. Avon Prods., Inc., No. 1:14-cr-00828 (S.D.N.Y. Dec. 17, 2014).

- A description of relevant compliance policies and procedures to evaluate;
- A list of relevant documents to review;
- A list of employees and others, such as independent directors, to interview;
- A list of proposed site visits (with proposed dates); and
- A list of tests, studies, and analyses to conduct and description of how they will be conducted.

In terms of scope, it is important that the company and the government understand not only the areas of the company (geographic and otherwise) on which the monitor will concentrate, but the monitor's methodology as well. For instance, if the monitor wishes to engage an external auditor to assist him or her in conducting tests, studies, or analyses of key controls, he or she should use the work plan to explain the reason for this (and why it is necessary to use an external auditor, instead of company resources).

A detailed work plan makes the process more understandable. It is important that the work plan reflect the tasks reasonably anticipated and that the monitor strives to adhere to it. This includes meeting the proposed dates for completion of fieldwork and submission of reports to the company and government. Even when unanticipated developments arise, the monitor should try to produce the report on time. Failure to do so can complicate the company's efforts to implement recommendations in a timely manner, as everything is pegged to the timeline in the settlement papers.

5.3.2 Written Reports

A monitor's initial written report should detail the scope of the review, the monitor's evaluation of the company's compliance program, and any recommended enhancements to the compliance program.

When detailing the monitor's evaluation, the report should catalogue the work that the monitor and his or her team performed and explain why this work was sufficient to gain the information needed to arrive at substantive conclusions. Thus, it is important that, during fieldwork, the monitor's team carefully documents all of its activities. Metrics included in the reports typically include the number of employees interviewed and their corresponding functions and levels, the number and nature of the site visits conducted, and any past or external work relied upon to reach conclusions.

The initial report also will provide recommendations. Because the recommendations are mandatory action items for the company, the monitor should present in the text of the report a sufficient evidentiary basis for each recommendation, in addition to vetting all recommendations fully in advance with the company (and allotting time in the work plan to do so).

5.3.3 Workable Recommendations

The company must work with the monitor to ensure that he or she crafts workable recommendations. During the course of the monitorship, the monitor and his or her team will develop an in-depth understanding of the company's anti-corruption compliance program. Without an appreciation for what the business does and how it does it, the monitor's work may consist of mere abstractions. What appears to be an ideal theoretical solution may not hold up when judged against the realities of the business. Substantive changes to a business to address a compliance problem, although sometimes necessary, should be a last resort. Whenever possible, recommendations should work within the company's existing compliance program, organization, business model, and culture.

Corporations may not always wish to accept the suggestions of their monitors, nor are they necessarily required to follow the monitor's recommendations. Typically, if a corporation "chooses not to adopt recommendations made by the monitor within a reasonable time, either the monitor or the corporation, or both, should report that fact to the Government, along with the corporation's reasons."[34] Monitors and companies should attempt to work together, however, to create workable recommendations and avoid having to escalate these issues to the government.

6. Confidentiality of Monitor Reports

In practice, FCPA monitors are given broad access to the facilities, personnel, and records of the companies they scrutinize. With this access to sensitive and confidential company information, the desire to preserve the confidentiality of the monitor's reports and other communications to the government is understandable. Two recent cases—*United States v. HSBC USA, N.A.* and *100Reporters LLC v. DOJ*—have placed into sharp focus the need to ensure that the work product generated by independent monitors appointed pursuant to an NPA or DPAs is kept confidential.

In *United States v. HSBC*, the government and HSBC have had to address the issue of potential public access to monitorship documents, albeit in a non-FCPA context. HSBC was required to engage a monitor in connection with resolving allegations of money laundering. Judge John Gleeson of the U.S. District Court for the Eastern District of New York initially required the government to submit a status report summarizing the monitor's conclusions following the first-year review.[35] Nearly one month after the submission of this six-page summary, Judge Gleeson ordered the government to submit the monitor's full "First Annual Follow-Up Review," consisting of a more than 250-page report and lengthy appendices, together totaling more than 1,000 pages.

After a document is filed in federal court, it is placed on the court's electronic docket and can typically be viewed, downloaded, and disseminated at will. In *HSBC*, both parties recognized the risk of putting a monitorship report on the court's electronic docket, and filed separate motions to place the report under seal permanently, to be reviewed by the court only in camera. After the government filed the report under seal, a former HSBC mortgage holder wrote a letter to the court requesting the release of the report. Following briefing and oral argument, on January 15, 2016, Judge Gleeson ordered the report unsealed, finding that it is a "judicial document" relevant to his judicial function, useful in the judicial process, and subject to the First Amendment and common law right of access.[36] Both the government

---

[34] Morford Memorandum, *supra* note 8, at 6.
[35] United States v. HSBC Bank USA, N.A., No. 12-CR-763, 2016 WL 347670, at *2 (E.D.N.Y. Jan. 28, 2016).
[36] *Id.* at *2–7.

and HSBC requested a stay of the unsealing order while they seek interlocutory appeal of the court's decision. On July 12, 2017, the Second Circuit blocked the release of the monitor report, including that it was not a "judicial document" because it was "not now relevant to the performance of a judicial function."

A recent Freedom of Information Act (FOIA) case—*100Reporters LLC v. DOJ*—has questioned the confidentiality protections available to monitor work product submitted to the government. The question stems, in part, from a context in which monitors are deliberately defined as "not the [monitored] corporation's attorney,"[37] and the attorney-client privilege is often expressly negated in monitorship agreements. Although DOJ guidance counsels that the monitor "is an independent third-party, not an employee or agent of the corporation or of the Government,"[38] recent scholarship has addressed the practical consequence of monitorships and argued that monitors serve as agents of both the corporations and the government.[39]

On July 23, 2013, 100Reporters LLC ("100Reporters"), a not-for-profit news media organization, submitted a FOIA request to the DOJ seeking six categories of documents relating to the Siemens FCPA plea agreement and the monitorship, including all documents authored or submitted by the monitor during the course of the monitorship pursuant to the settlement agreements. On July 23, 2013, The DOJ initially denied the request, on the grounds that, pursuant to FOIA Exemption 7(A), the materials sought by 100Reporters were exempt from disclosure because they were law-enforcement records whose disclosure could interfere with enforcement proceedings. On April 22, 2014, the DOJ further affirmed that denial on administrative appeal.

Almost exactly one year after the original FOIA request, on July 24, 2014, 100Reporters brought a FOIA action in the District Court for the District of Columbia, seeking an order requiring the DOJ to release the six categories of materials related to the Siemens plea agreement and the monitorship identified in its FOIA request. After becoming aware of the FOIA request in October 2014, Siemens and the monitor each brought motions to intervene in the action. On December 3, 2014, Judge Rudolph Contreras categorically granted the motions to intervene of both Siemens and the monitor over the opposition of 100Reporters, finding that both intervenors met all qualifications for intervention.

100Reporter's opposition to the monitor's intervention focused chiefly on an argument that the monitor lacked an interest in the underlying litigation—a crucial prerequisite for intervention as of right—and the court devoted the greatest amount of space in its consolidated opinion to this subject. As the court noted, intervention as of right requires that a prospective intervenor "demonstrate a legally protected interest in the action."[40] The monitor argued that he possesses "a substantial and independent interest" in the mandate

---

[37] Morford Memorandum, *supra* note 8, at 4–5.

[38] *Id.* at 4.

[39] *See, e.g.*, Veronica Root, *The Monitor-"Client" Relationship*, 100 VA. L. REV. 523,528 n.12 (2014) ("Despite [the] language in the [Morford Memorandum], the monitor is still perceived by the public and corporation as the government's agent and the monitorship agreements are structured to facilitate a monitor's role as government agent.").

[40] 100Reporters v. DOJ, No. 14-CV-1264-RC, 2014 WL 6817009 at *4 (D.D.C. Dec. 3, 2014) (quotation omitted).

established by the settlement agreements, and that "[c]onfidentiality between the Monitor and the DOJ—and the expectation that this confidentiality would be maintained—was vital to the Monitor's ability to carry out the Mandate."[41] The monitor noted that "it is only by protecting these materials from disclosure that the Monitor could ensure that [he] would have unfettered access to Siemens's sensitive information and to communicate the Monitor's findings in detail to the DOJ and the SEC."[42]

On March 31, 2017, Judge Contreras granted defendants' motions for summary judgment, in part, and denied in its entirety 100Reporters' cross-motion for summary judgment. The Court accepted the Monitor's position that the "consultant corollary" to the deliberative process privilege may extend to communications between a government agency and an independent monitor and thereby shield information from disclosure under FOIA Exemption 5—the first time a court has applied the consultant corollary to a compliance monitor. Judge Contreras denied summary judgment on these grounds because the DOJ did not specifically identify the deliberative process at issue with respect to each type of documents withheld by the DOJ, and left the door open for defendants to submit further affidavits to support this argument.

In response to the Court's order, the DOJ submitted two new declarations from DOJ personnel involved in the monitorship, an amended chronology of events supporting the deliberative process privilege, and the materials required for in camera review. The DOJ and 100Reporters filed renewed cross-motions for summary judgment.

On June 18, 2018, the Court granted in part and denied in part both sets of cross-motions for summary judgment. Ultimately, the Court determined that certain materials should be produced to 100Reporters; however, the Court determined that the DOJ properly withheld the core monitorship materials.

Fundamentally, these challenges to monitor confidentiality threaten to weaken the important role that monitors can play in post-resolution corporate reform. Confidentiality surrounding the monitor's work product plays an important role in allowing corporations to make their most confidential and commercially sensitive information available to the monitor so that he or she can comprehend the "full scope of the corporation's misconduct" and take the steps necessary to "reduce the risk of [its] recurrence."[43] Without such protections, a monitor is less likely to be an attractive or effective feature of DPAs or NPAs. If such confidentiality is significantly undermined, monitorships as a facet of corporate enforcement action resolutions will likely become less attractive both to the government and corporations.

7. Do Monitorships Work?

Some FCPA monitorships have been tremendously successful; others have proven challenging and disruptive experiences for the monitored corporation. The government continues to take steps to improve the process. For instance, in October 2018, Assistant

---

[41] Monitor's Mot. Intervene 7–8, 100Reporters v. U.S. Dep't of Justice, No. 14-1264-RC (D.D.C. Oct. 20, 2014).

[42] 100Reporters v. DOJ, No. 14-CV-1264-RC, 2014 WL 6817009 at *4 (D.D.C. Dec. 3, 2014).

[43] Morford Memorandum, *supra* note 9, at 4.

Attorney General Brian Benczkowski delivered a speech in which he emphasized that "it is incumbent upon [the DOJ's] prosecutors to ensure that monitors are operating within the appropriate scope of their mandate" and that the DOJ "absolutely want[s] to know or any legitimate concerns regarding the authorized scope of the monitorship, cost or team size."

An FCPA monitor wields tremendous power and discretion, and monitored companies frequently face a large imbalance of power. When executed poorly, a monitorship can make unreasonable demands on a company, lead to large bills, and saddle corporations with significant ongoing costs, often leaving the company without recourse.

When executed well, however, monitorships can make companies stronger. A corporate monitor can help to change the culture of a company and how it approaches compliance and ethics. Corporate monitors can motivate a company to direct attention and resources to compliance and ethics that were missing previously. This can lead to a stronger control system in the company. By helping the company adopt and implement strong anti-corruption compliance controls, a monitor can better position a company to comply with anti-corruption laws after the monitorship is over.

25 Voluntary Disclosures

IN THE COURSE of doing business, company managers may discover that the company has violated the law, thereby exposing the company to potential civil or criminal liability.[1] When this occurs, an inevitable question is whether the company should voluntarily disclose this information to the government. To be sure, the U.S. Department of Justice (DOJ), as detailed in Chapter 28 ("Department of Justice's New Revised FCPA Corporate Enforcement Policy") has strongly encouraged companies to self-report their misdeeds.[2] However, disclosure is not without serious risks and potential consequences. This chapter provides an overview of certain key considerations for companies deciding whether to self-disclose potential wrongdoing to government authorities.

First, this chapter examines the value that the government places on voluntary disclosure, from the perspective of when a company is being investigated,[3] prosecuted,[4] and sentenced.[5] Second, this chapter outlines the general benefits and risks of voluntary disclosure. Next, this chapter analyzes particular crimes and the more formal voluntary disclosure programs that have been established to handle them. Finally, this chapter addresses some additional disclosure concerns that are specific to publicly traded corporations.

---

[1] This chapter was contributed by T. Markus Funk and Andrew Boutros. This chapter has been adapted from *The ABA Compliance Officer's Deskbook*.

[2] *See* Chapter 28, *infra*.

[3] Chapter 19, *supra*.

[4] *Id.*; *see also* Chapters 26 and 28, *infra*.

[5] *See* Chapter 27, *infra*.

From Baksheesh to Bribery. T. Markus Funk and Andrew S. Boutros.
© Oxford University Press 2019. Published 2019 by Oxford University Press.

1. The Value of Cooperation

The decision to self-disclose actual or potential wrongdoing to the government is among the most difficult for a company to make. The decision is made in consultation with a variety of experts, including senior in-house attorneys (and almost always the general counsel and head of litigation or compliance), the board, the audit committee, and the company's top C-suite executives. Because the decision is so important, those involved in the process, including compliance officers, should be familiar with the formal value that the government places on such cooperation. Two primary sources outline how prosecutors and courts should interpret a company's decision to disclose sensitive information and cooperate with a government investigation:

- The DOJ's Principles of Federal Prosecution of Business Organizations
- Chapter 8 of the United States Sentencing Guidelines

The Principles of Federal Prosecution of Business Organizations (Principles) are set forth in the *Justice Manual*.[6] As the Principles acknowledge, a prosecutor generally has "substantial latitude" in determining when, how, and most importantly, whether to prosecute for violations of federal criminal law.[7] Nevertheless, among other things, the Principles set out that several important considerations that prosecutors must take into account when deciding whether to charge a companies or how to potentially resolve a case against a company once the decision to charge has been made. Among those considerations are a business organization's timely and voluntary disclosure of wrongdoing, as well as the organization's willingness to cooperate in any investigations of its executives and agents.[8] As a general rule of thumb, the government understands that cooperative organizations deserve to benefit from more lenient treatment as compared to non-cooperative organizations; today, cooperation includes providing all facts against all employees and executives, regardless of seniority, as required by the "Yates Memo."[9]

The United States Sentencing Guidelines[10] ("Guidelines") enumerate a series of considerations that a judge is to take into account when sentencing a convicted company.[11]

---

[6] The *Justice Manual* is available at https://www.justice.gov/jm/justice-manual.

[7] *Justice Manual* at 9-28.300, *available at* https://www.justice.gov/jm/jm-9-28000-principles-federal-prosecution-business-organizations#9-28.300 (last visited at Feb. 1, 2019).

[8] This factor is actually one of eight that a prosecutor is to consider. However, factor (A)(4) is the primary focus of this chapter, as it directly implicates voluntary disclosure considerations. Where relevant, other factors will also be discussed.

[9] More specifically, the government states that cooperation benefits a company "by presenting it with the opportunity to earn credit for its efforts." *Id.*

[10] The *United States Sentencing Guidelines Manual* is available at http://www.ussc.gov/guidelines-manual/2014/2014-ussc-guidelines-manual.

[11] *See generally* United States Sentencing Commission, *Federal Sentencing: The Basics* (2015), *available at* http://www.ussc.gov/sites/default/files/pdf/research-and-publications/research-projects-and-surveys/miscellaneous/201510_fed-sentencing-basics.pdf.

Although intended to guide judges, and although not mandatory, the Guidelines can also be a helpful barometer for companies and prosecutors in their dealings with one another, including during the negotiation stage. Specifically, chapter 8 of the Guidelines describes sentencing considerations for corporations.[12] A corporation that chooses to voluntarily disclose information, but is nevertheless charged, still stands to benefit at the sentencing stage if convicted. The Guidelines set out a formula by which the court can assign a convicted organization a culpability "score," with the general thrust being that the higher the score, the more severe the range of the monetary penalty. A corporation can significantly reduce its culpability score if the organization promptly discloses an offense before a government investigation has begun and is thereafter cooperative.[13] The benefits of such a reduction can be substantial: an organization facing a fine of $1 million could have its penalty cut by more than half if awarded full credit for self-reporting an offense.[14]

2. The Benefits of Voluntary Disclosure

There can be many tangible and intangible benefits to voluntary disclosure. Disclosure will likely improve the disposition of the prosecutor toward the company. In addition, voluntary disclosure may not only increase the likelihood of reaching a negotiated agreement, such as a deferred or nonprosecution agreement, but also generate better terms for such an agreement. If a company is prosecuted and misconduct was discovered through a compliance program, voluntary disclosure, as discussed in Chapter 28, may also help mitigate the ultimate sentence. If timed properly, voluntary disclosure will effectively preempt whistle-blowers and other third parties from disclosing to the government, most likely in a manner that will paint the company in a less favorable light.

3. Self-Reporting Portrays the Companny as a Good "Corporate Citizen"

Choosing to voluntarily inform the government of misconduct helps facilitate a good relationship with the prosecutor, painting the company as a good "corporate citizen."[15] This benefit can be significant, as ultimately the prosecutor holds significant leverage in deciding how and under what terms a resolution can be reached between the company and the DOJ. A company that discloses its violations, cooperates fully with an investigation, provides information against culpable employees, and employs proper remedial measures will likely be rewarded with leniency (or at least more leniency) from the government, potentially even with a decision not to prosecute.[16] Even if the government does decide to prosecute the

---

[12] USSG § 8C2.5.

[13] *Id.* Application Note 13.

[14] 1 Foreign Corrupt Prac. Act Rep. § 6:8 (2d ed.).

[15] *See* David Maria, *We Found Potential FCPA Violations: Do We Self-Report?*, In-House Def. Q. 34 (Winter 2015).

[16] *See* Chapter 28, *infra; see also* John J. Carney & Francesca M. Harker, *Disclosing Corporate Misconduct: When Does Voluntary Become Mandatory?*, N.Y.L.J. 3 (Oct. 12, 2010), *available at* http://www.bakerlaw.com/files/Uploads/Documents/News/Articles/LITIGATION/2010/NYLJ_Carney_Harker_October_2012.pdf.

company, disclosure and cooperation are likely to reduce the penalty imposed if the company is ultimately convicted.[17]

4. Cooperation Benefits

A company can gain favorable treatment for assisting the government in its prosecution of culpable individuals. In addition to considering a company's voluntary disclosure, the Principles also require a prosecutor to consider a company's willingness to cooperate in the investigation of its company agents.[18] Recently, the DOJ has even further sharpened its focus on prosecuting individuals for business crimes.[19] As a result, a company that facilitates a robust investigation of bad actors will likely be treated with some degree of leniency. Indeed, a company's voluntary disclosure and cooperation may not only garner leniency for the company, but in some cases may even result in a declination from prosecution.[20]

One example of a company that avoided prosecution is PetroTiger, Ltd.[21] PetroTiger decided to voluntarily disclose a scheme to secure a $39 million oil services contract by bribing Colombian officials, which violated the Foreign Corrupt Practices Act (FCPA).[22] Ultimately, the general counsel and a co-CEO were charged with bribery and fraud.[23] As for the company, because of PetroTiger's voluntary disclosure, cooperation, and remediation of payment, the DOJ ultimately declined to prosecute the company.

5. Nonprosecution Agreements

Voluntary disclosure increases the chances of receiving a nonprosecution agreement (NPA).[24] An NPA is a type of negotiated non-court-filed letter agreement where a business agrees to

---

[17] *See* Chapter 28, *infra.*

[18] *Justice Manual* at 9-28.300(A)(4), (6) ("the corporation's timely and voluntary disclosure of wrongdoing" and its "willingness to cooperate").

[19] *See, e.g.*, Remarks by Principal Deputy Assistant Attorney General for the Criminal Division Marshall L. Miller at the Global Investigation Review Program (Sept. 17, 2014), *available at* http://www.justice.gov/criminal/pr/speeches/2014/crm-speech-1409171.html. ("If you want full cooperation credit, make your extensive efforts to secure evidence of individual culpability the first thing you talk about when you walk in the door to make your presentation. Make those efforts the last thing you talk about before you walk out. And most importantly, make securing evidence of individual culpability the focus of your investigative efforts so that you have a strong record on which to rely.").

[20] *See* David Maria, *We Found Potential FCPA Violations: Do We Self-Report?*, IN-HOUSE DEF. Q. 34, 36 (Winter 2015).

[21] Press Release, U.S. Dep't of Justice, Former Chief Executive Officer of Oil Services Company Pleads Guilty to Foreign Bribery Charge (June 15, 2015), *available at* http://www.justice.gov/opa/pr/former-chief-executive-officer-oil-services-company-pleads-guilty-foreign-bribery-charge.

[22] *Id.*

[23] *Id.; see also* Joel Schectman, *Ex-CEO Sigelman of PetroTiger Sentenced to Probation over Bribery*, WALL ST. J., June 16, 2015, *available at* http://www.wsj.com/articles/ex-ceo-of-petrotiger-sentenced-to-probation-over-bribery-1434469990.

[24] *See* chapter 25 of this book, *infra.*

a combination of restitution, forfeiture, monetary sanctions, and other legal and structural governance reforms in exchange for the government's promise not to formally charge the company with a crime.[25] NPAs have been used across industries to resolve all varieties of crimes, including antitrust, fraud, domestic bribery, tax evasion, environmental violations, and foreign corruption cases.[26] A company that receives an NPA can avoid the negative repercussions that may result from being formally charged with a crime. These negative consequences cannot be underestimated. As already discussed, a company facing prosecution may suffer significant reputational harm, loss of shareholder value, and even prohibition from doing business with the federal government.[27]

In addition to fines, an NPA may also require a company to implement rigorous compliance program reforms and tighter accounting and internal control measures, appoint third-party monitors to oversee company operations, self-investigate and self-report criminal violations, and provide continuing investigative support.[28] In certain cases, an agreement can even contain provisions that alter the composition of a company's board of directors.[29] Still, as Section 6 discusses, voluntary disclosure may also mitigate these ramifications by allowing a company to engage in self-monitoring.

6. Voluntary Disclosure May Facilitate Self-Monitoring

Even if a company chooses to cooperate, the government may still require that the company be supervised at the time that the case is resolved. Company/corporate monitors are typically appointed as part of a negotiated settlement between a company and a government

---

[25] As discussed in chapter 25 of this book, there is a difference between a nonprosecution agreement (NPA) and deferred prosecution agreement (DPA). A company that receives an NPA is not formally charged with a crime, but may be charged if the company does *not* satisfy the terms of the agreement. In contrast, a company that receives a DPA is formally charged with a crime, but the charges will be dismissed if the company *does* satisfy the terms of the agreement. This chapter focuses on NPAs. *See* Cindy R. Alexander & Mark A. Cohen, *The Evolution of Corporate Criminal Settlements: An Empirical Perspective on Non-Prosecution, Deferred Prosecution, and Plea Agreements*, 52 AM. CRIM. L. REV. 537, 545 (2015).

[26] *Id.* NPAs are used with different degrees of frequency across the DOJ. For example, NPAs are rarely used by the DOJ's Environment and Natural Resources Division or the Antitrust Division. In contrast, NPAs are much more commonplace in the Criminal Division, especially in its Fraud Section. David M. Uhlmann, *Deferred Prosecution and Non-Prosecution Agreements and the Erosion of Corporate Criminal Liability*, 72 MD. L. REV. 1295, 1301 (2013).

[27] *See generally* Steven D. Gordon, *Suspension and Debarment from Federal Programs*, 23 PUB. CONT. L.J. 573, 574 (1994).

[28] *Id.*

[29] *See* Gibson, Dunn & Crutcher LLP, *2015 Mid-Year Update on Corporate Non-Prosecution Agreements (NPAs) and Deferred Prosecution Agreements (DPAs)* (July 8, 2015), *available at* http://www.gibsondunn. com/publications/Pages/2015-Mid-Year-Update-Corporate-Non-Prosecution-Agreements-and-Deferred-Prosecution-Agreements.aspx#_ftn12 (*citing* United States v. Aibel Grp. Ltd., Deferred Prosecution Agreement, H-07-005, at 6 (Jan. 4, 2007), which implemented a revised compliance and governance structure, including the appointment of an independent executive board member, the establishment of a compliance committee, and the engagement of outside compliance counsel).

enforcement agency, such as the DOJ or SEC.[30] The monitor's role is to supervise a company in order to ensure that the company abides by the terms of its negotiated settlement.[31] Monitors are given wide power and considerable discretion, although both arise out of the agreement itself.[32] The presence of a monitor can be taxing and restrictive for a company.[33] For example, a company must pay the monitor's costs and expenses, which may add "millions of dollars in costs on top of already steep fines and penalties."[34] In addition, the monitorship process can be "lengthy, expensive and intrusive."[35] Indeed, in this latter regard, the monitor may well receive access to sensitive and confidential information that the monitor may also ultimately pass along to the government.[36]

Rather than be subject to an external monitor, a company that self-reports its wrongdoing may instead be permitted to engage in self-monitoring, thereby circumventing these burdens.[37] For example, as part of FCPA resolutions, the government has allowed companies to self-monitor in cases where the company made a voluntary disclosure, has been fully cooperative, lacks a culture of corruption, and has demonstrated a genuine commitment to reform.[38] A company that self-monitors will avoid the significant expense it would otherwise incur from an external monitor.[39] Furthermore, self-monitoring will allow a company to control the scope of investigations as well as maintain greater control over its obligations.[40]

---

[30] Vikramaditya Khanna & Timothy L. Dickinson, *The Corporate Monitor: The New Corporate Czar?*, 105 MICH. L. REV. 1713, 1716 (2007). The practice of using monitors is not isolated to one particular area of regulation. *See* Russell Mokhiber, Editor, Corp. Crime Reporter, *Crime without Conviction: The Rise of Deferred and Non Prosecution Agreements* at the National Press Club, Washington, D.C. (Dec. 28, 2005), *available at* http://www.corporatecrimereporter.com/news/200/2005/12/.

[31] *Id.*

[32] For example, "[m]onitors are granted substantial power to oversee what the firm is doing; monitors cannot be easily replaced (indeed, even selling the firm does not necessarily terminate the monitoring obligation); monitors may be entrusted with making both important and day-to-day decisions; monitors may have the power to restructure a company's internal processes; and monitors' work may be protected by attorney work-product doctrine; among many other powers." *Id.*

[33] Laura Fraedrich & Jamie A. Schafer, *What Is in It for Me: How Recent Developments in FCPA Enforcement Affect the Voluntary Disclosure Calculus*, 8 GLOBAL TRADE & CUSTOM. J. 260 (2013), *available at* https://www.kluwerlawonline.com/abstract.php?area=Journals&id=GTCJ2013035.

In 2009, officials acknowledged, "monitors can be costly and disruptive to a business, and are not necessary in every case." *See* Lanny A. Breuer, Asst. Att'y Gen., U.S. Department of Justice, Prepared Address to the 22nd National Forum on the Foreign Corrupt Practices Act (Nov. 17, 2009), at 2, *available at* https://www.justice.gov/opa/speech/assistant-attorney-general-lanny-breuer-delivers-remarks-22nd-national-forum-foreign.

[34] *Id.*

[35] *Id.*

[36] Gibson, Dunn & Crutcher LLP, *2014 Year-End Update on Corporate Non-Prosecution Agreements and Deferred Prosecution Agreements (Part 2)*, 29 WESTLAW J. DEL. CORP. 1 (2015).

[37] Criminal Division, U.S. Department of Justice and the Enforcement Division, U.S. Securities and Exchange Commission, *A Resource Guide to the U.S. Foreign Corrupt Practices Act* (Nov. 14, 2012), *available at* https://www.justice.gov/sites/default/files/criminal-fraud/legacy/2015/01/16/guide.pdf.

[38] *Id.*

[39] *See* Fraedrich & Schafer, *supra* note 33, at 259.

[40] *Id.*

7. Effective Compliance Programs or Functions Can Help a Company Argue for a Reduced Sentence or a Pretrial Diversion Agreement

The Principles provide that "the adequacy and effectiveness of the corporation's compliance program" is an additional factor to be considered in determining whether to charge a company.[41] Although an effective compliance program will not necessarily absolve a company of its wrongdoing, it may reduce the ultimate punishment that is imposed as well as best position the company to argue for a DPA or NPA.[42] Of course, to gain credit under this factor, a compliance program cannot merely be a "paper program" that exists just for the purpose of attempting to mitigate punishment.[43] The compliance program must actually be effective in preventing and detecting wrongdoing by employees and company management.[44] Similarly, under the Sentencing Guidelines, the existence of an "effective compliance and ethics program" allows a judge to subtract points from the organization's Culpability Score.[45] In turn, this will result in a reduced sentence.[46]

8. Voluntary Disclosure Reduces the Likelihood That the Government Will Learn about Misconduct through Whistle-Blowers

One practical issue that a company must consider regardless of its decision to self-disclose is that a third party, such as a whistle-blower, may elect to make the disclosure decision for the company.[47] Naturally, a company is able to better control the message and better able to paint itself in the most favorable light possible when a company self-reports as opposed to when presented by a whistle-blower or competitor.[48] Also, if the government learns of a violation through a third party or its own government investigation, incriminating facts may be emphasized at the expense of cooperation.[49]

---

[41] *Justice Manual* at 9-28.300(A)(5); *see also id.* at 9-28.800 ("Corporate Compliance Programs").

[42] *Justice Manual* at 9-28.800(A) ("the existence of a compliance program is not sufficient, in and of itself, to justify not charging a corporation for criminal misconduct undertaken by its officers, directors, employees, or agents.").

[43] In evaluating the effectiveness of a compliance program, a prosecutor is to ask the following fundamental questions: "Is the corporation's compliance program well designed? Is the program being applied earnestly and in good faith? Does the corporation's compliance program work?" *Justice Manual* at 9-28.800(B).

[44] *Id.*

[45] USSG § 8B2.1.

[46] *See* Section 22.8, *supra.*

[47] *See* F. Joseph Warin & Maura M. Logan, *Disclosing Pending FCPA Investigations*, 46 Rev. Sec. & Comm., No. 6, 2013, at 65–66 (discussing voluntary disclosure in the context of violations of the FCPA), *available at* http://www.gibsondunn.com/publications/Documents/WarinLogan-DisclosingPendingFCPAInvestigations.pdf.

[48] David Maria, *We Found Potential FCPA Violations: Do We Self-report?*, In-House Defense Quarterly, 35, 35–36 (Winter 2015).

[49] Homer E. Moyer, Jr., *To Disclose or Not to Disclose–A Recurring FCPA Question, available at* https://www.millerchevalier.com/published-article/disclose-or-not-disclose-recurring-fcpa-question.

Whistle-blower disclosures have become significantly more likely since the passage of the Dodd-Frank Wall Street Reform and Consumer Protection Act.[50] The Dodd-Frank bounty system incentivizes whistle-blowers who may have original information relating to qualifying violations to come forward and report the misconduct to the U.S. Securities and Exchange Commission (SEC).[51] As previously discussed, under the bounty program, if a whistle-blower provides original, high-quality information leading to the successful prosecution of a qualifying offense resulting in the government collecting at least $1 million, the whistle-blower stands to receive 10 percent to 30 percent of the eventual recovery.[52] Due to the substantial financial award potentially at stake,[53] employees and third parties have a significant incentive to report violations to law enforcement, and the SEC in particular.[54] In 2014 alone, the Office of the Whistleblower received 3,620 whistle-blower tips, a more than 20 percent increase in the number of whistle-blower tips from 2012.[55]

Although the Office of the Whistleblower encourages whistle-blowers to report potential misconduct internally to the company first before going to the SEC,[56] there is no actual requirement that a whistle-blower do so. Furthermore, there are several reasons that a whistle-blower may choose to go to the SEC directly. First, unless a whistle-blower is familiar with the provisions or has knowledgeable legal counsel, he or she may not be aware of any incentives to first report a violation internally.[57] Whistle-blowers may, therefore, perceive a greater incentive not to report internally out of fear of losing their whistle-blower status if the company discloses to the government first.[58] Additionally, because penalties in cases involving voluntary disclosures may well be lower than non-voluntary disclosure cases, whistle-blowers may not have any incentive to cooperate internally with companies, because they want to maximize their whistle-blower reward.[59] A company considering disclosure should seriously consider the likelihood that the government will learn of its misconduct through someone else such as a whistle-blower.

---

[50] The Dodd-Frank Wall Street Reform and Consumer Protection Act, which was passed in July of 2010, is available at https://www.sec.gov/about/laws/wallstreetreform-cpa.pdf.

[51] 15 U.S.C. § 78u-6; *see generally* U.S. Sec. & Exch. Comm'n, *SEC Pays More Than $3 Million to Whistleblower* (July 17, 2015), *available at* http://www.sec.gov/news/pressrelease/2015-150.html.

[52] The SEC administers the bounty program. All payments are made out of an investor protection fund established by Congress that is financed entirely through monetary sanctions paid to the SEC by qualifying violators. No money is taken or withheld from harmed investors to pay whistleblower awards. 15 U.S.C. § 78u-6.

[53] For example, the SEC's whistleblower program paid more than $30 million in awards in 2014 and more than $14 million in awards in 2013. *See* U.S. Sec. & Exch. Comm'n, *SEC Announces Largest-Ever Whistleblower Award* (Sep. 22, 2014), *available at* http://www.sec.gov/News/PressRelease/Detail/PressRelease/1370543011290.

[54] Warin & Logan, *supra* note 47, at 65–66.

[55] *See* U.S. Sec. & Exch. Comm'n, *2014 Annual Report to Congress on the Dodd-Frank Whistleblower Program* 22 (2014), *available at* http://www.sec.gov/about/offices/owb/annual-report-2014.pdf.

[56] According to the Office of the Whistleblower, "[t]he whistleblower program was designed to complement, rather than replace, existing corporate compliance programs." *Id.* at 4; *see also* 240 C.F.R. §§ 21F-4(b)(7), 21F-6(a)(4), 21F-6(b)(3).

[57] *See* Fraedrich & Schafer, *supra* note 33, at 259.

[58] *Id.*

[59] *Id.*

9. The Costs of Voluntary Disclosure

The decision to voluntarily self-disclose misconduct is a lofty one. A company must not simply ask whether voluntary disclosure will provide some benefit, but whether disclosure will provide some benefit that outweighs any potential harm. For starters, the government may well not independently discover the misconduct in question, and so self-disclosure may result in an outcome that could have been avoided altogether. In addition, disclosure may give rise to civil "follow on" lawsuits that are all predicated on the same self-disclosed information. Liability for disclosure is not limited to the company, but may also implicate directors, officers, and employees. Finally, the cost of voluntary disclosure is not cheap—a company may be required to reveal information that would ordinarily be privileged or protected when gathered during the scope of the investigation. Each of these issues is addressed in greater detail in the following subsections.

9.1 THE GOVERNMENT MAY NOT INDEPENDENTLY DISCOVER THE MISCONDUCT IN QUESTION

From a cost-benefit analysis perspective, one reason a company may decide not to report potentially criminal conduct is simply the fact that the government may never learn of it. Thus, the voluntary disclosure of incriminating information may lead to a prosecution, pretrial diversion agreement, and the imposition of a penalty that otherwise would not have happened. Criminal prosecution often carries indirect consequences on top of criminal sanctions, including significant reputational harm,[60] loss of shareholder value,[61] suspension or debarment from doing business with the federal government,[62] and even the divestiture of assets.[63] Also, that a company chooses to self-disclose and cooperate does not guarantee leniency.[64]

9.2 COMPANIES THAT VOLUNTARILY DISCLOSE INFORMATION MAY BE SUBJECT TO ADDITIONAL LITIGATION

Exposure to additional "follow-on" litigation is a potentially significant consequence of voluntarily disclosing misconduct to the government. While under investigation, a company may be subject to a number of civil suits based on the same set of factual allegations that was the basis of the disclosure. These lawsuits include tort and contract law claims, unfair

---

[60] *See supra* note 27.

[61] *See supra* note 28.

[62] *See supra* note 29.

[63] *See generally* Gabriel Markoff, *Arthur Andersen and the Myth of the Corporate Death Penalty: Corporate Criminal Convictions in the Twenty-First Century*, 15 U. PA. J. BUS. L. 797 (2013).

[64] *Justice Manual* at 9-28.740 (specially noting that a decision to cooperate does not entitle a corporation to immunity); *see also* F. Joseph Warin & Andrew S. Boutros, *Deferred Prosecution Agreements: A View from the Trenches and a Proposal for Reform*, 93 VA. L. REV. IN BRIEF 107 (2007).

competition claims, whistle-blower and other employment lawsuits, and various other private actions.[65] The cost to litigate or resolve such follow-on litigation may greatly exceed the cost of settlement with the government.[66] Some examples include Nature's Sunshine Products settlement with the SEC for $600,000, followed by $6 million to civil plaintiffs;[67] Syncor International Corporation's settlement with the government for $2.5 million, followed by $15.5 million to civil plaintiffs;[68] and FARO Technologies' settlement with the government for $2.95 million, followed by almost $6.88 million to civil plaintiffs.[69] Even if no private parties file suit, a company may face claims from multiple government agencies, both domestic and foreign.[70] In this latter regard, and as discussed elsewhere, the emergence of foreign "carbon copy" prosecutions is particularly noteworthy. This involves one sovereign bringing a follow-on (or "carbon copy") action for conduct already resolved by another sovereign.

9.3 DISCLOSURE MAY PLACE COMPANY OFFICERS, DIRECTORS, OR EMPLOYEES IN A POSITION WHERE THEY COULD FACE CIVIL OR EVEN CRIMINAL LIABILITY

A company considering voluntary disclosure must also grapple with the harsh reality that disclosure may implicate individual employees, and perhaps even high-level company officers. Statements by senior DOJ officials have called for an increased emphasis on the prosecution of individual wrongdoers.[71] This sentiment was recently formalized in a September 2015 policy memorandum entitled "Individual Accountability for Corporate Wrongdoing,"[72] commonly known as the "Yates Memo," after the signatory of the memorandum, Deputy

---

[65] Warin & Logan, *supra* note 47.

[66] *Id.* at 63–64.

[67] *See* Judgment and Final Order, *In re* Nature's Sunshine Prods. Sec. Litig., No. 2:06-cv-00267-TS (D. Utah Feb. 10, 2010); SEC Lit. Rel. No. 21162, SEC v. Nature's Sunshine Prods., Inc., No. 09CV6722 (D. Utah filed July 31, 2009).

[68] *See* SEC Lit. Rel. No. 17887, *SEC Obtains $500,000 Penalty against Syncor International Corporation for Violating the Anti-bribery Provisions of the Foreign Corrupt Practices Act* (Dec. 10, 2002).

[69] *See* Raymund Wong & Patrick Conroy, NERA Econ. Consulting, *FCPA Settlements: It's a Small World after All* 12 (2009) (discussing FARO), *available at* http://www.mondaq.com/unitedstates/x/73626/Class+Actions/FCPA+Settlements+Its+A+Small+World+After+All; *see also* Nathan Vardi, *Plaintiff Lawyers Join the Bribery Racket*, FORBES, Aug. 16, 2010, *available at* http://www.forbes.com/sites/nathanvardi/2010/08/16/plaintiff-lawyers-fcpa-bribery-racket (discussing Nature's Sunshine, Syncor, FARO, and Immucor settlements).

[70] For example, because the FCPA is enforced by both the DOJ and the SEC, any unlawful conduct that the company discloses to one agency will likely come to the attention of the other, especially in this era of coordinated enforcement efforts. *See* Christopher A. Wray & Robert K. Hur, *Corporate Criminal Prosecution in a Post-Enron World: The Thompson Memo in Theory and Practice*, 43 AM. CRIM. L. REV. 1095 at 1133 (2006).

[71] *See* Daniel Chung & Edward Patterson, *DOJ's Newest Policy Pronouncement: The Hunt for Corporate Executives' Scalps*, Gibson Dunn Publications available at http://www.gibsondunn.com/publications/pages/Yates-Memo--DOJ-New-Posture-on-Prosecutions-of-Individuals--Consequences-for-Companies.aspx.

[72] *Individual Accountability for Corporate Wrongdoing*, Memorandum from Sally Q. Yates, Deputy Attorney General, to Heads of Department Components and United States Attorneys (Sept. 9, 2015), *available at* http://www.justice.gov/dag/file/769036/download.

Attorney General Sally Yates.[73] The memorandum states that in order for a company to receive any degree of cooperation credit—whether immunity, reduced charges, or recommendations for lighter sentences—a company must completely disclose all relevant facts about individual misconduct, regardless of employee seniority or rank.[74] This threshold requirement applies to both civil and criminal investigations.[75] The memo also provides that if a company does not know who is responsible for acts of wrongdoing, it must do its best to find out.[76]

9.4 A COMPANY MAY BE REQUIRED TO PROVIDE AUTHORITIES WITH PRIVILEGED OR CONFIDENTIAL INFORMATION

Government policies and practices promulgated by agencies such as the DOJ and SEC may result in a company that is seeking credit for cooperation to waive the attorney-client privilege in order to provide "relevant facts" to the government.[77] Officially, it is DOJ policy that credit for cooperation will not be based on a company's waiver of attorney-client privilege or work product protection, but rather will focus on the company's willingness to disclose "relevant facts."[78] However, the "relevant facts" that prosecutors often seek are frequently found in the very information gathered within the scope of an internal investigation, including through witness interviews conducted by company counsel. Accordingly, as a practical matter, companies that choose to make a voluntary disclosure and thereafter cooperate should expect to give up confidential information as a cost of cooperation. Given that all federal appellate courts except one do not recognize the selective waiver doctrine, by agreeing to share sensitive information with the government, a company should be prepared for the prospect that the very information it disclosed to the government may well become available to third parties, potentially giving rise to follow-on litigation and negative publicity.[79]

---

[73] *Id.*

[74] *Id.*

[75] *Id.*

[76] According to Deputy Attorney General Yates, a corporation must "investigate and identify the responsible parties, then provide all non-privileged evidence implicating those individuals." Press Release, U.S. Department of Justice, *Deputy Attorney General Sally Quillian Yates Delivers Remarks at New York University School of Law Announcing New Policy on Individual Liability in Matters of Corporate Wrongdoing* (Sept. 10, 2015), *available at* http://www.justice.gov/opa/speech/deputy-attorney-general-sally-quillian-yates-delivers-remarks-new-york-university-school.

[77] Carol Poindexter, *Recent Developments in Corporate "Cooperation" Credit: Opening Pandora's Box or Slamming the Privilege Waiver Lid Shut?*, 22 HEALTH L. 48 (2010).

[78] *Id; see also Principles of Federal Prosecution of Business Organizations*, Memorandum from Mark Filip, Deputy Attorney General, to Heads of Department Components and United States Attorneys (Aug. 28, 2008), *available at* https://www.justice.gov/sites/default/files/dag/legacy/2008/11/03/dag-memo-08282008.pdf.

[79] Other than the Eighth Circuit, all other federal appellate courts have rejected the "selective waiver" doctrine by holding that a disclosure to one (say the government) amounts as a disclosure to all (meaning, the full waiver of privilege or work product protection). Poindexter, *supra* note 77, at 50.

10. Formal Voluntary Disclosure Programs and Associated Crimes

The considerations discussed previously apply to voluntary disclosure more generally. However, the federal government has implemented more formal voluntary disclosure programs for certain types of offenses. The benefits of voluntary disclosure under these specific programs are more concrete, assuming that a company satisfies the stipulated conditions. However, even these formal programs have unique risks that should be taken into consideration.

11. Additional Concerns for Publicly Held Corporations

A public corporation's decision to voluntarily disclose actual or potential wrongdoing is subject to additional risks. For example, a corporation may be subject to mandatory disclosure requirements under the federal securities laws if it is being sued, investigated, or prosecuted, which in turn could negatively affect its reputation and share price.[80] In addition, publicly traded companies are subject to additional follow-litigation in the form of shareholder derivative suits and "stock drop" cases.[81] In a typical derivative suit, shareholders will sue directors or officers on behalf of the corporation for losses incurred under their management.[82] In a stock drop case, shareholders will allege that the misconduct should have been disclosed earlier and innocent stockholders were "tricked" into buying the stock.[83]

Additionally, publicly held corporations should also carefully consider whether they may be required to disclose misconduct in order to comply with SEC requirements.[84] SEC Rule 10b–5[85] prohibits (among other things) the omission of material facts that would otherwise make a corporation's financial statements false or misleading.[86] Despite the importance of the term "material," there is no clear definition.[87] The Supreme Court has explained that information is material if there is "a substantial likelihood that a reasonable shareholder would

---

[80] 17 C.F.R. § 229.103 (2018); *see also supra* note 24.

[81] Warin & Logan, *supra* note 47, at 62.

[82] *Id.* at 63.

[83] *See* Matt Levine, *There Will Always Be Stock Drop Lawsuits*, Bloomberg View (June 23, 2014), *available at* http://www.bloombergview.com/articles/2014-06-23/there-will-always-be-stock-drop-lawsuits.

[84] Carney & Harker, *supra* note 16, at 2 (noting that "[t]he decision of whether or not to disclose known misconduct based on its potential to have a material impact on corporate earnings cannot be underestimated after the passage of Sarbanes-Oxley (SOX) in 2002. Under SOX § 302, the CEO and CFO of a company must certify the accuracy of a company's financial statements. Therefore, undisclosed misconduct that has a material effect on the financial statements can heighten the liability for the certifying officers, with potential fines of up to $1 million and imprisonment of up to 10 years"); *see also* Sarbanes–Oxley Act of 2002, PL 107–204, July 30, 2002, 116 Stat. 745.

[85] 17 C.F.R. § 240.10b-5 (2018).

[86] *Id.*; *see also* Basic Inc. v. Levinson, 485 U.S. 224, 224 (1988).

[87] *Id.*

consider it important" in making an investment decision.[88] However, this test of materiality is difficult to apply in practice.[89] A corporation should consider both the probability and magnitude of the event contemplated.[90] If the event is extremely unlikely, it may be viewed as immaterial.[91] Similarly, if an event will have little, if any impact, it may also be viewed as immaterial.[92]

Furthermore, a duty to disclose misconduct may arise in order to comply with mandatory SEC filing requirements. For example, companies are required to "[d]escribe any known trends or uncertainties that have had or that the registrant reasonably expects will have a material favorable or unfavorable impact on net sales or revenues or income from continuing operations. If the registrant knows of events that will cause a material change in the relationship between costs and revenues . . . the change in the relationship shall be disclosed."[93] In other words, if management "reasonably expects" that information constituting misconduct will have a material impact on the company's financial statements, it must necessarily be disclosed.[94] So, for example, although a small bribe paid to a foreign official to obtain a large contract might be immaterial, the revenue stream derived from the bribe could be material (and thus subject to disclosure) and, of course, there is the fact that bribes to foreign officials are illegal under the FCPA.[95]

12. Conclusion

As the DOJ has articulated, there are good reasons that a corporation may decide to voluntarily disclose bribery and corruption-related (as well as other) misconduct to government authorities. A corporation is not only able to mitigate the implications of prosecution, but it can sometimes escape it altogether. At the same time, a corporation that is considering disclosure must be aware of the risks involved. Disclosing incriminating information can result in additional litigation, carbon-copy actions, follow-on litigation, reputational damage, significant monetary loss, and potential exclusion from federal programs or contracts.

In addition to the general benefits and costs, there are other factors that a corporation considering disclosure should take into consideration as well. Corporations should be cognizant of whistle-blower complaints. In this regard, there are lucrative rewards for those willing to go to the SEC or file suit under the False Claims Act, and these threats are likely

---

[88] TSC Indus., Inc. v. Northway, Inc., 426 U.S. 438, 449 (1976).

[89] 2 *Corporate Counsel Guidelines* § 5:22 (2014).

[90] *Basic Inc.*, 485 U.S. at 238.

[91] *Id.*

[92] *Id.*

[93] 17 C.F.R. § 229.303 (2018).

[94] Carney & Harker, *supra* note 16, at 3.

[95] *Id.* (providing a real-world example: "Global Crossing Ltd. Disclosed . . . that internal investigations had revealed $23,000 in payments that potentially could violate the Foreign Corrupt Practices Act. Despite the low dollar amount, Global Crossing Ltd. included these potentially improper payments in its SEC filings and the SEC commenced a preliminary investigation in response to this voluntary disclosure.").

to continue. In addition, companies should understand the disclosure framework for certain types of crimes or industries. Finally, publicly traded companies should be especially careful when disclosing information. If information that is disclosed (or not disclosed) to shareholders fails to conform to information that has been disclosed to the government, a company may be subject to liability for a securities violation.

26 Deferred Prosecution Agreements, Nonprosecution Agreements, and Corporate Integrity Agreements

COMPANIES—ESPECIALLY PUBLICLY TRADED companies—do not want to go to trial in criminal cases.[1] In fact, they do not want to be indicted at all. Among other reasons, the uncertainty of an indictment can be crippling to a public company's share price, business relationships, market activities, and reputation. Also, the collateral consequences of pleading guilty or losing at trial are just too great to risk. Historically, however, when a company (or an individual for that matter) committed a crime and the government thought it could prove it, there were three options on the table to resolve that criminal matter: (1) in the exercise of their discretion, prosecutors could elect not to file charges at all, an option known as a "declination"; (2) prosecutors could file charges and the case could proceed to trial with a determination of guilt or innocence by a jury (or a judge, if the parties elected); or (3) the company could plead guilty and by doing so, admit its guilt.[2]

With the dramatic increase in corporate criminal prosecutions over the last two decades,[3] a fourth option has emerged in the corporate criminal arena: deferred prosecution agreements (DPAs) and nonprosecution agreements (NPAs), which are alternatives to the traditional "guilty" or "not guilty" approach that the law has generally taken to charged crimes.[4] Collectively, these agreements are known as corporate pretrial diversion agreements.

---

[1] This chapter was contributed by T. Markus Funk and Andrew Boutros. This chapter has been adapted from *The ABA Compliance Officer's Deskbook*.

[2] Cindy R. Alexander & Mark A. Cohen, *The Evolution of Corporate Criminal Settlements: An Empirical Perspective on Non-Prosecution, Deferred Prosecution, and Plea Agreements*, 52 AM. CRIM. L. REV. 537, 537 (2015).

[3] *Id.* at 542.

[4] *Id.* at 538.

From Baksheesh to Bribery. T. Markus Funk and Andrew S. Boutros.
© Oxford University Press 2019. Published 2019 by Oxford University Press.

If a company satisfies the terms of a DPA or NPA—which commonly include fines, promises not to commit future crimes, compliance initiatives, corporate governance reforms, and virtually always a factual basis and cooperation in the government's investigation—the prosecutor dismisses the charges at the successful conclusion of the term of the agreement or the "diversion period" (in the case of a DPA) or does not bring charges at all (in the case of an NPA).[5] In this regard, DPAs and NPAs are essentially front-end probation agreements that allow a company to demonstrate its good behavior and prove that it is rehabilitated; if it does so successfully, it can emerge from the diversion period without a conviction at all.

In criminal proceedings in the healthcare industry, a corporation may enter into a corporate integrity agreement (CIA), a set of obligations that a healthcare provider agrees to fulfill with the Office of Inspector General (OIG) of the U.S. Department of Health and Human Services.[6] In exchange for the corporation's promise to fulfill these obligations, the OIG agrees not to pursue any course of action that would exclude the provider from participation in federal healthcare programs.[7]

This chapter will introduce each of these agreements and explain how they are used as prosecutorial and defense tools in the modern-day corporate criminal liability arena. It will then examine the factors that the government considers when deciding whether to use these agreements.

1. Defining DPAs, NPAs, and CIAs

DPAs, NPAs, and CIAs are three distinct types of negotiated agreements under which the government agrees to forgo prosecution in exchange for a corporation's agreement to fulfill a set of stipulated obligations.[8] These agreements allow both the corporation and the government to avoid the costs and uncertainty associated with an actual trial and protect the corporation from other negative repercussions of a trial and possible conviction, most notably the risks of being suspended or debarred from government contracting.[9] Although these agreements are similar in that they present alternatives to prosecution, they operate differently in practice.[10]

Though nomenclature debates continue, the major practical difference between a DPA and an NPA can be said to be whether and when charges are filed.[11] In a DPA, the government files a charging instrument (indictment or information) against the corporation in court, just as if it were initiating any other case against a defendant, whether an individual or corporation.[12] The prosecutor then agrees, however, to suspend its prosecution in exchange for the

---

[5] *Id.* at 544–45.

[6] Katrice B. Copeland, *Enforcing Integrity*, 87 INDIANA L.J. 1033, 1050–51 (2012).

[7] *Id.*

[8] Alexander & Cohen, *supra* note 2, at 544.

[9] *Id.*

[10] *Id.*

[11] *Id.* at 545.

[12] *Id.*

corporation agreeing to abide by the terms of the agreement.[13] If the corporation complies with these terms, then at the conclusion of the diversion period, the prosecutor dismisses the charges.[14] In an NPA, on the other hand, the prosecutor does not file any charges in court against the corporation; instead the prosecutor's office enters into an out-of-court letter agreement with the corporation, but reserves the right to file charges at some future date if the corporation does not comply with its obligations under the letter agreement.[15] In fact, in some cases, the letter agreement attaches a copy of an unfiled indictment as an exhibit. In doing so, the letter agreement contains a provision that states that in the event of a breach, the prosecutor will file the indictment in court and that the company agrees that there is a factual basis for the company's guilt as alleged in the indictment. The terms of every pretrial diversion agreement will be somewhat different, but are likely to include a sufficient factual basis and some combination of a monetary fine, a promise not to commit future crimes, a requirement to cooperate with the government, and corporate governance reforms.[16]

CIAs are similar to NPAs and DPAs in that they allow both the corporation and the government to avoid the time and expense of trial.[17] CIAs are, however, much narrower in scope. Generally, CIAs are only an option in cases of healthcare industry fraud.[18] A criminal

---

[13] The issue of what role the judiciary plays in approving DPAs is a hotly contested one. The D.C. Circuit, however, recently suggested that a court's role in reviewing a DPA is narrow. *See* United States v. Fokker Servs., B.V., 818 F.3d 733 (D.C. Cir. 2016). In *Fokker*, the parties entered into an 18-month DPA and, in connection with the DPA, filed a joint motion for exclusion of time under the Speedy Trial Act, which generally requires commencement of trial within 70 days of the filing of an information or indictment by the government but excludes periods of delay where necessary to "allow[] the defendant to demonstrate his good conduct." 18 U.S.C. § 3161(h)(2) (2018). The district court denied the joint motion on the basis that the DPA was "anemic" and "grossly disproportionate" in light of the charged violations of the International Emergency Economic Powers Act. United States v. Fokker Servs. B.C., 79 F. Supp. 3d 160, 166–67 (D.D.C. 2015) (criticizing the government for failing to prosecute responsible individuals, and further noting that certain employees were permitted to remain at the company, the DPA did not require an independent monitor, and the fine amount was inadequate). In asserting its authority to reject the DPA, the district court invoked the inherent supervisory authority of the court and the judiciary's power to protect the integrity of the judicial process. On appeal, the D.C. Circuit concluded that the district court overstepped its authority under § 3161(h)(2), which, in this circumstance, is limited to ensuring that the DPA serves the purpose of allowing the defendant to demonstrate its good conduct. Fokker Servs. B.C., 818 F.3d at 744–45, 747. In reaching that conclusion, however, the D.C. Circuit observed that courts have authority to reject DPAs that contain illegal or unethical provisions. *See* United States v. Saena Tech Corp., 140 F. Supp. 3d 11, 31–32 (D.D.C. 2015); United States v. HSBC Bank USA, N.A., 2013 WL 3306161, at *7 (E.D.N.Y. July 1, 2013)). Notably, in *HSBC*, the district court approved the DPA only after reviewing the merits of the agreement, and further concluded that it "retain[ed] the authority to ensure that the implementation of the DPA remain[ed] within the bounds of lawfulness and respect[ed] the integrity of" the court. HSBC Bank USA, N.A., 2013 WL 3306161, at *8–10.

[14] Alexander & Cohen, *supra* note 2, at 545; *see also* Rachel Delaney, *Congressional Legislation: The Next Step for Corporate Deferred Prosecution Agreements*, 93 MARQ. L. REV. 875, 878 (2009) (outlining the operation of DPAs).

[15] Alexander & Cohen, *supra* note 2, at 545; *see also* Leslie R. Caldwell, Assistant Attorney General, Department of Justice, Remarks at the New York University Center on the Administration of Criminal Law's Seventh Annual Conference on Regulatory Offenses and Criminal Law (Apr. 14, 2015), *available at* http://www.justice. gov/opa/speech/assistant-attorney-general-leslie-r-caldwell-delivers-remarks-new-york-university-center.

[16] Alexander & Cohen, *supra* note 2.

[17] 2 HEALTH L. PRAC. GUIDE § 36:17 (2015).

[18] *Id.*

conviction for an offense related to Medicare, Medicaid, or any state healthcare program results in a five-year mandatory period of exclusion from participation in any federal healthcare program.[19] The secretary of Health and Human Services may also exclude companies for other violations, including fraud related to other federal or state programs, kickbacks, claims for excessive charges or unnecessary services, and failure to disclose certain required information.[20] CIAs can help a corporation avoid these penalties.[21] So long as a corporation that enters into a CIA satisfies the terms of the agreement, the corporation will not be excluded from participation in federal healthcare programs such as Medicare and Medicaid.[22] CIAs typically impose more stringent compliance requirements upon a corporation than the law mandates; although these requirements can be onerous, they are generally better than the alternative, which is exclusion from government-funded healthcare programs altogether.[23]

A comprehensive CIA typically lasts three to five years and includes requirements to (1) hire a compliance officer and appoint a compliance committee; (2) develop written compliance standards and policies; (3) implement a comprehensive employee training program; (4) retain an independent review organization to conduct annual compliance reviews; (5) establish a confidential disclosure program; (6) restrict employment of ineligible persons; (7) report overpayments, reportable events, and ongoing investigations and legal proceedings; and (8) provide an implementation report and annual reports to the OIG on the status of the corporation's compliance activities.[24] As already noted, the requirements associated with a CIA are usually preferable to a trial and possible conviction, as well as to avoiding the OIG's power of exclusion from the healthcare industry.[25]

2. Eligibility Considerations

DPAs and NPAs provide prosecutors an important middle ground between declining prosecution and obtaining a conviction.[26] Whereas guilty pleas and trials are focused on punishment, DPAs and NPAs are focused on corporate rehabilitation and reforms. Because they offer an alternative to conviction, in the absence of an outright declination, they are highly sought after by corporate defendants and are becoming (and many would say, have become) an increasingly popular option for prosecutors.[27] Companies almost always prefer

---

[19] 42 U.S.C. § 1320.7(a) (2018).

[20] *Id.* § 1320.7(b).

[21] 2 HEALTH L. PRAC. GUIDE § 36:17 (2015).

[22] U.S. Department of Health and Human Services, Compliance, *Corporate Integrity Agreements, available at* http://oig.hhs.gov/compliance/corporate-integrity-agreements (last visited December 19, 2018).

[23] Sharon Finegan, *The False Claims Act and Corporate Criminal Liability: Qui Tam Actions, Corporate Integrity Agreements and the Overlap of Criminal and Civil Law,* 111 PENN ST. L. REV. 625, 655 (2007).

[24] U.S. Department of Health and Human Services, *supra* note 22.

[25] *See supra* notes 16–20.

[26] Department of Justice, *Justice Manual,* at 9-28.1000 (noting that while declining prosecution may allow a corporate criminal to escape without conviction, obtaining a conviction may result in serious third-party harms).

[27] Gibson, Dunn & Crutcher LLP, *2015 Mid-Year Update on Corporate Non-prosecution Agreements (NPAs) and Deferred Prosecution Agreements (DPAs)* (2015), *available at* http://www.gibsondunn.com/publications/Pages/2015-Mid-Year-Update-Corporate-Non-Prosecution-Agreements-and-Deferred-Prosecution-Agreements.aspx.

NPAs over DPAs because they do not want to be under the threat of a pending court-filed indictment or information,[28] even if it is diverted.[29] There are certain concerns associated with this threat, not the least of which is the fact that prosecutors almost always get to decide whether there is a breach of a DPA (or NPA for that matter).[30] Additionally, once filed, a charging instrument is almost always more easily activated, to say nothing of the risk that it is also subject to the inherent powers of a federal court.[31] As such, NPAs are almost always regarded as a superior option to DPAs from the corporation's perspective. And, as a widely accepted superior option, defense counsel routinely aim to earn an NPA (over a DPA) whenever possible.

Conversely, historically, prosecutors often allowed NPAs to be dangled as prized offerings, only available to the most deserving of corporate defendants who provided extraordinary cooperation or whose conduct was not especially egregious.[32] However, as federal courts have begun to more intensely scrutinize DPAs—and their terms and conditions[33]—a shift may be on the horizon; the government may elect in certain cases to proceed with an NPA rather than a DPA not because a defendant deserves it, but in order to avoid the scrutiny and potential pushback (or rejection) of a DPA by the judiciary. Some commentators have made this observation with respect to the U.S. Securities and Exchange Commission, which has filed an increasing number of cases in its administrative courts instead of the federal courts.[34]

Given the importance and desirability of DPAs and NPAs—as well as the power of the prosecutor to decline to file charges altogether—the Department of Justice's *Justice Manual* provides important guidance to prosecutors about factors to consider when deciding whether and how to charge a corporation.[35] These factors include the following:

- The nature and seriousness of the offense, including the risk of harm to the public
- The pervasiveness of wrongdoing within the corporation
- The corporation's history of similar misconduct, including prior criminal, civil, and regulatory enforcement actions against it
- The corporation's willingness to cooperate
- The adequacy and effectiveness of the corporation's compliance program at the time of the offense, as well as at the time of a charging decision

---

[28] *See supra* note 11.

[29] *See id.* (stating that in 2015, the government entered into 87 NPAs compared to 13 DPAs); *see also supra* note 13.

[30] F. Joseph Warin & Andrew S. Boutros, *Deferred Prosecution Agreements: A View from the Trenches and a Proposal for Reform*, 93 VA. L. REV. 121, 128–29 (2007).

[31] *See, e.g.,* Gordon Bourjaily, *How and Why Congress Should Bar the Use of Deferred and Non-Prosecution Agreements in Corporate Criminal Prosecutions*, 52 HARV. J. ON LEGIS. 543, 548 (2007); *see also supra* note 12, discussing United States v. Fokker Servs.

[32] *See* Bourjaily, *supra* note 31, at 545 (describing the government's offer of a DPA, but not an NPA, to Arthur Andersen LLP after its accounting fraud, and the firm's choice to reject the DPA because of the amount of "power and discretion" it would have given the government).

[33] *See supra* note 13.

[34] Debevoise & Plimpton LLP, *The Total S.A. Action: Are Administrative Orders the SEC's FCPA Resolution of Choice for the Future?* (2013), *available at* http://www.debevoise.com/~/media/files/insights/publications/2013/07/fcpa%20update/files/view%20fcpa%20update/fileattachment/fcpa_update_july_2013.pdf.

[35] *Justice Manual*, at 9-28.300.

- The corporation's remedial actions, including any efforts to implement an adequate and effective corporate compliance program or to improve an existing one, to replace responsible management, to discipline or terminate wrongdoers, or to pay restitution
- The collateral consequences, including whether there is disproportionate harm to shareholders, pension holders, employees, and others not proven personally culpable, as well as impact on the public arising from the prosecution
- The adequacy of remedies such as civil or regulatory enforcement actions
- The adequacy of the prosecution of individuals responsible for the corporation's malfeasance[36]

In this regard, the *Justice Manual* emphasizes that a DPA or NPA should especially be considered in cases where the collateral consequences of a corporate conviction would be significant for innocent third parties, such as nonculpable employees or consumers who benefit from the corporation's existence.[37]

Although no longer required—and indeed, although prosecutors are prohibited from asking for materials protected by work product protection or the attorney-client privilege[38]—as a practical matter, corporations may elect to waive these protections, at least partially, as part of their efforts to maximize the prospects of obtaining a DPA or NPA.[39] This is so because in determining whether a corporation "fully cooperated"[40] in accordance with the fourth factor listed above (as set out in the *Justice Manual*), prosecutors will assess whether the corporation disclosed all relevant, probative, underlying facts, information, and analysis, some of which may naturally be protected from disclosure by the attorney-client privilege or work product protection but waived upon disclosure.[41] Furthermore, now, as a condition to a corporation obtaining any cooperation credit at all, a corporation also must assist prosecutors in their efforts to identify and develop evidence against all culpable individuals.[42] That is, in order for a company to earn *any* credit for cooperation, it must identify all individuals involved in the wrongdoing, regardless of their position, status, or seniority in the company, and provide all relevant facts about their misconduct.[43] As stated

---

[36] *Id.*

[37] *See Justice Manual*, at 9.28-1100(B) (noting that "where the collateral consequences of a corporate conviction for innocent third parties would be significant, it may be appropriate to consider a non-prosecution or deferred prosecution agreement with conditions designed, among other things, to promote compliance with applicable law and to prevent recidivism").

[38] *Justice Manual*, at 9-28.710.

[39] *See* Alexander & Cohen, *supra* note 2, at 550.

[40] *See supra* note 35, at factor 4.

[41] Alexander & Cohen, *supra* note 2, at 593; Memorandum from Mark R. Filip, Deputy Attorney General, U.S. Department of Justice, to Heads of Department Components and United States Attorneys, *Principles of Federal Prosecution of Business Organizations* (Aug. 28, 2008), *available at* http://www.justice.gov/dag/readingroom/dag-memo-08282008.pdf.

[42] *See* "Individual Accountability for Corporate Wrongdoing," Memorandum from Sally Q. Yates, Deputy Attorney General, to Heads of Department Components and United States Attorneys (Sept. 9, 2015), *available at* http://www.justice.gov/dag/file/769036/download.

[43] *Id.* at 3.

in the words of the "Yates Memo," which established this Department of Justice (DOJ) policy: "in order to qualify for any cooperation credit, corporations must provide to the government all relevant facts relating to the individuals responsible for the misconduct."[44] This requirement applies to both civil and criminal prosecutions, and it reflects the DOJ's recent focus on holding individuals accountable for corporate wrongdoings.[45]

3. Obligations Imposed by DPAs and NPAs

As previously noted, DPAs and NPAs impose a variety of obligations on companies, including monetary fines and requirements to institute internal corporate reforms.[46] Obligations under DPAs and NPAs typically last one to three years, and for a median of exactly two years,[47] although they can be even longer and can be extended at the option of the prosecutor in those circumstances where the government has reason to believe (or has determined) that the corporation was not in compliance with the agreement or otherwise needs additional time for compliance reforms.[48] Whatever the diversion period, while a company is under the operation of a DPA or NPA, it will typically be required to provide regular reports regarding its progress toward compliance.[49] The nature of this required reporting varies, and depends on the terms of the agreement.[50]

At the end of the diversion period, the prosecutor agrees to dismiss the charges against the corporation (in the DPA context) or refrain from bringing them altogether (in the NPA context).[51] Either way, at the successful completion of the pretrial diversion process, a corporation emerges without a conviction on its record. This fact—and the benefit of avoiding a criminal conviction altogether—makes these agreements highly desirable. In turn, it provides prosecutors with tremendous power when deciding whether to extend them.

---

[44] *Id.* at 2–3.

[45] *Id.* at 4. The "all relevant facts relating to the individuals responsible" requirement is policy (1) in the Yates Memo, and the remaining Yates Memo policies state that: "(2) criminal and civil corporate investigations should focus on individuals from the inception of the investigation; (3) criminal and civil attorneys handling corporate investigations should be in routine communication with one another; (4) absent extraordinary circumstances or approved departmental policy, the government will not release culpable individuals from civil or criminal liability when resolving a matter with a corporation; (5) government attorneys should not resolve matters with a corporation without a clear plan to resolve related individual cases, and should memorialize any declinations as to individuals in such cases; and (6) civil attorneys should consistently focus on individuals as well as the company and evaluate whether to bring suit against an individual based on considerations beyond that individual's ability to pay."

[46] Peter J. Henning, *In Bank Settlements, Fines but No Accountability*, N.Y. TIMES (Dec. 12, 2012), *available at* http://dealbook.nytimes.com/2012/12/12/in-bank-settlements-big-fines-but-no-accountability.

[47] Alexander & Cohen, *supra* note 2, at 586; Richard S. Gruner, *Corporate Criminal Liability and Prevention*, L.J. PRESS (2005).

[48] *Id.*

[49] *Id.*

[50] *Id.*

[51] *Id.*

4. Monetary Fines

DPAs and NPAs often require defendant corporations to pay the government criminal fines that are tied to corporate losses or gains caused by the underlying conduct.[52] As of July 2015, the government had collected more than $4.2 billion in fines in 2015 alone from a total of 29 DPAs and NPAs.[53] A few agreements in 2015 involved eye-popping settlement amounts. For example, a DPA between Deutsche Bank AG and the DOJ settled for $2.369 billion,[54] a DPA between General Motors and the DOJ settled for $900 million,[55] and a DPA between Commerzbank AG and the DOJ settled for $642 million (Commerzbank paid an additional $808 million to New York authorities).[56]

5. Internal Reform Requirements

DPAs and NPAs often allow prosecutors to impose internal reform requirements on companies that may not otherwise be available in a traditional prosecution.[57] Such reforms include the following:

- Remedial measures and improved compliance and corporate governance policies and practices
- Cooperation in ongoing investigations, including investigations of responsible individuals as well as investigations with foreign authorities
- The imposition of monitors[58] and required periodic reporting to the prosecutor or a court.[59]

These internal reform requirements can be rigorous and extensive. They also can impose substantial costs on a corporation and require the attention and focus of the highest level of corporate management.[60]

---

[52] Gibson, Dunn & Crutcher LLP, *supra* note 27.

[53] *Id.*

[54] United States v. Deutsche Bank, AG, Criminal Action No. 3:15-cr-00061-RNC (D. Conn. 2015), *DPA available at* http://www.justice.gov/sites/default/files/opa/press-releases/attachments/2015/04/23/db_dpa.pdf.

[55] United States v. $900,000,000 in United States Currency (defendant in rem), Civil Action No. 1:15-cv-07342 (S.D.N.Y. 2015), *DPA available at* http://www.justice.gov/usao-sdny/file/772301/download.

[56] United States v. Commerzbank AG, Civil Action No. 15-cv-01825 (D.D.C. 2015), *DPA available at* http://www.justice.gov/sites/default/files/opa/press-releases/attachments/2015/03/12/commerzbank_deferred_prosecution_agreement_1.pdf.

[57] *Id.*

[58] *Id.*

[59] *Id.*

[60] Gibson, Dunn & Crutcher, *supra* note 27.

6. Monitoring

In some cases, prosecutors will require that third-party monitors be appointed to supervise corporate defendants who have entered into pretrial diversion agreements.[61] Companies are required to hire monitors and pay the expenses they incur.[62] These independent monitors oversee compliance with the terms of the corporate negotiated agreement, which often include following applicable laws and implementing policies and procedures that ensure compliance with these laws;[63] in essence, they embody the expression "trust but verify."[64] In doing so, while under the terms of a pretrial diversion agreement, third-party monitors are responsible for independently overseeing, among other things, company operations, required self-investigation and reporting, and continuing investigation support.[65] Monitors typically make an initial report to the government in the first year of the monitorship and then make annual follow-up reports.[66] Monitors are understood to act as independent third parties, not as employees or agents of the corporations or of the government; as such, companies that retain monitors typically agree that the monitor relationship does not create an attorney-client relationship.[67] This creates the potential that work product created by monitors during the course of their monitorship will not be protected from disclosure if an outside party attempts to access that information.[68]

In terms of whether the government may require a monitor in the first place, the most important factors in determining whether the government will insist upon a monitor are: (1) "the degree of ingrained corruption at the corporation," particularly whether management participated in the violation(s);[69] and (2) "the existence of an effective compliance program

---

[61] Warin & Boutros, *supra* note 30, at 375.

[62] *Id.* at 343.

[63] *Id.* at 321.

[64] Gibson, Dunn & Crutcher, *supra* note 27.

[65] *Id.*

[66] Warin & Boutros, *supra* note 30, at 348.

[67] *Id.* at 353.

[68] *Id.* This is because disclosure to nonprivileged parties typically constitutes a waiver of attorney-client privilege. In response, companies have negotiated with the government for a privilege nonwaiver agreement. Notwithstanding this, all federal appellate courts but one have rejected a "limited waiver of privilege," which allows otherwise privileged information to be selectively waived as to the government, but not third parties. The only appellate court to recognize such a limited waiver is the Eighth Circuit Court of Appeals. *See* Diversified Industries, Inc. v. Meredith, 572 F.2d 596, 611 (8th Cir. 1978) (en banc) (determining that a limited waiver of the attorney-client privilege occurred, because the corporation voluntarily surrendered material protected by the privilege in the context of a separate and nonpublic investigation by the SEC). The issue of the confidentiality of a monitor's work product is presently being litigated in two important cases, 100Reporters LLC v. DOJ, No. 14-cv-1264 (D.D.C. 2014), and United States v. HSBC Bank USA, N.A., No. 12-CR-763(JG), 2016 WL 347670 (E.D.N.Y. Jan. 28, 2016) (granting motion to unseal redacted version of monitor's report).

[69] Warin & Boutros, *supra* note 30, at 337; *see also* Final Judgment, SEC v. Siemens Aktiengesellschaft (D.D.C. Dec. 12, 2008) (No. 1:08-cv-02167), *available at* http://www.siemens.com/press/pool/de/events/2008-12-PK/SEC.pdf (requiring the appointment of a monitor where the company's fraud was pervasive, perpetrated through thousands of corrupt payments by employees at all levels, including management); *see also* Press Release, U.S. Dep't of Justice, Statoil ASA Satisfies Obligations under Deferred Prosecution Agreement and Foreign Bribery Charges Are Dismissed (Nov. 19, 2009), *available at* http://www.justice.gov/opa/pr/2009/November/

prior to the offense."[70] Other factors that have a significant effect on whether a monitor will be required include the nature and severity of the violation(s) and whether the company self-reported the violation(s).[71]

Selecting a monitor is a crucial consideration. The government requires the monitor selection process to ensure that (1) "a highly qualified and respected person or entity" is selected "based on suitability for the assignment and all of the circumstances," (2) "potential and actual conflicts of interest[]" are avoided, and (3) there is public confidence in the monitorship's effectiveness.[72] The government typically allows companies to propose their own monitorship candidates, subject to government approval.[73] Traditionally, it was only necessary for a monitor's selection and work plan to be approved by the government, and courts were not involved in the process.[74] More recently, however, some judges have exercised their judicial authority to participate in the monitoring process.[75]

Companies should carefully negotiate the terms of the entire pretrial diversion agreement in order to minimize the costs and burdens of a monitorship. The monitor acts in accordance with the terms of the settlement agreement,[76] so the less onerous the terms of the agreement, the less the monitor can impose his or her influence on the company. For example, Siemens successfully negotiated for its monitor to review only certain business lines, activities, and markets.[77] Companies should also attempt to negotiate for sunset provisions that allow for early termination of the monitorship under certain conditions, including demonstrated

---

09-crm-1257.html (requiring a monitor where management knew about and participated in the violations); *see also* U.S. Attorney's Office, S. Dist. N.Y., U.S. Announces Settlement with Hedge Fund Omega Advisors, Inc. in Connection with Omega's Investment in Privatization Program in Azerbaijan (July 6, 2007), *available at* https://www.justice.gov/sites/default/files/criminal-fraud/legacy/2011/02/16/07-06-07omega-settlement.pdf (not requiring a monitor where the violation was committed by a lower-level group of employees at a single branch office).

[70] Warin & Boutros, *supra* note 30, at 337; *see* Press Release, U.S. Department of Justice, Micrus Corporation Enters into Agreement to Resolve Potential Foreign Corrupt Practices Act Liability (Mar. 2, 2005), *available at* http://www.justice.gov/opa/pr/2005/March/05_crm_090.htm (requiring a monitor after noting that the company had no effective compliance program); GE InVision Inc., Security Act Release No. 51199, Accounting and Enforcement Release No. 2186 (Feb. 14, 2005), *available at* http://www.sec.gov/litigation/admin/34-51199.htm (also requiring a monitor after finding that the company had no effective compliance program); SEC Files Settled Charges against ITT Corporation, Accounting and Auditing Enforcement Release No. 2934, Litigation Release No. 20896 (Feb. 11, 2009), *available at* http://www.sec.gov/litigation/litreleases/2009/lr20896.htm (not requiring a monitor after finding that the company had an effective compliance program in place).

[71] Warin & Boutros, *supra* note 30, at 343.

[72] Memorandum from Craig S. Morford, Acting Deputy Attorney General, to Heads of Department Components and United States Attorneys (Mar. 7, 2008), *available at* http://www.justice.gov/dag/morford-useofmonitorsmemo-03072008.pdf.

[73] Warin & Boutros, *supra* note 30, at 350.

[74] *Id.* at 348.

[75] *See* United States v. HSBC Bank, No. 12–CR–763, 2013 WL 3306161, at *6 (E.D.N.Y. July 1, 2013) (expressing concern about the terms of the DPA surrounding the monitorship and requiring quarterly reports on its execution to be made to the court).

[76] Warin & Boutros, *supra* note 30, at 365.

[77] Final Judgment, SEC v. Siemens Aktiengesellschaft (D.D.C. Dec. 12, 2008) (No. 1:08-cv-02167), *available at* http://www.siemens.com/press/pool/de/events/2008-12-PK/SEC.pdf.

compliance and rehabilitation; as such, early terminations can save companies significant time, energy, and resources.[78] Other terms that companies should carefully negotiate include deadlines for annual review and reporting, budgetary limits for the monitor (absent exigent circumstances), the circumstances under which the company must adopt the monitor's recommendations, and completion of the monitorship.[79]

In selecting a monitor, a company should consider: (1) whether the monitor is likely to be acceptable to the government, (2) the monitor's background and experience as a monitor concerning the relevant laws and regulations, (3) the monitor's experience with similarly situated companies, (4) the monitor's view of the role as a monitor, (5) the monitor's likely rapport with management, and (6) the monitor's concurrent employment as a monitor with other entities or workload.[80]

Once a monitor is in place, companies should obtain a detailed budget and timeline from the monitor.[81] The company should also cooperate with the monitor and provide him or her with the necessary resources to avoid the monitor hiring outsiders at the company's expense.[82] Last, the company should ask to review the monitor's report before it is submitted to the government; doing so is permitted and will allow the company an opportunity to correct any mistaken facts and make suggestions for less onerous recommendations.[83]

7. Other Relevant Features of DPAs and NPAs

As previously noted, virtually all DPAs and NPAs require a company to provide a factual basis to support the government's allegations of criminal conduct.[84] In addition, there are instances where the government has extended the terms of these pretrial diversion agreements while it investigates claims of material breaches, thereby subjecting the corporation to the auspices of the agreement for a longer period of time than originally contemplated.[85] For example, in 2014, the government extended three separate DPAs or NPAs.[86]

Virtually all pretrial diversion agreements vest the DOJ with the exclusive authority to determine whether a corporation violated the terms of a DPA or NPA.[87] For example, in May 2015, the DOJ revoked its 2012 NPA with UBS because the company was said to have breached the agreement by manipulating benchmark interest rates.[88] Similarly, in 2004, the government also found that another company, this time, Stolt-Nielsen, breached its NPA

---

[78] Warin & Boutros, *supra* note 30, at 367.

[79] *Id.*

[80] *Id.* at 369–71.

[81] *Id.* at 371.

[82] *Id.* at 373–74.

[83] *Id.* at 375.

[84] *See supra* note 4.

[85] Gibson, Dunn & Crutcher LLP, *supra* note 27.

[86] *Id.* The government extended the terms of its agreements with Barclays Bank Plc., UBS AG, and Standard Chartered Bank in connection with its investigations of whether violations of the agreements had occurred.

[87] Warin & Boutros, *supra* note 30, at 128–29.

[88] *Id.*

and revoked the agreement.[89] To be sure prosecutors rarely exercise this option; indeed, the government has revoked a DPA or NPA only twice since 2000 due to alleged criminal conduct during the diversion period.[90] Still, the real existence of this option ought to provide defendants with a strong incentive to comply with DPAs and NPAs. And, a corporation entering into an agreement must be fully prepared and willing to comply with its terms.

8. CIAs

CIAs specifically apply to the healthcare industry, but they share many similarities with DPAs and NPAs.[91] In the absence of a CIA, the OIG, through the secretary of Health and Human Services, is authorized to exclude organizations that have committed certain healthcare-related offenses from participation in benefit programs such as Medicare or Medicaid.[92] Exclusion means that "items and services furnished, ordered or prescribed by a specified individual or entity will not be reimbursed under Medicare, Medicaid and all other federal health care programs until the individual or entity is reinstated by the OIG."[93] The OIG maintains a "List of Excluded Individuals and Entities," and anyone who hires an individual or entity on the list may be subject to monetary fines.[94] This can effectively prevent an excluded corporation from doing business under a federal healthcare program.

Under the terms of a CIA, the government agrees to forgo such an exclusion in exchange for the corporation agreeing to fulfill certain obligations, which are often very similar to those required by DPAs and NPAs.[95]

9. CIA Eligibility Considerations

The OIG has directed its staff to consider the following criteria when determining whether to enter a CIA, and, if an agreement is entered, the substance of that agreement: (1) whether the provider self-disclosed the alleged misconduct; (2) the monetary damage to the federal healthcare programs; (3) whether the case involves successor liability; (4) whether the provider is still participating in the federal healthcare programs or in the line of business that gave rise to the fraudulent conduct; (5) whether the alleged conduct is capable of repetition; (6) the age of the conduct; (7) whether the provider has an effective compliance program and would agree to limited compliance or integrity measures, and would annually certify such compliance to the OIG; and (8) other circumstances, as appropriate.[96] CIAs are often

---

[89] Stolt-Nielsen, S.A. v. United States, 442 F.3d 177, 180–81 (3d Cir. 2006).

[90] Id.

[91] Copeland, *supra* note 6, at 1072–73.

[92] 42 U.S.C. §1320a-7 (2018).

[93] 42 C.F.R. § 1001.2 (2018).

[94] Id.

[95] *See supra* note 16.

[96] *Justice Manual*, at 9-28.200.

entered into in proceedings involving "off-label" promotion of pharmaceuticals,[97] kickbacks, and overbilling of Medicare or Medicaid for health services.[98]

Just as DPAs or NPAs are desirable alternatives to prosecution for corporations, a CIA is almost always preferable to exclusion from federal healthcare programs. In practice, corporations are rarely convicted and subsequently excluded.[99] The OIG, however, has entered into hundreds of CIAs between 2010 and 2015.[100]

10. Obligations Imposed by CIAs

A standard CIA provides for a monetary fine (even exceeding $1 billion) and is often accompanied by a civil settlement,[101] and other requirements negotiated between the OIG and the offending healthcare organization.[102] These requirements can include: (1) hiring a compliance officer and appointing a compliance committee; (2) developing written compliance standards and policies; (3) implementing a comprehensive employee training program; (4) retaining an independent review organization to conduct annual compliance reviews;[103] (5) establishing a confidential disclosure program; (6) restricting the company's employment of certain individuals; (7) reporting overpayments, reportable events, and ongoing investigations and legal proceedings; and (8) providing an implementation report and annual reports to the OIG on the status of the corporation's compliance activities.[104]

---

[97] Off-label promotion occurs when manufacturers "promote or advertise their products for purposes, to users, in dosages, or in combinations other than the FDA-approved ones." Steven R. Salbu, *Off-Label Use, Prescription, and Marketing of FDA-Approved Drugs: An Assessment of Legislative and Regulatory Policy*, 51 FLA. L. REV. 181, 193 (1999). The extensive cost of FDA marketing approval, particularly at the end of a drug's life cycle, has provided some companies the incentive to engage in the practice. *Id.*

[98] *Id.*; *see* Copeland, *supra* note 6, at 1050.

[99] *See id.*

[100] A list of past CIAs is available at: http://www.oig.hhs.gov/compliance/corporate-integrity-agreements/cia-documents.asp (last visited Feb. 2, 2019).

[101] Press Release, U.S. Department of Justice, GlaxoSmithKline to Plead Guilty and Pay $3 Billion to Resolve Fraud Allegations and Failure to Report Safety Data (July 2, 2012), *available at* http://www.justice.gov/opa/pr/glaxosmithkline-plead-guilty-and-pay-3-billion-resolve-fraud-allegations-and-failure-report (announcing GlaxoSmithKline's agreement to pay $1 billion under a CIA to resolve its criminal charges arising from its unlawful promotion of prescription drugs and its failure to report certain safety data, and to pay an additional $2 billion to resolve its civil liability from the same activities as well as its alleged false price reporting practices); Press Release, U.S. Department of Justice, Eli Lilly and Company Agrees to Pay $1.415 Billion to Resolve Allegations of Off-label Promotion of Zyprexa (Jan. 15, 2009), *available at* https://www.justice.gov/archive/opa/pr/2009/January/09-civ-038.html (announcing Eli Lilly's agreement to pay a $515 million fine and forfeit an additional $100 million under a CIA and to pay an additional $800 million to settle its civil liability).

[102] Exact year-over-year figures for the fines generated by CIAs are unavailable, but fines can reach the billions of dollars. *See* http://projects.propublica.org/graphics/bigpharma (last visited Feb. 2, 2019).

[103] Unlike DPAs and NPAs, CIAs typically instruct the company itself to monitor compliance rather than require the appointment of a third-party monitor. *See* Copeland, *supra* note 6, at 1074 (asserting that CIAs instruct manufacturers to monitor their employees and then outlining the lack of enforcement of such monitoring requirements).

[104] U.S. Department of Health and Human Services, *supra* note 22.

The agreement delineates what parts of the company are subject to the CIA (including which subsidiaries, business units, and business activities fall under the agreement), the company's overall responsibilities arising from the agreement, and the responsibilities of individuals within the company.[105] CIAs often cover a defendant's subsidiaries.[106] This coverage prevents corporations from shifting production to their subsidiaries in an effort to shield themselves from compliance.[107] CIAs also set out a compliance mechanism, usually through an officer or a committee, as well as codes of conduct, reporting systems, and whistle-blower protection programs.[108] CIAs typically last for three to five years—much longer than the typical one- to three-year duration of DPAs and NPAs.[109]

Like DPAs and NPAs, CIAs often require executives to certify that the corporation is in compliance with the agreement.[110] These "Management Accountability and Certifications" often require certification related to training in compliance requirements, individuals' roles in the compliance scheme, and averments that the signee's department is fully in compliance.[111]

11. Conclusion

DPAs, NPAs, and CIAs provide the government with the means to pursue productive alternatives to criminal prosecution for corporate wrongdoers. Prosecuting corporate defendants can have the undesirable effect of impacting innocent third parties who are either employed by the offending party, rely on the offending party, or are otherwise invested in the performance of the offending party as is the case with innocent shareholders. By providing an option to accomplish meaningful corporate reform without exceedingly adverse consequences, these agreements can strike an important balance between conviction and exculpation and can protect innocent third parties from harmful, if not destructive, collateral consequences.

Corporations can also use DPAs, NPAs, and CIAs to avoid the devastating effects inherent in a criminal conviction. To be sure, these agreements often contain onerous requirements, but these requirements are almost always preferable to prosecution and conviction, which is why they have emerged as desirable alternatives to the traditional options for prosecuting and punishing criminal activity.

---

[105] Copeland, *supra* note 6, at 1051.

[106] Assistant Attorney General Stuart Delery, *Remarks at the CBI Pharmaceutical Compliance Conference* (Jan. 29, 2014), *available at* http://www.justice.gov/iso/opa/civil/speeches/2014/civ-speech-140129.html.

[107] *Id.*

[108] *Id.*

[109] *Id.*

[110] In 2008, a CIA with Cephalon, Inc., added new requirements that held management accountable for the agreement's terms. These "Management Accountability and Certifications" required certification as to training in compliance requirements, individual roles in the compliance scheme, and certification that the signee's department was in compliance. Copeland, *supra* note 6, at 1051.

[111] *Id.*

27 Company Cooperation and U.S. Sentencing Guidelines

THE U.S. SENTENCING Commission has changed how the U.S. Sentencing Guidelines calculate fines for certain defendant companies.[1] The amendments, effective November 1, 2010, make more readily available a long-standing three-level offense-level reduction. This change shifts the inquiry away from (1) the (mis)conduct of the company's high-level personnel and toward (2) the effectiveness of the company's compliance and ethics program. This move will surely benefit corporate defendants. Therefore, it is something for which compliance professionals and in-house legal counsel need to both understand and prepare.

Of course, crime prevention—that is, implementing and maintaining an effective compliance program—is a company's best chance to avoid ever having to consider the benefits of the three-point reduction in the first place. Thus, instituting and complying with the new amendments' requirements serves two corollary functions: it both *prevents* liability through deterrence and rapid response and *mitigates* the misconduct's impact should it nevertheless occur.

As the benefits of incentivizing companies to adopt proactive compliance, ethics, and self-reporting programs gain wider recognition, other countries eager to beef up their anti-bribery efforts can be expected to follow suit.

---

[1] This chapter was contributed by T. Markus Funk. This chapter has been adapted from *The ABA Compliance Officer's Deskbook*.

From Baksheesh to Bribery. T. Markus Funk and Andrew S. Boutros.
© Oxford University Press 2019. Published 2019 by Oxford University Press.

1. How the 20-Year-Old Categorical Bar on Fine Reduction Became History

As practitioners know, since the adoption of the Sentencing Guidelines some 20 years ago, Section 8C2.5(f) has permitted corporate defendants able to demonstrate that they, *at the time of the offense*, had an effective compliance program in place to significantly reduce their fines by way of a three-level reduction in their total offense level.

For a company that finds itself in the unenviable position of having to calculate its guidelines range, a three-level offense reduction translates into significant real-world results—effectively reducing the applicable fine by at least 50 percent. For example, at the lower end of the range, a three-level decrease drops the fine from $15,000 to $5,000; toward the higher end of the range, a three-level reduction moves the fine from $72.5 million (level 38) down to $36 million (level 35).

For the past two decades, however, companies seeking to benefit from a Section 8C2.5(f) reduction faced a considerable stumbling block in the form of an automatic bar in cases where "high-level personnel" participated in, condoned, or were willfully ignorant of the offense. As of this writing, however, the actions of high-level corporate personnel no longer foreclose the possibility of receiving a significant compliance credit.

2. Introducing the Four-Part Eligibility Test

Although the amendments may only provide cold, after-the-fact comfort to a charged company's shareholders or directors, the reality is that the three-level drop affords substantial benefits. Under new Section 8C2.5(f)(3)(C), a company with an effective compliance program, as defined in Section 8B2.1, can benefit from the three-level reduction if it meets four distinct criteria:

- The individual or individuals with operational responsibility for the compliance and ethics program have *direct reporting obligations* to the company's governing authority or appropriate subgroup thereof.
- The compliance and ethics program detected the offense *before* discovery outside the company or before such discovery was *reasonably likely*.
- The company promptly *reported* the offense to the appropriate government authorities.
- No individual with *operational responsibility* for the compliance and ethics program participated in, condoned, or was willfully ignorant of the offense.

The amendments respond to public concerns that (1) the categorical bar to the reduction operated too broadly, and (2) internal and external reporting of criminal conduct is, in appropriate cases, better encouraged by providing an exception to the general prohibition.

3. Effective Compliance Programs and Appropriate Responses to Criminal Conduct

Section 8B2.1(b)(7) requires that, in order to have an "effective compliance program," a company that has detected criminal conduct must take "reasonable steps to respond appropriately to the criminal conduct and to prevent further similar criminal conduct, including making any necessary modifications to the company's compliance and ethics program."

Application note 6 now helpfully explains what constitutes (1) an appropriate response to criminal conduct, as well as (2) proactive steps designed to avert similar conduct in the future. Specifically, the application note provides that such steps "may include the use of an *outside professional advisor* to ensure adequate assessment and implementation of any modifications" (emphasis added).

4. Answering Questions Raised by the Amendments

The amendments should be warmly received by companies making a significant effort to develop and implement effective internal compliance and ethics programs. Such proactive steps translate into robust compliance programs reducing corporate exposure to risk.

However, the appearance of the amendments also raises some important questions in need of answers:

(a) *What role, if any, can and should general counsel now play in internal investigations and in reporting offenses to the government? Are general counsel still able to instruct outside counsel on how to conduct internal investigations, or must such directions now principally come from the compliance/ethics officers?*

The amendments require that the company's compliance and ethics officers be *expressly* authorized to report their findings as it relates to actual or potential criminal conduct *personally* and *directly* to the company's executive leadership (the "governing authority"). This, however, does not require the company's general counsel to remain uninvolved in ethics and compliance issues. To the contrary, it is highly advisable that general counsel maintain a close, cooperative, and supportive relationship with the compliance and ethics officers. Likewise, the amendments do not preclude general counsels from instructing outside counsel on matters relating to the internal investigations. The only caveat is that the general counsel must take care not to function as a "gatekeeper," who filters information between the company's compliance and ethics officers and its executives.

(b) *Are internal investigations still privileged?*

There is no reason that the amendments' new reporting requirements should result in, or require, waiver or forfeiture of any attorney-client privilege. The amendments simply require unfiltered, direct reporting between the ethics and compliance officers and the company's executives, early and voluntary self-disclosure, and that the compliance and ethics officers remain free of culpability.

These objectives can be achieved without sacrificing the attorney-client privilege, and nothing in the text of the amendments (or its application notes) requires companies to waive the attorney-client privilege or work-product protections in order to qualify for a reduction.

(c) *Does a company's retention of outside counsel for an investigation impact the analysis of whether the three-level reduction is available?*

The use of outside counsel poses no obstacle, provided that they work through the company's compliance and ethics officers, and that it is the latter who report their findings to the company's executives. To the contrary, companies are well-advised to take advantage of outside counsel's independent investigation.

5. UK Bribery Act's Compliance Incentives Offer a Glimpse of the Future

With the passage of the UK Bribery Act of 2010, which outlaws bribery of both public and private officials, the United Kingdom is also placing an emphasis on unimpeded reporting, early detection, and self-reporting. Similar to Section 8C2.5(f)(3)(C) of the Guidelines, the UK Bribery Act of 2010 offers a defense for organizations able to demonstrate that, at the time of the offense, they had "adequate" compliance procedures in place to prevent the offense being investigated.

The UK's Serious Fraud Office—as part of its efforts to offer DOJ-style guidance "opinion releases" to companies—announced a non-exhaustive collection of measures likely required for companies to avail themselves of the "adequate procedures designed to prevent prohibited payments" defense, which in turn would allow companies to completely avoid criminal prosecution and instead face only civil liability or no liability at all. These measures include having the following in place:

- An effective compliance plan
- A formalized code of ethics
- Creation of an "anti-corruption culture" within the company
- The presence of direct internal corporate reporting systems
- Regular checks and audits
- Appropriate and consistent disciplinary processes
- Early detection of potential violations
- Voluntary self-referral
- Remedial actions to remedy past cases of corruption

However, the availability of such "home run" defenses for effective compliance and ethics programs appear to be the exception—not the rule—in most countries.

By way of brief comparison, Germany's 1998 Act on Combating Bribery of Foreign Public Officials in International Business Transactions, and the Turkish Law No. 4782 and the Turkish Criminal Code, while otherwise praiseworthy efforts to stem foreign bribery, afford companies no comparable codified "out" against criminal liability, even when companies can demonstrate good-faith efforts to prevent the bribery in the first place.

That said, as the benefits of incentivizing companies to set up effective compliance and ethics programs, reporting systems, self-disclosure, and whistle-blower protections become more widely understood, other countries can be expected to follow the United States and UK's lead.

6. Avoid Liability—and the Financial Consequences Thereof—in Four Easy Steps: Review, Revise, Hire, and Submit

Companies must take careful stock of their compliance and ethics programs to ensure that they are appropriately tailored to fit the amended guidelines. The four things that companies (through their compliance and legal departments) must do in light of the recent guidelines amendments are:

(a) *Review* their compliance and ethics program to ensure the compliance and ethics officers have direct responsibility, set forth in writing, to the board of directors' audit committee or similar subgroup to immediately inform them of suspected noncompliance or criminal conduct.

(b) *Revise* existing compliance policies and procedures to identify and promptly remedy potential internal control and compliance weaknesses.

(c) *Hire* outside counsel to investigate cases of suspected noncompliance and to suggest appropriate amendments to the company's compliance and ethics program to help stave off questions concerning whether the company took "reasonable steps" upon learning of the suspected criminal conduct.

(d) *Submit* an annual report assessing the implementation and effectiveness of the company's compliance and ethics program.

These four simple steps offer companies low-cost "insurance" against criminal conduct, as well as a means to mitigate—if not entirely avoid—the "parade of horribles" that unchecked conduct can have on a company's long-term future.

28 Department of Justice's New Revised FCPA Corporate Enforcement Policy

ON NOVEMBER 29, 2017, Deputy Attorney General Rod Rosenstein announced a new and significant shift in the U.S. Department of Justice's Enforcement Policy for the Foreign Corrupt Practices Act (FCPA).[1] The Policy, which has been written into the *Justice Manual*, is designed to provide more certainty to companies regarding the benefits of cooperating with federal enforcement officials investigating corrupt business activities abroad. Importantly, the Policy creates a "presumption that [a] company will receive a declination absent aggravating circumstances" where it has "voluntarily self-disclosed misconduct in an FCPA matter, fully cooperated, and timely and appropriately remediated." Significantly, a "declination" under the Policy is a case that would have been prosecuted or criminally resolved but for the company's full and complete satisfaction of the Policy's criteria. Regardless of whether a company qualifies for a declination or some reduced sentence short of a full declination under the Policy, any corporate participant in the Policy is "required to pay all disgorgement, forfeiture, and/or restitution resulting from the misconduct at issue." Under the Policy, all declinations (and, of course, any other form of a criminal resolution) will be made public.

---

[1] This chapter was contributed by Andrew S. Boutros and T. Markus Funk. This chapter has been adapted from an article authored by Andrew S. Boutros and John J. Schleppenbach that first appeared in *Bloomberg Law White Collar Crime Report*, 12 WCR 999 (Dec. 8, 2017).

From Baksheesh to Bribery. T. Markus Funk and Andrew S. Boutros.
© Oxford University Press 2019. Published 2019 by Oxford University Press.

1. Voluntary Disclosure

Defining what constitutes "voluntary disclosure," the Policy states that such disclosure must occur *prior* to an imminent threat of disclosure or government investigation and within a reasonably prompt time after becoming aware of the offense. The disclosure must also include all relevant facts known to the company, including facts about individuals involved in the violation of the law.

2. *Full* Cooperation

The Policy also expounds upon the (now-amended) meaning of "full cooperation," stating that a company must timely disclose all relevant facts gathered during its independent investigation, with attribution of facts to specific sources where it does not offend the attorney-client privilege. Companies are encouraged to make rolling productions of information. Cooperation, moreover, must be proactive rather than merely reactive and include timely notifications of any known opportunities for the government to obtain relevant evidence not in the company's possession. Document preservation and disclosure are also prioritized, with facilitation of overseas and third-party document production being favored. As part of their corporate cooperation efforts, companies should help make employees and former employees available to the government for interviews and make sure that their own internal investigations do not conflict with government investigations, a process known as "deconfliction."

3. Remediation

In terms of timely remediation, companies are expected to demonstrate a thorough analysis of the root causes giving rise to the misconduct and address remediation to those causes. Companies should also implement effective compliance programs, which will be gauged by a variety of factors including resources devoted, quality of personnel, and authority and independence. In addition, it is important that companies appropriately discipline employees and implement document retention programs, including by prohibiting employees from using software that generates but does not retain business records or communications. The DOJ will look at any and all steps that demonstrate recognition of the seriousness of the company's misconduct, acceptance of responsibility for it, and the implementation of measures to reduce the risk of recidivism.

4. New Definition of "Full Cooperation"?

Turning to a few additional in-the-trenches aspects of the government's enforcement approach, experienced federal practitioners know that, practically speaking, for some years there has been noticeable daylight between the policy on individual accountability on paper and how it was actually applied in real-word criminal cases. More specifically, the DOJ tended to only press the 'all-or-nothing' approach (formally requiring companies to disclose the names and conduct of every employee having any involvement with the potentially criminal conduct) on a case-by-case as-needed basis to gain leverage and certain tactical advantages.

As Deputy Attorney General Rosenstein in his November 29, 2018 'Yates Memo' speech candidly acknowledged, prosecutors loosened the policy as needed in individual cases so that it rarely, if ever, prevented DOJ prosecutors from achieving a desired resolution. Under the revised policy, then, the DOJ encourage more realistic cooperation efforts without compromising its reinvigorated policy of holding responsible individuals accountable.

Indeed, any policy that creates a no-grey bright-line can result in unintended—and typically unanticipated—consequences. And this is only more so in the context of criminal enforcement policies and approaches. Demanding that companies abide by an all-or-nothing binary rule of either identifying every employee who "may have played a role" in the conduct of concern, regardless of relative culpability, or receive no cooperation credit at all was both asking too much and perceived by most as unfair. And, the result was often counterproductive to encouraging cooperation.

Additionally, the previous individual-accountability policy effectively incentivized rank-and-file employees to refuse to cooperate in investigations because their attorneys reasonably told them that the results of any such cooperation would likely be handed over to the DOJ. This created de facto adversity between the interests of the individual employee and the interests of the company. The natural consequence was that companies were impeded in fully understanding what may have gone wrong, which, in turn, slowed cooperation with the government.

But there should be no mistake: As of this writing, the revised policy still requires companies seeking cooperation credit to turn over those individuals "*substantially* involved in or responsible for" the criminal conduct. Put another way, absent "extraordinary circumstances," resolutions with companies still will not insulate truly culpable individuals from criminal liability. Practitioners, however, appreciate that companies decide to cooperate for a number of reasons, and the actual or likely presence of a whistleblower of course is a significant one. Under the old policy, current and former employees fearing that the company will turn them over to the DOJ regardless of culpability at times preemptively rushed to the DOJ first. This, in turn, caused certain companies to err on the side of more immediate disclosure and cooperation. So in this sense, the more relaxed policy may actually slow down (if not disincentivize) the process in which companies rush to the DOJ doorsteps. On the other hand, the prospect of a more stream-lined investigation and more predictable cooperation credit makes corporate self-disclosure more palatable. As such, it will be interesting to see how time will treat this latest corporate policy development; after all, the predecessor policy from the prior administration (the Yates Memo from September 9, 2015) only survived about three years before the next administration scaled it back.

To be sure, the revised DOJ policy reflects a more nuanced and realistic assessment of the resource-allocation challenges of government enforcers and companies alike. But the most fundamental point of the cooperation-credit requirement remains entirely intact, namely, a company must still in good faith identify all substantially involved, responsible individuals if it wishes to receive any cooperation credit. And the government's understandable emphasis on holding the most senior persons accountable will continue to be front-and-center for all entering the Bond Building (home of the FCPA Unit), the Canada House (home of the UK Serious Fraud Office), and similar centers of enforcement power. Full and honest cooperation—and high-integrity internal investigations that help guarantee it—will continue to be a true precondition to alleviating penalties.

5. Staggered Punishments

Because some foreign bribery crimes are just so serious and aggravating that they do not lend themselves to a declination, under the Policy, a declination is not guaranteed, even for a fully cooperative company that voluntary self-discloses its misconduct. In cases where a company has voluntarily self-disclosed, fully cooperated, and timely and appropriately remediated, the Policy leaves open the possibility of charges where there are aggravating circumstances, such as involvement by executive management in the misconduct, a significant profit to the company from the misconduct, pervasive misconduct within the company, or criminal recidivism. But even in those circumstances, the Policy still seeks to incentivize cooperation—and preordains certainty—by stating that the DOJ will recommend a 50-percent reduction off the low end of the applicable U.S. Sentencing Guidelines fine range and generally not require appointment of a monitor, assuming in the case of the latter that the company has an effective compliance program in place at the time of the resolution.

In those cases where a company does *not* make a voluntary self-disclosure to the government, but otherwise fully cooperates with the government in its investigation and upholds the other standards of the Policy, the DOJ will recommend a sentencing reduction of up to 25 percent off of the low end of the applicable Guidelines range.

Importantly, culpable corporate executives and other individuals are *not* covered by the DOJ Policy and can still expect to be investigated and prosecuted for FCPA wrongdoing.

6. Conclusion and Parting Thoughts

Overall, the DOJ's new FCPA Corporate Enforcement Policy (and its 2018 amendment) is a breath of fresh air. It continues the government's movement toward incentivizing cooperation and corporate compliance and providing more certainty to what has often been criticized as an opaque and sometimes shadowy process. Companies doing business internationally should make sure that they have effective compliance programs in place and, when faced with a potential FCPA violation, the mechanisms to appropriately investigate, disclose, cooperate, and remediate. Doing so will exponentially increase a company's chances of obtaining a presumed declination under the DOJ's new Policy and reduce the likelihood that the new clear path forward will be blocked by lack of planning or unforced errors.

29 On the Anti-Bribery "Watchlist": Compliance and Labor/Anti-Trafficking Issues

1. New Challenges in Labor-Related Compliance

Those who practice in the international enforcement sphere are all too familiar with perennial compliance and enforcement "hot topics" such as the U.S. Foreign Corrupt Practices Act, the U.S. Travel Act, the UK Bribery Act, and carbon-copy prosecutions.[1] Perhaps less familiar, but substantively related—and increasingly demanding serious compliance attention and resources—is the emerging area of human anti-trafficking and forced labor laws and regulations as they relate to business supply chains. These mandates include the California Transparency in Supply Chains Act, the Executive Order on Strengthening Protections Against Trafficking in Persons in Federal Contracts, and the UK Modern Slavery Act of 2015. By enlisting or conscripting companies into the fight against human trafficking, child labor, and other "forced" or "coerced" labor practices, these laws introduce a wholly new compliance reality requiring accountability and supply chain compliance. What is more, few—if any—organized human traffickers are able to ply their dark trade without also bribing immigration officials, factory/labor inspectors, etc. In short, *there can be bribery without trafficking, but there cannot be trafficking without bribery*—which is why the two areas are inextricably intertwined, deserving mention in this book.

Today's companies—especially those that interface with, or rely on, overseas markets as part of their supply chains (and, these days, those are most companies)—must understand and prevent the myriad problems flowing from such labor issues. The costs for paying insufficient attention to these issues can include lawsuits (class action and otherwise), enforcement

---

[1] This chapter was contributed by T. Markus Funk. This chapter has been adapted from *The ABA Compliance Officer's Deskbook*.

From Baksheesh to Bribery. T. Markus Funk and Andrew S. Boutros.
© Oxford University Press 2019. Published 2019 by Oxford University Press.

actions, prosecutions/investigations, activist pressures, and brand-damaging negative media and other forms of publicity.

This chapter surveys today's trafficked/child/slave/indentured labor (collectively, "coerced" or "forced" labor) laws. By way of summary, the new—and increasingly important—"big three" forced labor regimes every attorney advising contemporary transnational businesses (whether in-house or as outside counsel) must understand are (1) the Federal Acquisition Regulation (FAR) anti-trafficking provisions, (2) the California Transparency in Supply Chains Act, and (3) the UK Modern Slavery Act of 2015. This chapter also includes a discussion of the Trade Facilitation and Trade Enforcement Act of 2015, which became effective in March 2016 (see Table 29.1).

2. The Federal Acquisition Regulations Anti-Trafficking Provisions

The U.S. government is the world's largest consumer of goods and services. As a result, its sheer buying power and leverage as an acquirer of goods and services puts it in the position of being able to change (or at least try to change) behavior, especially corporate behavior. It is no overstatement that the new FAR provisions relating to anti-trafficking have had an immediate and significant impact on the 300,000 or so direct suppliers (as well as countless sub- and sub-subcontractors/vendors) that do business with the U.S. government.

In moving our topic from the general to the specific, we note that in September 2012, President Obama signed an Executive Order on "Strengthening Protections Against Trafficking in Persons in Federal Contracts."[2] The final rule implemented by that Executive Order was published on January 29, 2015, and became effective on March 2, 2015.[3]

As of March 2015, implementation of that Executive Order applied to all government contractors (no de minimus exceptions).[4] The final FAR anti-trafficking provisions mandate that all federal contractors ensure that their supply chains are in no way tainted by trafficked labor. This subset of requirements also applies irrespective of contract type or contract value. In this regard:

Prohibited conduct. The key items of prohibited conduct are found at FAR 52.222-50(b),[5] which provides the prohibition that contractors, contractor employees, and agents may not:
   (a) *Engage* in severe forms of trafficking in persons during the period of performance of the contract;
   (b) *Procure* commercial sex acts during the period of performance of the contract;[6]
   (c) *Use* forced labor in the performance of the contract;

---

[2] Exec. Order No. 13,627, 77 Fed. Reg. 60,029 (Sept. 25, 2012).

[3] *Id.*

[4] *Federal Acquisition Regulation; Ending Trafficking in Persons*, 80 Fed. Reg. 4967 (Jan. 29, 2015).

[5] *Id.* at 4990.

[6] Although the rule is clear, the scope of the rule remains unclear. Are prime contractors now required to monitor the on- and off-hour conduct of sub- and sub-subemployees when it comes to commercial sex acts? What is actually expected of prime contractors and their subcontractors when it comes to this rule? Our best estimation is that the drafters of the rule recognize that the answers to these questions are not found explicitly in the rule's text, and as such, they must provide additional guidance to the business community on what is actually expected.

TABLE 29.1

Human Trafficking/Forced Labor Laws & Regulation Comparison Matrix

Enactment	Jurisdiction	Disclosure Requirements	Non-Disclosure/ Substantive Requirements	Penalties	Effective Date
California Transparency in Supply Chains Act (SB 657)	All companies that are: 1. Retail seller/manufacturer (based on tax status); 2. With annual gross worldwide receipts exceeding $100 million; and 3. "Doing business" in California (property or salaries in California exceeding $50K).	Disclosure must address what, if anything, done to: 1. Verify supply chain to evaluate/ address "risks of human trafficking and slavery." 2. Audit suppliers to evaluate compliance with company standards (and, if so, unannounced and through independent auditors)? 3. Obtain certification from direct suppliers that materials incorporated into goods comply with local anti-trafficking and slavery laws 4. Maintain internal "accountability standards and procedures" for those who fail to meet your standards. 5. Provide training to employees/ management with supply chain responsibility (focus on mitigating supply chain risks and identifying trafficking). Note: Disclosures must be on internet homepage.	None	• California Attorney General injunction for noncompliance. • Potential class action lawsuits for false or misleading declarations. • Consumer and advocacy group actions.	January 1, 2012

(Continued)

TABLE 29.1

Continued

Enactment	Jurisdiction	Disclosure Requirements	Non-Disclosure/ Substantive Requirements	Penalties	Effective Date
		Homepage disclosure must be through a "conspicuous" and "easily understood" link to full-text document			
Executive Order on Trafficking in Government Contracts (EO 13627) The final rule amends Federal Acquisition Regulation Subpart 22.17 and Contract Clause 52.222-50	Applies to all federal contractors for goods/services (size/nature of contract irrelevant).	For contracts for services or supplies that are not off-the-shelf items that (1) exceed $500,000 in value and (2) are to be performed outside United States, contractors and subcontractors must create and post at the workplace and on their company website a formal compliance plan including: • An employee awareness program about U.S. anti-trafficking policy • A process for employees to report activity inconsistent with zero-tolerance policy without fear of retaliation • A recruitment and wage plan • Available disciplinary actions for employees that violate the policy • Reciprocal expectations between company and supplier • A housing plan • Preventative procedures for subcontractors	Federal contractors, subcontractors, their employees and their agents prohibited from engaging in human trafficking, as evidenced through: • Using forced labor • Misleading/ fraudulent recruitment practices • Charging recruitment fees • Destroying, concealing, confiscating, or otherwise denying employee access to his or her identity docs	Imprisonment "Knowing and willful" false certification is a crime. Reckless disregard or conscious avoidance of truth qualify as "knowing." Consequences include up to five years' imprisonment and $250K fine. • False Claims Act: Government Fraud (31 U.S.C § 3729). • Trafficking Victims Protection Act (22 U.S.C. § 7104(g): Federal agency may terminate your contract.	March 2, 2015

- Each contractor and subcontractor must formally certify that it has a compliance plan in place, has conducted due diligence, and has an absence of misconduct, or if misconduct was observed, that appropriate remediation and referral actions were taken.

- Failing to pay return transportation costs
- Failing to provide employment agreement (if required) in employee's native tongue and prior to employee's departure from home country

Contractors and their subcontractors must agree to

- "Cooperate fully" with, and provide reasonable access to, agencies conducting investigations into, among other things, violations of this order
- Self-report, among other things, "activities that . . . are inconsistent with the requirements of this order or any other applicable law or regulation"

- Debarment: Business death knell for noncompliance (48 CFR 9.406-2).
- Loss of award fee or termination of contract

(Continued)

TABLE 29.1

Continued

Enactment	Jurisdiction	Disclosure Requirements	Non-Disclosure/ Substantive Requirements	Penalties	Effective Date
Business Supply Chain Transparency on Trafficking and Slavery Act of 2015 (*once-pending legislation*—H.R. 3226)	All companies that are: 1. Publicly traded *and* 2. Have annual gross receipts in excess of $100 million	Statement describing to what extent, if any, company: • Maintains policies to Identify/ eliminate risks of trafficking and slavery within supply chains, and actions taken pursuant to policies; • Maintains policies prohibiting employees/ employees of entities associated with supply chain from engaging in commercial sex acts with minors; • Evaluates and addresses risks of human trafficking and worst forms of child labor in supply chains; • Audits suppliers' working conditions/ labor practices; • Requires suppliers to attest that their product manufacturing/labor recruitments are carried out in compliance with trafficking and slavery laws, maintain internal accountability standards and procedures, train employees responsible for supply chain management, and recruit employees in compliance with company anti-trafficking policies; • Provides remediation to those who have been identified as trafficking and slavery victims	None	• Securities and Exchange Commission action for failure to adequately comply. • Potential class action lawsuits for false or misleading declarations. • Consumer and advocacy group actions.	Depends on if/when pending legislation passed

UK Modern Slavery Act of 2015 (Part 6 — Transparency in Supply Chains)	All companies that are: 1. Supplier of goods and/or services; 2. Corporation or partnership (wherever incorporated or formed) carrying on "a business, or part of a business," in any part of the UK *and* 3. With a total annual turnover exceeding £36 million.	Statement detailing steps taken during the past financial year to ensure slavery and human trafficking are not taking place in (1) any of company's supply chains, and (2) any part of its business. Approved/signed disclosure statement may include information concerning: • Company's structure/business/ supply chains • Anti-trafficking/slavery policies. • Anti-trafficking/slavery due diligence processes • Identification and management of higher-risk areas in business/ supply chains • Effectiveness assessment of measures, based on performance measures company considers appropriate. • Anti-trafficking/slavery trainings available to staff.	None	• High Court injunction (civil action brought by Secretary of State) • In Scotland only, action for specific performances of a statutory duty under § 45 of the Court of Session Act 1988.	Royal assent received March 26, 2015
Directive of the European Parliament and of the Council Concerning Various Disclosures	"The proposal provides that large companies should disclose non-financial information under a set of requirements devised to increasing transparency with the objective of strengthening the company's transparency and accountability, while limiting any undue administrative burden."	"Article 1 (a) of the proposal will require certain large companies to disclose a statement in their Annual Report including material information relating to at least environmental, social, and employee-related matters, respect of human rights, anti-corruption and bribery aspects. Within these areas, the statement will include (i) a description of its policies, (ii) results and (iii) risk-related aspects."	None	Uncertain	N/A

This chart was prepared by Perkins Coie Partner T. Markus Funk (MFunk@perkinscoie.com). Markus retains the copyright to this chart.

(d) *Destroy, conceal, confiscate, or otherwise deny access* by an employee to the employee's identity or immigration documents, such as passports or driver's licenses;

(e) *Use misleading or fraudulent practices* during the recruitment of employees or offering of employment (a number of examples are provided here); or use recruiters that do not comply with local labor laws of the country in which the recruiting takes place;

(f) *Charge* employees recruitment fees;

(g) *Fail to provide return transportation* to pay for the costs of return transportation upon the end of employment (a number of exceptions may apply);

(h) *Provide or arrange housing* that fails to meet the host country housing and safety standards; or

(i) *If required by law or contract, fail to provide an employment contract*, recruitment agreement, or other required work document in writing. (A number of more detailed requirements apply.)[7]

In rather stark contrast to this 2015 "new" version of the FAR's anti-trafficking provisions, the "old" (2009) version of FAR 52.222-50 prohibits a far narrower (and more "severe") set of conduct than does the current version of the regulation, in that the 2015 version also prohibits what fairly can be considered precursors and indicators of trafficking. More specifically, the 2009 clause prohibits three categories of conduct:

- Engaging in "severe forms of trafficking" in persons during the period of performance of the contract;
- Procuring commercial sex acts during the period of performance of the contract; or
- Using "forced labor" in the performance of the contract.

Also relatively clear are several requirements found at FAR 52.222-50(c)–(e), "Contractor requirements," "Notification," and "Remedies."[8] These requirements include the following:

- *Disclosures to all employees*: Contractors and subcontractors must notify their employees and agents of the U.S. government's policy prohibiting trafficking in persons and of actions that will be taken against employees or agents who violate the policy. "Such actions for employees may include, but are not limited to, removal from the contract, reduction in benefits, or termination of employment."[9]
- *Actions against employees*: Contractors must "[t]ake appropriate action, up to and including termination, against employees, agents, or subcontractors" who engage in the prohibited conduct contained in subparagraph (b).[10]
- *Immediate notification regarding violations*: Contractors must inform the Contracting Officer and Inspector General immediately of "[a]ny credible

---

[7] 80 Fed. Reg. at 4990–91.
[8] *Id.* at 4991.
[9] *Id.*
[10] *Id.*

Deconstructing Government Contractor Anti-Trafficking Provisions
(Federal Acquisition Regulation Subpart 22.17 and Contract Clause 52.222-50 – Effective 2015)

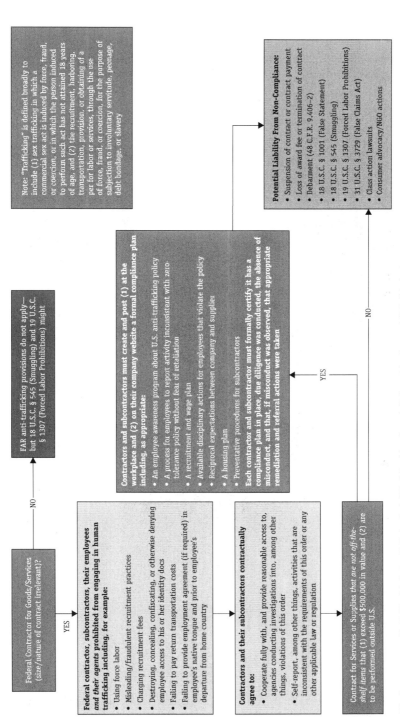

This chart was prepared by Perkins Coie Partner T. Markus Funk (Mfunk@perkinscoie.com). Markus retains the copyright to this chart.

FIGURE 29.1 Deconstructing Government Contractor Anti-Trafficking Provisions

information it receives from any source . . . that alleges a Contractor employee, subcontractor, subcontractor employee, or their agent has engaged in conduct that violates the policy in paragraph (b) of this clause. . . ."[11] In addition, the contractor must provide information concerning "[a]ny actions taken against a Contractor employee, subcontractor, subcontractor employee, or their agent pursuant to this clause."[12]

- *Remedies.* The government's remedies for noncompliance are also relatively clear. Noncompliance can result in:
  o Requiring the contractor to remove a contractor employee (or employees) from the performance of the contract;
  o Requiring the contractor to terminate a subcontract;
  o Suspension of contract payments;
  o Loss of an award fee;
  o Declination to exercise available options under the contract;
  o Termination of the contract for default or cause; and
  o Suspension or debarment.[13]

This is a non-exhaustive list of potential government remedies. Contractors must also consider the risk of False Claims Act liability, class actions, consumer boycotts, and possible criminal prosecution for fraud or false statements and certifications, such as criminal prosecutions under 18 U.S.C. § 1001 (false statements).

3. Compliance Plan, Certification Requirements, and Due Diligence

In addition to the requirements that apply to all contracts regardless of dollar value, there are other requirements, for certifications regarding compliance plans and due diligence, that apply above certain thresholds. Section 52.222-50(h)—compliance plan—provides that the regulation will apply to any portion of the contract that (1) is for supplies, other than commercially available off-the-shelf items, acquired outside the United States, or services to be performed outside the United States; and (2) has an estimated value over $500,000.

The clause requires that "annually after receiving an award," a contractor will provide the contracting officer a certification that it has implemented a compliance plan. A contractor must also certify that, after having conducted due diligence, either: (1) to the best of the contractor's knowledge and belief, neither it nor any of its agents, subcontractors, or their agents is engaged in any such activities; or (2) if abuses relating to any of the prohibited activities have been found, the contractor or subcontractor has taken the appropriate remedial and referral actions.

The relevant FAR provisions do not end with the above. Contractors must also (and, rather exceptionally) (1) affirmatively cooperate with, and provide access to, enforcement agencies investigating compliance with forced-labor laws; and (2) make a mandatory disclosure (or

---

[11] *Id.*

[12] *Id.*

[13] *Id.*

self-report) of potential anti-trafficking violations upon receipt of any credible information from any source that alleges a contractor employee, subcontractor, or subcontractor
employee has engaged in conduct that violates the new FAR provisions.[14] As experienced
practitioners will recognize, mandatory disclosure and required cooperation are no small
matters, and require immediate action in cases of even potential noncompliance.

The new FAR provisions notably raise the bar by requiring companies to ensure their entire supply chain is free from human trafficking and forced labor. Ensuring compliance, in
turn, will require considerable resources.

4. Imports Face New Level of Scrutiny: Closing the Tariff Act of 1930's Loophole with the Trade Facilitation and Trade Enforcement Act of 2015

The federal government took a significant step in February 2016 in the fight against slave,
trafficked, child, and indentured labor. President Barack Obama signed into law the Trade
Facilitation and Trade Enforcement Act of 2015.[15] This enactment, signed on February 22,
2016, and entered into effect on March 10, 2016, closed a critical loophole by amending the
Tariff Act of 1930 to remove the long-standing immunity for broad classes of goods made
with forced and prison labor.

The Tariff Act was passed in 1930. Since that time, the United States has made it illegal to
import any goods made with forced or prison labor. However, a controversial key carveout
provided that certain goods from abroad that met "the consumptive demands of the United
States" were exempt from the ban. So, for example, because the demand for cocoa or teak far
outstripped any domestic supply (after all, there is none), cocoa and teak imports were never
stopped regardless of how the cocoa or teak was harvested or produced.

The impact of the carveout is far more than academic. U.S. Customs and Border Protection
(CBP) and its predecessor agencies reported fewer than 40 instances in the last 85 years of
stopping shipments of goods suspected to have been made with forced or prison labor. Given
that forced and prison labor is commonplace in many parts of the world, this low number
speaks to the carveout's real-world impact. With the carveout a thing of the past, every indication is that scrutiny of imports, and the corresponding number of stopped shipments, is
likely to increase significantly.

In terms of specific enforcement mechanisms, as of this writing there is no concrete plan.
We assume that the first wave of enforcement will not come in the form of random shipments
inspections (after all, how does a random inspection of goods at a U.S. port reveal whether
that good was made with forced labor?). Instead, if enforcement of the Foreign Corrupt
Practices Act is to be a guide, we anticipate that business competitors, nongovernmental
organizations, disgruntled current or former employees, and activist groups can be expected
to provide substantiated/evidence-supported tips to CBP concerning specific shipments of
specific goods sent by specific manufacturers or through specific importers. Such targeted
whistle-blower complaints are the most likely source of successful enforcement actions.

---

[14] *Id.*

[15] Pub. L. No. 114-125 (2016).

5. California's Approach to Eradicate Slavery and Human Trafficking by Regulating the Direct Supply Chain

In response to increasingly vocal consumer calls for information about what products are made with forced labor, in 2011 the California legislature passed the California Transparency in Supply Chains Act of 2010 (S.B. 657).[16] The Act requires qualifying companies (and there are more than 3,200 of them) to disclose publicly the precise nature and scope of their efforts to eradicate human trafficking, slavery, child labor, and other forms of forced labor from their worldwide supply chains.

Although California's disclosure regime is now mandatory, compliance with the California Act has lagged (although early indications are that 2019 and beyond will see enforcement ramping up). This shortfall in compliance is animating advocacy groups to devise "naming and shaming" campaigns targeting those who ignore the California Act's disclosure requirements or whose disclosures are incomplete or, worse, inaccurate.

The arrival of such negative PR-generating, revenue-harming activism is intended to swiftly move corporate compliance from an item on the to-do list to a "to do right now" business imperative. Even more, the fact that 2015 witnessed a slew of federal class actions in California alleging violations of state consumer-protection laws because of false claims made about clean supply chains has only accelerated this dynamic (see Figure 29.2).[17]

For those subject to the 2010 California Transparency in Supply Chains Act, the law requires special attention from compliance officers. The California law applies to all (1) retailers and manufacturers (2) doing business[18] in California with (3) worldwide gross

---

[16] CAL. CIV. CODE § 1714.43 (2018).

[17] September and November 2015 saw a number of class action lawsuits based on theories (first aired in the UK *Guardian* newspaper) that companies' mandatory ("human-trafficking-free") disclosures under the California Transparency in Supply Chains Act were incomplete and/or inaccurate. The suits were premised on the claim that, contrary to company assertions, (1) there in fact was trafficked/forced labor in the company supply chains, and (2) had the class action plaintiffs/consumers known that the disclosures were false and misleading, they never would have purchased the product. On December 9, 2015, U.S. District Judge Cormac J. Carney in *Barber v. Nestle USA, Inc.* dismissed the plaintiffs' claims. As relevant here, Judge Carney ruled that the complained-about public statements concerning company compliance efforts were merely "aspirational" and, therefore, did not "mislead" consumers. Judge Carney also held that plaintiffs inappropriately asked companies to engage in certain affirmative conduct, rather than simply reporting the steps they have taken, as required by the California Act. This violated the Safe Harbor Doctrine. More specifically, plaintiffs claimed they were entitled to be informed of the "likelihood" that coerced labor tainted the products they purchased, whereas the California Act merely required companies to inform consumers of the steps the companies took to reduce the chances of such taint. Of course, to the extent a company issues statements stating facts ("we are 100% slave free"; "we have a zero-tolerance policy toward forced and child labor"; etc.) rather than aspirations, being on the wrong side of a class action continues to be a very real danger unless the declarations are carefully drafted (not to mention factually founded).

[18] "Doing business" in California means:
- Organized or domiciled in California;
- Sales in California exceeding $500,000 or 25 percent of total sales;
- Owns real estate or tangible personal property in California exceeding $50,000 or 25 percent of total real or tangible property; or
- Distributes employee compensation in California exceeding $50,000 or 25 percent of total compensation.

Breaking Down the California Transparency in Supply Chains Act

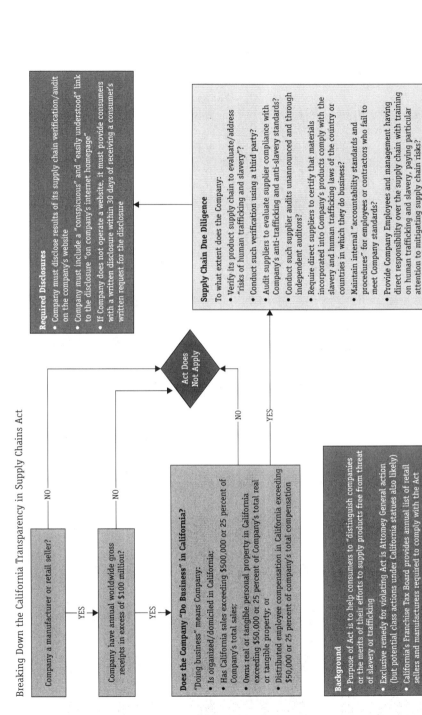

Required Disclosures
- Company must disclose results of its supply chain verification/audit on the company's website
- Company must include a "conspicuous" and "easily understood" link to the disclosure "on company's internet homepage"
- If Company does not operate a website, it must provide consumers with a written disclosure within 30 days of receiving a consumer's written request for the disclosure

Supply Chain Due Diligence
To what extent does the Company:
- Verify its product supply chain to evaluate/address "risks of human trafficking and slavery"?
- Conduct such verification using a third party?
- Audit suppliers to evaluate supplier compliance with Company's anti-trafficking and anti-slavery standards?
- Conduct such supplier audits unannounced and through independent auditors?
- Require direct suppliers to certify that materials incorporated into Company's products comply with the slavery and human trafficking laws of the country or countries in which they do business?
- Maintain internal "accountability standards and procedures" for employees or contractors who fail to meet Company standards?
- Provide Company Employees and management having direct responsibility over the supply chain with training on human trafficking and slavery, paying particular attention to mitigating supply chain risks?

Act Does Not Apply

Company a manufacturer or retail seller? — NO

Company have annual worldwide gross receipts in excess of $100 million? — NO

Does the Company "Do Business" in California?
"Doing business" means Company:
- Is organized/domiciled in California;
- Has California sales exceeding $500,000 or 25 percent of Company's total sales;
- Owns real or tangible personal property in California exceeding $50,000 or 25 percent of Company's total real or tangible property; or
- Distributed employee compensation in California exceeding $50,000 or 25 percent of company's total compensation

YES / NO / YES

Background
- Purpose of Act is to help consumers to "distinguish companies or the merits of their efforts to supply products free from threat of slavery or trafficking
- Exclusive remedy for violating Act is Attorney General action (but potential class actions under California statues also likely)
- California's Franchise Tax Board provides annual list of retail sellers and manufacturers required to comply with the Act

This chart was prepared by Perkins Coie Partner T. Markus Funk (MFunk@perkinscoie.com). Markus retains the copyright to this chart.

FIGURE 29.2 Breaking Down the California Transparency in Supply Chains Act

receipts over $100 million.[19] Those falling under its jurisdiction must answer a series of questions designed to reveal what, if anything, they are doing to ensure that their supply chains/products are free from the taint of human trafficking and other forms of forced labor. Specifically, they must answer what they are doing to:

- Audit suppliers to evaluate supplier compliance with anti-trafficking and anti-slavery standards and regulations
- Evaluate their product supply chains for risks of human trafficking and slavery (e.g., does the company use third-party auditors to conduct the evaluations?)
- Conduct such supplier audits unannounced and through independent auditors
- Require direct suppliers to certify that materials incorporated into the company's products comply with the slavery and human trafficking laws of the country or countries in which they do business
- Maintain internal accountability standards and procedures for employees or contractors who fail to meet company standards
- Train employees and management with direct responsibility over the supply chain regarding human trafficking and slavery

Those companies falling under the California Act's jurisdictions must (1) publicly disclose their specific answers to the foregoing, and (2) do so with a link on the homepage of the company's website. Although some say that this is a mere disclosure-only statute (true) that does not force companies to take any particular anti-trafficking action (technically true, but practically incorrect), such a view is shortsighted and does not recognize the realities in today's companies. Very few companies will be comfortable announcing "we are doing nothing" in their disclosure; instead, companies, realizing the questions, tend to put into place the asked-about activities/processes/trainings outlines so that they, in their disclosures, can accurately state that they are taking various steps to combat trafficking in their supply chains.

6. The UK Modern Slavery Act of 2015 Applies to Companies Doing "Any Business" in the United Kingdom

Multinational companies with business interests in the United Kingdom are now subject to another anti-trafficking regime by virtue of the UK's efforts to fight against global human trafficking. On the heels of the UK Bribery Act of 2010 (a close analog of the U.S. Foreign Corrupt Practices Act, but extending even further), the UK government has now borrowed significantly from the California Transparency in Supply Chains Act to impose its own disclosure framework.

The UK Modern Slavery Act (the "UK Act"), passed by Parliament in 2015,[20] requires certain businesses to make a slavery and human trafficking disclosure statement on their

---

[19] CAL. CIV. CODE § 1714.43(a)(1) (2018).

[20] Modern Slavery Act, 2015 ch. 30, *available at* http://www.legislation.gov.uk/ukpga/2015/30/pdfs/ukpga_20150030_en.pdf.

websites. The reporting obligation applied to financial years starting on or after April 1, 2016. Businesses with an annual turnover of 36 million British pounds (£36M) are subject to the reporting requirements of the UK Act. The UK Act became law in May 2016—setting forth certain attributes that would require companies to report—but deferred determining the annual turnover threshold, which is the annual revenue a business receives for its goods or services.

Those familiar with the California Act will recognize many of the UK Act's requirements. However, there are differences. Most notable, perhaps, is the UK Act's broader jurisdictional requirements. The UK Act's disclosure requirements extend to any company that:

(a) Carries on a business, or part of a business, in any part of the United Kingdom;
(b) Has a total turnover of no less than an amount to be determined by the UK secretary of state; and
(c) Supplies goods or services (in contrast to the California Act, which applies only to companies that are either a retail seller or manufacturer).

Additionally, unlike the California Act, which requires companies to expressly address a list of subject areas, the Modern Slavery Act merely provides a non-exhaustive list of suggested disclosure subjects.

Significantly, the Modern Slavery Act broadens the criteria on which businesses will be governed as set forth by the California Act (see Figure 29.3). The Modern Slavery Act's disclosure requirements extend to any company that meets all of the following criteria:

- Carries on a business, or part of a business, in any part of the United Kingdom
- Has a total turnover of no less than £36 (compared to the California Act's $100 million criteria); and
- Supplies goods or services (which stands in contrast to the California Act and its application only to companies that are either a retail seller or manufacturer).

In perhaps one of the most notable departures from the California Act, which requires companies to expressly address specific subject areas, the UK Modern Slavery Act merely provides that each fiscal year, a covered company must make a disclosure statement setting forth what it has done to ensure that trafficking is not taking place in its business or supply chain (leaving it up to the company to determine what areas to highlight/discuss). Alternatively, the company can make a statement that it has taken no such steps. In any event, it is critical that, as with the California Act, the disclosure be 100 percent accurate, neither overstating nor understating the company's actual activities.

6.1 WHAT IS A "SLAVERY AND HUMAN TRAFFICKING STATEMENT"?

Each fiscal year (ending on or after March 31, 2016), a covered company must make a statement setting forth what it has done to ensure that trafficking is not taking place in its business

UK Modern Slavery Act of 2015: Transparency in Supply Chains Disclosures (Part 6)

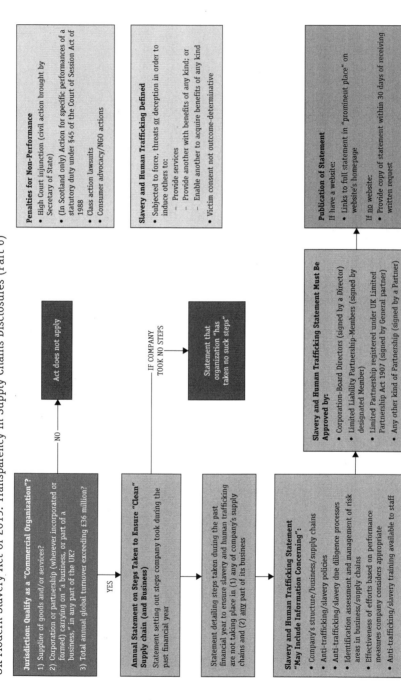

This chart was prepared by Perkins Coie Partner T. Markus Funk (MFunk@perkinscoie.com). Markus retains the copyright to this chart.

FIGURE 29.3 UK Modern Slavery Act of 2015: Transparency in Supply Chains Disclosures (Part 6)

or supply chain (a "disclosure statement"). Alternatively, the company can make a statement that it has taken no such steps. The disclosure statement can, but does not have to, include:

- The organization's structure, its business, and its supply chains
- Its policies in relation to slavery and human trafficking
- Its due diligence processes in relation to slavery and human trafficking in its business and supply chains
- The parts of its business and supply chains where there are risks of slavery and human trafficking taking place, and the steps it has taken to assess and manage those risks
- Its effectiveness in ensuring that slavery and human trafficking are not taking place in its business or supply chains, measured against such performance indicators as it considers appropriate
- The training about slavery and human trafficking available to its staff

6.2 WHO MUST APPROVE THE DISCLOSURE STATEMENT?

The UK Act attempts to promote accountability by requiring the disclosure statement be approved and signed in a specific manner. That is, corporations must have the disclosure statement approved by the board of directors and signed by a director; limited liability partnerships must get member approval and signature by a designated member; limited partnerships must get general partners' signatures; and any other partnership must get a partner's signature.

6.3 WHERE SHOULD THE DISCLOSURE STATEMENT BE MADE?

Closely aligned with the California Act, the UK Modern Slavery Act requires that any company with a website (1) publish the entire disclosure statement on its website, and (2) have a link to the disclosure statement in a prominent place on the website homepage. In the unlikely chance that a qualifying company has no website, it must provide its disclosure statement to a requesting party within 30 days of receiving a written request.

6.4 WHAT IF A COMPANY FAILS TO INCLUDE THE REQUIRED DISCLOSURE STATEMENT?

The UK secretary of state may bring civil proceedings in the High Court for an injunction if a company violates the UK Act's disclosure requirements. In Scotland, a proceeding may be brought for specific performance of a statutory duty under section 45 of the Court of Session Act 1988. Of course, civil litigation brought by shareholders, advocacy groups, consumer groups, etc. that focus on alleged inaccurate, incomplete, or misleading reporting of a company's efforts is, as has been the case with the California Act, in many ways one of the most concerning potential "penalties" facing companies under the UK Act.

7. A Parting Survey of the "Traditional" Anti-Trafficking Prohibitions

Labor-related certifications and prohibitions have an impact on the corporation. They are not just another bureaucratic paperwork diversion. If the compliance officer finds an executive with a reluctance to cooperate in assuring the company would comply with these labor-related federal requirements, a message to the person that includes these five federal laws and their punishments should capture the attention of a recalcitrant manager:

(a) **19 U.S.C. § 1307 (Forced Labor, Sex Trafficking):** "All goods, wares, articles, and merchandise mined, produced, or manufactured wholly or in part in any foreign country by convict labor or/and forced labor[21] or/and indentured labor under penal sanctions shall not be entitled to entry at any of the ports of the United States, and the importation thereof is hereby prohibited, and the Secretary of the Treasury is authorized and directed to prescribe such regulations as may be necessary for the enforcement of this provision."

(b) **18 U.S.C. § 1001 (False Statements):** "[W]hoever, in any matter within the jurisdiction of the executive, legislative, or judicial branch of the Government of the United States, knowingly and willfully 1) falsifies, conceals, or covers up by any trick, scheme, or device a material fact; 2) makes any materially false, fictitious, or fraudulent statement or representation; or 3) makes or uses any false writing or document knowing the same to contain any materially false, fictitious, or fraudulent statement or entry." **Penalty:** fine, imprisonment for not more than 5 years or, if the offense involves international or domestic terrorism (as defined in 18 U.S.C. § 2331), imprisoned not more than 8 years, or both.

(c) **18 U.S.C. § 545 (Smuggling):** "Whoever knowingly and willfully, with intent to defraud the United States, smuggles, or clandestinely introduces or attempts to smuggle or clandestinely introduce into the United States any merchandise which should have been invoiced, or makes out or passes, or attempts to pass, through the customhouse any false, forged, or fraudulent invoice, or other document or paper;" or "Whoever fraudulently or knowingly imports or brings into the United States, any merchandise contrary to law, or receives, conceals, buys, sells, or in any manner facilitates the transportation, concealment, or sale of such merchandise after importation, knowing the same to have been imported or brought into the United States contrary to law." **Penalty:** fine or imprisonment for not more than 20 years, or both.

(d) **18 U.S.C. § 1519 (Obstruction of Justice):** "Whoever knowingly alters, destroys, mutilates, conceals, covers up, falsifies, or makes a false entry in any record, document, or tangible object with the intent to impede, obstruct, or influence the

---

[21] " 'Forced labor,' as herein used, shall mean all work or service that is exacted from any person under the menace of any penalty for its nonperformance and for which the worker does not offer himself voluntarily. For purposes of this section, the term 'forced labor or/and indentured labor' includes forced or indentured child labor." 19 U.S.C. § 1307.

investigation or proper administration of any matter within the jurisdiction of any department or agency of the United States or any case filed under title 11, or in relation to or contemplation of any such matter or case." **Penalty**: fine, imprisonment for not more than 20 years, or both.

(e) **31 U.S.C. § 3729 (False Claims)**: "Any person who:

   (i) knowingly presents, or causes to be presented, a false or fraudulent claim for payment or approval;

  (ii) knowingly makes, uses, or causes to be made or used, a false record or statement material to a false or fraudulent claim;

 (iii) conspires to commit a violation of subparagraph (i), (ii), (iv), (v), (vi), or (vii);

 (iv) has possession, custody, or control of property or money used, or to be used, by the Government and knowingly delivers, or causes to be delivered, less than all of that money or property;

  (v) is authorized to make or deliver a document certifying receipt of property used, or to be used, by the Government and, intending to defraud the Government, makes or delivers the receipt without completely knowing that the information on the receipt is true;

 (vi) knowingly buys, or receives as a pledge of an obligation or debt, public property from an officer or employee of the Government, or a member of the Armed Forces, who lawfully may not sell or pledge property; or

(vii) knowingly makes, uses, or causes to be made or used, a false record or statement material to an obligation to pay or transmit money or property to the Government, or knowingly conceals or knowingly and improperly avoids or decreases an obligation to pay or transmit money or property to the Government." **Penalty**: "Liable to the United States Government for a civil penalty of not less than $5,000 and not more than $10,000."

8. Anti-Trafficking Compliance Program Guidelines

This section provides some basic guidelines for those compliance officers just getting started (or fine-tuning) a company's existing policies, and assumes a baseline familiarity with anti-bribery/anti-corruption (ABAC) compliance:

- *Introduce and Enforce Meaningful Policies* (or add policy language) focused on identifying and eliminating risks emanating from the various forms of coerced/forced labor within a business's supply chains (whether or not that risk is intertwined with ABAC concerns). Among other places, such internally consistent policies or policy language should be included in: (1) Codes of Conduct; (2) Annual Compliance Certifications; (3) Standard Contract Language; (4) Due Diligence Questionnaires; and (5) Supplier Statements of Conformity.
- *Adopt Standard Contract Language* among other key areas:
  o Indemnification;

- o Audit rights;
- o Requirement of full cooperation in the case of any internal investigation or review;
- o Requirement of immediate notification in the case of actual or potential nonperformance/problems;
- o Right to, as needed, contact the relevant authorities in the case of violation; and
- o Consent to follow company-developed action plan in case of any instances of noncompliance.
- *Design a Risk-Based Labor Verification/Audit Program* to evaluate and address risks of coerced and child labor in the company's supply chains, including:
  - o Designing features tailored to reduce, control, and eliminate those risks;
  - o Identifying the greatest risks existing within the supply chain;
  - o Deciding whether to employ independent third parties to conduct these verifications/audits;
  - o Considering including in the verification process consultations with independent unions, workers' associations, or workers within the workplace; and
  - o Ensuring that supplier audits evaluate supplier compliance with company standards for eliminating coerced and child labor issues.
- *Require Appropriate Certifications.* Suppliers in the supply chain should certify that, in addition to the above, materials incorporated into products comply with (1) the company's code of conduct, and (2) the laws against coerced and child labor in the country or countries in which they are doing business. Key substantive provisions should include representations and warranties that a supplier:
  - o *Complies* with all applicable national and international laws and regulations, as well as the company's code of conduct, including prohibition and eradication of coerced and child labor in its facilities, and that it requires its suppliers, including labor brokers and agencies, to do the same.
  - o Treats its workers with dignity and respect, provides them with a safe work environment, and ensures that the work environment is in compliance with applicable environmental, labor, and employment laws, and your code of conduct.
  - o Refrains from corrupt practices, and does not engage in human rights violations.
  - o Certifies that it has not, and will not, directly or indirectly, engage in certain activities connected to coerced and child labor. These activities should be expressly detailed in the certification.
- *Develop and Publicize Internal Accountability Standards*, including those related to supply chain management and procurement systems, and procedures for employees and contractors regarding coerced and child labor. Make sure you have procedures in place for employees and contractors who fail to meet these standards.
- *Assess Supply Chain Management and Procurement Systems* of suppliers in the companies' supply chains to verify whether those suppliers have appropriate systems to identify risks of coerced and child labor within their own supply chains.

- *Train Employees and Business Partners*, particularly those with direct responsibility for supply chain management, on the company's expectations as they relate to coerced and child labor, particularly with respect to mitigating risks within the supply chains of products.
- *Guarantee That Remediation Is Provided* for those who have been identified as victims of coerced and child labor.

The fight against human trafficking has without question entered a new phase, and has traditionally been part and parcel with bribery and corruption. Over time our summary of legal requirements will surely expand, both substantively and geographically, as consumers and governments come to expect that companies (and their compliance officers) will "do their part" to ensure that their supply chains and, ultimately, their products, are free from the taint of human trafficking and other forms of forced or coerced labor.

Conclusion

As we hope the foregoing chapters have underscored, it is high time that practitioners of the compliance, regulatory, and investigative arts recognize not only that other countries have credible anti-bribery/anti-corruption regimes—including ones with extraterritorial application—but also that new anti-bribery laws are being passed frequently. And from our perspective, even more importantly, is that the long-lagging enforcement of these laws is increasingly on the minds of prosecutors, regulators, judges, and politicians. As these key stakeholders and decision-makers gain a fuller appreciation of the wider fight against corruption, we believe they will feel emboldened to act positively to root out conduct that undermines democracy and the rule of law. We also believe these same stakeholders will be motivated to take steps that ensure that they do not fall behind their geopolitical "peers." As a consequence of today's increasingly polycentric fight against bribery and other forms of corruption, those advising companies will be expected to understand, and more importantly ward off against, this development's direct impacts on companies and individuals engaged in cross-border commerce, regardless of where in the world they are based or do business.

It is certainly true that contemporary practitioners have become attuned to the reality that foreign countries are sensitive to foreign bribery touching on their jurisdictions—and that their governments are doing something about it in terms of legislative enactments and enforcement actions. That is so even though in this evolutionary phase of the fight against bribery and corruption, the number of nations developing or fine-tuning their anti-bribery laws still far outstrips the number of nations actively pursuing suspected wrongdoers through enforcement actions. And, we are bullish on where this fight is headed. Put another way, gazing into our collective compliance crystal balls, we wager to predict that when the second edition of this book goes to print, we will be talking about which countries are

From Baksheesh to Bribery. T. Markus Funk and Andrew S. Boutros.
© Oxford University Press 2019. Published 2019 by Oxford University Press.

now enforcing laws focused on foreign and domestic bribery (both of government officials and in the commercial context) with a level of vigor that until now, or at least over the past roughly 10–15 years, only the United States has exhibited. In short, American dominance in the anti-bribery space will likely—and, in fact, should—sooner rather than later become a thing of the past. That, our friends, is not a bad thing, so long as fairness and due process are chief cornerstones of the international anti-corruption fight. After all, these ends should not justify any means.

Appendices

The 2018 TRACE Bribery Risk Matrix

The **TRACE Bribery Risk Matrix** measures the likelihood of bribe demands in 200 countries. It aggregates relevant data obtained from leading public interest and international organizations, including the United Nations, the World Bank, and the World Economic Forum, with the aim of helping companies assess the likely risk of bribe demands in each country and to design compliance and due diligence programs tailored to that risk.

The overall country risk score is a combined and weighted score of four domains, with higher scores indicating greater risk:

Domain One reflects the risk associated with *business interactions with government agencies*, including three subdomains measuring the frequency of government interaction, the degree to which bribery is expected and tolerated in such interactions, and the overall regulatory burden.

Domain Two measures a country's *anti-bribery deterrence and enforcement*. It comprises subdomains reflecting both societal attitudes and government enforcement.

Domain Three addresses *government and financial transparency*, relying in particular on measures of government budget transparency and transparency of financial interests.

Domain Four captures the *role played by non-governmental actors* in monitoring and controlling corruption, including the critical role of the media and a broad-based measure of the civil society capacity of a country's population.

From Baksheesh to Bribery. T. Markus Funk and Andrew S. Boutros.
© Oxford University Press 2019. Published 2019 by Oxford University Press.

Rank	Country Name	Total Risk Score	Domain 1	Domain 2	Domain 3	Domain 4
1	New Zealand	5	1	9	6	9
2	Sweden	5	7	10	1	3
3	Norway	7	13	5	1	1
4	Denmark	8	9	3	17	1
5	Finland	9	14	6	9	4
6	Netherlands	11	15	7	7	9
7	United Kingdom	12	17	10	7	9
8	Germany	13	20	12	10	7
9	Canada	15	25	9	10	8
10	Iceland	16	20	13	13	14
11	Luxembourg	16	22	1	16	18
12	Singapore	17	4	4	17	46
13	Switzerland	17	22	10	22	7
14	Hong Kong	17	7	13	18	38
15	Estonia	18	23	20	15	11
16	Australia	18	26	15	11	14
17	Austria	19	26	19	15	13
18	United States	21	32	23	11	12
19	Ireland	21	20	23	27	17
20	Portugal	21	25	25	21	13
21	France	22	34	18	8	17
22	Belgium	23	31	22	19	11
23	Lithuania	24	37	13	23	8
24	Taiwan	24	26	28	30	12
25	South Korea	24	25	25	22	26
26	Japan	25	30	21	27	18
27	Georgia	26	17	31	32	30
28	Monaco	29	–	–	14	16
29	United Arab Emirates	29	8	11	49	58
30	Israel	29	48	24	14	14
31	Slovenia	30	41	32	23	17

Rank	Country Name	Total Risk Score	Domain 1	Domain 2	Domain 3	Domain 4
32	Czech Republic	32	43	26	31	18
33	Uruguay	32	48	24	30	13
34	Chile	33	43	32	23	27
35	Andorra	34	–	–	29	13
36	Poland	35	41	34	35	25
37	Qatar	35	30	7	45	52
38	Spain	35	41	39	33	26
39	Latvia	36	46	13	55	14
40	Italy	36	49	54	18	21
41	Liechtenstein	38	67	–	12	8
42	San Marino	38	48	18	34	37
43	Slovak Republic	38	62	31	23	14
44	Malta	38	52	33	35	20
45	Oman	39	34	34	36	54
46	Bhutan	39	42	11	52	41
47	Cyprus	39	50	40	40	19
48	Costa Rica	40	60	32	36	12
49	St. Kitts and Nevis	40	39	45	54	24
50	Bahrain	40	42	16	31	61
51	St. Lucia	40	38	37	60	26
52	Jamaica	42	53	62	32	20
53	Croatia	42	55	41	35	29
54	Dominica	43	53	40	30	38
55	Samoa	43	44	30	63	30
56	Greece	43	51	52	40	25
57	South Africa	43	66	29	25	30
58	Kosovo	43	52	31	–	32
59	Tonga	44	47	46	50	30
60	Mauritius	44	53	29	57	27
61	Rwanda	44	34	29	54	64
62	Barbados	45	54	35	58	22

Rank	Country Name	Total Risk Score	Domain 1	Domain 2	Domain 3	Domain 4
63	Malaysia	45	44	32	43	57
64	Montenegro	45	57	44	40	29
65	St. Vincent and the Grenadines	45	51	40	48	35
66	Bahamas	45	55	32	56	26
67	Colombia	45	59	53	28	33
68	Romania	46	64	41	38	24
69	Seychelles	46	62	28	44	31
70	Cape Verde	46	54	39	51	32
71	Marshall Islands	47	38	39	72	43
72	Ghana	47	62	41	51	21
73	Jordan	47	44	42	42	60
74	Botswana	47	55	24	55	42
75	Macedonia	47	51	43	41	51
76	Grenada	48	53	56	53	28
77	Armenia	48	48	55	48	42
78	Puerto Rico	48	52	41	52	–
79	Bulgaria	48	62	44	41	34
80	Palau	49	64	51	53	16
81	Peru	49	62	53	41	30
82	Senegal	49	52	58	53	32
83	Namibia	49	64	30	45	38
84	Panama	49	57	60	51	28
85	Saudi Arabia	50	43	43	53	64
86	India	50	62	56	40	36
87	Serbia	50	60	42	47	42
88	Tunisia	50	59	51	53	32
89	Thailand	50	52	47	42	58
90	Micronesia	51	47	52	77	31
91	Albania	51	61	49	44	40
92	Indonesia	51	59	52	50	36
93	Hungary	51	56	49	51	44

Rank	Country Name	Total Risk Score	Domain 1	Domain 2	Domain 3	Domain 4
94	Antigua and Barbuda	51	59	53	54	33
95	Azerbaijan	51	52	43	43	63
96	Mauritania	51	57	64	40	45
97	Vanuatu	52	61	26	66	39
98	Mongolia	52	65	42	56	33
99	Fiji	52	63	57	49	34
100	Philippines	53	64	46	49	42
101	Kenya	53	66	50	46	39
102	Papua New Guinea	53	60	46	60	39
103	Nepal	53	56	63	49	47
104	Bosnia and Herzegovina	54	71	51	34	45
105	Ukraine	54	67	53	48	36
106	Maldives	54	61	56	45	47
107	Brunei Darussalam	54	56	33	57	60
108	Russian Federation	54	60	48	51	52
109	Benin	54	56	61	60	42
110	Zambia	54	64	27	57	53
111	Argentina	54	80	52	41	25
112	Brazil	55	78	54	36	33
113	Trinidad and Tobago	55	65	63	59	25
114	Belarus	55	48	43	61	68
115	Burkina Faso	55	62	66	55	36
116	Sao Tome and Principe	55	54	64	66	41
117	Niger	55	51	54	61	58
118	Kyrgyz Republic	55	63	58	53	42
119	Kuwait	56	76	37	48	40

Rank	Country Name	Total Risk Score	Domain 1	Domain 2	Domain 3	Domain 4
120	Togo	56	60	51	62	44
121	Morocco	56	54	57	57	57
122	Ivory Coast	56	61	63	56	42
123	Moldova	56	68	49	52	42
124	Solomon Islands	56	63	17	81	46
125	Guatemala	56	64	63	59	37
126	Mali	56	57	51	66	49
127	Kazakhstan	57	59	47	53	63
128	El Salvador	57	65	58	62	35
129	Dominican Republic	57	65	64	56	38
130	Turkey	58	56	47	57	70
131	Paraguay	58	63	61	57	47
132	Uganda	58	70	51	49	51
133	Mexico	58	70	55	49	49
134	Lesotho	59	58	44	78	53
135	Liberia	60	75	41	66	38
136	Ecuador	60	69	54	57	50
137	East Timor	60	66	62	65	43
138	Sierra Leone	60	72	49	58	49
139	Tanzania	60	70	56	57	49
140	Mozambique	60	67	64	49	57
141	Aruba	60	69	–	–	–
142	Vietnam	61	61	47	60	72
143	Gambia	61	55	60	57	78
144	Malawi	61	72	57	67	40
145	Suriname	62	68	48	82	38
146	Guyana	62	74	58	65	39
147	Lebanon	62	72	62	68	37
148	Sri Lanka	62	61	68	69	55
149	Kiribati	63	78	44	73	38
150	Belize	63	77	45	74	38

Rank	Country Name	Total Risk Score	Domain 1	Domain 2	Domain 3	Domain 4
151	China	63	65	51	54	76
152	Pakistan	63	78	62	50	52
153	Algeria	63	72	55	75	43
154	Cameroon	63	67	67	62	55
155	Bolivia	64	80	65	56	41
156	Iran	64	70	55	55	67
157	Gabon	64	72	66	54	57
158	Myanmar	64	66	62	70	55
159	Guinea	64	72	60	71	46
160	Honduras	64	71	67	65	50
161	Nigeria	65	79	61	59	48
162	Swaziland	65	66	41	73	69
163	Cayman Islands	65	74	–	–	–
164	Tuvalu	66	–	–	69	61
165	Cuba	66	74	50	65	63
166	Afghanistan	66	77	69	59	51
167	Comoros	66	57	84	79	57
168	Egypt	66	66	61	66	70
169	Tajikistan	68	65	63	70	75
170	Yemen	68	71	56	65	73
171	Syria	68	70	56	69	73
172	Haiti	68	74	83	67	49
173	Madagascar	68	72	70	78	52
174	Ethiopia	69	71	53	60	83
175	Iraq	69	70	62	79	60
176	Nicaragua	69	76	69	73	51
177	Uzbekistan	69	70	46	75	78
178	Sudan	70	72	78	60	70
179	Djibouti	70	61	51	87	81
180	Laos	70	58	70	80	81

Rank	Country Name	Total Risk Score	Domain 1	Domain 2	Domain 3	Domain 4
181	Republic of the Congo (Brazzaville)	70	77	68	72	59
182	Bangladesh	70	87	61	58	61
183	Central African Republic	71	72	78	75	58
184	Dem. Rep. of Congo	71	68	79	69	72
185	Zimbabwe	72	78	60	74	67
186	Bermuda	72	92	–	–	–
187	Angola	72	81	61	78	58
188	Guinea-Bissau	72	64	74	93	66
189	Macau	73	100	–	–	–
190	Cambodia	75	86	59	82	58
191	South Sudan	75	75	59	89	71
192	Eritrea	76	49	84	93	100
193	Burundi	78	61	80	92	92
194	Equatorial Guinea	79	74	85	91	74
195	North Korea	81	–	100	90	96
196	Turkmenistan	82	93	48	80	88
197	Chad	82	83	78	95	70
198	Venezuela	82	99	75	74	67
199	Libya	83	88	78	89	70
200	Somalia	92	90	89	100	88

9-47.000—Foreign Corrupt Practices Act of 1977

9-47.100—Introduction

This chapter contains the U.S. Department of Justice's policy regarding investigations and prosecutions of violations of the Foreign Corrupt Practices Act (FCPA). The FCPA prohibits both United States and foreign corporations and nationals from offering or paying, or authorizing the offer or payment, of anything of value to a foreign government official, foreign political party, foreign party official, or candidate for foreign public office, or to an official of a public international organization, in order to obtain or retain business. In addition, the FCPA requires publicly held United States companies to make and keep books and records which, in reasonable detail, accurately reflect the disposition of company assets and to devise and maintain a system of internal accounting controls sufficient to reasonably assure that transactions are authorized, recorded accurately, and periodically reviewed.

Further guidance on the FCPA is available in *A Resource Guide to the U.S. Foreign Corrupt Practices Act* (2012), published by the Criminal Division of the U.S. Department of Justice and the Enforcement Division of the U.S. Securities and Exchange Commission, *available at* https://www.justice.gov/sites/default/files/criminal-fraud/legacy/2015/01/16/guide.pdf.

[updated October 2016]

9-47.110—Policy Concerning Criminal Investigations and Prosecutions of the Foreign Corrupt Practices Act

No investigation or prosecution of cases involving alleged violations of the antibribery provisions of the Foreign Corrupt Practices Act (FCPA) of 1977 (15 U.S.C. §§ 78dd-1,

78dd-2, and 78dd-3) or of related violations of the FCPA's record keeping provisions (15 U.S.C. § 78m(b)) shall be instituted without the express authorization of the Criminal Division.

Any information relating to a possible violation of the FCPA should be brought immediately to the attention of the Fraud Section of the Criminal Division. Even when such information is developed during the course of an apparently unrelated investigation, the Fraud Section should be notified immediately. Close coordination of such investigations and prosecutions with the United States Securities and Exchange Commission (SEC) and other interested agencies is essential. Additionally, the Department has established a FCPA Opinion Procedure concerning proposed business conduct. *See* A Resource Guide to the U.S. Foreign Corrupt Practices Act at 86.

Unless otherwise agreed upon by the AAG, Criminal Division, investigations and prosecutions of alleged violations of the antibribery provisions of the FCPA will be conducted by Trial Attorneys of the Fraud Section. Prosecutions of alleged violations of the record keeping provisions, when such violations are related to an antibribery violation, will also be conducted by Fraud Section Trial Attorneys, unless otherwise directed by the AAG, Criminal Division.

The investigation and prosecution of particular allegations of violations of the FCPA will raise complex enforcement problems abroad as well as difficult issues of jurisdiction and statutory construction. For example, part of the investigation may involve interviewing witnesses in foreign countries concerning their activities with high-level foreign government officials. In addition, relevant accounts maintained in United States banks and subject to subpoena may be directly or beneficially owned by senior foreign government officials. For these reasons, the need for centralized supervision of investigations and prosecutions under the FCPA is compelling.

[updated August 2013]

9-47.120—FCPA Corporate Enforcement Policy

I. CREDIT FOR VOLUNTARY SELF-DISCLOSURE, FULL COOPERATION, AND TIMELY AND APPROPRIATE REMEDIATION IN FCPA MATTERS

Due to the unique issues presented in FCPA matters, including their inherently international character and other factors, the FCPA Corporate Enforcement Policy is aimed at providing additional benefits to companies based on their corporate behavior once they learn of misconduct. When a company has voluntarily self-disclosed misconduct in an FCPA matter, fully cooperated, and timely and appropriately remediated, all in accordance with the standards set forth below, there will be a presumption that the company will receive a declination absent aggravating circumstances involving the seriousness of the offense or the nature of the offender. Aggravating circumstances that may warrant a criminal resolution include, but are not limited to, involvement by executive management of the company in the misconduct; a significant profit to the company from the misconduct; pervasiveness of the misconduct within the company; and criminal recidivism.

If a criminal resolution is warranted for a company that has voluntarily self-disclosed, fully cooperated, and timely and appropriately remediated, the Fraud Section:

- will accord, or recommend to a sentencing court, a 50% reduction off of the low end of the U.S. Sentencing Guidelines (U.S.S.G.) fine range, except in the case of a criminal recidivist; and
- generally will not require appointment of a monitor if a company has, at the time of resolution, implemented an effective compliance program.

To qualify for the FCPA Corporate Enforcement Policy, the company is required to pay all disgorgement, forfeiture, and/or restitution resulting from the misconduct at issue.

2. LIMITED CREDIT FOR FULL COOPERATION AND TIMELY AND APPROPRIATE REMEDIATION IN FCPA MATTERS WITHOUT VOLUNTARY SELF-DISCLOSURE

If a company did not voluntarily disclose its misconduct to the Department of Justice (the Department) in accordance with the standards set forth above, but later fully cooperated and timely and appropriately remediated in accordance with the standards set forth above, the company will receive, or the Department will recommend to a sentencing court, up to a 25% reduction off of the low end of the U.S.S.G. fine range.

3. DEFINITIONS
a. Voluntary Self-Disclosure in FCPA Matters

In evaluating self-disclosure, the Department will make a careful assessment of the circumstances of the disclosure. The Department will require the following items for a company to receive credit for voluntary self-disclosure of wrongdoing:

- The voluntary disclosure qualifies under U.S.S.G. § 8C2.5(g)(1) as occurring "prior to an imminent threat of disclosure or government investigation";
- The company discloses the conduct to the Department "within a reasonably prompt time after becoming aware of the offense," with the burden being on the company to demonstrate timeliness; and
- The company discloses all relevant facts known to it, including all relevant facts about all individuals involved in the violation of law.

b. Full Cooperation in FCPA Matters

In addition to the provisions contained in the Principles of Federal Prosecution of Business Organizations, *see Justice Manual*, at 9-28.000, the following items will be required for a company to receive credit for full cooperation for purposes of the *Justice Manual*, at 9-47.120(1) (beyond the credit available under the U.S.S.G.):

- As set forth in the *Justice Manual*, at 9-28.720, disclosure on a timely basis of all facts relevant to the wrongdoing at issue, including: all relevant facts gathered during a company's independent investigation; attribution of facts to specific sources where such attribution does not violate the attorney-client privilege, rather than a general narrative of the facts;

timely updates on a company's internal investigation, including but not limited to rolling disclosures of information; all facts related to involvement in the criminal activity by the company's officers, employees, or agents; and all facts known or that become known to the company regarding potential criminal conduct by all third-party companies (including their officers, employees, or agents);

- Proactive cooperation, rather than reactive; that is, the company must timely disclose facts that are relevant to the investigation, even when not specifically asked to do so, and, where the company is or should be aware of opportunities for the Department to obtain relevant evidence not in the company's possession and not otherwise known to the Department, it must identify those opportunities to the Department;
- Timely preservation, collection, and disclosure of relevant documents and information relating to their provenance, including (a) disclosure of overseas documents, the locations in which such documents were found, and who found the documents, (b) facilitation of third-party production of documents, and (c) where requested and appropriate, provision of translations of relevant documents in foreign languages;
  - Note: Where a company claims that disclosure of overseas documents is prohibited due to data privacy, blocking statutes, or other reasons related to foreign law, the company bears the burden of establishing the prohibition. Moreover, a company should work diligently to identify all available legal bases to provide such documents;
- Where requested, de-confliction of witness interviews and other investigative steps that a company intends to take as part of its internal investigation with steps that the Department intends to take as part of its investigation; and
- Where requested, making available for interviews by the Department those company officers and employees who possess relevant information; this includes, where appropriate and possible, officers, employees, and agents located overseas as well as former officers and employees (subject to the individuals' Fifth Amendment rights), and, where possible, the facilitation of third-party production of witnesses.

c. Timely and Appropriate Remediation in FCPA Matters

The following items will be required for a company to receive full credit for timely and appropriate remediation for purposes of the *Justice Manual*, at 9-47.120(1) (beyond the credit available under the U.S.S.G.):

- Demonstration of thorough analysis of causes of underlying conduct (i.e., a root cause analysis) and, where appropriate, remediation to address the root causes;
- Implementation of an effective compliance and ethics program, the criteria for which will be periodically updated and which may vary based on the size and resources of the organization, but may include:
  - The company's culture of compliance, including awareness among employees that any criminal conduct, including the conduct underlying the investigation, will not be tolerated;
  - The resources the company has dedicated to compliance;
  - The quality and experience of the personnel involved in compliance, such that they can understand and identify the transactions and activities that pose a potential risk;

- The authority and independence of the compliance function and the availability of compliance expertise to the board;
- The effectiveness of the company's risk assessment and the manner in which the company's compliance program has been tailored based on that risk assessment;
- The compensation and promotion of the personnel involved in compliance, in view of their role, responsibilities, performance, and other appropriate factors;
- The auditing of the compliance program to assure its effectiveness; and
- The reporting structure of any compliance personnel employed or contracted by the company.
- Appropriate discipline of employees, including those identified by the company as responsible for the misconduct, either through direct participation or failure in oversight, as well as those with supervisory authority over the area in which the criminal conduct occurred;
- Appropriate retention of business records, and prohibiting the improper destruction or deletion of business records, including prohibiting employees from using software that generates but does not appropriately retain business records or communications; and
- Any additional steps that demonstrate recognition of the seriousness of the company's misconduct, acceptance of responsibility for it, and the implementation of measures to reduce the risk of repetition of such misconduct, including measures to identify future risks.

4. COMMENT

Cooperation Credit: Cooperation comes in many forms. Once the threshold requirements set out at the *Justice Manual*, at 9-28.700, have been met, the Department will assess the scope, quantity, quality, and timing of cooperation based on the circumstances of each case when assessing how to evaluate a company's cooperation under the FCPA Corporate Enforcement Policy.

"De-confliction" is one factor that the Department may consider in determining the credit that a company will receive for cooperation. The Department's requests to defer investigative steps, such as the interview of company employees or third parties, will be made for a limited period of time and will be narrowly tailored to a legitimate investigative purpose (e.g., to prevent the impeding of a specified aspect of the Department's investigation). Once the justification dissipates, the Department will notify the company that the Department is lifting its request.

Where a company asserts that its financial condition impairs its ability to cooperate more fully, the company will bear the burden to provide factual support for such an assertion. The Department will closely evaluate the validity of any such claim and will take the impediment into consideration in assessing whether the company has fully cooperated. As set forth in the *Justice Manual*, at 9-28.720, eligibility for full cooperation credit is not predicated upon waiver of the attorney-client privilege or work product protection, and none of the requirements above require such waiver. Nothing herein alters that policy, which remains in full force and effect. Furthermore, not all companies will satisfy all the components of full cooperation for purposes of the *Justice Manual*, at 9-47.120(2) and (3)(b), either because they decide to cooperate only later in an investigation or they timely decide to cooperate but fail to meet all of the criteria listed above. In general, such companies will be eligible for some cooperation credit if they meet the criteria of the *Justice Manual*, at 9-28.700, but the credit generally will be markedly less than for full cooperation, depending on the extent to which the cooperation was lacking.

Remediation: In order for a company to receive full credit for remediation and avail itself of the benefits of the FCPA Corporate Enforcement Policy, the company must have effectively remediated at the time of the resolution.

The requirement that a company pay all disgorgement, forfeiture, and/or restitution resulting from the misconduct at issue may be satisfied by a parallel resolution with a relevant regulator (e.g., the United States Securities and Exchange Commission).

Public Release: A declination pursuant to the FCPA Corporate Enforcement Policy is a case that would have been prosecuted or criminally resolved except for the company's voluntary disclosure, full cooperation, remediation, and payment of disgorgement, forfeiture, and/ or restitution. If a case would have been declined in the absence of such circumstances, it is not a declination pursuant to this Policy. Declinations awarded under the FCPA Corporate Enforcement Policy will be made public.

[added November 2017]

9-47.130—Civil Injunctive Actions

The SEC has authority to obtain civil injunctions against future violations of the record keeping and anti-bribery provisions of the FCPA by issuers. *See* 15 U.S.C. § 78u. Civil injunctions against violations of the anti-bribery provisions by domestic concerns and foreign nationals and companies shall be instituted by Trial Attorneys of the Fraud Section in cooperation with the appropriate United States Attorney, unless otherwise directed by the AAG, Criminal Division. *See* §§ 78dd-2(d), 78dd-3(d).

[updated November 2000]

Index

Printed in the USA/Agawam, MA
February 18, 2020

750365.003